ALSO BY RAYMOND ARSENAULT

The Wild Ass of the Ozarks:
Jeff Davis and the Social Bases of Southern Politics

St. Petersburg and the Florida Dream, 1888–1950

Crucible of Liberty:
200 Years of the Bill of Rights
(editor)

The Changing South of Gene Patterson:
Journalism and Civil Rights, 1960–1968
(coeditor with Roy Peter Clark)

Paradise Lost? The Environmental History of Florida
(coeditor with Jack E. Davis)

Freedom Riders:
1961 and the Struggle for Racial Justice
(2006; abridged edition, 2011)

The Sound of Freedom:
Marian Anderson, the Lincoln Memorial,
and the Concert That Awakened America

Dixie Redux:
Essays in Honor of Sheldon Hackney
(coeditor with Orville Vernon Burton)

ARTHUR ASHE

A LIFE

■

RAYMOND ARSENAULT

SIMON & SCHUSTER
New York   London   Toronto   Sydney   New Delhi

Simon & Schuster
1230 Avenue of the Americas
New York, NY 10020

First Simon & Schuster hardcover edition August 2018

SIMON & SCHUSTER and colophon are registered trademarks
of Simon & Schuster, Inc.

For information about special discounts for bulk purchases,
please contact Simon & Schuster Special Sales at 1-866-506-1949
or business@simonandschuster.com.

The Simon & Schuster Speakers Bureau can bring authors to
your live event. For more information or to book an event,
contact the Simon & Schuster Speakers Bureau at 1-866-248-3049
or visit our website at www.simonspeakers.com.

Interior design by Lewelin Polanco

Manufactured in the United States of America

1   3   5   7   9   10   8   6   4   2

Library of Congress Cataloging-in-Publication Data is available.

ISBN 978-1-4391-8904-7
ISBN 978-1-4391-8906-1 (ebook)

For the dearest of friends—
James Oliver Horton (1943–2017)
and Lois E. Horton

And for my beloved grandson—
Lincoln Hardee Powers

CONTENTS

PREFACE

For the past ten years, I have enjoyed playing doubles just about every Sunday morning on the soft courts of the St. Petersburg Tennis Center, where Arthur Ashe played his final match as an amateur in March 1969, the year I graduated from college. Playing under a high-blue, Florida sky with old friends: what more could one ask for, aside from a faster serve, a better backhand, and a little luck against left-handers? Of course, even Ashe had trouble against left-handers, especially his nemesis, the great Aussie Rod Laver. So I shouldn't have been surprised in January 2016, when a crafty left-handed opponent hit a drop shot that caught me off guard, causing me to lunge awkwardly, lose my balance, and fall to the ground—breaking my left wrist in two places. Embarrassed, I joked with friends that my clumsiness proved, once and for all, that "I was no Arthur Ashe."

Clearly, there is only so much a biographer can learn from his subject. As my doubles partners will attest, immersing myself in all things Ashe has not improved my tennis game, and I still play with more enthusiasm than skill. On the other hand, I feel my continuing encounter with Arthur (it took me several years to reach the point where I felt comfortable referring to him on a first-name basis) has been immensely helpful in other parts of my life. Of all the historical characters I have studied during my long scholarly career, he comes the closest to being an exemplary role model. He wasn't perfect, as the chapters following will demonstrate, and he, like everyone else, was a flesh-and-blood human being limited by flaws and eccentricities. Yet, through a lifetime of challenges large and small, he came remarkably close to living up to his professed ideals.

As the first black man to reach the upper echelon of a notoriously elitist and racially segregated sport, Ashe exhibited an extraordinary strength of character that eventually made him the most beloved and honored figure in tennis. He was the Jackie Robinson of men's tennis, but unlike the great Brooklyn Dodger star he was destined to soldier on alone throughout his playing career. On the men's tour of the 1960s and 1970s, there was no counterpart to Robinson's black peers—no Lary Doby, Willie Mays, or Hank Aaron. Though shy and generally reticent into his mid-twenties, Ashe took a sharp turn toward activism in 1968 and never looked back. By the close of his career, he had become a model of cosmopolitanism and a self-proclaimed "citizen of the world," earning almost universal respect as a forceful civil rights activist, an independent-minded thinker and writer, a humanitarian philanthropist, and an unrivaled ambassador of sportsmanship and fair play. More than any other athlete of the modern era—with the possible exception of Muhammad Ali—he transcended the world of sports.

Arthur had a positive impact on virtually every part of the world he touched by adhering to a stringent code of personal ethics, an uncommon generosity and empathy in his dealings with all who crossed his path, a passionate belief in the salvific power of education and intellectual inquiry, an extraordinary work ethic, and a deep commitment to social and civic responsibility. Add his zest for life and capacity for true friendship and you have the full package of commendable personal traits. He did not live very long—dying five months short of his fiftieth birthday—but he jammed as much meaningful activity into his relatively brief lifetime as was humanly possible.

Ashe's remarkable saga deserves a full biographical treatment that balances text and context, while paying careful attention to the multiple dimensions of his life. At its core, *Arthur Ashe, A Life* tells the story of an African American tennis player who overcame enormous obstacles to become one of the most successful and influential athletes of the twentieth century. Yet it also examines the lives of hundreds of other supporting characters—all connected in some way with Ashe's struggle and ascent. Written in the form of a braided narrative, the analysis twists and turns through a series of interrelated stories involving Ashe, his contemporaries, and the profound economic, social, cultural, and political changes that marked the half century following the close of World War II.

These stories developed against a complex backdrop that included militarization and the Cold War, the African American freedom struggle, major waves of feminism and antiwar sentiment, wrenching challenges to the industrial order, consumption on an unprecedented level, revolutionary changes in the role of television and mass media, and the maturation of celebrity, sports, and leisure as all-encompassing phenomena. Accordingly, this book presents an extended meditation on three of the most important themes in modern American history—the consequences of racial discrimination, the movement to overcome that discrimination, and the emergence of professional sports as a dominating cultural and commercial force.

The general outline of Ashe's life is well known. He has not been forgotten, and invoking his name still triggers recognition and respect among millions of tennis fans, especially among those who are African American. His legacy lives on in several organizations that he helped to found, including the Association of Tennis Professionals and the National Junior Tennis Learning Network. Indeed, with his continuing presence on television—either in the documentaries that often appear on ESPN, HBO, or Tennis Channel, or in the annual tributes accompanying broadcasts of the U.S. Open matches played at Arthur Ashe Stadium—the situation could hardly be otherwise.

What has been missing, however, is access to the intricate web of his life—to the tangled strands of experience accumulated over nearly half a century. Today, twenty-five years after Ashe's death in 1993, the absence of a full-scale biographical treatment is striking. With this in mind, I offer *Arthur Ashe, A Life* as an attempt to do justice to the nuances and subtleties of a personal saga worthy of our full attention. Such books were once a rarity in the historical literature on sports. But in recent years there has been a proliferation of carefully crafted sports biographies, several of which deal with African American athletes. The best of these "black" biographies—studies of Hank Aaron, Willie Mays, Jesse Owens, Joe Louis, Satchel Paige, Muhammad Ali, Roberto Clemente, Jackie Robinson, Sugar Ray Robinson, and Bill Russell—have placed individual experiences in the broader context of American history, illuminating the frequently overlooked cultural dimension of the national struggle for civil rights.[1]

Books on figures from the realms of baseball, basketball, and boxing dominate this list, while many other sports, including tennis, are conspicuous by their absence. The closest we have come to a major tennis biography are Frank Deford's groundbreaking *Big Bill Tilden* (1976), Susan Ware's excellent *Game, Set, Match: Billie Jean King and the Revolution in Women's Sports* (2011), and Chris Bowers's recently published *Federer* (2016).[2]

Fortunately, the tennis world has produced a number of candid and revealing autobiographies, including no fewer than four by Arthur Ashe. Each
of Ashe's published memoirs has been instrumental to my reconstruction of
his life, and collectively *Advantage Ashe* (1967), *Arthur Ashe: Portrait in Motion* (1975), *Off the Court* (1981), and *Days of Grace: A Memoir* (1993) provide
an indispensable view of his saga on and off the court. Spaced throughout his
adult life, they allow us to gauge change over time and the evolution of both
his private persona and expanding role as a public figure.[3]

Ashe's memoirs complement the wealth of archival material in the Arthur Ashe Papers located at the New York Public Library's Schomburg Center for Research in Black Culture—as well as the material gleaned from more
than one hundred interviews with individuals who knew him well. Together
these sources make it possible for a biographer to give voice to a man who has
been dead for a quarter century. Whenever possible, I have allowed Arthur to
speak for himself. Quoting liberally from his published writings, I have tried
to recapture the texture and meaning of his experiences, from his early years
in Richmond to his final days as a public intellectual and activist holding
forth on a range of important social and political issues.

After eight years of immersing myself in the details of Ashe's life, I am
more convinced than ever that his unique story is worth telling. As one of the
first black sports celebrities to be valued not only for his athletic accomplishments but also for his intellectual prowess and moral stature, he occupies
an important position in the interrelated history of race and sports. In his
ability to represent the best of what the sports world could offer to a nation
in dire need of real heroes, he had no peer during his lifetime. And sadly,
during the past twenty-five years—despite a measure of progress on several
fronts—no one has emerged to take his place. In this sense, he resembles the
irreplaceable Martin Luther King Jr., a man whom he revered and tried to
emulate. Uniqueness is a grossly overused word in the modern lexicon, but
sometimes it is appropriate. Sometimes remarkable individuals from unexpected sources such as the streets of Jim Crow Richmond or Atlanta soar
above the rest of us and point the way to a brighter future. Arthur Ashe was
such a man.

PROLOGUE

∎

I T WAS LATE JUNE 1955, and a boys and girls tournament sponsored by
the all-black American Tennis Association (ATA) was about to begin on
the public courts at Turkey Thicket Park, in the University Heights section
of Northeast Washington, D.C. One girl eager to play that day was Doris
Cammack—an up-and-coming fifteen-year-old harboring dreams of becoming the next Althea Gibson—the talented young woman from Harlem
who six years earlier had become the first black female to breach the color
line in competitive tennis. A victory in the Washington tournament would
solidify Doris's ranking as a regional star, but as the first round began she
faced an unexpected problem. On that sultry Saturday morning in June, her
dreams took a tumble when she learned an odd number of competitors had
registered for the girls draw, leaving her with no girl to play in the opening
round. Her only option, the ATA organizers explained, was to play a first-
round exhibition match against an eleven-year-old boy borrowed from the
male draw.

Though disappointed, Doris reluctantly agreed to the unusual arrangement. Yet when she saw how small and scrawny her opponent actually was—a boy with arms as thin as the handle of his wooden racket—she
balked. "I'm not playing against *him*," she sneered, convinced she had been

set up as a foil in what would almost certainly be a farcical match. Only after sensing that pulling out of the match would hurt the little boy's feelings—and after being assured by ATA officials that he was "pretty good"—did she agree to take the court against her four-foot-eight-inch, seventy-pound opponent.

What happened next stunned the small crowd of spectators that had gathered to watch an impromptu battle of the sexes. Brandishing amazing foot speed and a slingshot forehand that allowed him to hit the ball with surprising power and accuracy, the little boy took poor Doris to the proverbial cleaners. Losing only a handful of games, he needed less than an hour to win two sets and the match. Doris did her best to smile in defeat as she walked to the net and reached down to shake the boy's hand, but whatever confidence she had mustered before the match was gone. A few weeks later she gave up her ATA dreams altogether, disabused of any notion that she would find glory on a tennis court.

Little Art, as he was known then, was polite and respectful in victory, just as his parents had taught him to be. Yet he also felt the full flush of victory, even at the age of eleven. Soon his aspirations would move beyond mere victory as he began to dream of becoming a tennis star, but he never lost his manners or his sportsmanship—or, for that matter, his boyish enthusiasm for a game that brought him so much joy and satisfaction. Years later, Doris, who kept close tabs on her young conqueror's path to stardom, had difficulty keeping her composure when recounting her brief brush with a life ultimately marked as much by tragedy as by triumph. While laughing at the story of her own demise as a competitive tennis player, she could not help but tear up when recalling the fate of Arthur Ashe, a valiant and courageous man who would succumb to complications related to AIDS at the age of forty-nine.[1]

Nearly forty years after Doris Cammack's humiliation and more than a decade after the close of his storied career, Arthur found himself at the center of a more serious but equally telling scene unfolding in the nation's capital. This time he was in Washington to participate in a protest march outside the White House. The issue that had drawn him there was the mistreatment of Haitian refugees by immigration and law enforcement officials representing the administration of President George H. W. Bush. Randall Robinson—who grew up with Arthur in Richmond and later collaborated with him on issues related to Africa, race, and colonialism—had asked his old friend to come, and Arthur, loyal to a fault, could not in good conscience say no. Jointly sponsored by the NAACP and Robinson's twenty-year-old organization TransAfrica, the protest march drew a diverse group of two thousand participants and resulted in nearly one hundred arrests. Only one of those arrested was a sports celebrity. For years, Ashe had urged his fellow athletes to speak out on social justice issues, but relatively few had answered his call. In the Haitian protest, he was the lone representative of the sports world—a situation that did not surprise anyone familiar with American politics.

What was surprising, however, was Ashe's decision to take part in the protest even though he knew a terminal disease had reduced his medical condition to the breaking point. For nearly ten years, he had struggled with AIDS, a disease acquired from a blood transfusion administered during recovery from heart surgery in 1983. While he had first learned of his AIDS diagnosis in 1988—and his condition had only been public knowledge for five months at the time of the Washington march—his identification with this dreaded disease had already changed his life beyond recognition. Many of the changes were burdensome, and few observers would have blamed him if he had chosen to retreat from public view, spending what remained of his life with family and close friends.

But withdrawal was never an option for a man who had long identified with civic and social responsibility. Ashe followed his conscience even when it meant putting his comfort—or even his life—at risk. The racial prejudice that inspired the differential treatment of light-skinned Cuban refugees and their dark-skinned counterparts from Haiti was, in his view, simply too malevolent to ignore, whatever the personal consequences of an action against it might be.

Arthur's wife and doctors worried that the trip to Washington would tax his strength beyond acceptable limits—not an unreasonable assumption considering he had lost nearly 20 percent of his weight in the last year, reducing his body to a gaunt 128 pounds hanging on a six-foot-one frame. Unfortunately, his caretakers' fears were soon confirmed. The day after his arrest, and within hours of his return to his home in New York City, he suffered a mild heart attack. Only brief hospitalization was necessary, and his recovery was substantial enough to allow him to live for another five months before succumbing to pneumonia. The Washington episode spoke volumes about the depth of his commitment to active and responsible citizenship. Those who marched with him that day—or anyone else who read the newspaper accounts of his arrest—could not help but admire his determination to stand up for his belief in justice.[2]

These two anecdotes, separated by decades of history and experience, represent a small sample of the stories that make Arthur Ashe's saga one of the most distinctive in American history. No one, it seems safe to say, will ever duplicate his extraordinary life, which could have been conjured by an imaginative novelist. The stories that punctuate his biography are real, however, and both the nation and the world are better for them. The dynamic arc of his experiences—from a childhood of limited promise in the Jim Crow South to iconic status as a world-class athlete—followed an upward and sometimes soaring trajectory of maturation and growth. Never complacent, he had a restless spirit and an ever-searching intellect. Ironically enough, all of this philosophical and experiential turmoil was expressed in a reasoned, deliberate style that became his personal trademark. How he became this man, so calm and poised on the outside yet so driven and turbulent on the inside, is the subject of this book.

ONE

UNDER THE DOMINION

■

ARTHUR ROBERT ASHE JR. entered the world at 12:55 p.m., on July 10, 1943, at St. Phillip Hospital for Negroes, in the city of Richmond, the current capital of the Commonwealth of Virginia and the former capital of the Confederacy. His birth certificate recorded his arrival and clarified his assigned place within the hierarchy of Virginia's centuries-old racial caste system. As the son of Arthur Robert Ashe Sr. and Mattie Cordell Cunningham Ashe, both brown-skinned descendants of African-born slaves, he was classified as a "Negro." Under the laws of the commonwealth, he was a citizen with certain rights and privileges. But, in truth, he was legally consigned to second-class citizenship. Arthur Jr., like 700,000 other "colored" Virginians, had a special status defined by a long list of legal restrictions. Whatever his abilities and talents, there were places where he could not go and things he could not do. As he would learn, there were schools he could not attend, bus and streetcar seats he could not occupy, hospitals where he could not be treated, public parks he could not enter, and even tennis courts upon which he could not play. Born on the cusp of the civil rights revolution, he outlived these and other Jim Crow restrictions. But the indignities of his childhood and adolescence survived long enough to bruise his psyche and complicate his path to personal fulfillment and adulthood. To succeed, he would have to overcome.[1]

Variously known as the "Old Dominion" and the "Land of the Cavaliers,"

Virginia cultivated a distinct mythic identity rooted in a curious mix of aristocratic heritage and republican virtue. The commonwealth's assertive elite evolved from seventeenth-century Royalists into eighteenth-century revolutionaries, before rising and falling as Confederate defenders of slavery and state's rights—and later morphing into the post-Reconstruction and New South architects of Jim Crow. No one, black or white, could grow up in Virginia without acquiring a strong sense of place and a firm realization that history exerted a powerful influence over individuals as well as institutions. Vestiges of the past were everywhere, taking form in grand plantation houses and rustic shacks, historic churches and imposing county courthouses, Confederate monuments and memorialized battlefields. Living in Virginia in the mid-twentieth century as a white person was like living in a sprawling museum dedicated to an array of imposing ancestors, ranging from colonial and revolutionary ghosts to gallant Confederate brigadiers. Heritage and lineage were of paramount importance, especially in Richmond, where the statues of Robert E. Lee, Stonewall Jackson, and Jefferson Davis lined Monument Avenue in a sacred procession of marble reverence. All of this was refracted through the dominant cultural prisms of white supremacist and patriarchal ideology. The thought that a statue of Arthur Ashe, or anyone else of allegedly inferior stock, would ever grace the city's most hallowed avenue was inconceivable in 1943.[2]

Like all small children, Arthur Jr., or Art, as he was often called, had a vague sense of his place in the world during the 1940s. Only later did he learn the hard lessons of race, that his status as a "Negro" defined and limited his prospects for recognized achievement and personal fulfillment. His earliest experiences with whites were actually quite positive, limited as they were to Mr. Paul, the kindly Jewish owner of a nearby corner grocery store ("He even gave us free candy," Ashe recalled), and Claire McCarthy, his father's supervisor in the city parks and recreation department, who "always gave me all the pennies in her pocket" when she stopped by the house to talk with Arthur Sr.

Over time he became acutely aware that most whites were considerably less generous in their dealings with blacks. "Growing up black in the South, for survival and protection your antennae were always out," he observed in 1981. "My grandmother often used the phrase 'good white people' to describe those who helped us. She also talked about 'bad white people'; the ultimate bad people were the Klan—the Ku Klux Klan." He also came to appreciate the significance of his own mixed racial background, as he developed an increasing sensitivity to the nuances of color and class that often determined matters of identity and self-image in his community. "You knew there was something different about being black," he recalled years later, "and it even came down to gradations of skin color within the black community itself. The lighter your skin, the more status you enjoyed in the black community."[3]

He was always grateful to his mother's cousin, Thelma Doswell, for her dogged thirty-year effort "to piece our story together." No ordinary genealogist, Cousin Thelma had "the results of her research painted on a large canvas in her home in Hyattsville, Maryland," where Ashe and other family members sometimes came to marvel at her findings. The family tree carried a special meaning for Ashe, especially in his later years. "For black Americans," he explained in his 1981 memoir, *Off the Court*, "research into our origins is a kind of shield against a barrage of propaganda about our alleged inferiority, our supposed lack of history, our response to the challenge that we should prove ourselves before we can be treated equally."[4]

Ashe took a particular interest in his enslaved ancestors, the most difficult to track. While he was reasonably sure his cousin had correctly traced his maternal ancestry to a slave woman transported from West Africa on HMS *Doddington* and sold at auction in Portsmouth, Virginia, in 1735, it bothered him that "my first American ancestor didn't count enough to record-keepers in the eighteenth century to warrant a name." He knew she was sold to Robert Blackwell, a prosperous Virginia tobacco planter, but he couldn't help but wonder about her ordeal. "I have tried to imagine the terror, rage, and fear of my nameless ancestor," he wrote in *Off the Court*, "born free, captured and transported to a strange and brutal world. I would like to think that she tried to escape, as thousands tried, or that she joined one of the sporadic rebellions that were crushed harshly by masters who could not imagine that blacks were human beings. But along with her name, any record of rebellion or resistance has been lost."[5]

Fortunately, the record was somewhat clearer for the generations that followed, and Ashe was able to recapture the names of several pre–Civil War ancestors, including a Sauk Indian named Mike, who married Jinney Blackwell, the great-great-granddaughter of the nameless woman bought by Robert Blackwell a century earlier. Their son, Hammett Blackwell, born in 1839, would be the first of Ashe's ancestors to experience a measure of freedom after emancipation. By the end of Reconstruction, Hammett and his wife, Julia, had produced nearly two dozen children, including Ashe's great-grandmother Sadie, who raised a large family of her own. Sadie and her husband, Willy Johnson, lived on a small corn and tobacco farm near

Kenbridge, Virginia, fifty miles southwest of Richmond. Among the more fortunate members of the local black community, the landowning Johnsons had high hopes their children would be able to escape the grinding poverty that afflicted most of the black population in south-central Virginia. So they were less than pleased when their young teenage daughter Amelia married Pinkney Avery "Pink" Ashe, a man of questionable reputation almost twice her age.

Born in North Carolina in 1878 and descended from a slave family once owned by Samuel Ashe, the noted Revolutionary War leader and three-term governor of North Carolina, Pink was known as something of a local character in Kenbridge and nearby South Hill. A charming hustler and a restless roamer, he also turned out to be a serial bigamist who ultimately fathered twenty-seven children by a passel of women, some wives and some mistresses. "He was said to be half redskin and half Mexican," his grandson recalled in 1967, repeating family lore. "There could have been some white mixed in too, to make me as light-skinned as I am. Pink's hair was long and black and he wore a huge handlebar moustache. He loved drinks, hijinks, and girls. . . . He didn't mind fights either." For a time, Pink was a good provider, working fairly steadily as a carpenter and a bricklayer, and he stayed with Amelia long enough to father seven children, including Arthur Robert Ashe, born in 1920. But in 1932, just as the Great Depression was tightening its grip on rural Virginia, he abandoned his Lunenberg County family, reportedly to spend time with "another wife in Washington, D.C."[6]

Pink Ashe's departure made hard times even harder for his wife and children. Twelve-year-old Arthur had no choice but to quit school and look for work to help support his brothers and sisters. After three years of struggling to find steady employment in South Hill, he joined the Civilian Conservation Corps (CCC), which trained him as a carpenter, auto mechanic, and jack-of-all-trades. Though essentially illiterate, he gained enough confidence from his experiences in the CCC camps to move to Richmond in the late 1930s. The capital city of nearly 200,000 was also an industrial and commercial center and generally one of the best places in the state to find work. Obtaining gainful employment was never easy for a black teenager, and Arthur soon discovered that Richmond was among the most segregated communities in the South. Divided into racial residential zones, the city practiced an extreme form of codified Jim Crow that maintained cradle-to-grave segregation. The only force providing a measure of mitigation was a strong tradition of paternalism that sometimes benefited individual blacks fortunate enough to secure white patrons.[7]

One such individual was Arthur Ashe Sr., who found work as a chauffeur, butler, and handyman for Charles Gregory, one of Richmond's most prominent Jewish merchants. For five years he served Mr. and Mrs. Gregory, "driving them around the city, or answering the door as butler or waiting at table in a white coat." Eventually, with a little luck and a lot of hard work, he found supplementary employment with several other prominent Jewish families. By 1938, through his attachment to this network of Jewish merchants, he could claim a decent livelihood and a growing circle of influential friends. And he soon added a beautiful young wife to his blessings. One of his weekly tasks for the Gregorys was a laundry drop on Glenburnie Road, "just down the street from the Westwood Baptist Church," and next door to the house of one of Westwood's parishioners, Mattie Cordell Cunningham. Spying "a young, slender brown-skinned woman with long hair hanging her family wash on a clothesline," he somehow found the courage to strike up a conversation. Even though he was Presbyterian and she was Baptist, they soon discovered they had enough in common to form a relationship. A romance blossomed, and several months later they were married in the living room of her mother's house.[8]

The marriage of Arthur and Mattie was, by all accounts, a near perfect match, though it would take the young couple five years to bring their first child into the world. By then, the entire world was at war. On the very day that Arthur Jr. was born, Allied forces under the command of Field Marshal Bernard Montgomery and General George S. Patton landed on the shores of Sicily, initiating the long-awaited invasion of Axis-controlled Europe.

Mobilization for combat energized and transformed Richmond just as it changed virtually every American city. Only the most privileged local citizens carried on with their prewar lives without disruption, but Arthur Jr. was fortunate to be blessed with a family resilient enough to make the best of a turbulent and unsettling time. Like many African Americans, the Ashes dreamed of a "Double Victory"—a twin triumph over totalitarianism abroad and discrimination at home. Their new son, they hoped, would grow up in a postwar society where liberty and justice for all was more than an empty shibboleth.

During the final two years of the war, the Ashes suffered several anxious moments wondering if their frail and sickly son would even make it to the postwar era. Chronically undersized, with arms and legs that resembled pipe stems, Arthur Jr. looked more like a pitiable figure from a refugee camp than a boy destined to become a world-class athlete. In his preschool years, he contracted just about every childhood disease, any one of which might have overwhelmed his seemingly undernourished and unhealthy constitution.

Yet, despite these physical challenges, he was a reasonably happy child, nurtured as he was by a close and loving extended family. Bright and curious, he learned to read by the age of four, thanks to an attentive mother who engendered a lifelong attachment to books and the written word.[9]

Arthur Sr. worked long hours as a chauffeur and handyman to support his wife and child. Mattie, too, worked hard, not only at home but also as a cleaning lady at the Miller and Rhoads department store downtown. Even so, it was tough going financially. Like many young couples in Richmond's black community, the Ashes could not afford to live independently and had no choice but to rely on the kindness of relatives to get by. Until 1947, they shared a house on Brook Road with the family of a favorite uncle, Harry Taylor. This less-than-ideal arrangement allowed for little privacy, but it did ensure that their son would spend his preschool years surrounded by a swarm of cousins, aunts, and uncles.

Brook Road ran north and south along the western edge of Jackson Ward, an overwhelmingly black section of northeast Richmond celebrated as the birthplace of the famous dancer Bill "Bojangles" Robinson (1878–1949). Several blocks north of the Taylors' house, the southern edge of the lily-white neighborhoods of Ginter Park and Lee Ward served as a racial boundary beyond which local blacks rarely ventured. A quarter mile to the east—on the far side of Chamberlayne Avenue, a busy stretch of Route 1/301—the predominantly white neighborhood of Barton Heights marked Jackson Ward's northeastern border. Here the racial demography of the area was dynamic and sometimes even volatile.[10]

For the most part, the black enclave living along or near Brook Road was solidly working-class in its socioeconomic orientation, and there was enough light industry nearby to give the neighborhood a gritty, urban feel. The area was not, however, a slum. "I didn't live in a so-called ghetto situation," Ashe assured the journalist John McPhee in 1968, "I never saw rat-infested houses, never hung out on corners, never saw anyone knifed." Though clearly black and segregated, the northern part of Jackson Ward did not fit the stereotype of inner-city violence or pathology, perhaps in large part because it was situated close enough to Virginia Union College to provide a clear vision of middle-class alternatives.

With its sprawling eighty-four-acre campus and large stone buildings, Virginia Union was the pride of Jackson Ward, the second largest institution of higher learning in the city, surpassed only by the all-white University of Richmond. During the late 1940s, Virginia Union was home to scores of theology graduate students and several hundred undergraduates, including future Virginia governor Douglas Wilder. Symbols of black striving and accomplishment, their presence in the neighborhood would have a profound effect on Arthur Ashe Jr.'s childhood.[11]

Arthur Jr. spent the first seventeen years of his life in Jackson Ward, though his family circumstances changed dramatically in 1947, when his father found steady employment with the city of Richmond as a park manager and security guard in charge of the Brook Field Park, Richmond's largest black park. The job required the family to move a few blocks to the south and to live on the park grounds in what turned out to be splendid isolation. The Ashes' new home at 1610 Sledd Street—a five-room, one-story white-frame building constructed by Arthur Sr. during his first few weeks as a city employee—sat all by itself inside the park. Though modest, the Sledd Street house gave them access to a sprawling eighteen-acre complex that included baseball fields, four tennis courts, and a large swimming pool.

The recreational facilities at Brook Field Park were spartan and run-down by white standards, but for a boy who had never seen Byrd Park or any of the city's other whites-only enclaves, the Ashe family's new domain was, as he later put it, "an athletic paradise, a dream world for a kid who likes sports." The park was often full of black families, especially during the summer months when soaring temperatures drove people outdoors. "The field behind my house was like a huge back yard," Arthur recalled. "I thought it was mine. . . . There was really no reason for me to leave the place. Everybody came to me. The athletic equipment was kept in a box in my house." The biggest attraction was the pool; as one of the few places where local blacks could swim, it was "so full of kids in the summer you couldn't see the water." The park's tennis courts, just a few steps from the Ashes' front porch, were also popular, as were the baseball diamond, the outdoor basketball court, and the sprawling oak-ringed fields where both kids and adults tossed horseshoes and played football.[12]

In May 1948, young Arthur Jr. welcomed a baby brother, Johnnie. Arthur Jr. doted on his younger brother and by his sixth birthday was sharing a small bedroom with him. The five-year gap between the Ashe boys seemed to keep sibling rivalry to a minimum, even though it was obvious they had markedly different personalities. While Arthur was generally quiet and somewhat introverted, Johnnie was outgoing and more prone to mischief. They were also physically different. Next to his stocky and muscular brother, Arthur Jr. appeared rail thin with spindly arms and legs. Only when one looked closely at their faces was it clear they were brothers.

By all accounts, both brothers were happy, well-adjusted children, and the only serious upset in their lives during the first two years at Brook Field was the death of their grandfather Pink Ashe in 1949. Johnnie was too young to know what was going on, and Arthur Jr. had never known his grandfather, who had abandoned his wife and children in the early 1930s. But the old man's passing was a momentous occasion, nonetheless. The funeral at South Hill was Arthur Jr.'s first direct confrontation with death, and years later he recalled the scene as "a very personal and emotional experience for me." The raw images of a grief-stricken family stayed with him. "I don't think I cried," he recalled. "I was only five and a half years old. But I remember my Aunt Lola wailing uncontrollably, 'Daddy, Daddy.' I sat on my mother's lap through the long, highly emotional service, and I remember peering into the coffin at my grandfather. I can still see that thick mane of gray hair and the full mustache."[13]

With his wandering, self-serving ways, Pink Ashe had forfeited his status as the family patriarch. But his unusual saga remained an important part of family lore. He became a kind of antihero whose missteps reinforced parental lessons of propriety and self-control. Arthur Ashe Sr. represented the antithesis of the colorful wastrel Pink Ashe, but he, too, had his limitations as a father. Emotionally stern and largely consumed by work and the task of providing for his family, he did not supply much emotional support for his young sons. "There was little gray in my father's world," his son recalled years later. "His rules were black or white, right or wrong, without regard to race, and there was a time when I actually feared him. . . . Go get my belt, he would say if I returned late from school or forgot a chore. The belt could have been a strap in a barbershop; it was thirty-nine inches long, at least an eighth of an inch thick, and first-quality cowhide. Only grade-A leather would do for my behind." For a less severe male authority figure, six-year-old Arthur Jr. would have to turn to one of his uncles—or find someone outside the family, which is exactly what he did during the late summer of 1949.[14]

During the final weeks before he entered the first grade, Arthur Jr. had the good fortune to meet a young man by the name of Ron Charity, an eighteen-year-old Virginia Union student who frequented the courts that adjoined the Ashes' yard. Considered one of the best black tennis players in the Richmond area, Charity often played or practiced at Brook Field, where he sometimes gave lessons to younger players. Just a few yards away on the front porch where he liked to sit and read, Arthur Jr. could not help but notice the activity on the courts, especially when Charity was there with the Virginia Union tennis team or with members of the Richmond Racquet Club, a small but growing organization dominated by some of the city's most prominent black professionals. At first, the young boy was too shy to move close to the action, but on one memorable occasion he left the porch and joined a small crowd that had gathered to watch Charity and his Virginia Union teammates play an intercollegiate match. When Charity completely dominated his overmatched opponent, drawing loud cheers from the local rooters, even a six-year-old who knew next to nothing about the game of tennis was impressed. Exposed to the mystique of competitive tennis at such a tender age, he was all but hooked.

The fateful aftermath of Ashe's first encounter with Charity was seared in his memory:

> The next afternoon, he was out on the courts again, working on his serve. I watched for a while. Finally, he noticed me for the first time. "What's your name? Arthur Ashe, Junior. Your dad runs the playground? Yes, sir." He nodded and went back to his serve. His wooden racquet flashed high above his head in the late afternoon sun and sliced through the silence. White balls rocketed to the corners of the opposite court. After a while, he stopped and looked at me again. "You play tennis?" I shrugged. I had batted some old tennis balls around with the twelve-dollar nylon-strung racquet that had found its way into the wooden equipment box under my bedroom window. "You want to learn?" I nodded. At that age, any sport was a challenge I felt I could master. "You got a racquet. Go get it," he said.[15]

At first, Arthur Jr., a fifty-pound stripling who could barely hit the ball over the net, was in no position to master anything. But in the weeks and months that followed, he improved enough to sustain both his interest in tennis and the personal bond with his new friend and mentor. Charity came to regard him as his pet project, teaching his undersized but enthusiastic pupil the basic rules of the game, how to grip the racket Eastern forehand style ("the best grip for beginners"), and how to maximize his power by hitting the ball using a "slingshot" motion with an exaggerated backswing. Largely self-taught with no formal training as a coach, Charity had little concern for classic form. He simply wanted Arthur Jr. to play well enough to enjoy the game and feel good about his efforts on the court. Only later did he begin to realize that this scrawny little kid had the potential to become an accomplished player.[16]

Tennis was fun, but to please his coach Arthur Jr. had to adhere to regimen of concentration and studied practice. Indeed, the value and importance of practice and discipline were the primary lessons that he took with him to the first grade classroom at Baker Street Grammar School, where he soon became a model student. With Charity's encouragement and with his father's precepts ringing in his ears, he went off to school with strict orders to obey the teacher's commands without hesitation or questioning. Unfailing obedience was required at home, and his father expected nothing less when his son was under a teacher's supervision. As Ashe recalled, "Daddy expected me to bring top grades from school. I got straight A's to the sixth grade. The dark day I got my first B, I thought sure he would spank me." After he became an adult, Ashe loved to tell the story of how his father even monitored his daily trips to and from school: "When I entered Baker Street grammar school, Daddy walked with me at my gait, and timed how long it took: ten minutes. I had to be home every day 'immediately'—which meant ten minutes, not eleven, after school let out. This rule lasted through high school. I never dared break it." [17]

Fortunately, Arthur Sr.'s absolutist approach to parental guidance was tempered by the mediating influence of his warm and generous wife. Mattie Ashe, known to her friends as "Baby," seemed to bring out the best in her husband, smoothing his rough edges with patience and understanding. And she displayed the same gentleness with her sons, providing a sense of security and sweetness that enveloped the Ashe household. Blessed with a solid and loving marriage, the Ashes looked forward to raising a large family and growing old together.

But it was not to be. During the winter of 1950, the joy of Mattie Ashe's third pregnancy turned into a medical nightmare. A deteriorating gynecological condition compounded by high blood pressure led to an emergency surgery that triggered a massive stroke. When she died three days later, on March 23, her grief-stricken husband returned home to explain the unexplainable to his two sons. Their mother was gone, and she wasn't coming back. Years later Arthur recalled the image of his father "crying uncontrollably after he returned from the hospital. . . . He woke Johnny and me, picked us out of the bunkbeds we shared, put my brother on his knee, squeezed me tightly, and told us that Mama had died. 'This is all I got left,' he kept repeating. 'This is all I got left.'" The wake and public viewing held at the Brook Field house also left Arthur with a strong memory of a grieving family and community and a parting image of his mother: "Mama's coffin sat in the middle of our living room, open so mourners could pay their last respects. She lay inside, wearing her best pink satin dress and holding a red rose in her right hand. Roses were her favorite flowers, and Daddy had planted rose bushes around our little front porch to please her. He must have cut the funeral rose that morning, and put it in her hand. Daddy lifted me to kiss her on the forehead for the last time." [18]

Arthur Jr. chose not to attend the funeral, however, even though his father offered to take him. "I don't know why, but I said no," he explained with some puzzlement in his 1981 memoir. "It wasn't an emphatic or emotional response, just a matter of fact 'no.' I've tried to reach whatever feelings I had at the time, but all I can remember is a certain distance from the rush of unexpected events that turned our lives inside out." [19]

As an adult, Ashe repeatedly tried to recapture his feelings about his mother's death. "When I think of my mother, the strongest feeling I get is regret," he confessed in 1981. "I can remember her reading to me and encouraging me to learn. . . . But I can't remember her voice, I can't remember how she felt, smelled, or tasted. More than once, I've longed for a memory of my mother that seems just beyond my grasp." [20]

This longing ultimately drove him to seek out a psychiatrist's help, as he explained in his 1993 memoir, *Days of Grace*. "I knew I had to start with that figure of a woman dressed in a blue corduroy bathrobe who watched me eat breakfast one morning in 1950 and then went off to die and left me alone. In search of her, I found myself going where I would never set foot: into a psychiatrist's office." During several visits and nearly a dozen hours on the analyst's couch, he explored the mixture of shock and detachment that characterized his response to his mother's death and came to the conclusion that the cool, aloof quality that seemed to dominate his adult personality was rooted in childhood trauma. "For a long time now," he wrote a decade after the psychiatric sessions, "I have understood that this quality of emotional distance in me, my aloofness or coldness—whatever the name I or others give to it—may very well have something to do with the early loss of my mother. I have never thought of myself as being cheated by her death, but I am terribly, insistently, aware of an emptiness in my soul that only she could have filled.[21]

For a time, Arthur Jr.'s grieving father shared this emptiness. But an acute sense of responsibility for his children's welfare was a steadying influence. Above all else, he was a strong-willed man who kept his pledges, including a heartfelt promise to his wife the night before her operation. "I didn't bring them into this world to farm out," she informed him. "They're your children. I brought them into the world for you, so promise me that you'll raise them yourself." With a large extended family close by, the option of turning the children over to an aunt or a sister-in-law was tempting for a man with a full-time job. But, after a brief period of separation when Arthur Jr. and Johnnie went to live with an aunt and uncle, he honored his promise by scraping up enough money to hire a live-in housekeeper to manage the house and take care of his children. He needed a reliable helper, and a source of stability for his sons, and that is what he got in Mrs. Olis Berry, a childless widow in her early seventies who moved into the house in the spring of 1950 and stayed for fourteen years. A compassionate and good-natured woman, Mrs. Berry got along well with her employer and treated the Ashe children as if they were her own.[22]

Despite Mrs. Berry's efforts and strong support from friends and family, being a widower was tough for Arthur Sr., and his personality became more austere and inflexible following his wife's death. This harder edge did not detract from his working life at the park, where it was often advantageous to be an imposing authority figure. But at home his no-nonsense approach to life and his somber moods meant less laughter and more tears for his motherless sons. The impact on six-year-old Arthur Jr. was especially obvious, and some relatives became concerned he was becoming increasingly shy and withdrawn. "Arthur was so small and pathetic," one aunt lamented. "He looked like a motherless child. It about near broke my heart." There was no misbehavior and no acting out, and he continued to do well in school. But he talked less and read more, and his only source of solace seemed to be the pile of books that reminded him of his mother.

Three months after his mother's death, the only person who could reach him emotionally and draw him out of his shell was Ron Charity. Tennis, it turned out, was the antidote to the young boy's melancholy. The Ashe family did not know quite what to make of Arthur Jr.'s peculiar passion for a game that had little connection to their own lives and culture. But everyone was pleased and relieved that he had found something to ease his adjustment to life in a single-parent household. Arthur Sr. had never had much time for athletics, organized or otherwise, and preferred to spend his leisure time hunting or fishing. Yet he recognized the value of his son's new interest, which had the added benefit of keeping him close to home. Working hard, keeping busy, and staying close to home were the basic precepts of his parental advice. "There's to be no hanging around," he liked to say. "If you don't have to be somewhere you should be home."

As long as schoolwork and daily chores occupied most of his son's time, he was willing to tolerate a few hours of outdoor play on the nearby courts of Brook Field.[23]

By the time eight-year-old Arthur Jr. had completed the third grade, in June 1952, devotion to tennis had become an essential element of his identity. Along with his love of reading, it was his most distinguishing characteristic, the thing that separated him from the other boys and girls at the Baker Street Grammar School. He had become, as he later put it, "the little boy who could play tennis." No one else in his circle of friends was all that interested in tennis. Only "Little Ashe," as he was often called, spent almost every afternoon hitting and volleying with anyone, young or old, willing to join him on the court. And when he wasn't on the court or on the sidelines listening intently to Charity's instructions, he was often slamming ball after ball against a nearby backboard. "He was so eager to succeed," Virginia Union's longtime tennis coach John Watson recalled years later, "that he would get out of bed every morning at 5 o'clock, winter and summer, rain and shine, and before breakfast he would hit 1,000 tennis balls. One thousand. Think about that." According to Douglas Wilder, the future Virginia governor who grew up in Jackson Ward and who was twelve years older than Arthur, the young enthusiast's habit of monopolizing the backboard did not go over very well with some of the older boys in the neighborhood. On several occasions, he remembered with some embarrassment: "We told him to get out of the way and literally ran him off the court."[24]

All of this hard work began to pay off during the summer of 1952. Though still limited by his height and small frame—"the racket was almost as tall as he was," Wilder recalled—Arthur had clearly become the best nine-year-old player in the neighborhood and even found himself playing as well as or better than some of the older kids that he encountered in Charity's group lessons. Charity encouraged him to test himself against kids who were much larger and stronger than he was, assuring him that his quick reflexes and timing would prove to be an equalizer. Early in the summer, Charity convinced him to enter a Brook Field youth tournament, where Ashe got his first formal taste of defeat at the hands of eleven-year-old John Gordon Jr., the future tennis coach at Virginia Union. Though disappointed, he had discovered the allure of head-to-head competition. Soon thereafter he entered several similar tournaments at other black parks in Richmond and actually won some of his matches. Thrilled by this turn of events, two of his favorite relatives, his Aunt Marie and Uncle E. J. Cunningham, bought him an expensive racket for his ninth birthday.

The $22.50 price tag was steep by the standards of an economically pressed black community, and Arthur Sr. was not sure he approved of such extravagance. But this was only the beginning of an improbable adventure that would take his son well beyond the economic and social boundaries of the Ashe family's experiences.[25]

TWO

PLAYING IN THE SHADOWS

■

F OR GENERATIONS ASHE'S ANCESTORS had lived behind an
invisible wall of discrimination and prejudice, a barrier reinforced by
custom, law, and a long legacy of fear and intimidation. Arthur Jr. would become the first of his line to breach this barrier, primarily because he learned
to strike a white tennis ball better than just about anyone else. In the early
1950s, prior to the full flowering of the civil rights movement, no one but a
clairvoyant could have foreseen tennis as a means of escape into the white
world. Certainly no one in Richmond, black or white, would have made such
a prediction.

When Ashe first began to play, tennis courts were among the most segregated places in the city. Despite a long list of local segregation laws, casual contact between blacks and whites was relatively common—on public
sidewalks, in downtown shops, on factory floors, in the aisles of city buses.
But there were certain places in all Southern cities where blacks knew they
could not go. As far as tennis was concerned, blacks could play at Brook
Field Park or at several of the city's other black parks, or perhaps at one of
the two courts at Virginia Union. But that was it. The rest of the city's tennis
facilities, including the sixteen public courts at Byrd Park and the private
courts at the elegant Country Club of Virginia, were reserved for whites. The
whites-only policy had been in force as long as tennis had been played, and
no one in the black community seemed inclined to challenge these restrictive

practices—no one, that is, until Bill Taylor showed up at Byrd Park in the summer of 1952 with his eight-year-old cousin in tow. "Little Ashe," all fifty pounds of him, was interested in registering for the upcoming youth tournament at the park. Sam Woods, the director of the park, turned the boys away, though he reportedly did so as gently as he could. "I would love to have you," Arthur remembered him saying. "But the time isn't right. The tennis patrons won't allow Negroes." Too young to be angry or embarrassed, Arthur simply giggled and admonished his cousin: "I told you they wouldn't let me in." [1]

When Ron Charity heard about his pupil's disappointment at Byrd Park, he decided to press the matter with Woods. Known as "Mr. Tennis" in Richmond, Woods had been running the Byrd Park junior development program since 1943, earning a reputation not only as a successful coach, but also as a kind, respectful man. Born into a family of missionaries, he was the most approachable white official in Richmond's parks department and the most likely to bend the rules for a good cause. Unfortunately, even he did not dare challenge the sanctity of segregation. Later that summer, and in the years that followed, Charity would make repeated attempts to register Arthur in Byrd Park tournaments. Each time the application was politely but firmly turned down. Byrd Park remained segregated until 1962, the year before Woods's death, and Richmond's private tennis clubs held out for years after that. Even in the late 1960s, long after Arthur had left the city and achieved fame in the wider tennis world, Charity was still bumping up against the local color bar. Each year he submitted an application to play in the Richmond city tournament held at the Country Club of Virginia only to be rejected without explanation or apology. "I don't want to go into their clubhouse or their shower room," he once complained to his former pupil. "I don't want to buy a Coke at their refreshment stand. I just want to play in the tournament, see how many guys I can beat, then leave." [2]

As someone who had spent his entire life in the shadowy world of Jim Crow, Charity could not have been surprised by the intransigence of Richmond's white tennis establishment. He knew that tennis had always been among the whitest and most class-bound of games. Originally an indoor game played in stone cloisters by medieval monks, kings, and nobles, tennis evolved into the outdoor game of lawn tennis with little loss of status. Brought to the United States from Great Britain in 1874, late-Victorian lawn tennis was played almost exclusively at private clubs, where restrictive membership policies and stiff membership fees excluded all but the most privileged whites. By the end of the nineteenth century, the carefully manicured courts at Boston's

Longwood Cricket Club, the Philadelphia Cricket Club, and New York's West Side Tennis Club at Forest Hills had become important symbols of the Gilded Age elite's increasingly decadent sporting life.

The nature of the game reinforced its exclusivity. With no equivalent to sandlot baseball or impromptu football matches on vacant fields, tennis required special equipment and a special venue. Even so, with the introduction of low-maintenance concrete courts at the turn of the century, the game soon spread to public parks, schools, and colleges. The expanding popularity of the game over the next twenty years brought a measure of democratization, but much of this expansion was limited to recreational tennis. With few exceptions, the world of competitive tennis remained a bastion of upper-class, white Anglo-Saxon Protestant culture.[3]

Since the organization's founding in 1881, the United States Lawn Tennis Association (USLTA) had been the primary guarantor of exclusivity, especially at the upper levels of the game. The association's board, which oversaw the rules for tournament play, maintained strict standards of etiquette, attire, and admission. Among these standards was a strict color bar. When they stipulated a "whites only" policy, they were talking about more than proper court attire. Technically, the leaders of the USLTA did not have the power to bar blacks from the nation's public courts, except when USLTA-sponsored tournaments were involved. But they set an example of racial discrimination that often spilled over into the public sphere. In the early-twentieth-century South, blacks were legally barred from most public parks and shunted off to black-only facilities, very few of which had tennis courts. Even in the North, blacks often had difficulty finding places to play.[4]

Tennis had no mass appeal among African Americans during these years. Within the black middle class, however, there was a small but growing subculture of tennis enthusiasts. Mostly professionals and businessmen, the few blacks drawn to the game regarded tennis as more than an enjoyable pastime; it also had an alluring aura of elevated status and upward mobility. Playing the game that rich white folks played brought a certain satisfaction and a welcome opportunity to challenge the low expectations of black achievement. It would have been even more satisfying, no doubt, if black tennis players had been allowed to compete with whites and beat them at their own game.

Black players had no choice but to form their own parallel institutions. By the 1890s, private black tennis clubs had been established in several Northern cities, leading to an inaugural interstate tournament in Philadelphia in 1898. Other small tournaments followed, and in the decade prior to

World War I the largest clubs began to contemplate the creation of a national organization to promote black tennis. During the week following Thanksgiving, on November 30, 1916, representatives from more than a dozen clubs met in Washington, D.C., to form the American Tennis Association (ATA). The association's charter did not limit its memberships to blacks, but the clear intent was to hold an annual national tournament that would showcase the skills of the best black players in the nation, either at public parks in the North or at one of several historically black colleges.

In August 1917, thirty-nine players from thirty-three different clubs gathered at Druid Hill Park in Baltimore for the first ATA tournament. Both men and women competed, with Tally Holmes winning the men's singles championship, and Lucy Slowe the women's title. Holmes, who repeated as champion in 1918 when the tournament was held in New York City, went on to win two more ATA singles championships, in 1921 and 1924. White America took no notice of their skills or accomplishments, but as the ATA became an established entity, the black press reported every match, treating Holmes and other black champions as celebrities.[5]

Over time the ATA national tournaments became more than mere sporting events. By the 1930s they had become recognizable symbols of community and racial pride. As the players and their families turned the annual gatherings into major social events, incorporating everything from banquets to fashion shows into the mix of activities, black colleges vied for the right to host the tournament. Normally held in the North, the tournament moved to the South for the first time in 1927, to the Hampton Institute in Virginia. By 1940, the ATA represented 145 black tennis clubs.[6]

The leaders of the ATA had a lot to be proud of after twenty-five years of effort. Working within the limits of racial exclusion, the organization had created a structure that heightened the profile of tennis in a number of black communities across the country. Unfortunately, it had done so almost entirely within the narrow boundaries of the black middle class. Black tennis had acquired all of the trappings of the black bourgeoisie but no means of reaching out to the broader African American community. Even more disturbing to some, the organization had made relatively little headway in raising the overall caliber of play among its members. By the late 1930s Joe Louis had conquered the world of heavyweight boxing, Jesse Owens had won four gold medals in track and field at the Berlin Olympics, and Satchel Paige and his barnstorming Negro League all-stars had proven, at least to some, that they deserved to be on the same field with the best Major League ballplayers. There was no comparable evidence of progress or achievement in black tennis.[7]

While the ATA had established a small beachhead on the outer fringe of the tennis world, it had yet to penetrate the competitive core of the sport— or to advance the likelihood that black players would ever reach the upper echelons of the game. In tennis, far more than in baseball, the problem of restricted access was compounded by a chronic lack of readiness. Many black tennis players had superior athletic ability, mental toughness, and a love for the game. But success at the highest levels of tennis also required good coaching, attention to fundamentals, years of practice, and sustained competition against top-flight players on a variety of surfaces—all of which were in short supply in the world of black tennis. One of the biggest problems among black players was their delayed entry into the sport. Prior to the 1950s, there were no junior development programs for young black tennis players. By the time they became serious about tennis, most of their white counterparts had been playing for a decade or more.

There was little chance of overcoming these problems without first dismantling the rigid system of racial segregation that dominated both the game of tennis and American society at large. Regrettably, such a dismantling would not become a realistic goal until the maturation of a national civil rights movement in the late 1950s and early 1960s. Accordingly, ATA leaders rarely challenged the strictures of Jim Crow during the organization's early decades, though some of the most talented members yearned to test their skills against players of all races.[8]

Very few, of course, were able to do so. Prior to World War II, other than occasional casual matches on public courts in the North, integrated competitive tennis was limited to a few college campuses. The number of black players involved in mainstream intercollegiate tennis could probably be counted on one hand. Dick Hudlin, later one of Arthur Ashe's coaches, played for the University of Chicago in the mid-1920s, and Reginald Weir, the winner of five ATA national singles titles, played at the City College of New York in the 1930s. During the late 1940s, Weir competed in the previously all-white USLTA National Indoor Championships, and Bob Ryland of Wayne State University became the first black from an integrated college or university to participate in the National Collegiate Athletic Association (NCAA) tennis championships. Their experiences were certainly noteworthy, and Hudlin was even selected as captain of the University of Chicago team in 1924. But in general there was very little progress in opening NCAA tennis competition to black players prior to the 1960s.

For the vast majority of black collegians, the only option was to compete in the all-black Colored (later changed to Central) Intercollegiate Athletic

Association (CIAA). Founded in 1912, the CIAA organized competition among several dozen historically black colleges and universities, including Richmond's Virginia Union. While institutions such as Fisk and Howard had fielded intercollegiate tennis teams since the beginning of the twentieth century, tennis had always been a minor sport on black campuses. Underfunded and underappreciated, black intercollegiate tennis did not offer much in the way of coaching or financial aid. The on-campus tennis facilities at CIAA schools ranged from poor to nonexistent, and many teams were forced to play in public parks such as Brook Field. The level of competition suffered accordingly, but for many young black players, including Ron Charity, college tennis was literally the only game in town.[9]

The segregated world of black tennis that Charity entered in the mid-1940s offered limited opportunities for improvement or advancement. But there were hopeful signs of change as the nation approached mid-century. Nothing in the tennis world was as dramatic as the signing of the black football stars Woody Strode and Kenny Washington by the Los Angeles Rams in 1946, or Jackie Robinson's sudden ascent to the Brooklyn Dodgers a year later. But there were clearly cracks in the Jim Crow mold that had consigned generations of black tennis players to second-class status and exclusion.

One of the first hints of change came in 1939, when Bob Ryland won the Illinois state high school singles title, defeating Jimmy Evert, the future father of tennis great Chris Evert, in the finals. The product of an interracial marriage—his father was an Irish American—the light-skinned Ryland was a Chicago native who moved to Mobile, Alabama, as a small child. Returning to Chicago at the age of twelve, he soon became one of the city's best young players. His victory in the state tournament, the first ever for an African American, was a cause for celebration among his black peers. The timing of his unprecedented triumph was perfect, coming just a few weeks after Marian Anderson's groundbreaking concert at the Lincoln Memorial. While Ryland's achievement received much less attention than the black Philadelphian's symbolic triumph over the white supremacists of the Daughters of the American Revolution who turned her away from Washington's Constitution Hall, it was welcome news in the black tennis world.[10]

A second hopeful development occurred a year later, in July 1940, when the ATA-affiliated Cosmopolitan Club of Harlem hosted an interracial exhibition match between the reigning ATA singles champion, Jimmie McDaniel, and Don Budge, the nation's top professional player. Two years earlier, while still an amateur, Budge had become the first player to capture the Grand Slam, winning Wimbledon and the national championships of France, Australia, and the United States in the same year. One of tennis's first superstars, he had signed a lucrative endorsement contract with Wilson Sporting Goods Company, which sponsored the match against McDaniel. Fortunately, as a professional, Budge did not need permission from the racially conservative USLTA.

With an overflow crowd of more than two thousand in attendance, the match was a commercial success and a convincing triumph for Budge, who defeated the seemingly overmatched McDaniel in straight sets 6–1, 6–2. Budge was gracious in victory, assuring the crowd after the match that "Jimmy is a very good player. I'd say he'd rank with the first 10 of our white players. And with some more practice against players like me, maybe he could some day beat all of them." Predictably, some white observers interpreted the results as confirmation that even the best black players were not up to white standards. But others pointed out that the Cosmopolitan Club's clay court put McDaniel, a Californian accustomed to fast hard surfaces, at a distinct disadvantage. Writing in the *New York Herald Tribune*, veteran sportswriter Al Laney insisted, "it is not quite fair to McDaniel or to Negro tennis in general to judge by this one match. It must be remembered that he was playing before his own people as their champion against a man nobody in the world can beat."[11]

The Cosmopolitan Club event also featured a doubles match pitting Budge and former ATA champion Reginald Weir against McDaniel and Richard Cohen, the ATA's top-ranked doubles team. The spirited match reinforced the precedent of interracial play, setting the stage for a second exhibition match at the 1941 ATA national tournament in Tuskegee, Alabama, bringing organized interracial play to the Deep South for the first time.[12]

The idea of enlisting professional players to desegregate American tennis resurfaced three years later when the Cosmopolitan Club hosted a provocative exhibition featuring two of the world's best white female professionals, Alice Marble of California and Mary Hardwick of Great Britain. Each of the women was paired with a male ATA player, Hardwick with Weir, and Marble with Ryland. Since winning the Illinois high school title, Ryland had joined the Army, which issued him a special leave to participate in the exhibition. "I was the No. 1 seed in the ATA then, and the army thought it would be good publicity to send me to New York for the match," Ryland recalled. "It was two black men and two white women, but we were in Harlem, so the army didn't worry about anyone getting upset. We couldn't have done that in the South, though." He might have added that in 1944 playing mixed doubles across racial lines would have been frowned upon almost every-where in the United States, and the fact that Marble was a beautiful blonde widely regarded as professional tennis's most alluring female increased the potential for controversy.[13]

This daring social experiment would not be repeated for several years. But the immediate postwar era brought other signs of progress. In 1945, the recently discharged Ryland enrolled at Wayne State University in Detroit and promptly helped the university's tennis squad to qualify for the NCAA tournament. Advancing to the quarterfinals before losing, he returned to the tournament in 1946 but lost in the third round to future Wimbledon champion Bob Falkenburg of the University of Southern California (USC). Two years later, George Stewart of South Carolina State, the reigning ATA singles champion, became the second black player to participate in college tennis's most important tournament.[14]

The NCAA had no formal policy banning black athletes, just a long tradition that reinforced demographic norms on overwhelmingly white campuses. ATA officials were confident that black tennis players would eventually gain greater acceptance and visibility in the upper echelons of intercollegiate tennis, but they were less sanguine, however, about eliminat-ing the color bar in the much larger world of USLTA events. Even so, they found some encouragement in the postwar years from a selective relaxing of the USLTA's whites-only policy in some Northern and Western communi-ties. In New York and California a few blacks began to play in tournaments held in public parks, and in March 1948 Weir became the first ATA member to participate in a national USLTA tournament.

The historic breakthrough came at the National Indoor Champion-ships, held at the Seventh Avenue Armory in midtown Manhattan. "Here-tofore entries from players of the Negro race have never been accepted for a national tennis championship," *The New York Times* reported, carefully quoting Alrick H. Man Jr., the obviously nervous chair of the tournament committee. "We thought, in view of his showing in the Eastern champi-onship," Man explained, "that he should be permitted to play. This does not mean that we are speaking officially for the U.S.L.T.A. or that we are establishing a precedent to be followed necessarily in other tournaments. It is simply a decision of this group." With the national USLTA board looking the other way, Weir played two matches without incident, losing to the top-seeded Tony Trabert in the second round.[15]

Five months later, in August 1948, American tennis reached a second milestone when eighteen-year-old Oscar Johnson became the first black player to win a national USLTA-sanctioned title. Two years earlier, at the age of sixteen, Johnson had won the Pacific Coast Junior title in both singles and doubles and had gone on to repeat the feat twice. He also led his Los Angeles high school team to the Southern California interscholastic title. So it was no surprise when he breezed his way to the top of the field at the National Junior Public Parks tournament held in Los Angeles's Griffith Park.

Johnson's unprecedented victory in Los Angeles was encouraging, but he and other black players soon discovered that the apparent liberalization of USLTA policy did not prevent local tournament officials from upholding the color bar. When Johnson arrived at the National Junior Indoor tournament in St. Louis in December 1948, the tournament director summarily over- ruled the USLTA's acceptance of his application. After finding Johnson's name on the list of players, the director exclaimed: "Well, I'll be damned. But you won't play here boy." Fortunately, Dick Hudlin and a local black attorney were on hand to help, and a timely call to USLTA headquarters cleared the way for Johnson to play. Angered and a bit shaken by the con- troversy, the young Californian battled his way into the quarterfinals before losing to Trabert.[16]

The experiences of Weir, Ryland, Stewart, and Johnson were significant and visible advances in the desegregation of American tennis. But the greatest in- fluence on the world of black tennis was emerging behind the scenes during the mid- and late 1940s. The innovation that would eventually take the de- segregation of tennis beyond the stage of tokenism, that would propel black players into the competitive mainstream, and that would alter the lives of Arthur Ashe and scores of others, was the creation of a rigorous junior devel- opment program connected to the ATA.

Providing serious instruction for promising young African American tennis players was the consuming passion of one individual, Dr. Robert Wal- ter Johnson Sr., the man known to Ashe and many others as "Dr. J." A native of Norfolk who migrated to the Appalachian foothills town of Lynchburg after graduating from Meharry Medical School in 1932, Johnson was an un- likely choice to become "the Godfather of Black Tennis." As an undergrad- uate at Lincoln University in the 1920s, he was a star running back, earning the nickname "Whirlwind" with his exploits on the gridiron. Prior to begin- ning medical school, he spent several years coaching football, baseball, and basketball at a series of black colleges in Virginia, Texas, and Georgia. But he did not take up competitive tennis until he was in his early thirties. Essen- tially a self-taught player, he became a fixture of the ATA in the mid-1930s, especially after building a tennis court in his backyard in 1936. The court allowed him to become a full-fledged member of an informal circle of black doctors and professionals, each of whom had a private court that enabled the group to rotate the site of periodic weekend tennis gatherings. Stretching from Lynchburg to Wilmington, North Carolina, the circuit became the defining element of Johnson's social life. In the process, he sharpened his tennis skills, but mostly he became a close student of the game and "an astute judge of athletic talent," as his biographer later put it.

He also developed a keen interest in the younger players he encountered either at ATA tournaments or at the occasional informal tennis gatherings held in Lynchburg. By the early 1940s, he had adopted the practice of inviting outstanding ATA players to spend part of the summer at his home. He paid all of his guests' expenses, the only expectation being their willingness to play and talk tennis with him. Over time these arrangements evolved into the equivalent of a tennis camp, and black players looking for a summer haven began to clamor for a spot in Johnson's chosen circle. The Lynchburg court also became the site of an annual round-robin Labor Day tournament, an invitation-only event that capped off the ATA's summer schedule. Confirming his status as the unofficial social chairman of the ATA, Johnson enhanced the Labor Day gatherings by inviting celebrities such as the noted photographer Gordon Parks Jr. to share the court with his friends and top ATA players.[17]

The social side of all of this sometimes seemed to take precedence over the tennis. But beneath it all was a fierce determination to improve the quality of black tennis, particularly among younger players. Dr. Johnson and several of his closest friends were always looking for a promising star of the future, one that might even be able to cross over into the world of mainstream tennis once the poison of Jim Crow had run its course. The ATA had given him so much joy and fulfillment, yet he yearned for validation and respect in the wider world of tennis.

Dr. Johnson had a complicated take on the realities of race, class, and power. As the only black physician in Lynchburg, he probably gained certain economic benefits from segregation. And the source of his income also gave him a measure of independence and protection from the white power structure. As a leading figure in the local black community he sometimes served as a broker between black and white interests. Indeed, he even lived in a predominantly white neighborhood in a two-story house on Pierce Street that most local whites could not afford. Yet he was also a proud member of the National Association for the Advancement of Colored People (NAACP) who was not afraid to speak out against slum conditions and inadequate and underfunded public schools in Lynchburg's black neighborhoods, or to threaten legal action against segregated transit facilities. Though generally careful in his dealings with whites, he was determined to find a way to bring about needed change without sacrificing the benefits of his present position. In tennis, this meant improving the quality of black tennis by first reforming the ATA and later releasing the organization's best players into the mainstream of competitive tennis.[18]

Many of Johnson's ATA colleagues shared his ambivalence about the probable consequences of wholesale desegregation. But relatively few shared his unbridled enthusiasm for junior development. Many simply wanted to enjoy the game of tennis without spending too much time and energy worrying about future stars or collective improvement. One ATA insider who did share Johnson's concerns about the future of black tennis was his close friend from Wilmington, Dr. Hubert Eaton. Whenever the two men got together, at ATA tournaments or during the Virginia–North Carolina weekend gatherings, their conversations almost always included an evaluation of the strengths and weaknesses of promising young players followed by a discussion of the ATA's failings in the area of junior development.

One such conversation took place at Central State College in Wilberforce, Ohio, during the 1946 ATA women's singles final. Roumania Peters, a former champion, won the match in three tough sets. But Johnson and Eaton were more interested in her opponent, a tall, raw-boned, hard-hitting eighteen-year-old named Althea Gibson. They had seen her play before, as one of the ATA's leading Juniors, and they knew about her background as a tough kid growing up on the streets of Harlem. They had heard all the stories about her deprived childhood—that she had been born into poverty in South Carolina before migrating to New York at the age of three, that she had played more stickball than tennis as a kid, that her family was on welfare, and that she had dropped out of high school. So they were aware that she had a lot of issues to work through. Yet there was something special about her, something they saw that day in the way she combined ferocious competitiveness and powerful athleticism that drew their rapt attention.

Sitting in the grandstand analyzing the match, the two men came up with a plan to elevate her game. The first task, they decided, was to get her back in school and out of Harlem, where she reportedly spent much of her time hustling money in pool halls and bowling alleys. To this end, Eaton invited her to move to Wilmington, where she could live with his family and enroll in school. In the summer, Johnson chimed in, she could live with his family in Lynchburg, where she would have time to polish her game and where she would have little else to think about but tennis.[19]

Gibson readily agreed to this Pygmalion-like makeover, and over the next four years she underwent a profound transformation, completing high school and entering college, all the while refining her skills on the tennis court. In a regimen that became the model for the training that Ashe and others would receive in the 1950s, she took instruction in everything from court coverage to table manners. Though strong-willed and stubborn, she cooperated as best she could. While her singularly aggressive style of play remained unorthodox and her personality retained a certain edge, her life on and off the court took on a new sophistication as she blossomed into a poised and confident young woman.

Eaton and Johnson were justifiably proud of their pet pupil, who soon became the most successful female player in ATA history. From 1947 on, she was virtually unbeatable in ATA competition, winning ten consecutive national singles championships and nearly as many doubles titles. To Johnson's delight, she also joined her Lynchburg mentor in mixed doubles, capturing the national mixed title seven times between 1948 and 1955. By 1949, the year Gibson entered Florida A&M University as a twenty-two-year-old freshman, her dominance of the ATA women's division was so complete that some of her admirers began to speculate about an eventual climb to the top of the tennis world. In ATA circles, there was no longer any doubt that she had the potential to succeed in USLTA-sanctioned tournaments. The only question as the decade drew to a close was whether she would actually get the opportunity to prove that she could keep up with the world's top female players.[20]

With the recent desegregation of professional baseball and football, and with the continuing success of black athletes in boxing and track and field, the USLTA faced mounting pressure to open its tournaments to all races. During the past two years alone, Jackie Robinson had won Rookie of the Year honors, Larry Doby had become a star outfielder with the Cleveland Indians, black Americans had won eight Gold Medals at the 1948 Olympics, Sugar Ray Robinson had successfully defended his world welterweight title four times, and Ezzard Charles had replaced the retired Joe Louis as champion of boxing's heavyweight division. The traditional argument bandied about in the USLTA and elsewhere—that black athletes could never measure up to white standards—had clearly lost most of its force. For those who continued to defend the color bar, there was little basis for argument other than blatantly racist rationalizations that suddenly seemed out of place in the postwar American mainstream. With the exception of the Deep South, where the demands of assertive black veterans had provoked a severe reaction among white supremacists, the nation seemed to be moving toward increased racial tolerance in the immediate postwar era.[21]

What effect, if any, this general trend toward liberalization would have on the powerful inertial forces inside the USLTA was unclear. The emergence of the Ecuadoran Pancho Segura—who captured the U.S. Clay Court singles championship in 1944 as well as the U.S. Indoor title two years later—and of the Mexican American Pancho Gonzales, who shocked the tennis establishment with his 1949 triumph on the grass at Forest Hills, had already added a bit of color and ethnic diversity to the men's tour. But it remained to be seen whether a truly dark-skinned competitor could gain admittance to the pale world of the tennis elite.[22]

For a time, in late 1949 and early 1950, Gibson's chances of breaching the color bar did not look very promising. As she and her supporters soon discovered, the conservative racial attitudes that prevailed within the tennis establishment were buttressed by a complicated qualifying procedure that gave tournament directors and officials representing the most exclusive private clubs a virtual veto power. The tennis tour leading up to the U.S. National championships at Forest Hills was essentially a two-tiered affair, with a clay court and hard court tour played primarily at public facilities followed by an invitation-only grass court circuit played entirely at restricted private clubs. To qualify for Forest Hills, Gibson had to demonstrate her skills not only in the clay and hard court tournaments but also on grass. While the leadership of the USLTA privately assured ATA officials that they welcomed her participation at Forest Hills or anywhere else, no one, it seemed, was willing to lean on the grass court elite to make it happen.

During the spring of 1950, the USLTA allowed Gibson to play in the Eastern and National Indoor championships, and both times she played well enough to reach the quarterfinals. By all accounts, her white opponents treated her with respect, and there was little evidence of racial tension or hostility. Encouraged, ATA officials began to plan Gibson's participation in the invitational grass court tour, which they hoped would lead to an invitation to play at Forest Hills. When the invitations didn't come, they began to press USLTA officials for an explanation, and after a bit of nervous squirming, the USLTA central committee admitted that it did not have the power to overrule the restrictive policies of private clubs. Since her performance in two indoor tournaments was not sufficient to merit an invitation to Forest Hills, she would have to wait until the qualifying grass tournaments gave her the opportunity to demonstrate her skills.

This double-talk infuriated Gibson's supporters, including Alice Marble, who decided to do something about it. In an angry but eloquent letter published in the July 1950 issue of *American Lawn Tennis* magazine, Marble challenged the USLTA to break tradition and do the right thing:

> If tennis is a game for ladies and gentlemen, it's also time we acted a little more like gentle people and less like sanctimonious hypocrites. If there is anything left in the name of sportsmanship, it's more than time to display what it means to us. If Althea Gibson represents a challenge to the present crop of women players, it's only fair that they meet that challenge on the courts, where tennis is played. . . . She is not being judged by the yardstick of ability but by the fact that her pigmentation is somewhat different. If the field of sports has got to pave the way for all of civilization, let's do it. . . . The entrance of Negroes into national tennis is as inevitable as it has proven to be in baseball, in football, in boxing.

Delivered at a critical moment by one of the nation's most popular tennis stars, Marble's pointed words could not be easily dismissed, especially after an article in *Life* magazine echoed her call for reform, insisting that "it is about time that the U.S. tennis fathers, who have been drawing a de facto color line all these years, got over their ancient prejudices." Fearing an avalanche of negative publicity, USLTA officials soon found a way to get Gibson into two of the major qualifying tournaments. By drawing invitations to the South Orange, New Jersey, grass tournament and the National Clay Court tournament in Chicago, she had a legitimate shot at earning an invitation to Forest Hills, and after she made it to the quarterfinals of both tournaments, the USLTA quietly informed the ATA that an invitation was forthcoming.[23]

By the time the formal invitation arrived in late August, Gibson was at the ATA Nationals in Wilberforce, Ohio, where a wild celebration ensued after it was announced that the dream of breaching the color bar at Forest Hills was about to be realized. Bertram Baker, the ATA official who had spearheaded the behind-the-scenes negotiations with the USLTA, could hardly contain himself, assuring the gathering that "the year 1950 will . . . go down in the history of the American Tennis Association as the beginning of a new era." What he did not reveal at the time was that he had already begun negotiations with the USLTA to establish a quota system for black partici-pation in the U.S. National Championships. Over the next few months the two organizations hammered out a gentleman's agreement that allowed the ATA to funnel a limited number of black players to Forest Hills each year. Baker's handiwork would later prove to be controversial among those who thought the arrangement was susceptible to favoritism and cronyism. But only a few insiders knew this was in the works when Gibson made her his-toric debut at Forest Hills.[24]

USLTA officials tried to downplay the significance of Gibson's appear-ance at the West Side Tennis Club, and were relieved when the advance press coverage turned out to be less intense than the buildup to Jackie Robin-son's debut with the Dodgers three years earlier. In the black press, of course, there was considerable commentary and some expressions of concern, since it was well known that earlier in the year the West Side club had summarily rejected an application for membership submitted by the noted black dip-lomat Ralph Bunche. Fortunately, when Gibson took the court in her first-round match against Barbara Knapp of England, the crowd was respectful, and later when she walked off as a straight-sets winner the applause and cheers were reassuring.

The situation became much more tense in the second round when Gib-son unexpectedly pushed one of the tournament favorites, three-time Wim-bledon champion Louise Brough, to the brink of defeat. After losing the first set 6–1, Gibson rebounded to win the second set 6–3, and to take a 7–6 lead in the third before a violent thunderstorm suspended play. By that time, an overflow crowd of more than two thousand had gathered around the court to watch the unfolding drama. "I'll never forget that storm," Baker recalled years later. "Fans were shouting from the stands for Althea's opponent to 'beat the nigger, beat the nigger.' I'll always remember it as the day the gods got angry. A flash of lightning came and knocked down one of the statues of the eagles on the stadium court." It all proved to be a bit too much for Gib-son, who appeared jittery when play resumed the next morning. Seizing the initiative, the veteran Brough won three straight games and the match. This near miss haunted Gibson for months. But she took some consolation from the indisputable significance of what she had accomplished just by playing at Forest Hills. The American tennis establishment had finally opened a door that could never be fully closed again.[25]

THREE

DR. J AND THE LYNCHBURG BOYS

TENNIS BUFFS AND HISTORIANS will always remember the summer of 1950 primarily as the season Althea Gibson entered the mainstream of competitive tennis. But there was another, less well-known development. The first summer of the new decade was also a pivotal moment for Gibson's proud mentor and mixed doubles partner. With his prize pupil seemingly on the verge of greatness, Dr. Robert Johnson was primed and ready to expand and formalize his junior development program. He knew the ATA had no funds to underwrite the proposed program and that for the foreseeable future he would have to pay for it himself. But that didn't bother him. His medical practice was lucrative enough to support several prospects each summer, and there was plenty of room at his house in Lynchburg. All he needed was a crop of promising and cooperative recruits. Perhaps more than anyone else in the ATA inner circle, he dreamed of the day when the most talented black players would have the chance to compete against the nation's best.

For Johnson, Gibson's uncertain march to Forest Hills confirmed that the desegregation of tennis would be a difficult process. Yet, even with the vacillations of the USLTA, there was reason to believe that the pace of change was quickening. In June, just as the controversy over Gibson's access to the qualifying tournaments was heating up, Johnson made an important discovery. While driving back to Lynchburg from northern Virginia, he happened to see a sign directing visitors to the USLTA Interscholastic Tennis Championship on the University of Virginia's courts in Charlottesville. Intrigued, he spent several hours at the tournament watching some of the nation's best high school tennis players. All of the competitors were white, of course, which was no shock to Johnson. What did shock him, however, was the high quality of play. "To my surprise," he recalled years later, "the caliber of play in high school there was better than our colleges—frankly better than the best tennis we Negroes had to offer anywhere in the United States."[1]

This firsthand look at the effects of early training led to an impromptu conversation with the tournament director, Edmund "Teddy" Penzold. A well-connected figure in Virginia politics, Penzold was head of the Norfolk Port Authority and a close associate of Colgate Darden, a former Democratic congressman and governor who had assumed the presidency of the University of Virginia in 1947. Both Penzold and Darden were racial moderates open to the idea of gradual and limited desegregation, which was on the verge of implementation at the university in the summer of 1950. In September, Gregory Swanson became the first black student to enroll at the university's law school, though he was not permitted to live on campus. This grudging, halfway acceptance was as much as one could hope for in Virginia at that time, and it was in this context of limited expectations that Johnson approached Penzold with a proposition. If Penzold would allow a limited number of black high school players to compete, Johnson would make sure that the intrusion was as low-profile as possible. The black students would not use any of the campus facilities other than the tennis courts; they would not eat or stay on campus; and they would be out of town by sundown. To Johnson's amazement, Penzold agreed and promised to send him the necessary application forms later in the year.[2]

Penzold proved true to his word, and in the summer of 1951 the interscholastic tournament quietly desegregated. Johnson's only problem turned out to be his inability to find black high school players who could actually compete with the nation's best. The two black entrants in 1951, Victor Miller and Roosevelt Megginson of Lynchburg's Dunbar High School, were both, in Johnson's words, "annihilated in the first round." Neither boy won a single game, and Johnson left Charlottesville "embarrassed" and determined to do better the next year. For a time there was no certainty that there would be a next year, but with Darden's support Penzold managed to weather a storm of criticism. Despite considerable grumbling from conservative whites and even some talk of either removing Penzold from the directorship or giving up sponsorship of the tournament altogether, Johnson and his boys got a second chance in 1952.[3]

This time Johnson arrived in Charlottesville with a much stronger contingent, thanks to a year of careful preparation. Following the 1951 debacle, Johnson, at Penzold's suggestion, had organized a "Negro national interscholastic championship" that would act as a screening mechanism for entrants to the Charlottesville tournament. Run by a newly formed ATA junior development committee, the inaugural tournament was held at Virginia Union in May 1952. Twenty-three players representing ten black high schools participated, with Billy Winn of Wilmington, North Carolina, and Elton King, of Washington, D.C., facing each other in the finals. The finalists won the right to accompany Johnson to Charlottesville. Predictably, they were eliminated in the first round. But both boys played reasonably well, especially Winn, a lightning-quick left-hander who lost 6–1, 6–2 to the highly ranked Ohio star Barry MacKay.[4]

Encouraged, Johnson and his ATA colleagues made plans to expand the reach of the Lynchburg junior development camp. The goal of winning a match or two in Charlottesville was beginning to look more realistic, particularly if Winn and some of the other promising juniors could spend a good part of the summer training on Johnson's court. From 1952 on, the number of players spending at least part of the summer in Lynchburg increased to six or more, and with each passing year there was a noticeable improvement in the quality of play among the best recruits. It would be several years before one of the Lynchburg boys actually won a match and progressed beyond the first round at Charlottesville. But Johnson patiently laid the groundwork for future success by recruiting younger and younger boys.[5]

By the mid-1950s Johnson's belief that early development was the key to success in the tennis world had been confirmed by the apparent limitations of the best older players, including Althea Gibson. His star pupil had continued to play on the USLTA circuit and by 1953 had risen to a #7 national ranking. Yet she had been unable to break through against the nation's top players. When her ranking fell to #14 in 1954, she became so discouraged that she seriously considered dropping the game altogether, and in 1955 *Jet* magazine called her "the biggest disappointment in tennis." By then her token presence on the tour was no longer controversial, and in 1952 and 1953 three black male players—Reginald Weir, George Stewart, and Oscar Johnson—joined her as participants in the national championships at Forest Hills. But none of the male ATA stars fared very well against their white opponents, reinforcing Dr. Johnson's conviction that the only real hope for black tennis was the youth movement emerging on his Lynchburg court.[6]

An important element of Dr. Johnson's strategy was to give his young players the opportunity to test their skills against older and obviously superior players. Veteran ATA stars were frequent guests at the Lynchburg camp, where they often practiced with and competed against children less than half their age. Dr. Johnson also took the best young players on weekend outings to local and regional ATA tournaments, where they were encouraged to compete against stronger and more experienced opponents. Though bruising to the ego, being overmatched week after week toughened the Lynchburg boys and girls mentally and physically. It also weeded out those who lacked the discipline and drive that Johnson considered essential to long-term survival on the tennis circuit.[7]

Fortunately for Arthur Ashe and the game of tennis, Ron Charity was one of the older players invited to the Lynchburg camp. After watching Charity play at an ATA tournament in Richmond in 1953, Dr. Johnson asked the Virginia Union student to spend a few days at his home. Thus began a long friendship that would change both men's lives. When Johnson drove down to the ATA national tournament in Daytona Beach, Florida, in July, Charity went along, as did Althea Gibson. While it was too late for Charity to develop his talents beyond the middle range of ATA players, he became one of Johnson's unofficial junior development scouts, charged with looking for young talent appropriate for the Lynchburg camp.

For ten-year-old Arthur Ashe, the stage was set for a life-changing opportunity. In the spring of 1954, Virginia Union hosted the annual CIAA tournament, and both Charity and Johnson, who served as the tournament director that year, were on hand to watch the nation's best black collegiate players. Ashe was also there, and during a break between matches he wandered out on to one of Brook Field's empty courts to hit a few practice serves. After a few minutes, Charity approached the court and yelled out: "Somebody wants to meet you." Years later Ashe recalled what happened next:

> I followed him to a table that was under the tree outside the side door of my house. Seated at the table was the tournament director, recording scores and directing players to the proper court. . . . "Dr. Johnson," Ron Charity said, "this is Arthur Ashe, Junior." He shook my hand and looked me over quizzically. "I understand you're ten years old."

"Yes, sir."

"You've been playing three years."

"Yes, sir."

"You like tennis?"

"Yes, sir."

He nodded, asked a few more questions, and dismissed me. I went back to the empty court, but felt him watching me as I played. When I glanced over, he was talking to Ron. Later that day, he talked to my father for a long time.[8]

At this point, Dr. Johnson was skeptical that the scrawny, sixty-pound child that Charity was so high on deserved a spot at the Lynchburg camp. He wanted young recruits, but he wasn't sure a boy who looked like he was suffering from rickets had much of a future in a game that required strength and stamina. Charity continued to press Ashe's case, however, and a few weeks later Johnson consented to a tryout in Lynchburg. The audition revealed the boy's quickness and enthusiasm, but also a slingshot stroke obviously developed to compensate for his lack of size and strength. The camp would have to rebuild his game from scratch, breaking bad habits and instilling the fundamentals of proper form. But Johnson was intrigued enough by the challenge to agree to let Ashe come to the camp for a two-week trial.

The adventure began a few weeks later when Arthur Sr. put his excited son on the bus to Lynchburg. The three-hour bus ride turned out to be a memorable initiation for an innocent child with little knowledge of the world beyond his own neighborhood. As he remembered vividly two decades later, his educational experience began long before he reached Lynchburg. "Anyone who's ever sat in a Greyhound bus knows that the best seat is the one right across the aisle from the driver, the first seat on the right-hand side," he wrote in 1974. "You've got a clear vista looking out the front window. I sat there because I wanted to see the country. . . . The driver just looked over at me, and very nicely, he said: 'Now son, you know you can't sit there.' And so I got up and went to the back." With a less congenial bus driver, Arthur Jr.'s breach of racial etiquette might well have turned into a serious incident. The U.S. Supreme Court's controversial ruling in *Brown v. Board of Education* was barely a month old, and many white Southerners were on edge anticipating challenges to their authority.[9]

Even at the tender age of ten, Arthur had some sense of the formal restrictions imposed by the laws and customs of Jim Crow culture. "I can remember segregation," he later explained, "the hard, legal segregation of that time in Richmond. I suppose I was always aware of it, but it was not a concern to me. I can clearly recall the white line on the floor of the bus—it was just to the front of the rear door—and I understood that I was required to stay behind it. I don't ever remember discussing it; it was just understood." For him a more pressing reality was the code of behavior imposed by his father. Indeed, Arthur's initial excitement about the opportunity to spend part of the summer in Lynchburg undoubtedly involved a vision of temporary liberation from paternal control.[10]

The regimentation at Dr. Johnson's camp was, however, severe and unbending, even by the standards of the Ashe household. Dr. J, as he was known to the Lynchburg boys, had a detailed plan for each day's activities, on and off the court, and he expected all of his charges to follow his orders to the nth degree. As Willis S. Thomas Sr., the father of one of Ashe's camp mates, recalled, "He'd send you home in a minute if you didn't measure up to what he wanted." It was rare for a camper to get a second chance to challenge Dr. J's authority, and in Arthur's case a rude initiation into this closed system came on his second day in camp. Years later he described "the only disagreement I had with Dr. Johnson in eight summers at his home":

> I was the youngest and smallest of the six kids in camp—in fact, I was so tiny and skinny Dr. Johnson thought I had rickets—and the racket I'd brought from home still looked almost as big as me. Of course it was too heavy. But under Ronald Charity I had developed a knack of almost slinging it at the ball, like a midget Irishman tossing a caber. . . . On my second day, his son Bob was instructing me on how to hit. I kept using the swing Ronald had taught me, and Bob kept trying to correct me. But I got as stubborn as a mule. Finally I told Bob right out, "Mr. Charity told me to do it this way." I wouldn't change. Dr. Johnson wasted no time. He phoned my father. Daddy wasted no time either. He dropped everything and took the bus to Lynchburg that same afternoon. When he arrived he told me, "Son, Mr. Charity fixed it for you to come here so you could get better coaching. He's done all he can for you. Dr. Johnson has had more experience and isn't going to teach you wrong. If you don't want to obey him, come home." I stayed. "Mr. Charity" was never mentioned again in camp.[11]

Following this early confrontation, Arthur became a model of obedience and discipline. Once he learned the rules of the house, he began to develop a close bond with Dr. J and his son, as well as with his fellow campers. Their time together was as intense as it was carefully orchestrated, from the "machine that would fire tennis balls at us in a steady stream" to the "'dressing room' in the basement where the boys hung their clothes on hooks when they changed into tennis whites." As Arthur later explained, "Dr. Johnson wanted us always to look immaculate and correctly dressed when we played, even for practice." The daily regimen, as he remembered it, was jammed with organized activities:

> We'd get up about 8 every morning, cook our own breakfast, straighten our bedrooms, then hustle out on the courts by about 8:45. We'd take turns hitting with each other—four at a time, usually— all morning, without keeping any scores. . . . In the afternoon we'd drill on whatever Dr. Johnson had told each of us we needed to practice—like 100 serves or 100 backhands, overheads, crosscourts. During our turns off the court, we'd do chores around the house. Somebody had to cut the grass, tend the 150 roses. Somebody had to clean out the doghouse—with lye. That was the worst. . . . Dr. Johnson figured we didn't need an overseer standing by us with a whip. He trusted us to practice all day, mostly unsupervised, and to get the chores done. But now and then during the day he'd drop in to see how we were doing, and from about 4:30 he'd be with us constantly. . . . Dr. Johnson always fed us a hearty dinner . . . and . . . insisted on perfect table manners. . . . After dinner we were always too full or too tired to want to go out. We'd drift down to the basement party room where Dr. Johnson would talk to us about strategy, or show us tennis films. He had slow-motion pictures of all the strokes. Other evenings we'd listen to records, or read. There were hundreds of *World Tennis* magazines, and tennis rulebooks. We had to know all the tennis rules cold. Dr. Johnson gave us exams in them.[12]

This modified boot camp model posed a stiff challenge for all of Dr. J's pupils, but Arthur faced the added burden of being the proverbial runt of the litter during his first summer. This forced him to try "harder and harder," to compensate for his lack of size and experience. "If I couldn't outmuscle or outrun the other kids," he reasoned, "I could outwork them. I was first on the courts every morning, last to leave at night. And I was so enthused about the whole idea of the training camp that I took over odd jobs like cleaning up the court that weren't anybody's particular assignment." Enthusiasm aside, Arthur remembered the initial two-week stint in Lynchburg as "dull, and wearisome for me—especially since he didn't enter me in any tournaments." While Dr. J allowed him to join the older boys on two brief road trips, he gave him little encouragement. In Arthur's words, "that first summer, nobody would have thought I had any future in tennis." [13]

For an eleven-year-old boy about to enter the sixth grade, the Lynchburg initiation was a grueling test that might have soured him on the game of tennis, but fortunately Charity provided ample encouragement. During the fall of 1954, he continued to coach and counsel his young protégé, who was more determined than ever to excel on the tennis court. Even in his life off the court, Arthur seemed to be coming into his own, shedding some of his shyness and displaying more confidence. As a sixth grader in his final year at Baker elementary, he achieved a certain status, particularly after he was elected president of the student council. Studious and conscientious, with a quiet and polite manner, he stood out among his peers and was popular with his teachers. Nearly five years after his mother's death, he appeared to have overcome the trauma of his early loss, as his life had gained a certain stability and strength based on family, school, and tennis.

This stability would be shaken, at least temporarily, in the spring of 1955, by his father's remarriage. On March 20, three days before the fifth anniversary of his first wife's death, Arthur Sr. married Lorene Kimbrough, a widow with two small children: Loretta, born in 1952; and Robert, born a year later. Unbeknownst to his two sons, Arthur Sr. had been seeing Lorene since 1951, and Robert and Loretta were actually his children. Suddenly, Arthur Jr. and Johnnie had acquired a new family—a stepmother, a half sister, and a half brother. "At first, I was extremely upset," he recalled. "I was only eleven years old. Daddy moved back into his bedroom with Lorene, Mrs. Berry moved into our room—her snores replaced Daddy's—and we now had to call both women 'mother.'" Fortunately, both Ashe boys soon warmed to the new arrangement. Lorene proved to be a patient and caring stepmother, and Robert and Loretta, who lived with their grandparents twenty-five miles north of Richmond in Gum Spring, did not have much contact with Arthur and Johnnie until several years later.

The marriage also seemed to brighten Arthur Sr.'s personality, especially after Lorene's father gave the couple a five-acre tract of land in Gum Spring as a wedding present. Over the next decade, Arthur Sr., with the help of his sons, constructed a second home on the Gum Spring property. Built with odds and ends and scrap materials—many taken from the ongoing construction of an interstate highway running through east Richmond—this rural retreat would become a source of pride and an almost sacred haven for the Ashe family. It was also where Arthur Jr. first explored the great outdoors, traversing the woods and streams of Louisa County where his father taught him how to hunt and fish.[14]

During the spring of 1955, adjusting to a new family situation dominated Arthur Jr.'s life. But he was also worried he wouldn't be invited back to Lynchburg for a second summer of training. When he finally received the invitation in July, the summer was half gone. He was relieved and anxious to prove himself as a full-fledged camper, but once he arrived in Lynchburg, he found himself clinging precariously to the bottom of Dr. J's tennis ladder. He was still the youngest and smallest camper, and for a time Dr. J hardly seemed to notice that he was back.

In the intervening year between Arthur Jr.'s first and second camps, Dr. J and his son Bobby Jr. had become preoccupied with a sensational new prospect from California, fifteen-year-old Willis Fennell. At the 1954 ATA National tournament in Daytona Beach, Fennell had blasted his way to the 15-and-under championship without losing a set, convincing everyone present, including the Johnsons, that they had just seen the future of black tennis. Fennell obviously had a world of talent, and Dr. J wasted no time in recruiting him for the 1955 summer camp. The only question was whether the young Californian had the right temperament for success or even survival in Dr. J's authoritarian system. High-strung and cocky, Fennel sometimes had difficulty controlling both his temper and his ego. Things started well enough in June, when he became only the second Lynchburg boy to win a match at the Interscholastic tournament in Charlottesville. Although Fennell lost his second round match, Johnson predicted that he would eventually win the Charlottesville tournament—if he could stay focused and keep his ego in check.[15]

Playing at Durham, North Carolina, in July, Fennell justified Dr. J's confidence by winning both the ATA National Junior and 15-and-under titles, beating an overmatched Ashe in the latter division 6–1, 6–2. Indeed, Fennell's wins at Durham were so convincing that Dr. J decided to enter him in the upcoming adult men's singles competition at the ATA National tournament in Wilberforce, Ohio. His application, however, was rejected after the tournament's rules were amended to exclude Juniors from the adult competition, a move prompted by several of the ATA's older players who pressured the organization's leadership to preempt their probable humiliation by a fifteen-year-old upstart. Dr. J protested the decision, and Fennell angrily declared he was through with the ATA. But the decision stood. After returning to Lynchburg, Dr. J and his controversial protégé gained a measure of revenge a few days later when Fennell entered and won a USLTA Junior tournament in Wilmington, Delaware. But the young star could not contain his rage for long. During an August workout lesson in Lynchburg, he suddenly lashed out at Bobby Jr., who had been instructing him on the proper way to hit a lob. Tossing his racket, Fennell stormed off the court, never to return.[16]

Though saddened by the loss of his top prospect, Dr. J came to regard the Fennell fiasco as an object lesson in the supreme importance of emotional control and discipline. There was simply no place in his program for self-indulgent behavior, particularly in the increasingly dangerous atmosphere of the post-*Brown* South. As Leslie Allen, who spent two summers with Dr. J, later observed, "he was preparing us for a world that didn't want us." Virginia was a long way from the Deep South, but after a year of watchful waiting, Virginia's most powerful politician, Senator Harry Flood Byrd Sr., was actively pushing the state toward a more militant defense of segregation during the summer and fall of 1955. All across the region, racial moderates were in full retreat, cowed by the prospect of massive and even violent resistance to change.

Much of this resistance was political and judicial. But nothing symbolized the trend toward sectionalist defiance better than the brutal murder of fourteen-year-old Emmett Till in late August. When the young black boy's racially "inappropriate" remarks to a white woman led to his murder in Money, Mississippi, many Americans recoiled in horror. Black Americans especially were sickened both by the murderers' acquittal by an all-white jury and by the photographs of Till's mutilated body lying in an open casket at his Chicago funeral. For many blacks, including Dr. Johnson, the Till episode also served as a gruesome reminder that provocative behavior could have serious consequences in the Jim Crow South. Polite advocacy and pressing for orderly change were fine. But he certainly did not want any of his boys endangering himself or the race—or his junior development program—by acting out or causing needless controversy.[17]

Accordingly, he imposed a strict code of court behavior designed to forestall racial conflict. The code, as Johnson's biographer Doug Smith aptly concluded, amounted to "a variation of the turn-the-other-cheek philosophy that Brooklyn Dodgers general manager Branch Rickey urged Jackie Robinson to embrace in 1947." Smith, who spent time at the Lynchburg camp in the late 1950s, recalled Dr. J's rules as a means of keeping his players

out of "harm's way" and his integration-bound program on track. In Dr. J's
system, Smith explained, "court ethics meant more than extending common
courtesy and sportsmanship. He preached subservience. He instructed them
never to argue with the umpire, to pick up the balls and give them to the
opponent when changing sides. He insisted that balls hit close to the line be
called in favor of the opponent, even if the call is incorrect. He told them that
they must never argue with their opponents during a match."[18]

Dr. J felt compelled to spend part of each camp session reinforcing the
importance of court behavior. "We're going into a new world," he warned
again and again. "We've got to be extra careful. We've got to turn the other
cheek. All they want is an excuse to keep us out." Not everyone had the req-
uisite temperament and concentration to meet Dr. J's behavioral standards.
But for a select few, including Arthur Ashe, the inflexibility of the system was
tolerable and even beneficial. By the end of his second summer in Lynchburg, Arthur had become a model of composure and restraint, overcoming
his physical limitations and emerging as one of Dr. J's favorites.[19]

Win or lose, Arthur gave the game all he had without losing his cool. For
a boy so young, this was a major psychological feat. But, as he later acknowledged, his disciplined demeanor was hardly surprising considering his family
background. Adopting Dr. J's inflexible "training rules . . . wasn't so hard for
me," he concluded, "since Daddy had always been firm at home." Of course,
none of this would have mattered if he had not been able to demonstrate his
aptitude and passion for the game of tennis. "The kids who stuck were the
ones who kept winning in the tournaments," he remembered, explaining
that "Dr. Johnson's aim was to produce players who would be too strong to
be ignored in the white world of tennis. . . . So I knew I'd be dropped sooner
or later unless I kept winning. And I sure didn't want to be dropped. This
was what made me try so fiercely through summer after summer. I beat some
physically superior kids just because I was keyed up higher than they were,
or because I out-gutted them in long matches."[20]

At the end of the summer the only remaining champion in camp was
Arthur, who had won the national ATA 12-and-under singles title at the
Durham tournament, defeating his friend and fellow camper, Willis Thomas
Jr., 6–3, 6–4. Just before the final match, Arthur's parents and his brother
Johnnie drove down to Durham to surprise him, and he later claimed he
nearly lost his concentration and the match when he saw them in the stands.
But he was never in any real danger of losing. Though still too small to have
much chance of beating older players, he was virtually unbeatable in his age
group. Good black tennis players under the age of thirteen were scarce, and

he had beaten just about all of them by the time he entered Graves Junior High School in the fall of 1955.[21]

Winning a national championship was the thrill of Arthur's young life. But it was only the beginning of an ascending career that would lead to twelve more ATA national titles over the next seven years. His second title would come in July 1956, when he and Willis Thomas teamed up to win the doubles championship of the age 12–15 group. Playing in Durham, he lost the 12–15 singles final to fifteen-year-old Joe Williams, a much taller and stronger player. But Dr. J was pleased Arthur took the first set and pressed Williams throughout the match.

By this time, Arthur had become one of the Lynchburg camp's favored veterans, one of the fortunate few included in all of the weekend trips to ATA tournaments. Two or three times a month, he and two or three other kids piled into Dr. J's big Buick and headed out on the open road bound for Norfolk, Durham, Baltimore, or Washington. Years later he recalled the wonderful "camaraderie" of the hours on the road, the educational experience of listening to Dr. J's stories and moral lessons along the way, and the gracious hospitality of the black families that opened their homes to the doctor's wandering band. Along the way, he played an exhausting number of matches against a steady stream of opponents, many of whom were considerably older and bigger than he was. "By that third summer," he remembered, "Dr. Johnson was entering me in the juniors and men's divisions. I always got whipped. But I always won my own age division. These were all ATA tournaments. Dr. Johnson didn't think I was ready yet to go up against white boys with white umpires and white crowds, even though a few USLTA tournaments were now accepting Negro players."[22]

Though clearly encouraged by Arthur's progress, Johnson must have wondered if his diminutive pupil would ever be strong enough or tough enough to compete with full-grown adults, black or white; and despite a fierce determination to succeed, Arthur himself must have shared at least some of Johnson's concern. As he entered his teen years, he was beginning to see the faint outline of a bright future. With no firm sense of how far or fast he or any other black tennis player could rise in the world of mainstream tennis, he could only hope that the days of racially restricted play were numbered. The opening of the tennis world since the late 1940s amounted to little more than tokenism, but it was a start. And if the recent trajectory of racial change in other sports was any indication of what lay ahead for tennis, there was reason to be optimistic.

During the mid- and late 1950s, the pace of desegregation was quickening all across the sports world; indeed, by mid-decade the concept of the black sports hero had become an important element of American popular culture. This encouraging development was most obvious in boxing, where Sugar Ray Robinson and Floyd Patterson held sway, and in the national pastime of baseball. In 1954, Willie Mays and Monte Irvin, both born into poverty in Alabama, led the New York Giants to the team's first World Series title in twenty-one years. Moreover, the hitting star of the team the Giants defeated in the series, the Cleveland Indians, was the American League home run king and onetime Richmond resident Larry Doby. A year later, three black stars—Jackie Robinson, Don Newcombe, and Roy Campanella—led the Brooklyn Dodgers to the first World Series championship in the team's history. Campanella won three National League Most Valuable Player awards, and when Hank Aaron of the Milwaukee Braves was named National League MVP in 1957, he became the seventh black player in nine years to win the coveted award. By the end of the decade, future Hall of Famers Frank Robinson, Ernie Banks, and Roberto Clemente had joined the league's elite, preparing the way for the emergence of many more black stars during the 1960s and beyond.[23]

Black stardom was slower to emerge in professional football, but by 1957 the gridiron's dominant running back and most magnetic figure was Cleveland Browns rookie Jim Brown, who would soon become the National Football League's first superstar. In basketball, black stars were also elevating the game, as Bill Russell and Wilt Chamberlain ushered in the era of the dominating pivot man. Between them, Russell and Chamberlain led their college squads to three consecutive NCAA titles from 1955 to 1957, before transforming the style of play in the National Basketball Association (NBA) later in the decade. In 1957, Russell's rookie season with the Boston Celtics, his team won the NBA title, and during the next twelve years, with Russell at center, the Celtics dynasty would win ten more.[24]

Young Arthur Ashe, as an aspiring athlete and avid sports fan, found plenty of encouragement in the recent success of black male sports figures. But for him the most important sign of progress in the sports world was the rising fame of Althea Gibson. Along with Jackie Robinson and Pancho Gonzales, who dazzled Ashe at a professional tournament in Richmond in 1954, Gibson was his idol and role model. Ashe and the other kids at the Lynchburg camp followed the ups and downs of her career with rapt attention, so when her fortunes began to rise in late 1955 there was jubilation among the faithful. Reversing a long decline that had threatened to end her career, Dr.

J's most famous protégée reinvented her game after acquiring a new coach—Jamaica-born Sydney Llewellyn—and adopting a new Eastern-style grip.

Following a confidence-building 1955 international exhibition tour, during which she won eighteen of nineteen events, Gibson dominated the field at the 1956 French National Championships, capturing both the singles and doubles titles. Later in the summer, at Wimbledon, she finished second in the singles competition and won the doubles title. In less than a year's time, one of the biggest disappointments in women's tennis had become the hottest player on the tour. Soaring to the top of the tennis world, she won the Wimbledon women's singles and doubles titles in July 1957, which earned her a tickertape Broadway parade after her return to New York. Two months later, she won the U.S. National singles and mixed doubles championships at Forest Hills, and the following spring she was awarded the Babe Didrikson Zaharias trophy as Female Athlete of the Year for 1957. More accolades followed in the summer of 1958, when she repeated as the Wimbledon singles and doubles champion and as the U.S. National singles titleholder. By then she was acknowledged as the greatest player in women's tennis and one of the most accomplished athletes, black or white, in the world.[25]

This was a thrilling turn of events for Dr. J, Arthur, and everyone associated with the ATA and the Lynchburg camp. Foiling her early critics, Gibson had proven she had the talent and grit to overcome any obstacles to success on the tennis court. Unfortunately, it was a different story off the court. Gibson's belated rise to greatness at the age of twenty-nine brought her fame and put her in the celebrated company of black heroes such as Jackie Robinson, Willie Mays, and Jim Brown. But she was not always comfortable in the limelight, particularly when black journalists pointed out her responsibilities as a leader of the race. After being criticized for being self-centered and for ignoring pressing civil rights concerns, she lashed out at her detractors. "I am not a racially conscious person," she explained in her 1958 autobiography, *I Always Wanted to Be Somebody*. "I don't want to be. I see myself as just an individual." Statements like this only made matters worse, and her popularity in the black community gradually declined. Gibson's biggest problem, however—the one that brought her tennis career to a premature and disappointing conclusion—was financial. Despite her fame, she couldn't earn a living in the rarefied world of amateur tennis. Unable to secure steady sponsorship or lucrative endorsements, she turned professional in late 1958, immediately reducing her public profile to an appendage of the men's pro tour. By 1963 she had quit tennis altogether, turning to professional golf for her economic salvation.[26]

Gibson's bittersweet saga eventually became a cautionary tale for Ashe and other African Americans looking to tennis for economic opportunity and personal fulfillment. Even so, during the glory year of 1957 and 1958, Gibson's triumphs on the court repeatedly inspired Arthur, lifting his drive and ambition to new heights. "Politically, Althea's acceptance was crucial to my own," he later observed. "It made it easier for other blacks to follow." These were pivotal years in his development, a time of physical maturation and growing confidence. Having survived his testing time as the proverbial runt of Dr. J's litter, he "no longer got so many of the dirty jobs like cleaning the doghouse."[27]

In the early summer of 1957, Dr. J decided Arthur was ready to take on the pressure of an integrated USLTA tournament. He had interacted with whites before, but only on a casual basis, and never in a competitive situation. His first experience with integrated tennis took place at Clifton Park in Baltimore, a multiethnic, border-state city. Unlike most cities south of the Mason-Dixon line, Baltimore had begun the process of school desegregation, and the persistence of Jim Crow there had more to do with custom than codified discrimination. Confident that Baltimore was ready for integrated tennis, Dr. J registered several of the Lynchburg boys for the tournament. While he and the boys were a bit nervous, they were able to avoid open hostility by keeping to themselves. "We talked to white players," Arthur recalled, "but we didn't mix." On the court, the Lynchburg boys made a strong showing, winning several matches. Arthur fared the best, battling his way into the 15-and-under semifinals before losing to Hugh Lynch III of Bethesda, Maryland. The strategy against Lynch, dictated by Dr. J, was "to hit every ball to his backhand." At this point, Dr. J imposed strict rules as to what Ashe could or could not do during competitive matches; even after four years in camp, he was limited to the baseline area and not allowed to rush the net or serve and volley.[28]

Despite his disappointment following the Lynch match, Arthur left Clifton Park with a new understanding of the tennis world. The entire scene made a deep impression on him—especially the behavior and class background of the white players and their aggressive, hovering parents. "I noticed that most of the white boys were better dressed than we were," he later wrote. "Their folks drove up in big shiny cars or station wagons, and practically pushed Sonny Boy onto the courts. Some parents arrived late with their sons, and lit into the umpire if he had forfeited their match. . . . I heard them tell officials, 'Don't put my boy on an outside court. The crowd wants to see him.'"[29]

Later in the summer, Arthur would have other opportunities to test his skills against white players and to observe demanding tennis parents. At the 1957 Middle States Clay Court Junior Championships, held in Wilmington, Delaware, in late June, he and one of the older Lynchburg campers, Tom Hawes, fought their way through a tough field of white Juniors to face each other in the finals. Playing in front of a depleted crowd—relatively few of the white players and parents stuck around to see an all-black final—Hawes defeated Arthur for the title, the first USLTA tournament championship "ever won by a Negro boy" in the Middle States region. This unexpected triumph provided Dr. J with more than enough encouragement to enter both boys, plus Hubert Eaton, in the 1957 National Boys' Tournament in Kalamazoo, Michigan. At Kalamazoo, Herb Fitzgibbon of Garden City, New York, easily defeated Arthur in the first round. However, the slim fourteen-year-old from Virginia played well enough to impress several college coaches in the audience, one of whom, J. D. Morgan, would recruit him to play at UCLA four years later.[30]

Participating in his first two USLTA tournaments gave Arthur a taste of mainstream tennis, but he spent most of the summer of 1957 either practicing in Lynchburg or playing in segregated ATA events. Though still smarting from the Fennell controversy of 1955, as well as from ATA executive secretary Bertram Baker's refusal to include any of the promising Lynchburg boys in the U.S. Nationals at Forest Hills, Dr. Johnson continued to take Arthur and the other Lynchburg boys to as many ATA tournaments as possible. To his delight, Arthur, though barely fourteen, managed to win the 15-and-under ATA title in July 1957. "Suddenly everybody who was interested in Negro tennis took note of me," Arthur recalled. "When I went home to Richmond in the fall, my junior high school joined the Virginia Interscholastic Association (VIA) so it could enter me in the state high school all-Negro tennis tournament." Several months later the young star justified the school's faith in him by winning the VIA high school singles title—even though he was still technically a junior high school student.[31]

At this point, Arthur was beginning to look like a budding champion. During his final year at Graves Junior High—1957 to 1958—his appearance changed dramatically as he shot up in height and even put on a little weight. Though still rail thin, his weight was approaching one hundred pounds by June 1958, the month he left Richmond for his fifth summer in Lynchburg. He had come a long way. Now he had a clearer vision of where he was headed; and he was beginning to realize how hard he would have to work to get there. Most important, he had earned the respect of Dr. Johnson, who had begun to treat him as a rising star.

There were several young black players, in Lynchburg and elsewhere, who may have had more raw talent than Arthur. But with Dr. Johnson's help, he had turned himself into a paragon of emotional and physical control. Moreover, no one on the ATA circuit could match his determination and focus. Looking back on Arthur's rapid development during the mid-1950s, David Lash, the tennis coach at George Washington Carver High School in Durham, North Carolina, recalled: "He couldn't have weighed more than 80 pounds. But he loved to play. As soon as he finished his match he would find a good grassy spot and read a book. But the first question he asked when he came off the court was 'When do I play again?' Some boys didn't want to play many times a day, but Arthur did. He was always ready." [32]

FOUR

THE ONLY RAISIN IN A RICE PUDDING

◼

ASHE'S IMPRESSIVE CAPABILITIES AND enthusiasm were on full display during the summer of 1958. The "biggest thrill of the summer," he recalled, came at an ATA tournament in Norfolk, where he "beat Ron Charity for the first time." "It made me feel I was a man at last," he wrote in 1967. "And I guess Dr. Johnson also realized I was just about full grown, because that was the summer he quit practicing with me. He told me I'd gotten too good for him." Following this rite of passage, Ashe just got better and better. In June, he won the ATA Interscholastic singles title at a tournament in Durham, North Carolina, and two months later he won two more ATA championships at the national tournament in Wilberforce, Ohio, defeating Willis Thomas for the 15-and-under singles title before pairing with Thomas to win the doubles title. In between his ATA triumphs, Ashe competed in several USLTA tournaments, including the National Interscholastic tournament in Charlottesville, the Maryland Junior Championship (where he won the state title over 150 competitors), the New Jersey Boys' Tournament in Orange, which he also won, and the National Boys' Tournament in Kalamazoo, where he made it to the semifinals before losing.

Ashe's victories at Kalamazoo over several of the nation's best young players drew considerable attention—especially from a Wilson Sporting Goods representative who presented him with two free rackets, the first of many commercial gifts he would receive during his career. For an up-and-coming tennis player, receiving free equipment was an important milestone, the equivalent of being "knighted," as John McPhee once put it. Ashe's second visit to Kalamazoo was a triumph, and even his loss to future UCLA teammate David Sanderlin of California in a close semifinal match added to his growing reputation. Going into the match against Sanderlin, Ashe feared he would be completely overmatched. The "California boys," he later recalled, "were the power players. They'd grown up on those fast concrete courts, and they hit hard. The first time I watched Bill Bond I was scared. Big booming serve! Volleys like bullets! Dave Sanderlin and Dave Reed were almost as frightening." Ashe had a ways to go before he could give the powerful Californians a run for their money. Nevertheless, by the end of the year his national ranking in the 15-and-under Boys division had risen to number five, the best ever for a black male player.[1]

The only real disappointment of the summer occurred off the court, when officials of the Mid-Atlantic section of the USLTA rejected his application to compete for the section singles title. Since the racially restricted Country Club of Virginia was hosting the 1958 Mid-Atlantic Championships, Ashe was barred from playing, even though the tournament was being held in his hometown. The fact that he could live at home during the tournament and had no intention of using any of the Country Club's off-court facilities didn't matter to the local defenders of white privilege. By 1958, racially integrated tennis matches sanctioned by the USLTA had become commonplace in the neighboring border states of Maryland, Delaware, and West Virginia. But in Virginia the prospects for the integration of tennis—or of any other social or cultural institution—seemed dimmer than ever.[2]

Indeed, in 1958 racial lines seemed to be hardening all across Virginia as proponents of "Massive Resistance," the Old Dominion's self-professed brand of white supremacist reaction, encouraged outright defiance of the *Brown* school desegregation decision. Brandishing the doctrine of "inter-position" popularized by *Richmond News Leader* columnist James Jackson Kilpatrick, Virginia's attorney general, J. Lindsay Almond Jr., captured the governorship in November 1957 on a tidal wave of segregationist sentiment as the state capital became the vortex of the gathering political storm over integration.[3]

In this tense and uncertain atmosphere, Arthur entered Maggie Walker High School in September 1958 as a fifteen-year-old sophomore. Named for the nation's first black female bank president, his new school was within walking distance of Brook Field Park. Opened in 1937 as Richmond's first vocational high school for blacks, the large brick structure was a source of pride for the city's black residents. But with hordes of students coursing through its long corridors, the sprawling school could also be intimidating for new students accustomed to smaller institutions. While Arthur had no problem adjusting to the academic side of high school life, he felt somewhat out of place socially. "In high school I was pretty much alone," he recalled. "I'd been away every summer, and even when I was in town, I'd been on the tennis court most of the time. So I didn't get around much, didn't make many friends." Part of the problem was the severe restrictions his father placed on his social life. "Arthur didn't have a lot of friends," Ken Wright, one of his Walker High classmates, recalled. "His father had a reputation for being very strict, and there were only a few of us whom Arthur would hang out with. We'd ride our bikes, go swimming, he'd even eat dinner at my house. But whenever it started to get dark, he'd always get on his bike and take off."

Throughout his high school years, tennis continued to dominate Arthur's life, overshadowing the few personal relationships that punctuated his free time. Even so, during his two years at Walker, he made a concerted effort to become involved in activities beyond the tennis court. In addition to getting good grades, he joined several clubs, played second trumpet in the school band, developed a close friendship with the band director's son Joey Kennedy, and made the starting lineup of the junior varsity basketball team. Judging by his memoirs, he also discovered girls, including his first serious girlfriend, Pat Battles, the strikingly attractive daughter of a prominent black tennis coach from Stamford, Connecticut. After meeting at an ATA tournament in 1959, the young couple maintained an intermittent, mostly long-distance romance until 1967.

He was also an ardent Brooklyn Dodgers and Jackie Robinson fan, and in the spring of 1959 he enjoyed a brief stint as a second baseman and relief pitcher on the school baseball team. For several summers, he had spent many pleasant hours at a Brook Field baseball camp run by Maxie Robinson, a history teacher at Armstrong High School and the father of his friend Randall, who many years later would found the anti-apartheid organization TransAfrica. As a teenager Ashe was as passionate about baseball as he was about tennis, but his baseball career ended abruptly when the principal limited him to one spring sport. "I couldn't play both baseball and tennis," Arthur explained years later, "so I'd have to make a choice. . . . I never pitched again."[4]

Arthur never regretted his choice, but there must have been moments when he questioned the value of playing tennis for Walker High. In Jackson

Ward, as in most black communities, tennis was often dismissed as an insignificant sport. To many of Arthur's male classmates, tennis was a "sissy" sport, unlike football, basketball, and baseball, which were associated with the manly virtues of toughness and power. Perceived as a teachers' pet and "too much of a good thing," as one observer put it, he found it difficult to be just one of the boys. To make matters worse, the tennis scene at Walker High was less than inspiring. "Tennis wasn't much at Walker," he remembered. "The coach was just there because nobody else would take the job. None of the other guys on the team had trained under Dr. Johnson. They didn't know much about tournaments." For a serious and experienced player who had his sights set on a top national USLTA ranking, this was a formula for frustration.

He was also frustrated by a lack of playing time during the late fall and winter months, when cold and inclement weather often made it impossible to play outdoors. Many of the best young players—including the boys he had competed against at Kalamazoo—played all year round, either on the outdoor courts of Southern California or Florida, or on indoor courts. In Richmond, as in virtually all Southern cities, indoor tennis facilities were both scarce and rigidly segregated. While he was cooling his heels in Virginia, the rest of the tennis elite enjoyed the luxury of "off-season" competition.

Coupled with the difficulty and expense of traveling to more hospitable Northern venues, this race-based disadvantage constituted a serious impediment to Ashe's development as a top-flight player. As he once explained, by 1957 he had begun to realize what he was up against. Most obviously, he had no access to the "white Tennis Patrons Association in Richmond" which "sent white boys to all the national tournaments, with all expenses paid and all arrangements made." "For a while I felt a little bitter about that," he conceded, "—because by this time I was getting good enough to beat almost anybody my own age. . . . I was now ranked fourth among all boys in the Mid-Atlantic Section, and 31st in the nation. That was frustrating. I felt I could be ranked much higher if I ever played against those ranked above me."[5]

Arthur's first experience with winter play revealed what he had been missing. At Dr. J's urging, the organizers of the Orange Bowl International Junior Cup Tournament invited two Lynchburg boys, Arthur and Horace Cunningham, to participate in its December 1958 competition in Miami. This was a momentous development—the first time a USLTA-sanctioned tournament held in the South had included black players. The two boys were too young to comprehend the full significance of this milestone, but they were certainly happy to participate in a prestigious tournament that brought together young players from fifteen nations and served as a testing ground for the selection of the U.S. Junior Davis Cup team.

Arthur was thrilled by the invitation to play against international competitors, and even more by the prospect of becoming the first black player to represent the United States in Junior Davis Cup competition. He was, however, a bit disappointed to learn he and Cunningham would have to stay in a private home (owned by D.C. Moore, a local black tennis enthusiast) removed from their fellow competitors—all of whom were being housed in a whites-only hotel. Miami was racially segregated, yet, as Arthur sensed almost immediately, the Magic City's status as a tourist town made it more cosmopolitan and less obsessed with white supremacy than the cities of Virginia and the Deep South. A decade later, in the early 1970s, he would grow to love Miami and to consider it his second home. So it was fitting that one of his first major experiences with a measure of freedom took place among the swaying palms of South Florida.

Arthur's performance in Miami, though certainly creditable, was not quite good enough to earn him one of the two U.S. team positions in the Orange Bowl competition, or a spot on the Junior Davis Cup squad. Nevertheless, his spirited victories in the first four rounds of the Boys 15-and-under division turned more than a few heads before he ran into trouble in the semifinals against Charlie Pasarell, a talented fourteen-year-old from Puerto Rico. At this point, Arthur did not have the consistency or the experience to keep up with Pasarell, or with the ultimate winner of the Boys competition, Clark Graebner, whom he had met at Kalamazoo in 1957. But he left Miami with a much better sense of what to expect from the world's best young players.

Perhaps even more important in the long run, he had also acquired several budding friendships, including a special bond with Pasarell, his future college roommate. "He came from a lot of money, he was cultured and sure," Arthur later said of Pasarell, "and I was an insecure southern black kid out on my own. There were no blacks and no friends to speak of. And Charlie, I found out, was always there. I don't know whether he did it out of sympathy, but when I did seek out his friendship, he never refused it."

Known as "Charlito" in his native Puerto Rico, Pasarell was born into the island version of tennis royalty. His father, Charles Pasarell Sr., won the Puerto Rican singles championship no fewer than six times in the 1950s, his mother, Dora, was for a time the best women's player on the island, and as early as 1939 his uncle José Luis Pasarell won the island singles title. From early childhood, Charlito was groomed for tennis greatness, training not only with his father and uncles but also with Welby Horn, the celebrated teaching pro at San Juan's posh Caribe Hilton Hotel. By the time he was eleven, Charlito had already appeared on the cover of *World Tennis* magazine and was widely considered to be one of the most promising young tennis talents in the world. With his elegant strokes and strong serve, he could be a ferocious opponent on the court. But his off-court personality was famously warm and welcoming, so much so that he became "Possum" to his friends. He was a gentle, fun-loving soul destined to become Arthur's lifelong friend and confidant.[6]

The heady trip to Miami whetted Arthur's appetite for competition at the highest level. In July 1959, he would turn sixteen and move up to the Junior division. So he knew that in the near future he would have to step up his game to have any hope of entering the top echelon of mainstream tennis. His play that spring was limited to high school and ATA competition, which he dominated with little effort. As the ATA and Virginia Interscholastic Union champion, he was guaranteed one of the four black positions in the draw at the USLTA Interscholastic national tournament held in Charlottesville in mid-June. He had not fared very well in Charlottesville the previous year and was eager to demonstrate to himself, and to Dr. J, that he was now ready to compete at the highest level.

His first serious test of the year, however, came not in Charlottesville but in Baltimore in early June, when he competed in the Maryland State Junior Championships. Dr. J was banking on a good performance from Arthur in Baltimore, which he felt would guarantee an invitation to the Mid-Atlantic Junior Championships to be held at the Congressional Country Club in Bethesda, Maryland, in July. Still smarting from Arthur's exclusion from the 1958 Mid-Atlantic tournament held in Richmond, he was bound and determined to place him in the 1959 tournament. Arthur did his part, winning the Maryland state title in convincing fashion in a four-set final that saw him win 18 of the last 20 games. But to the dismay of both Dr. J and his talented protégé, the expected invitation to the Mid-Atlantic tournament did not materialize. Describing the incident eight years later, Ashe could not conceal his lingering bitterness: "They said my entry was filed too late and they had all the players they could handle. We knew that wasn't the reason. . . . To the tennis fathers there I was an untouchable, a nothing, and always would be."[7]

Before the summer of 1959 was over, the twists and turns of a society experiencing partial and involuntary desegregation [ ] down a roller coaster of emotions. For a sixteen-year-o[ ] on control and composure, the unpredictability and s[ ] white behavior was a continuing source of confusio[ ] of these emerging themes were on full display when [ ] and four other Lynchburg boys to the USLTA Interscholastic tournament in Charlottesville in mid-June.

This was the ninth year of black participation in the tournament, and Dr. J was still waiting for one of his boys to make a serious run at the title. Once again he would be disappointed, as all of the Lynchburg boys were eliminated in the early rounds of the 1959 tournament. Even so, he and his charges did witness progress of another kind, or so it seemed for a few hours. Earlier in the month, Robert Bland had become the first black student to receive a bachelor's degree from the University of Virginia, and this tentative move toward inclusion, however grudging, prompted a change in the tournament's housing policies. For the first time, Dr. J's contingent was invited to stay in a university dormitory rather than being forced to return home each night to Lynchburg. To Johnson's amazement, Arthur and the other boys were also invited to use the university's dining facilities, and even to take in a movie at the campus theater.

Unfortunately, but predictably, not everyone at the tournament entered into the spirit of this newfound tolerance. As one of the Lynchburg boys, Charles Brown of Durham, recalled, the "integrated" Charlottesville experience of 1959 turned into an almost tragicomic series of "strange happenings." "We arrived late that first night," he remembered. "They assigned us to a dormitory that had about 15 other guys who were already there and asleep. When we awoke the next morning, we were the only ones there. They had moved their beds out. Also, they gave all the players passes to go to the theatre, but we had to sit upstairs. Strange."[8]

Virginia's racial situation in the late 1950s was as tense as it was contradictory, even on the campus of a university claiming principles of moderation. The legally codified hegemony of white supremacist values was still very much in evidence everywhere south of the Mason-Dixon line. Segregation was also common in the North, of course, but as a matter of custom, not law. Arthur discovered the difference during the summer of 1959, when he expanded his range of experience beyond the familiar, traveling to the Northeast on three separate occasions. He had already been to Kalamazoo and Ohio with Dr. J, and to Chicago on a brief trip with his grandmother; and he had already played in one Northeastern tournament, the 1958 New

State Boys Championship held at the Berkeley Tennis Club in Orange. But the summer trips of 1959 represented his first meaningful experience with the metropolitan culture of greater New York.

Arthur's Northeastern adventure—and his official career as a Junior—
both began at the posh Berkeley club, where he competed for the New Jersey
State Junior singles title in mid-July, just days after his sixteenth birthday.
Seeded second behind Herb Fitzgibbon, he played well throughout the
tournament and ultimately defeated Fitzgibbon—all six feet, four inches of
him—in a grueling five-set final. But he had to play the match of his life
to do so. Having lost in straight sets to Fitzgibbon at Kalamazoo in 1957,
he was a heavy underdog. Prior to the match, Dr. J gave him strict instructions on how to foil his towering opponent. "Don't try to pass him," Johnson
counseled. "Try to hold him back from the net by hitting deep. When he
does get to the net, lob deep and try to retrieve every smash. Keep at it no
matter what."

Years later Arthur recalled the remarkable turnaround that launched his
career as a Junior: "I followed instructions and lost the first set 6–1. Still, I
kept lobbing. Soon the second set was gone too, 6–1. But I would no more
disobey Dr. Johnson than I would spit in his face. Fitzgibbon ran up a 4–1
lead in the third set and the spectators must have thought I was slaphappy,
because I'd reached the finals with my passing shots and now I wouldn't
try to pass Fitzgibbon. But finally he weakened, from all that running and
smashing, and began missing his overheads. That was my signal to begin
passing him. He took only one more game in the set, and I pulled it out 7–5.
He was through. I gobbled up the last two sets 6–1, 6–0." [9]

Arthur's unexpected triumph at the New Jersey Junior tournament was
thrilling, both for him and for Dr. J. But the Lynchburg upstarts had no
time to savor their victory. With only a week to prepare for the Eastern Junior Championships, held at the West Side Tennis Club in Forest Hills,
they settled in for a few days of practice in the Big Apple. Like all aspiring
tennis stars, Arthur had dreamed of playing on the hallowed grass at Forest
Hills, so he felt exhilarated by his first glimpse of what he later called "sacred
ground." But he couldn't avoid feeling he was out of place and not altogether welcome at Forest Hills. The atmosphere of white privilege had been
palpable at the Berkeley Tennis Club, but it was doubly so at the West Side
Tennis Club. Even though Althea Gibson had breached the local color bar at
the U.S. Nationals nine years earlier, racial exclusion was still the norm. The
week Ashe arrived in Forest Hills, Ralph Bunche announced he and his son
had once again been rejected for membership in the club.

With the Bunche controversy swirling in the headlines, Arthur took the court as both the number one seed and the only black in the tournament. Despite this diversion and a few catcalls from the crowd, he played well from the outset and fought his way into the finals against Hugh Lynch. A violent rainstorm forced a postponement and the relocation of the match to the North Shore Tennis and Racquets Club in Bayside, Queens, where Arthur won the first set 7–5. But after a shift in the weather forced a second postponement and a return to West Side, he lost the last three sets and the title. Even so, he won plaudits from his mentor. "He's going to be a good one," Johnson told a *Washington Post* reporter. "He has the perfect temperament for tennis. When he makes an error he just smiles. I can't use a boy unless he can control his emotions."[10]

A few days after Arthur's creditable showing, the Richmond public courts tennis director Sam Woods received a letter from the West Side club inviting him "to form a five-boy team that would play" similar teams from New York and other Middle-Atlantic cities. The letter suggested that the Richmond team should include the city's two best young players, Arthur and Tom Chewning. A white boy who would later cross the color line to play on the courts at Brook Field Park, Tom would become Arthur's closest white friend in Richmond after they met at a 1960 USLTA tournament in Wheeling, West Virginia. Before Wheeling, Tom had never heard of Arthur, even though they had lived and played in the same city all of their lives. Arthur, by contrast, was already familiar with Tom's exploits, having read about them in the Richmond press for several years. This incongruity embarrassed Tom, but he, like Arthur, welcomed the opportunity to participate in the intercity competition. Both boys were crushed when Woods declined the invitation. "Probably, he had to, if he wanted to hold his job in Richmond," Arthur later observed.[11]

Dr. J was also disappointed, but he took a measure of consolation from the West Side club's initiative. One of Johnson's long-standing goals was to see one or more of his Lynchburg boys play in the U.S. National Championships at Forest Hills. But for nearly a decade he had been stymied by ATA executive secretary Baker's policy of selecting only senior players as the ATA's designated participants at Forest Hills. Every year Johnson pressed Baker to change the policy, and every year he came away disappointed. Finally, in July 1959, Baker agreed to choose three of the ATA's most promising juniors—Joe Williams, Horace Cunningham, and Ashe. He even promised to arrange a week of practice on grass courts for the three Lynchburg boys. But in the end he reneged on both promises, tendering a lone invitation to

Ashe. This last-minute reversal brought the simmering feud between Johnson and Baker to a head, though at least Ashe got a second chance to appear
on the grandest stage in American tennis.[12]

Coming six weeks after his participation in the Eastern Junior Championships, Arthur's second appearance at Forest Hills was intoxicating
but brief. The luck of the draw pitted him against the most talented young
player in the world, the twenty-one-year-old Australian Rod Laver, in the
first round. A powerful left-hander with a devastating serve, "the Rocket,"
as he was known, would win three consecutive U.S. National singles titles
between 1960 and 1962 and ultimately prove to be Arthur's greatest nemesis,
winning 19 of 22 head-to-head matches. In 1959, Arthur reportedly "served
well and hit with good pace and length off the ground," but several mis-
played volleys gave the edge to Laver, who won in straight sets 7–5, 6–2, 6–2.
Though clearly overmatched, the young Virginian came away with his pride
intact—not bad for a sixteen-year-old about to enter his junior year in high
school. While Richmond's white establishment clearly had no regard for his
emerging talent, he drew considerable satisfaction from attracting attention
in the nation's largest city.[13]

Arthur returned from Forest Hills in early September, just prior to the opening of the school year. It was his second year at Walker High, and he settled
in like a veteran. His grades were excellent, and he got on well with his
teachers. He now had his driver's license and occasional use of his father's
pickup truck, and to his surprise the family rules were relaxed to allow him
to stay out until 11 p.m. on some weekend nights. Most of his friends had
much later curfews, but he didn't dare complain. He had a few casual dates,
one of which resulted in his first serious sexual experience, an impromptu
late-night front-seat seduction at the hands of a girl who knew what she was
doing. As Arthur recalled the scene, which amazingly enough took place in
a parking lot at the normally whites-only Byrd Park: "Soon my pants were
down, her dress was up and her panties pulled down and she shoved me
under the steering wheel. I just went along. . . . I could not let her think this
was my first time."

The excitement of sexual initiation was memorable enough to make it
into Arthur's 1981 memoir, *Off the Court*. But in 1959 he was fixated on his
continuing long-distance infatuation with Pat Battles. With her, he was a
perfect gentleman, happy to take things slowly. He was also reasonably content with his home life, having resigned himself to his father's strict ways and
having developed a close and loving relationship with his stepmother. Like

most adolescents, he suffered from periodic insecurities and mood swings, but, all in all, he seemed to have few complaints.[14]

What he worried about most was his future as a tennis player. Now that he had seen something of the world beyond Richmond, he realized that both time and place were against him. In the nation as a whole, the arc of history had begun to tilt toward increased tolerance and racial justice, but not in Virginia, where the fixation with racial segregation and white supremacy seemed stronger than ever. Years later, he recalled being deeply discouraged by the dark cloud of racism that threatened to blot out his potentially bright future: "I wondered if there was any point in keeping on with the grind of serious tennis. A Negro player didn't seem to have any future. Many players had lost hope and dropped out after a few summers with Dr. Johnson." Knowing that "some of those ex-players were driving cabs or mopping floors around Richmond and Lynchburg," he feared he would share their fate. "Did I want to go their way?" he asked himself. After considerable soul-searching, he decided to stick with tennis even in the face of racial discrimination and disadvantage. Reasoning that those "who had hung on even after the tournament gates slammed in their faces had at least gotten a better start in life," usually in the form of college scholarships arranged by Dr. J, the resilient sixteen-year-old "kept on."[15]

Arthur's persistence was rooted not only in the expectation of a college scholarship but also in his abiding love for the game and a determination to please his father and Dr. J, both of whom had made numerous sacrifices on his behalf. But there was no clear path beyond college. Planning a life around the game of tennis was a viable option for rich amateurs, not for those in need of gainful employment. Prior to the post-1968 Open era—a future virtually impossible to foresee at the beginning of the decade—the idea of achieving financial success, or even a modest living, solely through tennis was fanciful at best. While success on the tennis court might lead to a coaching career, the number of positions open to African Americans was limited, and many of those were part-time. As a top student, Ashe could envision other career choices—in law, medicine, education, or business. But a tennis-centered life was a dim prospect for a young black man coming of age in the early 1960s.

Arthur's motivations as a maturing adolescent were complex, and his continuing attraction to tennis involved varying calculations of risk and promise. Yet there was no sense of desperation. In later years, when journalists and others inquired about the trajectory of his life, he tried to counter the notion that he had used tennis to escape the alleged miseries of poverty and black life in Richmond. "We were never poor. Not even close," he insisted in 1968. "Things weren't that tough for me."[16]

What he did hope to escape, he freely acknowledged, was the stultifying racism that narrowed his options whenever he ventured outside the black community. Recalling his early childhood in Richmond, he insisted "the first whites I got to know—the insurance collectors, the Thalhimers, the Schillers, the Schwartzchilds—were nice people, so my first impression of whites was positive." "But I soon learned," he added, "that, collectively, white people didn't really like blacks. They kept us from going to school with them, worshipping with them, playing with them." The early realization that most white Virginians regarded him as less than fully human was reinforced by all manner of racial epithets. "I grew up aware that I was a Negro, colored, black, a coon, a pickaninny, a nigger, an ace, a spade, and other less flattering terms," he recalled with sadness in 1981.[17]

During the winter and spring of 1960, the racial situation in Richmond became increasingly volatile. In late February, several hundred students at Virginia Union joined the widening sit-in movement begun three weeks earlier by four North Carolina A&T students in Greensboro. On the first day of the Richmond protest, future Student Nonviolent Coordinating Committee (SNCC) field secretary Charles Sherrod led two hundred students down Chamberlayne Avenue, just east of the Ashes' house in Brook Field Park. Headed for a segregated Woolworth's lunch counter, they soon occupied a row of stools and waited patiently until closing time to be served. Two days later, the sit-ins spread to Thalhimers department store, where several students were arrested for trespassing. Picketing and mass rallies ensued, galvanizing much of the local black community and producing a seven-month-long boycott of Richmond's downtown business district. The crisis subsided somewhat in September, when several stores agreed to desegregate their lunch counters. The comforting fiction of local black complacency was gone forever.[18]

Tensions were also rising on the education front, where the NAACP was demanding belated compliance with the *Brown* decision. In early 1959 the federal courts had declared Virginia's Massive Resistance laws unconstitutional, paving the way for successful local desegregation suits in Richmond and other school districts. Pressured by a local civil rights organization known as the Crusade for Voters, the Richmond school board reluctantly endorsed token desegregation in the spring of 1960. Led by board chairman and future U.S. Supreme Court justice Lewis Powell Jr., who publicly advocated tokenism as the best means of avoiding "substantial integration,"

Richmond's pragmatic white establishment hoped to avoid the fate of nearby Prince Edward County, which had closed its entire public school system the previous fall. On September 7, 1960, the enrollment of two black students at the previously all-white Chandler Junior High School initiated a new era in Richmond's racial history. Two years later, Arthur's younger brother, Johnnie, would enroll as a freshman at the newly integrated John Marshall High School, becoming one of only 127 black students in Richmond enrolled in an integrated school.[19]

As the son of a conservative and protective father, Arthur did not dare to become involved in any of this agitation—commonly known among traditionalists as "the civil rights mess." But as a highly visible participant in predominantly white tournaments, he could not avoid the escalating racial tensions that permeated Virginia and the surrounding region. In the tennis world, even in times of crisis, racial discrimination tended to be subtler than in the world at large. As Arthur once put it, most tennis players were "too well mannered to express racism crudely." "No one ever refused to appear on court with me," he recalled. "No official ever called me a name. But the indirect rebuffs and innuendoes left their scars."

One such scar came from an incident at the June 1960 Maryland State Junior Tournament, after Arthur and his fellow Lynchburg camper Joe Williams dominated the draw and faced each other in the finals. In an obvious snub, the tournament officials canceled the normal award ceremony and simply "left the trophies" on a bench. A month later, at the Mid-Atlantic Junior Championships held in Wheeling, Arthur won the tournament that had excluded him the previous two years. As he later recalled with pride, the victory "made me the first Negro boy ever to win such an important tournament." Yet he was nearly disqualified when local officials falsely accused him of ransacking the cabins where the players were housed. After Dr. Johnson vouched for his protégé, the officials backed off. But the tournament's first black champion left town with a bitter memory of racial presumption.[20]

A third unfortunate incident occurred at the 1960 National Interscholastic tournament in Charlottesville, though this time Arthur was partially to blame. As the tournament's #8 seed, he had a legitimate shot at the coveted title that had eluded the Lynchburg boys for nearly a decade. This situation, coupled with the worsening racial climate, prompted Dr. Johnson to remind him and the other boys about the importance of avoiding any hint of racial conflict during the tournament. Reiterating his standard warning, Johnson stressed: "it was vital not to stir up any trouble." "A white player might throw a conniption fit about a linesman's decision," Arthur explained, paraphrasing his mentor. "Not us. In fact, during the early matches of a tournament on outside courts, where there were no linesmen and sometimes no umpires, and players called their own lines, Dr. Johnson warned us to give our opponents the benefit of the doubt on every close shot. If a ball landed slightly outside, we were to play it anyhow."[21]

As always, Arthur took Dr. J's advice to heart, which proved to be his undoing. Midway through a quarterfinal match against the tournament's #1 seed, Billy Lenoir of Atlanta, Arthur was up a set and leading 4–3 in the second, when an errant ball from a nearby court derailed his bid for an upset. On game point in the eighth game, he appeared to win the crucial point and the game with a drop shot beyond Lenoir's reach. But when he noticed another ball had rolled onto the backcourt well behind Lenoir, he reflexively asked his opponent if the ball had interfered with his play. Dr. J, sitting just a few feet away from the action, later described what happened next: "Lenoir looked back, saw the ball and said 'The referee said to always play a point over if the ball comes on the court.' The score would have been 5–3 in favor of Ashe if he had kept his big mouth shut. They played the point over, Lenoir won the point, the game, the set, and the next set because Ashe had lost his concentration, thinking about what it had cost him for opening his mouth, something he rarely does while playing. He did not win but two more games. He lost the biggest opportunity of his lifetime." "Maybe I carried the 'fair play' rule too far," Arthur later conceded. But perhaps only he, along with Dr. J and the other Lynchburg boys, could fully appreciate what happened that day.[22]

Race generally receded into the background when Arthur was at the Lynchburg camp—except when Dr. J uttered one of his favorite motivational reminders such as "Hit that to a white boy and you'll go home early" or "You're not going to beat those white boys playing like that." Race was never an issue at the all-black ATA tournaments, where the sole focus was competition. When Arthur became the youngest men's singles champion in ATA history in early August 1960, easily defeating six-time former champion George Stewart in the finals, he didn't dwell on his identity as a champion limited by race.

Everywhere else, however, racial identification and scrutiny seemed unavoidable. Even at the National Boys Tournament at Kalamazoo, in the hinterlands of western Michigan, Arthur caused a minor stir when he beat a white Rhodesian, Adrian Bey, in the second round. Both boys took their unexpected pairing in stride, but the racial politics of the scene, accentuated by Rhodesia's harsh system of racial discrimination, did not go unnoticed by others. Although he kept his feelings to himself, Arthur bitterly resented the almost constant racial commentary that surrounded his early participation in mainstream tennis. Like Althea Gibson, he wanted to be judged as an individual, not as the representative of a racial minority. While he acknowledged that he was "as noticeable as the only raisin in a rice pudding," the curiosity factor was a burdensome diversion for a serious athlete trying to keep his eyes, literally and figuratively, on the ball.[23]

FIVE

THE GATEWAY

∎

T O HAVE ANY HOPE of reaching his potential as a tennis player, Arthur needed professional coaching and sustained competition at the highest level possible, neither of which was available to him in his home state. "Anybody, white or Negro, who had a strong tennis game," he concluded, "had to get out of Virginia if he wanted to keep climbing."[1]

Encouraged by Dr. Johnson, Arthur had set his sights on securing a scholarship from one of the nation's top college tennis programs. But doing so was easier said than done, especially for a player from an all-black high school with a weak tennis program and a questionable academic reputation. As good as he was, he would have to continue to improve during his senior year to have a legitimate chance. Chasing a moving target, he had to find a way to keep pace with the California boys and the other nationally ranked Juniors who seemed to get better every time he played them. Nearing six feet, and a lean but solid 140 pounds, he was finally big enough to compete with the nation's best Juniors. But he also needed training conditions and competitive playing experiences that were comparable to those of his white opponents.

In tennis, timing is everything, not just in striking the ball but also in exploiting the opportunities of youth. And in the summer of 1960 Dr. J feared his seventeen-year-old star was running out of time. Frustrated with the racial situation in Richmond, and convinced Arthur could not afford another winter of enforced idleness or another spring of unproductive, high school play, Johnson, with the help of his old friend Dick Hudlin, concocted a plan for a transitional year at Charles Sumner High School in St. Louis, Missouri. Hudlin, the former University of Chicago team captain who had helped Oscar Johnson break the color line at the USLTA National Junior Indoor tournament back in 1948, was a teacher and longtime tennis coach at Sumner. Like Dr. J, he lived and breathed tennis, was passionate about Junior development, and had a private court in his backyard. He was also a strict disciplinarian, cut from the same cloth as Dr. J and Arthur Ashe Sr. Only after Arthur Sr. became convinced Hudlin would keep his son in line was the deal set. These three men, "the men who planned my life," as Arthur later called them, worked out an arrangement that provided for room and board at the Hudlins' house and a rigorous daily training regimen.

Arthur himself was never consulted about the arrangement and only heard about it definitively in late August, barely two weeks before the beginning of the school year. Earlier in the summer, during the Eastern Junior Championships in New York, Cliff Buchholz made an offhand comment about Arthur "moving to St. Louis," but at the time he assumed Buchholz "was kidding." A few weeks later, when he learned it was true, he could hardly believe it. "Near the end of the summer Dr. Johnson phoned me and said, 'I've made arrangements for you to live in St. Louis,'" he recalled, with a touch of resentment. "He didn't ask me, he just told me."[2]

The decision to send him to St. Louis made sense—from a strictly tennis point of view. As Dr. Johnson assured him, and as Arthur himself later confirmed, "There were good indoor courts. I could play year-round with stars like Cliff Buchholz and his brother Butch, Chuck McKinley, Dick Horwitz, and Jim Parker. It would be great for my tennis. And it would give me a better chance of getting into one of the good universities, which usually don't accept certification from segregated high schools." Even so, he wasn't happy about leaving his friends and family on the eve of his senior year. He had done well at Walker and fully expected to be named the class valedictorian at the spring commencement. Tennis considerations aside, he was concerned about how he would fare living as a boarder in a teacher's home and trying to fit in at a new school in a strange city.[3]

Despite his misgivings, Arthur decided, in characteristic fashion, "to make the best use of the opportunity" presented to him. Fortunately, his anxiety-filled trip to St. Louis was preceded by the diversion of a second appearance at the U.S. Nationals in New York. This time he was fortunate to draw a less formidable first-round opponent than Laver—Robert Bowditch, whom he defeated in straight sets. He was less successful in the second round, winning only eight games in three sets against Eduardo Zuleta of Ecuador. The loss to Zuleta confirmed what he already knew, that his patient baseline game was especially vulnerable on fast surfaces like grass. One of the advantages of relocating to St. Louis, Dr. Johnson had assured him, was the opportunity to play indoors on a fast, hard surface.[4]

The Hudlins gave Arthur a warm welcome and did their best to ease his transition to a new home, school, and community. But living with them proved to be less than ideal. To Arthur's dismay, the household situation in St. Louis allowed him little privacy or personal freedom. Coach Hudlin was a stern taskmaster with a controlling personality, even by the strict standards of Dr. Johnson and Arthur Ashe Sr. "He planned everything as if I had no brain," Arthur later complained. "He felt that tennis was the one big pleasure in life, so he gave me massive daily doses of it. I hinted a hundred times that I thought he was a bit domineering, but I never got through to him." The daily routine was grinding: "I did pushups every morning, went to school until noon, then played tennis all afternoon," and "every evening, after tennis, I ran a mile." The meals were plentiful enough, with "plenty of steak and rice," but they came with absolute restrictions—"no ice cream, no sodas, only fruit juice, only certain foods for breakfast." While Hudlin's rules all made sense as a boot-camp training regimen, this was not the way Arthur had hoped to spend his senior year. There was no escape, even on Sundays when he was required to attend mass with his devoutly Roman Catholic host family.

To make matters worse, he also had to deal with the Hudlins' troublesome ninth-grade son, Dickie. The Hudlins had hoped Arthur would serve as a role model for Dickie. But he had no luck in countering the boy's utter disdain for tennis or his mounting jealousy of the intruder posing as his surrogate older brother.[5]

"St. Louis," he later concluded, "was the worst nine months I ever spent." Part of the problem was the disappointing nature of the city itself. Prior to his arrival, he had envisioned his new home as a Midwestern river city located safely beyond the boundaries of the Jim Crow South. But it didn't take him long to detect the Gateway City's distinctively Southern tinge. Missouri lacked Virginia's codified statewide system of segregation, and there was a liberal faction on the St. Louis Board of Aldermen that actually managed to pass a local antidiscrimination ordinance in 1961. Nevertheless, St. Louis's traditional patterns of residential segregation, reinforced as they were by deep class divisions and pervasive economic inequality, produced a divided community that, in Arthur's words, "was de facto virtually as segregated as Richmond."[6]

Sumner High School, where Arthur spent much of his time during his year in St. Louis, was located in the heart of The Ville, an all-black neighborhood on the north side of the city. Originally known as Elleardsville, the area had once hosted an ethnically diverse population plus a sprinkling of former slaves. But in the years prior to World War I substantial black in-migration initiated a period of white flight that eventually transformed the area into a predominantly black community. Sumner High School, established in 1875 as the first all-black high school west of the Mississippi River, moved to The Ville from its original downtown location in 1910.

Soon thereafter the introduction of several black churches and the growth of a thriving black business district turned The Ville into St. Louis's most fashionable black neighborhood. The cornerstone of The Ville's development as a black cultural and commercial center was Poro College, established in 1913 by beauty products entrepreneur Annie Malone. By the 1930s, Poro College was just one part of a large cluster of important black institutions, most notably Homer G. Phillips Hospital, Lincoln Law School, and Stowe Teachers College. The bustling nightlife in The Ville's jazz and dance clubs added to the neighborhood's citywide reputation as the "cradle of black culture." By then, despite the advent of hard times, the Ville had become a tightly packed community of ten thousand; though nearly 90 percent black, the neighborhood was dominated by fully employed homeowners, many of whom considered themselves part of a rising black middle class.

Prior to the 1948 U.S. Supreme Court ruling in *Shelley v. Kraemer*, strictly enforced restrictive covenants made it all but impossible for blacks to buy homes in "white" neighborhoods. Yet once the Court forbade the use of such covenants, the halcyon days of neighborhoods like The Ville were numbered. During the 1950s, The Ville began to lose its critical mass of middle-class residents, a depopulation and "ghettoization" process that would only accelerate during the following decades, especially after the passage of the Fair Housing Act of 1968. By the time Arthur arrived in the late summer of 1960, the area surrounding Sumner High retained little of the vital character that had made it such a desirable place to live in the pre–World War II era.

Interestingly enough, one of the solid, middle-class citizens who had already moved away from The Ville was Dick Hudlin. Several years prior to Arthur's arrival, the proud University of Chicago graduate had bought a home in the virtually all-white, upscale suburb of Richmond Heights, originally named in the 1850s by Robert E. Lee, who found the township's topography to be strikingly similar to the environs of Richmond, Virginia. But whatever its etymological origins, Richmond Heights was demographically and culturally far removed from the inner city.

Hudlin faced stiff challenges as one of the first blacks to live in Richmond Heights. Despite his impressive educational background and his considerable accomplishments as a teacher and a coach, he encountered open resistance and cold stares among his white neighbors. Geographically, Richmond Heights was located eight miles southwest of The Ville, but racially it was a world apart. The daily drive to Sumner High took Hudlin and his young boarder past the sprawling grounds of Forest Park and through a variety of communities, white and black, suburban and inner city, all of which added to their worldly education.[7]

Arthur sensed The Ville's distinctive identity the moment he walked into Sumner High School. He had traveled eight hundred miles from Richmond only to discover that the South had no monopoly on racially segregated education. Even though the St. Louis school system was legally integrated, Sumner was an all-black school located in a virtually all-black neighborhood. "It was a different sort of neighborhood from Richmond's North Side," he observed. "The kids were more street-wise, and you had to be tougher to survive. There were more kids in the school, and you didn't get that feeling of community that you did at Maggie Walker."

All of this was disappointing for someone who had expected more from his new school. To his surprise, he encountered very few challenging courses at Sumner and easily finished the year with the highest grade-point average in the senior class—partly, according to him, because there was "little social activity to distract me from studying." As he put it, "I was almost a stranger in that school. I would have much preferred to graduate with my friends at Walker, I pined and sighed a lot." Aside from a brief stint on Sumner's cross-country team and his activities as captain of the tennis squad, he generally kept to himself. According to Cliff Buchholz, who grew close to Arthur during his year in St. Louis, the quiet, bookish kid from Virginia spent most of his off-court time reading in his room at the Hudlins' house.[8]

Looking back on the situation years later, Arthur concluded that the improvement in his game more than compensated for the social sacrifices and loneliness he experienced. During his first three months in St. Louis, he practiced on the outdoor courts at Washington University, an elite private institution located in one of the city's most fashionable neighborhoods. The opportunity to play almost daily with the talented Buchholz brothers, Jim Parker, and other highly competitive players gradually lifted the quality of his play. But the most noticeable change came a bit later, after the weather forced him to play indoors. St. Louis's only indoor tennis facility was the 138th Infantry Armory, a public facility legally open to all. As with many institutions in St. Louis, a long-standing tradition of de facto segregation informally barred blacks from playing on the armory's courts, and Arthur was not surprised to learn that he was "only the second Negro ever to play there." Fortunately, the armory's resident pro, Larry Miller, had assured Coach Hudlin and Dr. Johnson that their talented prospect would have full access to the armory's five courts. Later, after catching a glimpse of the young Virginian's potential, Miller volunteered to help coach him.[9]

Arthur worked with Miller on the armory courts throughout the winter of 1960–61. The first test of his St. Louis sojourn came in late November, just before the winter makeover, when he entered the National Junior Indoor Tournament held at the armory. This was the same tournament that had temporarily invalidated Oscar Johnson's registration twelve years earlier, but the times had changed and no one questioned Arthur's right to compete. Nevertheless, no one expected a baseliner to fare very well on the armory's slick surface against big hitters adept at the serve-and-volley game.

Both Miller and Hudlin were amazed when Arthur fought his way into the semifinals, where he faced the number three seed, Butch Newman of San Antonio. And even after he dispatched Newman in straight sets 6–2, 6–4, his chances of defeating the number one seed, Frank Froehling, seemed remote. Nicknamed the "Spider Man," the long-legged Froehling was four inches taller and two years older than Arthur—and he possessed the most powerful serve in Junior tennis. Arthur's only hope was to move Froehling around the court with passing shots and lobs, but to do so he had to adapt to a lightning-quick surface that played to his opponent's strengths. This was a tall order, but after winning the first two sets and losing the third and fourth, Arthur closed out the match 6–1 against a thoroughly exhausted Froehling. It was the longest match of his young career—a grueling four hours and ten minutes—proving that Hudlin's merciless conditioning regimen had paid off. The shocking upset victory over the towering Spider Man brought Arthur his first national USLTA title, which he later remembered as "the biggest thrill of my life up to then."[10]

Another unexpected development was Ashe's transition to a new style of play. Under Miller's guidance—with some added help from the

Buchholz brothers' father, Earl Buchholz Sr., the director of St. Louis's highly successful public parks tennis program—Arthur all but reinvented himself as a tennis player. "That winter in the Armory remade my whole game," he later acknowledged. The complete transformation from flat strokes and straightforward baseline play to a multidimensional combination of power serving and topspin artistry would entail several years of experimentation and trial and error. But the process clearly began in St. Louis. The catalyst, according to Arthur, was a "fast and slick" wooden surface that caused balls to "skid off the floor and accelerate after they bounce," which forced him to shorten his backswing. "With my old roundhouse backswing," he insisted, "the ball would have been in the back fence before I started moving my racquet forward." Stripping the choice down to its essentials, he explained on another occasion: "Wood is a fast surface, so I had to build the big serve-and-volley game. Playing for years on a clay surface had made me a retriever, a pusher. But you don't win by pushing the ball on hardwood or cement."

At his coaches' urging, Arthur also began "to lean forward and put more muscle into my service motion," and, in an effort to compensate for the speed of incoming serves, "to return serve differently." "Usually, I would stand just behind the baseline and wait for the ball," he explained. "Now I dropped back a yard and a half or so and charged the ball when my opponent served. I had never been comfortable charging the ball because of my clay-court background, but with my new aggressiveness, I developed new techniques to catch the ball on the rise. In the course of some weight-shifting drills suggested by Larry, I developed a topspin backhand, which worked very well for moving the ball cross-court as I charged forward." At the same time, he also changed from an Eastern to a Continental grip (also known as the "chopper" or "hammer" grip, where the player holds the racket as he or she would hold a hammer). When Tom Chewning hit with Arthur at Brook Field Park during the Thanksgiving and Christmas holidays, he noticed the differences right away. Though still slim, Arthur had become a hard-hitting beast on the court.[11]

By the time Arthur made his third annual trek to the Orange Bowl tournament in late December he felt reasonably comfortable with his new, more aggressive approach. Charging the net—a tactic all but prohibited under Dr. J's regime—was the most difficult challenge for a reformed baseliner, both physically and psychologically, and Arthur would continue to struggle with his inconsistent volleying throughout his career. In Miami he played well enough to reach the semifinals, overcoming a match point in his quarterfinal match against eighteen-year-old Rodney Mandelstam of South Africa, the 1960 Wimbledon Junior champion. Unfazed by the potential controversy surrounding a match pitting an African American against a white South African, both boys took Arthur's upset victory in sportsmanlike stride. And even though most of the fans were presumably segregationists of one stripe or another, there seemed to be at least grudging recognition that the black boy from Richmond possessed both grit and talent.

Arthur would need both of these qualities to carry the day in his semi-final match against the nation's #1 ranked junior, Bill Lenoir of Tucson, Arizona. Six months earlier, at the Interscholastic tournament in Charlottesville, Lenoir had outlasted Arthur by relying on a rock-solid two-handed backhand, and the same scenario unfolded in Miami. Bedeviled by poor net play, the upstart Virginian was eliminated in straight sets. Lenoir went on to win the tournament, and to lead the U.S. team to victory in the international team competition.[12]

The Orange Bowl competition attracted many of the world's best Junior players, and Ashe, making his third appearance in the tournament, took the opportunity to renew and deepen several friendships, notably with Charlie Pasarell, the talented Puerto Rican he had met in 1958. The pending selection of the U.S. Junior Davis Cup squad and future college plans were among the major topics of conversation in Miami, as Arthur and his friends took stock of their relative positions on the tennis ladder. All of this was a bit sobering for someone like Arthur who faced a questionable future compared to that of his white counterparts, especially Pasarell, who had numerous college options and the luxury of choosing between the nation's top two tennis programs, the University of California, Los Angeles (UCLA) and the University of Southern California (USC). Arthur, by contrast, had received only a few inquiries from major universities—the University of Michigan, Michigan State, and the University of Arizona—and one from the historically black Hampton Institute. At this point, he had no actual scholarship offers. Combined with a strong academic record, his #12 national Junior ranking clearly warranted a spot on a major college tennis team. But since only a handful of African Americans had ever played mainstream college tennis—and not one had ever received a financial aid package from a top program—he was not optimistic.[13]

When Arthur left Miami just before New Year's Day to spend a week with his family before returning to school in St. Louis, he had no idea where he would end up the following fall. He knew that Dr. Johnson and Coach Hudlin had been working feverishly on his behalf, exploiting every possible college contact, in an effort to secure the best possible position for him. Then he received an unexpected telephone call. The forceful voice at the other end of the line belonged to J. D. Morgan, the legendary tennis coach at UCLA. After introducing himself, Morgan got right to the point: "We're preparing to offer you a scholarship to come out and play for us." He then began ticking off UCLA's advantages: "a great education, year-round mild weather, perfect courts to play on, a flock of the nation's best amateurs and pros to practice with, a big city with every kind of fun you could name, and an unprejudiced student body." As Arthur later pointed out, this sales pitch was hardly necessary: "Offering me a chance to play there was like offering a football player a chance to play at Notre Dame." Morgan's words literally took Arthur's breath away. "You could have knocked me over with a feather," he recalled. "I was thrilled beyond belief. I said yes even before he finished his offer."[14]

Unbeknownst to him, Morgan had been monitoring his progress for at least three years. The UCLA coach was not in the habit of recruiting players from the East Coast; he preferred Californians familiar with the hard court game that dominated West Coast tennis. But as he watched Arthur play at the annual USLTA Junior championships at Kalamazoo, there was something about the young Virginian that intrigued him. While the slender boy often struggled against the Californians and other power hitters, there were flashes of brilliance that drew Morgan's attention. With proper coaching and more experience on hard courts, he might develop into a highly competitive college player, or perhaps even a star who could lead UCLA to future NCAA team championships.[15]

Morgan also hoped to lure Charlie Pasarell to UCLA, though he feared that the talented young Puerto Rican was headed for UCLA's cross-town rival, USC. Year after year, the two schools had gone head-to-head, vying for the NCAA team championship. Together they had won nine national tennis titles in the last eleven years, including UCLA's victory in 1960. And as the new decade progressed, there would be no letup in either the competition or the recruiting war between them. While UCLA was favored to repeat as champion in 1961, USC's powerful freshman squad led by Dennis Ralston and Rafael Osuna heralded a probable reversal of UCLA's dominance in the coming years. At the very least, Morgan faced an uphill struggle, which may have prompted his turn to the East for help.

What he didn't anticipate was the added bonus reaped from Arthur's friendship with Pasarell. When the Puerto Rican star learned Arthur had agreed to attend UCLA, he didn't follow suit immediately as Morgan had hoped he would. But he did lead Morgan to believe he was now leaning toward UCLA. Grateful that UCLA was still alive in the recruiting competition with USC, the coach could look forward to the very real possibility that he would soon have the services of a powerful duo of freshmen capable of advancing the UCLA tennis dynasty. Though nothing was certain, Arthur was confident that Charlie would ultimately choose UCLA. In fact, he was so confident that when Harvard later offered him a scholarship offer, in the hope of luring him away from UCLA, he resisted the Ivy League school's charms and never seriously considered severing his fate from that of his close friend.[16]

Arthur's enthusiasm for UCLA was tempered only by the school's remoteness from his family. As he put it, "I'd be a long way from the racial discrimination of Richmond. But I'd be a long way from my family, too." He knew his father would be reluctant to allow his oldest son to attend college so far away. But with Dr. Johnson's help, he was able to convince Arthur Sr. that the UCLA offer represented the opportunity of a lifetime, one that would lead, in all likelihood, to a bright future on and off the tennis court. In truth, while he was excited by the thought of attending UCLA, Arthur Jr. harbored some misgivings of his own. Living in St. Louis had already led to occasional bouts of homesickness, and he wondered what it would be like to live nearly three thousand miles from home.[17]

In the end, Arthur concluded traveling so far afield was well worth the risk. To him, UCLA was not just the host institution for an elite tennis program, or a university with an enviable academic reputation. It was also the alma mater of two of his most revered role models: Jackie Robinson, Class of 1942, and Nobel laureate Ralph Bunche, Class of 1927. Robinson lettered in four sports at UCLA before moving on to the Negro Leagues and eventually joining the Brooklyn Dodgers, and Bunche was a star guard on the university basketball squad for three seasons. Since the late 1920s, the UCLA athletic program had been a pioneer in recruiting African American athletes.

No black had ever played tennis for UCLA, and most of the university's black athletes either played football—as Woody Strode and Kenny Washington did in the 1940s—or participated in track and field, as the decathlon champion Rafer Johnson did in the late 1950s. But black athletes were hardly a novelty at UCLA by the time Morgan recruited Ashe. Indeed, two years earlier Johnson had served as president of the UCLA student body, the third black undergraduate to be elected to the position since 1948. Ashe had no reason to believe that his enrollment at the university, or his addition to the tennis team, would provoke even a ripple of controversy on campus. After all, he later wrote, "Negroes have been doing okay at UCLA for thirty years."[18]

With his college plans settled, Ashe returned to St. Louis in early January for his final five months of high school. He immediately found himself back in the grind, submitting to Coach Hudlin's tightly controlled training regimen and working on his game with Larry Miller, Jim Parker, and the Buchholz brothers at the armory. To his relief, the knowledge that he would be at UCLA in the fall—and that his stay in St. Louis wouldn't last forever—lessened the burden and lifted his spirits. "I came out of my shell in St. Louis," he recalled, "partly because they made such a fuss over me and nobody knew anything about me. I could be a different person, and nobody would ever know the difference. After growing up in a community where everybody knew who I was, either because of my father or because of my tennis, I could be anything I wanted in St. Louis." He was clearly straining at the leash and edging toward the independent state of mind that would later be his trademark. "Spending my senior year in St. Louis gave me the chance not only to change my tennis game but also my personality," he later insisted. "I was always rather shy and studious. I was good in baseball and tennis, but socially I was shy."[19]

Even with the tight discipline imposed by his hosts, the St. Louis experience accelerated Arthur's transition to adulthood. In addition to launching his new life beyond Virginia, it removed him from the routines of his adolescence: the normal activities with his circle of friends and schoolmates at Baker and Walker; the Sunday rituals of church and community; the extended family gatherings of uncles, aunts, and cousins; the occasional country outings to Gum Spring with his father, stepmother, and siblings; the long hours on the Brook Field courts; and the close mentorship of Charity and Dr. J. Everything seemed different in St. Louis, including the city's detachment from the surge of political change in the winter and spring of 1961. For all its faults, Virginia was closer to the center of things, especially to the excitement surrounding the early months of President John F. Kennedy's "New Frontier" administration and to the recent quickening of the civil rights movement.

In early May, Virginia was the backdrop for the first phase of the Freedom Rides, the Congress of Racial Equality's (CORE) daring direct-action campaign designed to test compliance with two U.S. Supreme Court decisions mandating the desegregation of interstate bus travel. One of the decisions, *Boynton v. Virginia*, stemmed from an arrest at the Richmond Trailways bus terminal in 1958, and the city was fittingly the first overnight stop of the Freedom Riders' planned two-week journey from Washington to New Orleans. Indeed, the interracial band of thirteen nonviolent activists spent their first night at a Virginia Union dormitory, almost within shouting distance of the Ashes' home. The Riders soon proceeded southward to Alabama, where they provoked a savage response from Klansmen and other militant white supremacists. A bus bombing in Anniston and mob violence in Birmingham and Montgomery truncated the original Freedom Ride, but this conflict soon spawned a mobilization of several hundred activists, including many Northern college students willing to board freedom buses bound for the Deep South. Most of the Freedom Rides concentrated on Alabama and Mississippi, but one Ride originated in St. Louis in mid-July, a month after Arthur left the city.[20]

What a seventeen-year-old Richmond native living in St. Louis thought of this unfolding civil rights drama is unclear. But by his own account, he had yet to develop the acute political consciousness and deep sense of social responsibility that dominated his later life. As a black Southerner approaching adulthood, Arthur obviously paid some attention to what was going on in the buses, lunch counters, courtrooms, and jails of the South; and Dick Hudlin reportedly did what he could to encourage his pupil's engagement with issues related to racial discrimination and civil rights. Nevertheless, actual participation in the movement—risking arrest or public identification with the protests—was out of the question for someone living under the tight regime imposed by his mentors and his father. Disciplined and obedient, he was not about to brook this disapproval, nor to jeopardize his career in any way. He had too much to lose, and his insurgent position in the mainstream tennis world was tenuous enough without being branded a troublemaker.

The closest he came to getting involved in a racial incident during his time in St. Louis occurred when he impulsively accompanied a white friend to a private tennis club traditionally reserved for whites. Predictably, as soon as he and his friend began to warm up, a booming voice ordered him off the court. "Hey, you!" a white staff member yelled out. "Get off there. We don't allow colored in this club." Hoping to avoid a major incident, Arthur complied immediately. But he never forgot his brush with the ugly side of St. Louis.

What Arthur could not avoid, of course, was public commentary on his status as "the first black" to enter the previously lily-white mainstream of men's tennis. "Those comments always put me under pressure to justify

my accomplishments on racial grounds, as if sports were the cutting edge
of our nation's move toward improved race relations," he complained in
1981. "The fact this kind of accomplishment by a black player got so much
attention was an indication that we still had so far to go." "I played in clubs
where the only blacks were waiters, gardeners, and busboys," he recounted,
adding with considerable understatement: "I knew there was apprehension
in some circles about my presence." Alone but hardly invisible, he had, in
his words, "moved into the world of tennis that had little in common with
the black experience. The game had a history and tradition I was expected
to assimilate, but much of that history and many of those traditions were
hostile to me." [21]

Whatever private thoughts young Arthur Ashe harbored on civil rights
matters, his dual preoccupations with tennis and schoolwork left little time
for social or political activism. Heeding Coach Morgan's warning that
UCLA would be academically demanding, he was determined to be as well
prepared as possible for the intellectual challenges ahead. So when he wasn't
on the tennis court, he was often studying or reading, even though the formal curriculum at Sumner did little to stimulate him. Realizing he "had
already taken subjects in Richmond as a junior that were being taught only
to seniors at Sumner," school administrators made arrangements for him to
take independent study courses. But, to his dismay, they could not overlook
the multiyear residency requirement when selecting the class valedictorian;
even though Ashe had the highest grade-point average in the class and was a
member of the National Honor Society, one year of work at Sumner was not
enough to establish his eligibility for the valedictory honor. [22]

This ruling, plus the absence of his family from the June graduation ceremony, brought Arthur's high school career to a disappointing end. But with
UCLA and a busy summer of tennis looming, he had little trouble putting
the difficulties of the past year behind him. "After graduation everything
changed," he later wrote. "I left the Hudlins and hit the tournament circuit
again—with some of my expenses paid by tournament promoters now, since
I was so highly ranked. I was somebody instead of nobody, and pretty much
my own boss."

The summer tennis season of 1961 marked an important turning point
in Arthur's young career. His status as a legitimate contender for national
preeminence was now undeniable. Displaying a new versatility and power
on the court, he was no longer just an object of curiosity who could be dismissed as a racial anomaly or as an overachiever with limited talent. Ranked

among the five best Junior players in the nation at the beginning of the summer, he was poised to rise even higher.

Two weeks after leaving St. Louis, Arthur fulfilled Dr. J's decade-long dream of seeing a Lynchburg-trained boy win the USLTA National Interscholastic singles championship. With his beaming mentor looking on, he won the title without losing a set, defeating Jim Parker, one of his St. Louis practice partners, in the finals. Arthur was jubilant, even though his triumph was preceded by an unfortunate incident earlier in the week. One evening three of his white friends—Butch Newman, Cliff Buchholz, and Charlie Pasarell—invited him to join them at a movie being shown at a downtown Charlottesville theater. "I turned them down because I knew I wouldn't get in," he recalled, "but the guys wouldn't take no for an answer. When we got to the theater, the reaction was predictable. 'You can't go in,' the woman in the ticket booth said. I wasn't surprised by her statement." He was, however, somewhat surprised by his friends' reaction. "Well, if he can't go in none of us will go," Buchholz declared. Asked about the episode years later, he remembered Arthur complaining to the ticket lady: "What do you want me to do, paint myself with whitewash?" The four friends left the awkward scene shaking their heads and nervously assuring each other that they had just undergone a bonding experience. Arthur would long remember the humanizing solidarity of that night, which confirmed not only the wisdom of leaving Virginia but also the potential for true friendship across the color line.[23]

If Arthur had any lingering doubts about his decision to leave the Old Dominion, they were probably gone by early July, when an article in *Sports Illustrated* revealed that several months prior to the 1961 tournament the University of Virginia had unexpectedly "asked to be excused from an agreement with the U.S. Lawn Tennis Association to hold the Interscholastic tennis championship on the University's courts through 1963." UVA officials, including the university's athletic director Gus Tebell, insisted their request was based on financial considerations and had nothing to do with Arthur's probable victory or the increasingly visible black participation in the tournament in recent years. But the editors of *Sports Illustrated*—who titled their editorial commentary "Tennis the Menace"—were not the only observers who suspected otherwise. Later in the year, when the USLTA announced that the tournament would be moved to Williams College in western Massachusetts in 1962, Virginia's well-deserved reputation for racial intolerance was intact. The relocation led the *Sports Illustrated* editors to speculate that in Williamstown "the sight of a Negro in white flannels does not upset white citizens as it apparently does in Charlottesville."[24]

Arthur himself did not dwell on the implications of the tournament's abrupt relocation. He was too busy traveling from city to city, and playing match after match against tough opponents. After Charlottesville, he only had time for a brief visit with his family in Richmond before heading for the Eastern Clay Court Championships in northern New Jersey. Though seeded fifth, he won the clay court singles title and finished second in the doubles. Four days later, he was in Omaha for the Missouri Valley Junior Championships, where he captured the singles title, defeating the number three seed, his friend Cliff Buchholz, in the finals. Three weeks later, in early August, he would face Buchholz again in the semifinals at Kalamazoo. This time the stakes would be much higher.

A year earlier, Arthur had been pleased to play his way into the fourth round of the USLTA National Junior Championships, where he lost to the heavily favored David Reed, his future UCLA teammate. But in 1961 he actually had visions of winning the tournament. Having already won two national championships in the last nine months, he knew winning the coveted singles title at Kalamazoo would, in all likelihood, catapult him to the top of the national Junior rankings. And if that happened, selection to the U.S. Junior Davis Cup squad would almost certainly follow. For Arthur, who was well aware that no African American had ever represented the United States in Davis Cup competition at any level, this was the real prize. In Charlottesville the guardians of Jim Crow could keep him from sitting where he pleased in a movie theater, and in Richmond they could still bar him from playing at Byrd Park. But, if he kept winning, he could experience something potentially much more important: official affirmation that a black man was good enough to represent his country in international tennis competition. Just as Rafer Johnson, Cassius Clay (later known as Muhammad Ali), Ralph Boston, and several other African American athletes were making their final preparations for the Summer Olympics in Rome, Arthur dreamed of sharing their formal inclusion in national life.

After several easy victories in the early rounds, he reached the semifinals at Kalamazoo with supreme confidence, having beaten Buchholz handily all summer. But the underdog from St. Louis rose to the occasion, playing the match of his young life. Arthur, in one of his weakest efforts of the year, managed to win only four games in two sets. When Pasarell defeated Buchholz for the title the next day, he, not Arthur, vaulted to the top of the Junior rankings. Despite all of his earlier victories, Arthur was still ranked fifth, a solid but disappointing showing for someone who had come so close to the pinnacle. Fortunately, he received more than a measure of solace a few days later when Tom Price, the head of the USLTA's Junior Davis Cup selection committee, overlooked his poor showing at Kalamazoo and put him on the national team.

Being tapped for Junior Davis competition was essentially honorific and only involved a commitment to a brief training period and the possibility of playing in one international tournament in late August. And only the top two players—in this case Pasarell and Buchholz—would actually represent the United States in the tournament. But Arthur was thrilled with his selection nonetheless. It gave him a powerful sense of inclusion, even though he suspected he would never completely shed his status as an outsider. When his Junior Davis Cup teammates tagged him with the nickname "Shadow," he laughed it off, insisting it was all in good fun. "If I didn't know these guys better," he admitted in 1965, "I'd be offended." Yet as he wrote two years later, "It never bothered me. I'd rather have people kid me about my race than pretend not to notice it." Perhaps because he never took obvious offense when it was invoked, the nickname followed him for several years. To many in the mainstream tennis world, he was indeed a shadow of sorts. But to the less visible world of the ATA and Dr. J—a world that he was about to leave—he was king of the court, plain and simple.[25]

Arthur spent much of August 1961 in the familiar surroundings of Dr. J's tennis camp. This would be his eighth and last extended stint in Lynchburg, and he enjoyed it to a degree he had never been able to experience before. Now, as the unchallenged king of the ATA's Junior development program— as the boy who had finally brought Dr. J the Interscholastic championship he had been hungering for—he could almost relax and bask in the glory of his accomplishments. In truth, no Lynchburg camper, not even Arthur, felt comfortable enough to relax around Dr. J for very long. But when Arthur accompanied him to the ATA National tournament at Hampton Institute in mid-August, he sensed that their relationship had entered a new stage of mutual respect and consideration. He now had the satisfaction of having given something back, something that no other Lynchburg boy had been able to muster.

At the Hampton tournament, Ashe found himself in the enviable but nonetheless awkward position of being treated as both a celebrity and the tennis version of the "Great Black Hope." As he blasted his way to his second consecutive ATA singles title, losing only thirteen games in a long week of matches, he couldn't avoid the feeling, at once exhilarating and vaguely troubling, that he had outgrown his origins. He was, however, able to mitigate at least some of the guilt by teaming with Charity in the doubles competition.

Now thirty-one and somewhat past his prime as a player, Charity had never won an ATA national title despite years of trying. But together he and Ashe engineered a blissful on-court reunion, defeating the defending doubles champions, Wilbur Jenkins and Thomas Calhoun, in four hard sets. Few victories ever meant more to Charity, or to Ashe, who later expressed his delight in sharing a moment of glory with the mentor who had "started me on the tennis escalator so long ago." Yet even a moment as emotional as this did not alter the realities of Arthur's situation. As he acknowledged a half decade later, "I'd gotten to the stage where there wasn't much competition for me in Negro tennis. So now it was time to make the big move into the white man's world."[26]

To this point, all of his experiences in the white world had been fleeting and carefully controlled. In virtually every instance either Dr. J or Coach Hudlin had been on hand to guide and watch over him. In California, for the first time in his life, he would be on his own, beyond the buffering influence of empathetic protectors who understood the psychological burden of crossing racial boundaries. In later years he would reflect at length on the difficulty of maintaining one's sense of self and identity while negotiating this crossing. But in the late summer of 1961 he had only a vague notion of the challenges and opportunities ahead.

At the end of August, Arthur squeezed in one final tournament—his third trip to the U.S. Nationals at Forest Hills—before saying goodbye to his family and heading to the airport for the longest and most important flight of his life. Normally his disappointing loss to the Frenchman François Godbout at Forest Hills would have occupied his thoughts for days. But his attention was elsewhere, fixated on his impending liberation from the confining realities of his hometown. "When I decided to leave Richmond," he later explained, "I left all that Richmond stood for at the time—its segregation, its conservatism, its parochial thinking, its slow progress toward equality, its lack of opportunity for talented black people." Turning away from it all, he opened his heart and mind to the uncharted wonders of the golden West.[27]

SIX

THE GOLDEN LAND

■

T HE LONG FLIGHT TO California was a revelation—the endless plains, the towering Rockies, the first glimpse of the blue Pacific. For an impressionable eighteen-year-old, the Western landscape was intoxicating and a bit frightening all at the same time. In a sense, Ashe had seen much of it before, either on television or in the movies, or in the pages of his favorite magazine, *National Geographic*. But by the time the plane touched down at LAX on the western edge of the sprawling metropolis of Los Angeles, he was beginning to sense just how far he had strayed from the sheltered environment of Richmond. St. Louis had been a comfortable way station; now he had arrived in a different world.

Ashe, like most westward migrants, came to California with great expectations and certain mythic conceptions of what he would find there. During its first century of statehood, California had attracted millions of American settlers drawn by its image as a golden land of promise and opportunity. These outsized expectations were seldom fully realized, but there was enough truth in the state's seductive image to sustain successive waves of mass migration, from the Gold Rush of the 1840s to the postwar booms of the second half of the twentieth century. Compared to many parts of the nation, California was relentlessly dynamic—a churning mix of economic growth, demographic change, and cultural innovation. The contrast with Virginia was striking and obvious.[1]

For Ashe, the strangeness of California resided not only in its gilded, metropolitan culture and arresting scenery, but also in its racial and ethnic demography. Los Angeles, in particular, was a vast, multicultural polyglot—an endlessly diverse city of Hispanics, Asian Americans, native white Californians, and all manner of transplants, white, black, brown, and yellow. Unlike the rigid racial divide of black and white in Richmond, the demographic mix in Los Angeles was complicated and unstable. In 1960, the population of Los Angeles County included five million whites, nearly two million Mexican Americans, approximately 470,000 blacks, and a slightly smaller contingent of Asian Americans, mostly of Japanese descent. The South Central area of Los Angeles had the largest concentration of blacks in the state, but even there the numbers were relatively small by Virginia standards.

In the state of California as a whole, blacks accounted for only 6 percent of the population. Many of California's black families had been drawn to the Pacific Coast in the 1940s by military assignments and wartime industries. Remaining in the state after the war, they spawned a continuing chain migration of family and friends. In Los Angeles, this migration eventually produced a distinct "black Angeleno" subculture rooted in several South Central neighborhoods. Hemmed in by de facto residential segregation and persistent employment discrimination, working-class black communities such as Compton and Watts had little to do with the city's white establishment, or with privileged enclaves such as UCLA.[2]

When Ashe arrived in the fall of 1961, blacks accounted for less than one percent of the university's total enrollment. The entire student body, graduate and undergraduate, included fewer than two hundred blacks, and many of them were either African exchange students or upper-middle-class coeds from the Baldwin Hills neighborhood, home of the city's small black elite. The number of students like Ashe—African Americans with working-class or Southern backgrounds—could probably have been counted on two hands.[3]

Arthur, of course, had some familiarity with white institutions. But nothing in his past had prepared him for full immersion in UCLA college life. Located in the tony neighborhood of Westwood, UCLA was a world unto itself. The campus, with its manicured grounds and massive brick buildings, was home to a relatively affluent student body of nearly nineteen thousand—mostly the sons and daughters of Southern California's comfortable upper middle class. Founded in 1881 as a two-year normal school, and later reorganized as the "south campus" of the University of California, the onetime stepchild of Cal-Berkeley had evolved into a major, independent university by mid-century. By the early 1960s, UCLA would merit a growing reputation as an academically rigorous, research-oriented institution, thanks in part to the efforts of its energetic new chancellor, Frank Murphy, who had come to the university in 1959 from the University of Kansas.

By the close of Murphy's presidency in 1973, UCLA would be a public university of the first rank, an institution with an enviable national profile. But in 1961, the year of Arthur's arrival, it remained a regional institution with limited national and international visibility. While the institution could claim several rising academic programs and a number of distinguished professors, UCLA's proximity to Hollywood and its chic social scene dominated its public image. Like Los Angeles itself, the university that bore the city's name was thought to be long on style and short on substance.[4]

Later in the decade, this showy image would be enhanced by the hoopla surrounding UCLA's intercollegiate athletic programs. Indeed, by the late 1960s, the Westwood campus became, first and foremost, the home of the Bruins, or the "Athens of Athletics," as proud UCLA sports boosters put it. This overweening sense of athletic pride was not yet a part of campus life when Ashe first arrived. While UCLA's big-time, Division 1 athletic program was decades old, its overall record was mixed, highlighted by its celebrated tennis teams and a few strong showings in track and field—but not much else.

In the year leading up to the Rome Olympics of 1960, the university gained fame as the training home of the world's two greatest decathletes, Rafer Johnson and C. K. Yang. But in the high-profile sports of football and basketball, especially, the Bruins were still overshadowed by instate rivals such as USC, Cal-Berkeley, and Stanford—and by the public universities of the Big Ten and the Southeastern Conference (SEC). UCLA would not win the first of its ten NCAA basketball championships until 1964, or the first of its five Rose Bowl victories until January 1966.[5]

In earlier times—prior to the glory years of Coach John Wooden and hardwood superstars such as Walt Hazzard, Lew Alcindor (later known as Kareem Abdul-Jabbar), and Bill Walton, and before the gridiron exploits of Heisman Trophy winners Gary Beban and Troy Aikman—the Bruins had often been noteworthy, but rarely for what they accomplished in the gym or on the field. What made UCLA special in the world of college sports was not success but rather the racial diversity of its athletes. This tradition—the Bruins' long history of recruiting black athletes—was one of the factors that drew Ashe to UCLA. He came primarily for the tennis—for the opportunity to develop his skills at the highest level, and to play on a team that would vie for the NCAA championship. But he did so with the expectation that he would be treated with a certain amount of respect, on and off the court.

Ashe was the first African American to play intercollegiate tennis at UCLA, but as he well knew, he was by no means the first black athlete to represent the university. In the mid-1920s Ralph Bunche was the starting point guard on the UCLA basketball team, and as early as 1939, the UCLA football team fielded no fewer than four black stars—Woody Strode, Kenny Washington, Ray Bartlett, and Jackie Robinson—making it the most integrated college football team of its day. Robinson went on to become the first UCLA athlete to earn varsity letters in four sports, and in the post–World War II era dozens of other lesser-known pioneers played for various Bruins teams. No other state university in the United States—other than historically black institutions—could match this heritage. Though predominantly white, UCLA offered Ashe inclusion in a tradition of racial integration that must have eased at least some of his apprehension about a strange new environment.[6]

Yet as Arthur soon discovered, this reputation for racial diversity and tolerance was not altogether deserved. The realities of campus life for UCLA's approximately two hundred black students were challenging at best, as institutional inertia and the weight of past injustices inevitably led to frustration and disappointment. Black students had been barred from living on campus as recently as the mid-1950s, and blatant racial discrimination in nearby neighborhoods continued to stymie the efforts of black students to find decent and affordable off-campus housing. As the civil rights movement raised everyone's consciousness, university officials did their best to keep up with the pace of social change and rising expectations. But progress was slow.

The future Olympian Rafer Johnson was elected president of the UCLA student body in 1958—the third African American to win that office, following Sherrill Luke and Willard Johnson, who would later collaborate with Ashe in the movement to abolish South African apartheid. But three years earlier, when Rafer first registered as a UCLA freshman, he had discovered that his only option was off-campus housing. Fortunately, this indignity had been eliminated by the time Arthur arrived in 1961. He, like hundreds of other incoming freshmen, was assigned a room in Sproul Hall, a one-year-old coed facility he later described as "a massive modernistic dorm on the edge of the campus near Sunset Boulevard."

Most Sproul Hall residents, including Arthur, were asked to share double rooms, but in his case there was the delicate matter of either pairing him with another black student or finding a white roommate who did not object to an interracial rooming assignment. After a bit of quiet deliberation, university administrators placed him in a room with Sam Beale, a Los Angeles–born Jewish sophomore known to be racially tolerant. As the drummer for the interracial UCLA Trio, the young biology major played music with the black bass player John Halliburton and the Czech-American pianist and vocalist Ray Manzarek, who later found stardom with Jim Morrison and the Doors. The son of a machinist father and an Iowa-born mother who often socialized with black friends, Beale had attended a predominantly white Los Angeles high school that had recently elected a black student body president.

As fellow "outsiders" on a WASP-dominated campus, Ashe and Beale were a good fit. Even though Beale had no interest in tennis, they hit it off from the outset, and with a year of college under his belt, the Californian proved to be a valuable mentor for the green freshman from Virginia. Both were serious students and the first members of their families to go college, so they shared a determination to improve their lot in life through education. A near perfect role model, Beale would go on to earn a PhD at UCLA and to enjoy a long and distinguished career as a professor of molecular and cell biology at Brown University.[7]

In the early weeks of the fall semester, Beale eased Arthur's transition to college life. But it didn't take long for Arthur to realize he would be spending most of his time with his teammates. His real home was the nearby Bruins Tennis Terrace, "a sort of Greek theater built especially for tennis, with elevated concrete seating for 1,500 people." Most of the time Arthur and his teammates found themselves practicing in front of empty seats, but the promise of future glory kept them motivated as they maintained the grind of practice hour after hour, day after day. Looking back on this regimen, Arthur acknowledged there was never any question he and his teammates were "in school primarily to play tennis." Yet he insisted "a UCLA tennis performer doesn't feel quite so different from other students as a big-time football or basketball workman does. The squad is too small for a special dormitory or training table. There are only six or seven of us. So we just melt into the student body. At times we feel almost like the kids who pay their own way."

As student-athletes at UCLA, Arthur and his teammates received a financial aid package that covered most of their expenses. But the level of support was modest by NCAA standards. UCLA provided its intercollegiate athletes with tuition, books, room and board, and guaranteed employment, but no scholarship per se. In Arthur's case, his job involved working at the UCLA tennis facility, mostly on custodial matters and equipment and court maintenance. "I picked up trash from tennis courts, swept and hosed them, maybe mended a net sometimes," he recalled. "Nobody cared when I worked, or how many hours a week, just so I logged 250 hours during the year. The pay was $2.50 an hour."[8]

Arthur had hoped to augment his financial aid package with a stipend from the Army Reserve Officer Training Corps (ROTC), which he and all other first- and second-year male undergraduates were required to join. But he soon learned that ROTC stipends were reserved for upperclassmen committed to an additional two years of training after their first two mandatory years. Even so, he had no problem donning a uniform and tolerating military discipline. He knew this would please his father, since in the Ashe-Cunningham family there was considerable pride that two of Arthur's uncles, Rudy and James Cunningham, had served as Marines in Korea, while a third uncle had been Admiral Chester Nimitz's valet during World War II.

Arthur relished the prospect of becoming an Army officer, a position of considerable status among black Americans. After completing four years of drills and military science classes, plus a six-week summer camp, he could expect to receive a commission as a second lieutenant with a two-year service commitment. During the spring of his sophomore year, when he was puzzling over the decision to sign up for the third and fourth years of ROTC, he turned to Coach Morgan and Bob Kelleher, a prominent Los Angeles attorney recently appointed U.S. Davis Cup captain, for advice. A World War II veteran who had commanded a PT boat in the Pacific, Morgan counseled him with a simple calculus: "You would be better off going in as an officer than an enlisted man." Kelleher agreed, declaring: "an officer's commission would look good on any resume." So Arthur signed up, setting himself on a path that would alter his life later in the decade.[9]

Uncertain about how much freedom he could handle, Arthur was receptive to just about any form of guidance—military or otherwise. With his family and Dr. J almost three thousand miles away, and with Coach Hudlin back in St. Louis, he could no longer rely on the authority figures that had given his pre-college life structure and direction. As a college student, he discovered his best option was relying on the wise counsel of Coach Morgan. For the next five years the man known as J.D. would be the most influential person in Arthur's life, and not only on matters related to tennis.

As a coach and mentor, Morgan paid close attention to what his players were doing on the court, but his greatest talent was his ability to identify and recruit young men with superior physical and mental potential. A case in point was his successful recruiting of Pasarell. As the first day of class approached in late September 1961, the young Puerto Rican was still wavering between his offers from UCLA and USC. The thought of joining Dennis Ralston and the powerful Trojan netters was enticing, but Morgan's persuasive charm decided the matter during a carefully orchestrated dinner at a fancy Sunset Boulevard restaurant. Arthur was on hand to help convince his friend to choose UCLA, but the wily coach did most of the talking. After a few minutes of casual conversation, Morgan, sitting between the two boys, suddenly grasped their forearms and pulled them toward him as if to seal a bond. "Glad to have both of you as Bruins," he declared with an air of assurance, and that was that. Though not quite sure what had just happened, Pasarell obediently nodded his assent, drawing a big smile from his new teammate.

Once Morgan had his recruits safely in the fold at UCLA, he didn't "try to teach them much about technique or strategy." Nor did he place much emphasis on physical conditioning or curfews. As Arthur recalled, the coach was not one to "tuck the boys in bed and say, 'lights out at ten.'" Nevertheless, whenever one of his players faced a personal crisis or needed advice on a serious matter he was always there.[10]

In Arthur's case, Morgan sensed immediately that his first black recruit could benefit from more than the normal "welcome to campus" orientation session. Wasting no time, he called Arthur into his office for a lengthy briefing during the first week of the semester. Accustomed to strong mentorship, the young freshman seemed to embrace the special attention. "From the first day I met J. D. Morgan," he wrote in 1981, "my antenna told me to trust him. After my arrival at school, he gave me the most complete rundown of a situation I ever received until General Creighton Abrams briefed the Davis Cup team in Vietnam seven years later. I didn't have to go to freshman orientation: J. D. knew everything and everybody."

Morgan's first task was to help Arthur choose a realistic set of courses compatible with his tennis responsibilities. When Arthur mentioned he "had thoughts of majoring in engineering or architecture," Morgan gulped before inquiring: "Are you prepared to study five hours a day?" "Five hours a day?" the young freshman asked incredulously. "Yes, Arthur. Engineering and architecture are very difficult disciplines," the coach insisted, adding: "I don't doubt you can do the work, but unless you have your heart set on a career in those fields, I suggest you try business administration."

As Arthur pondered this unexpected advice, Morgan offered a few more words of academic counseling. "Arthur, you're a big boy now," he said. "You're going to be here for four years. All my boys graduate. I'll know who your teachers are, and in some cases, I'll know if you're having trouble before you do. You're here on great recommendations. I know you'll do well. The most important thing for you to begin today is to learn to organize your time. It's difficult enough for freshmen who don't play varsity sports. It'll be tougher for you. Don't waste your time, plan ahead, and do your papers early. This is a tough school academically. Don't get behind." Before Arthur left, the coach gave him his home telephone number and an open invitation to ask for help: "If you think you've got a problem that you can't solve, give me a call any time. Don't worry about waking me. I only sleep six hours a night anyway."[11]

Less than a week later, as he faced the first crisis of his college career, Arthur took Morgan up on the offer. Like all incoming freshmen, he had been asked to write an essay to determine his English composition course placement. Having received considerable praise for his writing ability throughout his high school years, he had expected to score well on the placement essay. But to his shock the essay placed him in the lowest quartile of freshmen. With his confidence shaken, he phoned Morgan to report that he had been assigned to a low-level remedial English class. Unfazed, Morgan told him not to worry, that remedial assignments were common among freshmen coming from inner-city public high schools. Although the coach meant well, this revelation did little to lessen Arthur's feelings of anxiety and shame. Clearly, this was not the way that he had hoped to kick off his college years. After earning a solid B in the remedial course, he was elevated to the normal English course sequence during his second semester, and his overall performance in the classroom was well above average throughout his tenure at UCLA. But the remedial English assignment was not the last time he would have to overcome the limitations of a substandard Jim Crow education.[12]

Three weeks later, Arthur and J.D. faced a second crisis, and this time the resolution was not so easy. After calling Arthur into his office, the coach got right to the point: "Arthur, there's a weekend tournament at the Balboa Bay Club. Well, it's held every year and they usually send out invitations to the college teams. For some reason, they have decided not to invite you. So I've called you in to decide what you want to do about it." Arthur knew little about the Balboa Bay Club, but he knew enough about the whites-only tradition at elite private tennis clubs to realize immediately that race was the issue. "For a moment, I was too stunned to say anything," he recalled years later. "We don't have to send the team, Arthur," Morgan explained. "We can make an issue if you like. It's up to you." Caught off balance, Ashe tried to get his bearings. "I really don't know if I want to make a big thing of it just yet," he stammered. "I am not sure. I've only been in school a couple of weeks and I'm hardly in a position to start fighting the establishment. If the other players don't want me to play, I won't play. There are a lot of other tournaments I can play in."

Fearing his young freshman had misinterpreted the situation, Morgan immediately countered the suggestion that prejudiced white teammates were part of the problem. "The other players have nothing to do with it," the coach insisted before offering his best counsel. "You can't make a little issue," he advised. "If you want to fight something like that, you have to fight it to win it. And you have to prepare for it, get your ducks in order so to speak. There will always be clubs like that and people like that. If you want to make a career out of fighting them, your tennis is going to suffer. When you're more established, you can be a good tennis player and be in the position of fighting them on your terms." In the end, Ashe agreed to let the matter slide, and neither he nor Morgan told his teammates the real reason for his absence during the Balboa Bay Club tournament. Not even Pasarell knew about the racial exclusion until several years later.[13]

Coach Morgan helped Arthur to weather the Balboa Bay Club incident, but for the most part the young freshman had to chart his own course on matters of race. For the first time in his life, he found himself in a multiracial environment in which he had the freedom to associate with a racially diverse assortment of friends and acquaintances. All of his teammates were white, as were the vast majority of his classmates living in Sproul Hall. Yet he also spent time and developed friendships with a number of black students, including two prominent sophomore basketball players, Fred Slaughter and Walt Hazzard. In addition to playing center on the basketball team and competing as a sprinter for the UCLA track team, the Kansas-born Slaughter was the reigning campus table tennis champion until a skinny freshman named Ashe showed him what a highly coordinated tennis player could do with a paddle. Following Ashe's unexpected Ping-Pong conquest, he and Slaughter became fast friends, united by their common love of sports and shared educational interests. Similar in many ways (Slaughter later became a prominent attorney and sports agent, eventually serving as lead counsel to the National Basketball Association Referees Association), they would keep in close touch for decades.

Hazzard and Ashe were even closer, "drawn together," according to Ashe, "because we both came from families with modest incomes, and from segregated neighborhoods. Athletics was our big chance to make a name for ourselves. So we had pretty much the same outlook on life." The two black athletes could often be seen shooting baskets on the outdoor basketball courts adjacent to Sproul Hall. A year older than Arthur, Hazzard acted as his friend's social mentor, instructing him in the ways of college life. As an active member of UCLA's all-black fraternity, Kappa Alpha Psi, which maintained a small off-campus fraternity house on Crenshaw Boulevard, Hazzard urged Arthur to become a pledge. Having already been approached by Zeta Beta Tau, a more prestigious predominantly white fraternity, Arthur hesitated. He eventually decided that Zeta Beta Tau was too expensive and the chance to become Hazzard's "little brother" was too tempting to turn down—even though he was troubled by the racial implications of joining an all-black fraternity. Referring to Hazzard and his black fraternity brothers, he recalled, "They sort of pressured me into joining." [14]

Choosing between integrated and all-black institutions was a new experience for Arthur. Integration had never been an option in Richmond or St. Louis. Now he had choices to make as racial considerations complicated his social relationships. Arthur generally kept his freshman ruminations on race to himself—but not always. On several occasions, he discussed his "racial" options with Tebbie Fowler, a black sociology major who had grown up in the rough inner-city neighborhood of Compton and who had come to UCLA on a baseball scholarship. Fowler, who harbored strong feelings on the importance of racial pride and solidarity, warned Arthur about the limitations of racial assimilation. "If you're going to maintain your identity and your equilibrium," he insisted, "you can't associate too much, you can't assimilate. You can commingle, but not assimilate."

Behind this warning lurked the potentially perilous matter of interracial dating. For the first time in his life, Arthur found himself in the midst of white and Asian girls. Living in Sproul Hall, a coed dorm split into male and female wings, he couldn't avoid casual contact with "the forbidden fruit" of his Jim Crow past. And, as he later confessed, he didn't want to avoid them. He was quite literally fascinated by all manner of women, by the way they acted, looked, and dressed—and most of all by their enticing accessibility. [15]

Arthur's first college girlfriend, whom he met during his first month on campus and whom he dated steadily for six months, was Susan Ikei, "a Nisei, born in California of Japanese parents." The daughter of traditionalist parents who had moved to Van Nuys after spending several years in a World War II internment camp, she shared Arthur's growing curiosity about race and culture. "She had never dated a black before," he later pointed out. "She was just as intrigued with me as I was with her. We took classes together, studied together, went to football games and school dances together, we were crazy about each other."

Arthur's relationship with Susan prompted more than a few stares, but the fact she was Asian and not white seemed to shield them from more aggressive forms of disapproval. Even her parents, who invited him to their home on one occasion, seemed to take the relationship in stride. Arthur's relatively light brown skin color—he wasn't much darker than their daughter—may have softened her parents' reaction. Even so, he was well aware that race complicated his first real romance. "We spent hours talking about prejudice," he recalled, adding: "I could often sense the struggle between Susan, Nisei, and Susan, the college freshman." Although they remained friends throughout Arthur's years at UCLA, their daring interracial romance ended during the spring of 1962—to the obvious relief of many of his friends.[16]

Tebbie Fowler, for one, was pleased that Arthur had not taken the relationship with Susan to a serious level. "I go out with them," he said of white girls. "I may even sleep with a few, but I'd never marry one." At the time, Arthur was not sure that he agreed with his friend's calculating approach to interracial dating. But he had already surmised from the Balboa Bay Club incident and other more subtle signs of racial prejudice that Southern California was not nearly as tolerant as its boosters claimed. Near the end of his first semester, for example, he learned that several black members of the UCLA football team had received warnings from the athletic department that they should not bring "a white girl to the football banquet."[17]

Arthur's friendship with a Japanese American girl was just one part of his cultural awakening. His freshman experiences, both inside and outside the classroom, initiated an extended exposure to the wider world, a process of discovery that would continue for the rest of his life. In the fall of 1961 the allure of cosmopolitan culture was new to him, something he embraced without fully understanding just how far it would take him from the parochialism of his native Richmond. While the human diversity of UCLA had its limitations, the mix of students—Japanese and Chinese Americans, Mexican Americans, West Africans, East Africans, and even the native Californians of Anglo background—fascinated him.

Arthur did his best to absorb as much of this "family of man" mosaic as he could, but he soon developed a special interest in the cluster of African students who congregated in the student union. Prior to his freshman year, he, like most black Americans, had seldom thought about Africa—or about its historical connection to the African American diaspora. None of his teachers had ever encouraged him to reflect on his African antecedents.

Only after his encounter with the colonial accents, colorful native garb, and anticolonial political passions of UCLA's African contingent did he begin to appreciate the cultural crosscurrents of the Atlantic world. "My conversations with foreign students lasted for hours," he recalled. "Sometimes the Africans would talk loosely with the black American athletes. Accustomed to direct, unequivocal colonialism, they asked probing questions about our situation. 'Aren't you so-called student athletes exploited and underpaid?' By their reckoning, if five guys in uniform could fill the Sports Arena and all they got was tuition, books, and room and board, something was wrong."

Often the African students' criticisms focused on what they viewed as the cultural and ideological naïveté of most black Americans. "How can you Negroes call yourselves Afro-Americans?" one African student demanded. "You've never seen Mother Africa. You don't speak any African languages. You don't know our customs. None of you ever visit the Afro-Asian Cultural Center here. All I see you do is play cards and play pool when you're not in class." Arthur listened intently to what the African students were saying, but he often found himself questioning the validity of their complaints. "They were right about some things and wrong about others," he later concluded, "but the excitement for me was my first encounters with real Africans. To see their authentic clothes and their scarification marks and to discuss issues with them was pure intellectual and emotional pleasure."

Though initially hesitant to speak up, Arthur eventually gained enough confidence to offer a few criticisms of his own. "You don't have freedom of speech in Ghana and the Congo, do you?" he asked. As he later realized, he probably should have stopped there, since his next two questions betrayed an embarrassing ignorance of colonialism and its legacies. Displaying a condescension that must have infuriated the African students, he asked: "Why are there only thirty-six universities in all black Africa?" and "Why didn't you write your history down on paper?" According to Arthur, these blunt questions provoked "tremendous discussions about oral versus written history, origins and legacies, and the similarities between black people the world over." Right or wrong, at the age of eighteen he had entered the world of ideas, an intellectual arena that would ultimately provide him with countless challenges and much satisfaction.[18]

Interestingly enough, Arthur's newfound interest in Africa and the rapidly decolonizing Third World did not lead to engagement with the domestic civil rights movement. That would come later, in 1967—in the aftermath of the Civil Rights Act of 1964, the Voting Rights Act of 1965, and the emergence of Black Power the following year. During his time at UCLA, the campus witnessed an increasingly active student movement, beginning with a brave contingent of Mississippi-bound Freedom Riders in early August 1961. By the time Arthur arrived in mid-September, the local Freedom Riders had returned to campus, fresh from their experiences in Parchman Farm prison and full of energy and enthusiasm for the coming struggle. Soon a reinvigorated campus CORE chapter was challenging UCLA's older and more conservative student NAACP chapter for primacy among black students. Pushing for a more militant stance, the CORE activists joined forces with some of the same African students that Arthur had come to know through conversations in the student union. But they did so without the help or involvement of UCLA's black student athletes.[19]

In December, when a controversy erupted over a series of ugly incidents involving the basketball team's treatment by racist hotel managers and other whites in Houston, Walt Hazzard and Fred Slaughter consulted privately with the leaders of CORE-UCLA. But neither they nor Ashe, nor any other UCLA athlete, became actively or publicly involved in the ensuing campus controversy. In the wake of the Houston incident, the UCLA Student Legislative Council (SLC) urged Chancellor Murphy to adopt a university policy prohibiting "UCLA athletic teams from participating in events that allowed segregated housing or any form of racial discrimination" and requiring coaches to "withdraw their teams when confronted with any form of racial discrimination." Following a thorough investigation that technically exonerated John Wooden, who had come under fire for benching Slaughter and Hazzard during a game against Texas A&M rather than withdrawing his team from the tournament, Murphy announced the implementation of a policy that essentially met the SLC's demands. Interpreted as a major step toward racial equality on campus, the new policy undoubtedly pleased Ashe and UCLA's other black athletes. But other than a brief public statement by Hazzard, who agreed to speak to a black Los Angeles Sentinel reporter, the black athletes themselves played no public role in bringing about the new policy.

This was hardly surprising. As the sports historian John Matthew Smith has written, "In 1961 most college athletes kept their political views to themselves"—especially if they were black. "Black college athletes," Smith observed, "were expected to perform on the field, appreciate their educational opportunity, ignore racial insults and humiliations, and behave like 'good Negroes.'" Later in life Ashe would challenge this mandated silence, but during his UCLA years he was too focused on tennis and too intent on fitting in to voice his opinions on race or any other public issue. While he was intellectually curious enough to keep abreast of current events, he didn't feel he could afford to expend time and energy on matters unconnected to his formal courses or his competition on the court.[20]

Ashe was at UCLA for two reasons—to get a college degree and to display and develop his skills as a tennis player. Nothing else mattered nearly as much—including his social life. "As I think back," he wrote a year after his graduation, "I guess I never really felt a part of UCLA. I was gone a lot on lonesome tournament trips. Even when I was on campus, I was usually playing tennis, practicing tennis, or thinking tennis." At the time, long before the advent of Open Tennis, he had no expectation that this single-mindedness would lead to professional employment or financial security. Intellectually, he knew that eventually he would have to leave the tennis world to find a means of supporting himself. When contemplating the prospect of a long-term career, he had no reason to believe that the tennis world would rid itself of racial discrimination anytime in the foreseeable future. But even if it did there was little likelihood that life as a professional tennis player would be a viable financial choice for any aspiring player, black or white.

The professional tennis circuit had been around since Arthur's childhood, and some of the world's most talented players, including the great Australians Lew Hoad and Ken Rosewall and Arthur's idol Pancho Gonzales, had left the amateur ranks to play for pay. But even the best players had found it difficult to make a decent living on the pro tour. Despite the best efforts of the tour's tireless promoter Jack Kramer, the pro game limped along throughout the 1950s, disparaged by the national and international federations as a threat to the integrity of amateur tennis. One of the world's greatest amateur players in the late 1940s—and the first man to win the Wimbledon singles title wearing short pants (in 1947)—Kramer was both innovative and aggressive, so much so that he became public enemy number one among the guardians of the traditional tennis establishment. Nevertheless, by 1960 he had won over a number of influential converts to the idea of Open Tennis—a system that allowed all comers, amateur and professional, to play against one another.

To the horror of the old guard, a proposal to sanction between eight and thirteen Open tournaments per year was put to a vote at the 1960 annual meeting of the International Lawn Tennis Federation (ILTF). To the surprise of many, including the pro-Open delegations from the United States, Great Britain, France, and Australia, support for the proposal fell five votes short of the necessary two-thirds majority. Later in the meeting, the French federation introduced an alternative reform measure "calling for the creation of a category of 'registered' players who could capitalize on their skill by bargaining with tournaments for appearance fees higher than the expenses allowed amateurs," but this halfway measure was promptly tabled, in part because the USLTA opposed it. Roundly disappointed by the ILTF's rejection of Open Tennis, Kramer responded, as the tennis commentator Bud Collins put it, by "taking out his wallet and waving it in front of practically every player of moderate reputation." Before long, it was clear Kramer's all-out recruitment effort had backfired as the ILTF declared a virtual war on the professional tour.

Caught in the middle, Open Tennis seemed further away than ever by 1961, when a new proposal for a limited number of "experimental" Open tournaments lay buried in an ILTF committee and a USLTA-sponsored "home rule" proposal allowing individual federations to use their own discretion in sanctioning Open Tennis went down to defeat. Realizing his controversial reputation had become a sideshow hindering the cause of Open Tennis, Kramer stepped down in 1962. But this gesture only emboldened amateur tennis's old guard, especially the leaders of the USLTA, who in 1963 overruled the organization's pro-Open president Ed Turville, ordering its delegates to the annual ILTF meeting to vote against both Open Tennis and home rule.

The biggest losers were the fans, who would have to wait six more years for Open Tennis, and the players—the professionals who, more isolated than ever, took to small-venue barnstorming to survive—and the amateurs like Ashe who faced an uncertain future of inadequate under-the-table support. The prospects for Open Tennis did not look good in 1962, but having dedicated himself to the game since childhood, eighteen-year-old Ashe couldn't imagine any other life course.[21]

Tennis-wise, he entered UCLA with high hopes and more than a little pressure. But early bonding with his seven freshman teammates and Coach Morgan got him off to a good start. While the Balboa Bay Club incident was a temporary setback, it didn't seem to affect his performance on the court. As one of the two highest-ranked players among UCLA's freshman recruits, he was expected to play well, and for the most part he did. With the intercollegiate season scheduled to begin in January, the fall semester was devoted to long practices, conditioning sessions, and occasional participation in invitational tournaments. The first four months of Arthur's collegiate career were little more than a warm-up season designed to get the new recruits ready for the official dual meets to follow. He made good use of this time by demonstrating his work ethic to Morgan and by gaining confidence that he could more than keep up with the flashy, high-style California boys on the other side of the net.

Three weeks after his teammates traveled to the Balboa Bay Club tournament without him, he participated in a tournament at the equally famous Racquet Club in Palm Springs. This time the host club—known as a desert watering hole for Hollywood's show business elite—went out of its way to make him feel welcome. Charley Farrell, a movie actor and television personality who along with the actor Ralph Bellamy had founded the club in 1934, and Julie Copeland, the club's official hostess, made a point of approaching him before the first match. "We've followed your tennis, Arthur," they assured him, "and you're always welcome." Among the notables in the crowd were the singer Dinah Shore and model and showgirl Barbara Marx (the future wife of Frank Sinatra), both of whom invited him to play at the Beverly Hills Tennis Club. This was Arthur's first brush with celebrity, and he had difficulty keeping his mind on the match at hand. But he played well enough to impress the small crowd that had gathered to witness the club's voluntary desegregation. There would be many such moments in the years to come, but Arthur would never forget the kindness he encountered as a vulnerable college freshman breaching the barriers of race, class, and fame in the desert.[22]

As the fall semester progressed Arthur grew increasingly comfortable with his West Coast surroundings, and by the time intercollegiate play began in early January the quiet confidence that had always been his trademark was on full display. Ranked 28th in the nation—just behind Pasarell at #27—he wasted no time in demonstrating that the skinny kid from the East was a rising star with a bright future. In a four-month season of dual meets, he dominated the freshman singles competition without losing a match, and he was nearly as strong in doubles, teaming with David Sanderlin and occasionally with Pasarell to finish the season with only one loss. The high point came in late April when the UCLA freshmen beat archrival USC 9–0, losing only 11 games in nine matches, as Arthur won all of his matches without losing a game. By then, at least one sports reporter was calling Arthur and his teammates "one of the greatest college freshman teams of all time," and even predicting that the young star from Richmond would eventually become the "top U.S. net player."[23]

While such talk made Coach Morgan nervous, he couldn't hide his growing optimism about the future of UCLA tennis. As Arthur and his freshman teammates knew all too well, in less than a year Morgan would call upon them to sustain the Bruins' tradition of winning national championships. College tennis in Southern California had long been a pressure cooker stoked by the fierce rivalry between the Bruins and the USC Trojans. During the past twelve years, USC had won three national team championships in men's tennis, and UCLA had won seven, including the last two. Clearly, it was a thrilling time to be a Bruins tennis player, but the pressure to win a third straight championship—matching UCLA's great run of 1952–54—was fierce.

Even as a freshman, Arthur became deeply involved in the crosstown tennis wars, cheering for the UCLA upperclassmen from the sidelines and dreaming of the day when it would be his turn to do battle on the varsity level. While he and other Bruins rooters were cautiously optimistic, it was clear from the outset that the 1961–62 varsity squad faced an uphill struggle in its quest for a third straight NCAA championship. Led by captain Larry Nagler, the 1960 NCAA singles champion, the squad had been weakened by the graduation of Allen Fox, the 1961 singles champion. The loss of Fox, the #4 ranked men's singles player in the nation, left the Bruins vulnerable to the rise of several teams capable of challenging them for the 1962 title. Predictably, the most formidable challenger was the USC Trojans. Led by the sensational sophomores Ralston and Osuna, USC was expected to field one of the strongest teams in NCAA history.

Coach Morgan feared his team lacked the skill and experience needed to keep the Trojans at bay, and he was right. Despite the freshman triumphs that had brought Arthur a measure of glory, his first year at UCLA ended in bitter disappointment. Having lost both dual (two teams) matches to USC earlier in the season, the UCLA varsity went into the tournament as a clear underdog to its cross-town rival. No one, however, could have predicted the thorough thrashing the Trojans administered on the Stanford courts. USC dominated the nine-team field from start to finish, winning 22 points, an all-time NCAA-record. (Team points were awarded based on individual performance in singles and doubles.) UCLA finished a distant second with 12 points, and no UCLA player made it into the finals in either the singles or doubles competition. Osuna, USC's diminutive Mexican star, outlasted Marty Riessen of Northwestern for the singles title, and then teamed with Ramsey Earnhart to win the doubles title for the second straight year. When it was announced that no doubles team had won consecutive NCAA championships since 1925, Arthur and the Bruins knew that USC's victory was complete. The dream of a third straight team championship for UCLA had dissolved into the nightmare of USC's obvious superiority.[24]

Mercifully, Arthur had little time to think about the disappointing results at Palo Alto. School was out, and by June 24 he was making his way eastward to the first stop of the summer tennis circuit. Prior to his nineteenth birthday in early July, he was still technically a Junior, but he had already gained enough national attention to draw invitations and traveling money from tournament organizers eager to attract the nation's best players. With the recent liberalization of the USLTA's stance on racial integration, he was able to participate in the tour with little fear of outright hostility or official rejection, taking advantage of the fact that virtually all of the summer tournaments were held outside the South. As much as he missed his family, he had no desire to spend more than a few days in what he now realized was the confining, almost suffocating atmosphere of the Jim Crow South. Perhaps even more important, improvement on the tennis court was his number one priority, and the only reliable way to move to the next level was, as he later put it, "hard continuous tennis."

Arthur's financial situation had not reached the point where he could contemplate the ultimate summer tennis experiences—playing on the hallowed grass at Wimbledon or on the red clay at Roland Garros in Paris. But his disappointment in not joining Pasarell and several other American players on the trip to Europe was tempered by the prospect of traveling independently during a summer of personal liberation. Hackensack, New Jersey, the first stop on the summer tour, was a far cry from Wimbledon. But being there represented an important step on the path to both adulthood and full participation in the world of competitive tennis.

The Eastern circuit gave Arthur just what he needed, plenty of competition and a growing sense of inclusion and validation. Yet the summer of 1962 was also inevitably a season of confusion and some frustration for a young, relatively inexperienced player. The transition to the adult tour was not for the faint of heart, and Arthur faced additional barriers of race, class, and culture. He had played in integrated tournaments before, and after a year of intercollegiate matches he was accustomed to being the only black player in sight. But somehow playing on the summer tour was different. This was the real world, and he was on his own, without teammates, and without a coach to guide or protect him. The broad age range of older and younger players, the size of the crowds, the likelihood of daily interaction with a wide variety of players, officials, sponsors, reporters, and fans—all of these factors posed a challenge to a newcomer trying to establish himself.

For Arthur, racial isolation was often the toughest test. "To me those tournament trips were like exploring unknown country that could be unpleasant or even booby-trapped," he recalled. "Sometimes everything would be smiling and friendly on the surface, but I wasn't sure whether the friendliness was more than face-deep. I'd always been among my own kind when I was at home in Richmond or in Dr. Johnson's summer training camp. And at UCLA I had plenty of friends and no enemies. But the tournament trips were something else. There were weeks at a time when I never saw another Negro, except maybe waiters and locker-room attendants. You can imagine the feeling—traveling away from home and never seeing anybody of your own race. You're not scared but you're always on guard."

Although he knew it would take time and effort to adjust to the personal and social demands of the tour, he was less prepared for his lack of success on the court. Week after week, he found himself overmatched by older and more experienced opponents. He was fit, and at times seemed to be playing as well as he had ever played. Yet he discovered even his best wasn't quite good enough against the nation's top players. While he usually prevailed in the early rounds, he rarely made it beyond the quarterfinals. His first disappointment came at the beginning of the tour, in northern New Jersey, at the Eastern Clay Court Championships, a tournament he had won the year before. Coinciding with the first week of Wimbledon, the tournament traditionally drew a weak field of clay court specialists, and as the defending champion he was the number one seed. Brimming with confidence, he breezed through the first three rounds, but then ran out of steam against the former Princeton star Jim Farrin in the quarterfinals, 2–6, 7–5, 6–0. This "rude awakening," as *The Chicago Defender* put it, set him back on his heels.

The pattern continued throughout July, at the Detroit Invitational, where he lost in the semifinals, and at the prestigious United States Clay Court Championship in Chicago, where he lost in straight sets to Fred Stolle, a former Wimbledon doubles champion. At the end of the month, the tour moved to grass courts, a faster surface better suited to his game. But he continued to struggle, losing to Graebner in the second round at the Merion Cricket Club in Haverford, Pennsylvania. Teamed with Nagler, he won the doubles title at Merion, but a few days later he lost to Whitney Reed in the second round at South Orange, New Jersey.

His spirits rose temporarily in early August when he, Pasarell, and Reed were renamed to the U.S. Junior Davis Cup team, and when he took time out to participate in his last ATA national tournament, winning his third consecutive men's singles title. On the more competitive USLTA circuit, however, his fortunes continued to flag. By the end of the summer tour, he was roundly discouraged, but at least he now knew just how difficult it was going to be to climb the national tennis ladder.[25]

Before returning to UCLA to begin his sophomore year, Arthur had time

for an extended visit with his family in Virginia and a week of play at the U.S.
National Championships at Forest Hills. This was his fourth appearance at
Forest Hills, so breaching the color line at the West Side Tennis Club was no
longer a novelty. Even so, he was more determined than ever to play his best
at America's most famous tennis venue. In the first round, he defeated a familiar foe, Butch Newman, in a close match. But in the second round he had
the misfortune of coming up against the defending champion, Roy Emerson.

The Ashe-Emerson match took place on the Stadium Court, where
no black had played since Althea Gibson in 1958. The umpire was Titus
Sparrow, the first black person to preside over a Forest Hills match, and the
contest was the fifth and last match of the day on the Stadium Court. Only
a modest crowd was on hand to witness what was expected to be a rout, but
during the first two sets Ashe displayed flashes of brilliance, even though he
lost both sets. In the third and final set, Emerson kicked it up a notch, and
Ashe failed to win a game. The next day Al Danzig of *The New York Times*,
the dean of American tennis writers, praised Ashe as an erratic but talented
newcomer. "The slender youth is a stylist of imagination and daring," Danzig wrote, "with strokes that will be a real challenge once he has acquired
better control." [26]

Arthur had heard this type of criticism before—that he was as erratic
as he was talented. But he didn't mind, preferring the image of a flashy
risk taker to that of a plodding baseliner. At least some people in the tennis
world had begun to notice he was capable of creative and innovative play.
More than anything else, he wanted to be thought of as a young Pancho
Gonzales, a shotmaker with power who could invent dazzling new strokes
whenever he needed them. Gonzales had been Arthur's hero since he had
first seen him play in Richmond in 1954, and earlier in the year he had taken
instruction from the aging but still hard-hitting pro at the UCLA courts. At
Coach Morgan's invitation, Gonzales and other touring professionals sometimes practiced on the Bruins' courts, affording Arthur and his teammates
the rare opportunity to get to know and learn from some of the world's best
players. Arthur emerged from these informal workshops determined to hit
his serves and groundstrokes like Gonzales—harder than he had ever hit
them before. [27]

By mid-September, Ashe was back on campus and glad to be there, realizing
his second year of college would almost certainly prove less stressful than his
first. He now had a much better sense of what to expect both on and off the
court. No longer an innocent freshman, he had begun to embrace both the

responsibilities and freedom of early adulthood. While he still looked several years younger than his age, he was clearly growing up—intellectually as well as emotionally. Those who knew him best detected a new openness in his social and interpersonal relations. He was more confident and assertive, and less rigid in his daily routines. His sophomore roommate, teammate David Reed, actively encouraged this new attitude, and their oversized room in Sproul Hall soon became a gathering place for a widening circle of friends. "Our room was probably the best room in the place, intended originally for visiting big shots. It was extra large, with wood paneling," Arthur recalled. Putting the insecurities of his Virginia background behind him, he was fast becoming one of the self-assured "California boys" that he had once feared and envied as a young player.

Arthur's growing sophistication and maturation had a lot to do with the deepening bonds of trust among his teammates. As he reflected upon this part of his life several years later, he stressed the platoon-style "band of brothers" experience that created a surrogate family. "I guess being part of that small sociable squad," he wrote, "was the closest I've ever come in my whole life to feeling that I really belonged—even though we all were rivals for the top spots on the team." Race placed certain limits on this sense of belonging, he conceded, and at the deepest level he remained "different from the other tennis players." "I could always feel it," he recalled, "rather like being alone in a tribe of red Indians or South Sea Islanders." Nevertheless, he came to rely on several close interracial friendships that encouraged feelings of inclusion and eased his transition to adulthood.

His teammates still teased him about being "the Shadow," and there was no letup in the racial banter that punctuated courtside and locker room conversations. But over the years he had learned to fend off these casual indignities without anger, even though he seldom saw any real humor in them. Giving as good as he got, he was slowly but surely developing survival skills that would serve him well in the years to come. Here his even temper and cool demeanor proved useful, promoting an easy sociability that often protected him from the worst excesses of racial insensitivity and misunderstanding. Outwardly at least, he was just one of the guys, darker skinned to be sure, but safely inside the circle of friendship.[28]

As his sophomore year progressed, Arthur became increasingly relaxed and open in his dealings with other students, so much so that he eventually felt secure enough to challenge one of American culture's fundamental taboos. Interracial dating had become increasingly common on the UCLA campus since the mid-1950s, and Ashe himself had dated Susan Ikei during his freshman year. Nevertheless, as he was well aware, a romantic, interracial relationship with a white girl remained a daring and potentially dangerous transgression. The safest course, even at UCLA, would have been to suppress any urge to reach across the color line. But he was too curious to ignore the white coeds who sometimes smiled at him in class or at social gatherings, and he was too attracted to them to let race stand in his way for very long. In his earlier days, he had been afraid to approach or even make eye contact with a white girl. But as a red-blooded nineteen-year-old man about campus, he was ready to follow his emotions and take his chances exploring the unknown.

Arthur's first experience with living on the edge began innocently enough with a sideways glance at a beautiful girl standing on the edge of a dance floor in Sproul Hall. Two decades later, he recalled the excitement of the moment: "She was absolutely stunning, with coal-black hair, a tight green skirt, and dark green turtleneck sweater. And white. I was unable to take my eyes off her. She caught me looking at her and stared back boldly. . . . After twenty minutes of glances across the dance floor, I summoned enough nerve to go over and mumble the usual, 'Hello, What's your name?' It turned out she was a friend of a friend. I asked her to dance. I had never danced with a white girl before." Later, sitting in the moonlight on an outdoor patio, they talked for three hours, ending the evening with a peck on the cheek and a vow "to see each other again."

As Arthur walked back to his room alone, his mind raced with thoughts of how shocked his friends and family back in Richmond would have been to see him dancing with and kissing a white girl. "Talk about old southern taboos coming back to haunt you," he later wrote. "I was scared, thrilled, excited, sweating and numb—all at the same time." Looking back, he acknowledged the obvious: "the fact that she was different was part of my attraction to her." "Each of us brought our own perceptions and life experiences to UCLA," he continued. "We tried to mix and reconcile, probe and experiment with our different values and judgments. I don't think many of my white classmates ever dated a black woman. When you're in the majority, you don't feel you have to make any accommodation. Assimilation, if any, is for the minority. So is experimentation. . . . For someone like me, from the small stifling world of Richmond, the opportunity to try something new—unknown and forbidden—could not be squandered."[29]

Arthur's infatuation with his first white girlfriend, Phyllis Jones, lasted for several months, long enough for him to reflect upon the likely ramifications of their relationship. "At first, I worried about what my family would think, what J.D. would think," he recalled. "But everyone that mattered was so far away. I talked to Susan Ikei. She thought I was dumb to worry so much." Eventually Phyllis told her mother that she was dating Arthur Ashe, a member of the UCLA tennis team; somehow she failed to mention that her new boyfriend was black. Several weeks later, when Mrs. Jones happened to see him on a television sports report, the reaction was predictable. "You didn't tell me he was a Negro!" the devastated mother screamed. "I don't ever want him in my house, do you hear?" Phyllis sheepishly agreed but continued to date Ashe anyway, continuing the relationship until, as he put it, the novelty "wore off."

Arthur clearly knew that at one level he was defying convention, that in his words "a black man could have gotten killed for dating a white woman in Richmond," where antimiscegenation statutes still outlawed racial inter-marriage. But he also knew that sexual permissiveness, even across racial lines, was the norm at UCLA, where, as he later wrote, "the atmosphere was definitely anything goes." This was especially true, he insisted, for athletes: "Some women thought that a good athlete was also probably good in bed." "This fascination," according to Arthur, "was a powerful force," to the point where "most black athletes could have any woman they wanted, black or white." UCLA was an anomaly, of course: "Once you went away from West-wood . . . the situation changed. I had never been stared at like that before, as if was doing something morally wrong." He was so unnerved at one point that he bravely called his father to ask if it would be a serious problem if he happened to marry a white woman. "Don't make no difference to me," Arthur Sr. responded, "as long as she's a good person."[30]

As a new member of the UCLA varsity, Arthur found himself climbing up the tennis ladder. One of the secrets of his success was actually an off-campus opportunity that took him into a world where tennis, celebrity, and social privilege were conjoined. During their second year in Los Angeles, he and Pasarell began to spend more of their time at the Beverly Hills Tennis Club, where they cultivated a growing friendship with two of the world's most inventive and colorful tennis pros, Francisco "Pancho" Segura and Richard Alonzo "Pancho" Gonzales. Segura was the teaching pro at the club, and Gonzales, who was still playing on the professional tour, was a frequent visitor. Both Panchos developed a strong affinity for Arthur, whom they regarded as a fellow outsider. Taking considerable interest in his career, they considered him one of "the brown bodies," their term for players of color who had breached the barriers of race and class to enter the virtually all-white world of the American tennis elite.

Segura, a native Ecuadoran who had come to the United States in 1941 to play under the famed University of Miami coach Gardnar Mulloy, was a savvy pro known for his highly unorthodox two-handed forehand. Though often overshadowed by several of his contemporaries, he had his moments of glory, defeating Gonzales twice in consecutive U.S. Pro singles finals in 1951 and 1952.

A Californian, the hard-hitting Gonzales emerged from the barrios to become the reigning king of the professional tour throughout the mid- and late 1950s, winning the U.S. Pro singles title eight times between 1953 and 1964. In 1969, at the age of forty-one, he would somehow outlast Pasarell in the longest match in Wimbledon history, 112 games played over five hours and twelve minutes, an ironic twist considering that he had helped mentor his Puerto Rican friend for the past seven years.

Gonzales was sometimes as imperious as Segura was mellow, but both men were generous with their time and advice. Going beyond his flashy per-formances at the UCLA courts—which had demonstrated how to hit hard but not necessarily how to keep the ball between the lines—Gonzales worked on the technical aspects of the boys' shotmaking, especially their serves. "Toss the ball more to the right—into the court," he told them. "Lean into the shot. You serve with your body, not with your arm. If you serve with your arm, you'll get tired." In Segura's case, the help often went beyond technique and strategy as he introduced the two college boys to a host of tennis-playing Hollywood celebrities and sometimes even farmed out his scheduled lessons to provide them with a few extra dollars. "Segura charged fifteen dollars an hour," Arthur recalled. "I kept ten and gave him five."

The friendship's real payoff came on the court, where both he and Pas-arell began to strike the ball with greater force. They were soon hitting serves and groundstrokes "Gonzales style," which meant their pace rivaled that of the world's strongest power hitters. With this new pace came an inevitable decline in accuracy, but over time this became less of a problem.[31]

By the fall of 1962, it was clear that Ashe and Pasarell were already as good, and perhaps even a bit better, than any of the team's upperclassmen—and by the end of the year this was confirmed by their national rankings, #10 for Pasarell and #18 for Ashe. Once the spring semester season began, the two sophomores assumed the team's top two singles positions, playing ahead of several talented but envious teammates, including David Reed, David Sanderlin, Paul Palmer, and Thorvald Moe. Over the next four months, with Ashe and Pasarell leading the way, the 1963 Bruins managed to win the vast majority of their dual matches. But even with this infusion of talent they could not keep up with their crosstown rival USC. Led by Dennis Ralston and Rafael Osuna, the Trojans were more powerful than ever and virtually unbeatable on the fast concrete courts of Southern California.

On one occasion, during a mid-April dual match, the Bruins flirted with an upset as Pasarell upended Osuna, winning a marathon second set 21–19; and later in the day, after winning the first set, 9–7, Ashe seemed to be on his way to doing the same against Ralston. But the fiery Trojan from Bakersfield came back to win the final two sets. At the end of the singles competition the team score was 3–3, but after USC swept the doubles the day belonged to the Trojans.

Even though he lost to Ralston several times during his first varsity season and came to see him as a nemesis, Arthur gradually raised the level of his game during the winter and spring of 1963. He played especially well in special and invitational tournaments, winning both the singles and doubles titles at the first annual All-University of California championships in February, a week after upsetting the nation's #4 ranked player, Ham Richardson, in the third round of the Thunderbird Invitational tournament in Phoenix. UCLA's Athletic News Bureau soon began touting him as "one of America's coming amateur greats" and "the finest Negro prospect in the history of the game." "Ashe has fine speed and a flowing assortment of strokes, including a big serve and a solid backhand," a slightly hyperbolic press release explained. "Needs only to become physically stronger and to consolidate his game with emphasis on improving the consistency and 'percentage' of his play." In sum, the author of the press release concluded: "The sky is the limit for the personable Mr. Ashe." [32]

By early May the press was touting Ashe and Pasarell as likely selections to the U.S. Davis Cup team scheduled to play a first-round tie (the traditional term for a Davis Cup competition between two nations) against Iran in Tehran in mid-June. Both were eventually added to the team, along with Ralston and Chuck McKinley, but not before being drawn into a controversy that threatened Arthur's relationship with J. D. Morgan. With the exception of McKinley, all of the top American players selected by Captain Bob Kelleher were collegiate players scheduled to participate in the NCAA championship tournament to be held at Princeton University the same week as the U.S.-Iran tie. Since the contest against Iran was expected to be a walkover, UCLA and USC officials refused to release their top players from the obligation to play at Princeton. Arthur himself was not expected to be asked to play in Tehran, but Pasarell was Kelleher's clear choice as the "third man" to back up Ralston and McKinley in the singles competition.

Thrilled by the prospect of representing the United States, Pasarell made no secret of his preference to skip Princeton so he could play in Tehran. But Coach Morgan refused to grant him a release. This decision, as controversial as it was, probably would have been the end of the episode if an enterprising student journalist, the sports editor of the *Daily Bruin*, had not conducted an interview with Arthur, asking him what he thought about the Pasarell situation. Having little experience with the press, he did not hesitate to defend his closest friend, stating unequivocally: "I think the Davis Cup is far more important than any collegiate championship."

Predictably, Morgan exploded as soon as he read Arthur's words: "J.D. called me into his office and tore into me at the top of his voice for 45 minutes." "Sure the Davis Cup is more important," the coach pointed out. "But we'll beat Iran no matter who we send! So it is more important for Pasarell to play at Princeton!" A long lecture on school loyalty followed. As Arthur remembered the scene, Morgan was so forceful that "I didn't say three words." "As usual," he acknowledged in 1967, "J.D. was right." In the end, the U.S. team of Allen Fox, Donald Dell, and Gene Scott did not miss Pasarell—or Ralston and McKinley for that matter—as they dispatched the overmatched Iranians in short order.[33]

Arthur's verbal indiscretion was soon forgotten. By the time the UCLA team competed at Princeton, he was back in Morgan's good graces, especially after he played his heart out in a losing effort against Ralston in the semifinals. According to Al Danzig, who had been covering NCAA tennis for several decades, the Ashe-Ralston match had "hardly been surpassed for many years in this tournament in the quality of the play." To win, Ralston had to produce "the greatest tennis in his career in the fifth set." Ashe, after losing the first two sets, came back to win the third and fourth before simply running out of steam. Although losing such an important match was disappointing, he left the court with his head held high, knowing he had just played the best single set of his college career. "No other Negro player in the men's ranks," Danzig declared, "has ever remotely approached the tennis Ashe put forth." Ralston went on to win the singles championship, and several of his teammates also raised their game when it counted most. USC was once again the NCAA champion, scoring 27 points to second-place UCLA's 17.[34]

The loss to Ralston and USC stung, but in the immediate aftermath of the Princeton tournament Arthur was too excited to dwell on what had just happened. "That same night," he remembered, "it seemed that almost everybody from the two teams was on the plane to London." Having been left behind the previous year, he was ecstatic to be included in the American contingent headed for Wimbledon. As he put it, "even without winning the NCAAs, I was flying on several levels." Earlier in the year, he had been resigned to staying behind for a second time as many of his tennis-playing peers headed for the world's most prestigious tournament. Financially strapped as he was, there was simply no money to fund an expensive trip across the Atlantic. Indeed, at the close of the fall semester in December 1962, he had received a sobering reminder of his unenviable economic situation.[35]

Unable to scrounge up enough money to travel to Virginia over the Christmas break, Arthur had no choice but to remain at UCLA while the vast majority of his fellow students "went home for the holidays." "The campus became a ghost town with just a few of us left to haunt it," he later explained. "There was no meal service for several days and I was flat broke. For the first time since I left home, I did not have a cent in my pocket." Advised that Arthur was still on campus, J.D. invited him to have Christmas dinner at the Morgan house, but his lonely star declined the invitation, saying he had already made other arrangements. As Arthur described his embarrassing dilemma, "I really had no plans and I was too proud to ask my father to send me some money."

By Christmas Day, he was reduced to borrowing a dollar from his Haitian friend and future roommate Jean-Edouard Baker to pay for "some fruit and a sandwich from the vending machines in the basement of the dormitory." He later remembered this experience as "the worst" moment of his life as a college student, a low point that gave him "a sober regard for money." "Even five dollars," he explained, "would have meant I could walk to Westwood to see a movie. I wasn't tempted to run out and steal anything, but I thought long and hard about what it meant to have no money at all for an extended period. I was determined never to be in that situation again."[36]

Then an unexpected windfall in April changed his circumstances. As he and Pasarell left the court following an exhibition match at the California Club, a well-dressed, middle-aged white woman approached him and struck up a conversation about his tennis. After praising his play, she asked about his plans for the future. "I don't know," he told her. "If I can find the money, I'll go to Wimbledon next month. If not, I'll try to go back East and play the summer circuit there." When she asked how much it would cost for him to go to Wimbledon, he replied: "Oh, about eight hundred dollars would do it." After assuring him she thought he certainly deserved "a chance" to play at Wimbledon, she told him to "wait here just a moment . . . I'll be right back." Arthur assumed that the woman—who, he later learned, was Joianna

Ogner, the wife of a Beverly Hills auto dealer—"was going to get a business card." But instead "she walked about thirty yards down a long hall into a card room and shut the door behind her." For a few moments Arthur didn't know what to think, but "about three minutes later, she came striding back and put eight crisp hundred dollar bills" in his hand. "Here, this should do it," she declared with a smile. "Good luck. We'll be looking for your name in the *Times*."

As it turned out, the enterprising Mrs. Ogner "had gone into the card room, found eight guys around the table, and hit each one for a hundred dollars." In the years to come Arthur often cited this "act of kindness" as one of the turning points of his career. Not only did it fund his first trip abroad, but also it "balanced the Balboa Club incident" that had shattered his "image of California." "Now I knew," he explained, "there were warm and generous people out there who would give me a hand when they could." Coming at a critical point in his journey from Jim Crow to the wider world, the California Club episode gave him a glimpse of a bright future beyond the dark shadows of racial prejudice.[37]

SEVEN

TRAVELING MAN

■

D URING THE SPRING OF 1963, several other benefactors stepped
forward to help fund Arthur's first overseas adventure. "J.D. worked
hard to get me to Wimbledon," he later explained. "I wasn't eligible for
USLTA expense money abroad, because I hadn't yet been named to the
Davis Cup team, but J.D. got some of his high-powered alumni to put the
bite on various people for part of my expenses. Dr. Johnson also worked hard
on it. His junior development fund made a contribution toward my trip. So
did several Richmond people, white and black. And the Negro high schools
in Richmond took up a collection." Arthur was grateful for this tangible
show of support, which he took as a clear sign that he had finally "moved up
into the higher-flying level of players."[1]

In November, his new status would be confirmed by a cover story in
World Tennis magazine, his first real splash in the press. But the Wimbledon
trip was the milestone that meant the most to him, bringing the realization
of a lifelong dream. No African American man had ever graced the green
turf of the All England Lawn Tennis and Croquet Club, and now he would
be the first. Traveling outside the United States was a rare experience for
black Americans in the 1950s and 1960s. Indeed, few of his relatives and boyhood friends had ever traveled more than a hundred miles from home, and
the idea of crossing more than three thousand miles of ocean to play tennis
must have seemed preposterous to anyone growing up in the Jackson Ward

section of Richmond. In this context, Arthur's flight to London represented a radical new departure, literally for him, and vicariously for his friends and family. Sharing the flight with six Wimbledon-bound friends from the California tennis scene, he was sure he had embarked on the greatest adventure of his young life.[2]

Arthur's first visit to Great Britain was full of revelations. Even before his arrival at Wimbledon, he marveled at the multicultural mix streaming through the airport and along the streets of central London. Yet he couldn't help but notice the all too familiar signs of racial hierarchy. "The first thing I saw at Heathrow Airport after my arrival were the Indian and Pakistani women who cleaned the floor," he later commented, adding, "I quickly found that in London, like Richmond, black people did the dirty work." Noting that he "never saw a black face among the famous Guards" at Buckingham Palace, he concluded British colonialism had left a legacy of institutionalized discrimination manifested in a "class system" that "only made racism more oppressive."[3]

While London reminded him "of home in many ways," Arthur found Wimbledon to be "in a class by itself." As he gazed at Centre Court and its surroundings, the setting reminded him of "an Ivy League school, with ivy on the majestic walls," not unlike the Princeton campus where he had played two days earlier. Less grand was the gritty "B" locker room, the changing room to which he and the other "lesser-known players—the nobodies and qualifiers" were assigned. This manifestation of "the British class system" reminded him of "the 'separate but equal' cry of Virginia's Massive Resistance movement after the *Brown* decision."

One consolation was the tradition of dispatching Rolls-Royces and Bentleys to ferry all of the players to Wimbledon from their central London hotels. As Arthur recalled: "I'll never forget my first ride in a Bentley; it was the roomiest car I had ever been in and the driver addressed me as 'sir' or 'mister.' I was impressed but not fooled. I had learned early to be wary of strangers or whites bearing gifts. Still, I enjoyed the luxury; it made me feel important even though I wasn't." Being transported like a celebrity from the Westbury Hotel, where all of the American players were housed, "through meadows and trees to Wimbledon township, where the All-England [*sic*] club is," was a fantasy-like experience. The car "drove us around to the door of the locker room," he recalled. "People were crowded there getting autographs. We felt like movie stars."[4]

The celebrity treatment had actually begun the previous night. Writing in his memoir *Advantage Ashe* four years later, Arthur remembered the scene:

"We ate at a nice restaurant that first evening. Our waiter thought at first we were cricketeers, because some test matches were going on in London. When we told him we were tennis players, he gasped, 'Oh, you're playing at Wimbledon!' From then on he served us as if we were royalty." "Wimbledon in England," he pointed out to his American readers, "is like the World Series here. The matches are televised all over Europe. You go on the streets and people recognize you. Make a phone call and the operator knows your name."[5]

Once the visiting Americans arrived at Wimbledon, the special treatment continued. "There was a masseur available to rub us down," Arthur recalled with an enthusiasm that would seem quaintly innocent to future generations accustomed to overprivileged athletes, "and a TV so we could watch matches without going outside. We had the freedom of a cafeteria, a tea room, and a bar if we wanted it." "Outside," he continued, "I found that all courts—not just the main ones—were perfectly manicured. There were linesmen for every match, so no players had to call their own lines." Even more amazing was the dignified presence of umpires wearing "hard straw hats and carnations just as they did in 1880." As Arthur "wandered among the spectators" on his first morning at the site, he was, in his words, "awed by the ladies hats, which seemed to be topped with pink cabbages, velvet bows, and assorted feathers" and "by the nobility taking tea under impressive umbrellas." Wherever he looked, he saw "green everywhere—green ivy, green canopies, green doors and balconies and chairs," as "people stood around elbow to elbow, craning on tiptoe to look at aristocrats or to watch tennis."

Although he tried to remain calm and collected, he later confessed: "all the magnificence and efficiency dazed me a little," so much so that "I felt jittery when it was time for my first-round match." By the time he finished a nervous pre-match warm-up on one of the outside courts, he "was beginning to see why players say that no tournament in the world touches Wimbledon." Only after surviving his opening round match did he begin to feel that he belonged in such august surroundings.[6]

His first-round opponent, Carlos Fernandes of Brazil, was a clay court specialist unaccustomed to grass, but he gave the American serve-and-volley specialist all he could handle in a five-set thriller. After losing the first two sets, Arthur mounted a ferocious comeback, winning the last three sets 6–4, 6–4, 6–1. In the words of one reporter covering the match, "the first American Negro to play in the men's singles had acquitted himself with honor." His second-round match against the hard-hitting Aussie John

Hillebrand proved to be an even stiffer challenge, but Arthur ultimately prevailed in five long sets.

For Ashe, the twin victories—however narrow—represented a major milestone in his career. "Suddenly, in my first Wimbledon, I had reached the third round," he later explained. "I was so excited and nervous I could hardly contain myself. The first win over Fernandes had been the psychological hump. . . . For me, moving to the next round was like my first big win over one of those 'white boys' on the junior circuit."[7]

After playing two five-set matches in two days, Ashe was pretty much spent, and the Wimbledon schedule did not allow for any days off. Less than twenty-four hours after defeating Hillebrand, he found himself on the court with the #4 seed, Chuck McKinley, who had made it all the way to the Wimbledon final in 1961 before losing to Rod Laver. He had faced McKinley before with little success, and in his depleted state he was no match for the relentless five-foot-nine-inch dynamo. As he knew all too well, McKinley, a student at Trinity University in San Antonio, had been the clear favorite to win the recent NCAA singles title before withdrawing from the intercollegiate competition to focus on Wimbledon. In granting his request to skip the Princeton tournament, the president of Trinity had told him "you'd better win," and win he did, not only defeating Ashe in the third round but going on to win the 1963 Wimbledon singles title without losing a set. "We met on Court 6, next to the canvas-covered 'members' enclosure," Arthur recalled. "It is the noisiest court at Wimbledon because the members are talking, eating, and drinking right next to the court. But I couldn't blame the members for my game against McKinley. He was the best U.S. player, and I was talented but inexperienced."

Considering the circumstances, Arthur did not feel too bad about his elimination. "My arm seized up," he explained to the press after the McKinley match. "I wanted to quit halfway through." That he did not quit was a testament to a fighting spirit often camouflaged by his quiet demeanor. He wanted to win at Wimbledon as much as he wanted anything in his tennis life, a steely determination he would evidence on more than one occasion in the years to come.[8]

He also competed in the 1963 Wimbledon men's doubles competition teamed with the former UCLA standout Allen Fox. Though unseeded, the Ashe-Fox duo won two matches before losing in the third round to two Soviet players. The Cold War implications of the match attracted a larger than normal crowd, but the American cause received a boost in the next round when McKinley and Ralston defeated the Soviets.

Arthur's early elimination from the singles and doubles competition allowed him to concentrate on his pairing with Carol Hanks in mixed doubles. Hanks, an attractive twenty-one-year-old Stanford student, had grown up in St. Louis where she met Arthur during his year at Sumner High School. Ranked seventh in women's singles in the United States, she had won both the U.S. Hard Court singles title and the NCAA doubles title in 1962. She and Arthur constituted a formidable doubles team—and the first interracial pairing in Wimbledon history. Breezing through the early rounds, they ultimately lost in the quarterfinals to the veteran Darlene Hard of Long Beach and her partner Bob Hewitt, who along with Fred Stolle was the defending Wimbledon men's doubles champion.[9]

Arthur spent most of the Wimbledon fortnight's second week as a tourist. Flying home before the end of the tournament was not an option, thanks to the U.S. Davis Cup captain, Bob Kelleher, who had arranged a post-Wimbledon week in Sweden for three of his probable team members. Taking full advantage of the situation, Arthur explored central London, following a nightly routine that he and his California friends adopted. "Every evening on the first trip," he later recounted, "a group of us would walk up Conduit Street, turn right and walk half a mile to the little statue of Eros in the center of Piccadilly Circus. We ate dinner at Lyons Corner House and roamed Soho." By the time he left for Scandinavia, he felt he had experienced "the heart of London," and in the years to come he would repeat this "pilgrimage" to the center of what he termed "my favorite city . . . the most civilized city in the world."[10]

The trip to Scandinavia was brief because USLTA rules required all high-ranking American players to return to the United States within one week of the close of Wimbledon so they could begin play in the Eastern grass court circuit. Ashe and his traveling companions—Ralston and the McKinleys—made the most of their all-expenses-paid sojourn, flying to Copenhagen for a sightseeing day before traveling on to the Swedish resort town of Bastad, the site of an annual international tournament. With the pressure of Wimbledon behind them, the Americans were able to relax and enjoy the best of Swedish hospitality. The entire experience was exotic, from "playing one match at 9:30 in the evening—by sunlight," to being "a unique item" of attraction for the bevy of beautiful Swedish girls attending the tournament. With his attention obviously compromised by this seductive atmosphere, he didn't play very well, suffering an early exit in the singles competition. But he was able to combine tennis and pleasure in the mixed doubles competition, where he made it to the quarterfinals with a winsome Swedish partner,

Elizabeth Carlgren. "I hated to leave," he later confessed, but USLTA rules forced him to return to the real world.[11]

Two days later, thoroughly jet-lagged, he found himself in River Forest, Illinois, competing in the National Clay Court Championships. Somehow the weary traveler made it to the third round. A week later, he joined the Eastern grass circuit at the Pennsylvania lawn tennis championship held at the Merion Cricket Club. Having seen Wimbledon two weeks before, he was less intimidated by Merion's posh atmosphere than he had been during his earlier visits, which may help to explain why he played so well. After defeating Marty Riessen in the third round and Allen Fox in the quarterfinals, he played a valiant semifinal match against McKinley. After winning the first set 6–1, he seemed to be on his way to an upset victory, but McKinley fought back with an effective combination of "spin and twist" serves and "trigger sure" volleys—as a *New York Times* reporter put it—to win the next three sets. As in the past, Arthur's moments of brilliance were foiled by inconsistency and questionable shot choices. In the judgment of the reporter, "The Richmond youth showed that he is one of the greatest shot makers in amateur tennis. He also showed that his game is immature, erratic and risky."[12]

This type of criticism would dog Arthur throughout the summer and beyond, but it didn't have much impact on his style of play. While he acknowledged that risk taking sometimes led to squandered points and short-term failure, he maintained his resolve to take chances that few other players were willing to attempt. Developing a distinctive and innovative style of power tennis had become increasingly important to him, not only as a tactical matter on the court but also as a psychological mechanism of asserting his personal independence. Constrained for so many years by the strict mentorship of his father, Dr. J, and Coach Hudlin, he was finally free to make his own decisions. During the intercollegiate season, Coach Morgan often reined him in for the good of the team, but during the summer he was essentially on his own.

One of the things that Arthur liked best about tennis was the unpredictability of any given point—an unpredictability that dictated a wide variety of shots and split-second decision making. The thrill of responding to a challenging situation with a dazzling winner was not something he was willing to forgo, even if creative shotmaking sometimes got him into trouble.

For a tournament player to survive with this degree of self-indulgence required a measure of security born of confidence and success. As Arthur described the summer circuit, there were two basic types of players, those who "sail around enjoying life" and those who "work hard to be consistent winners." He judged himself to be in the latter, more serious group, but he knew climbing up the rungs of the national tennis ladder was an uneven process of fits and starts. "Once in a while somebody develops into a better-than-average tournament player," he explained. "Then he begins getting invitations to more important tournaments. And if he does well in these, eventually he starts beating nationally known players now and then. At that point he moves into a different orbit of tourneys and a different way of life. That happened to me." [13]

One of the most obvious benefits of moving into this higher orbit of tournament play was financial backing. Although technically amateurs, most successful players survived on a combination of private sponsorship and tournament guarantees, and within this system there was a hierarchy of support mechanisms. "If he's an also-ran," Arthur once explained, "he'll pay his own fares. If he has a sponsor who thinks he's a future champ, the sponsor will give him gasoline or air tickets. If he's a seeded player, the tournament promoters themselves will pay his transportation." Beyond these distinctions, virtually all players received additional support once they were on site: "No matter how he gets there, once he's at the tournament site he can just about make it for nothing. The tournament committee will have arranged for him to be put up in someone's home or at a hotel; and meals are usually free or can be mooched if necessary."

Prior to the summer of 1963, Arthur had lived on the lower margins of this system. "In my first years on the circuit I had to pay my own way from city to city, with the help of Dr. Johnson and my father and a few friends," he remembered. "While I was in a tournament the officials gave me a little money for 'living expenses' but the maximum allowable was $28 a day and only the top-seeded entrants got that. At Forest Hills when I was unseeded I didn't even get expense money, although the USLTA did arrange a special rate of $5 a night at the Hilton in New York." [14]

As a highly regarded seeded player, Arthur received what he called "full hospitality," which "meant better accommodations in most towns, and the legal maximum of $28 a day for living expenses, plus transportation money. And if I wanted to go some place during my free hours the tournaments usually provided a car for me." With a few exceptions, he was also accorded full participation in the social events that accompanied the weekly tournaments, especially after he joined the Davis Cup squad in early August. "That first summer as a top-seeded player was in some ways the most fun I'd ever had in my life up to then," he recalled. "I'd gotten over the strain of being a Negro alone in white men's clubs. Everyone had accepted me. I could relax a little. My tennis improved."[15]

As the first black player in the long history of the nation's Davis Cup competition, Arthur attracted considerable attention in the national press, which was searching for positive stories to offset the disheartening headlines marking the rise of violent resistance against an expanding and increasingly insistent civil rights movement. In his January inaugural address, Alabama's new governor, George Wallace, pledged to defend "segregation now, segregation tomorrow, and segregation forever," and in May, much of the nation was shocked by the arch-segregationist Bull Connor's use of attack dogs and fire hoses to intimidate nonviolent protesters, many of whom were adolescents or children, in the streets of Birmingham. A month later, on June 11, Governor Wallace defiantly stood in the "schoolhouse door" in a futile effort to prevent the desegregation of the University of Alabama, and the next day Mississippi NAACP leader Medgar Evers was assassinated outside his home in Jackson by a white supremacist extremist.[16]

Arthur's selection to the Davis Cup team was welcome news to Americans shaken by the racial turmoil and violence of recent events. Bob Kelleher had been hinting for several months that Arthur would eventually be put on the team, but when the selection became official the young UCLA star broke out into a broad smile that left no doubt how much this meant to him. His selection put him in the same category as Althea Gibson, who had played well in the Wightman Cup matches against Great Britain in 1957 and 1958. "I've got to live up to it," he acknowledged, and by "it" he meant the long American Davis Cup tradition of winning with style and sportsmanship. Whether he liked it or not, participation on the Davis Cup squad carried the special responsibility of representing both his nation and his race, and he didn't want to do anything on or off the court that might detract from what he regarded as an official elevation to full citizenship.[17]

Arthur's selection to the U.S. Davis Cup squad was not without controversy, and even he later questioned the merits of the choice. "Why was I picked over Frank Froehling, Ham Richardson, Allen Fox and Gene Scott, who were all higher ranked?" he wondered out loud four years later. "Was the committee tossing Negroes a crumb to make them happy?" At the time of the selection, W. Harcourt Woods, the chair of the Davis Cup selection committee, insisted racial considerations played no role in the committee's deliberations. "Ashe was picked on ability," he declared, "not because of the color of his skin." In defending the choice, Woods cited Ashe's recent victories over Richardson, Fox, and Riessen, and his blistering first set at Merion against McKinley, the nation's number-one-ranked player. But not everyone accepted this explanation.

Though friendly with Ashe, one vocal dissenter was Scott, the nation's #8 ranked player, who had been led to believe by a USLTA official that he would be on the team. Ranked ten positions higher than #18 Ashe, he demanded an explanation from the committee. "No wonder he was irked," Arthur later conceded. Inevitably a television interviewer asked him if he thought he had been "chosen because of race." "That was an insulting question," he later complained. "My impulse was to scream No! But . . . I know better than . . . to let my feelings show. So I just gave the TV guys a polite no."[18]

A month later Scott was added to the team, restoring his pride and preserving his friendship with Arthur. But a certain tension continued to surround the squad. As both men well knew, there was considerable pressure on the 1963 squad to win, since the United States had not won the Cup since 1954. Australia had won eight years in a row, eclipsing the United States team's seven-year winning streak from 1920 to 1926. Even more distressing, the 1962 U.S. squad had been eliminated in the semifinals of the Americas Zone, losing to Mexico for the first time in Davis Cup history. No one in the American tennis establishment wanted anything like that to happen again, but the same strong Mexican squad was scheduled to face the Americans in a semifinal rematch in mid-August.

The rematch would be played on a fast concrete surface at the Los Angeles Tennis Club, unlike the slow clay that had benefited the 1962 Mexican team playing at home in Mexico City. But neither Captain Kelleher nor anyone else on the American squad was taking anything for granted. If everything went according to plan, the team's two strongest players, Ralston and McKinley, would play both singles and doubles, leaving the remainder of the squad sitting on the sidelines as cheerleaders. The only possible hitch was a nagging hand injury that threatened to keep Ralston out of the competition. If Ralston couldn't play, McKinley would team with Riessen in doubles, leaving the hard court specialist Ashe as the likely singles substitute. When asked about how he thought he would fare against either of Mexico's singles specialists, Rafael Osuna and Antonio Palafox, Arthur expressed confidence. But the inner reality underneath his cool exterior must have tied his stomach up in knots. Barely twenty years old—and coming off a less than stellar summer season—he had little reason to be confident other than a faith in his ability to come through in the clutch.

For ten days prior to the tie, Arthur and his teammates lived at the Beverly Hilton Hotel, spending long hours working out under the watchful eyes of Captain Kelleher and Coach Pancho Gonzales. The practices honed Ashe's game, and on August 14 Kelleher told reporters the UCLA star "was a 20 per cent better player than he was two weeks ago. Gonzales has been chewing up all of our men and Ashe's game has benefited particularly." Ashe himself declared that he was "happy" about the recent improvement in his game, but when Ralston recovered in plenty of time to lead the American team to victory, his Davis Cup debut was postponed until the next round.[19]

In the meantime, Ashe headed east to play in the National Doubles Championships held at the Longwood Cricket Club before traveling to Forest Hills for the U.S. National tournament. Teamed with Larry Nagler at the Doubles Championships, he made it to the quarterfinals before being eliminated by Osuna and Palafox in a tightly contested marathon match 7–5, 9–7, and 17–15. Having played well, he left Boston for New York with renewed confidence. Still unseeded in his fifth appearance at Forest Hills, he survived the first two rounds. But he couldn't keep up with Riessen in the third. Playing on "a badly chewed up outside court," both men had difficulty keeping the ball in play, and in the end Riessen's superior volleying ability carried the day.[20]

A week later the two teammates were in Denver preparing for the upcoming tie against Venezuela, and once again they were competitors. This time they were vying to replace McKinley, who was temporarily unavailable for Davis Cup play. In view of Riessen's victory over Ashe in New York, it was no surprise when he got the nod from Captain Kelleher, even though the cement surface at Cherry Creek Country Club favored Ashe's game. Two years older than Arthur, Riessen had been on the American squad for three years but had never played a Davis Cup match. So Arthur did not resent his selection. Confident he would get his turn at some point in the near future, he cheered on Riessen and Ralston as they swept the Venezuelans in the opening day singles matches and two days later in doubles. With three points, the Americans had clinched the tie by Saturday afternoon, but Davis Cup tradition dictated that the final two singles matches would be played anyway, essentially "for fun only." As expected, Kelleher turned to Ralston for one of the Sunday singles matches, and with nothing on the line, he selected Arthur for the second. According to Gene Scott, who roomed with Arthur in Denver, Kelleher's first inclination had been to choose him for the second singles slot. But perhaps feeling remorseful about his earlier criticism of the selection process, he urged Kelleher to give the slot to Arthur.

"I'm going to Australia and Arthur isn't," he reportedly told the captain. "Let him play this one."

On September 15, 1963, after more than sixty years of Davis Cup play, an African American was finally on the court representing the United States. The match proved anticlimactic, as Arthur needed only 46 minutes to dispatch the Venezuelan clay court specialist Orlando Bracamonte, who won only two games in three sets. Later in the day, after Ralston closed out the tie with a win over Bracamonte's overmatched teammate Iyo Pimentel, Arthur joined in the victory celebration knowing he had achieved something that many members of the ATA had feared would never happen. Unfortunately, his pathbreaking appearance was not the only history made that day. That morning the 16th Street Baptist Church in Birmingham had been rocked with an explosion that killed four little girls and broke the hearts of many Americans, black and white, who had gained hope and inspiration from the March on Washington eighteen days earlier. This would not be the last time that Arthur would have to balance conflicting emotions born of a personal triumph forged in a broader context of racial hatred and human misery.[21]

The next round of Davis Cup play, only eleven days away, was the Inter-Zone semifinal against Great Britain, to be held on the grass courts at Bournemouth, England. But it had been decided that Ashe would return to UCLA to begin his junior year while the rest of the team traveled to Bournemouth. This meant he would also miss the Inter-Zone final— which, if the Americans defeated the British, would pit them against India in a tie played in Bombay in early November—and the expected Davis Cup final in Adelaide against the defending champion Australians in late December. Playing in India and Australia would require Ashe to withdraw from his fall semester classes, a sacrifice J. D. Morgan was unwilling to countenance.

Missing an extended tour of the British Commonwealth was disappointing, but Kelleher assured Arthur that his status as a Davis Cupper was secure. Beyond Kelleher's promise, there was also a noticeable shift in the way tennis officials and fans, and the press, treated him. Being a member of the Davis Cup team, he recalled in 1967, "definitely put me among the higher-level players, and I began to see what a difference it made." "Besides the prestige," he pointed out on another occasion, "I would be entitled to 100 pounds in expenses at Wimbledon the following year and also would escape the 'B' lockers." Playing in the Pacific Southwest Championship matches in Los Angeles the week after the Venezuela tie, he could already detect a change in his status. Suddenly he was no longer just another promising college player whose position as American tennis's "token Negro" made him an object of curiosity. Now he was identifiably a Davis Cup star and a legitimate national figure worthy of respect and public interest.[22]

Coming off a remarkable series of experiences during the summer—from Wimbledon and Sweden to his Davis Cup debut—Arthur returned to UCLA with a new attitude, one that allowed for a greater degree of self-indulgence and relaxation. His new spirit became manifest in his decision to live off-campus during his junior year. At first, he considered living alone, but after he had difficulty finding an affordable apartment, Pasarell and Jean-Edouard Baker, who as sophomores had shared a small one-bedroom apartment near Pico Boulevard, urged him to move in with them. Together the three friends soon found a two-bedroom in the Pacific Palisades about two miles north of UCLA.

Pasarell had long been Arthur's most trusted friend, and during the past year Baker had become the third member of a trio that mixed friendship with a love of tennis. A good prep school player who played briefly at UCLA but who could not keep up with Coach Morgan's rising standards, Baker came from a prominent mixed-race family in Port-au-Prince, Haiti. His father owned a large sugar plantation, and he had taken an early interest in the business aspects of the family's extensive landholdings. Cosmopolitan and sophisticated beyond his years, he served as Arthur's unofficial academic and social advisor during much of their time at UCLA. It was Baker who convinced him to specialize in marketing as a business major. "Baker has a lot of class. You can tell by the way he handles himself. He'll be cool in any situation. I learned a lot being around him," Arthur later explained. The fun-loving Haitian scion also urged him to let go and live a little, to enjoy life beyond the lines. Along with Pasarell, they began to explore what Arthur termed "various sports kicks": "Fall semester it was horseback riding. Then billiards and ping pong. In spring we got baseball mitts and a bat and played over-the-line."

With Jean-Edouard and Possum leading the way, it didn't take long for Arthur to loosen up. One sure sign was his decision to buy a new set of wheels to replace his small motorcycle—not just any wheels, but a 300cc. Honda motorcycle, the "biggest one they make" he proudly proclaimed. He bought the bike from Larry Nagler, who was a bit nervous about the sale, fearing the monster bike was more than his small-framed friend could handle. Somehow Arthur, who drove the bike to campus on a daily basis, managed to avoid a serious mishap, though years later Pasarell still cringed when he recounted how "dangerous and wobbly" his cycle-mad friend had been. Many of Arthur's friends—and especially his coaches—feared for his safety, and within a year the new Davis Cup captain George MacCall ordered him to get rid of it.

The motorcycle was Arthur's most dangerous indulgence, but there were other causes for concern. Before long, the strict discipline that had ruled his life since childhood lost some of its force. "Maybe I relaxed too much," he later acknowledged. "At home I'd lived by the clock, and by Daddy's strict rules. And when I lived on the UCLA campus I'd been under J.D.'s heavy hand most of the time. All my life I'd watched my words and my moves, so nobody would get sore and make trouble for me. Now I got a little careless, and let my mind wander more."[23]

By the end of the fall semester, the change in attitude was noticeable enough to draw Morgan's attention. As Arthur remembered: "Gradually J.D. saw that I was getting too free and easy. He sat down with me one day and we had a heart-to-heart talk, with his heart doing most of the talking. We talked about goals—not just in tennis, but in life. 'Self-discipline is the key to success in any line,' he told me. 'Why not start organizing your time, making it count?'" Arthur took this advice to heart. "I knew I fooled around a lot, wasted time," he later admitted, pointing to Morgan's habit of making every minute count as the model for his return to a productive, disciplined life: "Often I'd seen what he did with odd minutes, so I took his principles and began applying them. I started keeping a textbook in my car. Every time I stopped at a red light I read a few paragraphs. Between innings at a Dodger baseball game I read the entire *Wall Street Journal.*"

Later in life this near obsession with time management would become one of Arthur's personal hallmarks and an object of wonder among his friends. Morgan's example stayed with him, most obviously in his particular passion for keeping calendar notebooks. What became an uninterrupted tradition of writing everything down began at a press luncheon that he and Morgan attended in 1964. As they drove to the luncheon, Arthur "noticed a note pad on the front seat, and asked him about it." "Ideas come into my head and I jot them down," the coach explained. Arthur was impressed and a bit embarrassed he hadn't thought of this useful practice on his own: "Here I'd had business school training and a million appointments to keep with reporters, school authorities, tennis dignitaries and my own friends, but I was trying to carry them all in my head. I bought myself a calendar book, for appointments as well as ideas."[24]

Arthur's heart-to-heart talk with Morgan came early enough to ensure he would be more than ready to focus on the task at hand once the 1964 intercollegiate tennis season began. The upcoming varsity season figured to revolve around the parallel rivalries of UCLA and USC, and Ashe and Ralston. At the beginning of the spring semester, both schools had three legitimate stars—Ashe, Pasarell, and Reed for UCLA, and Ralston, Tom Edlefsen, and Bill Bond for USC. But USC soon lost Edlefsen to academic ineligibility, just after he had upset Ashe in the quarterfinals of the USLTA National Indoor Championships. Edlefsen's victory demonstrated how strong his combination with Ralston might have been, though USC remained formidable even without a rising star occupying the second singles spot.

By the third week of the intercollegiate season the UCLA Bruins had a growing sense they could challenge the Trojans' dominance. After UCLA overwhelmed Pepperdine College and the University of Redlands in the first two dual meets of the season, Ashe and Pasarell played extremely well in a narrow loss to Ralston and Chuck Rombeau in the semifinals of the Pacific Coast Men's Doubles Championships. At the Southern California Intercollegiate Championships in Pasadena, Ashe and Pasarell lost the doubles final to Ralston and Bond, but in the singles final Ashe defeated Ralston in a gritty match that stretched to 8–6 in the final set. Successfully defending his Southern California singles title and doing it against Ralston was no mean feat, and Arthur was understandably ecstatic in victory. By mid-March, the entire UCLA tennis team had reason to feel good about their prospects of winning an eighth national title for Coach Morgan. No other UCLA program had won even half as many national championships as the tennis team, and the university's athletic program was known first and foremost for tennis—or at least it had been until the recent, unexpected success of Bruins basketball.[25]

UCLA had long been a regional powerhouse in basketball, finishing first in the Pacific Coast Conference six times since John Wooden had taken over the Bruins' coaching duties in 1948. But the big break in the history of UCLA basketball came in the winter of 1963–64, a remarkable season that marked the dawn of a new era in UCLA sports. During the next twelve years, Wooden's incomparable Bruins enjoyed an almost unimaginable run of success on the basketball court, winning ten national championships. This near invincibility began in December 1963, and with each passing week of the season, as the victories piled up, the excitement among UCLA students and alumni grew to feverish proportions. By January the undefeated Bruins had somehow become the consensus number one team in the nation. Nothing in the university's history had ever gripped the campus with such emotional fervor, and the stars of the team—Walt Hazzard, Gail Goodrich, Keith Erickson, and Fred Slaughter—assumed godlike status among the Westwood faithful. From midseason on several sportswriters began referring to Wooden as the "Wizard of Westwood," a sobriquet that would follow him for the rest of his career.

In March, after finishing the regular season 26–0, Wooden's undersized but talented team had an opportunity to achieve something that only two teams in NCAA history had accomplished—winning a national championship with a perfect record. The final game, played against Duke, was close during the first half, as Arthur's good friend Fred Slaughter struggled against the Blue Devils' towering front line. But in the second half the Bruins pulled away, winning 98–83 in the highest-scoring championship game in NCAA history. Arthur was thrilled by the UCLA basketball team's storybook season, and as soon as the team returned to campus he celebrated with his deliriously happy friends Hazzard and Slaughter. Named the NCAA tournament's most valuable player, Hazzard, the slick ball-handling magician who made the team go, could hardly contain himself. The senior guard was a champion of champions, and no one could take that away from him.[26]

This was the kind of glory that Arthur and his tennis teammates dreamed about. Unfortunately, on March 21, the same day the basketball Bruins won the national championship, the tennis team lost a dual match to the Southern California All Stars, 6–3, despite Arthur's victory over Whitney Reed, once the top-ranked player in the nation. The mixed results continued a week later at the Thunderbird Invitational Tournament in Phoenix, where Pasarell won the singles title for the second straight year but Arthur lost badly to Ralston in the semifinals.

UCLA's prospects brightened considerably during the next two weeks, as the team won dual meets with the University of Arizona, Stanford, Cal-Berkeley, and USC. Played on April 11 before an overflow crowd at the UCLA courts, the upset victory over USC represented the Bruins' first head-to-head triumph over the Trojans in three years. It also snapped the Trojans' 32-match victory streak, but perhaps most amazingly, UCLA won even though Arthur lost to Ralston 6–4, 6–0. Two weeks later, at the Athletic Association of Western Universities (AAWU) tournament held at Ojai Valley, the Bruins once again defeated the Trojans, and this time they did so with Arthur outlasting Ralston in a tight match.

Arthur's win at Ojai Valley was one of the high points of the season, though it turned out to be his last victory over Ralston at the collegiate level.

Over a two-week period in early and mid-May, he lost to the USC senior three times in singles and once in doubles. No matter how well he served and volleyed, he couldn't seem to overcome Ralston's "piercing backhand" and steady play. In the end, Ralston was the only collegiate player to have a winning overall record against Arthur, who won only three of their ten college matches. Arthur took some consolation from the obvious benefits of a rivalry that made him a better player. But he nonetheless looked forward to Ralston's June graduation and was glad to see the last of his nemesis on the college circuit.

When the regular dual meet season ended in late May, Arthur and the Bruins had one more chance to bring Ralston and the high-flying Trojans down to earth. The traditional mid-June NCAA championship tennis tournament—held at Michigan State University in East Lansing in 1964— was the truest test of the crosstown rivalry, and if the Bruins could win there all of the recent disappointments would be avenged. Ashe and Pasarell would have to play the best tennis of their lives, while Ralston would have to falter. This was a tall order, and in the end it was beyond the Bruins' capabilities. While Ashe and Pasarell played well enough to make it to the singles semifinals, both lost, Ashe to Ralston in straight sets, and Pasarell to the Big Ten champion Riessen in four. When Ralston went on to defeat Riessen in the singles final and then teamed with Bill Bond to beat Ashe and Pasarell for the doubles crown, USC secured the team title over runner-up UCLA by a single point, 26–25.[27]

Coming so close but losing in the end to their archrival for the third year in a row was a bitter pill for the Bruins to swallow. But Ashe and Pasarell had no time to dwell on their disappointment. Within a few hours of the loss to USC, they were in Detroit boarding a jet bound for London. Though unseeded, they were scheduled to play both singles and doubles on the grass at Wimbledon in two days' time.

Arthur was thrilled to be back at Wimbledon, in part because as a member of the U.S. Davis Cup team he now received travel and expense money from the USLTA. During his first visit to Wimbledon, he had been all but overwhelmed by the Brits' pomp and pageantry. This time he had a better idea of what to expect, and he was ready to play.

Arthur's performance in the singles competition went well in the first three rounds, as he defeated Milan Holecek of Czechoslovakia in four sets, the Texan Cliff Richey after falling behind two sets to none, and his doubles partner Bill Bond in straight sets. But the luck of the draw turned against him in the fourth round when he faced the number one seed, Roy Emerson, who had defeated Arthur's friend Donald Dell in the opening round. Arthur would have loved to avenge Dell's loss, but Emerson, the eventual tournament winner, took full advantage of his young opponent's inexperience on grass to win in straight sets 6–3, 6–2, 7–5.

In the doubles competition, Arthur and Bond did not even reach the third round, yet their loss in the second round to the powerful Australian team of John Newcombe and Tony Roche was one of the most memorable matches of Arthur's career. This was his first opportunity to play on Centre Court, the most famous venue in tennis, and he did his best to make the most of it. "That famous dark-green Wimbledon stadium is round and the stands are roofed, since rain falls in England in June," he reported in his 1967 memoir, *Advantage Ashe*. "The stadium seats 18,000—more than Madison Square Garden—all around that one little center court. When it's full you think everybody in the world is there, and the court is like one postage stamp at the bottom of a big fishbowl." He was also impressed by the "ritual you go through if you're to play on the center court." As he explained, "You enter through a little back door, and when you step out on the grass you turn and bow to whoever is sitting in the royal box. I don't remember who was there that day. Bill and I were keyed up for a tough match. . . . We wanted to play the best tennis of our lives. That's how the Wimbledon center court hits you."

The wide-eyed and inexperienced Americans did not play well enough to win. But they gave all they had in a five-set marathon—the longest match yet in Ashe's career and one of the longest in Wimbledon history. With Ashe and Bond down two sets to one, the fourth set turned into a test of stamina ultimately won by the Americans, 22–20. Even though Newcombe and Roche won the fifth set and the match, Ashe and Bond also won a victory of sorts, establishing themselves as a legitimate threat to one of the best doubles teams in the world.[28]

Facing the mighty Australians in both singles and doubles was daunting, but for Ashe the greatest challenge of the 1964 Wimbedon tournament turned out to be political. Nothing taxed him more than a controversy surrounding white South African participation in the tournament. Prior to a scheduled match between Alex Metreveli of the Soviet Union and South Africa's best player, Cliff Drysdale, Metreveli defaulted "as a gesture of protest against South Africa's racial laws." And when István Gulyás of Hungary learned his assigned doubles partner was the South African Abe Segal, he dropped out of the competition. This coordinated protest by two Soviet bloc citizens attracted considerable media attention, inevitably drawing Wimbledon's only black player into the fray.

When asked about the controversy, Arthur made his opposition to the anti–South Africa protest crystal clear. "I don't think you want political protests of this kind in sports. . . . I would play Segal any time," he told the press. "I have to look at him as an individual. I can't look at his government and say because his country is that way he is that way also." Arthur's comments received plaudits in some quarters—including *The Pittsburgh Courier* and his hometown paper, the *Richmond Times-Dispatch*. But there was enough negative response to make him think twice before speaking out in public again. Sam Lacy, the veteran sports editor of the *Baltimore Afro-American*, issued a stinging rebuke, arguing: "It is unfortunate that Ashe couldn't have just gone on and played the role of a juvenile as a 19-year-old tennis player. . . . That he presumes to [be an] expert on international politics clearly demonstrates that he is either educationally puerile or politically naïve. . . . Ashe is quoted as saying 'I would play Segal any time.' Not if you were in Pretoria or Johannesburg or Cape Town, son."

A decade later as an anti-apartheid activist, Ashe would come to see the wisdom of Lacy's position, but for a time he defended the remarks he made during the Drysdale-Segal episode. "I never ask South African players their feelings about their government's racial policies," he wrote in 1967. "But I've kidded a lot with Segal and Drysdale, and with Rhodesian champ Roger Dowdeswell. If I had the chance, I'd play in South Africa. For one thing, I hear the expense money is generous. But I'm not crazy enough to try to go." [29]

Despite the unexpected South African diversion, Arthur regarded his second Wimbledon as a success, largely because he enjoyed himself immensely throughout the fortnight. With a little money in his pocket compliments of the USLTA, he spent several evenings at the Victoria Sporting Club, which in his words featured "gambling, lots of girls, and good food." He, Pasarell, and Dell played roulette, winning just enough to feed their habit, and later at the tournament's end he attended the "grand ball where the new men's and women's champs are the 'king and queen'"—and where they are accorded the honor of having "the first dance with each other." "I enjoyed the ball," he recalled, "imagining that some day I'd be king." Eleven years later he would get his wish.

Arthur's post-Wimbledon plans took him to Budapest, Hungary. He and two other Americans received "expense money, lodging, and transport" from the Hungarian tournament organizers. "But that was all," he later reported, adding: "You go behind the Iron Curtain for the new experience, not luxury or dough. We took a sightseeing bus all over the city, and wherever we went people would point and stare at us. I don't think they stared because I was a Negro. . . . It was our clothes that attracted their attention. 'We can tell Americans by the way they dress,' somebody said." While their tournament results were uneven, the visiting college boys had quite an adventure in Budapest, highlighted by Ashe's twenty-first birthday party, a raucous affair hosted by Suzy Kormoczy, Hungary's best female player, who gave him a beautiful crystal vase as a birthday present.

Arthur had such a good time in Hungary that he had mixed feelings about going home. Part of him, he later admitted, would have loved to join the lucky players who were setting out on "the plush European circuit" that featured "nice hotels, swimming pools, five-course meals" in tournament cities such as Baden-Baden in Germany, St. Moritz and Gstaad in Switzerland, and Bastad in Sweden. But his severely limited financial backing would not support an extended stay in Europe. His only realistic option— and even that represented a financial stretch—was to follow the Eastern United States summer circuit played on grass. He had never won a tournament on grass—in fact, he had never even come close. Nevertheless, he had gained some confidence from his respectable showing at Wimbledon. With his strong serve and topspin backhand, he had good reason to believe that sooner or later he would become comfortable enough to win on the slickest of surfaces.[30]

The 1964 Eastern grass circuit began in late July with the Pennsylvania lawn tennis championships held at the Merion Cricket Club. But Arthur's first stop of the summer was the National Clay Court Championships held in Illinois. Still jet-lagged from his European trip, he fought his way into the round of sixteen, only to lose to, of all people, Abe Segal, the white South African mentioned in his controversial Wimbledon statement. Even though the thirty-six-year-old Segal was nearing the end of his career, the crafty left-hander gave his inexperienced opponent fits on the soft clay.

Arthur fared somewhat better the next week when the play shifted to the fast grass at Merion. After breezing through the first two rounds and defeating Clark Graebner in the third, he came up just short in the quarterfinals against Chuck McKinley, who had eliminated him from the tournament the previous year. Playing in 90-degree heat, Arthur served and volleyed well and came within a point of winning the first set. But McKinley ultimately prevailed.

A week later Ashe had a second chance to show what he could do on grass when the tour traveled to South Orange for the Eastern Grass Court Championships. Here he began to hit his stride. After defeating Rod Susman of St. Louis in the third round, he came up against Ralston in the quarter-finals. The two collegiate rivals had never faced each other on grass, but as the number one seed Ralston was a heavy favorite. In the first set, the match went as predicted with Ralston winning 15–13, but in the second, won by Ashe 6–1, the underdog played inspired tennis. With the normally steady Ralston repeatedly double-faulting and committing numerous unforced errors, Ashe closed out the the match 6–4. Gracious in victory, he conceded he had taken advantage of a stale opponent suffering from fatigue and "the tournament grind." "He's only human," he told reporters, "he's got to take a rest." Equally gracious, Ralston countered that Ashe had carried the day primarily by hitting "great shots."

Whatever the reason, Ashe had just won one of the biggest matches of his career. And he was not done yet. In the semifinals, he defeated the defending champion Gene Scott, and in the championship match he dominated Graebner, winning three sets to one. The Eastern grass court title was not only his first triumph on grass, it was also his first tournament title of any kind since early June. The significance of the win, achieved at one of the most exclusive private clubs in America, transcended tennis.[31]

When the journalist Lincoln Werden pointed out the obvious fact that Ashe was the "first Negro" to win the Eastern, he must have had some sense of the incongruity between the black Virginian's triumph in an elite enclave and the dire news coming out of Mississippi. For six weeks, federal investigators had been searching for the remains of Andrew Goodman, Michael Schwerner, and James Chaney, three Freedom Summer volunteers who had disappeared in Neshoba County in late June. On August 4, two days after Arthur's victory at South Orange, their mutilated bodies were found buried in an earthen dam near Philadelphia, Mississippi.

Arthur never discussed the Mississippi murders in public or in print, but it seems highly likely he was aware of the struggles of the Freedom Summer campaign, since a number of UCLA students participated, and there was growing pressure on black students to become involved in the struggle. Arthur firmly resisted this pressure, but years later, after be became active in civil rights matters, he expressed deep regret that he had not responded to the call earlier.

Whatever his feelings about Freedom Summer and the broader freedom struggle in 1964, he was in no position to act upon his beliefs. As a relative newcomer to the exclusive world of the USLTA, he was too vulnerable and insecure to take any public stands that called attention to his status as a racial interloper, and he was not about to do anything that might hinder or derail his career.

While the black sharecropper Fannie Lou Hamer and other activists loyal to the Mississippi Freedom Democratic Party (MFDP) were meeting in Jackson to plan their challenge to the state's all-white delegation to the upcoming Democratic National Convention in Atlantic City, Arthur was defeating Richey in the third round at Glen Cove on Long Island. And later in the month, when Hamer was captivating the nation with her plea for justice before the Democratic Credentials Committee, Arthur was busy dispatching the British star Graham Stilwell in the third round of the Meadow Club International tournament held at nearby Southampton. While Southampton and Atlantic City were separated by less than one hundred miles, the respective dramas taking place in late August were worlds apart. Hamer and Ashe, two black Southerners breaking down the barriers of Jim Crow in decidedly different ways, probably had more in common than either realized. But at the time, politics and sports did not seem to have much to do with each other. He later remembered that prior to 1968 he had "always resented peer pressure from other blacks" who urged him to get involved in politics and protest. "What do black athletes, most of whom are not politically inclined, have to offer?" he asked rhetorically. "Speak out if you've got something to say," he reasoned, "otherwise say nothing."

So Arthur said nothing during the summer of 1964, as the nation witnessed Freedom Summer and the passage of the long-awaited Civil Rights Act. He preferred to "speak" with his racket—to advance the race through displays of talent, discipline, and sportsmanship, all of which confounded the white supremacist theories of racial inferiority that threatened blacks' access to equal opportunity. He already had a lot to be proud of on this score, including racial firsts in Junior and Senior Davis Cup play, in intercollegiate competition, and at Wimbledon, Forest Hills, and other prestigious tournaments. But he was still waiting for the truly big win, the breakthrough that would establish his credentials as a nationally recognized star.[32]

As he prepared for the 1964 U.S. Nationals, Arthur had hopes that his breakthrough year had arrived. With the grass court victory at South Orange under his belt, he felt he was finally ready to make a serious bid for the national singles title. This would be his sixth appearance at the U.S. National tournament—but his first as a seeded player. The tournament officials seeded him eighth behind Emerson, Ralston, the defending champion Osuna, McKinley, and three others. It was a formidable field, especially on grass, but Arthur's recent victories over Ralston and McKinley proved he belonged. No American had won the tournament since Tony Trabert in 1955, so Arthur naturally dreamed of being the one to snap the host nation's embarrassingly long losing streak.

Despite high hopes, the American contingent did not perform well at Forest Hills in 1964. Only McKinley and Ralston made it as far as the quarterfinals, and overall the results represented the host nation's worst showing in the tournament's eighty-three-year history. Arthur bowed out in the fourth round to Tony Roche. After splitting the first four sets, he surged ahead 3–1 in the final set only to fade at the end.

Arthur did not leave Forest Hills empty-handed, however. On the last day of the tournament, James B. Dickey, the president of the USLTA, announced that the UCLA star had been awarded the Johnston Trophy, an annual award given to the tennis player who best exemplifies the highest standards of "sportsmanship and excellence of play." Once again, the press pointed out the obvious, that he was "the first Negro to receive the trophy." But this seemingly obligatory racial categorization was only a minor distraction for the happy award winner. In his acceptance speech, he declared: "I hope I can be the exception to the rule that 'good guys always come in last.'" After years of disciplined and exemplary behavior, he finally had formal recognition of his efforts to live up to the highest ideals of sportsmanship.[33]

What a wonderful way to usher in his senior year at UCLA, yet Arthur was not quite ready to return to Los Angeles. An important Davis Cup tie against Australia was scheduled for late September in Cleveland, and he had just been chosen by Captain Vic Seixas to join McKinley, Ralston, and Riessen on the active four-man squad. The Americans were the defending Davis Cup champions, but after Forest Hills they were definite underdogs to the powerful Australians. Three of the four Americans—McKinley, Ralston, and Ashe—had just lost to Australians, and there was no reason to believe they would fare much better in Cleveland. Indeed, the Aussies—who had won the Davis Cup eighteen times, one fewer than the Americans—had the added incentive of matching the U.S. total. The Americans' best hope was that the visitors would become unnerved by the Cleveland venue, a strange concrete and steel structure constructed as a temporary site to be used for the Davis Cup tie and then dismantled. The second largest outdoor tennis arena in the United States, the seven-thousand-seat Cleveland site featured tall steel towers designed to accommodate television and radio broadcast equipment that would reach the far corners of the world for the first time in the annals of Davis Cup competition. Whatever happened on the court, the Cleveland tie was destined to make television history.

The battle on the court proved to be one of the most competitive Davis Cup finals in years. Sensing that there was no room for error, both captains used only two players, Ralston and McKinley for the Americans, and Emerson and Stolle for the Aussies. The other four players—Ashe, Riessen, Newcombe, and Roche—remained on the sidelines as cheerleaders. After splitting the opening singles matches, Ralston and McKinley teamed up to defeat Emerson and Stolle in the doubles match, giving the Americans a 2–1 lead. With one more singles victory the underdog Americans would repeat as champions, but on the final day of competition both Emerson and Stolle eked out narrow victories. The mighty Australians had won back the Cup, evening up the two nations' victory totals at nineteen apiece.[34]

Though disappointed by the loss—and by Seixas's decision to keep him on the sidelines—Arthur returned to UCLA in late September 1964 with a sense of purpose. With only one year of college eligibility left, he still had a lot to prove. Could he lead UCLA to an NCAA championship? Could he become the first African American tennis player to win the coveted NCAA singles title? He faced eight months of preparation during which he would have to maintain a tight focus and discipline, both on the court and in the classroom. It wasn't going to be easy to counter the many distractions of college life, especially in light of Pasarell's decision, prompted by Coach Morgan, to postpone his last year of tennis eligibility. Burdened with a marginal grade point average, Pasarell had good reason to interrupt his intercollegiate tennis in an effort to shore up his academic standing. But this decision put added pressure on Arthur, who would have to lead the Bruins to the NCAA tennis title without any help from his most talented teammate.

Perhaps even more disturbing was Arthur's suspicion that Possum would be in full party mode during his hiatus. Girls, dates, carousing, self-indulgent road trips, and periodic parties in their Pacific Palisades apartment—these were temptations that Arthur could ill-afford. To be sure, Coach Morgan would be watching him carefully during practice sessions and other on-court appearances, but Arthur himself would be the arbiter of his off-campus life. Self-discipline had always been one of his strengths, but the depth of his commitment to tennis would be sorely tested on more than one occasion during his senior year.

Arthur enjoyed his roommates' sociability and easygoing ways; and to a limited extent he began to change, even when it came to something as simple as taking time to eat a proper meal. "He said we helped him get a more relaxed attitude," Baker recalled. "Charlie and I have the Latin temperament—you know, take two hours to eat. When we first knew Arthur he'd eat in a hurry, take his last bite and want to get away and be doing something. And he'd eat anywhere—just eat and get it over with. But now he's learned to go out with us, take time, try new dishes."

Arthur also began to take advantage of an improving financial situation. He indulged in occasional shopping sprees, adding record albums and books, and even a few stylish upgrades to his notoriously spartan wardrobe. His biggest purchase, one that probably gave him more joy than any previous material possession, came in 1965 when he became the proud owner of a red Ford Mustang. Introduced at the New York World's Fair in April 1964, the sleek-lined Mustang soon became an enormously popular status symbol for Ashe's generation of college students. Driving around town or pulling up in style to park near the Bruins Tennis Terrace solidified his image as an enviable celebrity. Somehow the shy boy from Richmond had become a big man on campus.

By the time the 1965 intercollegiate season began in early February, he was ranked third in the nation and immersed in a rising tide of high expectations. During that winter and spring he experienced the most hectic and stressful tennis regimen of his life. With daily practices, weekly dual matches, and extended Davis Cup play, he had little time for anything else. Tennis, even more than in the past, dominated his life. After three years of playing in the shadow of USC and Ralston, UCLA was the preseason favorite to win the NCAA tennis championship, and Arthur was the odds-on favorite to capture the intercollegiate singles crown.

The UCLA basketball team was the reigning NCAA champion, and now it was time for Coach Morgan and the tennis Bruins to add to the university's newfound reputation as an athletic powerhouse. Midway through the spring semester, the pressure cooker of UCLA sports took on even more steam when the basketball team repeated as national champion in March, and the UCLA men's volleyball team followed with its own national title a few weeks later.[35]

The pressure to win was intense, but Ashe, who had grown in confidence and maturity during the past year, did not seem to mind. The spring 1965 term was his last semester of eligibility, and he was determined to make the most of it. The tennis could hardly been much better: UCLA won all eleven of its dual matches; Arthur lost only one dual singles match the entire season—to USC's Tom Edlefsen—and only one doubles match when he was teamed with his normal partner, Ian Crookenden. The team won the

AAWU championship with ease, capping the best overall conference season in the university's history, and the only remaining challenge was winning the NCAA team title in June.[36]

By his own admission, Arthur's performance in the classroom was somewhat less impressive. But he made sure he did well enough to avoid embarrassment or academic probation. During his college career he had settled into the pattern of a B student, reconciling himself to slightly above average grades as the price for athletic stardom. Even so, he hated to miss class. While his core business administration courses did not always offer the most stimulating material (his favorite area of study was anthropology), he remained intellectually engaged and did his best to keep up with his assignments, never an easy task for a Division I athlete. At several points he had found it necessary to take a reduced number of credits in an effort to accommodate his busy tennis schedule, so there was no chance of graduating with his class in June. Even at the end of the spring semester—his eighth at UCLA—he would still need to earn nine more credits for graduation.

Spending another semester, or even another year, at UCLA, where he had become increasingly comfortable and where the freedom of off-campus living suited his new lifestyle, was actually a welcome prospect. Where else could he find such challenging practice partners, girls as beautiful as the weather, a fairly relaxed racial atmosphere, and a convenient international airport to facilitate his travels to faraway tournaments? If not quite the Golden Land that he had envisioned four years earlier, Southern California was still an attractive option and something of a haven far removed from the intense racial turmoil of his native state and region, or so it seemed prior to the Watts uprising of August 1965. Los Angeles, he reasoned, was as good a place as any to prepare for life as an adult. An emerging cosmopolitan, he had embraced a lifestyle that would eventually transform his identity. The transition from parochial Virginian to international sophisticate would take years to complete, but the broadening was well on its way by the mid-1960s.[37]

Citizenship, full and engaged, was an important concept for a young African American looking for respect. From junior high school on, Arthur's drive to be taken seriously—especially by individuals in positions of authority—had been a hallmark of his personality, and this trait had only grown stronger during his college years. It affected all aspects of his life, from his dating patterns to his relationships with coaches and teachers to his behavior as a ROTC cadet, and it was never more apparent than during Davis Cup competition.

Pitting Americans against foreign players, the Cup matches created a special opportunity for national recognition and service, and no one embraced this opportunity more than Arthur. For a proud young man who often felt rejected by his home state, playing for the United States was an affirmation of self-worth and a powerful symbol of inclusion in American life. As he later insisted, no other tennis experience, not even a victory at Wimbledon, could match the satisfaction of winning the Davis Cup: "Segregation and racism made me loathe aspects of the white South but had left me scarcely less of a patriot. In fact, to me and my family, winning a place on our national team would mark my ultimate triumph over all those people who had opposed my career in the South in the name of segregation."

Arthur was eager to make a more significant contribution in 1965, especially since he had not been asked to play for his country the previous year. Though he—along with Froehling, Riessen, and Pasarell—had warmed the bench while Ralston and McKinley played all of the matches, this strategy did not work out very well, as the United States finished second to Australia for the sixth time in ten years. Vic Seixas, falling one victory short in his inaugural year as Davis Cup captain, resigned in frustration in March 1965, giving way to Los Angeles insurance man George MacCall, a close friend of 1962–63 captain Bob Kelleher.

The USLTA also authorized MacCall to hire a coach to supervise training and player development, and in March he chose Gonzales. With Pancho on board, and with Ashe, Scott, Richey, and the doubles specialist Riessen joining McKinley and Ralston on the 1965 squad, there was new enthusiasm and renewed hope that the United States could regain the Cup. Before the squad began to play, MacCall suspended both Richey, whose father had tried to interfere with the captain's handling of his high-spirited son, and Ralston, who had refused to follow through with a commitment to play in a warm-up doubles match in Houston. But the final roster still packed a lot of punch.

Named to the squad in mid-May, just as he was defeating Edlefsen for the Pacific Eight singles title and UCLA was edging USC for the conference team championship, Arthur was determined to justify MacCall's faith in him. Over the next decade, he would develop a reputation for intense commitment to Davis Cup competition, and for achieving a focus sometimes lacking in his normal play. "Playing Davis Cup tennis isn't like playing in any tournament," he observed. "There aren't the crowds of other players milling around and laughing it up with you in the locker room; there isn't the steady stream of news from a dozen courts about who's beating whom, nor the ebb and flow of people in the grandstand. . . . The whole horizon focuses down to a pinpoint on the one or two foreign opponents you'll be playing. And sometimes reaches inside and squeezes your heart when you hear the umpire call 'Advantage United States,' instead of 'Advantage Ashe.'" This intensity was already in evidence as Arthur prepared for the 1965 Americas Zone competition. During the last week in May, he was in Palo Alto for the California State Tennis Championships, where Ralston eliminated him in the semifinals. But he spent most of the week in nearby San Francisco "hitting with the pros"—including Gonzales, Ken Rosewall, and Rod Laver—in a frantic effort to get ready.[38]

Arthur's first test came in early June, when the American team faced off against Canada in the opening round. Held in the sweltering valley town of Bakersfield, a hundred miles north of the UCLA campus, the contest against the untried and lightly regarded Canadian team figured to be little more than a warm-up for the more challenging contests in the later rounds. MacCall warned his team about the peril of taking the Canadians lightly, but true to form the Americans won all five matches as Arthur completely dominated both of his singles opponents.[39]

With final exams and the NCAA tennis championships scheduled to begin in a week's time, he had no time to savor the victory. Rushing back to Los Angeles, he spent most of the next week in the library trying to catch up on his studies. But he also tried to get his mind and body ready for what he hoped would be the crowning achievements of his college tennis career: a national championship for the UCLA team and a national singles title for himself.

USC had dominated the NCAA tournament throughout Arthur's time at UCLA, winning three consecutive team championships. Along the way, Osuna had won the NCAA singles title in 1962 and Ralston had followed as singles champion in 1963 and 1964. Since his elevation to the varsity, Arthur had lost twice to Ralston in the national semifinals, and the UCLA team had finished a close second both years. Now, with Ralston gone and the NCAA tournament being played on the Bruins' home courts, he figured it was finally UCLA's year to shine. He was right.

UCLA controlled the tournament from start to finish, placing four players among the eight singles quarterfinalists, and all four players in the doubles final. After teaming with Crookenden to win the doubles title over Reed and Sanderlin, Arthur defeated the previously undefeated (20–0) Mike Belkin of the University of Miami in the singles final. The fifth UCLA tennis player to win the NCAA singles championship, he took his place beside Jack

Tidball (1933), Herbert Flam (1950), Larry Nagler (1959), and Allen Fox (1960). As impressive as he was in victory, Arthur was even more pleased with the team's performance—a staggering 31 points, more than double the total of second-place Miami. The USC Trojans, to his delight, finished a distant sixth with 10 points. After three years of frustration, the Bruins netters were back on top, and the skinny kid from Virginia was able to walk away from his collegiate career knowing he was the primary reason why.[40]

EIGHT

FROM DIXIE TO DOWN UNDER

■

W ITH HIS COLLEGE TENNIS career officially over, Ashe turned to other challenges. Aside from winning another Davis Cup or two, his fondest wish was to play well at Wimbledon. His first two visits to the hallowed British tournament had produced meager results, but after his recent NCAA triumph he had high hopes he could do better on his third try. Only two days separated the end of the NCAA championships and the beginning of Wimbledon, but somehow he and the rest of the American contingent arrived in London in time for the first round.

Without any time for warm-up play in the pre-Wimbledon grass tournaments, Arthur and the other Americans were at a distinct disadvantage. Pasarell, for one, had a terrible time on the slippery grass, repeatedly falling during a straight-set loss in the first round. Arthur fared somewhat better, though only after a slow start in the first set against Doug Kelso, a quirky young Australian who somehow managed "to serve without looking at the ball." Ultimately rallying to defeat Kelso in four sets, he had a similar experience in the second round against the Frenchman Pierre Darmon, losing the first set but winning the next three. In the third round, he won a tough match against Bob Carmichael, a twenty-four-year-old Australian from Melbourne. But in the fourth he ran out of luck against Osuna. Five years older than Ashe, the two-time Wimbledon doubles champion ended Arthur's dream, 8–6, 6–4, 6–4. Three Americans—Marty Riessen, Dennis

Ralston, and Allen Fox—reached the Wimbledon quarterfinals in 1965, the nation's best showing since 1954. Arthur would have to wait until 1968 to join such select company.[1]

Following his return from Wimbledon, Arthur traveled to the Western Open in Milwaukee, where he teamed up with Ralston to win the doubles title after losing a tough quarterfinal singles match to Riessen. The next week took him to the U.S. Indoor Championships in Chicago, where once again he came up short in the singles quarterfinals, losing to Mike Belkin, whom he had defeated for the intercollegiate crown in June. This disappointing showing against a younger, less experienced opponent was troubling. During the month since his NCAA victory, he "seemed to be just treading water," as he later put it. "I couldn't gain any momentum."[2]

He had a full two weeks to sharpen his game before the Americas Zone final against Mexico. Earlier in the year, after a period of solemn deliberation, he had recommitted himself to the goal of breaking into the top echelon of tennis. So he pressed on, motivated by dreams of personal glory, a burning desire to earn the respect of his peers, and the fear of disappointing Coach Gonzales.

During the last two weeks in July, Arthur turned his attention to getting ready for Osuna and the Mexicans. Mexico had won the Americas Zone only once—in 1962 when it defeated the United States squad for the first time in fourteen tries. But the 1965 Mexican squad was no pushover. The tie had originally been scheduled to take place in Mexico City, but the financially strapped Mexican Davis Cup Committee agreed to move the contest to Texas after Dallas businessman Jack Turpin offered them a $20,000 inducement. Dallas had never hosted a Davis Cup tie, and Turpin and other local tennis boosters were eager to put their city on the big-time tennis map in an effort to counter the stigma of the presidential assassination eighteen months earlier.

As Turpin had predicted, the matches against the Mexicans drew sellout crowds. Part of the attraction was watching Ashe in his first serious test as a Davis Cupper, but even more important was the obvious historical parallel with the vaunted spirit of the Alamo. This time, of course, the Texans held an advantage over the Mexicans, who were competing as decided underdogs on American territory. Texas was now officially and chauvinistically American, but unfortunately for Arthur, it was also a state with a strong commitment to racial segregation. There was considerable speculation about how he would fare in an ultraconservative town with a long history of racial intolerance.

Adding to the drama, the matches in Dallas coincided with the final days of congressional debate over the highly controversial Voting Rights Bill, a measure opposed by most Texas congressmen. Even so, there were few visible signs of protest against Arthur's appearance, partly because local leaders had wisely chosen to hold the Davis Cup matches on the public courts at the recently completed Samuell Grand Park. From the beginning Turpin had wanted to show off the new public facility, but others were motivated by the likelihood that Arthur would be turned away from the only alternative site, the all-white Dallas Country Club.

How much Arthur knew about the behind-the-scenes venue negotiations is unclear, but racial tensions were clearly part of the backdrop as he took the court in the highest-profile match of his life. He had not expected to play in the opening singles match against Osuna, Mexico's best player, primarily because he had just lost to him at Wimbledon. But Captain George MacCall surprisingly turned to Arthur for the marquee match. As an untested twenty-two-year-old, Arthur was understandably nervous about the entire scene. But his greatest challenge was the unusual style of his wily opponent. Osuna could slice and dice with the best clay court players in the world, and he had both the cunning and the stamina to frustrate and outlast the game's biggest hitters. The bituminous cement surface of the Dallas courts, substantially slower than grass, also favored the Mexican star. Having beaten Arthur handily the month before, he was the overwhelming favorite.

None of this seemed to matter, however, once the two men began to play. Osuna played poorly from the outset while Arthur was at his best, winning handily in straight sets 6–2, 6–3, 9–7. Serving up 15 aces, he simply overpowered Osuna with what *Time* magazine dubbed "the strongest serve in U.S. amateur tennis." Writing in *Sports Illustrated*, a gleeful Frank Deford reported: "In the very first match the show went haywire: a supporting player, not really a principal, decided to become a star." MacCall agreed, declaring: "Today Arthur became a man. He was under tremendous pressure, and he came through."

In the other opening day singles match, Ralston prevailed over Antonio Palafox, giving the Americans a comfortable 2–0 lead. But on the second day, the American doubles team lost to Palafox and Osuna, setting up a pair of potentially crucial singles matches on the third and final day. This time Arthur's opponent was Palafox. In another strong showing, Ashe served and volleyed his way to victory, giving the American team the three points needed to advance to the Inter-Zone Final against Spain. "It was his booming serve," commented Palafox after the match. "I tried to break his concentration, but I couldn't do it."

That night, the triumphant U.S. Davis Cup squad decided to celebrate at The Levee, one of Dallas's most popular nightclubs, later described by Arthur as "a sort of beer hall where they play Dixieland Jazz and bellow out songs that don't put Negroes in a favorable light." Sensing that he might not be welcome at the traditionally all-white club, Arthur tried to beg off but his teammates insisted that he join them. Walking into the club, they could not help but notice the giant Confederate battle flag hanging on the wall behind where a rockabilly band was playing. As soon as the band spied Arthur, the music stopped and a hush fell over the room. Alarmed, he was about to turn on his heel when the club manager rushed to the microphone to bellow a congratulatory welcome to the "winning" American team and "Arthur Ashe, the hero of the Davis Cup triumph over Mexico." Loud applause and cheers broke out, and Arthur and his teammates were soon sitting at a table accepting pats on the back and free drinks from a host of clubgoers. Perhaps at least part of the white South was redeemable after all, he thought, as he shared a night of triumph with men and women who, at least temporarily, seemed willing to put national pride ahead of racial prejudice.[3]

Arthur's ability to rise to the occasion in Davis Cup competition—a skill he would demonstrate over and over again in the years to come—established him as the hero of the moment in Texas. "All at once," he recalled, "I began to feel I could really get to the top." Even so, he learned a hard lesson during the next stage of Davis Cup play. When the U.S. team left for Spain on August 4, two days after the Dallas triumph, he was on the plane, though MacCall had no intention of tempting fate by putting him on the notoriously slow clay courts of Barcelona. Frank Froehling, the only American Davis Cupper with any experience on the European clay circuit, took Arthur's place in the singles rotation, and during the next two weeks, the star of the Dallas tie was reduced to the role of practice partner for Ralston, Froehling, and Graebner during the rigorous daily drills concocted by Coach Gonzales. "My recollections of Barcelona are dreary," he later wrote. "Gonzales worked us long hours every day to whip us into top condition. We always started with 15 minutes skipping rope. . . . Then tennis practice and then sit-ups, maybe 100. . . . We always finished with a run of several miles, with Pancho setting a fast enough pace so I was on the verge of throwing up." After all that, he sat on the sidelines.

MacCall's decision to bench Ashe was later questioned after the U.S. team struggled in Barcelona, losing 4–1 to Manolo Santana and the Spaniards. Ashe himself was philosophical, swallowing his pride for the good of the team. When he later described the scene, his sharpest memory of the Barcelona debacle was not his personal disappointment but rather the Spaniards' raucous victory celebration: "I'd never seen a crowd go as nutty as the people in Barcelona Stadium did after their team's clincher in the doubles. The air was full of hats and cushions, the screaming hurt my eardrums, and people were jumping over seats to hug each other. They paraded Santana and [Jose Luis] Arilla on their shoulders for half an hour. I wedged myself into a corner of the grandstand where I wouldn't get trampled." This was not how he had envisioned his first visit to Spain. But he was confident there would be better days ahead for the American Davis Cuppers, and that he would play an important part in the team's resurgence. As the unexpected hero of the victory over Mexico, he expected to be called upon once the Cup competition shifted to a faster surface. Indeed, his position on the team was enhanced by his noninvolvement in the Barcelona fiasco.[4]

Ashe and his teammates returned to the United States on August 18. But the homeland they returned to was not quite the same nation as the one they had left two weeks earlier. While they were away, the racial landscape had changed dramatically. On August 6 the long-awaited Voting Rights Act finally became the law of the land. With Dr. King and other civil rights leaders on hand for President Lyndon Johnson's signing ceremony, the new law signaled an end to black disfranchisement and a new departure in American electoral politics. Or so it seemed.

Five days later, the new era took an unexpected turn when a major race riot broke out in the Watts section of South Central Los Angeles. Somehow a routine traffic stop led to an explosion of anger in a black community suffering from chronic police misconduct and economic distress. During seven days of burning and looting, nearly a thousand buildings were torched, more than four thousand people were arrested, and thirty-four lost their lives. Major inner-city riots had occurred before—as recently as the summer of 1964 in New York City, Rochester, and Philadelphia—but no one had ever seen anything quite like the Watts uprising, where many residents seemed determined to burn an entire section of the city to the ground.

Arthur knew next to nothing about Watts, even though it was located less than fifteen miles from the UCLA campus. He, like most Americans, was genuinely puzzled by the dark spectacle of black protesters burning down their own neighborhood in a desperate cry for help. He would later be called upon to field questions about the infamous riot. "Well, you were in Los Angles, couldn't you see Watts coming?" people often asked. All Arthur could say in response was "I didn't know Los Angeles, even after several years."[5]

During the immediate aftermath of the riot, while the nation contemplated the meaning of what had just happened, Arthur was three thousand miles to the east preparing for the U.S. National Championships at Forest Hills. For the first time, he felt he had a legitimate shot at the coveted national singles title. It had only been a few short years since the breaching of the color line at Forest Hills, but now he had a realistic chance of becoming the first black man to win a national title on the fabled courts in Queens. Seeded fifth behind Emerson, Stolle, Ralston, and Santana, he would need a bit of luck and a favorable draw to come out on top. But he was definitely in the hunt.

For the most part, the draw went Arthur's way, though his participation in the tournament almost ended before it began. Following the tradition for seeded players, tournament officials did not declare a default when he arrived ninety minutes late for his opening match due to a traffic jam. Instead, after seeing the stadium court still occupied with another match, they moved his match against Gene Scott to the grandstand court for the first set. By that time Scott was steaming, and once they actually took the court he "couldn't seem to get his game under control, and lost 12 of the first 15 points." Arthur was embarrassed and apologetic, but that didn't stop him from rolling over his opponent in three quick sets.[6]

In the next three rounds, Arthur made sure he arrived in plenty of time, as he breezed through a series of relatively weak unseeded opponents. In the quarterfinals, however, he faced Roy Emerson, the number one seed. Generally considered to be the best amateur player in the world, the good-natured Aussie had already won nine Grand Slam singles championships, including the 1965 Australian and Wimbledon titles. He figured to make short work of the young collegiate star.[7]

Arthur, of course, had other ideas. He appeared surprisingly calm as, in his words, "he lazed around the locker room, playing bridge with Ralston and two sports writers." "I felt more confident than I ever had before," he insisted. "It was hard to explain, because I also knew that I'd never in my life played well enough to beat Emerson. . . . We'd played twice before and I hadn't taken a set from him." Nonetheless, Arthur was convinced he could put his strong serve to good advantage on the notoriously fast turf at Forest Hills, that the best way to play Emmo, as the great Aussie was called, was to reach back and unleash as much power as possible. Former Wimbledon champion Dick Savitt had said as much in a conversation the night before the match. "You've got to go for a winner when you return Emmo's service," Savitt had counseled. "Gamble and slam it back. When he weakens, his service is the first stroke to slip. But if you don't attack his serve you're setting yourself up. He'll come to the net behind it and kill you."

Arthur took Savitt's advice to heart—slamming return after return, breaking Emerson's serve in the first game of the match, and never letting up for the rest of the afternoon. Holding nothing back, he won the first two sets 13–11 and 6–4, forcing Emerson to mount a comeback to win the third, 12–10. After completing 66 games, both men were thoroughly exhausted by the 92-degree heat, but Arthur, seven years younger than Emerson, showed his superior stamina in the fourth, winning 6–2.[8]

With several members of his family cheering wildly from the stands, Arthur basked in the appreciation of a savvy New York crowd that could hardly believe what had just happened. The first person to congratulate him was his Aunt Marie, who, following their six-year-old tradition, planted a kiss on his cheek as he passed under the stadium court canopy. A few moments later, as he approached the entrance to the locker room, he was stunned to see Dr. Ralph Bunche, whom he'd never met, extending a hand and congratulating him on his amazing victory. Bunche and just about everyone else in the tennis world knew he had upset Osuna in Dallas five weeks earlier. But beating the mighty Emerson in a Grand Slam quarterfinal was something else again. "For 24 hours I was a hero," Arthur recalled, "the big hope to stop foreign domination of U.S. tennis. Remember, no American had won the Forest Hills title since Tony Trabert did it in 1955."[9]

When Arthur Sr. heard his son might be closing in on the coveted National singles title, he boarded a train for New York, and two days later Arthur Jr. did his best to make his father proud. But in his semifinal match against Santana, he could not overcome the Spaniard's accurate groundstrokes and soft spinning returns of serve. Although he got off to a great start, winning the first set 6–2, his Spanish opponent won the next three with relative ease. The next day Santana went on to win the title over Cliff Drysdale, but Arthur was not there to see the crowning of the tenth foreign U.S. national champion in a row. Following a family gathering at his Aunt Marie's house in Montclair, New Jersey, where his loss to Santana earlier in the day did nothing to dampen the heady talk of his coming stardom, he had flown to Chicago to play in yet another tournament.

Though disappointed by his loss to Santana, Arthur left New York with a sense of accomplishment. Losing in the semifinals did not negate the significance of his breakthrough, since few collegians, and certainly no black man, had ever gone so far in any of the four Grand Slam events. At the age of twenty-two, he had proved beyond a shadow of a doubt that he could play at the highest level. What Althea Gibson had accomplished on the women's side of the game a decade earlier now seemed possible, perhaps even probable, for the rising star from UCLA.[10]

At the gathering in Montclair, Arthur warned his giddy relatives not to read too much into his recent victories over Osuna and Emerson. But he, too, believed in his future—that he was finally on his way to bigger and better things. "I was like a hunting dog that sniffs something good," he later explained. "Beating Emerson showed me that I might be able to lick anybody in the wide world." As he contemplated a post-collegiate career, he became bolder and more adventurous, determined to "hit the trail harder," as he put it.[11]

In mid-September, he took the risk of accepting an unexpected invitation to the Colonial Invitational Tournament in Fort Worth, Texas. This would be his "first country club tournament in the South" and a very different experience from his Davis Cup journey to Dallas six weeks earlier. "Instead of traveling with the Davis Cup team, as I had on my first trip into Texas," he explained, "I went alone. The first thing I heard when I got off the plane was the genuine deep Suth'n drawl all around me. I felt as if I'd been kicked in the stomach. I hadn't heard many voices like that since I had left home years before. Unpleasant memories of growing up in Virginia came back. I was in the enemy camp, I felt."

Arthur's introduction to the posh Colonial Country Club a few minutes later did little to ease his anxieties: "When I walked into the Colonial Club, the Negro employees' eyes widened. They'd never seen a Negro guest there. Some of them thought I was a waiter who had dressed up and tried to sneak in the front door." Fortunately, the white Texans in the club proved to be "pleasant enough," though one man mistook him for a locker room attendant and yelled "Hey, boy, where's the bar?" They even made a point of addressing him as "Mr. Ashe," a courtesy title that surprised and pleased him. As the tournament progressed, he began to relax, bonding with several of the club's black employees, who took pride in his status as a black pioneer in a white world. "Every day," he reported, "the shoeshine man at the golf shop asked, 'How did we do, brother?'"

As Arthur advanced into the quarterfinals and beyond, several of the black waiters and caddies couldn't conceal their delight, telling him "you really took care of business." And later, after he won both the singles and doubles titles, upsetting Fred Stolle in the singles final and teaming with Ham Richardson to beat Stolle and Emerson in doubles, the waiters at the closing banquet made sure he received special service. "Frank Froehling was standing at the crowded bar," Arthur remembered, "and having no luck whatever in getting a drink. I stepped up and presto, I had my drink. At dinner, the largest piece of meat turned up on my plate. So the others began begging me to use my pull to get them better service." [12]

Rowland Scherman, a twenty-eight-year-old *Life* photographer assigned to cover Arthur's unprecedented Southern foray, captured much of the drama on film. During the tournament, he and Arthur became friends, and at the end of the week they decided to drive back to Los Angeles together. Traveling in Arthur's Mustang, they crossed 1,400 miles of plains, deserts, and mountains as the young tennis champion experienced the longest road trip of his life. After arriving in Los Angeles, Scherman spent several days taking additional photographs, including a memorable snapshot of Arthur's first encounter with UCLA's highly touted freshman basketball star Lew Alcindor. [13]

Although he was glad to be back in California, Arthur did not stay for very long. As he had recently revealed to his parents, alterations in the Davis Cup training schedule had forced a postponement of his graduation until June of 1966. Following the devastating loss in Barcelona, MacCall felt he had to do something dramatic to put the U.S. squad on the right track. With the backing of the American Davis Cup Committee, he decided to abandon the traditional pattern of bringing the squad together for relatively brief periods before and during the ties. The new regimen would involve a lengthy commitment spanning several months of preparation and team building, with the players receiving daily expense money.

The goal, as Arthur later explained, was "to upgrade the prestige of our Davis Cup team and weld it together." MacCall "arranged to pay each member $20 per day, all year round, and $28 for days we were in tournaments," he recalled. "This would add up to about $9,000 per year. We would no longer be allowed to accept any money from clubs or promoters. So we were financially under his thumb. He controlled our income and our travels. Any money we were given for exhibitions had to be handed over to him. We couldn't enter a tournament unless George said go." In effect, the U.S. Davis Cup team became "an elite corps of tennis players, offered to tournament promoters as a package." While he chafed at the loss of independence, Arthur accepted the necessity of commercializing the Davis Cup. "Big Tennis is basically show biz," he conceded, "and the top dollar in that industry comes with package deals and block bookings." He and his teammates stood to gain from a system in which "George has the bargaining strength of Sol Hurok in dictating terms." [14]

The first test of the new system came in late 1965 and early 1966. For three and a half months, from mid-October until the end of January, the American Davis Cuppers lived, practiced, and traveled together as they honed their skills in international tournament play, primarily in Australia. Hoping to enliven its traditional end-of-the-year tour, the Australian Tennis Federation had already invited several Americans to play as individuals, and MacCall seized the opportunity to turn the tour into a semiofficial practice season.

This brash scheme took them to a part of the world unknown to most Americans. Ashe had traveled to Europe three times since 1963, but he had never visited any place as exotic as Australia, New Zealand, or Fiji. The awesome Aussies, as he sometimes called them, had long been his primary tennis heroes and role models. No country in the world could match Australia's exuberant love for tennis, and no one played the game quite as well as they did. With Laver and Rosewall dominating the professional game and a seemingly endless string of talented amateurs winning nearly every major tournament in sight, the Aussies had never been more dominant. In 1965's four Grand Slam tournaments, six of the eight finalists and three of the four winners were Australian. "Never before had one nation dominated a tennis year so thoroughly," Bud Collins would later write. "This was the tennis version of the Holy Roman Empire, and Emerson, Stolle, Smith, Lesley Turner, John Newcombe, Tony Roche et al. were holy terrors."[15]

Embracing the opportunity to play against several of the world's best players week after week, Ashe couldn't wait to see how MacCall's experiment in extended play affected his game—even though the plan had certain drawbacks. He would miss seeing his family—and his many friends at UCLA, where exciting changes were in the offing. He would be far away when the university's new athletic arena, Pauley Pavilion, hosted its first basketball game in late November—an exhibition contest between the varsity and a freshman team that included the towering Lew Alcindor, the decade's most celebrated freshman athlete. And he would not be there in early January when the UCLA played in the Rose Bowl. Though not insignificant, these sacrifices represented a relatively small price to pay for the obvious benefits of a tennis holiday in the beautiful South Pacific.

Learning that their son's graduation would be delayed was a major disappointment to his father and stepmother, but he promised to return to school in the spring semester of 1966, remaining there until he earned his degree. The Ashe family would just have to wait a little longer to congratulate its first college graduate. Besides, he explained, postponing his graduation would also postpone his induction into the Army, giving him several additional months of civilian life devoted to honing his skills on the tennis circuit. With the recent escalation of the war in Vietnam, no one in his family was in any hurry for him to put on a uniform. The Ashes were already worried enough about Johnnie, who in July 1965 had left high school at the age of seventeen to join the Marines.[16]

Despite their disappointment, Arthur Sr. and Lorene trusted their oldest son's judgment. Highly motivated and disciplined, he had an aura of practicality and common sense that few twenty-one-year-olds could claim. Time and again, he had proven he was not one to choose immediate gratification over long-term goals. On the court and off, his commitment to self-improvement helped to define his character, and he never seemed to waver. He wanted to be the best tennis player in the nation—perhaps even the best in the world; and he wanted to do it without any loss of integrity or sportsmanship.

The ethical dimension of achievement was a matter of no small importance in the Ashe household, and Arthur Sr., as his sons well knew, never let down his guard on such matters. True achievement was tied to an old-fashioned sense of honor, as he made crystal clear when the journalist Frank Deford visited the Sledd Street house in 1966. "Look at these trophies," he told Deford, pointing to the accumulated symbols of his famous son's success. "I'd just as soon take them, the ones in the attic and that placard from the city, and throw them all in the junk heap if he ever did anything to disgrace me." For Arthur Jr. there was never any mystery about what his father valued most.[17]

Arthur Sr. actually had little to worry about when it came to misbehavior by his eldest son or any other member of his immediate family. His relationships with his second wife remained strong and loving, and their blended family continued to provide a nurturing enclave within the broader Ashe-Cunningham clan. Before going into the Marines, Johnnie had developed into a good student and a multi-sport athlete at the recently integrated John Marshall High School, where he earned letters in tennis, baseball, basketball, and football. When he left school after his junior year, the reason had little to do with race. His rebellion, he later explained, had more to do with living in the shadow of his famous brother. "While Arthur and I remained close," he recalled, "I got tired of being asked: 'Why can't you be like your older brother?'" "Leaving Richmond," he added, "was the only way I could establish my own identity."

The Ashe boys had no quarrel with their father's values, though they sometimes chafed at the autocratic manner in which he enforced family rules. Arthur's years at UCLA had prompted a gradual loosening of parental control, but by no means an end to it. The only time he felt reasonably free to make his own decisions was when he was traveling, especially when he went abroad and was generally inaccessible by phone. He was eager to see how he would fare during his extended stay in New Zealand, Fiji, and Australia.

When Arthur left for the South Pacific in late October 1965, he envisioned a three-month sojourn that would provide him with a measure of personal freedom, sharpen his game, and perhaps expand his understanding of the world. But he wasn't fully prepared for his sudden transformation into an international star. To his surprise, the New Zealanders and Australians embraced him as if he were one of their own. More than just another visiting American, he seemed to strike a chord of acceptance and approval in societies that had seldom been kind or welcoming to dark-skinned visitors.

The first stop was New Zealand, where the Americans played a week-long series of exhibition matches. Arthur was entranced by the spectacular landscape, which he later described as "the greenest place I'd ever seen," and by the exotic subculture of the Maoris, "the first South Sea Islanders I had ever seen." Struck by their distinctive physical appearance, he later confessed: "I looked at them and wondered, 'Where the hell did they come from?'"[18]

Arthur had a similar reaction to Fiji Islanders during a one-day stop-over on the way to Australia. After an impromptu set of tennis at the capital city's Nandi Tennis Club, where he encountered a multiethnic mix of Japanese, Indian, Australian, and "native Fijians with their bushy black hair," there was just enough time for a whirlwind visit to the countryside, where he caught his first glimpse of a sugarcane field before experiencing a harrowing horseback ride. Unaccustomed to a hornless English saddle, he hung on for dear life after the horse bolted down a rough-hewn path bordering the rows of sugarcane. "I landed on my side, bruised but unbroken," he recalled. "I had been scared, but there was no permanent injury. It would be a while before I went near another horse." It would also be a while before he leveled with MacCall about his close call. He suffered in silence during the flight to Brisbane.[19]

Arthur's brief encounter with the Maoris and Fijians stirred his curiosity, and in the years to come he would develop a keen interest in the native cultures of the South Pacific, including the downtrodden Australian minority known as Aborigines, a group that had just begun to express its discontent through social and political protest. Though numbering more than a million and representing approximately 7 percent of Australia's population, the Aborigines had limited visibility in the national scene.

With his travels limited to urban tennis venues and a few rural tourist spots, he came away believing that the nation's inhabitants were "almost 100% white people." "I was treated fine on my tours of Australia," he later acknowledged. "But living there would be out of the question. They're not too fond of Negroes or Asians. I'd heard this, and I could see that there weren't any dark-skinned people around." The Australian situation reminded him of London's "cold" attitude toward racial minorities. "Because I'm a tennis player, I'm welcome there," he concluded, "but the average Negro isn't. I've read about it. The British try to hide the prejudice, but it's there."[20]

Part of the Australians' attraction to him, Arthur soon discovered, stemmed from their fascination with an exotic object of curiosity: a black tennis player competing in an otherwise all-white sport. But beyond that there was a deep and unmistakable appreciation for his ability to combine talent and sportsmanship. The Aussies—who considered themselves to be among the most passionate and knowledgeable sports fans in the world— judged Arthur's character and performance to be the equivalent of sports nobility.

Within a week of his arrival in Australia, he had become the darling of the local and national press. The Americans' first stop on the continent was Brisbane, the site of the Queensland Championships, where Arthur unexpectedly dominated the draw. Prior to the tournament, most observers had expected Emerson and Stolle to show Arthur and the Americans what real tennis was like. As Arthur later explained, "Maybe they figured that Emerson had been off form when I beat him at Forest Hills, and that I'd get put in my proper place as soon as I played the big boys again." But the young American played some of the best tennis of his life, crushing Stolle, the Wimbledon runner-up, in straight sets in the semifinals. Serving 21 aces, he became "Aces Ashe" in one newspaper account, and the nickname stuck throughout his time in Australia. The final against Emerson was even more revealing, with Arthur outlasting the great Aussie champion, winning 6–1 in a fifth set where he lost only nine points. "That seemed to convince the Australian tennis experts," he recalled. "Suddenly I was a celebrity. I'd beaten the world's top-ranked player twice in a row."[21]

Arthur was almost giddy in victory, and once the Americans moved on to Sydney for the New South Wales championships he decided to celebrate. "Maybe it went to my head a little," he later confessed, but for once he abandoned his normal tournament discipline, spending "more time enjoying life" and "less time resting to get strong for the next match." During his first two weeks in Sydney, he took in several movies—always one of his favorite pastimes—and ate "heartily at the big barbecues and dinners given by Australian tennis officials and the U.S. consulate brass." Somehow he also found time to "hit a few music spots," to buy "kangaroo-skin rugs" and other Christmas presents for his family, to spend a day at the famous Sydney Zoo, to fish on the Hawkesbury River, and to pass "a lot of time with the rest of the squad at the big flat MacCall rented for his wife and two daughters, where there was a tremendous view of Rushcutters Bay."[22]

Arthur was having the time of his life, and during the early rounds he found he could still win after long days and nights of self-indulgent behavior. Later in the tournament, however, he learned a hard lesson about the importance of concentration. As he later described the situation, "Early in the tournament Ken Fletcher introduced me to two gorgeous airline stewardesses from Trinidad. Their names were Bella and Michelle. I sat at a table with them for an hour. I couldn't take my eyes off them. I found out Bella was going with Neil Hawke, a star Australian test cricketer, so I decided I'd better just admire from afar. But I began dating Michelle." "This was living!" in his estimation. But it was no way to win a major tennis tournament. When he faced John Newcombe in the championship match he lapsed into what Australians might have termed a dreamy but disastrous walkabout, thinking about girls and everything but tennis. "My mind drifted to Michelle and Bella," he confessed, "and the next thing I knew the tournament was over."[23]

Arthur had lost, and he had no one but himself to blame. In the postmatch press conference, after acknowledging his lack of concentration, he made the mistake of attributing Newcombe's victory to a fierce determination to secure a spot on the Australian Davis Cup squad. Newcombe himself ignored this rather ungracious assessment, but it prompted several Australian reporters to criticize Arthur's lackadaisical attitude. This was the only time he fell off his pedestal during the trip, but as he later acknowledged "the sting was good medicine. It sharpened my game and clamped my flapping jaw."[24]

Over the next month, Arthur continued to have fun, attending festive dinners and enjoying the dating scene, especially a night of revelry at the legendary Herman's Haystack nightclub on New Year's Eve when he "danced up a storm with an Australian airline stewardess." But along the way he managed to play some of the best tennis of his career. Relying on a strong, almost overpowering serve, he found a new consistency that put him ahead of the field week after week. Despite a bruised toe that inhibited his mobility, he won the South Australian tournament at Adelaide in mid-December, the Western Australian at Perth in early January, and the Tasmanian singles championship in Hobart a week later.[25]

Halfway through this run of success, he drew the attention of Harry Gordon, one of Australia's most prominent sportswriters. During the Christmas break, Gordon sat down with the young American star for an extended interview. The result, published in *The New York Times Magazine*, was the first in-depth profile of Arthur to appear in print. Characterized as a "Pioneer in Short White Pants," he expounded on a wide range of personal and public matters, from his boyhood in Richmond to his recent collapse during the match against Newcombe. Among the many revelations were: his distaste for practice and physical conditioning; his recognition that tennis had provided him with "a kind of apprenticeship in good living"; his reluctance to commit to a life of almost constant travel; and finally his long-term plan to retire from tennis, find a wife, work at a job that involves selling "either products or ideas," and settle down in Los Angeles.

Much of the article focused on race and Arthur's experiences as "the first male Negro to make it big in a game that has always been as 'white' as its players' togs." "I guess I'm just a sociological phenomenon," Arthur acknowledged. When asked about the rumor that certain white American players resented his intrusion, he insisted he "wasn't even interested enough to find out their names." He told Gordon about other indignities such as sometimes being mistaken for a locker room custodian and his exclusion from South African tournaments, where apartheid laws were in force. But he tempered his list of complaints with a certain resignation and an acceptance of reality. "I don't want to spend my life fuming," he declared. "What good would that do? It's like beating your head against a brick wall. If you go looking for discrimination, you can find it in a lot of places." Turning to a broader consideration of his racial heritage, he continued: "I could get mad about the fact that I don't know my own background beyond one generation. All I know is that we got our name, like all the other Negro families, from the slave masters who owned us. They sold you like cattle, and when you died, they'd throw you in the ocean, or use you for fertilizer if they were hard put. I could get mad, but what's the point?"

This was the first time he had expressed a measure of bitterness in a public statement on race, but he immediately reassured Gordon that he was "no militant Negro, no crusader." Staking out an independent path, he explained: "I want to do something for my race, but I figure I can do it best by example, by showing Negro boys the way. That's what Jackie Robinson and Willie Mays have done in baseball, Wilt Chamberlain and Bill Russell in basketball, Jim Brown in football. They're the three big money sports in the United States, and the Negroes have broken through." When Gordon pressed him, he acknowledged that the barriers of race and class in the tennis world were formidable. "Tennis in the States has always been a rich man's sport, and Negroes, generally speaking have not been rich people," he pointed out. "Look at it this way: It doesn't cost a boy anything to learn to run or jump or play football, but before he even takes on tennis he has to have a racket that costs $40. How many Negro kids can afford that?"

There were other, more confounding problems to overcome for any person of color trying to navigate the racial crosscurrents of the white tennis world. The situation was not always what it appeared to be, he insisted. "Even when I'm among pleasant white people," he observed, "they're usually bending over backward to be too nice. They want to keep making sure that I'm feeling good, just because I'm Negro, and that bugs me." Gordon interpreted this complaint as a simple request to be treated "as a human being first" and "a colored man second."

At another point in the interview, however, the Australian journalist extracted a concession that being the only black player in tennis had its compensations. "He knows," Gordon wrote, "that his color and his recent streak of world-beating form have made him a major drawing card. . . . This knowledge has caused a rather subtle but remarkable change in some of Ashe's attitudes during recent months. He used to be upset at the constant references to his color which appeared in newspapers. . . . Now, though, he rather enjoys being branded." As the UCLA business major put it, "Let's face it, being known as the only Negro in the game probably puts me a hundred dollars a week ahead of the others in market value. You have to be realistic. Every time I go out and beat one of the big ones, like Emerson, I can almost hear the cash register ringing up a higher figure. The amateur tennis market is like business anywhere—it's a question of supply and demand. People will usually pay a little more for a product that's different—and that's what I am."

As Arthur well knew from the courtside epithets that occasionally punctuated his matches, this racial dynamic could be a double-edged sword. But on balance he did not consider race to be an economic burden; on the contrary, he felt it had encouraged additional tournament invitations and funding and special consideration in the area of commercial endorsements, where he had been asked to represent Coca-Cola, Wilson Sporting Goods, and Fred Perry sportswear.[26]

Arthur was equally candid and upbeat about his value as an international symbol of improved race relations, citing his current rooming arrangement with Richey as a case in point. "People in other countries read a lot about race troubles in the U.S.," he reminded Gordon. "But when they see two guys from the South like Cliff Richey and me, one white and one colored, both sharing a room and being close friends, it must do a little good." This public display of diplomacy was new to Arthur in 1965, but in the years to come both the State Department and the U.S. Army would take full advantage of his success story, sending him on a series of goodwill missions to Africa and Asia. As he observed in 1967, "The State Department kept pointing to me as one of its answers to Red propaganda that Negroes are treated like dirt in the United States." Following in the footsteps of Louis Armstrong, Joe Louis, Althea Gibson, and other black celebrities, he was, for a time, a willing participant in this style of Cold War politics.

Only later, after his political consciousness moved leftward in the 1970s, would he conclude that he had been used for propagandistic purposes, and that the official trumpeting of his personal success had served to misrepresent and exaggerate the pace of change in American race relations. Making his way across Australia as a wide-eyed twenty-two-year-old, he still thought of himself as a tennis player, plain and simple, and as such he welcomed all of the public attention without much worry about how his newfound celebrity might be manipulated by political or ideological forces.[27]

As the Australian tour drew to a close, Ashe began to feel his career had entered a new stage. At the Australian National Championships, which began on January 22, he was the top-seeded foreigner and a legitimate challenger to the highest-seeded Australians—Emerson, Stolle, and Newcombe. Since he had beaten all three in recent weeks, and with the Australian press making a lot out of the fact that he was the first player to win four major Australian tournaments since Rod Laver in 1962, he believed he had a shot at the national singles title. Granted, this would be his eleventh Grand Slam tournament after seven tries at the U.S. National title and three appearances at Wimbledon, and the only time he had made it past the fourth round was at Forest Hills the previous September. But he seemed primed and ready for a dramatic breakthrough.

No American had won the Australian since Richard Savitt in 1951, and the last time an American had made it past the quarterfinals was 1959 when

Barry MacKay lost to Alex Olmedo in a memorable five-set semifinal match. So Arthur already felt he had accomplished a lot after breezing through the early rounds, manhandling Tony Roche in the quarterfinals, and outlasting Stolle in a semifinal match that ended with a grueling 10–8 victory in the fourth set. Now all that stood between him and his first Grand Slam championship was Emerson, the world's number one player, the winner of the Australian championship four of the last five years. He had already proven he could beat Emerson in other venues, and a few observers even judged him to be the favorite since Emerson was having something of a down year. But the betting odds suggested he was still a decided underdog.[28]

Emerson, as it turned out, had to play the singles final on the same day as the delayed completion of the doubles competition. The previous night he and Stolle had fought Roche and Newcombe evenly through four sets and 14 games of a fifth set before darkness brought the match to a temporary halt. The next morning Emerson and Stolle eventually took control of the final set, winning 12–10. But this belated victory left the defending champion with only a few hours to rest before taking the court against Ashe. Once they began to play, however, it was clear that he had more than enough energy—and skill—to keep his young American challenger at bay. After the Australian won the first set 6–4, Arthur came back to win the second 8–6. But after that it was all Emerson, 6–2 in the third, and 6–3 in the fourth. The only surprise turned out to be the match's bizarre ending. Serving at 30–40 in the ninth game of the fourth set and facing match point, Arthur was assessed a foot fault that brought the match to a close.

As the stunned crowd reacted with a mixture of cheers and boos, Emerson glared at Tom Addison, the linesman who had made the call, before tossing "his racquet under the umpire's stand in disgust," signaling he did not want to win "on a foul." Arthur didn't know quite what to do. After dropping his racket to the ground, he was, in his words, "on the verge of popping off, but got hold of myself in time." "I just walked up to shake hands with Emmo," he recounted years later, "who undoubtedly was the better player that day." Talking to reporters after the match, he expressed disappointment with Addison's call but stopped short of crying foul. "I just don't know what to say," he admitted. "I can protest but it won't do any good."[29]

The next day an exhausted and somewhat befuddled Ashe boarded a flight to Los Angeles. While most of the other American players were en route to Hong Kong for a few more days of touring, he "felt glad" to be "going home." The Australian trip had been a great adventure, but he had grown homesick during the closing weeks of the visit. As he later put it, "I began to run out of things to do" and even became "a little fed up with party food." "Gradually," he explained, "the tour stopped being fun." On the positive side, he had drawn considerable praise from the press and the Australian tennis establishment. Cliff Sproule, a former Davis Cup captain and one of Australia's most revered tennis officials, claimed Ashe had "done more for the Negro race than anyone in Australia." Though somewhat uncomfortable with the responsibility of representing an entire race, Arthur appreciated Sproule's comment enough to include it in his 1967 memoir. Yet in a later account of his first trip to Australia, written in 1981, he chose to avoid any association with such grandiose claims. Instead, he stressed the trip's tangible impact on his career. "Australia," he explained, "turned out to be as important to my tennis career as meeting Dr. Johnson and living in St. Louis during my senior year in high school. I had my first opportunity to play on grass for three straight months and won my spurs as an international player." [30]

Arthur returned from Australia with renewed confidence and an elevated game. But his experiences also gave him a more realistic view of what life was like for amateurs trying to make a living "from the weekly grind of ordinary tournaments." Life for the Aussie tennis players, whom he had long admired from afar, turned out to be far less glamorous than he had supposed. "Often they quit high school to take salaried jobs as 'representatives' of sporting goods companies," he wrote. "Their sponsors practically own them, and keep them slaving away in tank towns for a good part of the year. And Australian tourneys don't pay." [31]

When he arrived at LAX after the long flight from Sydney, Pasarell and Baker were there to greet him, and that night the three roommates attended a UCLA basketball game at the new Pauley Pavilion. Arthur cheered on the #10 ranked Bruins as they defeated the University of Arizona, but the evening took an unexpected twist when he had difficulty reading the numbers on the Pavilion's massive state-of-the-art electronic scoreboard.

The next day he called MacCall and asked him for the name of a good eye doctor, and within a week he was sporting a pair of prescription eyeglasses. Being diagnosed with myopia was a bit of a shock, but Arthur later claimed he "jumped for joy" after leaving the doctor's office. "I never realized that I had been living in a blur," he explained, "and I was actually high for a couple of days from the excitement of seeing everything so clearly. The glasses didn't have much effect on my tennis, but I had to adjust to the sharper and smaller images. Once I did, my confidence improved considerably." While it would be some time before he felt comfortable wearing glasses throughout the day, he and everyone else eventually became accustomed to the horn-rim spectacles that gave him a scholarly look. When he later adopted the practice of wearing aviator-style sunglasses, his appearance took on a more stylish mode. But in either mode, glasses were now part of his image.[32]

During his last semester at UCLA, Arthur was content to stay on the sidelines as his buddy Pasarell led the Bruins to an expected repeat victory at the national championships in June. Though no longer eligible for intercollegiate play, he still spent much of his time on campus at the Tennis Terrace, where he was either practicing with the varsity or helping to coach the freshman team, which included his first protégé, Luis Glass, the son of ATA stalwart Virginia Glass. With Arthur's encouragement, the hard-serving seventeen-year-old from Jackson Heights, New York, enrolled at UCLA in the fall of 1965 after he and his brother Sydney had spent several summers with Dr. J in Lynchburg. Following a stellar prep school career at Deerfield Academy, Glass won the 1965 ATA singles championship, which was enough to convince Coach Morgan to offer him a tennis scholarship. Pleased that he was no longer the only black tennis player on campus, Arthur tried to mentor Glass on and off the court. Tennis-wise, the young prospect flourished, leading the freshmen team with an unblemished 9–0 singles record. But off the court he was unable to adjust to the freedom of college life. Burdened with academic and social problems, he lost his scholarship and withdrew from UCLA at the end of his freshman year.

Drafted into the Army later in the year, Glass survived a tour in Vietnam working as a medic, and following his discharge in 1967 he managed, with Arthur's help, to secure a scholarship to Hampton University. Once again he fared well on the court, twice earning selection as a small college, Division III All-American in singles. But after two years at the Virginia school, behavior problems prompted university officials to cancel his scholarship. To Arthur's disappointment, his talented but troubled protégé never fulfilled his potential as a player, though he eventually became a successful teaching pro. The first of several promising black players to be touted as "the next Arthur Ashe," Glass was also the first, though certainly not the last, to succumb to the special pressures of following in Arthur's pioneering footsteps.

Arthur did what he could to keep Glass in school during the spring of 1966. But this was also a time for a certain amount of self-indulgence. Realizing that after completing his ROTC training in the summer he would be living the disciplined life of an Army officer, he tried to take advantage of every fun-filled opportunity that came his way. The combination of a busy class schedule and an ambitious tennis regimen took up much of his time during the week, but that left most nights and weekends open for an array of activities: cruising around Westwood in his Mustang; satisfying his passion for going to movies; playing recreational tennis with celebrities at the Beverly Hills Tennis Club; or just hanging out at his apartment with friends and roommates, which now included Andrew Ma, a graduate student from Hong Kong. As always, he also spent a lot of time reading and listening to music. Unfettered by the tight scheduling and competitive pressures that had dominated his life since leaving Richmond in 1960, he did pretty much what he wanted during his final months in Los Angeles. For the time being, he was like a bird on the wing flying high above the constraints of a grounded life.[33]

NINE

ADVANTAGE ASHE

■

B Y THE SPRING OF 1966, Arthur Ashe had begun to think of himself as an adult—as an autonomous individual with the freedom to make his own decisions. One sign of this new consciousness was his willingness to share the details of his unique life story with others, especially with his growing coterie of fans. Less guarded than in the past, he began to acknowledge his status as a public figure, and to the amazement of his friends, he even began to contemplate the idea of writing a memoir, a remarkable undertaking for a twenty-two-year-old college senior. The idea originated with Cliff Gewecke, a California sportswriter who had played baseball at USC in the 1950s. When Arthur proved receptive, Gewecke set up a series of interviews to serve as the basis for a narrative text. He also obtained a book contract with Coward-McCann, a small New York publisher best known for publishing Thornton Wilder's *Our Town* and William Golding's *Lord of the Flies*.

Gewecke's collaboration with Ashe eventually produced *Advantage Ashe*, a 192-page volume published in September 1967. Like most "as told to" books, *Advantage Ashe* was a hybrid creation filtered through the lens of a professional writer's literary and philosophical sensibilities. The text's unpretentious tone suggests that Gewecke had a light editorial touch, allowing his young protagonist to tell his story with a minimum of interference. Arthur's distinctive voice comes through as he reflects on his background and evolving identity—and on his experiences as a black man trying to succeed

in a white man's sport. Refreshingly direct, the narrative of his rise to prominence is punctuated with revealing passages of self-analysis, social commentary, and tennis lore. Throughout the book, he comes off as a charming if
somewhat naive young man, an introspective and intellectually curious person trying to understand himself and his place in the world.[1]

Arthur's candor begins in the opening pages of the first chapter, "Richmond Revisited," a bittersweet and telling account of a recent visit to his
hometown. He was there to participate in the first annual Fidelity Bankers
Life Invitational Tournament, an indoor tournament limited to eight players. The leaders of the Richmond Tennis Patrons Association (RTPA), an
organization founded in 1954 to provide funds for Sam Woods's program at
Byrd Park, had long dreamed of bringing a top-level tournament to the city,
so when they were approached in 1965 by the indoor tennis promoter Bill
Riordan—who was looking for a venue to complete his indoor circuit—they
jumped at the chance.

During its first decade, the RTPA limited its activities to the white community, but the organization's president in 1965–66 was Lou Einwick, a
racially liberal investment banker who had moved to the city in 1958. Einwick, who would oversee the Richmond tournament for nineteen years,
was determined to overcome the RTPA's segregationist past by reaching
out to Ron Charity and Arthur Ashe, who he hoped would anchor the new
tournament. Even though he had never been allowed to play in a racially
integrated tournament in Richmond, Arthur not only accepted Einwick's
invitation but also encouraged several of his friends to join him. At the same
time, Arthur Sr. agreed to transport an indoor canvas surface from Salisbury, Maryland, and to install it in Richmond Arena (renamed the Arthur
Ashe Tennis Center in 1982). Several days before the Richmond tournament began, a heavy snowfall complicated the transport from Salisbury, but
somehow Arthur Sr. found a way to retrieve the canvas on time. When the
all-black crew installed the surface, it established a tradition that would last
until 1984, the last year the tournament was held. Along the way Einwick
became a close friend to the Ashes, and over time his openness to change
and zeal for bringing big-time tennis to Richmond had a major impact on
both the local tennis scene and Arthur's relationship with his hometown.

Anticipating Arthur's return to Richmond to play in the new tournament, several white leaders active in the RTPA teamed with Charity to organize a civic celebration called "Arthur Ashe Day." Held on February 2, on
the eve of the tournament, the celebration involved a public greeting from
the mayor delivered on the steps of City Hall, a morning appearance before

the General Assembly, a formal resolution from the City Council naming the day in his honor, and a "grand banquet at the John Marshall Hotel." "This city is known around the world for many products," Mayor Morrill Crowe proclaimed, "—cigarettes . . . statesmen . . . and now Arthur Ashe, who has carried his country's banner around the world with dignity, honor, and skill." Just off the plane from Los Angeles, and barely two days removed from his return flight from Australia, an exhausted Ashe marveled at the hometown scene.

Underscoring the irony of the event, the interracial banquet was held at the same hotel where segregationist leaders had planned Virginia's Massive Resistance campaign twelve years earlier. Though legally desegregated by federal law in 1964, the Marshall had welcomed few black guests during the past two years, so Arthur was surprised and pleased when the Ashe Day committee reserved a room for him in the hotel. On this night more than two hundred guests, black and white, paid $10 each to honor Arthur and raise funds for the ATA's Junior Development Program. As a young man growing up under Jim Crow, he would not have thought of entering the stately Marshall Hotel through the front door, much less dining in the hotel's grand ballroom. But a lot had happened during the six years since he had left—namely, success and celebrity for him, and a growing realization in the city that the old ways of intransigent white supremacy were on the way out. Less than two years after the passage of the 1964 Civil Rights Act, whites and blacks could at least gather together in the same room to honor a favorite son. "There I was, in Richmond, Virginia," he wrote, "getting the big hello and the high-elbow handshake from folks who'd paid me no heed when I lived there."

Although Arthur was not sure about his new status as a hometown hero, he made a concerted effort to be gracious. "This is the biggest day of my life," he told the gathering, and he later insisted that he "meant it." Determined to steer clear of controversy, he kept his remarks brief and avoided any mention of race. But a year later, his memoir revealed what he had been thinking as he addressed the crowd in the hotel ballroom. "Times were changing," he wrote. "The one-time capital of the Confederacy was honoring a descendant of slaves. Racially-mixed tennis matches were now possible in the city that had barred me from going to school with white children, or from playing on tennis courts with whites. That's why I added in my speech, 'Ten years ago this could not have happened.'"

After the banquet, Arthur joined his father, stepmother, other family members, and a horde of friends at the Sledd Street house at Brook Field

Park. "That night I had quite a homecoming—cars and people were lined up solid around the house to greet me," he recalled. The joyous house party lasted into the morning hours, but since the honored guest was operating on three hours sleep, a less than ideal situation for someone facing an opening round match the next day, Arthur Ashe Sr. advised his son to retire early to get some rest at his hotel. Leaving the house, Arthur Jr. walked into the park, crossing "a long empty area that was full of memories." Strolling past the park's four tennis courts, located a mere "thirty steps from the side door of my house," he thought to himself: "Where would I be today if there hadn't been any tennis courts near me?"

Walking on alone through the moonlit grounds, he became nostalgic as he recalled his childhood experiences: "Crossing the three-block area . . . I thought of the happy days when it was my whole universe. I saw the basketball courts where I played on winter afternoons and the four ball fields where I played on summer mornings, and the Olympic-size pool where I swam for free on summer afternoons." His reverie ended, however, when he noticed the pool was closed—and not just for the winter. He had been told that the parks department had closed all of the city's pools in an effort to sidestep a court desegregation order, and actually seeing the empty pool saddened him beyond words. Despite the promising gestures he had witnessed earlier in the day, white Richmond clearly had a long way to go to overcome its segregationist legacy.

The next day Arthur could not get the image of the empty pool out of his mind. Amidst all the polite smiles, the bare concrete seemed to symbolize the emptiness of the Arthur Ashe Day celebration. Despite the kind words, there had been no apology and no real coming to terms with the indignities of the city's past and present. This was especially obvious to Arthur, but he was not the only one who felt something was missing. A hard-hitting *Richmond News Leader* editorial published that afternoon said as much. Referring to the City Council's official Arthur Ashe Day resolution, the editorial declared: "The resolution probably would have meant more if it had contained at least an implied regret that while he was growing up the inherited mores of the rest of us prohibited him from playing at Byrd Park."

This public rebuke was shocking, coming from an ultraconservative newspaper known for its strong segregationist stance. Arthur was both pleased and puzzled. But the buzz surrounding the controversial editorial did not help his concentration on the court. "Maybe those past years sort of clouded the air that Saturday in Richmond," he recalled. "Absent-mindedness, which sometimes comes over me on the tennis court, muddled me more than usual that day. While Frank Froehling was beating me, my mind kept wandering to my kid days." Expecting an easy victory by the hometown favorite and number one seed, the Richmonders in the stands were no less disappointed than Arthur when Froehling closed out the match. Teaming with Cliff Richey, he fared somewhat better in the doubles, reaching the final before losing to Chuck McKinley and Gene Scott. The previous day the USLTA had released its amateur rankings, which placed Arthur second in singles behind Dennis Ralston and fourth in doubles. Losing in front of his hometown friends took some of the joy out of the realization that he was approaching the top of the nation's amateur ranks. While he was confident he would have other chances to win in Richmond, he hated to squander the opportunity to put an exclamation point on his long-awaited hometown debut.[2]

Ashe's return to Richmond, with all of its racial overtones and ambiguities, coincided with a critical chapter in the ongoing story of race and sports in America, a saga he would later dub "a hard road to glory." During the early months of 1966, the racial contours of American sports shifted as the profile of black athletes became bolder and more visible. While three of the nation's major professional sports—hockey, tennis, and golf—would remain lily-white, or nearly so, for decades to come, several others—notably basketball, football, baseball, and boxing—had reached a turning point. After years of painfully slow progress, long-awaited changes were finally coming to fruition on several fronts.[3]

The first clear sign of a new era came at the college level in mid-March, when Texas Western University's all-black starting five shocked the nation by defeating the perennial college basketball powerhouse Kentucky in the final game of the NCAA tournament. The fact that the University of Kentucky team represented the all-white Southeastern Conference and was coached by the legendary Adolph Rupp, an avowed segregationist, underscored the significance of Texas Western's upset victory.[4]

Two weeks later, Major League Baseball finally made it to the Deep South when the Atlanta Braves, recently relocated from Milwaukee, played the team's first game in Atlanta Stadium in front of a racially integrated crowd. Prior to the Braves' move, the southernmost clubs had played in the border state and rim South cities of St. Louis and Houston. One of the most racially diverse teams in baseball, the 1966 Braves were led by four dark-skinned stars, the incomparable Alabama-born slugger Hank Aaron, Atlanta native Mack Jones, and the Dominicans Rico Carty and Felipe Alou.[5]

Professional basketball was also experiencing a significant shift in racial consciousness. In April the Boston Celtics overcame the Los Angeles Lakers to win their eighth straight NBA title. Only this time they did it with four black starters: Bill Russell, K. C. Jones, Sam Jones, and Tom "Satch" Sanders. Individual black stars such as Russell, Wilt Chamberlain, Elgin Baylor, and Oscar Robertson had been dominating the NBA for nearly a decade. But no championship team had ever featured more than three black starters. White supremacists must have wondered what was happening to a league that had been more than 80 percent white only a few years earlier, and later in the year their worst fears were confirmed when Russell was named the player-coach of the Celtics. Nearly twenty years after Jackie Robinson had broken the color line in Major League Baseball and sixteen years after Earl Lloyd had done the same for the NBA, a major professional sports team had hired an African American head coach.[6]

The racial situation in professional football was somewhat less promising, as whites continued to monopolize coaching positions and the high-profile, high-paying "skill position" of quarterback. But the winds of change were also gaining strength on the gridiron. Here the biggest news story of 1966 was the impending retirement of Jim Brown, the Cleveland Browns' black fullback who had won his third NFL MVP award and eighth rushing title in 1965. Widely acknowledged as the greatest running back of all time, Brown had announced that 1966 would be his last season. He had already begun an acting career, appearing in his first film in 1964, and during the summer of 1966 he was in London for the filming of a major World War II action film, *The Dirty Dozen*. The filming schedule called for completion in late June, giving Brown plenty of time to attend the opening of the Browns' training camp in mid-July, but delays kept him in London for several additional weeks. Despite Brown's stature, the Cleveland team's imperious owner Art Modell threatened to fine his star $1,500 for every missed week of camp. Incensed by Modell's disrespectful attitude, Brown, known for his strong sense of pride, announced his retirement on July 9.

The racial overtones of the Brown-Modell dispute were obvious, and some observers, especially in the black community, complained that the plantation mentality appeared to be alive and well in the NFL. Ashe, who had long admired Brown's outspokenness, applauded the football star's willingness to stand up to Modell. Self-respect, Ashe believed, was more important than any glory to be found on a football field. He could not yet imagine himself being so bold, yet he understood and empathized with Brown's circumstances. The tennis establishment, like the NFL, was the purview of wealthy white men, middle-aged or older, who ran their sport with an iron hand. The power relationships in tennis had more to do with class than race, but the result was the same. The power brokers called the tune, and the athletes danced accordingly.[7]

The racial dynamic of professional boxing—a sport that rivaled professional football as a bastion of imperious white management—was also changing. While black fighters had been welcome in the world of professional boxing since the 1930s, they had always been under the thumb of self-serving, and sometimes predatory, white promoters and managers. Even the great Joe Louis, the heavyweight champion from 1937 to 1951, had been constrained by a system of racial etiquette that demanded deference and obedience from black fighters, no matter how talented they might be. The notion of an independent-minded black boxer had long been a contradiction in terms, a legacy of Jack Johnson's controversial and tragic career during the first two decades of the twentieth century.

All of this began to change with the appearance of Louisville's Cassius Clay, the 1960 Olympic light heavyweight champion who proclaimed he was quite simply "The Greatest." After vanquishing reigning heavyweight champion Sonny Liston in February 1964, beating him again in May 1965, and pulverizing a host of white challengers in between, Clay altered the face of boxing, not only with his fists but also with his braggadocio style of verbal wit. Defying convention by joining the Nation of Islam and changing his name to Muhammad Ali in the immediate aftermath of the first Liston fight, the "Louisville Lip" became the most controversial figure in American sports by mid-decade.

Like many Americans, Ashe had conflicted feelings about Ali, bristling at his flamboyant and sometimes rude posturing while admiring his strong sense of self and his uncanny ability to follow through with even the most outrageous promises and predictions. To some whites, Ali was little more than an "uppity Negro," and a dangerous one at that, associated as he was with a black separatist cult. This view was especially prevalent after Ali humiliated "the good Negro," two-time former champion Floyd Patterson, with a twelfth-round technical knockout in late November 1965. After Patterson refused to call him Muhammad Ali, using instead his "slave name," Cassius Clay, taunts of "Uncle Tom" and "What's my name?" filled the ring as the champion pummeled the overmatched ex-champion into submission. It was a brutal display of speed and power that revealed Ali's darker side— winning him few friends outside the Nation of Islam.

By this time, Ali had become anathema to the white establishment, and many of his critics cheered when the Selective Service reclassified his draft status as 1-A in February 1966. With the troop buildup in Vietnam intensifying, this was tantamount to a direct ticket to the jungles of Southeast Asia. After he publicly announced his intention to avoid involvement in the war, stating, "I ain't got no quarrel with the Vietcong. . . . They never called me nigger," outraged boxing officials canceled his upcoming March title bout with Ernie Terrell. Effectively barred from boxing in the United States, he fought his next four bouts abroad. In the meantime the Louisville draft board rejected his application for conscientious objector status, a rejection upheld by the Kentucky State Appeal Board with the consent of the Justice Department.

In early 1967, Ali switched his state of residence to Texas but found no relief there as a four-judge panel of the federal district court ruled unanimously that he had no legitimate claim to conscientious objector status. Scheduled for induction on April 28, he showed up at the Houston induction center at the appointed hour, but when asked to step forward for formal induction he refused, even after being warned that his refusal constituted a felony punishable by five years in prison and a $10,000 fine. Later that day, the New York State Athletic Commission suspended his boxing license and the World Boxing Association stripped him of his heavyweight title. Seven weeks later, on June 20, an all-white jury in Houston convicted him of draft evasion, assessing the maximum penalty possible. While the case was on appeal, Ali managed to stay out of prison, but he would not reenter the ring until October 1970, when his conviction was overturned by the U.S. Supreme Court in a unanimous decision that found the government's rejection of his application for conscientious objector status to be lacking in specifics.[8]

Two decades later, Ashe and Ali would develop a warm friendship. But in the mid-1960s, the two men were about as far apart, emotionally and politically, as two African American athletes could be. Ashe was as quiet and polite as Ali was loud and brash. While he may have had strong feelings about Ali's conversion to Islam or his draft evasion, he did not say so publicly. What he did say during these years gave no hint of his later opposition to American involvement in Vietnam. In early November 1965, he revealed his support for the war. "Those bullets don't have much appeal to me, I'll admit," he told the *Los Angeles Times*. "But if there's a job to do over there, the sooner it's over the better. I'll be proud to serve." Later the same week, a pro-war reporter for the *Redwood City Tribune* judged Ashe to be "just as conscientious as any marcher. . . . And he's showing considerably more patriotism and courage. We need more Arthur Ashes."[9]

These early statements in support of a war that would soon divide the nation represented Ashe's first public commentary on a subject of controversy. With this one exception, he did not speak out on any of the era's swirling controversies prior to the publication of *Advantage Ashe* in the fall of 1967. In truth, he was seldom asked about such matters. But even on the rare occasions when he was asked to comment on a controversial issue, he rarely said anything forthright or revealing. Over the next decade he would become increasingly comfortable with his role as a vocal public figure—the "thinking man's tennis player" as some called him. But as late as 1966 he was still wary of voicing his opinions in public, even on matters of deep personal concern.

Ashe's reticence was based partly on self-interest—he didn't want to say anything that would damage his career. But he was also inhibited by self-doubt and a measure of intellectual and political confusion. While he had certain predilections, he had not fastened upon a consistent frame of reference that would help him assess the flow of issues and events with any degree of certainty or clarity. Like most college students, he was a work in progress. On important matters such as war and peace, economic opportunity, and civil rights, he was still trying to refine his core beliefs in the forge of education and real-life experience. It was not that he didn't think about such things, or that he didn't care. He just wasn't ready to commit to a position that he might want to retract later.

Deliberative by nature, Arthur did not want to be hurried or to become involved in controversies that might complicate his life. Part of the problem was a lack of time. As a college athlete trying to manage a hectic schedule of practice sessions, matches, classroom assignments, and personal activities, he found it challenging to get through the average week even without the added pressure of active political involvement. As his college years drew to a close, he was busier than ever, and when he returned from Australia in late January 1966 after three and a half months abroad, he was already seriously behind in his classes. Even though he was no longer eligible for intercollegiate play, his tennis schedule for February and March was relentless. When he wasn't working out with Pasarell and the UCLA varsity on the home courts, he was often away playing tournaments to satisfy George MacCall's determination to maintain his players' sharpness on the court.

As soon as Richmond's Arthur Ashe Day concluded, he made his way to Philadelphia for an invitational indoor tournament. He lost the Philadelphia singles final to Pasarell, despite serving up 20 aces, but together the two roommates won the doubles title. Two days later they were both in Salisbury, Maryland, competing in the U.S. National Indoor tournament, where Ashe lost in the quarterfinals to South African Cliff Drysdale, and where Pasarell won his second singles title in a row. From there they traveled to New York to play in the first annual Vanderbilt Athletic Club invitational round-robin tournament, which showcased eight highly ranked amateur players. Despite flashes of brilliance, Ashe finished fourth in the round robin, two places ahead of Pasarell, who finished sixth.[10]

Ashe had expected a higher finish, but fortunately his brief visit to New York proved successful in other ways. During the week, he was introduced to Joseph Cullman III, a noted tennis enthusiast who served as chairman of Philip Morris Incorporated. The giant tobacco-based conglomerate had extensive holdings in a number of subsidiaries, including Clark Gum and American Safety Razor, and Cullman had recently taken advantage of his contacts in the tennis world by hiring several top players to represent Philip Morris's interests, notably Rafael Osuna in Central America, Roy Emerson in Australia, and Manolo Santana in Spain. Impressed by Ashe's clean-cut and well-spoken manner, Cullman offered to do the same for him once he finished his two-year stint in the Army. Thus began a personal relationship that would become increasingly important to Ashe over the coming years, despite his misgivings about indirectly associating with a potentially lethal product like tobacco. With tobacco companies moving into sponsorship roles in the tennis world, he simply went with the flow, but his primary reason for agreeing to work for Philip Morris's nontobacco divisions was his deep respect for Cullman. The corporate executive "became a second father to me," he declared in 1992, as well as "an invaluable mentor" in the ways of the business world.[11]

The other highlight of the week was the time he spent with his girlfriend, Pat Battles. Working as a telephone operator in nearby Stamford, Connecticut, Battles had long hoped Ashe would ask her to marry him. But she was stunned when he actually proposed during the New York tournament. In what he later acknowledged to be an impulsive set of decisions, he asked and she accepted. His closest friends were shocked, including ex-roommate Jean-Edouard Baker, who later described Ashe's romantic folly: "While he was in New York City on a tennis tour he went out a couple of nights with this Negro girl he'd met a long time ago. They'd been writing each other for several years. She was a telephone operator. They had a good time and Arthur asked her to marry him. Right like that! Took ten minutes to make the decision. She accepted, so they were engaged. When he got back to Los Angeles she phoned every day." [12]

True to form, Ashe "the traveling man" was not always there to take his fiancée's calls. In early March, he was back at UCLA, where puzzled friends quizzed him about his surprise engagement, but he was there for only a few days before heading for the Pacific Coast Doubles tournament in La Jolla. Two weeks later, while he was winning the singles title at the annual Thunderbird tournament in Phoenix, Arizona, news of his engagement finally hit the press. The young couple, Pat's proud mother announced, would be married in Richmond on June 5. The announcement in *The New York Times* added that Ashe would graduate in late June and upon completion of his ROTC training later in the summer would receive a commission as a second lieutenant in the Army.

On the surface Arthur's immediate future seemed set, yet from the beginning his closest friends had serious doubts he would go through with the marriage. "Gradually," Baker recalled, "we could see Arthur getting bored with her," which had been his pattern over the last two years. "He'd get interested in some girl, then get bored—or scared, maybe—and wouldn't want to see her," Baker observed, adding: "I told him, 'Better not get married, you'll be bored with your wife.'" [13]

In late March and early April, Arthur spent a week in San Juan, Puerto Rico, participating in an international tournament at the Caribe Hilton resort, where Pasarell had played since he was a small boy. For years the man known as Charlito in San Juan had been regaling Arthur with tales of his beautiful native island, and now Ashe had a chance to see for himself. This was his first visit to the Caribbean, and he was immediately charmed by the tropical lushness of the landscape and the warm welcome he received from the Pasarell family. The range of skin color, the blurred racial lines, and the appearance of congenial social relations were outside his experience, and he came away fascinated with the overall contrast between the harsh biracialism of the Jim Crow South and the more diverse and open culture of Puerto Rico. The Caribe Hilton was obviously not the best place to explore the deeper realities of race and class on a poverty-stricken island. But Arthur took in what he could, peppering his hosts with questions about local life. He also managed to win the tournament, defeating Cliff Richey in the singles final. [14]

Ashe's impressive victories in Phoenix and San Juan drew the attention of the press, including *Look* magazine, which ran a feature story titled "Arthur Ashe: Hottest New Tennis Star." The text by senior editor Chandler

Brossard was complimentary, and to Arthur's delight it broke new ground by focusing more on his tennis than on his role as a racial pioneer. Frank Deford had followed this line in a brief article published the previous August in the wake of Arthur's Davis Cup victory in Dallas. But Brossard's was the first in-depth profile to play down his singular status as a black tennis star.

During his college years Arthur found it difficult to explain why he resented press coverage that stressed his race. He finally began to level with the press corps in May 1966 in a forthright *Sport Magazine* interview titled "Arthur Ashe: I Want to Be No. 1 Without an Asterisk." Years later he clarified his views, lamenting that "there was a great deal of fuss about being the 'first black' Junior Davis Cup player, the 'first black' to get a tennis scholarship to UCLA, the 'first black' to win at Charlottesville, etc. Those comments always put me under pressure to justify my accomplishments on racial grounds, as if sports were the cutting edge of our nation's move toward improved race relations. The fact that this kind of accomplishment by a black player got so much attention was an indication that we still had so far to go."[15]

The persistent problem of being measured and identified according to race-based standards went well beyond press coverage. It was also part of a society being challenged and reshaped by an increasingly influential civil rights movement. To black Americans striving for racial justice and equal opportunity, and to the embattled white conservatives resisting the movement, Arthur was more than just a talented tennis player. Whether he liked it or not, his career was also a marker of racial progress.

Spending most of his time outside the South during the critical years 1961 to 1966 shielded Arthur from some of the pressure to become actively involved in a struggle centered below the Mason-Dixon line. As he later recalled, "At UCLA, I was geographically removed from most of the major activities of the civil rights movement. The marches and sit-ins and arrests were on the front pages every day, but I was a long way from them." Even so, geography did not absolve him of the responsibility to take a stand on issues related to race and civil rights. Nor did it remove him completely from the sounds and sights of the struggle. Both before and after the trauma of Watts, UCLA witnessed vigorous campus debates over questions of racial integration, cultural nationalism, and what came to be known as "Black Power." "It would have been difficult," if not impossible, he acknowledged, to avoid racial politics altogether. "Growing up in the South in the 1950s, studying at UCLA in the 1960s, even playing tennis," he pointed out, "planted seeds of confrontation."[16]

One such confrontation occurred during Arthur's last year at UCLA,

when he encountered Ron Karenga, a militant Black nationalist holding
forth outside the entrance to the student union. Karenga, as Arthur described
him, "was a short, bald-headed graduate student who headed a group called
US, which meant 'us slaves.' He wore great big dark glasses, a Fu Manchu
mustache, bright dashikis, and was known as the heaviest, baddest black
dude on campus." For nearly thirty minutes Arthur stood in a small crowd
of students listening to Karenga's take on the importance of "self-defense
for the black community" and the need to inculcate respect for African traditions. Eventually the rest of the crowd slipped away leaving Arthur and
Karenga to carry on a one-on-one discussion. "We talked about the black
struggle, California-style," Arthur recalled, with Karenga making a plea for
cultural awareness of the African past: "If black people didn't start learning
and enjoying their culture, Karenga argued, they would become 'white Europeans.' I'd never heard this doctrine before. And with my southern background I wasn't sure he understood where I had come from and what I was
up against."

Arthur never forgot Karenga's parting words: "It's attitudes like yours
I'm trying to change. Look, you're the cream of the black crop, you're in college, you're going to do fairly well in life. If I can't convince you, then what
do you think about the black masses?" This was a hard sell for someone who
had become adept at blending in with his surroundings, even though both
men knew this routine was becoming more challenging as the fear of black
militancy grew. "In 1966, I secretly felt uneasier, what with all those riots and
talk about 'white backlash' and 'black power,'" he confessed in *Advantage
Ashe*.[17]

During the past year, several "tennis incidents" had given Arthur cause
for concern: "In one Southern town people on the streets yelled 'Nigger!' at
Luis Glass, the young Negro player from UCLA, and the situation got so
edgy that he withdrew from the tournament." Even in Richmond, where Arthur Ashe Day had promoted a measure of interracial harmony in February,
a distressing racial confrontation occurred four months later when regional
officials of the Middle Atlantic Boys Division of the USLTA scheduled a
tournament at the whites-only Hermitage Country Club. Four years earlier, Byrd Park had hosted an integrated Middle Atlantic tournament, but
breaching the color bar at the Hermitage club proved much more difficult.

When Weldon Rogers, the thirteen-year-old son of the Reverend Jefferson Rogers, a well-known Washington, D.C., civil rights leader, showed
up unexpectedly and tried to register for play, he was turned away by the
tournament director, who explained that the registration period had long

passed. Convinced that enforcement of the pre-registration rule was a smoke screen for racial discrimination—a reasonable conclusion in light of the director's declaration that "Club policy doesn't allow a Negro to take part in any of its athletic or social events"—the Reverend Rogers forcefully pleaded his son's case but to no avail. In an earlier time, this would have been the end of it. But in the spring of 1966, there were signs of change. To the Rogerses' amazement, thirteen white players, later dubbed "Thirteen Young Heroes" by *World Tennis* magazine, refused to play and walked out in protest. Unfortunately, the USLTA officials on-site were unmoved by this show of courage and refused to suspend the tournament.[18]

Arthur faced his own challenges in the South that spring. Trying to capitalize on the success of the 1965 Davis Cup tie against Mexico, the Dallas Country Club organized an invitational tournament scheduled for April. Contacting Captain George MacCall, the organizers made it clear that they planned to invite several members of the Davis Cup squad, but not Arthur. MacCall shot back an ultimatum: "Take all the players I send you or none." After the organizers reluctantly agreed to MacCall's conditions, everything seemed set. But the country club soon threw a monkey wrench into the deliberations by accepting Arthur while refusing to admit black spectators. To circumvent this complication, the tournament was soon moved to the Samuell Grand Tennis Center, the public park that had hosted the 1965 U.S.-Mexico tie. Though wary of what he might face once he arrived in Dallas, Arthur managed to avoid any troubling incidents, and by the end of the week he had won both the singles and doubles titles.

Arthur later pointed out with considerable satisfaction that he had "yet to lose a match in any big Southern tournament." But he had to admit that to date he hadn't "played in many." "I've never been asked to the Blue-Gray at Montgomery, the Atlanta Open, or the Sugar Bowl in New Orleans," he observed in 1967, adding that fortunately "most Southern tourneys don't count for much." Even so, he freely admitted he "sometimes felt a little resentful at seeing swanky Southern tournaments ignore me in favor of white players I know I can beat."

Yet he was not willing to make a public issue of these racially motivated snubs. "Some people tell me I should ask other players not to compete in the South unless I can too," he reported. "There's been pressure on me to make a big stink about it, or to tell Martin Tressel and Bob Kelleher, the past and present USLTA presidents, 'In effect you're sanctioning race prejudice when you sanction these Southern tournaments. If you don't make them drop the color bar, I'll put out public statements blasting you.'" Putting out public statements was not Ashe's style during these years. As he explained, "I'm not getting militant as long as I'm the only player shut out. When more Negroes want to play in Southern tournaments and have the skill to be worth watching, then maybe I'll go along with an organized protest if one is needed." [19]

This tentative openness to participation in a protest movement sometime in the future was one of the first hints Ashe was beginning to rethink his position on the civil rights struggle. As a public figure on the verge of celebrity—and as the only identifiable African American in the upper echelons of tennis—he found it increasingly difficult to remain mute on matters of race and civil rights. Privately he had been trying to make sense of the evolving civil rights scene for some time, but his first extended public commentary on such matters came in 1967 when he and Gewecke collaborated on *Advantage Ashe*.

Written against the backdrop of intense ideological debate over nonviolence, Black Power, and racial separatism, Arthur's statements as a twenty-three-year-old memoirist suggest a temporary retreat into the lost world of Booker T. Washington. While not quite an accommodationist, he expressly endorsed leaders whom he considered to be moderate centrists: Dr. Ralph Bunche, Secretary of Housing and Urban Development Robert Weaver, Senator Edward Brooke of Massachusetts, Solicitor General Thurgood Marshall, and Dr. Martin Luther King Jr. The inclusion of Marshall and King indicated he understood the necessity of struggle, both in the courtroom and in the streets. But he also expressed serious doubts about the utility of extended mass protests. "I know Dr. King has the best interests of Negroes at heart," he wrote, "but I doubt if his tactics will work indefinitely. It looks to me as if a Negro's best chance to advance is to get himself an education somehow and prove his worth as an individual. I've seen many Negroes do this—even in the South. Then they're accepted voluntarily because people appreciate them. But all the civil rights in the world won't help the lazy ones or the soreheads."

Continuing his critique of the movement, Arthur distanced himself from the philosophy of nonviolent direct action advocated by the Southern Christian Leadership Conference (SCLC), CORE, and SNCC. He also revealed his political naïveté by lumping nonviolent and violent protesters together. "By crusades and protest marches and rock-throwing we seem to try to ram ourselves down people's throats," he observed. "Sometimes a demonstration is the best way of getting headlines about a bad deal, but I don't think demonstrators should try to make trouble for anyone. We'll never advance very far by force, because we're outnumbered ten to one. Quiet negotiation and slow infiltration look more hopeful to me." Sensing this view might be unpopular with many of his black readers, he asked rhetorically: "Does this make me an Uncle Tom? If so, okay. I'm not the crusader type. I pay my $3 yearly dues in the National Association for the Advancement of Colored People, and tend to my tennis. I feel the way Joe Louis does. When somebody asked why he wasn't active in the civil rights fight, he said, 'some people do it by shouting, some march, some give lots of money. I do it my way—behaving. All ways help.'"[20]

Ashe would eventually disavow the tone and much of the substance of the conservative positions expressed in *Advantage Ashe*. In retrospect, he and others came to see that his early remarks on civil rights reflected the continuing influence of his father and the perceived necessity of avoiding the pitfalls of white backlash. He was also pushing back against mounting pressure to become more militant. As in-your-face activists such as Stokely Carmichael and H. Rap Brown gained currency—and as the Black Panther Party made its presence felt in inner-city neighborhoods and even on college campuses such as UCLA, where two student members of the Panther Party would be killed by police in January 1969—Arthur resisted what he termed the "don't trust the white man" philosophy. "It bugs me," he complained, "when Negroes give me the African-type advice."[21]

This was how he felt in 1967. Yet by the end of the decade he had become much more sympathetic to the strivings of black activists of all stripes. While he never subscribed to what he saw as the self-defeating principles of racial separatism, he developed a greater appreciation for the sacrifices and frustrations of individuals and groups agitating for radical change. This appreciation, which surfaced during the tumultuous year of 1968, would become more apparent in the 1970s and 1980s, and by the end of his life his assessment of the responsibility of speaking and acting out on behalf of racial justice had come full circle, placing him solidly in the camp of W. E. B. Du Bois, Booker T. Washington's archrival.

Written in 1992, Ashe's final statement on the protest tradition was tinged with guilt and suffused with admiration for "the black men, women, and children who risked their lives during the civil rights movement." As he pointed out with obvious regret, "While blood was running freely in the streets of Birmingham, Memphis, and Biloxi, I had been playing tennis. Dressed in immaculate white, I was elegantly stroking tennis balls on perfectly paved courts in California and New York and Europe. Meanwhile, across the South, young men and women of my age were enduring pain and suffering so that blacks would be free of our American brand of apartheid."

He acknowledged he had "certainly been offered more than one opportunity to stand up for the movement" and that his refusal to seize these early opportunities could no longer be explained away by the dictates of his rising career on the court. "Some of my friends tried to assure me that I, too, was playing my part in the revolution," he recalled, "but they never convinced me of it, not completely. There were times, in fact, when I felt a burning sense of shame that I was not with other blacks—and whites—standing up to the fire hoses and the police dogs, the truncheons, bullets, and bombs that cut down such martyrs as Chaney, Schwerner, and Goodman, Viola Liuzzo, Martin Luther King, Jr., Medgar Evers, and the little girls in that bombed church in Birmingham, Alabama. As my fame increased, so did my anguish."[22]

In the late spring and early summer of 1966, Ashe's anguish, in so far as it existed, was well hidden beneath his carefully measured detachment from the passions of the day. But it wouldn't be long before the shifting nature of the struggle for freedom and equality forced him to reevaluate his lack of involvement. The shift, which had begun the previous year when the divisions and disagreements among SCLC and SNCC leaders surfaced during the voting rights campaign in Alabama, was exacerbated by differing responses to a series of developments, notably the Watts riot, the escalating war in Vietnam, the legislative initiatives of President Johnson's Great Society program, and SCLC's decision to move the epicenter of its antidiscrimination campaigns to the North. Arguments over political philosophy, strategic priorities, the strengths and weaknesses of nonviolence, and the advisability of racial integration led to organizational fragmentation and hard feelings that threatened to tear the movement apart along class, race, and generational lines.

At issue was the apparent emptiness of the legal and legislative victories of the past decade. Among many working-class and younger blacks there was a growing suspicion that long-awaited civil rights advances, though welcome, had failed to address many of the most pressing problems related to economic and social inequality and systemic discrimination. This disillusionment fueled a new, if often unfocused, militancy that found expression in several forms, ranging from urban riots and cultural nationalism to racial separatism and the emerging political persuasion of Black Power.

The first clear sign of the new era came near the end of Ashe's last semester at UCLA, in May 1966, when the nonviolent champion and former Freedom Rider John Lewis lost his bid to serve a fourth term as SNCC's national chairman. Lewis's successor, Stokely Carmichael, was a freedom fighter of a different stripe—a brash and assertive New Yorker who refused to rule out violence as a legitimate means of struggle. Born in Trinidad, in the West Indies, Carmichael had grown up on the streets of the Bronx before enrolling at Howard University in 1960. After participating in the Freedom Rides and serving time in Parchman Farm prison in the summer of 1961, he became increasingly disenchanted with interracial cooperation and nonviolence. This growing alienation from much of the movement's leadership set the stage for his spectacular debut as SNCC's national chairman in June 1966.[23]

The backdrop for Carmichael's launching of SNCC's Black Power phase was the "March Against Fear," a 220-mile journey from Memphis to Jackson, Mississippi, organized by James Meredith, the courageous Air Force veteran who had desegregated the University of Mississippi in 1962. On June 6, the day after Ashe flew to London to participate in the Beckenham, Kent, grass tournament, Meredith and a small group of companions crossed the Mississippi state line and headed south into the Delta on Highway 51. Twelve miles down the road he was gunned down by a forty-year-old white supremacist named Aubrey James Norvell. Three shotgun blasts put Meredith in the hospital, provoking enough outrage to mobilize a large contingent of civil rights leaders determined to continue the march all the way to the state capital in Jackson.

Carmichael and SCLC's chairman, Martin Luther King Jr., were among the leaders responding to the call, and as the three-week-long march progressed, they had ample opportunity to air their differences at the nightly mass rallies held at campsites and other venues along the route. King and his lieutenants preached the gospel of nonviolence, invariably including a ritualistic call-and-response. "What do we want?" they asked, and the crowd roared back "Freedom." For King and the SCLC this was a tried-and-true method of generating mass enthusiasm, but this time the message of nonviolence did not go unanswered.

When the march reached the mid-Delta town of Greenwood on June 16, Carmichael, taking full advantage of King's temporary absence from the state, came up with a rhythmic and dramatic call-and-response ritual of his own. Following the lead of Willie Ricks, a SNCC activist who had experimented with rhetorical references to "Black Power" earlier in the march, Carmichael used the provocative slogan to seize the initiative for his militant stance on the issues dividing the movement. Having spent most of the summer of 1962 in Greenwood, he knew his audience, and he knew what they wanted to hear. "We want black power!" he told them. Repeating the phrase four times, he declared: "From now on when they ask you what you want, you know what to tell 'em." "What do you want?" he asked over and over again, and each time the crowd roared "Black Power!"

When King returned to the march the next day, he tried to dissuade Carmichael from using an ambiguous phrase that would inevitably raise the specter of black supremacy and "racism in reverse." But the proverbial genie was out of the bottle. For the next two weeks, the reporters covering the march talked of little else, fueling a media frenzy that sparked a national debate focused largely on the perceived dangers of Black Power. On June 19, Carmichael flew to Washington to appear on the Sunday morning television show *Face the Nation*, where he was asked to clarify his controversial slogan's implications for the future of American democracy and racial harmony. Ranging across a wide variety of issues, he soothed few nerves with his comments on political self-determination for blacks and the irony of a government "dropping bombs in Vietnam to ensure free elections there" while refusing to intervene in Mississippi to protect the voting rights of ordinary black people.[24]

For the remainder of the summer, Carmichael toured the nation as a spokesman for Black Power, delivering speeches that inspired hope in some circles and outright fear in others. Hailed by some as the new Malcolm X—the Black Muslim leader assassinated in 1965—he grew increasingly militant in his advocacy of everything from racial separation to the antiwar movement. He condemned the recent carpet bombing of North Vietnam while pointing out the bitter irony of asking black soldiers to fight for freedom abroad when they were routinely denied it at home. Appearing on *Meet the Press* on August 21, he clarified his personal objection to the hypocrisy of current American military policy. "No, I would not fight in Vietnam, absolutely not, and would urge every black man in this country not to fight in Vietnam," he declared.[25]

Ashe, like most Americans, took all of this in from afar and didn't quite know what to make of it. When he first learned of the March Against Fear, he was in England, and when the Greenwood drama inaugurated the Black Power debate ten days later, he was at Forest Hills in New York. He had hoped to fly to Miami to root for Pasarell and the UCLA Bruins at the NCAA men's tennis championship. But other commitments prevented him from witnessing his best friend's triumph in the NCAA singles competition.

MacCall, who ruled the Davis Cup squad with unbending authority, had ordered Arthur to join his American teammates Riessen and Graebner at Beckenham during the second week of June as a final warm-up for their upcoming tie against Mexico. Scheduled to report for basic training at Fort Lewis, Washington, on June 23, Ashe did not have the option of remaining in England long enough to join the draw at Wimbledon. Traveling across the Atlantic for such a brief stay was hardly worth the effort in his view, and adding insult to injury on the very day of his graduation he was eliminated from the Beckenham tournament by Ray Ruffels, a twenty-year-old unranked Australian.[26]

With tennis dominating the final weeks before his stint at Fort Lewis, Arthur did not comment publicly on the emerging Black Power controversy coming out of Mississippi. What he thought about it at the time is subject to speculation, and even a year later, when he discussed a variety of racial issues in *Advantage Ashe*, he made no mention of Carmichael or the politics surrounding the March Against Fear. He also failed to discuss the matter in his 1981 memoir, *Off the Court*. Only near the end of his life, as he reflected upon "The Burden of Race" in his final memoir, *Days of Grace*, did he have his say on the "brilliant harangue in Greenwood, Mississippi, from which, in my opinion, black America has never adequately recovered." He offered a searing indictment of Carmichael's approach to the freedom struggle: "In promulgating Black Power, Carmichael wittingly or unwittingly (the former is much more likely) turned his back on the moral emphasis and genuine nonviolence of King's leadership and moved toward a radically secular philosophy of racial emancipation." In Ashe's view, this was "the beginning of the end of dominance of morality in African American culture. Instead, the amoral quest for naked and vengeful power would rule thereafter."[27]

When Arthur reported to Fort Lewis in late June, the March Against Fear was still in progress, and Carmichael's controversial comments decrying black participation in the war were still percolating. But he soon discovered that Fort Lewis was its own world, cut off from the tumultuous political landscape beyond its borders. From the outset of basic training, he, in his words, "plunged immediately into the simplistic, disciplined, and physical world of the military." An all-encompassing experience, "it had all the harassment and dehumanization which seem to be required ingredients for creating soldiers."

As a trained athlete accustomed to a disciplined life, Arthur did not anticipate any difficulties adapting to Army regulations or to the physical and psychological demands of boot camp. But he encountered an unexpected challenge the very first day when he was thrust into the role of cadet brigade commander. Appointed deputy brigade commander, he was unexpectedly forced to step up when his immediate superior suffered an injury.

"We hadn't gone fifteen yards beyond the gate when the cadet brigade commander stepped into a pothole and sprained an ankle," he later explained. "He had to be taken to the infirmary; suddenly I was in charge of an entire unit of eight hundred men."

Relatively unfazed, Ashe oversaw the brigade without incident for several hours, but the situation went south at the end of the day when he was ordered to march his troops "back to the barracks and line them up in the courtyard so they could be dismissed." Once they were in the courtyard, he noticed the entire unit was lined up facing the wrong direction, as did one of the training officers, who bellowed "you've really got it fucked up, mister." Forced to march his troops out of the square, "turn them around, and bring them back the way they were supposed to be," he ended up "terribly embarrassed because I was already in the spotlight over my tennis."[28]

Arthur was not the first sports celebrity to train at Fort Lewis; nor would he be the last. But he stood out nonetheless—not only as one of the few black men in the camp but also as one of the camp's most popular cadets. Despite his inauspicious beginning, it didn't take long for him to win the respect of his brigade and most of the camp's officers. With his low-key, unaffected personality and strong work ethic, he was able to blunt potential animosity related to racial prejudice or personal envy. Blessed with athletic prowess, a fastidious appearance, and a strong, ramrod-straight military bearing, he looked and acted like an Army officer from the outset. Knowing they were almost certainly headed for combat in Vietnam, some of his fellow cadets undoubtedly resented the likelihood that his celebrity status would place him in a cushy stateside assignment. Yet few of his peers seemed to blame Arthur for his privileged position. During his six weeks in camp, he never asked for special treatment of any kind, and he never seemed to complain about anything. He did his share of KP duty and ended up as the second highest rated soldier in his platoon. Though relieved when it was over, he looked back on his time at Fort Lewis as a worthwhile experience. Even in this austere setting, he embraced the opportunity to learn "about weapons, tactics, map reading, and other useful skills," and he valued the "good friends" that he made along the way.[29]

Arthur's positive attitude reflected his perception that the situation could have been much worse: he could have been assigned to a training camp in the Deep South; and the timing of his induction into the Army could have been set for a date in the immediate aftermath of his basic training. Instead, Army officials had granted him a six-month delay, setting his induction date for February 1967. Most important, he had been assured earlier in the summer that his probable assignment would be at the U.S. Military Academy at West Point. While visiting the Orange Lawn Tennis Club in northern New Jersey, he was approached by Bill Cullen, the longtime tennis and squash coach at West Point. Well aware that Arthur would be on active duty within a few months, Cullen presented the young Davis Cup star with an intriguing proposition. "We'd be interested in having you as an assistant tennis coach at the Point," he declared, adding that the Academy also needed "a data-processing officer." "The two posts could be combined," he explained. All Arthur had to do was to apply for data processing training as soon as he received his commission. "I'll take care of the rest," Cullen promised.

Thrilled by Cullen's offer, Arthur could now look forward to a two-year stint in the Army compatible with his long-term goals as a tennis player. Without making any guarantees, the Army had unofficially informed him that he could expect special leaves to participate in Davis Cup play as well as a limited number of invitational tournaments. While he would miss a majority of the tour, there would be ample opportunity to stay in shape and keep his competitive edge. That was more than he had expected, considering the rising pressure on the Army to maintain a large combat force in Vietnam. Even though he had announced publicly that he was willing to fight in Vietnam, he was in no hurry to make good on his pledge.[30]

In the meantime, as he waited for the onset of active duty, Arthur had nearly half a year to solidify his position as one of the top amateur players in the nation. Ranked second behind Dennis Ralston at the beginning of 1966, he had visions of moving higher by the end of the year. The opportunity was there with Ralston planning to turn professional by early 1967—and with American tennis at its lowest ebb in years. Moreover, many of the world's best players had joined the pro tour during the past four years and thus were ineligible to play in amateur tournaments.[31]

Coming out of basic training in mid-August, he expected to be a little rusty. But he played surprisingly well in his first post-camp outing, fighting his way into the semifinals of the Hall of Fame tournament in Newport, Rhode Island, before losing to Ralston. He played even better the following week at the U.S. National Doubles Championships in Brookline, where he and Marty Riessen lost a tough semifinal match to the defending champions Roy Emerson and Fred Stolle. With only a few days before the opening of the U.S. National tournament at Forest Hills, he had just enough time to travel to Philadelphia for an ATA benefit event heralded as "National Arthur Ashe Day." Held at the Philmont Country Club, the event featured exhibition matches between the American and Australian Davis Cup teams, and additional singles matches involving Santana, Drysdale, and other Ashe admirers.

That night three hundred people filled a banquet hall to hear several speakers praise Arthur's character. Emerson, who had just vanquished the honoree in Brookline, assured the crowd that "all the players of the world have a great regard for Arthur on and off the court." Speaking with uncharacteristic emotion, MacCall declared: "I hope if I have a son, he could be like Arthur Ashe." Though a bit embarrassed, Ashe appreciated the $2,500 raised that evening to support Dr. J's junior development program.[32]

Arthur's character was also the subject of an admiring profile published in *Sports Illustrated* the same week. Frank Deford had written two earlier pieces on Arthur, but his August 29 cover story, "Service, But First a Smile," went well beyond his earlier efforts. Assigned to preview the upcoming tournament at Forest Hills, Deford decided to focus on Arthur, who in his view represented America's best hope to recapture the National singles title.

Later one of Arthur's closest friends, Deford marveled at the young star's poise and grace under pressure. Predicting he "may someday be the best player in the world," Deford concluded that "the only Negro player in a white tennis world" had figured out how "to endure the capriciousness of a time that so arbitrarily gives and takes from his race." Beyond dealing with the daily challenges and slights of racial discrimination, Arthur inevitably found himself in the position of serving as "an image, that of the American dream, minority division." "It is a difficult role for a 23-year-old," Deford declared, "but Ashe bears it all with ease."[33]

The article went on to sketch the outlines of Arthur's life and career. The dominant theme throughout was Arthur's ability to mix an inner vitality with an outwardly calm detachment. "The most impressive thing," according to Pasarell, "is that he is so able to take things as they are. He can be absolutely objective." Along the same lines, Arthur told Deford: "I'm always thinking. I don't care how tired I am, once I get in bed I can't go to sleep for an hour. There's just so much to think about." Ashe's UCLA coach, J. D. Morgan, who had come to regard Arthur as an adopted son, stressed his former player's fertile imagination, which he acknowledged was a potential problem on the court. According to the coach, "the biggest thing he has going for him is also his biggest fault—his imagination." Arthur's "intellectual meandering" during matches had become notorious, and Deford duly reported, "most players agree that the best way to beat Ashe is just to hang with him until his concentration starts to wander." Gonzales, who had sometimes criticized

Arthur on this score, chose instead to stress his integrity and constancy of purpose. "I don't know how the Army, the two years, will affect Arthur's tennis career," he told Deford, "but I know this. He is at peace in his mind. He won't duck a thing, and he won't let anybody down."[34]

With all of this praise ringing in his ears, Arthur arrived at Forest Hills more determined than ever to play up to his potential. Having reached the semifinals in 1965, he expected to do even better after an additional year of seasoning. The Australian tour had elevated his game, especially on grass, and his eight tournament wins in the last twelve months boosted his confidence. Seeded fourth, with only the defending champion Santana, Emerson, and Ralston ahead of him, he felt no ill effects from his six-week hiatus at Fort Lewis.

In the first round, Arthur got off to a rough start, barely outlasting Lamar Roemer of Houston 15–13. But he came on strong in the final two sets, winning 6–2, 6–0. His next opponent, New Yorker Ron Holmberg, was much tougher. After losing the opening game at love and splitting the first two sets, Arthur eventually took charge, but he had to survive a forty-five-minute rain delay before closing out the match. His third-round opponent was John Newcombe, an unseeded twenty-two-year-old Australian who had first attracted attention in 1963 as the youngest Aussie ever selected to play Davis Cup. Two years later he would team with Tony Roche to win the Wimbledon doubles title, but his prowess in singles play was only beginning to show in 1966. A rangy player whose powerful serves rivaled those of the world's best amateurs, Newcombe was destined to be one of the dominant players of his era, winning three Wimbledon singles titles (1967, 1970, and 1971), two U.S. National singles titles (1967 and 1973), and five Wimbledon doubles championships.

By the end of 1967, Newcombe would be the number-one-ranked amateur in the world. But there was only a hint of this future success in September 1966. Nearly everyone expected Ashe to make it through to the round of sixteen. But on a day of upsets, when both Roche and Drysdale lost to lightly regarded, unseeded opponents, Ashe suffered one of the most disappointing defeats of his career. "Thoroughly outplayed," in the estimation of one reporter, he was never really in the match, which barely lasted an hour. His only consolation was that he was hardly the only American star to suffer an early exit. When the dust settled at the end of the round of sixteen, Clark Graebner was the only American to advance to the quarterfinals. This was the nation's worst showing in the eighty-six-year history of the U.S. National Championships. As recently as 1963 half of the eight quarterfinalists had been American. But now no fewer than five of the quarterfinalists were from Australia. The long-standing rivalry between the world's two tennis super-powers seemed totally out of balance, even before Stolle defeated Newcombe in an all-Aussie final to become the first unseeded Forest Hills champion since Mal Anderson in 1957. Adding insult to injury, Stolle also teamed with Emerson to run away with the doubles title, easily defeating Graebner and Ralston in straight sets.[35]

America's chance of seeing an American champion at Forest Hills any-time soon or of recapturing the Davis Cup suddenly seemed remote. The pressure to shake up the American Davis Cup squad was now intense, but MacCall refused to panic. "We're just going to have to work harder," he told the press on the last day of the tournament, adding: "Everybody seems to for-get that our boys, particularly Ashe, did very well against these same Aussies during our tour of Australia last winter."

Ashe appreciated MacCall's comment, but he also feared the rising tide of Australian dominance had yet to reach its crest. The first test came two days after the closing match at Forest Hills when five members of the Aus-tralian Davis Cup squad squared off against five of the Americans in a pre-view series held in Cleveland. To the surprise of almost everyone, Ashe and his teammates won all five matches, though the significance of the rout was tempered by the absence of Emerson and Stolle. Later in the week, a sec-ond series of matches was held in Toledo, followed by two more contests in west central Texas. In each case, the results were mildly encouraging for the Americans, especially in Odessa, Texas, where Ashe defeated Emerson in a tough three-set match. The following week, several of the Australian stars stopped off in Berkeley to play in the Pacific Coast International Champion-ships before returning home. This time the Americans clearly dominated the competition, with both Ashe and Pasarell making it to the semifinals. Five of Australia's best players—Emerson, Newcombe, Roche, Kerry Melville, and Owen Davidson—were eliminated in the earlier rounds after finding Berke-ley's concrete courts less than ideal for their style of play. While Stolle ulti-mately overcame Pasarell to win the title, the Aussies' overall performance was lackluster at best.[36]

None of these exhibition matches had any direct impact on the fight for the Davis Cup, but the boost to American morale came just in time. The American squad's first official tie was scheduled for November 5 in Porto Alegre, Brazil, against a weak Brazilian team that bore no resemblance to the powerful Aussies. MacCall was concerned nonetheless, knowing the Porto Alegre matches would be played on slow clay with a raucous crowd of Brazilian fans cheering on their countrymen. The American Davis Cup Committee had tried to move the tie to Los Angeles, but was rebuffed by the designated arbiter, the Australian Lawn Tennis Association. The fact that the captain of the Brazilian Davis Cup team, Paolo da Silva Costa, was also the president of the International Lawn Tennis Federation (ILTF) did not help the American cause. But it was the Australians who turned the knife.

Taking nothing for granted, MacCall arranged for the American squad to arrive in South America a full two weeks beforehand to acclimate his players to the slow clay. Entering Arthur and his four teammates in the South American tennis championships held in Buenos Aires in late October, MacCall did what he could to neutralize the Brazilians' advantage. In the Buenos Aires warm-up, the Americans performed surprisingly well, with all five advancing to the third round or beyond. Arthur made it to the semifinals before bowing out to Brazil's best player, Thomas Koch, in a five-set marathon, and Richey defeated Koch for the South American title the next day.

It was a different story once the team arrived in Porto Alegre. Influenced by Richey's strong performance in Buenos Aires, MacCall generated considerable controversy by substituting the nineteen-year-old Texan for Arthur in the second singles spot behind Ralston. Considered to be relatively weak on clay, Arthur was limited to a pairing with Ralston in the doubles. At a purely technical level, the move seemed to make sense, but after Richey lost to José Edison Mandarino on the first day of competition the second-guessing began. Playing in 100-degree heat, Richey won the first set but faded noticeably thereafter, suggesting that Arthur's superior fitness could have led to a different outcome. Ralston had no trouble disposing of Koch in the other opening day singles match, and he and Arthur followed up with a decisive victory over Koch and Mandarino in the doubles match to give the Americans a 2–1 lead going into the final day of play.

To advance to the next round, the Americans had to win only one of the two closing singles matches. But neither Richey nor Ralston was up to the challenge. Richey was the first to go down, so unnerved by the crowd and the heat that he was almost hapless against Koch's steady game. The overmatched Texan won only seven games in three sets. Now all of the pressure was on Ralston. As the crowd rallied behind the home team, baiting the fiery American with jeers and catcalls, Mandarino rose to the occasion, playing the match of his life. Somehow Ralston managed to win two of the first three sets, but after that the Brazilian took charge. Arthur, who watched helplessly from the sidelines, later recalled the shock of his old rival's unexpected loss:

"Twice Ralston went ahead in sets, but twice Mandarino pulled even. We could see Ralston fade after the rest period. The fifth and deciding set was no contest." Worst of all, he wrote, "it was the fifth time in seven years we'd been put out before the challenge round."

Giddy in victory, the Brazilian captain da Silva Costa attributed the upset victory to the "fiber and courage" of his players. But Arthur expressed a different view, arguing the Americans had no one but themselves to blame. "Probably our team's worst trouble," he wrote, "was that we hadn't worried. It just never crossed our minds that Brazil might win. All our talk was about 'after we beat Brazil.'" Some American tennis officials and many irate fans called for MacCall's dismissal, but Arthur stood by his coach, who was uncharacteristically quiet after the defeat. "We felt real low afterward," he remembered. "George didn't bark at us. It was too late for that. We just brooded, then gradually began to bury the memories and look ahead." Perhaps so, but it seems more likely that the memory of the Porto Alegre debacle lingered just below the surface of his mind, a cautionary affirmation of the sin of pride he had first encountered in the Sunday school lessons of his youth.[37]

Once MacCall realized his job was not in jeopardy, he began to rally his players around his chosen strategy of rigorous training and continuous play. In short, he wanted to repeat the experiment of seasoning his players on the tough Australian circuit. Initially, he had hopes that his entire squad would be available for a second dose of extended play Down Under. But in the end only Ashe and Richey were able to commit to the entire tour. Pasarell, still enrolled at UCLA, agreed to come for the first month but informed MacCall he would have to return to the United States before the end of the year. The team's unofficial alternates, Allen Fox and Jim McManus, made a similar commitment, temporarily fleshing out the American contingent. This made Ashe and Richey the stalwarts, especially after Ralston, the nation's top-rated player, left the team to join the professional ranks in late December.

Ralston's departure dealt a serious blow to the American squad's chances of keeping up with the Australians, but it opened up new opportunities for Ashe. Making the most of the Australian tour suddenly became an even higher priority than it had been when he had arrived in Melbourne in late November. From the outset, he had been eager to return to the scene of his triumphant run the previous year. He also looked forward to reengaging with Australia's lively social scene, a prospect that did not please his fiancée. Since announcing their engagement in March, the couple had seen relatively little of each other, their relationship having definitely cooled since Arthur's impulsive proposal. Within four months he would break off the engagement, confirming his roommates' prediction.

The Australian trip, Arthur reasoned, would not only sharpen his game and keep him in MacCall's good graces; it would also enable him to have a bit of fun and adventure before submitting to the constraints of military life. Despite their continuing rivalry for the Davis Cup singles spot, he and Cliff Richey were on good terms, and their relationship got even better after Cliff's sister Nancy, one of the top female prospects in American tennis, joined them on the Australian tour. For two months the three Americans were nearly inseparable as they made their way from Melbourne to Adelaide, the site of both the South Australian and Australian National Championships. Both the tennis and the camaraderie had more than a few high moments, even though Arthur was unable to repeat his wildly successful run of the previous year. At the Victorian tournament in Melbourne, he lost to Newcombe in the quarterfinals, and at the mid-December South Australian championships, where he was the defending champion, he suffered a second early exit, losing in the third round to young Ray Ruffels, who had defeated him at Beckenham in 1965.

Three weeks later, following the Christmas break, Arthur's situation went from bad to worse when a strained hip muscle forced him to withdraw from the singles competition at the West Australian Championships in Perth. Nursing the injury, he recovered enough to join Richey for the doubles competition. A week later, at the Tasmanian Championships in Hobart, Arthur was finally on the mend, defeating the hot Australian prospect Bill Bowrey in a tough semifinal match that went four sets before the American prevailed 13–11. Though upended in the singles final by Tony Roche, he and Richey managed to win the doubles title, signaling he was ready to take on the challenges of the final two weeks of the tour: the Australian-American International round-robin tournament at the famous White City courts in Sydney, and the Australian National Championships in Adelaide.

Arthur played well at White City, even though the final team score was a disappointing 6–3 in favor of the Australians. Rounding into top form, he was optimistic about his chances at the Australian National tournament. While Emerson had won the Australian singles title five of the past six years, Arthur's near miss the previous January, plus his multiple victories over the great Emmo at the U.S. National Championships and other venues, gave him hope that he was on the verge of winning his first Grand Slam title.

As expected, Arthur made his way through the first three rounds with relative ease, though he and Richey suffered an upset in the third round of the doubles competition, losing to the unheralded "pick-up team" of the young Australian Bill Coughlan and the Indiana collegiate star Dave Bloom. Arthur faced Coughlan again in the fourth round of the singles, extracting a measure of revenge, and he went on to crush Owen Davidson in the quarterfinals. In a semifinal match against Newcombe suspended by darkness in the second set, Arthur played one of the greatest matches of his career. With both players at the top of their game, the momentum went back and forth during most of the two-day struggle. After Arthur won the first set 12–10, Newcombe came back with a marathon 22–20 victory in the second. Only in the third set did Arthur begin to pull away, serving ace after ace to win the last two sets convincingly, 6–3, 6–2. Though thoroughly exhausted, he had earned a rematch against Emerson for the coveted title.

Predictably, Arthur's epic victory over Newcombe proved to be pyrrhic. With only a few hours to recover after his grueling semifinal endurance test, he found himself overmatched by Emerson, who had enjoyed a day of recovery after a semifinal match against Roche. The first eight games of the match were closely contested, but after that Emerson made short work of his young American challenger. In the 1966 final Arthur had managed to take a set from the perennial champion, but this time the Australian's dominance was total.[38]

Arthur was philosophical in defeat, knowing he had lost to one of the game's all-time greats. But he also felt the enduring power of the Australian mystique. A month earlier Emerson had led the Australian Davis Cup team to its third straight title, and, even more amazingly, its eleventh title in the last twelve years. The Americans' 1963 triumph had proven to be an anomaly, and Arthur wasn't sure if he and his teammates would ever catch up to the all but invincible Aussies. Back in November, an American friend had approached the Australian journalist Harry Gordon with a disturbing question: "How can our boys learn to play tennis like the Australians?" Other than suggesting that the Americans should kidnap Harry Hopman, Australia's legendary Davis Cup captain, Gordon had no easy answers for his friend. His only serious suggestions were to urge the Americans to adopt Hopman's "Spartan approach to training and discipline," and to open up the American tennis scene to a wider spectrum of its population. "In Australia," Gordon reminded his readers, "'Anyone for tennis?' means just that: anyone. Not just people who ski and play polo, or people who went to college, or people with white skins."[39]

Ruminations on the stifling limitations of race and class were always part of the mix for Ashe. But he had more mundane things to think about as he ended his sojourn in Australia. Leaving Adelaide on the last day of January, he had just enough time to fly home for the second annual Richmond Invitational Tennis Tournament. This time there would be no Arthur Ashe Day, only a welcome reunion with family and boyhood friends. The Richeys were also on hand, having accompanied Arthur on the flight back to the States, as were George MacCall, Cliff Drysdale, and four American Davis Cup veterans—Pasarell, Riessen, Froehling, and McKinley. For a fledgling tournament, the draw was impressive—a tribute to Arthur's stature among his peers. With little fanfare, several of the world's leading amateurs had come not only to compete but also to support their friend.

Pasarell and Ashe were teamed up in the doubles, but both hoped to challenge the defending singles champion, McKinley. Playing indoors on a fast canvas court, the two former roommates ran through the field. Facing each other in the final, they put on a serve-and-volley show that wowed a biracial crowd of 3,300, most of whom were disappointed when Pasarell emerged victorious. Later in the day, there was some recompense when the two singles finalists joined forces to overwhelm Drysdale and Ron Holmberg in the doubles final. Overall the hometown favorite made a good showing, but the tournament's most important achievement was the degree to which a still divided city had adjusted to interracial competition.[40]

Arthur took all of this in with a mixture of skepticism and relief, realizing that the orchestrated scene in the public arena masked a darker reality. While he could sense the subtle changes sweeping over Richmond in the wake of the civil rights acts of the mid-1960s, he also knew that, with few exceptions, the traditional patterns of racial segregation and economic and social stratification still held sway. The local code of Jim Crow segregation had loosened with respect to public accommodations, and there seemed to be more respectful dialogue across racial lines. Yet some by-products of the civil rights revolution were hard for Ashe to swallow, notably the closing and bulldozing of Brook Field Park.

The parkland had already been cleared by the time of Arthur's visit, and by the end of 1967 the area surrounding his boyhood home would be completely transformed into a sprawling federal post office complex. Redevelopment of the broader Jackson Ward neighborhood had begun several years earlier with the construction of the Richmond–Petersburg Highway (later part of the I-95 Interstate), which removed many historic structures and effectively bisected the northeast corner of the city. Arthur hardly recognized much of the streetscape that had been so familiar to him at the beginning of the decade. Most of his extended family was still there, but Jackson Ward's status as a viable residential community was under siege, threatened by un-savory real estate speculation and physical deterioration.

Arthur was pleased, however, to discover that his father, now past fifty, had survived the Brook Field demolition by diversifying his employment and being more entrepreneurial than ever. When Deford interviewed him in August 1966, Arthur Sr. not only had a job with the city but also a thriving two-truck landscaping business. The enterprising leader of the Ashe clan owned "a car and a 21-foot motorboat" and had "just built a new house out in Louisa County with virtually nothing but his own two hands." When the journalist John McPhee visited the house in Gum Spring, Arthur Sr. was commuting to Richmond, supervising eight employees, and juggling three jobs, including a special police officer pool and tennis court supervisor po-sition with the Richmond Department of Recreation and Parks, and a jan-itorial business specializing in office buildings, banks, and medical centers.

Somehow Arthur Sr. also found time to oversee the annual court in-stallation at the Richmond Invitational, and to spearhead an effort to build a tennis complex in northeast Richmond's Battery Park neighborhood as a substitute for the Brook Field courts lost to the post office development. He even owned four rental properties in addition to the Gum Spring house. A seemingly tireless worker, he had achieved economic security while some-how finding ample time to fish and hunt on the weekends. His only major concern seemed to be the likelihood of his two sons finding themselves in harm's way on the battlefield.[41]

Arthur shared his father's concern for Johnnie and was haunted by the thought that his little brother might not make it back from Vietnam. He was less worried about his own situation, having been assured that the Army planned to keep him away from the war. While he had yet to receive formal orders, West Point's Coach Cullen, with MacCall's blessing, had quietly ar-ranged a stateside assignment. Slated for a position in the Adjutant General's Corps, which he termed the "chairborne infantry," he would report to the Adjutant General's School at Fort Benjamin in Lawrence, Indiana, during the last week of February, and would remain there for nine weeks before moving to West Point. As he explained in the final chapter of *Advantage Ashe*, written just before he went on active duty, he did not want to shirk his duty by accepting "special soft spots," yet at the same time he was willing to go along with the Army's decision "to put me on tennis courts as a sort of showpiece." While the moral ambiguity of his position was obvious, he had no choice but to accept his good fortune.

During his final weeks of civilian life, Arthur was confident the Army would fulfill its promise to place him at West Point. His brother Johnnie, who was all too familiar with the vagaries of military life, was not sure. Accordingly, without telling his older brother, he hatched a plan to extend his tour in Vietnam in exchange for a promise that Arthur would remain stateside. After broaching the idea with several of his superiors, he received assurances that military policy would not allow two brothers to serve in the same combat zone at the same time. While there is no evidence that Johnnie's noble gesture had any impact on his brother's assignment, the effort spoke volumes about the Ashe brothers' devotion to one another. The fact that Johnnie made sure his older brother knew nothing about his behind-the-scenes maneuvering until many years later made his selfless act all the more remarkable.

Despite Arthur's physical separation from his family in the years since 1961, the familial bond had remained strong. So he was grateful for the opportunity to spend time with his father, stepmother, and other close relatives before going off to the Army. By the time he left Richmond on February 9, 1967, bound for Philadelphia's annual indoor international tournament, he felt emotionally renewed and ready for the challenges ahead. The most pressing challenge, other than playing well in Philadelphia and in the upcoming national indoor championships in Salisbury, Maryland, was to put the finishing touches on the final chapter of *Advantage Ashe*. Writing a memoir at the tender age of twenty-three had proven more difficult than he had imagined when he and Gewecke had begun the project in early 1966. But his ability to express himself in print, and his willingness to reveal his thoughts and opinions to the public, had grown during the past year. Gradually overcoming his natural shyness, he felt more comfortable speaking out on issues that mattered to him.[42]

One such issue was the American Davis Cup team's perennially poor showing on clay, a point he made clear in a lengthy interview published in *The New York Times* in February. The team's failures on clay, he maintained, could be traced to a lack of practice on the slow surface—and to the USLTA's refusal to address the problem. "I sometimes wonder," he confessed, "whether the United States Lawn Tennis Association wants to win the cup back, after what has been happening to us." "How," he asked plaintively, "are we going to beat these guys—Mandarino, Koch, Santana—on the slow courts they practically live on when we play only two or three clay tournaments a year?" The root of the problem was the long-standing USLTA policy prohibiting extended summer play in Europe. "When Wimbledon ends in early July," he pointed out, "we are required to be back home within a week so that there will be somebody to play in our own grass tournaments. Our clay court season is a joke." Considering that more than 90 percent of the recent Davis Cup ties had been played on clay, the USLTA's policy was, in his view, tantamount to surrender.[43]

Arthur knew this sharp criticism would generate considerable consternation in the higher circles of the USLTA. American tennis officials rarely countenanced open dissent by players, and no one expected the most well-mannered player on the tour to be the one to lead the charge against the grass court crowd. There was less surprise, however, among the people who knew him best, those who had watched him mature into a confident and strong-willed young man. "Arthur's gone a long way in four years from the guy I first knew," Jean-Edouard Baker assured Gewecke during a 1966 interview. While Baker conceded that his former roommate was still "basically shy" and an "introvert," the new Arthur Ashe was "a lot more sophisticated" than the innocent, wide-eyed eighteen-year-old freshman he had met in 1962. In another interview, Luis Glass marveled at Ashe's "internal strength" that was beginning to surface for all to see. Much of his behavior was still ruled by a determination to maintain a clean image, to avoid, as his sophomore roommate David Reed put it, "the least little thing that might offend people." But there were now enough exceptions to this reticence to suggest he was on the path to purposeful assertion, and perhaps even to full-blown activism.[44]

In the closing chapter of *Advantage Ashe*, titled "Looking Ahead," he provided a hint of things to come in a lengthy commentary on the dismal prospects for black tennis players aspiring to join him on the tour. The heart of the problem remained the lack of opportunity for young blacks to develop their skills at an early age. "Many of them are born with the reflexes, stamina, and desire that a top player must have," he insisted. "But where will they get the financing and coaching?" he asked. As for the problem of funding, he pointed out that "a coach costs $10 or $15 an hour" and "rackets and stringing come to $750 a year." "Where can Negro families get that kind of money?" he demanded. "Tennis is still mostly for the country-club types," he concluded, predicting "it will probably stay that way for another generation."[45]

As Arthur acknowledged, part of the problem was tennis's lack of popularity in the black community. "Negro boys look up to Willie Mays, Lew Alcindor, Bill Russell, Floyd Patterson, Bob Hayes—and try to follow them," he wrote with more than a touch of regret. "I don't think Negro boys are impressed that much by what I've done. I'm the only one. If there were a bunch of us it would be different." At this point, his lament was limited to a few pages in a memoir. But within two years he would join forces with Pasarell to do something concrete about the barriers of race and class that plagued the game he loved. Together—along with the former University of Virginia tennis star Sheridan "Sherry" Snyder—the two UCLA alums would found the National Junior Tennis League (NJTL) in 1969.

The NJTL was designed "to gain and hold the attention of young people in the inner cities and other poor environments," but Arthur made sure the organization's charge went well beyond tennis instruction. He and his partners promised to teach aspiring players "about matters more important than tennis," and from the outset the NJTL's local chapters stressed the importance of education, self-discipline, and personal growth. One of Arthur's most important legacies, the NJTL would eventually attract hundreds of thousands of members, transforming the profile of tennis in inner-city neighborhoods across the nation. At the time of his death, a quarter century after its founding, the organization's impact on the racial and class makeup of professional tennis was not all that Arthur had hoped it would be. But this disappointment was tempered by victories elsewhere. Consistent with the founders' ideals, the NJTL's most important accomplishments took place off the court.

The NJTL's emphases on education, character development, and the cultivation of skills that enhanced economic opportunity grew out of the fear that single-minded dedication to sports had become a serious problem in African American culture. As Arthur later put it, many black children were spending too much time on the playing field and not enough time in the library. One remedy for this imbalance was to use tennis as an entry point for involvement in off-court programs promoting educational and personal growth. Putting this strategy into action changed many lives, including Arthur's. Over time his activities on behalf of inner-city children led him down a path dedicated to service and philanthropy. Indeed, this commitment to public engagement, which first emerged during the waning years of the turbulent 1960s, would eventually become the driving force of his life. While he was still determined to excel on the court and to encourage young black players to follow his lead, his priorities began to shift dramatically in 1967 and 1968. More and more, he came to see his own athletic success as a means of acquiring moral and social influence, as a source of leverage rather than an end in itself. During his years in the Army, and in the decades that followed, he would demonstrate time and again that his greatest gifts transcended the game of tennis.[46]

TEN

OPENINGS

∎

ASHE'S LAST HURRAH BEFORE reporting for duty was the final round of a new international invitational indoor tournament held at the Concord Hotel in Kiamesha Lake, New York, a little more than an hour's drive from West Point. The title match, won by Ashe over Thomas Koch, was held on Wednesday, February 22, two days before he was scheduled to begin his training assignment at Fort Benjamin Harrison. Flying to Indianapolis, where he caught a bus to the base, he arrived on time—a bit breathless but ready for duty. After checking in on Friday, he received word he was free to travel to Cleveland the next day to compete in the Western Indoor Championships. And after that, a second leave would allow him to participate in the second annual Vanderbilt invitational tournament in New York City scheduled for the first week of March.

The Army's apparent willingness to go out of its way to accommodate Ashe's tennis schedule went beyond his expectations. He decided to make the most of it before his superiors changed their minds. On Tuesday, the last day of February and his fifth day of military service, he defeated Clark Graebner for the Western title before returning to Indiana. Unable to reach New York in time for his opening round-robin match on Thursday, he convinced the Vanderbilt tournament officials to delay his first match until Saturday. Harried by all of this back-and-forth travel, he arrived in New York just in time to play back-to-back matches, one of which he somehow managed to win. During the next twenty-four hours, he played six matches in an attempt to catch up with the field. But on Sunday evening, he ran out of time and defaulted his final match in order to catch a 9:45 flight back to Indiana. Arriving in Indianapolis after midnight, he took an early morning bus to Fort Harrison, no doubt collapsing in exhaustion when he finally reached his barracks. A few hours later he stumbled into class for his first full day of instruction. Though accustomed to tight schedules and competing commitments, he had never experienced anything quite like his first ten days in the Army.

The previous year, the Vanderbilt tournament had shaken up his life in the span of a week as he impulsively proposed to Pat Battles. But he hadn't expected so much excitement this time. Just a quiet send-off and perhaps a mock salute or two from his fellow competitors would have been fine. But his military status had driven him to attempt a balancing act that bordered on the impossible.[1]

He found time the following week to settle in at the fort. Yet a few days later he was off to Puerto Rico to participate in a tournament at the Caribe Hilton. With a week's leave, he invited his fiancée to join him in San Juan, where she could meet Pasarell, who was home on spring break from his last semester at UCLA. Ironically, the trip actually ended his romantic entanglement. "We took separate rooms," he recalled, "and planned to have a nice week while I played the tournament. But I began to have second thoughts about getting married." Before the week was over, he told Pat he couldn't go through with the marriage. Though disappointed, she was not surprised. Their courtship had been tepid from the beginning, and it was obvious he had never fully committed to the relationship. Describing the breakup years later, Arthur confessed: "Pat took it all rather calmly, more calmly than I did." For a time, he "felt ashamed of the breakup," knowing how much embarrassment it brought to both families. But he soon "realized it had been the right decision."[2]

In truth, after his return from Puerto Rico Arthur was so busy with tennis and his data-processing classes that he didn't have much time to think about his love life. As March drew to a close, he was back on the court, first in Indianapolis, where he faced Koch again in an exhibition of international team competition, and later at Brookville on Long Island. At Brookville, he finished first in the round-robin format, dispatching a series of formidable challengers including Froehling, Scott, and McKinley. Before rushing back to base, he had just enough time to accept the winner's trophy from the tournament director and former University of Virginia tennis ace Sherry Snyder, who would later help him found the NJTL.[3]

Ashe's first two months of active duty would have been even more hectic if he had participated in the first round of the 1967 Davis Cup competition. But when his teammates traveled to Trinidad in late April for the opening Americas Zone tie against the British West Indies team, he stayed behind in Indiana. MacCall—who felt his team had little to fear from the West Indians—decided to save Arthur for the future rounds. While the Army had promised his availability for Davis Cup play, the nervous captain knew there were limits to the amount of leave the Army was willing to grant. With Ralston out of the picture. Arthur was the obvious choice to fill the number one singles slot. The safest path was to let others carry the load in Trinidad, leaving Arthur to join the team in the second round, when the likely opponent would be the powerful Mexican team. The Americans eliminated the West Indians without losing a match, confirming the wisdom of MacCall's strategy.

While the American squad was vanquishing the West Indians, Arthur was spending his final days at Fort Harrison. With the completion of his nine weeks of training, he was ready to begin his assignment at West Point. But the Army responded favorably to a special thirty-day leave request from MacCall and postponed the West Point reporting for a month. The second-round tie against Mexico was scheduled for the last week in May, and the long leave gave Arthur time to prepare to face Rafael Osuna and the Mexicans' newest star, nineteen-year-old Marcelo Lara. Since the tie would take place on slow clay in Mexico City, preparation figured to be especially important. Arthur spent most of May getting ready for the Mexicans, but he also took some time to conduct an inner-city clinic in Brooklyn and to visit with relatives still puzzling over why he had canceled his engagement.[4]

Part of his preparation involved getting acclimated to extreme exertion in a hot climate, a goal that took him to Atlanta during the first week in May. Joined by the entire American squad, he played in the Atlanta Invitational tournament, where he was the top seed. This was his first appearance in a Deep South city, and he was understandably nervous about how he would be received in a state that had just elected the white supremacist demagogue Lester Maddox to the governorship. Well aware that virtually all of Atlanta's private tennis facilities still barred blacks from membership, he feared the worst. But he made it through the week without any major incidents; playing well, he reached the semifinals before faltering against Marty Riessen. Thankful for the supportive presence of Pasarell, who knew what his close friend was going through, he left town with a sigh of relief and renewed confidence that he could face any challenge, even in the haunted land of Rhett Butler and Scarlett O'Hara.[5]

By the time Arthur and his teammates arrived in Mexico City, both his nerves and his backhand were under control. A week earlier MacCall had announced that the second lieutenant on leave from West Point would play the first singles match against the Mexicans on May 27. Having withheld Arthur from the singles competition on the clay courts of Porto Alegre with disastrous results, he was not going to make the same mistake again. The previous August, while Arthur was still at Fort Lewis, the American Davis Cup team had defeated the Mexicans 5–0 on a hard court surface in Cleveland. But MacCall anticipated that it would be much more difficult to beat the Mexicans on their familiar home clay.

Despite MacCall's concern, the high altitude in Mexico City actually lessened the Mexicans' advantage. While the light air at 7,400 feet posed a conditioning challenge for anyone accustomed to lower altitudes, it also quickened the clay, making the pace not nearly "as slow as it is on this surface at sea level." Osuna admitted as much the day before the tie began. "The game here is different from tennis anywhere else," he assured reporters. "It is different from clay and it is different from grass and cement."

Whatever the balance of advantages and disadvantages, the tie did not begin well for the Americans. In the first singles match played at the cavernous Chapultepec Sports Center, Osuna fought back from a 2–1 set deficit and a service break in the fourth to overcome Richey. Though eight years younger than Osuna, the Texan ran out of gas by the middle of the fourth set, losing nine games in a row and dropping the fifth set 6–1. Down 1–0 as a team, the Americans looked to Ashe to even the score in the second match against Marcelo Lara. Having never played against the young Mexican, or even seen him play, he did not know what to expect. Within minutes of taking the court, he realized Lara was no pushover. With the crowd urging him on, Lara hit several backhand winners that seemed to unnerve Ashe, who served up several double faults before a rain delay gave him time to regain his composure. Eventually he gained control, winning the first set 7–5 and the second 6–2. Lara came back strong in the third, but after a second rain delay Ashe closed out the match 7–5. The team score was now tied.

On the second day, Graebner and Riessen won a surprisingly easy victory over Osuna and his young partner, Joaquín Loyo-Mayo, putting the American team into the lead going into the final day. Facing Osuna in the second round of singles matches, Ashe got off to a strong start in the first set and withstood a spirited comeback by Osuna to win 8–6. After that Osuna faded noticeably; unable to counter Ashe's big serve and exhausted by several long rallies, he managed to win only five games in the last two sets. Looking fresh without "the slightest sign of fatigue," according to one observer, a smiling Ashe marked the victory by walking over to the American bench and embracing MacCall, who must have been the happiest man in the stadium. For the time being, at least, the monkey was off his back, and the quest for the Cup was alive and well. A few minutes later Richey and Lara took the court to play the now meaningless final singles match, but a violent rain and hailstorm postponed the formal end of the tie until the following morning. Richey eventually won the match in five sets, but Ashe was not there to see it. With his leave about to expire, he rushed to the airport to board his return flight to New York.[6]

The next round would be played in mid-June at the Pancho Segura Tennis Club in Guayaquil, Ecuador, but Ashe had already informed MacCall it was highly unlikely he would be available. During the month of June, he would be busy getting squared away and learning his new job at West Point, and it was doubtful the Army would grant him another extended leave only three weeks after his return from Mexico. Neither he nor MacCall expected his absence in Guayaquil to pose much of a problem. Ecuador, in only its sixth year of Davis Cup play, had never had much success in international competition and had only reached the Americas Zone final by upsetting Argentina. So it didn't appear that Ashe's presence would be necessary for the heavily favored Americans to advance to the next round.

Even so, MacCall, who knew from his bitter experience in Brazil that anything could happen on clay, decided to request another leave for his top singles player. To his surprise, the Army granted his request on June 8, nine days before the opening matches in Guayaquil. Arthur soon joined his teammates in Ecuador, but not before honoring his commitment to play Pasarell in a high school stadium in the Bronx to help launch a Philip Morris–backed inner-city tennis program. In characteristic fashion, he was trying to do it all, keeping faith with his principles while representing his nation and advancing his tennis career.

Arthur had never been in Ecuador, and he was a bit surprised by the gritty character of the port city of Guayaquil. Pancho Segura, for whom the city's prime tennis venue was named, had told him a few things about his home country during their sessions at the Beverly Hills Tennis Club. But he had never mentioned the Ecuadorans' embattled sense of national pride born of colonial exploitation and condescension from the larger states of South America. In the nation's tennis circles and elsewhere there was a passion to be taken seriously and to achieve respectful inclusion in the international scene. They had been waiting for a breakthrough, and the Davis Cup battle with the mighty Americans provided them with a golden opportunity to enhance their national profile, as Arthur and his teammates would soon discover.

The tie began well enough for the Americans, with Richey overpowering Ecuador's second-best player, twenty-one-year-old Francisco "Pancho" Guzmán, in four sets. But the expected American victory in the second singles match, which pitted Ashe against twenty-seven-year-old Miguel Olvera, was in doubt from the opening games of the second set. After winning the first set 6–4, Ashe lost control of his normally reliable serve, committing a cluster of double faults that provided Olvera with an opening. Seven years earlier, as the first unseeded winner of the Cincinnati Masters tournament, the Ecuadoran had shown flashes of brilliance, and he seemed to return to his top form against Ashe. The slightly built, almost gaunt Olvera had only recently recovered from a serious bout of tuberculosis, yet the favored American was down two sets to one by the time a local curfew suspended play at 6 p.m. That night Ashe huddled with MacCall, and Gonzales to come up with a strategy to counter Olvera's momentum. But when the match resumed the next morning, Arthur was uncharacteristically flat and unable to quiet the crowd as it cheered Olvera's crisp and accurate shotmaking. The final score in the fourth and decisive set was 6–2, leaving Ashe with his first defeat in nine Davis Cup singles matches. Overcome with emotion, Danny Carrera, the Ecuadorans' captain, raced onto the court and tried to jump the net, but caught his foot on the tape and ended up with a broken leg.

The next day, with their injured captain cheering from the sidelines, Olvera and Guzmán lost the first set at love before rallying to win three of the next four. Suddenly the American squad was down 2–1 and in danger of suffering one of the biggest upsets in Davis Cup history. To avoid elimination the Americans would now have to win both single matches on the final day of play. After a sleepless night punctuated by vomiting related to a stomach disorder, Arthur took the court against Guzmán in the first match of the second round of singles. Despite some lingering queasiness, he quickly established his dominance, winning the first set 6–0. But Guzmán came back to win the next two sets 6–4, 6–2. Fighting for his life, Arthur took advantage of Guzmán as the Ecuadoran tired in the fourth, winning for a second time at love. At this point, the extreme swings in momentum had created a bizarre stalemate, leaving the frenzied crowd with an almost unbearable string of highs and lows as the match and the tie hung in the balance.

In the end, Guzmán proved to be the man of the hour, outlasting Arthur 6–3 in the final set. The Americans watched in stunned silence as deliriously happy fans stormed the court and carried Guzmán around the arena on their shoulders. Moments later, officials of the Segura club doused their hero in champagne, kicking off a celebration that lasted into the night and beyond. The next morning the headline in one of Ecuador's most popular dailies, *El Universo*, trumpeted the shocking upset as "*La Victoria para Historia*," which even the linguistically challenged Americans could decipher as "A Victory for History." Later in the day, Harry Hopman chimed in with the speculation that Ashe had not played nearly enough in recent weeks "to bring him to his peak." "Obviously," the Aussie captain concluded, "his army duties have restricted his match practice and general condition."[7]

Such statements put Ashe in a difficult position. He did not want to make excuses or blame the Army for a weekend of mediocre play; and with more than eighteen months of service to go, he did not want to do anything to endanger the gentleman's agreement that split his time between tennis and his military routine. Yet he knew better than anyone that there was probably some truth to Hopman's observation. As he later conceded, it was not easy to navigate the "delicate path between my roles as Lieutenant Arthur Ashe, U.S. Army, and Arthur Ashe, tennis player." When the Ecuadoran tie was over, his teammates flew off to Wimbledon while he returned to his duties at West Point.[8]

Arthur was sad to miss Wimbledon, but considering the alternatives, he did not view his commitment to the Army as a heavy burden. With so many of his fellow soldiers slogging through the jungles of Vietnam, he didn't feel right questioning the terms of his arrangement or complaining about his relatively cushy duty on the banks of the Hudson. After he got the hang of it, his life at West Point was at worst tolerable and at best a good fit with his personal interests and skills. He was good at his job at the data processing center, and he enjoyed his collaboration with Coach Cullen and the late afternoon practice sessions with the freshman team. Relatively busy but hardly overworked, he had plenty of free time to read, listen to music, or take in a movie. He also had a new girlfriend, with two photographs of her proudly displayed on his work desk. Since his arrival at West Point he had accumulated a variety of new friends among the staff, and from the summer of 1968 on he enjoyed numerous weekend outings with his buddy Pasarell, who was serving as an enlisted man at Stewart Air Force Base, located a mere ten miles up the Hudson from the Military Academy. On other occasions, he visited relatives in New Jersey or Virginia, taking advantage of his return to the East Coast after six years west of the Mississippi.[9]

All in all, Arthur had few complaints about his circumstances in the weeks and months leading up to his twenty-fourth birthday. He and Pasarell were still ranked first and second in the nation, and the Army continued to keep a loose rein on his comings and goings. Spending pretty much the entire second half of July on the road, he traveled first to the National Clay Court Championships in Milwaukee, where he was the top seed and the defending champion. Fearing he would be a little rusty after six weeks away from the tour, he was surprised how easily he advanced through the field, ultimately meeting and defeating Riessen in the title match. Normally he would have left Milwaukee and circled back east to play in the Pennsylvania grass championships. But instead, at the Army's insistence, he flew to Winnipeg, Manitoba, to represent the United States in the Pan American Games.[10]

The situation in Winnipeg was less than ideal, with the American tennis contingent missing virtually all of the nation's top players. Arthur had no choice but to be there, but the rest of his peers were off playing the grass circuit, uninterested in participating in a struggling international competition dominated by track and field. "Of the two other American men there," the sportswriter Frank Litsky pointed out, "one is ranked 36th nationally and the other is unranked. None of the three American women is ranked in the top 20." Indeed, Arthur told Litsky that the team was a "joke," though he did his best to soldier on. Eliminated from the medal competition in singles by Koch, he rebounded by teaming with twenty-year-old Janie Albert, the daughter of the famed Stanford quarterback Frankie Albert, to win the Gold Medal in Mixed Doubles.[11]

Following the Winnipeg appearance, Ashe's competitive tennis would be limited to a few benefits and exhibition matches for the remainder of the year. With the defeated American Davis Cup team on hiatus until the following spring, there was less incentive for the Army to grant him leave. So for the better part of a year he stayed close to home. While he often practiced with the cadets at West Point in an effort to keep sharp, he had little chance to test himself against top-flight competition. One exception was the Nassau Tournament held on Long Island in mid-August, when he played and lost badly to Chuck McKinley in the quarterfinals. Adding insult to injury, *The New York Times* reporter covering the match remarked that Ashe had done pretty well for someone who is "only a week-end player now."[12]

To Arthur's dismay, he missed the 1967 U.S. National Championships at Forest Hills, a mere two-hour train ride from his bachelor officer's quarters. Unable to secure a two-week leave that would allow him to play in the most important tournament of the year, he had to settle for a one-day pass and a special exhibition appearance. Joined by Emerson, Drysdale, and Osuna, he conducted a clinic for 1,800 kids from all over New York. The unprecedented event was cosponsored by several corporations, most notably the Pepsi-Cola Company and the Clark Gum Company division of the Philip Morris empire headed by Joe Cullman. Having already hired Osuna, Cullman was signaling to Ashe that the job offer they had discussed in 1966 was still on the table. Sharing a common commitment to inner-city youth and uplift through tennis instruction, the two men enjoyed a deepening relationship that would bear considerable fruit in the years to come.

Three weeks after the Forest Hills clinic, Ashe joined Froehling, Scott, and two other players for a two-day benefit tournament held at a high school in the town of Lawrence on the south shore of Long Island. To participate in the benefit, Ashe had to reorganize his work schedule and rush back and forth between West Point and the high school. But these small-scale charity events were becoming increasingly important to him. They made him feel good about himself and took some of the sting out of his temporary absence from competitive tennis. Moving from words to action, he had found a way to translate his tennis skills, and the social and economic opportunities they had afforded him, into community involvement. His memoir *Advantage Ashe* was released the same week as the Lawrence benefit, and he was beginning to regret some of the more conservative passages in the book. In a sense, his rising consciousness was moving so fast he couldn't keep up with himself. Increasingly aware of the distance between his privileged life and the difficult circumstances facing the vast majority of African Americans, he was developing a determination to give back, not just to succeed. The transition from self-absorbed athlete to committed activist had begun.[13]

Ashe's emerging consciousness of an imperfect social order in need of radical reform was not the only change affecting his life that year. As he adjusted to his growing awareness of the world beyond the baseline, as well as to the limits imposed by his military status, powerful forces were moving into position to change the game of tennis forever. In the halcyon decades to come, 1967 would be remembered as the seedtime of Open Tennis. After nearly a decade of false starts, a system compatible with the commercialization of modern sports was becoming a realistic prospect. The age of the "shamateur" and the concomitant demonization of playing for money was finally coming to a close, heralding the impending arrival of a brave new world of opportunity for Ashe and other talented tennis players.[14]

Ironically, the man most responsible for this turn of events was Herman David, the chairman of the All England Club, generally considered the most hidebound of tennis institutions. A bona fide member of the British elite and a former captain of his nation's Davis Cup team, David was determined to preserve Wimbledon's status as one of the premier sporting events in the world, and surprisingly enough he was willing to dispense with tradition to do it. Alarmed by the failure of tennis to keep pace with the major sports that had already adapted to commercialization and the media opportunities of the television era, he became, in the journalist Richard Evans's words, the "brave man" who "kicked Open Tennis out of the womb."

David had been touting some form of Open Tennis since the late 1950s, but the birthing process began in earnest at Wimbledon in the spring of 1967 when he agreed to sponsor a professional tournament played on the hallowed grounds of Centre Court. Held in mid-July, the precedent-setting tournament featured eight of the world's finest players—including Rod Laver, who had not played at Wimbledon since turning professional in 1962. The final match, a thrilling struggle between Laver and Ken Rosewall, drew a capacity crowd and was broadcast in color on the BBC2 television network. It was all a huge success, and the public's obvious enthusiasm and the sizable profits gained from the event were more than enough to convince David and many of his colleagues on the British Lawn Tennis Association's (LTA) central committee that the time had come to initiate a new, more inclusive era of competitive tennis.

By November, David had gathered enough support to push through a resolution committing the LTA to an Open Wimbledon in 1968. The decision shook the tennis establishment to its foundation as David declared in so many words that the revolution had begun. As Evans later paraphrased the declaration: "The All England Club Championships would be open to all categories of player and that if the ILTF didn't like it, they could lump it." "From that moment on," Evans continued, "life in tennis was never quite the same again." [15]

The overall reaction of the various national tennis federations was mixed, but the support for radical change gathered considerable momentum after Bob Kelleher, the former Davis Cup captain who had just ascended to the presidency of the USLTA, convinced a majority of delegates at the USLTA's national meeting to empower him "to break with the ILTF if necessary." This was a brash move, considering that the British LTA was already under the threat of expulsion, but Kelleher's diplomatic skills proved decisive when he traveled to Paris for a special ILTF meeting in early March. At that crucial

meeting, he worked out a tentative compromise that ratified national auton-
omy on the issue of Open Tennis.

An unfortunate element of the compromise, one that would later complicate the implementation of the new system, was acceptance of a formula
that placed players in four separate categories ranging from full-blown professional to registered (or "authorized") player. The creation of the latter
category, which stipulated that certain players could only accept prize money
at a limited number of tournaments, represented a desperate attempt by traditionalists to hang on to an ethos of amateurism controlled by the national
federations. Even with this complication, however, the basic agreement
coming out of the Paris meeting supported the idea of Open Tennis, an advance ratified at a second ILTF meeting at the end of the month. Faced with
the prospect of a full-scale revolt by the powerful British, American, and
Swedish federations, the delegates at the second meeting approved a plan for
twelve experimental Open tournaments in 1968.[16]

Ashe, like everyone else in the tennis world, watched with amazement
as this drama unfolded. While he still had a year of military service to go, his
plans for the future now had to be reevaluated in light of the extraordinary
developments of the past six months. Ranked second among American amateurs at the beginning of the year, just behind Pasarell, he stood to gain from
Open Tennis—if he could regain the level of play he had reached before
entering the Army. Not yet twenty-five, he had every reason to believe his
best years were ahead of him, even though the competition from younger
players was getting stiffer. At the Sugar Bowl tournament in New Orleans
in late December, he had barely survived his opening round match against
the reigning NCAA singles champion from USC, twenty-year-old Bob Lutz.
When he faced the twenty-eight-year-old Yugoslavian star Niki Pilic in the
title match, he felt relieved to be playing someone with a few years on him.[17]

Ashe managed to defeat Pilic, but he worried he was losing ground every
week he languished at West Point. Some rivals—like Ralston, Newcombe,
and Roche—had already turned professional, and the remaining amateurs
had the advantage of playing week after week against tough competition.
Fortunately for Ashe, he would do far less languishing during the winter
and spring of 1968 than he had expected. Benefiting from a very liberal leave
policy, he spent much of January and February playing in a series of tournaments that took him from Puerto Rico to Long Island to Richmond, where
he won the singles title on his third try—and later to Philadelphia, Salisbury,
and upstate New York's Kiamesha Lake resort.

In between the Salisbury and Kiamesha tournaments, Arthur stopped

at West Point just long enough to learn he was being promoted to first lieutenant. March was only slightly less hectic as he traveled to California for the
Pacific Coast Doubles tournament before ending the month with appearances at the Mexico City International Championships and the Madison
Square Garden Challenge matches in New York City. In the final match of
the Madison Square Garden tournament, he defeated Emerson in straight
sets, in what turned out to be the Australian's last amateur competition. The
day after the final, Emerson signed a pro contract with George MacCall's
recently organized National Tennis League (NTL), a rival to a similar pro
tour associated with Lamar Hunt, the Texas oil baron who had helped to
found the American Football League in 1959.[18]

In 1967, Hunt joined forces with the New Orleans promoter Dave
Dixon to form a new professional tour known as World Championship Tennis (WCT). Offering an unprecedented level of prize money, WCT would
have a major influence on the evolution of Open Tennis. The new age began
with the signing of a cluster of players known as the "Handsome Eight," a
talented group that included three of the four semifinalists from the 1967
Wimbledon singles competition. Bankrolled by Hunt, WCT held its first
tournament in Sydney in January 1968 and followed up a month later with
its first American tournament, held in Hunt's adopted hometown of Kansas
City.

A spate of WCT tournaments soon followed, and when the first event
of the Open era was held at Bournemouth, England, in late April, Roche,
Newcombe, Drysdale, and the other members of the Handsome Eight were
off playing pro tennis somewhere else. The quality of the draw at Bournemouth did not match the significance of the occasion, and most of the professionals present were affiliated with the NTL and George MacCall, who
had abandoned amateur tennis and the Davis Cup wars with obvious relief. There was considerable interest in how the amateurs would fare against
professionals, especially after two of the world's best pros, Roy Emerson
and Pancho Gonzales, lost to Mark Cox—an unheralded twenty-four-year-
old left-hander from Cambridge. In a later round Laver dispatched Cox in
straight sets, avenging the pros' honor, and the eventual tournament winner
was Rosewall, who took away the Open era's inaugural top prize of a little
over £2,000.

Though paltry by the standards that would soon rule the game of tennis, Rosewall's windfall represented a small fortune to Ashe, who had been
earning less than $4,000 a year as a second lieutenant. The allure of finan-
cial gain had never been a primary motivating force for him, but he began

to consider the option of turning professional once his military career was over. His primary reservation about committing to a future on the pro tour was uncertainty about how it would affect his eligibility for Davis Cup play. Under the current rules, professionals were barred from Davis Cup competition, and there was no clear indication that this rule would change. Sacrificing his right to represent his country was unthinkable for Ashe, especially after Donald Dell replaced MacCall as Davis Cup captain in March 1968.[19]

Five years older than Arthur, Dell had been a star collegiate player at Yale and a member of the American Davis Cup squads in 1961 and 1963. Their paths first crossed in 1964 at Wimbledon, but other members of the Dell family—Donald's younger brother Dickie and their father—had known Arthur since the early days when Dickie and Arthur were competing in the same USLTA Junior tournaments. On at least one occasion, the Dells gave Arthur a ride back to Washington, where he caught a bus to Lynchburg. Dickie and Arthur kept in touch, and after Donald completed law school at the University of Virginia in 1963 and joined the tour, he and Arthur struck up a friendship that would change both of their lives. Donald had ambitions beyond the mastery of tennis and didn't remain on the tour very long. Although he eventually developed an extremely successful career in sports management, he turned first to law and politics, securing a position as an aide to Sargent Shriver, the head of the Office of Equal Opportunity and the brother-in-law of the recently slain President John F. Kennedy. Eventually, as a member of the Kennedys' inner circle, he became close to former attorney general Robert Kennedy, who asked him to serve as his advance man in California during the 1968 presidential primary campaign.

During the turbulent spring that saw President Johnson's unexpected withdrawal from the race on March 31 and Dr. Martin Luther King's assassination in Memphis five days later, Ashe's and Dell's like-minded politics, combined with their shared passion to reclaim the Davis Cup, drew them together. Dell encouraged his friend to get more involved in politics, but he was not the only person pressing the young lieutenant to assume an activist stance.[20]

Two years earlier, the Reverend Jefferson Rogers, the pastor of the Church of the Redeemer, Presbyterian, in Washington, D.C., whom Arthur had known since childhood, had reentered his life after Rogers's son had been barred from integrating the 1966 Mid-Atlantic tournament in Richmond. Over time Rogers became something of a father confessor as Arthur wrestled with the responsibility to speak out against social and racial injustice—and a morally questionable war in Southeast Asia that Dr. King had been condemning since 1965.

Ever since his arrival at West Point, Arthur had harbored doubts about the wisdom of waging an all-out war in Vietnam. In the spring of 1968, in the wake of the devastating Tet Offensive earlier in the year, he became disillusioned with the war effort. To him, the reason for fighting was too murky, and the cost in lives was just too high. "During one stretch," he later recalled, "it seemed there was a funeral every day at West Point. I was saddened to see so many young men, so young they had not even been promoted to first lieutenant, brought back in boxes that reminded us of the consequences of our business. I never thought this war made sense." Adding to his sadness was the obvious connection between the senselessness of the war and racial inequality. "Seeing the dead and knowing that a disproportionate number of young blacks were paying the ultimate price for faulty American policy," he wrote in 1981, "moved me toward firm opposition to our involvement in Southeast Asia, even with my military status."[21]

On issues ranging from war and peace to civil rights, the Reverend Rogers saw himself as a liberal counterpoint to the conservative counsel of Arthur Ashe Sr., whom he knew and didn't especially like. He had come to regard Arthur Jr. as almost a surrogate son, even though he detected few signs of religious faith in his young friend. He knew all too well how stultifying the ritualistic but often empty emotionalism of some forms of African American religion could be—including, he suspected, the kind of religion Arthur had been exposed to in his youth. More than anything else, the reverend wanted to infuse him with the uplifting spirit of the Social Gospel, the powerful force that animated his own life. A towering bear of a man with a deep and mellifluous voice persuasive enough to suggest divine origin, Rogers possessed a natural charm that often proved irresistible to anyone ensnared in his moral orbit. Certainly this was the case with Arthur, who could not say no when the reverend asked him to address the Church of the Redeemer's public forum on social issues.

After recovering from the shock of accepting an assignment well outside his comfort zone, Arthur decided to speak on the proper role and responsibilities of black athletes in the era of civil rights. The speech was scheduled for March 10, but several days before he traveled to Washington, *The Washington Post*, for whom he would soon be a special correspondent, ran a story with the provocative headline: "Ashe Becomes Activist, Plans Speech Here on Civil Rights." That was embarrassing enough, but even worse was the story's subheading: "Negro Tennis Star Emerges from Shell."

By the time Arthur arrived at the Church of the Redeemer, he was as nervous as he had ever been. His anxiety turned into near panic when a smiling Reverend Rogers introduced him to the radical SNCC leader, Stokely Carmichael, who was scheduled to deliver his own speech to the forum the following week. Feeling "hemmed in," as he later put it, between the ideology of Black Power and the constraints of being on active duty, he now feared his prepared remarks would alienate both ends of the political spectrum and probably embarrass his host in the process.

Since he had never given an extended speech in public before, his heart was in his throat as he began. Somehow the words came out, a bit halting at first, but eventually with rhythm and composure. Most of the speech proceeded as planned, nothing "revolutionary or militant," just a straightforward discourse on the social responsibilities of black athletes. As he later recounted the message, he told the capacity crowd he believed "the black athlete, whether of average ability or a superstar, must make a commitment to his or her community and attempt to transform it." Citing Bill Russell and Jackie Robinson as role models, he argued for a long-term strategy that recognized meaningful reform as a gradual process. "What we do today may or may not bear fruit until two or three generations," he insisted. The most important thing was to begin the process in earnest, and to remain engaged over the long haul. He could have stopped there, and probably should have, but he couldn't resist adding a few remarks about the negative effects of black laziness and complacency. "There is a lot we can do and we don't do because we're lazy," he declared. "This may be brutal, but poverty is half laziness." This seemingly gratuitous feint to the right raised more than a few eyebrows. But generally speaking the audience seemed to like what he had to say. At the end of the speech he received a standing ovation, and there were pats on the back and handshakes all around as he left the church.[22]

The next morning the *Washington Post* reporter covering the speech stressed Arthur's candor, a virtue that did not impress his superiors at West Point. Upon his return to duty, he was subjected to a stern reprimand and a warning "not to make any more speeches of even a vaguely political nature." In point of fact, West Point officials could have blocked his outburst in Washington if they had been more observant of his rising political consciousness. Back in late January, *New York Times* reporter Neil Amdur, later the coauthor of Ashe's 1981 memoir, *Off the Court*, had published a lengthy article profiling the preparation for the Church of the Redeemer appearance. "This is the new Arthur Ashe: articulate, mature, no longer content to sit back and let his tennis racket do the talking," Amdur announced, and Arthur concurred. "I guess I'm becoming more and more militant," he told the reporter, who felt the need to add a caveat for his readers. "Ashe's 'militancy' is subtle," he explained, "like his sense of humor." Later in the article, however, Amdur acknowledged that this subtlety had recently undergone a significant transformation. "Ashe's confidence," he assured his readers, "contrasts with the reticence associated with his past."[23]

Solid proof that Arthur had indeed turned a corner in his slow march toward activism came a week later when he returned to the Church of the Redeemer to hear what Carmichael had to say. After the speech, Carmichael gave him "two pieces of advice: boycott the Davis Cup because of South Africa's participation and buy a gun." Ashe's immediate reaction to the words of a true militant went unrecorded, but he later expressed admiration for Carmichael's forthright advocacy of black insurgency. As he explained in 1992, "something of Stokely's militancy may have rubbed off on me." Despite important differences on a number of issues, there was a bond between them. "Viscerally, emotionally, I admired Carmichael," he recalled. "His raw courage inspired me."[24]

Earlier in the day, several hours before Carmichael's speech, Arthur had joined Dell for a youth tennis clinic held in the gymnasium of McKinley High School, an inner-city school with an overwhelmingly black student body. After the two Davis Cuppers entertained 150 students with a dizzying exhibition of serve-and-volley tennis, Arthur gave an interview to Phil Finch, a young reporter for the *Washington Daily News.* "The second-ranked amateur in the U.S. and undoubtedly the best Negro tennis player in history," Finch explained to his readers, was also "a man of startling candor who is quite aware of his position in life and quite unafraid to discuss it." This was in keeping with the article's headline, "Ashe Isn't Afraid to Tell It Like It Is, Baby," but Finch went on to emphasize the tennis star's distinctive style of activism. As the admiring reporter put it, "He possesses an intriguing levelheadedness and states his case without the polemics that sometimes seem to have become associated with the civil rights movement, pro and con."[25]

Confirming this point, Arthur did not flinch when Finch inquired about a proposed Olympic boycott being organized by controversial San Jose State sociology professor Harry Edwards. While Edwards wanted a boycott that would bring attention to racism in the United States, the primary issue at hand was apartheid-plagued South Africa's probable readmission to the Olympics, a development that spurred the Supreme Council for Sport in Africa (SCSA) to call for a boycott. The International Olympic Committee (IOC) had barred South Africa from participation in the 1964 Tokyo games, and the SCSA wanted the ban to remain in place for the 1968 Mexico City games scheduled for October. So did a number of prominent African American athletes, including Ashe, Jackie Robinson, Bob Gibson, K. C. Jones, Dave Bing, and more than twenty others who signed a petition in early February. Despite this show of concern, on February 15 the IOC voted to reinstate the South Africans. Angered, the SCSA and its allies stepped up the pressure, forcing Ashe and others to decide just how far they wanted to go to make their point.

In his conversation with Finch, Arthur did not discuss the proposed African boycott. But he walked a fine line between support for Edwards's boycott by African American athletes and skepticism that it would have much effect. "I think Edwards has shaken the guilty consciences of a lot of Negro athletes," he told the reporter. "Take me, for example. Why should I complain? I've got it made, nothing to worry about. . . . Negro athletes have got to realize that they may be cheered during a game, but as soon as they take a shower, it's just the same old story. So, I think Edwards is doing good, if only for bringing the problem before the public." That said, Ashe warned: "there's a bit of egoism involved. Everybody likes his name in the papers. And progress is going to come, too. It's coming already. But it's going to come piecemeal, despite all the shouting and demands for equality 'now.'"

In this roundabout way, Arthur expressed his continuing reservations about radical protest and revolutionary change. In the wake of his controversial speech the week before, he was on his way to becoming an activist, though definitely one with a light touch. At the end of the month, he was noticeably reticent when asked if he would boycott Davis Cup play that involved South Africa. "I'm thinking about it," he told reporters, "but I want to stay within the confines of Army policy. I'll do what they let me do. But even so, I'm wondering if it would be worth it. If I'm one lone voice in the wilderness, it might not accomplish anything."[26]

Ashe would never relinquish his attachment to careful deliberation and rhetorical understatement, even when the issue at hand tapped his deepest convictions. But in an important sense the Church of the Redeemer speech and its immediate aftermath represented a major milestone in his life. Although he had no way of appreciating its full significance at the time, his later reflections emphasized the importance of the speech and the Army's subsequent disapproval. For one of the first times in his life, he was playing the role of a rebel. Clearly, it was not a role that he could assume with complete comfort, at least not yet, and for a while he had second thoughts about his public speaking debut. "After the rebuff," he recalled in 1981, "I felt I had been used by the Reverend Rogers. But I gradually admitted to myself that I had a strange sense of satisfaction for speaking out. I knew there would be trouble if I made the speech, but I accepted the rebuke as my way of paying dues to the cause. After all, I had done nothing in the sixties but play tennis and enjoy life." In his view, "the speech released a great deal of anxiety and guilt I had repressed and marked the beginning of a period of political activity—in and out of tennis. I became more serious and started to notice political elements I had ignored in certain situations."

One expression of Arthur's new approach to politics was his deepening concern about South African apartheid and the movement to combat it. On April 12, he was one of sixty-five athletes to endorse the American Committee on Africa (ACOA)'s call for an Olympic boycott to protest South Africa's inclusion in the 1968 summer games. Led by former CORE activist George Houser, ACOA was in the forefront of the small but growing American anti-apartheid movement. Another example of Arthur's rising political consciousness was a greater concern for what he was witnessing at West Point. Suddenly he saw the rough treatment of first-year cadets in a different light, and over time he came to deplore the "beast barracks," where the Army employed "an intensely dehumanizing experience designed to break them down so they could be reconstructed into military men."[27]

He was also developing a profound respect for Martin Luther King, whose fight for freedom and equality had recently expanded into the realm of economic justice. Captivated by the Memphis sanitation workers' struggle, Ashe suffered a devastating blow on April 4 when King was gunned down. He learned of the assassination while driving across the George Washington Bridge into Manhattan, and the image of shock and horror stayed with him for years. "I wanted to pull over," he remembered, "but I was in the middle of the bridge. Once I got off, I pulled to a stop on Amsterdam Avenue. A number of black people had done the same thing and were listening to the bulletins. Some got out of their cars and talked about the shooting. Their reactions ranged from sorrow to anger."

Arthur felt the loss deeply and personally, having established a relationship with King earlier in the year. While they had never met, the Nobel Prize winner and civil rights icon had sent him a warm letter on February 7. "Dear Mr. Ashe," the letter began, and the brief text that followed moved from a boilerplate expression of gratitude—a "personal appreciation and that of my co-workers in SCLC for your expression of support and solidarity in the fight for justice, freedom, and dignity for all people in this country"—to a more intimate reference to the Reverend Rogers's belief in Arthur's potential value to the civil rights struggle. Rogers, whom King described as "a long-time and staunch freedom fighter," had "spoken to us several times of your basic devotion and dedication to the movement." "Your eminence in the world of sports and athletics," King continued, "gives you an added measure of authority and responsibility. It is heartening indeed when you bring these attributes to the movement." The letter ended with a tantalizing invitation to a personal meeting sometime in the future, followed by the salutation: "Yours for freedom, Martin Luther King, Jr."

Filed away with Arthur's most cherished possessions, the letter later served as a comforting reminder of King's grace and power to inspire. While he never felt worthy of consideration as one of King's lieutenants, he did his best to follow the civil rights leader's lead, partly through his friendship with the Reverend Andrew Young, whom he met in 1970 during a chance encounter at LaGuardia Airport. Young was running for a seat in Congress representing Atlanta, and Ashe impulsively offered the former King aide a $500 campaign contribution. He would later make more substantial, nonmonetary contributions to the cause, but this early gesture was his way of reconnecting with the spirit of the fallen leader whom Young had served so well.[28]

In November 1970, Ashe was disappointed when Young lost his congressional race. By that point, he had developed a deep interest in politics, having cut his political teeth two years earlier when he became absorbed in Robert Kennedy's run for the White House. Spurred on by Donald Dell's close friendship with the Kennedys, he supported the former attorney general in every way he could. They first met in Washington in 1967, and in early June 1968, he saw him again in Sacramento after Ashe and some of his teammates participated in the Central California championships. The American squad was still in California after sweeping a tie against Mexico in Berkeley the previous week, and Dell seized the opportunity to introduce his players to the man he hoped would become the next president of the United States. Ashe would meet President Johnson and Vice President Hubert Humphrey when the Davis Cup team was invited to the White House later in the year, but meeting the charismatic brother of a departed hero was one of the greatest thrills of his life. For someone who had grown up under the yoke of Jim Crow, Johnson's folksy Southern twang was off-putting, and Humphrey's continuing vacillation on the war was problematic at best. But Ashe felt comfortable with the political style and rhetoric of a Northeastern liberal like Kennedy, especially after the New York senator espoused a progressive platform promising an end to the war as well as serious attention to the plight of the urban poor.

After the encounter in Sacramento, Kennedy traveled on to Los Angeles while the Davis Cup squad flew to Charlotte, North Carolina, to prepare for an upcoming tie with Ecuador. The Americas Zone final began on June 7, but by that time the nation was reeling from the shock of RFK's assassination two days earlier. When Ashe's newfound political hero died twenty-six hours after being gunned down by Sirhan Sirhan, a young Palestinian Arab with Jordanian citizenship, he could hardly believe it. Barely two months after the loss of Dr. King, the Democrat with the best chance to put some of King's ideas into practice was gone. Dell was devastated and Ashe only slightly less so, as the U.S. Davis Cup tried to keep its composure during the attempt to avenge the unexpected loss to Ecuador the previous year.

Despite the unfortunate circumstances—before the opening match Ashe confessed to being "extremely nervous"—the Americans won both singles matches on the opening day. On the second day, with Pasarell substituting for captain Dell, who was in New York attending Kennedy's funeral, Graebner and Lutz defeated Pancho Guzmán and Miguel Olvera to clinch the tie. The next day Graebner and Ashe completed the sweep with two singles victories, bringing Arthur's Davis Cup singles record to 16–2.

Back in early May, Arthur had begun his 1968 Davis Cup winning streak in the opening round tie against the British Caribbean team. Held at Richmond's Byrd Park—formerly a forbidden venue for Ashe—the tie produced little drama on the court as the Americans won all five matches with ease. Dell had chosen the Byrd Park venue as part of his plan to reduce the Davis Cup's elitist, private club orientation. As he explained to reporters on the eve of the tie, "We're taking tennis to the people and putting the matches where they can be seen and appreciated." Despite its history as a whites-only facility, the recently desegregated Byrd Park represented a step toward democratization. But as Dell well knew, playing there would be an emotional experience for his friend. Arthur's earlier exclusion from the park still rankled and would continue to be a sore subject for years to come. "What infuriated me most," he wrote in 1981, "was having a white Richmond type come up to me somewhere in the world and say, 'I saw you play at Byrd Park when you were a kid.' Nobody saw me at Byrd Park, because when I was a kid it was for whites only."

For Arthur, playing the March 1968 tie at Byrd Park was definitely bittersweet, though he tried to make the best of it. In his judgment, "it was a homecoming of sorts, because the city made a big deal of my return. I could

have held a grudge for all the previous injustices Richmond blacks had suffered, but I began to forgive the city for its past injuries. After all, they were
trying to right some of those wrongs. I felt that I should meet them more
than halfway. I had an obligation to make things better for those who would
follow me." Besides, he added: "My family still lived there." [29]

After Richmond, Sacramento, and Charlotte, the next round of Davis
Cup play was scheduled for Cleveland in mid-August, when the Americans
would face Spain, the last obstacle before the expected confrontation with
the defending champion Australians. Fortunately, Arthur and his teammates had two months to prepare, and thanks to West Point's increasingly
liberal leave policy, he was now on the court far more often than he was in
his office. Army officials had been told that the United States had the best
chance in years to win the Davis Cup, and they did not want to do anything
to hurt their national team's chances. America's image in the world was bad
enough, they reasoned, without squandering an opportunity to enhance the
nation's prestige away from the battlefield.

By the summer of 1968 Arthur had become too important as a symbol
of African American success to be sacrificed at the altar of military discipline
and duty. Some of the parents of the young men who were fighting and
dying in Vietnam probably questioned the fairness of this arrangement, but
Army officials were willing to take the heat in the hope that winning the
Davis Cup would justify their decision to treat Arthur as they did. With a
brother fighting on the front lines, Arthur had considerable sympathy for the
parents who objected to his special status. But he felt the most appropriate
response to this perceived inequity was to expend every ounce of his energy
to achieve athletic excellence. His personal challenge, whether he liked it or
not, was to represent his race, and more importantly, his nation with all the
integrity and dignity he could muster. [30]

All of this was swirling around in Arthur's head when he and Pasarell
left for England on June 10, the day after their emotional victory in Charlotte. He hadn't played at Wimbledon since the summer of 1965, when he
had lost to Osuna in the fourth round. Now three years older and vastly more
experienced, he was eager to see how far he could go on the English turf.

In a pre-Wimbledon warm-up tournament in Bristol, he fought his way
through a tough draw, winning the right to play Cliff Richey in the semifinals
by beating the transplanted Hawaiian Jim Osborne in the quarters. Though
Richey was playing well, his infamous temper got the best of him after several verbal altercations with the umpire Harry Evans. With the match even
at one set apiece and with Arthur leading 3–2 in the third, the fiery Texan

reacted to a questionable line call by swatting a ball into the stands in disgust and vowing to do it again in defiance of Evans's warning. A heated exchange followed, which soon led to Richey's disqualification by tournament referee Hugh Kerridge, who pronounced Arthur the winner.

The next day, with Richey still fuming and his Davis Cup teammates trying to calm him down, Arthur defeated Graebner to win the tournament. Taking advantage of a teammate's outburst was not the way he wanted to win the title, and certainly not the way to build solidarity among the American Davis Cuppers. But he went on to the Queen's Club tournament in London with hopes for a less volatile experience. For him, as for most of the American amateurs entered in the draw, the 1968 Queen's Club competition would be the first Open tournament of his career. Many of the world's best pros were there, including the number one seed Laver and his fellow Aussies Roy Emerson and John Newcombe. It was an intimidating field, to say the least, and no one was all that surprised when Arthur was eliminated in the second round by the fleet-footed Dutchman Tom Okker.[31]

Crushing Okker 6–1 in the first set before fading, Arthur had reason to think that with a little luck he might fare better at Wimbledon. But when he read through the list of names in the Wimbledon draw, he wasn't so sure. Thirty-two of the 128 entrants were pros, accounting for thirteen of the sixteen seeds. The number one seed and the odds-on favorite to win the men's singles title was Laver, who had won the title in 1961 and 1962, the last two years he had played in the tournament as an amateur. The highest seeded amateur, Manolo Santana, the 1966 champion, was #6, and the only other amateurs among the seeded players were Okker at #12 and Ashe at #13.

Ashe's chances of beating the higher-seeded pros seemed remote, and his situation appeared to get much worse after he strained a leg muscle during a warm-up with Pancho Gonzales. Arthur pronounced himself "70 per cent fit," but no one thought that was good enough to win the tournament or even get past the first or second round. With nothing to lose, he decided to relax and enjoy what time he had on the grass surface he had come to love. This low-key approach seemed to work, as he quickly dispatched Eduardo Zuleta of Ecuador in the first round, dropping only six games in three quick sets. In the second and third rounds he played even better, beating the tough young Egyptian Ismael El Shafei and the Swede Ove Bengston in straight sets.

The competition got much tougher in the fourth round when Ashe faced his first professional opponent, Newcombe, the defending Wimbledon champion. Prior to the Ashe-Newcombe match, one of several pitting an amateur against a professional, Fred Tupper of *The New York Times* took stock of the situation. "It's been a long time coming, this first open Wimbledon," he wrote. "At the halfway stage, it still prompts a question that has the tennis world agog in anticipation. Who is to win it? Will it be professional or amateur?" With five of the thirteen pros already eliminated, eight amateurs were still in the hurt, including Ashe, Graebner, Okker, and Tom Edlefsen. Of the eight, Okker seemed to have the best chance of advancing beyond the quarterfinals. But Ashe, gaining confidence with every round, had other ideas.

Newcombe, seeded fourth, was in top form and had every reason to believe he would dominate Ashe in their quarterfinal match. But Ashe played the match of his young life, serving 19 aces and hitting clutch shot after clutch shot. Before the Aussie pro could catch his breath, the American amateur had won the first two sets. After Newcombe came back to take the next two sets, it looked like Ashe might fall short in the end. But somehow he summoned up the stamina and skill to stymie Newcombe's closing parries. Leading 5–2, he nervously squandered three match points in the eighth game, but a few minutes later he served out the match with an ace. In the first Open Wimbledon, he had made history by conquering the defending champion.

As it turned out, the historic fairy tale did indeed end in the next round when Ashe faced the prohibitive favorite Laver. Playing on July 3, a week before Ashe's twenty-fifth birthday, the two semifinalists—one right-handed, one left-handed, one black, one white—presented the Centre Court crowd with a study in contrast. But both left the court with a sense of genuine satisfaction. Laver won in straight sets, proving he was the better player that day, and he then went on to win his third Wimbledon singles title. For Ashe there was no title and no prize money. Yet the boost to his confidence was incalculable. He now knew he could compete with the best players in the world, pro or amateur. Graebner enjoyed a similar boost, losing narrowly to Santana in the other semifinal match, and two months later they would build upon their near misses at Wimbledon by waging an epic semifinal match at the first U.S. Open.[32]

Before returning to the United States, both Ashe and Graebner received congratulations from their proud Davis Cup captain. But Ashe received something more from Dell, something that would affect the rest of his life. Earlier in the week during a break in a practice session, the two men had what Arthur later described as their "first lengthy conversation about life and tennis." Dell was older and presumably wiser, but he had the wisdom to listen as his young friend revealed his feelings. Arthur talked about the controversy surrounding his recent flirtation with activism, the speech in Washington, and his evolving views on Harry Edwards's proposed Olympic boycott and South Africa.

The land of apartheid, in particular, was on his mind, primarily due to a disturbing conversation with Cliff Drysdale two weeks earlier during the Queen's Club tournament. As Arthur recalled the scene, a group of players was sitting in the Queen's clubhouse "talking primarily about the possibility of forming an association of professional tennis players, a kind of trade union, and about the reception we could expect from various governing bodies around the world." Suddenly, Drysdale, a native South African, interjected that he was excited about playing in the first South African Open in the fall. Turning almost reflexively to Arthur, he counseled with a smile, "They'd never let you play." Startled, Arthur asked rather innocently, "is it *that* bad?" In response, Drysdale backed up a little bit, acknowledging that the South African Lawn Tennis Union "would let you play." "I'm pretty sure of that," he added. "In fact, they would love to have you come. But you would need a visa to enter South Africa, and the government would never let you have one." After Arthur asked incredulously if Drysdale was serious, the South African suggested: "Try them. You'll see."

When Arthur sat down with Dell two weeks later, Drysdale's challenge was still burning in his mind, and the fire of indignation would continue to burn over the next five years until he finally obtained a South African visa. In the near term, Dell's willingness to discuss this and related issues openly and honestly helped seal a personal bond that transcended race and political ideology. It was a bond that Arthur would treasure for the rest of his life, and the subsequent triumphs and adventures the two men shared had a lot do with the trust that solidified during the 1968 Wimbledon fortnight.

Despite Dell's preppy image, he and Arthur had more in common that most people realized. Like Arthur, he had experienced life-changing upward mobility, an ascent based on a first-class education made possible by the sacrifices of his lower-middle-class parents. During their seminal conversation at the first Open Wimbledon, he revealed that his parents had even "skipped much-needed dental work to send their kids through school." This story, which Dell only learned as an adult, gave him new respect for his parents, and in turn his willingness to share the story with one of his players heightened Arthur's respect for him. For much of his life, Arthur had yearned for true friendship based on mutual respect embedded in the emotional and intellectual tissue of head and heart, and in his relationship with Dell, as in his relationship with Charlie Pasarell, he had found such a friendship.[33]

Nothing captured the meaning of Dell and Ashe's friendship better than their common passion for the pursuit of the Davis Cup, and this passion would be on full display when the American squad took on Spain in mid-August. But first there would be five weeks of preparation, first in Sweden, a week later at the U.S. National Clay Court Championships in Milwaukee, and finally at the annual grass court tournaments in Haverford and South Orange.

Ashe's second visit to the Swedish resort town of Bastad, where he celebrated his twenty-fifth birthday in style, was every bit as satisfying as his first. The competition was stiff, with Graebner, Santana, and Koch in the draw, and the Swedish girls were as friendly and alluring as ever. Fortunately, Dell was there to keep his singles star out of trouble and make sure he spent at least some of his time on the practice court. Midway through the week, Dell and his doubles partner, Ion Tiriac of Romania, actually gave Ashe and Graebner a scare in the doubles competition before fading in the second set. For once, Ashe felt reasonably comfortable on clay, though the clay court specialist José Edison Mandarino of Brazil outlasted him in the quarterfinals.

The only downside in Bastad for Ashe was the international reporters' insistence on pressing him with essentially unanswerable questions about his future, and even more disturbingly, about South Africa. During and immediately after the Wimbledon fortnight, there was considerable speculation and more than a few rumors about lucrative professional contract offers being waved in the faces of Riessen, Okker, Graebner, and Ashe, either by WCT or its rival, MacCall's NTL. While it was generally assumed Ashe would remain an amateur until after his discharge from the Army in February 1969, his attractiveness to professional recruiters was obvious.

It was the questions about South Africa's participation in Davis Cup competition that made him sigh the most. What would he do "if the United States had to face South Africa in the Davis Cup at Johannesburg?" His tentative answer was that he would probably give up his position on the U.S. squad. "Perhaps I better withdraw," he told reporters on his first day in Bastad. "Maybe I risk violence because I'm a Negro. The white South Africans don't like to watch a Negro on the court, and nonwhites don't like me to appear together with whites. I don't know what to do." This would not be the last time Ashe found himself struggling with the dilemmas of engagement with South Africa. But at least he was beginning to recognize the importance of addressing the many issues related to apartheid and South Africa. All he asked, at this point, was enough time to figure out the best positions to adopt. He was already engaged, but not yet knowledgeable about the complexities of the South African situation.[34]

Between his tennis future and the troubled state of the world, Arthur certainly had plenty to think about in the weeks after his return to the United States. His immediate challenge was to sharpen his game on the clay courts in Milwaukee. As a Southern boy, he felt like a stranger in the Midwest, but he had always fared pretty well in Milwaukee, where he had actually won the tournament in 1967. As the defending champion, he had high hopes for a second singles title, but he ran into the equivalent of a Chilean buzz saw in the third round. After winning the first set against Patricio Cornejo and holding a match point in the eighteenth game of the second, he lost his edge and his chance to advance. He did better in the doubles, making it all the way to the semifinals before he and Richey were upended by the tournament favorites Stan Smith and Bob Lutz.[35]

The penultimate warm-up before the tie against the Spanish took place at the Merion Cricket Club. On the first day of the tournament, Ashe received a boost when the mid year "Tennis Player of the Year" standings were released. According to the ballots cast by an international panel of eleven sportswriters, he was the fourth best player in the world with only the three top Aussies—Laver, Rosewall, and Roche—ahead of him. Another powerful Aussie—Newcombe—finished fifth in the balloting. Strikingly, Ashe was the only amateur in the top five; the next highest amateurs were Okker and Graebner at #7 and #8.

The entire American Davis squad was at Merion, and most, including Ashe, were happy to be back on grass. Ashe was in top form, vanquishing the Indian Davis Cup star Premjit Lall in the quarterfinals and the Australian Allan Stone in the semis. At the same time, he and his partner Riessen were advancing through the doubles field, hoping to get by the top-seeded team of Smith and Lutz in the semifinals. After Riessen defeated the South African Ray Moore in the other singles semifinal, the doubles partners faced each other in the title match. All during the week, there had been rumors that Riessen planned to sign a WCT contract as soon as the tournament concluded, and at one point the former Northwestern star said plainly, "I want to make a living playing tennis," suggesting the rumors were accurate. All of this drew attention to the match between the two friends.

Riessen had never had much success in his singles matches against Arthur, and the 1968 Merion final was no exception. Playing in front of an overflow crowd of 3,500, Arthur ran over his doubles partner—with whom he would have to finish a suspended doubles semifinal later in the day. Punctuated by 14 service aces, it was one of the most impressive performances of Arthur's career. "I think he played the best I've ever seen him play," Riessen remarked after the match. "I've never seen so many balls go by me when I thought I had a chance." A few minutes later, he was back on the court to complete the doubles match against Smith and Lutz, which he and Arthur eventually won thanks to a hand injury to Lutz, who had to retire. The biggest development of the day, however, was the professional contract Riessen signed that afternoon. The pro tour now had "The Handsome Eight plus One," with plans for the future addition of Okker, Graebner, and Ashe. All of this left Dell with a sinking feeling, since the current rules of Open Tennis did not allow professionals to participate in Davis Cup competition.

The dismal prospect of eventually losing his best players to the professional tour gave Dell more than a few sleepless nights. But his immediate challenge was to complete his team's preparation for the tie against Santana and a tough Spanish squad. He had hoped to have his entire team on hand for the final warm-up tournament in South Orange, but a dental emergency put Arthur temporarily out of commission. While his teammates competed in the Eastern Grass Championships, a tournament won by Pasarell in a thrilling come-from-behind victory over Graebner, he was still recovering from minor surgery. Fortunately, after the close of the tournament in New Jersey he would have twelve full days to get ready for the Spaniards.[36]

By the time Arthur arrived in Cleveland, following a week of rest at West Point, he was back in good health and ready to play. The long-awaited tie was held on a hard surface in front of a wildly enthusiastic home crowd. On the first day of play, Graebner faltered in the opening singles match against Santana. But the Americans were back on track after Arthur followed with an easy victory over Juan Gisbert. After Graebner and Pasarell—Dell's controversial substitutes for the successful Smith-Lutz duo—won the doubles match, the U.S. team went into the final day leading 2–1. Needing one more singles win to clinch the tie, Dell turned to Graebner and Ashe to close the deal. Graebner, who played first, sealed the team victory with a clutch performance against Gisbert, and Ashe followed with a difficult but satisfying five-set win over Santana. Advancing to the next round, the American squad was now halfway to its goal of wresting the Cup from the mighty Australians.[37]

In Arthur's life, as in the nation and the world at large, 1968 was turning out to be a year of extreme highs and lows. The winter had brought his belated political awakening, followed by a spring of assassination and heartbreak, and now the summer was becoming a season of largely unexpected personal triumphs. In the political realm, the rising political fortunes of the demagogic Republican candidate Richard Nixon and the bitter conflict in the streets of Chicago during the Democratic National Convention were disheartening.

But set against these troubling developments was an upward personal trajectory that took Arthur to a new level of fulfillment.

Less than twenty-four hours after the Davis Cup tie victory in Cleveland, Arthur rushed to Boston for the U.S. Amateur Championships. Despite the tournament's title, no American had won the U.S. Amateur singles title since 1955. The 1968 event was the 88th annual U.S. Amateur tournament but the first played at the Longwood Cricket Club. Though seeded number one, Arthur had not come close to winning the title in eight tries, and considering the lingering effects of his extended play in Cleveland the day before arriving at Longwood, he didn't expect to win. The grass surface at Longwood was to his liking, but that was about all he had going for him, or so it seemed.

Arthur's ninth appearance at the U.S. Amateur began in disastrous fashion when he failed to win a game in the opening set of his first-round match against Chris Bovett, an unseeded British player. But he soon righted himself, winning the next three sets in short order. "Different balls, different court surface, lack of pressure and three hours of sleep" was his explanation for the slow start. The important thing, he pointed out to reporters, was that he had survived to play another day. Pasarell, seeded just below Arthur, was not so fortunate, losing in the first round to seventeen-year-old Eric Van Dillen.

Arthur had little trouble advancing through the next three rounds, and after he defeated Allan Stone in the quarterfinals he began to think he had a chance to win it all. His unseeded opponent in the semifinals was Jim McManus of Berkeley, a left-hander he had played many times before, and the familiarity seemed to work to Arthur's advantage. While it took four sets to dispatch McManus, with Arthur losing an exhausting third set 14–16, the victory put him in the final match against Lutz, who had upset Graebner in the other semifinal match. Arthur had beaten Lutz twice earlier in the year, but the young USC student from San Clemente, previously known as a doubles specialist, was playing the best tennis of his life.

Playing in 90-degree heat and gusty wind, both players had trouble keeping the ball inside the lines. Early on Lutz was the steadier of the two, and after three sets he was leading 2–1. But in the end Arthur's strong serve proved to be the difference. Before the match was over, he had served 20 aces, one more than Lutz's dispiriting 19 double faults. Closing out the fifth and final set 6–4, after blanking Lutz in the fourth, the new U.S. Amateur champion raised his arms in triumph before receiving a standing ovation from the crowd and warm embraces from several of his Davis Cup teammates. Pasarell and the others knew how much this victory meant to their friend. Not only did it virtually assure him a number one ranking for the year

among American amateurs; it also set him up as the amateurs' best hope to
challenge the pros' expected dominance of the first U.S. Open. With the first
matches at Forest Hills less than a week away, Arthur carried considerable
momentum into the tournament.[38]

He was also dead tired, emotionally as well as physically. Talking to reporters immediately after his victory, he announced plans to "take three days
off and fish and hunt before practicing" for the Open. Four days later, after
following through with his plan, he sat down with *New York Times* columnist Arthur Daley to discuss his "rugged assignment" at Forest Hills. Anticipating that Ashe would face Laver in the quarterfinals, that "if all goes well
for each in the preliminary stages" the king of the American amateurs would
square off against "the paladin of the pros," Daley asked him about his prospects. Having lost to Laver in the recent Wimbledon semifinals, Ashe had
"no illusions" about the difficult path ahead of him. "Playing tennis against
Rod," he confessed to Daley, "makes you feel like Don Quixote tilting at a
windmill. He can so overwhelm you that you can't get started. He makes
quite a few errors but an awful lot of winners. He goes for broke and comes
out swinging. He reminds me of Arnold Palmer, a great shot maker with a
ferocious gambling instinct."

Ashe obviously admired Laver's aggressive style of play, which he had
studied since he had first played the Aussie at the U.S. National tournament
in 1959. But he feared he hadn't learned "very much about him at Wimbledon," explaining "I wasn't in there long enough." In any event, Laver was
not the only major obstacle in his way. "All the pros will be tough now,"
he predicted. "When they went to England for those first few open tournaments, they just weren't in condition. . . . Besides, they'd come off playing on
all kinds of surfaces and grass was so new to them that they were disoriented.
This time they'll all be ready."

The seeding order at Forest Hills, determined before Ashe's victory at
Longwood, was consistent with his judgment of the top pros' readiness. Seeds
one through four went to four Australians—Laver, Roche, Rosewall, and
Newcombe—and overall professionals eligible to win the top prize money
of $14,000 filled twelve of the sixteen seeded positions. Ashe, seeded fifth,
was the highest seeded amateur, followed by Graebner (seventh), Okker
(eighth), and Pasarell (twelfth). The #13 seed was forty-year-old Pancho
Gonzales, who could not resist trying his hand at winning the historic and
potentially lucrative inaugural U.S. Open.[39]

Ashe's greatest obstacle was clearly Laver. His best, and perhaps only,
chance for survival was an early-round upset that would take the Rocket out

of the tournament. That didn't seem very likely as the tournament got under way on September 1, yet the improbable almost became reality in the second round when the Wimbledon champion lost the first two sets to Koch before mounting a furious comeback to win the last three. Ashe, by contrast, had no trouble in the early rounds, easily defeating Frank Parker, a fifty-two-year-old pro who had come out of semiretirement in search of previously unavailable prize money, and Paul Hutchins, the unseeded captain of the British Davis Cup team.

Neither Ashe nor Laver had any trouble in the third round, but lightning struck in the fourth. While Ashe won a surprisingly easy straight-set victory over Emerson, Laver waged a futile struggle to stay in the tournament. In a stunning upset, Drysdale, the #16 seed, outlasted the greatest player in the world, winning the last two sets at 6–1. A member of WCT's Handsome Eight, Drysdale was no slouch. But the victory over Laver was easily the greatest triumph of his career.

Though pleased that Laver was out of the way, Ashe did not take Drysdale lightly. He knew the South African's two-handed strokes could be confounding, and that proved to be the case in the first set. After Drysdale won the first set 10–8, Ashe knew he was in for a long and difficult fight. Relying on his superior serve, the U.S. Amateur champion won the last three sets and the match, but the margin was narrow throughout. Well into the fourth set, the result was still in doubt, and even after winning he sheepishly told reporters: "I don't think I'm playing that well." When the reporters pointed out that he had accumulated quite a streak of wins going back to early August, he still insisted: "I'm surprised at being in the semifinals."[40]

Surprised or not, he was now two victories away from winning the first U.S. Open singles title. The victory over Drysdale set up a semifinal match against Clark Graebner, a struggle destined to be one of the most famous matches of Ashe's career. Much of the fame stemmed from John McPhee's extraordinary dissection of the two semifinal combatants in a remarkable series of *New Yorker* articles later published as the book *Levels of the Game*, widely considered one of the most perceptive tennis books ever written. As McPhee pointed out, the stark contrast between the two Davis Cup teammates—one black, Southern, and quietly determined to make his mark; the other white, Midwestern, and seemingly self-satisfied with his upper-middle-class life—added color, literally and figuratively, to the already considerable drama surrounding the first U.S. Open. Even their equipment clashed, as Graebner used a Wilson T-2000 metal racket, introduced to the tour the previous year, while Ashe still relied on a traditional wood-frame racket.

Born only four months apart, but different in so many ways, including their style of play, the two men were perfect representatives of the emerging eclecticism of American tennis. As amateurs, neither man was eligible to collect prize money, but their primal contest made good copy and good television. The recent infusion of money into the game of tennis explained part of the public excitement generated by many of the matches at Forest Hills, but the fascination with the Ashe-Graebner match was about something else. In a sense, the match was a throwback to the gladiatorial ethic that had dominated competitive tennis since its nineteenth-century origins. While the era of full-blown commercialization had dawned, Ashe and Graebner were not yet part of it.

By teasing the meaning out of the match game by game, McPhee enshrined the 1968 semifinal confrontation as a classic in the annals of tennis. Yet in pure tennis terms the match was nothing special. Graebner was quick out of the gate, defeating a noticeably sluggish Ashe 6–4. But after that Ashe was in control, winning the next two sets 8–6 and 7–5. During a required ten-minute intermission prior to the fourth set, Dell found himself in the strange position of counseling both of his Davis Cup players. For Graebner, his advice was to play all out: "Look, go out there and play him 100 per cent. You don't want to wake up tomorrow morning and know that you didn't give 100 per cent to win." The advice for Ashe, in contrast, focused on mechanics: "you can't play stiff-legged against Clark, you know that. You've got to bend your knees. You've got to pick up your feet and bend your knees on the return." After this Solomonic performance, the captain mumbled to Pasarell, who had walked into the locker room midway through the dual counseling session: "I feel like a schizophrenic. It's a shame they couldn't have been in opposite halves. They would've been in the final together." Pasarell, who had no reservations about taking sides, counseled his former roommate to "wake up," and then added with emphasis: "You were asleep in the first set."

When the friendly rivals came out for the fourth set, Ashe was definitely the fresher of the two, and less than a half hour later it was all over. By a score of 6–2, he won the fourth set—and the match. Later in the day, Ken Rosewall—the diminutive but venerable thirty-three-year-old pro who had won the first French Open singles title back in June, the man known in the locker room as "Muscles"—suffered a mild upset in the second semifinal match. In a victory of youth over experience, twenty-three-year-old Tom Okker surprised just about everyone by winning in four sets to advance to the final against Ashe. Technically still an amateur, the Dutchman had chosen the hybrid status of registered player, which meant he could accept prize money in Open tournaments. So win or lose, he would take home the top prize of $14,000 after playing against a true amateur in the title match.[41]

Another oddity was an unexpected hitch in the coordination of the doubles and singles schedules. Since Ashe and his partner, the Spanish pro Andrés Gimeno, were still alive in the doubles competition but had yet to finish their semifinal match against Graebner and Pasarell—a match suspended because of darkness—Ashe faced the prospect of playing three matches in less than twenty-four hours. Trying to facilitate a live television broadcast of the singles final, the tournament organizers scheduled the singles final for 3 p.m. on Monday, even though this meant Ashe and Gimeno would have only a few minutes of daylight in which to complete their semifinal doubles match. Predictably, the doubles semifinal had to be suspended for a second time early Monday evening, pushing its completion into Tuesday morning. After Ashe and Gimeno pulled out the match after playing 42 games over three days, the exhausted duo still had to play the doubles final, which not surprisingly they lost to the formidable team of Smith and Lutz.

The delayed completion of the men's doubles competition was embarrassing for Forest Hills officials eager to show they knew how to put on an Open tournament. But the real culprit was the marathon, 65-game singles final that consumed most of Monday afternoon. When the first set lasted almost an hour, ending in a 14–12 Ashe victory, the crowd at Forest Hills Stadium suspected they were in for a long day. Over the next two hours the momentum swung back and forth with no one gaining the upper hand until Ashe surged ahead in the fifth set. All through the match Ashe used pinpoint backhands and blistering serves—he had 26 aces—to neutralize Okker's speed and mobility, and in the end he had too much firepower for the Dutchman.[42]

Arthur would never forget the scene after the final point. "After two hours and forty minutes," he recalled in 1981, "I could hardly believe it was over. I spun, stood at crouched attention like a well-drilled West Point Cadet and aimed my racquet handle at the tarpaulin-covered stadium wall. I walked slowly behind the umpire's chair, clasped my hands, and then held them up as if a fifteen-round decision had just been announced in my favor." For Arthur, not given to on-court displays of emotion, the release came during the award ceremony that followed. "My father came on to the court with me," he recounted, "and it felt wonderful to share that moment with him. Dr. J was in the stands. Bob Kelleher introduced me as 'General Ashe,' as I laughed and hugged my father. He was crying. . . . I hadn't seen him cry that much in years. When he said, 'Well done, son,' I knew how much that moment must have meant to him."[43]

The next day, one journalist commented: "Perhaps with more than 7,000 fans standing and applauding yesterday, his father's arms wrapped around his shoulders. Arthur Robert Ashe Jr. finally believed he belonged." Nevertheless, during the press conference following his victory, the new champion stressed his unique experiences as the only black in Open tennis. He embraced the opportunity to discuss his recent turn to a more activist stance, startling reporters by insisting "this country could use another three or four Browns and Carmichaels," a reference to the black militants H. Rap Brown and Stokely Carmichael whom he had criticized in the past. At another point he alluded to his bond with Gonzales, "whose skin was closest to mine" in the overwhelmingly white tennis world.

Finally, before joining friends and family for a celebration, he turned to his passion for Davis Cup play. As he told the reporters, knowing that his words would get back to Dell: "It's nice to hear the announcer say, 'Point . . . Ashe.' But I'd rather hear him say, 'Point . . . United States.'" Avoiding any mention of South Africa or Harry Edwards's proposed Olympic boycott, he focused on the primacy of representing his nation.[44]

In an opinion piece in *The New York Times* the next day, Arthur Daley emphasized the importance of the Ashe-Drysdale match, applauding Ashe's decision to share the court with a white South African. When asked about his feelings on the matter, Ashe responded: "Sure it entered my mind that Cliff is from South Africa. I couldn't help but think of it." Nevertheless, by taking the match in stride, he provided Daley with a perfect opening to strike a blow against advocates of the boycott. "If Arthur Ashe had defaulted to Cliff Drysdale as a protest against South African racial policies," Daley assured his readers, "he would not have accomplished a fraction as much as he did by meeting, and beating him in direct confrontation."[45]

Ashe agreed with Daley's argument. But as much as he would have liked to, he could not hang around in New York to discuss the fine points of the boycott debate with Daley or anyone else. Prior to the U.S. Open, Dell had arranged for the Davis Cup team to participate in the Desert Inn Invitational in Las Vegas, Nevada, scheduled to begin one day after the close of the Open. By the afternoon of September 11, Ashe was under the scorching Nevada sun playing a singles match against Dell, a strong player who could still give his players a run for their money on the court. The twenty-five-year-old won the match against his thirty-year-old captain, and went on to win the tournament, beating Graebner in the final.

After enjoying his brief visit to Las Vegas's adult playground, Ashe headed back to West Point to resume his duties at the data processing office. He had hardly been there since the late spring, so he wasn't sure what to expect from the colleagues he had all but abandoned. His fellow officers, it turned out, could not have been happier for him and warmly congratulated him for winning the Open. But the best part of his West Point homecoming was the reception he received from the cadets. "I was invited to dinner in the Great Hall," he recalled with emotion years later. "I'll never forget the 3½-minute ovation they gave me. Only a few people have been so honored by the entire corps at mess. I knew how special this outpouring was, and I was grateful." As he waited for the applause to die down, Lieutenant Ashe also knew how fortunate he was to live in an era of expanding horizons, when someone from the Jim Crow streets of Jackson Ward could experience such a moment.[46]

ELEVEN

MR. COOL

■

ASHE'S DOUBLE VICTORY IN the U.S. Amateur and the U.S. Open changed his life beyond recognition. During the fall of 1968, the twenty-five-year-old Army lieutenant discovered what it was like to be a true celebrity. As a top-flight tennis player and the only African American on the men's tour, he was accustomed to a certain amount of attention. But he had no previous experience with the intense media scrutiny and public exposure that accompanied national acclaim. Suddenly, his off-court activities and opinions were a matter of public interest as privacy gave way to influence and visibility. "Being thrust on center stage," he later recalled, "gave me a great opportunity to reach people."[1]

Ashe's new life of interviews, cover stories, and public appearances began in earnest a week after the Open when he appeared on *Face the Nation* hosted by Martin Agronsky. *Face the Nation* featured interviews with prominent politicians and newsmakers, and Ashe was the first athlete to be interviewed on the show since its debut in 1954. Poised and articulate, he handled Agronsky's questions with surprising ease for someone so young. In rapid succession, he held forth on a number of issues related to race, civil rights, and the civic responsibilities of black athletes.

He returned to these themes later in the week as a guest on *The Joey Bishop Show*, a late night talk show on ABC, and he also appeared on *The Dating Game*, trumpeting his status as an eligible bachelor. In early October, he joined several other black celebrities as a guest on *Soul*, a new Ford Foundation–funded variety show aimed at New York City's black community. Sitting onstage with the likes of Malcolm X's widow, Betty Shabazz, he could hardly believe his good fortune. Life as a celebrity was becoming fun.[2]

Ashe's accomplishments soon made the pages of magazines ranging from *The New Yorker* to *Vogue*, and in late September he even found himself on the cover of *Life*. The cover photo captured a steely-eyed Ashe charging the net, and inside the magazine a flattering, five-page photo essay concluded with a brief but revealing interview by David Wolf. "Detachment—that air of icy elegance—is part of Ashe's image now," Wolf insisted. "It is an extra piece of identification that will enhance his celebrity. Paul Hornung had his harem. Ty Cobb his uncontrollable rage. Arthur Ashe has his cool."

Arthur himself seemed to agree, declaring: "What I like best about myself is my demeanor. I seldom get ruffled." But when asked to explain his recent success on the tour, he steered the conversation in an entirely different direction. In the past, he told Wolf, he had lacked a secure sense of racial identity and a realistic connection to the world around him. Sheltered and protected by his father, he had been "preconditioned to think in a segregated environment." "There were places we couldn't go, but we just accepted it," he explained. "Now I realize that has a deep effect. You grow up thinking you're inferior, and you're never quite sure of yourself."

His newfound confidence and assertiveness on the court, he reasoned, had a lot to do with his recent decisions to assert himself off the court. During the last two years, following his graduation from UCLA, he had been inspired by "a social revolution among people my age. I finally stopped trying to be part of white society and started to establish a black identity for myself." That evolving identity had led him to support the Olympic boycott movement, to become involved in the Urban League's inner-city programs, and to try to make up for years of inattention to social and racial issues. "I'm not the favorite person of a lot of people in the black community," he confessed. "I'll be the first to admit that I arrived late. I've got a backlog of unpaid dues."[3]

In November, Arthur's newfound activism found further public expression in a lengthy profile in *Ebony* magazine. Although "in the early days black militancy was not his bag," feature writer Louie Robinson Jr. reported, "a different Arthur Ashe speaks today . . . his attitude on his responsibilities in the cause of black justice has changed. . . . Ashe sees himself as 'definitely more militant' today, and believes his old idea of simply achieving as much as one can individually and 'setting an example' is not enough." "It's changed mostly because I'm older and wiser," Arthur insisted, adding, "Then there's outside pressures. What was liberal five years ago may be moderate now." In keeping with the spirit of the times, he had moved beyond the guiding principles of his carefully controlled Richmond boyhood, summarized by Robinson as "be neat and clean, work hard, mind your manners and don't cause trouble." While Arthur still adhered to the first three principles, he no longer put much stock in the fourth. As a freethinking adult, he was determined to do what he could to advance the cause of social justice, even at the risk of being labeled a troublemaker.[4]

Arthur did not, however, go looking for trouble, at least not yet. If he felt sure of himself when addressing an issue, he did not hesitate to speak his mind. Yet on a number of issues related to race and politics he was still mulling over his options. A case in point was his mixed response to the Olympic boycott controversy. The proposed boycott by African nations had become moot in April when the IOC sustained South Africa's banishment from the Olympics. But the continuing agitation by Harry Edwards and the Olympic Project for Human Rights (OPHR) placed considerable pressure on African American athletes either to stay away from the Summer Olympics in Mexico City or to make some sort of gesture on behalf of black solidarity once they were there.

On October 16, two black American Olympians, Tommie Smith and John Carlos, shocked Olympic officials and much of the sporting world by doing just that. After placing first and third in the 200-meter dash, the two San Jose State runners, both OPHR members, appeared at the medal ceremony wearing black socks but no shoes. When the American national anthem began to play, each man bowed his head and raised an arm with a black-gloved hand held high, a gesture widely interpreted as a Black Power salute. Suspended from the American delegation, Smith and Carlos immediately became symbols of racial pride to some and objects of derision and outrage to others. Ashe couldn't decide quite how to react to their provocative violation of the Olympic ban on political protest. Years later he would praise Smith's and Carlos's courage, but at the time he made no public statement on the matter. What Edwards called "the Revolt of the Black Athlete" had begun, but Ashe wasn't sure he was ready to join the revolution.[5]

At this point in his life, he was having too much fun to be an ideologue. The *Life* and *Ebony* profiles both noted his jet-setter lifestyle and the fun-loving side of his character, especially when it came to women. According to Wolf, Arthur's Davis Cup teammates envied "his collection of beautiful girls of all colors," and Robinson pointed out that in Arthur's "part of the tennis world, the food is good . . . the accommodations are comfortable, and the girls are plentiful. And while Arthur's sense of restraint prevents his qualifying as a playboy . . . the pleasures are considerable." To make the point, Robinson ended the piece with the image of Arthur being picked up at the Los Angeles airport by a chauffeured Cadillac limousine, compliments of the comedian Bill Cosby. "Arthur eased himself inside," Robinson wrote admiringly, "and glided off into the velvety blue of the California night. He never lost his cool."[6]

Arthur could hardly be blamed for enjoying the moment and taking a measure of pride in his new status. He was, after all, a black man born and raised under the dominion of Jim Crow—the first of his race since Althea Gibson to become a Grand Slam champion and bona fide tennis celebrity. He had reached the mountaintop, and the climb up had not been easy. He had also arrived at the pinnacle of American tennis under less than ideal conditions as a wartime Army lieutenant on leave. Somehow, the tumultuous months of 1968—a time rent with political protests and assassinations and deep social divisions—had proven to be his breakthrough year.

Arthur's achievements during this time—his last full year as an amateur—were nothing short of remarkable. Playing in only 22 tournaments, he won 10, including both the U.S. Open and the U.S. Amateur. His overall match record of 72–10 represented a winning percentage of 87.8, one of the highest figures in the history of competitive tennis. A semifinalist at Wimbledon, he made the finals of the U.S. Open doubles and led the American Davis Cup team to victory, winning 11 of 12 singles matches. When the final American rankings for the year were released, no one was surprised that Arthur was ranked number one.[7]

Public acknowledgment of his stature came in many forms, from magazine cover stories to laudatory comments by his peers. But one sure sign of his new status during the fall of 1968 was the hovering presence of the journalist John McPhee. A leading practitioner of an emerging genre known as creative nonfiction, McPhee had gained considerable fame as an essayist for *Time* and *The New Yorker*, producing a series of memorable biographical profiles, including several on Princeton basketball star Bill Bradley. Published collectively in 1965 as *A Sense of Where You Are*, the Bradley pieces demonstrated McPhee's interest in the cerebral side of athletic competition. Raised as the son of the Princeton athletic program's staff physician, he was fascinated by the higher-order mind-body connection displayed by Bradley and other true student athletes.[8]

Tired of writing individual profiles, he had begun to toy with the idea of writing a dual profile, and in early September 1968 the televised U.S. Open

semifinal match between Ashe and Graebner presented him with just what
he had been looking for—two talented and complex individuals worthy of
joint study. His goal was to produce a detailed narrative that would reveal
hidden truths about a seemingly transparent subject—in this case, competitive tennis. Anticipating the "thick description" technique perfected by
the noted anthropologist Clifford Geertz in the 1970s, McPhee undertook a
comprehensive study of the text and context of the Ashe-Graebner match.[9]

The result was a series of *New Yorker* essays that ultimately became *Levels of the Game*, a sports book like no other. After securing Ashe and Graebner's cooperation, McPhee acquired the kinescope of the match from CBS.
He also obtained a large but portable Bell and Howell projector that allowed
him and his protagonists to watch the match frame by frame. Throughout
the fall of 1968, he dragged the projector from site to site, wherever Ashe or
Graebner, or in some cases their family members, happened to be. From
West Point and the Graebners' New York apartment on East 56th Street to
Gum Spring and San Juan, the questions and observations never flagged.

McPhee wanted his readers to feel the rhythm and logic of the match, but
he also wanted to present richly textured biographical portraits that ranged
across space and time. There was the match, with its physical architecture
of serves and volleys, and there was human behavior, personal and quirky,
decisions of the moment rooted in years of parental guidance and coaching,
repetitive practice, and real-life experiences both good and bad. There were
also cultural and political contrasts—an avowedly liberal black man from
Richmond, a disinherited son of the South, ranged against the privileged
son of a conservative Cleveland dentist, a proud representative of the white
Republican establishment.

Life magazine's Donald Jackson described *Levels of the Game* as "probably the best tennis book ever written," and Robert Lipsyte of *The New
York Times* speculated that McPhee might have reached "the high point of
American sports journalism." Many readers found the taut narrative to be
reminiscent of Ernest Hemingway's prose—sparse but gripping. Some were
undoubtedly hooked before finishing the first paragraph, which describes
the physics of Ashe's serve:

> Arthur Ashe, his feet apart, his knees slightly bent, lifts a tennis ball
> into the air. The toss is high and forward. If the ball were allowed to
> drop, it would, in Ashe's words, "make a parabola and drop to the
> grass three feet in front of the baseline." He has practiced tossing a
> tennis ball just so thousands of times. But he is going to hit this one.

His feet draw together. His body straightens and tilts far beyond the
point of balance. He is falling. The force of gravity and a muscular
momentum from legs to arm compound as he whips his racquet up
and over the ball.

With this opening description of mechanical artistry, McPhee set the
stage for a searching exploration of the physical and psychological aspects
of competitive tennis. Ashe was fortunate to be one of the two individuals
caught in McPhee's penetrating gaze, which magnified his emerging stardom, ensuring he would never again live as an ordinary private citizen.[10]

Successful, attractive, and famous, twenty-five-year-old Arthur Ashe had all
the attributes of celebrity but one: money. Despite all the hoopla, he still lived
on his modest Army salary supplemented only by the small allotments of
travel money sanctioned by the USLTA. How long this situation was likely
to last was the subject of considerable speculation during the fall of 1968. For
a time, much of the press interest in Ashe revolved around his prospects for
landing a lucrative professional contract. Following the U.S. Open, the double shock of the winner's empty payday and Tom Okker's windfall fueled
the expectation that financial considerations would eventually force all of the
highly ranked amateurs to turn professional.

In Ashe's case, the decision was complicated by his military status—
and by a bizarre development in mid-October. Motivated by the obvious
unfairness of awarding the winner's prize money of $14,000 to the defeated
runner-up, an anonymous fan compensated Ashe with a donation of one
hundred shares of General Motors stock worth an estimated $8,900. Since
the gift was unsolicited, the USLTA's amateur rules committee chairman
Lawrence Krieger announced Ashe could accept the stock without jeopar-
dizing his amateur status. "It's like 'The Millionaire' TV show," a grateful
Ashe exclaimed, though he acknowledged his attorney and former UCLA
teammate Larry Nagler was already conducting preliminary negotiations
with two professional organizations, WCT and the NTL, for much larger
sums.[11]

In the early months of Open Tennis at least one major obstacle to professionalization remained. Professionals were still barred from Davis Cup
play, forcing the leading amateurs to choose between patriotic loyalty and
personal financial gain. And it wasn't clear when—if ever—this traditional
prohibition would be lifted. Australia had won the last four Davis Cups, but
the recent professionalization of the top Aussie players had decimated the

defending champions. Their declining chance of repeating as champions in 1968 was a welcome development for the rest of the field. Yet there was also the fear that the Davis Cup was losing its legitimacy as a prestigious world championship. If the best players in the world were forced to sit on the sidelines, public interest in the competition would surely fade away.

For a time, the ILTF's registered player category—a middle ground between amateurs and contract pros—provided a partial solution to the Davis Cup eligibility problem. As registered players, Ashe and others retained their amateur status as far as Davis Cup competition was concerned, yet they could also choose from week to week whether they wanted to accept an appearance guarantee or compete for prize money. This hybrid existence appealed to Ashe, but in the weeks following the 1968 U.S. Open, the future of Open Tennis was thrown into question when both WCT and the NTL threatened to boycott all seven of the Open tournaments planned for the 1969 American tour. Unless the USLTA abandoned its endorsement of the registered player category, the real pros would stay home.

The so-called registered players were nothing more than "shamateurs," insisted Jack Kramer, the longtime spokesman for professional tennis. "How can a country allow a man to collect prize money and then call him an amateur when they want him to play for them in the Davis Cup? It's ridiculous. The pros don't mind being beaten, but they object to registered players taking prize money. . . . They reckon a man who wants to play for money should become a pro."[12]

At this point, Arthur denied he had definite plans to turn pro, protecting his eligibility to play on the American Davis Cup team, which was expected to beat the Australians for the first time in five years. He was also preoccupied with balancing the fall tour with his responsibilities at West Point. On the days when he was actually at the Military Academy, he put in a full day of work at the data processing center. But thanks to a very liberal personalized leave policy, he spent much of his time traveling to tournaments and playing competitive tennis. In mid-September, he finished first at the Desert Inn Invitational in Las Vegas, and the following week he played well at the Pacific Southwest tournament in Los Angeles, running his winning streak to 30 matches before losing to Rosewall in the semifinals. He suffered a pinched nerve in his neck during a September 24 exhibition match with Bob Lutz and was forced to withdraw from the Pacific Coast tournament in Berkeley. But, after a restful month at West Point limiting himself to light workouts, he was ready for the resumption of Davis Cup play.[13]

The last hurdle before facing the defending champion Australians was a tie against a pesky team from India. The U.S.-India matchup took place in Charlie Pasarell's hometown of San Juan, and the American Davis Cuppers turned the event into a Caribbean vacation. Under the supervision of Dell and Ralston, they played hard, on and off the court, growing closer as teammates and as friends. John McPhee was also on hand with his Bell and Howell projector, vying for as many free minutes with Ashe and Graebner as he could. Over the course of the week the Princeton writer became something of a team mascot and good luck charm.

Fortunately, the powerful American team didn't need much luck. Even though several of the matches were played in sweltering 90-degree heat that seemed to favor the Indians, the Americans prevailed 4–1, with Ashe winning two singles matches in convincing fashion. His three-set victory over Premjit Lall inspired one hyperbolic reporter to write: "Except for the second set, Ashe played with the fidelity of an IBM 1040. Lall programmed the shots and the slim Army lieutenant responded with the pinpoint accuracy of a computer." Not known for his consistency, Ashe appreciated the metaphor.[14]

From Puerto Rico, the American Davis team flew to London for the British Indoor championships, which Dell and Ralston viewed as a tune-up for the upcoming matches in Australia. Billed as a confidence booster, the trip was a bitter disappointment from the start. Trailing 6–1, 5–1 in a first-round match against Keith Wooldridge, Graebner pulled a back muscle and was forced to withdraw, and by the end of the third round Pasarell, Smith, and Ashe had all lost to virtual unknowns. In his second-round loss to Gerald Battrick, an unheralded twenty-one-year-old Welshman, a noticeably listless Ashe managed to win only seven games in three sets.

The team remained in London for a week of practice and a second indoor tournament, but the situation went from bad to worse when Graebner's back strain persisted and Ashe developed severe tendinitis in his right elbow. Doctors prescribed extended rest for both players, and it wasn't clear that either would be ready for the Challenge Round in late December. With the team on edge and feeling the weight of the coming challenge, Dell decided a relaxing tour of France was in order. Traveling to Paris and out into the French countryside proved to be just what the doctor ordered. For Ashe, who had never been to France, the weeklong trip was eye-opening, especially after Dell arranged for the team to spend Thanksgiving with Sargent Shriver, the recently appointed American ambassador there. Shriver's mother-in-law, Rose Kennedy, was staying at the embassy residence for the holidays, and Ashe managed to engage her in an extended conversation about everything from her family's roots in Ireland to the imperiled state of the world. The experience was unforgettable. "As far as I was concerned," he later wrote, "my formal schooling was complete."[15]

The enchanting French sojourn did not produce a miracle cure for Ashe's ailing elbow, but it did produce a storm of controversy surrounding a verbal indiscretion. At a press conference featuring the visiting American Davis Cuppers, several reporters pressed Ashe to reveal how he felt about his rumored snub by South African white supremacists. When one reporter asked him about his apparent exclusion from the South African Open, he tried to steer the conversation to a broader discussion of racial discrimination by private tennis clubs in the American South. But when the reporter demanded to know what he would do about "the South Africa problem," Ashe suddenly blurted out in jest: "Oh, I'd drop a Hydrogen Bomb on Johannesburg!" Though clearly intended as a joke, this brash declaration provoked sensational headlines, especially in South Africa. To Owen Williams, a liberal white South African who later facilitated Ashe's quest to play in the land of apartheid, the facetious hydrogen bomb threat was the "exasperated quip that would reverberate around the world."

The hydrogen bomb statement left many Army and State Department officials shaking their heads in disbelief and sullied Ashe's image among white South Africans. Dell, always protective of his team's image, was not happy about his friend's misstep and the ensuing controversy. Yet, as the U.S. Davis Cup captain, he was more concerned about Ashe's physical condition. For a while the situation was touch-and-go, and in early December nagging injuries forced both Ashe and Graebner to withdraw from a scheduled benefit tournament in Chicago. A week later, however, there was enough improvement to justify putting both of them on the plane to Brisbane. After two weeks away from the court, they were, to Dell's relief, finally ready to play.[16]

Arthur's performance at the Queensland tournament in Brisbane—a tournament he had won during his first trip to Australia in 1965—confirmed his readiness. Showing few signs of tendinitis, he paced himself through the early rounds before going all out against Ray Ruffels in the semifinals. Winning handily, he drew high praise from Harry Hopman, who proclaimed "the young Army lieutenant" to be "the best player in the world, amateur or professional." Ashe had lost enough times to Laver to know this wasn't true, and it was clear the wily Aussie coach was setting him up for a fall. But the words were nice to hear anyway. Two days earlier, the USLTA's ranking committee had elevated him to the number one ranking among American players, so his mood was soaring. Feeling more confident than he had felt in weeks, he went on to win the Queensland tournament by outlasting Stan Smith in a grueling but exhilarating five-set final.[17]

The Americans left Brisbane brimming with confidence, especially Arthur, buoyed not only by his Queensland victory and number one ranking but also by the news that, thanks to the generosity of several "Richmond tennis enthusiasts," his father was flying to Australia for the Challenge Round. He was thrilled for his father, who had rarely traveled outside Virginia, and appreciative of his hometown's unexpected philanthropy. It had meant so much to have his father at the U.S. Open, and now Arthur Sr. would be able to see his son represent his country on the world stage.[18]

The Americans were heavy favorites to take back the Cup from an inexperienced Australian team missing its greatest national players—Laver, Newcombe, Rosewall, and Roche. But with the memory of past years' upsets still fresh, Dell and his squad were not taking anything for granted. Though unproven, the Aussie squad's young players were proud and fit and itching to prove themselves. The uncharacteristically small crowds in Adelaide confirmed that just about everyone was anticipating an American triumph. Yet the wild enthusiasm of the Australian fans who did show up was a bit unnerving for the Americans as play began on December 26.

Playing in a cold, gusting wind against Bill Bowrey, Graebner lost the first set 8–10, but came back to win three of the next four. Later in the day, Ashe also had a slow start against the left-hander Ruffels, losing the first set 6–8; however, he won the next three easily, giving the Americans a commanding 2–0 lead in the best-of-five series. That evening, he had dinner with his father, his teammates, and USLTA president Bob Kelleher, who had been parlaying with his Australian counterparts trying to convince them that the Davis Cup should be open to all players, professional and amateur. The mood was joyous, especially for Ashe, a self-styled Davis Cup "junkie."

"On Friday morning," he recalled, "I couldn't stand to watch the doubles match. I was too nervous. Graebner and I rode around Adelaide in our team car, turning the radio on and off following the fortunes of Stan Smith and Bob Lutz as they tried to finish it off. The reality of winning was beginning to sink in. I thought of sitting in the dollar seats as a twelve-year-old in Richmond, watching the Aussies play. I was so close to getting my name on the old bowl. Now, in an automobile, on the other side of the world, too anxious to be in the tennis stadium with seven thousand tennis-mad Australians and a handful of Americans, I heard the winning point over the radio. The dream had come true."

After Smith and Lutz clinched the Cup with a victory in the doubles, the final day of singles competition was anticlimactic. Playing out the string, the two teams split the second singles matchups, with Graebner beating Ruffels and Ashe losing to Bowrey in four sets. The unexpected loss to Bowrey snapped Ashe's 12-match Davis Cup win streak, and in an unusual show of emotion on the sidelines after the match he burst into tears. But his disappointment didn't last long. Surrounded by his teammates, and with his father looking on, the American ace was full of smiles at the presentation ceremony. After five years of struggle, the giant silver bowl was back in American hands.[19]

Ashe and his teammates remained in Australia for two weeks, opening the 1969 tour with an appearance at the Victoria Open in Melbourne. He had played in the Victoria tournament twice before, losing both times in the later rounds, and he fell short again in 1969, losing to Stan Smith in a tough four-set final. This was Ashe's third loss in four tries against the often overpowering twenty-two-year-old, and he was disappointed by his erratic play and inability to take advantage of Smith's numerous double faults. At several points during the match, Ashe's mind appeared to be elsewhere, which was hardly surprising since he had just received word that the United States Jaycees had selected him as one of the ten Outstanding Young Men of America.

The Jaycees award surprised and pleased him, and he was grateful to Lou Einwick, the Richmond tournament director who had nominated him for the award. Yet he recognized the irony of being honored by an organization that only eight years earlier had imposed a color bar banning him from their tournaments. The biggest problem, however, was that the Jaycees expected him to accept the award in person at a ceremonial banquet to be held in Syracuse, New York, in late January. The timing of the Jaycees banquet fell right in the middle of a scheduled two-week tour of New Zealand, Southeast Asia, and Japan. Fortunately, Dell and the State Department worked out an arrangement for him to interrupt the tour with a whirlwind visit to upstate New York.

At the banquet, Arthur did his best to justify all the hard work that it had taken to get him there. Determined to offer the Jaycees some thought-provoking words of substance in his acceptance speech, he startled many in the crowd with an internationalist perspective on American strengths and weaknesses. Referring to his recent conversations abroad, he presented a troubling refrain: "They say sure, Apollo 8 was great, the Davis Cup was great, our collection of medals in the Olympics was great, our color TV is great, our Peace Corps is great. But what of John Kennedy, and Malcolm X, and Medgar Evers, and 4 little girls in a Birmingham church, and Robert

Kennedy, and Dr. King, and what of Harlem 10 miles from Westchester County, abject poverty 5 minutes from the White House and polluted air and rivers, and people starving in Mississippi and Appalachia." What the Jaycee leaders thought of Arthur's provocative speech went unrecorded, but clearly this was an "outstanding" young man with more than tennis on his mind.[20]

The first stop on the tour was Christchurch, New Zealand, where Ashe made headlines by announcing his intention to turn pro as soon as he was discharged from the Army in February. He was not ready, however, to become a contract pro under the auspices of either WCT or the NTL. The rival promoters Lamar Hunt and George MacCall had both offered him "big money," but he did not want to give up his independence. "I like being my own boss, to go where I want and do what I want," he told reporters. Whether the tennis establishment would continue to allow this degree of freedom, he conceded, was an open question.[21]

The vagaries of the so-called tennis wars would eventually determine the fate of the semipro, registered player option. But at the second stop on the Asian tour Ashe and his teammates found themselves in the midst of a real war. For nearly a week in mid-January 1969—the same week Richard Nixon entered the White House—the Davis Cup champions crisscrossed South Vietnam visiting hospitals and entertaining American troops with tennis exhibitions. It had been a year since the jolting disruption of the Tet Offensive, and the new normal among the American forces was frustration and confusion, a reality diplomatic and military officials did their best to hide.

Throughout the tour of Vietnam, Ashe felt a bit strange as an Army lieutenant out of uniform, and his fervent opposition to the war did not help matters. With a younger brother who had served two year-long deployments on the front line of the conflict, he viewed the war in highly personal terms, and nothing he saw or heard in Vietnam provided any reassurance that the sacrifices his brother and others had made were justified. As he listened to a series of glowing assessments of the American war effort, he sensed his official hosts were offering little more than self-serving propaganda.

In Saigon, the team spent a memorable—and for Arthur a thoroughly disillusioning—lunch listening to American ambassador Ellsworth Bunker hold forth on the march to victory. "His manner at his home . . . was more like that of a businessman who had just shot 80 on the golf course," Arthur recalled years later, adding that his most vivid memory of the visit to the embassy residence was that Bunker "lived just across the back alley from 'the best little whorehouse in Saigon.'"

The mood was more somber when the team received a briefing from General Creighton Abrams at the "Pentagon East" headquarters of the Military Assistance Command. The overall commander of American forces in Vietnam, Abrams proudly described the current strategy of "sweeps" and "search and destroy" missions. When Arthur questioned the advisability of the search and destroy technique, which often led to massive civilian casualties, Abrams grew defensive. "Well, we're trying to contain communism here," the general growled. "If we don't, you'll wind up fighting them on our shores. Take your pick."

After an awkward pause, the briefing turned to the subject of declining morale among American soldiers. "Morale is my biggest problem, even among the officers," Abrams conceded. Yet when Arthur asked him about the special problems facing black soldiers, the general sidestepped the issue of racism by launching into a discussion of drug abuse. Not all of the serious drug users were black, he acknowledged, but the implication of racial pathology was clear. After Arthur blurted out, "Soon, I'll have a brother over here," Abrams offered the consolation that "hopefully, we'll finish by then." Unconvinced, the young lieutenant left the briefing with a heightened skepticism about the rationale and leadership of the American war effort.[22]

The next stop, the military hospital at Long Binh, was even more eye-opening. Here, during a series of exhibition matches played on the hospital grounds, Ashe had his first brush with actual combat. Midway through a doubles match pitting Ashe and Pasarell against Smith and Lutz, several mortar shells landed somewhere near the base, not in close proximity to the hospital but close enough for the players to see puffs of smoke. "We became quite nervous," Ashe recalled, "and at one point Lutz dropped his racquet and started to run off the court. The soldiers in the bleachers were amused and watched the mortar rounds without moving. We were embarrassed, but we had not gone through the initiation to real war."

Later that day, as they visited the Long Binh hospital wards, the tennis delegation came face-to-face with the consequences of the real war. "We were stunned by what we saw," Arthur reported. "For the first time, the full impact of the war was brought home. We saw GIs who had lost their eyes, part of a face, arms or legs. We saw jaws wired shut or eyes closed and greased to keep the lids from being shut. It was difficult to absorb, especially so for Lutz. Bob had been happy-go-lucky, but the experience in Vietnam had a visible effect on him."[23]

Arthur was shaken by what he saw in Vietnam, and by the time he left the war-torn nation in late January he had concerns about the dangers his brother, who had already experienced two years of combat, would face during a third deployment. This sense of foreboding lingered, but he did his best to fulfill the assigned goodwill mission as the Davis Cuppers made their way across Burma, Laos, Cambodia, Indonesia, Thailand, Hong Kong, the Philippines, and Japan. As tennis "ambassadors," he and his teammates did their best to be upbeat and friendly, cheerfully representing American openness and optimism in a part of the world that had ample reasons to be wary of American power.

This was not always an easy task. Navigating the customs of so many countries in such a short span of time was a serious challenge for young men who had some familiarity with Europe, Latin America, and Australia but no previous experiences in Asia. Yet somehow they managed. For Arthur, the most intellectually inquisitive of the bunch, the final week and a half of the trip was an educational treasure, especially when it came to matters of race. "You might wonder about my fascination with the issue of color," he later acknowledged. "It is something related to my past and something I saw wherever I went. I had to catalogue the phenomenon and make sense of it for my own value system."

His particular interest in Asian cultures dated back to his UCLA days, when he had first explored comparative cultural and racial mores while taking an anthropology course. Now he had the opportunity to observe firsthand the complex racial hierarchies of Asian life. "My tour of Southeast Asia and Japan confirmed the universal nature of the color problem," he explained. "The racism of Asia was a fascinating counterpoint to that of America and the British Commonwealth. . . . The Japanese and the Chinese sat at the top of the pecking order, with the Burmese, Laotians, Cambodians, and Vietnamese at the bottom and the Koreans and Thais somewhere in the middle." Indeed, after observing that the rickshaw drivers and airport baggage handlers in Hong Kong "were not likely to be Chinese at all," he came to the sad conclusion "that the entire world was stratified by color."[24]

Ashe had plenty of time to think about his impressions of Asia during the long flight back to the States. After a brief stopover in Hawaii, the team flew to California and then on to Washington for a celebratory luncheon at the White House arranged by Robert Kelleher, the president of the USLTA. When the plane arrived at National Airport at eight in the morning, Kelleher was there to greet the Davis Cuppers, who, to his disappointment, had returned home wearing blue jeans and sporting scraggly beards and unkempt hair. After Kelleher, with Dell's help, marched them to the barbershop and monitored their choice of luncheon outfits, the team arrived at the White House looking fairly respectable. Even so, President Nixon, who was reputed to loathe the game of tennis, turned out to be a stiff host. After an hour of awkward chatter, the president presented each player with a set of gold cuff links and a box of golf balls stamped with the official White House seal. Puzzled, the Davis Cuppers soon departed, thankful for the presidential invitation but wondering if he actually knew what game they played.[25]

From Washington, Ashe traveled to Richmond, arriving just in time to play in the Fidelity Bankers Invitational in front of a hometown crowd. Exhausted and jet-lagged, he lost a semifinal match in straight sets to Tom Koch. Later in the day, he and Pasarell suffered a second embarrassment in the doubles when they lost to a team that included a fresh-faced, eighteen-year-old Junior from New York. The tendinitis in Ashe's elbow had returned, and it was even worse the following week at the Philadelphia Open (the world's first indoor Open tournament), where he lost in the first round to the young Czech Jan Kodes. "It only hurts when I serve," Ashe told the press, but he admitted he was considering withdrawing from the upcoming National Indoor Championship tournament scheduled for mid-February.[26]

This was not the way he had envisioned his post–Davis Cup homecoming, but he had bigger concerns than nursing a sore elbow. The leadership of the USLTA was meeting in Belleair, Florida, in an effort to forestall a threatened pro boycott of Open Tennis. Also at issue was the future of the registered player category that would allow Ashe and others to turn professional without losing their Davis Cup eligibility. If the USLTA voted the right way, he would retain the option of becoming an "independent" pro able to accept prize money without signing a contract with either WCT or the NTL. Whatever ruling the USLTA came up with could be rendered meaningless by the ILTF board, which was scheduled to meet in July to consider granting "self-determination to each nation with regard to open tournaments." But voting to change the current USLTA policy, which allowed noncontract pros to play in Open tournaments but not in invitational pro tournaments, was an important step in the process.

The USLTA's unanimous ruling on February 8 sanctioned the continuation of the registered player category, but conflicting statements regarding the new rules made the situation more confusing than ever. "Can American tournaments, other than the five sanctioned opens, offer prize money to the new category of player," *New York Times* tennis writer Neil Amdur asked; "or must these tournaments again face the task of dealing with the delicate matter of appearance money or expense money?" Unfortunately, the various answers to this question issued by the individual members of the USLTA governing committee provided no clear guidance for tournament officials or for players like Ashe facing difficult career decisions.[27]

The only certainty for Ashe was that he was about to leave active duty in the Army. His honorable discharge on February 24 made it official: even though he would remain in the inactive Army reserves for another decade, Lieutenant Arthur Ashe was essentially a civilian again. Aside from the March 1968 reprimand for speaking out at the Reverend Rogers's forum, the Army had been good to him, giving him the time and freedom to play Davis Cup and to raise his game to a new level. Along the way he had developed several close friendships at West Point. Despite his strong feelings about the war, he reentered civilian life with a deep respect for the traditional military values of discipline and honor. In this respect, he was still his father's son.

Even so, he felt a great sense of liberation. "I'm as excited as hell," he told a group of reporters on his first day as a civilian. "Some of the strains have been cut. I'm a tennis player with one hat on, and I can be a businessman with another hat on. I've got the whole world at my feet and I can pick and choose." When asked to provide specifics, he mentioned business opportunities with the Philip Morris Company and the Hobson-Miller Paper Company, as well as plans to buy a coin laundromat. Reiterating his reluctance to become a contract pro, he once again stated his preference to play as an independent—to be, in effect, his "own boss." Calling himself a "maverick," he stressed the importance of freeing up time to continue his civil rights–related work with the Urban League. "Talking and working with kids is important to me," he explained. "I just think that for me my freedom to do what I want and play where I want is more important than money." Two days later, George MacCall of the NTL confirmed that earlier in the year Ashe had spurned his offer of a $400,000 five-year contract.[28]

In late March, during a tournament in St. Petersburg, Florida, Ashe elaborated on his decision to turn MacCall down. It wasn't that he didn't want to make money from tennis; on the contrary, like all tennis professionals he looked to the game for his livelihood. "I am a pro," he declared. "I'm out to earn all the prize money I can, not as a contract pro but as an independent businessman." What set him apart was his determination to maintain both his independence and a balance between financial success and the pursuit of excellence in other areas of life.

His motivations, he freely acknowledged, were complex and by no means entirely altruistic: "I just got out of the Army and I relish my freedom. For the first time in two years I can go where I want and do what I want.

If I were under contract, I would have to go where I was told to go. This way I can play one week, lay off the next and even make a trip to the moon if anyone invites me. . . . Most of all, I want to win at Wimbledon. I'd play there even if there were no prizes because the prestige of winning is beyond calculation. That's what also is so attractive about not becoming a formal pro but remaining eligible for Davis Cup. Again prestige is involved. How else could I have luncheon at the White House with the President?"

In an age when big money was asserting its dominance over the sporting world, Ashe's comments on the limits of pecuniary motivation were unusual to say the least. But even more unusual was his forthright commitment to social action on behalf of the black community. "Another reason for retaining my independence as a player is that I have commitments in an area that means so much to me, the black area," he explained. "I'm working with Whitney Young in the Urban League. . . . I guess we'd be classified as moderates, but we get the job done. One of our aims is to get jobs for dropouts, and we are meeting with success. I can do something no social worker, no matter how well intentioned, can do. I can walk into any poolroom in Harlem, and those kids listen to me. I talk their language and they know who I am and what I've done. I'm also buying a Laundromat in a Jersey ghetto area, and I am investing in a Negro insurance company." [29]

Ashe's brash claim to what would later be termed "street cred" was dubious at best, but his assertion of racial solidarity was revealing. Public identification with the civil rights struggle clearly had become important to him and would become even more so in the years to come. When his Davis Cup teammates teasingly called him "our little militant," he laughed. Yet his personal interest in the plight of the black community was serious business. After years of relative passivity, he was now fully engaged in the struggle, though he continued to avoid racial conflict whenever possible.

Before Arthur left St. Petersburg, for example, he was involved in an ugly incident at the private, all-white Lakewood Country Club. When all of the courts at the tournament venue—a public facility located in a predominantly black neighborhood—were full and could not accommodate his practice session, he moved the session to Lakewood at the suggestion of Paul Reilly, a fifteen-year-old white ball boy who insisted the pro at the private facility wouldn't mind. But as soon as Arthur and Paul began to volley, a golf cart from the nearby Lakewood course raced toward their court with the driver screaming, "Get the nigger off the court!" Embarrassed, Paul stepped forward, ready to confront the racist intruder. But Arthur immediately intervened to defuse the situation. "Let's just go," he advised, putting himself between the boy and the golfer. "I don't want you to get in trouble because of me." So they left, leaving the desegregation of the country club for another day. This was certainly not the way Arthur had envisioned the closing moments of his amateur career, but in characteristic fashion his concern for others took precedence over his own urge to vent or strike back. In the struggle for the long haul, he could not allow one ignorant man to get under his skin or cause him to lose his cool.

"His militancy is the quiet kind, without flamboyance," Arthur Daley observed later that week, but it was "extremely effective" nonetheless. Impressed by Ashe's levelheaded, practical approach to life, he predicted the young tennis star would ultimately have the best of both worlds—the satisfaction of helping his race and the benefits of financial security. "He'll make it all right," Daley insisted, "because he's a smart and resourceful independent businessman, who is currently disguised as a player." During fifteen years of amateur competition, Ashe had received college scholarships, travel and expense money, innumerable trophies and plaques, and even a few gifts. Yet not a penny of prize money had come his way. That situation was about to change.[30]

On March 25, 1969, Ashe traveled to New York to begin his new life as a noncontract professional tennis player. The inaugural Madison Square Garden Open was offering $25,000 in total prize money, with $5,290 going to the tournament champion. But to walk away with serious money, Ashe would have to overcome a top-notch field featuring many of the world's best players, including the great Australians—Laver, Roche, Emerson, and Newcombe—and the forty-year-old legend Pancho Gonzales. Playing on a new rubberized indoor surface called Uni-Turf and still nursing his aching right elbow, Ashe entered the tournament with low expectations. Yet somehow he managed to fight his way into the final, beating Scott, Moore, Pasarell, and Emerson.

The other finalist was Andrés Gimeno, the thirty-one-year-old Spaniard who had served as Ashe's doubles partner at the U.S. Open. The two men had never faced each other, but Ashe suspected he was in for a long day against a veteran pro known for his exhausting baseline game. In the early going it appeared that Ashe—who only managed to win three games in the first two sets and lost his serve seven consecutive times—would be dispatched in straight sets. But he rallied to win the third and fourth sets, setting the stage for a showdown in the fifth. Trailing 0–4 in the final set, Ashe surged back again, eventually drawing even as the match approached the three-hour mark. In the end, after Ashe fought off six match points, Gimeno prevailed 9–7. Even so, the rookie's valiant effort delighted the New York crowd, earning him considerable respect and a $3,690 paycheck.[31]

Two days later, Ashe was in San Juan for the Caribe Hilton International, an amateur tournament that temporarily put him back in the position of accepting expense money. Once again he made it to the final match, and this time he won, outlasting Charlie Pasarell in five sets. It had been six months since his last tournament victory, and he hoped this breakthrough was a sign he had put the sore elbow and the slump behind him.[32]

Ashe's first challenge after San Juan, however, was getting to New York in time for an important luncheon at the 21 Club. For several weeks, he had been consulting with Sidney B. Wood Jr., the 1931 Wimbledon singles champion and president of the Town Tennis Club, a posh indoor tennis facility on East 56th Street. Wood was also the head of the Tennis Development Corporation, the manufacturer of a synthetic surface called Supreme Court. At the luncheon, he introduced Ashe as the new director of the Town Tennis Club and as the product evaluator of Supreme Court, purportedly a durable and relatively inexpensive option to traditional grass courts.

Accepting the position at the Town Tennis Club, which maintained two rooftop courts "high above Sutton Place," represented Ashe's first major venture into the potentially lucrative world of product endorsement. This was a milestone in his career, as was his association with an elite private club that would have excluded him from membership a decade earlier. The irony of the situation was not lost on Ashe, who reminded the guests that he had come "a long ways" from the segregated facilities of Richmond, where he spent seven years on the public courts before being granted permission to play at a private club.

His allusion to past exclusions caused a minor stir, but the story of the day was the disclosure that he and several other players had decided to form an organization of independent professionals. With WCT and the NTL making threats and demands, the players needed some means of "protecting their interests in major open events against domination by the two American-based groups of contract pros." As he explained, "the 16 contract pros are holding up all the money in the major tournaments. They get prize money, plus so much expense money. We don't get expenses. In a draw of 128, why should 16 guys get all the money?"[33]

Why, indeed, but there would be a lot of off-court volleying before the matter was settled. Three days after his appearance at the 21 Club, Ashe was off to the Monaco Open for the beginning of a three-month stint on the European tour. This was his sixth trip to Europe, but all of his previous visits had been limited to three weeks or less. The 1969 trip, stretching across six nations, would provide him with his first extended experience with slow, European-style clay courts. His prior performances on European clay had been less than stellar, and the uncertain status of his right elbow did not bode well for his chances for success this time. But he could not resist the double lure of making serious money at the various European Opens and traveling across Britain and the Continent with Pasarell and Graebner. Rome, Paris, Madrid, Berlin, and London beckoned, and sore elbow or not, he was determined to make the most of the situation.

Culturally, the grand European tour of 1969 was a great success, but tennis-wise it proved to be thoroughly disappointing. Even when his elbow behaved, he felt awkward on clay and never really got his rhythm. In Monaco, he lost to Newcombe in the quarters; at the Italian Open in Rome, he lost badly to Jan Kodes in the third round; and at Bournemouth in late April he suffered a humiliating first-round loss to a young, unheralded Frenchman, Jean-Claude Barclay. "I could have stayed in the States, but I came here for experience," a disconsolate Ashe commented after the Bournemouth match. "I sure got it. Right now I have no confidence at all." [34]

The quality of his play picked up in early May, and he made it to the semifinals in Madrid. But at the West Berlin Open a week later, in the final warm-up for the French Open, he played erratically, losing in the third round. Played on the famous red clay of Roland Garros stadium, the French Open was the biggest event on the 1969 Continental tour with first-place prize money of $7,000. Seeded sixth, Ashe was the highest-seeded American in the singles competition, and he and Pasarell were also considered a serious threat in the doubles. No American, however, had won the French national singles championship since Tony Trabert's consecutive victories in 1954 and 1955, and during the past decade only one American, Gonzales in 1968, had made it as far as the semifinals.

In 1969, three Americans—Ashe, Stan Smith, and Cliff Richey—made it into the round of sixteen, but none advanced to the quarters. Playing in a rain-delayed match against the unseeded Australian Fred Stolle, Ashe suffered one of the worst defeats of his career. Unable to gain secure footing on the damp clay, he sprayed forehand after forehand into the net or beyond the baseline, and managed to win only six games in three sets. He and Pasarell fared much better in the doubles, losing a close semifinal match to the top-seeded Australians John Newcombe and Tony Roche. But overall Ashe's first encounter with Roland Garros was sobering at best. The City of Light might be dazzling outside the stadium, but on the inside the red clay did nothing for him.[35]

Ashe left Paris in early June with only a few hundred dollars in prize money to his credit. Fortunately, the next stop on the tour, the Wills Open in Bristol, England, would be played on the more comfortable surface of grass. Even his elbow seemed to perk up on the lawn at Bristol, and he won three matches without losing a set before succumbing to the always tough Ken Rosewall in the quarterfinals. By the time he arrived at Wimbledon in mid-June, his confidence was on the rebound, and he seemed ready for the biggest challenge in tennis.[36]

This was Ashe's fifth appearance at Wimbledon but the first as a high seed. As the reigning U.S. Open champion and the top-ranked American, he drew considerable media attention, fueled in part by the recent publication of John McPhee's flattering profiles of him and Graebner in *The New Yorker*. Even before they took the court, the men's locker room at the All England Club was abuzz with congratulations for the two young Americans. Once the tournament was under way the center of attention shifted to Rod Laver—the winner of the last two majors, the Australian and the French, and the heavy favorite to win his second consecutive and fourth overall Wimbledon crown. Ashe continued to draw secondary attention as a player worth watching.[37]

The biggest topic of conversation at the 1969 Wimbledon, however, was the recent founding of the International Tennis Players Association (ITPA). Announced at a June 16 London news conference by John Newcombe, the new organization had been in the works for several weeks as Ashe, Pasarell, Marty Riessen, and other members of the organizing committee played and talked their way across Europe. With Ashe taking an active role in the ongoing discussions of strategy and purpose, Newcombe stepped forward to serve as the ITPA's temporary chairman and spokesperson. "The world tennis situation is in a turmoil," Newcombe told the reporters in London, "and the players think they can help if organized. We want to raise the standards of the tournaments we play in. . . . If necessary we will act as one to discipline players who misbehave, and we will also fight to protect players who are unjustly treated. We want better communications between all the people concerned with the game." Anticipating opposition from the traditional movers and shakers of the tennis world, he added: "We are not politicians. We do not intend to get involved in nation-to-nation controversy. Nor do we intend to strike. But we do feel that we should express our opinions."[38]

By the time the ITPA held its first general meeting on June 19, three days before the start of Wimbledon, there were signs that several parts of the tennis establishment felt threatened by the players' assertive stance. Ashe and his colleagues were determined to force the issue of players' rights, and over the pre-Wimbledon weekend they approved five recommendations, including the demands "that all members receive in writing conditions for their participation in a tournament" and "that a player representative be assigned to each country where major tournaments are held."

Elected ITPA treasurer, Ashe spoke to the press during the first official day of Wimbledon, a rain-soaked Monday that forced the postponement of the first-round singles matches, including his scheduled match against Riessen. "We can't tell anybody what to do," he conceded, "but we can advise and recommend. And we want observer status at the I.L.T.F. meeting next month." Earlier in the day, he and other ITPA representatives had been granted a meeting with Wimbledon officials, which he viewed as a good beginning for the organization. "That's almost de facto recognition, already," he said with a wry smile.[39]

Once the rain stopped and the tournament began, Ashe was all business, proclaiming he was "90 per cent fit" and claiming his elbow had healed to the point where he could "go all out on his service." All he needed was the opportunity to soak his arm "in hot water every day" plus a bit of "hot weather." In typical London fashion, the weather remained cool and windy, but Ashe managed to dispatch Riessen in four sets anyway, despite losing the opening set 6–1 and double-faulting five times in his first two service games. He had a similarly slow start in a second-round match against the South African Terry Ryan, losing the first two sets. But he came back to win the last three. In the third round, he once again needed five sets to overcome a nonseeded opponent, Graham Stilwell of Great Britain.

In the round of sixteen, Arthur finally found his stride, winning an emotional four-set victory over his childhood idol Pancho Gonzales. Three days earlier, the forty-one-year-old Gonzales had outlasted Pasarell in the longest match in Wimbledon history—112 games played over five hours and twelve minutes. So after he lost to Arthur the crowd gave "the old lion" a thunderous standing ovation. No one appreciated Gonzales's effort more than Arthur, yet avenging his best friend's loss was sweet nonetheless.[40]

Arthur had two days' rest before facing Lutz in the quarterfinals, but maintaining his focus proved difficult. When London *Times* reporter John Hennessy got wind of a rift in the ITPA ranks, Arthur offered a candid and full disclosure that put him in the middle of a public controversy. The issue was South Africa and the ITPA's willingness to issue a strong statement against apartheid. Arthur had raised the matter at a closed meeting of the ITPA earlier in the week. After informing his fellow members that he had been denied a visa by the South African government in March even though the South African Lawn Tennis Union (SALTU) had approved his application to play in the nation's annual championship tournament, he argued strenuously that South Africa should be banned from Davis Cup competition and expelled from the ILTF.

While Arthur did not call for an outright boycott of South Africa by the ITPA, he did ask for a public statement condemning racism and apartheid. A month earlier, he had been one of thirteen black athletes to join more than a hundred other black leaders and intellectuals in the sponsorship of an American Committee on Africa (ACOA) statement calling for the revocation of a U.S. government permit allowing South African Airways to schedule commercial flights between Johannesburg and New York. Filling a full page in *The New York Times*, the ACOA statement urged the U.S. government "to support U.N. action against apartheid instead of aiding the South African government and its representatives like South African Airways." It also mocked the airline's tourist brochure slogan "We'd like the pleasure of your company" by pointing out that "any 'welcome' to South Africa is reserved for *whites only* under your government's laws."

This direct, public condemnation of apartheid was what Arthur was looking for from the ITPA. The ensuing discussion revealed that, with the exception of the South African Bob Hewitt, all thirty-six members at the meeting opposed apartheid and generally sympathized with Arthur's views. Yet when Arthur called for a vote as to whether the ITPA should issue a formal anti-apartheid statement, his proposal went down to defeat 19–17. Where this left Arthur and the ITPA was unclear, but when a reporter asked several ITPA members if they would refuse to play in South Africa "as a gesture of solidarity," he found few takers.[41]

The Wimbledon rift was the first of many unexpected twists in Ashe's long involvement in the South African liberation movement. Over the next twenty years he would experience the inevitable highs and lows of political struggle and grow accustomed to the fits and starts of uneven progress. But in 1969 he was a novice activist who found it difficult to accept complacency, or worse yet hypocrisy, masquerading as caution. When he took the court against Lutz in the quarterfinals, he was still angry, though he tried to avoid taking out his frustrations on his friend and Davis Cup teammate. Whatever his mood, he played his best tennis in months, winning the first two sets in less than fifty minutes and eliminating Lutz in four sets.

This victory advanced Ashe to the semifinals against Laver, the defending champion, who had beaten him in the semis the year before. No one expected Ashe to do much better in the rematch, but when he took the first set 6–2 the Centre Court crowd began to stir. Unfortunately for Ashe, both men soon returned to form, with Laver winning three straight sets, the last at 6–0. Once again Ashe had come up short, failing to make the finals of the tournament that meant more to him than any other.[42]

Distressing as it was, the loss to Laver was not the worst news of the day for Ashe. While the semifinal match was in progress, delegates from forty Davis Cup nations were meeting less than a hundred yards away. The delegates had gathered to consider two major issues—a French proposal to open up Davis Cup competition to contract and teaching professionals and a Polish-Hungarian proposal to expel South Africa from the competition. Though supported by the United States, Australia, and most of the larger tennis powers, the French proposal went down to defeat 21–19, falling well below the necessary two-thirds majority. Bitterly disappointed, Ashe insisted the vote—orchestrated by the smaller nations—made "no sense at all" because "it's the smaller nations who will suffer most from it." To complete the fiasco, as far as he was concerned, a procedural maneuver prevented the South African expulsion proposal from even coming to a vote. For the time being, the buck had been passed to the ILTF, which was scheduled to consider a similar proposal in July.[43]

Ashe's involvement in the controversy surrounding South Africa's participation in Davis Cup competition became a subject of public discussion in the weeks following Wimbledon. While in Washington for the inaugural *Washington Star* International Open in early July, he faced tough questions from reporters who wanted to know what he would do if South Africa and the United States faced off in the Davis Cup Challenge Round scheduled for September in Cleveland. Would he agree to play against the avowedly racist nation, Neil Amdur asked, or "would he protest that country's apartheid policy by sitting out the series?" Ashe's murky response betrayed the difficulty of his situation. "Either way I guess I'm a target," he acknowledged. "If I play in the Davis Cup, some people might protest. If I don't play as a sign of protest, that may only help South Africa win the cup, which would be twice as bad for everyone." When pressed to be more specific, he refused to be pinned down. "I want the International Lawn Tennis Federation to make the first move this week at their meetings in Prague," he insisted. "If they don't do anything, then I think you'll see some things happening."

While Ashe waited for the ILTF to act, he joined Dell and several other ITPA members for a series of inner-city youth clinics. Following the morning clinics, some of the world's best independent pros began tournament play at a public court facility located in a predominantly black working-class neighborhood. All of this had been carefully planned by Dell as a demonstration of the ITPA's vision of truly open tennis. Ashe, who had been the first person to urge Dell to place the tournament at a public, inner-city venue, couldn't have been more pleased. "It's great to see tennis getting out of the country clubs at last," he told reporters.[44]

Two days later, in the same spirit of innovation, Ashe celebrated his twenty-sixth birthday by starting his quarterfinal match with an experimental metal racket. But after four games of erratic play, he went back to his tried and trusted wood racket. Some forms of change, it seemed, were more risky than others, especially when thousands of dollars of prize money were at stake. Ashe eventually reached the final round, where he lost a tough five-set match to Tom Koch, who had beaten him at Richmond in February. Sporting shoulder-length hair, Koch symbolized the new freedom of competitive tennis, and the match, played in front of a racially diverse crowd that included several members of President Nixon's family, was a testament to the changes sweeping across the tennis world. For his part, Ashe walked away with the runner-up prize of $3,000, the second largest paycheck of his career.[45]

The 1969 *Washington Star* tournament kicked off the first U.S. Summer Circuit of Open play. The two American Opens of 1968 had been expanded to fifteen Open tournaments offering a total of $440,000 in prize money. Open Tennis was clearly becoming the norm, despite the uncertain future of the registered player classification and the continuing tensions between contract pros and the major tennis federations. At its July meeting, the ILTF withdrew its endorsement of the registered player concept, but the USLTA refused to follow suit. It would take another two years to clear up the confusion. In the meantime Open Tennis gained an increasingly secure footing among fans and players alike.[46]

In mid-July, Ashe was heartened by the unexpected news that Great Britain had eliminated South Africa from the 1969 Davis Cup competition. Played in front of raucous crowds in Bristol, the Britain–South Africa matches were disrupted by anti-apartheid demonstrations featuring protesters lying down on the court as flour bombs were tossed from the stands. Ashe, as a steward of sportsmanship, was ambivalent about the disruptions, but mostly he was relieved that he no longer faced the prospect of boycotting the Davis Cup final.

Under growing pressure to abandon its racial restrictions, SALTU pledged to do just that in late July. "There will be no color bar in South African tennis," SALTU president Alf Chalmers announced. "And that means in the selection of South African players for the Davis Cup squad and in foreign teams participating in matches in this country. . . . Furthermore, I would be very happy to welcome a team, like the United States squad, that included a Negro star like Arthur Ashe." Chalmers insisted that the South African government had "given its approval to these matters," but Ashe and many others remained skeptical. When asked if the South African government would grant Ashe a visa, Chalmers began to hedge, claiming he could not speak for the government. "All I can say," he admitted, "is that we would do our very best to assist him." [47]

Ashe did not waste any time in calling the South Africans' bluff. On July 29, he announced his intention to reapply for a South African visa. His first application had been informal, forwarded quietly through private channels. "This time I won't be silent," he vowed. "I'll go right to the South African embassy in New York. If they want to turn me down, they'll have to do it right there in front of all of you. . . . As long as the Government's silent, nothing's changed." Ashe also reported he had just spent three hours consulting with Owen Williams, the legendary South African tennis promoter who earlier in the summer had been hired to manage the second U.S. Open. Williams was a close friend of Joseph Cullman, the tournament chairman and president of the Philip Morris Company, and Gladys Heldman, the influential publisher of *World Tennis* magazine. A controversial choice because of his South African ties, Williams nonetheless drew high praise from Ashe, who cautioned against "guilt by association." "He's really a great guy," the black American declared, who is "all in favor of my coming over to play in the South African open." Williams expressed some doubt that the South African government would give Ashe a visa but confirmed he would "love to have Arthur in the draw." [48]

In August, Ashe temporarily turned his attention away from South Africa and the ongoing tennis wars to focus on his preparation for the U.S. Open. With his elbow problem seemingly behind him, he was eager to defend his title—and to vie for the first-place prize money of $16,000, the largest payday in tennis history. In the final warm-ups before Forest Hills, he lost to Stan Smith in the semifinals of the Eastern Grass Court championships, and a week later he came up just short in his attempt to defend his national "amateur" title at Longwood. In the Longwood semifinals, he lost a tough five-set match to Lutz, whom he had defeated in the final the year before. This was

Ashe's first loss to his young Davis Cup teammate in four career matches, but he played well enough to pronounce himself ready to face the world's best at Forest Hills.[49]

In truth, Ashe knew his chance of repeating as U.S. Open champion was slim. Laver, who had dispatched him with relative ease at Wimbledon, was the overwhelming favorite, and even if the Rocket faltered there were other powerful Australian grass court specialists to overcome. And beyond them there was Stan Smith, who had won on the grass at Longwood the week before. Seeded fourth, Ashe found himself on the same side of the draw as Laver, which meant that barring any major upsets they would face each other in the semifinals. First, however, he had to contend with a serious threat to his concentration.

On the eve of his opening round match against eighteen-year-old Dick Stockton, who would later serve as his colleague in the broadcast booth, Ashe received telephone calls from two anti-apartheid groups considering setting up a picket line to protest Williams's involvement in the Open. Ashe did his best to dissuade them, in part because he did not want to embarrass the host West Side Tennis Club, which had just voted "to reward all U.S. Open singles champions with honorary memberships." As the 1968 singles champion, he had become the first black member in the club's history, and he did not want to face a picket line on his first day as a member. "I told them, you'll have to trust me for another year," he informed reporters. "I said, we think we can lick this problem, and that if nothing's done by next year, I'd join the picket line myself." While he didn't specify what "the problem" was—his application for a South African visa, Williams, or apartheid itself—his pledge was enough to forestall the anti-apartheid demonstration.[50]

With one potential crisis avoided, Ashe promptly ran into a second when Gonzales publicly criticized his work ethic, comparing him unfavorably to Laver in a *New York Times* interview. "Arthur Ashe has ease of movement, stamina and speed," Gonzales opined. "He has all the equipment to convince you that his potential is unlimited. But I don't like his inclination to loaf in practice. He could—and should—learn from Rod Laver. . . . What I admire most in Rod is his determination and concentration. He carries that determination even into practice, because he chases every ball as if it were match point in a championship. It's a wonderful habit to get into. Ashe would become better if he were to do the same." This was not what Ashe wanted to read on the eve of a tough third-round match, but part of the sting came from the recognition that Gonzales was right.[51]

Despite all the diversions, Ashe managed to maintain his composure and a string of impressive victories through the quarterfinals. The real test came when Laver joined him in the semifinals. Ashe was the only independent pro and one of only two Americans to reach the quarterfinals. The other six were all Australians, and after his old friend from St. Louis Butch Buchholz was eliminated, the defending champion stood alone against a fearsome trio of Australian contract pros: Rod Laver, Tony Roche, and John Newcombe.

The pride of America and the ITPA were clearly at stake in the match against Laver, and Ashe was determined to give it all he had. It was a competitive, seesaw match from the start, with Ashe pulling ahead in the first set only to lose 8–6. He also led in the early going in the second set, surging ahead 4–2, but once again he faded and lost 6–3. The third set was an all-out slugfest that went to 12–12 before the referee suspended play on account of darkness. After a night's sleep, Ashe was still hoping for an upset. But after a rare foot fault led to a service break in the 25th game, Laver quickly closed out the match 14–12.

It was Laver's 29th consecutive singles victory, and in the championship match against Roche the next day he extended the streak to 30, becoming the first player in tennis history to win a second Grand Slam (he first won all four major singles championships in 1962). Ashe was still number one in the United States, but the Rocket was undeniably the world's best tennis player. Before presenting the championship trophy at center court, USLTA president Alastair Martin turned to Laver and exclaimed: "You're the greatest in the world . . . perhaps the greatest we've ever seen."[52]

In the immediate aftermath of the second U.S. Open, Ashe did not have much time to think about the implications of Laver's dominance. He was too busy getting ready for the Davis Cup Challenge Round tie in Cleveland. The surprise challenger was an upstart team from Romania led by the mustachioed veteran Ion Tiriac and a brash twenty-three-year-old shotmaker named Ilie Nastase. Known for his courtside antics and outsized personality, Nastase presented a clear contrast to the cool and collected Ashe, whom he faced in the opening singles match on September 19.

Ashe had never played Nastase, but he knew he was in for a fight, having watched the young Romanian defeat Smith in four sets at the U.S. Open. Fortunately, he got off to a strong start on the fast asphalt surface, winning the first set 6–2. Battling a stiff wind, he managed to fight off a series of furious Nastase rallies to win the next two 15–13 and 7–5. At one point in the third set, the referee stopped play when two antiwar demonstrators ran through the stands waving a North Vietnamese flag. Later in the week, demonstrators affiliated with the Students for a Democratic Society (SDS) marched around the outside of the stadium chanting "Ho, Ho, Ho Chi Minh," and clashes with police led to seventeen arrests. Nothing, however, could stop the Americans from sweeping the series and retaining the coveted Davis Cup. After defeating Tiriac in five tough sets in the third singles match—his 22nd win in 25 career Davis Cup matches—Ashe embraced Dell in a joyous celebration. For the first time since 1949, the American squad had won back-to-back Davis Cups, and Dell and Ashe were two of the main reasons why.

The joy of victory was muted only by the undeniable decline in the status of the Davis Cup competition. There was no national television coverage as there had been in 1964, the last time a Challenge Round had been played in the United States, and press and public interest in the Cleveland matches seemed lukewarm at best. The message was clear: as long as Laver, Newcombe, and the other contract pros were excluded from the competition, winning the Cup would mean far less than it had in the past. Even though a record number of countries—fifty-one in all—had entered teams in the 1969 competition, the Davis Cup was no longer a wholly legitimate world championship. As one Cleveland fan explained to his son, "Romania is here because the best players like Rod Laver, John Newcombe, and Tony Roche aren't." Neil Amdur agreed, pointing out the hard truth that Romania's "appearance generated more interest from the Students for a Democratic Society than from any major television network."

Nearly everyone acknowledged that major adjustments to the Davis Cup's eligibility rules were in order. But the arcane procedural requirements of the Davis Cup committee insured it would take at least two years to enact meaningful reform. In the meantime, the excluded contract pros would have to console themselves with prize money, and players like Ashe—those passionately devoted to Davis Cup play—would have to wait for the tennis bureaucrats to work out a compromise that would restore the Cup's prestige.[53]

TWELVE

RACKET MAN

■

RESTORING THE DAVIS CUP to its former glory was important to Ashe. But his first priority as a rookie tennis professional was finding a way to earn a decent living. To his dismay, throughout the summer and fall of 1969 the future of Open Tennis—the source of his livelihood—looked uncertain at best, especially after WCT announced its plan to hold fourteen invitational tournaments in 1970 with no provision for including independent pros like him.[1] During his first nine months as a pro, Ashe had managed to earn a few thousand dollars by scrapping his way into the quarterfinals and semifinals of several open tournaments. But his inability to win the top prize money—his biggest paycheck was $5,000 for finishing second at the Las Vegas Open in October—forced him to look elsewhere for much of his income.[2]

Fortunately, the combination of Arthur's reputation as a consummate gentleman and his success on the court—especially his U.S. Open and Davis Cup victories—allowed him to take advantage of the lucrative field of celebrity product endorsement. With rare exceptions, black athletes had traditionally been considered unmarketable as product endorsers. But with the help of Dell's public relations and negotiating skills, he was able to defy both prejudice and conventional wisdom. Arthur had come to rely on the young Yale-educated laywer for advice and counsel, and by late 1969 they had become more than friends.

As Arthur tried to make sense of the choices before him—most notably, whether to remain a registered player or become a contract pro—Dell
urged him to entrust his future to Mark McCormack, a Cleveland lawyer and sports agent who had founded International Management Group
(IMG) in 1960. The first agent to recognize the almost unlimited potential
of celebrity product endorsement, McCormack had turned golf stars Arnold
Palmer, Gary Player, and Jack Nicklaus into moneymaking icons. In the
weeks following America's Davis Cup victory in Cleveland, Dell arranged
no fewer than three meetings between Ashe and McCormack. Each time
Arthur came away with an uneasy feeling about the slick-talking Cleveland
lawyer, and after the third unsuccessful attempt to get him to sign a contract
with IMG—at a breakfast meeting in New York—he asked Dell plaintively:
"How many more times are you going to do this? You keep taking me to
McCormack because you think he's the best, but why don't *you* do it? Why
don't *you* manage me and be my lawyer? Just think about it, if I turned pro
and Stan did . . . we could all do it together, you could join us and it could be
a lot of fun and we could start a business."

At that point, Dell was nearing the end of a two-year leave from the
Washington law firm, Hogan & Hartson. Having restored America's Davis
Cup fortunes with the first two championships since 1963, he was ready to
return to his law practice. Becoming a sports agent, he later insisted, had
never entered his mind before Arthur's plea. After initially laughing off the
suggestion, he soon broached the idea with Hogan & Hartson's senior partner, who, surprisingly enough, urged him to follow Arthur's advice. That
was enough to convince Dell to take a risk, and by the spring of 1970 the
sports agency law office later known as ProServ was up and running, albeit
with only two clients, Ashe and Smith. Thus began one of the most successful sports agencies of the twentieth century.[3]

Sealed with a handshake, the Dell-Ashe partnership radically altered the
careers of both men. While Dell made the deals, Ashe became an active partner in the highly personal "packaging" process. As he wrote tellingly many
years later, "A star athlete could make more money off the field than on—if
he or she was packaged properly. . . . I had to sell a product—me—and the
product had to be of high quality to get a high price. The yardstick, then and
now, was Arnold Palmer."[4]

Marketing a black tennis player with only two major titles to his credit
was obviously much more challenging than drawing upon the exploits of
a legendary white golf champion from the heartland of America. But Ashe
and Dell reasoned that in the wake of the civil rights movement a clean-cut

and physically attractive athlete of any color was potentially appealing to enterprising capitalists looking for consumers. "I had a good image—U.S. Army, Davis Cup, acceptable manners," Ashe recalled, adding: "My experience indicated I was acceptable to white Americans, who bought the racquets, shoes, and tennis clothes I hoped to sell." What else could anyone ask for other than lighter skin and straighter hair? That was the unanswered question as Dell and Ashe approached their first potential business partners.[5]

They began early in 1969 with Wilson Sporting Goods, the leading manufacturer of tennis rackets and the largest sporting goods corporation in the United States. Ashe had used a Wilson "Don Budge" racket, named for the sport's first Grand Slam champion, since the age of thirteen, and he had always dreamed of having a Wilson model with his own name on it. Dell arranged a meeting with Wilson executive Gene Buwick, and the three men sat down in the Polo Lounge of the posh Beverly Hills Hotel. From the outset, Buwick was enthusiastic about offering Ashe a contract, but the deal hit a snag as soon as they began to talk about money. Protracted negotiations followed, but in the end Dell was unable to procure the six-figure contract he thought Ashe deserved.[6]

Though disappointed, Ashe encouraged Dell to look elsewhere, and they soon found themselves in the eccentric company of Howard Head, the Baltimore-based aeronautical engineer who had invented laminate skis in the late 1940s. Founded in 1950, the hugely successful Head Ski Corporation had recently moved into the tennis racket business with the hope of expanding upon Wilson's success with the innovative T-2000 metal racket. Seeking legitimacy in the tennis world, Head wanted to hire a leading professional player willing to experiment with and promote a new line of metal rackets. In Ashe, who was also seeking legitimacy of a kind, he found the perfect match for his unconventional product. On April 21, 1969, the two men signed an endorsement agreement authorizing Head to market "Ashe tennis products."

Head would eventually join forces with the Prince Company to produce a metal racket with an oversized head. But the 1969 prototype featured a normal-size head made of fiberglass and honeycombed aluminum. Ashe's early experiences with the prototype, which he considered to be much too light, were an exercise in frustration. The later, heavier models, however, suited him well and quickly became one of the world's most popular rackets, making the names Ashe and Head virtually synonymous by the mid-1970s. Along the way, both Ashe and Head made a great deal of money. Under the terms of their five-year contract, Ashe received a 5 percent royalty on every

Head racket sold, which amounted to several hundred thousand dollars a year during the 1970s. At the time, the Head contract represented one of the most lucrative deals in sports history. Suddenly the poor boy from Richmond was rich.[7]

In the fall of 1969, Ashe signed a second major endorsement contract, this time with Catalina Sports Clothes. A year earlier, the USLTA had granted Catalina a license to "market a line of color-coordinated tennis clothes" bearing the USLTA logo, and subsequently a number of players, including Ashe, had traded in their traditional tennis whites for flashy pastels. This break with tradition did not sit well with certain members of tennis's old guard, and during the 1969 U.S. Open, Bill Talbert, the tournament director, refused to allow Arthur to take the court wearing a yellow Catalina shirt. Arthur protested that the shirt was USLTA-endorsed apparel, but Talbert remained firm. Incensed by Talbert's decision, Catalina's president, Alex Lawlor, promptly canceled the USLTA contract and hired Arthur as the company's official spokesman. As tennis's fashion renegade, he was soon making appearances at department stores, and whenever tournament officials looked the other way—brazenly taking the court clad in one bright color or another.[8]

Over the next year, Dell arranged additional endorsement contracts with the noncigarette division of Philip Morris, American Airlines, and All-American Sports, a Florida tennis academy run by Nick Bollettieri. For the most part, Arthur posed for magazine advertisements and made store appearances sandwiched between tournaments. The standard routine involved signing autographs and answering questions, a format he soon mastered. "One of the first things I did," he recalled, "was to throw out the staid approach of my fellow athletes and inject a little theater into the appearances. I would get customers involved by using them in demonstrations. I would turn the tables and ask the audience questions." It was an easy game for a bright young man who liked to display his natural wit—and who eagerly embraced any opportunity to dispel negative racial stereotypes.[9]

Arthur's positive image and attitude were crucial elements of his commercial viability. But these attributes wouldn't have amounted to much without Dell's skillful direction. A trusted personal friend for nearly a decade, Dell also proved to be a rock-solid advisor and the primary architect of Arthur's financial security. In addition to arranging and managing endorsements, he and his partner Frank Craighill convinced Arthur and four other players—Lutz, Pasarell, Ralston, and Smith—to form Players Enterprises, Inc. (PEI) in October 1969. Organized as a collaborative investment and

pension-earning mechanism and managed by Dell and Craighill, PEI provided the players with an efficient means of financial planning. Eventually
expanded to include six other players, PEI became involved in a wide range
of commercial enterprises, from tennis camps and shops to condominium
developments and tournament sponsorships. For a time in the 1970s, Arthur
served as president of PEI, and he played an active role in the corporation's
multifaceted affairs until its dissolution in 1986.[10]

PEI was a complex and formal corporate entity with myriad legal intricacies. But for Arthur, PEI's primary foundation—as in his relationship
with Dell—was mutual trust. As he explained years later, "My whole career
has been built, I now see, on seeking and following good advice, and on
working with other people rather than striking out on my own into territory
others knew better. In starting out, I invested, literally and metaphorically, in
a community effort with other tennis players who were as uncertain as I was
in 1968 where professional tennis was going. All that we were sure about was
that we had one another, and wanted to help shape the future of the sport."[11]

Ashe and Dell often bragged that their close personal relationship allowed them to work together for more than a decade "without a formal
agreement between us." In 1986 a change in the federal tax code forced them
to sign a written agreement. Yet years after Arthur's death, Dell was still
insisting that their twenty-three-year partnership rested on "little more than
a handshake." Arthur expressed essentially the same sentiment in 1992, but
in a different way. "I did not start off with a total commitment to Donald as
a lawyer and manager," he wrote. "Trust has to be earned, and should only
come after the passage of time. Eventually that trust in Donald became like
granite."[12]

Ashe's reliance on Dell—a preppy white attorney with degrees from Yale
and the University of Virginia law school—raised more than a few eyebrows
in the African American community. But Ashe refused to countenance such
criticism. When one black friend questioned how he could consider himself a
"role model for young blacks" when he had a "white man" handling his money,
he responded: "I don't have a white man handling my money. I have Donald
Dell, who happens to be white." The distinction was important to Ashe, who
felt comfortable discussing just about anything with Dell—including race
and racism. Race notwithstanding, Dell developed a sensitive and empathetic
understanding of Ashe's unique position in the overwhelmingly white tennis
world. In many ways, they became more like brothers than business associates, anticipating each other's preferences and predilections and sharing a
deep bond sealed with good-natured ribbing and knowing glances.

Cloaked in friendship, Dell's influence and guidance were instrumental to Ashe's groundbreaking career as an African American endorsement icon. Prior to Ashe, no other black athlete had entered the mainstream endorsement market with such ease. In the early going, both Head and Catalina reported a handful of canceled retail contacts, and Dell made sure his client avoided any personal appearances in the Deep South. But with very few exceptions, customers of all races seemed to embrace Ashe as an appealing and credible spokesman.[13]

Ashe's ability to break racial barriers without making whites uncomfortable had become so obvious by the late 1960s that he soon found himself working for one of the nation's most exclusive employers. In October 1970 he became the director of the tennis program at the posh Doral Resort and Country Club in greater Miami. Nine years earlier, during the Orange Bowl tournament, he had been unwelcome at the nearby Admiral Hotel because of his race. But race didn't seem to matter to Howard Kaskel and Al Schragis, the co-owners of both the Doral resort in Florida and the Tuscany Hotel in New York. When Ike Bomzer, the doorman at the Tuscany, overheard a conversation between Kaskel and Schragis about the need to upgrade the Doral tennis program, Bomzer put in a good word for Ashe. A few days later, Ashe flew to Miami for an interview, and the job was soon his.

When Ashe held his first clinics at Doral in December, he became the first black athlete in American history to serve as the home pro at an elite country club. As he commented with considerable understatement at a reception marking his hiring, "It's rather novel being associated with a southern organization in this capacity, when I can't even play at the country club in my hometown of Gum Springs, Virginia." For the next two decades, he would spend several weeks a year conducting Doral clinics, playing golf, enjoying the comforts of the Doral Hotel and a condominium nestled behind the sixteenth green, and eventually luxury home ownership in a nearby subdivision. In the process, he and Schragis became close friends and golfing buddies.[14]

The most remarkable aspect of Ashe's status as a commercially viable celebrity was his popularity among mainstream white Americans during a time when he was becoming more outspoken and politically active. Most professional athletes—especially those who hoped to garner and maintain lucrative endorsement contracts—shied away from taking public stands on controversial issues. There were a few notable exceptions in the late 1960s, nearly all of whom were black. Among black sports figures, Muhammad Ali,

Jim Brown, Bill Russell, Curt Flood, and Bill White were the most active and outspoken advocates of social change. But none of them had much success in augmenting their salaries with endorsement contracts.

As members of an embattled black community they felt pressure to become actively involved in the civil rights struggle. This pressure had increased dramatically since the summer of 1968, when Ashe and other black athletes were challenged to endorse the proposed Olympic boycott. And from October on some athletes drew inspiration from the symbolic raised fists of John Carlos and Tommie Smith in Mexico City. Yet even in this changing context noninvolvement in social and political activism remained the norm among black athletes.

This reticence was understandable. To speak out on matters of race and civil rights was to risk censure and alienation. The political and racial issues they faced were often confusing, and young men who had spent most of their lives mastering a sport were seldom adept at navigating the crosscurrents of Black Power and white backlash. The political order was polarized, everything related to race was in flux, and language and behavior acceptable to certain groups one day might well be problematic the next. There was no easy means of dealing with this baffling situation, other than remaining silent in public. Ashe was one of the few who had the poise and confidence to speak out, and even he did so with considerable trepidation and caution.[15]

Ashe's personal survival formula—still in the trial-and-error stage in 1969—was to leaven candor with pragmatism. He spoke his mind but invariably in measured tones. He was an idealist, yet he rarely went looking for controversy. Most emphatically, he adopted an open-minded, intellectually inquisitive approach to public policy. This independent posture became his trademark, one that many came to respect and admire. But it also led to inevitable clashes with organizational and ideological orthodoxy. In particular, his self-professed commitment to racial integration—a philosophy that historian Eric Hall has dubbed "militant integrationism"—prompted considerable criticism from both ends of the political spectrum. Black nationalists frequently attacked him as an "Uncle Tom," while black conservatives tended to view him as a naive and meddling liberal. As Ashe explained to a California reporter years later, "Those were the frenetic, psychedelic, schizophrenic '60s, when the moderate progressive's hero could be the reactionary's nigger and the revolutionary's 'Uncle Tom.'"[16]

Fortunately for Ashe, there was a wide swath of moderation between these extremes. Most of the general public, black or white, gave him a measure of approval, or at least a pass. Interestingly enough, Ashe himself

suspected he was more popular among whites than blacks, and impression-
istic evidence suggests he was right. Very few whites, it seems, regarded Ashe
as a menacing figure, even when he was beseeching them to change their
ways and be more tolerant. Perhaps if he had played another sport, if he had
been a physically intimidating brand of athlete—a brawling boxer or a bruising running back—or if he hadn't looked like a bespectacled teacher, the
white response might have been different. But as the cool and calm paragon
of tennis sportsmanship, he did little to arouse the fears of white America.

Staying in the good graces of black Americans was considerably more
complicated. When African Americans placed their hopes in him—when
they looked to him as a symbol of racial pride and progress—the pressure to
address the serious social and economic problems afflicting the black community sometimes became overwhelming. From the spring of 1968 on, Ashe
publicly accepted the responsibility to be an active leader of his people, to do
what he could to foster civil rights and economic and social justice. But early
on in his activist phase the shifting realities of race and identity politics led
him away from a tight focus on domestic affairs. While he did not abandon
the problems in his own backyard, he often looked abroad for clarity and
purpose. Indeed, as he confessed on more than one occasion, his chosen refuge from the minefield of American racial politics was South Africa. "I was
too confused about what was going on among the leaders of black America,
especially the younger leaders, to know precisely where to tread," he recalled
in 1992. "South Africa was a clearer issue, and I turned to it almost with
relief."[17]

Ashe's deep interest in South Africa became obvious when his visa application first hit the headlines. On December 3, Cliff Drysdale and the
members of a newly formed South African tennis players association made
a public appeal for a visa that would allow Ashe to play in the 1970 South
African national tournament. "We would not try to disrupt the championships or embarrass anyone," Drysdale declared, "but the eventual outcome of
barring Ashe could be catastrophic for South African tennis." Two days later,
Fred W. Waring, South Africa's Minister of Tourism, Sport and Recreation,
and Indian Affairs, announced his nation had no intention of granting Ashe
a visa. He and other South African officials had not forgotten that two years
earlier, in a moment of unexpurgated anger, Ashe had talked of dropping an
H-bomb on Johannesburg. Waring interpreted Ashe's intemperate rhetoric
as proof that his primary intention was "not to play tennis but to engage in
political activity." Unfazed, Ashe responded with the warning that denying
his visa application would have "profound implications."[18]

Playing in Paris at the time, Ashe consulted with Secretary of State William P. Rogers, who took time out from a diplomatic mission to France to assure him that the State Department would do everything in its power to obtain the visa. As a representative of the Nixon administration, Rogers was eager to advance the president's "constructive engagement" (sometimes derided by critics as the "Tar Baby" policy) approach to South Africa. To Nixon, who took a personal interest in the Ashe case, the visa controversy was a means of expanding communication with white South Africans as a prelude to a relaxation of economic sanctions, all in the interest of protecting "American economic and strategic interests." In late January 1970, Nixon dispatched William Rountree, the U.S. ambassador to South Africa, to Port Elizabeth for a discussion of the visa controversy with Prime Minister John Vorster.

Ashe was only vaguely aware of the administration's efforts on his behalf and did not expect much from Rountree's mission. After his return to the United States in mid-December, Ashe, with Dell by his side, held a press conference during which he read a carefully worded statement insisting he would "come not to expound my political beliefs about South Africa, but simply to play my best possible tennis." This clarification was reassuring enough to draw the public support of ten South African provincial "tennis chiefs," plus an approving endorsement from the normally noncommittal South African golf pro Gary Player. But the South African government remained implacable.[19]

The visa controversy would continue to draw press coverage over the next three years. But it did not seem to interfere with Ashe's widening role as a commercial spokesperson for Head and other corporate entities. Corporate executives undoubtedly winced from time to time, yet they stuck with him, even when his growing frustration led to heightened rhetoric. Sometimes grudgingly, and sometimes with a measure of pride, they accepted his independent spirit, recognizing that his passionate concern for the liberation of South Africa, like his commitment to the players' union, had become an indelible part of his public image.

A far bigger concern was his performance on the court. As the reigning U.S. Open singles champion and the nation's top-ranked player, he was an eminently marketable commodity. Yet within weeks of entering the endorsement market, his ranking began to slide. During his first ten months as a professional, he won only two tournaments, and despite moments of brilliance, he often seemed outmatched by the leading Australians and his countryman

Stan Smith. Reaching the semifinals of Wimbledon and the U.S. Open, and leading the U.S. team to a second consecutive Davis Cup title, were impressive achievements. But his lingering elbow problem and tendency to fade in the late rounds cast doubt on his future. By the end of 1969, he had fallen behind both Smith and Richey in the U.S. rankings, and his world ranking had slipped to #8. Fittingly, he ended the year with a loss to Smith at the Honolulu Davis Cup Classic.[20]

The Honolulu tournament was a way station to Australia and the opening of an exciting new decade of competitive tennis. Eager to return to the scene of America's glorious 1968 Davis Cup triumph, Ashe entered the 1970s in desperate need of a confidence-building victory. But neither the trip nor the decade began well. Though seeded number one in the Tasmanian championships, a tournament he had won in 1966, he lost in the third round to unseeded Bob Carmichael. A week later, he played much better in the Victoria Open in Melbourne. But he couldn't overcome Roche in the semifinals, losing a close match that lasted more than three and a half hours. Disappointed and exhausted after the loss, Ashe worried his body might not have enough time to recover before his opening match at the Australian Open.[21]

Ashe and his Davis Cup teammates had bypassed the first Australian Open in 1969, which Laver won in a walk. This time the field was missing several of the world's best players, including several NTL pros under George MacCall's management—most notably Laver, who had announced in October that he would not defend his title. When Open officials refused to meet MacCall's financial demands, he simply canceled his players' tournament registrations.[22]

In the depleted draw, Ashe was the #4 seed, but few observers expected him to make an impressive showing. No American had won the Australian national title since Alex Olmedo in 1959, and after Smith lost to the unheralded Aussie Dick Crealy in the second round, it looked like the American drought would continue. The only two Americans to reach the quarterfinals were Ashe and Ralston, and when the top three seeds all lost their quarterfinal matches, the Americans' chances suddenly brightened. In the semifinals, Ashe and Dennis Ralston battled through three and a half sets before a pulled muscle forced the former USC star to withdraw.

Somewhat improbably, considering his problems in recent months, Ashe now found himself in the finals of the Australian championship for the third time. Having lost to Emerson in the 1965 and 1966 finals, he had the good fortune in 1970 to face Crealy, who was playing in his first major championship match. At six-foot-four, Crealy was a powerful player who had already dispatched two of the world's best players—Stan Smith and Tom Okker—in the early rounds. But the Australian's hot streak fizzled against Ashe.

Playing in a steady "drizzle with swirling wind" that forced him into a routine of either wiping off or shielding his glasses, Ashe overcame his vision problems to win the championship in straight sets. The previous day, Smith and Lutz had won the doubles title over John Alexander and Phil Dent, so Ashe's victory completed a rare American sweep against the powerful Aussies. After a joyous late night celebration in Sydney, a beaming Ashe headed home with his $3,808 winner's share in hand. Since it had been nearly a year since he had won a tournament, he decided to continue celebrating back in the States with a skiing vacation at Sun Valley, Idaho. Having been on skis only once in his life, he promised Dell he would avoid any major risks and stick to "the little slopes."[23]

Two days later, Ashe's Idaho idyll was rudely interrupted by the news that the South African government had turned down his request to play in the upcoming South African Open. The only condition under which the government would grant him a visa was the unlikely possibility of his participation in a Davis Cup match in South Africa. As Minister Waring explained, the government's decision was a simple matter of law and racial self-preservation. "He is aware of the accepted practice in South Africa," Waring said of Ashe, and "his application is, in his own words, an 'attempt to put a crack in the racist wall down there.'" In response, Ashe parried: "I thought I was doing them a favor," an oblique reference to South Africa's possible expulsion from the sporting world. While it remained to be seen whether the anti-apartheid forces would ever have enough political muscle to expel South African athletes, the likelihood of such an action was certainly greater in the wake of Ashe's visa denial.[24]

One option short of expulsion was a players' boycott of the South African Open. But there was no consensus on this matter among the members of the ITPA. "There are three basic views within the association," ITPA president John Newcombe reported. "Some of the players seem to feel that it's Arthur's personal business, some feel that it's political and some think that the Government's action was a dirty deed." To Ashe's dismay, Newcombe himself, though strongly opposed to apartheid, had real misgivings about a boycott. "Boycotting the South African open is not going to help the South African Lawn Tennis Union," the Aussie insisted. "I don't see why we should make tennis suffer in South Africa for something the Government has done." Ed Turville Sr., a former president of the USLTA and the incoming captain of the U.S. Davis Cup team, disagreed. While he stopped short of calling for a full boycott, the St. Petersburg, Florida, attorney announced he "could not encourage" any American Davis Cup players "to play the South African circuit this year."[25]

In the meantime, the momentum for outright expulsion continued to build. Alastair Martin, the president of the USLTA, urged the ILTF to suspend South Africa's membership for violating rule 19, "which forbids racial discrimination." He also called for a special meeting of the Davis Cup nations to consider expelling South Africa from Cup play. In mid-February, the powerful Australian Lawn Tennis Association voted to support any American motion calling for expulsion.[26]

This was welcome news for Ashe, who took time out from his practice rounds at the National Indoor Open in Salisbury, Maryland, to explain his position to reporters. A week earlier, at the urging of U.S. representative Charles Diggs—an African American from Detroit who had experienced a disillusioning visit to South Africa in 1969 under a restricted visa—Ashe had testified before the House Foreign Affairs subcommittee on Africa. During the hearing, he announced that he opposed the imposition of political sanctions against the entire nation of South Africa. But, as he insisted in Salisbury, that did not mean he had any reservations about expelling South Africa's white athletes from the ILTF and Davis Cup competition. "I'll keep on trying to have South Africa kicked out until it happens," he vowed. "I just don't want the punishment to fall on the wrong people." He went on to dismiss the South African government's gesture of allowing him to play in South Africa as a member of the Davis Cup team as "ridiculous." "I view it as an affront to my humanity," he declared. "They'll accept me as a piece of the American flag but not as an individual human being."[27]

Getting this off his chest proved cathartic, but it did not seem to have much effect on his peers. In a poll conducted by the Voice of America, players offered a wide range of opinions on Ashe's effort to use the visa denial issue to bring about social change in South Africa. A few voiced strong support for his position. Tom Koch of Brazil vowed to bypass the South Africa circuit as long as apartheid was in effect, declaring: "Arthur Ashe is my brother"; and Ingo Buding of West Germany said he "would do anything Ashe asked him to do regarding . . . sanctions against South Africa." But most of those polled—including Roche and Laver—rejected Ashe's call for action.

Some of the most critical comments came from Ashe's Davis Cup teammates. "Ashe should be a tennis player," Richey declared, "not a politician." Graebner argued, "The South African situation is very complicated" and complained "Arthur thinks he can solve everything by just saying 'Give it to me.'" Even Riessen, who shared Ashe's revulsion for apartheid, was unwilling to support a boycott. "I can't change anything," he explained. "It's not worthwhile to protest if you have to break your contract and go to jail, which even Arthur wouldn't want me to do." Though disappointed and even hurt by these remarks, Ashe was philosophical about the situation. "It's not that they don't care," he observed, "but tennis players as a group are apolitical, independent, even egotistical, perhaps, and each goes his own way. Their view is that it's my problem and has nothing to do with them." When asked if conducting an almost solitary fight against tennis apartheid was a burden, he responded: "Problems such as these hurt tennis, but I enjoy my role. . . . If it does good in the world, it is not a burden." [28]

Ashe was less sanguine in private, but the ongoing controversy did not seem to affect his tennis. During the winter and spring of 1970, he played some of the best tennis of his career. After the first four tournaments of the indoor tennis circuit, he was the leading money winner among independent pros, with $6,400 in earnings, and his national ranking had improved from third to second. At Richmond, in mid-February, he combined a welcome visit with his family with a rare double victory, defeating Smith in the singles final and teaming with Pasarell to win the doubles. In Macon, Georgia, in early March, he lost a tough final round match to Richey, but as the tour progressed his confidence grew. With the erratic play and elbow problems of the previous year safely behind him, his future looked bright. [29]

The only other dark cloud on the horizon was the continuing organizational struggle between the contract pros and the ILTF. The players themselves, often caught in the middle, had formed the ITPA in June 1969. But during its first year the fledgling players organization had faltered, the victim of tension and conflict between independent and contract pros. To counter the bargaining position of the contract pros, Ashe and thirty-one other independent pros announced the formation of the Association of Independent Tennis Professionals in March 1970. The plan was to hire a nonplaying administrator to manage their contractual arrangements and financial affairs. But no one was confident that any organization, however well intentioned, could bring solidarity and peace to the warring tennis world. [30]

While all of this was brewing, Ashe and his Davis Cup teammates flew to Boston for another new twist in the evolution of Open tennis, a special three-day charity event called the World Cup. Playing for $20,000 in prize money, tennis's two national powerhouses, the United States and Australia, competed in a series of seven Davis Cup–style matches. The designated beneficiary was the Sportsmen's Tennis Club, a local organization raising funds for a Roxbury inner-city tennis center. The event's secondary goal was to get the attention of Davis Cup national delegates and encourage them to rescind the ban on contract pros. The inaugural World Cup, won by the Aussies 5–2, drew large crowds and helped fund the center. But it would be nearly three years before the Davis Cup delegates came around on the contract pro issue.[31]

The tennis establishment was more tractable on the question of South Africa's participation in Davis Cup competition. On March 23, at a special meeting in London, the delegates suspended South Africa from Davis Cup play for two years. Halfway across the world in Melbourne when he heard the news, Ashe termed the suspension "a pretty sad but just decision." Personally, he confessed, "I feel that I have gained an empty victory from which I will get about five minutes emotional satisfaction. I would rather see South Africa change its ways instead of seeing them excluded from Davis Cup competition." He worried about its secondary impact on individual South African players such as Drysdale and Ray Moore, both of whom were outspoken opponents of apartheid.[32]

In mid-April, Ashe elaborated on his feelings during testimony before a special eleven-member United Nations Committee on Apartheid. Coming off back-to-back wins in Puerto Rico and Bermuda, he was on an emotional high as he addressed the United Nations delegates. Continued "pressure from the top" was essential, he insisted, and addressing the perverse racial discrimination in South African sports required nothing less than expulsion from the ILTF. With the ILTF annual meeting scheduled for July, anti-apartheid forces had less than three months to ratchet up the campaign for expulsion. "If we isolate South Africa completely—athletically, legally, culturally, physically—will they change?" he asked rhetorically, his voice cracking with emotion. "Maybe they will say the world really hates us. Maybe they will change. We've tried everything else."[33]

At the time, South Africa was in the midst of a bitter national election campaign that was pushing the ruling regime of Prime Minister John Vorster to the right. Dr. Albert Hertzog, a former minister in Vorster's cabinet, had launched a splinter party known as the Reconstituted Nationals in an effort to forestall any dilution of the apartheid system. Vorster's decision to approve a visit to South Africa by a touring New Zealand rugby team that included dark-skinned Maoris had enraged Hertzog, forcing the prime minister to renew his support for apartheid. "We are building a nation for whites only," Vorster proclaimed. To bring home this point, the government had recently decreed that black South Africans would no longer be tolerated in a wide range of clerical jobs, including receptionists, telephone operators, cashiers, and typists. To the dismay of Ashe and others trying to open South African's sporting world, the racial strictures of the apartheid system were hardening.[34]

The tennis wars were also experiencing a hardening of lines. On April 8, the ILTF announced it was following through with the creation of an "experimental Grand Prix circuit" consisting of Wimbledon, the U.S. Open, and at least sixteen other tournaments. First suggested by Jack Kramer in September 1969, the Grand Prix was lavishly sponsored by Pepsico and featured a point system that led to cash awards and a possible berth in a season-ending Grand Prix Masters tournament. Participants in the Grand Prix shared a bonus pool of $150,000, and the top six point accumulators went on to vie for an additional $50,000 in the Grand Prix Masters.[35]

These figures, extraordinary for 1970, were clearly designed to prevent independent pros like Ashe from signing with either of the contract pro groups. This forced the hand of the contract pro administrators, and after WCT absorbed the NTL in May, expanding its stable of players to thirty, it was only a matter of time before the leaders of the combined and strengthened organization created a Grand Prix–style circuit of its own. The "declaration of war," as Bud Collins later described it, came during the U.S. Open in September, when Lamar Hunt, the multimillionaire backer of WCT, announced plans for the 1971 World Championship of Tennis, a twenty-tournament circuit limited to the world's best thirty-two contract pros. Selected by an international panel of tennis writers, the participants would compete for a million dollars in total earnings, and the top eight point winners would square off in a season-ending playoff worth $50,000.

The ILTF immediately countered by raising its Grand Prix prize money to $1.5 million, but WCT's advantage in the ensuing "bidding war" soon became clear. When combined with the guaranteed payments that came with WCT contracts, the extra prize money became an almost irresistible lure for independent pros. Even Ashe, who had been vocal about his desire to remain independent, could not resist the temptations of the enhanced WCT. At first, he responded cautiously, acknowledging the WCT plan "was great for tennis" but warning that the contract terms might be "too restrictive" for him. Although Hunt had promised that the top independent pros would be eligible for inclusion in the field of thirty-two, Ashe was not sure it would be worthwhile to participate in the WCT tour as an independent. "I'd have to play it with no guarantee," he explained, "when the contract pros are playing it with a guarantee."[36]

Whatever his reservations, Ashe rocked the tennis world on September 17 with the news that he had agreed to a WCT contract worth $750,000. The five-year deal included guarantees and deferred payments for Ashe and similar but less lucrative packages for Pasarell and Lutz. "I'm glad everything is finally settled," Ashe told reporters. "I didn't sign for the money. I was offered more in the past to sign. I just felt now was the time." His primary motivation for signing with WCT, he insisted, was his continuing frustration with the Davis Cup and the USLTA.

Ashe had already warned Davis Cup officials he would not play for the U.S. team in 1971 unless the competition was opened to contract pros. Now he wanted to send a strong message to the USLTA, which he felt had mismanaged the expansion of Open tennis. "I appreciate everything the U.S.L.T.A. has done for me," he declared. "But they just move too slowly. . . . They make bad appointments, their hands are tied by antiquated rules and they don't want to assume a role of leadership." At the 1970 U.S. Open, the USLTA had finally relaxed the rules enough to allow pastel shirts and shorts alongside the traditional whites, and it had instituted an innovative nine-point (first player to win 5 points wins the set) sudden death tiebreaker system to close out 6–6 sets. But for Ashe it was too little too late. By contrast, in his view, WCT would almost certainly "move the game in the right direction." [37]

Dismissing money as a primary motivation was in keeping with Ashe's image. But it did not change the fact that the WCT contract established him as one of the wealthiest athletes in the world, putting him on a par with the best-paid stars of the NFL, NBA, PGA, and Major League Baseball. In only his second year as a professional athlete, he had achieved a degree of financial security few Americans could even imagine. In 1970, he was one of three tennis players to earn more than $100,000 in prize money, trailing only Laver and Rosewall in on-court earnings. And when hundreds of thousands of dollars in endorsement money were added in, he had money to burn.

For the first time in his life, he could buy just about anything he wanted, and for a while he was tempted to test the limits of his enviable situation. After lavishing his family with gifts, he bought a vintage Rolls-Royce that he shipped home from Australia, as well as indulgences such as expensive clothes, jewelry, and golf clubs. He also added to his growing record and book collections. The shopping spree did not last long, and he soon returned to his frugal ways. Yet he confessed he often felt like a parvenu susceptible to money worship. "This is terribly embarrassing to admit," he wrote in June 1973, "but money makes me happy. I'm not as secure about money as people like Pasarell and Graebner who always had the damn stuff. But I don't mean I just sit on it. I'm a pretty good giver to the causes I'm really interested in, and I love to play with money to gamble. . . . Maybe if you never had money you're more inclined to use it just to remind yourself that you've got some." [38]

Money helped to make 1970 a breakthrough year for Ashe, but for him the most important development of the year was proving his 1968 U.S. Open victory and number one ranking among American players were more than flukes. The erratic ups and downs of 1969 had given way to a string of successes in the first year of the new decade. Staying healthy enough to play in thirty tournaments, he won 82 percent of his matches, reached fourteen finals, and won eleven titles. After starting the year with the Australian Open title, he finished a close second to Richey in the final Grand Prix standings, winning $17,000 in bonus money. Even though he stumbled at Wimbledon, losing to Andrés Gimeno in the fourth round, and at the U.S. Open, where he dropped a close quarterfinal match to Newcombe, losing two sets 7–6 under the controversial new tiebreaker system, he seemed to play at or near the top of his game week after week.

Ashe's year-long record of consistency—achieved while he was devoting considerable time and energy to off-court concerns such as South Africa and the tennis wars—should have put to rest the notion he could not combine top-flight tennis with social and political responsibility. But it did not do so. The charge that his tennis suffered because he spent too much time on such matters would dog him for years, though Ashe himself found ample compensation in using his skills for a higher purpose than mere tennis glory. [39]

For him the most meaningful experience of the year was not winning the Australian Open in January, or helping the U.S. win a third straight Davis Cup by defeating West Germany, or even signing the lucrative WCT contract. His event of the year took place in late October and early November when he participated in a State Department–sponsored tour of six African nations. The entourage included Stan Smith, Frank Deford of *Sports Illustrated*, Bud Collins of the *Boston Globe*, the British freelance writer Richard Evans, and a United States Information Agency–sponsored documentary film crew. [40]

Ashe had been fascinated with Africa since his UCLA days, and now he finally had the opportunity to gain firsthand experience in the recently decolonized continent. The "Good Will" exhibition tour began in Nairobi, the sprawling capital of the East African nation of Kenya. Independent since 1963, the former British colony had been the scene of the violent Mau Mau uprising during the 1950s. The highlight of the Americans' brief visit was a meeting with President Jomo Kenyatta, a noted Pan-Africanist intellectual. This was a heady experience for young tennis players on their first trip to Africa. But Kenyatta, known for his charm and eloquence, graciously put them at ease and even impressed them with his knowledge of tennis. Years later Ashe recalled Kenyatta's sharp intellect, but couldn't resist adding, somewhat insensitively, that the African leader bore a striking physical resemblance to Joel Chandler Harris's Uncle Remus.[41]

From Nairobi, the American ingenues flew south to Dar es Salaam, the capital of Tanzania, a sprawling nation only nine years removed from semicolonial U.N. trust status. Once a part of German East Africa prior to being transferred to British control at the close of World War I, Tanzania was a complex and fascinating nation led by President Julius Nyerere, who had recently developed a close relationship with Mao Tse-Tung and the People's Republic of China. Troubled by postcolonial Africa's propensity for one-party rule, Ashe took a special interest in Nyerere's attempt to combine a one-party system and socialism. "I didn't agree with this principle," he wrote several years later. "How would there be enough room for dissent? Wouldn't you end up with 'strongmen' running everything and possibly becoming corrupt? I read Nyerere's book on African socialism and began to seriously question how countries were organized."

Tanzania was a revelation in several ways. Though carefully briefed before their arrival in Dar es Salaam, Ashe and Smith were not prepared for the grilling they received during a meeting with university students. Ashe found them "starved for information" about the United States, but also highly critical of everything, from American policy in Vietnam to the lack of activism among African American celebrities. "What are you and other famous Americans doing for the struggle in the U.S.?" they asked. When Ashe tried to turn the tables by asking troubling questions of his own—such as "Why does your government lock up political prisoners?" and "Why can't you come up with an orderly way to change governments?"—the students became defensive and refused to answer. He later learned that, fearing government retaliation, they had simply been afraid to answer his questions in public. Africa, he was beginning to realize, was a complicated puzzle.[42]

The next stop was Lusaka, the capital of Zambia, formerly the British colony of Northern Rhodesia. Zambia's President Kenneth Kaunda was a leading critic of the white supremacist governments of nearby Rhodesia (formerly known as Southern Rhodesia) and South Africa, so it was not surprising when the Zambian press peppered Ashe with questions about the visa controversy. Startled by the directness of the questions, he insisted he no longer had any interest in playing in South Africa. When asked if he would "give up tennis to oppose apartheid," he responded: "Yes, the liberation of black people is more important."[43]

After a brief stop in Kampala, Uganda, the tour headed to West Africa for a visit to Lagos, the capital of Nigeria. The most populous and diplomatically the most important nation in sub-Saharan Africa, the former British colony had just emerged from a brutal civil war that had led to more than a million deaths, mostly Ibo tribesmen supporting the secession of Biafra. When Ashe and Smith arrived, ten months after the cessation of hostilities, the nation was still under the control of Major General Yakubu Gowon, a military dictator regarded as a hero by some and a war criminal by others. Prior to holding an exhibition match and youth tennis clinic, the Americans spent more than an hour with Gowon. Despite a few awkward moments, Ashe came away with a generally positive impression of the Nigerian ruler, who "laughed very easily, talked freely and spoke of the need to return Nigeria to civilian rule as soon as possible." "Nigeria feels a great kinship with Afro-Americans," Gowon insisted. "We are the two most important groups of color in the world today." Pleasantly surprised to encounter a military leader who "talked like a statesman," Ashe was dismayed a few months later when Gowon "was deposed in a bloodless coup."[44]

Ashe later complained that the State Department should have known better than to put novice envoys in such a vulnerable and potentially embarrassing situation. But he wisely kept these feelings to himself during his stay in Nigeria. The tour ended in Ghana, the former British colony that had initiated the decolonization of sub-Saharan Africa by gaining its independence in 1957. Formerly known as the Gold Coast and British Togoland, Ghana provided a hopeful ending to Ashe's on-site African education. After touring the capital city of Accra and meeting with Ghana's legendary president Kwame Nkrumah, Ashe and Smith played a two-set exhibition match and conducted a clinic for a group of aspiring tennis players. By the time the two Americans left Ghana and Africa on November 6, bound for the French indoor championships, they had a treasure trove of African memories but few illusions about the harrowing challenges of postcolonial politics.[45]

In mid-November, Ashe spent a glorious week in Paris that ended with a convincing straight-set victory over Riessen in the final. Speaking to reporters after the championship match, he credited his sharp play to his recent tour of Africa. "Every time we saw a kid do something wrong at one of the clinics we gave," he explained, "we'd say 'do this or do that,' then I started to realize that I should have been telling myself to do the same things."[46]

This back-to-basics approach did not work quite so well a few days later when Ashe lost to Drysdale in the first round of the Wembley indoor tournament. But he was back on track the following week, teaming with Smith to win the doubles championship at the Swedish Open in Stockholm while finishing second to his African touring partner in the singles. Stockholm was the last tournament of the ILTF's inaugural Grand Prix series, and Ashe's runner-up showing was good enough to give him a second-place finish behind Richey in the final point standings. The second-place bonus prize money of $17,000, the largest payout of his career, pushed his annual on-court earnings over the $100,000 mark.[47]

Tennis's big-money era had arrived, yet no one at the time could be sure how long it would last. A $210,000 Tennis Champions Classic to be held in New York City and featuring Ashe, Laver, Rosewall, Roche, Newcombe, and Gonzales was scheduled for January 1971. But the alluring prospect of unprecedented earnings could not hide the fact that the very future of Open tennis was in question as its third year came to a close. Long before Ashe returned to the United States in mid-December, the tennis wars had entered a new phase, moving through a deep crisis to an uneasy truce.[48]

On November 6, while Ashe and Smith were en route from Africa to France, USLTA officials moved to bar contract pros from playing in all 1971 USLTA-sanctioned "prize money" tournaments, including the U.S. Open. Pending ratification by the USLTA's administrative committee at an upcoming meeting in Cleveland, the proposed ban would also exclude Ashe and other contract pros from national rankings. Citing the recent WCT contracts signed by Ashe, Pasarell, and Lutz, USLTA executive director Bob Malaga declared, "We have no choice but to go our own way." This declaration underscored the predicament in which the divided world of competitive tennis found itself. As journalist Neil Amdur pointed out, "Unlike other organized professional sports, tennis has no single leader or commissioner to deal with such internal strife. The international complexities of the sport and the reluctance of all parties to trust completely the decision of one mediator has created the confusion at a time when tennis is enjoying record participant popularity and renewed spectator appeal."[49]

At the Cleveland meeting on November 12, Malaga pushed for an immediate ban, but in the end cooler heads prevailed and the decision was postponed. Three weeks later, behind-the-scenes negotiations between the ILTF and WCT produced a joint statement promising that all concerned—the national and international tennis federations and the representatives of the contract pros—would "work together toward the development and spectator appeal of the game throughout the world." In addition, a parallel statement announced contract pros would be eligible to play in the 1971 French, Wimbledon, and U.S. Open tournaments. For the time being at least, the tennis world had stepped back from the brink.[50]

While all of this was going on, the first year of the 1970s—a decade that Bud Collins would later characterize as "a new era for tennis" and "the decade of its most rapid growth"—came to a dramatic close with the first Grand Prix Masters tournament. Held in Tokyo, the $50,000 round-robin competition opened somewhat awkwardly on December 7, the twenty-ninth anniversary of the Japanese attack on Pearl Harbor. Richey, the top point getter in the season's Grand Prix series, had withdrawn after contracting hepatitis, but the other Grand Prix stars provided the overflow Japanese crowds with seven days of top-flight tennis. Hampered by a minor ankle injury, Ashe finished in fourth place with a 3–2 record. But even with this disappointing finish he took home $5,000 in prize money. The surest sign of the tennis world's newfound wealth, however, was the $9,000 second-place money that pushed Laver's earnings over the $200,000 mark for the year. No previous player had ever approached, much less surpassed, that level in earnings, and Ashe and his peers could only marvel at the Rocket's good fortune while wondering what bounties lay ahead.[51]

THIRTEEN

DOUBLING DOWN

■

DURING THE FIRST THREE months of 1971, the big money continued to ripple across the tennis world. Using a winner-take-all match format, the $210,000 Champions Classic, a round-robin competition held in seven different cities, brought together nine of the world's best contract pros. Each weekly match was worth $10,000 to the winner, with the loser going home empty-handed, a format that allowed the ultimate winner of the series to win as much as $170,000. Prize money of this magnitude was unprecedented, and the Champions Classic organizers added to the drama by imposing a special tiebreaker rule and stipulating that all matches would be played on a new acrylic fiber surface called Sportface. Every aspect of the series was designed to maximize its commercial impact, and the opening match, fittingly enough, was held in New York's Madison Square Garden.[1]

Ashe played his first Champions Classic match—which also happened to be his first match as a contract pro—in the Garden on January 28. His opponent was Laver, who had already picked up $40,000 by winning four Classic matches. Arthur, by contrast, was coming off a month of rest, having last taken the court in Tokyo in December. In a pre-match interview, he was philosophical about his career record of 0–5 against the Rocket, citing rest and relaxation as a possible key to breaking the losing streak. "I am fairly eager, if that counts for anything," he offered whimsically. "I'm mentally rested. Between now and Thursday, I'll go easy on the pie and cake. We'll see what happens." When asked about his involvement in the high-stakes series, he was surprising candid about his motivation. "American players are more money conscious," he explained. "I guess it's our culture. Americans look for money every waking hour."[2]

When it came to the actual match, however, neither relaxation nor candor was much help. With the crowd solidly behind him, Ashe—wearing canary yellow tennis clothes that sent a message to the stuffy leaders of the USLTA—played reasonably well. But once again he could not match Laver's powerful ground game, losing in straight sets, two by tiebreaker. "I just can't seem to win tiebreakers," he complained after the match, speculating that the new system favored more patient players. "It presupposes conservatism," he insisted, acknowledging that his somewhat reckless style of play put him at a disadvantage.[3]

Not everyone appreciated Ashe's nontraditional approach to tennis, but to many of the sportswriters covering the tour he was good copy and a welcome respite from the sameness that dominated the men's game. To Robert Lipsyte, Ashe was a godsend. "At its highest tournament level," Lipsyte wrote in the wake of the Ashe-Laver match, "tennis is a combative game, the racquet an extension of the total man. One of the most interesting players is Arthur Ashe, whose brilliant, quirky game has been disappointing. He will gamble on a shot, he will swipe at the ball, he will fall into periods of inattention, he will explode into games of wild artistry." Laver, by contrast, was "a working saddle pony to Ashe's skittery thoroughbred."[4]

Ashe's flashiness was partly a matter of style unrelated to shot selection. During the two years since his discharge from the Army, his physical appearance had undergone a dramatic transformation. His once close-cropped haircut had been replaced with a modified Afro style—one less flamboyant than the bulbous cut popularized by the radical activist Angela Davis but identifiably ethnic nonetheless. At the same time, his mode of dress—especially his casual street clothes and aviator sunglasses—had taken on a hip, funk quality. Like the young African American dancers on the popular television show *Soul Train*, he often wore open-collared shirts that exposed a string of beads hanging around his neck; and following his first trip to Africa, he favored brightly colored African-style dashikis. From his on-court tennis clothes to his suits and sport coats, he was, as Nick Bollettieri once observed, always "meticulous in his dress." Years later, Seth Abraham of Home Box Office (HBO) television aptly attributed this fastidiousness to Arthur's chosen role as "a man of symbolism."[5]

Now in his late twenties, Arthur had clearly entered a new, more confident phase of his life. While his basic demeanor was as cool and calm as ever, he had become more forthright in his determination to employ images— both visual and verbal—to express his personal feelings, especially on matters of racial pride. Although he eschewed the excesses of cultural nationalism, he wanted the world to know that he was unmistakably and unashamedly black. As he wrote in 1992, "I think of myself as being in some respects a 'race man,' an expression that black Americans use to describe someone committed to his people and vigilant about racial injustice." Where his particular version of the "race man" role would lead was not altogether clear in the early 1970s. But he seemed to be finding his footing on the pathway to a secure and fulfilling racial identity.[6]

One memorable episode in the spring of 1971 illustrates the challenge that Ashe faced. During a visit to Atlanta, he attended a party at the home of Walt Hazzard, his old UCLA friend in his third year as a starting guard for the Atlanta Hawks of the NBA. Dell accompanied Ashe to the party, but everyone else in the room was black, including SCLC leaders Andrew Young and Jesse Jackson. As Ashe remembered the scene, "a warm discussion of race, politics, and protest" led to an awkward moment when he defended his gradualist principles. Without warning, Jackson "stuck" him "with a needling comment," as Ashe put it. "The problem with you Arthur," Jackson offered, "is that you're not arrogant enough." The response was classic Ashe—cool but firm. "You're right, Jesse," he acknowledged. "I'm not arrogant. But I don't think that my lack of arrogance lessens my effectiveness one bit."[7]

Arrogant or not, Ashe had become a controversial figure in some circles. As he became more identifiably black and moved toward positions that might be construed as militant, his public image took on a sharper edge. This became apparent in early 1971 when the South African Lawn Tennis Union invited Evonne Goolagong to participate in the upcoming South African championships but reaffirmed Ashe's exclusion. On February 24, Theo Gerdener, South Africa's minister of interior, announced that as a supporter of black liberation movements in Southern Africa Ashe was "persona non grata." After rejecting Arthur's visa application for the third time, Gerdener confirmed that two "acceptable" nonwhites, Goolagong and Kazuko Sawamatsu of Japan, had been granted permission to play in the South African Open.[8]

An up-and-coming nineteen-year-old Australian star of Aboriginal background, Goolagong was reportedly welcome because, unlike Arthur, she had refrained from publicly criticizing South African apartheid. Raised in a small sheepherding community west of Sydney, the light-skinned and attractive Goolagong possessed a winning smile and a carefree, graceful manner that made her the new darling of the women's tour. From the white South African perspective, her apolitical persona made her a perfect counterpoint to a black American determined to "make political capital" out of his visit. A nonwhite according to the law of apartheid, she could be used as a symbol of a new, more tolerant South Africa without posing a threat to the racial status quo. This strategy of indirection drew a sharp response from Ashe, who warned the South Africans that they couldn't hold back the tide of liberators forever and that "there will be more after me." Though initially careful to absolve Goolagong of any blame, he would later question her judgment.[9]

Their names were paired again two weeks later when they both played in the singles finals of the Australian Open. With Ashe as the defending men's champion and Goolagong playing in her first major final, their contrasting roles in the continuing South African Open controversy added an interesting twist to the tournament. When both lost—Ashe to Rosewall, and Goolagong to Margaret Court—their pairing seemed almost fated.[10]

Their common fortunes did not last long, however. Goolagong went on to win the 1971 French Open and Wimbledon singles championships, earning the nickname "Sunshine Supergirl" and enjoying one of the most extraordinary runs by a teenaged tennis star. Ashe, by contrast, had a disappointing year. Playing in only nine finals in thirty-two tournaments in 1971, he won three minor titles, and his winning percentage in singles matches fell to 71 percent, a drop of 11 percent from the previous year. He made it to the singles quarterfinals of the French Open, and to the semifinals of both the Italian and U.S. Opens. But his twin goals of recapturing the number one U.S. ranking and winning a third major title went unfulfilled.[11]

If there was a saving grace in Ashe's third year as a pro, it was that he was playing the best doubles of his career. For him, as for many of the tour's top singles competitors, playing doubles was part practice, part relaxation, and a good way to pick up some extra prize money. Known as a good, though not necessarily great, doubles player, he was a sought-after partner on the tour. But he had never thought of himself as a doubles specialist.

Ashe's newfound success in doubles had begun at the 1970 French Open, when he and Charlie Pasarell made it all the way to the doubles final before losing in straight sets to the colorful Romanians Nastase and Tiriac. In 1971 he paired with Marty Riessen, who had become one of his closest friends on the tour. An accomplished doubles player who often teamed with Tom Okker, Riessen had nearly won the 1969 Wimbledon doubles title with the Dutchman, losing a tight championship match to the defending champions, Newcombe and Roche.[12]

At the March 1971 Australian Open, the Okker-Riessen team once again finished second to Newcombe and Roche. But two months later at the French Open, Riessen found himself in need of a new partner when Okker remained in the Netherlands to help his wife care for their new baby. Fortunately, Ashe was available. After breezing through the early rounds, the two Americans faced Brian Fairlie of New Zealand and Frew McMillan of South Africa in a semifinal match complicated by McMillan's recent comments on the South African visa controversy. Earlier in the week, McMillan, whom Ashe liked and admired, had spoken out against his country's myopic policies, urging the South African government to grant his friend a visa. Commenting on the South African leaders' fear of letting Ashe into the land of apartheid, he declared: "I can see the Government's reason for not letting Ashe into the country, but I think eventually they are going to have to pocket their pride and let him in." [13]

McMillan's courageous dissent gave the press something to talk about when he and Fairlie faced Ashe and Riessen. The match saw the Americans win the first two sets with ease only to lose the next two. Ashe and Riessen eventually regained control, winning the fifth set 8–6, and when Ashe and McMillan shook hands after the last point, pressing black flesh to white, many in the crowd knew they had witnessed more than a tennis match.

The championship match was anticlimactic by comparison, but an overflow crowd—unusual for doubles—turned out to see Ashe and Riessen take on fellow Americans Stan Smith and Tom Gorman. The result was a five-set victory for Ashe and Riessen, "a 3-hour-15-minute battle of serve and volley" rarely seen on a slow, red clay court. A "struggle of brute strength," according to one reporter, the match was a harbinger of the future in a sport that would soon see the proliferation of oversized metal rackets and muscle-building training regimens.[14]

Smith, who had teamed with Ashe to win the U.S. Indoor doubles title in 1970, was the prototype of the new power tennis star. At six-foot-three, he towered over most of his opponents, many of whom came to fear his "cannonball service." Some sportswriters even began to refer to him as "the leaning tower of Pasadena" after he burst upon the tennis scene in 1968, winning both the intercollegiate singles title and the first U.S. Open doubles championship with Lutz. In many ways, however, 1971 was his breakthrough year. By the time the tour reached Wimbledon, he was already the top-ranked

American player, even though he had missed more than two months of play after entering the Army in January.[15]

At Wimbledon, Smith's strong showing against the defending champion Newcombe in the singles final catapulted him to a top-five world ranking. Watching from the stands, Ashe pulled hard for his friend and former doubles partner. But he had difficulty concentrating on the match because he had more important concerns.[16]

On June 27, four days before the doubles final, Ashe's mentor, Dr. Robert Johnson Sr., passed away in Lynchburg at the age of seventy-two. A lifetime of fast living had finally caught up with the man known as the Whirlwind. Johnson had been sick for months, and his relatively early death was hardly a shock to Ashe or anyone who knew him well. But this did not save Ashe from a profound sense of loss. He owed the man he called Dr. J a debt beyond calculation. There were so many memories of the Lynchburg camp and of the long car rides through the Virginia and North Carolina countryside. Indeed, only nine years earlier they had shared the joy of pairing up during the ATA national doubles competition.

It was all very emotional, and Arthur wanted to pay proper respect to the man who had changed his life. Yet he faced the dilemma of deciding whether he should remain at Wimbledon for the next round of doubles competition or withdraw and fly back to Virginia for the funeral. Would Dr. J, always a stickler for following through, want him to honor his commitment to his partner? Or should he break the rules just this once?

In the end, Arthur decided to forgo the funeral, hoping that the Johnson family would understand. The choice was a difficult one, in part because he already suffered from a difficult relationship with Bobby Jr., who had always resented his father's close relationship with the interloping surrogate son from Richmond. Arthur's suspicion his decision to stay in England would lead to trouble was fully warranted. Even after Arthur explained that he hated funerals, Bobby Jr. refused to let him off the hook. "Nobody likes to go to funerals," he insisted, with more than a touch of anger, "Dr. J would have wanted him there . . . and I think he deserved it. My father literally picked this boy up from nothing and made him what he is today." Arthur knew nothing of Bobby Jr.'s hurt feelings until after his return to the United States in mid-July. But worrying about the likelihood of such a reaction was clearly a distraction during the closing days of Wimbledon.[17]

Arthur had a number of troubling matters on his mind throughout the Wimbledon fortnight. On June 23, the day before he faced Riessen in the third round, the South African golf star Gary Player made headlines by announcing that Lee Elder, America's best-known black golfer, had accepted his invitation to play in the previously all-white South African PGA championship tournament in November. "A lot of people are under the impression that a black man cannot play in South Africa," Player declared, "and that is not true. One of the things this invitation can do is clear up that misimpression." Since the press reports of Player's announcement pointed out the obvious inconsistency between South Africa's treatment of Ashe and Elder, Arthur's stigmatization appeared to be deliberate and personal. Faced with this added insult, he had difficulty focusing on his third-round match, losing to Riessen for the first time in five years.[18]

Ashe was also troubled by the continuing turmoil plaguing the business side of tennis. During the spring leading up to the French Open and Wimbledon, the uneasy truce between WCT and the ILTF had produced an unstable separation of contract and independent pros. There were two parallel circuits: WCT's contract pro series comprised of 20 tournaments played in nine countries; and the USLTA-sponsored U.S. indoor series for independent pros, managed by the flamboyant promoter Bill Riordan. Adding to the confusion were several hybrid tournaments, such as the Italian and French Opens, co-promoted by WCT but open to independent pros.

Viewed as a temporary solution, this hodgepodge version of Open tennis all but collapsed when half of the contract pros decided to skip the French Open. The primary reason was reportedly their exhaustion after five months of weekly WCT tournaments, with most of the contract pros deciding it was sensible to play in either the French Open or Wimbledon but not both. Among the leading WCT pros, only Ashe, Smith, and Richey chose to play both tournaments in 1971. The explanation for the absences did not wash with the leaders of the ILTF, who suspected that Lamar Hunt had arranged the "boycott" in an effort to undercut the national associations' stature and influence. To them, it was a power play, plain and simple, designed to increase Hunt's leverage over everything from player appearances to television contracts.[19]

During and after Wimbledon, ILTF leaders mobilized to counter Hunt's aggressive moves. In mid-July the federation voted overwhelmingly to ban WCT's thirty-two contract pros from participating in ILTF-affiliated events, effective January 1, 1972. The era of Open tennis, after three and a half years of experimentation, appeared to be all but over. Despite all of the money and popular interest that had flowed into the sport since 1968, the competing factions struggling for control of professional tennis had seemingly chosen high-risk brinkmanship over compromise.

According to a recent poll, tennis had never been more popular, with a record 10.6 million players on the court and a total of $400 million spent annually on tennis-related equipment and activities. Much of this growth stemmed from the game's newfound presence on television. Historically, tennis had lagged far behind the other major sports as a source of televised entertainment, and as late as 1968 televised tennis matches were a rarity. Live broadcasts of tennis matches began in 1967, when Bud Collins convinced the local Public Broadcasting System affiliate to let him send a film crew to Longwood. This successful experiment soon led to the historic five-year contract signed by CBS and the U.S. Open in 1968. Once the U.S. Open was put on the screen, other tournaments followed suit, producing a broadening culture of televised tennis by the early 1970s.

In the process, tennis commentators such as Bud Collins, Buddy MacKay, and Jack Kramer became identifiable and important ambassadors of the sport, and the top players became recognizable sports celebrities, public figures who fostered an explosion of interest in the tour and the game at large. None of this, however, did much to enhance the structural and organizational integrity of competitive tennis. "For the most part," Neil Amdur lamented in July 1971, "the power politics of tennis has continued to overshadow the artistic performance and engaging personalities of the bright, fresh faces on the tour."[20]

All parties eventually stepped back from the brink. But it would take another year of negotiation before a stable and enduring peace emerged. In the meantime, Arthur and his fellow touring pros played on, hoping somehow Open tennis could survive amidst the chaos of money-driven maneuvering.

Ashe was fully engaged in the tennis wars that affected his livelihood. But his highest personal priority was the ongoing fight against racial discrimination and inequality—especially in South Africa. Having embraced the struggle late in the game, near the close of the classic civil rights era, he was determined to make up for lost time. In addition to continuing his work promoting and conducting inner-city tennis clinics and working with the National Urban League, he became the honorary chairman and chief fund-raiser for the Howard University Mississippi Project (HUMP). The goal was to raise $500,000 for medical care for the poor in Quitman County, Mississippi. After learning of the project's frustrations, Ashe agreed to boost the fund drive by exploiting his contacts in the tennis world. "As a middle-class black involved with a sport connected with the socially elite," he explained, "I know a lot of people with a lot of money."[21]

In 1971, and in the years that followed, Ashe became involved in a number of antipoverty and racial uplift projects. But his greatest passion remained the liberation of black South Africans from the cruelties of apartheid. Despite two visa denials, he was more determined than ever to break the color bar in South African tennis. He knew full well that his appearance in a previously all-white tournament would represent little more than a symbolic victory over apartheid, a tiny crack in a towering wall of prejudice and racial separation. Yet he also felt that, as the most prominent black tennis player in the world, he had both the opportunity and responsibility to use his talent and position for a higher purpose than fame or personal gain.[22]

For Ashe, both personal redemption and social justice were at stake—and for once he found himself ahead of the curve on a civil rights issue. At this point, no other American athlete had publicly identified with the anti-apartheid movement, which was still in its infancy in the United States. Despite the obvious risks, he took enormous satisfaction in being out front and leading the way, though it proved difficult to convince other American athletes to follow his lead. Even so, he took comfort from the growing number of Americans from other walks of life who were involved in the struggle.

It would take until the mid-1980s, after more than a decade of organizing in the United States and years of rising resistance in South Africa, for the American anti-apartheid movement to come of age. But the early 1970s was the movement's seedtime. In February 1971, thirteen black members of the U.S. House of Representatives founded the Congressional Black Caucus, the first legislative initiative of which was an anti-apartheid bill calling for trade restrictions against the white supremacist regime. Introduced by Representative Ron Dellums, a first-term Democratic congressman from Oakland, California, the bill initiated a campaign that grew into a national movement for corporate divestment in South Africa.[23]

Trade restrictions and divestment rested on the idea of effecting change through economic deprivation and isolation, a strategy with the unfortunate side effect of punishing black as well as white South Africans. The vast majority of anti-apartheid activists, including Ashe, would eventually endorse this approach. But in 1971 he was among those who preferred engagement to isolation. Even though he supported the effort to banish South Africa from Davis Cup competition, he hoped to change South Africa primarily through increased contact and dialogue with the outside world. Most of all, he wanted to go to South Africa to serve as a role model, to provide a concrete example of racial integration.[24]

Despite repeated warnings from other anti-apartheid activists that South

Africa's white leaders would turn his proposed visit to their advantage, Ashe persisted. In August 1971, the visa controversy took on new life after *The New York Times Magazine* ran a feature on Evonne Goolagong. When asked about Goolagong's recent participation in the South African tennis championships as "an honorary white," Ashe could not hide his contempt. Identifying one's race correctly was "not a matter of personal preference," he insisted. "If you're born black you're committed in the race war." John Newfong, a spokesman for the Australian Aborigines' Advancement League, agreed. Commenting on Goolagong's "honorary white" status, he declared, "One shouldn't have to elaborate on what an insult this is to her, to her people at home, and to black people everywhere."

Prior to her visit, Goolagong declared: "I don't want to talk about apartheid. . . . I'm going to South Africa to play tennis and to see the country. That's as far as it goes." And after her return from Johannesburg, she complained about the press's preoccupation with race: "It's as though all that matters is that I'm aboriginal. I'd much rather people knew me as a good tennis player than as an aboriginal who happens to play good tennis. Of course I'm proud of my race, but I don't want to be thinking about it all the time." Ashe had made similar statements earlier in his career and shared her sentiments. Yet he could not accept this as a rationale for avoiding her responsibility to speak out on matters of race and equality. He hoped she would come to the realization, as he had, that there was no honorable retreat from the struggle for racial justice.[25]

Ashe freely acknowledged that his situation was different from Goolagong's, that he could take advantage of cultural and historical connections unavailable to her. While she could only cling to the vestiges of a fragmented and dispossessed Aboriginal culture, he could draw upon the racial heritage of a broad African diaspora and the emerging nations of sub-Saharan Africa. His first visit to Africa had stirred his soul, and he could hardly wait to return.

During the final weeks of 1971, the WCT tour imposed a grueling intercontinental travel schedule beginning in Berkeley and continuing on to British Columbia, West Germany, Spain, Belgium, Sweden, Italy, and Texas before returning to California. By Thanksgiving, all of the contract pros were travel weary and ready for a break. But this did not stop Arthur and three of his friends—Pasarell, Okker, and Riessen—from packing their bags on November 28 and heading off to West Africa for a three-week tour of Senegal, Cameroon, Gabon, and Ivory Coast. Before their departure, Pasarell even managed to squeeze in a Los Angeles wedding to his longtime girlfriend

Shireen Fareed, the daughter of the U.S. Davis Cup squad's team physician, Dr. Omar Fareed. After the ceremony, the wedding party took a red-eye flight to New York where, compliments of Arthur, the newlyweds spent their wedding night at the Doral-on-the-Park Hotel. A few hours later, they were on their way to Dakar, Senegal, the first stop on their West African adventure.[26]

The 1971 junket, like the 1970 tour, was a State Department goodwill mission that mixed tennis with public diplomacy. The four countries were all former French colonies that had gained independence in 1960. Among the most prosperous nations in West Africa, all four had ethnically diverse populations with historical ties to the Atlantic slave trade. Senegal was predominantly Muslim, Cameroon and Ivory Coast had large Muslim minorities, and Gabon was largely Roman Catholic. Politically, each was a one-party state controlled by an authoritarian chief executive, and in Senegal, President Léopold Senghor—one of Africa's most prominent leaders and the proponent of a philosophy known as "Negritude"—presided over an ideologically driven socialist regime.

All of this provided a fascinating backdrop as Arthur and his friends made their way across fifteen hundred miles of West Africa. After conducting tennis clinics in Dakar, they traveled to Abidjan, Ivory Coast's largest city, where they competed in a mini-tournament. From there, they flew south and east to Yaoundé, the sprawling capital of Cameroon. A cosmopolitan city with a heavy residue of French colonialism, Yaoundé boasted several tennis clubs, one of which produced an unexpected benefit.[27]

While driving on the grounds of the city's premier tennis club, the visiting Americans spotted a young boy on a roadside court practicing his serves and volleys with a handmade wooden paddle. Impressed by the boy's strength and athleticism, Arthur inquired about his identity. Coincidentally, the boy had written him a letter three weeks earlier, hoping that he might meet the American star during his visit. Later in the day, Arthur hit with him and came away impressed. "First, he serves right down the middle past me," Arthur recalled. He was also dazzled by the boy's agility. "His strokes were good," he observed, "but what impressed me was that he seemed to be awfully good with his feet. In young kids, that's what you look for first."

The "little brown-skinned kid," as Arthur described him, turned out to be eleven-year-old Yannick Noah, the lyrically named, mixed-race son of a Cameroonian father and a French mother. Yannick's father, Zacharie Noah, had been a prominent soccer player in Sedan, France, until he was sidelined by a serious injury in 1963. Yannick's mother, Marie-Claire, was a teacher and amateur tennis champion, and a former captain of the French national women's basketball team. Born in Sedan, in 1960, Yannick moved to Cameroon with his family at the age of three.

A few hours after the encounter, Arthur mentioned the boy during a telephone conversation with Philippe Chatrier, the president of the French Tennis Federation. Intrigued, Chatrier asked about the boy's age and skill level. "You say he's good?" the Frenchman queried, and Arthur responded, "Excellent, but he's not going to go very far if he doesn't get out of the Cameroon. I'll pay his way to France for you to take a look at him."

With this impulsive act, Arthur launched a career that would alter the history of French tennis. Chatrier accepted the American's offer, and Noah soon found himself living at the French Tennis Federation's training center in Nice. After becoming a leading Junior and growing to a strapping six-foot-four, he turned pro in 1979 and soon became a member of the French Davis Cup squad. Four years later, he became the first Frenchman in thirty-seven years to win the French National singles title. Reaching his peak as the world's #3-ranked singles and #1-ranked doubles player in 1986, he ultimately won 23 singles and 16 doubles titles. After leading France to two Davis Cup championships, in 1991 and 1996, he retired at the age of thirty-six as perhaps the most beloved and admired figure in French sports history. Later, he became one of Europe's most popular singers and recording artists, as well as a noted philanthropist devoted to underprivileged children and AIDS victims.[28]

Quite naturally, Ashe took a certain pride in Noah's many accomplishments, and the two became good friends, with Ashe occasionally acting as an informal counselor. Yet Ashe was adamant that he was not personally responsible for Noah's rise to glory. "Yannick Noah is not my protégé," he insisted in 1982. "I didn't teach him a single stroke. We played doubles together at Wimbledon, and I arranged practice courts for him one year at Eastbourne, before Wimbledon. But Yannick and I are not that close. I see him, I say hello, and maybe we'll have a five-minute conversation here and there. But that's it."[29]

Ashe's determination to distance himself from Noah reflected the burden of being America's only black male tennis star. From the early 1970s on, tennis commentators frequently speculated on the likelihood of other black players joining Ashe in the upper ranks of the game. Who would be the next Arthur Ashe? Would there ever be another Ashe? Such speculation inevitably placed added pressure on aspiring black tennis stars—and on Ashe, who was expected to have a special relationship with any black person climbing up the tennis ladder.

Noah posed a particularly thorny problem because he was French and African, not American. "I'm sure people would like to believe that Yannick and I, because we're black and I supposedly 'discovered' him, are tight," Ashe observed, with some testiness. "There was a lot of resentment over this issue among some black American players on the circuit. . . . Their rationale was, 'Well, Arthur's a brother and he should be helping us out more than he's helping Yannick Noah.' What they didn't realize was that I wasn't helping Yannick that much."[30]

Ashe's venting on the Noah issue came more than a decade after his trip to West Africa. But in 1971 he was already troubled by the burden of smoothing the way for young black players. Generous by nature, he rarely missed an opportunity to conduct clinics for inner-city blacks, and his support for the National Junior Tennis League never flagged. Yet he often had difficulty striking the right balance in his individual relationships with promising black players. He wanted to help his younger "brothers"—and "sisters"—as he often called them, but not if his friendship and intervention led to a sense of entitlement. He sometimes practiced tough love by withholding help when he questioned the potential recipient's work ethic. While he agreed almost everyone needed a boost now and then, the only true roads to success, in his view, were self-reliance, discipline, and playing by the rules.

Ashe gave tennis advice freely, and he often dispensed loans for tuition payments and other emergencies. But he did not believe in favors that opened a shortcut to the top. Early in his life, thanks to his father and Dr. Johnson, the principle that success had to be earned had become a personal article of faith. Predictably, this attitude sometimes produced hard feelings among young players who looked to Ashe for assistance.[31]

As early as 1967, after Arthur had helped UCLA recruit Luis Glass, the young back star's failure to live up to his potential led to accusations that Ashe had not done enough to help the struggling teenager. Similar charges dogged his relationship with Arthur Carrington, a talented African American player sometimes touted as "the next Arthur Ashe." Four years younger than Ashe, Carrington grew up in an inner-city neighborhood in Elizabeth, New Jersey, before becoming one of Dr. Johnson's prized pupils. After meeting in 1962, Carrington and Ashe sometimes practiced together, and they kept in touch during Carrington's stellar college career at the Hampton Institute. After winning the 1973 ATA national singles title, Carrington seemed poised for stardom. But it didn't happen.

Carrington turned professional in the spring of 1974 and was assigned a world ranking of 241, but after losing his first four matches he abruptly left the tour, never to return. The primary reason, he later explained, was racial: "I had an identity crisis on the pro tour. I couldn't relate to white people." Try as he might, he couldn't turn off his militant, streetwise toughness; nor could he pretend to be Arthur Ashe. Many years later, after Carrington had become a successful tennis coach, he recalled that "Arthur presented one kind of image and I presented another one, a kind of urban thang." Ashe was never militant enough or "black" enough for Carrington, who once criticized him for "not trying to identify with blacks" and for "not showing any courage." "I know he's not Muhammad Ali," Carrington acknowledged, "but he could be standing taller."

Most observers attributed Carrington's on-court troubles to a bad attitude, but Sydney Llewellyn, the legendary African American coach who nurtured Althea Gibson in the 1950s, placed much of the blame on Ashe's shoulders. According to Llewellyn, Carrington was one of several young black players ill-served by Ashe. "He only gave a handout here and there," the veteran coach complained, adding that Ashe "never sincerely helped any of those kids. A white man asked Ashe what he thought of Carrington and he said, 'Carrington is ghetto in dress and talk.' Ashe wiped Carrington out with one sentence."[32]

The truth was that Ashe was highly selective in his patronage of up-and-coming players. Those who exhibited discipline, good sportsmanship, and a consistent work ethic could generally count on his support. Those who appeared to be lazy or who approached him with a sense of entitlement were out of luck. During the 1970s, he went out of his way to mentor a number of young black players, including Rodney Harmon, Chip Hooper, Juan Farrow, Horace Reid, Kim Sands, and Leslie Allen. But the subsequent relationships did not always produce the intended results.

In the case of Farrow, the "last highly touted junior" trained by Dr. Johnson, Ashe provided considerable financial assistance and encouragement but only until he discovered Farrow was a chain-smoker. Convinced the high-strung prospect was "too undisciplined to become a champion," Ashe severed their relationship. In a 1982 interview, Farrow attributed their falling-out to a mismatch of personal style and culture: "I just feel that Arthur feels that I'm not the kind of guy that he would like to see up there. I'm not the one to do the smiling, the patting on the back and going about saying things the way he would. He probably thinks I get high all the time and I'm running around after every tournament thinking this is a joyride." Three years later, at the age of twenty-seven and with a world ranking of 227,

Farrow retired from the tour as yet another talented black prospect unable to fulfill the promise of becoming the "next Arthur Ashe." [33]

Ashe also had a falling-out with Horace Reid, a talented prospect from Atlanta who had enjoyed his sponsorship as a teenager. After Reid secured a tennis scholarship to UCLA in 1975, Ashe promised to provide him with "$100 a month and all the tennis equipment you need," but the young star never fulfilled his potential. After dropping out of UCLA, he played in only eleven pro tournaments and never made it past the round of sixteen. His highest world ranking, 272 in 1978, was a bitter disappointment for him and Ashe, and the two became estranged after he quit the tour. Reid had regarded Ashe as his hero and role model, but their personal relationship could not bear the emotional freight of unmet expectations. "I felt like damaged goods after dealing with Arthur," he recalled many years later, insisting his unreliable mentor "never took the time to know me as a person." [34]

Having grown up without a father in the house, Reid was clearly looking for something more than financial patronage or an occasional boost. But the role of father figure did not fit Ashe's personality or philosophy. Indeed, he had little patience with those who were chronically needy or emotionally demanding, or who were unwilling or unable to adapt to the realities of competitive tennis. As Rodney Harmon once observed, Ashe concentrated on helping "people help themselves." At the same time, according to Chip Hooper, Ashe believed he could not afford to devote too much time or effort to any single individual. Instead, he felt the need to focus on "the big picture for black athletes." [35]

Ashe's most successful male protégés were, in fact, Chip Hooper and Rodney Harmon, both of whom reflected his general approach to tennis and life. The son of a surgeon, Hooper was a tall, rangy serve-and-volley specialist who trained with Dr. Johnson before meeting Ashe at a Richmond tournament in 1970. Impressed by the twelve-year-old's combination of power and control, Ashe became Hooper's sponsor and later supported his career, first at the University of Arkansas, and later on the pro tour, where he rose to a career-high #17 world ranking in 1982. [36]

Arthur was even closer to Harmon, a Richmond native who grew up less than a mile from Brook Field Park. In 1969, at the age of eight, Harmon met Ashe at an NJTL clinic held at Battery Park. He later served as a ball boy at several tournaments and trained with Willis Thomas, Arthur's boyhood doubles partner. In 1973, Harmon was named the nation's most promising young player after Arthur nominated him for the $1,000 award. The two remained close, and five years later Arthur arranged an even larger scholarship that allowed Harmon to attend the Nick Bollettieri Tennis Academy in Florida. In 1980, after Harmon experienced a disappointing freshman year at the University of Tennessee, Arthur facilitated a successful transfer to Southern Methodist University, where Ralston was the tennis coach and where Harmon eventually became an All-American. "Arthur assisted me in making the transition," Harmon recalled, "by helping me with the cost of some of my tuition. . . . His deal was that I would only have to worry about paying him back if I didn't graduate. It was really important to him that I graduate, so I graduated."

Harmon's decision to finish his degree, which meant delaying his professional career, was complicated by his unexpected success at the 1982 U.S. Open. After defeating eighth-seeded Eliot Teltscher in a memorable fourth-round match, Harmon became the first African American since Ashe to reach the quarterfinals of a major tournament. Although he lost to the eventual tournament winner, Jimmy Connors, his moment of stardom rekindled hopes that a new Arthur Ashe had finally emerged. But it was not to be. Slowed by a series of injuries, Harmon managed only three years of part-time play on the pro tour, winning less than $10,000 in prize money and never rising above a world ranking of 56.

Harmon was, however, a winner in every other way. Despite the pressure to become a full-time touring pro, he remained at SMU, graduating in 1983 with a degree in communications. With Ashe's help, he soon became a successful men's tennis coach at the University of Miami and went on to serve in a series of important coaching and executive positions with the USTA before returning to college coaching at Georgia Tech in 2012.[37]

Throughout his career, Harmon identified Arthur as his inspiration and role model. "They don't make them like Arthur anymore," he lamented in 2001, "someone who suffered a lot and then wants to help others the way he did." On one occasion, after a youth clinic at the Doral club in Miami, Harmon asked Arthur why he spent so much time instructing kids. "When you do something for someone else," Arthur explained, "you bring more joy to yourself than anything else you do. It really means a lot to me helping other people." In Harmon's experience, "Arthur was not the kind of person who would publicize what he was doing to help other black players. That was not his way. He did what he thought was right in a quiet, thoughtful way."

To Harmon, Arthur's most striking trait was the ability to listen: "What I remember about him is that he was such an active listener. He would listen to what you had to say to completion. He never would rush you or interrupt you, or even give you the impression that he didn't want to hear what you had to say." Harmon also liked to repeat one of Arthur's favorite sayings—"You've got to realize that the Lord blessed you with two ears and only one mouth, so He wants you to listen twice as much as you talk."[38]

This was good advice, worthy of an experienced elder, but Ashe was hardly a gray-bearded sage. The man who advised and inspired Harmon was himself a young man. When Harmon watched in awe as Ashe battled Laver in the semifinals of the 1972 Richmond tournament, his idol was only twenty-eight years old. Still in his prime as an athlete, he was not yet the worldly public intellectual he would become in the 1980s. Fortunately—for him and for the many individuals who benefited from his friendship and wise counsel—he would continue to evolve, thanks to an ever-widening intellectual curiosity nourished by civic engagement and voracious reading. It wouldn't be long before his dedication to learning became an obsession, symbolized by his collection of first editions and his determination to complete the *New York Times* crossword puzzle every day. A black tennis star who turned himself into an amateur philosopher, philanthopist, and social critic, all before the age of thirty—who could have imagined such a thing in an age dominated by self-absorbed and intellectually disengaged sports celebrities?[39]

FOURTEEN

RISKY BUSINESS

■

A SHE ENTERED HIS FOURTH year of professional tennis with a lot on his mind. Back home in Virginia family matters were testing his emotions. Whenever he managed to spend a few days in Richmond or Gum Spring, as he did just after his return from West Africa in December 1971, he was reminded of how much his extended family meant to him—and of how several of those dearest to him were growing old and fragile. "I think the more family you have the closer you are," he once wrote, and he regretted that his merciless travel schedule never allowed him enough time to spend with the ones he loved the most.[1]

He especially missed his brother, Johnnie, who remained in the military as a gunnery sergeant and engineer shuttling between posts in California, Okinawa, and Japan. Though passionately devoted to the Marine Corps, Johnnie was still trying to adjust to what he had seen and experienced in the jungles of Southeast Asia. In many ways Arthur and his brother were closer than ever, but not on their views of the war. While Johnnie continued to embrace his role as a soldier, Arthur had grown to hate the war that had divided the nation.

President Nixon's failure to extricate American forces from Vietnam, among his other failings, had convinced Arthur that the current administration was politically and morally bankrupt. He had opposed Nixon and the Republicans in 1968, and nothing he had seen since had changed his mind.

As the 1972 election approached, he adopted a left-of-center liberal posture. Disillusioned with the complacency of mainstream politics, he donated to the campaign funds of several antiwar Democrats, including Andrew Young of Georgia, who won a seat in Congress after having lost his first bid for office two years earlier. Arthur's earlier donation to Young's unsuccessful 1970 campaign represented a milestone in his move toward active political involvement, initiating a relationship that would have an impact on both men's lives.

Arthur was also an early and enthusiastic supporter of the 1972 antiwar presidential candidacy of Senator George McGovern of South Dakota. Like many members of his generation, he was tired of the hidebound style of politics that had stymied the causes of peace and social justice, and he had grown increasingly impatient as the war dragged on. President Nixon's groundbreaking trip to China in late February 1972 raised hopes for a new departure in East-West relations and a possible end to hostilities in Vietnam, but by late spring the war was once again in full tilt with the resumption of B-52 bombing raids on Hanoi and Haiphong and the mining of North Vietnamese ports. The Paris peace talks were stalled, and peace seemed further away than ever.[2]

The other "war" in Arthur's life—the one between WCT and the ILTF—was also dispiriting in early 1972. The ILTF's banishment of contract pros went into effect on January 1, and during the long winter that followed there was no letup in the struggle to control the men's tour. Despite record crowds and unprecedented prize money, Open tennis—split as it was between two warring factions—was teetering on the brink of collapse. In mid-March, WCT, in an act of calculated escalation, countered the ILTF ban with the creation of a $50,000 tournament during the Wimbledon fortnight. Since the contract pros were unwelcome at Wimbledon, they would hold their own concurrent tournament in a major American city. Wimbledon and ILTF officials feigned indifference, but all knew the breakdown of recent talks was a portent of disaster.

Arthur knew that Dell and Kramer, representing the USLTA, were working behind the scenes to craft a long-term arrangement that would satisfy both WCT and the ILTF. But the swirl of rising prize money and potential television contracts kept raising the stakes, making all parties less inclined to compromise. Even before WCT's bold move, Kramer had admitted that the two sides were further apart than ever. Speaking of the contract pros, he confessed, "They don't need us. And for sure, we don't need them." That same week, when Arthur uncharacteristically fell to his knees and pounded the hard court floor after losing a second-set tiebreaker to Ken Rosewall in the semifinals of the Philadelphia indoor championships, his friends knew his off-court frustrations were as much to blame as his last errant forehand. At that point, he and everyone else had good reason to fear that the days of Open tennis and hefty paychecks were numbered.[3]

Fortunately, Dell and Kramer's negotiating skills prevailed during a final series of talks in April. Cliff Richey's long-awaited decision to sign a contract with WCT earlier in the month had weakened the ILTF's position, preparing the way for a comprehensive agreement. Though subject to ratification at the ILTF's annual meeting at Helsinki in July, the document signed in London in late April brought peace to the tennis world. "The war is over," Allan Heyman, the Danish president of the ILTF, declared. While the agreement did not come soon enough to reopen the 1972 French Open and Wimbledon to Arthur and the other contract pros, the men's tour would be fully united in time for them to play in the U.S. Open in September.

The April 1972 agreement did not affect the women's tour, which was undergoing its own evolution and growth thanks largely to Billie Jean King and popular young stars such as Evonne Goolagong and Chris Evert. And some of the agreed-upon arrangements would undergo modification after the wildcat promoter Bill Riordan filed a successful antitrust suit against the tennis establishment. But the basic terms of the agreement ratified in July 1972 would remain in effect for the rest of Ashe's playing career.

Under the new rules, the distinction between contract and independent pros was eliminated; all WCT tournaments became ILTF-sanctioned events; once the present WCT contracts expired, all pros would compete for prize money under the same conditions with no guaranteed contract payments; the schedules of WCT and non-WCT events would be coordinated to avoid direct conflict or competition; the WCT circuit—consisting of two parallel, eleven-tournament tours, each with thirty-two players—would conclude in April, prior to the beginning of the ILTF's Grand Prix and Masters circuit; the WCT finals would take place in May; and all WCT players would be strongly encouraged to participate in all four Grand Slam tournaments.[4]

The only major unresolved issue was the nagging problem of Davis Cup participation, which was under the purview of the national Davis Cup committees. In 1971, the committees had voted to eliminate the traditional Challenge Round structure, which guaranteed the defending champion a place in the final competition. Beginning in 1972, the defending champion—at that time, the United States—would have to compete in the zonal competition along with all the other nations. The U.S. team did so successfully—winning a fifth straight Davis Cup over a tough Romanian squad playing at home in Bucharest—but without the help of Arthur and the other leading American contract pros. The "professionalization" of Davis Cup competition would not come until 1973, when Australia recaptured the Cup thanks to the eligibilty of Laver, Newcombe, and Rosewall.[5]

Ashe, though pleased with America's successful defense of the Davis Cup in 1972, was not happy about another development in the Davis Cup saga: the movement to readmit South Africa to Cup competition. The primary rationale for readmittance was South Africa's recent loosening of racial barriers in women's tennis—most notably Goolagong's participation in the 1972 Federation Cup tournament held in Johannesburg, and the appearance of several nonwhite women at the trials held to select South Africa's team.

None of the nonwhite women made the team, but several influential ILTF and Davis Cup leaders interpreted the girls' eligibility as an "encouraging gesture." When several of the girls were allowed to register for the upcoming South African Open, USLTA president Robert Colwell and British LTA secretary Basil Reay praised South Africa's new attitude, and Colwell even called for sanctions against nations refusing to play South Africa in Davis Cup competition.

The idea that these cosmetic changes represented a meaningful break from apartheid seemed ludicrous to Ashe, who was still effectively barred from playing in the South African Open. But with few exceptions Davis Cup officials felt otherwise. In July, at a special committee meeting in Helsinki, delegates voted 5–2 to readmit South Africa to Davis Cup competition, with only the Soviet and Indian delegates opposing readmittance. Two years later, an all-white South African team would actually win the Cup after the Indian government refused to let its team take the court in the final round.

All of this left Ashe deeply conflicted. While he did not want the world to be fooled by misleading propaganda or manipulated by a South African government determined to misrepresent what was happening inside its borders, he did not believe in isolating the apartheid regime from the rest of the world. He still preferred engagement and dialogue to banishment and enforced silence, though his patience was growing thin. For him and the growing number of activists dedicated to the liberation of South Africa, the prospects for a true resolution of the troubled nation's racial dilemmas appeared dimmer than ever.[6]

It was a strange summer for Ashe, who had more time on his hands than usual. Temporarily relieved of the frenetic international travel schedule imposed by the French Open and Wimbledon, he stayed closer to home. In between brief tournament trips to Connecticut, Missouri, New Hampshire, Washington, D.C., and Kentucky, he found time for family, politics, and other passions. He attended political rallies for George McGovern and even raised money for him by offering to hit a few volleys with anyone willing to donate $100 to the campaign chest.[7]

He also spent time promoting the NJTL and other inner-city tennis programs. He was thrilled the NJTL was finally catching on and that the game of tennis was losing some of its elite image. "After all these years as a country-club sport played by the very rich," he announced in late July, "tennis is now moving into the mainstream of the American sports scene. Just think, 30,000 kids, black and white, learning the game."

His own game had been subpar for most of the summer, but at the end of July he broke out of his slump with a singles title at the First National tournament in Louisville. A week later, at the U.S. Pro championships in Boston, he lost a close semifinal match to Okker in singles and teamed with Lutz to reach the doubles final against Roche and Newcombe, who won. He played even better in Cleveland and Fort Worth—the last two tournaments leading up to the U.S. Open—and pronounced himself ready to tackle the world-class field at Forest Hills.[8]

Just prior to the Open, Ashe participated in a pro-celebrity tournament benefiting the Robert F. Kennedy Memorial Foundation, an organization that aided underprivileged children living in inner cities, Appalachia, Chicano communities, and Indian reservations. Held at the Forest Hills Stadium and billed as "A Day of Stars and Tennis," it was the kind of high-profile fund-raising event he had been advocating for years. The participants included Laver and other leading pros, plus a host of celebrities ranging from Bill Cosby and Dustin Hoffman to Goldie Hawn and Dinah Shore. The entire Kennedy clan was on hand, from Robert Kennedy's widow, Ethel, to Senator Edward Kennedy of Massachusetts. It was a glorious day for Ashe, who talked tennis and politics with Ethel Kennedy and her sister-in-law Eunice Shriver while helping to raise nearly $100,000 for a good cause.[9]

The entire affair put Ashe in a good mood, just what he needed on the eve of the Open. It had been nearly a year since the contract and independent pros had competed in a Grand Slam tournament, and the pre-tournament excitement was palpable. The crush of players seeking entry into the tournament had prompted an increase in the men's draw from 128 to 148, and in the women's draw from 64 to 80. Advance ticket sales had broken all records, delighting tournament director Bill Talbert. "I've been around tennis for forty years," he exclaimed. "I've had some very exciting moments. But the family has outgrown the house."

Seeded sixth behind Smith, Rosewall, Laver, Nastase, and Newcombe, Ashe faced the Pakistani star Haroon Rahim in the first round. Easily advancing to a second-round match against Bob Maud of South Africa, he played on the Grandstand Court, where an earlier match had pitted the 1971 U.S. Open runner-up, Jan Kodes, against Alex "Sandy" Mayer Jr., an unheralded twenty-year-old amateur from nearby Wayne, New Jersey. When Mayer upset Kodes in five sets, winning the final set 6–1, the fans sensed they were in for a wild tournament.

Later in the afternoon Ashe defeated Maud in straight sets, and he went on to defeat the Australian Ross Case and Lutz in the next two rounds. But all around him the top seeds—notably Laver, Rosewall, Newcombe, and Okker—were falling. Ashe himself was involved in a minor upset when he outlasted Smith, the number one seed, in the quarterfinals. Trailing two sets to one and facing match point in the fourth, Smith double-faulted to end the match. Afterward one reporter described the upset as the return "of the Ashe of yore, the one with only tennis on his mind." In recent years, the reporter explained, the 1968 Open champion had paid a price for "dividing his time between tennis and social concern." He had become "an articulate spokesman for minority groups" and had taken "on hundreds of personal interests," but in the process he had lost his number one ranking among American players. Now he was back, the dominating "Mr. Cool, with a repertory of a whippy forehand and a bludgeoning serve."[10]

This interpretation made good copy, but it did not reflect the truth. Ashe was actually busier than ever attending to his off-court interests. On September 8, the day after his victory over Smith, he helped to launch the newly formed Association of Tennis Professionals (ATP), which replaced the ITPA. In the works since mid-April, the ATP brought together fifty male players from sixteen different nations, all willing to pay $400 a year in dues for the services of Kramer as executive director and Dell as legal counsel. Cliff Drysdale was elected the ATP's first president, and Ashe agreed to serve as vice president. Following the formal announcement of the group's founding, Ashe explained to the press that he and his peers were "tired of being stepped on by two elephants," WCT and the ILTF. ATP would "unite, promote, and protect" the common interests of the players.[11]

The founding of the ATP was the biggest story to come out of the 1972 U.S. Open. But the unexpected success of several ATP stalwarts was also noteworthy. Teamed with Roger Taylor, Drysdale won the doubles title, and three of the four singles semifinalists—Ashe, Richey, and Gorman—were American ATP members. The only non-American to survive the quarter-finals was the Romanian bad boy Ilie Nastase. After Ashe defeated Richey in the first semifinal match and Nastase defeated Gorman in the second, the final presented a striking contrast of styles and personalities. The frequently outrageous Nastase was as hot as Ashe was cool, and even his close friends never knew what "Nasty," as he was often called, was going to do next. Asked prior to the match how he would beat Ashe, he wisecracked "with my racquet—over his head."

In the actual match, Nastase's antics stopped short of violence, but just barely. During the first set, which Ashe won 6–3, the Romanian repeatedly dropped his racket in exasperation—once after Titus Sparrow, a black service linesman, called a foot fault. Later in the set, when a close service call went against him, Nastase feigned disbelief and threw a towel at one of the linesmen. At that point, it looked like Ashe was on his way to a second U.S. Open title, but as the match progressed Nastase ratcheted up his game. Always formidable on grass, he eventually took command with a remarkable display of shotmaking. Although Ashe rallied to win the third set in a tie-breaker, Nastase closed out the match with convincing wins in the two final sets.

At the presentation ceremony, Ashe graciously accepted the $12,000 second-place prize money and praised Nastase's artful play. Yet he couldn't resist offering a few words of advice. "When Nastase brushes up on his manners," he counseled, "he'll be an even better player." "Ilie and I are good friends off the court," he added teasingly, "although I must say his table manners are just like his court manners."

Two weeks later, Ashe and Nastase ran into each other again, this time on a walkway at the Los Angeles Tennis Club. Lost in thought about an upcoming match, Ashe walked right past the Romanian without acknowledging him. Always a talker, Nastase could not let the incident pass without a bit of gentle needling. "Hey, Negroni," he yelled, using the Romanian term for black man. "I thought you were my friend. How come you tell those reporters that I need manners? Can you believe, in Romania they ask me 'What kind of man is this Arthur Ashe?' and I tell them, 'Fine fellow.' Now what am I going to say if you tell reporters that I need better manners on court. Bad manners? Not me! Hey, Negroni, let's be friends again." After a brief double take, Ashe laughed and walked on. Over the years he and Nastase would have a series of run-ins, but he could never stay mad at the Romanian rogue for very long.[12]

For Ashe, losing to Nastase at Forest Hills was, ironically, one of the high points of 1972. In addition to earning him one of the largest paychecks of the year, making the finals restored his confidence and led to a noticeable uptick in his play. One week later, he defeated Emerson in the championship match at the Montreal International tournament. It was only his second tournament title of the year—and his first in nearly six months.[13]

The quality of Ashe's play slipped noticeably in late September and early October, darkening his mood and temporarily shaking his confidence. Then, on October 24, just as he was about to leave for a month-long tour of Western Europe, he received news that his boyhood idol Jackie Robinson had passed away at the age of fifty-three. After twenty-five years of bearing the burdens and responsibilities of being Major League Baseball's racial pioneer, Robinson had succumbed to heart disease and diabetes. Since Ashe shouldered similar burdens and both men were UCLA graduates, he felt a special affinity for the great Dodger infielder. He couldn't help but ponder his own mortality, wondering what the possible consequences of his own solitary struggle might be. Even so, he refused to let Robinson's early death get the best of him. His best option, he decided, was to seize the day and not worry too much about a medical future largely beyond his control.

Refocused, Ashe soon began to hit his stride on the European circuit. Mercifully, he was in Sweden in early November when George McGovern suffered a landslide loss to Richard Nixon. Feeling more comfortable with the socially progressive politics of Western Europe than with the seemingly reactionary majority of his own country, Ashe had several weeks to commiserate with friends and acquaintances beyond America's borders. From Sweden, he traveled to the Netherlands, another nation that shared his opposition to the Vietnam War. Playing in Rotterdam, he made it all the way to the finals before losing to Dutch favorite son Tom Okker.

A week later he was in Rome, where he celebrated the end of the European circuit and the Thanksgiving holiday by defeating Lutz in the championship match. The first-place prize money of $25,000 was the largest payday of his career, raising his 1972 on-court earnings to nearly $120,000 and making him the second biggest money winner on the tour. In terms of victories, it had been a disappointing year, with only three tournament wins and only six championship match appearances; and for the first time in his career his overall winning percentage had dipped below 70 percent. But, as he told the press in Rome, it was "nice to end the season on a positive side." He also took the opportunity to express his—and the ATP's—commitment to sharing the wealth. "That chunk of money made this my biggest payday," he informed the reporters. "But the present prize-money breakdown gives too much money to a man at the top."[14]

Ashe began the new year of 1973—his fifth on the professional tour—with high hopes. Although he was approaching thirty—a forbidding milestone in the tennis world—he was confident his best years lay ahead. Perhaps most important, the game of tennis as both a profession and a sport appeared to be entering a golden age of open competition and popularity. With the ATP securely in place, the tennis wars in abeyance, prize money rising, and the popularity of the game soaring to unprecedented heights, a bright future beckoned.

It was, after all, the long-awaited Centennial year of modern tennis. A century earlier, the modern game had reportedly been born in Wales thanks to the efforts of a British soldier, Major Walter Clopton Wingfield. Although later research would bring this claim into question, the designation of 1973 as the official centennial was uncontroversial at the time. It was to be a year of renewal and unity, with everyone coming together to celebrate the occasion. "This May Be the Year for Tennis Without Politics," a January 7 *New York Times* headline proclaimed. Unfortunately, the realities of life and labor soon intervened. As Bud Collins would later write, "1973 was the game's most peculiar year," a period of expansion marked by bitter, internecine conflict and "unprecedented labor strife." Before the year was over, the tennis world would be ripped apart by boycotts, lawsuits, and both real and ritualistic battles over gender and racial inequities.[15]

The year of tumult began quietly enough with the introduction of WCT's new January-through-May format. Sixty-four pros divided into two groups of thirty-two competitors played in parallel tours, designated A and B, with each tour consisting of eleven $50,000 tournaments. Ashe was assigned to Tour B, the weaker of the two tours, while several of the strongest players—including Smith, Laver, and Emerson—played in Tour A. Ashe's toughest opponents turned out to be Rosewall, Riessen, and Roger Taylor, who joined him in Tour B's top four finishers. In May, they squared off against the top four in Tour A in a $100,000 WCT Masters tournament in Dallas.[16]

While he eventually finished among the top four, Ashe's performance during the inaugural Tour B season was inconsistent and generally disappointing. Following an especially bad patch in January and February when he was eliminated in the first round at Milan and Copenhagen, and in the second round at Cologne, he finally won his first tournament of the year in Chicago in early March. The following week, at the World Cup tournament in Hartford—sponsored for the first time by Ashe's future employer, the Aetna Insurance Company—he lost convincingly to Emerson in singles, and he and Riessen later lost to Emerson and Newcombe in doubles, insuring that the Aussies would win the Cup for the second straight year. Always keen on beating their archrivals, Ashe and his disappointed teammates were jolted by their 5–2 loss, which did not bode well for the Americans' chances of retaining the Davis Cup later in the year.

A week later Ashe gained a measure of revenge by beating Rosewall in the semifinals at Merrifield, Virginia, even though he went on to lose the championship match to Okker in a third-set tiebreaker. After six weeks of play, WCT's Tour B had six different winners, demonstrating a remarkable parity. At both Houston and Cleveland, Ashe lost to Rosewall in the quarterfinals. In Charlotte, he made it all the way to the finals only to lose to Rosewall for a third straight week, once again running afoul of the tiebreaker format by losing the last six points.

Going into the final week of the tour, Ashe had only one victory to his credit. Yet his overall play put him in second place behind Rosewall. In the eleventh and final tournament, held in Denver, he fought his way into the championship match. But in the final he suffered one of the worst defeats of his career, losing 6–1, 6–1 to Mark Cox, a twenty-nine-year-old Cambridge-educated Englishman whom he had defeated handily on several occasions.[17]

Following the discouraging loss, few observers thought Ashe would be much of a factor at the WCT Masters tournament. But he surprised almost everyone by returning to top form and nearly taking home the top prize of $50,000. In the Masters semifinal, he outlasted Rosewall in a grueling five-set match, winning the final set 6–2 after losing the fourth 1–6. Although he lost his edge in the championship match against heavily favored Stan Smith, the winner of six of Tour A's eleven tournaments, taking home the second-place prize money of $20,000 took some of the sting out of the loss, as did the fact that the championship match featured two Americans after two years of dominance by Rosewall and Laver.[18]

From Texas, Ashe traveled to Las Vegas for the Alan King–Caesars Palace Classic, a $150,000 tournament co-sponsored by the ATP. Billed as "the world's richest single tournament," the Classic was designed as a showcase for the ATP's rising importance to the game of tennis. Unveiled in January 1973 along with plans to set up ATP "tournament bureaus" in the United States and Europe as liaisons "between the players and promoters," the lucrative tournament sent a clear message to the ILTF and WCT: the ATP could not be ignored or taken for granted.[19]

To Ashe and his colleagues, the Classic was a demonstration of the ATP's power and legitimacy. With its first-place prize money set at $30,000, the tournament attracted many of the world's best players, including Smith, Laver, and Newcombe. Surprisingly, Ashe was the only seeded player to reach the semifinals. With all of the other top players falling in the earlier rounds, his semifinal match pitted him against Roscoe Tanner, a tall twenty-one-year-old left-hander from Lookout Mountain, Tennessee, reputed to have the fastest serve in tennis. Wildness and inconsistency had plagued Tanner since he had turned professional in 1970, and Ashe had beaten him in their previous three meetings. But on any given day Tanner's extraordinary serve could test the return skills of the world's best.

During the first set, Tanner gave Ashe all he could handle, pushing him to a 22-point tiebreaker, the longest of his career. Trailing 6 points to 4 and facing two set points, Ashe rallied, eventually winning the tiebreaker 12–10. He went on to win the second set 6–2, advancing to the final where he expected to face Richey. But to nearly everyone's surprise, Richey lost the other semifinal to Brian Gottfried, an unheralded twenty-one-year-old rookie pro from Fort Lauderdale, known primarily for his distinctive Fu Manchu mustache. Ashe had never faced Gottfried, but the way the young Floridian had dominated Graebner, Riessen, and Richey served warning that he was not to be taken lightly.

Playing before a nationally televised audience for what was potentially the largest prize money of his career, Ashe was full of confidence prior to the match. But nothing went right once he took the court. From the outset, he had trouble handling wind gusts of up to twenty miles an hour, and he couldn't seem to adjust to Gottfried's deep cross-court backhands and passing shots. After dropping the first set 6–1, and double-faulting on game-ending points in the fifth and seventh games of the second, he managed to win only three games in the deciding set.

Described as a rout by the press, Gottfried's victory received less attention than Ashe's loss. For the fifth time since January, he had fought his way through the draw only to lose in the championship round. Predictably, questions about his lack of a killer instinct reemerged. Having heard all of this before, Ashe responded with unusual sharpness during the post-match press conference. "I don't like losing these finals," he confessed to the reporters. "I don't like to read those things—that Ashe can't win the big ones." [20]

Ashe clearly was troubled by the growing suspicion that he lacked whatever it took to capture tournament titles on a consistent basis. But he didn't have much time to ponder this or any other nagging criticism. After Las

Vegas, he was off to Paris for the beginning of a six-week stint playing on the clay and grass courts of Europe. Competing in the Paris-Rome-London circuit had been part of his annual cycle since the late 1960s, but this time would be different. Earlier in the spring, he had decided to take on two additional "responsibilities," both of which complicated his European tour.

The first was Meryl (pronounced Merle) Carr, a strikingly beautiful Jewish woman from Toronto whom he had been dating for more than a year. For several years, he had been playing the field, dating a wide variety of women and studiously avoiding any long-term relationships. His first and only serious romantic entanglement, his year-long engagement to Pat Battles, had ended awkwardly in March 1967, and he had been wary of commitment ever since. His deepening infatuation with Meryl, however, led him to reconsider his aversion to lengthy relationships.

Ashe's romantic involvement with Meryl marked his first extended experience with interracial dating, although he had dated white women before on a number of occasions, beginning as early as 1962. He had gone out several times with the Swedish tennis star Ingrid Löfdahl, had enjoyed a fling with an Iranian woman in 1972, and had even engaged in an illicit affair with a married white woman from Dallas. Indeed, in 1967, the year the U.S. Supreme Court finally struck down bans on interracial marriage in the landmark *Loving v. Virginia* ruling, he had talked openly about his liberal views on interracial dating and intermarriage. "If I see a white girl who fascinates me I'll make a play for her," he declared in his surprisingly candid memoir *Advantage Ashe*. "I've taken white girls to parties just to watch the reactions. Some of my acquaintances look shocked or embarrassed, and I feel slightly sorry for them." Later in the book, he discussed his experiences with Swedish girls in the "swinging" resort town of Bastad: "Girls from all over Sweden save up for a year to go to Bastad and meet the tennis players. The ratio is about two girls to every fellow, and I didn't see a bad looking girl the week I was there." "I had two girl friends," he bragged.[21]

Ashe was well aware this kind of boastful talk would not play very well back in the States—and that it was potentially explosive in places like Richmond. But he didn't seem to care, refusing to trim his sails to fit the racial conventions of narrow-minded traditionalists, black or white. "It doesn't bother me when I see a Negro woman with a white man," he insisted. "That riles a lot of Negroes. But I feel sorry for Negroes who feel that way. They're even more narrow-minded than some whites. I'll go out with a white girl if we happen to like each other. Some Negroes think I don't like Negroes. I just laugh when they tell me this. Or I give them a silent stare. I've had some of them ask me, 'Ashe, do you think you'll ever marry a Negro girl?'"

While he conceded he was "more likely to fall for a girl of my own race," he refused to rule out the possibility of intermarriage, even though he recognized the obvious difficulties an interracial union would entail. "If I did have a white wife I know I wouldn't be too popular in American tournaments," he acknowledged. "I couldn't live in Richmond, or even in most other places." Nevertheless, he took some solace in the fact that Senator Edward Brooke of Massachusetts, the first black United States senator elected since Reconstruction, had "married a white wife, and it didn't stop him from getting elected Senator in a state where only 3% of the voters are Negro."[22]

At the same time, Ashe was well aware of the furor over the popular entertainer Sammy Davis Jr.'s eight-year marriage to the Swedish film star May Britt. A decade earlier, the singer and actress Pearl Bailey's 1952 marriage to the celebrated white jazz drummer Louis Bellson endangered both of their careers. Earlier still, during the so-called Progressive Era and the Roaring Twenties, the heavyweight boxer Jack Johnson's successive marriages to three white women led to pariah status and several near riots. Indeed, throughout the post–Civil War era, in custom and often in codified law, the intermarriage taboo applied to celebrities as well as ordinary citizens, and even a figure as distinguished as Frederick Douglass could not escape mass ridicule and scorn following his marriage to the white abolitionist Helen Pitts.[23]

To date, most of Ashe's interracial dating had taken place outside the borders of the United States, either in Australia or Europe, where attitudes toward miscegenation tended to be somewhat more tolerant and forgiving than in America's hypersensitive racial climate. Thus, his extended involvement with Meryl presented him with new and potentially uncomfortable situations. Cold stares and ugly incidents were inevitable challenges for any interracial couple living in the United States, where according to an October 1972 Gallup poll only 29 percent of Americans "approved" of interracial marriage between blacks and whites.

Although Meryl's parents were Canadian, they initially expressed strong disapproval of their daughter's interracial relationship. Fortunately, after she stood firm and refused to break off the relationship, her family came around and more or less accepted Arthur as a worthy suitor. Even so, he never felt completely comfortable in their presence. For the Carrs, as for most white families in the 1970s, traditional stereotypes and fears related to race and sex were a fact of life, and Arthur's celebrity status did not shield him from this reality. On the contrary, his visibility probably heightened his vulnerability. Whenever he and Meryl went out in public, they could be sure that somewhere in the room someone was commenting on their relationship, perhaps only in a whisper, but usually with an air of disapproval.

One solution, though temporary and imperfect, was to escape to a more tolerant cultural setting, a place where they could be together without shouldering the heavy burden of America's racial baggage. This is the path Arthur chose in the spring of 1973. Risking censure from his family and throwing caution to the wind, he invited Meryl to accompany him on the European tour. A freelance commercial artist with an open schedule, she gleefully accepted. For nearly six weeks, from mid-May until the end of June, she would be his companion. Running from the French Open to Wimbledon, it was, as Arthur wrote in mid-June, "the longest time I've ever spent with one woman."[24]

The second added responsibility was an ambitious book project undertaken in collaboration with Frank Deford, the Princeton-educated sportswriter who had written two of the earliest *Sports Illustrated* articles on Ashe and who later joined him on the 1970 goodwill tour of West Africa. During his last year at UCLA, Ashe had collaborated with Cliff Gewecke on the memoir *Advantage Ashe*, and he was eager to write a sequel. The project with Deford was a bit different, however. This time the plan was to keep a year-long, Wimbledon-to-Wimbledon diary—a daily chronicle written in Arthur's own words to be edited by Deford at the end of the year. As Deford later revealed, Arthur "would tape his thoughts every night into a recorder and then send me the tape. A tape would arrive every three weeks. Plus we would see each other regularly too, so it wasn't like this was done just by tapes."

The primary goal, as Arthur later wrote in the preface to the book, published in 1975 as *Arthur Ashe: Portrait in Motion*, was helping the public "to understand tennis, to appreciate the matches you see and the players who participate in them." But he couldn't resist adding a secondary goal, the prospect that "the book might even make it possible" for ordinary fans "to understand tennis politics."

With a bit of luck, the diary would end with Arthur's first Wimbledon title, or so the editors at Houghton Mifflin hoped. Alas, this storybook ending did not happen, and the narrative closed not with a triumph but rather with a third-round loss to unseeded Roscoe Tanner. Even so, there was more than enough drama along the way—from tennis wars to family funerals to broken romances.[25]

The book might have been even more interesting if Arthur had begun his diary a bit earlier. His first daily entry was written on June 11, a full month after he arrived in Paris for the French Open. By that time, a rush of events had enveloped him and the tennis world, though most of the action was outside the lines. In Arthur's case, the lack of on-court success was hardly a surprise. Though seeded fourth by French Open officials, he was not expected to be much of a factor on the slow red clay of Roland Garros. In doubles, he had fared fairly well at the French Open, reaching the championship round with Charlie Pasarell in 1970 and winning the championship with Marty Riessen the following year. But the singles competition was another matter. While he had reached the singles quarterfinals twice, in 1970 and 1971, he had failed to advance on both occasions, losing tough five-set matches to Zeljko Franulovic and Frank Froehling. Having won only one tournament so far in 1973, he didn't hold out much hope of surprising his critics with a victory in Paris.

True to form, he survived the first three rounds only to be eliminated in the fourth by the Italian clay-court specialist Paolo Bertolucci. For Ashe, once again most of the fun in the City of Light took place far away from Roland Garros. But he tried to keep the situation in perspective, recalling his modest Richmond origins and remembering there were worse fates than having a few extra days to sample the museums, cafés, and nightclubs of Paris with a beautiful woman on his arm.[26]

A week later, with Meryl at his side, Ashe flew to Rome for the Italian Open. Once again he suffered an early exit, losing in the fourth round to Pasarell. After the loss, he was subjected to a chorus of friendly ribbing from Pasarell and others, but he soon found himself dealing with matters more troubling than another clay court defeat. As the newly elected treasurer and former vice president of the ATP, he was thrust into a resurgent controversy involving Niki Pilic of Yugoslavia.

Earlier in the year the Yugoslav Tennis Federation had suspended Pilic for breaking a commitment to represent Yugoslavia in a Davis Cup tie in New Zealand. The ATP came to Pilic's defense, arguing the Yugoslav federation's action constituted an arbitrary abuse of its disciplinary power. Threatening to withdraw all of its members from the upcoming French Open if Pilic's suspension remained in force, the ATP solved the immediate problem by filing a partially successful appeal with the ILTF's Emergency Committee. Reducing the suspension from three months to one, the Emergency Committee made it possible for Pilic to play in the French Open, where he made it all the way to the championship match before losing to Nastase.

This temporary solution, while helping Pilic, failed to satisfy Ashe and other ATP leaders, who insisted they should have full disciplinary authority over their members. They were also furious that the one-month suspension included the Wimbledon fortnight. As Bud Collins later observed, the ATP leaders were convinced that the timing of the one-month suspension "was devised by the ILTF to demonstrate its muscle, believing the players would never support a boycott of the world's premier tournament. Thus, the 'Pilic Affair' became a test of the will and organization of the new association. Many ATP leaders felt if they gave in on this first showdown, they would never be strong, whereas if they held firm and proved to the ILTF that even Wimbledon was not sacred, the ATP's unity and power would never be doubted in the future."[27]

Beginning in Rome, when the Italian Federation broke ranks with the ILTF and ruled that Pilic's suspension was inoperative until after the Italian Open in May, the controversy came to a head in the weeks leading up to Wimbledon. Ashe was often in the thick of it, but there was a brief interlude in mid-June when he took leave to attend to a personal matter. On June 11 he and Meryl flew from Yugoslavia to London, where they planned to celebrate her birthday with a night on the town. Following dinner at Trader Vic's and an hour or so of gambling at the Playboy Club, they returned to their room at the Westbury Hotel. Twenty minutes after Ashe's head hit the pillow, he was awakened by a long-distance call from his Aunt Marie in Richmond. His grandmother Cunningham—Big Mama as he called her—had passed away. The matriarch of the family—the mother of ten children and a powerful woman who had outlived her husband by nearly four decades—was gone.

Despite the uncertain situation surrounding Pilic, he felt compelled to fly home for the funeral. Big Mama was special; the strongest direct link to his mother, she was his favorite relative. In his words, she was "a strong, dear, fine woman" who "kept the family together, all the while working full-time in the kitchen at a white public school." Two days later, he flew home, where his father met him at Byrd Field. By the time he arrived at his Uncle James's house, a wake was in progress. All of Big Mama's surviving eight children were there, along with dozens of cousins, nieces, nephews, and in-laws. In the Cunningham-Ashe family, there had not been a gathering like this in more than twenty years, not since Mattie Ashe's funeral.

For Arthur, the reconnection with his extended family at Big Mama's funeral was a highly emotional experience. As he sat in the sanctuary of Westwood Baptist Church, where he had spent countless Sundays as a child, he lost all of his legendary coolness. Even though he had become "a closet agnostic" as an adult, the physical closeness of his family and the spirit of the preacher's "tremendously moving service" touched something deep inside of him as he "was plunged into the warm, familiar world of my childhood again: the minister, sweating and singing and preaching, and the choir." As he recalled years later, "I tried to keep my reserve through the service and almost did. But when my Uncle Rudy cried, 'Good-bye, Mama,' I broke down and emotions poured out of me, totally out of control. I cried like a baby for several minutes. When it was over, I was drained of tensions I didn't even know had been inside. But it was all right, I was among family and old friends. I was 'Arthur Junior' again."

Earlier in the day he had declined an opportunity to peer inside the open casket for one last look at his grandmother, but he took in everything at the Woodland Cemetery gravesite where they laid her to rest next to his mother's grave. "It was warm and the sky was high clear blue when they buried her," he noted in his diary. "Then I got a flight back to New York and was on the nine P.M. Pan Am to London." [28]

The emotions stirred by family and a life well lived had drawn Ashe in, temporarily overwhelming his normal air of reserve. But once he was back in the real world of London, he realized it would take a cool head to deal with the fast-developing Pilic crisis. On June 15, the day he returned to the tense pre-Wimbledon scene, ATP's lawyers asked Great Britain's High Court for an injunction ordering the All England Club to approve Pilic's participation in the upcoming tournament. Four days later, less than a week before the start of the first round, the High Court judge, Sir Hugh Forbes, ruled that Pilic and Wimbledon were outside his jurisdiction; there would be no injunction against Pilic's suspension by the ILTF. Effectively validating the suspension, Forbes ordered a stunned Pilic to pay several thousand pounds in court costs.

That evening, the ATP executive board held an emotional meeting at the Westbury Hotel. "We talked and argued for hours, restrained, remarkably civil, but always on edge," Ashe wrote in his diary, "for we realized that we were in the process of declaring war." Sometime after one o'clock in the morning, Drysdale called for a vote on a proposed boycott of Wimbledon. Two board members, including Pilic, abstained, and the Englishman Mark Cox voted no, but the other seven voted in favor. It was two o'clock before Ashe fell into bed, and it was later still before he calmed down enough to sleep. But several hours later, in the cold light of morning, he recorded his thoughts on one of the most turbulent days in the annals of tennis. To his knowledge, this "was the first time any athletes in any sport had voted, on principle, to withdraw from their championship of the world. I could hardly believe what we had done." A week earlier, he had predicted that the Pilic affair would become a milestone in the history of tennis. "Ban him, lose us all," he had written on June 11. "Tennis is exactly a century old, and this, at last, will be the moment when the players stand up for themselves."

The actual withdrawal required the approval of a majority of ATP members, and a morning meeting on June 20 took care of that. According to Ashe, after the board presented its recommendation to the full membership, "they accepted it with hardly a dissent." In the end, seventy-nine ATP members withdrew from the tournament, including Ashe and thirteen of the top sixteen seeds. Only three ATP members—Nastase, Roger Taylor, and Ray Keldie—remained in the draw.[29]

For a time, it appeared that many of the top women's players would join the boycott, partly as a show of support for Pilic and the ATP, but mostly as a demand for narrowing the gap between men's and women's prize money. But Billie Jean King's effort to mobilize the women's draw fell flat after Goolagong and Evert, among others, refused to join the boycott. "I've come over here to play tennis, and that's all I'm interested in," Evert declared. Ashe and the ATP would have to fend for themselves.[30]

They also had to face a furious reaction from the British tennis establishment, as the national press rushed to the defense of the hallowed All England Club and excoriated the boycotters for putting their personal interests ahead of the public good. One television reporter, Peter Wilson, who sparred with Ashe in a confrontational interview, described the absent players as "brash," "ill-mannered," "overpaid," and "spoiled." Wimbledon, he and other reporters insisted, was too important to be brought down by a petty labor dispute. Accordingly, they urged British tennis fans to buy Wimbledon tickets as a demonstration of patriotism. The result, to the ATP's dismay, was a series of near record crowds.

Much of what the fans saw was not up to Wimbledon standards, but the fortnight also witnessed moments of rare drama, especially in the highly competitive women's draw, where King won her fifth Wimbledon singles title, outlasting Evert in the championship match. On the men's side, the first Wimbledon appearance of the popular "young guns"—Bjorn Borg and Jimmy Connors—gave the fans and the press something positive to talk about. But the excitement didn't last. After the prohibitive favorite Nastase lost to Sandy Mayer at the close of the first week, and after both Borg and Connors were eliminated in the quarterfinals, the men's singles competition lost much of its punch. In the end, Jan Kodes of Czechoslovakia defeated

Alex Metreveli of Russia in a lackluster men's singles final that revealed just how much damage the ATP boycott had wreaked.[31]

It would be many months before the hard feelings and post-boycott recriminations subsided, and Ashe and others were well aware that the Wimbledon boycott—essential as it was to the stature of the ATP—entailed certain costs. Decades later, he speculated that the boycott, along with the infusion of big money, led to a coarsening of the game in the early and mid-1970s. Betraying a measure of guilt, he wrote: "For many of us, the deluge of money led to confusion and an unholy scrambling after dollars. Certain values and standards that had bonded players in my earlier years—certain codes of honor and a spirit of cooperation and camaraderie—disappeared." "I wonder," he added, "how much we, the leaders of the players during this transition, contributed to the fall."

The anger and divisiveness that enveloped the game of tennis in 1973 saddened Ashe. But neither he nor anyone else at the time could find a workable solution to the age-old dilemma posed by reform—how to avoid throwing out the baby with the bathwater. The ATP needed money and power to counter the stifling influence of the ILTF and its national federations, yet the path to power threatened some of the game's most laudable traditions. The players were fighting on so many fronts it was difficult to keep track of allies and enemies or to maintain a steady course of responsible and ethical behavior.[32]

The confusing battle over World Team Tennis (WTT) was a case in point. The collective brainchild of Larry King, the enterprising husband of Billie Jean King, and three other sports promoters—WTT offered intercity team competition involving men and women in an innovative coed format. Announced with great fanfare during the week leading up to Wimbledon by Jerry Saperstein, the former owner of the Harlem Globetrotters and a co-owner of New York's WTT franchise, the new league was scheduled to begin play in May 1974.

In its original form, WTT play called for teams of six players, two of whom had to be female; a four-color court; a forty-four-match season running from May to August; equally weighted matches in five categories— men's singles and doubles, women's singles and doubles, and mixed doubles; and a no-ad scoring system in which match victories required five winning games with nine-point tiebreakers invoked after a 4–4 deadlock. No one had ever seen or even proposed anything like it, and tennis traditionalists groaned with contemptuous skepticism.

Lamar Hunt, the primary sponsor of WCT, didn't see any conflict with his organization and welcomed the formation of WTT. But Ashe and many of his ATP colleagues had serious concerns about Team Tennis's compatibility with Open tennis. Speaking to reporters in Miami, Ashe questioned the wisdom of WTT's plan to offer individual salaries. "As of now, the concept of salaries is against our constitution," he explained. "Our players compete 'solely for prize money,' that's the phrase in our constitution." He also expressed concern that the WTT summer schedule "would conflict with the Wimbledon, French and Italian tournaments." Among the ATP's top players, only Rosewall had endorsed WTT, in sharp contrast to the strong opposition expressed by his fellow Aussies. "Rod Laver said W.T.T. would wreck international tennis in May, June, and July," Ashe reported, adding: "I agree with him. I can understand why Rosewall would want the security of a salary at his age, but I don't think it would be good for the A.T.P. players as a group."[33]

This stance put Ashe squarely at odds with a number of influential figures, including Billie Jean King, whom he would come to admire as much as anyone in the world of sports. On different sides of the gender equity issue, the two were not yet close friends, largely because Ashe shared many of the chauvinistic attitudes common on the men's tour. "Women's Lib has been very trying," he confessed in August 1973, adding: "I don't know if, all of a sudden, I could psychologically handle a fifty-fifty split in my house. I mean: who breaks the tie? I do want to be up-to-date and fair and all that, but the truth is that I also don't want any woman telling me what to do with my life (and vice versa too). So all right, if that sort of thinking makes me a male chauvinist, then I'm a male chauvinist."

Ashe would later come to regret these words, but in 1973 his consciousness level did not allow him to ally with King and other feminists. While her primary loyalty was to any movement or innovation that challenged the hidebound traditions of male dominance, his was to the boys club known as the ATP. Only later, after years of separate struggle, would they become comrades in arms bound by a common commitment to social justice, racial equality, and gender equity. Looking back on the WTT controversy from the perspective of the early 1990s, Ashe acknowledged: "Although both Billie Jean and I resented the stodginess and snobbery of the international tennis establishment, we had different ideas about how best to proceed."[34]

In June 1973, in the heat of battle, Ashe claimed there was an anti-WTT consensus in the ATP. But he almost certainly overstated the case. Speaking for WTT, cofounder Dennis Murphy effectively disputed Ashe's contention.

"Ashe has been saying that from day one," Murphy insisted, "but when the A.T.P. held a vote, there were seven against us, nine for us and 29 who wanted more information."

In truth, attitudes toward WTT were in flux and undoubtedly changing from day to day. Yet the unprecedented amount of money dangled in front of the players by the new league virtually insured that Murphy's view would prevail over Ashe's. By early August, ten players had signed WTT contracts authorizing individual teams to "bid for their services." The league also conducted a twenty-round draft, with the New York team picking Ashe, an unlikely signee as the league's most vocal critic, in the fifth round.

At this point, WTT was technically an outlaw league operating without validation from the ILTF or the ATP. But once the league floated the rumor that Newcombe's WTT salary guarantee was $75,000 and that King's exceeded $100,000, a number of players were poised to sign up. The only thing stopping them, it seemed, was the possibility of being banned, either by the ILTF, or its American affiliate, the USLTA. "World Team Tennis officials insist they want peace and harmony with other organizations," Neil Amdur observed. "But unless a broad accord is reached between now and next May, there may be as much activity in a courtroom as on the tennis court." For a time it appeared that WTT contract players would be turned away from the U.S. Open by the USLTA. But an emergency meeting convened on August 27, two days before the Open's first match, led to a tentative truce forestalling any banning. Even so, the legal situation surrounding WTT would remain murky for the remainder of the year.[35]

For Ashe, the 1973 U.S. Open was a distracting jumble of organizational complications that left little time for concentration on his on-court performance. Just as the immediate WTT crisis was subsiding, a second and even more troubling controversy emerged. The ATA, the organization that had nurtured Ashe during his early years in tennis, had always had a complicated and somewhat troubled relationship with the USLTA and Forest Hills. In recent years, the hard feelings had been smoothed over by an agreement to guarantee the ATA singles champion a spot in the U.S. Open draw. Yet somehow, through a combination of negligence and indifference, 1973 ATA champion Arthur Carrington had been left out of the draw.

When USLTA officials informed Carrington that his only avenue into the draw was to compete for an alternate position as a wild card, he exploded. "There's a reason why there's not many blacks in tennis," the first-year pro protested. "We can't say Althea Gibson or Arthur Ashe have opened the doors because no one has followed them up. We have to do it all over again."

The USLTA president, Walter E. Elcock, was unmoved by Carrington's complaint, or by the ATA's insistence that an agreement had been breached. "I told them that, to my knowledge, there used to be an understanding that the A.T.A. annual singles champion was given a spot in the draw," Elcock explained. "But since the advent of the open championships, with so many good players, they've gone into qualifying tournaments."

Despite intervention by Ashe and others, Elcock refused to soften his racially insensitive stance, and only after John Paish of Great Britain withdrew at the last minute did Carrington receive a place in the opening round of 128. A host of loyal ATA stalwarts turned up at courtside to cheer Carrington on, but the young star, playing for the first time on grass, had an off day and lost his hard-earned first-round match to Ove Bengston of Sweden.

Distracted by the Carrington controversy, third-seeded Ashe also seemed off his game. He had been looking forward to the 1973 U.S. Open as a special occasion after agreeing to team up with Althea Gibson in the mixed doubles competition. But the twenty-third anniversary of Gibson's Forest Hills debut did not turn out the way he had hoped it would. In the singles competition, he kept his focus long enough to win his first two matches, but on September 2 he suffered a double defeat, losing a third-round match to the seventeen-year-old Swedish phenom Bjorn Borg and suffering a straight-set loss in the mixed doubles. "This was the worst day of the year," Ashe wrote in his diary. "I don't want to think about it. . . . Jesus, I feel like an old man. I'm thirty years old and teeny-boppers are upsetting me. It takes something like this to make you aware of how really short an athlete's life is. It seems like the day before yesterday that I was the kid, beating the old man."

To make matters even worse, Ashe had to excuse himself immediately after his loss in the mixed doubles and rush off to an important ATP board meeting in midtown Manhattan. After arriving at the meeting, he assured Meryl that the directors could finish their business in an hour, so she agreed to wait outside the meeting room. Three hours later she was still waiting, angrily cooling her heels and wondering why her boyfriend had abandoned her. "I just forgot about her being there," Ashe confessed in his diary. "I just forgot. You can imagine how that went over." Meryl soon forgave him for his uncharacteristic thoughtlessness. But the entire scene reminded him that real life is a challenge, even for famous athletes with beautiful girlfriends.[36]

The U.S. Open was the biggest show in tournament tennis in 1973, easily outshining the boycott-tarnished Wimbledon. But even the excitement at Forest Hills was upstaged by the buzz surrounding a single match in late September. Promoters heralded the upcoming "Battle of the Sexes" between twenty-nine-year-old Billie Jean King and the fifty-five-year-old hustler Bobby Riggs as the "match of the century," and it was difficult to argue with the claim. Four months earlier, Riggs had crushed the Australian star Margaret Court in the first male-female confrontation, winning 6–2, 6–1 in fifty-seven minutes. Held on Mother's Day, before a crowd of 3,500 at the San Vicente Country Club in Southern California, the nationally televised $10,000 winner-take-all match left Riggs itching for more fame, namely a confrontation with King, the biggest name in women's tennis. "I want her, the Women's Libber leader," Riggs chortled. "She can name the place, the court and the time, just as long as the price is right."[37]

The place and time turned out to be the Houston Astrodome on September 20, and the price was a staggering $100,000 in prize money plus nearly $200,000 more in appearance guarantees. This time the crowd exceeded thirty thousand—the largest crowd in tennis history—and millions of others watched the television coverage, which reached tennis fans in thirty-six nations via satellite. What they saw was a spectacle befitting Barnum and Bailey. King entered the arena lounging on a "Cleopatra-style gold litter" held aloft by four toga-clad male track-and-field athletes, and Riggs followed "in a gold-wheeled rickshaw pulled by six professional models in tight red and gold outfits." Meeting at center court, the two combatants exchanged gifts: a large candy cane for King and a baby pig for the self-styled "chauvinist pig" Riggs. Eventually, they actually played tennis, and in the end King overcame Riggs's clownish antics and chauvinistic bluster, winning handily in three straight sets. Almost immediately, there was talk of a rematch, leaving some tennis traditionalists to wonder if the circus atmosphere would ever subside.[38]

Ashe, surprisingly enough, did not add his voice to the chorus of criticism, even though he had spoken out against the corrupting power of big money and show business hype in the past. The fact that his good friend Jack Kramer was scheduled to be one of the match's courtside television commentators (at King's insistence, Kramer, a notorious male chauvinist, was ultimately replaced by Howard Cosell) may have colored his attitude. He seemed to take genuine pleasure from all the hoopla. As he wrote in his diary three weeks before the match, "Among some of the players, there is grousing that the whole thing is a detriment to the game of tennis, but myself, I love it. I don't see how it can fail to generate more publicity for the whole sport— and besides, how can anyone not favor the one thing in the whole big bad world that is just good clean fun?"

In mid-September, a week before the big show in Houston, he found himself paired with King at a television taping on Hilton Head Island in

South Carolina. During their mixed doubles matches, the "odd couple" got to know each other. "I hear she's really been coming down on my case lately," he wrote. "Here's a recent published quote from Mrs. King: 'Don't tell me about Arthur Ashe. Christ, I'm blacker than Arthur Ashe.' Hmmmm. I let it pass today, mostly because I suspect that she's really not personally mad at me, only in dispute because I've been opposed to World Team Tennis. . . . Also, I've been against her contention that the women should get prize money equal to the men at tournaments where they both play." In the end, they "made a pretty good team" in Ashe's estimation, and he came away from the experience with renewed respect for the woman known as "the Old Lady" on the tour. "I'll tell you one thing I've learned playing with Billie Jean King," he declared. "She is a much better player than I imagined, and I now honestly believe that she has an excellent chance to beat Bobby Riggs."[39]

Ashe was right, of course, and he even won a last-minute wager on the match, which he watched on television in a crowded bar in Los Angeles. "As soon as I saw Billie Jean play that first game I knew she had it," he reported in his diary. "There was no choke there. She was moving so easily, and . . . she just wasn't scared the way Margaret had been. And I knew Billie Jean could hit the ball, from playing with her at Hilton Head. So, I called out for a bet. . . . When you've got one player who can't move and the other can hit the ball and isn't nervous, you have got a sure thing in tennis. So I won $80 on The Old Lady."[40]

Some commentators hailed the King-Riggs match as a historic turning point in women's sports, but Ashe was not one of them. Neither his public comments nor his diary betrayed much concern for the politics of gender or feminist consciousness. While he prided himself on being relatively enlightened and progressive on women's issues, his major public policy interests lay elsewhere. Racism, poverty, war, and barriers to political democracy and postcolonial self-determination—these were the issues that drew his attention. During the fall of 1973, there was too much going on in the world to waste any time on "the Bobby Riggs nonsense," as Ashe called it. He and other public-minded citizens were busy keeping abreast of a number of ongoing historical dramas, including the Yom Kippur War in the Middle East, the OPEC oil embargo, Watergate and the "Saturday Night Massacre," Vice President Spiro Agnew's resignation, a coup d'état in Chile, and the election of Coleman Young and Maynard Jackson as the first black mayors of Detroit and Atlanta.[41]

On October 1, Ashe's social conscience took him to "darkest Mississippi," to Jackson, where he gave a speech at a National Urban League luncheon.

Arranged by his Aunt Lola, who lived in Gulfport, the speech focused on the need for black economic empowerment and voter registration. Ashe also conducted a clinic and played an exhibition match at Jackson State, the site of a brutal police riot three years earlier. To his surprise, James Meredith, who a decade earlier had desegregated the University of Mississippi, was in the crowd.

After the match, the two men talked about the climate of fear that still pervaded many parts of Mississippi, a discussion that led to a brief diary entry on the general state of black politics in America. "Jackson must be one of the toughest places in America for black franchise," Ashe wrote. "—It really takes you back in time when you hear about blacks being *afraid* to vote in the 1970s—but then, everywhere I go in the U.S. I find that we are still politically unsophisticated, just now coming into our own. . . . Blacks will not really have arrived in politics until we start publicly disagreeing with each other." Independence of mind had long been a cherished virtue to Ashe, but it carried special force for a thirty-year-old black activist trying to find his way through the uncertain racial politics of the early 1970s.[42]

FIFTEEN

SOUTH AFRICA

■

ASHE'S COMMITMENT TO INDEPENDENT thinking was especially evident in his determined effort to play tennis in South Africa. Ever since his first application for a South African visa had become public in 1969, he had received sharp criticism from several leading anti-apartheid organizations. Any contact with the white South African regime, they warned, would almost certainly backfire, redounding to the interests of white supremacist propagandists. Though recognizing the potential pitfalls of providing white South Africans with an opportunity to misrepresent superficial change as something substantial, he continued his struggle to desegregate South African tennis.

After three visa refusals, Ashe's stubborn determination to play in South Africa appeared moot. But, to his delight, the situation shifted in his favor in late June 1973. On the eve of the Wimbledon fortnight, just as his chance of cracking the South African color bar seemed all but gone, new hope emerged during a private meeting with Owen Williams. Having befriended Ashe during the 1969 U.S. Open, the liberal South African promoter had been working behind the scenes for more than a year urging officials of the Vorster government to reverse their decision. Prodded by Gladys Heldman, the editor of *World Tennis* magazine and a strong proponent of all manner of good causes, Williams was determined to see Ashe play in the South African Open.

Once one of his nation's most gifted amateur players, Williams was an active member of the anti-apartheid Progressive Party, a small party holding only one seat (held by Helen Suzman) in the South African parliament. Yet, as the successful promoter of the South African Open, he was in a position to influence several of the government's most powerful figures. In particular, he had access to Piet Koornhof, the Minister of Mines, Immigration, Sports, and Recreation. Widely considered to be the heir apparent to Prime Minister John Vorster, Koornhof was the primary architect of a three-year-old policy that had opened South Africa to "a carefully audited handful of world-class black athletes," most notably Goolagong, the golfer Lee Elder, and the racially integrated New Zealand rugby team. In Ashe's estimation, "it was all strictly window dressing, since there was no comparable integration (if any at all) permitted at the lower-levels of sport," though he acknowledged "at least it was a start."[1]

As Koornhof's experimental policy became almost standard practice, Williams began to plot a breakthrough for Ashe. "The more enlightened Nationalists believe that the white Afrikaners, the party's main constituency, are ready to accept Koornhof's policy," Williams assured Ashe, adding, "If so, it becomes petty and foolish to let in a lot of other athletes and continue a vendetta" against you. After listening intently to Williams's assessment of the situation, Ashe reaffirmed his willingness to play in South Africa. But he would only do so, he told Williams, if four conditions were met:

> First, that I would come and go as I pleased, anywhere in the country. Second, that the stands . . . at Ellis Park, in Johannesburg, would be "totally integrated," with no special sections for racial groups. Third, that a conscientious effort would be made to try and arrange a meeting for me with Prime Minister Vorster. And fourth, that I would be accepted for what I happen to be—a black man. I would not permit the issue to be avoided by supplying me with any temporary "honorary white" status.

Williams carefully wrote down the four conditions, which he acknowledged were reasonable and potentially acceptable to the Vorster government. Predicting Ashe would be playing in South Africa before the end of the year, he promised to call as soon as the arrangements were set. After four years of frustration, Ashe remained skeptical. "It is my guess that nothing more will ever come of it," he noted in his diary.[2]

Even so, just in case he was wrong, he began to prepare for a South African journey. Back in New York on July 4, he devoted most of Independence

Day to the writing of "letters to several friends, black and white, asking them for their views on any possible trip of mine to South Africa." Although he wanted to go in the worst way, he was also "deeply concerned with how other blacks might take such a trip." The recipients included Representatives Andrew Young and Barbara Jordan, the noted black poet Nikki Giovanni, the expatriate South African anti-apartheid activist Dennis Brutus, and UCLA's J. D. Morgan.

The responses were mixed. Three advised him not to go; four urged him to go; two others said yes, but only if stringent stipulations were imposed; and Barbara Jordan was noncommittal, assuring him she trusted his "good judgment." None of this mattered, however, since his July 4 diary entry indicates he had already made up his mind long before the letters were mailed. "There are two basic avenues used to approach the South African question," he wrote. "One is more a roadblock than an avenue, a militant, all-or-nothing policy, which maintains that nobody should have anything to do with the dreadful place: boycott it, freeze it out, ignore it and wait for its millennium from a respectful distance. The United States wasted a generation on that philosophy toward China; it still operates its Cuban policy that way. The other avenue is a gradualist one—result-oriented. It assumes that progress can only come in small chunks; that you deal for your advances as you can. Surely, it is less emotionally satisfying this way, but, I'm certain, more realistic and more successful."[3]

Ashe associated the gradualist approach with the nonviolent movement led by his hero, Dr. Martin Luther King Jr., and with the wisdom of the nineteenth-century abolitionist Frederick Douglass. Quoting Douglass's famous aphorism, "Power concedes nothing without a struggle—never has, never will," Ashe insisted, "you must be prepared only to chip away at power and injustice." In late July, he received reinforcement for this view from Giovanni. "I should imagine in the modern world information is the key to freedom," she wrote. "We have very little information coming from that country. A lot of emotion, a lot of rhetoric but very little first hand reports. I should think an intelligent young man like you will be able to absorb not only what is said but what is not said. . . . We know, of course, that one visit won't change a government but it's a start." Coach Morgan agreed. "I believe that your presence there would be another important factor in breaking down the walls of racial bias against the black community," he told Ashe on July 12, adding, "positive, constructive representation by you would have a far greater impact on the white South African government than anything else you could do."[4]

Sharing Giovanni's passion for information, Ashe had schooled himself in the intricacies of South African history, politics, and culture. During the past four years, he had been reading everything South African he could lay his hands on—dozens of books and scores of journal articles and newspaper accounts. He absorbed it all, from the Afrikaner Trek of the early nineteenth century and the Bantu, Xhosa, and Zulu migrations to the rise of the African National Congress (ANC) and the recent hard-line politics of Vorster. He studied the legal history of apartheid, from the Population Registration and Group Areas Acts of 1950 to the Black Homeland Citizenship Act of 1970, poring over documents that few native South Africans had taken the time to read. If the chance to visit South Africa actually did materialize, he wanted to be ready to make the most of it.

As he waited for Owen Williams's internal diplomacy to yield a visa, Ashe kept close tabs on what was happening on the ground in South Africa. There were a few scraps of good news—signs of hope that at least some white South Africans were turning away from the most rigid forms of apartheid. But there was no real movement toward freedom for black South Africans. Indeed, in some areas the noose of apartheid was tighter than ever. In April, an Afrikaner extremist named Eugene Terre'Blanche had founded the Afrikaner Resistance Movement (ARM), with the express purpose of convincing all white South Africans that blacks were not only racially inferior but also an imminent threat to the "Afrikaner volk." As ARM's influence spread, Prime Minister Vorster faced increasing pressure from the right, which didn't bode well for Ashe.[5]

In mid-October, Williams sent word that the South African cabinet was about to meet and that a breakthrough might be in the offing. But once again Ashe's hopes were dashed. "No word from South Africa," he reported in his diary on October 17. "If the cabinet met last night, they either tabled me or aren't prepared to let me know their answer yet." During the next two weeks, Ashe followed the European tour from Spain to Germany to France, ending up in Paris at the end of the month. It was there, after surviving a Right Bank shopping spree with Meryl, that he received the long-awaited good news. "Let the record state that it was on Halloween," he declared, "when they finally agreed to let Arthur Ashe into South Africa. Owen Williams called me at nine this morning with the official word, and it was on the radio this afternoon. Even before then, I had a call from the South African embassy. They told me I could pop around and pick up my visa any time."

Whether he was being offered a treat or a trick remained to be seen, but the Halloween surprise gave him a measure of hope. Once Arthur actually saw the visa, he discovered there was indeed a trick of sorts: unbeknownst to Williams, the embassy had issued a visa that described its black American holder as an "honorary white." As he had done many times in the past, Arthur laughed off this latest indignity. Nothing, not even a gratuitous insult, he told himself, was going to stop him from going to South Africa. Williams marveled at how his American friend sidestepped this unexpected affront. "Arthur handled it like the joke it was," he observed, "and proceeded to carry himself with an aura of quiet dignity throughout his visit that was the mark of the man." [6]

Ashe received several messages of congratulation, including one delivered in person by Blen Franklin, the president of the all-white South African Lawn Tennis Union (SALTU). Ashe thought nothing of it at first, but he soon learned their "pleasant little chat" had been a prologue to a clever maneuver of South African sports diplomacy. "It turned out at the ILTF meeting," Ashe reported, "that he used me as one of the 'eight points' explaining why South Africa should be allowed back in the Davis Cup. So they're ahead; they've already hooked something very big with me as part of the bait." Though disappointed, he did not let Franklin's indirection dampen his enthusiasm for the upcoming visit. Reasoning that "it can work both ways," he explained: "My going to South Africa is a trade. They've already gained something out of me, and I'll gain something too. If nothing else, my presence signals a pause in apartheid."

Ashe, bracing himself for a barrage of criticism, had prepared a response that he hoped would fend off the sharpest blows. "People who do not want me to go point out to me that I will be a tool of an illegal government, one chosen by a minority electorate," he wrote on November 2. "Unfortunately, this is true; also unfortunately it is the only government South Africa has got." [7]

"There are a lot of reasons why I'm going," he admitted. "The South African Open is the sixth most prestigious in the world. I want to play in it, and I want to win it. And I'm curious. I probably know as much about South Africa as any person in the world who has never been there, but I wonder how secondhand impressions will square with reality. I'm human: I just want to see the damn place with my own eyes and my own mind."

While not denying he harbored a few "selfish, personal reasons" for going, Ashe expressed confidence his visit to South Africa would do more good than harm. "Whereas I don't see myself as Jackie Robinson or even as Rosa Parks, neither trailblazer nor pawn of history," he explained, "I do think I'm just a little bit of progress. Ellis Park will be integrated, and I will be a free black on display." His potential role in the movement to end white dominance in South African sports was too important to ignore. "South African blacks have never had one of theirs become a national sports hero," he pointed out, adding: "their idols are restricted to neighborhood status, and when you must limit your idols, surely you must limit all the dreams and aspirations, and you remain, perforce, a limited man."

Using this calculus, he offered himself as the black South Africans' surrogate champion, the value of which depended on how well he played on the courts of Johannesburg. "If I lose in the first or second round, I have no platform," he conceded. "I'm just an interested tourist—who happens to be black—gallivanting around South Africa." Dell had reminded him of this hard truth during a recent telephone conversation. "Remember," he advised, "nobody listens to losing quarter-finalists." Ashe still had two weeks of play on European clay to sharpen his game before flying to South Africa. But the consistently poor quality of his recent performances—"I have been playing worse and worse," he complained on October 21—did not bode well. The last thing he wanted to do was to embarrass himself in front of a crowd of gleeful white South Africans gloating in front of their black servants. "I'm already starting to worry," he confessed on November 9, "that I'll go down to South Africa next week to make history and get wiped out in the first round." [8]

Ashe had one more tournament to play—a two-site tournament in Nottingham and London—before leaving on November 16. Once again his performance—losing to Tiriac in the second round—was anything but a confidence builder. A week earlier, he had put Meryl on a plane to Toronto, thinking a little less romance and a bit more concentration would help his game. But even this sacrifice didn't seem to help. To make matters worse, during the twenty-four hours before his departure he had to endure a last-ditch intervention by several members of Dennis Brutus's anti-apartheid group, the South African Non-Racial Olympic Committee (SANROC). The heated discussion went on for hours, with the SANROC stalwarts pulling out all stops to convince Ashe to cancel his trip. In the end, an exhausted Ashe remained firm. Later that night, while walking out of the Westbury Hotel lobby to catch a cab to the airport, he couldn't avoid a sendoff from Nastase, who waved him through the door with a salutary "Hey, Brown Sugar, don't let them put you in jail." [9]

The long flight to Johannesburg took a full day, with a brief stopover in Nairobi. Though nervous, Ashe had plenty of time to compose himself before setting foot on South African soil, and he had considerable help from his traveling companions Donald and Carole Dell, the ATP's press officer Richard Evans, and Frank Deford, who was covering the trip for *Sports Illustrated*. The sixth member of the party, Bud Collins of the *Boston Globe*, was scheduled to meet the others in Johannesburg, after flying in from Australia. These trusted friends and colleagues would be with Ashe for the entire two weeks, sharing his experiences but also watching his back and keeping him out of trouble. On the flight to Nairobi, Dell and Evans prepped him on how to deal with the South African press. Mostly, they reminded him of his promise to avoid any public criticism of the South African regime. As Ashe acknowledged, "I had agreed as part of the deal that I would keep my counsel and hold any substantive opinions for my departure. This would also serve to keep the press from hounding me, so that I would be able to concentrate on playing tennis."[10]

Upon his arrival in Johannesburg, Ashe got off to a good start by assuring reporters he intended to fulfill his part of the bargain. "I'm here in a spirit of cooperation," he told them. "I've come as a man, nothing more, nothing less, and I look forward to a fascinating twelve days." The scene at the airport afforded Ashe "a mellow welcome," and even before the plane touched down a stranger came up to him with an unexpected greeting: "Mr. Ashe, I'm one of those horrible South Africans, and I just want to wish you the best of success. I promise you we're not all as bad as we're supposed to be, and you mark my words: three fourths of the people will be pulling for you."

The stranger turned out to be a government official assigned to escort Ashe to the customs bureau, where in Ashe's words, his passport and visa were examined by a man who "looked like he just came in from the Boer War," complete with "starched, short-pants, long-socks uniform; swagger stick; bushy mustache." After being waved through, Ashe spotted the friendly faces of Owen Williams and his wife, Jennifer, who had come to drive the American party to the home of Brian Young, a liberal Jewish businessman who had offered to house Ashe, Deford, and the Dells during their stay. Evans and Collins were housed in private residences nearby in the same upscale neighborhood of Sandton. Young was in Swaziland for the weekend, so their welcoming host was Gordon "Forbesy" Forbes, a former South African tennis star and Cliff Drysdale's brother-in-law.

Even before his arrival in plush Sandton, Ashe experienced a few surprises. "My first impression," he reported, "was that apartheid was a much more subtle proposition than I had anticipated. . . . During the entire trip from the airport, nearly an hour's drive, I saw only two blacks driving cars.

All you see are Africans walking—and walking slowly, as if they really have no place to go." [11]

Subtle or not, the power of apartheid became obvious during his first meal at the Young mansion. When he asked one of the house servants for a cold drink, she dropped her eyes and said: "Yes, master." Unnerved, Ashe recognized and later commented on the irony of his situation: "So here is little Artie Ashe, the skinny black kid from the capital of the old Confederacy, all set up in a mansion, carrying on jes' like white folks, and gettin' himself called Master." In the days that followed, Ashe made a concerted effort to equalize his relationship with the woman whose name, he learned, was Anna. He also learned she came from a "homeland" village more than two hundred miles from Johannesburg and was able to see her family only twice a year. In a series of long conversations, they compared notes about black life in South Africa and the United States, and on Ashe's last day at the house she finally addressed him as "Arthur."

Arthur's experience with Anna betrayed a deep ambivalence about his luxurious accommodations. "I knew in advance," he acknowledged, "that a lot of people would call me a hypocrite for living in a white man's house." But he also knew the only viable alternative was a much too public stay in a first-class hotel where he would be treated as an "honorary white." The suggestion that he should have arranged to stay in Soweto—which he termed a "grim 'black' city"—was, in his view, unrealistic for someone preparing to play competitive tennis. "I did not come to South Africa in sackcloth and ashes to serve penance," he explained. "I know damn well how badly the Africans in this country live, but I cannot see how it would serve any useful purpose to live like one myself. I know I'll catch a lot of heat for this, but I think it's best this way." [12]

On his first night in Johannesburg, Ashe and his friends attended a Saturday-evening cocktail party hosted by several of the breweries sponsoring the South African Open. Ashe couldn't help noticing that the invitees included whites, blacks, Indians, and others officially classified as "Coloureds." With its racial mingling, the party was clearly illegal under the laws of apartheid, which prohibited whites from providing "drinks for persons of any other race." Yet no one seemed to care. Later, Ashe joined Williams for dinner at an exclusive restaurant, and once again he marveled at the way everyone seemed to wink at an obvious breach of racial etiquette. "If I had been a native nonwhite," he observed, "I would have not been permitted in the place. Hell, if I had been a native nonwhite, I wouldn't have even be permitted to be up that late in Johannesburg. There's a curfew for all nonwhites at 10 P.M." [13]

On Sunday morning, Ashe made his initial visit to the Ellis Park tennis courts, where he saw his first "WHITES ONLY" signs, something he hadn't seen in America for nearly a decade. He was there to begin his preparation for his opening round match, and to "hit with some of the country's best black players." Right away, he realized that "none of them" was very good, an obvious reflection of being denied access to decent tennis facilities and systematic coaching. This would have to change, he decided, if there were to be any meaningful progress toward equal performance. "You can't just bring a handful of them into the Open, beat them love and love in the first round and then send them back to nowhere till the next year's Open," he insisted. "We've got to obtain the right for the best players to compete on the Sugar Circuit." Of course, the first order of business was for him to lead the way by winning the Open, the Sugar Circuit's biggest prize.[14]

By Monday, his third day in South Africa, Ashe was beginning to get a better feel for the realities of apartheid, and he didn't like what he was seeing and hearing. In a private meeting with black journalists held in the players' lounge at Ellis Park, he received an earful about the pass laws and a racially repressive criminal justice system. "Apartheid is handled with such sophistication," he noted after the meeting, "that it is sometimes easy to forget that South Africa is nothing less than a police state. The injustices here go far beyond the seminal matter of racial inequality. . . . Arrest is arbitrary, incarceration capricious, and there is an execution, on the average, every nine or ten days. Without any trial, you can be imprisoned for three months at a clip—and they can repeat that each and every three months, ad infinitum."

The South African regime also made diabolically effective use of house arrests, better known as "banning." This practice, Ashe reported in his diary, "permits you to exist but not really to live. If the government bans you, you cannot publish, attend a university, visit a library, travel or even meet with more than one person at a time." He had long been aware of the most blatant aspects of South Africa's system of social and political control, including the incarceration of Nelson Mandela and other ANC leaders at Robben Island. But in recent years the counter image of what Ashe called "well-publicized 'liberal' breakthroughs" had obscured the reality of "increased repression." After listening to the black journalists talk about what was happening beneath the veil of propaganda, he offered an apt metaphor for the regime's disingenuous claims. "It is as if they have unscrewed the top of one bottle of apartheid and given the rest of the world a good heady whiff of that," he observed, "but then screwed the lid even tighter on all the other bottles—and tightest of all on those that are concerned with men's minds: the schools, the press, the churches." [15]

In addition to giving Ashe a sobering introduction to life on the ground in black South Africa, the journalists informed him that much of the black community resented his visit. "Many blacks don't want me here," a distressed Ashe reported, because "they feel my being here legitimizes the government and lends it some credence." This was not what he wanted to hear. He could only hope his critics would keep an open mind as he moved through his two weeks in South Africa. This hope received an immediate boost from Don Mattera, an aspiring poet and *Johannesburg Star* correspondent who had a private conversation with him after the other reporters had left.

Classified as Coloured, the light-skinned Mattera was an independent thinker who had his own take on Ashe's visit. When Ashe asked him if he approved of the visit, Mattera responded with a resounding yes. "Oh, I'm glad you're here," he exclaimed. "We need some contact, we need to be periodically assured that people in the rest of the world still understand and care. Committed black Americans should visit South Africa." He was adamant, however, that they had to come for the right reasons. Bob Foster, a black American boxer scheduled to fight a white South African opponent in Johannesburg later in the month, had already worn out his welcome as far as Mattera was concerned. From the outset Foster had studiously avoided the local black community while publicly praising white South African hospitality. Claiming that he "loved" South Africa, he talked of building a vacation home somewhere in the nation, presumably far away from Soweto and other black enclaves. "Someone like Foster only hurts us," Mattera told Arthur. "That kind of person should stay away." [16]

When the tournament began the next morning, Arthur was eager to see who would show up to see the first interracial match in the long history of South Africa's top-flight men's competition. Although the stands were "not quite filled," he could see that a significant number of blacks—perhaps as many as two hundred—had turned out to see him play. Mostly, he was pleased there was some intermingling between blacks and whites, though the scene stopped short of the fully integrated seating arrangements Williams had promised. [17]

The opening day crowd included Mark Mathabane, a skinny, thirteen-year-old boy from Alexandra, an impoverished, nonwhite shantytown located in the Witwatersrand mining area north of Johannesburg. Five years later, with the help of Stan Smith, he would migrate to the United States to attend college, and in 1986 the publication of his searing memoir, *Kaffir Boy*, would establish his reputation as a leading critic of apartheid. But in November 1973 he was an aspiring young tennis player awestruck by Ashe's example. "The more I read about the world of tennis, and Arthur Ashe's role in it," he recalled in *Kaffir Boy*, "the more I began to dream of its possibilities. What if I too were someday to attain the same fame and fortune as Arthur Ashe? Would whites respect me as they did him? Would I be as free as he?"

Pro-boycott activists could have given Mathabane an earful of objections, but the boy from Alexandra was hardly alone in embracing Ashe's visit. "His coming meant so much to blacks," he insisted, "who literally worshipped American blacks who proved they could triumph in a white man's world, a world that many of us believed was booby-trapped with all sorts of obstacles designed to sink blacks deeper into the mire of squalor and servitude, where white people wanted them to belong." [18]

Mathabane's fascination with Ashe was common knowledge at the Barretts Tennis Camp, one of the few places in South Africa that occasionally allowed blacks and whites to play on the same court. The owner of the camp—a liberal German immigrant named Wilfred Horn—provided Mathabane with a ticket and bus fare to the first-round matches at Ellis Park. Once he arrived at the park, the wide-eyed boy took it all in, noticing that "the few black people at the tournament, much to my surprise, mingled freely with whites, as the two groups walked about the courts, eagerly seeking autographs from the tennis stars." He saw a different situation, however, in the bleachers at Centre Court, where Ashe was about to play. There "most black people kept to themselves, sitting in a cluster in the northeast section of the stands, an area without a canopy and fully exposed to the torrid Transvaal sun." Exercising the brashness of youth, Mathabane "tried, along with a couple of friends from Soweto to 'integrate'" the more comfortable, shaded section inhabited by whites, but "the atmosphere became so tense that we abandoned the effort," and rushed back to the safety of "the black section."

A few minutes after noon, Mathabane and the rest of the crowd watched Ashe open a new era of South African tennis with a crisp forehand winner down the line. His opponent, a tall, bearded Texan named Sherwood Stewart, could only smile. Having flown in from Sydney on Monday night, he told his seatmate Bud Collins that, win or lose, he simply wanted to be a part of history. Ashe went on to win the match in three straight sets, delighting most of the crowd as well as a bevy of reporters looking for a good story. Whenever Ashe won a point, Mathabane recalled, "black spectators rent the stadium with clapping and cheering. I chuckled at catching subtle expressions of disdain on several white faces as a black man trounced a white man."

He also noted—to his amazement—that many white spectators appeared to be rooting for Ashe.

This surprise only added to the surreal quality of the experience, which became obvious as Mathabane headed home to the stark realities of Alexandra. "Throughout the entire day at Ellis Park," he wrote, "I had been existing in a different world, a sort of make-believe world. I had breathed fresh air, walked on paved roads, mingled freely with white people, rested upon green grass and eaten free hot dogs given to me by whites. But as the packed bus rattled along Louis Botha Avenue, leaving behind the city of gold with its neon lights for a ghetto of darkness, smog, fear and violence—and all around me I saw sullen, worn, tired and sad faces of black workers—my spirits sunk."

The shock of such sharply contrasting worlds made Mathabane question the reality of what he had experienced. "Now that I had seen Arthur Ashe play," he explained, "I found it hard to believe that he was a black man. How could a black man play such excellent tennis, move about the court with such self-confidence, trash a white man and be cheered by white people? . . . How did Arthur Ashe get to be so good in a white man's sport? . . . Were the blacks in America really like us?" [19]

This self-deprecating question was not the kind of query Ashe had hoped to provoke during his visit to South Africa. But he had his own questions about the cultural distance between black Americans and black South Africans. Reading historical and contemporary accounts of racial challenges and civil rights struggles had given him some basis for comparison. Yet he yearned for firsthand knowledge of black South African life. He didn't want to miss any opportunity to get beyond the surface realities and reductionist stereotypes obscuring the human potential of black South Africa.

Accordingly, within minutes of his win over Stewart, he left Ellis Park for an impromptu tour of Soweto, the infamous black township located seventeen miles southwest of downtown Johannesburg. Williams had provided him with a car and a driver—a black Mozambiquan named Solomon—and had encouraged him to explore Johannesburg and its environs. [20]

Solomon, who turned out to be an extremely knowledgeable and perceptive guide, provided Ashe with a rare inside look at life in one of Africa's densest ghettos. The tour was almost too much for Ashe to endure. Almost no one worked or shopped in Soweto, he discovered. Instead, Soweto blacks had to travel by train or bus back and forth from work and "to buy most of their goods from the white man." Though it had a population of more than a million, Soweto, in his estimation, was "not a city so much as . . . an urban reservation." As he reported with some shock in his diary, "the government owns all the houses. No public transportation within the city. One fire brigade, one hospital, one switchboard for 500 phones. Plumbing is rare, and perhaps a tenth of Soweto has electricity." The almost total lack of educational institutions was perhaps the worst of it: "Unlike the whites, who have free education, the blacks, who can least afford it, must pay tuition, so that thousands of kids never go to school, and roam the streets, idly passing all the formative hours of their lives." Jim Crow Richmond, even at its worst, had done better than this.

As Solomon steered through Soweto's crowded streets, Ashe saw it all. "The best of it," he concluded, "is endless rows of tiny little cottages; the worst, shacks of paper, wood, and tin." Before returning to Sandton, he witnessed a parting scene that touched him as few experiences had ever done. "It was late afternoon now," he wrote, "and the thousands of workers were coming home from the long day in Jo'burg. Many had risen before dawn, and many were burdened with food and other items they had to buy in the city. There was the train station, and before it, a great field, maybe half a mile wide, which they had to cross. . . . We watched as they came, hundreds, thousands of them, filing toward us as the sun fell across their backs. Suddenly it occurred to me that I had seen something very much like this once before, and then I remembered that that scene was in Africa too, a time in Kenya when I saw hordes of wildebeest crossing a broad savanna." Turning away from this "last tableau . . . the most vivid, and the most heartless," he told Solomon it was time to leave.[21]

The next morning, while he was still trying to make sense of what he had seen in Soweto, Ashe learned his new friend Don Mattera had been banned. The only consolation was that the banning order had apparently originated before their conversation at Ellis Park. Considering what he had already experienced since his arrival, he was hardly in need of any additional guilt. In an afternoon match against the Australian Barry Phillips-Moore, he was able to hold his concentration long enough to win. That evening he ran into Mattera just prior to a reception for black journalists sponsored by the United States Information Agency (USIA). Guarded by a stern-looking agent from BOSS, the South African Bureau of State Security, Mattera explained he could not attend the reception, even though he had organized it. Before leaving he shook Ashe's hand and vowed to continue his fight for freedom. "They have banned me, but they cannot stop me," he insisted.[22]

Though unnerved by Mattera's situation, Ashe gathered himself for the dialogue with the black journalists. Jammed into a small, cramped hall were seventy-five black and Coloured South Africans, several of whom—Ashe later learned—were paid informers. The BOSS agent was also there, silently presiding over a scene charged with what Arthur interpreted as "fear and passion." "I did not really understand how scared the people were though until I looked over at one of the group's officers and saw that his hands were trembling," he confessed. Somehow the trembling man screwed up his courage and opened the session with a tribute to Mattera. "He has spoken out for the common brotherhood," the man declared. "So our time must be short too, for so do we." Suddenly, there were cries of "Power, power!" and "Shame, shame!"

This seemed to signal that the dialogue could begin in earnest, but to Ashe's chagrin, much of what followed was sharply critical of his visit. One man called him an "Uncle Tom," and another bluntly told him to go home before he did any more damage: "You stay away, all of you. All right, Arthur?" When Arthur responded that this advice made him "very sad," another critic jumped in. "Your presence delays our struggle," the man explained. "You go back to New York. Stay away, Stay away. You come here and save their tennis. Soccer is dying here because of the sanctions placed on it." Arthur then made the case against sanctions, arguing they simply "won't work" in a world where money is valued more than morality. But one of the few female journalists in the room would have none of it and scolded him for thinking like a naive American. "We don't just want equality, as you do," she explained. "We were dispossessed. We want our land back."

Ashe fought back with a brief history lesson taken from the American civil rights movement. "History," he pointed out, "shows that progress does not come in huge chunks. It comes bit by bit. There was the lady Rosa Parks on the bus in Montgomery, and she was tired, and she said, *No, I'm not moving*, and the whole thing for us started from there." But the mention of Parks only fueled the fire. "She would have been banned here," one man shouted out, "and Martin Luther King would have been put on Robben Island." Another challenged his credentials, asking, "What role did you play in the civil rights struggle in the United States?" and "Were you in the 1963 march on Washington?"

Frustrated but refusing to give up, he made one last effort to make his point. "Please, I know these things," he said as calmly and diplomatically as he could. "Of course I know it's infinitely harder here than it is in the States. But I still see my being here as a start. You've got integrated seating out at Ellis Park. It was never there before. And we're trying to get black players on the Sugar Circuit. There will be something left when I'm gone." The best way to bring about change, he added, was to choose the path of rationalism over emotionalism: "Maybe I'm naïve, but I think, when you're mapping out a plan for progress, emotion cannot be allowed to play a large role, except for drumming up support." Reaching back to his early training, he ended with his favorite quotation of Dr. J's: "Those whom the gods wish to destroy, they first make mad."

When Arthur recalled the scene years later, he was proud that somehow he had managed to follow his own advice. "I didn't lose my temper," he wrote in 1981, pointing out "this was one of the few places they could meet in public and vent some of their anger." At the time, Arthur was uncertain about what had transpired. His best guess, however, was that by the time he left the room he had gained the support of roughly half of the black journalists. "You know they tell me I can't sleep on the white man's sheets because I'm black," a journalist named Patsy complained, "but they let you come and they find you the best beds, and if you're black and good enough to sleep on sheets, then so am I. Every time they do something like this, they kick their own policies in the backside." Another thanked Ashe for inspiring a sense of empowerment: "I see you and other free blacks who come here, and it is a challenge to me to be like you, free, and if not me, my sons." [23]

On Thursday—Thanksgiving Day back in the United States (and coincidentally the tenth anniversary of President John Kennedy's assassination)—Ashe faced another major challenge when he squared off in the quarterfinals against Bob Hewitt. A notoriously ornery competitor, Hewitt was a transplanted Australian who had resettled in South Africa after marrying a Johannesburg model in the 1960s. Among the South African players, he stood out as the staunchest defender of the status quo. "Hewitt and South Africa were made for each other," Ashe once quipped. The two men had barely spoken since a 1970 argument over apartheid. "The conversation ended rather abruptly," Ashe recalled, "when Hewitt informed me that he didn't want to talk about it anymore since I didn't even know that South African blacks preferred apartheid because 'they're happy.'"

All of this personal history raised the stakes for the match, which not surprisingly drew a capacity crowd. Ashe guessed roughly half of the fans were pulling for him, and he was pleased there was a large contingent of blacks on hand. He was less pleased, however, with the seating arrangements. While a few blacks were scattered throughout the stadium, most were seated in a segregated section. Even though he appreciated the swell of support from that section, which cheered "brazenly for me, without a great deal of concern for the niceties of evenhanded tennis crowd etiquette," he worried about the mixed message that the seating patterns communicated.[24]

Three days earlier the *Rand Daily Mail* had reprinted an article he had written for the London *Sunday Times* that reiterated his expectation that there would be "no special sections reserved for Blacks and Whites only." But he also recognized he had no choice but to accept a partial victory over segregated seating. Tacitly acknowledging this fact, he made a point of saluting the nonwhite section as he left the court after trouncing Hewitt in straight sets. "I saw a 'force' in the faces of the black spectators that helped my game," he conceded, adding: "They shouldn't have cheered Hewitt's mistakes, but I understood their feelings. It was comparable to some of my black friends talking about 'those white boys' during my junior days, an opportunity to defy the system." By his admission, after less than a week in South Africa, he had learned that in this strange land "you negotiate the truth along with everything else."[25]

Despite Ashe's busy schedule at Ellis Park—which included playing doubles alongside Tom Okker—his handlers managed to fit in a dizzying round of social events. On Friday, he attended a party hosted by John Burns, the director of the South African bureau of the USIA. Among the invited guests was the noted liberal South African writer Alan Paton, the author of *Cry, the Beloved Country*. Formerly banned for his militantly anti-apartheid views, Paton had flown in from Durban just to meet Ashe. The two had an extended conversation during which they compared notes on the paradoxes of South African society. "The whole world thinks we are odd," said Paton, a comment Ashe took as "a spectacular understatement." A number of black students were also at the party, some representing banned organizations such as the South African Students' Association and the Black People's Convention. Several of the students made it clear they disagreed with Ashe's decision to come to South Africa, but this time he was ready for the onslaught.[26]

The next morning he was back at Ellis Park for a semifinal match against Cliff Drysdale. Some members of the crowd were well aware of the bond between the two men, but others seemed to view the match as a racial showdown tinged with ideological overtones. Indeed, at several points in the match the referee found it necessary to ask the fans in the black section of the stands to tone down their cheering for Ashe. Coming off a series of lingering injuries, Drysdale was never really in the match as Ashe won handily in straight sets. Meeting at the net for a warm handshake, the two men who had been present at the conception of Ashe's South African quest exchanged knowing smiles of recognition.[27]

Tennis-wise, Ashe was nearing his goal of winning a South African championship. He and Okker were still alive in the doubles competition, with two matches to go, and he had won 12 straight sets in singles. Only Jimmy Connors, the brash young left-hander from Illinois, stood between him and the singles title. They had played only once before, in the final at the U.S. Pro Championships in Boston the previous July, and Connors had won. Though only twenty-one, Connors had already earned a formidable reputation as a talented battler and a lone wolf, both on and off the court. Playing on Bill Riordan's semi-renegade indoor circuit, he had refused to join the ATP and had generally thumbed his nose at Ashe and the tennis establishment. He was an opponent Ashe would enjoy beating, but it wouldn't be easy. After being trounced by Connors in the semifinals, Okker told Ashe he had never competed against a stronger player.[28]

One of Ashe's biggest challenges was to keep his mind on tennis. There was so much else going on, so much to do and see. As he recalled years later, "activities off the court intrigued me more. I wanted to see and do everything. I wanted to visit every tribe, talk to everybody, find out firsthand how this bastion of Western civilization could still fervently believe in apartheid." Moreover, everyone seemed to want a piece of his time. "The press interest in him was insane," Connors remembered. "They followed him everywhere, shoving microphones in his face and demanding a comment on every political issue. Arthur stayed cool throughout the whole tournament, but how he managed to concentrate on tennis I'll never know."[29]

Typically—less than an hour after finishing the Drysdale match—Arthur received an urgent message from Williams. The national sports minister, Piet Koornhof, wanted to meet with him as soon as possible. Arthur had asked to meet with Prime Minister Vorster, but it looked like he was going to have to settle for Koornhof. A few minutes later he was face-to-face with the tall Afrikaner, who agreed to talk "candidly but off the record." Encouraged by Koornhof's concession that the days of apartheid were numbered, he secured a promise that a future discussion would take up the issue of desegregating the Sugar Circuit. Yet when Ashe recounted the meeting years later, his strongest memory was of Koornhof's conservative indirection. The Afrikaner "skirted issues," Ashe recalled, and though "sympathetic to the plight of blacks," he "stopped short of saying that apartheid was wrong." Most distressingly, "he offered almost no hope of one-man, one-vote rule," prompting Ashe to comment: "So much for Western civilization."[30]

The next day was Sunday, the day before the Connors match, and Arthur used the time away from the tournament to conduct a youth tennis clinic in Soweto. To his delight, more than 1,500 black South Africans (including Mark Mathabane) showed up, mostly just to watch. Some came to catch their first glimpse of a black tennis star. Many others, he surmised, "had probably never seen tennis played before."

As soon as the clinic was over, he spoke to the crowd through a large megaphone. But his words were soon drowned out by a combination of enthusiastic fans rushing forward for autographs and hecklers carrying anti-Ashe placards. After several angry students confronted him with cries of "Go home, brother, and leave us alone. You're doing more harm than good by coming to South Africa" and "sellout and stooge," other members of the crowd came to his defense. A brief melee ensued, but he was able to escape unharmed. "Gingerly, I kept moving and smiling," he recalled, "and managed to reach a car."[31]

On Sunday evening, he remained in Soweto for a lavish yard party hosted by one of the community's few physicians. Nearly two hundred guests crowded into the house and yard, where they listened and danced to a native band and feasted on a buffet provided by Williams. It was a joyous scene that he had not expected to see in Soweto, and he was almost overcome with emotion when the evening ended with a series of gracious toasts honoring his presence. "You are the pride and idol of us all," Renee Ngcobo, a leading black lawyer and the head of a black tennis association, exclaimed. "You epitomize sportsmanship, for the essence of sportsmanship is to experience happiness in the happiness of others—and to feel their pain and their suffering too. God bless you for coming, Arthur, our Arthur." After calling for three cheers from the crowd, Ngcobo placed a traditional luck-bearing amulet around Arthur's neck and pronounced that the visiting American's new nickname was *Sipho*—which meant "a gift" in the Xhosa language.[32]

Arthur couldn't have asked for a better sendoff on the eve of his big match with Connors, and when he actually took the court on Monday, he discovered that virtually all of the fans in the stadium were solidly behind him. The crowd was so much in his favor that during the second set he had to "plead with the fans not to applaud when Connors made mistakes." Reflecting on the crowd's behavior, he later concluded it was difficult to interpret the actual meaning of the cheers, especially among the whites. "Cheer for the black man and assuage your guilt feelings," he suggested rhetorically, speculating that "some of the people who supported me so warmly on center court today will tomorrow behave despicably toward some poor black man."

Whatever the mix of fan motivation, the cheering didn't seem to bother Connors, who dominated the match from start to finish. Although Arthur played reasonably well and even forced a tiebreaker in the second set, Connors's ground strokes—especially his whiplashing two-handed backhand—were too much to overcome. The young left-hander won in straight sets, leaving Arthur to comment: "They will have to wait another year for a black man to be champion of South Africa." Actually, this wasn't quite accurate. On Tuesday, he and Okker defeated the Australians Rob Maud and Lew Hoad in the doubles final. While this wasn't exactly what he had come for, the doubles title provided some consolation. "In a way," he observed, "this might have been the most important doubles match I ever won, for now a black man's name rests on the list of South African champions. Etched. Forever."[33]

With the close of the doubles competition Ashe was done with the tennis scene at Ellis Park, but not with South Africa. He still had two days before his flight to New York, and he was determined to make the most of the time he had left. On the afternoon of the 27th, he and the rest of his entourage—except for the already departed Bud Collins—flew to Durban, on the Indian Ocean. Their real destination, or so they thought, was the remote bush town of Ulundi, where they were scheduled to meet with Mangosuthu Buthelezi, a Zulu chief described by Ashe as "probably the most powerful black man in South Africa." Unfortunately, after chartering an early morning plane, the Americans flew into a powerful storm that forced a return to Durban. Ashe later reached Buthelezi by phone, but the failure to meet the chief in person was "as great a disappointment as losing to Connors."[34]

Later in the day, the stalwart travelers flew west to Cape Town, where Ashe met with a group of graduate students and their teacher, Christopf Hanekom, a distinguished professor of anthropology at Stellenbosch University. Hanekom and his students represented the cream of the Afrikaner intellectual elite, and Ashe was eager to sound them out on matters related to democracy and apartheid. He later claimed to appreciate the general candor of the Afrikaners, as opposed to the hypocrisy that characterized British South Africans, many of whom professed liberal anti-apartheid beliefs that they rarely practiced. "It is one thing to express righteous indignation," he observed, "it is another, quite obviously, to vote against this dandy arrangement that provides you with cheap servants, cheap labor and complete superiority."

At Stellenbosch, however, Ashe encountered about as much racist candor as he could tolerate. Early on, Hanekom revealed the racial roots of his politics by offering Ashe a backhanded compliment. "You are an exception," he insisted, commenting on his guest's virtues. "You are not completely black; you have some white blood in you." Later, one student used urban America's racial troubles as a counterpoint to South Africa's alleged balance between limited freedom and order. Soon another student jumped in, "delighted," Ashe noticed, to cite "U.S. faults and inconsistencies to support their own injustices." After patiently listening to a litany of empty claims, including the assertion that "we don't have the riots that you suffer," Ashe got right to the point. "Perhaps riots are a small price to pay for freedom of expression," he suggested. "And besides, every day that goes by with apartheid increases the chances that the riot that does come will be even more violent, a huge conflagration."

Ashe then turned toward Hanekom and asked: "Tell me, professor, are you scared?" After an awkward pause, Hanekom shook his head and said no, providing Ashe with a perfect opening. "Boy, I'd be, if I were you," he said, following up with a quick laugh "to take the edge off." Hanekom and the students, Ashe noted, just sat there stone-faced and silent, "loath to even admit the violence, both casual and one-sided" that permeated their racist social system.

Later on, Professor Hanekom maintained that a new form of apartheid was emerging, "a voluntary multiracialism" placing South Africa "on the road to diverse equality." Before Ashe could respond, one of the students added it was all a matter of timing. "We are not so static a society as it may seem," he insisted. "But at the moment, we just do not believe that racial equality would benefit the whole society." When Ashe asked how they could "justify the whites making all the decisions," another student offered differential stages of "evolution" as the primary basis for legal inequality.

Unaccustomed to such unvarnished condescension, Ashe made one last attempt to bring his hosts out of the darkness. Speaking of apartheid, he asked: "All the sophisticated evolutionary arguments aside, all the intellectual and political position papers forgotten—in your heart, do you think it's right?" When the students hesitated to respond, their professor jumped in with a rehash of his earlier arguments. Growing impatient, Ashe cut him off with a real-life example. Pointing to Conrad Johnson, a prominent Coloured businessman and tennis official who had come to observe the discussion, he turned to Hanekom and said: "Forget all that. Just what about this man? Why can you vote and this man can't? Why are you free and this man isn't?" Looking distressed, Hanekom glanced nervously at Johnson and then looked downward as if in defeat. "Mr. Ashe," he confessed meekly, talking barely above a whisper, "that is an ace up your sleeve. I cannot defend that."[35]

Later in the afternoon, Ashe encountered a different side of the South African establishment when he visited the famous heart surgeon Christiaan

Barnard at the Red Cross Hospital in Cape Town. Barnard, Ashe discovered, was a jumble of contradictions. He was proud of his hospital's biracial facilities and open about his personal distaste for apartheid. Yet he opposed a South African democracy that followed a one-man, one-vote model, and he was unapologetically paternalistic in his attitude toward nonwhites. They remained cultural "children" in his view, and the government had no choice but to treat them as such. The only sane policy, he insisted, was to "take a child's hand to help him cross the road." Thanking Barnard for his honesty, Ashe left the hospital with more questions than answers, and a new appreciation for the complexities of South Africa's problems.[36]

Before flying back to Johannesburg, Ashe held a youth tennis clinic at the home of Leon Norgarb, one of the Western Cape's most liberal coaches, and at the Cape Town airport he had a private meeting with Hassan Howa, a prominent Coloured leader who served as president of the South African Cricket Board of Control (SACBOC). Known as an uncompromising "all or nothing" opponent of apartheid, Howa had publicly criticized Ashe for playing in front of largely segregated crowds at Ellis Park. After a surprisingly amicable meeting, Howa stunned reporters with the revelation that Ashe had been given assurances by government officials that "South Africans may be playing mixed sport in three years." According to Howa, Ashe told him that while "the government was working in the direction of mixed sport," broad changes could not be implemented until after the next general election. Ashe had asked Howa to keep this information to himself, but the flamboyant activist could not resist making headlines.

All of this complicated the final stop of Ashe's trip, a meeting with Koornhof in the capital city of Pretoria. Held in the seat of power, this second meeting offered both men a chance to clarify their positions and expectations related to the desegregation and democratization of South African sports. The conversation was blunt but cordial, and by the time Ashe left for the Johannesburg airport he felt cautiously optimistic.

Once he arrived at the terminal, he read a prepared statement, a version of which had already been distributed to reporters. Written by the journalist Richard Evans, the original statement began with a "strongly worded" condemnation of apartheid, but Ashe decided to soften the first paragraph. "Gentlemen, you were handed a statement prematurely, which is a mistake on my part" he told the reporters. "I would like to change the statement—the first paragraph—and I trust you will do this as a favour to me."

He then read the revised statement. "Having read a great deal about your country before my visit," he began, "nothing I have seen or experienced in South Africa has surprised me. . . . However, after talking to and exchanging views with people of every political persuasion, from my brothers in Soweto to students at Stellenbosch, I believe the first breezes of change may be reaching the Southern tip of Africa. I am optimistic that progress can be made in the immediate future and I fervently hope my presence here over the past 12 days will be of benefit to all concerned." He went on to acknowledge that the desegregation of the South African Open was "only a beginning" and ended with a thank-you to "all the many people for the cordial and friendly way they received me." [37]

Ashe worried then and later that his statement was too sanguine, but thankfully, just before boarding the plane, he learned that a few minutes earlier Koornhof had announced the Sugar Circuit would soon be open to all races. Minutes later, with the plane still sitting on the tarmac, the man now called Sipho in Soweto received three additional parting gifts. The first two, concealed in a rolled-up newspaper and smuggled onto the plane by Carole Dell, were a poem by Don Mattera and a picture of Winnie Mandela, the wife of Nelson Mandela, the imprisoned ANC leader serving a life sentence on Robben Island. A handwritten message on the back of the photograph delivered a farewell message of thanks and advice. "The best you can do," Mrs. Mandela counseled, "is ask the South Africans what you can do to help in their struggle." Mattera's poem, titled "Anguished Spirit—Ashe," brought the departing tennis star to tears. Written ten days earlier on the day of Mattera's banning, the anguished verses would haunt and inspire Ashe for the rest of his life. They began:

> *I listened deeply when you spoke*
> > *about the step-by-step evolution*
> > *of a gradual harvest*
> > *tendered by the rains of tolerance*
> > *and patience.*
> *Your youthful face*
> > *a mask*
> > *hiding a pining, anguished spirit, and*
> > *I loved you brother,*
> > *Not for your quiet philosophy*
> > *But for the rage in your soul*[38]

The third gift was a large bouquet of flowers rushed onto the plane just before takeoff. The accompanying card was from Koornhof. Genuinely surprised, Ashe didn't quite know what to make of this gesture. Did the gift simply reflect good manners? Or had the wily cabinet officer been playing him for a fool all along? Did the white South Africans believe they had foiled his best efforts? What, after all, had black South Africans gained from his controversial and exhausting trip? On the long flight to New York via Dakar, he had a full day to reflect upon these and other troubling questions.

Ashe's diary entry for November 29, written for the most part on the plane, registered his initial assessment of his experiences in South Africa. All in all, he was proud of what he had accomplished. "I still have the resolve," he wrote, "that contact with an adversary is better than isolation of him." The progress he witnessed—and the likelihood of more to come— had proved his critics wrong. "I believe that the criticism applied against my trip," he argued, "is more emotional than logical, and more frustrated than anything, and I'm convinced that my way can produce results. Arthur Ashe is not going to topple a government, but the very nature of sports is such that I believe that progress can be made in this frivolous area first. . . . Cliché or not, sports can bring change." Even something as simple as white boys and girls clamoring to get his autograph at Ellis Park provided real hope for the future. "South Africa cannot be a lost cause," he insisted. "Not from what I saw at Ellis Park."

Several days before his departure, Ashe and Williams had discussed the possibility of jointly underwriting a foundation dedicated to developing the tennis skills of young nonwhite South Africans. During the flight, he decided he would definitely follow through with this idea. "Those who show promise will get money for equipment and coaching," he promised. "Also, all the used rackets and clothes and any paraphernalia that I have left over will go to black South African players." He anticipated that this decision would draw some criticism from black Americans who expected him to give priority to the needy in his own country. But he reasoned the desperate situation in South Africa warranted special attention.

"Tennis, or boxing, or any sporting event can, if only for a moment, in that cursed, bizarre place, bring a diversion," he speculated. "Maybe that is what South Africa needs above all—a little escape. The place is so intense, so scared." Much of what he wrote on the plane expressed his belief that the liberation of black South Africa was going to take time; it would be years, he feared, before anything approaching racial equality could be achieved. Nevertheless, he ended his diary entry declaring it was "just a matter of time" before black South Africans experienced this liberation. "Sooner or later, the black man is going to rule South Africa," he wrote, "and the white man knows it. But more important, the black man knows it." [39]

Ashe's first trip to South Africa had proven to be an all-encompassing experience. "I felt strange touching down at JFK and reentering the 'real world,'" he recalled. "My stomach had been knotted the entire time and I was tense and taut." Even growing up in Virginia had not prepared him for South African apartheid. In 1973, following two decades of advances in civil rights, it was "incredible" to him that white South Africans "still thought in terms of racial supremacy." He knew all too well, of course, that America was still struggling with the vestiges of Jim Crow and white supremacist ideology. But he returned from South Africa with a newfound appreciation for the progress that had been made since his childhood. [40]

Ashe saw tangible proof of this progress within hours of his early morning arrival in New York. After an emotional press conference where he vented about his hatred of apartheid, and after saying goodbye to the Dells, he boarded a flight for Raleigh, North Carolina. Several months earlier, he had agreed to speak at Duke University in Durham, conduct a youth clinic, and play an exhibition match against Roscoe Tanner. Having hardly set foot in North Carolina since his early ATA days, he was amazed at the relatively relaxed racial atmosphere in the Raleigh-Durham area. Indeed, he was astonished to learn that a month earlier Raleigh had actually elected a black mayor, a funeral director and city councilman named Clarence Lightner. [41]

After a breathless and jet-lagged day in North Carolina, Ashe flew to Newark on December 1. Meryl, whom he hadn't seen in nearly a month, was there to greet him and drive with him down to Princeton, where he was scheduled to play in another series of benefit exhibition matches. Though still exhausted from his intercontinental travel, he did not want to disappoint the Princeton event's chief organizer, Margie Gengler, the star of Princeton University's undefeated 1973 women's tennis team and the girlfriend and future wife of Stan Smith. In an attempt to raise funds for the Youth Tennis Foundation of Princeton and the Friends of Princeton Tennis, Gengler had enlisted several pros—including Ashe, Tanner, and Bob Lutz—plus the actor Dustin Hoffman and the songwriter Burt Bacharach, for a round of celebrity doubles.

Ashe had first visited Princeton in 1963 when it had been the site of the NCAA tennis championships. At that time, the Princeton student body was virtually all white, and the local black community, the boyhood home of Paul Robeson, was isolated from the university and the town's upscale neighborhoods. Culturally, Princeton had long been considered the south-ernmost of the Ivies, and in its entire history prior to the mid-1960s the uni-versity had enrolled fewer than a dozen black students. Ashe had felt like an intruder in 1963. But a decade later—as he mingled with celebrities and signed autographs for fans, black and white—he could see that the town and the university had changed. Not only had the university's black enrollment increased dramatically, but also when he was introduced to the mayor of Princeton township he found himself shaking hands with longtime black community activist Jim Floyd Sr.[42]

Racial progress, it seemed to Ashe, was beginning to take hold in all regions of the country. But there were some things he hoped would never change. Whenever he became disoriented or uneasy, as he did after his re-turn from South Africa, he felt the pull of his family and the nurturing folk culture of his childhood. Nothing soothed his nerves or restored his spirit more than a visit to Gum Spring, still the source of his sense of place, and that is where he headed a few days after the Princeton fund-raiser. "My par-ents and I live such completely contrasting life-styles," he wrote on Decem-ber 7, "that it is necessary for us to see each other every now and then to get to know each other again. I don't mean that I have to come down here to love my parents again, but we all have to get together every so often so that we can remember how much we do share and how much we love each other."

As a kid, Ashe had helped his father build the house at Gum Spring, and some of his fondest memories were of fishing and hunting with his fa-ther and brothers in the streams and woods of rural Louisa County. On this particular visit, he became philosophical about the impact of Gum Spring on his life. "When I think back on it," he concluded, "I sort of lived a dual life as a boy. I was city, but I was raised country by an old-fashioned country father. Maybe that's why I can manage so well as the black in a white world. It's the same sort of experience. I've never been the kind of sonuvabitch you ever could put in any particular niche."

Perhaps so, but Ashe's country upbringing was sorely tested on his first morning home when his father woke him up early to go deer hunting. This deer hunt, he soon discovered, was no casual walk in the woods. In addi-tion to the Ashes, there were eighteen other hunters in their party, fifteen of whom were white. Cultural change had clearly come to rural Virginia, and nothing he had seen in Raleigh or Princeton could match this taboo-breaking interracial gathering. "Just four or five years ago," he insisted, "you never would have gotten blacks and whites hunting together in Virginia, especially out in the sticks like this."

The Louisa County hunters, Ashe's father explained, were just ordinary folks who had come not for sport but rather "to put meat on the table." The hunting party turned out to be "a very well organized, efficient operation" in Ashe's estimation, but before the day was over he was picking shotgun pellets out of his leg from a stray shot. The wounds turned out to be superficial, but he still had quite a tale to tell. Whether his friends back in New York and Miami would actually believe it was another matter.[43]

A week later, he traveled to Kingston, Jamaica, for another kind of shooting. A film crew was working on a documentary about his recent trip to South Africa, and the director John Marshall wanted to film Ashe in Jamaica "in a place where there are a lot of blacks around in a natural setting." At one point, the crew left Kingston to do some filming in the small town of Lucea, where Ashe met with a group of high school students who were encouraged to talk about their views on race and South Africa.[44]

After a brief respite with Meryl in Miami, he rejoined the film crew in Pennsylvania, where Marshall had arranged for him to have an on-camera conversation with Muhammad Ali at his training camp at Deer Lake. Having never met Ali, he was thrilled to to spend time with the man known as "The Greatest." Although their personalities could hardly have been more different, the two men hit it off, especially after Ali praised Ashe's decision to go to South Africa. After the camera was turned off, he even confessed he too had planned to go to South Africa but had called the trip off after being pressured by several Islamic ambassadors to the United Nations. "Me representing the whole Islamic world," he told Ashe, "I had to listen to these people. But you going as an individual, Arthur—I support everything you did as an individual."[45]

That night Ashe flew back to Miami for the opening of Doral's holiday tennis program. Spending Christmas in Miami had become a treasured part of his annual routine, a time to relax in the sun, play a little golf, and get ready for the beginning of a new WCT tour. He also liked to spend at least a few hours at the Orange Bowl Junior tournament, where he had gotten his start in the late 1950s. In 1973, there was the added attraction of seeing his old coach from St. Louis, Dick Hudlin, who had accompanied the latest hot ATA prospect, Juan Farrow, to the tournament. A native of Lynchburg, Farrow had recently followed Ashe's example in leaving Virginia and enrolling at Sumner High, where he would soon win the first of three consecutive Missouri state scholastic singles championships. Ashe was impressed with Farrow's tennis, but he worried about how the funky young Virginian would be received on the tour. "I can hardly wait till he gets on the circuit,"

Ashe declared in his diary. "Juan wears big apple caps, the flashy clothes, the two-toned high heels, the works. I can just see the day when he shows up at some country club like Longwood. All those tennis officials are going to be walking around saying, 'Whatever happened to that nice little colored boy Arthur Ashe?'"[46]

Ashe himself often pondered the same question. What had happened to the relatively simple life he had led in his teens and early twenties? Success had brought excitement and financial security, but it had also placed him at the mercy of almost ceaseless travel and seemingly impossible demands. At the age of thirty, he didn't really have a home he could call his own, and at times he wasn't quite sure where he was or where he was headed. The primary blessing—and perhaps the ultimate curse—in all of this was the stimulation that pervaded his life. Before leaving South Africa, he told the press that the last few days had been "the most interesting week in my life." But after a month back in the States, he wasn't so sure. Considering his recent, post–South Africa experiences, he was beginning to think his entire adult life resembled a fantastical movie script. What new adventures lay in store for him in the coming years, he could only imagine.[47]

SIXTEEN

PROS AND CONS

∎

I N THE WORLD OF tennis, 1974 was the year of Jimmy Connors. As Ashe and others looked on in envy and awe, he won 99 of 103 singles matches, a record unmatched in the modern era. Along the way he won no fewer than fifteen tournaments, including three of the four Grand Slam events. Ashe, in comparison, won 85 of 112 matches and three tournament titles, a very good year by almost any standard but far short of Connors's amazing run. Any comparison was skewed somewhat by Connors's decision to forgo the standard WCT tour, where the weekly competition was decidedly tougher than on the makeshift circuit arranged by Connors's agent, Bill Riordan. But the young left-hander's dominance at the Grand Slam tournaments quashed any doubt that he was the best singles player in the world.

In January, Connors took the Australian Open title, defeating Phil Dent in the final. In July, he won the Wimbledon final in straight sets over Ken Rosewall, matching his fiancée, Chris Evert's, easy victory on the women's side. And in the final match at the U.S. Open in September, it took him barely an hour to vanquish Rosewall again. Outclassed from the start, the thirty-nine-year-old Australian managed to win only two games.[1]

Week after week, Connors played almost flawless tennis. No one on the men's tour had enjoyed such dominance since Laver a decade earlier, and once Connors achieved the world number one ranking in late July he did not relinquish it for a record 160 weeks. He might even have equaled Laver's and Don Budge's achievement of winning all four Grand Slam tournaments in a single year had he not been banned from playing in the French Open. When Connors signed a contract with the Baltimore Banners of World Team Tennis (WTT) in mid-January, complicated negotiations regarding the new league's impact on scheduling and player compensation were just beginning. During the following three weeks, all of the major parties—the ILTF, the ATP, WCT, and WTT—hashed out an agreement tolerable to everyone but the leaders of the French and Italian tennis federations.[2]

On February 15, one day after ILTF president Allan Heyman announced the agreement, Philippe Chatrier declared the French federation had no intention of abiding by the ILTF's decision. There were similar rumblings from a representative of the Italian federation, which shared Chatrier's concern that WTT's summer schedule would wreak havoc with the European national championships held in June and July. Under the terms of the agreement, French and Italian tennis officials were given two options designed to guarantee that participation in team tennis would not prevent the world's top stars from playing in Paris and Rome. But Chatrier rejected both options, including a proposal to offer certain players guaranteed earnings and a place in the draws without having to survive a qualifying round. Defying the ILTF, he vowed that "the French championships, both indoor and outdoor, would be closed to any men or women players who sign contracts with the W.T.T."[3]

Chatrier kept his promise long enough to deny Connors the chance to win three Grand Slam tournaments in a row and to insure a somewhat depleted field at the 1974 French Open. Even so, virtually all of the non-WTT stars, including Ashe, showed up in Paris. Always a bit uncomfortable on the slow red clay at Roland Garros, Ashe nonetheless had won the doubles championship with Riessen in 1971, and he harbored some hope he could win a second French Open doubles title with his new partner, Roscoe Tanner. But the two hard-hitting Americans succumbed in the third round to the exotic and unheralded team of Ismail El Shafei of Egypt and Zeljko Franulovic of Yugoslavia.

In the singles competition, he won a tough first-round match against Ivan Molina of Colombia, who had defeated him as recently as August 1973; and in the second round he outlasted Antonio Muñoz of Spain, despite losing the first set. His third-round match against Muñoz's countryman, Manolo Orantes, one of the world's premier clay court shotmakers, was a different matter, however. In his diary, Ashe described Orantes's 6–1, 6–2, 6–2 victory as "an assassination." At one point in the second set, after Ashe hit "a beautiful approach shot and followed it to the net," he was "passed so cleanly" that all he "could do was stand there and laugh—out loud."[4]

Almost no one was surprised when Ashe lost to Orantes, who went on to test the ultimate champion, Bjorn Borg, in a five-set final. Like any serious competitor, Ashe hated to lose, but two weeks in Paris was ample compensation for a Francophile who could never get enough of the City of Light. Ashe loved Paris almost as much as he loved London, and nothing—not even Chatrier's prolonging of the WTT controversy—could sour him on the French. The red clay he could do without. But the rest of it—the food, the wine, the women, the cosmopolitan culture—was intoxicating.[5]

On this visit the Parisian women were less distracting than in the past because Meryl was with him. They had been in Paris together before, but this time it was different. After nearly two years of dating, their relationship had reached a critical stage. There was talk of a long-term commitment and even marriage, and Ashe was feeling the pressure. On their second night in Paris, they had a pleasant dinner at the historic Left Bank restaurant Le Procope. But later in the week they had an uncomfortable discussion about fatherhood and what she alleged to be an unhealthy American preoccupation with status and ego. The inevitable challenges of an interracial and interreligious relationship had been on his mind for some time, but now it appeared there were other potential problems to consider. He wasn't sure they wanted the same things out of life, or that she could find happiness as the wife of a touring tennis professional.[6]

The latter point was driven home their ninth day in Paris, when they had dinner with two recently married tennis couples, the Lutzes and the Tanners. Months earlier, a sober reflection in Ashe's diary had focused on Nancy Cook Tanner's "identity crisis." "She is trying to understand that she is no longer Nancy Cook," he explained, "but she is not even Nancy Tanner; primarily she is just Roscoe Tanner's wife. In the tennis world, nobody really bothers to sort out the wives as people; they are just tolerated as appendages. It's not right, but that's the way it is." He predicted this would "change in time," but nothing during the Paris dinner suggested mitigation would come anytime soon. At that point, he had no way of knowing that the Tanners' marriage would end in a bitter divorce, but the signs of trouble were already in evidence.[7]

On June 13, Meryl and Arthur flew to London before driving northward to Nottingham, the site of a pre-Wimbledon warm-up tournament. On the way over both caught serious colds, complicating their plans for a romantic week in the English Midlands. Arthur managed a few hours of practice on the grass courts, but mostly they stayed in their room sneezing and coughing. By the third day, both were "going stir crazy," with the only excitement being an anti-Semitic incident in the hotel bar. When the bartender pointed to a slot machine and called it "a Jew box," Meryl exploded, which did nothing to improve the struggling couple's mood. The next day, rain postponed Arthur's opening match, sending him back to the same bar, where this time he received a jolt of a different kind. An old friend from UCLA was getting a divorce, he learned from a conversation at the bar. At first, he professed shock, but later that night he speculated in his diary "that marriage as an institution is on its way out." Whether marriages have to contend with the tennis tour or not, "very few people seem to be able to handle it anymore."[8]

Over the next two days, he passed through a confusing range of emotions that he apparently kept to himself. After losing a close match to Guillermo Vilas on Wednesday afternoon, he spent most of the evening on ATP paperwork and reading the early chapters of Hermann Hesse's then popular novel, *Steppenwolf*. Others had found wisdom in Hesse's tale of an existential hero, and now it seemed to spur Arthur into action. On the morning of June 20, his last day in Nottingham, he awoke with a sense of clarity. His cold was gone, but so was his passion.

As his diary entry that night explained: "I don't want the responsibility of worrying about her, and us, anymore, and the chemistry has ebbed. I don't know when it did, but it has, and if there's one thing you can't fake, it's a feeling, especially if the feeling has been there before. So I just said, well I think we had better call it off, and she knew I meant it, so there wasn't really much for her to discuss. She knew I had made up my mind." Putting a tearful Meryl on the train to London later in the morning was "one of the hardest things I had ever had to do," he acknowledged. Still, he had done it, decisively closing an important chapter in his life.[9]

The clean break gave Arthur's personal life a fresh start. Fresh and exciting, as it turned out: following his second-round match at Wimbledon, he received an unexpected call from Diana Ross, the great Motown artist and actress who had achieved international fame as the lead singer of the Supremes. Married to music executive Robert Silberstein and the mother of two young daughters, she had no romantic interest in Arthur. But she had wanted to meet him for some time. A big fan of her music, he was happy to accommodate her, especially after she volunteered to make a special trip to Wimbledon from her central London hotel.

"Her record company drove her out to Wimbledon in a burgundy Rolls-Royce," he recalled. "We met in the foyer and went up to the tea room. I had already played and won my match that afternoon. When she walked into the room, all eyes turned to us." After watching a late afternoon match from the Tea Room roof, they hopped into the Rolls and headed for the Mayfair Hotel, where she was staying. Following a couple of drinks in the lobby bar, she left for a dinner engagement and he returned to his hotel, but not before arranging to meet in Washington two weeks later. As Arthur later explained: "I was going to play in the *Washington Star* tournament and she would be performing at the Carter Baron Amphitheater next door. It turned out that we unknowingly were on the same floor of the Washington Hilton and had dinner together on a couple of evenings. One night, my family came up from Richmond with some home-cooked food and we all ate in her suite. She seemed lonely at the time and really enjoyed the warmth of the family gathering."[10]

Arthur was learning that life as a celebrity had its privileged moments. But there was no guarantee fame would do anything for his tennis game. Wimbledon 1974—his eighth appearance at the world's most prestigious tournament—turned out to be a disappointment on the court. Seeded eighth, he breezed through the first two rounds only to lose to Tanner in the third as the big left-hander wore him down on a hot and blustery afternoon.[11]

At several points during the match, he had trouble with the wind and appeared to lose his concentration, none of which surprised his closest friends. Those who knew about the recent breakup with Meryl, not to mention his platonic dalliance with Diana Ross, had worried about his state of mind going into the match. And all of them were well aware that love lost and friendship found were not the only diversions dividing his attention at Wimbledon. A week earlier, on June 23, he had been elected president of the ATP, replacing Cliff Drysdale. Assuming the presidency was both an honor and a burden, but an unexpected development earlier in the day put immediate emphasis on the latter.[12]

Just hours before Ashe's election, the ATP was informed that WTT, along with Evonne Goolagong and Jimmy Connors, had decided to file a $10 million lawsuit against the French and Italian tennis federations, the Commercial Union Assurance company (the primary sponsor of the Grand Prix series, which included the French and Italian Opens), and ATP executives Donald Dell and Jack Kramer. Claiming that Dell and Kramer had "conspired with the French and Italians" to bar WTT players from the European grand slams, the suit promised to reheat the tennis wars. Ashe, who rarely lost his temper, was furious. "Every time I passed Connors in the locker room today," he wrote in his diary, "it took all my will power not to punch him in the mouth. It's sickening. He and Riordan could be such a good part of tennis, but will they only be satisfied when they have wrecked the whole game?"[13]

Publicly, Ashe was more circumspect. "Now that I'm president," he acknowledged, "I've . . . got to watch what I say and differentiate between Ashe the player and Ashe the ATP president. But I'm going to devote myself to this job. When I give it up a year from now, I want ATP firmly established as a responsible force in the game." Yet he already knew it wasn't going to be easy to balance success on the court with administrative responsibility. "This job is going to be tough for me," he conceded, adding, "Cliff has not done well as a player since he assumed the presidency."[14]

Eight days later on Court Seven—after presiding over two tense meetings of the ATP board—he got a taste of just how difficult it was going to be to keep his eye on the ball. The loss to Tanner hit Ashe especially hard. "I take defeat harder all the time," he confessed. "I just wanted to be left alone after the match. The girls kept jamming their autograph books at me, and I turned them away. 'I'm sorry, I really don't feel like signing now,' I said. I rarely do a thing like that. I saw the press, but I didn't want to. After a defeat, they make me feel as if I'm on trial." His only consolation was that his loss paled in comparison to the biggest tennis story of the day, El Shafei's shocking upset of Borg. In any event, most of the attention was focused on Connors and Evert as they marched toward twin victories at Centre Court. After Ashe and Tanner were eliminated in the third round of the doubles competition, both men slipped away unnoticed.[15]

Tanner, at twenty-two, was confident his best years at Wimbledon lay ahead. But Ashe faced a different prospect. Still looking for his first Wimbledon title at age thirty, he was beginning to fear it might never happen. Having reached the semifinals in two of his first five visits to the All England Club, he now appeared to be falling back into the pack. This was not what he had envisioned in early 1973, when he had agreed to keep a Wimbledon-to-Wimbledon diary. He and the editors at Houghton Mifflin had hoped to close his chronicle with a strong showing—perhaps even a victory—at Wimbledon. Instead, he ended with failures on and off the court amid speculation that he was nearing the end of the road professionally.

In the final entry, he denied he was contemplating retirement. "Hell, I've got a lot of years left," he insisted. "Look at Rosewall. I keep myself in good shape and I don't have any weight problem. I do hate the practice. That's the only negative. But I don't mind the training. I love to run, and I love this life, even if I take the losing too seriously now." Sometime in the distant future, he would put down his racket and, before moving on to a new career, "take a year off and do nothing—just read all the books I've always wanted to and go to all the places I've never been." But for now he was still in the hunt.[16]

After the emotional roller coaster of the 1974 European tour, Ashe retreated to the calm of Doral. He was very fond of southern Florida. "Miami is especially nice," he wrote in 1973, "because it's so tourist-conscious that they don't permit any industry to speak of, so there's almost no smog. And it seems to me there's still space to move around in here." His stay at Doral gave him a chance to decompress before moving on to the annual crush of mid- and late-summer tournaments. During the previous year, he had found the routine of keeping a daily journal "therapeutic." "Writing," he explained, "has forced me to take a closer look at my life and myself." And now he had at least a few days reserved for light workouts, relaxation, and reflection.[17]

Working with aspiring tennis players, especially children, was never a dreaded chore for Ashe. Not only did he enjoy the role of a teacher, but also the clinics at Doral and elsewhere helped him maintain a sense of perspective and balance. "To watch him with the children—that was really something," an admiring Rodney Harmon once observed. "He took time to try to hit balls with each of the kids, and what really impressed me was how he would try to make every kid at the clinic feel important. . . . He stayed so long we told him that he probably needed to go for the sake of his own busy schedule."

Looking at the flailing arms and legs of his students, virtually all of whom were white in 1974, reminded Ashe that his athletic talent was a special gift not to be taken lightly. His accomplishments as a tennis player had brought him fame, respect, and a certain amount of power. Yet recent experience had confirmed he needed to be more than a great athlete. Success on the court, however glorious, was not enough to sustain his spirit.

Nor was it enough to be popular and well liked. He also wanted to make a difference in the world, to prove his life had a deeper purpose than striking a tennis ball better than anyone else. He had suspected as much for years, but the visit to South Africa in 1973 affected him in ways that were still bubbling to the surface a year later. He now realized that while he had seen enough of the good life to know he liked it, the role of a decadent tennis playboy did not suit him. He liked to have fun, and he felt reasonably comfortable in the posh surroundings of Doral and other elite enclaves. But he couldn't block out his responsibilities as an informed citizen painfully aware that poverty, discrimination, and vestiges of colonialism shackled much of the world's population. "From what we get, we can make a living," he wrote in his 1993 memoir, *Days of Grace*. "What we give, however, makes a life."

A pure athlete would have spent almost every waking moment practicing and preparing for the next big match. But that was not Ashe. On any given day, his attention was likely to be divided between tennis and a host of other interests, from the administrative details of the ATP to a developing situation in South Africa to whatever he happened to be reading that day. Although the transition to a second career as a social activist and public intellectual was far from complete in 1974, he was clearly on his way. Ashe bristled whenever sportswriters insinuated that outside interests had compromised his performance on the tennis court, but in private he sometimes conceded there might be a measure of truth in such criticisms. Even so, his grudging recognition of limitations did not stop him from trying to prove his critics wrong.[18]

During the second half of 1974, Ashe had to deal with a wide range of off-court distractions—everything from Richard Nixon's resignation on August 9 to South Africa's Davis Cup participation to the continuing controversies surrounding Connors and WTT. Yet somehow he managed to stay on top of his on-court responsibilities. His results were respectable, especially for one of the oldest players on the tour. He made it to the quarterfinals at the *Washington Star* International, the WCT tournament in Louisville, the U.S. Pro Championships in Boston, and the U.S. Open.

The competition was stiff at every stop, especially at the Open, where he lost a close match to John Newcombe. Over five grueling sets, Ashe played some of the best tennis of his life, serving and volleying with power and precision and wowing the crowd with backhand winners. Only a brief lapse in the third game of the fifth set let him down, when two double faults gave Newcombe an opening. Despite the loss, Ashe was justifiably proud of his performance—even if it was soon obscured by the hoopla surrounding Connors and Evert. Once again, as at Wimbledon, the fiancés (scheduled to be married on November 8) appeared to be fashioning parallel victories on a grand stage. This time, however, Evert lost to Goolagong in the semifinals, temporarily disrupting the fairy-tale story line. Unfazed, the reporters covering the Open hardly blinked as they fixated on the "love match" between the "princess" of Fort Lauderdale and the "riverboat gambler" from Illinois.[19]

Ashe did not begrudge Connors his latest victory or his rising celebrity. And he felt nothing but admiration for Evert, despite what Ashe considered her questionable taste in men. Yet as ATP president he could not abide Connors's callous disregard for his fellow players. He did not like Connors personally, but that was not the issue. He was convinced the players on the professional tour had to pull together to protect their common interests. Promoters and sponsors and tennis federation officials all had their own agendas and could not be trusted to look out for the players' well-being.

In this context, Connors's self-serving independence was no small matter, especially after he joined the WTT lawsuit. Ashe believed, with some justification, that Connors was allowing himself to be used by Bill Riordan, a suspicion that took on new life after a French court ruled against the suit as it applied to the European federations. To many observers, the decision to continue the legal action against the ATP executives and Commercial Union Assurance seemed more personal than anti-monopolist. Connors and Riordan always put on a good show and deserved at least some of the credit for tennis's booming popularity. But now their determination to go their own way threatened the livelihood of other players and the future of Open tennis.[20]

Connors and Riordan, of course, did not see it that way, pointing out that the ATP's legal problems represented only one of many complications challenging the tennis world in the fall of 1974. Chief among them was a developing situation in the Davis Cup competition. In January, the United States had been eliminated by lowly Colombia, but Ashe and his teammates received some consolation when all of the other world tennis powers, including mighty Australia, also fell by the wayside. Hampered by a cumbersome schedule and competing events, many of the world's best teams were forced to play critical matches with second-line players. The result was a series of shocking upsets that ultimately reduced the field to two unexpected finalists, India and South Africa. After South Africa defeated Italy at Ellis Park in Johannesburg in early October, the championship match against India was scheduled for the same site later in the month.

In sixty-three years of competition, only four nations—the United States, Australia, Great Britain, and France—had ever won the Davis Cup, so both India and South Africa were closing in on an unprecedented feat. India, however, faced a dilemma. Should a nation populated by darker-skinned people participate in an athletic competition hosted by a racially discriminatory regime? The fact that hundreds of thousands of Indians had resettled in South Africa during the past century and that as early as 1919 Mohandas Gandhi had led a nonviolent struggle against racial discrimination in South Africa complicated the situation. As recently as July, the Indian delegate to the Davis Cup Committee on Management had voted to expel South Africa from the upcoming 1975 competition. The expulsion vote, which required a two-thirds majority of the seven-member committee, fell one vote short at 4–3. But India's inclinations were well known long before the match with South Africa became a distinct possibility.[21]

On October 5, following South Africa's victory over Italy, R. H. Khanna, secretary of the All-India Tennis Federation (AITF), announced India had decided to default. "The principle of opposing apartheid," Khanna insisted, "is more important than a tennis championship." Officials representing the South African Lawn Tennis Union, which controlled the "choice of ground" for the final, promptly telegrammed Khanna with an offer to play the championship at a neutral site, or "even in a black African state." But Khanna held firm, even after Basil Reay, secretary of the Davis Cup Nations Committee, threatened India with expulsion from future competition. The default drew both praise and ridicule. While some lauded the AITF for standing on principle, Ashe and others who favored engagement over isolation, including the subcontinent's leading tennis stars, Anand and Vijay Amritraj, saw nothing but folly in the default.

On November 7, Davis Cup officials not only awarded the cup to South Africa by default, but also surprised almost everyone by giving the rogue nation a spot on the powerful management committee. New to the committee but hardly bashful, the South African delegate immediately moved to expel his Indian colleague from the meeting and the committee. Fortunately, he later withdrew the motion, and by the end of the meeting W. Harcourt Woods, the American chairman of the committee, had restored order by summarily moving South Africa to the North and Central American Zone competition for 1975. India and South Africa would never have to worry about facing each other again, except in the committee.[22]

All of this had important implications for the American Davis Cuppers— and for Ashe. In early October, Ashe and the American team had defeated the Commonwealth/British West Indies team in the first round of the 1975 North and Central American Zone competition. In the next round they would face Mexico, and after that, if they won, would advance to the main draw, where thanks to the Davis Cup committee's decision of November 7, their opponent would be South Africa. This was a nightmare scenario for American tennis officials who hoped to avoid controversy and depoliticize the Davis Cup.[23]

Much of the speculation concerned Ashe and how he would respond to the challenge of facing the white South Africans in international competition. On October 16, at the height of the Indian default controversy, Owen Williams announced that Ashe had agreed to play at Ellis Park for the second straight year. Arthur soon confirmed he was eager to return to South Africa to see if conditions had improved during the past twelve months. But playing South Africa in the Davis Cup was potentially a different matter. When asked if Arthur would be willing to participate in a U.S.–South Africa match, Dennis Ralston, the embattled captain of the U.S. team, was hesitant to say anything definite. "Arthur said he wanted to play Davis cup," Ralston told a *New York Times* reporter on October 25, "but I don't know that he would want to play against South Africa. We haven't discussed that yet."[24]

Ashe, fearing the Davis Cup issue would spoil his upcoming visit to South Africa, hesitated to comment. At the time he was far away in Tehran, Iran, where, ironically, he was in the process of losing a tough match to Andrew Pattison, a twenty-five-year-old white Rhodesian who had migrated from South Africa as a young boy. From Tehran, Ashe traveled to Paris for the French Indoor Championship, and then on to Stockholm, where he won his first tournament since March, and finally to a Dewar Cup tournament in England, before heading for South Africa. With hardly a moment to catch his breath, he had neither the time nor the inclination to say very much about the Davis Cup question prior to his arrival in Cape Town on November 14.[25]

In the meantime, he received a good bit of unsolicited advice. When several observers speculated that Ashe and the Americans might prefer to play the South Africans at a neutral site, the American Committee on Africa's special projects director Ray Gould erupted. "The playing at a neutral site is what we really condemn," he explained. "It's a cosmetic cover-up of the real issue." Ashe agreed that apartheid was an evil system and that South Africa should never be treated as just another nation. But, as in years past, he took the position that engaging white South Africans in an open dialogue held out more promise than forcing them into isolation. In a letter made public on October 26, he reiterated his belief that international engagement fostered the liberation of black South Africans. "In light of the recent developments in Guinea-Bissau, Angola and Mozambique," he wrote to M. N. Pather, secretary of the multiracial SALTU, "I, more than ever, think that further contact with politically active American blacks is essential to speed up South Africa's transition to normalcy." Ashe was aware that Pather had already condemned his participation in the South African Open, insisting the white sports establishment was using him. But he remained convinced that sealing off white South Africans from the rest of the world would make things worse not better.[26]

Unmoved by Ashe's letter, Pather scolded the American tennis star for his naïveté: "Arthur Ashe must realize that tennis in this country is played

on racial lines, and if he was a citizen of South Africa, he might not have
got to his present stage." The entire exchange was distressing, but Ashe remained hopeful his critics would respect his right to do what he thought
was best for black South Africans. He felt he had so much to offer, having
collaborated with Williams on an ambitious plan to create expanded opportunities for black athletes through the Black Tennis Foundation. Following
the South African Open, a special "Tennis Day" exhibition featuring some
of the world's top players would be held at Ellis Park, and Williams predicted the benefit would raise at least 30,000 rand for the new foundation.
Under the original plan, much of the money would have been funneled to
SALTU, but Pather made it clear he would reject the donation as "tainted
money." Ashe claimed to be acting in the best interests of black South Africans, but, according to Pather, he was actually "trying to buy the friendship
of the Black people after sacrificing them."[27]

These harsh words gave Ashe pause as he prepared for his return to South
Africa. But at least he had a better sense of what to expect than on his first
visit, and this time there would be no restrictions on his political commentary during the visit, or so he thought. Of course, once he was actually there
making his way across a labyrinthine landscape of tribal and racial complexity, he discovered surprises around every turn. For most of the journey, he
was accompanied by three fellow travelers: Dr. Robert Green, SCLC's former national education director, who served as dean of the College of Urban
Affairs at Michigan State University; Michael Cardoza, Dell's assistant at
ProServ; and Andrew Young, who had just won a second term representing
Georgia's Fifth District.

Together the four men—three black and one white—encountered a dizzying array of South Africans. In Cape Town, they met with Dr. Christiaan
Barnard, who unintentionally provided a sobering reminder of the limitations
of white South African liberalism. Distancing himself from the harsh racialism of the Afrikaners. Barnard was eager to show off a pediatric cardiac unit
where black and white babies lay side by side. "We don't discriminate here,"
he proudly explained. But minutes later he confessed, somewhat sheepishly,
that he did "not believe yet in one-man one-vote in South Africa."

Disappointed, Ashe suspected "an implicit quota system loomed in the
back of Barnard's mind. He believed logically that all men were equal, but
evidence led him to the conclusion that his country would be better off not
immediately putting the ballot in the hands of his African maid or his illiterate gardener." The Barnard visit dampened Ashe's hopes for change in

South Africa. "Those who claim there is white support for equality inside South Africa exaggerate their claims," he concluded. "The white liberals there are not as liberal as they'd have you believe. . . . I have come to the conclusion that white South Africa will have to be forced to change." [28]

A lesson of a different sort emerged from a social gathering hosted by a group of prominent Coloured South Africans. After a few minutes of pleasant conversation, Ashe was taken aback when one of the Coloured leaders upbraided him for concentrating on the plight of the black majority. "You're spending a lot of time with the Africans, and that's fine," the man declared, "but when are you going to help us a bit?" Somewhat flustered, Ashe tried to explain that black Americans were unaccustomed to sharp differentiations based on color as opposed to race, but his host would have none of it. "Hell," he exclaimed, "you're colored yourself. You should help your own kind." [29]

Solidarity was an unrealized ideal even in the black community, and Ashe and his colleagues had to be careful as they divided their time among black South African leaders. Many leaders of the ANC, including Nelson Mandela, were in prison and unavailable, but Ashe made a special effort to meet with Robert Sobukwe, Mandela's counterpart in the rival Pan-African Congress. Sobukwe, who had been released from prison in 1969 after nine years of solitary confinement, was still under house arrest in Kimberley, the North Cape mining town made famous by Cecil Rhodes and the De Beers Corporation. Banned from all political activity and anything but local travel, he agreed to meet with the Americans even though he knew it was a clear violation of his parole. At age forty-nine, the freedom fighter turned law student was physically broken. But "the professor," as his admirers called him, had lost none of the personal charm and courage that had made him a respected figure in black South Africa.

Sobukwe was little known outside South Africa, and Ashe, Young, and Cardoza did not know what to expect before arriving in Kimberley. The meeting easily exceeded all of their expectations. Despite years of privation, Sobukwe showed no trace of anger or bitterness. Warm and gracious, he expressed admiration for Young, King, and the SCLC, and thanked Ashe for returning to South Africa. Encouraged, Ashe asked how the trip might benefit black South Africans. Without a moment's hesitation, Sobukwe "launched into an hour-long discussion on South African race relations and the role of the outside world in bringing about equality." As the three Americans sat transfixed, he uttered the words they had been waiting to hear. "A lot of good could result from your trip," he offered. "We have many problems here and not too many black Americans really know our situation. If you could help explain our predicament to your countrymen, that in itself would be a help."[30]

Unfortunately for Ashe, the meeting in Kimberley proved to be the high point of his two weeks in South Africa. At almost every other stop, from Cape Town to Johannesburg, he became enmeshed in a web of racial and political tension that kept everyone on edge. While there were moments of inspiration, including an encouraging interview with the Zulu chief Mangosuthu Buthelezi in Nongoma, for the most part he encountered skepticism and suspicion.[31]

The tournament itself was a disappointment, even though he was gratified by the number of blacks in the stands who cheered wildly whenever he appeared on court. He played well in the early rounds, defeating the tough Mexican Raúl Ramírez in the semifinals, and for the second straight year faced Connors in the final. In the first set of the title match, Ashe pushed his cocky young opponent into a tiebreaker before losing 7–6. But from then on it was all Connors, who closed out the match 6–3, 6–1.

Losing to a man he didn't like or respect, especially in such an emotional setting, was a bitter pill for Ashe to swallow. But the worst of it was the negative press coverage following the match. The South African press could not resist playing up the simmering feud between the two Americans, and when Ashe made the mistake of breaking tradition and leaving the court while Connors was being photographed with the championship trophy, enterprising reporters made the most of it. Even before the match took place, several reporters speculated that Ashe's failure to include Connors on a three-man American team scheduled to face three South Africans on Tennis Day was a deliberate snub. After his victory Connors confirmed that Ashe's decision had made "me want to beat the pants off him." When asked about the matter, Ashe shrugged his shoulders and explained he had chosen Marty Riessen and Brian Gottfried over Connors simply because they were two of his "closest friends." Unconvinced, local white reporters continued to talk about the "bitter personal feud between the two American tennis stars."[32]

Sensationalist journalism of this kind irritated Ashe, even though in this case there was more than a grain of truth in the "grudge match" stories. But his biggest problem with the press had nothing to do with Connors. In a meeting with black journalists held several hours after the final match, he was shaken by a series of hostile statements that challenged his understanding of South African racialism. At first, the black reporters welcomed Andrew Young's interest in South Africa and showered him with praise and applause. They seemed especially interested in Young's background as an aide to Dr. King and in his reasons for accompanying Ashe. "I have come to South Africa because I have realized that unless my brothers in Africa are free I can never be completely free," Young told them. "In America we often get a completely wrong picture of what is going on here. For instance a banned journalist is vilified as a sort of vicious communist. Well, today I had lunch with one and found him to be one of the finest, gentlest people I have ever met. That is why it is important for us to come to South Africa to find out the truth."

This statement drew loud applause, but Ashe's participation in the white-run South African Open was another matter. Didn't he realize, one reporter asked plaintively as Ashe winced, that playing in the Open implicitly supported the existing system of "racial" sport? When Ashe tried to counter with an explanation of how the Black Tennis Foundation would open up new opportunities for black South African athletes, his words were drowned out by cries that the Tennis Day money would only legitimize SALTU's black and Coloured affiliates.

One reporter claimed that, despite good intentions, Ashe had allowed the South African government to turn his visit into pro-apartheid propaganda. Others asked about his stands on corporate divestment and a proposed expulsion of South Africa from the Olympics. For nearly two hours the questions kept coming. How could he associate with a hypocrite like Owen Williams? Was he really impressed with the cosmetic changes and half-baked desegregation of Ellis Park? Through it all, Ashe kept calm and listened far more than he spoke. The anger in the room did not surprise him, since he had experienced a similar grilling in 1973. But somehow this gathering seemed more desperate than the group at his first encounter. The education he received that night would percolate in his mind for years to come, and he would never forget the scene at the end of the meeting when the journalists rose as one with clenched fists as they sang the militant anthem "Nkosi Sikelel' iAfrika."[33]

Two days later, a somewhat chastened Ashe presided over the Tennis Day event. The crowds were smaller than he and Williams had anticipated, and the money raised for the Black Tennis Foundation, 10,645 rand, was barely a third of Williams's early estimate. But it was a start, and no major disruptions or protests spoiled the day. Before his featured match with Ray Moore, Ashe presented an autographed racket to Shepherd Mojanaga, a promising young black tennis player whose obvious delight signaled how important the black American star was as a role model. It was a great moment for Ashe who, despite all the disappointments and difficulties of the past two weeks, remained committed to cultivating and liberating the talent of young black South Africans.[34]

As both Ashe and Young noted at a press conference two days later, just before departing for New York, South Africa's future, not its past, was what really mattered. They talked of a new South Africa and of emerging leaders like Sobukwe. "There are people who shape history," Young informed the reporters, "people with limited or no physical resources who fight injustices through the sheer force of their personalities. Like Martin Luther King, Robert Sobukwe is one." Sometime in the not so distant future, he predicted, "the South African Government may have to go to Sobukwe like the British went to Kenyatta." Ashe agreed, calling his new friend "a real leader of the African people." No one that day had any way of knowing that Sobukwe would be dead within three years, and that it would take another decade and a half before Mandela would enact the scenario laid out by the two Americans. But there was a prescient wisdom in their long-range vision.[35]

Once he was back in the United States, Ashe talked openly about his recent experiences in South Africa and tried to clarify his views without riling his critics. In a press conference on December 16, he made it clear that he believed India—which he pointed out "had its own problems, such as the caste system"—had erred when it defaulted in the Davis Cup competition. "By not playing," he insisted, "India set back normalization of racial tensions two or three years." How he had calibrated this precise assessment was left unexplained, but he went on to justify his decision to participate in the South African Open. "South Africa and its apartheid policy is something I like to monitor," he explained. "I don't say anything inflammatory and I don't burn my bridges behind me. . . . I guess the government knows that we both use each other, for different reasons, but that's all right. There is progress being made. They like to say to the world, 'We're not so bad, we let Arthur Ashe play here.' I say to them, 'You're still pretty bad.'"[36]

Such candor did not assuage Ashe's critics on the left, who continued to question his judgment. But he soon turned to other, less controversial matters. For the first time in months, he focused on private concerns of mind and body. December was almost always a quiet month for tennis players, a time to rest and relax. Ashe played in only one tournament during the final weeks of 1974, traveling to Caracas, Venezuela, for the Galaxy Cup competition. And to his delight he won, taking home the top prize money of $12,000. Otherwise, he had plenty of time to reflect upon the recent past. All in all, it had been a good year. Despite several major aggravations—the tennis wars and the Connors suit, continuing criticism of his stance on South Africa, and inconsistency on the court—he had reason to be pleased. He had managed to sort out his personal life without becoming enmeshed in an emotionally draining and potentially loveless marriage; he had fulfilled his pledge to return to South Africa; and he had begun to earn the respect of his peers for his work as president of the ATP.

Admittedly, his performance on the court had not been what he had hoped for. During the past twelve months, despite fighting his way into nine finals and emerging with three championship trophies, he had seen his U.S. ranking slip from third to fifth, and his world ranking from ninth to tenth. He couldn't seem to beat Laver or Connors, and his volley and forehand were maddeningly inconsistent. Yet he took considerable satisfaction in being the third oldest player in the world top ten, just behind Laver and Rosewall. At age thirty-one, he was no longer a kid, despite his youthful looks and trim build. But he didn't feel old—or even marginally over-the-hill. Although he was growing accustomed to being edged out by younger players, he was still competitive at the highest levels of tennis.

Ashe was deeply introspective about aging and stages of life, and he always seemed to be assessing where he was in the scheme of things—where he had been, where he was going, and what he should expect out of himself. Keeping the year-long diary had encouraged this, and when Houghton Mifflin settled on *Portrait in Motion* as a subtitle, he must have laughed. When had he stopped long enough for a portrait? Perpetual motion was more like it. But that's the way he preferred to live. Who knew how long anyone would be around, so it was wise to live every day to the fullest. He intended to be around for a long time, but with his mother's early death in the back of his mind, he wasn't taking any chances.

Intellectually, he knew he was probably past his prime as a tennis player. But emotionally he couldn't relinquish the dream of winning at least one more Grand Slam title, of beating the world's best when it counted the most. Perhaps he could even win at Wimbledon, though the only man past the age of thirty to have done so in the last twenty years was Laver in 1969. And even Laver hadn't been able to repeat the feat. Like the Rocket, Ashe had not given up on becoming number one. Amidst all of his administrative burdens, social concerns, and hopes for a better world, he still yearned to be the champion of champions. Simultaneously reaching for the stars and searching for the inner strength that would both set him apart and sustain him was what Dr. J had taught him to do two decades earlier. And he had learned the lesson well. As 1974 drew to a close, the boy turned man who had traveled so far from Jackson Ward was more determined than ever to prove to himself and the world that he could go a good bit further.[37]

Ashe believed in the power of positive thinking. Yet he knew he could not simply will himself to the top of the tennis world. As a seasoned veteran, he knew that getting to the top would require something new and different, perhaps even a fundamental change in his approach to the game. Merely changing the arc of his backhand or deciding to charge the net more often would not be enough. After contemplating his situation following his return from South Africa, he became convinced he had two basic options. The first—and perhaps the most direct—means of improving his game was to concentrate on tennis while downsizing his numerous off-court interests and commitments. The second was to try to upgrade his stamina and athleticism.

Theoretically, he could forget about the moral imperative of responsible citizenship, jettison his social, political, and business interests, resign as president of the ATP, and spend just about every waking moment thinking about or playing tennis. In other words, he could follow the lead of the dazzling young Swede Bjorn Borg, who had mastered the systematic, corporate approach to competitive tennis. "Borg has a coach, Lennart Bergelin, and a manager, Bob Kain, from the International Management Group," Ashe observed, with more than a touch of envy, "and all he has to worry about is hitting the tennis ball."[38]

Ashe realized, of course, that he could never equal Borg's single-mindedness. As he later confessed, "I knew that I would go nuts if I only played tennis." So for him the second option was much more realistic. The idea of adopting a rigorous and scientific physical fitness regime was both appealing and practical. Athletes in other sports, especially track and field, had benefited from performance-enhancing fitness programs, and Ashe didn't see any reason why tennis players shouldn't follow suit. He had always taken good care of himself, but with the exception of the winter of 1967–68 when he had maintained a daily weight-training program at West Point, he had never been compulsive about fitness. Since 1968 proved to be his breakthrough year, he reasoned that a regimen of vigorous workouts might do the trick once again.[39]

Ashe did not expect miracles. Unlike many leading African American sports figures, he had never been blessed or burdened with the label "natural athlete." With his slight build, he did not have the commanding physical presence or bearing of his counterparts in other sports, where belief in the natural superiority of black athletes had gained considerable currency. By the mid-1970s, there was more than enough talent, from O. J. Simpson to

Kareem Abdul-Jabbar to Muhammad Ali, to sustain a virtual cult of black athleticism.

Primed as much by romantic racialism as by actual statistical dominance, popular explanations of black athletic achievement often relied on stereotypic images and pseudoscientific assertions and rarely included factors related to intellect or disciplined training. Thus, when Bill Russell became the NBA's first black coach in 1966, or when Frank Robinson became Major League Baseball's first black manager nine years later, or when Ashe became president of the ATP in 1974, they clearly were operating outside the expected parameters of African American life. In later years, Ashe would write about all of this with a spirit of passionate indignation. But in early 1975, as he carefully plotted a strategy for elevating his career, he was more concerned with overcoming the vagaries of his own mind and body.[40]

To this end, he turned to a friend who had been urging him to pay more attention to physical training, balance, and body positioning. In early 1974, during a tournament in Japan, he had the good fortune to meet Henry Hines, a world-class long jumper and two-time NCAA champion who enjoyed a considerable reputation as an expert on footwork and agility. "Tennis players have never been great athletes," Hines observed. "The top players in the past have been the ones with the best strokes, not the athletic talent." Even Ashe, who was widely thought to be an athletic player, struck Hines as an underachiever: "There were a lot of balls that Arthur was just out of position to hit. He'd be up on one leg with his weight distribution totally off, and it made it difficult to hit the ball." Hines envisioned a new style of tennis, more athletic and more powerful. "The level of the game is going to rise," he predicted. "The athletes are taking over. Can you imagine if a guy like Dr. J [Julius Erving] had played tennis instead of basketball? That's what's coming: guys who can fly and get to every ball on the court, no matter where it is, and nail it."

Ashe was intrigued by Hines's critique, and the two men soon planned a collaboration that took them to Puerto Rico during the winter of 1975. Prior to participating in the CBS Classic tournament, Ashe, Pasarell, and several others flew down early for a week of agility drills and serious exercise. As Hines put them through their paces, Ashe became convinced the track star was right, that tennis players had a lot to learn about movement and proper physical conditioning. Unfortunately, he was so eager to meet Hines's expectations that he overdid it, straining his left heel. While he remained in the tournament, he lost to Laver in the title match, 6–3, 7–5.[41]

Over the next month, the heel continued to hamper Ashe's performance on the court. In late January, at the U.S. Indoor Championships in Philadelphia, he lost in the quarterfinals to the Chilean Jaime Fillol. A week later in Richmond, the heel seemed to be improving and he was a little steadier on his feet. But he faded in the final, losing to Borg 4–6, 6–4, 6–4.[42]

This was hardly the way Ashe had envisioned his ascent to the heights of greatness. During the previous two years he had reached nineteen finals, but he had lost fourteen of them, leading several sportswriters to dub him the tour's "perennial bridesmaid." And now he was at it again, playing well but losing the big matches. He could blame the Puerto Rico and Richmond losses on his sore heel, but in truth he wasn't sure that the injury was his biggest problem. He knew he had to learn to bear down when the going got tough, to keep his focus on winning rather than simply competing, and to pace himself during long matches against younger opponents. The failure to close and the tendency to wear down in the late going were both in evidence against Borg, who had worn out opponents much younger than Ashe. But at thirty-one he was not ready to admit that age had caught up with him. He simply had to redouble his efforts, he told himself: train harder, keep fighting, and above all, win—which he began to do in March.

The first sign that Ashe's season was turning around came in Rotterdam, where he wrested a Grand Prix Masters title from Tom Okker. Ashe almost always had Okker's number, having won 15 of their 23 previous meetings. But this time the mastery was different. Ashe was in complete control from start to finish, serving up 19 aces and hitting clear winners almost at will. And Okker's annhilation was only the beginning. During the next two months, he played inspired tennis, beating Borg in the final at Munich in mid-March and Okker again in Stockholm at the end of April.

Even at his best, Ashe did not win every match. Playing on the clay at Monte Carlo, he lost to Manolo Orantes. And he succumbed to both Newcombe and Laver at the Aetna World Cup in Hartford. In the doubles, he teamed up with Dick Stockton to beat Ken Rosewall and John Alexander. But in the end the Aussies won the annual team competition 4–3, defeating the Americans for the fifth time in six years. Following the final match, Ashe was philosophical in defeat. "We had a plan," he said with a shrug, "but it didn't work out too well. We think we know how to beat Rod, but it's not easy." When pressed for specifics, he added: "It's his left-handedness that gets me. It makes me reverse my thinking." Inevitably the questioning moved on to Connors's noticeable absence from the team. Would Ashe and Captain Ralston be open to Connors's participation on next year's squad?

"All Jimmy has to do is accept the invitation," Ashe insisted. "That goes for Davis Cup as well. We'd all welcome him to the team."[43]

Despite the loss to the Aussies and the Connors situation, Ashe was in an upbeat mood by the end of March. Not only was he playing well, but he was also making a great deal of money. With earnings of nearly $70,000 in three months, he was first on the WCT money list, far ahead of second-place Borg. During the same period, Connors made even more on the independent circuit, earning an additional $100,000 by beating Laver in the so-called Heavyweight Championship of Tennis challenge match in Las Vegas on February 2. But Ashe was not concerned about that. His own life was going about as well as he could hope for, both on and off the court. In early April he became the first player to qualify for the WCT Masters Championship playoffs in Dallas. He had qualified for the playoffs four times before but had never won. Perhaps, he began to think, this might be his year.[44]

During the second week of April, Ashe's attention shifted for a time to Africa. As a board member of the philanthropic Phelps Stokes Fund, he had long supported the African Student Aid Fund, underwritten by a celebrity tennis exhibition held in Queens. A primary sponsor of the event, he played an exhibition match against Kenny Lindner, a recent Harvard graduate and the 1974 Ivy League singles champion, and he later teamed up with Walter Cronkite to play a spirited set against actress Dina Merrill and Gene Scott. It was the kind of event Ashe enjoyed but one that also reminded him of what was really important in the broader scheme of life. The Student Aid Fund, he explained to reporters, was essential to the future of Africa and had already made a difference: "Kwame Nkrumah, the leader of Ghana, had a grant. So did Eduardo Mondlane of Frelimo, the Mozambique liberation movement. And there are dozens of diplomats and cabinet officers." The grants were small, never more than $1,000 per year, but the money raised by the tennis exhibition always went to deserving students who might otherwise be unable "to pay their way here."[45]

The day after the benefit in Queens, Ashe flew to Johannesburg to play in a WCT Green Group tournament (WCT's original A and B tours were now split into three touring groups, Red, Blue, and Green). There were several white South Africans in the draw, and Ashe played two of them, Derek Schroder and Rauty Krog, in succeeding rounds. He won both matches with ease and felt surprisingly comfortable at Ellis Park. He still couldn't find a decent hotel in Johannesburg that would accommodate a black man, so once again he stayed at the home of Brian Young. Playing in South Africa was becoming routine, and he now had a retinue of friends to welcome him back and cheer him on. His loss in the quarterfinals was disappointing, and he continued to ache for a singles title on South African soil. Yet, win or lose, he was glad to be back in a nation that had become an important part of his life. Asked why he was so eager to subject himself to the indignities of what he acknowledged was "a hell of a repressive place," he laughed and cleverly put the onus on white South Africans: "It's good for their education. They think blacks are stupid, that they can't make decisions. I shoot down their theories."[46]

Ashe knew, of course, that not all white South Africans were racist reactionaries. One prime example was his friend Frew McMillan, who alongside his partner, Bob Hewitt, had developed into one of the world's premiere doubles players. In late April, within days of his return from Johannesburg, Ashe found himself defending their right to play in the World Doubles Championship in Mexico. Despite being the defending champions, Hewitt and McMillan—along with McMillan's family—were taken into custody after their arrival in Mexico City. A month earlier President Luis Echeverría had removed Mexico's national team from Davis Cup competition after learning their next opponent would be South Africa, and he was now ready to expel Hewitt and McMillan as a further expression of his nation's opposition to apartheid. The government's official rationale was that the two men had entered the country illegally using tourist visas, as opposed to the required work visas; thus they lacked authorization "to play professionally" in Mexico. But nearly everyone on the scene knew what was really at issue.

McMillan was actually traveling on a British passport, and Hewitt, a native Aussie married to a South African woman, was carrying an Australian passport. These details didn't matter to Echeverría, who, along with the visiting President Julius Nyerere of Tanzania, issued a joint statement condemning the South African government and by implication the two tennis players as well. Ashe was appalled. "Nobody hates apartheid more than I do," he insisted, "but this is ridiculous." Eventually international tennis officials worked out a compromise of sorts that put Hewitt and McMillan in a special "runoff" tournament in Dallas, where they played the Mexico City doubles winners, Ross Case and Geoff Masters, who had eliminated Ashe and Okker in the semifinals. The mixture of tennis and politics, Ashe now realized, was becoming more volatile with every passing week.[47]

Late April also brought the release of the final point standings in the four-month-long WCT tour, and to no one's surprise Ashe headed the list of eighty-four players. Compiling the best singles record was a coveted honor marked by the awarding of a thirteen-pound solid-gold tennis ball worth

$33,333. Ashe, along with everyone else, was wide-eyed at the presentation ceremony as two women in gold dresses flanked by armed guards presented him with the gleaming ball. But he knew even a solid-gold tennis ball would feel hollow if he failed to follow up with a strong performance in the upcoming WCT Masters in Dallas.[48]

The WCT playoffs, though only five years old, had taken on the status of a major sporting event. The total prize money had risen to $100,000, with the winner taking home $50,000, more than twice the winner's share at Wimbledon. Ashe felt he had a reasonably good shot at the top prize, but it wasn't going to be easy. Although defending champion Newcombe was not part of the field of eight, Laver, Borg, and Raúl Ramírez—who had dashed the American Davis Cup team's hopes earlier in the year—were primed and ready to give him a run for his money. As the WCT point leader, Ashe received much of the press attention prior to the tournament, and there was also a considerable buzz about his recently released diary, *Arthur Ashe: Portrait in Motion*. Dubbed "the thinking man's tennis player" by Bud Collins in an enthusiastic *New York Times* review, he came in for a lot of good-natured ribbing in the Dallas locker room. The irony of this characterization was inescapable, considering that many observers believed thinking too much was Ashe's greatest limitation as a player. People were always telling him to be more instinctual, to just relax and hit the ball.[49]

Whatever the truth of the matter, Ashe's dazzling play in Dallas temporarily silenced even his toughest critics. In the first pairing, he had to overcome a 6–1 first-set loss to Mark Cox before serving his way to victory in the final three sets. And in a semifinal match against John Alexander he followed the same pattern, losing the first set and winning the next three. In the final pairing he faced Borg, who had survived a tough five-set semifinal match against Laver. Once again, as if by design, he lost the first set but closed out the match and the championship with three sets of brilliant tennis. In the final set, Borg failed to win a single game, losing the last three games at love.

The triumph in Dallas was Ashe's biggest win in five years, and his friends knew how much it meant to him. In characteristic fashion, he tried to downplay the significance of what had just happened. But Dell would have none of it. "Go ahead, Art," he yelled out during the post-match press conference, "come right out and say you're happy." Managing a wry smile, Ashe did admit that a "gypsy in Stockholm" had predicted his victory two weeks earlier. Mostly, he confessed, he was "relieved." After all, it had been a long time since his win at the 1970 Australian Open. When the reporters peppered him with questions about how he had handled the pressure to win the WCT crown, he couldn't resist offering a sense of perspective and putting in a plug for his beloved Davis Cup. The final against Borg had tested his composure, but he insisted: "there is nothing that approaches the pressure of playing for the Davis Cup, not even this." It was vintage Ashe—cool, collected, and rational.[50]

For him the significance of Dallas was not so much that he had won but how he had won. At the age of thirty-one, he had outlasted three younger opponents, including a nineteen-year-old. Part of the explanation, to be sure, was Borg's condition after playing an exhausting five-set match against Laver in the semifinals. And there was the international travel issue. "It was not surprising that Borg wilted," Leonard Koppett claimed in *The New York Times*. "Last Sunday he played a Davis Cup match for Sweden in Warsaw. He flew here Monday, competed and reached a rare emotional peak in the grueling Laver match, so he was pretty worn out mentally as well as physically by the time things turned against him today." Perhaps so, but Ashe had survived a tough semifinal match of his own and had not wilted in the final. While he did not want to claim too much in the wake of his victory over Borg, he later revealed his confidence "soared" after the match. "Winning WCT made me think about Wimbledon," he recalled. "Much of the decorum had gone out of tennis, and the respect for tradition that was promoted by Laver, Rosewall, Emerson, and the other Aussies was fading. But Wimbledon remained special."[51]

SEVENTEEN

WIMBLEDON 1975

W IMBLEDON WAS NEARLY SIX weeks away, and Ashe did not want to get ahead of himself. But in mid-May he began to prepare for what he hoped would be the tournament of his life. In years past, he had spent the late spring in Europe playing the often frustrating clay court circuit, which included the Italian and French Opens. This time he decided to play only in the Italian Open and forgo the French. Skipping Paris was a personal sacrifice, but it allowed him to spend more time on the grass courts of England. The previous year he had tuned up for Wimbledon at Nottingham, where he had said goodbye to Meryl. In 1975, he began his grass court preparation a week earlier at Beckenham, in County Kent.[1]

While Bjorn Borg and Guillermo Vilas were slugging their way into the finals at the French, Ashe was reacquainting himself with the speed and odd bounces of tennis played on turf. He played well, beating Sherwood Stewart in the quarterfinals and Andrew Pattison in the semis. In the final, he faced Roscoe Tanner, who loved playing on grass and who was hitting the ball harder than ever. But somehow Ashe managed to win the title match in straight sets. Both men soon moved on to Nottingham, where the last tournament before Wimbledon began on June 16–and where Connors, Vilas, and several other top contenders joined them.[2]

Connors's presence at Nottingham gave the warm-up tournament an added intensity. The reigning Wimbledon champion and the odds-on favorite to repeat at the age of twenty-two, he seemed almost invicible. Predictably, when the official Wimbledon seedings were announced on the 16th, he was seeded first; Rosewall was second, followed by Borg, Vilas, Nastase, and Ashe. Connors, like Ashe, had skipped the French Open, and he had by-passed the Italian as well, serving notice that all of his energy was directed at Wimbledon. Most observers expected him to breeze through the field at Nottingham. But the tournament took an unexpected turn when Tanner upset him in the quarterfinals. Ashe also failed to advance, losing to Tony Roche in straight sets. The Australian left-hander had been away from the tour for three months recovering from an Achilles tendon operation, but he played almost flawless tennis against Tanner in the semifinals, so Ashe didn't feel too bad about being upended. Connors also refused to panic and credited his loss to bad luck. After insisting he was striking the ball about as well as he ever had, he promised that at Wimbledon there would be no hitting the ball "just a tiny fraction out," as he had at Nottingham. "By Monday," he predicted, "the ball is going to be meeting the line." [3]

Ashe winced when he read Connors's statement in the newspaper. It was just the kind of arrogance that had made him a near pariah among his peers. Neither Ashe nor anyone else was surprised that Connors was the number one seed. But the air of condescension and sense of entitlement that enveloped his persona irked Ashe as few things ever had. To him, Connors's attitude was ultimately self-defeating in terms of the things that mattered most—personal honor and earned respect—and he couldn't imagine anything more destructive to the game of tennis and sportsmanship than Connors's win-at-any-cost approach to the sport. [4]

Or at least he thought he couldn't until the week before Wimbledon. On June 21, two days before the opening round, the world learned what Ashe had known for several days. Standing before a gaggle of reporters, Connors's manager, Bill Riordan, announced that his famous client had recently filed two libel suits in an Indianapolis court. The first sought $3 million in damages from Ashe for characterizing Connors as "brash, arrogant and unpatriotic" in a letter sent to the ATP membership. The second suit asked for $2 million more from Kramer, Dell, and ATP secretary Bob Briner, for sanctioning a disparaging magazine article written by Briner. The frivolous nature of the suits left many observers shaking their heads, but for Ashe the timing of the announcement was the worst of it. [5]

Ashe, like all serious tennis players, had dreamed of becoming a Wimbledon champion since he was a boy. Winning a title on Centre Court would be the experience of a lifetime, and he wanted it more than he cared to admit.

Arthur Ashe's mother, Mattie Cordell
Cunningham Ashe, c. 1946.

Arthur (right) and Johnnie Ashe
with Mrs. Olis Berry, their live-in
housekeeper and nanny, c. 1952.

Twelve-year-old Arthur Ashe
Jr. poses with his trophies in
front of his Sledd Street home,
Brook Field Park, Richmond,
Virginia,1955.

Lynchburg campers breach the color bar at Forest Hills; Ashe (right) and Hubert Eaton shake hands with John Botts (far left) and Herbert Gibson, their doubles opponents at the Eastern Junior Tennis Championships, July 18, 1959.

4

5

Ashe reminisces with his mentor, Dr. Robert W. Johnson Sr., c. 1966.

6

Ashe with Richard Hudlin, his tennis coach at Charles Sumner High School, St. Louis, Missouri, 1961.

Ashe, the first African American to play Davis Cup tennis for the United States, with his Davis Cup teammate Marty Riessen and Coach Pancho Gonzales, September 11, 1963.

Ashe serves to Orlando Bracamonte of Venezuela during a Davis Cup match, Cherry Hills Country Club, Denver, Colorado, September 15, 1963.

The UCLA Bruins, winners of the 1965 NCAA national tennis team championship. Left to right: Ian Crookenden, David Sanderlin, Coach J. D. Morgan, David Reed, and Ashe.

10

Ashe stretches to hit a forehand during his Davis Cup match against Antonio Palafox of Mexico, Dallas, Texas, August 2, 1965.

11

Ashe meets UCLA freshman and future Hall of Fame basketball star Lew Alcindor (later Kareem Abdul-Jabbar), September 1965.

12

Standing on the steps of Richmond's city hall, Mayor Morrill M. Crowe presents Arthur with a proclamation naming February 2, 1966, "Arthur Ashe Day" in Richmond.

Ashe, his doubles partner, Senator Robert F. Kennedy, and their opponents, Charlie Pasarell and Donald Dell, at an exhibition match in Washington, D.C., August 3, 1967.

Ashe instructs young players at an inner-city tennis clinic, Washington, D.C., July 23, 1968.

Ashe stands arm in arm with his father after winning the first U.S. Open men's singles title at Forest Hills, New York, September 9, 1968.

16

15

Charlie Pasarell and Ashe: Davis Cup teammates, best friends, and fishing buddies, Maroubra Beach, near Sydney, Australia, January 2, 1969.

1968 Davis Cup champions at a White House luncheon with President Richard Nixon, February 11, 1969. From left to right: Ashe, Clark Graebner, Dennis Ralston, Nixon, Captain Donald Dell, Bob Lutz, and Stan Smith.

Friends and rivals, c. 1969. From left to right: John Newcombe, Tom Okker, Ashe, and Rod Laver.

Ashe, clad in a West African dashiki, en route to the Tasmanian Tennis Championships in Hobart, Australia, January 1970. Later in the month, he won the men's singles title at the Australian Open in Sydney.

Ashe appears before the United Nations General Assembly's Special Committee on Apartheid to advocate the expulsion of South Africa from the International Lawn Tennis Federation and Davis Cup competition, April 14, 1970.

Ashe and Bob Lutz with World Championship Tennis (WCT) founder Lamar Hunt (center), after both players signed lucrative five-year contracts with WCT, September 9, 1970.

Ashe and Ilie Nastase pose with the U.S. Open men's singles trophy, September 10, 1972. Nastase defeated Ashe in the final.

Association of Tennis Professionals (ATP) leaders discuss a proposed boycott of the upcoming Wimbledon championships, June 18, 1973. From left to right: Cliff Richey, Ashe, Niki Pilic, Stan Smith, and Jack Kramer.

Ashe talks with young fans in the black township of Soweto, South Africa, November 23, 1973.

A moment of rest for Ashe and a ball boy at the WCT Masters Tournament, Dallas, Texas, May 11, 1975.

Ashe and Bjorn Borg poke fun at their celebrity status with dueling cameras, 1975.

Ashe and Jimmy Connors just prior to the men's singles final at Wimbledon, July 5, 1975.

Ashe stretches for a backhand volley during the third set of his Wimbledon match against Connors.

Ashe holds up the Wimbledon men's singles silver-gilt trophy as the crowd roars its approval.

Paired as Wimbledon singles champions, Ashe and Billie Jean King walk onto the dance floor at the Wimbledon Ball.

Black tennis pioneers Ashe and Althea Gibson, with ten-year-old tennis prospect Derek Irby, at the United Negro College Fund celebrity benefit tournament in New York, October 8, 1976.

Fiancés Arthur Ashe and Jeanne Moutoussamy, four days before their wedding, February 16, 1977.

Ashe and Jeanne on their wedding day, flanked by best man Johnnie Ashe and matron of honor Diane Elliston, with the Reverend Andrew Young officiating, United Nations Chapel, New York, February 20, 1977.

Ashe and his doubles partner, Senator Ted Kennedy, at the Robert F. Kennedy Benefit tournament, Forest Hills, New York, August 1974.

Ashe counsels an overheated John McEnroe during a Davis Cup tie against Czechoslovakia, New York, July 10, 1981.

Captain Arthur Ashe, flanked by his victorious team, holds the Davis Cup during the award ceremony in Grenoble, France, after the U.S. team repeated as champions by defeating the French, November 28, 1982. Left to right: Eliot Teltscher, Gene Mayer, Ashe, John McEnroe, and Peter Fleming.

Ashe during a mentoring session with several young African American tennis pros, c. 1982. From left to right: Ashe, Leslie Allen, Chip Hooper, Renee Blount, Lloyd Bourne, and Kim Sands.

Ashe and other celebrity activists announce the formation of Artists and Athletes Against Apartheid during a press conference at the United Nations building in New York, September 14, 1983. From left to right: Gregory Hines, Tony Randall, Ashe, Ruby Dee, Randall Robinson, Ossie Davis, and Harry Belafonte.

Ashe and presidential candidate Jesse Jackson at the opening of Jackson's state campaign headquarters in Brooklyn, New York, December 17, 1983.

Working as a broadcaster for ABC Sports, Ashe interviews Jimmy Arias at the 1984 Summer Olympics in Los Angeles, California.

Ashe is arrested during a protest in front of the South African embassy, Washington, D.C., January 12, 1985.

42

Ashe and Jeanne at the podium during the AIDS announcement press conference at the HBO building, April 8, 1992.

43

Jeanne, Ashe, and their daughter, five-year-old Camera, at the Arthur Ashe AIDS Tennis Challenge, USTA National Tennis Center, Flushing Meadows Corona Park, Flushing, New York, August 30, 1992.

Standing in front of the White House, Ashe and others protest the Bush administration's mistreatment of Haitian refugees, September 9, 1992. Ashe is flanked by Mary Frances Berry (left) of the United States Commission on Civil Rights and Sylvia Hill (right) of TransAfrica.

45

In one of his final public appearances, Ashe speaks on the AIDS crisis at a symposium sponsored by the World Health Organization, World AIDS Day, United Nations headquarters, New York, December 1, 1992.

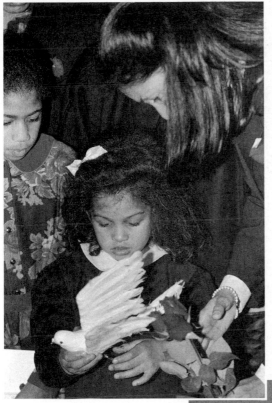

Jeanne looks down at six-year-old Camera as she examines a paper dove taken from the floral arrangement at the graveside service for her father, Woodland Cemetery, Richmond, Virginia, February 10, 1993.

Ashe Memorial on Monument Avenue, Richmond, Virginia, created by the Richmond sculptor Paul DiPasquale and dedicated on July 10, 1996.

Eric Fischl's controversial nude sculpture of Ashe, *Soul in Flight*, installed in the commemorative garden near the entrance to the USTA National Tennis Center, Flushing Meadows Corona Park, Flushing, New York, in August 2000.

Jeanne and Camera pose next to a poster of the newly dedicated Arthur Ashe postage stamp (issued in 2005) on Arthur Ashe Kids Day at the U.S. Open, August 28, 2004.

But now, even more than wanting to win himself, he wanted Connors to lose. He had no reason to believe he could stop him; in three meetings—twice in South Africa and once at the U.S. Pro Championships in 1973—Connors had thrashed him.

Ashe had every intention of breaking this pattern. But if he couldn't do it someone else had to step up. Who that might be was a puzzle, however. Laver and Rosewall were probably too old, Newcombe, described by one observer as "the one man whose power could worry Connors on the fast grass," was sidelined with an injury; Nastase was out of shape; Vilas was still unsteady on grass; and young Borg wasn't quite ready. Anything could happen on any given day, but the prospects for stopping Connors's march to a second title didn't look very promising as the Wimbledon fortnight began on June 23.[6]

The London bookies certainly didn't think there was much chance that anyone but Connors would hold up the coveted silver-gilt trophy at the close of the tournament. For the first time in Wimbledon history authorities had allowed a betting tent to be set up on the tournament grounds, and there was an almost frenzied anticipation of playing the odds at Centre Court. The betting scene was complicated by a recently imposed ban on players placing bets on the Wimbledon competition. At Nottingham, several players had made a killing after discovering the bookies had made mistakes in setting the odds, and Wimbledon officials did not want the world's most famous tournament to be sullied by a betting scandal. Ashe and the ATP board endorsed the ban, but there was some grumbling among ATP members, particularly those who had placed winning bets at Nottingham. Ashe, who liked to gamble from time to time, regarded the betting controversy as a minor matter. But it was still an annoying distraction on the eve of the tournament. He knew that to have any chance of making it into the late rounds, he would have to focus on tennis and nothing else.[7]

With a costly libel suit hanging over his head, that was not going to be easy. But a favorable draw helped him ease into the tournament. His opponent in the first round was Bob Hewitt, a strong doubles player but no match for the #6 seed in singles, especially on grass. Hewitt played well, taking a set, but Ashe's serve-and-volley game was too much for him the rest of the way. Ashe breezed through the next two rounds, beating Jun Kamiwazumi of Japan and Brian Gottfried in straight sets. Getting by Gottfried was a relief, since he had once crushed Ashe in a tournament in Las Vegas. Ashe anticipated a tough fourth-round match against Alexander, the tenth seed, but the Australian lost unexpectedly to the unseeded British veteran Graham Stilwell.[8]

Talented but inconsistent, Stilwell had grown up on grass courts and at one time or another had beaten many of the world's best players, including Ashe. This would be his last Wimbledon, and he put everything he had into the match against the favored American. After losing the first set 6–2, Stilwell rallied to win the second 7–5. With Ashe in unexpected trouble, the British fans surrounding Court 1 began to stir. But to their disappointment Ashe pulled himself together and won the last two sets easily.[9]

Having lost only two sets in the first four rounds, he was pleased with his performance so far. Confident and relaxed, he felt somewhat detached from the hoopla that always surrounded Wimbledon. At this point, the British press had hardly paid him any notice, as all eyes were on the defending champions, Connors and Evert. The speculation and the betting odds predicted a "love-bird double" for the young couple, and reporters and fans couldn't get enough of one of the most romantic stories in Wimbledon's long history. The story line took a strange twist during the second week, however, when the tabloids revealed the tennis romance was over. Between matches, Connors was out on the town, not with Evert, but with the beautiful British actress Susan George. "We're just good friends," George insisted, but tongues continued to wag as the tournament progressed.[10]

For serious fans, Connors's performance on the court was the real story. No man had run through the Wimbledon field without losing a set since Chuck McKinley in 1963. But Connors's dominance in the first four rounds put him on track to do just that. His matches against John Lloyd, Vijay Amritraj, Mark Cox, and Phil Dent turned out to be mismatches as he unleashed powerful groundstrokes from both sides. During the Lloyd match, Connors slipped on the grass and hyper-extended a knee, but even that didn't seem to slow him down. In the next round Amritraj forced him into one tiebreaker, but that was as close as anyone came to taking a set from him. The first man since Emerson in 1966 to make it through the first four rounds without losing a set, Connors was drawing raves even from old Wimbledon hands who thought they had seen it all.[11]

Connors's mastery continued in the quarterfinals against eighth-seeded Ramírez, whom he vanquished in three quick sets. Meanwhile, Ashe was engaged in a brutal quarterfinal match against Borg. Determined to avenge his loss in Dallas, Borg came out smoking, winning the first set 6–2, and cruising through the first three games of the second. Ashe's dream of winning Wimbledon, it appeared, was all but gone. But somehow he hung on.

After barely managing to hold serve in the fourth game, he won four of the next five games and evened the match with a backhand winner that caught Borg off balance. When Borg's missed volley gave the second set to Ashe 6–4, the fans settled back in their seats for what looked to be a long struggle. For a while, Borg steadied himself, and the advantage went back and forth in the third set until Ashe eked out a close 8–6 victory. After that Borg faded just as he had done in Dallas. Winning 6–1 in the final set, Ashe was on to the Wimbledon semifinals for the first time since 1969.[12]

The victory over Borg should have been a confidence builder, but after the match the Swedish star revealed he had strained a groin muscle during an early morning practice. "I continued to play because I thought that perhaps I was just a little stiff," he told reporters. "It got worse and I had problems moving up and down the court. . . . You have to get under the ball on grass, but I couldn't do it. There was no way I could bend my knees, there was so much pain." This was not what Ashe wanted to hear, but he knew Borg was telling the truth. During the match he had sensed the Swede wasn't quite right. For once the tennis gods had given him a break. He was in the semifinals, and he was not going to worry too much about how he got there. Mostly, of course, he didn't want to think about how easy it had been for Connors to get there.[13]

Ashe's unlikely opponent in the semifinals was Tony Roche, the colorful thirty-year-old from Wagga Wagga, Australia. Seeded sixteenth, Roche had entered the Wimbledon singles competition at the last minute after playing so well at Nottingham. Considered a threat in the doubles competition but largely unheralded as a grass court singles player, Roche went into his quarterfinal match against Okker as the clear underdog. Most of Roche's success in singles had come on clay, where he had won both the French and Italian national titles in 1966. But on occasion he could exhibit flashes of brilliance on any surface, as in 1968 when he made it all the way to the Wimbledon finals, where he lost to Laver. In the early going against Okker, the match held to form, with the Dutchman leading two sets to one. But Roche stormed back, taking the final two sets 6–4, 6–2.[14]

Clearly, Roche was dangerous, and Ashe did not take him lightly. He knew it would take his best tennis to win. And yet he couldn't avoid being somewhat philosophical about the situation. It had been six years since he had played on Centre Court, and he was thrilled to be back, win or lose. The stands were filled to capacity, as always, and the age-old Wimbledon traditions held sway. And, as several commentators pointed out, this year the atmosphere had an added touch of newness. Most obviously, there was the betting tent and all its attendant activity, the soap opera surrounding Connors and Evert, and the strange dominance of left-handers in the men's draw. For the first time in living memory, three of the four male semifinalists were southpaws. Only Ashe hit from the starboard side. And if the seeds held true to form in the semifinals—if Ashe made it through to play either Connors or Tanner—Wimbledon would have its first "all-American tennis final" since Jack Kramer had squared off against Tom Brown in 1947. This made Roche the last hope of the British Commonwealth and an even bigger sentimental favorite than might normally be expected.[15]

Ashe had plenty of supporters in the stands, but he wasn't accustomed to assuming the role of a heavy, even among a minority of fans. This, along with Roche's topspin forehand, unnerved him a bit, and he saw the first set slip away 7–5. He came back to win the next two sets, but lost the fourth in a tiebreaker. In the fifth set, his strong serve began to desert him when he needed it most, and Roche continued to volley well. But in the end Ashe prevailed 6–4. It had taken more than three hours to wear Roche down, but he had done it. After six long years of waiting, he would get his third and probably last chance to compete in a Wimbledon final. The only thing left to be determined, other than the championship itself, was the other finalist. Would it be his friend and doubles partner Tanner—or Connors, the only man in professional tennis who came close to being his sworn enemy? Shakespeare himself couldn't have devised a more dramatic choice.[16]

The Connors-Tanner match promised to be a hard-hitting affair, offering tennis fans a rare exhibition of unbridled power. Several of Tanner's serves had been clocked at more than 140 miles per hour, and Connors's fabled returns often came back just about as fast. So whatever the outcome, the first semifinal match would be power tennis from start to finish. Tired as he was, Ashe was not about to miss it. After a shower and a few words with the press, he settled into a chair to watch the slugfest on the BBC.

Ashe, like almost everyone else, expected Connors to win. He was not prepared for what he saw on the court that day. Tanner was at the top of his game, hitting big serves and volleying well. Yet it didn't seem to matter. Every time Tanner came close to gaining an advantage, Connors kicked his game up to a higher level. At several points, the sheer power of Connors's groundstrokes and returns drew gasps from the crowd, and with each game his dominance and swagger became more obvious. The whole thing was over in eighty minutes. Connors was the reigning king of Wimbledon, and he had served notice that anyone who hoped to take away the crown had better be ready to play the best tennis of his life.

The line score— 6 4, 6–1, 6–4—did not begin to capture the magnitude of Connors's victory, and after the match commentators and reporters strained to find the right superlative to describe what they had just seen. Statistics detailing past glories "pale into insignificance in comparison with Connors' performance today," Fred Tupper wrote in *The New York Times*. "Did anybody ever see a ball hit so hard? Possibly Ellsworth Vines did so in his great years of 1931 and 1932, when his service ripped the turf at Forest Hills. Nobody else." Never one to hide his accomplishments with false modesty, Connors himself offered a similar judgment, though he stressed the scrappiness, not the power, of his performance. "Today my form was my best ever," he told reporters. "Even better than last year. I was diving, jumping, sliding, slipping and getting balls I could get to."

Recalling the match years later, the tennis writer Richard Evans had difficulty coming up with superlatives to match Connors's remarkable performance. "Connors did things to a tennis ball in that match that made people wince," Evans wrote in 1990. "No matter how far he had to run, no matter how awkwardly the ball came to him, no matter how much off balance he was when he swung into his stroke, Connors belted ball after ball into Tanner's court with barely credible accuracy. The harder Tanner hit the ball, the better Connors liked it. He devoured power, swept it up inside him and then exhaled it like some dragon breathing fire. Poor Roscoe simply got scorched." [17]

Whatever the source of Connors's dominance, Ashe was impressed—and more than a little concerned. He had less than twenty-four hours to recover from his match with Roche and to figure out some way to counter Connors's all-around brilliance. He wanted to beat Connors in the worst way, especially after watching him strut around like the cock of the walk. But how any mortal was going to do it remained a mystery as he left the stadium for his hotel. The ride back to the Westbury gave him some time to think and reflect on the challenge ahead, but when he walked into the lobby he was still uncertain about how to neutralize Connors's combination of speed, agility, and power.

Even so, Connors's annihilation of Tanner had confirmed Ashe's suspicions and made one thing crystal clear: it would be foolish to try to overpower him. As Evans later put it, "Feed Connors pace and you are dead. He had tried it. He knew. But everyone else knew that Arthur's whole game was based on power. How many times had we seen him go down hitting, seemingly unable to change the magical pattern of that beautiful flowing game of his. It was magical when it worked, but anything that allowed so little margin for error was liable to come apart at the seams and Ashe's game had often done just that. The way Connors took the ball early and stepped into those howitzer drives of Ashe's spelt doom for the black American and there didn't seem to be anything Arthur could do about it. At least that was what everyone believed." Everyone, that is, but Ashe and a few of his friends—and surprisingly enough Bill Riordan. Unbeknownst to Ashe, Connors had aggravated a foot injury during the Tanner match, after which Riordan took the ailing star to Chelsea Hospital for an examination. The doctors at Chelsea recommended withdrawal from the tournament, counseling that his failure to do so might result in a career-ending injury. Unmoved, Connors brushed off their concerns and vowed to play on. Riordan, always looking for the main chance, also played on—leaving Connors at their hotel while he visited his bookmaker to place a large bet on Ashe.

Later in the evening, Arthur gathered a group together to discuss strategy. More than friends, they represented some of the best minds in tennis: Dell, Riessen, Pasarell, Erik Van Dillen, and Freddie McNair. These were men who knew his game almost as well as he did, and who probably wanted Connors to lose as much as he did. While he didn't expect any of them to come up with a perfect plan, he hoped for some sage advice as well as moral support. It made him feel better just to have his trusted friends close at hand. Although Connors might win, as a lone wolf he would probably never enjoy the kind of camaraderie and mutual respect that Arthur's circle of advisors provided.[18]

Fortunately, Arthur found more than consolation that evening. As his friends peppered him with suggestions, a clear course of action began to take shape. McNair started it off with the admonition: 'You've got to play through his strengths to his weaknesses." When Arthur responded, "That's easy enough to say," Dell jumped in: "You can do it if you put your mind to it. But it involves changing your style of play." Predictably, Arthur's first thought was that the night before the Wimbledon final was hardly the time to reinvent oneself. But he was willing to listen and learn. As he recalled the scene, "We broke down Jimmy's game, shot by shot. His major weakness was the low forehand approach shot. Also he liked pace, and he loved opening up the court hitting cross-court. If you tried to open up the court, he would try to open it wider. I had to go wide on both sides with my serves and keep as many balls as possible down the middle. Keep the ball low. And pray." Several hours earlier Ralston had called to offer the same advice. Always the coach, he boiled it all down to a single maxim: "Chip the ball. Don't hit over.

Chip it. You want to make him hit up all the time. . . . Don't hit the ball hard. No pace. No pace."[19]

By the time the gathering broke up a few minutes before nine, Ashe had a definite plan in mind, one that involved hitting shots seldom seen on the grass courts at Wimbledon. "I could hit a slice forehand," he later explained. "But sliced forehands were a shot that players used in the 1920s; we saw it more at the club level, on clay courts, than on the tour. But I knew I could use the sliced forehand if I had to. I also had a backhand slice, and I made up my mind that slices were going to be my bread-and-butter shots. . . . When he served, I would chip the ball down the middle and short because the grass was worn down the middle, the ball wasn't going to bounce very high. . . . If he came to the net, I would lob to his backhand side."[20]

It was all very exciting to think about, but no strategy would mean much if he were too tired to play at full tilt. By all rights, he should have retired for the night after the strategy session ended. But he didn't. His friends were going to the Playboy Club for a late dinner and a bit of blackjack, and he went, too. When he finally went to bed around one in the morning, he felt a few pangs of guilt. But he doubted that anything he did prior to the match would matter very much.[21]

He arrived at Wimbledon around midday expecting to experience one of two extremes—either complete humiliation or the sweetest of triumphs. He suspected the former was much more likely, especially after walking past the betting tent. There on the big board were the current odds: Connors, 3 to 20 to repeat as champion, and 9 to 10 to win in straight sets. At least he now knew what the oddsmakers thought of his chances—not much. On the positive side, he expected most of the crowd to be with him. Perhaps the most adventuresome among them might even take a risk and bet on him. But no amount of support would mean very much if the chip-and-lob strategy let him down.[22]

Strangely enough, the long odds had a calming effect during the final minutes before the match. For once, Ashe decided he had nothing to lose, even by adopting what might appear to be a foolhardy strategy. He felt loose and supremely confident as he joined Connors for the traditional Centre Court walk-on. "I had the strangest feeling that I just could not lose," he insisted in a 1985 interview with *World Tennis* magazine.[23]

Taking the ceremonial bow before the Royal Box, the two finalists made quite a pair—Connors, short and compact with his mop of hair and freckled skin; Ashe, tall and lean with his Afro and chocolate brown skin. The sharp contrast extended even to their warm-up clothing, with Connors wearing a red, white, and green sweater designed by his friend the former Italian star

Sergio Tacchini, and Ashe wearing a dark blue Davis Cup pullover emblazoned with the letters "U.S.A." in red. Some observers later suggested Ashe was trying to needle Connors by wearing the Davis Cup apparel, and they were probably right. Ashe was in no position to overlook any potential advantage, and reminding Connors that he and Riordan were on the unpopular side of the Davis Cup controversy couldn't hurt.[24]

Riordan himself was sitting in the friends box along with professional tennis's most infamous stage mother—Gloria Connors—and Susan George, looking beautiful as ever but also appearing as the "other woman" who had edged Evert aside. Always a sentimental favorite at Wimbledon, Evert had lost in the semifinals to Billie Jean King, and now it was clear that she had lost Connors, too. Since most of the crowd had no idea that she and Connors actually had parted ways weeks earlier, seeing George as the girlfriend unfairly reinforced Connors's image as the bad boy on the court. Ashe, of course, didn't care about any of this. He was just glad to see that Dell and his other ATP friends were on hand, clustered in the stands as an unofficial rooting section.[25]

The match began on time at two o'clock under a gray sky, with Connors serving first. He held serve, as did Ashe in the second game. So far there were no surprises and no hint of what was about to happen. In the third game Ashe took Connors to add out and, after a furious rally, appeared to have broken serve when Connors hit the ball beyond the baseline. But to Ashe's astonishment the linesman called the ball good. Fortunately, the venerable umpire, George Armstrong, who knew the shot had floated long, soon announced, "The ball was out, game to Ashe." Connors grimaced and pointed an index finger to the sky, but the game was over. Now leading 2–1, Ashe went on a tear, winning the last four games of the first set and the first three of the second. The fourteen thousand fans at Centre Court, and the millions watching on television, could hardly believe what they were witnessing. The great Jimmy Connors, the prohibitive favorite, had lost the first set 6–1, and he was being bageled in the second.[26]

After a disappointed patron shouted "C'mon Connors" during the changeover between the third and fourth games, Connors yelled back, "I'm trying, for Christ's sake." He went on to hold serve in the fourth game, breaking Ashe's string. But after that he had no consistent answer to Ashe's off-pace returns and steady serve-and-volley game. Ashe handily won the last three games of the set. Having not lost a set in his first six matches at Wimbledon, the number one seed had now lost two in a row, winning only two games.[27]

Connors played much better in the third set, using every shot in his arsenal to fight his way back into the match. Ashe knew Connors was nothing if not a scrapper—and was certainly young and strong enough to wear down an older opponent. So this was no time to play cautiously or sit on a lead. Ashe made a valiant effort to close out the match in straight sets, but he couldn't do it. He was on serve at 5–6 and serving to even the set when Connors broke through to win the third. With the crowd murmuring and sensing a momentum shift, Ashe tried to compose himself. But it wasn't easy with Connors suddenly coming on like a thrashing bull. After Connors broke Ashe's serve in the second game and held in the third, the defending champion was up 3–0. Describing one winning exchange by Connors as "a rally for the gods" and commenting that the defending champion might be "an arrogant young man but what a tennis player," the BBC television commentator prepared his audience for a classic comeback.[28]

At that point, it looked like nothing short of a miracle could stop Connors from winning the set and squaring the match at two sets each. He had come back from the dead before, and now it seemed he was doing it again. And certainly no one could be surprised that Ashe—one week from his thirty-second birthday—was running out of gas. Besides, tennis fans were accustomed to seeing him finish second; always a bridesmaid but never a bride, as more than one sportswriter put it. After two hours of disbelief, there were smiles and knowing looks among the bookies at the betting tent and among Connors's loyal friends and supporters. Dell and the ATP crowd could hardly watch as Ashe walked out to hit his first serve in the crucial fourth game. Years later, Richard Evans recalled the palpable sense of impending doom as Ashe's triumph seemed on the verge of slipping away: "Now what price for Ashe's brave tactics? Would Arthur's nerve hold? Would he continue with the pre-match plan to slow-ball Connors into oblivion or would he find, as danger loomed, the wholly natural desire to resort to type and play his normal game too tempting? At change-overs, Ashe was still sitting motionless in his chair, eyes closed like some meditating Buddha, letting his whole mind sink into a state of complete relaxation for 30 seconds."

Once he was back on the court with his eyes wide open, Ashe showed no signs of panic—or of abandoning his chip-and-lob strategy. He won the first point and lost the second, before forcing Connors to hit the ball wide. At 30–15, Ashe served an ace wide to the left, and suddenly he had a chance to stop Connors's run. At game point, he missed his first serve but spun the second one in, hoping somehow Connors wouldn't crush it. Taking advantage of the short second serve, Connors stepped forward and hit a blistering forehand to Ashe's right. For a split second it looked like a sure winner, but Ashe managed to lunge and hit a low backhand volley beyond Connors's reach. The game score was now 3–1 in Connors's favor.

"We are really watching a tremendous battle here," the BBC announcer exclaimed at the beginning of game five, and both men soon proved him right. The advantage went back and forth, with Connors finally moving to game point with a strong first serve that Ashe barely touched. But Ashe fought back, winning one point on a great chip shot to Connors's left and another on a backhand volley. At break point, Ashe hit a spectacular fore-hand passing shot that had Connors flailing. Suddenly, the game score was 3–2, and the set was back on serve. Ashe held serve in the sixth and eighth games, and Connors did the same in the seventh, thanks to three backhand errors by Ashe.

In the ninth game, Connors served with new balls, and Ashe couldn't handle the tremendous kick on the first serve. On the second point, Connors again hit a powerful first serve, forcing Ashe into a desperate backhand lob return. Thinking the lob was out, Connors pulled his racket down at the last second, but the ball grazed the baseline. This "error in judgment," as the courtside commentators called it, drew a murmur from the crowd that seemed to unnerve Connors. He failed to win another point, giving the game and the lead to Ashe. As improbable as it seemed, one more game and the championship was his.[29]

In the tenth game, with Ashe serving for the match, Connors managed one cross-court winner. But otherwise Ashe was in command. On the final point, he served hard and wide to Connors's backhand, and the soft return barely made it to the net, where the new champion swatted it down. "He has done it. He really has done it," the BBC announcer cried out, momentarily abandoning his British reserve as a crescendo of applause filled the stadium. "What a terrific scene. That's a final we shall never forget."[30]

For Ashe, after nearly three hours of frenzy and a lifetime of anticipation, it was a moment of almost pure joy. "When I took the match point," he recalled, "all the years, all the effort, all the support I had received came to-gether. My first thought and only sad moment was that Dr. Johnson had not lived to see my greatest victory." In the past he had sometimes felt pangs of remorse after drubbing an opponent, but not this time. As soon as the final point was over, he turned to the section where Dell and his friends were sitting and raised a clenched fist. Some were surprised by this expression of emotion, and he later confessed this was "the only time in my career that I would feel such an urge." But as he told one reporter after the match, "That was for the friends who have stuck with me. It was for Donald Dell and Jack Kramer and Bob Briner, and the whole ATP board."[31]

Some observers, then and later, saw something different in Ashe's gesture. To their eyes, he had given a Black Power salute reminiscent of the clenched fists raised by Tommie Smith and John Carlos at the 1968 Olympics in Mexico City. Though much briefer than the Mexico City incident— Smith and Carlos kept their arms fully extended and their black gloves raised high throughout the playing of the American national anthem—Ashe's salute represented, in the words of tennis historian Sundiata Djata, "a black power symbol . . . an action that seemed 'momentous' for some whites who thought of Ashe as being quiet and shy." Ashe himself denied any political intent, dismissing any direct association with Black Power, but this did little to dispel the myth that his behavior was racially motivated. According to one account written in 2007, the 1975 Wimbledon champion had "displayed the second most famous clinched fist ever by a black athlete."[32]

Whatever it was, the gesture was over in a flash. Lowering his arm, Arthur walked slowly to the net for a quick handshake. He then took a seat to wait for the presentation of the trophies. During the ceremony that followed, he and Connors both did their best to avoid each other, and there was no pretense of affection. When asked about the apparent awkwardness a few minutes later in the interview room, Arthur made no attempt to sugarcoat the situation. "He didn't say anything, and I didn't say anything," he confessed. A barrage of other questions followed, but Arthur remained, as one reporter put it, "as outwardly cool as ever." When one questioner suggested this had to be the Wimbledon champion's greatest day in tennis, he shocked almost everyone by shaking his head from side to side. "No, winning the Davis Cup in '68 would be first," he replied. "And winning Forest Hills in '68 was second until this one."[33]

The candor continued. Responding to a reporter who wanted to know if the win over Connors had surprised him, Arthur stated matter-of-factly: "When I walked on the court, I thought I was going to win. I felt it was my destiny." When asked the obvious follow-up question—was he surprised by the ease with which he had dispatched Connors—Ashe paused, but after thinking about it for a moment, he threw caution and false modesty aside. "If you're a good player," he advised, "and you find yourself winning easily, you're not surprised." Later, when one reporter asked for an evaluation of Connors's performance, he did not hesitate to characterize his opponent's failings as partly psychological, noting that roughly two thirds of Connors's errors had fallen "into the middle of the net." "He hardly ever put the ball behind the baseline," Arthur explained. "That's a sign of choking."[34]

Understandably, this explanation did not sit well with Connors. "Any guy has to play out of his mind to beat me," he told the reporters a few minutes later, after learning of Ashe's comments. "I'm not going to lose the match. Got to beat me. And he beat me today." After a pause, he repeated the word "today" with emphasis, suggesting the outcome would be different the next time. "I don't choke, my friend," he added, glaring at the reporter who had quoted Ashe. "I've been playing too long to choke." Prompted by another reporter, he turned to the Davis Cup controversy and his feud with Ashe and the ATP. Reasserting he was his own man and that no one should expect him to go along with the crowd, he was feisty to the end. Asked if he planned to attend the Wimbledon Ball that evening, he quipped: "If I can have the first dance," an honor traditionally reserved for the men's and women's singles champions.[35]

Connors skipped the Wimbledon Ball, but Arthur arrived early and stayed late. Beaming for the cameras and accepting congratulations from a bevy of friends and admirers, he celebrated in style, on and off the dance floor. Following tradition, he danced the first dance with the women's champion, Billie Jean King. Though disappointed with his less than courageous stand on women's issues in the past, King couldn't have been happier for Arthur after his triumph over Connors. She wasn't alone. Congratulatory telegrams and letters poured in over the next few days, and Arthur, enjoying a rare week away from the court, spent several hours, including part of his thirty-second birthday, reading them.

One letter, written by Barbara Jordan—the eloquent, deep-voiced African American congresswoman from Texas—praised his "humility" as well as his performance on the court. But Arthur knew she was being too kind, that in fact he had not been especially humble in the flush of victory. Nor had he been especially gracious to Connors in the post-match interview, though he soon tried to make amends. In a July 7 interview, he insisted Connors was not only "the best tennis player in the world," but also "basically a nice guy." He also denied the Wimbledon final had been a "grudge match" and minimized Connors's role in the controversial libel suit. "I don't really think Connors is doing it, filing the suit," he told a group of reporters in Pittsburgh. "I think it's his manager, Bill Riordan. A 23-year-old kid doesn't go around suing people. If left to his own devices, I don't think he would be saying the things he's saying."[36]

Arthur had never had much respect for Riordan, whom he had known since the late 1950s, but he had more reason than ever to be contemptuous of the slick promoter's way of doing things. Two days earlier Riordan had tried to explain away Connors's loss with the claim that his client had suffered a serious injury during the first week of the tournament. "The doctor had a good look at Jimmy last night and said he was amazed he was able to walk, let alone play tennis," said Riordan. "Something about torn ligaments in his right shin area. Jimmy didn't want anybody to know because it might sound as if he were making excuses."[37]

Whatever his physical condition, Connors didn't think much of Riordan's post-Wimbledon commentary. Ashe had been trying for months to drive a wedge between Connors and his manager, in the hope of deescalating the tennis wars, and in the aftermath of Wimbledon the strategy began to succeed. In mid-July, at Connors's request, Riordan reluctantly dropped the libel suits against Ashe and the ATP directors. For the time being, Connors remained Riordan's client, and the suit against the Commercial Union Assurance Company was still pending. But there was a definite thaw in the icy relationship between Connors and the tennis establishment.[38]

The key element in what would later be called the tennis "détente," aside from Ashe's efforts, was a changing of the guard on the U.S. Davis Cup team. Although Ashe, Dell, and others urged the American Davis Cup committee to give Dennis Ralston another chance as captain, three straight years of losses (1973–75) were too much disappointment to ignore. On July 31, Tony Trabert replaced Ralston as the U.S. Davis Cup captain, triggering widespread speculation that Connors would soon join the team. He had sworn he would never play for Ralston, who was closely associated with the ATP, but Trabert, the 1955 Wimbledon champion, was thought to be more independent. "I plan to talk to Jimmy personally," Trabert announced, "and tell him what I have in mind to clear the air. I think we can work things out. . . . I hope he plays. It would be sad if he didn't, sad for the team, sad for the country, and sad for Jimmy himself."[39]

On a personal level, Ashe was sorry to see Ralston go, but he was pleased that Trabert's appointment opened up new possibilities for compromise with Connors. Riordan, by contrast, called Trabert's appointment "an American tragedy," predicting that the new captain, who had publicly criticized Connors earlier in the year, would be no more acceptable than Ralston had been. As it turned out, Ashe was right and Riordan was wrong. When Trabert named the 1976 U.S. Davis Cup team on September 6, Connors was on it. Asked about Riordan's earlier prediction, Connors displayed the kind of independence that Ashe had been hoping for. "I guess Bill thought it was best to say that," he told the press, "but I like to speak for myself."[40]

Connors had reason to be in a good mood. Two weeks earlier he had accepted a lucrative out-of-court settlement from Commercial Union, ending
the WTT lawsuit. And Trabert had acceded to his demands related to his
participation in the Davis Cup competition. Connors had sought assurance
he would "play no matter what the situation or surface," and Trabert had
agreed: "I told Jimmy that I want to use the best team I can from start to finish and win the Cup. I told him he's the only player we have who deserves to
play in every match on every surface." This blanket promise did not sit well
with the rest of the team, including Arthur, who was left off the squad scheduled to play Venezuela in the opening round of the North American Zone
in mid-October. But he came around to the view that it was a small price to
pay if Connors's participation did indeed make a difference. The important
thing was not who played where or when, but rather to bring the Cup back
to the United States.[41]

EIGHTEEN

KING ARTHUR

—

THE CONTROVERSIAL AGREEMENT BETWEEN Trabert and Connors did not amount to much in the end. By the time the U.S Davis Cup team took the court against Venezuela in October, the tennis world was no longer held hostage by Connors's ego. Nor was it dominated by the specter of an unmatchable talent. Connors was still the most feared player in the game, and he would remain so until John McEnroe's meteoric rise in 1979. But he was clearly beatable, as Ashe had proven at Wimbledon, and as Manolo Orantes would demonstrate in the finals of the 1975 U.S. Open in September.[1]

As both Connors and Ashe discovered, it was a new day at the U.S. Open. The 1975 tournament was the first U.S. national championship at Forest Hills to include night play, and the first to use the 12-point, win-by-two tiebreaker, as opposed to the dreaded, sudden-death nine-point version. Most jarringly, earlier in the summer the newly named USTA (the L for Lawn had finally been dropped) had removed the traditional grass from Forest Hills and replaced it with a claylike surface called Har-Tru, confounding grass and hard court specialists like Ashe. A year earlier, when officials had introduced the idea of a new surface at Forest Hills, Ashe had opposed the soft-court option, predicting a "catastrophe" for serve-and-volley specialists. He proposed putting down a "medium-fast" surface instead and warned, "No American will win his own country's championship if we don't." Ignoring the warning, USTA officials installed the Har-Tru courts anyway.[2]

Ashe didn't expect to fare very well on the new surface, and he didn't, losing to Eddie Dibbs in the fourth round—in straight sets in ninety-eight minutes. On the same day, Laver, another aging serve-and-volley star, lost almost as convincingly to Borg. Connors, thought to be nearly invincible on all surfaces, played well enough to make the final. But Orantes, a twenty-six-year-old Spaniard who had grown up on clay courts, tore Connors up in three quick sets. One observer, amid cries of "Olé! Olé! Olé!" and "Viva Orantes," likened Connors to a hapless bull being taunted by a matador, while another quipped: If Orantes wins, "do you think they'll give him one of Jimmy's ears?"[3]

Ashe was not amused and even felt a little sorry for his fellow American. He was convinced that more than an unfriendly surface had brought Connors down. Writing in 1981, he viewed the 1975 Wimbledon upset as a pivotal moment, not only in Connors's career, but also in the broader scheme of top-level competitive tennis. "Looking back," he concluded, "I believe my victory over Connors that day was the most significant singles match of the seventies. I fully believe that if Connors had beaten me, he would have also won the U.S. Open that fall . . . and that Bjorn Borg would not have won five straight Wimbledons. If Jimmy had won our match, he might have found a way to beat Borg, and Borg's ascendancy would have been delayed, or maybe it wouldn't have happened at all. If the time isn't right, many balloons get burst in sports."[4]

As smart as he was, Ashe was not a trained historian. So it is hardly surprising his analysis reflected a certain amount of reductionist oversimplification. Yet, in an important sense, his assessment of Wimbledon 1975 was correct. His victory over Connors was not just another athletic accomplishment to be stored away in the record books and the memories of serious tennis fans. It was also, as Richard Evans wrote in 1990, "a triumph that spread happiness and satisfaction throughout the sporting world because it turned a good man and fine sportsman into a great champion."

In a retrospective essay written in 1985, *World Tennis* magazine columnist Steve Flink offered a similar judgment: "Not only was Ashe's triumph the most astonishing verdict in modern times at Wimbledon, but his glorious . . . performance was met with universal acclaim by a sporting public that had long appreciated his elegance of style on and off the court. I've been involved in tennis in different capacities for 20 years and can think of no event that has brought such joy into so many lives." Ashe's personal experiences confirmed Flink's assessment. "I might be standing in an elevator or walking down a street, and somebody comes up to me and says something about it," he reported. "Among whites, they say it was one of their most memorable moments in sports. Among blacks, I've had quite a few say it was up there with Joe Louis in his prime and Jackie Robinson breaking in with the Dodgers in 1947."

On a more functional level, Ashe's Wimbledon victory came at a time when the trajectory of his career was in doubt. Whether the upset at Wimbledon changed Borg's, or even Connors's, life in any fundamental way is debatable. But there can be no doubt that it changed Ashe's life almost beyond recognition.[5]

Most obviously, the public—and even many of his colleagues on the tour—treated him differently after the Wimbledon victory. Suddenly he seemed to be an object of public and private fascination. He had always stood out physically—and to some extent culturally—from the majority of touring tennis professionals. And he had long been accustomed to being in the public eye. But now he was no longer just a star athlete. In the wake of Wimbledon he was a bona fide celebrity, with a face and story line worthy of magazine covers. Now even nonsports journalists wanted to interview him, to inquire about what he was thinking and doing both inside and outside the lines. Suddenly he couldn't go anywhere without being noticed or asked for an autograph or a snapshot with a fan. Two days after his Wimbledon victory, he appeared at a shopping center in Pittsburgh as a representative of Catalina sportswear. Expecting a modest turnout, he was genuinely shocked when "fifteen hundred fans mobbed the store." Later in the week, he encountered similar scenes in Cleveland and in St. Petersburg and Tampa. "All these trips were planned long before I won Wimbledon," Ashe told a *St. Petersburg Times* reporter, "but the interest in me has suddenly mushroomed."[6]

Ashe and Catalina made a lot of money that week, and as the summer progressed he began to realize fame at the highest level involved considerable material benefits. He had anticipated enhanced respect after joining the "very exclusive club" of Wimbledon champions. But it took him a while to grasp the monetary implications of his new status. "Like many other athletes," he later explained, "I had clauses in my contracts that provided for extra compensation if I reached the semifinals or finals of important events, including Wimbledon. My exhibition fees almost doubled, which meant I could make the same money in half the time."[7]

Ashe never complained about making too much money. But he could not help but notice the disjunction between his new wealth and status and

his performance as an athlete. He found his post-Wimbledon life more than
a little puzzling, because on the court he was essentially the same man who
had entered the 1975 draw as the #6 seed. While he was clearly one of the
world's best players, he had not separated himself from the field or even
achieved a number one ranking. He still thought of himself as essentially
a challenger—a confident and talented player, but certainly something less
than a dominating champion. There was pride in the Wimbledon triumph,
but no swagger. He still embraced a realistic and measured sense of his
strengths and weaknesses; he was capable of brilliant shotmaking, but, as he
knew all too well, he remained erratic and susceptible to lapses in concentration. And he continued to depend on a unique style of play that combined
physical ferocity and psychological control. He still hit the ball hard whenever possible, and he was as polite and gentlemanly as ever.[8]

He also continued to come up with roughly the same results. Despite his
lingering heel problem, he had played well during the six months prior to
Wimbledon, and he did the same afterward. He spent the rest of 1975 playing and often winning on the Commercial Union Grand Prix, a lucrative
forty-two-tournament circuit that had begun in May. Offering $4 million in
total prize money, the 1975 Grand Prix stretched across nineteen different
countries, ending in December with the Grand Prix Masters round-robin
championship in Stockholm. The top eight players qualified for the Masters
tournament, and by the end of September, when Ashe defeated Guillermo
Vilas at a tournament final in San Francisco, he was second in the total
point standings. The $16,000 in prize money raised his 1975 on-court earn-
ings to $256,850, one of the highest figures in tennis history. And he was not
done yet.[9]

Scheduled to play in five more tournaments before the end of the year,
he now had the $300,000 milestone in his sights. But it wasn't going to be
easy. The 1975 Grand Prix was one of the most grueling and tightly packed
tours in the annals of tennis, and Ashe and his rivals were growing weary
by the time they arrived in Paris in late October. Week after week, the competition was as rigorous as the travel schedule, even though only half of the
best players were present at any one tournament. While Ashe was playing in
Paris, for example, Rosewall and Newcombe were playing halfway across the
world in Manila.[10]

In Paris, Ashe expected Ilie Nastase to be his toughest competition. In
the semifinals, he tried to outlast the Romanian baseliner in a contest of
"long rallies from the backcourt" but soon found himself two sets down.

Switching to a serve-and-volley strategy in the third set, he turned the tide and pulled off one of the greatest comebacks of his career, winning the last three sets 6–3, 6–3, 6–4. By the end of the nearly three-hour match, both men were exhausted, and it showed the next day when Ashe faced Tom Okker in the final. After winning two of the first three sets, he faded noticeably and lost in five.[11]

A week later, at the Swedish Open, he once again played well but lost to Adriano Panatta of Italy in the quarterfinals. From Stockholm, he traveled to Edinburgh and then on to London, where he lost to Eddie Dibbs in the semifinals. A late addition to the schedule and sandwiched between Stockholm and Johannesburg, the London tournament led to frayed nerves and a general unraveling of the tour's traditional decorum. Nastase, after losing his passport in a Stockholm nightclub, arrived in Edinburgh twenty-four hours late, and Tanner, who arrived after midnight and suffered a forty-one-minute straight-set loss to Buster Mottram later the same morning, labeled the tight scheduling "ridiculous," accusing the sponsors of "clearly breaking the rules by scheduling play on weekends at both the beginning and end of tournaments." Surprised by his easy win, Mottram happily went on to the next round, where he questioned so many line calls during his victory over Ray Moore that the two men almost came to blows in the locker room after the match. "If you behave like that against me again," the normally mellow South African told Mottram, "I'll stick my steel racquet down your throat."[12]

In Johannesburg, there was no sign of such ragged nerves, only the normal strains and stresses of the apartheid-afflicted nation. After coming up short in his first two efforts at the South African Open, Ashe was more determined than ever to win a major singles title in the troubled land that had tested his civility. With the defending champion Connors bypassing the tournament, Ashe was the top seed. Yet after a few minutes of erratic play in a third-round match against the unseeded South African Pat Cramer, he was out, eliminated in three sets. Paired with Brian Gottfried, he fared better in the doubles, making it to the semifinals before losing to Charlie Pasarell and the West German Karl Meiler.[13]

After coming up empty in South Africa, a weary Ashe took the long flight back to Europe for the Commercial Union Grand Prix Masters round-robin playoffs. By the time he arrived in Stockholm, he was noticeably out of sorts and uncharacteristically negative during a pre-tournament press interview. Acknowledging he was dead tired, he confessed he was simply "not interested in playing tennis now." In the future, he would cut down his schedule to more manageable proportions. He saw his upcoming opening round match against Nastase as a "damn near impossible task," a statement more prophetic than he knew.[14]

Playing against Nastase was always a trial. But in Stockholm the Romanian's antics actually began in the hotel bar the night before the match. Already holding forth for a group of journalists, Nastase started in on Ashe as soon as he entered the bar. "Ah, Negroni," he exclaimed, "how you feeling? Good, I hope. Tomorrow night you will need to feel good." Having heard this kind of needling before, Ashe simply smiled and sat down on the bar stool next to Nastase. But the Romanian couldn't leave it at that. "Such a good serve you have, Negroni . . ." he continued. "But it does not matter because I beat you anyway. Tomorrow I do things to you that will make you turn white. Then you will be a white Negroni." As the bar filled with nervous laughter, all eyes turned to Ashe, who calmly slid his drink toward Nastase, telling the bartender, "That'll be on Mr. Nastase's check." As Richard Evans described the scene, Ashe then "slipped gently off his stool; tapped Ilie on the shoulder by way of recognition and, with a satisfied grin on his face, walked out. It was the kind of exit only Arthur Ashe could have pulled off with quite so much dignity and timing."[15]

Unfortunately, Ashe's smooth exit simply set the stage for a major confrontation the following evening. "Twenty-four hours later the contrast was total," Evans recalled. "From the serene, understated, imperturbable human being I had always known, Ashe had been reduced to a screaming, nerve-ruined wreck. I have never seen him like it before or since. And the cause of it was, of course, Nastase." Once he was on the court, it was clear Ashe was in no mood to put up with the Romanian's clownish antics. Periodically throughout the match, Nastase received warnings from the referee Horst Klosterkemper, but he blithely ignored the West German and continued to hold up play by bantering with the crowd.

With the match even at one set apiece, Ashe began to pull ahead in the third and was leading 4–1 in games and 40–15 in the sixth game when Nastase started in again with his crude comments and stalling tactics, delaying his serve by more than two minutes at one point. Ashe had finally had enough, and after looking at the referee and waiting for a few seconds for Nastase to be disqualified, he took matters into his own hands and shouted out: "I claim a default. I'm leaving." The normally unflappable American star then zipped up his racket bag and disappeared into the locker room.

This was the first time in Ashe's long career he had done anything like this, and the crowd was stunned. So was the referee, who issued an immediate disqualification. A few minutes later, Klosterkemper explained to reporters that Ashe's impulsive departure had actually preempted Nastase's ouster. "I had made up my mind to disqualify him," he insisted. "But I had no chance because Arthur Ashe left the court."

In the locker room, Ashe continued to vent his anger. "I'm not taking any more of that crap," he screamed at one point. "There's no goddamn way you're getting me back on that court. He's broken the rules, goddamn it. I helped write them. I ought to know." After ripping off his sweat-drenched shirt and flinging it toward his locker, he vowed: "That son of a bitch isn't going to get away with it anymore. I'll damn well see him run out of the game before he tries that stunt again." Ashe's emotional outburst shocked everyone in the room, including Nastase, who was hiding behind a row of clothes and towels before "sheepishly" venturing out to issue an apology. Stonily silent by this point, Ashe simply ignored Nastase's gesture.[16]

Following the match, Klosterkemper announced that both players had been disqualified but both would be allowed to continue in the round-robin competition. Under this ruling, both men still had a shot at the $40,000 first-place prize money, but this solution did not sit well with Ashe. Vowing to file a formal protest against the double disqualification, he declared, "I know the rules were broken; it's as simple as that." While he conceded walking off the court was a mistake—that he had allowed himself to get "mad for the first time in 10 years"—he insisted enough is enough: "I've felt like walking off the court against Nastase many times before but never did . . . but I won't take that from him anymore."

To his surprise, an ad hoc committee headed by ILTF president Derek Hardwick upheld the protest the next day. After Ashe was awarded the first-round victory, Nastase complained: "If you're not an American in this game, you don't count." With the dual disqualification overturned, the "travesty," as Arthur called it, was over, and his quests to secure the year's number one world ranking and to set the all-time record in earnings remained intact. All he had to do was defeat several of the world's best players at a time when he was almost too tired to care.[17]

This feat, as it turned out, was too much for Ashe to manage. After playing well in the early rounds, he came up short against Borg in the semifinals, losing three sets to one. Playing one of his worst matches of the year, he double-faulted seven times and, as one observer commented, "was consistent only in hitting the ball into the net." It was a disappointing end to a great year, even though the $10,000 check for making it to the semifinals raised his 1975 earnings to $315,550, the highest in tennis history to date.[18]

Despite the earnings record, this was not the way Ashe had hoped to close out his most successful year. But he won a major victory off the court on December 8 when the Men's International Professional Tennis Council (MIPTC)—a tripartite committee representing the ILTF, the ATP, and tournament directors across the world—voted to implement Open tennis's first formal code of conduct. Ashe himself was a member of the MIPTC, and for several months he had been calling for such a code, largely in response to Nastase's increasingly outrageous behavior. During the past year, the Romanian star had incurred more than $8,000 in fines, including a hefty assessment for mocking the social pretensions of British tennis. When he and Connors added bow ties to their tennis outfits and drank champagne between games during a London tournament, British officials were not amused. The new Code of Conduct did not expressly prohibit the courtside consumption of alcohol, but there were strict standards and fines for just about every other possible offense, starting with "$50 for "throwing a racquet or hitting or kicking a ball out of the court in anger." [19]

The largest fine, $10,000, was reserved for the general category of "conduct detrimental to the game." No one, including Ashe, was altogether confident that the Code—often referred to as the Nastase Code—would bring decorum back to the game. Yet he and many others thought it was worth a try. One critic, Ed Meyer, a New York lawyer who had recently represented Connors, Riordan, the Women's Tennis Association (WTA), and WTT in court, insisted what tennis really needed was a "czar" in the mode of the National Football League's powerful commissioner Pete Rozelle. But few people shared his belief that a single person could bring order to the money-driven "mixed-up tennis world." [20]

The drama in Stockholm symbolized the continuing fluidity of professional tennis, a jumble of uncertainties that extended to the annual determination of world rankings. "Who is No. 1?" Charles Friedman asked in a provocative *New York Times* essay on December 10. "That question pops up in tennis at the end of every year. Sometimes the answer is clear as who deserves to be rated the best player in the world, sometimes it's not." According to Friedman, the top ranking for 1975 was still unclear, although he judged Ashe to be the leading contender in a strong field that included Borg, Connors, and Nastase. A week later, the USTA named Ashe the top-ranked American player as determined by its new computerized ranking system. But there was no such clarity at the top of the world rankings. Just before Christmas, *World Tennis* magazine rated Ashe as the world's best, followed closely by Connors, Borg, Orantes, and Nastase. During the coming weeks, however, some unofficial year-end evaluators would reverse the top two positions and put Connors first.[21]

The uncertainty about the world number one ranking, though a problem for some, did not seem to bother Ashe, who harbored a healthy skepticism about athletic superlatives. While he was as competitive as ever, he took great satisfaction in being the first thirty-two-year-old during the Open era to challenge his younger rivals for the top ranking. Laver was thirty-one in 1969, the year of his last number one ranking, and Rosewall, the other great Australian, was already thirty-five and past his prime at the beginning of the Open era. Thus, Ashe could legitimately claim that he was making tennis history at an age when most of his peers were winding down their careers. Whether his ranking was first or second, he was defying conventional wisdom about life as an aging tennis player.[22]

Ashe's late-career resurgence—along with his close identification with good sportsmanship at a time when the sports world was growing coarser and more crass—was one of the major reasons the press and the public began to embrace him as an iconic figure. In the months since his Wimbledon victory, his fame had grown exponentially. Some journalists had even begun to refer to him as King Arthur. To others using more contemporary language, he had become a "superstar."[23]

Ashe's sudden elevation to superstar status can be attributed, in part, to the sheer drama of his upset victory over Connors, an unexpected reversal of fortune performed at one of the world's premier sporting events. But there were other powerful forces at work, forces much less in evidence when Ashe had won his first Grand Slam tournament seven years earlier. In the mid-1970s, his rising fame was amplified by a maturing culture of celebrity that was transforming American life in the closing decades of the twentieth century. Fueled by a consumer culture that fostered everything from competitive narcissism to an entertainment-based search for identity, personal fulfillment, and vicarious experience, the American public of the 1970s exhibited an obsessive fascination with an ever-expanding array of movie idols, television personalities, rock stars, and sports heroes.

An emergent version of this cult of fame had existed since the development of motion pictures and radio in the 1920s, with a noticeable expansion in the early years of television and economic recovery following World War II. But it took the social challenges and technological innovations of the 1960s to bring about the celebrity-saturated popular culture of what some called the "Me Decade" of the 1970s. Only then, in the wake of the turbulent

1960s, did hyper-individualism and preoccupation with self-discovery and self-fulfillment morph into a relentless drive to identify with the rich and famous.[24]

No American institution embraced the media-fueled culture of celebrity more enthusiastically or more emphatically than the world of spectator sports. Driven by a preoccupation with winning and superior performance—a quest enhanced by unprecedented media coverage, increasingly sophisticated training regimens, and all manner of statistics and quantitative measurement—the American sports establishment of the 1970s wasted few opportunities to stimulate popular interest in the private and public lives of the nation's most accomplished athletes. No detail was too trivial or too intimate to escape public scrutiny. Every aspect of an athlete's life—what he or she did on or off the field, from the locker room to the bedroom, from the training table to the courtroom—was fair game. The more famous the athlete, the deeper the curiosity, it seemed, as Ashe would discover in the months following his Wimbledon victory. Tennis fans had always paid close attention to the ups and downs of their favorite players. But by the mid-1970s the range and intensity of public interest in tennis personalities had reached unprecedented levels.[25]

In less than a decade, professional tennis had become big business and the object of considerable popular attention. With the emergence of WCT and WTT, the resurgence of interest in Davis Cup competition, the triumphant swagger and outsized personality of Jimmy Connors, the hoopla surrounding the 1973 "Battle of the Sexes" exhibition match between Billie Jean King and Bobby Riggs, and the growing popularity of female tennis stars such as King, Evert, and Goolagong, tennis had belatedly joined the ranks of the nation's major spectator sports. It finally had its share of glamorous and controversial personalities, personal rivalries, internal power struggles, and plenty of money on the line—all requirements for the sports celebrity sweepstakes. By the end of the decade, the drama—some might say soap opera—of professional tennis would take on new dimensions with the ongoing rivalry and contrasting styles of Borg and Connors, the tantrums of McEnroe, the WTA's continuing fight for equity, and the controversy surrounding the transgender status of Renée Richards. But in the mid-1970s there was already enough grist to keep tennis's celebrity media mill churning.[26]

Ashe was just one of several tennis superstars who benefited from the enhanced status and visibility of Open tennis. But he was the only one who also faced the challenge of meeting the special responsibilities of a black celebrity. In the post–civil rights movement era of the 1970s, black celebrities

were no longer strange and rare curiosities. After decades of underrepresen-
tation in American popular culture, black artists, entertainers, and sports
figures were becoming commonplace. From Diana Ross and Aretha Franklin to Ray Charles and Louis Armstrong, from Sidney Poitier and Sammy
Davis Jr. to Bill Cosby and Cicely Tyson, black celebrities populated the
nation's airwaves, movie screens, and concert halls. Some had even risen to
superstar status, placing themselves among the nation's most popular and
revered artists.[27]

This phenomenon affected all aspects of African American culture, including Ashe's love life. In the wake of the Wimbledon victory, his eligible
bachelorhood took on a heightened profile. One of his admirers was Beverly
Johnson, the Ford Agency supermodel who created a sensation in August
1974 by becoming the first black woman to appear on the cover of *Vogue*.
Ashe, who had seen Johnson's face on several covers, found her beauty captivating. As he recalled in 1981: "I thought her photographs were stunning,
had wanted to meet her for some time, and kept asking Gene Barakat, a New
Zealander who worked at the Ford Modeling agency, 'When are you going
to introduce me to Beverly Johnson?'" Eventually Barakat came through,
awkwardly relaying Ashe's request for a dinner date in New York.

Initially Johnson declined his invitation but later reconsidered after a
friend upbraided her for missing a great opportunity. Rejecting her argument that Arthur was too "squeaky clean" for a woman accustomed to dating
edgy bad boys, he urged her to reconsider, which she did. On the first of
what would become many dates, Beverly found herself falling for Arthur's
gracious and courtly manner. "We shared a charming dinner, then went to
see a funny movie starring Richard Pryor," she recalled. "Arthur was a bit
shy and . . . kissed me on the cheek at the end of the night and asked if he
could call again. I felt like a schoolgirl after a drive-in movie." She remembered thinking, "Was this my real Prince Charming at long last?" Before
long, she was smitten and harbored hopes he would come to feel the same
way about her. Soon news of their relationship reached the pages of *Ebony*
and *Jet*, which made Arthur a little nervous. He did not want the pressure
of publicity to push him into an arrangement that would be difficult to end
without considerable embarrassment. Yet this did not stop him from dating
her for more than a year.[28]

Beverly Johnson's fame was global in scope, but during the mid-1970s the
mystique of African American celebrity was perhaps most evident in the
world of sports. Indeed, Ashe's celebrated victory at Wimbledon was only

one of several signal achievements that marked 1975 as a breakthrough year for black athletes and coaches. All across the sports world, it seemed, blacks were reaching unprecedented levels of success, visibility, and acclaim.

In Major League Baseball, the 1975 season began with Frank Robinson assuming the helm of the Cleveland Indians as the national pastime's first black manager and ended with Hank Aaron breaking Babe Ruth's all-time RBI record and extending the major league career home run record to 745. In between, Rod Carew became the first hitter since Ty Cobb to win four consecutive batting titles, and Joe Morgan—the National League's Most Valuable Player—led the Cincinnati Reds to a memorable World Series victory over the Boston Red Sox.[29]

The rising profile of blacks was even more obvious in basketball, especially in the NBA where African Americans accounted for more than 75 percent of the league in 1975. A quarter century after desegregation, professional basketball had become largely a black man's sport. At the NBA All-Star Game in March, only three of the ten starters were white, Walt Frazier of the New York Knicks was named the Most Valuable Player, and for the first time the coaches of both the East and West squads were black. The two coaches, K. C. Jones of the Washington Bullets and Al Attles of the Golden State Warriors, squared off again in the NBA finals in June, the same month that black stars Marques Johnson and Richard Washington led Ashe's alma mater UCLA to a record tenth NCAA championship.[30]

Black numerical superiority did not extend to the gridiron, where whites accounted for roughly two thirds of the nation's college and professional football players. Yet black players more than held their own at the star level. In professional football, the most celebrated superstar was unquestionably O. J. Simpson, who led the National Football League in rushing with 1,817 yards gained in 1975, while setting the single-season touchdown record of 23, one more than Chuck Foreman of the Minnesota Vikings, another African American. The NFL's dominant team, the Pittsburgh Steelers, on its way to a second straight Super Bowl victory, was led by the bruising Afro-Italian running back Franco Harris and the all-black front four of its vaunted "Steel Curtain" defense: Joe Greene, L. C. Greenwood, Ernie Holmes, and Dwight White. With the exception of James Harris of the Los Angeles Rams, all of the NFL's starting quarterbacks—the gridiron's most glamorous position— were white. But at the other positions the achievements and stardom of black players were undeniable.[31]

Finally, in boxing African Americans had achieved a hard-earned dominance by the mid-1970s, especially in the heavyweight division where

Muhammad Ali, Joe Frazier, and George Foreman held sway. A decade earlier, Ali's outsized personality, politics, and skills had made him one of the most important sports figures of his time. But with the carefully staged championship bouts of the mid-1970s—most notably the "Rumble in the Jungle" against Foreman in Zaire, held in October 1974, and the "Thrilla in Manila" against Frazier a year later—he took celebrity to a new level, becoming one of the most recognizable individuals on the planet.[32]

The proliferation of black sports celebrities in the 1970s was a sure sign that Jim Crow culture was on the wane. But for Ashe the situation was decidedly bittersweet. On the one hand, he now belonged to a fraternity of shared experience and privilege. Yet the growing number of elite black athletes all across the sports world made the racial tokenism of professional tennis all the more conspicuous. The oddity of his solitary status as the nation's only black tennis star became more obvious with every passing year. During twenty years of struggle the modern civil rights movement had brought substantial change to almost every corner of America, opening up institution after institution. But somehow the revolution had all but bypassed the world of competitive tennis. After more than a decade on the men's tour, and after eight years of Open tennis, Ashe was still alone. The boy from Richmond had become King Arthur, but there were no black knights in—or indeed on—his court.[33]

Over the next decade and a half, Ashe would devote considerable time and energy trying to remedy this problem, either by sponsoring and counseling young black prospects at the college or Junior level, or by developing youth tennis programs in inner-city black neighborhoods. But during the heady winter of 1975–76, when he finally reached the pinnacle of being ranked number one in the world, his primary concern was maintaining the quality of his own game. In early 1976, *Tennis* and *World Tennis* magazines, the French sports monthly *L'Équipe*, and the USTA all placed him at the top of the tennis rankings, and the Martini and Rossi corporation named him Player of the Year, an award that came with a $7,500 check and a ceremonial gold-plated racket.[34]

This was a remarkable situation for a thirty-two-year-old veteran with a bum left heel. In the Open era, only Ashe and Laver had achieved a number one ranking after the age of thirty, and even the seemingly ageless Aussie star had eventually slipped in the rankings. Ashe knew he was living on borrowed time, and despite his recent accolades, few observers expected him to sustain the level of play that had brought him nine tournament titles and a

Wimbledon crown in 1975. But in the early weeks of the 1976 winter circuit he seemed almost unbeatable. Playing consistently good tennis, he compiled a 12-match winning streak and won the first two tournaments of the year. He then flew to Denver for a special exhibition match with Tony Roche and came away with a straight-set victory and $15,000. Only on January 29 did he finally come down to earth, suffering an upset loss to Tom Gorman at the indoor pro championships in Philadelphia. A week later, however, he was soaring again with a victory at Richmond, his third tournament win in less than thirty days.[35]

From Richmond, Ashe traveled to Lagos, Nigeria, to play in that fifteen-year-old nation's first professional tennis tournament. But just before the tournament was scheduled to start, the Nigerian capital plunged into chaos when an attempted coup d'état against the government of General Murtala Mohammed left the general dead and the nation wondering who was in charge. Ashe and his racket-bearing friends spent the next three days "holed up in the U.S. Embassy compound waiting for events to sort themselves out." By the third day, the players were getting antsy and wondering when their ordeal would be over. When they asked to leave the country, Nigerian officials informed them they would not be paid unless they honored their commitment to play in the tournament. The players then pressed the officials to start the tournament, and by the next morning, with the antigovernment forces in retreat, the situation seemed calm enough to allow play to begin.

After the tournament proceeded through three rounds without incident, Ashe found himself facing former UCLA star Jeff Borowiak in a semifinal match that drew a small crowd. Otherwise the situation appeared normal until the third game of the second set. Then, seemingly out of nowhere, chaos enveloped the stadium. As Ashe later described the scene, "I was in the middle of my service motion, up one set over Jeff Borowiak and tied 1-all in the second, when a group of soldiers brandishing machine guns burst into the tennis stadium. 'What the hell is going on here?' shouted the soldier in charge. 'What are you doing? You're playing games while we're mourning the death of our president.' They were enraged."

At this point, much of the crowd "panicked and began to flee," leaving Ashe, Borowiak, the referees, and the ball boys to deal with the soldiers. "One of the soldiers stuck his machine gun in my back and shoved me off the court," Ashe recalled. "I could feel the cold steel in my back through my wet shirt and there was a sinking feeling in my stomach. I waited for the weapon to go off as I scrambled from the court. Once I was off and it seemed clear I had no intention of returning, the soldier let me go and directed his attention toward some of his countrymen. Four minutes later, we climbed into a government car to go back to the Embassy residence, but right in the middle of the road was the soldier who had shouted at me. He was mercilessly beating a Nigerian who had been trying to get away on a motorcycle. Jeff and I decided to pass up the car and head the other way on foot. One hundred yards away, a large official limousine stopped in front of us. It was the Hungarian ambassador, who had been a spectator. He recognized us and offered us rides back to the U.S. Embassy." A few hours later, State Department officials and a squad of U.S. Marines escorted nine players to the airport and put them on a plane to Rome, the next stop on the WCT tour.

In Italy, after Ashe and the other evacuees regaled the international press with tales of their brush with revolution, the touring pros managed to play several days of tennis without armed interruption. Once again Ashe won the tournament, defeating Lutz in the championship match. Amazingly, it was only six weeks into the year, and Ashe had already won four tournaments, nearly half the number he had won in all of 1975. "Arthur Ashe," *The New York Times* reported, "is on a rampage."[36]

The streak would continue for another full month, with Ashe eventually winning thirty-two of thirty-three matches. From Rome he went on to Rotterdam, where he won his fifth tournament of the year. After beating Laver in a tough semifinal match—his third victory over the great Australian in twenty-five tries—he needed only fifty-nine minutes to dispatch Lutz in the final.

A week later, Ashe led the American squad to a surprisingly easy victory over Australia in the seventh annual Aetna World Cup competition, held in Hartford. The United States had won the best-of-seven series only once before, in 1971, but the 1976 contest was a mismatch from the outset. With Laver absent due to a family medical crisis and with Connors added to the American team for the first time, the Aussies managed only one victory in seven matches. Ashe won both of his singles matches, beating Newcombe for only the second time in six years and outlasting Roche in a tough three-set contest. He then partnered with Ralston to defeat Phil Dent and John Alexander, one of the world's most formidable doubles teams.

Winning the World Cup with Connors on the team was doubly sweet for Ashe in light of his earlier criticism of the left-hander's lone-wolf ways; and Connors himself was all smiles after the victory. "Team competition has always been difficult for me," he conceded. "I've always been a loner, a rebel. But I'm all finished with the feuding now. The more I play for a team, the more I like it. I hope they invite me back next year." This was welcome news to Ashe, who went out of his way to praise his new teammate. "I never really knew Jimmy until we played together at Hartford last weekend," he told reporters. "We had dinner together. We talked in the locker room. We made a date to play golf. . . . I found that Jimmy is a lot like me; he is independent and has a lot of pride." When asked about a possible challenge match against his new friend, he insisted he had "no objection so long as it does not interfere with the regular tournament schedule," and "Bill Riordan is [not] involved."[37]

Ashe and Connors had not played since the 1975 Wimbledon final, but pressure for a rematch had been building for months, especially since the beginning of Ashe's winning streak. With his street-fighter style, Connors was the most exciting figure in tennis, and despite Ashe's number one ranking, the young star was still widely regarded as the best player in the game. Praise for Ashe was tempered by the realization he had dominated only one section of WCT's split-tour format. With up to three concurrent tournaments a week, WCT events had experienced a noticeable dilution of talent. In any given tournament, the competition typically included only one third to one half of the tour's best players. While Ashe was facing Laver and Lutz in Rotterdam, for example, Tanner and Vilas were playing in another WCT tournament in St. Louis. In many instances, WCT tournaments also had to compete with Davis Cup and special exhibition challenge matches, all of which further diffused the talent pool.[38]

The proliferation of tournaments and so-called celebrity matches reflected the ongoing commercialization of Open tennis. The age of big-money tennis had finally arrived, and players and sponsors alike were nervously adjusting to new realties and expectations. New opportunities had inevitably brought new problems, and many tennis insiders, including Ashe, were concerned that monetary considerations had widened the gap between an elite group of stars and the majority of touring professionals. Ashe himself was not above taking advantage of the new system and was currently participating along with seven other top players in the $320,000 Avis Challenge Cup competition held in Kona, Hawaii. But as a leader of the ATP, he worried about the long-term impact of celebrity tennis on the overall tour.[39]

The celebrity problem came to the forefront in late February when two untelevised WCT events were overshadowed by a glitzy, nationally televised celebrity challenge between Connors and Manolo Orantes, the two singles finalists from the 1975 U.S. Open. While the WCT participants drew modest crowds and competed for a top prize of $17,000, Connors and Orantes shared

$400,000 of television revenue and competed for a $250,000 winner-take-all purse. After 21 games and fewer than ninety minutes on the court, Connors walked away with the biggest paycheck in tennis history, which, according to one astonished reporter, amounted to more than $2,700 per minute.[40]

Ashe, as a member of the elite "Millionaire's Club" in career earnings, was not in the best position to complain about Connors's windfall. But in the spirit of fairness, he felt compelled to condemn anything that threatened the livelihood of his fellow ATP members. Lucrative challenge matches were all right to a point, but not when they systematically diverted attention and funding from the tour. "I confess I wear two hats," he acknowledged, "the first being that of Arthur Ashe the player, who loves the thought of being paid to play, at the rate of $250,000 for a few hours' work. The second hat, however, is that of Arthur Ashe the president of the Association of Tennis Professionals, who knows that such matches can kill the incentive for top professionals to play in the long and exhausting tournaments that made them what they are in the first place."[41]

A week later, Riordan expressed a decidedly different view, criticizing Ashe for being naive and hypocritical on matters of money. "We have tried to infuse big-money matches into tennis. The sport is, after all, entertainment, and if it isn't we are all in trouble," he pointed out. "We wanted, and still want, to make the sport accessible to all those nonpurists out there who flip on their TV sets for a look. In the process we try to land big paydays for tennis stars. I'm old-fashioned enough to believe that a sport isn't truly big time unless its athletes realize big money." He went on to attack "the Tennis Establishment," and by implication Ashe, for trying "to keep the sport in a wax museum." Traditionally, tennis had been an "old school tie and only club members allowed. Not until the dust was kicked off the sport did the public realize what a big, handsome stud it was and how much fun you could have playing it or watching it. Tennis, despite lead weights on its back, is now big money. It will grow even bigger provided the striped-tie Neanderthals keep their distance."[42]

Riordan's words stung, but Ashe must have taken some satisfaction from the irony of being lumped with the "Neanderthals" of tennis. A black touring pro, once the ultimate outsider, had somehow become a stodgy insider worthy of attack by a roguish insurgent. Ashe and just about everyone else associated with professional tennis knew Riordan's characterization was at best a half-truth. Yet Ashe had to admit the men's tour had been especially good to him as of late.

Ashe's hot streak on the court finally came to an end in early May at the WCT Masters, where he lost to Harold Solomon in the first round. A week later, he lost to Brian Gottfried in the quarterfinals of the Las Vegas Tennis Classic. Even though he and Pasarell managed to win the Las Vegas doubles title, it was clear he was slipping back into the pack in singles play. Though disappointed, he couldn't feel too sorry for himself, since win or lose he was now earning most of his income from the sale of Head rackets, especially the increasing popular "Arthur Ashe Competition 2" model.[43]

Of course, he still preferred to make as much money as possible on the court, and during the spring of 1976 his best chance to do so came in late May when he traveled to Kona, Hawaii, for the late rounds of the Avis Challenge Cup. After defeating Rosewall in the semifinals, his earnings in the round-robin competition reached $80,000, by far the largest paycheck of his career, and he stood to earn $100,000 more if he could defeat Nastase in the final. In light of their earlier confrontation in Stockholm, the Ashe-Nastase matchup drew considerable attention and one of the largest television audiences in tennis history.

A week earlier, Nastase had renewed his bad boy image during a WTT match between the Hawaii Leis and the San Diego Friars. Whenever the Friars' female star Terry Holladay served, Nastase rang a cowbell, inciting the Leis' fans and angering her male teammates Laver and Ross Case. Before the contest was over, Case and Nastase engaged in a brief shoving match and had to be separated.[44]

During the big match against Ashe, Nastase picked up where he left off, entertaining the crowd with outrageous "clowning" and needling his opponent with "non-stop talking." At several points, he harangued Ashe, and near the end of the second set, he called him a "bloody nigger." Ashe later claimed he couldn't hear anything coming from beyond the other baseline, but a courtside microphone picked up Nastase's voice, allowing hundreds of thousands of NBC television viewers to hear it all too clearly.

After the match—which Nastase won in five sets—Ashe tried to downplay the incident. "I didn't hear anything he said," he insisted. "But even if he said it, I don't think he's a racist." Graciously giving Nastase the benefit of the doubt, he let the matter drop. In the end, there was no disciplinary action, and Nastase walked away with the $100,000 prize money. Under the championship match's winner-take-all format, Ashe received only a consolation prize—a black coral ring reportedly worth $400. Considering the nature of Nastase's transgression, the symbolism was perfect.[45]

Ashe did not dwell on the unfortunate incident in Hawaii, which he chalked up to Nastase's personal demons. Yet he later saw it as a bad omen that ushered in a season of disappointment and discontent. On the court, his performance dropped off sharply during the summer of 1976. At the French Open in early June, he was seeded third but struggled from the outset, eventually losing in the round of 16 to a young unseeded Hungarian, Balázs Taróczy, who had first met Ashe as a nine-year-old ball boy in Budapest. A week later at Nottingham, he was upset in the first round by Roger Taylor, and at Wimbledon, where he was the defending champion and the number one seed, he lost to Vitas Gerulaitis in the fourth round. Ashe, who had never lost to Gerulaitis in four matches, managed to win the first two sets. But his long-haired, twenty-two-year-old opponent wore him out in the final three. "I was just dead," a weary and disappointed Ashe commented after the match. Fortunately, before the tournament was over he took some comfort from the news that Connors also suffered an upset, at the hands of Tanner in the quarterfinals—and that Nastase lost to Borg in the men's final.

For Ashe, the 1976 Wimbledon was memorable mostly for a personal drama outside the lines. When he arrived at the All England Club on the first day, Lois Wise, a twenty-two-year-old former Miss Hawaii, was on his arm. As Ashe explained to curious reporters, they had met several years earlier in Honolulu during a reception sponsored by her employer Aloha Airlines and had dated off and on ever since. But after she sat in the friends box at Centre Court wearing a bright red and white carnation in her hair, the British press had a field day speculating about her relationship with the Wimbledon champion. Described by one reporter as Ashe's "now-constant beauty queen companion," she politely dismissed any suggestion that marriage was in the offing. "Arthur and I are just very good friends," she insisted. "I don't know why people always ask about marriage."

At it turned out, Lois was not the only woman to complicate his stay at the 1976 Wimbledon. The movement to equalize prize money for men and women that had begun in earnest five years earlier with the creation of the Virginia Slims circuit was approaching a crisis point, and the WTA was threatening to boycott future Wimbledons unless equal prize money was guaranteed. As president of the ATP, Ashe felt compelled to make a public statement on the proposed boycott. After warning the WTA that "Wimbledon isn't the sort of event to which you issue demands," he countered the claim that equalization was justified: "Equal prize money at Wimbledon is basically two questions for me. The first is the quality and the depth of the field. The other is the number of drawing cards the women have. I think on both counts that they would do better not to compare themselves with the men but to look at the women's situation as it really is. They have been piggybacking on us for a long time." These strong words would come back to haunt him in later years; indeed, within a year he would reverse his position, much to the delight of Billie Jean King and other committed feminists. But in 1976 he was in solid agreement with his ATP colleagues, very few of whom had much sympathy for the equalization cause.[46]

The WTA's negative reaction to his comments troubled him, and he hoped that eventually all concerned could agree on a reasonable compromise. But he had more immediate problems to attend to as the summer of 1976 progressed. In a series of post-Wimbledon tournaments, he continued to struggle, losing to unseeded opponents on several occasions. He had not reached the quarterfinals of a single tournament since May, and the situation showed no signs of improvement in early August, when he traveled to North Conway, New Hampshire, to play on red clay in the Volvo International tournament. At the Volvo, after losing to Zeljko Franulovic in straight sets in the second round of the singles competition, he teamed with Connors in the doubles. The press welcomed this surprise partnership as proof that Ashe and Connors had "mended" their feud, noting the two men had actually double-dated earlier in the week. But even the dream pairing ended in defeat as the heavily favored 1975 Wimbledon finalists were upset in the third round by two young, unseeded Chilean players.[47]

By the time Ashe arrived at the U.S. Open in early September, his confidence was at its lowest ebb in years. Seeded a disappointing seventh, he lost to Jan Kodes in the second round, his earliest exit in nine U.S. Opens. He won just nine points and one game in the first set, and the entire match lasted only fifty-one minutes. "It really wasn't much of a match," he conceded. "Jan played well, and I didn't offer much resistance. I couldn't keep the ball on the court. This summer has been a disaster for me. That's life." When asked if this was the worst he had ever played at the Open, he muttered disconsolately, "Don't know. Don't care. It's over."[48]

Unfortunately, the slump was not over, and he played out the year without winning another tournament. While his overall match record for the year was a more than respectable 64–23, he could not seem to win when it really mattered. In late September, he made it to the finals of the Pacific Southwest Open in Los Angeles but lost badly to Gottfried in the championship match. Two weeks later, he managed to defeat Nastase in a tough semifinal match at Hilton Head Island, South Carolina, but with his foot situation worsening he was no match for Borg in the finals. In late October he eked out two early-round victories in Vienna, but a week later his foot injury forced him to withdraw from the Stockholm Indoor Open.

Ashe would not play again competitively until December 17, when he represented the United States in a Davis Cup match against Roberto Chavez of Mexico. The Mexican team had upset the Americans the two previous years, but not this time, as Ashe and Tanner both won their singles matches and Smith and Lutz followed with a doubles victory that gave the U.S. an insurmountable 3–0 lead. In the second round of singles matches, Raúl Ramírez defeated Ashe in straight sets, depriving the Americans of a clean sweep. The U.S. squad would go on to face Argentina in the 1977 Davis Cup Americas Zone final, but Ashe, who underwent foot surgery in February 1977, would not be part of the team that lost to Guillermo Vilas and the Argentines 3–2 in May.

By the time of the U.S.-Mexico match in December 1976, Ashe's U.S. ranking had fallen from first to third, his only consolation being that for a record twelfth straight year he found himself ranked among the top five Americans. Even more disturbing, his world ranking, according to *Tennis* magazine, had slipped from first to twelfth in a single year. This rapid descent from the top of the rankings could be explained, in part, by his persistent foot problems, and consoling friends assured him there was no reason to panic. But, at age thirty-three, he feared his best performances on the court were behind him.[49]

While Ashe did his best to maintain an optimistic frame of mind during this tough time, he was hampered by a series of setbacks off the court. Both during and immediately after the 1976 U.S. Open, the tennis world remained sharply divided over the concerted effort by the WTA to force the Wimbledon organizing committee to equalize the prize money for men and women. The U.S. Open had adopted an equal prize money policy in 1973, and many other tournaments had followed suit, but not Wimbledon. The issue troubled Ashe more than ever, and there were signs he had become conflicted over the matter. But as of September he still stood in public solidarity with his traditionalist male colleagues. "It's a question of market value," he told the press, insisting that among the women only Evert and Goolagong belonged in the same prize range as the men.[50]

The state of tennis politics was bad enough, but in the broader political arena—an area of increasing interest to Ashe—nothing seemed to be going very well. President Nixon's replacement, Gerald Ford, had proven to be a disappointment on matters of race and economics, and Ashe worried that four more years of Republican rule would undo many of the gains achieved during the 1960s. Mercifully, the Vietnam War was no longer a major distraction for progressive Americans interested in social change and racial justice, yet the civil rights community remained fragmented and ineffective. Indeed, racial liberalism appeared to be in decline, as battles over "forced busing" and affirmative action fueled a powerful white backlash.

It was the Bicentennial year, and there was considerable fanfare and celebration commemorating the nation's democratic origins. But the prospects for a true renewal of democratic values—one that advanced the civil rights agenda of racial justice and equal opportunity—seemed dim during the months leading up to the national election of 1976. In the early stages, Ashe enthusiastically embraced the liberal-minded presidential campaign of his friend Sargent Shriver, but he became discouraged after Shriver dropped out of the race in late March.

Initially, the eventual Democratic nominee, Jimmy Carter, did not excite Ashe, largely because of the Georgian's mixed record on matters of race. Only after Carter received Andrew Young's endorsement did Ashe feel comfortable in the Carter camp. Ashe and Young had been friends since their first meeting in 1970, but their friendship deepened after spending time together at the *Washington Star* tournament in July 1974 and traveling to South Africa later in the year. Their mutual admiration was obvious and, following Carter's inauguration in January 1977, Ashe was thrilled to be invited to the White House to attend Young's swearing-in as the U.S. ambassador to the United Nations.[51]

Carter's victory over Ford in November 1976 gave Ashe some hope that the years of conservative Republican dominance and political backlash were over. But, in truth, his focus was not on the American political scene during that summer and fall. From mid-June on, South Africa, not the United States, dominated his thoughts and prayers. After the Bantu Education Department began enforcing a long-forgotten law requiring secondary education to be conducted in Afrikaans in the spring of 1976, black students engaged in a series of protests and strikes that brought a brutal response from white policemen. On June 16, in Soweto, where more than twenty thousand students had gathered for a protest march, the police fired indiscriminately into the crowd, killing several marchers. The protests soon spread to other black townships, prompting more police violence. Before the confrontations gave way to an uneasy peace in late June, an estimated 360 students were dead, and waves of outrage galvanized anti-apartheid forces across the world. A partially successful worldwide boycott of South African exports followed, but no one knew quite what the future held in the wake of the "Soweto uprising."

During his most recent visit to South Africa, in November 1975, Ashe had sensed that something like this might happen in the near future. Among

South African whites there was a stubborn refusal to embrace meaningful change, he noted, and among blacks there was a new militancy and a growing determination to resist the worst excesses of apartheid. "You could not tell by looking around the streets," he recalled six years later. "You had to talk to people. Black people were bolder about the things they didn't like; they were more vocally open. . . . You could feel the tension underneath. The superficial changes in petty apartheid only whetted the appetites of black South Africans for more and faster change."

In early 1976, Ashe had warned his South African friends on the tour that the deadly combination of black protest and white repression could erupt at any moment, and as soon as the Soweto uprising appeared in the press, he called Ray Moore to say "I told you so." Ashe and Moore monitored the soul-sickening spectacle from London, where they were awaiting the start of Wimbledon, and as the reports of escalating violence trickled in, both men trembled for the future of a nation that appeared to be spinning out of control.

What worried Ashe most, aside from the savagery of the police, was the apparent isolation of South Africa's black activists. Among the white liberals who professed to oppose apartheid there were few signs of support for the protesters and even fewer expressions of outrage directed at the government. The white liberals, it seemed, preferred order to freedom, and at this critical moment there was little evidence of interracial activism, a factor crucial to the success of the American civil rights movement in the 1960s.

Ashe also observed there had been almost no black-on-white violence. As he recalled in 1981: "One startling, sobering statistic fascinated me: in all of the racial unrest, not even a handful of white South Africans were killed. The Africans talk in symbolic terms of destroying the system they hate, yet almost no white South Africans were killed. That wouldn't happen in the United States under similar circumstances. South African blacks were punishing themselves more than anybody else. Even when they had those riots, nobody in the lines had any weapons; the people were all unarmed, with nothing more than sticks and stones."

At the time, Ashe didn't know what to make of this restraint, and he neither criticized nor praised the black South Africans' refusal to engage in all-out warfare. Years later, however, he looked back on the 1976 Soweto uprising as a major milestone in modern South African history. As he put it, "that one incident changed values within the country. . . . There was more unanimity of feeling about apartheid. The black reaction . . . showed that blacks were not going to settle for the life that white South Africa had been promising them."

The Soweto uprising also raised the international profile of the broader struggle against apartheid. "South Africa internationally could no longer hide from the problem as it tried to do in the past," Ashe insisted. "Even the investment atmosphere changed. Outsiders like me had to change our approach. We could not rely on an occasional letter to a congressman or senator. We too had to raise our ante. I had to get bolder just to keep up." He would indeed become bolder in the years to come as the anti-apartheid struggle evolved into a powerful worldwide movement. But in the early aftermath of the white crackdown in Soweto, the liberation of black South Africa seemed further away than ever.[52]

NINETEEN

AFFAIRS OF THE HEART

S OUTH AFRICA'S PLIGHT AND other troubling public issues were not the only things disrupting Ashe's peace of mind in 1976. His private life was also a source of anxiety and uncertainty. As long as he remained on the tour, the pattern of nonstop travel and the commitment to compete at the highest level would be the controlling influences in his life. But what would he do with himself when he retired? Though only a year removed from his greatest triumph, the precipitous decline in the quality of his tennis forced him to contemplate the second phase of his adult life. With hard work and a bit of luck, he might be able to extend his career for a year or two, but surely he would be off the court before the end of the decade.

Perhaps more than any other touring pro, Ashe had prepared for this day, diversifying his interests and building social capital. He could, he reasoned, develop a second career in business, or television, or coaching, or writing and public speaking, or perhaps a combination of all of the above. Already financially secure, he had the luxury of reorganizing his life with more than money in mind. Yet this wide range of choices kept him up at night. For a man who had seen so much of his life determined by forces beyond his control—by his father, by Dr. J and Coach Morgan, and later by the dictates of the tour—this freedom to choose was a new experience.[1]

Ironically, in another important area of his life, Ashe was troubled by the prospect of giving up his freedom. For fifteen years or more, he had enjoyed his bachelorhood. As his envious friends could attest, he had certainly made the most of it, dating dozens of talented and beautiful women, including his current girlfriend, Beverly Johnson. Along the way, he had survived one engagement and one near miss, but for the most part he had avoided entangling relationships. He attributed this blissful freedom to both good luck and careful planning. "Marriage and the idea of marriage were always rather frightening to me," he once confessed. "What bothered me was not so much marriage as divorce. . . . I thought people in general got married for the wrong reasons and turned to divorce not because they couldn't get along but because they didn't try hard enough." [2]

Despite this fear, Ashe denied he was a confirmed bachelor. For him, it was primarily a matter of timing. "Keeping my promise to myself to stay single until I was thirty was easy enough," he insisted. "I had plenty to do and there was much about life I wanted to enjoy." But this all changed in 1973. "When I reached thirty," he revealed, "I literally started to look for a wife. I was ready to open up—to share my life with someone. Before then, I would have resented the restraints, not with respect to other women but restraints on my time. This may seem to be a cold-blooded approach to marriage, but I wanted to take a logical and rational view of the institution and to make sure it would work for me." [3]

For three years, Ashe searched for the right woman to share the rest of his life. His dates were almost always beautiful, and many were talented and accomplished women, yet not one came close to being "THE ONE," as he put it. By the fall of 1976, he had become discouraged and wondered if he would ever feel the emotional spark that would bond him to a woman for life. For the better part of a year, he had dated Beverly, and she had begun to broach the subject of marriage. But, despite their stimulating physical relationship, he did not feel quite the same way about her. As sexually exciting and beautiful as she was, Johnson had a history of drug abuse that gave him pause. As a practical matter, he also worried about the daunting challenge of simultaneously accommodating the demands and pressures of two high-powered careers. As one of the world's most sought-after models, Beverly always seemed to by flying off to one photo shoot or another. How could they raise a family or have any kind of meaningful life together under such circumstances? The more he thought about it, the more he realized he just couldn't see himself in a permanent relationship with her.

Frustrated and disappointed, he had just about given up. Then, on October 16 and 17, he participated in a United Negro College Fund Pro-Celebrity tournament held at the Felt Forum in New York. Over the years he had taken part in dozens of similar benefit events, but this time donating a weekend to a worthy cause would change his life. One of the photographers assigned to cover the event and take his picture was a young woman wearing blue jeans and a beige sweater. There was something about her—the way she looked, the way she carried herself—that grabbed his attention. She was beautiful, to be sure. But there was something else about her, something magnetic that drew him in.

As the shutters clicked, Arthur tried to initiate a conversation. His opening line, "Photographers are getting cuter these days," drew a terse response. "Well, thank you," the woman replied in a tone that let him know his lack of originality had failed to impress. Clearly, he had gotten off on the wrong foot, and a few seconds later, as the photographers scrambled for a good position, she literally stepped on his foot. Undaunted, he approached her later in the afternoon and managed to get her name. "Jeanne Moutoussamy," she told him, slowly spelling out the last name when he looked puzzled. Moments earlier she had been in conversation with an acquaintance of Arthur's, the famous African American photographer Gordon Parks, and Arthur feared they were a couple. But a later conversation with Parks in the men's dressing room revealed there was no attachment other than friendship and a work connection with NBC.[4]

That evening, at the post-tournament party, Arthur screwed up his courage and approached her again. This time they talked for several minutes, after which he asked her out on a dinner date. His open invitation referred to "some future date," but she wanted to pin him down. "When?" she asked. "How about tomorrow?" he responded, and she agreed.

The first date—a leisurely dinner filled with conversation—took place at Thursday's restaurant on West 58th Street. They met in the lobby of 30 Rockefeller Plaza, the building where Jeanne worked, and where Arthur started the evening with a flourish by presenting her with a single red rose. Since he hardly knew her at this point, he had no way of knowing how she would react to the rose or anything else he had to offer. But that evening, in a few short hours punctuated by laughter and knowing glances, he learned a great deal about Jeanne Moutoussamy.

Most obviously, he found her to be extremely bright and articulate. Within minutes he discovered they had a number of common interests— literature, music, art, and Africa. He even discovered that their birthdays were only one day apart—hers on July 9 and his on July 10. It also didn't take much time for him to realize she was an independent woman with strong opinions, some of which did not match his. Recalling their rambling chatter

on a range of issues, he conceded she "more than held her own." Cosmopolitan in her tastes and unusually poised, she proved to be charming even when
making a disputable point. By the end of the evening, he was exhilarated and
all but hooked.

Soon thereafter, he called Beverly to break the news that he had met
someone special. "I'm really sorry about this," he told her, "but it's pretty
serious, so I can't see you anymore." Unaccustomed to being dumped, especially on the phone, she was, to put it mildly, floored. But even over the
phone, she sensed almost immediately that nothing could change his mind.
From the tone of his voice, nervous and embarrassed as he was, she could tell
that something profound had happened to him.[5]

Deeply in love for the first time in his life, Arthur was certain that Jeanne
was the one for him. She had it all, from a breathtaking smile to a set of
experiences and interests that drew him to her. Part of the attraction was
her unusual background. Born in Chicago in 1951, she was the product of
a multiethnic Roman Catholic family—part East Indian, part Caribbean,
and part African American. Her father, John Warren Moutoussamy Sr., was
a prominent Chicago-born architect who helped to design several notable
buildings, including the skyscraper that housed the offices of the popular
black magazines *Ebony* and *Jet*. His father, the son of an Indian couple from
Pondicherry, was a native of Saint Francois, Guadaloupe, who had migrated
to Louisiana as a young man in the 1920s before moving on to Chicago.
Jeanne's mother, Elizabeth Hunt Moutoussamy, was an interior designer
born in Hot Springs, Arkansas, of mixed racial background ranging from
African American to Cherokee. Raised as a Baptist, Elizabeth converted
to Catholicism during her engagement and later became a strict follower
of her husband's lifelong faith. Together, John and Elizabeth raised three
children—Johnny, Claude, and Jeanne.

As Arthur would soon learn, Jeanne remained close to her mother, father, and brothers, even though she had come to regard her upbringing as
too rigid and confining. The family's protective regimen during her girlhood
had not even allowed her to go to summer camp as her brothers did. Indeed,
she had rebelled at age nineteen, impulsively marrying an aspiring twenty-
one-year-old copywriter named Michael Lloyd. The marriage, which lasted
a mere three months, was annulled in January 1971. By that time—after
declaring, "marriage is not for me"—Jeanne had fled from Chicago to New
Rochelle, in suburban Westchester County, New York, where she lived for a
time with a favorite aunt while she attended the College of New Rochelle. A
year later, she transferred to the Cooper Union School of Art in Manhattan,

where she developed a passion for graphic design and photography. With its unlimited possibilities, Manhattan proved to be the perfect backdrop for a strong-willed young woman seeking personal reinvention.

During her junior year, Jeanne spent several weeks in West Africa taking photographs she later presented in three extensive portfolios. Skilled well beyond the typical undergraduate, she drew the attention of NBC, which hired her as a graphic designer and photographer during her senior year. Only twenty-five when she met Arthur, she was already one of New York's most promising young photographers.[6]

Ambitious and proud of her work, Jeanne was a committed civil rights activist and feminist who had no tolerance for sexist condescension. So she was thrilled when at that first dinner Arthur asked to see some of her work. Back at her NBC cubicle at 30 Rockefeller Plaza, he seemed to take a genuine interest in her portfolios, asking lots of questions about her choice of photographs. "He got big points for that," she recalled years later. More than enough points to warrant a second date, it turned out. The following night they attended a benefit at a New Jersey tennis club frequented by Arthur's uncle E. J. Cunningham. Arthur's beloved Aunt Marie was also on hand to meet her nephew's new girlfriend, so it wasn't long before the family grapevine was buzzing about his budding romance.[7]

Whatever was stirring was soon interrupted by Arthur's commitment to play in two European tournaments in late October and early November. It would be almost three weeks before he returned to New York, but he did his best to keep his new relationship alive. "I kissed her on the cheek in the lobby of 30 Rockefeller Plaza . . . and was off," he remembered. "I called from the airport and from Vienna. I called every day from Europe and talked to her on election night as Jimmy Carter went over the top. By the time I got back, we were in love; at least I was."[8]

Nurturing a romance through transatlantic communication was a new and not altogether satisfying experience for Jeanne. But her new boyfriend was so attentive—albeit at long distance—that she tried not to complain. For a time Arthur feared she would grow tired of the phone calls and break off their relationship. But fear turned to joyous relief when she invited him to come to Chicago to have Thanksgiving dinner with her family. The visit with the big-hearted and welcoming Moutoussamy clan went well, so well that Jeanne's relatives began to press her about wedding plans. "Has Arthur asked you to marry him yet?" one aunt asked, drawing a swift denial from Jeanne. "No, God," she exclaimed, "I've only known him a month!"[9]

In truth, both Arthur and Jeanne were already contemplating a long-term relationship, perhaps even marriage. But before that could happen they had to overcome the lingering psychological effects of her first marriage. From the beginning of her relationship with Lloyd, Jeanne had sensed something fundamental was not quite right. She had felt the need to leave Lloyd, but she was also fleeing from the sometimes stifling atmosphere surrounding her parents' close circle of devout Catholic friends. She loved her family, but her life in Chicago had not allowed for much freedom or independence.

Early on in their relationship, Arthur became aware of Jeanne's independence of mind—and of her long-standing disillusionment with aggressive men. She was especially distrustful of black men who, in her experience, were long on seductive talk and short on substance. He knew she was hesitant to commit to anyone—even someone to whom she was deeply attracted. So he proceeded as slowly as he could, despite his depth of feeling. He was "more distant with her" than with previous girlfriends. During the early dates there was "no kissing, no holding hands, not even privately." He didn't want to do anything to scare her off.[10]

All of this began to change, however, after the Thanksgiving visit. The couple's deep mutual affection was becoming more obvious with every passing day—both to them and to everyone around them. Now that he had met Jeanne's family, it was time to introduce her to Arthur Ashe Sr. He was confident his father would see the same sterling qualities in Jeanne that he did. But he wasn't prepared for his father's reaction. "For an instant, I thought he would faint," Arthur Jr. recalled. "He just stood there and stared at Jeanne. I had never seen him so stunned."

A few moments later, when he had the chance to ask his father what was going on, he learned what should have been obvious. "She looks just like your mother," Arthur Sr. whispered. "Later that day," Arthur Jr. recalled, "I looked again at an old photograph of my mother, taken when I was just four years old. Indeed, there was a strong resemblance: the straight brown hair, the high cheekbones, the large eyes, the light brown complexion." He "hadn't noticed" the resemblance until that day, but after his father's prompting he began to see it as a sign of something deeper: "I sensed that somehow, my mother had managed to reach from beyond and influence my choice of the woman who would share my life."[11]

Before long Arthur was plotting a marriage proposal. But the demands of the tour temporarily complicated matters. Diverted by two trips, one to Tucson for a Davis Cup tie against Mexico, and a second and much longer trip to

Australia, he had no choice but to put his love life on hold. In mid-December, he helped the U.S. squad defeat Mexico 4–1, though he lost his second singles match to Raúl Ramírez. There were some days when his heel problem wouldn't allow him to play anywhere near his best, and Ramírez caught him on one of those days. Although the heel didn't seem to be getting any better, he reluctantly agreed to honor his commitment to play in the Australian Open in early January. The Australian sojourn actually began with a preliminary tournament on December 26, which meant he and Jeanne would not be together for the Christmas holidays. Once again he tried to make up for his absence by calling her every day.[12]

Once the Australian Open began he concentrated on the task at hand. Despite the pain in his heel, he managed to win his first four singles matches before losing to John Alexander in the quarterfinals. His loss came on January 6, the day of the Epiphany, and he was tempted to truncate his tour and fly home. But he and Roche were still alive in the doubles competition, so he decided to stay a bit longer. Amazingly, he and Roche actually ended up winning the doubles title. His left heel was still painful and increasingly unreliable, but this unexpected victory was enough to convince him to stay another week to play in the South Australia championships in Adelaide.

He had always played well in Adelaide, and he managed to win his first two matches. His luck ran out, however, in a third-round match against Pasarell. By the end of the four-set match, he was limping noticeably and some observers wondered how he had managed to remain on the court so long. This time he knew there was no point in prolonging the tour and within a few hours he was on a plane bound for the United States.[13]

The long plane ride home gave him plenty of time to ponder his personal and professional circumstances, and by the time he reached New York he had made two important decisions: "I would have heel surgery and get married." Both decisions involved considerable risk, though he was fairly confident Jeanne would agree to marry him. Even so, he couldn't seem to manage a traditional proposal. Instead he surprised her by putting an engagement ring "in an envelope in her medicine cabinet." As a result, he experienced more than a few anxious moments when "it took her three days to find the envelope." Despite this hiccup, Jeanne said yes, making Arthur— and both families—deliriously happy.[14]

The wedding date was set for February 20, ten days after Arthur's scheduled heel surgery. Since he expected to be on crutches for at least six weeks, the couple decided to simplify matters and hold the wedding in New York.

Their plans crystallized on January 30 when he went to Washington to attend the swearing-in ceremony of Andrew Young. Held in the East Wing of
the White House, the ceremony gave him the chance to meet both President
Carter and Supreme Court Justice Thurgood Marshall, who administered
the oath to Young as the new U.S. ambassador to the United Nations.

Young was pleased that his former African traveling companion had
taken the time to come to Washington for the ceremony, and he went out
of his way to offer his congratulations on the upcoming marriage. Indeed,
when Arthur asked if he would be willing to officiate, Young not only said
yes but also suggested the United Nations Chapel as the perfect venue for
the blessed event. Located in midtown Manhattan, the small but beautiful
ecumenical chapel was a perfect fit for a couple determined to avoid a showy
wedding.[15]

But before there could be any ringing wedding bells, Arthur had to get
beyond the surgery scheduled for February 10. The procedure entailed "a
carving of his heel bone, designed to relieve pressure from his Achilles tendon, where years of calcium deposits had built up." Deemed a success, the
surgery left him pain-free for the first time in more than four years. He had
not spent a night in a hospital since he had undergone a tonsillectomy at
the age of ten, but spending a week in bed gave him time to think about his
future.

Not surprisingly, he vacillated between optimism and resignation. "If I
was 20, I wouldn't give the operation a second thought," he told one reporter,
adding: "sitting here I've been thinking about it for three days. If I had to
quit tennis now, I'd be fairly satisfied" since "there are only five active players
with records equal to mine. So, what the hell?" Minutes later, however, he
expressed a totally different outlook: "I'm going to really want to play again.
Maybe I'll be like a colt out there all frisky. I won't be afraid to run on my
heel, and the other guys won't be able to play me wide and know they've got
me. I bet you I play at least four more years—*four more years*. They're not
going to get rid of me that fast."[16]

As the wedding day approached, Arthur's mood brightened. When asked
about his fiancée, he could not resist beaming. "I think we have very compatible life styles," he offered at one point, adding half jokingly: "We're Africa
freaks. She likes West Africa and I'm keen for East Africa, which means we'll
probably end up in the Central African Republic." On a more serious note,
he spent much of the last week of his bachelorhood dealing with a controversy surrounding an opinion piece he had recently written for *The New York
Times*.[17]

Titled "An Open Letter to Black Parents—Send Your Children to the Libraries," his highly provocative essay pulled no punches. "Since my sophomore year at University of California, Los Angeles," he began, "I have become convinced that we blacks spend too much time on the playing fields and too little time in the libraries. . . . I don't have children, but I can make observations. I strongly believe the black culture expends too much time, energy and effort raising, praising and teasing our black children as to the dubious glories of professional sport."

This style of parenting, he insisted, was bound to lead to disappointment, disillusionment, and unfulfilled lives. "There must be some way to assure that the 999 (out of a thousand) who try but don't make it to pro sports don't wind up on the street corners or in the unemployment lines," he wrote. "Unfortunately, our most widely recognized role models are athletes and entertainers. . . . While we are 60 percent of the National Basketball Association, we are less than 4 percent of the doctors and lawyers. While we are about 35 percent of major league baseball players, we are less than 2 percent of the engineers."

While acknowledging that "racial and economic discrimination forced us to channel our energies into athletics and entertainment," he maintained "parents must instill a desire for learning alongside the desire to be Walt Frazier. . . . We have been on the same roads—sports and entertainment—too long. We need to pull over, fill up at the library and speed away to Congress and the Supreme Court, the unions and the business world." He closed with a personal note about his grandmother's pride in his educational accomplishments—and her relative lack of interest in his tennis exploits. "What mattered to her was that of her more than 30 children and grandchildren, I was the first to be graduated from college, and a famous college, at that," he explained. "Somehow, that made up for all those floors she scrubbed all those years."

Ashe had been expressing this point of view to high school audiences for several years, but this was the first time he let loose in a major public forum. Clearly, he had other things on his mind besides tennis; facing the possibility that his playing career was over, he was preparing for the coming transition to life after tennis—a life that would include a role as a public intellectual.[18]

Jeanne was wholly supportive of his intellectual ambition, as were the close friends and family members who gathered at the United Nations Chapel to witness one of the most joyous days of his life. To those who knew him best, Arthur's intellect and independence of mind were two of his most endearing and impressive traits. More than his whiplike backhand, perhaps even more than his polite and gentle demeanor, the quality of his mind—the intellectual curiosity and seriousness of purpose with which he approached the world—made him special. That was why Jeanne and the others were not overly concerned about his heel or about whether he had a future on the court. They were confident he would make the most of the rest of his life in all the best ways. So as he stood next to Jeanne and said his vows, there was joy all around, and not even the cast on his left leg could diminish the occasion.

The night before the wedding, Young and his wife, Jean, invited the young couple to have dinner in their sprawling suite at the Waldorf Towers. Whenever Young presided at a wedding, he took the time to offer prenuptial counseling to the couple at hand. But with a "celebrity" couple like Arthur and Jeanne, he sensed that counseling was especially important—that whatever the depth of their affection there would be difficult challenges related to public image and personal ambition. The Youngs knew Jeanne was a professional woman with a proud sense of personal identity—that she, like Arthur, was a strong-willed, independent-minded individual. Creating a mutually satisfying and equal partnership was not going to be easy, considering the cross-pressures of their busy lives and Arthur's status as a celebrity.

Young urged them to deal honestly and openly with the complexities of their public and private lives. "When a couple marries," he told them, "six people are really involved. There are two people—yes, but they are different people at different times. First, there is the person you are. Then there is the person you think you are and then finally there is the person others think you are. Most of the time, these three people are not the same." To Arthur, who was averse to opening up emotionally, these words did not carry much weight at the time. But in the months and years that followed, he would come to recognize the wisdom of Young's counsel.[19]

Following a brief honeymoon in Haiti, the newlyweds moved into a duplex apartment on East 72nd Street, in the heart of Manhattan's trendy Upper East Side. For the first month of their marriage, Arthur was pretty much confined to the apartment. During this period, he and Jeanne spent a great deal of time together, more time than he had spent with anyone since he and his brother had been inseparable as children. Thus, along with the normal adjustments to married life, he had to deal with inactivity and inevitable boredom. This lack of mobility left him with plenty of time to read. By the time his cast was removed in mid-March, he was more than ready to resume his normal life—at least psychologically. As he soon discovered, he was still physically a long way from being ready to play again.

Facing a longer period of convalescence than he had expected, he began

daily workouts at the Nautilus Sports Medical Institute in an effort to accelerate his recovery. Working with a team of physical therapists, he swam,
rode an exercise bike, and lifted weights. It would be several weeks before
his doctors gave him the okay to run, but by early April he was walking well
enough to consider a brief trip to South Africa.[20]

The producers of ABC television's *Wide World of Sports* had asked him to
host a documentary on sports and the prospects for racial integration in
South Africa, and he eagerly accepted the challenge. He had not been to
South Africa for eighteen months, and he wanted to see firsthand how the
1976 Soweto uprising had altered the political climate. The trip would also
give Jeanne a chance to take some photographs, to meet Owen Williams,
Don Mattera, and other liberal reformers, and to have her first look at the
country that meant so much to her husband.

Within minutes of landing in Johannesburg, Arthur sensed South Africa
was in deeper trouble than ever, and during five days of interviews he encountered nothing to dispel this view. Conservative figures in the government had
stymied Minister of Sports Piet Koornhof's reform measures at every turn,
and Koornhof himself had shown little willingness to take any real risks on
behalf of black South Africans. In a meeting with the minister, Arthur challenged him to provide evidence of meaningful change. "You say mixed sport
in South Africa is a reality, but where is it?" he asked. "You show me where
it's being done." In response, Koornhof implored him to "understand how
things work here." "We can't force these things," he insisted. "They're purely
voluntary." He went on to cite a few examples of progress—Indians playing
cricket alongside whites, a series of interracial boxing matches, and an integrated professional soccer match—but it was not enough to convince Arthur
that the government had authorized anything more than tokenism.

In a closing press conference at the Johannesburg airport on April 9, he
expressed his profound disappointment. In view of what he had seen, it was
no longer advisable for him to play tennis in South Africa. Yet he refused to
give up on the nation that had become his second home. He promised that
following his return to New York he would solicit contributions from American corporations with economic interests in South Africa—contributions
that would fund "a million-dollar tennis stadium to be built in Soweto."
He also promised to press those same corporations to make good on their
pledges of "equal opportunity in employment."

What he was not willing to do was to support the all-out sports boycott of South Africa advocated by several black African nations. "I know the

Africans would kill me for saying this, and probably the militant blacks at home as well," he acknowledged, "but I know I'm right in saying that if you isolate them completely, the progress will come to a stop, a dead stop. Isolation can be effective, but it has to be selectively used." Constructive engagement was still his preferred path, and he vowed to return to South Africa on a regular basis. "I've become emotionally involved with South Africa and its problems," he insisted. "I guess I'll just keep coming back here until blacks have the vote." [21]

Ashe was correct when he speculated that his refusal to endorse the all-out boycott would lead to sharp criticism in some quarters. A few weeks after his return, he was shouted down during a speech at Howard University. Early in the speech two South African exchange students standing in the back of the hall began to yell: "Uncle Tom! Uncle Tom! Arthur Ashe is an Uncle Tom and a traitor! You betrayed us in South Africa! You betrayed your black brothers! Shame on you, Arthur Ashe! Sit down and shut up!"

When the shouting continued, Ashe stopped in mid-sentence and allowed the protesters to speak. But their words offered nothing he hadn't heard before, and his shock soon turned to anger. "Will you answer just two questions for me?" he demanded. "Just two questions? Why don't you tell everybody in this hall tonight why, if you are so brave and militant, you are hiding away in school in the United States and not confronting apartheid in South Africa, which is your homeland?" When they failed to answer, he continued his retaliation: "And also tell us how you as radicals expect to win international support for your cause when you give vent to your anger and rage as you have done here tonight in disrupting my speech. What do you expect to achieve when you give in to passion and invective and surrender the high moral ground that alone can bring you victory?" Once again there was silence in the back of the hall, and he was able to finish his speech without further interruption. [22]

Nevertheless, he had to face the reality that public pressure for a boycott banning South African athletes from international competition was on the rise. In late May, a coalition of fifteen organizations, including the SCLC and Jesse Jackson's Operation PUSH, founded the American Coordinating Committee for Equality in Sport and Society (ACCESS). The new organization's plan was to "hammer away at the issue of apartheid," primarily through an escalating boycott strategy. The coalition had the support of Ambassador Young, who during a recent visit to Johannesburg had urged black South Africans to mount "an economic boycott against apartheid." Where all of this left Ashe and his strategy of constructive engagement was unclear, but the growing impatience with the white South African government was forcing everyone, including him, to rethink their positions.[23]

From July 1976 on, Ashe's activities on behalf of South African liberation were entwined with a new organization known as TransAfrica. Conceived a year earlier at a conference on the African diaspora sponsored by the Congressional Black Caucus, TransAfrica advocated a human rights–oriented American foreign policy that would promote justice and liberation in Africa and the Caribbean.

The guiding force behind the organization's activities was its first director, Randall Robinson, a boyhood friend of Ashe's. In the 1950s, Robinson's father had been black Richmond's most celebrated baseball coach and "a fixture at Brook Field." As young boys Robinson and Ashe played baseball together, and they later kept in touch. After graduating from Harvard Law School in 1970, Robinson spent five years as a Boston-based civil rights attorney before stints as an assistant to two black congressmen, Bill Clay of Pennsylvania and Charles Diggs of Detroit, in 1975 and 1976. During these years, he worked to cement the relationship between the Black Caucus and anti-apartheid activists, including Ashe. The subsequent collaboration between the two men, based on a close personal and political bond, was essential to TransAfrica's growing visibility and influence, and Ashe eventually helped Robinson to establish the TransAfrica Forum, the fund-raising arm of the organization.[24]

For Ashe, the liberation of South Africa—and TransAfrica's lobbying efforts—would become consuming interests. But in June 1977, he temporarily refocused his attention on a matter of growing concern within the ATP. Tension between American players and their European, South American, and Australian colleagues had arisen over an imbalanced schedule that seemed to favor American tournaments. Since the United States was the source for most of the prize money and corporate sponsorships, and a large majority of the television coverage, there were frequent complaints about the "Americanization of Pro Tennis." Representing the American members of the ATP, Ashe acknowledged the problem but countered with the claim that sometimes the geographic imbalance worked to the detriment of Americans. "Some American players, particularly guys in college," he pointed out, "have been complaining about Europeans coming over to the United States and taking spots in our satellite tournaments." Even so, he added: "you can't have a protection policy."[25]

Resuming an active role as an ATP leader gave him a sense of satisfaction, but more than anything else he wanted to get back on the court. In late June, his doctors finally gave him the go-ahead, albeit a bit reluctantly, to return to competition. It was too late to enter the draw at Wimbledon, where he had to confine himself to the role of television commentator. But at least he was there for the dramatic men's single final that saw Borg defeat Connors to win a second straight Wimbledon title. Ashe admired the Swede's skill as well as his sportsmanship, which stood in sharp contrast to Connors's notorious gamesmanship, and he could not conceal his delight after Borg's victory. Watching Borg at his best stirred Ashe's competitive impulses, making him more eager than ever to get back on the court.[26]

In early July, he was not quite tournament ready, and he gave up his spot in the WCT Tournament of Champions to Alexander. But a week later, he decided to enter both the singles and doubles competition at the *Washington Star* tournament. As soon as he took the court for a few minutes of practice prior to the first round, he knew he had made a mistake. Withdrawing just before the match started, he let Dell, the tournament co-chairman, deliver the bad news to the press. "Arthur tried to play today," Dell reported, "but the swelling in his foot forced him to stop. The heel doesn't seem to be responding to treatment." Ashe valiantly promised to see if his heel would allow him to remain in the doubles competition with his partner Stan Smith. But even that proved to be too much for his ailing body.[27]

A week later, he tried again, and this time he did a little better. Playing at a WCT event in Louisville, he won his first-round match against Sashi Menon, a lightly regarded pro from India. In the second round, however, he lost a close match to thirty-eight-year-old Irion Tiriac. Ashe hated losing to someone even older than he was, but at least his heel had proven steady enough for serious play. Encouraged, he entered the Volvo International Tournament in late July, and once again he managed to win his first-round match, against Jai DiLouie, an eighteen-year-old Texan. He played even better in the following rounds, but in the round of sixteen he lost to fifth-seeded Harold Solomon. Limping noticeably after the match, he knew he had pushed himself too far.[28]

The next time he took the court was at the Robert F. Kennedy Pro-Celebrity benefit in late August. The heel still hurt, but he felt comfortable enough to try his luck at the U.S. Open the following week. Realizing this would be his last opportunity to play at Forest Hills—the Open was scheduled to move to a new facility in Flushing Meadows in 1978—he registered for the singles draw. Unseeded, he drew an unheralded first-round opponent, twenty-seven-year-old Zan Guerry of Lookout Mountain, Tennessee.

He was anxious to play Guerry, but it didn't happen. On August 27, the disappointed former champion was forced to withdraw from the tournament after a brisk but painful practice session. "I think I tried to do too much too soon," he explained. "My left heel acted up again and now I will have to postpone my comeback until 1978."[29]

He was also suffering from a lingering eye infection, but that did not stop him from serving as a commentator for ABC television. To his delight, Jeanne—who had quit her job at NBC—would also be working at the Open as a photographer for several sports magazines. As a *New York Times* headline put it, "Ashe Is Back at Forest Hills—With a Wife but Without a Racquet."[30]

As it turned out, Arthur didn't need a racquet to exert an impact on the tournament. At the end of the first week of play, he was drawn into an ugly controversy surrounding the racially insensitive remarks of William J. McCullough, a retired New York police officer who presided over the West Side Tennis Club's officials. When the Open moved to Flushing Meadows in 1978—a move that the West Side club was hoping to stop—McCullough predicted the majority-black population of the Flushing neighborhood would create serious problems. "Now let's talk about moving from a friendly, cooperative environment and going to an unknown," he suggested. "I say this: that when they move from here to a park, they are going to find that they will not only have trouble in making the tennis fans come but in getting the community to work with them." As the West Side club's only black member, Arthur was asked to comment on McCullough's statement, and he responded without hesitation: "My first impression is that what he said sounds institutionally racist. It sounds like a racial slur if I ever heard one."[31]

Without setting foot on the grass courts of Forest Hills, Arthur was seemingly everywhere at the 1977 Open. On Friday, September 9, he was one of three figures honored at a Waldorf-Astoria luncheon "marking the merger of the National Tennis Foundation and the International Tennis Hall of Fame." During his remarks to the assembled leaders of the tennis world, he couldn't resist scolding them after a year of nearly constant organizational squabbling. "We should hermetically seal them in here," he declared, motioning across the ballroom, "until they solve their problems." While he still yearned to get back out on the court, he was clearly enjoying the role of a plain-speaking tennis graybeard.[32]

That evening, he assumed an even more public role when he appeared in an hour-long CBS special titled *Super Night at Forest Hills.* Billed as an "all-star entertainment salute," the comedy-variety show pushed tennis to the background as Ashe, Billie Jean King, and Ilie Nastase shared the stage with Sammy Davis Jr., Andy Williams, Alan King, Minnie Pearl, Kelly the Chimp, and others. One television commentator complained the show took "the word 'super'" to "still another dimension of meaninglessness," but Ashe, who hadn't had much to smile about in recent weeks, enjoyed a much needed night of fun cavorting with the comics and other celebrities.[33]

Two days later, just minutes before the Sunday afternoon championship match between Vilas and Connors, he took part in a much more serious affair. Switching from celebrity to activist, he became a willing though somewhat conflicted participant in a protest organized by ACCESS. Outside the entrance to the West Side club, approximately two hundred protesters passed out leaflets either condemning South African apartheid or challenging the right of South African players to participate in the Open. Ashe, who supported the first position but not the second, decided to address the crowd anyway. Amid chants of "Sports, yes; apartheid, no: tennis with South Africa's got to go!" he endorsed the protest, saying, "I just wish there were 10,000 people out here." Prior to speaking, he held an impromptu news briefing in which he called for South Africa's banishment from Davis Cup competition. With so many withdrawals by countries unwilling to play South Africa, the nation of apartheid had "made the competition ridiculous."[34]

Ashe and his ACCESS allies served warning at Forest Hills that the tennis establishment could not turn a blind eye to the South African situation without incurring public embarrassment. But Ashe himself was the first to admit that the way forward was murky at best. In early October, he contributed an opinion piece to *The New York Times* focusing on the question "South Africa's 'New' Interracial Sports Policy: Is It a Fraud?" Recalling his recent visit to South Africa, he cited several experiences that confirmed his worst fears. "The one 'mixed' soccer game we went to film," he reported, "turned out to be an all-black team playing an all-white team." The government's determination to maintain "separate development" and an uncompromising "homeland policy," he insisted, made a mockery of its professed policy of racial equity in sports. "I was even refused tickets when I tried to buy five for South African kids who recognized me," he recalled. "It seems I stumbled by mistake upon the 'white' ticket window."

The obviously fraudulent nature of the South African government's new policy left Ashe in a quandary. On the one hand, the fraud seemed to justify continuing the boycott of South African athletes imposed in 1976 by the SCSA, the Supreme Council for Sport in Africa, the primary organization representing black Africans. Yet the boycott left Ashe's philosophy of engagement and dialogue through sports in shambles. "The great pity," he concluded, "is that the most powerful and visible vehicle for peaceful change in South Africa is sport. Not 'playing ball' with South Africa may needlessly prolong the system the world is trying to dismantle."[35]

Ashe's interest in South African liberation and other social issues remained strong in the closing months of 1977, but many of his fans were more interested in his private life with his beautiful bride. The newlyweds did their best to retain a modicum of privacy, but in September, during the first week of the Open, they agreed to a *New York Times* interview. Much of the article described the inevitable adjustments that Jeanne had experienced. "Since the marriage," the *Times* reporter observed, "she has traveled a lot more than usual." Even with her husband's injury, they had hardly spent a weekend at home. As Jeanne reported: "We've been to London, Paris—if you ever have to see Paris in five hours, do it with Arthur—Colorado, Miami three times, Richmond twice, and then South Africa."

The trips to South Africa and London were especially eye-opening for a woman unaccustomed to the glare of publicity or the life of a celebrity. After one young woman jumped on Arthur's back during an attempt to get an autograph at Wimbledon, Jeanne confessed: "I've never seen people like that before. It's a madhouse. Just like what you see in the old Beatles movies. You know, the screaming girls, they just go bananas."

Despite such scenes, she insisted life with her new husband was manageable. "I'm not overwhelmed by his world. I pretty much create my own world in his world," she explained. "When I get itchy and want to come back to New York, when there's something I've got to get done, I just say 'see you later.'" When they were in New York together, their favorite pastimes were riding bicycles, catching a movie, or visiting museums and art galleries. Jeanne's passion—frequenting the New York fine art scene—was new for Arthur. Even so, "she doesn't have to drag me," he insisted. "I go along," he said. "I have a layman's interest in art—particularly black Africa art. I even find myself going to these places when she doesn't go."

Compromise, they had already discovered, was the secret to a happy marriage. Both of them loved music, for example, but favored different styles. He did his best to accommodate her love of jazz, developing his own passion for Chick Corea and Miles Davis, and she returned the favor by embracing his love of rock idols such as the Beatles, Eric Clapton, and the Moody Blues. Another minor source of tension was Jeanne's aversion to cooking; she preferred to eat out, something Arthur had experienced more than he cared to remember. During the interview, after she exclaimed, "I love going out," her husband countered with a wistful reference to "homemade sweet potato pies." "We have little wars when she wants to go out," he explained. "Sometimes we get food from the Chinese restaurant across the street. It's one way to compromise. You're eating out but eating in." On many of the most important matters, there was no need for compromise. Both of them, for example, expressed the desire to have children, though early in the marriage Jeanne resented the familial pressure from members of the Ashe clan urging the young couple to have a baby as soon as possible.[36]

Some compromises took more than a little effort to reach. One serious strain on their relationship during the first year or two of their marriage was Jeanne's fiercely independent nature. She did not want to be treated as "Mrs. Arthur Ashe," a label she formally rejected at the outset of the marriage. In an increasingly common gesture among young feminists, she had decided to retain her maiden name after marriage, a decision Arthur accepted but didn't like very much. As he recalled in his 1981 memoir, " 'Fine,' I said, 'Don't change your name.' But at social functions or tennis matches, people would still come up and say, 'Oh, hello, Mrs. Ashe,' and Jeanne would do a slow burn." After much discussion, she finally settled on the hyphenated "Jeanne Moutoussamy-Ashe."[37]

Beyond the name problem was her determination to advance professionally without any help from her husband. "She felt uncomfortable with me trying to do things for her career; she wanted to do things on her own, not as Mrs. Arthur Ashe," he recalled. "She realized that I could pull a string here and there to help her career along a little faster. But she did not want her contemporaries in photography to feel that she had gotten this assistance without merit." Nothing infuriated her more than a meeting with a photo editor who showed more interest in her famous husband than in her portfolio. "You have to be a very secure, mature person to handle that properly," she later conceded. "At twenty-five, and not being fully established and totally secure in my work, that was very difficult for me to deal with. And I had gone from making $22,000 a year at NBC to absolutely nothing. I had quit my job and become a wife, and it was traumatic."[38]

Fortunately, the psychological insecurities related to freelance work and marriage to a celebrity became less of a problem for her after she and Arthur took a memorable trip to South Carolina in late 1977. After a few days in Charleston, they rented a car and drove south along U.S. Highway 17 through the heart of the Carolina low country, skirting the barrier Sea Islands. Prior to the 1960s, this part of South Carolina, once an empire based

on chattel slavery and rice and cotton cultivation, had resembled the proverbial land that time forgot. But by the time the Ashes arrived, the forces
of modernization had brought enough resort development and tourism to
make one wonder how long the area would be able to retain its distinctive
look and feel.

A few miles north of the Georgia border, enterprising developers had
already created the Hilton Head Plantation, an alluring cluster of manicured
golf courses, tennis courts, swimming pools, marinas, and condos, one of
which would be the future home of Arthur's close friend Stan Smith, who
would establish the Smith Stearns Tennis Academy on the island in 1985.
While there were many such resorts under development or in the planning
stages, enough of the vernacular architecture and folk culture remained in
1977 to set Jeanne off on a photo mission with her camera "clicking away,
recording old churches, courtyards, fishermen mending nets, and other types
of coastal folk."

As she told her friends in New York the following week, she found the
unpainted shacks and unprepossessing people to be hauntingly beautiful
and photogenic. She was drawn especially to the human side of the island
scenes—the local history and culture that had accumulated over centuries of
physical isolation and economic deprivation. The dignity of land and labor
cast in the midst of poverty spoke to her, perhaps in part as an echo of the
Louisiana family stories she had heard as a child. So it wasn't long before she
was back in the islands looking for more subjects and scenes to photograph.

On her second visit, she searched for a reasonably undisturbed island
where people still lived as they had earlier in the century. She soon found
Daufuskie Island sitting only a few hundred yards across the Calibogue
Sound from the yacht-filled Hilton Head marina. With its overwhelmingly
black population, its unpainted shacks set amidst towering and twisted live
oaks, and its linguistic reliance on the creolized dialect known as Gullah,
Daufuskie was just what Jeanne had been hoping to find—an authentic link
to the past.

Several trips to the island—and hundreds of photographs—later, she
had the makings of a remarkable photo essay detailing the remnants of a
vanishing culture. Published as *Daufuskie Island, A Photographic Essay* in
1982, her book used visual images to communicate a sense of place as well as
a deep connection between history and memory. In the estimation of more
than one reviewer, it was a triumph of documentary and artistic expression
created by a master photographer. But to Arthur and Jeanne it was most
valuable as a pathway to marital equity. In a marriage of high achievers,

Jeanne had produced something that, in terms of honesty and artistry, rivaled the most important achievements of her talented husband.[39]

Both before and after the publication of *Daufuskie*, Arthur did his best to accommodate his wife's feelings on matters of independence. But it would be several years before they put this problem completely behind them. In the meantime, he had to deal with identity problems of his own. Facing his declining fortunes on the court and the possibility of involuntary retirement, he hoped for the best and prepared for the worst. One serious disappointment was Catalina's decision to terminate his contract after eight years of successfully representing their line of sports apparel. Since he was no longer at or near the top of the tennis world, the company reasoned he was no longer worth substantial royalties. "I was terribly hurt by their decision," he later admitted. "I had helped them build their image in tennis; now that I was no longer at the very top they seemed to have little use for me."[40]

Losing the Catalina contract was a psychological blow, but fortunately his other endorsement contracts and business interests ensured he and Jeanne would have plenty of money for the foreseeable future. Head rackets were selling better than ever. (In October 1978, Head did not renew the option on his contract, but six months later the company reversed course and offered him an even more lucrative deal.) He was earning money as a television commentator and as a spokesperson for several corporate sponsors; he still had his seasonal teaching position at Doral; and in 1978 he branched out into several additional commercial activities. Under the auspices of *Tennis* magazine, he wrote a series of instructional articles; he made television commercials for the National Guard; he signed a major endorsement contract with Le Coq Sportif tennis wear; and he became a consultant for the Aetna Life and Casualty insurance company.[41]

Several years earlier Aetna had assumed sponsorship of the annual World Cup competition between the United States and Australia, and it was at the first Aetna-sponsored tournament in Hartford that Ashe finally beat Laver. He subsequently became friends with Aetna's president, Bill Bailey, and their relationship led to a consultancy involving minority recruitment in which he facilitated the hiring of up-and-coming minority managers and executives. The program proved to be a striking success, and in 1982 he became the youngest member of Aetna's board of directors.[42]

This was a time of deep transition for Ashe, not only in terms of his adjustment to married life, but also in his evolving sense of priorities. Despite his hopes of regaining his stature on the tennis tour, he no longer thought of himself as a tennis player with an array of side interests. As he later explained, "I had to hasten my readiness for retirement. I worried less about my tennis results and more about my business involvements. Meetings that once had been a nuisance now took on new importance." Though still a professional athlete, he was growing more comfortable with his status as a celebrity and as a man about town in New York. Part of the change grew out of his association with corporate executives and with Jeanne's friends in the art world, as he now found himself in social situations he could not have imagined earlier in his life. One example, which drew a few gibes from his tennis buddies, was his participation in a December 1977 fashion show at the World Trade Center. As four hundred patrons of the Northside Center for Child Development looked on, he joined Muhammad Ali and five other top athletes on a runway where they modeled a line of fur coats. No one back in Richmond, he was convinced, would have known what to make of this ostentatious display, but it was all for a good cause.[43]

Once again he ended the year at Doral. Having Jeanne with him to enjoy the Doral Hotel's lavish amenities made this the most special winter sojourn to date. He had always appreciated the restorative powers of balmy weather and a good round of golf, but never more so than in December 1977. Other than a few light workouts and an early October United Negro College Fund benefit—where he played doubles with Andrew Young, newsmen Walter Cronkite and Harry Reasoner, and several other celebrities—he hadn't been on a tennis court for nearly four months. During the layoff his world ranking had slipped to a lowly 257, but on the positive side the pain in his heel had dissipated to almost nothing by Christmas. While he now realized his footwork would never be what it once had been, he felt ready to resume his comeback.[44]

A month earlier, the sportswriter Tony Kornheiser had predicted as much in an article profiling the rehabilitation efforts of both Ashe and Billie Jean King. "Ten years ago they were the best tennis players this nation had," Kornheiser reminded his readers. "Billie Jean was fire. Ashe was ice. Now, at the athletically advanced age of 34, they are rolling the dice again, shooting for 7-come-11 on the world tour." The article went on to discuss why the two aging warriors refused to retire. "Neither needs the money," Kornheiser pointed out. "Both have career options. Ashe could become a diplomat; certainly he has the intellect and the demeanor. Billie Jean has proven herself a giant in the crusade for women's rights. Part of it, obviously, is their love of center stage, the smell of the liniment and the roar of the crowd. But most of it is enlightened self-interest." Both know "there is still time before they have to surrender."

It was, Arthur confirmed, as simple as that. "The idea of cutting it off like a guillotine, of going cold turkey," he told Kornheiser, "well, I don't want to suffer the withdrawal. . . . I don't know whether I can play again, but for my own peace of mind I need to find out. I don't care about reaching No. 1; I just want to play. I just like hitting tennis balls." The joy of the game he had learned to love as a child was obviously still there, not only in his head, but also in his heart and spirit.[45]

TWENTY

COMING BACK

■

A SHE BEGAN 1978—HIS TENTH year as a pro—with modest expectations and a reasonable plan to ease into the tour with a few test matches. After spending early January in New York, where he watched the Grand Prix Masters, he was off to Evansville, Indiana, for a singles challenge match against Orantes. Although he lost, the match went well enough to spur him on, and two weeks later he traveled to Richmond to test himself in tournament play. With several members of his family in the stands, he drew Nastase in the first round and somehow managed to outlast the tough Romanian in a three-set battle. A consistently strong serve was the difference, compensating for his noticeably rusty groundstrokes. "I'm not in top form yet," he told reporters with a smile, "but I'm back." The next day he lost to Rosewall in straight sets, but he felt he had crossed an important threshold. With no pain in his heel, he was ready for the next challenge.[1]

In mid-February, he entered a tournament in Palm Springs, California, but lost in the first round. A week later, however, he played much better in a WCT event in Denver, fighting his way into the semifinals before losing to Smith. He did not play again until March 11, when he faced the eighteen-year-old sensation John McEnroe in a benefit match at a high school gymnasium in Morningside Heights, on the edge of Harlem.

In the meantime, all eyes in the tennis world were fixed on Nashville, where the U.S. Davis Cup team was scheduled to play South Africa on March

17. In early March, Ashe had applauded his friend Ray Moore's decision to leave the South African team. Though not a member of the U.S. team, Ashe reiterated that had he been asked to play against South Africa he could not have done so "in good conscience." As for the anti-apartheid protests planned for Nashville, he would support them "as long as they did not disrupt play."[2]

He was also one of several black leaders trying to forestall a plan to hold a heavyweight championship boxing match between Muhammad Ali and Leon Spinks in the South African "colony" of Bophuthatswana. Since Bophuthatswana's status as an "independent enclave" was suspect at best, Jesse Jackson claimed the fight "would only serve to sanction the conduct of the South African government." "I doubt very seriously that Ali would go through with such a fight," Jackson predicted. "No black fighter in this country could fight there and gain respect at the same time Arthur Ashe is endorsing the boycott of the South African Davis Cup team." Jackson was correct, and to his and Arthur's relief, the bout was moved to New Orleans, where Ali regained his title in a unanimous decision.[3]

The Davis Cup controversy was a different matter, however. Fielding one of its strongest teams in years, the U.S. Davis Cup committee was not inclined to withdraw even in the face of worldwide condemnation. So the Americas Zone match went on as planned, despite several thousand protesters gathered outside the Vanderbilt University courts where the match was being played. In an effort to blunt criticism, South African officials had belatedly added a Coloured player, Peter Lamb, to their squad before it arrived in Nashville. A Vanderbilt sophomore who had come to the United States courtesy of the Black Tennis Foundation founded by Ashe and Owen Williams, Lamb had already played on the university team for a year. But when the talented nineteen-year-old did not see any play during the tie, Ashe and other critics cried foul, dismissing the South Africans' gesture as blatant tokenism. The U.S. squad won the tie 4–1, advancing to the Americas Zone final against Chile, and a few months later the South Africans were banished from Davis Cup play by the ILTF. They would not return until 1992.[4]

While the Americans and South Africans were playing tennis—and politics—in Nashville, Ashe was at a Washington tournament. In singles, he suffered elimination at the hands of Gottfried, but in doubles he and McEnroe made it all the way to the championship match before losing to Smith and Lutz. A week later, he played well enough to reach the singles semifinals in Dayton, Ohio, but once again he lost to Gottfried. In late April, at the Santa Clara Valley Grand Prix tournament, he won his first title in two years by outlasting the white South African Bernie Mitton in the final.[5]

With this victory, he finally felt ready to tackle the big European tour naments. His first stop was the Italian Open in Rome, where he beat the young Italian clay court specialist Vincenzo Franchitti in the first round. "I'm getting better every day," he told reporters after the match, adding: "I hope to be in the first 16 seeds at Wimbledon." Unseeded in Rome, he won his second-round match but could not keep up with fleet-footed Harold Solomon in the third. After splitting the first two sets, he tired noticeably, losing the last set 6–0.[6]

At the French Open in late May, he was once again unseeded. Ecstatic to be part of the French championship's golden anniversary, he beat the Australian Phil Dent in the opening round. "I'm just trying to catch up to everybody," a beaming Ashe reported. "No problems with my foot. It feels fine." He went on to defeat José Luis Clerc of Argentina in the second round and Jan Kodes in the third. To beat the Czech star, he had to overcome a severely cramped right leg, but there was no sign of cramps when he faced Guillermo Vilas in the fourth round. Even so, the defending French Open champion made short work of his older opponent, losing only six games in three sets. Ashe was good-natured and whimsical in defeat, attributing his loss to age and a lack of speed. "I wasn't fast enough on the clay and he was quicker than I was at net," the thirty-four-year-old would-be comeback kid explained. "If I were 10 years younger, I'd handle him with ease."[7]

Ashe's showing at the French Open was good enough to earn him a fifteenth seed at Wimbledon, just behind Alexander and just ahead of Newcombe. Borg, the winner of the previous two Wimbledons, was the heavy favorite to repeat, so no one took much notice of the lower seeds. Even so, Ashe was determined to make his presence felt in what he feared would be his last Wimbledon. Prior to the tournament, he spent a week at Devonshire Park, where Ralston guided several American players through a series of grueling grass court workouts.

Eager to recapture the glory of his 1975 Wimbledon triumph, he received a good omen on the eve of the opening round when he learned the West Side Tennis Club had finally elected its first black member. As a U.S. Open champion, he enjoyed honorary member status, but the club had never accepted a regular black member prior to its acceptance of William Cammack, a well-known local NAACP official and the older brother of Doris Cammack, the crestfallen girl defeated by Arthur in 1955. Remembering the rude treatment accorded Ralph Bunche and his son in the 1960s, he was more than pleased.

Having never lost prior to the third round in any of his ten previous

Wimbledon appearances, he fully expected to survive his first-round match against Steve Docherty, a towering six-foot-five-inch Australian who had played football at Washington State. But the match, an up-and-down marathon played on one of Wimbledon's outer courts, ultimately favored the younger player. The afternoon match went on and on, ending just before darkness with a Docherty victory in the fifth set.

Disappointed and exhausted, Ashe found little consolation in the fact that, along with Smith and Kodes, he was one of three former Wimbledon champions to go down to defeat that day. This string of upsets, according to Neil Amdur, "was another indication that an era might have ended in tennis." When asked about the level of his frustration, an emotional Ashe confessed: "It's pretty big. You figure you key your whole year around this one tournament" only to "go down to ignominious defeat in the first round, 7–5 in the fifth on court 14, the last court at Wimbledon." Publicly, he vowed Wimbledon had not seen the last of him, but privately he must have wondered if he would ever play singles again on the hallowed grass.

In the meantime, he at least had the doubles competition, where he teamed with Yannick Noah, his eighteen-year-old protégé from Cameroon. The sight of two black players on the same court, unusual enough in itself, was compounded by the identity of their first-round opponents, Bernie Mitton of South Africa and Andrew Pattison of Rhodesia. Despite this racial subtheme, the match was a good-natured affair that went five sets before Ashe and Noah closed it out 14–12. They went on to lose in the next round to Riessen and Stockton, but their pairing remained the high point of the fortnight for Ashe.[8]

A week later, he was back in the States for the Tennis Hall of Fame tournament in Newport, Rhode Island. Surprised but pleased he was seeded number one, he was primed to win his second tournament of the year. But this comeback scenario did not pan out, as Mitton upset him in straight sets in the round of sixteen. In mid-July, Ashe suffered another early round loss, this time to Solomon in the *Washington Star* tournament. But he continued on the tour for the remainder of the summer, hoping he would eventually round into top form and perhaps even earn enough points to qualify for the eight-person Grand Prix Masters tournament scheduled for January 1979.[9]

By the time the U.S. Open started in late August, Ashe was tournament tough. Seeded sixteenth, he was eager to play on the hard courts of the new National Tennis Center at Flushing Meadows after several years of struggling on the slow clay at Forest Hills. With Jeanne looking on, he breezed through the first three rounds, losing only two sets along the way. In the fourth round, however, he came up against the always tough Raúl Ramírez. He had played Ramírez many times before, with mixed results. The Mexican was ten years his junior and much more likely than he to survive a long, drawn-out match. After Ashe lost the first set but won the next two, Ramírez won the fourth in a tiebreaker and the fifth going away. The thirty-five-year-old ex-champion didn't know it at the time, but this would be his last appearance at the U.S. Open.[10]

Following the Open, the U.S. Davis Cup team was scheduled to play Chile in Santiago, and there was some speculation that Captain Tony Trabert would select Ashe as one of the two American singles competitors. He had always been at or near his best in Davis Cup play, and as recently as December 1976 he had won a singles match against Mexico. That win had come on a hard surface in Tucson, however, and the Santiago matches would be played on clay, Ashe's weakest surface. For that reason, Trabert bypassed him in favor of Solomon and Gottfried, a decision later questioned after they won only two singles matches between them as the U.S. team barely edged the Chileans 3–2.

Under increasing pressure in the weeks leading up to the next tie—a tough contest against a Swedish squad that had won the Davis Cup in 1975—Trabert decided to shake things up. Since the tie would be played in Göteborg, Sweden, on a fast indoor carpet, he turned to Arthur as the logical choice to join Vitas Gerulaitis in the singles competition. Delighted, the "old man" was ready to give his all for the U.S. squad. But even that was not enough against Borg, the consensus number one player in the world. Although Arthur played as well as he had in months, he lost in straight sets. In his second singles match, he fared much better, easily defeating against Kjell Johansson. This victory not only clinched a 3–2 American triumph, but also marked the 27th Davis Cup singles win of Arthur's career—an American record.

Davis Cup exploits were a matter of great pride to Arthur, making it all the more painful when Trabert left him off the team in the next and final round. When the United States beat Great Britain for the Cup at Rancho Mirage, California, in early December, the 4–1 victory came on a hard court just to Ashe's liking. But in preparing for the tie, Trabert decided to go with Gottfried, essentially depriving Ashe of the chance to close out his Davis Cup career with a victory in the spotlight. He had good reason to feel slighted, having beaten Gottfried on the same surface in the final match of the Pacific Southwest tournament in September. But he kept his feelings to himself. True to form, he was as polite as ever even in the face of disappointment.

The only thing that mattered, he insisted, was America regaining the Cup after a six-year drought.[11]

As 1978 drew to a close, Ashe took stock of his comeback. Since the beginning of the year, he had won three tournaments and made the final in a fourth, winning more than 70 percent of his matches. For someone who two years earlier had feared he might never play competitive tennis again, these were no mean accomplishments. Yet he wanted more. As he later explained, his record put him "within striking distance of the top eight players who would qualify for the Grand Prix Masters tournament at Madison Square Garden. I had qualified for the eight-player season-ending events before, but this one took on new importance for me. I had a feeling it would be my last chance to win the Masters."

By early December, he was in eleventh place in the Grand Prix points standing. The odds that he would make the cut were low, but the rumor that Borg and Connors were planning to bypass the tournament gave him some hope. The only problem was his commitment to spend the Christmas holidays at Doral conducting clinics. Since his only chance of qualifying depended on earning points in several late-December and early-January tournaments in Australia, his fate was in the hands of his Doral employers, who understood his dilemma and agreed to let him skip the clinics.[12]

Even so, getting to Australia in time to play was a near miracle. After playing a match in Stockholm, he flew to Brisbane via Zurich, Bahrain, Singapore, and Sydney. Arriving in the morning, he played his first match at 5:30 that afternoon. After he managed to win that one and several others before bowing out in the semifinals, it looked like he might have enough points to qualify for the Masters. But, taking no chances, he went on to play two more tournaments, the New South Wales Open in Sydney and the Australian Open in Melbourne.

Third-seeded in Sydney, he lost to Allan Stone in the fourth round. In Melbourne, he played some of his best tennis in years and cruised into the semifinals. The possibility of actually winning a second Australian Open had hardly occurred to him. Yet there he was on the verge of facing Vilas in the final. The only person in his way was twenty-six-year-old John Marks, an unheralded but heady Australian.

The match against Marks proved grueling. Playing before a crowd of twelve thousand fans, the two men went back and forth for nearly four hours. After Marks won the first two sets, Ashe fought back and won the next two 6–2, 6–1. In the fifth set, Marks took a 3–0 lead and appeared to be coasting to victory. Once again Ashe refused to give up. Fighting off five break points in the fourth game, he won that game and the next four, for a 5–4 lead. By this point, both players were so exhausted that neither could hold serve. In one game Ashe had two match points, but in the end Marks prevailed 9–7. For the loser the extended standing ovation that followed was bittersweet, but there was no longer any doubt he had come almost all the way back.[13]

After Vilas went on to defeat Marks in the final, the Argentine star decided to forgo the Grand Prix Masters, joining Borg on the sidelines. With this decision, Ashe became the eighth qualifier. The last time he had played in the Masters was 1975, when Nastase's antics had pushed him to walk off the court. This time Nastase had failed to qualify, but Ashe faced an even bigger problem when he drew John McEnroe in the first round. A few weeks earlier Ashe had praised the young New Yorker as the best player in the world. At a tournament in Stockholm the previous fall, he had watched McEnroe "destroy" Borg. "McEnroe just sliced Borg up like Zorro," he recalled. "Just a cut here, a nick there. It was unbelievable. Borg did not know what to do."[14]

Unfortunately for Ashe, McEnroe did pretty much the same thing to him in the opening round at Madison Square Garden. The left-hander's 6–3, 6–1 victory took only fifty-five minutes, and incredibly he committed only one unforced error in the entire match. Early in the second set, with Ashe trailing 0–2, a woman in the crowd yelled out "Remember 1975!" A smiling Ashe tipped his racket in acknowledgment, but there would be no repeat of the Wimbledon miracle.

Fittingly, Ashe's scheduled opponent in his second match was none other than Connors, the odds-on favorite to win the Masters title. Humiliation at the hands of a cocky rival was a late-career experience Ashe hoped to avoid, and fortunately for him a severe blister forced Connors to withdraw from the tournament a few hours before their match. Advanced to the semifinals by default, Ashe reached the final by outlasting Gottfried after a long struggle. Though disappointed, Gottfried praised Ashe after the match. "He should be commended for what he's done," the young Floridian declared. "For him to maintain eagerness and put as much work into coming back is phenomenal."[15]

He was eager all right, but no one expected that to make much difference in the final against McEnroe. When asked about his chances, Ashe responded: "He can be had as well as anyone else." Perhaps so, but almost no one expected a competitive match. What they didn't factor in, however, was Ashe's willingness to adapt. Following McEnroe's victory over Eddie Dibbs in the other semifinal match, Ashe spent several hours at his Manhattan apartment poring over a videotape of the contest. He then came up with a strategy of positioning, dink shots, and defensive lobbing designed to blunt McEnroe's wide kicking serves and powerful overheads.

Through four sets, the strategy worked. Ashe won the first set 7–6 in a tiebreaker, but McEnroe came back to win the second 6–3. They also split the next two sets, pushing the match toward an unexpected and rare drama. As the fifth set progressed, Ashe hung in against his heavily favored opponent, setting the stage for a possible upset. With the game score 4–5 and McEnroe serving at 15–40, Ashe actually had two match points, and the $100,000 first-prize check was almost in his grasp. But the miraculous upset was not to be. After McEnroe fought off the two match points and held serve, the last two games and the match were his.

McEnroe took home the big prize, leaving Ashe with the $64,000 second-prize money. Yet much of the glory adhered to the runner-up. Humble in victory, McEnroe declared: "I don't know how I won the match." In truth, both men emerged as winners. "The final," Amdur observed, "saved the $400,000 event, which had been wracked by the absence of Bjorn Borg and Guillermo Vilas, the early loss of an injured Jimmy Connors and otherwise routine round-robin matches. It was Ashe who made the occasion, saying he felt more like 28 and playing as if his last hurrah was still years away."[16]

With such encouragement, Ashe could not help but look forward to the 1979 tour. His world ranking had risen into the top fifteen, while his American ranking now hovered around number five, not bad for a thirty-five-year-old who had all but disappeared from the rankings a year earlier. He felt reasonably fit, and even though he continued to wrap his left heel and ankle and stretch his legs strenuously before every match, he was confident he could still play at the highest level.

In his first regular tournament appearance of the year, the U.S. Pro Indoor championship in Philadelphia, he proved his performance in the Grand Prix Masters final was no fluke. After upsetting second-seeded Vilas in the fourth round, and engineering a comeback five-set victory over Geru-laitis in the semifinals, he was the talk of the tournament. "Suddenly, Arthur Ashe has become the most exciting player on the men's tennis tour," wrote Amdur. "Not the best, not even the most consistent but certainly the most dramatic mix of maturity and talent." Dramatic was indeed the word when he faced Connors in the final. They had not played each other since Ashe's Wimbledon victory in 1975, and Connors went all out to extract a measure of revenge, which he accomplished with brutal efficiency. Still recovering from the Gerulaitis match, Ashe put up little resistance in the final. "I think Arthur may have been a little bit tired," Connors observed, leaving his defeated opponent to quip: "I feel like somebody beat me with a stick."[17]

A week later, Ashe was in his hometown of Richmond for a WCT tournament, and this time he played well, eventually losing to Vilas in the semifinals. But at a Palm Springs tournament in mid-February, he was forced to withdraw prior to the opening round. While getting up from a training table just prior to the match, he strained his neck, which soon became too stiff for him to play. This sure sign of aging drew a few gibes from the younger pros in the locker room, but he soon recovered enough to play in the National Indoor championship in Memphis, where he made it all the way to the championship match against Connors. Ashe had never won the National Indoor, the only major American title to elude him, so he was fired up to play Connors for the second time in a month. The rematch was a close contest, as Ashe used his strong serve to counter Connors's superior speed and court coverage. But the left-hander ultimately prevailed, winning a record fifth National Indoor title.[18]

After his unexpectedly strong start in the winter of 1979, Ashe cooled off in the spring. There were no championship matches, no titles, and to his dismay, no invitation to play Davis Cup. Nevertheless, the press continued to marvel at his spirit and longevity. In April, *Ebony* ran a feature story titled "Arthur Ashe: The Man Who Despite Age and an Operation Refused to Quit; He Comes Back as a Top Star." The author, Louie Robinson Jr., described Ashe's comeback as "the game's most exciting development of the year." Tennis fans were excited, he explained, "not just because a great champion has gained extended life" but also because tennis could still claim "a respected celebrity in a sport which now seems to have more prima donnas than an Italian opera company."[19]

At the same time, Ashe's interest in politics and social issues was as strong as ever. In a series of speeches and newspaper articles, he expressed his opinions on a wide range of issues, from the questionable value of sports boycotts to the educational and moral challenges facing black college students to his doubts about the wisdom of affirmative action. He did not shy away from controversy, and there was a direct, no-nonsense quality to many of his public statements. Speaking at Atlanta University in April 1978, he chided an audience of black students for squandering the gains of the civil rights movement. "Your older brothers and sisters got their heads busted in," he complained, "but you're not utilizing the tools it took a lot of people a lot of time to get." He pleaded with them to eschew a sense of entitlement, to assume responsibility for their own actions, and to avoid putting their faith in professional sports as a means of advancement.[20]

In October 1978, Ashe wrote a provocative piece for *The Washington Post* objecting to a proposed boycott of the 1980 Moscow Olympics—a position consistent with his opposition to the movement to boycott the 1968 Mexico City Olympics. The morale and competitive spirit of the world's best athletes, he insisted, were more important than using sports to make a questionable political statement. In late December, just before he left for Australia, he returned to Atlanta to speak at Morehouse College on the virtues of careful career planning and the shortage of black students preparing for careers in the sciences. Nothing, it seems, was beyond his capacity for social and philosophical commentary.[21]

Six weeks earlier, in November, a rumor that Ashe planned to run for public office had resurfaced after his friend, the former New York Knicks star Bill Bradley, was elected a United States senator from New Jersey. Ashe did not deny he had thought about running for office, but such a venture would have to wait, he insisted, until after his tennis career was over. He also feared he was too honest—too much of a truth teller—to survive as a politician.[22]

A case in point was his appearance at Howard University in March 1979. Representing Aetna, he was there to lay the groundwork for the future recruitment of black employees. While his prepared speech ruffled few feathers, during the question-and-answer period he alienated much of the crowd by endorsing the recent *Bakke* decision. After being rejected for admission to the University of California, Davis, School of Medicine in the early 1970s, a white applicant named Allan Bakke had filed suit against university officials charging them with reverse discrimination. Widely viewed as a test of the constitutionality of using racial quotas as a form of affirmative action on behalf of black applicants, the case went all the way to the U.S. Supreme Court, which in November 1978 issued a complicated 5–4 ruling that simultaneously upheld both the general principle of affirmative action and Allan Bakke's case for admission. Despite a measure of confusion, the ruling inspired considerable anxiety among affirmative action supporters, and few liberal Democrats found anything good to say about it.

Ashe was an exception. In his view, the ruling served a useful purpose in striking down the use of formal racial quotas by university admissions officers. Speaking as a firm believer in meritocratic self-reliance, and as a corporate representative of the Aetna insurance company, he offered the Howard students a stern warning. "The day will come," he told them, "when you're going to have to stand on your own two feet and make it. . . . You have to come to the realization you're going to go through the door because you're fully qualified not because you're part of a quota." In a properly constituted society, he insisted, the only acceptable roads to success were education, hard work, and earned respect; equal opportunity, not entitlement, was the key to a brighter future for black Americans. When a chorus of boos and angry objections followed, he retreated to another topic, but many students left the hall disappointed and disillusioned.

Later he rarely mentioned the *Bakke* controversy in public. In private, however, he continued to struggle with the issues of racial entitlement and self-reliance. In his last public statement on the matter, written in 1992, he confessed he still had strong misgivings about any policy that favored one race over another. "If American society had the strength to do what should be done to ensure that justice prevails for all," he insisted, "then affirmative action would be exposed for what it is: an insult to the people it is intended to help. What I and others want is an equal chance, under one set of rules, as on a tennis court. . . . Affirmative action tends to undermine the spirit of individual initiative. Such is human nature: why struggle to succeed when you can have something for nothing?"[23]

Ashe lived his entire life according to this standard of hard work, and he never worked harder than during the comeback spring of 1979. As he had learned early in life, there was no guarantee even the most strenuous efforts would pay off, and over the next few months this hard truth would become all too evident. Earlier in the year, against Dell's advice, he had entered into a risky business partnership with an old friend from Richmond. Sharing an interest in Africa, he and his partner formed a trading company, International Commercial Resources, with the intention of establishing trading links across the continent. "We were cautious, very cautious," Ashe later insisted. "We began our venture by negotiating with the government of Liberia, which seemed to be the safest, most stable place in Africa for an American to do business. . . . Our main dealings were with an efficient and apparently principled government administrator, Charles Taylor, who was himself a confidant of the president of Liberia at that time, William R. Tolbert." Unfortunately, within a year Tolbert's regime would be toppled by a violent coup, rendering the investment worthless. Ashe "never saw a penny of the money again."[24]

Arthur's fortunes on the court weren't much better. In early May, he began an extended tour in Europe, the scene of many of his greatest triumphs and potentially the perfect backdrop for his return to form. The first stop was the Nations Cup tournament in Düsseldorf, West Germany, where the United States team beat the West Germans but lost badly to both the Australians and the Italians. Arthur, who did not play particularly well, hoped his fortunes would improve once he arrived in Paris for the French Open, where at thirty-five he would be the oldest player in the field, two years older than Rosewall when he won the French Open in 1968. As the ninth seed he had every expectation of playing his way into the later rounds. But in the third round he lost in four sets to an unseeded nineteen-year-old Czech by the name of Ivan Lendl. Seventeen years Ashe's junior, Lendl would go on to become one of the world's greatest players. But in 1979, the loss to a boy who had won the French Junior championship the year before was crushing.[25]

A bitter factional feud that threatened to destroy the ATP in the weeks preceding Wimbledon added to his despair. Unhappy with Bob Briner, the ATP's executive director, and wary of Briner's ally and patron Donald Dell—who was thought to represent the original core of ATP stalwarts while neglecting other members—Cliff Drysdale and Ray Moore led a revolt to elect an anti-Dell majority to the board of directors. Arthur had close friends on both sides, but since he was personally closer to Dell than anyone else, he became a marked man during the lobbying campaign preceding the board election. As Richard Evans, himself an ATP insider, described the situation, "The anti-Dell faction needed Ashe's position on the Board to go to one of their own men and Arthur, understandably, was terribly hurt at being opposed by colleagues he had always considered to be his friends."

When the ballots were counted during the pre-Wimbledon Queen's Club grass court championships, Ashe retained his seat on the board by a narrow margin, and the power of Dell and his management company Pro-Serv emerged essentially undiminished. But the battle for control of the board scarred or destroyed several close friendships. While Briner's departure and replacement by Butch Buchholz had a healing effect, the turmoil in the organization sickened Ashe, who already had enough challenges in his life.[26]

The following week, he was in London for the Stella Artois Wimbledon warm-up tournament. Once again he played well in the early rounds before losing to the #30-ranked Víctor Pecci, a flamboyant six-foot-three-inch Paraguayan. In the pre-Wimbledon press coverage, Ashe drew some attention as a potential spoiler in the upcoming tournament. But in the opening round at Wimbledon, Chris Kachel, a virtual unknown from Australia, eliminated him in straight sets, the second straight year he had bowed out early.[27]

Following Arthur's unexpected exit, Jeanne decided they should take advantage of the situation. "You need a vacation," she told him, clearly implying she needed one, too. "Let's just get away from everything and ev-erybody." Angling for a real vacation for some time, she reminded him he had not taken any time off since their brief trip to South Carolina. "When-ever we travel, you're playing tennis and I'm looking for a Laundromat," she complained. "I would like to be able to sit down at a dinner table and not have someone come over and sit in a chair next to us and start a conversa-tion."

Still smarting from his loss, Arthur was out of sorts and initially cold to her idea. But he soon came around. As the second week of the Wimbledon fortnight began, they flew to Paris and then on to the French Riviera, where they stayed in the Château St. Martin, near the quaint village of Vence. Their time in Vence proved restful and therapeutic for Jeanne, while Arthur—"not the vacation type," as he put it—did his best to relax. Try as he might, it wasn't easy for him to forget his recent reverses and nagging doubts, even in the beautiful setting of southern France.[28]

Back in New York, he reflected on his prospects. "The end was clearly in sight," he conceded. "Nevertheless, I saw no reason why I couldn't continue to play professionally, with mixed success to be sure, for at least two or three more years." Fortunately, he did not have to worry about losing his elevated standard of living. Unlike less successful touring pros, he enjoyed the luxury of having other sources of income, ranging from an array of endorsements and investments to an exciting new career as a broadcaster.

As in other aspects of his life, he brought a special quality of perspective and experience to the broadcast booth. He knew the sport inside and out, and demonstrated both a wry sense of humor and an impressive command of the English language. In the ABC booth with Howard Cosell covering the round-robin matches at the Forest Hills Invitational in mid-July 1979, he more than held his own with one of broadcasting most colorful figures. As one television critic described the scene, "In the friendliest of manners, Mr. Ashe kept puncturing his broadcast partner's pomposities. When Mr. Cosell managed to turn 'architecture' into a verb, Mr. Ashe laughingly said, 'I'll have to look that up in my Funk and Wagnalls.'" It was classic Ashe—subtle, whimsical, and on point.[29]

TWENTY-ONE

OFF THE COURT

■

E VEN THOUGH HIS TRANSITION to the broadcast booth ensured
gainful employment for the foreseeable future, Arthur was not quite
ready to hang up his racket. A week after the July 1979 Forest Hills broadcast, he entered a tournament in Kitzbühel, in the mountains of west Austria.
The beautiful setting and luxurious accommodations were simply too alluring to pass up. As he explained to Jeanne, if he managed to make it into
the late rounds, which he fully expected to do, they could turn the trip into
an extended Alpine vacation. Unfortunately, this anticipated Austrian idyll
soon fell victim to two unexpected developments: a second-round loss to an
unheralded French player, Christophe Freyss; and a call from Arthur's sister
Loretta, who informed him their father had been hospitalized after a severe
attack of angina.[1]

Although Arthur Sr. soon recovered and lived for another ten years, the
angina attack warned of troubles to come. Indeed, within a few days of his
return from Austria, Arthur Jr. suffered an attack of his own. On Monday,
July 30, still feeling the effects of jet lag, he went to bed in his and Jeanne's
New York apartment around half past ten while she was still downstairs
working in her darkroom. A little over an hour later, he was, in his words,
"jolted awake by the most intense chest pain I had ever suffered. After about
two minutes, the pain subsided. Telling myself that I was suffering from
nothing more than a severe case of indigestion, I tried to go back to sleep. I

was almost there when the pain returned even more intensely than before. Breathing hard, I sat up in bed. I could not remember an attack of indigestion so acute. Again, the pain subsided; again I relaxed; and again, after about fifteen minutes, I was jolted by an excruciating pressure in my chest. Finally the pain ebbed and I returned to sleep."[2]

When Arthur awoke the next morning he felt fine, so he decided to honor his commitment to conduct two youth tennis clinics, one at Crotona Park in the Bronx and a second at the East River Tennis Club in Queens. After playing an eight-game pro set against the club pro Butch Seewagen and signing a few autographs, he "stepped under a large courtside umbrella to escape the sun." Almost immediately the chest pains from the night before returned, this time with much more intensity. He later described the pain as a "sledgehammer" hitting his chest. "My breastbone," he remembered, "felt like it would cave in." Without telling anyone, he tried to "walk off the pain" in a nearby parking lot.

At that point Seewagen looked out the window of the pro shop and saw his friend in distress. Rushing over to help, he yelled out to Dr. Lee Wallace, a New York Hospital staff physician who happened to be playing on a nearby court. Following a few quick questions from the doctor, Arthur was whisked away to New York Hospital for an examination. "I'll never forget the ride," he later wrote. "Thank God, we just happened to be near the 59th Street Bridge, and it wasn't busy. . . . Butch drove. I sat in the front clutching my chest. Dr. Wallace was in the back. We made small talk, touching on everything except the pain." Fortunately, it only took seven minutes to reach the emergency room.[3]

Arthur was shocked when Dr. Wallace told the emergency room doctor: "I want Mr. Ashe admitted as a possible heart attack patient." While Seewagen called Jeanne to tell her what was happening, the hospital staff wasted no time. "Within 10 minutes of the time we left the club," he recalled, "I had an oxygen mask over my face, IV needless in my arm, and an EKG machine monitoring every beat of my heart." Even before they were sure he had suffered a heart attack, the doctors gave him morphine for pain and medication to prevent arrhythmia. "All of this took about five minutes," he estimated. "Meanwhile, my mind was racing as fast as the medics. I thought of all sorts of things—all bad, debilitating and permanent. Stroke. Bypass operations. No-salt diets. No more tennis. Worse yet, dying."[4]

By that time Jeanne had arrived. Four years earlier she had watched her father nearly succumb to two heart attacks suffered in a single day, so she was experienced enough to know her husband could draw comfort from her strength. "Jeanne's grip on my hand was reassuring," Arthur would later write. "I listened for beeps from the EKG machine. Were they faster or slower? How serious was my condition? What was happening to me? I tightened my grip on her hand." At one point, after detecting shivers, she grabbed his arm and with what he remembered to be "a studious, controlled calm" asked "Are you cold?" "No, just scared to death," he replied, in a moment of vulnerable but endearing honesty. If "partners in a marriage have to feel like they're needed," as he later insisted, Jeanne was about to enter a new phase in their relationship. Earlier in their marriage, she had sometimes chafed at his self-sufficiency, voicing doubt that he really needed her in his life. That problem would never trouble them again.[5]

An examination soon confirmed Arthur had indeed suffered a heart attack, the result of myocardial ischemia—"a lack of oxygen in the blood going to the heart muscle." The initial assessment by the attending cardiologist, Dr. Stephen Scheidt, suggested the scale of the attack was moderate and that the heart had suffered only limited damage. Nevertheless, Arthur was clearly unnerved. As one early visitor—the journalist Carole Kranepool—reported: "When I first visited Arthur in the hospital, he looked despondent and he seemed frightened. He wasn't the Arthur I knew, always outgoing and happy. He was withdrawn."

Less than a week later, however, a second visit revealed a dramatic change of spirit. Now "he was keeping constant charts of his condition: hoping to explore and explain the reasons for his heart attack," and he had become "an incessant reader of books on heart diseases." One of the attending physicians told her Arthur probably "knew more about his condition than most doctors know about heart disease." Following two days in intensive care, "Dr. Ashe" spent nearly a week in the coronary care unit before being sent home with strict orders to rest.[6]

Arthur's heart attack shocked the tennis world. As soon as they heard the news, fans across the globe asked the obvious question: how could this happen to a world-class athlete still in his mid-thirties, a man so thin and seemingly so fit he had managed to keep pace with younger opponents barely half his age? That he looked considerably younger than his years made it even more difficult to believe he was seriously ill. For Arthur, the heart attack "shattered a myth that every professional athlete has about invincibility." Writing in 1981, he recalled he had once shared the public's naïveté on such matters: "Athletes, especially those involved in aerobic sports, are in great shape. If they catch cold or sneeze, they consider it a personal affront." But "when you do get sick, it brings you back to life, to reality."[7]

Ashe's first public statement on his illness came four weeks after his attack, in an article written for *The Washington Post*, where he had been writing opinion pieces for two years. Both personal and philosophical, the article asked the question: "Why me?" After describing the whirl of confusion and fear he had experienced during his first few minutes in the hospital, he revealed that "during the entire episode—in the car on the way to the hospital, in the emergency room and during the four days in the intensive care and cardiac care unit—one thought recurred: Why me?" This question, he insisted, "was more than just a complaint from someone who felt cheated by fate."

To prove his point, he went on to analyze his recent experience, turning a personal story into a discourse on fitness and fate. "I'm not your typical heart attack patient," he explained, stating the obvious. "My blood pressure is below normal. I don't smoke or take drugs. I'm thin. My serum cholesterol is low. I'm not hypertense. I have no trouble absorbing sugar. And with all the tennis I play, I'm about as physically fit as a 36-year-old man can be." All of this helped to explain why he "didn't pay much attention at first to the chest pains." As he recalled his reasoning: "I had started to sweat, but I wasn't short of breath. I felt some pain in my arms and I made a vague connection to my father's recurring symptoms. But I'm a pro athlete—no way I'm having a heart attack." Only after hospital tests confirmed the attack did he begin to acknowledge his situation. "The answer to my big question— why me?" he eventually concluded, "—seemed to boil down to family history and random chance."

Ashe's family history should have alerted him to his own vulnerability, considering his mother's death from cardiovascular disease at the age of twenty-seven, his father's two heart attacks—the first suffered at age fifty-five—and the high blood pressure and hypertension rife among his aunts, uncles, and cousins. But it didn't occur to him that professional athletes had to worry about such things. "I never thought about it in terms of myself, really," he later confessed, "because I was an athlete, and I figured I was immune." Eventually he became convinced the rigorous physical regimen of competitive tennis, while giving him a false sense of security, had also softened the blow. "The doctors tell me," he reported, "that my physical condition probably kept the attack from being more severe. It may even have saved my life." No amount of physical conditioning, it seemed, could completely offset the combined influence of bad genes and bad luck. But four weeks after the attack he already felt his body regaining its normal energy and rhythm.

Barring any unforeseen problems, he assured the *Post*'s readers, the prognosis looked good. "Some time in the next two months an angiogram will be performed on me," he explained. "Assuming I pass the test, a graduated conditioning program will be mapped out for me around the beginning of November. In the meantime I am walking about normally, eating what I want, taking French lessons and going to the Sports Training Institute here every day for about 40 minutes." While acknowledging that a full recovery was less than certain, he made the startling announcement: "right now I plan to start playing competitive tennis again at the U.S. Pro Indoor tournament in Philadelphia the third week in January. It will then be five months since my attack, and I'm looking forward to re-establishing myself where I left off—among the top 10 tennis players in the world."[8]

A month later, to Arthur's shock and dismay, the test revealed the damage to his heart was extensive, much greater than his cardiologists, Drs. Mike Collins and Virginia Bouchard Smith, had first thought. He was suffering from a 95 percent closure of his left anterior descending artery, a complete closure of his circumflex artery, and 50 percent closure at two places along his right coronary artery. "The amazing thing," he later conceded, "was that I had been playing professional tennis like this." The doctors acknowledged the damage from the August heart attack could have been even worse, but they strongly recommended coronary bypass surgery. When he asked about his prognosis without surgery, they responded with sobering news: "Sorry, Arthur. Unless you have an operation, you can forget about playing tennis again. Certainly not professional tennis." Since these were not the words he wanted to hear, he tried his best to ignore them. For a time, nothing the doctors said seemed to dampen his optimism—or his determination to achieve a full recovery without surgery.[9]

Throughout the fall of 1979, he clung to the hope of proving his cardiologists wrong. Given enough time for proper rehabilitation and conditioning, he reasoned, he could avoid surgery, gradually recover his strength and skills, and eventually come back stronger than ever. The main problem with surgery, as he saw it, was that his doctors could not cite a single case of a patient returning to competitive athletics following open-heart surgery.

By late November, he had grown confident he had made the right decision—and that it was time to think about returning to the tennis court. During a recent trip to Iowa to campaign for Senator Edward Kennedy, he had shown considerable stamina and had returned to New York ready to tackle additional physical challenges. After consulting with his doctors, he agreed to start slowly with an exhibition match scheduled for December 9. The match was part of a United Negro College Fund benefit event featuring celebrity doubles and an exhibit of Jeanne's photographs taken during a 1978 trip to the South Carolina Sea Islands. Held at the Art Salon on East 62nd Street, the photography exhibit represented a new beginning for Jeanne's career and a perfect complement to Arthur's return to tennis.[10]

The Ashes' planned participation in the UNCF benefit signaled a resumption of normal life. But, unfortunately, the tennis side of the plan never materialized. On December 6, three days before the event, Arthur developed chest pains after watching *Monday Night Football* in a Jacksonville hotel room with several of his ATP tennis buddies. He refused to panic, but after a restless night punctuated by heart palpitations, he asked Pasarell, who always seemed to be there when he needed him most, to take him to Jacksonville Memorial Hospital.

After two days of tests and bed rest, the doctors released him with the reassurance he had not suffered a second heart attack. Prior to his release, however, he had a lengthy conversation with another patient—a man "who had just undergone a triple bypass two days before." To his amazement, the man "was in great shape: no blood, one tube in his arm, no oxygen, all he had was a simple dressing. He said all the pain was gone, and that he wasn't even on medication anymore." This, as it turned out, was enough proof to dispel Arthur's fear of heart surgery. "So I went back home," he recalled, "and resolved that I would get this done myself." Though still wary of going under the knife, he said, in effect: to hell with the odds against a postoperative return to the tour. He had beaten the odds all of his life, and he was confident he could beat them again.[11]

One of the city's leading heart surgeons, Dr. John Hutchinson III, happened to be a fraternity brother, and Arthur was fortunate to find an opening in Hutchinson's schedule on December 13, only five days away. The surgery turned out to be a quadruple coronary bypass involving the removal of several veins in his legs. The veins were then implanted in his chest as a replacement for the clogged arteries threatening his life.

Dr. Hutchinson had performed this operation many times with great success, and Arthur's experience was no exception. In the recovery room, the surgeon informed his famous patient he could now look forward to a long and reasonably normal life. When Arthur asked him if the prognosis pointed to a possible return to the tour, Hutchison was equivocal. Perhaps hearing only what he wanted to hear, the anxious patient interpreted this as a green light and began planning an ambitious rehabilitation program designed for a return to the court.

A week later, just before his discharge, Arthur discussed his future at a press conference held in the hospital solarium. With Dr. Hutchinson at his side, he began by showing off his surgical scars. After pulling "open his powder blue pajama top," he "puffed up his chest and proudly exhibited the incision bisecting his upper body; then he rolled up his trousers to display scars running from knee to ankle." Don't be fooled by these surface wounds, he told the reporters; he was supremely confident he would be "back in the gym next week." After explaining he "would begin with light workouts under the supervision of a team of cardiologists and sports medicine specialists from New York Hospital," he predicted that within a few months he would be back on the court playing his best tennis in years, adding "I think you'll see me playing Wimbledon in June."

Dr. Hutchinson, who had performed more than four thousand open-heart operations in the last twelve years, confirmed "Mr. Ashe has a lot of things going for him." But the circumspect doctor stopped far short of predicting that his famous patient, still suffering from postoperative anemia, would ever see a successful return to Wimbledon.[12]

Jeanne was just happy to see him breathing and on the mend. Though outwardly supportive of his dream of returning to tennis, she quite naturally feared he was setting himself up for failure and unnecessary disappointment. Whatever her true feelings, she knew she was absolutely essential to his chances of recovery. "Jeanne understood what I was going through," Arthur later wrote. "She saw me lying on the table in New York Hospital that August day and knew that she had to assume control of the situation. She was frightened for me but also sensed that I was most comfortable in a calm, controlled environment. If I read panic in her eyes, she reasoned, it would not help my attitude."

To some extent, Jeanne had been through this before, having dealt with her father's serious heart attacks in 1974 and her aunt's open-heart surgery four years later. Moreover, she had started her marriage with a husband on crutches, and for more than two years she had lived with his ongoing convalescence—first from his heel problem and later from his heart condition. While all of this had placed inevitable strains on their relationship, the beleaguered couple seemed to grow closer during the six months leading up to Arthur's surgery, and the bond between them became even tighter in the weeks and months that followed. The rehabilitation process was demanding and often frustrating, and sometimes Arthur felt and acted like a caged lion. There were also times when Jeanne was nearly overcome by feelings of anxiety and dread. But mostly she feared Arthur was driving himself too hard in a potentially dangerous and self-defeating effort to get back on the court.[13]

Many of Arthur's closest friends shared Jeanne's concerns and wondered why he was so determined to return to the tour. With all the other things he had going for him, why, they asked, did he feel the need to prove himself on the court at an age when most players had already retired? Among all the players of his generation, he had seemed the most likely to fashion a graceful transition to an active and fulfilling retirement. Yet he insisted on waging a last-ditch effort to extend his career.

As Arthur later explained, his primary motivation was fairly simple. "I had enjoyed a wonderful career and didn't want it to end," he recalled in 1992. It was difficult to imagine a life without tennis. The game had dominated his life since childhood, and he had never tired of the basic rhythms and physical and psychological dictates of the sport—the challenge of hitting a bouncing ball or running down a difficult shot, the endless gamesmanship of risk taking, recovery, and composure.

He also loved the tour, with all its faults and complications, and he cherished the lifestyle that came with it. "When I played tennis," he wrote in 1981, "I loved the idea of waking up, feeling nervous about the consequences of winning or losing, enjoying the pressures of staying on top." On another occasion, he contrasted the void of retirement with the continuing allure of the tour: "I missed the travel to foreign lands, the camaraderie of the players, the excitement of the matches themselves." "Where would I be?" he wondered, without "the glitter and glamour of the tennis world . . . the endless stroking of the ego, the copious episodes of pampering and privilege."

He also fixated on his last chance to counter certain negative characterizations that had dogged his career. From time to time, critical observers had charged he lacked a killer instinct, that he often lacked focus as his wandering mind led him into erratic play, and that his many off-court interests ensured he would never reach the top of the tennis world. These charges still rankled him, and he remained determined to dispel them. Many observers saw his grand plans as unrealistic, even outlandish. But, as he reminded them, there had been similar expressions of doubt before his great victory at Wimbledon in 1975—and before his unexpected Australian Open doubles title two years later.[14]

During the early months of 1980, as the wounds of the operation healed, he acted as if he had every expectation of resuming his career. Eager to shed his invalid status, he acted more like his normal energetic self with every passing day. Although Jeanne did her best to slow him down, he soon felt confident enough to raise the level of his physical activity and, on occasion, to leave the security and familiarity of his cardiologists and the New York medical enclave. At this point, his only major concession to his medical condition was to avoid long-distance travel.

Resuming most of his normal activities, he was often out and about in New York attending to ATP and endorsement business, giving press interviews on the current state of the tennis world, campaigning for Senator Kennedy, visiting friends, and working out at the Sports Training Institute on 49th Street. He even found time to resume his writing for *The Washington Post*, penning articles on subjects as varied as sports betting and the proposed Olympic boycott. All of this activity in the face of adversity gained notice and earned him serious consideration for the International Award for Valor in Sport, presented in London on February 5. In the end, he lost out to an intrepid French hang-glider blinded during an ascent of K2, the world's second highest peak. But the nomination enhanced his image as a stalwart figure worthy of respect and admiration.

One exception to his temporary travel ban was a sad mid-January journey to Westport, Connecticut, where he served as a pallbearer at the funeral of Alex Deford, Frank Deford's eight-year-old daughter, who had succumbed to cystic fribrosis. Deeply attached to Alex and her family, Arthur later described the funeral as one of the most "harrowing" experiences of his life. His only other midwinter venture outside of New York came in February, when he flew across the country to attend an ATP board meeting in Palm Springs. As a morale-boosting gesture, the reunion with his ATP comrades turned out to be just what he needed. Staying with the Pasarells, he even got the chance to meet their new baby daughter, Fara.[15]

After his return from California, Arthur started swimming almost daily, and he even began a series of semisecret tennis workouts at the East River Tennis Club in Queens. Butch Seewagen, the same club pro who had witnessed his attack the previous summer, reportedly put the former U.S. Open champion through his paces without any apparent ill effects. By early March, he was encouraged enough to schedule more on-court workouts. But first he and Jeanne, accompanied by their longtime friend Dr. Douglas Stein, flew to Cairo, Egypt, for a late-winter vacation. Having missed his annual Doral sojourn in December, he was eager to feel the warmth of the subtropical sun. Encouraged by the Egyptian star Ismail El Shafei, who promised that a few days of balmy North African weather would do wonders for mind and body, he boarded the long flight to Cairo with high expectations.

Part of Egypt's attractiveness for Arthur was the softening of its relations with Israel since the signing of the August 1978 Camp David Accords, an agreement that produced a joint Nobel Peace Prize for Prime Ministers Anwar Sadat and Menachem Begin. Having heard about the "new Egypt" from both El Shafei and Andrew Young, who had defended the Accords before the General Assembly of the United Nations, he wanted to see it for himself.

The first day in Cairo was everything he had hoped for, but on the second day his Egyptian vacation ended in near tragedy. After leaving his hotel near the Great Pyramid for an afternoon run, he suffered an attack of angina. "I was loping along gently, easing into the main phase of my run," he recalled, "when the angina struck. It hit me relatively softly, but hard enough to stop me dead in my tracks. I felt the world come to a halt. I walked slowly back to the hotel." A few minutes later Doug Stein did a cursory examination, taking his friend's pulse and listening to his heart. He then asked Arthur to do a few jumping jacks. Almost immediately the angina pains returned. "You were right to stop running," Stein told him. "Your heart wants no part of it." He advised his ailing friend to return to New York for a full examination. Arthur now knew he had come to a crossroads. "As we flew out of Cairo," he later confessed, "I knew one thing for sure: My career as a competitive tennis player was over."[16]

Surprisingly enough, he and Jeanne did not fly directly back to New York. Instead, they lingered in Europe for a few days, mostly in Amsterdam. A trip to the famous Rijksmuseum was his gift to Jeanne in compensation for their ruined trip to Cairo. Her love of art exceeded his, but he had a special attachment to Rembrandt. He was especially fond of Rembrandt's most celebrated painting, *The Night Watch*, but on this particular visit he found himself concentrating on another Rembrandt masterpiece, *The Prophet Jeremiah Lamenting the Destruction of Jerusalem*. As he pointed out to Jeanne, Jeremiah's obvious depression spoke to him. The painting's "power over me," he later explained, "had much to do with what had happened to me in Egypt . . . my ill-fated attempt to jog near the Nile and the collapse of my dreams of returning in glory to the tennis court." Somehow this great piece of art helped the frightened couple to put their fate in context, allowing them to share the burden of a difficult but inevitable decision.[17]

Over the next month he had a few second thoughts about his decision, but after consulting with his cardiologists he realized he had to face reality. During the second week of April, just after publishing a poignant *Washington Post* piece on the life and recent death of the Olympic hero Jesse Owens, he composed a letter and mailed it to twenty-two of his closest friends and associates. "Long ago in my Sunday school classes," he began the letter, "I learned that 'for everything there is a season.' . . . After many hours of hard thought and soul-searching, I have decided from today on, to end my nonstop globetrotting odyssey in search of the perfect serve and retire from competitive tennis. In its place, I hope to begin another exciting season of writing, talking, listening, reading, and assisting." [18]

A week later, on April 16, he followed with a formal public announcement. "I won't be entering any more tournaments," he told a group of reporters, assuring them "there will be no great transition because I have been in the process of doing this for years." When asked "why now?" he explained: "It is time. Health is a factor, but that's not the only reason." In fact, he added: "I feel pretty good. My doctors say I will live to be 100, but they won't put it in writing." [19]

The reaction to Ashe's retirement was swift. Within days his mailbox overflowed with expressions of affection and respect, and almost immediately glowing tributes began to appear in the press. Some reporters pointed to his gaudy statistics: ten years as a professional; 304 tournaments played and fifty-one singles titles earned during the Open era; a finalist in 32 percent of the Open tournaments in which he played; a career match winning percentage of over 75 percent; eleven years in the American top ten; three Grand Slam singles titles and two Grand Slam doubles titles; one NCAA team championship and one NCAA national singles championship; ten years as a Davis Cup team member and the highest percentage of Davis Cup singles victories, 84.4, of any American player in history. Others stressed his leadership roles in the ATP and the development of Open tennis, and still others highlighted his gritty and heroic effort to extend his career.

Nearly all, of course, mentioned the strength of his character, his exemplary sportsmanship, his commitment to social justice, and his determination to make a difference in the real world. One of the most moving tributes, penned by Barry Lorge of *The Washington Post*, praised Ashe as "a self-proclaimed 'citizen of the world.'" "Thoughtful and knowledgeable on numerous subjects," Lorge wrote, "Ashe has long been respected as much for his sportsmanship, eloquence, and deportment as for his electric serve and backhand. In a sport overpopulated with crybabies and greedy opportunists, he became a millionaire without ever forgetting his sense of responsibility to the public and the game." [20]

Lorge and other admirers set the stage for formal recognition of an extraordinary life and career. To Ashe's embarrassment, special awards and accolades began to pile up. The first came from his hometown of Richmond, where the school board named a new $3 million school gymnasium after him and where he received the city's Community Service Award. At a racially integrated awards banquet held on May 9, Arthur Ashe Sr. was on hand to accept the award on behalf of his son, who was en route to Europe to cover the Italian and French Opens for ABC television.[21]

In Paris, on May 31, Arthur's old friend Philippe Chatrier hosted a special dinner for Arthur, Jeanne, "and some friends" at Tour d'Argent, one of Paris's finest restaurants. "They gave me a silver plate very suitably inscribed: 'To Arthur from the French. Thanks for the memories,'" he reported rather drolly, "which is about as close as I'm going to get to winning anything here." He was touched by Chatrier's kind gesture, but the high point of the French Open was watching their shared protégé, twenty-year-old Yannick Noah, fight his way into the fourth round.[22]

A week later, Arthur was back in the States at Dartmouth College, where he received an honorary Doctor of Arts degree, the first of more than a dozen such degrees he would acquire over the next decade. In July, he received a tribute of another kind when the American Heart Association asked him to be the chairman of its national fund-raising campaign, and later in the summer a poll of professional tennis players identified him "as the person who has made the greatest contribution to the game."[23]

Arthur undoubtedly appreciated all of the plaudits that marked his retirement. But in general such things, he confessed, didn't do much to soothe his soul. On the surface he appeared to be a reasonably happy person, yet, as his close friends came to realize, he also harbored a complicated inner life of struggle and striving. He had always been a person of substance and independent mind. But during the 1970s, he had become increasingly engaged with social and political issues, especially matters of race and class. Indeed, by the time of his retirement, he had become what would later be known as a public intellectual—a role that, for him, carried a heavy burden of social responsibility.

Since his mid-twenties his conscience had become ever more prodding, to the point where he could no longer turn away from perceived injustice. His days as a self-defined, and sometimes self-absorbed, athlete were over, and he now saw himself, first and foremost, as a truth seeker, albeit one who was not above leveraging his sports celebrity on behalf of worthy causes. As such, he often felt he carried the weight of the world on his shoulders. Accordingly, his inner life took on a somber complexity born of unmet expectations. This dissatisfaction—nourished by self-criticism and seemingly at odds with his calm, easygoing demeanor—was brought to the surface by the health crisis that precipitated his retirement.

Yet, to some extent, his complicated new persona simply represented an amplification of a seriousness that had always been a part of his character. "The abrupt end of my tennis career only accelerated my search for another way I can make a contribution," he wrote in 1981. "I don't want to be remembered mainly because I won Wimbledon." As a convalescing thirty-seven-year-old facing his own mortality, he found himself embracing social action and engaged citizenship with a new urgency and a new sense of purpose. Despite all of his accomplishments and accolades, he knew he could do better, both as a role model for African Americans and as a caring human being worthy of the "Citizen of the World" moniker that appeared on his favorite T-shirt.[24]

Having only a vague sense of what lay ahead, he dedicated the late spring and early summer of 1980 to reflection and repurposing. He later remembered this season of soul-searching as an attempt "to negotiate the middle passage between the old and the new," a negotiation prompted by a profound sense of incompleteness. Looking back on this crisis of confidence twelve years later, he wondered why he had been so discontented. "How could I be dissatisfied, even subtly, with my life to that point?" he asked rhetorically. "I had lived, many would say, a fantasy of a life. I had won a measure of international fame many people would die for. I had traveled all over the world, and often in grand style. Relatively speaking, I had made a great deal of money. I had won a large number of friends. How could I be dissatisfied?"

During the past decade, Arthur had created extremely high standards for achieving a fulfilling and meaningful life, and so far, in his view, he had failed to meet them. It was as simple as that. "Who knows what force gnaws at us," he quipped in 1992, "telling us that our accomplishments, no matter how sensational, are not enough, that we need to do more?" What he did know was that his sense of dissatisfaction in 1980 had little or nothing to do with failing to accomplish all that he had hoped for on the tennis court. Instead, his lament was that he had not done nearly enough off the court, that his belated commitment to public service had been a case of too little too late. Denying that his dissatisfaction was rooted in an ego-driven "rage for immortality," he insisted he just "wanted to be taken seriously."[25]

Being taken seriously, in his view, meant he would be allowed to transcend the professional athlete's traditional role as an entertainer. As he put it, "professional athletes were the modern counterpart to minstrels or *jongleurs* in the Middle Ages. All we needed, I sometimes believed, was the pointed hats and the curved shoes tipped by little balls to be complete fools. From start to finish we were entertainers, with essentially clownish roles assigned to us." While he loved the game of tennis and sports in general, he could not accept or endorse the intellectual and political impotence that characterized most of the sporting world's top figures.[26]

He admired the few athletes who had broken out of this mold—most notably Muhammad Ali, Jackie Robinson, Bill White, Curt Flood, Bill Russell, Kareem Abdul-Jabbar, Jim Brown, Bill Bradley, Billie Jean King, Tommie Smith, John Carlos. The courage to stand up for their beliefs even at the risk of damaging their careers, was, to his mind, cause for celebration and emulation. Looking back a quarter century, he recalled the stalwart defiance of Smith and Carlos, "the somber, black-gloved athlete-protestors," who, in his words, "turned the victory stand at the Olympics in Mexico City in 1968 into a sacrificial altar, as they surrendered their victory to the greater good of downtrodden black people." For Arthur, who was not one to endorse Black Power or radical politics, the heroism of these athletes had less to do with the content of their political ideology than with their willingness to be engaged citizens. "Although I did not always agree with everything these men had said and done," he declared, "I respected the way they had stood tall against the sky and had insisted on being heard on matters other than boxing or track and field, on weighty matters of civil rights and social responsibility and the destiny of black Americans in the modern world."[27]

Doubting his own status as an activist, he sought both clarity and moral renewal by conducting an exhaustive examination of his first thirty-seven years. He started small, jotting down a few notes during his early convalescence. But with Ashe nothing ever remained small, and before long his exercise in memory and reflection led inexorably to an ambitious book project. By late spring he was working away on a memoir—not a standard memoir, he hoped, but rather an autobiographical and philosophical exploration of identity, race, ethics, and public policy.

He had already produced two books of personal and collaborative narrative—*Advantage Ashe* with Cliff Gewecke Jr. in 1967, and *Portrait in Motion* with Frank Deford in 1974. Both books, in his view, had served a useful if limited purpose in providing him with opportunities to speak his mind. But he wanted his third book to reach beyond the pleasantries and banalities of life on the tennis tour.

The manuscript began as a solitary project, but following the pattern of his first two books, it soon became a collaborative work. Feeling he needed someone to serve as both a sounding board and a writing coach, he hired Joel Dreyfuss, a thirty-five-year-old Haitian-born journalist who had written for *The Washington Post*, the *New York Post*, and *Black Enterprise* magazine. Dreyfuss had just completed a book on affirmative action, *The Bakke Case: The Politics of Inequality*, coauthored with Charles Lawrence III, a law professor at the University of San Francisco. A talented writer with a passionate interest in African American history, Dreyfuss appeared to be an ideal collaborator for Arthur, and for a time their work went smoothly. Eventually, however, Arthur began to worry that Dreyfuss's editorial work was undercutting the manuscript's autobiographical voice. Dreyfuss had strong opinions on a host of matters, and they did not always coincide with his views. After a few months of work, the two men parted company, leaving Arthur to search for a new collaborator who could bring the project to completion with Arthur's voice.

This time he chose the *New York Times* tennis writer Neil Amdur, a journalist he had long admired. An unobtrusive partner, Amdur had a light but effective editorial touch that ensured the final product would bear the marks of Ashe's distinctive style and character. Together, they produced a surprisingly candid and wide-ranging book that became one of the most influential tennis autobiographies of the Open era. Aptly titled *Off the Court*, the 230-page memoir appeared in bookstores in September 1981. Several favorable reviews followed, but for Arthur the primary reward was the self-knowledge he had gained from a year of research and writing. While he was still searching for just the right balance between personal and public concerns—and he would continue to do so for the rest of his life—writing *Off the Court* led to a new awareness of what was really important to him.[28]

Years later he revealed that another book had also proved essential to his midlife transformation. In the fall of 1978, Jeanne gave him *The Seasons of a Man's Life*, a sophisticated study of life's transitions written by Daniel J. Levinson and four other members of the psychiatry faculty at Yale's School of Medicine. Sensing her husband was having great difficulty facing the inevitable transition to midlife, she hoped he would absorb Levinson's declaration that a fulfilling life does not have to decline after the age of forty. To her delight he took Levinson's message to heart, especially the dictum: "Each phase in the life cycle has its own virtues and limitations." As Arthur read and reread the book, it became a kind of secular bible in the Ashe household.

One of Levinson's key insights was the significance of a "culminating event" as a perceived capstone experience. In the mind of someone approaching old age, Levinson suggested, this event "carries the ultimate message of his affirmation by society." Arthur regarded this truth as an unsettling challenge. "My 'culminating event,'" he wrote tellingly in 1992, "could never be physical, never something athletic. My 'culminating event' had to be less personal and materialistic, more humanitarian and inclusive. As I approached forty, I could think of nothing important that I had ever achieved of that sort. I had been a professional athlete, strictly defined and recognized as such."[29]

Arthur worried he might never experience "that truly satisfying" culminating event. But while he was mulling over this sad prospect, he took several important steps toward adding new meaning to his life. On a personal level, he had much more time to spend with Jeanne. With their life as a couple replacing tennis as the primary arbiter of their daily activities, they grew closer and more interdependent. As Jeanne later commented, they now shared "a healthy dependency." She still had her work as a freelance photographer and had begun work on a book, *Viewfinders: Black Women Photographers*, which would be published in 1986. And they each had their own circle of close friends. But increasingly they shared a connection with their neighborhood and the broader New York community. While travel was still part of their lives, Arthur no longer spent half of his life on a plane. Now they were together in a way that had been all but impossible when the demands of competitive tennis had dominated his life.

Arthur still devoted much of his time to the off-court activities that he had developed over the past decade: personal appearances related to endorsements of Aetna Life Insurance, American Airlines, Head rackets, and the French sportswear company Le Coq Sportif; periodic broadcasting assignments for ABC Sports; board meetings of the Council of International Tennis Professionals and the ATP; and fund-raising for the United Negro College Fund, the NJTL, and other philanthropic organizations. He even spent some of his post-retirement time on a tennis court conducting holiday clinics at Doral—though most of his days in Florida were now devoted to golf, the only competitive sport his doctors would allow him to play. "There, in the sun, I worked at my tennis responsibilities for the resort, and on my golf game for myself," he would later write. "With my heart condition, golf had superseded tennis as my main sport; with every year I had become more and more entranced by the fairways and the greens."[30]

At the same time, intellectual pursuits began to play a larger role in his life. In addition to undertaking a serious regimen of French lessons, he doubled the time he spent reading. He had always been a bibliophile, but now he became an avid collector of first editions. His daily reading—mostly works of nonfiction dealing with public affairs and history—deepened his interest in the state of the world and nourished his passion for writing and public commentary. "I have always been in love with the English language and the power of the pen," he insisted in the final chapter of *Off the Court*; and now he had the time to indulge this passion.

He had been writing opinion pieces for *The Washington Post* since June 1977, but in 1979 and 1980 he both stepped up the pace and widened the scope of his columns. During this two-year period, he contributed twenty-three articles to the *Post*. All dealt with sports in some fashion, but they also touched upon such diverse topics as South African apartheid, parental pressure on young athletes, racial quotas in the NBA, the proper role of sports agents, Title IX and gender equity, sports gambling, Olympic boycotts, and the rights and responsibilities of student-athletes. In addition to his semi-regular columns in the *Post*, he also penned occasional pieces for a wide variety of newspapers and magazines ranging from *The New York Times* and the Cape Town *Times* to *People* and the London *Observer*. *Tennis* magazine hired him to write instructional articles, a number of which later appeared in two collections aimed at young readers, *Getting Started in Tennis* (1979) and *Arthur Ashe's Tennis Clinic* (1981).

"I'll continue to write," he predicted in 1981. "I'm not sure what but I enjoy writing. My *Washington Post* bi-weekly column has forced me to learn how to say concisely what I'm thinking. I feel fortunate to have a forum like the *Post* in which to air my views. There are several more books in me. I learned from John McPhee and Frank Deford that writing is an art. If you know how to do it and can do so with passion and conviction you can write and write and write. I would never run out of subjects because my life and experiences are always changing."

He also ramped up his speaking schedule. Hardly a week went by without at least one speaking engagement, often at an inner-city venue where he thought he could exert some influence on behalf of education and personal responsibility. He also maintained a presence on the college lecture circuit, offering his views on everything from South Africa to chronic unemployment and economic inequality. In many instances, he was speaking as a recruiting consultant for Aetna, and in that capacity alone he spoke to thousands of college students. Often finding himself in front of predominantly black audiences, he mixed the rhetoric of empowerment with blunt words of advice. Refusing to pull his punches, he tried to be honest and prescriptive without being preachy. After nearly twenty years in the spotlight, the shy little boy from Richmond had become an enthusiastic and assertive public speaker.[31]

Another sign of his renewed dedication to public service was his increasing involvement in partisan politics. For several years he had toyed with the idea of running for public office only to draw back each time after calculating the inevitable impact on his career. Now he had more latitude to throw his hat into the ring, perhaps in a race for a congressional seat. But two primary factors kept him on the sidelines—the uncertainty of his health and Jeanne's reluctance. Unlike his close friend Senator Bill Bradley of New Jersey, he ultimately decided to limit his political activity to endorsements, fund-raising, and an occasional campaign appearance. This decision was also based in part on his growing frustration with the rise of image-dominated and money-oriented politics. "Candidates are now packaged rather than being allowed to be themselves," he explained in 1981. "They take a poll, find out what the people are thinking, and then change their views to suit the results. . . . I don't really have the temperament for all that now."

Despite his disillusionment, he became increasingly active and vocal in a number of political campaigns: for Ted Kennedy during the 1980 Democratic presidential primaries; for Jimmy Carter during his unsuccessful reelection battle with Ronald Reagan; for David Dinkins in several races for Manhattan borough president; for the reelection of two of the nation's most prominent black mayors, Tom Bradley of Los Angeles and Wilson Goode of Philadelphia; for Charles Robb in the 1982 Virginia senatorial race; and for Bill Bradley in his 1984 reelection campaign.

During these years, Ashe's support for the Democratic Party was firm and consistent, especially when highly qualified black candidates were involved. Though discouraged by what he viewed as the backlash politics of Reagan Republicanism on the national level, he took heart from the progressive turn in local politics in cities such as New York, Philadelphia, and Los Angeles. There were even hopeful signs in his home state of Virginia, where his friend, the Richmond attorney Douglas Wilder, had overcome the power of the Byrd machine to become an influential state senator. Elected to the Senate in 1970, Wilder moved up to lieutenant governor in 1985, the first African American elected to statewide office in Virginia. Four years later, with Arthur's help, he would become the first black governor in American electoral history. As Arthur later wrote, "I never dreamed that one of the older boys who came to play at Brook Field on the courts my father tended could become governor of our state. But Doug Wilder did so."

The content and tone of Arthur's political views underwent little change during these years. His ties to the Kennedy clan, originally forged during his political awakening of 1968, were stronger than ever—especially with Ted Kennedy and Robert Kennedy's widow, Ethel. In February 1982, he would even serve as one of the official hosts for Ted Kennedy's fiftieth birthday party. His close relationship with the Kennedys went well beyond politics, as did his cherished connection with Andrew Young.

He did not, however, become an ideological or partisan gadfly. When it came to staking out a position on individual issues, he always insisted on making up his own mind. As the journalist Peter Bodo once observed, "he was an inquisitive, open-minded, practical thinker—a keen social observer rather than a mere partisan." This resistance to orthodoxy sometimes had its downside, but he didn't seem to care. "There are a great number of people who don't like me," he declared in 1981, "who feel that I haven't done enough for certain causes or that I've chosen the wrong ones to support." A case in point was his continuing support for the 1978 *Bakke* decision, an unpopular position in liberal Democratic circles. Refusing to adopt a standard position, either pro or con, on affirmative action, he was determined to find a middle way that balanced meritocratic goals with the historical reality of racial discrimination.

A second issue separating Arthur from his liberal friends and allies was minimum-wage legislation. While he supported the basic principle of a government-mandated living wage, he had serious misgivings about the Carter administration's effort to raise the minimum hourly wage to $3.50 and beyond. "I fully believe that the minimum-wage law works to the detriment of the inner city," he declared. "My father, who is always attuned to the street, tells me that $3.30 an hour is keeping a lot of blacks out of work. Some people want to hire kids, black or white, but can't afford $3.30, he says. He is right. . . . I know all about the argument of the lower tier putting semiskilled adults out of work, but it's time to try something different."[32]

Sometimes Ashe took positions to the right of the Democratic lodestar, and sometimes to the left. Dialogue and deliberation were his watchwords, especially on matters of deep concern such as South Africa. Since 1977 he had undertaken a searching reconsideration of his constructive engagement approach to South African liberation. Influenced by TransAfrica and the noticeable tightening of apartheid following the Soweto uprising of 1976, he had moved slowly but surely toward a liberation policy of isolation and exclusion. Taking advantage of white South Africans' obsession with demonstrating their prowess in international sports competition, he joined the widening movement to deprive them of this nationalistic outlet. "Not only did I play a major role in having South Africa banned from Davis Cup play," he declared with a measure of pride, "I also worked hard to convince individuals not to play there."

For a time, under the influence of Young, the Carter administration appeared to be headed in the same direction in developing more assertive policies toward South Africa. But to Ashe's dismay, this hopeful trend all but disappeared after Young's resignation in August 1979. Young's behind-the-scenes efforts to negotiate with the Palestine Liberation Organization—he met secretly with a PLO representative in Manhattan on August 2—were exposed by the Israeli security force Mossad, and an embarrassed President Carter had no choice but to ask for Young's resignation. In the wake of what came to be known as "The Andy Young Affair," Carter administration officials paid little attention to South Africa, though they did provide Ashe and other anti-apartheid activists with some hope by giving support and formal recognition to the newly independent nation of Zimbabwe (formerly Southern Rhodesia) in April 1980. If majority rule could be instituted in Zimbabwe, where a racial "bush war" had raged for several years, perhaps the same kind of transformation was possible in neighboring South Africa.

Any concern he had about the current administration's policies, however, paled in comparison to his fear of what Carter's opponent Ronald Reagan would do in Southern Africa. Throughout the 1980 Republican primary campaign, Reagan promised to institute a hard-line foreign policy stressing anti-Soviet vigilance. In his view, any ally willing to stand up to Soviet expansion deserved America's unqualified support. For South Africa, this meant no interference with the system of apartheid.[33]

During the early summer of 1980, the Reagan threat became all too real. Carrying the burden of an unpopular boycott of the Moscow Olympics and a deepening hostage crisis in Tehran, Carter seemed unable to counter the image of a failed presidency. His approval ratings were in steep decline, and after Reagan secured the Republican nomination in mid-July the situation only got worse. When Carter won the Democratic nomination on the first ballot in August, Arthur was disappointed, convinced that Kennedy was the only Democrat with a reasonable chance of defeating Reagan in November.[34]

By late August Arthur had turned his attention back to tennis and the upcoming U.S. Open. As the political winds blew in the wrong direction, he drew more than a little consolation from the surging popularity of his favorite game. Working as a commentator for ABC Sports, he participated in one of sport's greatest spectacles. Twelve years after he had won the first

U.S. Open, he could still experience the rush of excitement he had always felt being in the presence of the world's best players. This time the focus would be on McEnroe and Borg, the 1980 Wimbledon finalists headed for an epochal championship-round rematch. Some observers were anticipating a match for the ages, and Ashe felt fortunate to be there to see it. The life of a sports-celebrity-turned-broadcaster-and-public-intellectual had its moments, even in the face of forced retirement and political turmoil.[35]

TWENTY-TWO

CAPTAIN ASHE

■

D URING THE FIRST WEEK of the 1980 U.S. Open, Ashe got word that Marvin Richmond, the new president of the USTA, wanted to speak with him. Sensing this might have something to do with the Davis Cup team, a subject dear to his heart, he immediately went in search of Richmond, whom he had known for several years. Richmond got right to the point: "Tony Trabert wants out. He can't take it anymore." "Take what?" Ashe asked a bit coyly, knowing that Captain Trabert was frustrated by his team's early exit from the 1980 competition, and by his players' lack of discipline. "The behavior of the players. McEnroe. Gerulaitis. Fleming. They are driving him nuts," Richmond explained. Realizing his dream of captaining the American squad might be in the offing, Ashe asked: "Am I on your short list?" "No," Richmond responded, "because we don't have a short list. We want you."

Ashe could hardly believe his ears, but he maintained enough composure to ask for twenty-four hours to think it over. He later confessed he really didn't need any time to make the decision; he just wanted time to prepare for "the inevitable onslaught of the press." From the moment Richmond made the offer, he knew he wanted the captaincy as much as anything in his life. "I felt so happy and proud I could have jumped into the air," he recalled, "—the job meant that much to me."

Ashe—who respected Trabert, having played for him on the 1977 and

1978 Cup teams—wanted him to be the first to hear the news. "I'm happy for you, Arthur," the outgoing captain exclaimed. "You would have been my first choice, too." Yet he couldn't resist offering a few words of warning: "good luck to you with some of these guys. It's just not the way we were brought up. . . . I can take high-spirited. But what's been going on is really offensive. I find too much of the behavior distasteful. It's just not fun anymore, Arthur."[1]

Ashe placed part of the blame on the generational gap between fifty-year-old Trabert and his players, and on Trabert's "law-and-order" persona. Perhaps a younger coach (Ashe was thirteen years younger than Trabert) would have better luck modulating the players' behavior. As he told *Tennis* magazine, "I'm a little closer in age to the players so I'm hoping that my brand of friendly persuasion will work."

Richmond and his USTA colleagues shared this hope. Arthur's demeanor, combined with his knowledge of the game and his superior Davis Cup record as a player, made him an obvious choice to replace Trabert. Indeed, his selection was universally popular aside from the rants of a few extreme white supremacists. As soon as the selection was announced on September 8, letters of congratulation flooded the Ashes' mailbox.

The outpouring of support and affection continued for months, including heartfelt letters from two former Davis Cup captains, Ed Turville and Donald Dell. "I don't believe I have ever been more pleased in my life," Turville wrote in mid-November, "when Marvin Richmond came up to me in September and said you were to be the next Davis Cup captain. . . . It has always been my opinion since our Davis Cup days that you would be a logical choice for the job."

Two weeks later, Dell expressed similar sentiments while adding a few words of caution. "I think you will make an outstanding Captain, Arthur," he wrote, "but believe me these new players will test your patience, determination, and character. . . . Never lose sight of the big picture in dealing with the USTA, the press, the players, and the public: As Davis Cup Captain you and your Teammates represent 220,000,000 Americans above all else. Davis Cup is the Olympics of Tennis and therefore everyone on the Team must act accordingly or he shouldn't be on the Team." Over the next four years, Dell's words would come back to him again and again.[2]

His serious challenges began during the first month of his captaincy, a full six months before the first round of the 1981 Davis Cup competition. Even before he announced the members of the U.S. team, he had to deal with a major controversy surrounding John McEnroe. In the aftermath of the thrilling Borg-McEnroe championship matches at Wimbledon and the U.S. Open, a promoter named Sol Kerzner seized a golden opportunity. With McEnroe losing to Borg in five tough sets at Wimbledon, and Borg returning the favor at Flushing Meadows, the idea of a rubber match became irresistible—both as a potential moneymaker and as a means of determining the best player in the world.

The biggest problem for Ashe was that Kerzner owned and operated a South African hotel chain that included Sun City, a year-old luxury resort and casino located in Bophuthatswana, "one of the phony 'independent' states set up by South Africa." Hoping to promote his resort while circum-venting the objections of anti-apartheid activists, Kerzner planned to hold the match in Sun City's new fourteen-thousand-seat stadium. To seal the deal, he offered Borg and McEnroe a total of over $1.5 million ($600,000 each in appearance money plus an additional $150,000 to the winner, plus a share of an estimated $200,000 from television rights) for a five-set match—one of the largest one-day paychecks in sports history. The two tennis stars readily accepted the lucrative terms, and Kerzner scheduled the televised match for December 6.

Ashe was apoplectic when he heard the news. The ink on his Davis Cup contract was hardly dry, and he was already faced with a major crisis. With the United Nations preparing a blacklist of entertainers and athletes who had performed in either South Africa or one of its homelands, McEnroe's decision to play in Sun City could have dire consequences. An upcoming heavyweight championship fight between the American boxer Mike Weaver and the South African Gerrie Coetzee, scheduled for October 25 in Sun City, had stirred up a storm of controversy, and Ashe knew the Borg-McEnroe match would be even worse. "The outcry against Weaver was nothing com-pared to what would probably be visited on McEnroe," he recalled. "Weaver might claim that he needed the money; but most people would think that John had already made a fortune in prize money and endorsements or would do so soon. The huge sum of money might make playing there excusable, but it also seemed to put a price on McEnroe's integrity."[3]

Feeling the need to protect the honor and reputation of the U.S. Davis Cup team, Ashe intervened in early October. "Determined to stop the match," he later explained, "I approached John McEnroe, Sr., who is a lawyer and his son's principal adviser. I did not want to make a public fuss about the matter. However, I let the McEnroes know that a public fuss was bound to ensue if the match were played." Signing the Sun City contract was not only morally wrong; it would also tarnish John Jr.'s reputation. Others, including

Franklin Williams, the former U.S. ambassador to Ghana, approached John Sr. and voiced similar objections to the match. "I relayed the problems and concerns to him as expressed by some very responsible people," John Sr. told Ashe.

The combination of pressure and persuasion worked, and after John Jr. called Ashe to discuss the matter, John Sr. announced on October 16 that his son had withdrawn from the Sun City match. "John and I felt it was neither the right time, nor the right place, for that match," he informed the press. Ecstatic, Ashe seized the opportunity to explain why he felt so strongly about boycotting any event involving Sun City and the "phony homeland" of Bophuthatswana. During an interview on the cable television program *Sports Probe*, he declared: "I would have less objection if it were in Johannesburg. I still don't like it, but at least South Africa is a legally constituted nation."

Later in the afternoon, Ashe dashed off a short piece that appeared in *The Washington Post* the next day. Calling the McEnroes' decision "a rare triumph of morality over money," he went on to explain that the creation of "phony independent nation-states" such as Bophuthatswana had "been forced upon unwilling black South Africans in the last seven years by the white-minority government." "The object of this 'independent' scheme by the South African government," he continued, "is to one day have a country with no black South Africans. The country's 22 million black citizens are to be stripped of their native-born citizenship and granted new passports from new governments that no one recognizes."[4]

Ashe survived the Sun City episode without any noticeable damage to his relationship with McEnroe. But the episode left him with a measure of uneasiness about mixing racial politics with the fortunes of the U.S. Davis Cup team. While he welcomed the chance to educate the public on the evils of apartheid and South Africa's duplicitous homeland policy, he was wary of even the appearance of taking advantage of his race or color. He went out of his way to downplay race when asked how it felt to be the first black Davis Cup captain, but his racial status was always lurking in the background. He was, after all, the first black coach of a national team. For a race seldom valued for its intellectual and leadership skills—a race seldom seen on the tennis court much less in the coaching box—this was a momentous step forward.

Ashe was under considerable pressure to succeed. But he faced the added pressure of assuming the captaincy at a time when, as he later put it, the Davis Cup's "national and international prestige [was] waning." "The best players did not care to play," he recalled, "and attendance had dwindled at many matches." The U.S. team, in particular, had closed out the 1980 competition in March with an embarrassing 4–1 loss to Argentina in the Americas Zone final. While the U.S. had won the Cup as recently as 1979, the likelihood of winning in 1981 was an open question.[5]

There were, however, signs of an impending resurgence of the Davis Cup's importance and popularity. In October 1980, the Nippon Electronic Company (NEC) of Japan became the first international sponsor in eighty years of Davis Cup competition. Signing a contract for three years, NEC promised to provide $1 million in prize money in an effort "to maintain the quality and tradition of the event." Player compensation would no longer be limited to expense money, a change that would encourage the game's best players to participate. Patriotism, it was hoped, would no longer have to compete with the allure of the big money on the regular tour.

There would also be a new format for Davis Cup play in 1981. Under the new rules, the top sixteen nations would play in a series of elimination matches in March, with the final two nations squaring off for the Cup and $200,000 in first-place prize money in December. The schedule would be compressed to minimize conflicts with tour events, and the format would be further refined in 1982, producing much more manageable and player-friendly competition. "The main pieces were now clearly in place for a re-vival of the Davis Cup," recalled Ashe, a strong supporter of the new system.[6]

Captain Ashe's first official task was to choose a squad to play Mexico in the first round. Since the tie would take place in Carlsbad, California, in March 1981, there was plenty of time to select and train the team. He had several of the best players in the world at his disposal—if they agreed to play. Predictably, his biggest problem was convincing Connors, the world's third best singles player, to join the team. Connors had not played Davis Cup since 1976, when he had suffered an upset at the hands of Mexico's Raúl Ramírez. To Ashe's dismay, Connors—still smarting from that loss, which had eliminated the U.S. from the 1976 competition—refused to join the team for the first round. He might play Davis Cup later in the year, he hinted, but he would not play against Mexico. Years later McEnroe, the 1981 team's number one singles player, characterized this recalcitrance as selfish and indefensible. "Connors hemmed and hawed," he remembered, "he said he had scheduling conflicts, his toe was hurting—whatever. What else was new? For Jimmy, tennis meant money, and Davis Cup wasn't money."

Connors's absence left Ashe with a difficult decision regarding a second singles player. After some deliberation, he chose his old friend Roscoe Tanner, another left-handed ace known for his powerful serve. Selecting the U.S. squad's doubles competitors also involved some complicated maneuvering. The obvious choice was the team of Stan Smith and Bob Lutz, who had represented the United States off and on since 1968, winning fourteen of fifteen Davis Cup doubles matches over the years. Unfortunately, after Smith developed arm trouble several weeks before the tie with Mexico, Ashe was forced to go with his second choice, Marty Riessen and Sherwood Stewart, leaving the U.S. with a strong but less than invincible squad for the first round.[7]

He also soon discovered his job involved more than mere coaching. Faced with "a collection of individuals, each of whom was something of a star in his own right," he found it necessary to cater to ego-driven and seemingly petty demands. "I found myself being called upon to apply both diplomacy and psychology to keep everyone happy," he recalled. "I also found that I did not enjoy this aspect of my job much. Dutiful myself, I disliked being a nursemaid or a babysitter for my fellow adults." Keeping McEnroe focused and under control was Ashe's biggest challenge, but each team member had some measure of personal quirks and demands.[8]

In the matches against Mexico, however, most of the problems were on the court. After McEnroe easily defeated seventeen-year-old Jorge Lozano in the first singles match, Tanner lost to Ramírez in the second. With the team score 1–1, Ashe expected Riessen and Stewart to gain a point in the doubles, but they faltered, losing to Ramírez and Lozano in five sets. This put the United States in the unenviable position of having to win the last two matches to avoid a humiliating defeat in the first round. Fortunately, both McEnroe and Tanner came through in the final singles matches, giving their team a 3–2 victory.

Ashe's debut had turned out all right, even though an ugly spat between McEnroe and Ramírez tarnished the victory. During the match, McEnroe repeatedly questioned line calls, forcing Ashe to get up from his courtside seat to calm his volatile star. In a post-match interview, Ramírez charged that McEnroe had deliberately disrupted play with his complaints. "I think he complains too much," the Mexican star insisted, "and I think he does it on purpose." Feisty as ever, McEnroe shot back that Ramírez was no one to talk about questioning close calls: "He's the best in the world at that."

Arthur wisely stayed out of the fray; he was just happy to get out of Carlsbad with a win. But he did not escape entirely unscathed. Following the unexpected loss in doubles, Pancho Gonzales took him aside for more than a few words of stern advice. The decision to play Riessen and Stewart when McEnroe could have substituted for either of them was a serious mistake, Gonzales declared. "You should play your best doubles players even if they are playing singles," he insisted. "If they are fit, they are not going to be too tired. McEnroe would not have lost that match." More pointedly, he urged Arthur "to be more involved in what's going on on the court." When the rookie captain claimed he *was* involved, that his heart "was thumping away out there," Gonzales tempered his criticism a bit: "Well, we don't want your heart to thump too much, Arthur. But you have to *look* more involved, I guess."[9]

Arthur knew Gonzales's advice had merit. Yet he could not bring himself to act upon it. He was more than willing to counsel his players behind the scenes and during practice, but not out in the open for the world to see. "I did not want to interfere with the play of international tennis stars by seeking to coach them on camera," he later explained, adding: "At courtside, I tended to be restrained. I did not intend to leap up at every point during a match merely to assert my presence or authority. And I was determined not to join the players automatically in their protests and tantrums, as football and basketball coaches routinely do. I would back the players if I thought they had a point, but I wouldn't become enraged on demand."[10]

The challenge of balancing restraint and engagement sorely tested Ashe during a second-round tie against Czechoslovakia at the National Tennis Center in July. Led by Ivan Lendl, the world's fourth best player, the Czechs were the defending champions; and, to Ashe's dismay, McEnroe, the Americans' best hope to defeat Lendl, "arrived at Flushing Meadows with his nerves sorely frayed and his emotions drained." Fortunately Connors, who had finally joined the team, was on hand to pick up some of the slack. The source of McEnroe's discontent was an acrimonious struggle with Wimbledon officials over his court behavior. His repeated tantrums over line calls had led to $2,250 in fines, and the Wimbledon committee had threatened to bar him from future All England tournaments if he didn't stop. The committee had already broken tradition in refusing to offer an honorary club membership to the Wimbledon singles champion. This snub was a first in Wimbledon history, but one that the British press endorsed with savage delight.

While McEnroe claimed he couldn't care less about his censure by the British establishment, he was not himself during his opening round match against Lendl. Playing before nearly eighteen thousand fans, the largest Davis Cup crowd in American history, he lost in straight sets, though remarkably he did so without misbehaving or losing his temper. After the match, he conceded he was mentally worn out from the Wimbledon controversy. Nonetheless, he proved his mettle two days later, thrilling a rousing crowd of fellow New Yorkers with a crushing victory over Tomas Smid. Combined with Connors's earlier win over Smid, and Smith and Lutz's triumph in the doubles, this impressive effort eliminated the defending champions.

Ashe was thrilled not only by the team's victory over the Czechs but also by McEnroe's grit and poise under pressure. It was perhaps the happiest moment he had experienced since his retirement fifteen months earlier, and it was all the better because Jeanne was there to share it with him. Connors, by contrast, was in no mood to celebrate—despite his two singles victories. By his own admission, he was never happy when he failed to capture the limelight, and all the hoopla surrounding McEnroe the hometown hero apparently spoiled the scene for him. Prior to the tie, he had promised he would be part of the Davis Cup squad for the remainder of the year. But, as Ashe later put it, "in the hour of victory . . . he packed his bags and strolled away from us." Connors would not play against Australia in the next round; in fact, he would not play Davis Cup tennis again until 1984.[11]

Connors's abrupt departure forced Ashe to put Tanner back in the second singles slot behind McEnroe. Fortunately, the team had more than enough punch to handle a weak Australian team. Played in Portland, Oregon, in October, the semifinal tie drew large crowds, nearly 35,000 over three days of play. The result, as expected, was a 5–0 sweep for the Americans, but the most memorable aspect of the Portland competition had nothing to do with the score.

To the horror of much of the American tennis establishment, McEnroe and his partner, Peter "Flam" Fleming, set a new standard of uncouth behavior during a doubles match against Peter McNamara and Phil Dent. "McEnroe and Fleming behaved so badly and uttered so many profanities, and so insulted their opponents, the officials, and some spectators," Ashe observed, "that I was left embarrassed, enraged, and bitter. When I told the two of them that they had behaved disgracefully, they were unapologetic. I found myself withdrawing even more from them." In the days leading up to the match, McEnroe had made it clear that he bitterly resented Ashe's attempts to maintain a consistent protocol of decorum. The temperamental star, Ashe concluded, "hated any form of authority, at least in tennis. I wasn't a linesman or an umpire or a referee, but as captain I represented authority, and he clearly felt an obligation to rebel."[12]

Now Ashe faced the difficult task of getting his team ready for the final against Argentina, which would be played in Cincinnati in mid December. The fallout from the misbehavior in Portland was considerable, with some observers speculating that the root of the problem was the poor fit between the U.S. squad's high-strung players and their "low-key" captain. *World Tennis* columnist Richard Evans concluded McEnroe "was operating at a pitch of emotional endeavor that Ashe could barely understand." Ashe himself later acknowledged as much, but like Trabert before him, he could not bring himself to accept the coarse behavior of some of the younger players. Nor could he see himself as an on-court cheerleader willing to follow the lead of rabid win-at-any-cost players. Consequently, he seemed passive and emotionally unsupportive to McEnroe and several other players who saw his commitment to sportsmanship as a cover for his lack of intensity.[13]

Whatever the truth of the matter, Ashe knew he had strong backing from the American tennis establishment. With the USTA celebrating its centennial year, there was considerable pressure on American tennis to show its best face to the world. Bringing the Davis Cup back to the United States would go a long way toward achieving this goal but only if the U.S. squad adhered to the accepted rules of sportsmanship and decorum. Ashe took this dual challenge seriously, and prior to the tie in Cincinnati he vowed publicly to default if any of his players dishonored the U.S. team by misbehaving during the upcoming matches. When asked to comment on this declaration, McEnroe chose to attack the reporters for manufacturing a controversy. "Why do you guys write about that stuff?" he growled, claiming: "All you want to do is sell newspapers!"

This was not a good sign as the Americans prepared to take the court against a tough Argentine team led by Guillermo Vilas and José Luis Clerc. For a time in late November, Connors led Ashe to believe that he was seriously considering rejoining the U.S. squad for the Davis Cup final, but he eventually begged off. Ashe's biggest problem, however, was finding a way to win that did not sully the nation's honor. He later recalled he could sense "a great tension among the players in Cincinnati," as both teams featured players with highly temperamental court personalities. Vilas and Clerc had been feuding for years, "egged on by their Latin brand of vanity," as Ashe put it. On the American side, Fleming insisted he didn't need any coaching from Ashe or anyone else, and McEnroe arrived in Cincinnati looking for "blood." At the 1980 Davis Cup tie held in Buenos Aires, he had lost to both Vilas and Clerc amidst a "tumultuous, heckling crowd," so to him the rematch in Cincinnati was a personal grudge match.[14]

Ashe feared that all of this angst—combined with the lingering anger from Portland—would prove explosive, and he was right. In the opening singles match, McEnroe punished Vilas with a dominating straight-set victory. As Ashe recalled, "Vilas was so wounded by this thrashing that he refused to come to the interview room. Instead, he pouted and sulked in his tent." Later in the day, Tanner lost to Clerc, evening the team score at 1–1 and setting the stage for a crucial doubles match pitting McEnroe and Fleming against Vilas and Clerc.

The doubles match played on Saturday, December 12—almost two years to the day after Ashe's bypass surgery—turned out to be one of the most exciting matches in Davis Cup history. The huge crowd at Riverfront Stadium witnessed a high quality of play from the start and more than the usual gamesmanship as the two teams tested each other's patience and composure. After the teams split the first two sets, the third set, eventually won by the Americans, became a near donnybrook. As the fading Argentines resorted to delaying tactics, all four players began to trade insults and obscenities.

By the beginning of the fourth set, tempers were on edge, and as McEnroe walked out to hit the opening serve, Vilas and Clerc suddenly "packed their bags as if on their way to the locker room." The referee had canceled the traditional ten-minute break following the second set because there had been an unexpected earlier delay involving the repair of the stadium's synthetic surface, but apparently Vilas and Clerc had not gotten word of the cancellation. Convinced the confusion was actually a deliberate provocation, McEnroe yelled out sarcastically: "Let me know when you're ready, all right? We got all afternoon." Taking this as an insult, the Argentines angrily walked toward the net, and within seconds all four players appeared to be close to blows, as they stood almost toe-to-toe. Instinctively, Arthur rushed out onto the court to defuse the situation.

In all the years Arthur had been playing tennis, he had rarely raised his voice above a polite conversational tone, but this time he practically screamed: "John, get to the line and serve! Now!" McEnroe and Fleming seemed stunned by his forceful intervention, and, for the moment at least, the tension eased as the players separated and McEnroe trudged over to the baseline to serve. The Americans went on to win the first game, but as the teams changed ends before the second game Clerc and McEnroe "went at it" again, slinging verbal barbs. Fleming soon joined in, forcing Arthur to intervene once again. "John, Peter. You have to quit now. This is a disgrace," he pleaded. "You cannot continue like this. I do not want to hear another obscenity out there. You are playing for the United States. Remember that!"

For a brief instant, the captain thought there was a chance the message had gotten through, but as soon as McEnroe walked onto the court a taunt from Clerc elicited an impassioned "Go fuck yourself!" loud enough to be picked up by television and radio microphones. "I was stunned," Arthur recalled. "I stormed onto the court, and John and I exchanged some bitter words for a few seconds. This time I thought I might punch John. I have never punched anyone in my life, but I was truly on the brink of hitting him."

This loss of control in public represented a dark moment for Ashe. But the unruly scene in Cincinnati did not seem to bother the spectators in the stadium, many of whom seemed to relish the spirited disruption of a sport once known for its politeness. The limits of propriety in professional tennis had been expanding since the beginning of the Open era, and only the old-timers could remember when unrestrained aggression and self-indulgent behavior were not part of the game. One observer old enough to recall the traditions of an earlier era was Arthur's friend Philippe Chatrier, who was attending the Davis Cup final as president of the ITF. Thoroughly disgusted by what he saw and "embarrassed for my hosts," the Frenchman left the stadium in the middle of the doubles match.

Virtually everyone else, of course, stayed to the end, ultimately witnessing a remarkable display of tennis artistry. Once the U.S. captain and his hot-blooded star cooled down enough to allow the match to continue, the magic of competitive tennis played at the highest level took over. For several hours, the momentum shifted back and forth, as every winning volley seemed to draw an equally spectacular counterpunch from the opposing side. After Argentina won the fourth set to tie the match at 2–2, the fifth set became a war of attrition. For much of the set, Vilas and Clerc appeared to be the fresher team and to hold a slight advantage. But for more than an hour McEnroe and Fleming kept it close. In the fourteenth game, with Argentina leading 7–6, Vilas served for the match. With the Americans on the verge of defeat, the crowd exhorted them to hold on, and they responded with a flurry of well-placed volleys that ultimately broke Vilas's serve. An hour later, in the twentieth game, they did the same to Clerc (who had held serve in the 12 previous service games), winning the set 11–9 and bringing the marathon match to a close.[15]

In his post-match comments, Arthur tried to calm the waters with a matter-of-fact description of what had just happened. "I'm happy they won and I kept them out of trouble," he declared with a hint of a smile. "That's what I am supposed to do." Privately, however, he was still seething. "My anger wouldn't abate," he recalled years later. "It was so powerful it

astonished me." After a fitful night, he felt he had to do something dras-
tic to convince McEnroe and Fleming that he wouldn't tolerate a repeat of
their disgraceful behavior. Placing two early morning calls to USTA president Richmond and Gordon Jorgensen, the chairman of the U.S. Davis Cup
committee, he stated his concerns. "I've had it," he told Richmond. "This
cannot continue. What John and Peter did out there was absolutely inexcus-
able. In thirty years of competitive tennis, I have never seen anything like it.
Even *close* to it. It makes us look bad, all of us, including the United States as
a nation. I want to forfeit the match if McEnroe acts anything like that again.
I need your support." Knowing that a forfeit might well mean the loss of the
Davis Cup, both men nonetheless gave him their backing.

Several hours later, just prior to the final singles matches, Arthur delivered the news to McEnroe in a private meeting. Speaking in a stern voice,
he warned him that a repeat of the previous day's behavior would lead to
default. Explaining that the "national honor was at stake," he looked in vain
for a sign that McEnroe understood the seriousness of the situation. After sitting in stony silence as his coach presented the equivalent of an ultimatum, a
sullen McEnroe eventually grumbled, "Is that all?" When Arthur said "Yes,"
McEnroe left the room without saying another word.

Later in the day, when McEnroe took the court to play Clerc, Ashe had
no confidence that any of his words had sunk in. But as the match progressed he realized his young star was making a concerted effort to control
his emotions. The hard-fought contest included plenty of difficult moments,
any one of which might have pushed McEnroe over the edge on a normal
day. But on this day, to Ashe's relief, he kept his composure. "On Sunday,"
Sports Illustrated writer Barry McDermott observed, "everyone was talking
about McEnroe's racket, not his mouth." Showing flashes of utter brilliance,
he played what Ashe would later call "an extraordinarily, gutsy, magnificent
match," winning 6–3 in the fifth set.

Recalling the hyper emotionalism of the match in his 2002 memoir,
You Cannot Be Serious, McEnroe wrote: "When Clerc hit that last volley in
the fourth game long, I jumped a foot in the air and pumped my fist; the
crowd jumped to its feet, yelling 'U-S-A! U-S-A!' That gave me goosebumps.
I couldn't squander the rare opportunity of having an entire arena full of
people all on my side, and I knew I wouldn't let my country down." The
winning point, he remembered, triggered a rare outburst of joy: "I leaped
into the air, let out a victory cry, then jumped the net to shake Clerc's hand.
I threw myself into Arthur's arms, and then Bill Norris's. [Norris was U.S.
Davis Cup trainer.] I turned to the crowd and stuck both my index fingers

into the air. Then I hugged every guy on the team. I was a hero: a very strange sensation for me, let me tell you. . . . I was on top of the mountain."[16]

Despite all the recent turmoil, the Davis Cup was back in American hands. During the victory celebration, a beaming McEnroe held the cup aloft for the crowd to see, and later in the press room he exclaimed; "This is by far the best Davis Cup victory I've ever had." In the post-match press conference, both he and Ashe tried to keep the focus on the quality of the tennis—and on the triumph itself. But several reporters broadened the focus with questions about Ashe's troubled relationship with McEnroe—and about his future as a Davis Cup captain.

Even Neil Amdur, the *New York Times* columnist who had grown close to Ashe during the past eighteen months, speculated about the difficulties ahead. "Whether McEnroe and Ashe can continue their silent partnership remains to be seen," he counseled his readers. McEnroe, while agreeing that differences in attitude and perspective could sometimes make courtside relationships "uncomfortable," put a positive spin on the situation. "When you win the cup," he declared, "a lot is forgotten." Arthur seemed to agree. When Amdur asked him if he had thought about resigning, the answer was an emphatic no. "I don't want to leave. I love it," he insisted.[17]

Having won the Davis Cup on the first try, Arthur was reasonably sure his position as captain was secure. Yet, even in victory, some observers speculated he might not be the best man for the job. Perhaps, it was suggested in some quarters, the Virginia gentleman's leadership style was too passive to keep the "Superbrat" and his ill-mannered partner in line. In the weeks following the Davis Cup triumph, he received advice from all sides: from tennis columnists, most of whom seemed to appreciate the difficulty of his situation; and from letter-writing fans, some of whom urged him to throw McEnroe and Fleming off the team. "I have always admired your tennis and your attitude toward the game," one man wrote from California. "Tennis is the most exciting and enjoyable sport in the world, and I love it passionately. Please do not let it be demeaned by a great player of low moral stature." Another fan, writing from Indiana, pointed out that McEnroe was "the absolute image of the 'Ugly American.'"

For the most part, both the press and the public seemed hesitant to place the blame squarely on Arthur's shoulders. But there were a few exceptions. "With no visible joy," *Seattle Times* editor George Meyers wrote with a measure of sarcasm, "Arthur has answered one of the burning questions of the day: When victory, and profits, are paramount, do superlative skills absolve outrageous, unforgivable conduct? Obviously, yes." In a similar vein, a tennis-playing doctor from Philadelphia scolded Arthur for tolerating "deplorable tactics on the court." "If you can't control your players," he wrote, "it is your responsibility to select other players who are gentlemen and who will reflect the best interest of the team and of the United States in international competition."[18]

Arthur took these charges of complicity very seriously. In fact, Dell, whose judgment he trusted as much as anyone's, had been expressing similar sentiments for months. In the aftermath of the Portland melee, Dell advised him "to think long and hard before ever again naming McEnroe and Fleming to represent America," reminding him: "You have spent your entire life trying to convey by example just the opposite of their behavior. You have always said, 'Winning is not the only thing.' In my opinion, were either McEnroe or Fleming, or *both*, left off the next Davis Cup match by you, setting such an example by you would do more in one gesture for American tennis than a lifetime of . . . Code of Conduct fines." "At least," he added, "America could be proud of its athletic representatives."

When Arthur ignored Dell's advice, he entered uncharted territory. For the first time in his career, he found himself being taken to task for a major mistake in moral judgment. As the most celebrated sportsman in tennis, he was unaccustomed to public censure that questioned his integrity. While he was no stranger to controversy, the Davis Cup debacle was different. Any suggestion he had compromised his ethical principles for the sake of winning the Davis Cup cut him to the core.

Dell and others close to Arthur knew that for him the Davis Cup triumph was decidedly bittersweet. They could see that the captaincy had already taken a toll on a man who valued his reputation for decency and sportsmanship above all else, and some even worried his health might suffer—or that he might even sink into depression—if the McEnroe controversy continued for much longer. Dell, for one, knew Arthur needed a bit of timely help to find a way forward. In a letter written in the spirit of true friendship less than a week after the victory in Cincinnati, he avoided any mention of his earlier advice, offering instead words of appreciation and encouragement. "I wanted to write and congratulate you on winning the 1981 Davis Cup," he wrote. "It was a real achievement and tribute to your sensitivity and leadership ability in light of the many controversies and difficult circumstances throughout the year. Working with some of your players, particularly McEnroe and Fleming, is not easy and I thought you handled it with dignity and grace." In closing, he added: "I hope in 1982 it will get easier based on your

1981 experiences. Certainly, if you can communicate more with McEnroe where he will learn to respect and listen to you, that is a step forward for everyone, and pro tennis as well." [19]

Ashe began his second year as the U.S. Davis Cup captain with Dell's advice in mind. Establishing a better relationship with McEnroe, he knew all too well, was the key to success. If they could find a way to work together—and a way to bring McEnroe's intensity to bear on the points at hand, while drawing it away from the verbal sniping at opponents or linesmen—the U.S. team could repeat as champions in a manner that would make all Americans proud.

Ashe had already decided McEnroe would remain on the team "He'll be back with us against India the first week in March," the captain announced on December 14. "We're learning how to communicate. He wants to play. I want him to play. He know he's got to behave. He's trying. . . . He doesn't have any choice. He either must overcome his temper or be perpetually suspended." When asked to elaborate, he explained: "It upsets everybody. John knows that. It disrupts but he doesn't do it to be disruptive. He can't help himself. It's not intentional and it's not gamesmanship. It's just the way he reacts naturally. We're trying to get him to change that." Getting control of his emotions might even bring new life to McEnroe's career, Arthur ventured. "In Davis Cup, there's more at stake," he reminded the reporters. "You play harder, prepare longer and better. They expect court decorum. National pride and national honor are at stake. . . . I think Davis Cup play can be the vehicle by which he learns to control himself." [20]

The first test for McEnroe came in early March, when the U.S. squad faced India on the hard courts at Carlsbad, California. In the opening singles match, he defeated Vijay Amritraj in straight sets, but along the way he was assessed a penalty point for arguing a line call with the umpire. The penalty was warranted since under Davis Cup rules all complaints had to be relayed through the team captain. But to Arthur's relief, McEnroe kept his cool and finished the set without incident. After Eliot Teltscher won the other opening day singles match, McEnroe and Fleming went on to clinch the tie with a win in the doubles. During the match, McEnroe yelled out a couple of choice comments, but since they were not directed at anyone in particular the umpire gave him a pass. [21]

So far so good, but Arthur knew the true test would come when McEnroe found himself in a high-pressure match, possibly when the U.S. squad faced a powerful Swedish team in July. Led by seventeen-year-old Mats Wilander, who had just shocked the tennis world by winning the 1982 French Open, the Swedes figured to give the Americans all they could handle. Fortunately for the Americans, the tie would be played in St. Louis on indoor carpet, not on slow Swedish clay.

Most tennis observers predicted the Americans would eliminate the Swedes and advance to the semifinals, but concerns about the erratic play of Teltscher and Gottfried forced Ashe to consider possible replacements for the second singles spot. He was still mulling over his options when he arrived at Wimbledon in late June to serve as a color commentator for BBC and HBO.

One of the major stories to emerge during the first week of the 1982 Wimbledon Championships was the unexpectedly strong play of Chip Hooper, a towering six-foot-five Ashe protégé from Southern California. Three weeks earlier at the French Open, Hooper had fought his way into the round of sixteen, the first African American male to do so since Ashe in 1975. Although Connors ended Hooper's Paris run, his world ranking rose to #23 by the time he arrived at Wimbledon. Even so, since he had never played on grass prior to the Queen's Club tournament the week before Wimbledon, no one could have predicted his first-round mauling of the #8 seed, Peter McNamara. On a day when rain postponed most of the opening matches, Hooper's upset win over Australia's best player was the big news.

After commentators marveled at the speed of Hooper's serve, estimated at nearly 130 miles per hour, Ashe was asked about the possibility of adding the young serve-and-volley specialist to the Davis Cup team. Without painting himself into a corner, Ashe ventured there was indeed "a reasonable chance" he would turn to Hooper as a replacement for Teltscher or Gottfried—if Hooper continued to play well on the Wimbledon grass. Two days later, after Hooper played a sloppy losing match against unseeded Russell Simpson of New Zealand, Ashe reluctantly concluded his young friend from California was not quite ready for Davis Cup play.

Ashe regretted he had raised Hooper's hopes only to deflate them. But knowing the tough twenty-three-year-old as he did, he was confident that there wouldn't be any lasting damage to his promising career. He was more worried about the fragile psyche of another young star. Still only twenty-two years old, McEnroe had suffered through a tough early summer. Eliminated in the early rounds of the French Open, he fought his way into the final singles match at Wimbledon only to lose to Connors in five sets. Squandering a 2–1 set lead, he couldn't overcome Connors's pinpoint service returns in what was then the longest Wimbledon final on record, four hours and fifteen minutes. A day earlier, he and Fleming, the defending champions, had lost the doubles final to Australians Peter McNamara and Paul McNamee.[22]

When McEnroe showed up in St. Louis a week later, he was in a foul mood, still smarting from his European defeats. But somehow he found a way to channel his frustrations into a superior performance on the court. In the opening singles match, he made short work of Anders Jarryd, with the only glitch coming when he momentarily lost his composure and angrily swatted a ball into the roof. In the second singles match Teltscher lost a tough five-set struggle to Wilander, suffering an acute muscle strain in the process. This loss, plus the injury, put added pressure on McEnroe and Fleming to win the doubles competition, and they rose to the occasion with a solid win over Jarryd and Hans Simonsson.

Prior to the tie, Ashe had considered replacing the McEnroe-Fleming duo with the Mayer brothers—Gene and Sandy—to reduce the pressure on his young star. But at the last minute he decided to stick with his talented but temperamental doubles team, whose strong performance soon confirmed the wisdom of the decision. After Gottfried lost a second-round singles match to Jarryd, the team score stood at 2–2.

This set the stage for a dramatic winner-take-all battle between McEnroe and Wilander. With both men playing at the top of their game, the result was one of the longest matches in Davis Cup history: seventy-nine games and five sets stretching across six hours and thirty-five minutes. After McEnroe won the first two sets, Wilander came back to win the third and fourth. The third set lasted two hours and thirty-eight minutes, with the Swede finally prevailing 17–15—though not before McEnroe, in the words of one observer, vented "his frustrations at every line call he felt was wrong." At one point, he kicked one of ESPN's courtside cameras, and after one alleged missed call he sent a ball whizzing by a startled linesman's head. Cool and reserved, Wilander did his best to ignore his opponent's outbursts, but standing nervously on the sidelines Ashe worried that McEnroe would go over the edge before the match was over. To his relief, McEnroe held it together and eventually outlasted Wilander 8–6 in the fifth set.

The picture of the exhausted winner embracing Arthur at center court and then resting his head on the relieved captain's shoulder was worth a thousand words. "At one point I thought it was going to go on forever," McEnroe confessed. Pushing aside any objections to his star's emotional outbursts, Ashe was exultant in victory. "That's the best match you've ever played in your life," he told the man who had single-handedly saved America's chance of retaining the Davis Cup.

Speaking to Amdur in New York the next day, he had nothing but praise for McEnroe: "It was a very satisfying weekend . . . seeing John overcome what was an obvious emotional, trying situation for him." His relationship with McEnroe would always be complicated, he explained, but he had great respect for him both as a player and as a human being. "We'll always have differences," he acknowledged. "But that doesn't stop us from working together. It's hard for the public to understand John. He's 23 years old. People expect the maturity of a 30-year-old because he's No. 1 in the world. They ask the guy to dig deeper than anyone else. He had to go deeper than he'd ever gone before yesterday because he'd never gone that long before."[23]

Not everyone was willing to cut McEnroe so much slack. In the aftermath of the St. Louis tie, there were renewed calls for his removal from the team. "When the match between Wilander and McEnroe determined the outcome we accepted 'victory' with shame," a man from New York City informed Ashe. "To be ashamed of McEnroe's behavior on court is nothing new, but . . . to see you, our coach, smiling in amusement, that hurt the most." One letter writer called McEnroe "a disgrace to the American people," and another claimed his tantrums were "at best embarrassing: at worst, repulsive." "Surely," she reminded Ashe, "winning is not the sole goal of the Davis Cup competition."

USTA and Davis Cup officials tended to be more forgiving than traditionalist fans. After a decade of allowing Nastase, Connors, and others to test the limits of on-court behavior, the tennis establishment had lost its innocence, choosing notoriety and commercial success over adherence to rigid rules. What had once been shocking was becoming an acceptable form of entertainment that boosted television ratings and exploited celebrity. The only holdouts, it seemed, were the keepers of tradition at the All England Club and several national Davis Cup committees. Now even the world of Davis Cup was adopting a more permissive approach to player behavior, the irony being that one of its most celebrated traditionalists, Arthur Ashe, was caught up in the transition.[24]

Arthur had plenty of time to puzzle over all of this as he waited for the next round of Davis Cup in the fall of 1982. For the Americans, the semifinal tie would take place in southwestern Australia, in the isolated seaside city of Perth. The opponent, an Australian team that the United States had defeated 5–0 the previous year, did not figure to put up much resistance. But Arthur was taking no chances. In early September, he added the Mayer brothers to the team as replacements for Teltscher and Gottfried. Though controversial, the move seemed to give Arthur more options since the Mayers were adept at both singles and doubles.

Even so, he remained uncertain about the team's overall strength in singles, and a week later he made a last-minute attempt to recruit Connors. Now thirty, Connors had just won his fourth U.S. Open singles title, defeating Lendl in the final, and his stock had never been higher as far as Ashe was concerned. "I think I understand Jimmy," he told one reporter, implicitly referencing his own background. "His mother and his grandmother raised him with the idea that they were from the other side of the tracks. They were never part of the country-club set and they will never feel they are. . . . Jimmy works at his image. He relishes it. He's just like Pancho Gonzales, who right to the end relished the role of the tough Mexican-American. It works and it sells. It distinguishes him from everybody else." Arthur was even willing to overlook Connors's notorious on-court antics and unrestrained gamesmanship. "Eighty percent of it has been good for tennis," he insisted. "We were stuck in an emotional straightjacket for 50 years. Nastase made it easier for everybody and then Jimmy came along. He doesn't do much harm except maybe to a few ladies in the front row."[25]

For those familiar with Arthur's long-standing advocacy of gentlemanly behavior, this praise for Connors sounded like pandering, and perhaps in part it was. In any event, his plea to Connors went unanswered, and the public statement praising the notorious "bad boys" of tennis could not be taken back. This is fortunate for those searching for clues to Arthur's inner life, as his statement reveals a complex position on the dictates of tennis etiquette. It seems he may not have been as much of a tennis traditionalist as his public image suggested. When it came to on-court behavior, he maintained a strict, inviolable standard for himself but not for others. He recognized that the game of professional tennis, as a commercially viable enterprise, benefited greatly from colorful characters that could attract fans and light up a crowd with their expressive personalities. At the same time, he knew he could never become one of these characters. Formed early in his career under Dr. J's mentorship, his primary role would always be to uphold the best traditions of sportsmanship.

This double standard not only made commercial sense; it also saved Arthur from an isolating, priggish absolutism. Despite his strong opinions and sense of purpose, he never took himself too seriously. His openness to different points of view was a key element of his popularity among his fellow touring pros, including McEnroe and the other bad boys of tennis.

Arthur's take on all of this is instructive. From his perspective, the roots of what amounted to a love-hate relationship with McEnroe were psychological as well as pragmatic. As Davis Cup captain, he stuck with McEnroe because he needed his skills, and he wanted to win. But there was also something deeper sustaining their partnership. The bond between them, at least for him, involved an inner transference of roles. As he explained near the end of his life, the "Superbrat" expressed his own deeply hidden impulse to be wild and free to experience a vicarious escape from his persona of coolness and control.

"Far from seeing John as an alien," he wrote in 1992, "I think I may have known him, probably without being fully aware of my feelings, as a reflection of an intimate part of myself. This sense of McEnroe as embodying feelings I could only repress, or as a kind of darker angel to my own tightly restrained spirit, may explain why I always hesitated to interfere with his rages even when he was excessive. . . . Now I wonder whether I had not always been aware, at some level, that John was expressing my own rage, as I could never express it; and I perhaps was even grateful to him for doing so, although his behavior was, on another level, totally unacceptable."

Ashe's relationship with Connors was different. While he respected his skills, he couldn't abide his selfishness and lone wolf ways. Unlike McEnroe, who thrived on Davis Cup play and who could always be counted on to give his all for the team, Connors rarely showed interest in anyone but himself. Although Connors's standoffishness obviously had a lot do with his background and upbringing, Ashe grew tired of self-serving excuses. Thus, any disappointment that the talented left-hander would not be part of the squad in Perth was tempered by the likelihood that his presence would pose a threat to team morale.[26]

When the Americans traveled to Perth, the only bad boys on the squad were McEnroe and Fleming, and for a few anxious hours over the Pacific there was some doubt that either of them would actually make it to the tie. After McEnroe defeated Connors in a Grand Prix final in San Francisco, he and Fleming boarded a Boeing 747 for Australia with a refueling stop in Honolulu. Leaving Honolulu, the plane experienced an aborted takeoff and later, during a second attempt to take off, a blown tire that wasn't discovered until the plane had already flown two hours to the west. The plane eventually returned safely to Hawaii, and McEnroe and Fleming, with nerves frazzled, boarded another plane that made it to Perth without incident, delivering the Americans two days late. Ashe greeted the weary travelers at 9:30 p.m. with open arms and a sigh of relief. But with McEnroe's first match scheduled for the following morning, the captain insisted on a few minutes of practice before bedtime. When McEnroe didn't put up a fight, other than mumbling about being exhausted, Ashe sensed their relationship had entered a new, more cooperative stage.

The next day, braving jet lag and a raucous Aussie crowd, the intrepid American star defeated McNamara in four sets. But along the way he was assessed a conduct warning and a penalty point by the umpire, Patrick Flodrops of France. At one point, he argued vehemently with both Flodrops and referee Jacques Dorfman after an alleged missed call on the baseline cost him a service break. Although Ashe agreed with McEnroe, he pleaded with him to accept the ruling and move on.

Following the match, McEnroe acknowledged he and his captain had radically different "philosophies concerning conduct in Davis Cup matches." "I really felt I got some bad calls," he insisted. "At break point in the fourth set I thought the ball was well inside the line, and Arthur thought so, too. But he didn't say anything. I wanted his support." Ashe also had to deal with carping from Gene Mayer, who, after defeating John Alexander in the other singles match, complained that his "ranking and record" justified a much earlier selection to the team. "I always made myself available," he pointed out, "but Ashe picked others." The U.S. team went on to blank the Australians 5–0, but clearly Ashe had some fences to mend before the Americans squared off against the French in the final tie scheduled for late November.[27]

Fortunately, the Davis Cup schedule allowed Ashe to spend a few days away from the pressures of his captaincy. But, in typical fashion, he used the time to attend to several of the other commitments that marked a frenetic lifestyle beyond anything one would expect of a man with a recent history of heart disease. "Consider Arthur Ashe," Joseph Durso wrote in *The New York Times* on November 10, two weeks before the final tie. "There may be busier people in sports . . . but probably not many. His tennis-playing career . . . was shortened by heart surgery. But he returned to become captain of the United States Davis Cup team, which meets France in the final round, starting Nov. 26 in Grenoble. So, Captain Ashe will fly to Europe next week for that. First, though, he must return from Japan, where he gave a series of clinics on tennis. He will do that today. Then, he can sit in front of a television screen to catch himself in yet another role: star on a daytime soap opera, 'The Doctors,' on NBC-TV."

The soap opera appearance was a one-time thing and a passing fancy. But Durso's brief profile captured only a fraction of Ashe's public life. His ongoing commitments ranged from the Aetna board and Le Coq Sportif appearances to the NJTL and TransAfrica, with seemingly every activity receiving conscientious attention. As a member of the NAACP's Prison Advisory Council he lobbied against misuse of the death penalty, and as part of the National Advisory Council of NIH's National Heart, Lung, and Blood Institute, he tried to apply his hard-earned knowledge of heart disease. In July he traveled to Richmond to accept the "Virginian of the Year Award" given by the Virginia Press Association, and he also found the time to deliver lectures at Princeton, West Point, and several other universities By the end of the year, he had even taken on a semester-long teaching assignment at Florida Memorial College, a century-old black institution in Miami.[28]

Following his retirement in 1980, Arthur had reconnected with his old friend and mentor the Reverend Jefferson Rogers, who had recently moved to Miami to become the director of Florida Memorial's Center for Community Change. The Ashes were now spending more time in Miami as Arthur conducted clinics at Doral during the Christmas, Easter, and Thanksgiving holidays. In 1981 they had finally put down roots in Florida, buying a house located a short distance from the entrance to Doral. In this large and comfortable second home, he and Jeanne had room to relax and entertain friends such as Rogers and Al and Carol Schragis, the Doral owners to whom they had grown close.

Spending time with Rogers, in particular, soon led to a host of new activities that transformed Arthur's life in Florida. From now on he would have a closer connection to the black communities of Dade and nearby Broward County, as well as several other black enclaves located further north along Florida's Atlantic coast. After enlisting Ashe in an effort to save the historic Daytona Beach home of the noted black theologian Howard Thurman, Rogers arranged for him to become a member of Florida Memorial's board of trustees. One thing led to another, and Ashe soon found himself in front of a weekly two-hour honors seminar on "The Black Athlete in Contemporary Society."

Fitting this commitment into his schedule was no mean feat, but he was determined to teach the course, which had few counterparts in American higher education. "Loving books myself," he later wrote, "I knew that I would enjoy being a teacher." Even so, his classroom experience at Florida Memorial failed to meet his expectations as he struggled to motivate students woefully unprepared for serious academic work.[29]

In preparing to teach the course, Ashe discovered both his own ignorance of the historical record and the paucity of assignable books and articles dealing with the past and present experiences of black athletes. After an exploratory trip to the New York Public Library uncovered only two book-length studies of African American athletes—Edwin B. Henderson's *The Negro in Sports* (1938), and A. S. Young's *Negro Firsts in Sports* (1963)—he confessed he "was baffled by this poverty of information." This lack of published resources stiffened his resolve to recover a lost history essential to any reconsideration of American attitudes toward race and athletic achievement. By November, he was emotionally and intellectually committed to the idea of researching and writing a "handbook on the Black American Athlete," and on December 8 he completed a four-page proposal that he would later submit to more than twenty publishers.

The proposal outlined plans for a comprehensive chronicle that would combine a historical narrative covering 350 years divided into seven eras with a reference section listing the names and accomplishments of "all black men and women who distinguished themselves" in athletic competition. All Ashe needed was a skilled staff of collaborators, several hundred thousand dollars of funding, an appropriate publisher, and enough time to bring the project to fruition. Realizing he faced a steep learning curve, he envisioned the handbook as requiring "a minimum of two man-years of constant research, writing, and rewriting," plus recognition that this was no ordinary book project. "All parties involved," he insisted, "must be spiritually committed." As the overall coordinator and primary author, he was a model of intellectual engagement and commitment, and his near obsession with the project would prove essential to its ultimate success. But it would still take six long years to reach the publication stage.

Amazingly, all of this activity—learning and teaching about a neglected subject, and writing a work eventually encompassing three volumes and more than a thousand pages—took place while he was attending to an array of business and philanthropic interests and guiding the U.S. Davis Cup team. When asked how Ashe managed to accomplish so much in his later years, his friend and boss at HBO, Seth Abraham, commented: "I think he lived every day as though it could be his last." Other friends and colleagues agreed, marveling at his determination to take advantage of every meaningful opportunity that came his way—to do it all and to do it well.[30]

Like most busy people, Ashe had a clear set of priorities. Most obviously, he took a special interest in anything associated with the Davis Cup. Genuine patriotism explained part of his deep commitment to the American team, but his attachment was also elemental and visceral. As captain he was able to recapture much of the spirit and excitement of his playing days; nothing else in his public life stimulated him in quite the same way. The thrill of competition was like an addictive drug, one that hadn't lost its allure since his retirement from the tour. Perhaps that is why he was so determined to stick it out as captain regardless of how many uncomfortable moments McEnroe and Fleming put him through. He felt the vibrant heat of life when he was with his players, and despite his cool exterior, he wanted to win the Cup every bit as much as they did.

Ashe was a keen student of Davis Cup history, and he knew that winning consecutive victories in his first two tries would place him in rare company. Dell had coached the victorious U.S. team in 1968 and 1969, his first two years as captain, and Ashe was on the verge of matching this feat. The only remaining obstacle was a French team representing a nation that had not won the Cup since 1932.

On paper the 1982 American squad appeared to be a heavy favorite. But Ashe feared it was not going to be easy to beat the French in Grenoble. With some justification, he worried that McEnroe and his teammates would be handicapped by the special indoor clay surface the host country had chosen for the final tie. Fifty years earlier, in an infamous Roland Garros final known as "The Great Cup Robbery," the French had defeated a superior American team by tampering with the court, deadening the tennis balls by cooling them in a freezer, and resorting to creative officiating.

The venue in Grenoble had served as an ice rink during the 1968 Winter Olympics, and to get the site ready for Davis Cup competition the French Tennis Federation "trucked in about three tons of rock, soil, and crushed brick to simulate the clay at Roland Garros stadium in Paris." The clear intention was to create a slow surface that would neutralize the Americans' power game, but as late as ten days before the tie one observer claimed the court was so moist that walking on it "was like walking on mashed potatoes." By the time the Americans arrived, the surface had hardened, and a relieved Ashe announced: "The court is fabulous." But he remained concerned about the speed of the court and playing indoors where "the applause will be deafening," a likely boost for the host country.[31]

None of this would matter, of course, if the Americans played up to their potential. Whatever the conditions, the young French team appeared to be overmatched, despite the formidable presence of their rising star, twenty-two-year-old Yannick Noah. It had been eleven years since Ashe had chanced upon Noah in Cameroon, and the young man had blossomed into one of the world's best players. Ranked ninth in the world, he had twice made it to the quarterfinals of the French Open and seemed on the verge of joining the top echelon of Connors, McEnroe, Borg, and Lendl. An imposing figure at six-foot-four, he had recently gone through a dramatic physical transformation after putting his hair in dreadlocks to honor his sister's wedding. "The classically featured Yannick now looked like a Rastafarian, rather fierce," Ashe observed, adding that McEnroe, Noah's opening match opponent, "was not about to be intimidated by anyone." When asked if he was "afraid of Noah and his home court," McEnroe replied, "I'm more afraid of his new hairstyle."

A consummate gentleman who patterned his court manners after Ashe's, Noah presented a sharp contrast to McEnroe's bluster. After the draw determined that Noah would play McEnroe in the opening match, the Frenchman seemed unnerved. The only French player to skip the post-draw news conference, he returned to his hotel room, either to rest up for the match or to prepare for the worst. Sensing that Noah, who had never played McEnroe before, was intimidated by the American star's dual reputation as a gritty competitor and a masterful shotmaker, Ashe was pleased with the matchup. His prediction that McEnroe would win no matter how well Noah played proved correct, though Noah was both brilliant and tenacious in losing the first set 12–10 and then winning the next two. With the American down two sets to one, the French crowd roared its approval, urging Noah to finish him off. But he couldn't pull it off. During the fourth and fifth sets, it was all McEnroe, and when Gene Mayer defeated Henri Leconte in the second opening day singles match, the Americans had a comfortable 2–0 advantage. The next day, McEnroe and Fleming won in straight sets over Noah and Leconte, capturing their ninth consecutive Davis Cup doubles match and clinching an American victory.

With the overall result settled, the Americans began to celebrate, even though they would return to the court the next day to play two inconsequential singles matches. After McEnroe defeated Leconte, Mayer barely went through the motions in losing to Noah 6–1, 6–0. The final match score was 4–1, good enough to inspire a beaming Ashe to address the presentation ceremony crowd in French. He knew the French would appreciate the effort no matter how many mistakes he made, and he wanted to show Jeanne, who was in the crowd, that three years of language lessons had not been wasted. "The crowd loved it," he recalled years later, "and even laughed at my jokes."

In victory Ashe was almost giddy. Leading the U.S. team to a second consecutive Davis Cup triumph was, to him, one of the high points of his career, ranking with his 1968 U.S. Open and 1975 Wimbledon titles. It was not just that the Americans had won but how they had won, overcoming adversity with grit and class. The team chemistry and camaraderie were exemplary, and they behaved themselves on and off the court. It was just what he had hoped for, a classic team victory with each individual making a difference and contributing to the result. He was especially pleased with Gene Mayer, who seemed to have forgotten his grievances against the Davis Cup selection process, and who not only played well when it counted but also assumed the role of a "happy chatterer, who lifted his teammates' spirits with his endless stream of talk." Mayer was all smiles in the locker room after the match as he and his father, Alex Mayer Sr., a Davis Cup veteran who had played for Hungary in the 1960s, toasted the victory with French champagne.

Ashe saved his greatest praise for McEnroe. When asked about his star's surprisingly strong performance on slow clay, he responded: "This is normal. The guy's the most talented player ever to play the game." Unaccustomed to hearing such an expansive superlative from Ashe, the reporters immediately asked him to elaborate, which he was happy to do. "He's the best doubles player I've ever seen," he declared. "He has more shots than anybody, he has more control over his body physically. His hand-eye coordination is probably the best of anybody except Rosewall. He also has great foot-eye coordination, and he can do anything with the ball. . . . He can hit with topspin. He can hit it flat. He can hit a drop volley. He can put the serve any place. And he has that intangible—true self-confidence. He genuinely believes that he can always raise his game if he has to."

Watching McEnroe at his best, keeping the Cup, enjoying an emotional reunion with Noah and Chatrier, temporarily abandoning his heart-healthy diet and eating elegant French food—what else could he have wished for, other than grabbing a racket and returning to the court as a rejuvenated thirty-nine-year-old ready to play. He knew the euphoria wouldn't last, and he wasn't one to expect miracles. Yet after three years of putting his life back together—of overcoming illness and learning the value of patience, he wasn't about to rest on his laurels. He was still in the game, thankful for what he had accomplished but always looking forward to the next win.

When Ashe flew back to New York in late November for an extended holiday vacation, he had no way of knowing that Grenoble would be the high point of his tenure as Davis Cup captain. While he would continue to lead the U.S. team for three more years, there would be no third victory and few moments of celebration. Most distressingly, the Davis Cup reverses would soon become the least of his problems. As 1982 drew to a close, he entered a new phase of his life—a testing time fraught with challenges both frightening and mysterious.[32]

TWENTY-THREE

BLOOD LINES

∎

J EANNE'S OLDER BROTHER, John Moutoussamy Jr., was just a few months older than Arthur. A successful lawyer employed by the Chicago district attorney's office, Johnny was one of Arthur's favorite in-laws. Happily married and the father of two small children, David and Jay, he seemed to have it all. But on Friday evening, December 17, 1982, he suffered a massive heart attack while attending a benefit dinner. The Ashes, who had just arrived in Chicago, were staying with Jeanne's mother and father. After they heard the news, Jeanne accompanied her parents and Johnny's wife, Penny, to the emergency room while Arthur stayed behind to take care of the children. Hours later Jeanne called Arthur from the hospital with the bad news: "Arthur, Johnny didn't make it." The next morning, with Jeanne and her family "almost overcome with shock and grief," part of the sad task of telling the boys about their father's death fell to Arthur. He had rarely experienced a more trying and difficult moment than when he sat down with David, the younger boy, and when the older boy, Jay, went into hysterics it brought back "my father's tearful reaction to my mother's death in 1950."[1]

Following the funeral, the Ashes flew to Miami. Jeanne hated to leave her grieving family, but Arthur had commitments at Doral. In addition to the Christmas season clinics, his honors course at Florida Memorial College (FMC) was scheduled to begin in less than a month. On New Year's Day, he spent three hours with Jeff Rogers, who briefed him on what to expect from the dozen students enrolled in the course. As he put the finishing touches on his teaching plan and syllabus, he felt eager and ready for the semester to begin, but he had to interrupt his preparation in mid-January with a whirlwind trip to New York, where he attended an array of board meetings and social functions, including a banquet honoring the legendary sportswriter Red Smith.[2]

By the time he returned to Miami for the first day of class, he was grateful for the relatively slow pace and orderly decorum of a college classroom. He soon found he enjoyed lecturing and, even more, the seminar-style back-and-forth with students during the course's weekly two-hour meetings. Unfortunately, the situation soon soured. "For the first two or three meetings, my dozen students seemed bright and alert enough," he recalled a decade later. "Then I received their first papers, and the first shock. Three students, all women, handed in well-researched, finely written papers. Almost all of the others, in varying degrees, upset me so profoundly that my hands shook with disbelief and anger the first time I read their prose. Their command of English was so abysmal, their sense of organization so weak, their mastery of logic and argumentation so pathetic that I could not believe that these young students would ever graduate from college."

After sharing several of the most garbled passages with Jeanne, he knew the students' problems were serious. Still, he worried about overreacting. "The last thing I wanted," he later confessed, "was to be perceived as a snob come down from New York City eager to heap scorn on the students, or for blacks to think that I had been socializing with rich white people for so long that I had lost touch with reality. Maybe I have, I told myself." A few days later an awkward conversation with Rogers left him chastened. "Arthur, I know what you are saying is true," Rogers conceded. "I've seen some of those papers, too. But you have to understand what these kids have been through, what their families have been through, just for them to get to this point. This is not UCLA." When Arthur reminded Rogers he had done well at UCLA after attending all-black schools, his friend countered with a plea for empathy and patience: "All I know, Arthur, is that we at this college . . . have to look out for all the young men and women out there. . . . Sure, we give the benefit of the doubt to some of the kids we admit. But somebody has to give them the benefit of the doubt, after what they have been through in this country. You know the white man isn't going to do that."

Arthur promised Rogers he would do his best to embrace the spirit of "remedial instruction." But it wasn't long before his commitment to high standards and personal responsibility got in the way. "When some of the

students drifted in late to class," he recalled, "or stayed away altogether without an excuse, or made feeble, trifling excuses to explain why they hadn't
read this book or finished that paper, I felt my indignation rise again." "At
some point," he insisted, "each individual is responsible for his or her fate. At
some point, one cannot blame history. Does the legacy of slavery explain why
Mr. Jones eased into class ten minutes late this morning? Why Mr. Smith
yawned in my face and claimed that he had not known about the assignment?"

In the end, Arthur stuck by his guns. There was no lowering of standards and no tolerance of poor attendance, late submissions, or disrespectful
behavior. Several students responded with renewed commitment. But others
simply dropped the course. "On the whole I was rather disheartened," he
later confessed, ultimately judging the semester to be "one of the more discouraging seasons of my life." Even so, his first semester was an important
learning experience. "Its main virtue," he concluded, "was to make me even
more determined to try to make a difference in the area of education, in particular. Certainly it was the major reason for the uncompromising position I
took on the question of higher academic standards for athletes governed by
the NCAA."[3]

Another salvation was a busy schedule that often diverted his attention
from the problems at FMC. During late January and eary February, for example, he attended Aetna and AMF-Head board meetings, huddled with his
New York literary agent, appeared on the *Sportsbeat* radio show, and played
golf at the Bing Crosby Pro-Am at Pebble Beach. He was also busy preparing
for the upcoming Davis Cup tie against Argentina and thinking about how
tough the Argentines would be in front of a raucous Buenos Aires crowd.
The only two times the Americans had played in the Argentine capital, in
1977 and 1980, they had lost. It had been tough enough to beat them in Cincinnati in 1981, and this time they would be stronger than ever. In the past
two years, Vilas had risen to number four in the world and Clerc to number
five, and the tie would be played on their favorite surface, the notoriously
slow clay of the Buenos Aires Lawn Tennis Club.

Ashe, too, would have a strong squad, with now third-ranked McEnroe
and seventh-ranked Gene Mayer as his singles players, and McEnroe and
Fleming in the doubles. Unfortunately, no one on the American team was a
clay court specialist, though the win in Grenoble had demonstrated some capacity to adapt to a slow surface. Ashe could only hope that lightning would
strike twice.[4]

The mounting pressure to defeat the Argentines was palpable. But on

February 9 and 10, less than three weeks before the Buenos Aires tie, Ashe enjoyed a welcome respite on the Ivy League campus of Yale University. Awarded the Kiphuth Fellowship, named for the legendary Yale swimming coach and athletic director Bob J. H. Kiphuth, Ashe was only the third recipient following the British runner Sebastian Coe and Ireland's Lord Killanin, the former president of the International Olympic Committee. Established to honor "men and women distinguished in the fields of physical training, sport, sports writing, physiology, literature and the arts," the award required the recipient to deliver a public lecture dealing with an issue of major importance.

If Ashe was nervous, he didn't show it, perhaps because he already knew so much about the school, having listened to Donald Dell's endless tales about his alma mater. "During his brief visit," commented Steve Flink of *World Tennis*, "one discovered that Ashe would probably fit comfortably into the intellectual landscape of campus life as a teacher, if he ever chose to do so." Henry Louis "Skip" Gates Jr., a young assistant professor of English destined for academic stardom, was similarly impressed. After watching Arthur interact with a group of students during a campus tour, Gates asked the visiting tennis star if he had ever thought about pursuing a PhD. He also tried to recruit him to teach a multiweek course at Yale, perhaps on sports, race, and education. Arthur was flattered and told Gates he would think it over.

Arthur's visit included a press conference held at the Payne Whitney Gymnasium. Accompanied by his old friend Benny Sims, the first black teaching pro at Longwood Cricket Club, he strode to the podium to answer a bevy of questions posed by a mixed crowd of students and reporters. Relaxed but focused, he offered a full measure of constructive advice. "It's very important to learn another language and to speak it like English," he declared. "Second, take a course in computer science. Third, take one in public speaking to give you self-confidence. . . . Last, I urge you to get to see as much of the world as possible. You can't learn enough about it from the *New York Times*, Dan Rather or Tom Brokaw. You've got to see it for yourself."

Predictably, someone in the crowd wanted to know his opinion on Proposition 48, the new NCAA policy that raised the existing requirements for Division I and II scholarship eligibility. Beginning in the fall of 1986, freshman athletes receiving scholarships would have to have a score of at least 700 (out of 1600) on the Scholastic Aptitude Test (SAT), and a 2.0 or better high school grade point average in eleven academic courses.

Prop 48 was approved despite considerable opposition, mostly from historically black colleges and universities. From the moment it passed, there was pressure either to lower the standards or to allow exceptions to accommodate disadvantaged and minority students. Eventually the NCAA worked out a compromise—essentially a "partial qualifier" category providing scholarship possibilities in the sophomore year (they could not play as freshmen) for marginal and underperforming students if they met one of the two requirements—either the minimum acceptable score on a standardized test or the required high school grade point average. This amendment would later spawn a countermeasure known as Prop 42, which sought to restore the original strict standards of Prop 48.

Ashe, who was in the process of writing an opinion piece on Prop 48 for *The Washington Post*, confessed he was no fan of the SAT as a determining factor in college admissions. "The intent of the proposal is commendable," he acknowledged, but he did not like Prop 48's rigid and inflexible standards. "Many athletes are in college to play ball and not to get an education," he pointed out, before resorting to a mixed metaphor: "but the remedy is too broad a brush. You need to do it with finely chiseled tools, not with a sledgehammer. Basically, what you are saying is you will keep someone out of college on the basis of what they did one Saturday morning on an S.A.T. test." By the end of the press conference it was obvious to everyone in the room that the speaker was no ordinary tennis jock.

That night, Arthur, accompanied by Jeanne and Dell, attended a dinner party at the home of Yale president A. Bartlett Giamatti, a literary scholar who later served as the commissioner of Major League Baseball. The next morning he toured the campus with Professor Gates before lunching at Mory's, the famous Yale eating and drinking club. After lunch he met with the men's and women's tennis teams and fielded a variety of questions, including one about Connors's refusal to play Davis Cup. "Why doesn't he play?" one student asked, and Ashe responded candidly: "It's a matter of money, priorities and his age."

Candor was also in evidence when Ashe delivered his formal Kiphuth Fellowship speech later that afternoon. Billed as a lecture on "College Athletics: A Reappraisal," his forty-minute talk was both down-to-earth and philosophical. Professor Michael Cooke's introduction set the tone. "The important thing is not that Arthur won, but how he won," Cooke declared. "He has a rare level of spiritual class." Arthur began by reflecting on the lasting influence of his Jim Crow upbringing in Richmond. "Being black you take certain baggage everywhere you go," he told the crowd of five hundred. He then turned to issues related to collegiate sports and education but would revisit the "upbringing" theme during the question-and-answer period. "When I grew up I had to say 'Yes, sir' 'No, sir' to my father," he recalled. "You do it for a while and it stays with you. . . . But I've got to admit that for a long time I've had this urge to walk out on Centre Court at Wimbledon and for just one match act like McEnroe."

When asked about the future of tennis, he placed himself in a dying breed. "Tennis is going to be changed by a new breed of athlete," he predicted. "By 1990 there will be a large number of players who are 6 feet, 3 inches, weigh 185 to 190 pounds. They will be fast and will be the kind of athletes who could have gone into the NBA. It will change tennis completely. Until very recently we had great players but not the best athletes in terms of foot speed and hand-eye coordination. Soon the best athletes will be playing tennis and it will be at a level like you've never seen." The prototype of this new breed, he pointed out with some pride, was Yannick Noah.

At the Kiphuth awards dinner that evening, the guest of honor found himself blushing as Dell addressed the gathering. "Arthur has a quiet confidence in himself," Dell explained. "Underneath that quiet exterior lies someone who is very forceful, always changing, ever different, very much a leader. He believes in striving for excellence by example, not by what he says but by what he does." Later, when Arthur rose to accept the award, he expressed his gratitude with gracious humility. "Awards like this Kilputh Fellowship increase the pressure not so much to prove myself but to live up to the ideal," he insisted. "But each time something like this happens, it makes me feel my philosophy of life is right." The concluding ovation was long and loud, leaving him with a feeling of optimism that had been difficult to muster since Johnny Moutoussamy's death.[5]

Ashe departed from New Haven with a renewed sense of hope and purpose— two assets he would surely need in Buenos Aires. He knew the Argentines were slight favorites, but he wasn't prepared for an injury to McEnroe three weeks before the tie. Just as injury-plagued Gene Mayer was rounding into the best shape of his career, McEnroe suffered a shoulder injury that impeded his serve. He could still play but not with his normal abandon. The American squad's best option, at this point, was to recruit Connors, and both Ashe and McEnroe pleaded with him to come to the aid of his national team. But Connors refused, leaving Ashe with little choice but to stick with his injured star. If anyone could overcome physical adversity and gut it out, Ashe reasoned, it was McEnroe.

The opening singles match between Gene Mayer and Vilas did not bode well for the Americans. Mayer had lost to Vilas the first five times they had played, and the sixth meeting, framed by a boisterous Argentine crowd, led to the same result. Then it was McEnroe's turn. He knew Clerc would be tough, but neither he nor Ashe was fully prepared for the hostility that pervaded the small, bandbox stadium. From the outset, as one observer noted, the crowd "whistled and jeered . . . sang soccer cheers, waved blue-and-white Argentine flags and chanted the names of the Argentine players." Clerc, in addition to playing well, did everything he could to whip up the crowd, lapsing into a mock victory dance "after winning key points" and delighting in the frequent chants of "la batata" (the Spanish word for sweet potato), his favorite nickname.[6]

Part of the fans' intensity was almost certainly a response to the support the United States had given to the British during the recent Falklands War. Having suffered a humiliating defeat at the hands of the British navy in June 1982, Argentina was in desperate need of a victory that would restore some of its national pride. For a nation where tennis was second only to soccer in popularity (reportedly more than 3 million of Argentina's 28 million citizens played tennis), the notion of exacting a bit of revenge from the U.S. Davis Cup team—especially from the brash young star dubbed "El Irascible" by the Argentine press—was irresistible.

To the Argentines' delight, this notion became reality on a hot and humid weekend in March. Unsteady and seemingly unnerved, McEnroe won only two games in the first two sets, losing a set "at love for the first time in six years of cup play." Somehow he battled back to win the next two sets, but in the fifth set he fell behind 5–2 before play was halted by darkness. After a night's sleep, McEnroe returned to the court hoping for a miracle, and for a while the miracle appeared to be in reach as he fought back to tie the set at 5–5. But after two sessions and nearly five hours of play, Clerc closed out the match 7–5. Though disappointed, McEnroe had no time to think about what might have been. Later that afternoon, he and Fleming took the court against Vilas and Clerc with the tie on the line. This time the American side was fortunate enough to prevail in an exhausting five-set war of attrition.

By staving off elimination in the doubles, the Americans could still win the Cup by taking both singles matches on the final day of competition. But this was a highly unlikely prospect considering McEnroe's tender shoulder and the 10 exhausting sets he had already played. After McEnroe broke Vilas's serve in the first game of their match and went on to take a 4–2 lead, Ashe detected a glimmer of hope. But it soon faded as Vilas subjected McEnroe to a humiliating drubbing. Dropping the first set 6–4, and the second

6–0, the American star lost the first five games of the third. McEnroe's losing streak ultimately stretched to an incredible 15 games, the longest drought of his career. He lost the third set 6–1, but not before initiating a strange moment of bonding with Ashe. "Well, captain," he asked during the last changeover of the match, "do you have any pearly words of wisdom for me?" Ashe could only smile and wave him back out onto the court and certain defeat. "I thought it was our finest moment together," he wrote years later. "Sometimes a defeat can be more beautiful and satisfying than certain victories."

McEnroe, in Ashe's estimation, had once again demonstrated the heart and guts of a lion. "In front of all those hostile, jeering fans," the grateful captain recalled, "he seemed a lonely figure, yet brave and brilliant, heroic." Neither man would ever forget this experience, and it became part of the deep bond between them. In the short run, of course, they were less philosophical. In March 1983, McEnroe's strength of character was less evident than the stark reality of defeat and disappointment. Back among the American people, both he and Ashe had difficult questions to answer and crucial decisions to consider. Personal development and team spirit notwithstanding, the Davis Cup was lost, and for the first time in nine years the United States had been eliminated in the first round. There would be no third consecutive victory for Captain Ashe.[7]

Losing the Cup was bad enough, but an even more troubling problem soon emerged. On March 10, *The New York Times* announced the sports management group led by Dell, Ray Benton, Frank Craighill, and Lee Fentress was about to split up, with Dell and Benton on one side and Craighill and Fentress on the other. While his relationship with Dell was special, he liked and respected all four of the major partners. Their firm had served him well and had been instrumental in the maturation of Open tennis. He hated to see them break up and worried that a whole web of friendships and mutually beneficial relationships was in danger of collapsing. "I was upset by it all," he told a *Washington Post* reporter in early May. Though "not completely surprised," he had hoped "that the family would figure out a way to stay together."

The biggest issue dividing the partners was the proper role of ProServ, the firm's marketing and television subsidiary. Under Dell's direction, ProServ had undertaken the promotion of several tournaments, despite Craighill's and Fentress's opposition. Dell's disagreements with his partners, both personal and professional, ran deep—too deep, as it turned out, to be resolved amicably. In April, the split became formal with Dell and Benton staying with ProServ and Craighill and Fentress forming a new management firm, Advantage International.

Arthur stuck with his buddy Dell, of course. Their friendship was stronger than ever, and the business partnership they had sealed with a handshake more than a decade earlier was as inviolable as it was successful. Still, the firm's dissolution hit Arthur hard. He had never thought of himself as a pessimist, but he was beginning to fear an uncertain future. Bad news, it seemed, was becoming a pattern in his life. Ever since Johnny Moutoussamy's death four months earlier he had suffered one setback after another, with the exhilarating visit to Yale being the only exception. Johnny's death, the loss of the Davis Cup, ProServ's breakup—he must have asked himself: what matter of misfortune would be next? He would find out in short order.[8]

While attending an Actna board meeting in early April, Arthur began to experience angina-like pain in his chest. He had felt a few pangs in late March but hadn't thought much of it. This time, however, the pain was too strong to ignore. Over the next eight weeks, as his doctors ran a series of tests, he tried to maintain his normal schedule of activities, including his teaching and his increasing attention to the book project.[9]

On April 13, he held a midday press conference at the Palm restaurant in Washington, where he announced Howard University Press had agreed to publish his manuscript, *The History of the Black Athlete in America*. For several months his agent, Fifi Oscard, had been trying to secure a contract from a major publishing house. But editors at more than a dozen commercial presses had rejected Arthur's proposal, largely because they doubted the capacity of a former tennis player with no training as a historian to pull off such an ambitious project.[10]

The first editor willing to see beyond this obvious deficiency was Charles F. Harris, the executive director of Howard University Press. The press itself was a relatively unimpressive operation with few major publications to its credit, but Arthur was swayed by "the intellectual tradition of Howard University," the "philosophy of the Howard University Press publishing program," and the university's renowned repository of black history, the Moorland-Spingarn Research Center. For the press, as for Ashe, the project represented a financially daring initiative. "It is estimated that this project will require an expenditure of $500,000," the university soon revealed, "half of which will be provided by Howard University Press and Arthur Ashe. The remaining $250,000 will be solicited from public and private philanthropic sources."[11]

Even before the contract signing, Arthur had expended significant funds on the project. By the end of March he had rented office space on Lexington Avenue and hired a clerical assistant, Derilene McLeod, and two researchers—Kip Branch, an English professor at Wilson College in Pennsylvania, and Sandra Jamison, a professional librarian. With their help, he soon filled the office with as many relevant books and articles as he could find. After compiling a preliminary bibliography, Branch and Jamison created an interview questionnaire, contacted a number of black historians, enlisted the help of student interns at several colleges and universities, and sent out information requests to more than one hundred athletic departments. Meanwhile, Arthur focused on reading books on sports and black history and "outlining his research needs." [12]

All of this preliminary work was exhausting and exhilarating, and keeping busy helped to take his mind off his health problems. As Jeanne looked on with amazement and some concern, he never stopped moving. The day before the news conference in Washington, he was in New York, bouncing between a morning doctor's appointment and other commitments before serving as the master of ceremonies at the Paul Robeson Scholarship Dinner held at Columbia University that evening. He even managed to call his sister Loretta's house to wish his niece La Chandra a happy fifth birthday.

There was no letup in his frenetic schedule, but in early May he reluctantly obeyed a doctor's order to cancel a fishing trip in New Brunswick, Canada. He also relinquished his position on the Men's International Professional Tennis Council. Later in the month, he decided to forgo a trip to Athens, Georgia, where he was inducted in absentia into the newly opened Men's Collegiate Tennis Hall of Fame. Staying close to home, he found time to write a blurb promoting his friend Vic Seixas's new book *Prime Time Tennis* and to publish a *Washington Post* article on Calvin Peete's recent experience as one of the first black golfers to participate in the Masters tournament played at the historically all-white Augusta National Golf Club. [13]

In early June, he traveled across town to St. John's University to accept an honorary degree. But as his doctors continued to evaluate his condition, he was warned not to travel much beyond the five boroughs of New York. To his dismay, he missed both the 1983 French Open—where Noah became the first black man to win the French singles title—and his annual broadcasting stint for HBO at Wimbledon. Skipping the trip to Europe proved to be the right decision. By the end of the second week of play in Paris, his doctors were already preparing him for bypass surgery. [14]

"My doctors tell me I'm in no danger of keeling over tomorrow," he reassured reporters on Friday, June 17, and on Sunday morning he was admitted to the hospital to await surgery. Play began the next day at both Wimbledon and the Gordon's Gin–Arthur Ashe Tennis Classic, a United Negro College Fund benefit tournament held at the National Tennis Center. But Ashe's two favorite tournaments would have to proceed without him. On Tuesday morning, he went under the knife at St. Luke's-Roosevelt Hospital, the site of his 1979 surgery. The surgeon performing the procedure, Dr. John Hutchinson III, the hospital's chief of cardiothoracic surgery, was familiar, having presided over his first heart operation. The procedure turned out to be a relatively simple double bypass.

Going into the surgery, Arthur had great confidence in both Dr. Hutchinson and the hospital. During the surgery the only complicating factor was the difficulty of cutting through "the tough scar tissue" left over from his first operation, and the surgical team finished in ninety minutes. A hospital spokesman soon announced the famous patient was in "satisfactory and stable" condition, and on Wednesday, the same spokesman predicted he would be strong enough to leave the hospital in "a week to 10 days." [15]

In truth, Arthur was not doing as well as he or the doctors had expected. Unlike his condition during the early recovery period following his first operation, he "felt weak, even anemic." A bit shaken by this lethargy, he asked Dr. Hutchinson if there was anything that could hasten his recovery. For starters, Dr. Hutchinson prescribed two units of blood. "This transfusion," Arthur recalled, "indeed picked me up and sent me on the road to recovery from my surgery."

What he did not know then, and what he would not discover for five long years, was that the transfusion "also, unwittingly, set in motion my descent into AIDS." No one at the time had any inkling that blood transfusions could be contaminated with the human immunodefficiency virus (HIV). Patients suffering from acquired immunodefficiency syndrome (AIDS, a term used by the Centers for Disease Control for the first time in September 1982) had been under clinical observation since 1981, but the existence of HIV was virtually unknown until the findings of the research teams led by Drs. Robert Gallo and Luc Montagnier were published in *Science* magazine on May 20, 1983, exactly one month prior to Ashe's surgery.

Medical knowledge of this and related viral agents was still in its infancy, and no one at the time believed any form of routine blood screening—for HIV or any other virus—was necessary (or even possible) for the maintenance of public health. The first practical blood test would not be developed until 1984, and American blood banks would not begin to screen their blood supplies until a year later, two years after Ashe's exposure to HIV. By early 1985 more than eight thousand AIDS cases had been identified in the United States, and more than four thousand Americans had died from complications related to AIDS.[16]

In late June and early July 1983, Arthur's doctors—unconcerned about tainted blood—were preoccupied with trying to get him back on his feet with a reasonably healthy heart. Following the transfusion, he was stronger with each passing day and generally in good spirits—in part because he was able to take in more than a week of televised Wimbledon matches. The highlight, for him, was when a twenty-four-year-old Nigerian, Nduka Odizor—who as an eleven-year-old had attended an Arthur Ashe–Stan Smith tennis clinic in Lagos—upset Guillermo Vilas, the Americans' Davis Cup nemesis, in the opening round. If this couldn't lift Arthur's spirits, nothing could.

By the time Arthur left the hospital on July 6, he seemed to be on the road to recovery, yet Jeanne could sense her normally optimistic husband's unease about the future. "My second operation, coming as it did only four years after the first, was a major physical and psychological setback," he later explained, "one that left me on the brink of depression. I had assumed that my quadruple bypass surgery would be far more effective and lasting than it turned out be: was the second but a presage of a decline that would virtually cripple me? More than ever, I became aware of my mortality."

He was also facing his fortieth birthday on July 10, not a happy prospect for any man in a youth-obsessed culture. Needing something to break the mood of encroaching decrepitude, Jeanne decided to treat him with a small but special birthday party. In addition to inviting Dr. Doug Stein, the Dells, and a few others, she hired a stripper to liven up the evening. "The main surprise of the party," the birthday boy recalled, "was a performance by a striptease artist who proceeded to bump and grind her way around my living room, dressed in precious little, while I hung my head in sheepish embarrassment." He understandably assumed that Dell or one of his other male friends had arranged the "entertainment." But once the bumping and grinding ended and the woman read the birthday message, he discovered "the real culprit" was Jeanne.[17]

One of the things he loved most about her was her sense of humor, which could brighten even his darkest days. After more than six years of marriage, their relationship was stronger than ever, strengthened by their shared experiences both good and bad. The one cloud over their marital horizon, other than Arthur's heart condition, was their inability to have children. They both loved kids, and Jeanne was never more proud of him than when he frolicked with his nieces and nephews, or when he worked with youth organizations such as the NJTL and the Black Tennis and Sports Foundation (BTSF), which sponsored after-school and weekend programs in several cities. Co-founded by Ashe and his old Lynchburg tennis camp friend Bobby Davis in the 1970s, the BTSF was hampered by perennial financial and local management issues. But its goals embodied Ashe's concern for inner-city kids. Similarly, the NJTL's summer programs—with their focus on personal growth and character development—remained one of his most passionate interests. Fittingly, just after his birthday, the National Council of Juvenile and Family Court Judges Association honored him for his "Meritorious Service to the Children of America." While both he and Jeanne appreciated the award, it also reminded them of their unfulfilled efforts to have children.

These frustrations would soon take them to Virginia Beach, to the Jones Institute for Reproductive Medicine. Established by the husband-and-wife team of Drs. Howard and Georgeanna Seegar Jones in 1978, the institute had pioneered studies of in vitro fertilization and had produced the nation's first "test tube baby" in 1981. The in vitro process was expensive and cumbersome, and it had limited likelihood of success. But the Ashes decided to try it anyway. Over the next two years, Jeanne and Arthur made numerous trips to the Institute, hoping to be among the fortunate few to conceive with the new technology.

At the same time, their health and fertility problems had taught them there are no guarantees in life, a realization that prompted both of them to become more spiritual and philosophically reflective. Jeanne, a lapsed Catholic for more than a decade, returned to the Roman Catholicism of her childhood, and though both she and Arthur prided themselves on being analytical and rational thinkers, they figured a measure of faith in a higher power couldn't hurt.[18]

By September of 1983, the Ashes seemed to be on the rebound. The special fortieth birthday party had raised Arthur's spirits, and before long he was back in the swing of things, resuming his frenetic schedule of activities and even adding a few new twists. While Jeanne worried he might overdo it, she knew her husband would never be content with a sedentary life. Despite certain risks, she felt she had to allow him do the things that made him feel alive. His close friends agreed. "This successful operation will enable you to lead a much happier and fulfilling life in the future," Donald Dell wrote from Wimbledon on June 22. "Arthur, I do believe that many good things come out of adversity. . . . In tennis you know the phrase 'You only learn from losing,' and unfortunately sometimes this is true in life. You have had several serious and difficult health problems these past five years," but "as a result of these various illnesses you have grown as a human being in stature, understanding, patience and tolerance."

Arthur appreciated the encouragement and concern for his welfare expressed in Dell's letter. Throughout their long relationship, his friend and agent had acted as both a mentor and a cheerleader. Six weeks before the surgery, Dell sent Arthur a handwritten note expressing his affection and respect—and his optimism: "Lieutenant, you have made a real *impact* on those around you these past 39 years—by your love, caring, intelligence, loyalty, and in a word—*FRIENDSHIP*. Never forget all the joy and good feeling you have brought to *so many*. Your future lies ahead, and it will be challenging, hard working, energetic and successful."

The respect and concern went both ways. Throughout that difficult spring, Arthur worried about Dell's state of mind during the messy aftermath of the management group breakup. He knew how ugly the situation had gotten because virtually everyone involved had approached him with their side of the story, even after he formally re-signed with Dell and Pro-Serv. Much of the haggling and backbiting involved competing attempts to recruit Rodney Harmon as a client. A promising young black player from Richmond, Harmon signed with ProServ on May 25. But Advantage International cried foul, claiming Dell had secured the contract by secretly offering him $10,000 under the table. Dell and his ProServ colleagues vehemently denied they had offered Harmon any special inducements, but the controversy dragged on for months.[19]

Arthur welcomed Harmon to the ProServ team, but beyond that he had no time for recriminations or awkward conversations he regarded as little more than petty squabbling among former friends. For one thing, he was too busy working on his book. Since his return from Buenos Aires, the task of writing a history of black athletes had dominated his thoughts. While he maintained other commitments, recovering the lost stories and statistics related to more than four centuries of black athletic achievement had become his greatest passion. "It did more than energize him," his brother Johnnie observed, "It gave him a new purpose"—and a new understanding of his connections to black history. As Johnnie recalled, "He'd say, 'The same problems I went through, Jack Johnson went through, Joe Louis went through.'"

Arthur wanted to know more, and early in the project he reached out to the public for help. On June 27, he made his needs known in a pointed interview conducted by a *New York Times* reporter. "Get-well cards are nice, and flowers are even nicer," the reporter told his readers, "but if you really want to cheer up Arthur Ashe during his recuperation from last week's heart surgery, you might want to rummage through the attic to see if you have any old scrapbooks or letters telling of the exploits of obscure black athletes." He went on to relay Arthur's specific requests. "I'm having tremendous difficulty finding source material on the early days," Arthur revealed. "The kind of material I need just isn't found in libraries or bookstores, not even in the best college libraries. A lot of it was never written. People didn't write books or articles about black athletes, and even the black newspapers missed it. I need to find people who have old scrapbooks, photographs, or letters, or who can remember something about relatively unknown black athletes."

He would eventually turn his attention to the twentieth century, but the initial focus was the pre-colonial era through the nineteenth century. "We're starting with games that black people played in West Africa in the days before the slave trade," he explained, "moving to what games they brought with them to America, and then on through history, to people like Isaac Murphy, the black jockey who won the first Kentucky Derby." The reporter, a veteran obituary writer accustomed to fact-checking, could not resist pointing out that Murphy won no fewer than three Kentucky Derbies between 1884 and 1891, but not the first one held in 1875. That honor belonged to another black jockey, Oliver Lewis, and his horse, Aristides.[20]

Ashe was well aware he would have to improve his research skills to have any chance of producing an "authoritative" work on black athletes. But he also knew it would take several years to complete what almost certainly would be a multivolume project. So he was willing to start small and gradually work his way up to serious historical reconstruction. His first attempt at historical writing was "Tennis Everyone?"—an amateurish and rather inauspicious article written for the July 1983 issue of United Airlines' in-flight magazine, *Hemispheres*. In less than two pages, he covered 110 years of tennis history, from the invention of lawn tennis in 1873 to a forecast of the upcoming competition at the U.S. Open. But the article said nothing about the sport's long history of racial discrimination—or about women's tennis. After Leslie Allen—a rising star among black players on the women's tour—read the article, she complained to Arthur, whom she considered one of her mentors, that she was "a little disappointed, and a lot annoyed." Her primary complaint was that he had focused on the men's game while completely ignoring the women's. "If one writes about the A.T.P.'s formation and the politics of tennis," she insisted, "certainly there is a place for the formation of the W.T.A." "It seems to be a grave omission," she added, "for King, Court and Goolagong to go unnamed!" This would not be the last time Arthur stumbled over matters of gender balance, but to his credit he was always willing to listen and learn.[21]

Thanks to the American Davis Cup squad's early elimination, he had plenty of time for research. He now had an expanded staff, which included Charles Harris's son Francis and Ocania Chalk, a former reporter and amateur sports historian who had already published two books on black athletes—*Pioneers of Black Sport* (1975) and *Black College Sport* (1976).[22]

By August, Arthur and his staff were conducting oral history interviews and fanning out to libraries, archives, and private attics. It was often slow, tedious work, but he never seemed to tire of the subject. One interesting development intersecting with his personal history, and with his research, was Yannick Noah's rise to a new level of stardom during the summer of 1983. As Noah's discoverer, Arthur was inevitably drawn into the media circus accompanying the Frenchman's victory at the French Open in June. Finally, a man of color other than Arthur had won one of the four majors.

Noah, it turned out, was a man of color in every sense of the word, an outsized personality who radiated youthful exuberance and telegenic chic. And unlike many of the celebrities of men's tennis—McEnroe, Connors, Nastase, and the other bad boys—he was almost always nice and polite. "Noah has never understood why players act any other way," Barry Lorge observed in *Sport* magazine. As Noah himself put it, "We should all realize how lucky we are, how nice our life is. We are doing something we like, we get so much money, we travel all over the world, we can be very popular. What we do is not very important, but I receive thousands of letters from kids and I have to realize that for them I am somebody, and I shouldn't disappoint them. You should be polite on the court. It's a game and you don't have to act crazy or cheat."

All of this sounded very much like something Arthur would say, and Noah often credited the Virginian with being his role model. Yet he was very much his own man, a much edgier character than Arthur, and one who favored social and cultural experimentation over political activism or institutional involvement. Adorned with his Jamaican-style dreadlocks, he cultivated an image of freewheeling fun that included recreational use of hashish. He owned two racehorses and six cars, and a seemingly endless array of expressive clothing, and unlike Arthur he apparently felt no need to apologize for his extravagant self-indulgence or lack of social activism.

"My politics are to play on the court and win," he told Ray Kennedy of *Sports Illustrated* in August 1983. "I don't know anything about the other kind of politics, and I'm not interested in learning. . . . I am not an ambassador for any race or any country. My mother is white; my father is black. So inside me I don't feel like I'm black or white. I think I do more for people by winning Roland Garros than I could by going to South Africa and having meetings. Maybe when I'm 35 I'll change, but I don't think so."[23]

This was not what Ashe wanted to hear, yet he knew from personal experience that Noah had a good heart that would eventually lead the young star to a more mature and statesmanlike posture. Noah's later philanthropic endeavors would confirm this judgment, but during the late summer of 1983 most of the attention was directed at his skills on the court—specifically his chance of winning his second major at the U.S. Open. It had been fifteen years since the first U.S. Open, and there was even more hoopla than usual in the days leading up to the tournament. The top two seeds were McEnroe and Lendl, but Noah as the #4 seed was considered a potential spoiler. Noah did not win the U.S. Open that year, losing in the quarterfinals to nineteen-year-old Jimmy Arias. Nevertheless, the excitement he generated helped make the tournament a special experience for Ashe.[24]

As a commentator for HBO, a tennis historian, and the first U.S. Open champion, Ashe was called upon to take stock of the tournament's first decade and a half. When Bud Collins asked him to reflect on his unique double victory in the 1968 U.S. Amateur and U.S. Open tournaments, the legendary tennis journalist reminded him he had been "a curiosity." Collins set the scene for his readers: "As he mounted the U.S. Open victors' podium at Forest Hills 15 years ago, Arthur Ashe stood out like a Brooks Brothers suitor at a nudist colony or a go-go dancer in 'Swan Lake.' It was strange enough that he was black and an American. What made him an even greater oddity was his status: Ashe was an amateur. Practically a missing link."

The U.S. Open had changed dramatically since then, Ashe acknowledged, and mostly for the better. They had not yet named the stadium court for him—that honor would come posthumously in 1997. But there were already enough honors to assure him his accomplishments at the Open had not been forgotten. At one benefit banquet held during the second week of the tournament, he received the Omega Award, given annually to a tennis player "who has shown determination of spirit and ability in overcoming significant physical obstacles." A few days earlier, he had been on the giving end of an award ceremony, presenting the Arthur Ashe Award for NCAA Division II to a young college player from Pennsylvania in recognition of combined athletic and scholarly achievement.

The 1983 U.S. Open—later remembered mostly for its "record crowds" and "record temperatures"—ended on September 11 with Connors defeating Lendl in the men's singles final for the second straight year. Connors had won five U.S. Open singles in the past ten years, but at age thirty-one he was clearly entering the downslope of his career. Lendl would go on to win three Open titles, and Connors would never win another. Nevertheless, Ashe was convinced even a somewhat diminished Connors would be a welcome addition to the 1984 U.S. Davis Cup team. That Connors was now a Dell and ProServ client gave him hope that the left-hander would agree to play Davis Cup. But as the opening round tie against Ireland approached, there was no sign Connors would come around anytime soon.[25]

The root of the problem, as Ashe saw it, was a selfish attitude all too common among the tour's leading players. "It's time that some of the older players—guys like Connors—started to help out the sport," he declared just prior to the beginning of the Open. "I think nothing burns in the gut of ex-top players more than to hear players like Connors say, 'We are the game.' Connors doesn't mean the players in general, he means just the three or four top players." This straight talk was hardly calculated to soften Connors up— and true to form he kept his distance from Ashe and the Davis Cup. But Arthur was not one to mince words when the good of the game was involved.[26]

Once the Open was over he still had three weeks before turning his attention to preparations for the 1984 Davis Cup competition. In addition to preparing materials for his second semester of teaching at Florida Memorial, on September 14 he joined the singer Harry Belafonte and several other celebrity activists—including the dancer Gregory Hines, the white actor Tony Randall, and the husband-and-wife activist duo Ossie Davis and Ruby Dee—at the United Nations headquarters in midtown Manhattan for an important announcement regarding South Africa.

Ashe and Belafonte, with the help of TransAfrica's Randall Robinson, had taken the lead in organizing Artists and Athletes Against Apartheid (AAAA). The goal of the new organization was to convince artists and athletes to boycott venues in South Africa proper and in the so-called native homelands. Their chosen weapon, Ashe announced, was persuasion. "John McEnroe was offered seven figures to play tennis in Sun City," he reminded reporters. "Once we explained why he shouldn't go, he decided not to." It was a critical time in South African history, he explained; during the past week the all-white South African parliament had approved a new constitution that would allegedly "give nonwhites a role in the national Government for the first time in the country's history."

Ashe and other activists staunchly opposed the new constitution, which they feared would preempt any real move toward a true democracy based on universal suffrage. Since it would be submitted to the white electorate for approval in a November 2 referendum, the time to step up was now, and Belafonte insisted that celebrities had an important role to play. "Artists have had a powerful impact on many issues in recent years—Vietnam, civil rights," he insisted. "We're part of people's lives." Unfortunately, Ashe could not say the same for celebrity athletes, though he hoped that was about to change.

Just prior to the referendum, the AAAA initiated a joint effort with the United Nations Committee on South Africa to institute a cultural boycott of the nation that had given the world "the evils of apartheid." At an October 8 press conference, Ashe insisted the boycott was in compliance with a 1968 resolution passed by the U.N. General Assembly, and that for both political and moral reasons professional athletes and entertainers, indeed all Americans, should boycott all things South African. This was a hard sell at a time when Frank Sinatra was being paid $1.6 million for performing at Sun City, but Ashe and his allies were determined to push the American anti-apartheid movement to a new level. Fortunately, the AAAA was only one part of a multipronged effort to bring the anti-apartheid cause to the forefront of the debate on American foreign policy toward South Africa. In recent months the so-called Sullivan Principles—a plan first introduced in 1977 by Philadelphia minister and civil rights activist Leon Sullivan to require strict fair employment and nondiscrimination standards for all American corporations doing business in South Africa—had gained new life as an alternative to complete divestment.[27]

The AAAA's efforts were important to Ashe, but for much of September he was absorbed in his book project. In the weeks following the U.N. press conference, he began to write and rewrite the early chapters of what would be the first of three volumes. Once he had produced a rough draft of a chapter, he generally sent it out to professional historians asking for feedback. Those who responded included several of the nation's leading black scholars, notably John Hope Franklin and Benjamin Quarles. Well aware that the academic world had contributed next to nothing to the history of black athletes, most of the scholars who looked at the early drafts offered encouragement and the mildest of constructive criticism.

The major exception was Quarles, the author of *Black Abolitionists* and several other well-received books on African American history. To him, Ashe's efforts were too amateurish to be of much value. Lacking analytical focus and synthetic reach, the early drafts were, in his view, chronicles worthy of antiquarian interest but not consideration as true history. Washing his hands of the whole enterprise, he informed Sandra Jamison in May 1984: "Hence please do not consider me for any further role in the endeavor." Though somewhat disheartened by Quarles's critique, Ashe and his staff pressed on, realizing they had plenty of time to make major adjustments to the form and content of the manuscript.[28]

In the late summer and early fall of 1983, Ashe's most immediate challenge was not academic credibility but rather the restoration of the American Davis Cuppers' confidence. The early elimination by Argentina and Connors's continuing recalcitrance had cast a shadow over Ashe's captaincy. The Americans' best hope of regaining momentum was to defeat the Irish squad in a tie that determined which country would compete in the World Group, rather than in the less desirable Zonal Group. On paper, the U.S. team appeared to be a heavy favorite, but the fact the tie would be played in Dublin was cause for concern. When Ashe and the Americans left for Ireland on September 24, they feared anything could happen once they took the court on the enigmatic Emerald Isle. Jeanne, who accompanied her nervous husband on the trip, did her best to dismiss any talk of Irish mysticism. But on the first day of play Eliot Teltscher's loss to lightly regarded Matt Doyle almost made the Americans believe in wily leprechauns and the proverbial luck of the Irish. A native Californian playing for Ireland by virtue of a single Irish grandparent, Doyle took advantage of a wildly enthusiastic home crowd and a fast surface ill-suited to Teltscher's game.

Oddly enough, the other Irish singles player, Sean Sorensen, grew up in Maine with Irish-born parents before moving to West Germany. None of this mattered to McEnroe, who had his own Irish ancestors. Acknowledging his lineage, one Dublin newspaper's headline counseled: "Relax, John, You're at Your Granny's." Noticeably unsentimental about his Irish roots, McEnroe downplayed his ethnic heritage and at one point went out of his way to insult his hosts. Dublin, he announced upon his arrival, "looks like London to me, only drearier. I hope the people are nicer." This statement did not endear him to the Irish faithful, but for many local fans the rudest gesture was his merciless dismantling of Sorensen. Playing in front of a record crowd that included his parents, he set the tone for the American dominance that ruled the rest of the week. The next day, he and Fleming overwhelmed Sorensen and Doyle in the doubles competition, and the American team went on to win the tie 4–1. In defeating Sorensen, the New Yorker equaled Ashe's American record of 27 Davis Cup singles victories, and two days later he broke the record by beating Doyle. Relinquishing the record in this fashion did not bother Ashe one bit, and he returned from Ireland in good spirits with renewed faith in his team.[29]

Ashe's mood got even better during the next three months as one of the toughest years of his life closed on a series of high notes. He derived a great deal of satisfaction from working on a black athletes exhibit to be displayed at the 1984 New Orleans World Fair, and from waging a successful campaign to add tennis to the upcoming summer Olympics in Los Angeles. Tennis had been eliminated from the Olympics after the 1924 games, and from the 1940s on periodic attempts to restore it had fallen flat. But during the Open era there was renewed hope the sport might eventually achieve Olympic status commensurate with its booming popularity.

During the early 1980s, Ashe worked closely with ILTF president Philippe Chatrier on the Olympics issue, and together they helped to disentangle the thorny issue of professionalism and Olympic eligibility. This involved delicate negotiations with the International Olympic Committee (IOC) and scores of national tennis federations. After a series of close IOC votes and compromises in 1983, tennis was accepted as a demonstration sport for the 1984 games in Los Angeles, with the expectation of a return to full medal status at the 1988 games in Seoul, South Korea. Ashe only wished Olympic tennis had come ten years earlier when he would have been eligible and eager to represent the United States.[30]

Fortunately, as a forty-year-old retiree he had other opportunities for glory. In October 1983, he traveled to the Sea Pines Plantation on Hilton Head Island to accept the first annual Du Pont Tennis Hall of Fame Award. The award, which carried a $5,000 charitable contribution to the NJTL, was presented during USA Cable's television coverage of the Stan Smith Du Pont Classic, a tournament named for his close friend and longtime Davis Cup teammate, who had moved to Hilton Head following retirement from the tour in 1981. Arthur was delighted to spend a couple of days with Stan and his wife, Margie, two of his favorite people, and he was only sorry that Jeanne, who was in Norfolk for a fertility consultation, couldn't be there for the reunion.[31]

Following the festivities at Hilton Head, Arthur felt better than he had in months. The worst by-products of the bypass operation were now behind him, and his energy level seemed to have returned to normal. In mid-October, he held Aetna minority recruiting sessions at Georgetown, Howard, and the University of Virginia, and at the end of the month he joined Chris Beck in Philadelphia for a ribbon-cutting ceremony at the Arthur Ashe Youth

Tennis Center. Beck, who had known Arthur since the late 1950s, had been instrumental in securing a large bequest that funded the creation of the new facility. Combining character training and after-school educational opportunities with tennis instruction, the center modeled Arthur's vision of the best that youth athletic involvement could offer.[32]

By November, Arthur was also back in the swing of his business and philanthropic activities, traveling to Palm Springs for a Le Coq Sportif sales meeting, convening BTF board meetings and attending an Urban League fund-raising dinner in New York, delivering motivational speeches in Tuskegee, Alabama, and Winston-Salem, North Carolina, and conducting his weekly classes at Florida Memorial. As Thanksgiving approached, he slowed down a bit, settling in at Doral, where he played as many rounds of golf as his busy schedule would allow. "I think golf is a release for him," Jeanne told one reporter. "He needs the golf because he is really still a very competitive guy." Whenever he could, he played in a foursome with celebrated resident pro Seve Ballesteros, with whom he was often paired in meet-and-greet sessions with the Doral guests. Golf had become a passion for Arthur, and he loved to talk about his game. "I have this fantasy," he once quipped. "And I'm the only one who could do it—win the U.S. Open in tennis and golf." He knew better, considering he was playing with a mediocre 14 handicap. But anything seemed possible when he was teeing off under a glorious, high blue sky at Doral.

While there were periodic trips to New York to attend board meetings and to look in on the activities of his book project staff—and one visit to Richmond for a hunting and fishing trip with his father—Arthur spent the remainder of the year in South Florida, mostly on the golf course. All the while, he tried to keep tabs on his public responsibilities while finding time for himself. Sometimes he found a way to satisfy both private and public enthusiasms, as on December 29 when he traveled to the Woodmont Country Club in Tamarac, an hour north of Doral. He was there to participate in a benefit golf tournament organized to raise funds for the Hunger Project, a six-year-old nonprofit organization dedicated to ending hunger and starvation in the Third World. Trying to save the world while playing a game he loved—it was classic Arthur Ashe.[33]

TWENTY-FOUR

HARD ROAD TO GLORY

■

AFTER HIS APPARENT RETURN to relatively good health in late 1983, Ashe seemed stronger and more focused than ever. Rehabilitated for the second time by a miraculous medical procedure, he now expected to be around for many years to come. He had not only cheated death; he had also learned important lessons about the human condition, and about what was important in life. Most obviously, as he turned from a quite natural preoccupation with his own condition to an almost obsessive interest in his embattled black predecessors, he reevaluated his own experiences in the light of history. Engaged with the past, he became more inquisitive about the roots of contemporary social and political reality, especially the perseverance of racism and prejudices related to class and gender.

He had already completed three memoirs, but his examination of the lives of others raised his awareness of the shifting and complex patterns of continuity and discontinuity. With this new awareness came a more forceful approach to public affairs, a boldness that valued actions over words. While he remained a deliberative intellectual committed to evolutionary change, he was growing more impatient—and more forthright about what needed to be done to make the world a better place. Though still respectful of civil discourse, he now prized truth telling above all else. The political imperative of using knowledge to promote justice and equality had taken on a new urgency. After fifteen years, the activist sensibility that had first stirred in him in 1968 now dominated his view of the world and his place in it. In this spirit, he would later write: "I know I could never forgive myself if I elected to live without humane purpose, without trying to help the poor and unfortunate, without recognizing that perhaps the purest joy in life comes with trying to help others."[1]

He equated service with leadership and applied this perspective to all aspects of his life, including his Davis Cup captaincy. In January 1984, the American squad received a boost when Connors finally agreed to join the team. The self-absorbed star was now a ProServ client and directly exposed to the powerful persuasive charm of Donald Dell. The turning point was a conversation with Connors and his mother, Gloria, during which Dell convinced them "that no American had ever achieved legendary status in tennis without playing Davis Cup." This appeal to ego overcame Connors's reservations about playing under Ashe's low-key captaincy, which seemed a poor fit with his aggressive style. His Davis Cup debut came in Bucharest, Romania, in March, but several weeks earlier he felt the need to clear the air with the man who had embarrassed him at Wimbledon in 1975.

As Ashe remembered it, the conversation between the two former rivals was tense but productive. "Look, Arthur, I don't need anyone sitting on the sidelines telling me how to play tennis," Connors began. "One thing I want to know though, Arthur," he continued. "Are you going to fight for me?" "What do you mean, Jimmy?" Arthur asked. "I mean, am I going to be out there by myself? Will I be doing my own arguing?" Connors demanded. "I'm out there, Jimmy," the captain reassured him. "I'm on your side. I'm going to be working for you." Later, when Connors took the court in Bucharest, Arthur made a show of vocal support. "Twice during Jimmy's first match," he recalled, "I made sure that I jumped up and made my presence known. . . . I am not sure what I accomplished by these moves, except for making Connors happy. But that was reason enough, I suppose."[2]

In Bucharest, Connors helped the Americans blank the Romanians 5–0, while reveling in teasing the home crowd as it hooted and hollered for its favorite son Nastase. The entire Romanian team was overmatched, winning only one set in five matches. Along the way Connors even seemed to get along with McEnroe, whom he had long resented as a publicity hog, but this fragile camaraderie did not last long. True to form, Connors soon lost interest in a team that did not recognize him as its biggest star. While he participated in the subsequent ties against Argentina, Australia, and Sweden, eventually his "old discomfort with the Davis Cup began to surface," as Arthur later put it. "To Mac and me, that silver cup was the Holy Grail," Arthur added. "To

Jimmy, it seemed that it might have been made of Styrofoam, he had so little sense of, or interest in, Davis Cup legend and lore."[3]

Despite a spate of distracting on-court antics and boorish outbursts by Connors, McEnroe, and Fleming, Arthur was able to keep the team on track against the Argentines and Aussies, winning both ties 5–0. But during the final tie, held in Göteborg, Sweden, in December, the American cause went completely off the rails. Arthur later described it as "one of the more dismal points of my tennis career." The final tally was 4–1 in favor of the Swedes. But that wasn't the worst of it. What hurt the most, he recalled, was "the way we had lost to Sweden. . . . From our arrival, nothing seemed to go right. . . . We needed to accustom ourselves to the surface, but none of us seemed ready to make the supreme effort. Meanwhile, everyone on the Swedish team except Mats Wilander [who was competing in the Australian Open] diligently arrived in Göteborg ten days before the tie and worked out hard for four hours daily."

The Americans, especially McEnroe and Connors, seemed "badly off their stride." To Ashe, McEnroe "looked exhausted and depressed, which was understandable since he "had recently been suspended for twenty-one days for outrageous behavior in a tournament in Stockholm. Viewers around the world had seen the film clip of McEnroe engaging in a vile, murderous tirade, smashing racquets and cups and abusing officials. Now, rusty from his enforced rest, he had to return to Sweden to play Davis Cup tennis. With the press he was first testy, then surly, and finally bitter and contentious." Connors's mood wasn't much better. Distracted by the impending birth of his second child, he had received Ashe's permission to arrive in Göteborg a day after the rest of the team. Ashe later conceded this accommodation was probably a mistake. By the time Connors arrived, "all his hostility to the Davis Cup and to team play seemed to return. Everything about our arrangements appeared to anger him, and nothing I said made any difference."[4]

Connors would eventually direct most of his hostility toward the umpires and referees, but he reserved some of his barbs for Ashe. As the captain walked onto the court to oversee a practice session, he was greeted with a "FUCK YOU" message "scrawled in large letters in the soft clay." Angry that Ashe had arrived ten minutes late, Connors had expressed his displeasure as only he could. Though stunned, Ashe kept his composure. "I felt exactly as if he had slapped my face," he recalled. "I wanted to replace him on the spot and send him home, but I knew our chances of winning would have dropped precipitously. I swallowed my pride and endured the insult."

Ashe's restraint, as it turned out, did little good. In his opening day singles match against Wilander, Connors played poorly and lost in straight sets. Most distressingly, at the end of the first set, he unleashed his frustration, resorting to what Ashe later characterized as "unspeakably vile language cursing both the umpire and referee Alan Mills." After the match, an outraged Mills fined Connors $2,000 and let it be known he was considering recommending at least a temporary banishment from Davis Cup competition. This threat vanished when Connors, at Dell's insistence, apologized profusely to both Mills and the umpire. But the whole ugly scene gave the Americans a terrible start in their final thrust for the Cup. When McEnroe followed with a loss to Henrik Sundström, injuring his wrist in the process, Ashe could see the chances of winning a third Cup slipping away. The next day the feared loss became reality when the young but talented Swedish doubles team of Anders Järryd and Stefan Edberg upended McEnroe and Fleming in four sets.

The Cup was lost, and only two meaningless "dead rubber" singles matches remained. With his wife about to give birth, Connors had no interest in sticking around. Though still fuming, Ashe granted Connors's request to leave before the closing singles matches. This opened up an opportunity for Jimmy Arias—who had "made it clear that he did not enjoy being a backup player, even to Connors and McEnroe." But the young clay court specialist failed to take advantage of the situation, losing to Sundström—and ending the American fiasco with a whimper. The humiliation was not quite over, however. At the closing awards banquet, USTA president Hunter Delatour apologized to the Swedes for his countrymen's outrageous behavior, a gesture unique in the annals of Davis Cup play.[5]

In the aftermath of Göteborg, Ashe braced himself for a barrage of criticism. As he was the first to admit, his team had not only failed to win the Cup but had also embarrassed the American tennis establishment. In the view of many observers, he had lost control of his players. "We had prepared shabbily, and had paid the price accordingly," he readily conceded. "For this I bear most of the blame." Even so, he was surprised by the magnitude of the fallout. J. Randolph Gregson, the incoming USTA president, vowed to undertake a thoroughgoing investigation of the nation's Davis Cup program, and one of the program's primary sponsors, Louisiana-Pacific corporation chairman Harry Merlo, threatened to "withdraw our sponsorship" unless "constructive changes" were implemented. William Simon, the former secretary of the treasury and an avid tennis fan, condemned McEnroe's and Connors's "disgusting and vulgar displays of childishness" in a column titled

"America's Punks," and other journalists called for the dismissal of the players who had acted so shamelessly.

Ashe also had to endure a torrent of correspondence from fans asking him to throw McEnroe and Connors off the team. The most troubling reaction, however, was Gregson and Merlo's move to require all American Davis Cuppers to sign a contract to "abide by a list of guidelines for good behavior." Implemented in January 1985, the pledge drew sharp criticism from the players and a mixed reaction from Ashe, who wanted to find some way to foster decorum but who disliked the Draconian nature of the new requirement. As he later conceded, "I couldn't bring myself to a resolutely hard line against the players even if . . . they behaved in ways that I detested." The root of the problem, as he saw it, was a new spirit of self-indulgence that had replaced sportsmanship and the best traditions of the game. He also believed the recent crisis had a lot to do with the technology of televised matches. Cursing on court had always been a part of the game, but its effect had changed with the use of highly sensitive microphones. Television cameras captured every outburst and tirade, producing a spectacle that drew the rapt attention of some fans and the disgust of others.

Without endorsing either the pledge or the misbehavior that inspired it, Ashe tried to find a middle ground. "Tennis players are not going to stop cursing," he declared, "but they are going to have to learn to do it *sotto voce* or else they will be defaulted. In the future, audible coarse language will not be tolerated from our team members."[6]

Though sympathetic to Ashe's position, McEnroe adamantly refused to sign the pledge. He had already announced plans to sit out the March 1985 tie against Japan, but now he vowed not to return to the team as long as the pledge was mandatory. Connors also rejected the pledge requirement as unnecessary and insulting and promptly dropped off the team. "Connors's refusal was more symbolic than substantial," Ashe concluded. "He had never really been one of us." Connors admitted as much in a revealing statement to reporters. "I've never been a team man," he confessed.[7]

With McEnroe, Fleming, and Connors out of the picture, Ashe was hard pressed to find suitable replacements. Eliot Teltscher was the only carryover from the 1984 squad, and the best the embattled captain could do to fill the other three slots was Aaron Krickstein in singles and Ken Flach and Robert Seguso in doubles. Seventeen-year-old Krickstein was years away from fulfilling his considerable potential, and Flach and Seguso, who had played together at Southern Illinois University, were twenty-one-year-olds with less than two years of experience on the professional tour. Talented and full of youthful enthusiasm, the squad was nonetheless a pale imitation of the powerful American teams of the early 1980s.

In March 1985, the team had little trouble defeating the Japanese on indoor carpet in Kyoto, winning all five matches and losing only one set. The true test would come later in the year when his young squad faced the world's strongest teams. But in a sense it didn't really matter. He had already begun to lose hope, though publicly he continued to put up a confident front. Hamstrung with the bitter conflict between McEnroe and Connors and the continuing squabbles over the new Code of Conduct, he no longer felt he could do his job effectively. Despite his best efforts, he knew the Cup was not coming back to America anytime soon.[8]

This unwelcome turn of events was discouraging, but Arthur had other deep and consuming interests that kept him afloat emotionally. First and foremost was his life with Jeanne and their continuing efforts to have a child. By 1985, after two years of unsuccessful fertility treatments, they had become roundly discouraged, so much so that they abandoned the in vitro process and turned to adoption.

By that point they had already initiated a major lifestyle change by buying a home in suburban Mount Kisco, forty miles northeast of New York City. Approximately an hour's train ride from the city, Mount Kisco offered a quiet, bucolic contrast to the bustling urban scene of Manhattan. After eight years of married life in an urban environment where they could not walk down the street without being recognized, the Ashes had decided to seek a bit of privacy in the gently rolling hills of upper Westchester County.

Home to a number of celebrities—including *New York Times* publisher Arthur Ochs Sulzberger Sr. and Ilie Nastase—Mount Kisco featured sprawling, farmlike estates. The house and seven acres of land the Ashes purchased in the spring of 1985 was adjacent to a farm owned by James Wood, who told the press he was pleased to sell the house and land to "a really nice neighbor." Built just prior to the Civil War, the Italianate-style house featured thick stone walls, thirteen rooms, and, in the words of one awestruck visitor, a view "so picturesque that people sometimes park their cars across the street and admire the landscape." After completing the first phase of extensive renovations—which included a darkroom for Jeanne and an office for Arthur—the Ashes moved into the house in the fall. For the next six years they would split their time between Mount Kisco and their Florida home near Doral.[9]

Beyond the Davis Cup captaincy and family matters, Arthur continued to embrace a wide range of passions that took up a great deal of his time, from overseeing the black athletes book project to writing occasional columns for *The Washington Post* to working with TransAfrica and AAAA on South African liberation to supporting the expansion of the NJTL. As the sports columnist Thomas Boswell quipped in January 1985: "With only nine different careers, the former tennis ace says he's itchy."[10]

All of these varied public activities were extremely important to Arthur, and all in some way involved issues of racial equity and social justice. As he later put it, "my Cup captaincy did not fully satisfy my desire to make the most of my retirement years, or give me an entirely settled perspective on my new life. . . . Even the most important record in tennis would not have stilled certain disquieting feelings that ran deeper in me than patriotism or sporting fame. I am an African American, one born in the iron grip of legal segregation. Aside from my feelings about religion and family, my innermost stirrings inevitably have to do with trying to overcome racism and other forms of social injustice. . . . Not the tennis court but the arena of protest and politics would be the single most significant testing ground for me in the middle years of my life."[11]

His signature role as an activist remained his involvement in the anti-apartheid movement, a commitment that reached a new level in mid-January 1985 when he was arrested while participating in a protest march in front of the South African embassy in Washington. The march was part of an ongoing protest campaign led by Randall Robinson, who had organized the Free South Africa Movement two months earlier. Beginning with a November 21 sit-in at the embassy by Robinson, District of Columbia congressional representative Walter Fauntroy, and Mary Frances Berry, a member of the United State Commission on Civil Rights, the movement soon enlisted a number of public figures as picketers, including Harry Belafonte, Coretta Scott King, Jesse Jackson, and Ashe. During a six-month-long campaign, the protests spread to more than a dozen cities, and several thousand marchers were arrested. On the day Ashe was arrested, sixteen others were taken into custody, including trade union officials, municipal employees, and teachers. Many were seasoned protesters who had been arrested before, but this was the first arrest for Ashe,

As he confessed, "Because I had spent my life making sure no one would ever have cause to arrest me for anything, the experience of being handcuffed, carted away, and booked was daunting." The night before joining the picket line, he telephoned his father to warn him of the likelihood of an arrest. This was not good news in Gum Spring, but Arthur Sr. knew his eldest son lived in a different world than his. "Well, son, I don't know," he offered.

"South Africa's an awful long way from us here. But if you think you have to do it, then I guess you have do it." "Just be careful," he added.

In point of fact, Arthur Sr. should not have been too concerned. His son had no intention of risking his physical well-being or of running up a lengthy criminal record. While Arthur Jr. was convinced it was important for him to take a stand on that particular January day, he did not take breaking the law lightly. Despite his continuing involvement in the anti-apartheid movement, he would not be arrested again for several years. He came close in late 1985 when he joined Belafonte and Jackson on an anti-apartheid picket line outside the U.S. mission to the United Nations in New York. But he and his fellow protesters escaped with a warning.

Ashe's reservations about going to jail were twofold. First, he did not want to be seen as a grandstanding celebrity protestor. "Much as I admire certain well-known entertainers who are quick to respond to calls to the barricades," he later explained, "I did not want to become a fashionable protestor giving photo opportunities, as they are called, to journalists." Second, he was sometimes suspicious of his own motives when it came to advocacy on South African issues. "To what extent was I trying to make up, with my anti-apartheid crusade, for my relative inaction a decade or more earlier during the civil-rights struggle?" he asked himself. Indeed, he had doubts about the legitimacy of protests such as those in front of the South African embassy. "No one knew better than I that a demonstration such as the one in Washington, when I was arrested, was mainly a staged or token affair, a piece of political choreography," he insisted. "I did not feel in any way like a hero for taking part in it. Indeed, I was painfully aware of the difference between . . . the symbolic punishment that I had allowed myself to be subjected to, and . . . the terror that the Ku Klux Klan and thousands of white Southern vigilantes and law officers imposed on black men, women, and children who risked their lives during the civil-rights movement." [12]

Captain Ashe did not shirk his activist responsibilities, even though he was aware that the Davis Cup Committee and the USTA frowned upon such activities. One controversial issue that drew his rapt attention in late 1984 and early 1985 was the reorganization of the NJTL. For fifteen years he had hovered over the NJTL's summer camp programs like a protective parent, volunteering his time on numerous occasions as he urged local chapters to expand their mission beyond mere tennis instruction. Whenever and wherever he was asked to appear at an NJTL workshop or fund-raiser, he made an effort to adjust his schedule—and he never accepted fees or reimbursements from local chapters, many of which were strapped for funds.

The financial solvency of the individual NJTL chapters had always been a concern, but successive sponsorships by the Clark Gum division of Philip Morris (1969–70), Coca-Cola (1970–79), and Congoleum (1980–82) had alleviated some of the pressure on local boosters. But in 1983, with no corporate sponsor willing to step up to replace Congoleum, the NJTL faced a major financial crisis. This set the stage for an extended negotiation with USTA officials, many of whom had long advocated a merger between the NJTL and USTA junior development programs. The NJTL needed help, but Ashe and others worried that a formal merger would eventually weaken the organization's core commitment to inner-city and minority youth. Despite its recent moves toward a more progressive public stance, the USTA, Ashe feared, was far more interested in consolidating and strengthening the nation's junior development programs than in serving the interests of racial equity and equality of opportunity. When the merger became official in early 1985, Ashe's doubts remained, but he had little choice but to wish the USTA well and hope for the best.

Ashe shared the USTA's concerns about the overall state of American tennis. As he told a reporter in July 1985, "It's a shame that in the U.S. there's only one McEnroe. We should have half a dozen." A month later, he offered a sobering evaluation of the American tennis scene: "I don't want to cast aspersions on the ability of solid professional players, but none of them is the next John McEnroe. We'll always produce our share of journeymen in the top 60, but as for a new superstar, I don't see that type around."

The USTA's biggest challenge was overcoming the traditional barriers of class and race. "We have not done enough to sell the sport at the grassroots level," he insisted. "The typical tennis family profile is upper middle class. If a family doesn't earn at least $35,000 to $40,000, you can almost forget it. . . . There are really good athletes at the lower and middle class level who just can't afford to play tennis." For poor blacks, of course, the situation was compounded by the lack of facilities and high-level instruction in inner-city neighborhoods. "In essence, a young black has to leave the community and go to a 'white club,'" he pointed out, but "there aren't enough of them at those clubs for blacks to feel comfortable."[13]

Earlier in the year, Ashe's singular ability to overcome these obstacles had garnered considerable attention. In March, the International Tennis Hall of Fame selected him as one of 1985's three inductees, and two months later he was honored at *Tennis* magazine's twentieth anniversary party as one of the sport's "top 20" players and "most influential" figures of the past two decades. "During his time in tennis," the sportswriter Dave Anderson wrote, "he has been the 'first black' American male in everything he has done—so much so that there has not yet been a second American black to do what he has done. To appreciate what Arthur Ashe has accomplished, imagine if Jackie Robinson were still the only black to have been voted a most-valuable player award in the major leagues, much less the only black to have been voted into the baseball Hall of Fame."[14]

Ashe appreciated the accolades but found the absence of black peers profoundly depressing. "I take no satisfaction in such exclusivity," he wrote in 1992. "I take no pride in the fact that twenty-five years after winning the U.S. Open, I am still the only black American man to have won a Grand Slam event." As of 1985, only one other African American man, Chip Hooper, had won a professional tennis tournament of any kind, Grand Slam or otherwise. In 1982, the year his world ranking peaked at #18, Hooper captured a doubles crown in Munich, and two years later he won a second doubles title in Florence. But his best showing in singles, other than two losses in the finals of minor tournaments in France and New Zealand, was making it to the fourth round of the 1984 French Open.

Hooper's only serious rival among black males on the tour was Rodney Harmon, but his career seemed to fizzle after a promising debut at the 1982 U.S. Open. Other than Ashe, no African American had ever made it as far as the U.S. Open quarterfinals, and this feat would not be equaled until James Blake played Andre Agassi in 2005. The other African American men following in Ashe's footsteps in the 1980s—Marcel Freeman (#46 in 1986), Todd Nelson (#58 in 1986), Bruce Foxworth (#146 in 1979), and Juan Farrow (#227 in 1985)—generally exhibited more potential than performance. But there was much more success on the women's side of the tour, starting with the former UCLA star Renee Blount's singles victory at a 1979 tournament in Columbus, Ohio. She went on to have some success at Wimbledon, reaching the third round of the singles competition in 1981 and the quarterfinals of the doubles three years later.[15]

Leslie Allen, a former USC star from Cleveland, fared even better, reaching the fourth round of the French Open three consecutive years (1979–81), and achieving a #17 world ranking in 1981, the year she won the singles title at the Avon Championships in Detroit. An accomplished student, Allen was the first black female player to make the transition to the world of tennis administration, preceding Katrina Adams, another Ashe favorite, by several years. Retiring in 1987 at the age of thirty, Allen later served on the WTA's board of directors and eventually established the Leslie Allen Foundation, which prepared inner-city kids for careers in off-court occupations related to professional tennis.[16]

To Ashe's delight, the most successful black female players of the 1980s came out of a public parks program connected to the NJTL. At the age of ten, Zina Garrison and Lori McNeil began playing at the McGregor Park Tennis Center in Houston, where the former ATA standout John Wilkerson ran a tennis program that became a major recruiting ground for talented young black players. Soft-spoken and folksy, with a world of patience, Wilkerson recognized early on that both girls had an enormous amount of raw talent as well as a rare level of grit and determination. Carefully crafting them into powerful serve-and-volley players, he had them ready to play at the U.S. Open by the age of fifteen. Two years earlier, Wilkerson, who first met Ashe in 1965, had invited the Wimbledon champion to conduct a clinic at McGregor Park. As soon as Ashe saw the girls play, he realized their potential was unlimited. Over the next few years, he kept in close touch with both girls and helped Wilkerson—and their other coach, his boyhood friend and doubles partner Willis Thomas—to shepherd them into the world of professional tennis.

Garrison was the first to make a splash, winning both the Wimbledon and U.S. Open Junior singles titles and ending the year as the world's number-one-ranked Junior. After turning pro in 1982, she promptly reached the singles quarterfinals of the French Open, and followed up with an even stronger showing at the 1983 Australian Open, where she made it to the semifinals. Hailed as "the new Althea Gibson," she was ranked #10 in the world by the end of the year, even before she won her first singles title in Zurich in early 1984. Many more titles followed—14 in singles and 20 in doubles—before she retired in 1997. After winning two Olympic medals in 1988—a bronze in singles and a gold in doubles—she reached her highest world ranking, #4, in 1989.

Garrison's greatest triumph, however, came a year later when she defeated the defending champion Steffi Graf in an epic Wimbledon semifinal match. In the final, she lost to the powerful left-hander Martina Navratilova, leaving Ashe as the only African American to win a Grand Slam title during the Open era. But her near miss foreshadowed the later achievements of Venus and Serena Williams.

Lori McNeil, Garrison's close friend and frequent doubles partner, rounded out the top echelon of black female players during the 1980s. One month younger but two inches taller than Garrison, McNeil took longer to develop her skills, but neither Ashe nor Wilkerson ever doubted her potential for stardom. After turning pro in 1983, she won 33 WTA doubles titles and 10 singles championships, rising to a #9 world ranking by 1988. Her one Grand Slam title came that year when she paired with Jorge Lozano to win the mixed doubles competition at the French Open. But her greatest claim to fame came several years later when she twice shocked Graf with first-round upsets, at the 1992 WTA Tour Championships and at Wimbledon in 1994—the first time a defending Wimbledon singles champion was defeated in the opening round.

Like Allen and Garrison, McNeil grew close to Ashe, whom she considered a trusted friend and role model. Following her retirement from the WTA tour in 2002, she worked for three years at the Junior Tennis Champions Center in College Park, Maryland, before accepting a position as the national coach of women's tennis for the USTA. She also continued to work with Wilkerson and the youth programs of the NJTL and the ATA, and along the way she established the Lori McNeil Foundation.[17]

In late May and early June 1985, both Garrison and McNeil were in Paris for the French Open, Garrison as the sixth seed in women's singles and McNeil as the doubles partner of Kim Sands, a tall twenty-eight-year-old who, with Ashe's help, had become the first African American woman to win a tennis scholarship at the University of Miami. Born and raised in the Little Haiti section of Miami, Sands had developed her skills through the local NJTL and had later worked closely with Ashe at Doral. "I couldn't have had a better teacher," she later said of Ashe.[18]

Ashe was there, in part, to root for his friends and protégés, but also as a coach scouting prospective Davis Cup players. Realizing the American squad's next Davis Cup tie would be played on the clay courts of Hamburg, he wanted to see how well Teltscher, Krickstein, and Arias handled the notoriously slow red clay and eccentricities of Roland Garros. The trip to Paris was also a vacation of sorts, a chance for him and Jeanne to enjoy the City of Light without the pressure of either performing on the court or formally coaching his Davis Cup players. She could revisit the city's art museums and take pictures of some of Europe's most beautiful streetscapes, and he could spend time with old friends like Chatrier and Noah.

The opportunity to spend time with Noah was especially welcome. Ashe knew he would see Noah in New York later in the year, both at the U.S. Open and at the scheduled late-November opening of Guignol, the Frenchman's chic new midtown Manhattan restaurant. But there was something special about a Paris reunion with the man who, more than anyone else, deserved the mantle of "the next Arthur Ashe." Now twenty-five, Noah had won the French Open singles title in 1983 and the doubles title the following year. In 1985, however, his close friend and perennial doubles partner Henri Leconte eliminated him in the fourth round of the singles competition. Though disappointing, this early exit gave him more time to spend with Arthur and their mutual friend the jazz musician Dizzy Gillespie, who joined them at the stadium's Le Coq Sportif lounge.

Arthur had good reason to commiserate with his friends that night. Among the American Davis Cup prospects only Krickstein survived beyond the third round, and his tournament soon ended with a devastating straight-set loss to Lendl in the fourth. With three of the eight quarterfinalists from Sweden, Ashe could not help but have flashbacks of the 1984 disaster at Göteborg. As long as the American squad was forced to play without McEnroe and Connors, the future of the U.S. Davis Cup program looked bleak.[19]

After Paris, Ashe was committed to spending two weeks at Wimbledon as a color commentator for HBO. But first he returned to New York to deliver the commencement address to the graduating class of the United Nations International School. Addressing 102 seniors representing forty-one different nations and twenty-seven different languages, and their families, was not a burden for a man who styled himself as an internationalist, even if it required him to cross the Atlantic twice in one week.[20]

This grueling international travel schedule was a bit insane for a man who had already suffered two heart attacks. But nothing could have kept him away from Wimbledon during the tenth anniversary of his epic victory over Connors. Pretty much everyone he encountered at the All England Club, or in downtown London, wanted to reminisce about the remarkable decade-old triumph, and in most cases he politely indulged their curiosity. Billie Jean King—who as the winner of the 1975 Wimbledon women's singles title had danced the first dance with Arthur at the post-tournament ball—was no exception. In recent years she had grown increasingly close to Jeanne and Arthur, who had come to revere her not only as an all-time great on the court but also as a heroic bisexual feminist willing to stand up for the rights of women and the LGBT community.

Both considered her to be a model of personal courage and integrity virtually unequaled in the world of sports. "As far as I am concerned," Arthur would write in 1992, "Billie Jean King is the most important tennis player, male or female, of the last fifty years." While he admired her skills as a player, he felt her true greatness could be found in her ability to combine athletic accomplishment and social activism. "Billie Jean brings energy and imagination to just about everything she does," he observed. "She is rare in combining unquestionable brilliance and success as a tennis player with the passion of a crusader for justice."[21]

For Ashe the best aspect of the 1985 Wimbledon fortnight, other than sharing a broadcast booth with King and Barry McKay, was the appearance of three African American men—Harmon, Hooper, and Todd Nelson—in the singles draw. While only Hooper made it beyond the first round, losing to Edberg in the third, the unprecedented black presence at Wimbledon was encouraging.

On the negative side, virtually all of Ashe's leading Davis Cup prospects suffered a repeat of their disappointing performances in Paris. One of the few Americans to survice beyond the opening round was the doubles specialist Robert Seguso, who surprised Ashe and everyone else by making it to the fourth round in singles. The biggest surprise among the "American" entrants, however, was twenty-seven-year-old Kevin Curren, a white South African who had become an American citizen earlier in the year. Though unseeded, Curren made it all the way to the championship match, upsetting both Connors and McEnroe in the process.

Although Curren lost in the finals to the seventeen-year-old German sensation Boris Becker, his near miss captured just about everyone's attention. Aside from his performance on Centre Court, Curren's ambiguous status—along with that of Johan Kriek, another white South African who had recently obtained American citizenship—was a major topic of conversation and controversy both during and after the Wimbledon fortnight. The question of their eligibility for selection to the U.S. Davis Cup squad was unclear, and there were sharp differences of opinion on the matter.

Ashe, in a *Washington Post* essay published on the last day of the tournament, took the position that the former South Africans should receive the same consideration as any other American players. This judgment, at odds with the view held by many anti-apartheid activists, was in keeping with his long-standing insistence that banning South African national teams from international competition was warranted but the routine banning of individual athletes was not. Only in Kriek's case was Ashe's support somewhat surprising, since the South African had embarrassed himself in an ugly incident involving Arthur Sr. during a practice session at the 1980 Richmond Open. Unaware that the black man working courtside was

Arthur's father, Kriek spoke rudely to him and ordered him around like a child. That Arthur Jr. did not hold a grudge undoubtedly surprised Kriek, but the decision to take the high road was a matter of personal pride and integrity. His support for individual South Africans was not unconditional, however. If a South African player refused to repudiate his government's policies on apartheid, the player, in Ashe's view, no longer had the right to play internationally.[22]

Following the close of Wimbledon on July 7, Arthur and Jeanne flew home to New York, where two days later they celebrated their birthdays—his forty-second and her thirty-fourth. The next day he took the train to Washington, where he joined Dell, Pasarell, and six other members of the Player's Enterprises, Inc. board of directors for a bittersweet meeting. Since its inception in 1969, PEI had amassed an array of tennis-related businesses, but everyone agreed the time had come to sell virtually all of its properties and interests in preparation for the liquidation of the corporation. The financial arrangements agreed upon at the meeting were complicated, providing for the sale of the Le Coq Sportif sportswear company and the Potomac Tennis Club, reimbursements to ProServ, and the transfer to Charlie Pasarell of the rights to run the La Quinta Super Series Tournament.

After the meeting adjourned, Ashe and his fellow board members retired to a local watering hole to discuss their many years of collaboration and what they had just done to bring it to an end. Over the next three days, several board members remained in Washington to participate in a "35 and Over" mini-tournament connected to the Sovran Bank Classic. But Ashe was not one of them. He had just enough time to pick up Jeanne in New York and drive to Newport, Rhode Island, where his induction into the International Tennis Hall of Fame was scheduled for Saturday, July 13. When he arrived in Newport on Friday, a dozen members of his family—including his parents, Jeanne's parents, his two brothers, his sister, and assorted nieces, nephews, and cousins—were already there.[23]

Normally, Ashe would have been embarrassed by all this fuss; indeed, he had never put much stock in awards and honors. The previous week at Wimbledon, he had told Bud Collins: "I'm not a guy for trophies. You wouldn't know I have a tennis background if you came to my apartment in Manhattan. You'd have to look hard to find a small replica of the Davis Cup and the Wimbledon trophy." Instead, he revealed, "My wife's pictures are all over the place." When Collins had a follow-up conversation with Ashe in Newport a few days later, the honoree conceded that being inducted into the Hall of

Fame was "a great honor," but he insisted "these things are celebrations of the past, and I don't give much thought to the past. I'm more interested in the future." Collins found this to be a strange statement for someone who had spent the past two years working obsessively on a comprehensive history of black athletes, but he chalked it up to nervousness about the impending ceremony.

On the day of the induction there was no escaping the historical magnitude of the moment. The scene at the venerable Newport Casino, built in 1880 with Victorian excess and aptly characterized by Collins as "a delightful antique playpen," was dripping with history. In his brief acceptance speech, Ashe reflected on his curious journey to the Hall. "Twenty years ago, if I told anybody I'd be in the Hall of Fame," he declared with a wry smile, "an awful lot of people would have given me some very strange looks." He had gotten there, he acknowledged, through a combination of hard work and faithful mentoring from several dedicated coaches and advisors. Two days earlier, in a conversation with a UPI reporter, he had singled out Dr. J as the key figure in his rise to stardom: "If there is any one person I wish could be there at Newport, it would be Dr. Johnson. He is not alive now, but he would be very pleased about it." [24]

While Ashe's famous coolness was on display, he could not hide his satisfaction that he "had been elected to the Hall both as a player and as a contributor to the game." As he told one reporter, "I always made a conscious effort not to have wins and losses on the tennis court determine my self-esteem." He was also proud he was being inducted in his first year of eligibility—only five years after retirement—a special tribute that he acknowledged repeatedly in his remarks to reporters. In the three decades since the establishment of the Hall, only a handful of players had been so honored.

Earlier in the decade, several of the greatest players of the post–World War II era, including Santana, Segura, and a trio of legendary Aussies—Rosewall, Laver, and Neale Fraser—had entered the Hall, and now he was there with them. The other three 1985 inductees were the British tennis writer David Gray, his fellow Briton Ann Haydon Jones—the winner of seven Grand Slam championships—and Fred Stolle, the towering Australian who had won a record 10 Grand Slam doubles titles plus the 1965 French and 1966 U.S. national singles championships. Ashe was the only American inductee and, as a throng of reporters pointed out, the first African American to achieve this status since Althea Gibson in 1971. The two racial pioneers would remain the Hall's only black members until Dr. J's posthumous induction in 2009.

Following the ceremony, Ashe sat down with a group of reporters. Steering them away from both the racial and commercial aspects of his career, he emphasized his joy in playing tennis for so many years. "To hell with the bank account, even though I've profited handsomely from tennis," he exclaimed at one point. "I hope that everyone at the end of their playing career, at whatever level, can say the one thing I can say: 'It was fun.' That's what means the most."

Eventually Arthur turned to the special difficulties facing aspiring black players. "Tennis is still a rich kid's sport," he told Marion Collins of the New York *Daily News*, before addressing her question on the Code of Conduct controversy. "Sure I get fed up being the nice guy," he confessed, "but back in the '60s, if you were black and the first one, you simply had to behave yourself. I couldn't have gotten away with coming on like Ali—it wouldn't have been tolerated." He then added: "I genuinely believe that if McEnroe were black, he wouldn't be allowed to do some of the things he does." This comment prompted Collins to explain: "If behavior weighs heavily on him, it is because his main task as captain of the U.S. Davis Cup squad isn't showing its millionaire members how to hit the ball, but keeping their notorious tempers in check, something he has tackled with restraint and loyalty."[25]

In the days and weeks following the Hall of Fame induction, Ashe's challenge was no longer reining in McEnroe and Connors but rather assembling a strong team without them. When the Americans came up against Boris Becker and the West Germans on the clay courts of Hamburg in early August, it became clear just how much the team missed its biggest stars. Three weeks earlier Becker, still technically a Junior, had shocked the tennis world by winning the Wimbledon singles title. After the tall redhead crushed Teltscher in the opening singles match, the Americans' hopes rested with Krickstein, but the steady baseliner lost a tough five-set match to Hansjorg Schwaier. The Americans mustered a spirited comeback, winning the doubles and the first singles match on the final day. But Becker closed out the tie in style with a convincing victory over Krickstein. As Ashe later recalled with a shrug, the young German hardly broke a sweat; from the start of the match, he wore a sweater "and never bothered to take it off."[26]

Ashe was crestfallen after the Hamburg defeat. "For the third straight year," he later explained, "I had led the United States to defeat in the Davis Cup. I understood that my days as captain were numbered." After nearly five years as captain, he could be philosophical about his fate. He had been given his shot, and he had made the most of it, becoming only the second

American captain in thirty years to win back-to-back titles. When the axe fell in mid-October, he was disappointed but not surprised. At a meeting in Manhattan, Randy Gregson and Gordon Jorgensen, the chair of the U.S. Davis Cup Committee, delivered the bad news. Although Arthur "made it clear" he "wanted to stay on," the decision was final.

On October 22, *The New York Times* announced Ashe would soon "be dropped" as captain, reportedly "for a perceived lack of discipline and organization on the team." Later in the day, he submitted his resignation. Grateful for his cooperation, Gregson and Jorgensen offered him the ceremonial position of Davis Cup Committee vice chairman. In the interests of a smooth transition, he accepted, but after Tom Gorman was named as his replacement in December, he quickly faded into the background. At the same time, the USTA quietly dropped the requirement to sign the Code of Conduct, paving the way for McEnroe's possible return to Davis Cup play.

Ashe's own assessment of his record as captain was mixed. As he later pointed out "with some pride," his overall record was 13 wins and only three losses, a highly respectable showing in any context. Nevertheless, he freely acknowledged his shortcomings, stating: "as I had led some of the most talented teams ever fielded by the United States, we should have done better, and some of the blame must rest on my shoulders." He knew his critics were right when they faulted him for failing to keep his players in line: "To be more effective, I suppose I should have been more gregarious at times, and at other times more aggressive. I should have tried harder to impose my will on the players. But I couldn't do that, and I have to live with the consequences. I accepted the fact that as much as I want to lead others, and love to be around people, in some essential way I am something of a loner." [27]

The silver lining in the cloud of dismissal was the recognition that "to be effective, I would have to step up more boldly into the spotlight, especially if I wished to be effective in the crucial area of social and political progress." Looking back on the ups and downs of his five-year tenure, he later wrote: "My Davis Cup captaincy was a rich, challenging, and also satisfying experience, not least of all because of that simple lesson." [28]

His only complaint concerned the Davis Cup committee's discomfort with his activism. Two days after his resignation, he granted an interview to *Jet* magazine, and the resulting story ran under the provocative headline: "Ashe Says Activist Role May Be Part of His Ouster as Davis Cup Team Captain." When asked if "politics had anything to do with it"—specifically his opposition to apartheid—Ashe had responded: "I think so. . . . Some people probably think I've gone too far. . . . No one at the USTA said so to my face. But I've heard so from other sources." Nearly a decade later, he remained convinced "Gregson and others in the USTA saw me as someone far more concerned with politics than a Davis Cup captain should be. And by politics, I'm sure they meant 'radical' politics."[29]

Beyond the arrest and his high-profile role in the anti-apartheid movement, Ashe's involvement in electoral politics clearly disturbed some members of the American tennis establishment. While he had resisted the temptation to run for office, his vocal support for Jesse Jackson during the 1984 presidential campaign became a subject of controversy at the highest levels of the USTA. Even though he was not especially enamored with the flamboyant Chicago-based civil rights leader's grandstanding, Ashe overcame his reservations and founded an organization known as Athletes for Jesse Jackson in late 1983. Soliciting funds and endorsements from professional athletes representing a range of sports, he boosted Jackson's support in the Democratic primaries, where he finished third behind Vice President Walter Mondale and Senator Gary Hart of Colorado.

Even though he knew some USTA officials disapproved, Ashe never tried to hide his support for Jackson, which continued through the 1988 primaries. He also embraced Douglas Wilder's historic 1985 campaign for the lieutenant governorship of Virginia, just as he had done in the early-1980s campaigns of Senator Bill Bradley of New Jersey, Senator Chuck Robb of Virginia, Mayor Andrew Young of Atlanta, and Mayor Wilson Goode of Philadelphia. None of this went over very well at USTA headquarters, but as long as Ashe's squad remained a viable contender for the Davis Cup no one dared to voice any strong objections. Only when the squad began to lose did Ashe's political activity contribute to his expendability.

While Ashe conceded there were legitimate arguments for his ouster, he nonetheless felt wronged by the tennis establishment. "Many people in the tennis leadership, as in other points, are terrified of taking a stand on political affairs, or on controversial questions of social justice," he observed. "Although certain exceptions come to mind, the prevailing political ambience of tennis has always been a wealth-oriented conservatism of the kind associated in this country with staunch Republicanism and exclusive country clubs." Perhaps more to the point, civil disobedience was anathema to the tennis elite regardless of the issue at hand. "The idea of apartheid in South Africa undoubtedly is abhorrent to some of these people," granted

Ashe, "but the idea of demonstrating in the streets against it might be even more abhorrent, in practical terms." Once one of the sport's most orderly figures, he had come to reject this amoral calculus. Near the end of his life, he put the matter as simply as he could: "I hate injustice much more than I love decorum."[30]

Whatever its origins, Ashe's ouster as Davis Cup captain had a silver lining. During the next three years—relieved of the pressures of his captaincy—he redoubled his efforts to bring the book project to completion. Expanding his staff to seven, he presided over a beehive of activity. With Ocania Chalk and Kip Branch doing most of the research, and others attending to the compilation of statistics, he concentrated on writing the sport-by-sport narratives. He hoped to deliver a first draft to Howard University Press by early 1986. But having exhausted his $10,000 advance during the first year of the project, and having subsequently invested more than $200,000 of his own money, he didn't know how much longer he could provide such a high level of funding.

Ashe's determination to press on with the book did not stop him from attending to other aspects of his life. He still fulfilled his commitments to Doral, showed up at periodic NJTL events and Aetna board meetings, wrote columns for *The Washington Post*, visited family in Virginia, lobbied for TransAfrica, worked with Jeanne on advancing the adoption process, and even served as a cheerleader for the Davis Cup squad when it traveled to Ecuador in March 1986. But, for the most part, his daily routine was dominated by hours of poring over research reports and trying to bring the black ghosts of the past back to life on the page. "*A Hard Road to Glory* was an emotional experience for me," he recalled, "because it dealt so intimately, at almost every stage, with both the triumph and tragedy, the elation and the suffering, of blacks as they met not only the physical challenges of their sport but also the gratuitous challenges of racism. No sport was exempt from this painful double history, so that compiling the record was a fairly relentless exposure to disappointment."

He was on a mission, determined to draw attention and respect to the black athletes who had come before him—the forgotten as well as the famous. He told himself he had stood on their shoulders and owed it to them to cast a light on the dark shadows of the past. So he was more than a little upset in December 1985 when Charles Harris resigned as executive director of Howard University Press. Fourteen years earlier, Harris had left Random House to found a new university press at Howard, and most observers had expected him to finish his editorial career there. But over the years he had become increasingly frustrated by a chronic lack of funding and had lost confidence in the press's capacity to publish high-quality books on African American history and culture.

Harris explained all of this to Ashe, who must have wondered why his editor hadn't revealed any of these concerns two years earlier. For a time, Ashe was afraid Harris's departure from Howard would make it difficult if not impossible to produce the substantial, groundbreaking book they had envisioned. But by mid-February 1986, there was cause for optimism. One reason was the recent success of a television documentary version of *A Hard Road to Glory* broadcast on February 1. With Ashe as host and the deep-voiced actor James Earl Jones as narrator, the sixty-minute film used rarely seen archival footage to recapture the experiences of Jack Johnson, Jesse Owens, Jackie Robinson, and several others who had overcome racial discrimination to become world-class athletes. Later in the year it received an Emmy.

The other hopeful signs were Harris's creation of a new press dedicated to publishing high-quality books on African American topics, and his belief that Ashe's history of black athletes was the perfect book to launch his new enterprise. Crossing over from a strictly academic audience to a broader range of lay readers, the press would facilitate Ashe's goal of reaching as wide a readership as possible. There would also be financial advantages for Ashe, who would receive a much larger advance against royalties than the $10,000 he had received from Howard University Press. He would have to return the Howard advance, but Harris assured him he would come out ahead in the long run.

In July 1986, with Ashe listed as a member of the board of directors, Harris established Amistad Press, Inc., named for the famous slave ship redirected to the Connecticut coast by mutinous slaves in 1839. Soon thereafter Harris entered into a co-publishing agreement with Dodd, Mead and Company, a venerable New York publishing house founded the same year as the *Amistad* revolt. By the time Amistad Press's first books appeared in print in November 1988, Harris had replaced Dodd, Mead with another co-publisher, Warner Books. Throughout the period of Ashe's involvement, the fledgling press maintained strong ties to financially and editorially sound publishing houses.

Although it took him two years to pay back the advance, Ashe's faith in the project was fully restored by late summer. With more than a thousand pages of the manuscript completed, he could see the light at the end of the tunnel. Most of the narrative was finished, and the major task remaining was fact-checking and filling in gaps in the encyclopedic chronicles of each sport. He could now spend more time with Jeanne at the Mount Kisco house. Earlier in the year, he had been troubled by a nasty feud between Dell and Craighill over the transfer of the La Quinta tournament rights from PEI to Charlie Pasarell. But the PEI dissolution storm had blown over by late summer.[31]

For the remainder of the year, life in general was probably as good for Ashe as it had been in years. In June he was finally able to vent his frustrations about the lack of black participation in competitive tennis by writing a *New York Times* opinion piece titled "Why There Aren't More Blacks Playing Tennis." The reasons, he told his readers, were threefold: "money, accessibility, and peer pressure." While he expressed pride in the efforts of the NJTL, he warned "no real breakthrough can be achieved . . . until more black coaches are trained." In closing, he predicted: "It may take until the 21st century before a black player again wins at Wimbledon or the United States Open."

Despite this dire prognosis, Ashe knew the situation was improving on the women's tour. The previous summer Zina Garrison had made it to both the singles semifinals at Wimbledon and the doubles semifinals at the U.S. Open, setting a new standard for her male counterparts to emulate. She did not fare as well in 1986, reaching only one quarterfinal of a Grand Slam tournament—at the Australian Open in January. Yet Ashe remained hopeful about her future—and his. In August, just before the first round of the U.S. Open, he actually picked up a tennis racket and played in a celebrity benefit match at the National Tennis Center. And in another highlight of the summer—one that had little to do with tennis—he joined his fraternity brother Walt Hazzard in early August at the annual Kappa Alpha Psi convention in Indianapolis, where he received the fraternity's highest honor, the Laurel Wreath Award.

Not everything was going smoothly, of course. At the Open, he witnessed the continuing decline of American male contenders—only one American man made the quarterfinals—as well as Ivan Lendl's second straight Open singles title. The final weekend of the tournament marked a low point in American tennis, and before it was over he wished he had accepted an invitation to South Africa to attend the September 4 investiture of the anti-apartheid activist Desmond Tutu as Archbishop of Cape Town. His broadcast duties kept him in New York, but South Africa would have provided welcome relief from the American tennis scene, which included the continuing controversy over McEnroe's banishment from Davis Cup play. In the meantime, the American squad suffered a crushing defeat at the hands of the Australians, winning only one match on the grass courts of Brisbane. For the fourth straight year, the Americans had failed to win the Cup, though it was no longer Ashe's problem.

In November, Ashe was in the news for another reason. After the basketball superstar Michael Jordan's lucrative contract with ProServ put Dell and all of his clients in the spotlight, *The New York Times* ran a story titled "The Selling of Michael Jordan," in which the agent offered a comparative perspective. "Michael Jordan has a charisma that transcends his sport," Dell declared. "He belongs in a category with Arnold Palmer or Arthur Ashe." Later in the article, the author, Phil Patton, discussed Jordan's desire "to be seen as 'neither black nor white'" when it came to endorsements. "The black star is often caught in a dilemma," Patton explained. "Conventional advertising wisdom holds that it is very hard for a black athlete to be convincing to white middle-class consumers. There are, of course, those who have crossed this boundary, such as the former football star O. J. Simpson and ProServ client Arthur Ashe. They are both charismatic and articulate, and marketing surveys show they are perceived as 'beyond race.' ProServ is betting that Jordan has this elusive quality also." [32]

Ashe appreciated the kind words, but since the early fall he and Jeanne had been lost in a fog of anticipation, preoccupied with the impending adoption of a child. The agency that had approved their application could not give them an exact date, but they were hopeful their baby would arrive before the end of the year, preferably before they were scheduled to be at Doral. Arthur and Jeanne had longed for the day when they could call themselves parents, and they now knew the big day was coming soon. But as Christmas approached the waiting became almost unbearable.

Finally, on December 21, 1986, they got the word. Their baby—a little girl—had been born earlier that day. They had already picked out a girl's name—Camera, in honor of her new mother's profession—and when they saw her for the first time two days later they were overcome with emotion. Brown-skinned with delicate features, she looked very much like what they had imagined their hypothetical birth child would look like. All of that was an unexpected bonus, of course; they were just grateful for a healthy baby. Arthur later described the scene as he and Jeanne nervously prepared for Camera's first night in Mount Kisco: "We pulled out a bureau drawer in a walk-in closet and that's where she slept her first night home. Like many first-time parents, we were obsessed by the possibility of sudden infant death (also called crib death) or another mysterious ailment that would take away from us the fragile little body that represented our hopes and dreams of the past few years. We kept popping up in bed and going over to the bureau drawer to make sure she was well—to make sure, I think, that she was still there."

Several days later, they had calmed down enough to bundle her up and board a plane for Miami, where they spent the next few weeks keeping her safe and warm but out of the sun. Neither Jeanne nor Arthur had ever romanticized parenthood, but both embraced their new roles as mother and father without reservation. Camera was now the center of their universe. "From the first day, she altered the pattern of our lives," Arthur recalled. "We knew that her coming would do so, but the extent to which she changed things was nevertheless something of a shock." Another surprise, he confessed, was the intensity of his paternal feelings. As he commented a few weeks prior to her sixth birthday, "I had no idea that I would love fatherhood as much as I do. I have an acute sense of responsibility for her—to help her, teach her, protect her, and (most of all) to love her." [33]

As Camera grew into a crawling infant and later a wobbly but adventurous toddler, the Ashes experienced the normal ups and downs of parental apprenticeship. Gradually, they adopted a loose and indulgent style of parenting at odds with their own upbringings. "In matters of discipline, I know I can't go the way of my father," Arthur acknowledged. "He was of the old school; his word was law, and he enforced the law with his thick police belt."

In a 1980 interview, Jeanne commented that her famously calm and collected husband had once told her he wanted "to be more emotional, more open, more outgoing." This was a tall order for a man accustomed to restraint, but Camera's arrival opened up new possibilities. Several family members later insisted she changed him. From the outset, there was a deep emotional bond. When he was with her, there were no hyper-rational calculations or measured moments of intellectual reserve. He was, in his words, "ecstatic about her." Citing his brother Johnnie's tender relationship with his daughter, Luchia, and his sister Loretta's relationship with her children La Chandra and David, as models, he wanted Camera to experience the same nurturing love as his nieces and nephews.

Just about everyone in the Ashes' inner circle noticed Camera's impact on her father. In a 2005 interview, Billie Jean King even credited Camera with deepening Arthur's belief in gender equality. As women's rights and his daughter's welfare became entwined, the feminism that had emerged under Jeanne's influence early in their marriage took on new meaning. "What put him over the edge," King recalled, "was . . . when they adopted Camera. . . .

He was totally gone. He was all for girls. . . . You could see that the whole paradigm of his life . . . had been challenged. . . . Everyone noticed it, how much he changed when Camera came into his life."

Arthur's tendency to indulge Camera was perhaps inevitable. But, as he acknowledged, it was clearly enhanced by a sense of insecurity born of his recent medical experiences. "With all my own physical problems," he wrote in 1992, "her positive robustness has been a godsend to me, a daily reaffirmation of the power of life." As he thought about his current good fortune as a father, he couldn't help but recall his earlier visits to children's hospital wards. "Children seem immortal," he observed. "But I know how quickly they can be taken away. . . . Often you meet kids who are going to be well, but just as often you meet kids who you know are going to die soon. It is heartbreaking." With this in mind, he did not take Camera's good health "for granted."[34]

His own health appeared to be holding up well. To Jeanne's surprise, he seemed to have more than enough energy to keep up with both his lively daughter and the considerable demands of his public life. Throughout 1987 and the first half of 1988, there was no letup in his work. He even accepted a new assignment as co-chair of the USTA's Committee on Junior Development.

He also joined the executive committee of Harry Edwards's new National Organization on the Status of Minorities in Sport (NOSMS), which focused on one of Ashe's greatest passions—the need to expand opportunities for minorities in managerial and behind-the-scenes positions in the sporting world. Edwards's June 1987 appointment by Major League Baseball commissioner Peter Ueberroth as a part-time consultant charged with the task of finding "jobs in the sport for black and Hispanic former players" was an encouraging development. But there was still so much left to do along these lines in every major sport.

One of NOSMS's strongest supporters was Jesse Jackson, and for a time in late 1987 and early 1988, Ashe became marginally involved in his second campaign for the Democratic presidential nomination. Ashe liked Jackson's platform, which combined elements of the New Deal and the Great Society with the interracial ideal of a "Rainbow Coalition." But he was less enamored with the candidate's flamboyant personality, and he had never fully trusted him since his refusal to repudiate the anti-Semitic, black separatist leader Louis Farrakhan.

Pitted against Governor Michael Dukakis of Massachusetts, Jackson won seven primaries and four state caucuses—an unprecedented showing for a black candidate. But in the end Dukakis won the nomination; this left Ashe in a difficult position. Though a lifelong Democrat, he disliked Dukakis, and after a period of soul-searching he decided to vote for the Republican nominee George H. W. Bush. It was a decision he later regretted, and by 1992 he would find himself walking a picket line in front of the White House.[35]

Both before and after the election, Ashe made a concerted effort to maintain his status as a public intellectual. Expressing his opinions on a variety of issues related to sports, education, race, and equal opportunity, he continued to contribute occasional columns to *The Washington Post* and *The New York Times*. He also remained active as a guest lecturer at colleges and universities, and occasionally at high schools, youth centers, and public libraries. Almost all of his public comments tried to balance contemporary concerns with a historical perspective on the roots of inequality and injustice. In November 1987, for example, he delivered a lecture at the New York Public Library, presenting not only a preview of his forthcoming book but also a stinging commentary on the continuing lack of black coaches and executives in professional sports.

The book project was never far from his mind, as work on the final revisions and edits proceeded apace. Month after month, he attended to matters of content and style, often shuttling back and forth between Mount Kisco and the Lexington Avenue office. Packaged under the title *A Hard Road to Glory: A History of the African-American Athlete*, the roughly 1,400-page manuscript was now divided into three prospective volumes organized chronologically: 1619–1918; 1919–1945; and 1946 to 1988. Originally scheduled for publication in February 1988, the three volumes ultimately required editorial tweaking that delayed release for nine months.

After nearly six years of research and writing, Ashe was more excited than ever about the project. But he was also nervous about how the books would be received. Not normally given to boasting, he betrayed his insecurities by assuring *Tennis* magazine's Barry Lorge that *A Hard Road to Glory* would be a smashing success. "There is no question in my mind," he told Lorge, "that it will be the bible on the subject. . . . The record section alone will blow people away."[36]

While he waited for his magnum opus to hit the bookstores, Ashe kept busy with a multitude of activities, including a mid-July Aetna board meeting held at the Sagamore Resort on the shores of Lake George in upstate New York. Normally the board met at Aetna's corporate headquarters in

Hartford, but company president Bill Bailey had decided that a change of scenery might trigger a much needed burst of creativity.

Arthur in particular was captivated by the resort's physical beauty and calming atmosphere, so much so that he returned to the Sagamore a month later for a family vacation. With a week to go before the start of the 1988 U.S. Open, a few days of lakeside relaxation proved irresistible. Jeanne, who was recovering from a case of Lyme carditis that had forced her to miss a recent family reunion in New Orleans, loved the idea, and she and Arthur decided to invite the Dells to join them. For three glorious days, the four friends who had been through so much together could temporarily escape the pressures of the real world—the rhetorical combat of the national election, the latest outrage in South Africa, the constant demands of ProServ's clients, the seemingly dismal prospects for American men at the upcoming U.S. Open. All of this seemed far away as they sipped drinks on the Sagamore's grand veranda, pretending not to have a care in the world.[37]

TWENTY-FIVE

DAYS OF GRACE

■

THE FIRST TWO DAYS at the Sagamore were full of laughter and easygoing companionship, marred only by Jeanne's lingering illness. Bouncing twenty-month-old Camera on their knees and trying to keep up with the boundless energy of a toddler, the Ashes and the Dells could not help but feel the fullness of life. Arthur had felt this way many times before, yet he knew from experience that health and happiness were fragile commodities susceptible to change at a moment's notice. He had encountered this truth repeatedly during the past nine years, and on the third day at the Sagamore—August 24, 1988—he learned yet another cruel lesson about the vagaries of life.

Following a pleasant and uneventful breakfast, Arthur, Jeanne, and Camera returned to their suite. While Jeanne attended to Camera, Arthur walked over to the telephone to call home to see if he had any messages on his answering machine. Grabbing the wall phone with his left hand, he started to dial the numbers with the fingers of his right hand. What happened next surprised and shocked him. "My fingers made an attempt to respond to my will," he recalled, "but they struggled in vain to do what I asked. I was trying to put my index finger on the buttons, but the finger wasn't working very well." Frustrated, he yelled out to Jeanne, "Something is wrong with me. . . . My fingers. I can't get them to work well." "Maybe they are numb because you slept on them?" she suggested. "Yes, that must be it," Arthur responded, but a few moments later he told her, "No, they aren't numb. I can feel them, definitely. I just don't seem to be able to use them." Thinking he was suffering from a pinched nerve or some other temporary condition, Jeanne dialed the numbers for him and went back to tend to Camera.

As the day progressed, Arthur tried to stay calm and patiently waited for his fingers to return to normal. But by late afternoon he began to worry that he had suffered a small stroke. At one point he suggested it might be best if they packed up the car and immediately returned to Mount Kisco, where he could see his internist, Dr. William Russell. After some discussion they decided to spend Wednesday night at the Sagamore and drive home in the morning. Arthur later remembered he had gone to bed that night with the expectation that he would "awake to find my fingers back to normal." But Thursday morning brought no such relief, and by the time he checked out, his "right hand was hanging from the wrist, almost completely limp."[1]

Alarmed but not sure he was facing an emergency, Arthur made an appointment with Dr. Russell for Friday afternoon. A morning appointment wouldn't work because a film crew from the *CBS This Morning* television show was scheduled to arrive at the Ashes' house by 9 a.m. to conduct one of its celebrity home interviews. Both Arthur and Jeanne thought about canceling, but in the end they decided to proceed as scheduled—and to avoid any mention of Arthur's hand problem.

As Arthur recalled the experience, "The television interview was pleasant in most respects, but also something of an ordeal. No matter how hard I tried, I could not move a digit up, down, or sideways. My right hand, now completely limp, literally hung dead from my wrist. As I answered questions and talked about the house, I tried to act as nonchalant as I could; I certainly told no one from CBS that something was wrong. The truth is that I had to prop up my right hand with my left. I still have no idea how I got through the interview without anyone on the crew taking notice. I answered the questions with as much charm as I could muster, but my mind was elsewhere."

By early afternoon, both his mind and body were at Dr. Russell's office. Arthur had been Russell's patient for several years, and he had grown to trust the man he once characterized as "someone almost out of Norman Rockwell's America of a bygone age." Russell was also an avid tennis player who relished caring for one of the tennis world's most prominent figures. Accustomed to worrying about Arthur's heart, he was initially caught off guard when he saw his patient's limp right hand. After examining the fingers, palm, and wrist, he asked if Arthur had been dizzy or short of breath. Had he had a fever? Had anything struck his right hand? When the answer to all of these questions was no, he suspected his famous patient was suffering from a potentially serious condition. "Something is interfering with the signals from your brain to the hand," he told Arthur. "The interference is almost certainly in the area of the brain, because I can't think of any other likely reason for your hand to stop working."[2]

Minutes later Arthur, with Jeanne by his side, traveled across the street to a CAT scan facility. When the twenty-minute procedure was over, the Ashes joined Dr. Russell and a radiologist in a nearby room where the CT images of Arthur's brain were displayed on a light box. As the doctors examined and reexamined the images, their concern became apparent. They didn't say much at first, leaving Arthur and Jeanne to stare at the images in a frantic attempt to see what they were seeing. "I had never seen CAT-scan images of my brain before," he later revealed. "Then I saw that the two hemispheres of my brain, which should have been nearly identical, were not. The right side of the brain was clear. The left side showed an irregularly round shape—a splotch. . . . What was it doing on my brain?"

Clearly shaken by what he had seen, Dr. Russell spoke as calmly as he could. "Look," he said, "I don't want to steer you wrong. I am not a neurologist or a neurosurgeon." The radiologist nodded in assent, prompting Russell to ask Arthur if he could "find someone at New York Hospital?" Arthur answered "of course," but he left the CAT scan facility uncertain about his future. "The drive back home, although it took only eight minutes, was pretty awful," Arthur recalled. "Up until the moment of seeing the CAT scan, I had not felt extreme anxiety. What had triggered my anxiety now was not the CAT scan itself but the jolting effect of the image on Dr. Russell. Obviously he thought I had something to fear."[3]

Back at home, Arthur and Jeanne agreed he should get a second opinion as soon as possible. Later that afternoon, he walked into the New York Hospital office of Dr. John Caronna, a distinguished neurologist with almost twenty years of experience in his field. After looking at the CAT scan images, Dr. Caronna confirmed Arthur's fears without being alarmist. "Something is in there," he acknowledged. "We can see that. But what? I don't think we can know for certain without a biopsy. . . . We need to look at the tissue, examine it. I think we have to talk to a neurosurgeon. He can explain your options."

A few minutes later, Dr. Russell Patterson, a neurosurgeon, and Dr. Stephen Scheidt, Arthur's cardiologist, joined the consultation. Patterson tried to soften the blow by offering two options. "We don't have to do anything right away," he insisted, adding: "Obviously something is going on, probably an infection of some sort. We can simply wait and see what happens next." Faced with the specter of an entire arm going dead, or worse, Arthur inquired about the second option. "We could go in right now," Dr. Patterson told him. "As soon as possible. That way, we would know exactly what we are dealing with. And we can get as much of the infected tissue out as we can." Gulping hard, Arthur reluctantly chose the second option.

The next day, an MRI confirmed Dr. Patterson's general diagnosis, and later in the week a consultation with doctors at the Brunswick Hospital in Amityville, where his good friend Dr. Doug Stein conducted his practice, provided further confirmation that surgery was the best option. On Wednesday, August 31, the third day of the 1988 U.S. Open, Arthur entered New York Hospital for a "fresh battery of tests, including a spinal tap and a blood test." All of this was prep work for the biopsy and brain surgery to follow, but it turned out to be much more than that.[4]

The doctors at New York Hospital received the test results on Thursday, but they could not bring themselves to deliver the news to their famous patient right away. The results were far worse than they had anticipated, so they decided it would be best if Arthur and Jeanne learned the hard truth from personal friends. The go-betweens were Stein and Eddie Mandeville, close friends who had been making daily visits to Arthur's bedside. After talking to Arthur's doctors, Stein gathered himself for what would almost certainly be the most difficult conversation of his life. On Friday morning, he asked Mandeville to join him, and together they waited solemnly for Jeanne to arrive at the hospital. When they told her the news, she gasped and nearly fainted.

When he saw his wife and two of his closest friends enter the room, Arthur knew something was up. After a nervous greeting, Stein fought through his tears and uttered words no one wants to hear: the blood test results indicated that Arthur was HIV-positive. Like most Americans, Arthur had paid intermittent attention to the AIDS pandemic during the past five years, and he knew enough about this frightening new disease to know that contracting it was tantamount to a death sentence. In early 1988, he had heard the stark warning issued by C. Everett Koop, the surgeon general of the United States: "If you contract AIDS, you will die." For a few seconds, he remained silent before asking plaintively, "What does this mean about Jeanne?" Before anyone could answer, she leaned forward to embrace him. As he later described the anguished scene: "She reached out quickly, put her left arm around my shoulders, and squeezed my hand hard. 'You and me, babe,' she said. 'You and me.'"

At this point, Jeanne's blood had not been tested for HIV, and it would be several days before she received a clean bill of health. When Arthur discussed the situation with his doctors, they explained he had probably received tainted blood during one of his two bypass operations, either in 1979 or 1983. Their best guess was that the two units of blood administered when he was recovering from the 1983 procedure were the culprits, but there was no way of knowing for sure. The only certainty was that he was HIV-positive. Whether he had full-blown AIDS was another matter. In all likelihood, the infection in his brain was a sign that he did, but they couldn't be certain until after performing a biopsy.[5]

Performed six days later, just as the U.S. Open was drawing to a close, the tissue removal and biopsy operation identified the infection as toxoplasmosis, a once rare condition that had become a common marker of AIDS. Arthur responded to the news with a simple "Aha," as Jeanne grabbed his hand, "squeezing it hard and long, as if she would never let go." Over the next few days, before Arthur's release from the hospital on September 15, they talked about virtually every aspect of their perilous situation. "I wasn't frightened or nervous," Arthur later insisted. "The public hysteria over AIDS was probably then at its zenith, but I would not become hysterical."

They also decided to focus on the present and the future, not the past. Nothing could be gained, they reasoned, from casting blame or indulging in self-pity. "As for my AIDS," Arthur concluded, "I was simply unlucky to have had a couple of units of transfused blood that may have been donated in 1983 by some gay or bisexual man, or some intravenous drug user who perhaps had needed the money badly. I will never know for sure, and this is not an issue I dwell on."[6]

A more pressing and inescapable problem was the likelihood of public disclosure in a nation terrified by the threat of AIDS. "Pulling ourselves together after the shock, Jeanne and I talked about who should be told, and when," he recalled. "Of course, we were sure that half of the hospital staff already knew these results. . . . But if the story could be kept out of the newspapers and magazines, and off the radio and television, then who should we tell? Almost certainly we would not tell my father; I did not think his heart could take news like that." In the end, he decided to limit news of his condition to a trusted circle of close friends, roughly a dozen people who along with his doctors would share the difficult journey ahead.[7]

Ten years earlier Arthur had responded to his first heart attack by turning himself into an expert on cardiology, and he did the same with AIDS. As one of his doctors recalled, "he always had something to read in hand." His first task was to read everything he could find on toxoplasmosis. The source of his infection, he soon learned, was the parasite *Toxoplasma gondii*, a relatively common pathogen. For most people with toxoplasmosis, the period of infection is relatively brief and inconsequential, especially when it is treated with antibiotics. But for HIV-positive patients, it is a clear sign of trouble to come; during the progression of AIDS, the brain is vulnerable to a number of infections, including several that lead to dementia, and once the brain is affected by one of these infections there is a strong possibility others will follow.

Though understandably alarmed, Arthur also learned his current condition could have been much worse. Many AIDS sufferers begin their descent not with toxoplasmosis but with PCP, a devastating form of pneumonia. Indeed, most of the AIDS patients who had died from infection had succumbed to PCP. Contracting toxoplasmosis was no picnic, and despite the extraction of the diseased brain tissue, the condition was likely to return at some point. But if it did return, treatment with antibiotics rather than surgery would be the probable protocol.[8]

There were, of course, other horrors to worry about. Many AIDS patients eventually contracted Kaposi sarcoma, a form of skin cancer characterized by reddish purple blotches. If this disfiguring condition attacked Arthur's body, there would be no way of concealing his condition from the public other than complete isolation. In the emerging popular culture of AIDS, Kaposi sarcoma was thought to be a sign that an infected individual's HIV-positive status probably stemmed from sexual contact associated with homosexuality.

As Arthur and his doctors examined and reexamined his skin during the weeks and months following his brain surgery, they found no evidence of this skin cancer. But Arthur knew that as soon as his condition became public, he would have to face a barrage of humiliating interrogation: "Had I been shooting up heroin over the years? Or was I a closet homosexual or bisexual, hiding behind a marriage but pursuing and bedding men on the sly?"

Despite the fact that several thousand people had contracted AIDS through blood transfusions, there was widespread skepticism that a significant number of individuals had been infected in such an innocent and blameless way. After all, at the dawn of the crisis in July 1983, Margaret Heckler, the secretary of health and human services, had declared emphatically, "The nation's blood supply is safe." Prior to 1986, Surgeon General

Koop was under strict orders from President Reagan to say little or nothing about the AIDS crisis. And when he did break his silence with an official report, Koop placed a heavy emphasis on the connection between AIDS and homosexuality. When the gay actor Rock Hudson became the first major celebrity to die of AIDS in October 1985, there was open discussion in the press about the homosexual roots of his illness. From then on, the assumption that AIDS was primarily a homosexual disease was a mainstay of public thought.

With no clear direction from the nation's leading medical and health authorities, it is little wonder that rumors, oversimplifications, and false claims came to dominate the public understanding of AIDS. Sooner or later, any man who had the disease had to deal with suspicion of his homosexuality, and Ashe was no exception. When he wrote his memoir *Days of Grace* several months after his condition became public, he felt compelled to address the question of sexual orientation. "I can look anyone in the eye," he declared, "and say two things about my sex life: in almost sixteen years of marriage, I have never been unfaithful to my wife, and I have never had a homosexual experience. Many people may not believe me, but I cannot do anything about their skepticism, or their malice."

Navigating around the fears and falsehoods inspired by the AIDS crisis occupied Arthur's attention from the moment of his diagnosis. For several reasons he felt he had no choice but to keep his condition hidden from the public, government authorities, and his employers. He worried that if his condition became known, his passport would be taken away, and there would no more trips to Wimbledon or the French Open. Would he be welcome at NJTL events, where parents might fear their children would become infected if they came in contact with him? Would he be able to continue his activities on the college lecture circuit? Would he be able to remain on the Aetna board? Work with kids at Doral? Retain his endorsement contracts? Interact with his friends and neighbors, and even his extended family, without feeling like something of a pariah? All of these questions haunted him as he looked to the future.[9]

Even without public exposure, Arthur faced daunting challenges. First and foremost, he had to keep his equilibrium and avoid panic. One of his first decisions was to rule out suicide, a common path among AIDS victims. "For me, suicide is out of the question," he revealed in *Days of Grace*. "Despair is a state of mind to which I refuse to surrender. . . . The news that I had AIDS hit me hard but did not knock me down." Those close to him during this time marveled at his ability to escape what he later called an "avalanche of deadly emotion." "I cannot say that even the news that I have

AIDS devastated me, or drove me into bitter reflection and depression even for a short time," he insisted. "I do not remember any night, from that first moment until now, when the thought of my AIDS condition and its fatality kept me from sleeping soundly."

Even for a man known far and wide for his stolid composure, this assertion of quietude in the face of death is startling. Arthur's explanation pointed to the decade of high anxiety he had already experienced: "My first heart attack, in 1979, could have ended my life in a few chest-ravaging seconds. Both of my heart operations were major surgeries, with the risks attendant on all major surgery. . . . Mainly because I have been through these battles with death, I have lost much of my fear of it. . . . So AIDS did not devastate me. AIDS was little more than something new to deal with, something new to understand and respond to, something to accept as a challenge." [10]

Arthur knew AIDS would ultimately end his life, probably within three to five years. But he was determined to stick around as long as he could. By the end of 1988, he was taking an array of drugs designed either to ease his pain or prolong his life. Before starting this protocol, however, he had to deal with two postoperative conditions. Since he was allergic to penicillin, his doctors prescribed a sulfur-derived alternative, Daraprim, a powerful antibiotic that left him with severe and painful kidney stones. Once the kidney stones passed through his system, he thought he was in the clear. Yet he soon discovered the antibiotic had also triggered a skin disorder known as Stevens-Johnson syndrome. The condition, as described by Dr. Henry Murray, the AIDS specialist assigned to Arthur's case, resembled "a dramatic life-threatening sunburn" that left a "striped ocelot" pattern on the victim's skin. Though it did not last very long, the Stevens-Johnson syndrome also attacked the inside of Arthur's mouth. "For five days I could neither talk nor eat," he recalled, "because my mouth had become painfully sore."

By early October, with the Stevens-Johnson episode behind him, Arthur began to work with his doctors on a long-term medicinal plan. Under the care and supervision of Dr. Murray—a forty-five-year-old Cornell Medical School graduate with a specialty in infectious diseases—he soon became, in the doctor's words, "the most well-informed patient that I ever had." He read every relevant source he could get his hands on, including the special AIDS issue of *Scientific American* that appeared a month after his surgery. One particularly disturbing article in the magazine claimed "90 percent of AIDS patients die within three years of being diagnosed." Arthur, who knew the date of his diagnosis but not the date when his blood had been infected with HIV, did not know where he stood in respect to this morbid piece of data.[11]

Tempted to ask Dr. Murray for an estimate of how long he had to live, Arthur opted instead for a simple question: "Will you tell me when I have about three months left?" "We'll do our best," Murray promised, but he couldn't say any more than that. Part of the uncertainty rested in Arthur's dual status as a patient afflicted with both AIDS and a serious heart condition. Keeping him alive required a joint effort by Dr. Murray and the cardiologist Dr. Scheidt. As Arthur explained, the two doctors "had to coordinate their different treatments to be careful that the side effects of certain therapies in one area do not jeopardize my health in another."

This coordination proved difficult, largely because both of his conditions required a complex set of medications. The resultant burden was considerable, even though Arthur was reportedly a model patient who almost followed his doctors' orders. A firm believer in medical science, he was also psychologically averse to taking any medication beyond the minimum required. So he wasn't pleased when his daily pill consumption rose to two dozen and beyond. For his heart condition, he was already taking five medications plus several natural vitamins, and he kept amyl nitrate in his medicine cabinet in case he suffered another serious attack.[12]

His daily regimen of anti-AIDS medicines was even more daunting. Chief among them was azidothymidine, commonly known as AZT. Introduced in 1987, AZT had become the medical profession's primary weapon against AIDS by the time Arthur was undergoing treatment. Unfortunately, across the full range of AIDS patients it affected individuals in radically different ways. For some it was a "miracle drug," but for many others it was toxic and dangerous. Arthur, as it turned out, was one of the fortunate AIDS sufferers who tolerated AZT "fairly easily." Yet like almost all AZT users, he discovered it could take months and even years to determine the optimal daily dosage. At the outset, he was taking ten AZT capsules per day, but after several reductions his dosage was down to three per day by the fall of 1992.

The reduction of his dosage was typical among AIDS patients, as doctors learned less was often more when it came to AZT. Once this became obvious, Arthur worried that taking the high dosage had already shortened his life. Since experimentation was common in AIDS treatment, his entire regimen of medicines evolved over time. Eventually Dr. Murray prescribed Cleocin, an antibiotic Arthur took four times a day, leucovorin (folinic acid) and Daraprim (pyrimethamine) as brain seizure inhibitors, nystatin pills to combat thrush infections in the throat, and didanosine (ddI) as an additive to AZT. All told, the annual cost of his prescriptions was approximately $18,000, only part of which was covered by insurance.[13]

Despite periodic blood tests, Arthur had no way of knowing how much effect the barrage of pills was having. But within six weeks of his surgery, he felt strong enough to resume most of his normal activities. Throwing himself back into the swirl of board meetings, lectures, workshops, and other public appearances was essential to shielding his bout with AIDS from public view and consistent with his nature. If death was destined to come early, he reasoned, he wanted to make the most of every minute he had left. In the words of Dr. Murray, who marveled at his patient's resilience, "he did it all." [14]

Arthur's return to public life began with the long-awaited launch of *A Hard Road to Glory*. On November 13, one day before the official publication date and one week after a full-page advertisement appeared in *The New York Times Book Review*, the *Times* ran a sports section essay written by the proud author. Titled "Taking the Hard Road with Black Athletes: Success in Sports Became a Matter of Cultural Pride," the promotional piece offered a tantalizing précis of the five-year-old project's findings. "Records aside, black athletes have had a major impact on black history," Ashe insisted, claiming that "proportionately, the black athlete has been more successful than any other group in any other endeavor in American life . . . despite legal and social discrimination that would have dampened the ardor of most participants." [15]

Earlier in the week, Ashe had said essentially the same thing during a phone interview with Barry Lorge. "The book has been an obsession for almost six years," Ashe told Lorge, adding: "I learned so much that was not in my history books. I kept asking myself, 'Why didn't I know this before?' . . . There was so much human-interest raw material that had never been compiled before. To me, it put into perspective the contributions black athletes have made to black life in this country, which was much greater than I had imagined. . . . I think this book will change the way black historians look at sports." Lorge encouraged his readers to take a look at what Ashe had produced, though he warned that the three volumes were "primarily a reference work." As he put it, "Ashe knows he is not James Michener, and his topic was not aimed at the best seller list." [16]

Perhaps not, but Amistad Press projected sales of 40,000 to 45,000 for each of the three volumes during the first two years after publication. To meet this goal, Ashe and his publisher would need the help of enthusiastic reviewers. By Thanksgiving, *A Hard Road to Glory* had received one full-scale review in the *Chicago Tribune*, plus a brief shout-out from Dave Anderson of *The New*

York Times, who declared Ashe's "three-volume history of the black athlete tells more about his dedication to a purpose than his Wimbledon and United States Open tennis championships." The *Tribune* review, written by Skip Myslenski, praised both the text and the author while stressing the books' revelation of just how hard the road to glory had been. "Arthur Ashe, once a tennis champion, now one of sport's consciences," Myslenski wrote, "recounts the closed minds, narrow thinking, and the endless prejudices encountered by Blacks as they strove to become part of America's sporting fabric." [17]

The major review Ashe had been waiting for appeared in *The New York Times Book Review* on December 8. Titled "Champions We Never Knew" and written by the noted journalist and author David Halberstam, the review described *A Hard Road to Glory* as "a fascinating three-volume study." Though not a trained professional historian, the author, in Halberstam's judgment, had "done nothing less than put together a remarkable history of the Black athlete in America from 1619 to the present."

The review went on to point out that "this work is more than a history. It is a cry of protest in which ancient sins are revealed. Mr. Ashe is not merely a historian, he is a witness as well. And the story he tells is in many ways a melancholy one . . . a history of races never run, fights never fought and dreams deferred. For decades and decades blacks were barred by whites from whatever sport existed, and then they were defamed by those very same whites for lacking the guts, ability and intelligence to compete." Halberstam saluted Ashe for turning "endless rumors and previously documented stories into fact, a considerable achievement." The three volumes represented nothing less than "a compelling history of prejudice and meanness, of honor and dishonor," a discourse "both about sports and not about sports." In closing, he maintained that "for any reader trying to understand the relationship between sports and society and why there are so many blacks on the field but so few coaching and in the front offices and the news media, I cannot commend 'A Hard Road to Glory' too highly. Mr. Ashe's accomplishment is monumental." [18]

Ashe hoped Halberstam's tribute would be the first of many glowing reviews, but it soon became apparent only a handful of newspapers had any interest in his book. One newspaper that acknowledged the book's appearance was *The Washington Post*, but the *Post*'s reviewer, Dan Nicholson, had few good things to say. "No one seems to have been able to make up his mind what sort of book—encyclopedia, reference book, coffee table book—*A Hard Road to Glory* should be," he complained. "As a result, it is a little of each, and not enough of any one."

Ashe had expected the black press to embrace his effort to tout the achievements of black athletes while exposing the tawdry history of racial discrimination in the world of sports. But by and large he encountered indifference from black as well as white journalists. Part of the problem was Amistad Press's inexperience with the process of getting books to potential reviewers. Yet a more fundamental obstacle seems to have been a general disdain for sports history, not only in the academic world but also in the broader arena of public affairs.

In March 1989, Nicolaus Mills wrote a decidedly mixed review of the book in the progressive magazine *The Nation* commenting: "Too often Ashe writes in a dreary prose that belongs in an encyclopedia, but the story he tells is nonetheless riveting." Surprisingly, neither the *Journal of Negro History* nor the *Journal of Sport History* reviewed the book, and only two academic reviews appeared before the second edition was released in 1993.[19]

By the spring of 1989, it was becoming clear that the public's response to the book was not what Ashe or his publisher had hoped it would be. Sales were relatively small for a book touted by David Halberstam in *The New York Times Book Review*. The number of copies sold for each volume did not reach ten thousand until the summer of 1990, and Ashe's obvious disappointment became a concern among friends, who worried an emotional deflation might affect his health. Consequently, several friends—Dr. Eddie Mandeville and his wife, Harriette, the noted psychologist Kenneth Clark, and Clark's daughter and son-in-law, Kate and Donald Harris (a former SNCC field secretary)—decided to sponsor a book-signing party designed to boost Arthur's spirits. Held at the posh Hudson Valley Tennis Club in Hastings-on-Hudson, the party drew an overflow crowd, and Arthur left the gathering with renewed hope that a widening readership was in the offing.[20]

This brightening mood did not last. On Palm Sunday, March 19, one week after the book party, Arthur's father passed away at Humana St. Luke's Hospital in Richmond. After collapsing during a dinner at his daughter Loretta's house in the Richmond suburb of Glen Allen, he was rushed to the hospital. Having battled serious heart disease for more than a decade, he succumbed to cardiac arrest seven weeks before his seventieth birthday. Devastated, Arthur Jr. struggled to keep his composure. "My heart withstood the shock but I cried and cried when I heard the news," he later wrote. "Dominating, stern, protective, my father had loved me when I needed him most." During the funeral service held at the New Line Baptist Church in Louisa, only a few miles from the house in Gum Spring where father and son had shared so many good times, the tears flowed again as the loss became real.

The stern taskmaster of Arthur Jr.'s youth had become a close companion and trusted friend in recent decades, and it was difficult for family members to imagine one without the other. The father was the son's primary link to the past, to a beloved mother absent for nearly forty years, and to a deep family heritage that he felt down to his bones. Surviving his own challenges would be harder from now on, and he would need Jeanne and Camera more than ever. Fortunately, he still had his stepmother, Lorene, his brothers Johnnie and Robert, his sister, Loretta, and a passel of aunts, uncles, cousins, nieces, and nephews to share both the grief and family pride. "He's a family person," Loretta stated proudly, knowing her older brother never forgot a family member's birthday or failed to offer financial help or words of comfort in times of need. "He hasn't changed since the day he started playing tennis," she insisted. "I really love and admire him for that. . . . He's a wonderful person. And I'm not saying that because I'm his sister." [21]

Staying close to his family helped Arthur deal with grief and anxiety about his own mortality. But he also coped by embracing a whirl of activity. Not only did he continue the public life he had led since his turn to activism in 1968; he also sought new experiences. Serious illness, he assured one reporter, "makes you feel a bit more pressed for time. And I'm always looking for new challenges, the challenges I feel are worthwhile and interesting." One was the Ashe-Bollettieri Cities program, also known as ABC. Hatched at the French Open in 1987 but not begun until August 1988, ABC was based on the idea tennis could be used, in Arthur's words, "as a way to gain and hold the attention of young people in the inner cities and other poor environments so that we could teach them about matters more important than tennis."

His collaborator was Nick Bollettieri, the flamboyant director of the famous Bollettieri Tennis Academy in Bradenton, Florida. While agreeing with Arthur on the need to encourage education and character development among disadvantaged kids, Bollettieri was also interested in expanding the recruitment of talented Juniors beyond the country club elite and creating a national tennis academy that could compete with the state-supported training programs in Europe. Determined to make all of this happen, he enlisted the cooperation of Bob Kain—CEO of International Management Group (IMG), the owner of the Bollettieri Academy—to expend most of the seed money needed to initiate ABC.

The ambitious goal was to make ABC self-sufficient within two or three years and eventually to acquire public funding from municipal governments. The first camp opened in the summer of 1989, in Newark, New Jersey, with

Arthur's old friend Bobby Davis in charge of the tennis instruction. Davis—who had helped Arthur to develop the Black Tennis and Sports Foundation's tennis workshops—soon had more than 1,500 kids in the program, an office in the Newark City Hall, and a board of directors that included the mayor.

In 1990, a second ABC program opened in Kansas City with Kevin Dowdell, a young black Princeton graduate, as director, and a year later a third program was added in Albany, New York. By the time the Kansas City program became operational, Bollettieri and IMG were in the process of disengaging from ABC, which had shown no sign of becoming self-sufficient. With the Bollettieri Academy hemorrhaging money in an effort to keep ABC afloat, Nick and Arthur, who had known each other since the late 1950s, decided to go their separate ways.

This split allowed Arthur, working closely with Dowdell, to reconfigure ABC as a true nonprofit, which he renamed the Safe Passage Foundation (SPF). From the beginning, Arthur had considered ABC to be a welcome alternative to the NJTL. Convinced that many NJTL programs under USTA influence had become fixated on competition, he wanted to establish a network of inner-city tennis centers that allowed kids to experience the sheer joy of the game. Under his leadership, the SPF developed a formula based on a strict division of time and effort, with half devoted to competition and the other half to off-court life skills. Utilizing indoor gymnasium courts, shortened rackets, and low-compression balls, SPF programs allowed kids to ease their way into full-scale competitive tennis. Traditional one-day workshops typically left participants with a day of memories, a T-shirt, and little else, but Arthur wanted a program that changed kids by "teaching them the game of life."[22]

In 1991, Arthur turned over the operational leadership of the SPF to Dowdell. Though highly successful, the three SPF centers required constant attention, especially after they became affiliated with the Athletes Career Connection (ACC), an organization Ashe had founded several years earlier. The ACC's efforts were directed at college students and athletic programs in an attempt "to redress the terrible attrition rate among black college athletes."

Initially, ACC worked with only seven colleges and universities—Seton Hall, Fordham, and Penn in the Northeast; American and Howard in Washington; and Morehouse and Spelman in Atlanta—but Arthur had plans to expand across the nation. Unfortunately, the organization—which sponsored lectures and workshops designed to stimulate academic achievement among black athletes—went into decline as financially strapped institutions began cutting nonessential programs during the economic recession of 1990.

But this did not blunt its founder's determination to prepare black athletes for "the full range of career options open to them after college." [23]

Such preparation, in his view, had to begin at the K–12 level well before admission to college, and his strong feelings on the issue of minimum standards for college admission put him at odds with several of the nation's most prominent coaches. On January 11, 1989, by a vote of 163–154 the NAACP adopted Proposition 42, the hotly debated measure that strengthened the freshman admission standards mandated by Proposition 48. Beginning in August 1990, freshman athletes would have to satisfy *all* of the minimum requirements outlined in Proposition 48: a 2.0 average in a core curriculum of eleven high school courses; a 2.0 cumulative grade point average, and a score of either 700 on the SAT exam or 15 on the ACT.

Fearing this new standard would block the admission of many black athletes, opponents wasted no time in voicing their outrage. Perhaps the most vocal opponent, John Thompson, the celebrated men's basketball coach at Georgetown University, stormed off the court prior to his team's game against Boston College, vowing he "would not coach again" until the NAACP agreed to reconsider Prop 42. Harry Edwards, Ashe's old ally, supported Thompson, calling Prop 42 "an elitist, racist travesty," and Thompson's counterpart at Temple University, the fiery African American coach John Chaney, condemned the misguided reform measure as "racist and absurd." All of this intimidated the NAACP, which soon declared it was willing to convene a special conference to reconsider Prop 42. On the other side of the issue, delegates representing several of the 163 institutions supporting Prop 42 vowed to defend the measure. [24]

With no sign the controversy was going away anytime soon, Ashe entered the fray with a provocative *New York Times* opinion piece titled "Coddling Black Athletes." After quoting a *Newsweek* reporter's conclusion that "there's got to be a better way" than instituting Prop 42, Ashe begged to differ. "Well, there may indeed be a better way," he wrote. "But so far we haven't found it. The rule still contains the most powerful inducement yet for high school athletes to abandon their cynical belief that they'll get a scholarship even if they don't bother to study." While he acknowledged "it is conceivable that some college administrators see Proposition 42 as a convenient cover for a racist policy of reducing the numbers of black athletes who receive scholarships," he maintained "most probably see it as I do: the only way to establish unequivocally the idea that a scholarship is a reward for academic as well as athletic skills and efforts, not an entitlement granted for athletic prowess alone."

As on other occasions, Ashe targeted a pervasive sense of entitlement as the most insidious problem facing young black athletes. "We need to address the deep-seated cynicism of coddled, black public school athletes, many of whom are carried through school with inflated grades and peer group status that borders on deification," he insisted, adding: "they learn early that they don't get the idolatry, attention, and, ultimately, Division I scholarships for their intellectual promise." The long-term benefits of Prop 42 were, in his view, undeniable. "We should either get serious about academic standards," he argued, "or cut out the hypocrisy and pay college athletes as professionals." It was time for fundamental reform, he insisted, closing with a dire prediction that "Black America stands to lose another generation of our young men unless they are helped to learn as well as play ball."

For Thompson, Ashe's commentary on Prop 42 was tantamount to racial treason, and he could not let it pass without a response. Within hours of the article's publication, the strong-willed coach phoned to voice his displeasure, and a candid and sometimes heated conversation ensued. But neither man changed his position. Thompson continued his campaign against Prop 42, and Ashe wrote an article for *Ebony* describing his recent visits to predominantly black high schools where "the obsession with sports borders on pathology."[25]

Ashe's crusade against entitlement was part of a larger effort to combat what he viewed as the damaging mentality undergirding calls for reparations and affirmative action. He knew this position was not popular in many black communities, especially among young people. But he refused to bend to popular sentiment. After one disillusioning experience with students at Stamford High School in Connecticut, he went away with a new sense of what he was up against. As he later wrote, "On display was the increasingly dominant African American adolescent ethos of entitlement, of 'You owe me,' which I consider monstrous." On the question of reparations specifically, he argued self-respect and a strong work ethic would do more for black Americans than belated payments or handouts, however much they were warranted. "We may indeed be entitled to something," he acknowledged in 1992. "But our sense of entitlement has been taken too far. One of the major tasks of my teachers as I grew up was to make sure that no black kid gave up the struggle to do better because of despair in the face of segregation."[26]

Ashe's concern about entitlement was only one part of his ongoing consideration of the social and economic impact of racial exploitation and discrimination. In the summer of 1990, for example, he interjected himself into a major controversy surrounding racially restrictive membership policies at private country clubs. When the Shoal Creek Country Club in Birmingham was selected to host the national PGA Championship, PGA officials pressured the club to break with its whites-only tradition. The grudging response was to grant an honorary membership to a prominent black businessman, Louis Willie. Ashe, who knew tokenism when he saw it, nonetheless accepted this gesture as a welcome sign of change. "This is a breakthrough of monumental proportions," he told *The New York Times*. "It's difficult to overestimate it. One of the benchmarks of a breakthrough is that it reaches far beyond sports. What happened at Shoal Creek is only 20 percent about sports. It's about society, commerce, and culture. It's the upper echelon of white society finally being forced to say, 'All right, it's time.'"[27]

A month later, when the Augusta National Golf Club followed suit and accorded membership to Ron Townsend, the black president of the Gannett Television Group, Ashe felt vindicated. "When they first said they had been looking for someone for some time, none of us believed it," he acknowledged. "But in actual fact, they really were. I'm not sure why they thought it was finally time. Maybe it was like what Bear Bryant was thinking in 1970 when he decided 'we'd better recruit some of those colored boys.'"

Following up on the developments at Shoal Creek and Augusta, a *Tennis Week* reporter asked Ashe if "any pro tennis tournaments" were still being "staged at clubs that discriminate against blacks," Ashe said no, primarily because "very few pro tournaments now are played at private clubs." The real problem, he pointed out, was at the amateur level, at the "hundreds and hundreds of tournaments and clubs where discrimination had its "greatest exposure." "Just go down the USTA Yearbook pages and throw a dart and you'll hit one," he advised, adding: "it wouldn't take a Pulitzer Prize–winning reporter to find problems here if he really wanted to do it."[28]

To combat this problem, Ashe—in cooperation with the BTSF—enlisted Earl Graves, the African American media magnate in charge of *Black Enterprise* magazine and the BET network, in an effort to reach out to corporate sponsors and advertisers who might fund an array of activities designed to expand black participation in the world of tennis. Instructional videos featuring black players, summer camps at historically black colleges, and special travel packages to tennis tournaments were just three of the proposed elements of a broad, multifaceted marketing strategy aimed at a black audience.[29]

As this activity suggests, Ashe's illness had done nothing to dull his interest in political and social dialogue related to black Americans. During the

mid- and late 1980s, he had participated in a series of retreats held either
in Miami or on Hilton Head Island, where black political figures such as
Andrew Young and Douglas Wilder engaged in wide-ranging discussions
of current issues. These extended conversations, which often involved cri-
tiques of the quality and character of black leadership, propelled Ashe into
renewed political involvement. Despite all that was going on in his life, he
found time to campaign for his friend David Dinkins during the 1989 New
York mayoral race. And a year later he was a vocal supporter of Harvey Gantt
during his unsuccessful bid to unseat North Carolina's reactionary U.S. senator Jesse Helms.

Ashe despised Helms and his ilk, and on the college lecture circuit he
often expressed his contempt for white supremacist demagogues. But he was
equally hard on demagogic black leaders. He had no respect for men such
as Louis Farrakhan of the Nation of Islam or Professor Leonard Jeffries of
the City College of New York who indulged in anti-Semitic tirades. And he
did not hesitate to criticize the Reverend Al Sharpton and other publicity
seekers who seemed to promote their own narrow interests over the interests
of the broader black community. He even took popular black icons such as
Malcolm X to task. Sweeping and unrestrained condemnations of whites
saddened him, and he felt he had to speak out against irresponsible outbursts
by misguided black leaders. "I am appalled by the level of irrationality in our
community," he wrote in 1992, "and especially by the complicity of some
newspapers and radio stations in encouraging this excess."

To his mind, hyper-emotionalism and racial scapegoating were the
enemies of social progress. Mass violence—whether in America, South Africa, or anywhere else—sickened him, and he came to feel that Gandhian-
Kingian nonviolence was the only true path to freedom for blacks and other
oppressed groups. His heroes were men like Andrew Young and the former
Freedom Rider John Lewis, who became a congressman from Gergia in
1987. Both of these leaders preached the gospel of the "beloved community,"
combining faith with a pragmatic realism designed to move the black community forward.[30]

During the last five years of his life—after decades of unfocused spiritual
exploration—Ashe adopted a faith-based philosophy that gave him comfort
and a considerable amount of moral and psychological sustenance. Following the obligatory worship of his childhood, he generally kept his distance
from organized religion, preferring the posture of "a practical Christian," as
he put it. But now he embraced a deeper commitment, something beyond
the basic "loyalty to the Golden Rule" that had anchored his earlier approach

to ethical and spiritual life. One outward symbol of this new attitude was a renewal of his childhood affinity for gospel music, which he claimed had eclipsed jazz and 1960s-era rock 'n' roll as his favorite kind of music.

Arthur confessed he wasn't sure whether his ill health had precipitated his new attitude toward religion and gospel. But he hoped not. "Have I become more and more concerned about morality and God as I find myself closer to death?" he asked himself in 1992. "Perhaps. But I don't think my poor health is the reason. I think I am simply being faithful to the way I was brought up, and that I would feel this concern even if I expected to live to be a hundred years old."[31]

He was also heavily influenced by the renewal of his friendship with Jeff Rogers, who led him to the writings of the recently deceased Howard Thurman, the Reverend Martin Luther King Jr.'s longtime spiritual advisor. With Rogers's guidance, Arthur became an enthusiastic disciple of the great theologian's teachings, reading and rereading Thurman's *Jesus and the Disinherited* and *Meditations of the Heart*, two almost mystical disquisitions on life and death drawn from multiple religious traditions ranging from Quakerism to Zen Buddhism. Infused with practical advice on how to face death without fear, this eclecticism appealed to Arthur's internationalist approach to moral discourse. "Aside from the Bible," he revealed, "Dr. Thurman's two dozen or so volumes are the most important books to me in my moments of crisis and in my extended struggle with disease." He was especially taken with Thurman's conception of achieving a state of serenity by "centering down," a process akin to Zen meditation, and with "the idea of the sacrament of pain."

The latter concept helped Arthur to deal with the perplexing question: "Why does a benevolent God tolerate or even encourage the presence of suffering in the world?" "What did we do to deserve slavery?" he asked. "What did we do to deserve a century of segregation?" Thurman's answer advanced the notion that "pain has a ministry which adds to the sum total of life's meaning and, more importantly, to its fulfillment." Arthur found considerable solace and wisdom in this statement. "Believing that pain has a purpose," he declared, "I do not question either its place in the universe or my fate in becoming so familiar with pain through disease." For him, this insight was an immeasurable help in dealing with a terminal illness. "I do not brood on the prospect of dying soon," he explained. "I am not afraid of death. Perhaps fear of death will come to haunt me when the moment of death is closer. On the other hand, perhaps I will be even less fearful, more calm and at peace."[32]

Even so, Arthur was in no hurry to take his final breath. He was still in the game, one manifestation of which was his insistence on playing an active role in monitoring and adjusting his treatment regimen. He regularly interrogated his doctors with medical questions, either about his current protocol or alternative therapies. In the summer of 1990, he became enthused about Kemron, touted by Daniel arap Moi, the president of Kenya, as an anti-AIDS wonder drug. The reported results among African patients did, indeed, seem promising, but a series of clinical trials by American doctors soon called the African findings into question. After Dr. Murray expressed considerable doubt about Kemron's efficacy, a disappointed Ashe decided to forgo treatment with the drug, even though he suspected the Western medical establishment had not given Kemron a fair shake.[33]

During these years, the search for a cure for AIDS, or even a reliable means of slowing the progress of the disease, proved elusive, and the annual toll of AIDS-related deaths continued to climb, reaching forty thousand by 1994. By then, it was the leading cause of death among Americans twenty-five to forty-four years old. Perhaps even more horrifying was the manner of death for AIDS sufferers; the long list of excruciating and eventually fatal symptoms ranged from the cancerous Kaposi sarcoma to the parasite-induced cryptosporidiosis, a devastating gastrointestinal condition that often ended in starvation. But even worse was the public's insensitivity to the plight of those infected. The association of AIDS with homosexuality destroyed most of the empathy that might have been expected in a national culture that fancied itself as humane and compassionate. As the journalist Andrew Sullivan has written, gay victims of AIDS "were surrounded by a culture that emphatically believed that they had asked for this, that mass death was, as *National Review* put it, 'retribution for a repulsive vice.'"[34]

Mercifully, Arthur's medical experience was surprisingly benign for a considerable period of time. For a full four years after his diagnosis, he avoided lengthy hospitalization. Dr. Murray, for one, marveled at his patient's resilient capacity to maintain a normal life in the face of AIDS. While Arthur lost some weight during these years, his energy level, general health, and outward appearance underwent little change. "There's a bit of age on his face, as you might expect," one reporter observed in 1989, "but by and large he looks as fit as any surgically repaired man of 45 has a right to." Inside, of course, he was experiencing changes that would ultimately precipitate his death. But this did not prevent him from living life to the fullest, making numerous public appearances, both in person and on television, where there was no letup in his broadcasting career.

He was also able to exercise as strenuously as his heart condition would allow. While he no longer played tennis, other than an occasional racket-testing session for Head or a brief demonstration at a youth clinic, he maintained a rigorous daily regimen of sit-ups, walking, and spending time on an exercise bike. "I know what I can and can't do, how much I can lift, how fast I can walk, how hard I can push myself on the bike," he assured Barry Lorge in a 1988 interview. When he was in Mount Kisco, he could often be seen taking long walks—traversing, as he described it, the "3.2 miles from my house to the Croton Reservoir and back—15 minute miles, which is 120 steps a minute, up and down hills, with my Spanish language tape and earphones." He was also active on the golf course, where his midrange handicap remained steady. In November 1990, he even scored his first hole-in-one during the Bryant Gumbel/Walt Disney World Pro-Am in Orlando.

Most of his many golf outings took place at Doral, where he, Jeanne, and Camera spent part of each winter. South Florida was their second home for at least two months a year, and they reveled in the outdoor activities there, especially after they sold their bucolic Mount Kisco retreat in 1990. Wherever he found himself, Arthur kept busy. His intellectual pursuits were more ambitious than ever, his voracious reading habits continued unabated, and he was almost always engaged in one writing project or another.[35]

His involvement in philanthropic activities also seemed to expand with every passing year. In 1988, he estimated he devoted 20 percent of his time to pro bono commitments of one sort or another; and the actual figure probably increased after the AIDS diagnosis convinced him he had no time to waste. While he generally reserved weekends for family activities, he spent a good part of every week trying to turn words into action on behalf of his many chosen causes. For example, during the early 1990s—in an effort to complement the work of the Safe Passage Foundation and the Athletes Career Connection—he founded and promoted the African American Athletic Association, a New York–based organization devoted to elevating academic achievement among black student-athletes. At the same time, he also spearheaded an ambitious effort to open an African American Sports Hall of Fame in downtown Richmond.[36]

On top of everything else, Arthur also managed to sustain a large number of business interests, from product endorsements to entrepreneurial initiatives. His endorsement clients now ranged from Head rackets and Le Coq Sportif sportswear to Bristol-Myers pharmaceuticals, Volvo, and Unisys. And his many investments included shares in several radio stations, a telephone company, and the all-black ownership group of the Denver Nuggets

NBA franchise. Combined with his broadcasting salary, the steady income from endorsements and investments supported a comfortable lifestyle, even though not all of his entrepreneurial ventures were successful.

Arthur's most notable business failures were his short-lived partnership with Doug Stein in an ill-fated wholesale clothing business called STASH ("a combination of Stein and Ashe") and a longer but ultimately unfortunate partnership with his brother Johnnie, who had sought help in the financing and construction of an apartment complex in Jacksonville, North Carolina, in 1988. Named Cordell Village, after their mother's middle name, the sixty-five-unit complex was designed to accommodate the families of Marines stationed at nearby Camp Lejeune. But as Arthur recalled: "When President Bush ordered the buildup of forces in the Persian Gulf in August 1990, we, the owners of Cordell Village, were on our way to ruin. Overnight, half of the apartments at Cordell Village emptied as our resident marines headed for the sands of Saudi Arabia and Kuwait."[37]

Despite these reverses and his HIV status, Ashe held his head high during the four years following his diagnosis. As the journalist Marvin Martin later observed, he "carried on with his various projects, still keeping many balls in the air at once. He just considered AIDS one more ball he had to juggle." Prior to late 1992, he did not have the look or demeanor of a dying man. Externally he appeared to be as strong, psychologically and emotionally, as ever. Whatever was happening inside his body, there was no outward sign that he was entering the final stage of an abbreviated life.

He had a multitude of interests, but beyond that he passionately embraced his continuing role as an activist. His involvement in strengthening and refining African American political sensibilities remained a high priority, as did his commitment to using tennis as an entering wedge in the struggle against despair among inner-city children and adolescents. And most obviously, there was the goal of black liberation in South Africa. Nothing stirred his soul more than encouraging news from Cape Town or Soweto, though such news was in short supply during the 1980s.[38]

Finally, at the beginning of the 1990s—a decade Arthur knew would be his last—there was South Africa news worth celebrating. After almost eighty years of struggle by the ANC—and after twenty years of personal commitment to the anti-apartheid cause—he now had reason to believe that victory was in sight. For Arthur, as for millions of black South Africans, Nelson Mandela's sudden return to active political life in 1990 represented a triumph of incalculable proportions. He had been an admirer of the legendary ANC leader since the late 1960s, when his white South African friend Ray Moore told him that Mandela was "the one man in South Africa capable of leading my country out of this mess." Moore even predicted Mandela would some-day become president of South Africa, but Arthur discounted his friend's optimism until the events of 1990 changed his mind. During the past year, he had followed the statements and nervous political maneuvers of South Africa's Afrikaner president, F. W. de Klerk, who seemed to be considering some form of transition from pro-apartheid intransigence to a democratic opening that might someday lead to racial equality. But Mandela's release from prison on February 10 caught him by surprise.[39]

Ronald Reagan's second administration and the first year of George H. W. Bush's presidency had been a discouraging period for the anti-apartheid movement, and there were moments when Arthur wondered if he would live long enough to see black South Africa's liberation. One such moment was January 1986, when his hopes hit bottom during an impromptu visit to the campus of Dartmouth College, in Hanover, New Hampshire. Six years esarlier he had spent a wonderful weekend at Dartmouth as an honorary degree recipient, but his second visit would not be so pleasant. In recent years, the Dartmouth campus had witnessed an upsurge of right-wing militancy promoted by *The Dartmouth Review*, a five-year-old newspaper staffed by students and funded by a national consortium of conservative activists. Predictably, the newspaper led the reaction when a group of liberal students constructed a small shantytown of shacks on the campus green to "dramatize the plight of black South Africans." The immediate issue at hand was a call for the divestment of the college's investments in South African companies, but as the college's board of trustees mulled over the request on January 16, the day after Martin Luther King Jr.'s birthday, the activists at *The Dartmouth Review* took matters in their own hands. Calling themselves the Committee to Beautify the Green, a dozen sledgehammer-wielding students attacked the shantytown at three o'clock in the morning. After dismantling three of the four wooden shacks, they carted off the pieces of lumber on a flatbed truck, to the shock of the campus.

The perpetrators would eventually be brought before a campus judicial review board that convicted them of violating Dartmouth's Code of Conduct. But Randall Robinson of TransAfrica was more concerned about the morale and future prospects of the campus's beleaguered anti-apartheid movement. Despite the bitter cold enveloping New Hampshire in late January, Ashe agreed to accompany his friend and colleague on a mission of mercy. Speaking outdoors on the green in sub-freezing conditions, they assured the small group of students and faculty that they "were not alone in their struggle." Sadly, despite the recent attack, there was no evidence of a groundswell of anti-apartheid activity at Dartmouth, and Ashe and Robinson left the campus with heavy hearts. "Seldom have I felt so embattled and outnumbered in the struggle against South Africa," he later confessed.[40]

What a difference four years made as Ashe contemplated the coming era of change. Even before Mandela's release, there had been a few signs of encouragement. Numerous letters from Ashe's friends in South Africa documented a rising spirit of resistance, and the divestment movement was clearly catching hold on a number of American college campuses. Unfortunately, there were also moments of backsliding, as in September 1989 when the ATP board appeared ready to endorse participation in two upcoming tournaments in Johannesburg. At a meeting held at the United Nations Plaza Hotel, Ashe—accompanied by Mark Mathabane, the expatriate South African author of *Kaffir Boy*, who sixteen years earlier had journeyed to Ellis Park to see a free black man play tennis—pleaded with the board to honor Mandela's request to maintain the boycott of South African sports teams. With Mathabane nodding in agreement, Ashe convinced the board there had been no real softening of the apartheid regime, despite recent false claims by the de Klerk government.[41]

Coming only a few days after Arthur's release from the hospital, the ATP decision to exclude the two South African tournaments from the tour was a welcome victory. But the real triumph played out over the next three years as Mandela fought for the imposition of a one-man, one-vote democracy. In the early stages of this process, he visited the United States and Canada in an effort to drum up support for his efforts. On June 20, 1990, the South African leader arrived in New York, and Ashe was on hand to witness one of the most joyous scenes of his life. "I thank God that I lived long enough to see Nelson Mandela come to the United States and be welcomed with a ticker tape parade through the canyons of Wall Street in New York," he later wrote. "I was seldom more proud of America and my fellow Americans than when I saw the way we welcomed him as a hero. The success of the parade was a sure and gratifying sign that many people, black and white, rich and poor, recognize his sacrifice and applaud the almost superhuman way he preserved his dignity, his humor, and his unquenchable moral sense through the nearly three decades of his imprisonment."

For Ashe, the high point of Mandela's visit was an ABC television town hall moderated by Ted Koppel. David Dinkins made sure Ashe had a reserved seat in a special section near the podium where Mandela was speaking and after the program was over, the mayor, at Ashe's request, introduced him to the speaker. As Ashe later described the scene, "I watched David go over to Mandela and whisper in his ear. I saw Nelson's head raise abruptly, and he broke into a beautiful smile. 'Arthur is here?' he asked, with obvious surprise and delight. 'He's right here,' David said turning to me. 'Oh, my brother,' Nelson said, looking straight at me. 'Come here!' He threw his arms around me and held me for a moment in a most affectionate embrace." To Ashe's surprise, Mandela began their conversation by praising *A Hard Road to Glory*, which he had received as a gift from Yusuf Surtee, a fellow ANC leader, and which he had managed to read before his release from prison. As Mandela exited the hall, Ashe moved "up the aisle and into the lobby, talking with him all the way." "I could scarcely believe he was there at my side," he recalled.[42]

Sixteen months later, in November 1991, Ashe saw Mandela again, this time in Johannesburg. Visiting at Mandela's request, he was part of a "Democracy Now" delegation of black leaders and celebrities that included the composer Quincy Jones, the publisher Earl Graves, and Randall Robinson. The highlight of his brief stay was what he later termed "several stirring conversations" with Mandela, but he also visited several old friends, including the poet Don Mattera, and held a "private lunch with a group of whites, who peppered me with questions about President Bush's attitude to the changes that were beginning to sweep their country."

During their flight back to the United States via London, Ashe and the other African American delegates discussed what they had just experienced, and they all agreed the situation seemed to be moving faster than they ever could have imagined. Their mood was almost euphoric, but Robinson eventually broke the spell with a disturbing caveat. "We are all getting excited," he said, "and yet I keep thinking about one thing. . . . For all the changes we have seen, Nelson Mandela still cannot vote in his own country." It would take two and a half years of additional negotiation and struggle before that democratic milestone became a reality. On April 27, 1994, Mandela not only cast his vote; he was also elevated to the presidency of South Africa by the votes of millions men and women realizing full citizenship for the first time.[43]

Arthur would miss the long-awaited moment of jubilee, but he saw Mandela one last time, in New York, in July 1992. The Democratic National Convention was then in full swing, and the two men had no shortage of things to discuss. Arthur told the man he now called Nelson that a lot had happened to the Ashe family since they had last met. He and Jeanne had sold their house in Mount Kisco and moved back to an apartment on the

Upper East Side of Manhattan. Camera had grown into a lively and confident five-year-old kindergartener. And, perhaps most important, Arthur had revealed to the world that he was suffering from AIDS. Nelson had already heard the sad news, but he wanted to know more about his friend's perilous condition—and how he and Jeanne were coping. "Our main topic was now AIDS," Arthur recalled, "both as it affected me personally and as an international scourge. I was pleased to see that he knew a great deal about the subject and was free of the prejudices that prevent many political leaders from confronting it." [44]

Arthur was with the African leader long enough to tell him the story of how he had been forced to make his condition public three months earlier. On Monday afternoon, April 6, 1992, the Ashes received a visit from an old friend, Doug Smith, a former ATA tennis player now writing for the national daily newspaper *USA Today*. When Smith called to arrange the visit, Arthur assumed he wanted to do a news feature on *A Hard Road to Glory*. But after a brief conversation about the book, Smith turned to a more serious matter. *USA Today* had gotten a tip—a "lead" on a potential story—concerning Arthur's health. "We have heard that you are HIV-positive, that you have AIDS," he blurted out. Though stunned, Arthur immediately shot back: "Can you prove it?" Smith acknowledged he couldn't, but quickly added: "That's the point. My editor wants to know, is it true? They sent me to find out. Is it true?" Trying to stay calm, Arthur nonetheless felt his ire rising. As he recalled: "The anger was building in me that this newspaper, *any* newspaper or any part of the media, could think that it had the right to tell the world that I had AIDS."

After several awkward silences, Arthur demanded to speak with Smith's editor. Smith gave him the phone number of Gene Policinski, the managing sports editor for *USA Today*, and a few minutes later the editor was on the phone trying to explain his position. He asked Arthur point-blank: "Are you HIV-positive, or do you have AIDS?" Without fully considering the implications of his words, Arthur responded with a coy "Could be." "I could not lie to him," he later explained. "Sometimes, indirectly, I had to lie about AIDS. Now and then, I had to lie about it directly. In November 1991, when I wanted to go to South Africa, I lied on the application for my visa and said that I did not have an infectious disease. But I never lied without a sharp twinge of conscience, even in lying to the government of South Africa."

After informing Policinski he "had no intention . . . of confirming or denying the story," Arthur asserted "the public has no right to know in this case." While he knew public figures forfeited a blanket right of privacy, he insisted he was no longer a public figure: "I don't play professional tennis anymore. I officially announced my retirement in 1980. I am not running for public office, so my health is no one's legitimate concern except my own." Policinski thought otherwise. "You *are* a public figure," he maintained. "And anytime a public figure is ill, it's news. If he has a heart attack, as you did in 1979, it's news. We have no special zone of treatment for AIDS. It's a disease like heart disease. It is news."

Suspecting that Policinski was right in a legalistic sense, Arthur retreated to an effort "to control the announcement." He asked the editor for "a little time, say, thirty-six hours, to call friends, talk to other journalists, and prepare a public statement." Policinski was noncommittal. He would not publish the story without additional confirmation, but neither would he back away from the ongoing investigation. "Policinski and I ended the conversation without coming to any agreement," Arthur recalled, "except that I stood by my refusal to confirm the story, and he stood by his determination to continue to investigate it, as well as his right to publish it if he could find confirmation. I fully expected to see the story in the next morning's edition."[45]

When the story did not appear the next morning, he knew he had at least twenty-four hours to prepare and deliver an announcement. Both he and Jeanne had long feared this day would come, and they had already discussed their options. Now the force of circumstances was upon them. Canceling all of his appointments, he sat down with Jeanne to figure out how they could best handle the situation. There were few precedents to guide them. In November 1991, the basketball star Magic Johnson had called a press conference to announce both his HIV status and his retirement from the NBA, but most celebrities suffering from full-blown AIDS—including the actor Brad Davis and the African American clothing designer Willi Smith—had failed to reveal their condition prior to their deaths. Arthur and Jeanne were essentially entering uncharted territory.

April 7, 1992, was one of the most difficult days of their life together. With considerable justification, they feared revealing Arthur's condition would reach well beyond simple embarrassment and an end to the family's privacy. In addition to the inevitable rumors of closeted homosexuality, there would also be severe restrictions on employment and international travel. "I wondered if I would ever see Wimbledon again," Arthur later wrote. "I wondered about my commercial connections, my consultantships and other jobs in television, in the manufacture and sale of sports equipment in clothing, and in coaching. All of these connections went back a long way, and represented a tremendous investment on my part as well as on the part of those companies. Would these connections survive the news?"[46]

Their first test was a call to Seth Abraham, the president of HBO Sports's parent company Time Warner Sports. Over the years Abraham had become a close friend, and he was one of the few who already knew about Arthur's battle with AIDS. After describing his conversation with Policinski, Arthur asked Abraham for permission to hold a press conference at HBO's headquarters at 1100 Sixth Avenue. Abraham agreed without hesitation and reserved a room on the fifteenth floor large enough to handle a throng of reporters.

With the venue set, Arthur began calling friends and family members to warn them about the upcoming announcement scheduled for the following afternoon. In the eleven hours between 3:15 Tuesday afternoon and 2:45 Wednesday morning, he made nearly three dozen calls, many to those learning about his condition for the first time. "Hearing the news that I had AIDS, two or three people burst into tears," he recalled. "I hastened to tell them, and others that I was fine, that my spirits were up, that they should not worry about me." Among the calls were one to Dr. Louis Sullivan, the secretary of health and human services, and another to the head of the National Commission on AIDS, who was asked to invite medical reporters to the news conference. But most of the calls were to close friends and long-standing colleagues—people like Donald Dell, Charlie Pasarell, and Frank Deford, all of whom agreed to be part of Arthur's official entourage on Wednesday afternoon.

Deford also volunteered to edit Arthur's draft of the opening statement to the press. The celebrated *Newsweek* feature writer and his best friend from the world of tennis had been through a lot together—coauthoring a book, traveling to Africa, and mourning the loss of Deford's daughter Alex—but putting the AIDS statement together represented the toughest challenge of their many years of friendship. Both men were veteran writers, but nothing either had ever written seemed as important as these few paragraphs.[47]

As Arthur composed the first draft, he was interrupted by a series of calls. Even without the help of a press conference, news of his condition was spreading. Andrew Young called from Atlanta, David Dinkins from the New York mayor's office, Doug Wilder from Richmond, and even President Bush from the White House. All expressed their support and sympathy, and promised to stick by him. The support that counted most, of course, came from Jeanne, who remained a tower of strength as the day's events unfolded. And there was also five-year-old Camera, prancing around the apartment with only a vague sense of what was happening. So far she had been shielded from the knowledge that her father was seriously ill, but both parents realized it was time to tell her what was going on. As Arthur later explained, "We had to tell her before someone, most likely some other child, taunted her with the fact that her father has AIDS."

The dreaded conversation with Camera would have to come soon, but Arthur could not bring himself to do it prior to the news conference. "I could hardly look at her," he remembered, "without thinking of how innocent she was of the import of this coming event, and how in one way or another she was bound to suffer for it." At one point, she interrupted his writing with a hug around his knees and an outstretched but closed right hand hiding something special. When she opened the hand to show her father the gift, the "bright silver wrapper" of a Hershey's chocolate Kiss was revealed. Fighting back tears, he kissed her cheek before returning to his keyboard.[48]

Several hours later, long after Camera had gone to bed, he completed a draft and ended what seemed to be the longest day of his life with a final round of phone calls. Crawling into bed a few minutes before three in the morning, he closed his eyes to try to get as much rest as he could. But he found it impossible to sleep "except in fits and starts." Mostly, he twisted and turned, periodically opening his eyes and aimlessly gazing through the darkness. "From my windows on the fourteenth floor of my apartment building in Manhattan I saw the lights of the city, and watched for the sun to come up through the murk and mist of Brooklyn and Queens to the east," he recalled. "Before six o'clock, with the sky still dark, I was dressed and ready to go, ready to hunt for a newspaper, to discover if my secret was out, exposed to the world."

Walking across the street to a small shop, he found a freshly printed copy of *USA Today*. A quick scan of the front page and the sports section, the logical places for a sensational story about a sports celebrity, told him his secret was intact. "There was not a word about me," he later reported. "I felt a great relief. And then I knew that the relief was only temporary, that it was now up to me to take the matter into my own hands and break the news to whatever part of the world wanted to hear it. And I would have to do it that day, Wednesday, because the days—maybe the hours—of my secret were definitely numbered. I had to announce it to the world that, I, Arthur Ashe, had AIDS."[49]

Returning to the apartment, he spent part of the morning making changes to his prepared statement. He then shared the changes with Jeanne and Frank, both of whom gave their approval to the revised draft. Soon Doug Smith came by to record an interview. The focus was supposed to be AIDS, but Arthur began by demanding to know the names of both the reporter who took the call at *USA Today* and the paper's informant. He suspected the informant was Dr. J's son, Bobby Jr., who had long held a grudge against him. But Smith refused to divulge any information. Eventually Arthur let the matter rest and turned to an account of his illness, and later in the morning Jeanne granted Smith a second interview. A hurried lunch followed, after which Arthur took a few minutes to get ready for the ride to the press conference.[50]

The press conference was scheduled for 3:30, and the Ashe entourage arrived at HBO headquarters just a few minutes before the appointed time. Ross Levinsohn, HBO's head of publicity, met them in the lobby and accompanied them to the fifteenth floor. As the elevator whisked them up to the room, Arthur, perhaps looking for a bit of encouragement, read the first paragraph of his statement out loud. But when he got to the end of the paragraph, which revealed that he was "HIV-positive," Dr. Murray offered a stern correction: "No, Arthur, you have AIDS. That's what you have to tell them." After an awkward silence, the chastened patient nodded his assent, and by the time they reached the room he was more or less ready to say what had to be said.[51]

Familiar to fight fans, the room had hosted many pre-fight announcement events over the years, a fact Arthur wryly judged to be morbidly appropriate for what he was about to do. When he entered the room accompanied by Jeanne, Dell, Dinkins, and three doctors—Mandeville, Scheidt, and Murray—he saw a packed house of reporters. As he later put it, "I half expected to hear the bell sound for Round One."

Hoping to lighten the mood, he began with a joke. "George Steinbrenner has asked me to manage the Yankees," he said with only a hint of a smile. "But I graciously declined." When "nobody laughed," he knew he couldn't delay any longer. He began by reminding the reporters that "rumors and half-truths have been floating about, concerning my medical condition since my heart attack on July 31, 1979." He then went right to the heart of the matter: "I had my first bypass operation six months later on December 13, 1979, and a second in June 1983. But beginning with my admittance to New York Hospital for brain surgery in September 1988, some of you heard that I had tested positive for HIV, the virus that causes AIDS. That is indeed the case."

As a murmur of reaction filled the room, he continued with a brief description of the origins and evolution of his condition, from a transfusion of HIV-infected blood to toxoplasmosis to four years of treatment for AIDS. Anticipating being asked why he had not revealed his condition to the public in 1988, he tried to explain and justify the delay. "The answer is simple," he argued. "Any admission of HIV infection at that time would have seriously, permanently, and—my wife and I believed—unnecessarily infringed upon our family's right to privacy. Just as I am sure that everybody in this room has some personal matter he or she would like to keep private, so did we. There was certainly no compelling medical or physical necessity to go public with my medical condition."

He then thanked those who had kept his condition a secret. "I have it on good authority," he declared, "that my status was common knowledge in the medical community, and I am truly grateful to all of you—medical and otherwise—who knew but either didn't even ask me or never made it public." He acknowledged this "silent and generous conspiracy to assist me in maintaining my privacy. That has meant a great deal to me and Jeanne and Camera." With this mention of family, he was overcome with emotion and began to cry. As he later described his momentary breakdown, "I felt the tears flooding my eyes, and my throat simply would not open to let out the words." The silence in the room deepened his embarrassment, but try as he might he was unable to regain his voice.

Seeing her husband's distress, Jeanne moved to the podium, and Arthur stepped aside and handed her his prepared text. Somehow Jeanne managed to fight back her own tears as she read a section on the announcement's probable impact on Camera. With Arthur's words, she told the gathering: "Even though we've been preparing Camera for this news, beginning tonight, Jeanne and I must teach her how to react to new, different, and sometimes cruel comments that have little to do with her reality." Seeing Arthur had regained his composure, she stepped back from the podium to let him finish. For several minutes, he held forth on a series of matters, including his displeasure with *USA Today*. The paper's editors, he pointed out, "put me in the unenviable position of having to lie if I wanted to protect our privacy. *No one should have to make that choice.* I am sorry that I have been forced to make this revelation now."

In closing, after assuring the audience that both Jeanne and Camera had tested negative for HIV, he talked about his past—and his future. "I have been an activist on many issues in the past—against apartheid, for education and the athlete, the need for faster change in tennis," he said. "I will continue with those projects in progress, and will certainly get involved with the AIDS crisis." After promising to work on AIDS education and fund-raising with other HIV-positive individuals, including Magic Johnson, he ended with a few sobering remarks. "The quality of one's life changes irrevocably when something like this becomes public," he insisted. "Reason and rational thought are too often waived out of fear, caution, or just plain ignorance. My family and I must now learn a new set of behavioral standards to function in the everyday world, and sadly, there was really no good reason for this to have to happen now. But it has happened, and we will adjust and go forward."

Forty-five minutes of questions followed. The reporters wanted to know about his current physical condition, about his medication, and about whether or not he planned to sue the hospital that had given him infected blood. One reporter asked if he had been forcibly outed by *USA Today*. "Absolutely," he responded. "If the person hadn't called the newspaper, I'd still be leading a normal life." When asked if he had any advice for fellow AIDS patients, he counseled perseverance and continued hope—"because you never know what breakthrough lies around the corner." On this positive note, he brought the most difficult public experience of his life to a close.

The news conference had been painful, to be sure, but as he later revealed, he also felt "a certain sense of relief." Earlier in the day he had predicted as much in a conversation with Doug Smith. Comparing his impending revelation to a Roman Catholic confession, he hoped for the same feeling of release that many parishioners experience coming out of a confessional booth. "You're supposed to come out feeling better," he told Smith, adding: "there's a self-imposed burden when you keep something like this to yourself. It's one of those things that cry out for revelation, just to tell someone." Of course, Arthur had not told *someone*; he had, in effect, told the whole world. And for better or worse, he and those he loved would have to live with the consequences of that expansive revelation.

As he and Jeanne left the room to begin their new life, the confessional metaphor came back into his mind. Despite all the distractions of the moment, he could not resist contemplation of moral lessons to be learned. Even in situations that drove him to tears, or that tested his faith in himself, he continued the quest for wisdom of the highest order—something he would surely need in the coming weeks and months.[52]

TWENTY-SIX

FINAL SET

∎

I N THE IMMEDIATE AFTERMATH of his AIDS announcement, Arthur Ashe discovered just how public his private life could be. The magnitude of the national and international press reaction troubled him, but he decided his best option was to add some additional public comment of his own as a prophylactic against misinformation. On Thursday, April 8, 1992, he appeared on both the NBC *Today* show and ABC's *Nightline* to express his outrage over *USA Today*'s invasion of his family's privacy; and on Friday evening Barbara Walters interviewed him on the *20/20* news and entertainment program, during which he described the involuntary disclosure of his struggle with "the 1990s version of leprosy" as "demeaning." Taking advantage of an opportunity to educate the public, he assured Walters and her national audience that he posed no danger to those around him. "You can kiss me," he told his host. "You can hug me. You can shake my hand. You can drink out of the same glass. I can sneeze on you. You're not going to get it from me."[1]

Few newspapers commented on the issue of contagion, except as it applied to the safety of the nation's blood supply, and there was even less discussion of AIDS victims as societal pariahs. Instead, editors and reporters focused on Ashe's personal saga as a physically and emotionally wounded celebrity and the issue of "weighing privacy against the public's need to know," as Alex Jones of *The New York Times* put it. On the latter issue, many journalists—despite considerable sympathy for Ashe's predicament—sided with *USA Today*. An informal poll of a half dozen editors attending the national convention of the American Society of Newspaper Editors revealed that all but one favored disclosure. Speaking for many of her colleagues, Jane Healy of the *Orlando Sentinel* declared: "I can't imagine knowing that information and keeping it quiet. I think a lot of it comes down to whether there is a real public issue there rather than just titillating the public." [2]

A surprisingly large number of editors and reporters, however, disagreed with Healy, and a thoroughgoing debate over Ashe's right to privacy soon made its way into editorials and journalism school classrooms, where it is still being studied twenty-five years later. In the first few days following the announcement, Ashe welcomed the supportive comments of several prominent journalists, including the syndicated columnist Ellen Goodman, who described *USA Today*'s action as "the medical equivalent of an outing," using the popular term for dragging gay men and women out of "the closet." Jonathan Yardley of *The Washington Post* condemned *USA Today* for pursuing the story "with all the fury of a cur attacking a T-bone. . . . That Ashe had long ago ceased to be a 'public figure' as anyone in his right mind would interpret the term was entirely beside the point; the point was that red meat was there to be eaten." [3]

Raymond Coffey of the *Chicago Sun-Times* wrote a biting commentary under the headline "Media Double-Faulted on Ashe Story," and Michael Olesker of the *Baltimore Sun* characterized "Ashe's agony" as "journalism's shame." "Sometimes the scoop is a shame on us all," he wrote. "It's gossip pretending to be investigative journalism. It's invasion of privacy masquerading as the public's right to know. This time it's nobody's business but Arthur Ashe's, only now it's been turned into everybody's business." [4]

New York Times sportswriter Robert Lipsyte began his April 10 column with the simple question: "Do we need to know that Arthur Ashe has AIDS?" "My first answer to myself," he continued, "was an emotional No. Here was a man whose public life has been about fairness, responsibility, respect and self-control. For the last three years he had tightly gripped the fraying corners of his life. Now they were being torn from his hands." [5]

Other commentators writing in the nation's most influential newspaper took a more measured stance, seeing merit on both sides of the privacy issue. The noted feature writer Anna Quindlen confessed she was conflicted and "disquieted by the Arthur Ashe story." "I can't help but feel that in the medical sense we outed him, a practice that, in the sexual sense, I deplore," she wrote with candor. "That's the human being talking. The reporter understands:

public figure, big news." The *Times* editorial board took a somewhat differ-ent tack, expressing sympathy for Ashe while scolding him for attacking "the wrong target." The real culprit was not an overly aggressive and invasive newspaper but rather "the cruel and benighted public attitudes that com-pelled Mr. Ashe to keep his disease secret for three years."[6]

Several other major papers followed the *Times* editorial board's lead, in-cluding *USA Today*, which had to deal with an avalanche of criticism from angry readers—481 phone calls, mostly negative, and sixty canceled sub-scriptions in the first thirty hours after Ashe's announcement. Eventually the paper received over six hundred protest letters, a situation the paper's editor, Peter Prichard, tried to preempt with an April 13 editorial defending his disclosure policy. "Generally, I think it is a mistake for journalists to keep secrets—or to protect some friends who happen to be public figures, but not others," he contended, citing misguided press suppression of two presiden-tial maladies—Franklin Roosevelt's paralysis and Woodrow Wilson's 1919 stroke—as classic examples. Neither "conspiracy of silence," Prichard in-sisted, "served the public." And in Ashe's case, he argued, sustaining such a conspiracy could have especially dire consequences, since "sweeping Ashe's secret under the rug would have contributed to the public ignorance of AIDS and done nothing to reduce the disease's stigma." *USA Today* had actually done Ashe a favor by forcing him to share his story with the public. Thanks to the disclosure, "Ashe and his family are free of a great weight."[7]

Carl Rowan, the acclaimed African American journalist who knew and admired Ashe, made the case for disclosure even more forcefully, writing: "The self-glorifiers in the media who claim they would have joined in the secret-keeping apparently have not thought about the possible gains to mil-lions of people and the nation because Ashe has told his story however reluc-tantly." To Rowan, it was obvious "the monstrous threat of this killer disease AIDS is multiplied when current victims hide it, succumbing to the bigotry of those who call AIDS 'God's punishment of bad people' or to the fears of those who think someone with AIDS is 'untouchable.'" "We need more unsenti-mental reporting about this disease," he insisted, "not journalistic copouts in the name of 'privacy' or 'friendship.' AIDS education was far more important than any man's privacy, even if that man was Arthur Ashe." "Ashe may still be angry that some friend 'ratted' on him and told USA *Today* that he has AIDS," he argued in closing. "Yet, having stepped forward with class, Ashe may now see that secrecy did not become him nearly as well as his recent actions to rip the 'leper' label off the victims of a terribly wretched disease."[8]

Ashe would eventually see the wisdom in Rowan's words, but only after his anger about being outed began to subside. It would not take him long to embrace his new role as an advocate for AIDS sufferers, confirming Bud Collins's prediction that he would "treat AIDS as any other task or foe—straightforwardly and with grace and courage." First, however, he had to confront the day-to-day challenges of dealing with public suspicions and ignorance of his disease, beginning with two appointments the day after the announcement. "I made sure to keep the two appointments," he recalled, "because I was anxious to see how people would respond to me. . . . I was thinking not only about the people I knew personally, even intimately, but also about waiters and bartenders, doormen and taxi drivers. I knew all the myths and fears about AIDS."

The first two tests—a morning fund-raising appointment at the New York Community Trust's development office and an evening black-tie gala celebrating his friend Joe Cullman's eightieth birthday—went better than he expected. He was pleased with the genuine warmth and the absence of awkwardness at both events. Cullman, the former CEO at Philip Morris, had known about Arthur's condition for some time, as had all of his major commercial employers—Aetna, Head, Doral, Le Coq Sportif, HBO, and ABC. Yet "none of those companies had dropped me after I quietly revealed to their most important executives that I had AIDS," he reported. For a time following the public disclosure, he wasn't sure they could withstand the inevitable pressure from nervous stockholders or executives to cancel his contracts. But as he noted in the July 1992 issue of *Tennis*: "Not only have companies reaffirmed their allegiance, I have had new offers."[9]

Judging by the torrent of supportive letters, he had reason for optimism. Yet the situation on the ground remained uncertain and threatening, at least in his mind. When Sally Jenkins of *Sports Illustrated* interviewed him in mid-April, she found a man extremely anxious about what he was likely to face in the real world. The questions she inferred were troubling: "Will the world be a friendly place when he steps out of his apartment building and people wonder if he's headed to New York Hospital for his monthly blood test to check the status of a disease that is most frequently transmitted by homosexuals and intravenous drug users? Will it be a friendly place for his five-year-old daughter, Camera, a radiant child who attends an elite private school? Will it be a beautiful place for him and his erudite wife, Jeanne, the next time they dine out? Ashe is not at all certain."

He told Jenkins his "first order of business" was to "destigmatize" a disease that loomed as "the modern-day equivalent of leprosy." But he also reported he had encountered very little of the ugly and standoffish behavior accorded many AIDS victims. "I have not yet walked into a restaurant where I might feel that they really don't want me in there," he told her. On the contrary, he had experienced numerous acts of kindness, some expressed in letters and others in more tangible gestures of affection. "On the street, strangers wish him good luck," Jenkins wrote. "Elizabeth Taylor, whom he has never met, sends a glorious spray of tulips. A neighbor gives him a box of chocolates, shakes his hand and then reaches up to give him something more, a kiss."[10]

During the critical time of adjustment in April and May, as Ashe became acclimated to his new situation, the outpouring of love and affection was beyond anything he had ever experienced. The kindness coming from his closest friends was to be expected. But dozens of his other ATP colleagues—including Rod Laver, Tom Okker, Brian Gottfried, and Jeff Borowiak—took the time to send him personal cards and letters expressing their concern. Chris Evert, Steffi Graf, Pam Shriver, Tracy Austin, and several other members of the WTA also reached out to him, as did a number of athletes and coaches from other sports, including Magic Johnson, Pelé, Sugar Ray Leonard, Lynn Swann, John Thompson, and even the South African Gary Player.

From beyond the sports world came letters from people of all ages and walks of life—from elementary school children and retired teachers, from white Mississippians and black South Africans—all sharing a bond of attachment to someone they respected and admired. "I've watched all the interview shows you've been on, read all the columns which say only superlatives about your grace, strength and intelligence," a woman from Larchmont, New York, wrote. "So I can't add to that. All I can say is . . . when I think about the one person whose fame is deserved, you are it."

A Brooklyn woman dealing with her sister-in-law's struggle with AIDS expressed her admiration and empathy: "I know that I am only one of many to offer you support and applaud your courage and dignity. . . . I hope that the publicity you are receiving now does not hamper the quality of your life. . . . I hope as well that if you feel prepared to do so, you will speak out on AIDS issues as eloquently and effectively as you have on civil rights, apartheid, and heart disease. Voices like yours send powerful messages." There were hundreds of letters like these, confirming Barry Lorge's judgment that "of all the champions in sports, few have earned more respect and affection than Arthur Ashe."[11]

Ashe felt his widening circle of supporters deserved the best he could give them, which in the short term meant resuming his normal range of activities.

He wanted to repay their faith in him by remaining strong and active—by living up to the high standard that Pancho Gonzales had set for him years earlier, that of a man who "won't duck a thing" and "won't let anybody down." So within days of the disclosure he was back at it, handling his multiple responsibilities as a philanthropist, businessman, and public intellectual. He wouldn't allow himself to skip a single meeting or miss a single deadline, as he shuttled from one public function after another. As he kept saying, "I am not sick," and he was determined to prove it by maintaining a breakneck schedule. "I never worried as much about being a social outcast as I did about not being able to maintain my life's schedule," he insisted.[12]

Instead of slowing down, he immediately embraced a whole new set of responsibilities as an advocate for AIDS victims. Less than twenty-four hours after the announcement at the HBO building, he stood next to Mayor Dinkins at a second gathering called to announce the appointment of the city's first municipal coordinator of AIDS policy. The new coordinator, Ronald S. Johnson, the executive director of the Minority Task Force on AIDS, had often criticized the city's handling of the AIDS crisis, and after accepting the appointment as coordinator he surprised the crowd of reporters—and the mayor—by announcing he was not only gay but also HIV-positive. Dinkins took the announcement in stride, claiming: "I didn't know he was H.I.V.-positive," but "had I known I would have leaped more quickly to make the appointment." Unimpressed, William Dobbs, a leading member of the radical AIDS advocacy group Act Up, insisted there was "no substance to the appointment of an AIDS czar who has no real power" to increase the city budget's paltry allocation for solving AIDS-related problems. "It makes one wonder," Dobbs continued, "if the Mayor is only doing this in response to his good friend Arthur Ashe getting AIDS."[13]

For Ashe, this was an eye-opening entry into the battleground of AIDS politics. And he would encounter more of the same the next day when *The New York Times* reported he planned to remain on the board of directors of Aetna Life and Casualty Company "despite the company's refusal to sell new policies to people with AIDS or to people who test positive for the virus that causes AIDS." Aetna's board chairman, Ronald Compton, insisted the policy was "appropriate" considering "the social context of this devastating disease," though he acknowledged Ashe's recent announcement "might make the board more sensitive to AIDS." While this statement held out some hope Ashe could work from within to liberalize the company's seemingly harsh policy, his current situation on the board was awkward at best.

Aetna's position on HIV/AIDS patients later received blistering criticism from *The Village Voice*, which condemned Ashe for his involvement with a company wedded to corporate greed. "I was accused of colluding with the company despite my own condition," he recalled. This charge, he insisted, had no basis in fact: "The truth is that I would never have remained on the Aetna board if it had such a policy; but I have certainly voted in support of prudent and sensible changes in connection with individual life-insurance policies. At a certain point, Aetna decided to stop selling *individual* health-insurance policies to anyone. . . . We did so for a simple, sufficient reason: we were losing money on individual policies. . . . We insure groups of people. We absolutely do not require these groups to test its members or its prospective members for AIDS. And most groups do not require tests for basic individual coverage, only for excessive amounts of coverage." While it is doubtful that this capitalistic justification satisfied the company's critics, Ashe's faith in Aetna's good intentions was undoubtedly sincere. Later in the year, he declared: "I am proud of Aetna and of my association with the company."[14]

As the spring of 1992 wore on, Ashe demonstrated that he was ready to tackle the AIDS crisis with conviction and determination. Wherever he found himself, from college lecture halls to the National Press Club, he felt compelled to address one aspect of the crisis or another. At the same time, he also recognized there were still important non-AIDS-related issues to address. "I am not going to drop everything else I do in life just to be a single-focus, single-minded AIDS activist," he told a reporter in April. Accordingly, he kept his hand in a wide variety of activities, including broadcasting for HBO and ABC and writing for *Tennis* magazine and *The Washington Post*. He also weighed in on ongoing controversies such as the proposed expansion of the National Tennis Center in Queens, Nelson Mandela's plans for democracy in South Africa, and the shocking acquittal ("It defies logic" and "the standards of Common decency," he told the press) of the white police officers responsible for African American Rodney King's brutal beating in Los Angeles. Whenever possible he mixed his AIDS work with other commitments, and in his own estimation he had developed a knack for "putting things together and seeing relationships between things that" had once "seemed disparate."[15]

In early May, he honored a long-standing commitment to conduct a youth clinic at Byrd Park in Richmond. Returning to his hometown was always emotional for Ashe, but Byrd Park, in particular, flooded his mind with memories both good and bad. It had been forbidden ground for him as a young tennis player, yet it was also where he had lost his virginity. He yearned for reconciliation with the local power structure, primarily as a means of affirming his identity as a Richmond native. In November 1982, Richmond officials had made a tangible gesture of respect by naming the city's new six-thousand-seat, multipurpose arena the Arthur Ashe Athletic Center, and ever since he had wanted to respond in kind. He also appreciated the Richmond City Council's unanimous resolution (passed four days after his AIDS announcement) commending him "for his courageous statement to the world about his own personal fight against AIDS and for taking on a leadership role in advancing the cause of AIDS education, prevention, and treatment." Clearly, Richmond was no longer just Harry Byrd's town, or the "holy city" of the "Lost Cause." It was also Doug Wilder's town, and to some degree it was Arthur Ashe's town, too.

Ashe's urge for rapprochement became manifest during the May 1992 visit. In his first public statement, he declared: "It's nice to be home." But he also wanted to reach out to the city in a more concrete and lasting way. For several years, he had quietly harbored a desire to create an African American Sports Hall of Fame that would reflect the accomplishments he had chronicled in *A Hard Road to Glory*. He envisioned a museum that would not only reenshrine the black athletes already inducted into existing Halls of Fame—such as those in Cooperstown, Springfield, Canton, and Newport—but also memorialize the achievements of the many other black champions who, because of racial restrictions, had never attained this status. Initially, he thought the best prospects for the host city were Atlanta, Indianapolis, St. Louis, or Durham, but after a discussion with Joseph James, the director of Richmond's Office of Economic Development, he decided he wanted to put the museum in his hometown.

For three decades and more, Richmond officials had been searching for ways to combat what one local historian called "the city's gritty rust-belt realties," but a series of high-profile urban renewal and redevelopment projects had not solved the problems of a decaying downtown. Richmond officials had not given up, however, and by the early 1990s historical and heritage-based tourism had emerged as the city's best hope for economic renewal. So when Ashe told James about his dream of building an African American Sports Hall of Fame, there was considerable enthusiasm about building the Hall in Richmond, where adding African American historical sites to the city's traditional Confederate venues was an increasingly attractive option.

Ashe and James agreed the best means of getting started was to "hold a Gala Benefit Dinner to honor every African-American ever inducted into a major pro-sports Hall of Fame." On June 17, Ashe ran the idea by Walter

T. Kenney Sr., Richmond's black mayor, who as a city councilor since 1977 had allied with Henry Marsh, the city's first black mayor. It would be a "black-tie affair," and he anticipated "inviting over 600 national leaders in business, communications, entertainment and the arts as well as over 130 African-American Hall of Fame inductees."

It would be several months before Ashe received official approval and seed money from the City Council, and by the time the date for the gala was scheduled—for November 1993—he wasn't sure he would be around to attend. But that didn't stop him from doing everything he could to advance the project. He was convinced the hall would serve as an important legacy perpetuating the influence of *A Hard Road to Glory*, especially after the City Council agreed to place the proposed 68,000-square-foot building in Jackson Ward, three blocks away from the site of Ashe's boyhood home on Sledd Street.[16]

The campaign for the Hall, as important as it was to Ashe, did not push his AIDS work to the side. For better or for worse, he had joined Magic Johnson as a poster boy for the campaign against the dreaded disease. "To many people, especially to people who meet me or even those who merely find themselves in the same room with me," he explained, "I probably personify the problem of AIDS. When I am there with them, they can avert their eyes but not for long, and must face the problem that has been facing them for years, and will face them even more boldly in the future. I do not like being the personification of a problem, much less a problem involving a killer disease, but I know I must seize these opportunities to spread the word. Talking to audiences about AIDS has become, in some respects, the most important function of my life."[7]

To serve this function, he had to maintain a certain level of health and emotional well-being, and he had no way of knowing how long he would be able to do so. As he told the journalist B. Drummond Ayres Jr. in May, he knew sooner or later his blood tests would tell him he was on the " 'downhill' side of the disease," that, in effect, he was nearing the end and would have to "reassess" what he could do in the public arena. But he preferred to focus on his present condition. "I've been rock solid with my tests for the past three and a half years," he told Ayres, "and I'm not down yet." Ayres came away from the interview marveling at Ashe's capacity to maintain a positive attitude in the face of adversity. The ailing tennis star, he concluded, "seems anything but angry and focused on himself. In the worst year of his life, so far, he is pushing on, promoting tennis, talking up racial equality, spreading the word about the killer disease he carries."[18]

By late spring, Ashe was growing increasingly confident in his ability to develop an agenda for attacking the disease. Sharply critical of the Bush administration's unwillingness to address the crisis in any meaningful way, he aligned himself with Governor Bill Clinton of Arkansas, the leading contender for the Democratic presidential nomination and a strong advocate of a national health care system that would, among other advantages, facilitate extended treatment of AIDS victims. Ashe had grown increasingly disenchanted with Bush on a number of fronts, but the president's refusal to take a strong and consistent position on AIDS issues was especially disappointing.

He made this point in no uncertain terms in a commencement address delivered at Harvard Medical School in early June. After Magic Johnson, the scheduled commencement speaker, had been forced to cancel, Arthur volunteered to take his place. The expected topic was AIDS, and he did not disappoint his audience of medical school graduates and their families on that score. Demonstrating his command of the subject, he cast his speech as broadly as possible placing the AIDS crisis in the context of a woefully inadequate national health care system.

Describing himself as "a thirteen year professional patient," he took the system to task for being unnecessarily expensive, ethically corrupt in its billing practices, too dismissive of patients' concerns, and inattentive to the needs of the poor and much of the middle class. In the future, he counseled, physicians' salaries and hospital fees would have to be reduced to accommodate a larger proportion of the public, "especially if AIDS continues to spread as expected." Terming "the absence of a coherent national healthcare policy" as "one of the major disgraces of American life," he prescribed a set of initiatives that would transform American medicine into a more compassionate and caring institution, one driven not by greed but by the urge to serve. "Through a prudent combination of federal assistance and private enterprise," he maintained, "America will ensure appropriate, adequate, and sufficient physical and mental health care for all its citizens." In his idealized conception, American medicine would also acknowledge "its preeminent moral position in leading combined global efforts to assist, share information, and seek solutions for our common medical concerns."[19]

This final point was of great importance to Ashe. Behind the scenes, he was already laying the basis for an organization later known as the Arthur Ashe Foundation for the Defeat of AIDS (AAFDA). The foundation's charter mandated that at least 50 percent of its funds would be sent abroad. Since the magnitude of the AIDS crisis was especially appalling in Africa, he felt that it should receive a significant proportion of whatever funds could be raised.

The AAFDA's initial goal was to secure between $2.5 and $5 million within two years, and by mid-August the structure of a foundation with that capacity was in place. Ashe leaned heavily on his friend Margaret Mahoney, the executive director of the Commonwealth Fund, for advice and direction, and together they put together an impressive board of directors that included Dr. Irving Chen of the UCLA AIDS Institute; Dr. Machelle Allen, an AIDS specialist at New York's Bellevue Hospital; and Dr. Michael Merson, the director of the World Health Organization's Global Programme on AIDS. Ashe and the board hired Jackie Joseph, a former Stanford tennis star with an MBA from Columbia, as executive director. A talented journalist and publicist who later created the popular website TennisCountry.com, Joseph would remain at the helm of the foundation for several years.

Eager for the AAFDA to begin its work, Ashe acknowledged he and Jeanne had discussed the eventual creation of such a foundation long before his April 1992 AIDS announcement; and now that he had revealed his condition, he wanted to make up for lost time. While he soon discovered it would be several weeks before his fledgling foundation was ready to launch its first official appeal for funds, he looked forward to the eventual kickoff—a daylong benefit tournament held at the National Tennis Center in late August.[20]

The summer of 1992 brought other important developments for Ashe. In late June, while at Wimbledon, he made a fateful call to Arnold Rampersad, a Princeton English professor he had met eight months earlier at a children's book fair. A native of Trinidad and Tobago who had migrated to the United States in 1965 at the age of twenty-four, Rampersad had recently won a prestigious MacArthur Foundation fellowship, largely on the basis of an award-winning two-volume biography of the black poet and intellectual Langston Hughes. Impressed by the literary excellence of the Hughes biography and by Rampersad's personal charm, Ashe left their first meeting hoping they would reconnect in the near future.

For several months, Ashe had been thinking about writing a final memoir that would supplement and supersede his 1981 autobiography, *Off the Court*. He now felt ready to go beyond the standard narrative genre by recasting his life story as a moral and philosophical journey. He wanted to explicate "his views on certain issues of importance to him, such as race, education, politics, and sports." And with the end of his life drawing near, he also wanted to devote part of the time he had left to a searching discussion of his experiences as an AIDS sufferer. To do so would require a collaborator, one who could start immediately and work under considerable time pressure. When

Ashe asked Rampersad if he would be willing to join him on this breathless autobiographical and philosophical adventure, the Princeton professor said yes, commencing a successful collaboration that would produce one of the decade's best-selling autobiographies, *Days of Grace, A Memoir.*

Ashe would not live long enough to see the book in print or even to complete the manuscript, which ultimately stretched to nearly five hundred pages. But a series of lengthy taped interviews conducted during the summer and fall of 1992—combined with Rampersad's skilled writing—fashioned most of the content and structure of what would become a book of distinction. Working without a formal contract from July to November, Rampersad turned Ashe's recollections and reflections into polished prose.[21]

Organized thematically rather than chronologically, Ashe's memoir begins with an interpretive account of his April 1992 outing, before flashing back to two chapters on the 1980s, one commenting on his heart problems and the aging process, and a second detailing his experiences as captain of the U.S. Davis Cup squad. The fourth chapter, titled "Protest and Politics," traces his turn to civil rights activism in 1968 and the subsequent evolution of his interest in South Africa, and the fifth and longest chapter, titled "The Burden of Race," drills deeper into the sometimes baffling and confounding connections among race, politics, power, education, and sports. The sixth chapter, "The Striving and Achieving," discusses matters of money, commercial endorsements, and board service as a potential contribution to social justice and equal opportunity, whether the service is on a corporate board such as Aetna's or on nonprofit, philanthropic boards such as those overseeing ABC and SPF.

The final five chapters, accounting for a little more than a third of the text, offer a highly personal perspective of the AIDS crisis, from Ashe's 1988 diagnosis to a closing letter to "My Dear Camera." The letter—perhaps the most poignant section of the book—presents a familial and moral legacy to a beloved daughter who will soon be without a father. It begins: "By the time you read this letter from me to you for the first time, I may not be around to discuss with you what I have written here. . . . You would doubtless be sad that I am gone, and remember me clearly for a while. Then I will exist only as a memory already beginning to fade in your mind. Although it is natural for memories to fade, I am writing this letter in the hope that your recollection of me will never fade completely. I would like to remain a part of your life, Camera, for as long as you live."[22]

Writing passages like this may have been therapeutic, but pushing the project forward was an enormous challenge. Fortunately, unlike many of his

commitments, preparing *Days of Grace* did not take him away from home—
or unduly complicate his effort to maintain a balance between family time
and the demands of his public life. "I travel a great deal now, sometimes flying three times or even more in a single week," he explained. "But I seldom
stay away more than a single night from my family. I cannot bear to be away
so long from Jeanne and Camera."

Spending time with Camera was his highest priority, and he seemed to
find pleasure in the simplest and most mundane parental activities. "I love
getting Camera ready for school in the morning, or helping her go to sleep at
night," he wrote. "I love sitting on the floor with her and her coloring books
or playing games or simply talking with her." Most of their time together was
spent at home, but as a proud father he also liked to take her to public events,
perhaps in part to show her off but mostly to enrich her childhood. Two days
after the AIDS announcement, with Jeanne home sick, he took her to the
Essence magazine awards show as his date. "I entered the hall with her on
my shoulders, so she could see everything and everyone," he recalled, "and
the crowd kindly gave us a standing ovation as we made our way to our seats
near the front. At one point, Denzel Washington, who has four daughters of
his own, came down from the stage to say hello to Camera, and she slunk in
embarrassment to the floor."

While Camera was probably too young to appreciate the full meaning of
such experiences, they meant the world to him. "I feel strong when I am with
her," he insisted, "I feel the power of her youth and vitality. She taxes me at
times, to be sure, but I pay the tax willingly." He also derived strength and
comfort from Jeanne, whom he termed his "co-patient." The bond between
them had never been stronger, as she gracefully adjusted to the ceaseless demands of her multiple roles—wife, lover, mother, nurse—demonstrating an
unusual combination of strength and tenderness, discipline and empathy, realism and hope. "What may have rent apart other marriages," Arthur observed
in June, "has only strengthened ours," which made him "feel better already
about Camera's future." Thanks to Jeanne's patient guidance: "She knows
that Daddy has AIDS and she knows what to say if the subject comes up."[23]

During the months following the disclosure, Arthur and Jeanne also
drew upon the love and support of their extended family. In early May, they
traveled to Chicago to celebrate Mother's Day with Jeanne's mother and
other members of the Moutoussamy clan, and in mid-August they hosted
an Ashe-Cunningham family party at the Manhattan apartment. Originally planned as a small gathering, the party, in Arthur's words, "grew and
grew, out of love and caring for me, and I was glad for that. I had no way of

knowing when I would see many of them again." Eventually the crowd of twenty-four became a bit much for the host, who, by his own admission, was beginning to wilt with exhaustion, prompting two aunts—as the reigning family matriarchs—to bring the festivities to a close.

The following weekend, Arthur and Jeanne and Camera traveled south to Gum Spring to spend a few days with his stepmother, Lorene. Returning to the house his father had built with his help was an emotional experience, heightened by the possibility that this would be his last visit. He had nothing but fond memories of his years with Lorene, the woman who had done so much to nurture his transition from childhood to adolescence. He tried to write a little while he was there, thinking that being close to home and hearth would inspire him, and at one point during the weekend he visited the graves of his mother and father. But mostly he just relaxed, as he and others "rocked and reminisced easily on the porch."[24]

Surprisingly enough, the six months following the AIDS announcement— especially June through August—was a period of relative contentment for Arthur. "Apart from those few days when my medical problems sapped my strength, when my mornings were an ordeal of listlessness and diarrhea," he revealed, "the summer of 1992 was a joy." Adjustments in his medication gave him renewed hope and boosted his mood as the season progressed. He felt strong enough to exercise regularly, and he played a lot of golf that summer— usually in Scarborough-on-Hudson at the Sleepy Hollow Country Club, where he had been a member since March.[25]

Arthur had begun to take an almost childlike delight in his golf game, partly because he was shooting the lowest scores of his life. Maintaining some meaure of athletic skill was important to him as a symbol of vitality and normalcy, and he took pride in his continued involvement in the sports world, both as an amateur golfer and an influential figure among retired tennis stars. In June, when a nominating committee advanced his name as a candidate for a spot on the U.S. Olympic Committee, he did not object. And later in the month, he insisted on fulfilling his contract as a color commentator for HBO at Wimbledon. Returning to Wimbledon, probably for the last time, meant a great deal to him. "I left New York with a happy heart," he later explained, "because I thought of this trip as a true bonus. The previous year I had flown to London for Wimbledon thinking that it would surely be my last visit to the scene of my greatest triumph in tennis." Prior to his arrival in 1992, he expressed concern that the infamous British tabloid press would pander to curiosity about his medical condition. But he was pleasantly surprised by the tabloids' uncharacteristic restraint.

Determined to enjoy his last hurrah, Arthur made the rounds from Centre Court to the broadcast booth to the locker rooms as if he were on a holy pilgrimage. It had been three decades since his first visit, and some of the traditions that had made Wimbledon so special were no longer in evidence. But for him the glorious green expanses of the All England Club had lost none of their charm. Even a spate of heavy rain failed to dampen his enthusiasm; indeed, the rain delays were welcome in that they gave him more time to reconnect "with old friends."

He even managed to squeeze in an appearance on the actress Lynn Redgrave's televised interview show, *Fighting Back*. Deeply interested in health and human rights issues, Redgrave asked him questions about his "life with AIDS," and about his views on the fight against the disease and the prospects for a cure. Was he resigned to an early death? Had he given up hope? His response was an unequivocal "I will never quit," though he was quick to add that personal pledges were far less important than institutional responses to AIDS. Even if "there is no cure for AIDS in time for me," he declared, there is certainly "hope" for those who have not yet made the transition from HIV-positive status to full-blown AIDS.[26]

After this televised interlude, he returned to the tournament with a measure of relief, but also with a sense of accomplishment, hoping his candor had opened up a few minds. Back in the broadcast booth, he was pleased to spend several days with Billie Jean King, the person he admired most in the contemporary sports world. Born three months apart, Arthur and Billie Jean had known each other since they were teenagers, and they had worked together in the broadcast booth off and on for several years. Their mutual respect was obvious and genuine and never stronger than during the 1992 Wimbledon fortnight. Since they had not had the chance to spend any extended time together during the three months since the AIDS announcement, they had a lot to talk about when they were off the air.

They discussed everything from presidential politics to Arthur's outing, but mostly they reminisced about the past, including an episode at the 1991 Wimbledon tournament that had touched Billie Jean's heart. Introducing Camera to the sprawling Wimbledon complex, Arthur had, in his words, "strolled with her from one green court to another, telling her (as if at four she could understand me) about my matches on this court and that." What Billie Jean saw that day was a loving, solicitous father who "couldn't wait" to hold Camera's hand and "take her around." "He loved her, he really loved her," she concluded, with renewed affection for her old friend. A year later he returned the favor. "More than ever," he wrote, "I savored the terms of our long friendship, and admired the sharpness of her mind and the resilience of her spirit."[27]

The 1992 Wimbledon fortnight left Arthur with a good feeling about his place in Wimbledon history. "When I left England this time," he wrote, "I did not feel nearly as pessimistic about my chances of returning . . . as I had in 1991. Perhaps I will be back next year, and even the year after." Another source of optimism was the healthy state of American tennis. In 1992, three of the four men's semifinalists were American: the veteran John McEnroe; twenty-two-year-old Andre Agassi; and twenty-year-old Pete Sampras. When Agassi won the title on the closing day of the tournament, he became the fifth American in the last eleven years to capture the singles championship. By contrast, during the decade prior to Arthur's victory in 1975, only two other American men won the singles title. American tennis was clearly on the upswing, a trend confirmed by Sampras's unprecedented run of six Wimbledon triumphs between 1993 and 2000.[28]

For Ashe, the only discouraging aspect of the competition was the continuing absence of an African American star who could extend his Wimbledon legacy. He did hold out some hope that the highest-ranked black player on the ATP tour, eleventh ranked MaliVai "Mal" Washington, would eventually make a name for himself at Wimbledon. Four years later, in 1996, Washington would indeed become the second African American to reach the Wimbledon finals. Though he lost the championship match to Richard Krajicek of the Netherlands, this near miss represented an impressive achievement, one that the 1975 Wimbledon champion would have appreciated had he lived long enough to see it.

Washington's remarkable fortnight was as close as American tennis would come during the 1990s to finding the long-awaited black successor to Ashe. But regrettably Washington's promising career would be cut short by a severe knee injury, and he would never reach another Grand Slam final. For nearly a decade no one emerged to take Washington's place, but in 2006 the former Harvard All-American James Blake sparked memories of Ashe when he achieved a #4 ranking and reached the quarterfinals of the U.S. Open. The son of a white British mother and an African American father, Blake played eight years of Davis Cup competition and even upset the great Swiss champion Roger Federer in the quarterfinals of the 2008 Olympic singles competition in Beijing.

Blake was a class act on and off the court, and he rarely missed an opportunity to thank Ashe for serving as an exemplary role model. "It's an honor any time I hear my name linked to Arthur Ashe," he once declared. On the court, he fell short in his effort to follow in Ashe's footsteps, but otherwise he fulfilled his famous predecessor's goals, compiling a public service record that earned him ATP's Arthur Ashe Humanitarian of the Year Award in 2008. Nearly a decade later, he honored Arthur's legacy with *Ways of Grace*, an inspiring book of essays on activist athletes courageous enough to speak out on public issues. "Ashe taught me that despite the situation you are in, no matter how grave, how embarrassing, or how devastating," Blake wrote movingly in the introduction, "you can try to find a positive way to affect the world."[29]

Tennis-wise, neither Blake nor any other African American male has approached the success of the incomparable Williams sisters, Venus and Serena, who together won 30 Grand Slam singles championships in a nineteen-year span from 1999 to 2017. But no one could have predicted in 1992 that the duplicable black tennis champion was Althea Gibson, not Arthur Ashe. During Arthur's lifetime, the dream of sharing the limelight with other male tennis stars arising out of the black community remained alive, if largely unfulfilled.

Failure almost always leads to a certain amount of recrimination, and the unsuccessful search for the next Arthur Ashe was no exception. Some of the most disgruntled black tennis players, those who had fallen short of their expectations, sometimes complained that Arthur had done little to help them, intimating that he secretly enjoyed his singular status as America's only black tennis champion. Expecting support based on racial solidarity, they felt entitled to personal intervention that would hasten their climb up the tennis ladder. Such expectations misjudged the motivations of a man who believed all success should be earned. Arthur knew from experience that there were no shortcuts on the road to true success; that is why he placed so much faith in hard work—and so little in any form of favoritism, racial or otherwise.

At the end of his life, Ashe still believed in virtually all of the precepts he had learned many years earlier either from his father or Dr. J. To be successful at the highest level, an aspiring player had to develop both the right attitude and the right skills early on in the educational process. That is why he put so much emphasis on the work of the NJTL and other tennis institutions designed for children and adolescents. Even when health considerations might have dictated less involvement with kids, he honored all of his commitments to youth organizations.

On July 20, less than two weeks after his return from Wimbledon, he presided over a benefit match in northern New Jersey between Bjorn Borg and Guillermo Vilas, two Ashe admirers who had agreed to do what they could to raise funds for the Safe Passage Foundation program in Newark. A testament to Ashe's elevated stature, the Borg-Vilas match raised more than $10,000 for the Newark program and helped set the stage for a $100,000 sponsorship granted by the Nestlé corporation later in the year.

Nothing could have made Ashe happier. He believed in the SPF mentoring program, which valued education and character development above all else. "We use tennis to attract the kids," he explained, "but we make sure that we spend about one-third of our time talking about other, more serious matters. I always try to lift the sights of the youngsters to new heights. Trying to be the next Michael Jordan is fine, I tell them; but why not also aim for the goal of owning the team that employs the next Michael Jordan?"[30]

The Borg-Vilas benefit match boosted Ashe's morale, as had his meeting with Nelson Mandela a week earlier. But the high point of the summer came on August 30, when the professional tennis community rallied behind his effort to raise funds for his new foundation, the AAFDA. Held the day before the first round of the U.S. Open, the Arthur Ashe AIDS Tennis Challenge drew a huge crowd and the participation of nine of the game's biggest stars. The outpouring of support was unprecedented, leading one reporter to marvel: "The tennis world is known by and large as a selfish, privileged world, one crammed with factions and egos. So what is happening at the Open is unthinkable: gender and nationality and politics will take a back seat to a full-fledged effort to support Ashe."

Celebrity participants included Mike Wallace of CBS and Mayor Dinkins, who read a pronouncement designating August 30 as Arthur Ashe Day in New York. Agassi and McEnroe later entertained the crowd by clowning their way through a long set, and, to Ashe's delight, the man once known as Superbrat "even staged a mock tantrum against the umpire." Several days earlier, on a more serious note, McEnroe had spoken for many of his peers in explaining why he felt passionate about Ashe's cause. "It's not something you can even think twice about when you're asked to help," he insisted. "The fact that the disease has happened to a tennis player certainly strikes home with all of us. I'm just glad someone finally organized the tennis community like this, and obviously it took someone like Arthur to do it."

Arthur was thrilled with the response to the AIDS Challenge, which raised $114,000 for the AAFDA. And that was only the beginning. During the Challenge, one man walked up and casually handed him a personal check for $25,000, and later in the week the foundation received a $30,000 check from an anonymous donor from North Carolina. Such generosity was what he had hoped to inspire, and with his encouragement, the AAFDA staff began to plan fund-raising events connected to the 1993 Wimbledon and U.S. Open tournaments. Perhaps the lofty goal of raising $5 million by the end of 1993 was realistic after all, he thought. And when virtually all of the players in the 1992 U.S. Open draw complied with the foundation's request to attach a special patch—"a red ribbon centered by a tiny yellow tennis ball"—to their tennis outfits as a symbolic show of support for Arthur and other AIDS victims, he knew he had started something important.[31]

The willingness of so many individuals to answer the call to action on AIDS issues was gratifying. Arthur's belief in active citizenship was a bedrock principle that had guided his life since the late 1960s, and before the Open was over he was able to demonstrate just how seriously he regarded calls for personal commitment to social justice. When Randall Robinson asked him to come to Washington to participate in a joint TransAfrica/NAACP protest march scheduled for September 9, he immediately said yes.

The issue at hand was one with which he had become increasingly concerned—the Bush administration's racially discriminatory treatment of Haitian refugees seeking asylum in the United States. Along with more than two thousand other protesters, Ashe marched in front of the White House to seek justice for the growing mass of Haitian "boat people" being forcibly repatriated to their native land without a hearing. In stark contrast to the warm reception accorded Cuban refugees fleeing Fidel Castro's communist regime, the dark-skinned boat people had fallen victim to the administration's harsh policy of denying refuge to individuals and families adversely affected by conditions in Haiti.

The blanket ruling that the Haitians, unlike the Cubans, were essentially economic refugees undeserving of political asylum seemed to fly in the face of the political realities of both islands. To many observers, including Ashe and the organizers of the White House protest, this differential policy smacked of racism. "The argument incensed me," Ashe wrote. "Undoubtedly, many of the people picked up were economic refugees, but many were not. According to U.S. law, all were entitled to a hearing, and this step was routinely denied them."

Arthur knew a great deal about Haiti: he had read widely and deeply about the nation's troubled past; during his college years one of his closest friends had been Jean-Edouard Baker, a light-skinned islander who would later chair the Haitian Olympic Committee; he had visited the island on several occasions; and he and Jeanne had even honeymooned there in 1977.

More recently, he had monitored the truncated career of President Jean-Bertrand Aristide, a self-styled champion of the Haitian poor whose regime had been toppled by a military coup. The Bush administration's collusion with the anti-Aristide forces was obvious, highlighted by its policy of interdiction on the high seas. All of this was too much for Arthur, who felt compelled to speak out against the administration's blatant disregard for freedom and fairness. "I was prepared to be arrested to protest this injustice," he stated bluntly.[32]

Considering his medical condition, he had no business being there; certainly no one would have blamed him if he had begged off—no one, that is, but himself. At the appointed hour on Wednesday morning, September 9, there he was standing in Lafayette Square clad in jeans, T-shirt, and straw hat. The big, bold letters on his shirt read: "Haitians Locked Out Because They're Black." He did his best to blend in with the crowd, a near impossibility for a man so famous and so revered. He didn't want to be treated as a celebrity protester; he simply wanted to make a statement about the responsibilities of democratic citizenship. While he knew his presence at the protest was largely symbolic, he hoped to set an example for others to follow. Putting yourself at risk for a good cause, he assured one reporter covering the march, "does wonders for your outlook. I am sure it released a torrent of endorphins. Marching in a protest is a liberating experience. It's cathartic. It's one of the great moments you can have in your life."

Despite the promising signs at the recent AIDS challenge, the scene in Washington repeated a traditional pattern. When he arrived at the Shiloh Baptist Church, the staging ground for the protest, he saw no other professional athletes, active or retired, black or white, among the protesters. The throng did include a handful of celebrities from other walks of life, most notably wheelchair-bound black dancer and choreographer eighty-three-year-old Katherine Dunham, a longtime resident of Haiti who had just completed a forty-seven-day hunger strike in protest of American interdiction policy. But Arthur alone represented the sports world.

Since federal law prohibited large demonstrations in close proximity to the White House, the organizers expected arrests even if the picketers remained peaceful. Following the nonviolent direct-action tradition of the 1960s, they welcomed mass arrests as a means of publicizing their cause. The District police did not disappoint them. As soon as the crowd assembled in Lafayette Park, the police ordered them to disperse. But no one moved. At first the police did nothing, but a few minutes later, following a second refusal to disperse, nearly a hundred demonstrators, including Arthur, were

arrested, handcuffed, and carted away in a convoy of paddy wagons. At the
U.S. Superior Court building in southwest Washington, each defendant was
assessed fines of $50 before being released. Arthur, despite his physical con-
dition, asked for and received no favors as he went through the same process
as everybody else. After paying his fine and calling Jeanne to assure her he
was all right, he took the late afternoon train back to New York with a sense
of personal satisfaction—but also with limited expectations that the Bush
administration would change its policies. Politics, like life, he had learned
early on, was a never-ending struggle carrying no guarantees of success.

The next night, while sitting on his couch watching the nightly news,
he felt a sharp pain in his sternum, and later in the evening, when the pain
intensified, he asked Jeanne to take him to New York Hospital. Tests soon
revealed he had suffered a mild heart attack, the second of his life. Prior to
the trip to Washington, Jeanne had worried something like this might happen if he didn't scale back his schedule. But she knew her husband was never
one to play it safe when something important was on the line.[33]

On the tennis court, he had always been prone to fits of reckless play,
going for broke with shots that sometimes defied logic or good sense. Similarly, in his life off the court, particularly in his later years, he almost always
went full out, filling every day with as much activity as he could. He did so,
not because he craved activity for its own sake, but rather because he wanted
to make a difference in the lives of others. He wanted to be a great and good
man, to live a virtuous and productive life, and to leave a legacy of independent vision and moral purpose that transcended the world of sports. While
tennis was the primary source of his celebrity, the pursuit of greatness on a
much larger stage was the force that ultimately propelled his life.

That is why he embraced a dizzying array of roles beyond his career
as a tennis star. Social justice and civil rights activist, athletic administrator, coach, author, historian, teacher, lecturer, philanthropist, entrepreneur,
diplomat, and public intellectual—he was all of these things and more.
Even near the end of his life, when his body was ravaged with AIDS, he still
wanted to do it all. That is why he felt he had to be there at Lafayette Park
to make yet another gesture on behalf of simple justice and human rights.

While nearly everyone was justifiably concerned about this latest physical setback, both Arthur and his cardiologist tried to downplay the gravity
of the situation. "He really isn't very sick," Dr. Stephen Scheidt told reporters, adding that the recent heart attack had nothing to do with his patient's
struggle with AIDS. The doctor foresaw an early release from the hospital
and announced Arthur was already "on the telephone conducting his affairs

as usual," albeit from a hospital bed. Betraying a wry smile, he described his indefatigable patient as metaphorically "charging the net."[34]

Released from the hospital three days later, Arthur resumed his busy schedule. On the evening after his morning release, he was sitting at the desk in his home office when the phone rang. Despite the demands of his presidential campaign, Bill Clinton had taken time to wish Arthur well and "to express the hope" they would meet in person in the near future. This unexpected gesture renewed the spirit of a man who had every reason to be discouraged. "As I sat in my office after hanging up," he recalled several weeks later, "I thought of him and Hillary Rodham Clinton and the grueling, sometimes humiliating, and still unfinished campaign, they were pursuing simply to have his message heard and believed and his integrity accepted, and I was encouraged to carry on my own campaign. I decided to strike nothing from my schedule but to plunge ahead."

During the next ten days, he demonstrated both his energy level and continuing commitment to public service. As he recounted in *Days of Grace*, the second half of September was one of the busiest periods of his life: "Four days later [after the Clinton phone call] I flew to Atlanta to speak to a gathering of officials of community health centers on 'Health Concerns of the Uninsured.' Just after my return, I engaged a lively call-in audience on WLIB, the New York radio station. I then flew to Gainesville for a lecture at the University of Florida. The next day I was in Hartford, Connecticut for an Aetna board meeting, then dined on September 24 at a fund-raiser in Manhattan for Governor Clinton, where I had the opportunity to meet and talk with him. The next day I returned to Hartford by company helicopter for another Aetna meeting, then I flew to Duquesne University in Pittsburgh to give a speech. The last day of September found me in Richmond, discussing with the mayor of the city a project dear to my heart—an African American Sports Hall of Fame to be located there. Then I returned to New York to attend a special showing of the Matisse exhibition of the Museum of Modern Art before heading out that evening to Baltimore, where I was to speak the following day."[35]

October brought no letup in his schedule. After joining the Olympic swimming champion Donna de Varona as the co-master of ceremonies for a fund-raising dinner for the Women's Sports Foundation, an event held in midtown Manhattan, he and Jeanne flew to Ponte Vedra Beach, Florida, to attend a gala celebrating the twentieth anniversary of the ATP. Proud of his leadership role during the early years of the ATP, he was thrilled to take part in a reunion that probably would be his last opportunity to see many of his fellow pioneers. The list of attendees was a virtual who's-who of ATP veterans—Laver, Emerson, Rosewall, Stolle, Drysdale, Borg, Nastase, Smith, Pasarell, and Lutz, among others. But throughout much of the evening Arthur was the center of attention. "I could not help notice, after a while," he recalled, "that I was obviously one of the special attractions of the hour, that my old tennis comrades were seeking me out and spending time with me. I seldom sat down without a small group gathering around my chair."

Everyone knew, of course, that this might well be their last chance to spend time with a man they loved and admired, a suspicion that tinged the reunion with bittersweet moments. But it did not stop Arthur and his buddies from indulging in the boys club ritual of poking fun at each other. After thanking his friends for allowing him to use the gala as an AAFDA fund-raiser—the gathering raised $50,000—and after receiving a standing ovation from the crowd, he could not resist teasing his old rival Nastase, commenting that he had never seen him "participate in a standing ovation on behalf of anyone except Nastase." The Romanian just smiled and waved, but Drysdale later extracted a measure of good-natured revenge by roasting Arthur's golf game. "Arthur could practice his swing in a telephone booth," Drysdale offered with a grin, "and even with that short of a swing, I've never in my life seen anyone lose more golf balls." [36]

While nothing could quite match the camaraderie of the ATP reunion, Ashe seemed to value and enjoy all of his public appearances during the closing months of 1992. In early November, he received the Helen Hayes MacArthur Award, an honor recently established by a New York hospital foundation to recognize "the achievements of individuals who help and inspire other people to live their lives to their fullest potential." Ashe took great pride in receiving the Hayes award, in part because the presentation ceremony coincided with Magic Johnson's reluctant decision to abandon his effort to rejoin the NBA as an active player. Some players, it turned out, were not comfortable having him on the court. During the ATP reunion, Ashe had acknowledged Johnson's activism as a model "paradigm of living with AIDS," so the Hayes Hospital Foundation's recognition of his own attempt to live a fruitful life free of despair was welcome.

In mid-November, Arthur traveled to Richmond to help Governor Wilder preside over the annual banquet of the Virginia Heroes sixth-grade mentoring program, an organization he had helped found two years earlier. From there he flew to Boston to receive the AIDS Leadership Award from the Harvard AIDS Institute. A month earlier, he had become a member of the institute's international Advisory Council, in recognition of his force-ful advocacy of confronting the AIDS crisis on a global scale. In the seven months since his original AIDS announcement, he had emerged as one of the nation's most knowledgeable and articulate commentators on the dis-ease, and the institute wanted to acknowledge his contributions.

Senator Edward Kennedy said as much in his keynote address at the awards ceremony in Cambridge. Privacy issues and other personal concerns had delayed Arthur's engagement in the public fight against AIDS, but once his engagement began, Kennedy assured the audience, the level of his com-mitment was virtually unparalleled. As if to prove the point, the Common-wealth Fund, a private foundation devoted to improving access to health care around the world, named Arthur to its board of directors the following week.[37]

December began with notification that two leading universities—Yale and New York University—planned to honor him with honorary doctoral degrees. But far more important in his view was the World AIDS Day ad-dress to the United Nations General Assembly that he delivered on Decem-ber 1. Invited to speak by Secretary-General Boutros Boutros-Ghali, Arthur made the most of his opportunity to speak his mind on AIDS. "I considered that speech one of the most significant of my life, perhaps even the most significant," he wrote a few weeks later. Most of the speech was a passion-ate plea for greatly enhanced government action against a disease that had precipitated a worldwide crisis. Unfortunately, he pointed out, "It has been the habit of humankind to wait until the eleventh hour to spiritually commit ourselves to those problems which we knew all along to be of the greatest ur-gency." In his view, AIDS was one of those problems, and the situation was complicated by a woefully unequal distribution of medical resources: while developing countries would account for an estimated 80 percent of future AIDS cases, the current proportion of funds spent on AIDS patients in those countries was only 6 percent of worldwide expenditures.

He insisted this imbalance was an intolerable disgrace—a needless risk that represented a danger to the entire world. "All of us world citizens—Eastern and Western, developed and developing, regardless of ethnicity, national, or geographic origin—must see AIDS as *our* problem," he main-tained. AIDS is a formidable enemy, he acknowledged, but "we must suc-ceed or our children and grandchildren will one day rightfully ask us why in the face of such a calamity we did not give our best efforts. What shall we tell them . . . if we don't measure up? How shall I answer my six-year-old daughter and what do we say to the estimated ten million AIDS orphans by the year 2000?"[38]

He knew expanding the fight on a global scale would take time—and that it was unlikely he would be around to see it. In the meantime, his strategy was to focus on small but significant initiatives that might serve as models for progress elsewhere. Two days after delivering the U.N. speech, he appeared at the State University of New York Health Science Center in Brooklyn to announce the establishment of the Arthur Ashe Institute for Urban Health (AAIUH). Several months earlier, he had toured the Health Science Center with the Reverend Paul Smith, a former student of Howard Thurman's who served on the board of the Thurman Trust. Ashe had met Smith through Jeff Rogers in the late 1980s, and the Brooklyn minister had become his trusted friend and spiritual counselor since the discovery of his AIDS affliction.

Through his affiliation with the Health Science Center, Smith familiarized Ashe with the center's innovative approaches to medical care in an inner-city setting. In particular, their tour of a ward for children suffering with AIDS left Ashe in tears but also with renewed determination to do something concrete to help the youngest and most vulnerable of those stricken with the disease. Perhaps the work of the Arthur Ashe Institute in Brooklyn would inspire similar efforts in other cities. With this multiplier effect in mind, he also began to lay the financial foundation for the establishment of a chair in pediatric AIDS research at the renowned St. Jude's Hospital in Memphis. Everyone had to step up before it was too late, he told his friends and anyone else who would listen.[39]

Ashe refused to view his fate in tragic terms. "You have to stop thinking of yourself as a victim and become a messenger," he told a reporter in August; and that is exactly what he accomplished during the ensuing months. As Robert Lipsyte observed in early December, "it's hard enough to fight a lethal disease without trying to satisfy people who want to build role models." But Ashe was more than up to the task. According to a reporter for *Tennis*, instead of fading from view and losing public favor after his AIDS announcement, he became larger than life as his "influence and power . . . increased geometrically."

Being honored for surpassing all reasonable expectations of a role model was not something Ashe sought. But he recognized that each awards ceremony and its accompanying publicity gave him an added opportunity to spread his message. At the annual banquet of the American Sportcasters Association, held in Manhattan on December 5, he received the Sports Legend Award as several hundred sports industry luminaries looked on. The association had traditionally dedicated its fund-raising activities to elementary school antidrug programs, but Ashe urged the organization to broaden its efforts to include AIDS education.[40]

Later in the week, *Sports Illustrated* announced the magazine's editors had selected Arthur Ashe to be 1992's Sportsman of the Year. Arthur had known about his selection for some time and had already granted a lengthy interview to Kenny Moore, a *Sports Illustrated* feature writer assigned to write a cover story that would appear later in December. As the first retired athlete to receive the award since its inception in 1954, he was, in his words, "literally floored" when he received word. Two tennis players—Billie Jean King in 1972 and Chris Evert in 1976—had previously received the award while still active on the tour. But Arthur was the first athlete in any sport to be honored by *Sports Illustrated* for nonathletic accomplishments.

Despite some embarrassment, he welcomed his selection as an affirmation of the value of former athletes such as Jackie Robinson, Senator Bill Bradley, and Justice Byron "Whizzer" White, individuals who had demonstrated a "lifelong commitment to political and social causes." As he told Richard Finn of *USA Today*, "They were people who after their active days as an athlete were finished decided they were not finished. They were not going to rest on their athletic laurels and decided to do what they could do in society."

By all indications, Ashe was an extremely popular choice as Sportsman of the Year, and Moore did his best to dispel the notion that the magazine was honoring him as "a good victim." "To give it to him for that reason, to somehow use the award as a eulogy while there is still time diminishes what Ashe has been," concurred Mike Lupica of the New York *Daily News*. "Here is Arthur Ashe, who could sit it all out now, who could spend his remaining time with his wife and daughter and let others try to make everything right, still out there. . . . He goes from one podium to another, one city to another. He fights. He fights AIDS and racism and poverty."

Bernie Miklasz, writing in the *St. Louis Post-Dispatch*, agreed: "This wasn't a gesture of sympathy from the magazine but the recognition of a lifetime of achievement." Among the hundreds of like-minded endorsements, perhaps the most emphatic came from Mike Celizic of the Bergen County *Record*, who claimed: "it's impossible to argue against Ashe receiving any award. Whatever they give him isn't enough for what he's given—and continues to give—us."

This outpouring of affection and respect touched Arthur deeply. Appearances on ABC's *Good Morning America* and *NBC Nightly News* allowed him to express his thanks to *Sports Illustrated*, the press, and the public at large for lavishing him with praise that he wasn't sure he deserved. But the best way to repay these kindnesses, in his view, was to carry on with his public life for as long as he could. At this point, there was no indication his medical condition would worsen anytime soon, so he continued to make plans for activities that would take place well into the next year. Despite the inevitable problems facing him down the road, he felt strong and confident. "As Christmas drew near," he recalled, "I had every reason to be happy."[41]

Arthur knew this situation could not last indefinitely, but the jolt that shattered his hopes came much sooner than he expected. On December 21, he helped Jeanne coordinate the celebration of Camera's sixth birthday. It was a joyous occasion, a family milestone that he decided to capture on videotape. He assumed the role of videographer, a task that unexpectedly tested his strength and endurance. "Walking through the streets lugging the videocamera proved more onerous than I had thought," he confessed, adding: "I was left feeling weak and tired, so that I did little for the next two days."

The realization his fatigue had little to do with carrying a heavy camera came on Christmas Eve, when he braved the cold to take a walk around his Upper East Side neighborhood. "I was startled by how freezing cold the air was," he remembered. "I walked for about twenty minutes, but after five minutes I began to regret having come out at all. I was frozen to the bone and gasping for air." The next day—as he, Jeanne, and Camera celebrated the Christmas morning ritual of opening presents—he remained concerned about his breathing. Not wanting to spoil the day, he kept his fears to himself as Camera tore open her brightly colored packages and Jeanne delighted in the Hasselblad camera he had picked out for her. But in the late afternoon, when it was time to resume a cherished family tradition of taking toys to needy families, he had to beg off.

"When I was a boy, on Christmas, my father always took me late in the day to visit families who were less fortunate than we were," he explained. "We brought food and toys—and Daddy always insisted that we give away not simply old toys but one or two of the new toys we had just received." Continuing this generous tradition with Camera meant a great deal to him, and for the preceding three Christmases he had taken her to Harlem hospital wards to distribute toys. But on what he suspected would be his last Christmas, he just couldn't manage it. While he felt terrible about skipping what he regarded as "the most important ritual of the day," he had to face the fact that he simply "was not well enough" to risk going out into the cold.[42]

His best hope, at this point, was to recover his strength in Florida, where

he was scheduled to close out the year. The day after Christmas, the Ashes
flew to Miami for a week of golf and relaxation interrupted only by a series
of tennis clinics at Doral. The weather was ideal, and Jeanne's parents and
brother Claude joined them to help ring in the New Year. For the first few
days, Arthur seemed to be on the road to recovery, but this trend didn't last.
While playing one of his last golf games of the year in a foursome that included his father-in-law, he noticed his breathing had become strained and
irregular. He suddenly felt very tired even though he was "riding comfortably from tee to green in a golf cart." Even more alarming, he soon began
to cough. As he recalled, "the cough persisted," and by the time he reached
the seventh green he was on the verge of panic: "As I waited to putt, I took
out my cellular telephone and called my main AIDS physician, Dr. Henry
Murray, in New York. He advised me to see a doctor as soon as possible."

Thus began a trying week of uncertainty and worrisome medical exam-
inations. A few hours after the call, he was at the office of Dr. Barry Baker,
an AIDS specialist, who immediately ordered a chest X-ray. When the X-ray
proved inconclusive, Ashe made an appointment with Dr. Michael Collins
at Miami Baptist Hospital. Fourteen years earlier, Collins had been one of
the New York cardiologists who treated his heart disease. At this point, Arthur doubted his shortness of breath had anything to do with AIDS, and he
hoped Collins would confirm that his current problem could be traced to
a partial blockage of the arteries leading to the heart. Back in September,
following his heart attack, tests had revealed a blockage that would have to
be addressed sooner or later, probably via an angioplasty. So he assumed his
current problem could be alleviated in that manner.

An echocardiogram soon proved otherwise, however. The problem did not
reside in his heart but rather in his lungs, though it would take additional tests
to determine the exact source of his shortness of breath and persistent cough.
Relieved that the doctors at Miami Baptist did not seem especially alarmed by
his condition—not enough, at least, to admit him to the hospital—he spent the
afternoon playing golf with Butch Buchholz and two other friends. Though
still short of breath, he began to think that perhaps he was just suffering from
an ordinary cold. That evening he and Jeanne had a great time at Joe's Stone
Crab in Miami Beach, one of their favorite South Florida eateries, and by the
time he went to bed he felt "pretty fine," as he later put it.

The next day, however, brought him back to a sobering reality. It was
New Year's Eve and the closing day of his Doral tennis clinic. He managed
to finish the clinic without incident, but during an afternoon golf game he
found it difficult to walk more than a few steps from his golf cart. By the end

of the round, it was clear "that in addition to angina discomfort, the mere act of drawing air into my lungs was causing me some pain." Though alarmed, he did his best to keep up with the family's New Year's Eve festivities— dinner with Jeanne's parents, her brother Claude and his wife, and a few friends, followed by a small house party at Claude's home. But long before midnight his labored breathing prompted Jeanne to call an end to the day. Fearing Arthur's condition was worsening, she convinced him it would be advisable to shorten their stay in Florida and return to New York.

At first, Arthur thought she was being too cautious, but at five the next morning he bolted up sweating profusely with a high fever. Later in the morning, he called Dr. Murray, who advised him to see a doctor in Miami before flying home. After a dose of Tylenol brought his fever down, he and Jeanne decided to take the first available flight to New York. Several hours later, he underwent an examination at New York Hospital, where Murray made a tentative diagnosis that he was suffering from an unusual form of pneumonia. Prescribing the antibiotic azithromycin, he allowed Arthur to go home for the weekend. But over the next two days the powerful drug had little effect, as his fever spiked and his coughing grew worse.

On Monday, he returned to the hospital to see Dr. Thomas King, a pulmonary specialist, who immediately ordered a bronchoscopy. This unpleasant diagnostic procedure involved pushing a thick tube with a small video camera into the lungs through a nostril. After a half hour of monitoring the camera, Dr. King concluded his diagnosis. Arthur had all the signs of suffering from *Pneumocystis carinii* pneumonia, or PCP. The presence of PCP, a deadly disease rarely seen in patients without AIDS, was a clear indication Arthur's luck had run out. "Thus far," he explained in *Days of Grace*, "aside from the toxoplasmosis that uncovered the fact that I have AIDS, I had avoided every one of the opportunistic diseases that, in combination with the presence of HIV in the body, define the condition known as AIDS. Now I had one of the most feared." [43]

While the general prognosis was bleak, Dr. Murray reassured Arthur he would survive the current bout of PCP. The fever, chills, shivering, and coughing would continue for a time until his condition could be stabilized with a combination of Tylenol and pentamidine. While not in immediate danger of dying, he would have to remain in the hospital. A few days later, he moved to a long-term private room on the sixteenth floor. Named for the Greek shipping tycoon Stavros Niarchos, the luxurious room had once housed John F. Kennedy, a fact Arthur loved to recite when visitors came to call.

Other than Jeanne's multiple visits each day, there were a limited number of visits to his room. He welcomed members of his extended family, as well as several friends, notably Donald Dell, Frank Deford, Eddie Mandeville, and Andrew Young. Camera also visited him, but only twice. Arthur's stated rationale for keeping her away was the desire to sustain her normal daily schedule. But one suspects he also worried about the emotional impact of repeated visits. As much as he wanted to spend time with her, he did not want her to remember him as an invalid.

A few friends such as Stan Smith, Chris Beck, and Randall Robinson received calls from his hospital room phone, but at Jeanne's suggestion, he left his cell phone at home, thus limiting the drain on his energy. While the calls he did make were mostly personal in nature, he also used them to maintain some connection with his public life. During the call to Robinson, for example, he lobbied for more activism on behalf of Haitian refugees. It was imperative, he told his old friend, "to press the initiative we had won with President Clinton's election," and for "the African American community . . . to extend its arms in welcome to the refugees." Robinson, who agreed with everything Arthur said, could only marvel at his friend's tenacity—fighting the good fight even as his life slipped away.

Arthur and Jeanne were able to keep his grave condition "out of the news," thanks to the discretion of the journalists and friends who knew but did not disclose what was transpiring at New York Hospital. All through January and early February, he continued to receive invitations to various public events, including Clinton's inauguration on January 20. But he begged off as graciously as he could without any reference to his hospitalization. Most of his waking hours were spent reading or listening to music, and each day he devoted as much time to the *Days of Grace* manuscript as his energy level would tolerate. Back in December, he had told Kenny Moore of *Sports Illustrated* that he believed in living a full life, that the best course was to "pound away as hard as you can at what you care about until it's over." And that is what he did within the limits his failing body imposed.[44]

In mid-January, he felt a bit stronger, and his doctors gave him the good news that he was well enough to be released from the hospital. Returning home where he could have the semblance of a normal family life boosted his spirits. For the time being, at least, his cough had subsided and his breathing was less labored. He even began to think ahead, anticipating things he wanted to do and projects he wanted to complete. One event he looked forward to was a father-daughter Valentine's "red dress" dance at the Sleepy Hollow Country Club scheduled for Saturday, February 13. While he had no way of knowing how long he would live, the recent lull in his struggle with PCP suggested he would almost certainly survive long enough to experience the joy of accompanying Camera to the dance.[45]

A second project that drew his interest in January was a proposed Arthur Ashe statue to be placed in front of the proposed African American Sports Hall of Fame. At this point there was no guarantee that the Hall of Fame would be built in the forseeable future, and Arthur doubted he would live long enough to witness its completion. But the idea of erecting a statue of his likeness appealed to him, especially if he could have an influence on its design. In a limited but significant way, he reasoned, the statue might enhance a positive legacy in his hometown. The imagery had to be just right, however—a representation of his ideals, something that would communicate his faith in education, equality, and active citizenship.

The proposal to erect an Ashe statue originated with Paul DiPasquale, a Richmond sculptor known for his marble and stone representations of Native American figures. A chance meeting with Ashe during a tennis workshop in April 1992 led DiPasquale to discuss the statue idea with Clarence Townes, a Richmond economic development official spearheading the city's effort to find a site and funding for the Hall of Fame. One of DiPasquale's Native American sculptures had already been installed near the city's new minor league baseball stadium adjacent to the Arthur Ashe Center, and a second piece of public art—a large bronze statue of "The Headman," a figure commemorating the African American role in constructing the city's canal system—was nearing completion. Through Townes, the sculptor provided city officials with a letter urging the addition of an Ashe statue to the Hall of Fame plan.

After Ashe saw the letter, he called DiPasquale on January 21 to express his approval and to discuss the specifics of the statue's design. Earlier in the month, the sculptor had sent Ashe a package that included a letter and photographs showing examples of his work. "I had asked him in my letter what he wanted to portray, what sort of message did he want to send," DiPasquale recalled. "He had this shopping list of ideas. He wanted children, he wanted himself but not to be the center of attention; he wanted to share the podium with the children. He wanted books . . . 'to portray that knowledge is power.' And he wanted to be in his warm-up suit, in his tennis shoes, and he said 'I want to be as I am today.' . . . And as a closing, almost an aside, he said 'Oh, and I suppose a tennis racquet should be in there somewhere.'"

After assuring Ashe he would abide by his wishes, DiPasquale requested a few items to help him produce an accurate representation of reality: "I asked him to send me photos, not posed, but informal, candid shots. Pictures of how he held himself, walked, stood." Knowing Ashe's reputation for efficient attention to detail, the sculptor expected to receive the photos within a week. But two weeks later he was still waiting for them to arrive at his Richmond studio.

Scheduled to visit New York in mid-February, he called Arthur on Friday the 5th to see if they could meet in person, but no one answered the phone. On Saturday, he called a second time, but once again there was no response. Only when he read the Sunday morning headlines did he understand why Arthur had not answered. Readmitted to the hospital on Friday morning, Arthur was put on a mechanical ventilator that kept him alive but also made it impossible for him to speak. As resourceful as ever, he found another way to communicate by writing notes on a tiny pad of paper. Most were to Jeanne, but a few were more public in nature, including a message to President Clinton urging the appointment of a civil rights–minded attorney general. Watching her dying husband as he struggled to scratch out a few meaningful words, Jeanne could only nod her head in love and admiration. His condition had improved slightly during the morning, and he refused to give up. Only on Saturday, February 6, his second day in the hospital, did he begin to slip in and out of consciousness. At 3:13 that afternoon he took his last breath.

When the package of photos finally arrived in Richmond the following Wednesday, the day of Arthur's funeral, DiPasquale wept uncontrollably for the man who had not forgotten him after all. Two weeks later, when the sculptor contacted Jeanne to see if she wanted to proceed with the statue project, she revealed that getting the photos ready to mail "was the last thing he did before going to the hospital." Even at the end of Arthur's life, when the mere act of breathing was a major struggle, he somehow managed to follow through with his promise. A man determined to fulfill pledges large and small, a man of uncommon integrity and responsibility—that is who he was, and it was this nobility of spirit that DiPasquale's sculpture would try to capture.[46]

SHADOW'S END

■

PAUL DIPASQUALE WAS NOT the only one caught short by Arthur Ashe's unexpected death. As Arthur's medical situation worsened during the first week of February, only a few hospital workers, close friends, and family members knew what was happening. For everyone else his passing came as a shock. Even though his AIDS diagnosis was widely recognized as a death sentence, his ability to maintain a strenuous schedule of public activities during the past ten months had given the false impression that he was in no immediate danger. Since his disclosure in April 1992, he had grown noticeably thin, but otherwise he appeared to be relatively healthy.

Those following his case closely knew he had been HIV-positive for nearly a decade, and that he had suffered from full-blown AIDS for at least half of that time. But neither the public nor the medical establishment had a clear idea of how long an AIDS patient was likely to live. Much of the nation—including a large number of politicians and physicians—was still in a state of ignorance when it came to AIDS, even though AIDS-related deaths had been a daily occurrence since the early 1980s. With the development of reliable blood testing in 1985, AIDS deaths stemming from blood transfusions declined precipitously, leaving gay men and intravenous drug users as the most identifiable victims of the disease. Unlike the other celebrities who died of AIDS during the first decade of the pandemic—notably the actor Rock Hudson, the dancer Rudolf Nureyev, the pianist Liberace, and the artist Robert Mapplethorpe—Ashe, as a drug-free heterosexual, seemed anomalous.[1]

On Sunday, February 7, the day after Arthur's death, Jeanne issued a press release that emphasized the special quality of his life, making only brief mention of the cause and manner of his death. "Arthur was the ultimate competitor in tennis and in life," she proclaimed. "He fought hard on the last days of his life and even though he lost his battle, as in his tennis days, it was always how he played the game. He will be greatly missed by Camera and me and our entire family." The release also contained a moving tribute from Donald Dell. "Arthur was so special because of his quiet courage and selflessness, which made a lasting impact on those he touched," declared his friend of thirty years. "Arthur set an example and standard of personal conduct for all of us who loved him to try and emulate in our lives. The world will never experience another sportsman like Arthur Ashe." In closing, the family requested that individuals interested in paying respect to the deceased should make contributions to the Arthur Ashe Foundation for the Defeat of AIDS in lieu of sending flowers.[2]

When the press reports of Arthur's death ran that morning—most appearing on the front pages of newspapers all over the United States and beyond—the coverage was both massive and reverential, an outpouring more befitting a head of state than a mere sports hero. *The New York Times* led the way with two stories on Sunday and five more the next day. The lead piece in the *Times*, titled "Ashe, a Champion in Sport and Life," reported that when the news of his death reached Madison Square Garden on Saturday night, just before the start of a heavyweight fight between Riddick Bowe and Michael Dokes, the stunned crowd stood in silence as a bell rang ten times in Arthur's honor. Three thousand miles to the west, at a tennis tournament in San Francisco, another crowd stood for an extended moment of silence. "I have always admired his courage, respected his integrity and have been impressed by all he has done for so many," tournament director Barry MacKay declared, fighting back tears. "Arthur's passing represents a tremendous loss for tennis and the world beyond."[3]

Bill Rhoden, a prominent African American sportswriter for the *Times*, offered a tribute titled "Arthur Ashe: A Hero in Word and Deed." The two men had scheduled a lunch for the following week, Rhoden reported, but now he would have to go on without the benefit of a final meeting. "He has left a tremendous void," Rhoden wrote, "but also has issued a tremendous challenge to those who feel—like he felt—that sports is merely a point of departure, that sports can be more, must be more than what it is. That is

Arthur Ashe's legacy. And I'll think of that every time I remember that lunch date we will never keep."[4]

Another friend who missed the chance to say goodbye was David Dinkins, who was on vacation in Puerto Rico. "Words cannot suffice to capture a career as glorious, a life so fully lived or a commitment to justice as firm and as fair as his," Dinkins told the *Times* by phone. "From his very early youth, Arthur Ashe has always kept his eye on the ball, not just on the tennis court, but in every single aspect of his life. He celebrated the many championships he won, the many records he set. But day in and day out, always he wondered about and worried for those less fortunate than he." Governor Douglas Wilder, who had known Arthur even longer than Mayor Dinkins, voiced a similar tribute: "Not only have I lost a dear friend, but America has lost a moral giant. His leadership . . . was totally committed to improving the lives of those yet to enjoy the full fruition of rights and opportunities in this country."

Governor Wilder made sure Richmond and the rest of Virginia paid due respect to its fallen favorite son. Following an autopsy on Monday, Arthur's body was transported to Richmond to lie in state at the Virginia Executive Mansion, the stately yellow brick home with massive columns that stands behind the commonwealth's capitol. If anyone objected to this special public tribute, no one said so out loud. But nearly everyone was aware he or she was witnessing a scene unimaginable in an earlier, less tolerant era. The last Virginian to be so honored was General Stonewall Jackson in 1863. Yet here was a governor and a local hero—both black and both born and raised under the shadow of Jim Crow—sharing a sacred space in a house built by slaves in 1813, a house symbolizing the political and racial heritage of the Old South.

On that Tuesday evening the line of mourners stretched along five blocks, and some waited as long as four hours for their turn to pass by the open mahogany casket resting on a burgundy-draped bier. Out on the lawn the governor held an impromptu news conference, assuring reporters the massive turnout marked the beginning of an enviable and unprecedented legacy. With Camera by her side, Jeanne roamed the grounds and the first floor of the mansion, sometimes snapping photos of the crowd but mostly visiting with friends and family members. By nine o'clock, when the capitol police closed the door leading to the viewing room, more than five thousand people had walked by the casket to say goodbye, many pausing for "a few reflective moments," as Ira Berkow of *The New York Times* observed. Moved by the seemingly endless line of mourners, black and white, Berkow noted the irony that it had taken Arthur "49 years to travel the two miles from where he grew up on Sledd Street here to the Governor of Virginia's Executive Mansion."[5]

The next morning the memorialization moved to more familiar ground—to the Arthur Ashe Center, North Richmond's cavernous gymnasium. The memorial service was scheduled to begin at one o'clock, but some members of the crowd were already lined up in front of the entrance at 7 a.m. By the time the service began with a ten-minute-long version of "When the Saints Go Marching In"—a choral tribute accompanying a lengthy procession of Arthur's relatives—there were more than six thousand people in the seats. According to one estimate, more than 90 percent of the crowd was African American, but the nearly six hundred whites in attendance were noteworthy, representing the largest white turnout at a predominantly black gathering in Virginia history.

For the most part, the pageantry and spirit of the service transcended race as tearful mourners—black and white—looked down on the open casket "topped with two cotton doves and 275 red roses." The Reverend Wallace Cook of Ebenezer Baptist Church set the tone by proclaiming, "We've gathered to celebrate the life of a great humanitarian who has come home." Readings from the works of Howard Thurman and several gospel selections followed, punctuating a sequence of more than a dozen speakers who eulogized the departed as a hero among heroes. Jesse Jackson reminded the crowd that Arthur was a profoundly influential force, a man who "knocked down walls and built bridges." "Most athletes limit themselves to achievements and contributions within the lines," he declared, "but Arthur found greatness beyond the lines," as "he turned anger into energy and stumbling blocks into steppingstones." David Dinkins, after insisting "Arthur Ashe was just plain better than most of us," declared: "If ever there was a man who proved civility is not a weakness, it was Arthur." Wiping tears from his eyes, he acknowledged: "Words cannot suffice to capture a career as glorious, a life so fully lived, or a commitment to justice as firm and fair as his." In equally emotional terms, Governor Wilder foresaw a powerful legacy, noting "loving kindness survives even death."

Throughout the three-hour service, the themes of civil rights and racial justice were in the air. Two of the eulogizers, Richmond's mayor, Walter Kenney, and Andrew Young, made direct and forceful reference to the freedom struggle that had animated Arthur's life. After pointing out that Richmond's white establishment had not always embraced the city's most famous black citizen, Kenney praised Arthur's forgiving and generous spirit:

"Instead of writing off Richmond for good, he came back to give, to share, to encourage the young people of this city." Young was even more forthright, describing his old friend as a "race man" and "a black man in a white game" who "had to deal with the race question every day," gracefully shouldering "the burden of race" and somehow finding a way to "wear it as a cloak of dignity."

At the close of the service, Dell, Yannick Noah, Sherry Snyder, and five other pallbearers carried the casket to a hearse that moments later led a cortege to the burial site at Woodland Cemetery, where Arthur was to be interred alongside his mother. All along the three-mile route to the cemetery, individuals and families stood in tribute, some waving or calling out to the passing cortege, and others standing in reverent silence. The burial ceremony that followed was semiprivate, limited to family members, close friends, and a few dignitaries, including Senators Bill Bradley and Chuck Robb and Secretary of Commerce Ron Brown, who was representing President Clinton.

During the past three days, a large crew of city employees had worked feverishly to clean up the cemetery, which had fallen into disrepair, a tangible metaphor for the belated embrace of a native son who had fled the city in discouragement three decades earlier. But no one seemed to pay much attention to the recently manicured grounds and gravesites. The focus was on Arthur and what he had given to the world. After a round of prayers and moving tributes, the service closed with a rousing rendition of the civil rights anthem "We Shall Overcome." Swaying in the twilight with arms interlocked, those closest to Arthur gave him a salutation befitting a man of hope and glory.[6]

Two days later, many of those present at the burial joined more than five thousand other mourners at the Cathedral of St. John the Divine, in the Morningside Heights section of Manhattan. The first athlete to be so honored, Arthur joined the ranks of the great African American artist Romare Bearden, the musical giants Dizzy Gillespie and Duke Ellington, and the noted jurist Thurgood Marshall, all of whom had been memorialized at the cathedral. The choice of venue was highly appropriate, presiding Canon Joel Gibson explained, commending Arthur's forty-nine years as "a grand life that commands a grand space."

The date of the memorial service—coincidentally the 184th anniversary of Abraham Lincoln's birth—accentuated the historic feel of the moment. The weather was stormy, with ice and snow blowing through the streets in bracing gusts. To Bill Rhoden, the mood in the hall seemed somber and sad until Dinkins admonished the crowd, declaring: "This is a memorial tribute, not a wake, so feel free to come alive."

With the dark mood broken, the service, according to Rhoden, took on "the feel of an intimate gathering . . . despite the cathedral's cavernous sanctuary with its 12-story ceiling, and despite the almost eerie chill that hung in the air." This intimacy reflected the deeply personal expressions of love and respect voiced by an array of friends speaking from the cathedral's ornate raised pulpit. In contrast to the Richmond gathering, this time, Rhoden observed, "there was less focus on what Arthur Ashe meant to the world than [on] what he meant to friends. One by one the friends came up to tell stories about how Ashe . . . had touched their lives." Charlie Pasarell, Stan Smith, Billie Jean King, Bill Bradley, and several others gave testament to Arthur's rare talent for deep and abiding friendship. One of the most poignant moments came when Pasarell paid tribute to his fallen friend. "No man has ever loved his friends more than Arthur loved his friends," he insisted, choking back tears. "And yes, it can be said that no man loved all humankind more than Arthur did. That gift of Love is Arthur's great virtue. So on this day, I simply want to say to my great friend, 'I love you, Arthur,'" Later in the service, Arthur's favorite niece, Luchia, Johnnie's eldest daughter, challenged the audience to follow her uncle's lead, to go "beyond platitudes and praise" in the struggle to "eradicate man-made fences."[7]

The hope and camaraderie forged during the New York memorial service would be a topic of conversation in tennis circles for months, and anyone fortunate enough to have been there sensed they had experienced something special. Neil Amdur, among many others, was hit hard by his friend's death. "I don't think Ashe realized how many people truly loved him," he wrote the day after the service. "Maybe he wondered but wasn't sure. After all, he was shy and had been away from the competitive limelight for a decade before being forced back into the public arena last April. No matter. People cared because he made everyone a part of his life. Rich. Poor. Old. Young. Black. White. Americans. Africans. South Africans. Europeans. Australians. He was as comfortable in a board room as a press room, a tennis court or a court of law, Wall Street and Main Street. Muhammad Ali, Pelé, Magic Johnson and Michael Jordan were the fiery comets in the sports galaxy, but Arthur Ashe was the guiding light."

Amdur chose his metaphor carefully, remembering Arthur had once carried the nickname "Shadow." Created in jest by his friends, this appellation nonetheless set him apart from his white peers, the young stars fortunate enough to inhabit tennis's brightest firmament. In the early years and throughout the decade of the 1960s, Arthur alone was *on* the tour without being *of* the tour, and gaining full acceptance would take years of patient effort. As Amdur noted, the heartfelt testimonials he and others witnessed at the cathedral confirmed the depth of feeling and commitment that Arthur inspired and shared. "It is not surprising that so many peers considered Ashe their 'best friend,'" he concluded. "He had a knack for putting himself in other people's shoes, without cramping that person's style." So in the end, what truly set Arthur apart was not race or color, but rather his unsurpassed ability to maintain a healthy balance between friendship and competition.

In trying to explain Arthur's unique achievement, Amdur turned to an aphorism attributed to the Romanian star Ion Tiriac: "a true champion is that person who enriches a sport by his presence and leaves the game better for having been in it." Using this standard, Amdur placed Arthur a notch or two above the best tennis players of his or any other generation. "There was no better world champion than Arthur Ashe," he observed, "because he not only enriched a sport with his presence but also left a wondrous legacy—true to all, but most important, true to himself."[8]

The prediction that Arthur would leave a "wondrous legacy" was borne out within weeks of his death. His transcendent value as a role model drew much of its strength from an improbable life story marked by barrier-breaking upward mobility, grace under pressure, unblemished ethical behavior, and an almost selfless concern for others. But as Arthur knew all too well, none of this would have mattered if he had not been excellent at his chosen craft. He first came to public attention because he could hit a tennis ball just about as well as anyone, and it was this success that gave him the opportunity to showcase his other strengths—intellectual, literary, political, and moral.

This attractive package—unprecedented in the American sports scene—lost none of its luster after his death. If anything, it took on mythic overtones as his many friends and admirers tried to adjust to a world without him. "Has any athlete, not to mention *former* athlete—ever been lionized so at his death?" Frank Deford wrote in a *Newsweek* essay in late February. "It wasn't as if Arthur was the best player ever; why, he wasn't even the best of his time. Rather, he was just a very good tennis player who had come to be recognized as an altogether exceptional human being. I think that, by the time he died, Arthur Ashe had become everybody's favorite athlete." This canonization, as Peter Bodo later pointed out, had a lot to do with Ashe's struggle with AIDS.

"Ironically, if it were not for his illness — his specific illness—Ashe probably never would have gotten the popular widespread recognition and accolades that he deserved," Bodo observed in 1995. "Not until he disclosed that he was suffering from AIDS did Ashe earn universal recognition as a 'role model.'" In his earlier life, his image had been too "oblique," too "owlish, complex, dispassionate and even remote" to engender deep attachment or affection in the public mind—even among African Africans, who "respected his achievements without embracing him wholeheartedly."[9]

In Arthur's case, a certain amount of glorification was probably inevitable, considering the tragic death that framed his saga. But his outsized legacy took on added strength from its embodiment in a seemingly endless string of posthumous honors and awards and accompanying ceremonies. "Almost every week, it seems, some organization or institution wants to celebrate the memory of Arthur Ashe by initiating a scholarship program or renaming a stadium or conferring an honorary degree," Rachel Shuster of USA Today observed in late May 1993, noting that "more than 1,000 worldwide requests, from street names to leadership awards, have arrived at ProServ offices since Ashe's death."

In May and June alone, he received numerous honors, including posthumous honorary degrees from Yale, Columbia, and NYU; John Henry "Pop" Lloyd Humanitarian Award for Service to the Youth of America (named in honor of a Negro League baseball star); the prestigious Olympic Order from the IOC; the Congressional Medal of Honor, awarded in a ceremony at Ellis Island; and the Presidential Medal of Freedom, conferred by President Clinton at a National Sports Awards ceremony held at Constitution Hall.[10]

On July 10—which would have been Arthur's fiftieth birthday—members of his family joined a large gathering of his friends to dedicate a memorial adjacent to his grave at Woodland Cemetery. Young and Wilder, among other dignitaries, were there to hear the poet Maya Angelou's tribute to "this man superb in love and logic," who, she predicted, would be remembered for "the lives grown out of his life." Later the same week, the International Tennis Hall of Fame in Newport paid special tribute to its 1985 inductee during its annual induction ceremony. Recounting his exploits on and off the court, the Hall pledged a generous donation to the AAFDA, a gift he would have appreciated even more than the kind words.[11]

The printed word also played an important role in shaping and sustaining the legacy. Feature stories by newspaper and magazine writers who admired him continued to appear during the weeks and months following his funeral, confirming his status as an unrivaled darling of the press. Journalists celebrated his virtues for a number of reasons, including the sense that he was one of them—"a man of artistry and letters" and "a journalist and social scholar," as Amdur put it.

Ashe's own writing was crucial to his continuing influence, a fact that became obvious during the first Grand Slam tournament after his death. His absence was conspicuous during the 1993 Wimbledon fortnight—the first time in twelve years he had not held forth in the HBO broadcast booth at Centre Court. But the publication of *Days of Grace* on June 23, combined with the nearly simultaneous release of a revised edition of *A Hard Road to Glory*, produced an unprecedented wave of interest in his life. *Days of Grace* soon rocketed toward the top of the best-seller list, reaching number one among nonfiction titles by mid-July and remaining among the top fifteen until October. No "tennis" book had ever gained such popularity, as tens of thousands of readers gained a new appreciation for what he had gone through—and for what he had accomplished.

In addition to recounting the milestones of a remarkable life, the book featured a number of revealing and even shocking statements about racism, suffering, and survival. One observation that stunned even some of his closest friends was his claim, voiced initially to a reporter for *People* magazine, that "AIDS isn't the heaviest burden I have had to bear." "Race is for me a more onerous burden than AIDS," he reported. "My disease is the result of biological factors over which we, thus far, have had no control. Racism, however, is entirely made by people, and therefore it hurts and inconveniences infinitely more." Continuing in this vein, he insisted that, despite all of his success and good fortune, "a pall of sadness hangs over my life and the lives of almost all African Americans because of what we as a people have experienced historically in America, and what we as individuals experience each and every day."[12]

The unblinking honesty of *Days of Grace* made it an indispensable coda to the Ashe canon. But other publications also helped to illuminate the shadows of his complicated life. One such piece was Pasarell's moving tribute to his dear friend, published as "Unforgettable Arthur Ashe" in the September 1993 issue of *Reader's Digest*. "A life ends, but values endure," he maintained, and Arthur's values were the kind worth remembering and following. "Arthur Ashe was the most courageous man I ever knew," he wrote, "holding himself and others to the highest standards. . . . Ours was a friendship based on more than tennis. If I marveled as he scaled the heights of professional sports, what impressed me more was how he used dignity and restraint as weapons against opponents, whether childish tennis players or the cruel purveyors of racism. With his poker-faced courage, he stared down social injustice, three heart attacks and AIDS, and became a conscience for a nation."[13]

A literary tribute of a different kind appeared on December 1—World AIDS Day—in the form of *Daddy and Me*, an extended photo essay featuring Jeanne's family photographs. Conceived in 1992 with the expectation that Arthur would live long enough to see it in print, *Daddy and Me* was, in Jeanne's words, "a family project from the beginning." As she explained: "We were sitting at the dinner table when Camera was about 5, talking about the best way to describe to her friends what it is like to live with someone who is ill. We decided to explain it in her words and use the photographs I had been taking of their relationship to illustrate to kids that you can love someone with an illness, that you can live with them and have a full happy life." The result was a touching reminder of an innocent child shielded by an indomitable and generous spirit cloaked in fatherhood. Despite the inevitable tears of loss and remembrance, the book helped Jeanne and Camera to get on with their lives.[14]

Twelve years later, on the eve of the 2005 U.S. Open, the U.S. Postal Service issued an Arthur Ashe postage stamp bearing his likeness. But of all the tributes to Arthur's memory, the most exotic was undoubtedly the tattoo that appeared on the left biceps of the former heavyweight boxing champion Mike Tyson in late 1993. As Robert Lipsyte reported, "Arthur Ashe's likeness gazes somberly at us from books, awards, solicitations and now from Mike Tyson's arm." Serving a six-year prison sentence for rape, Tyson vowed to earn an early release by channeling the virtues of a man he had come to admire. Bemused, Lipsyte observed: "what could be a greater symbol of rehabilitation for a parole board hearing than Ashe's face and the title of his book, 'Days of Grace,' tattooed on a convicted rapist's biceps?" What Arthur would have made of this gesture is anyone's guess, but it seems likely he would have found some way to give the troubled ex-champion the benefit of the doubt.[15]

In 1994, Arthur's public profile received another boost when his longtime employer HBO produced a stirring documentary on his life. Titled *Arthur Ashe: Citizen of the World*, the ninety-minute telefilm featured narration written by Deford and dozens of interviews with a range of people representing all aspects of Ashe's life. Interviews with Arthur himself provided some of the film's best footage, especially when he talked about his struggle with AIDS. Produced under the aegis of Seth Abraham, the HBO Sports president who had hired Arthur as a broadcaster in the early 1980s and who later became one of his most trusted friends, *Citizen of the World* captured the essential elements that made his life so meaningful: the improbability of his rise to stardom, the nobility with which he conducted himself, and the courage displayed as he approached the end of his life.[16]

The real key to sustaining Arthur's legacy was institutional longevity. If his life were to have a lasting influence, at least some of the institutions that he helped to create and foster would have to survive. The continuing strength of the National Junior Tennis League (NJTL), the Association of Tennis Professionals (ATP), the Safe Passage Foundation (SPF), and the Arthur Ashe Foundation for the Defeat of AIDS (AAFDA), among other Ashe-related organizations, would be the best index of his continuing presence in American life.

Keeping all or even part of this philanthropic and organizational empire going was an enormous task, and much of the burden fell, at least initially, on Jeanne's shoulders. Fortunately, she proved to be a highly effective steward of her late husband's social capital. A beloved figure in her own right, she was also able to draw upon the skills of a number of talented and committed individuals willing to do almost anything for her. This was especially true of the AIDS- and health-related initiatives—the AAFDA, the Arthur Ashe Institute for Urban Health, and the Arthur Ashe Student Health and Wellness Center established at UCLA in 1995—which required personalized fund-raising efforts. Jeanne and her many friends were crucial, especially after she established the Arthur Ashe Learning Center (AALC) in 2007. Essentially a clearinghouse for all things Arthur Ashe, the AALC maintains both the website www.arthurashe.org and a popular booth open during the U.S. Open. Among other initiatives, the AALC distributed educational materials inspired by Arthur's writings and sponsored exhibitions featuring personal and historic photographs.[17]

Many of the organizations associated with Arthur—notably the ATP, TransAfrica, and the NJTL—were well established and on a strong footing, administratively and financially. And each in its own way continued to identify with Arthur's professed ideals. Even the ATP, which represents a diverse clientele of professional tennis players, has presented an annual Arthur Ashe Humanitarian Award since 1983. The NJTL, now under the umbrella of the USTA, still features Ashe in its promotional and training materials, a continuing connection that has helped to sustain a network of more than 350 local programs serving nearly 230,000 mostly inner-city youngsters.

The Safe Passage Foundation also survived Arthur's death, expanding to ten cities after moving its headquarters from Newark to Los Angeles in

1995. And so did several other institutional manifestations of his outreach to inner-city communities, notably his minority recruitment activities at Aetna, which honors his legacy with an annual Arthur Ashe Voice of Conscience Award; the Arthur Ashe Children's Program, established in 1992 as an extension of Willis Thomas's Washington Tennis and Education Foundation; and the Virginia Heroes sixth-grade mentoring program founded by Arthur and Wilder in 1990. Encompassing two of Arthur's basic beliefs—the power of forgiveness and the importance of nurturing children—Virginia Heroes remains worthy of its name twenty-eight years after its founding, an enduring symbol of his reconciliation with the hometown that had once rejected him.[18]

Several of Arthur's lesser-known initiatives did not fare so well, however. The Black Tennis Foundation of South Africa (BTF), and the Black Tennis and Sports Foundation (BTSF) proved unsustainable and became defunct soon after his death. The BTF had been floundering since the mid-1980s, when co-founder Owen Williams moved from South Africa to Dallas after accepting a position with Lamar Hunt's WCT, and the BTSF had never enjoyed a secure financial base.[19]

Another unsuccessful initiative—one that had once seemed so promising but which foundered after Arthur's death—was the African American Sports Hall of Fame. Despite strong support from local officials and corporate sponsors willing to donate a downtown building, the project lost momentum and came to a dead stop in 1997 when the city's economic development staff moved on to other alternatives. Part of the problem was insufficient fund-raising, but there was also the complicating factor of dealing with a continuing controversy surrounding the placement of Paul DiPasquale's sculptural tribute.[20]

Hall of Fame or no Hall of Fame, DiPasquale remained committed to producing a statue that would honor Ashe as one of Richmond's most distinguished citizens. And from early 1993 on, he had the support of Jeanne, Governor Wilder, the city's African American city manager Robert Bobb, several city councilmen (including future senator and vice presidential candidate Tim Kaine, who joined the council in July 1994), the *Richmond Times-Dispatch*, and a substantial proportion (though probably not a majority) of the city's residents. What he did not have was solid support from Richmond's artistic community. Per Arthur's request, he designed a statue that incorporated children, books, and a sculpture of a people's champion wearing a warm-up suit and untied tennis shoes. After sending a preliminary sketch to Jeanne in mid-February, he spent two months in his studio sculpting a ten-foot-high, two-thousand-pound clay statue, the first solid step toward the completion of a monument that, in his words, would inspire "reverence, inspiration and awe for everyone who sees it."

Jeanne, Johnnie, and other members of the Ashe family soon visited Di-Pasquale's studio to view the clay statue, and their enthusiastic approval encouraged the city's Ashe Memorial Committee to move forward. DiPasquale had worried about Jeanne's reaction, knowing her endorsement was crucial to the success of the project. But his fears evaporated when she put her hands on the clay surface of the statue's face and began to cry. Feeling the molded clay, she whispered through her tears that the likeness of Arthur was almost eerily accurate.[21]

On February 8, 1994, the City Council authorized placing a finished version of the statue on city property at a site to be determined later. The project's estimated $400,000 cost was a stumbling block, but the Virginia Heroes group—led by former Governor Wilder, who had left office in January, Arthur's old friend Tom Chewning, now a successful businessman, and Marty Dummett, a former editor for Prentice Hall who served as the group's executive director—stepped up to lead the fund-raising effort. During the next ten months, DiPasquale crafted a plaster-cast proof version of the statue, which Virginia Heroes presented to the public on December 6. At the presentation ceremony, Wilder, who had already privately expressed his site preference, announced he wanted to place the statue among the Confederate hero figures on Monument Avenue. As he later put it, "These are heroes from an era which would deny the aspirations of an Arthur Ashe. He would stand with them, saying, 'I, too, speak for Virginia.'"[22]

Jeanne and many others continued to favor a placement adjacent to the future site of what was now being called the Hard Road to Glory African-American Sports Hall of Fame, but the Monument Avenue proposal advanced by Wilder and the Virginia Heroes group ignited a firestorm of controversy that consumed nearly three years of public debate. Even though several official bodies—including the City Council and its Site Selection Committee, the City Planning Commission, and the City Urban Design Committee—ultimately endorsed the Monument Avenue site, there was spirited opposition to the proposed invasion of the city's most sacred thoroughfare.

Many local whites—especially residents of the elite neighborhood running along Monument Avenue—were appalled by the thought of desegregating the line of heroic statues memorializing Jefferson Davis, Stonewall

Jackson, Robert E. Lee, Jeb Stuart, and other Confederate icons. Much of the opposition was voiced in the name of local control, historic preservation, and defense of tradition, but thinly veiled—and sometimes even overt—racism also became a factor in the debate. Not only did DiPasquale, Chewning, and other statue proponents receive hate mail and threatening phone calls from die-hard white supremacists, but also Confederate reenactors representing the Sons of Confederate Veterans routinely attended City Council meetings as self-appointed defenders of Monument Avenue's racial purity. "Some people will never acknowledge Richmond's prize, Richmond's world-loved man," DiPasquale explained in a letter to Jeanne in July 1995, but he assured her "their children will grow up knowing his message just as green means go and red means stop."[23]

While a number of liberal whites spoke out in favor of the proposal, popular support was heavily concentrated in the black community. One of the leading figures working behind the scenes to secure the Monument Avenue site was John Charles Thomas, the city's leading black attorney and the first African American to serve on the Virginia Supreme Court (1983–1989). Another was Chuck Richardson, an outspoken black city councilman who chastised those among the opposition who refused to face the real issue at hand. "Everybody's dancing around the question, which is 'Do we put a black man on Monument Avenue?'" he declared. "The hand-me-down ideals those individuals represent is the very thing that chased Arthur out of this city. The Civil War is a part of our history. Now we have another part: Civil Rights."

Diametrically opposed to Richardson was Ray Boone, the influential editor of the *Richmond Free Press*, the city's leading black newspaper. Along with Mayor Leonidas Young, he opposed the Monument Avenue site while pressing for the statue's inclusion in the Hall of Fame project. "Identifying Arthur Ashe with racist generals of The Lost Cause would scandalize our hero's shining memory," Boone editorialized in 1995. "Subordinating him to a solid line of Confederate figures would intensify injustice, unfairly equating Arthur Ashe to a bronze row of history's most traitorous villains."

Mayor Young, who later served time in prison for mail fraud and influence peddling, vacillated from one position to another until former Justice Thomas explained the facts of political life to him during a private meeting held at Thomas's house on Monument Avenue. The Ashe statue will be "erected on Monument Avenue, period," Thomas told Young, "and if necessary it will be done over your political corpse." One of Young's plans—to abandon the Monument Avenue statue site in favor of a site at Byrd Park, with the renaming of a downtown street as Arthur Ashe Boulevard thrown in the bargain—was struck down by the City Council after a six-hour public forum held on July 17, 1995. Before adjourning, the council endorsed the DiPasquale design and the Monument Avenue site, drawing considerable praise from the press and seemingly bringing the controversy to a close. But, in actuality, wrangling over the Ashe monument was far from over.[24]

Independent of the site controversy, DiPasquale's design drew considerable opposition on aesthetic grounds. This criticism took on new life during the summer of 1995, when a local gallery owner named Betty Reynolds organized Citizens for Excellence in Public Art (CEPA), a cultural advocacy group that endorsed the Monument Avenue site but not DiPasquale's statue. Speaking at the July 17 public hearing, Reynolds—a politically connected member of a wealthy Richmond family—called for a government-sponsored international competition to select a more appropriate design. Though rebuffed by the City Council, Reynolds and CEPA persisted in their criticism. "Many individuals are hesitant to speak out about the quality of the statue itself and the lack of a competition because of the high emotions surrounding the site, sensitivity to the Ashe family, and the fear of criticism being taken in racial terms," she claimed in a letter to the editor of the *Richmond Times-Dispatch*. "But the fact remained," she continued, "there is widespread feeling throughout the city that the current piece is of very limited artistic merit and many feel that this current statue is more appropriate for mall art than Monument Avenue."

In August, the city went forward with what one observer called "a quiet groundbreaking ceremony" at the intersection of Monument Avenue and Roseneath Road, four hundred yards north of the monument dedicated to Confederate naval hero Matthew Fontaine Maury. The site of the Ashe statue now seemed set, yet that did not stop Reynolds and CEPA from organizing a petition drive and letter-writing campaign to pressure the city's Committee on Architectural Review (CAR) to sanction a design competition. In December, CAR held a public hearing on the matter, but at the end of the evening a solid majority voted to retain DiPasquale's design.[25]

Having worked on the Ashe statue on and off for nearly three years, DiPasquale finally had permission to proceed to completion and installation. But the resolution came too late for Jeanne, who had grown tired of the bickering. She was also disgusted by the insulting, backdoor efforts to preserve Monument Avenue's racial sanctity, and she said so in an eloquent op-ed piece published in the *Times-Dispatch* on New Year's Day 1996. She began: "Richmond, can you remember that the 'Arthur Ashe monument,' as you call it now, was never meant to be a monument just to Arthur? Rather it began with Arthur's own dream of creating an African-American Sports Hall of Fame. . . . He saw it as a culmination of his life's work to leave behind a lasting memorial to all African-American athletes. That it would be in Richmond, where he was born and raised, left him even more proud. It was in this context that Arthur agreed to cooperate with the sculptor, Paul DiPasquale, for a statue that would go in front of the Hall of Fame."

She had nothing but praise for DiPasquale, whom she described as a "wonderful artist." "It distresses me," she wrote, "that he has in any way been criticized when I know that his intentions were to honor my husband with his talent. Likewise, I can certainly understand that Arthur's family wants to name as many things after him as is possible. No one appreciates more than I how very much there is about Arthur to be proud of! But, somehow, what *Arthur* wanted has been lost in the shuffle." From there she moved to the heart of the matter: "No, I am not in agreement with the decision to place the 'Arthur Ashe monument' on Monument Avenue. My reasons are not politically driven; nor are they artistically or racially motivated. I have always felt that in all this controversy, the spirit that Arthur gave to Richmond has been overlooked. I am afraid that a statue of Arthur Ashe on Monument Avenue honors Richmond, Virginia, more than it does its son, his legacy, and his life's work."

"Why can't we return to Arthur's original dream for his hometown?" she asked. "As 1996 begins, my wish for the new year is that there can be a national effort to build a Sports Hall of Fame in Richmond that is a place of honor for all the great people Arthur saluted in *A Hard Road to Glory*. Arthur returned to his roots. Let his legacy grow in your soil. Water it, nurture it, and it will be the shining star that Arthur was for all of us. For that dream, you have my support. And with that, Richmond would have something dear and significant—much more than another statue on a boulevard of statues."[26]

These words drew an immediate response from city officials, including Mayor Young and the City Planning Commission. Nearly everyone professed surprise that Jeanne harbored serious misgivings about placing the statue on Monument Avenue, but Young and others scrambled to accommodate her position. On January 2, the Planning Commission voted 6–2 to postpone final approval of any Ashe statue site for at least sixty days, while the mayor proposed a compromise plan calling for the temporary installation of the statue on Monument Avenue to be followed by eventual removal to the Hall of Fame grounds.

Jeanne's op-ed also refocused attention on the Hall project, which had been limping along for more than two years. In late February, she joined the basketball star Ralph Sampson and other celebrities at a reception at Richmond's Jefferson Hotel, hoping to kick-start an ambitious campaign to raise the estimated $23 million needed to construct the Hall. Harrison Wilson, the father of future Seattle Seahawks quarterback Russell Wilson, had been hired as executive director of the project, and for a time Jeanne gained renewed hope that under his leadership the Hall would eventually become a reality. But the necessary funds never materialized, even though the city pledged $1 million as seed money.[27]

On February 26, when the City Council met to render a final judgment on the Monument Avenue site, some observers feared a majority of the nine-person council was prepared to vote no, having reportedly succumbed to the pressures of recent behind-the-scenes maneuvering. But during an open forum prior to the vote, Tom Chewning turned the tide with a clever response to Vice Mayor John Conrad's leading question. Why should a statue of a tennis player be placed among the great heroes of the Confederacy—all distinguished leaders known for their sterling character, Conrad asked? Chewning, after conceding that Monument Avenue should indeed be reserved for public men of high character, proceeded to read a biographical sketch of such a man—without revealing the man's identity. Caught off guard and obviously flustered, Conrad reluctantly acknowledged that the character sketch "fit Arthur Ashe to a tee." Only then did Chewning reveal that the sketch had been taken from an encyclopedia entry on General Robert E. Lee. This startling revelation sent a murmur of recognition through the council, which a few minutes later voted 8–1 in favor of placing the Ashe statue on Monument Avenue. Conrad, unmoved by Chewning's clever ploy, cast the only negative vote.

When the Monument Avenue statue was unveiled and dedicated four months later on July 10—on what would have been Arthur's fifty-third birthday—feelings of relief and triumph enveloped those who had fought long and hard to honor perhaps the only local hero whose legacy held the power to liberate the city's from its stifling Confederate heritage. The symbolic importance of the statue was undeniable, even among those who opposed it, turning a vision of social and cultural change previously considered to be fanciful into something viable. Adding to the air of unexpected fulfillment, Mal Washington had reached the men's singles final at Wimbledon four days earlier—the first African American to do so since Arthur in 1975. As Arthur's life had proven, seemingly impossible dreams could be achieved if enough heart and soul and determination were brought to bear on the task at hand—even in the rarefied sanctums of Monument Avenue and Centre Court.

Unconvinced that the Monument Avenue placement was a good idea, Jeanne quietly boycotted the ceremony. But Arthur's brother Johnnie, Wilder, and Chewning stepped up to headline the festivities, which included a rousing performance by the Harlem Boys Choir. Deviating from his sister-in-law's position, Johnnie told the interracial gathering of fifteen hundred: "Arthur Ashe Jr. is a true Virginia hero. He belongs here. We expected the profound from Arthur Jr., and he gave it to us. A man from humble beginnings who rose to great heights. It is out of love, respect and appreciation for a true humanitarian that we gather here today." Long one of the strongest proponents of the Monument Avenue site, Wilder declared: "Today is not just any day in Richmond. Monument Avenue is now an avenue for all people." Chewning—citing his friend's "character and respect for his fellow man"—struggled to keep his composure as he spoke in the statue's shadow, and those in the crowd old enough to remember Richmond in the 1950s understood the significance of his presence. Richmond's two best tennis prospects of that era, once separated by the barriers of Jim Crow, were now figuratively joined as one on a day of hope and long-delayed redemption.

To those who had fought for the placement of the statue on Monument Avenue, and who had beaten the political odds, the installation of DiPasquale's artistry was cause for jubilation. Justice John Charles Thomas spoke for many of Ashe's local admirers when he composed a poem titled "In Proportion" soon after he left the dedication ceremony. The poem closed with the stanza:

> And so it was, cast as it is in bronze
> A monument to a man and his faith
> A symbol of hope and a sign of a new era
> An appropriate coda to hysteria
> And all in proportion to the sky
> As the world passes by[28]

There were, of course, many individuals who failed to appreciate the uplifting message so obvious to Thomas. As recently as late February, a *Richmond Times-Dispatch* poll had revealed that a substantial majority of local whites opposed the placement of the Ashe statue among the Confederate heroes. One white observer speaking before the City Council claimed that putting a statue of Arthur Ashe on Monument Avenue was equivalent "to putting a commode in your living room." While a certain segment of the white community probably agreed with this sentiment, only a dozen or so Confederate-flag-waving protesters showed up at the unveiling. One protester held up a sign attacking the invasion of Monument Avenue as a "hate crime," but most of the rest of the crowd, black and white, seemed to appreciate the shining new monument. There it stood for all of Richmond to see, with its twelve-foot bronze statue of Ashe holding books in one hand and a tennis racket in the other, four bronze children extending their hands upward, and an 87,000-pound block of Georgia granite supporting the figures. A verse from the Book of Hebrews was etched in the granite. "Since we are surrounded by so great a cloud of witnesses," the inscription read, "let us lay aside every weight, and the sin which so easily ensnares us, and let us run with endurance the race that is set before us."

The Ashe statue, for all its critics and complications, soon became a major tourist attraction and a symbol of pride and hope for many Richmond residents, especially in the black community. Ultimately producing more racial healing than resistance, it has stood as a testament to the emergence of a more united and tolerant city. But its location still inspires controversy. Jeanne Moutoussamy-Ashe, for one, has never reconciled the Monument Avenue site with the original goal of paying tribute to Arthur's life with a statue placed in front of the proposed African American Sports Hall of Fame.[29]

Much more important than placing the statue on Monument Avenue, in Jeanne's view, was the USTA's decision to put Arthur's name on the new stadium being built at the National Tennis Center in Flushing Meadows. The decision came after a display of resistance by the USTA board of directors, who voted unanimously to use the name USTA Stadium as a starting point for a lucrative corporate naming opportunity down the line. The board reversed its decision in February 1997, bowing to a pro-Ashe petition campaign initiated by *Inside Tennis* editor Bill Simons and supported by Bud Collins, Nick Bollettieri, and key members of the USTA staff and sectional presidents, among others. Seven months after the dedication ceremony in Richmond, USTA president Harry Marmion, with Jeanne standing by his side, held a news conference to announce the organization's intention to honor Arthur's legacy. "We are naming our new stadium in his honor because Arthur Ashe was the finest human being the sport has ever known," Marmion declared. Though no one knew it at the time, Arthur's name would eventually be linked to his cherished friend Billie Jean King, for whom the National Tennis Center was renamed in 2006.

The new stadium—which had been in the works since March 1995, when the USTA began a major upgrade of the National Tennis Center— was not just any stadium. With more than 23,000 seats, it was the largest tennis venue in the world when it opened in late August 1997. Replacing the 18,000-seat Louis Armstrong Stadium—the primary venue for the U.S. Open since the center's founding in 1978—Arthur Ashe Stadium was constructed at a cost of $254 million, part of which paid for a DecoTurf cushioned acrylic surface and all manner of state-of-the-art sound and broadcast technology. It had everything but a retractable roof, which would be added with great fanfare in 2016. Fittingly, the stadium was built on the former site of the Corona Ash Dumps, immortalized in F. Scott Fitzgerald's *The Great Gatsby* as the "Valley of Ashes." At the stadium's opening ceremony, held just before the first round of the 1997 Open, USTA officials showered praise on tennis's one-and-only Ashe.

On the eve of the 2000 Open, the USTA honored him further with the placing of the Arthur Ashe Commemorative Garden on the approach to the stadium. Featuring *Soul in Flight*, a striking bronze statue depicting a nude figure reaching up to serve a tennis ball, the garden included a marble base inscribed with one of Arthur's favorite sayings: "From what we get, we make a living; what we give, however, makes a life." For a time, the anatomically correct figure designed by Eric Fischl sparked considerable controversy, but eventually the statue became an accepted fixture of the National Tennis Center.[30]

Of course, the most significant element of Arthur's legacy—more important than any stadium or statue—has been the continuing relevance of his ideals and life story to new generations of athletes, especially among young inner-city and African American tennis players. Through the efforts of the NJTL and other youth tennis programs that use Arthur as a model, hundreds of thousands of young boys and girls have been inspired to make more of their lives than they might otherwise have done. Many have aspired to follow his lead as a tennis champion, but the example that often mattered most was his capacity to combine athletic excellence with sportsmanship, education, and social responsibility.

For a quarter century, the challenge to be like Arthur Ashe has reverberated through countless inner-city tennis workshops, the annual Arthur Ashe Kids Day activities at the U.S. Open, and the ESPN Arthur Ashe Courage Award presented at the nationally televised ESPY Awards show each summer. Given to individuals whose influence "transcends sports," the Courage Award has honored recipients as varied as Muhammad Ali, Billie Jean King, Nelson Mandela, and Caitlyn Jenner. While some of the selections have been controversial, no one has ever challenged the appropriateness of naming the award for Ashe, who continues to be one of the most revered figures in sports history.[31]

While the tennis world is still waiting for "the next Arthur Ashe" to rule *inside* the lines, the game and the nation at large have already benefited greatly from his acolytes' achievements *outside* the lines. Many of those fortunate enough to experience his mentorship have felt a need to give back to society in some meaningful way, and the long list of philanthropic foundations established by his most successful protégés is unique in the world of sports.

The ongoing activities of foundations initiated by black tennis stars such as Yannick Noah, Zina Garrison, Lori McNeil, Leslie Allen, Mal Washington, and James Blake testify not only to personal altruism, but also to the power of Ashe's exemplary generosity. While Arthur also influenced many white players, the black commitment to extending his legacy has often carried a special force. Rooted in shared experience, this devotion represents a collective debt to a racial pioneer who labored long and hard not only to desegregate competitive tennis but also to open up economic and social opportunities for blacks in the broader community.[32]

Race has not defined Ashe's legacy, however, and during the past two decades whites as well as blacks have both followed and fostered his model, especially among children. The materials distributed by the Arthur Ashe Center for Learning, and the workshops and camps run by the NJTL, the SPF, the USTA, and a miscellany of Arthur Ashe urban tennis centers have reached a diverse population of youngsters who never had the opportunity to see him play or to witness his acts of moral courage and responsible citizenship.

Perhaps the most prominent and influential Ashe surrogate is Katrina Adams, a Northwestern graduate once ranked as high as #67 in the world. A mainstay of the Harlem Junior Tennis and Education Program for more than a decade, she eventually found her true métier in the upper levels of national tennis administration. In 2015, she became the first African American to serve as president of the USTA, the most powerful position in American tennis. Passionately devoted to Ashe and his legacy, she has worked to expand the USTA's connections to a diverse set of constituents and communities, a goal that has eluded the organization throughout most of its history.[33]

There are, of course, many other Ashe surrogates whose names are all but unknown outside of tennis circles. Willis Thomas, Bobby Davis, Lenny Simpson, Sherry Snyder, Jean Desdunes, Kim Sands, Skip Hartman, D. A. Abram, Kevin Dowdell, Chris Beck, Traci Green, John Wilkerson, Rodney Harmon, Bryan Shelton, Mal Washington, Benny Sims, and Karin Buchholz—just to name a few—have devoted much of their lives to spreading the Ashe "gospel." Like the man who inspired them, they have tried to persuade young and old, black and white, male and female, that athletic excellence should be viewed more as a means than an end in itself. Without the accompanying virtues of education and social conscience, they argue, success on the court—or any other playing field—can become an unhealthy diversion from the important things in life.

A quarter century after his death, the proponents of Ashe's legacy now find themselves in an era prone to crass commercialism, overblown media images, and winning at any cost. While the world of athletics in the twenty-first century still produces many moments of unscripted drama and joy, such unsavory topics as sexual assault, spousal abuse, cheating through steroid use or blood doping, and trash talking now punctuate sports coverage in newspapers across the world.

Fortunately for its participants and fans, tennis, among all major sports, seems to have had the most success bucking this trend. The game's best players—Roger Federer, Rafa Nadal, Andy Murray, and Novak Djokovic on the men's side; and the Williams sisters, Serena and Venus, on the women's—are all among tennis's best ambassadors—individuals as impressive off the court as on. None is as politically or socially active as Ashe was during the second half of his career, and none has reached the level of a true public intellectual. Indeed, tennis has generally lagged behind the other major sports in the willingness of its players to take a public stand on controversial political issues. Nevertheless, virtually all of tennis's top players—along with many of their less successful colleagues—share a commitment to some form of community engagement, usually through unpaid public appearances or donations to private foundations. This is also true of many retired players, especially those once close to Ashe—loyal friends and admirers such as Pasarell, Smith, Drysdale, Noah, King, and McEnroe. All but King are less political than Ashe, but in every other way they reflect his legacy.[34]

The power of Ashe's legacy is still palpable. This became evident in October 2016, when President Barack Obama discussed the subject on a televised forum held on the campus of North Carolina A&T University at Greensboro, the birthplace of the 1960 sit-in movement. Billed as "A Conversation with the President: Sports, Race and Achievement," the forum featured questions from an audience of students and alumni primed with an aphorism from Maya Angelou: "We may encounter many defeats, but we must not be defeated."

Twenty minutes into the show, Sam Hunt, a starting guard on the school's basketball team, rose to ask a question about mixing activism and sports. "Many athletes have taken a stand on social issues of today," he posited. "What do you think is the most effective way for professional and collegiate athletes to make a change?" In response, the president acknowledged "there are so many ways to make an impact" but went on to offer two competing models of activism—one associated with Muhammad Ali and the other with Arthur Ashe. Looking back at the era of his youth, he identified these two black men as the sport figures he admired above all others. They were, he explained, "the most influential" athletes affecting "how I thought about what it meant to be a man."

President Obama described Ali as a bold and brazen champion who terrified much of white America in the tumultuous 1960s before gaining acclaim as a national treasure later in the century. "Ali was all personality and loud and noisy and truth telling, and self-promoting and brash, just a bigger-than-life personality," he told the audience. But eventually his principled stands on issues of importance won the respect of millions, many of whom came to see him as a "grandfatherly, lovable figure."

The President deftly captured the differences in style and tone that separated his two heroes. In sharp contrast to Ali, "Arthur was button downed, spoke proper English, and conjugated his verbs, and looking all like a professor or something, and was perceived—because he was in a white sport—as always being gentlemanly and humble in how he spoke." Yet both the boxer and the tennis player were highly effective activists who pushed the nation down the same path to freedom and democracy. "Ali gave people enormous pride," the president recalled, "and ultimately convinced not just black Americans but white Americans to question what their government was doing and how they were thinking about racial justice." "Arthur, in his own way," Obama insisted, was no less "transformational in getting people to recognize the dignity of African Americans despite whatever might be thrown at them." Moreover, on the international level he worked tirelessly to liberate black South Africans from the scourge of apartheid, "helping to create an entire movement here in the United States."

Closing out the segment on activism, the president declared: "How you do it is less important than your commitment to use whatever platform you have to speak to the issues that matter." With more time, he could have elaborated on the heroic milestones of both men's lives. But even his brief remarks—at least in Ashe's case—captured the essence of a life that echoed the wisdom of Angelou's sage dictum. Arthur Ashe suffered many defeats, including a cruel and untimely death. Yet he was undefeated in the realms that mattered most—heart, soul, integrity, and character. In this important sense, there is no shadow to darken his legacy. What remains is the radiance of a good and great man whose inner light shines outward for all to see.[35]

ACKNOWLEDGMENTS

This book is rooted in a friendship that began on the tennis courts of Brandeis University during the fall of 1971. At the time, tennis was the game of choice among the faculty and students of the university's History of American Civilization graduate program, and no one availed himself of this choice more often than James Oliver "Jim" Horton, an African American student from Newark, New Jersey. Born in March 1943, Jim was three months older than his idol Arthur Ashe, to whom he bore a striking resemblance. They were the same height and weight, they shared the same coloring, and they both took the court dressed in tennis whites with Ashe-model Head rackets in hand. In 1972, during a professional tournament at the Longwood Cricket Club in Chestnut Hill, Massachusetts, a crowd of Ashe fans waiting for him to leave the locker room to begin a match against Tom Okker rushed over to get an autograph from their hero only to discover they had just surrounded Jim Horton, who coolly signed several programs before his real identity became apparent. This was undoubtedly one of the great moments of Jim's life, and in later years he loved to tell the story of the accidental "autograph scam" at Longwood.

Jim and his wife and perennial coauthor, Lois, were scholars of community life among Free Blacks in the antebellum North, a speciality that focused their attention on such notables as Frederick Douglass and Harriet Tubman. But when it came to the contemporary scene Ashe was their guiding star. Jim's personal admiration for his role model, both as a tennis player and as a human being, knew no bounds, and he communicated this feeling to all of his friends on and off the court. As his close friend and frequent doubles partner, I was drawn inexorably into the Ashe-Horton orbit. My tennis skills, unlike Jim's, never reached the level where I could realistically pattern my serve and backhand after Ashe's signature strokes. But I came to share Jim's interest in and respect for one of the sports world's most admirable figures.

Years later, as our professorial careers matured and as our common interest in the history of civil rights took a cultural turn, we talked about coauthoring a journal article, or perhaps even a book, on Ashe. Unfortunately, our proposed collaboration was scotched by a rare brain disorder that curtailed Jim's career in 2007 and ended his life a decade later. When I began this book in 2009, Jim was my inspiration, and as the research and writing progressed, his deep connection to Ashe was often in my thoughts. At the outset, I decided to dedicate the book, if and when I ever finished it, to Jim and Lois Horton. Now, after nine years of work, I am pleased and honored to do so as a small token of my debt to two cherished friends who dedicated their life together to the same ideals that Arthur Ashe held dear—honesty, justice, and equality.

I also owe an incalculable debt to Arthur's widow, Jeanne Moutoussamy-Ashe. Her cooperation, encouragement, and support have been indispensable throughout this long project, and I can never repay her many kindnesses. She generously shared memories of her seventeen years with Arthur—and of the quarter century she has devoted to sustaining his legacy. Her command of detail and nuance saved me from numerous errors, and her skill and experience as a professional photographer proved invaluable.

Other members of the Ashe family graciously shared their memories of Arthur. I especially want to thank Arthur's brother Johnnie, his sister, Loretta Ashe Harris, and his niece La Chandra Harris Pace for their help. Their collective portrait of a closely knit extended family was instrumental to my reconstruction of Arthur's private life, especially during his early years.

In the early stages of my research, I was fortunate to receive help and encouragement from two of Arthur's closest friends, the great sportswriter Frank Deford and the legendary agent Donald Dell. Together, they facilitated my initial contact with Jeanne, and in a series of interviews Dell provided essential information about Arthur's career. Through his comprehensive Rolodex, Dell also provided me with contact information for figures throughout the tennis world, and I am very grateful for his willingness to do so. At several points I relied heavily on Deford's writings, including the script for the remarkable 1994 documentary film, *Arthur Ashe: Citizen of the World*. But his serious illness and untimely death in May 2017 prevented me from conducting a formal interview with him.

Fortunately, I *was* able to interview three of the collaborators who helped craft Arthur's published memoirs: Cliff Gewecke, Neil Amdur, and Arnold Rampersad. I am grateful not only for their writing and editing skills, but also for their willingness to elaborate on the nature and details of their work with Arthur. Without their contributions, which provide vital access to Arthur's voice and thoughts, this book would have been virtually impossible to write. As an analyst of Arthur's life, I stand on their shoulders.

I would also like to acknowledge the important efforts of those who have either authored or edited book-length studies of Ashe. Louie Robinson Jr., John McPhee, Marvin Martin, Richard Steins, Mike Towle, Eric Hall, and Peter Bodo plowed the biographical ground before I did, unearthing and examining important elements of Arthur's life. Particularly noteworthy in this regard is Eric Hall's 2015 book, *Arthur Ashe: Tennis and Justice in the Civil Rights Era*, a revised Purdue University dissertation written under the direction of the noted sports historian Randy Roberts. Hall's insightful analysis of Arthur's involvement in the struggle for civil rights aided my own effort to make sense of this challenging topic, and I thank him for his groundbreaking work. I would also be remiss if I failed to acknowledge the value of John McPhee's sports classic *Levels of the Game*, as well as the 2014 interview he granted me, conducted in the strangest of circumstances—in the midst of my raucous forty-fifth class reunion at Princeton.

In addition to the books noted above, three studies of the history of African American tennis—Doug Smith's *Whirlwind*, Cecil Harris and Larryette Kyle-DeBose's *Charging the Net*, and Sudiata Djata's *Blacks at the Net*—include valuable chapters on Arthur Ashe's rise to prominence. In various ways, each of these authors provided historical context, informing my understanding of Arthur's role as a racial pioneer.

Interviews represent a critically important part of the research base upon which this book rests. Many of the interviews were formal attempts at oral history, but others began as casual impromptu conversations about Ashe. Their length and importance varied widely, but each in its own way contributed to my evolving understanding of Ashe's saga. I conducted many of the formal interviews, but a large number involved the participation of graduate and undergraduate research assistants. Arranging and conducting these interviews was often demanding and challenging, and I owe a great deal to my talented research assistants Erin Hughes, Jackie Inman, Rachel Sanderson,

Arielle Stevenson, Nano Riley, and Dara Vance. Working out of the Snell House at the University of South Florida, St. Petersburg, they formed an indispensable team that helped me when I needed it most.

The interviewees themselves deserve special mention and my unwavering gratitude for the gift of their time and knowledge. By sharing their memories, experiences, and perspectives, they added immeasurably to the texture and fiber of the book. My thanks to: Seth Abraham, D. A. Abram, Katrina Adams, Leslie Allen, Neil Amdur, Susan Anderson, Johnnie Ashe, Sam Beale, Chris Beck, Timothy Bent, Alex Bloom, Renee Blount, Steve Bond, Nick Bollettieri, Litten Boxser, Butch Buchholz, Cliff Buchholz, Karin Buchholz, Granville Burgess, Trey Burpee, Doris Cammack-Spencer, Lucretia Carrico, Arthur Carrington, Clayborne Carson, Tom Chewning, Bud Collins, Ian Crookenden, Billy Davis, Bobby Davis, Jonathan Davis, Patricia Battles Davis, Donald Dell, Jean Desdunes, David Dinkins, Paul DiPasquale, Steve Dittmann, Kevin Dowdell, Veronica Drake, Cliff Drysdale, Deb Ebner, Harry Edwards, Lou Einwick, Roy Emerson, Bob Farrell, Judith Ferszt, Carlos Fleming, James Floyd Jr., Allen Fox, Marcel Freeman, Marcus Freeman, Frank Froehling, Zina Garrison, Henry Louis Gates, Cliff Gewecke, Brian Gottfried, Clark Graebner, Reginald Green, Traci Green, James Grossman, Shema Grover, Rodney Harmon, Don Harris, Loretta Ashe Harris, Ralph Harris, Skip Hartman, Kate Henchman, Chip Hooper, Lee Irby, Dennis Jenken, Willard Johnson, Lynda Kaplan, Leslie Kelen, Ann Koger, Phil Lucas, Rodney Mandelstam, Eddie Mandeville, Gene Mayer, June Mayfield, Javier Maymi-Perez, John McEnroe Jr., Kay McGuire, Kevin McGuire, Lori McNeil, Steve McNichols, John McPhee, Will Michaels, Ray Moore, Chris Morris, Jeanne Moutoussamy-Ashe, Toby Muir, Henry Murray, David Myers, Gary Nash, Todd Nelson, John Newcombe, Butch Newman, Jim Nicholson, Steve Northup, Mary Beth Norton, La Chandra Harris Pace, Charlie Pasarell, Martha McMasters Pearson, Gene Policinski, Connie Price, Dennis Ralston, Arnold Rampersad, David Reed, Horace Reid, Mike Reilly, Paul Reilly, Steve Reilly, Cliff Richey, Nancy Richey, Barbara Ricks, Marty Riessen, Randall Robinson, Jefferson Rogers, Robert Ryland, Jeffrey Sammons, David Sanderlin, Kim Sands, Joan Sanger, C. J. Savage, Rowland Scherma, Al Schragis, Bryan Shelton, Charles Sherrod, Diane Shropshire, Bill Simons, Lenny Simpson, Fran Sims, John Sims, Bob Singleton, Fred Slaughter, Bruce Smith, Jolyn Johnson Smith, Paul Smith, Stan Smith, Sherry Snyder, Jack Spong, Dick Stockton, Roscoe Tanner, John Charles Thomas, Willis Thomas, Doug Thompson, Tony Trabert, Pat Turner, Rick Tuttle, Bill Wallace, Sally Wallace, Mal Washington, John Wilkerson, Charles Williams, Owen Williams, Robert

Woodrum, Eric Yellin, and Andrew Young. Among these many interviews, my sessions with Tom Chewning, Donald Dell, Cliff Drysdale, Lou Einwick, Loretta Ashe Harris, John McEnroe Jr., Jeanne Moutoussamy-Ashe, Charlie Pasarell, Paul DiPasquale, Jeff Rogers, Al Schragis, John Wilkerson, and Andrew Young were especially instructive and eye-opening.

Archival research lies at the heart of this book—which literally could not have been written without the help and expertise of numerous archivists and librarians. I am greatly indebted to the staffs at the Nelson Poynter Library at the University of South Florida, St. Petersburg; the Arthur Schomburg Center for Black Culture, a branch of the New York Public Library; the International Tennis Hall of Fame (ITHF) Library in Newport, Rhode Island; the Kenneth Ritchie Library at Wimbledon; the UCLA Sports Information Office; the Charles E. Young Research Library at UCLA; the Olympic Studies Center in Lausanne, Switzerland; the Richmond Public Library; the St. Louis Public Library; and the Library of Congress. Special thanks to Meredith Miller Richards of ITHF and Meri and Dave Hartford of Artworks Cape Cod for help with the photographs.

I also received strong institutional support from the University of South Florida, St. Petersburg, which granted me three semesters of sabbatical leave—the fall semester of 2009, and a full academic year in 2016–17—to work on this book. Generous travel funds attached to the John Hope Franklin Professorship of Southern History were also instrumental to the numerous research trips I was able to undertake during the last eight years. Frank Biafora, the Dean of the USFSP College of Arts and Sciences, supported my work at every turn, and I can't thank him enough for his faith in my sports history adventure. I would also like to acknowledge the support of Associate Dean Susan Toler and the CAS stalwarts Jennifer Woroner, Jason Morris, Harriet Fletcher, Drew Thomas, and Paul Schulz. I am also very grateful for the support and encouragement I received from Regional Chancellors Margaret Sullivan and Sophia Wisniewska, Vice Chancellors of Academic Affairs Noreen Noonan, Mark Durand, and Martin Tadlock, Dean Bill Heller of the College of Education, and Interim Dean Jeff Cornelius of CAS.

As always, my colleagues in the Department of History and Politics, which I served as chairman from 2012 to 2016, were always there to back me up when I needed it most. I owe a special debt to Professors Richard Abato, Sheramy Bundrick, Michael Francis, Peter Golenbock, Arturo Jimenez-Bacardi, Peyton Jones, Catherine Koziol, Hugh Lafollette, Felipe Mantilla, Judith Anne Scourfield McLaughlin, Chris Meindl, Elisa Minoff, Gary Mormino, and Thomas Smith. Thanks also to Veronica Mathews, Daun

Fletcher, and Amy Anderson, three outstanding academic program specialists who kept the office running smoothly when I was away. Peter Golenbock deserves special mention as my most enthusiastic cheerleader, perennial doubles partner, and fellow Rays fan during the past fifteen years. Rounding out the Snell House gang is the incomparable Director of Special Events, Joan "Sudsy" Tschiderer, whose interest in the Ashe book went above and beyond what anyone could reasonably expect from a non-tennis-playing soccer fan.

For many years—and especially during the past decade—a wide circle of friends has provided me with encouragement, intellectual engagement, and countless moments of pleasant diversion from my labors as a historian. Part of this circle goes back as far my graduate school days in the 1970s, when I first became interested in Arthur Ashe. Many thanks to my loyal Brandeis friends John and Virginia Demos, David Hackett and Judy Fischer, Jennifer Gallop, David and Elaine Gould, the late Jim Green, Mike and Tina Grossberg, Ted and Nan Hammett, Dirk and Nancy Hartog, Jim and Lois Horton, Fred and Holly Hoxie, Mickey and Phyllis Keller, Liz Pleck, Bob and Jan Randolph, Mitchell Snay, David Starr, and Steve and Lee Whitfield. The Goulds deserve special thanks for graciously allowing me to share their Brooklyn home during my periodic research trips to New York. The indispensable man, Steve Whitfield—my dearest friend and most trusted historical advisor for more than forty years—gave me many hours of wise counsel and a close reading of several chapters.

Another special group of friends—the Sunday morning tennis gathering at the historic St. Petersburg Tennis Center—has boosted my spirits, if not my tennis game, throughout the past decade. Playing on the same soft courts where Arthur Ashe ended his career as an amateur in March 1969, they have never wavered in their determination to put me through my paces on the court while supporting my effort to reconstruct an important part of tennis history. I am grateful for the many hours I have spent either talking or playing tennis with Ann Sackett, CeCe Keeton, Michael Miller, Peter Golenbock, Gary Mormino, Norris Rickey, Peter and Jeanne Meinke, Rich and Mimi Rice, Felipe and Olivia Mantilla, Tracey Maher, Burton and Ellen Hersh, Dave and Marg Radens, Ajay Verghese, Jim Wightman, Babs Ringold, and Kimberley Oliver.

I would also like to acknowledge the support of a number of other friends who helped me to frame the right questions as I rummaged through the details of Ashe's life. Some may have grown weary of hearing me talk about Ashe, but I haven't forgotten their many kindnesses and contributions during my long journey to publication. My sincere thanks go out to: Merle

Allshouse, Kristy Anderson, Ellen Babb, Colleen Bancroft, Dave and Patty Barnicle, Reba Beeson, Peter Belmont, John Belohlavek, Randy Berg, Susan and Peter Betzer, Bob Bickel, Judy Blake, Jim Bledsoe, David Blight, Russ Buchan, Lonnie Bunch, Georgeanne and Vernon Burton, Donald Carey, Rick Cesa, Roy Peter Clark, Spencer Crew, Theresa Collington, Carol Dameron, Jack Davis, Jamie Day, Eric Deggans, Adam Estevez, Rebecca Falkenberry, Janine Farver, Laurens Grant, Wendy Grassi, Jim Grossman, Sheldon and Lucy Hackney, Steve Hahn, Joyce Haines, Eric Hall, Woody Hanson, Bill Harris, Rob Heinrich, Earl Hitchcock, Tamika Hobbs, Mike Honey, Jim Howell, Allen and Bobbie Isaacman, Bob Devin Jones, Charles Joyner, Herb Karl, Jon and Monica Kile, Richard King, Susan King, Jeff Klinkenberg, Bernard and Kate LaFayette, Lin LaPointe, Rob Lorei, Laurie Macdonald, Janice Marks, Randall Miller, Eric Morgan, Lynne Mormino, Harvey and Nancy Nelsen, Lauren Prestileo, Nano Riley, Marc Samels, Jim Schnur, David and Dawn Shedden, Howard Simon, Herb Snitzer, Jay Sokolovsky, David Starr, Bill Stokes, Rose Styron, Pat Sullivan, Jon Tallon, Mills and Brenda Thornton, Susan Turner, Daniel Tyson, Milly and Don Vappie, Jim Verhulst, Maria Vesperi, Albert Vogt, and Chris Warren.

This book also benefited from several public presentations that elicited helpful comments and constructive criticism. In April 2014, I spoke on Ashe as the annual Harold Seymour Lecturer in Sports History at Cornell University, where my hosts were Mary Beth Norton, Glen Altschuler, and the golf and baseball historian George Kirsch. In October 2016, I delivered a second paper on Ashe at the 17th International Conference on Sports, held in Lille, France; and in May 2017, I presented a third Ashe paper at the annual meeting of the Florida Historical Society, held at an even more exotic location—on a cruise ship en route to Cozumel and Tulum. While few of the fun-loving passengers took notice, the subject was Ashe's role in the desegregation of tennis in Florida.

I am also heavily indebted to the staff of Simon & Schuster. During the course of this project, I have worked with five editors in succession: Marty Beiser, Dominick Anfuso, and Web Younce at Free Press, and Thomas LeBien and Bob Bender at the parent company, Simon & Schuster. Corporate upheaval of this magnitude, which has become commonplace in the publishing world in recent years, puts strains and stresses on authors and editors alike. But from start to finish I have had the good fortune to work with some of the best editors in the business. Bob Bender, the sage veteran who inherited this project five years after its inception, has provided exemplary oversight during the home stretch. He is a consummate professional, as is his associate

Johanna Li. I thank them for their patience and editorial acumen. I am also grateful to Fred Chase, a superb copy editor who saved me from making many errors, and to Elizabeth Gay for her stellar publicity work. Peter Ginna, my former editor at Oxford University Press and Bloomsbury USA, also deserves acknowledgment and thanks for his continuing interest and involvement in my work. He has been both a good friend and an invaluable advisor.

Fortunately for the creative evolution of this book, I have been able to rely on the skills and judgment of my extraordinary agent, Wendy Strothman. She has been with me from the intial planning to the last revision, prodding and guiding me through the rough patches while never losing faith in the ultimate value of reconstructing Arthur Ashe's remarkable life, and serving as both agent and editor. Spending time with Wendy and her husband, John, either in their Greenwich Village flat, or at their coastal retreat in Maine, has been a great pleasure, and I thank them for their gracious hospitality and friendship. I also greatly appreciate the work of Wendy's gifted associate Lauren MacLeod.

Last, but by no means least, I want to acknowledge the love and support of my wonderful family. During this book's nine years of gestation, the personal circumstances of virtually every member of my family underwent substantial change, including my mother, who passed away in 2012 at the age of eighty-six. My wife, Kathy, retired after more than thirty years as a university librarian, the last ten as a library dean; my daughter Anne completed her law degree and became a successful attorney and federal law clerk; and my daughter Amelia and her partner, Shawn Powers, finished their dissertations, became professors, got married, and bore a child. Yet they all found the time and energy to lend considerable aid, comfort, and technical expertise to a struggling historian in need of help on all fronts.

Kathy was especially valiant, offering her talents as an editor when severe cuts in the manuscript were required. Initially, I hesitated to accept her offer, hoping to save her from an onerous and thankless task. But she insisted and ultimately prevailed, demonstrating after fifty years of marriage that she is still the best writer in the family. After several painful but productive months of line-by-line editing, we came to the end of our combined effort in early June 2017, just in time to enjoy a much anticipated Golden Wedding Anniversary in Ireland. The highlight of this joyous celebration was spending a glorious week with two daughters, a son-in-law—and our impish and precocious twenty-one-month-old grandson, Lincoln.

Back home in Washington, D.C., Lincoln has an old-style wooden tennis racket and an oversized, bright orange U.S. Open tennis ball in his room.

He loves to drape himself over the ball and roll around, though he doesn't know what to make of the racket other than to chew on its strings. But someday soon, I predict, he will figure it out, and later yet he may even read his grandfather's book on one of the greatest tennis players of the modern era. I certainly hope so. Like everyone else, he will need inspiring role models to help him find his way in life—and I can't think of any better example to follow than the young boy from Richmond who moved from athletic achievement to enlightened service as a "citizen of the world." Beyond identifying with Arthur Ashe, sharing this book's dedication with Jim and Lois Horton is an additional honor that, I trust, Lincoln will someday appreciate in full measure.

ARTHUR ASHE'S TENNIS STATISTICS

American Tennis Association

Boys 12 and Under Singles (1955)
Boys 15 and Under Doubles (1956, 1958)
Boys 16 and Under Singles (1957, 1958)
Interscholastic Singles (1958, 1959, 1960)
Boys 18 and Under Singles (1960)
Men's Singles (1960, 1961, 1962)
Men's Doubles (1961)

USLTA

U.S. National Indoor Junior Men's Singles (1960, 1961)
U.S. National Interscholastic Men's Singles (1961)
U.S. Hard Court Men's Singles (1963)
U.S. Clay Court Men's Singles (1967)
U.S. Indoor Men's Doubles (1967)
U.S. National Amateur Men's Singles (1968)

NCAA

NCAA Singles, Doubles, and Team Championships (1965)

Open Era

U.S. Open Men's Singles (1968)
Australian Open Men's Singles (1970)
U.S. Clay Court Men's Doubles (1970)
U.S. Indoor Men's Doubles (1970)
French Open Men's Doubles (1971)
Wimbledon Men's Singles (1975)
Australian Open Men's Doubles (1977)

OPEN ERA STATISTICS (SINGLES)

YEAR	TOURNAMENTS	TITLES	FINALS	MATCH RECORD	WINNING PERCENTAGE	U.S. RANK	WORLD RANK
1968	22	10	12**	72–10	.878	1	2
1969	26	2	8	83–24	.776	2	8
1970	30	11	14	91–20	.820	3	9
1971	32	3	9	77–31	.713	2	6
1972	31	3	6	69–30	.690	NR*	5
1973	31	2	9	68–29	.701	3	9
1974	29	3	9	85–27	.759	5	7
1975	29	9	14	108–23	.824	1	4
1976	28	5	9	64–23	.736	3	2
1977	5	0	0	6–5	.545	NR	130
1978	28	3	4	65–25	.722	9	10
1979	13	0	2	30–13	.698	5	7
TOTAL	304	51	96	818–260	.751		

Sources: *OTC*, 220–30; *BCHT*, 543–44; "Arthur Ashe," atpworldtour.com.

*As a contract player, Ashe received no ranking from the USTA in 1972.
**Estimate.

According to atpworldtour.com, Ashe's Open Era tournament prize money totaled $1,584,109.

GRAND SLAM TOURNAMENTS, SINGLES

Australian National Championship (1966–67), Australian Open (1970–1978)

1966: (finalist, l. Roy Emerson)
1967: (finalist, l. Roy Emerson)
1970: (champion, d. Dick Crealy)
1971: (finalist, l. Ken Rosewall)
1977: (quarterfinalist, l. John Alexander)
1978: (semifinalist, l. John Marks)

French Open

1969: (4th round, l. Fred Stolle)
1970: (quarterfinalist, l. Zeljko Franulovic)
1971: (quarterfinalist, l. Frank Froehling)
1973: (4th round, l. Paolo Bertolucci)
1974: (4th round, l. Manolo Orantes)
1976: (4th round, l. Balazs Taroczy)
1978: (4th round, l. Guillermo Vilas)
1979: (3rd round, l. Ivan Lendl)

U.S. National Championship (1959–68), U.S. Open (1968–78)

1959: (1st round, l. Rod Laver)
1960: (2nd round, l. Edward Zuleta)
1961: (2nd round, l. François Godbout)
1962: (2nd round, l. Roy Emerson)
1963: (3rd round, l. Marty Riessen)
1964: (4th round, l. Tony Roche)
1965: (semifinalist, l. Manuel Santana)
1966: (3rd Round, l. John Newcombe)
1968: (National Amateur champion, d. Bob Lutz)
1968: (Open champion, d. Tom Okker)
1969: (National quarterfinalist, l. Bob Lutz)
1969: (Open semifinalist, l. Rod Laver)
1970: (quarterfinalist, l. John Newcombe)
1971: (semifinalist, l. Jan Kodes)
1972: (finalist, l. Ilie Nastase)
1973: (3rd round, l. Bjorn Borg)

1974: (quarterfinalist, l. John Newcombe)
1975: (4th round, l. Eddie Dibbs)
1976: (2nd round, l. Jan Kodes)
1978: (4th round, l. Raúl Ramírez)

Wimbledon

1963: (3rd round, l. Chuck McKinley)
1964: (4th round, l. Roy Emerson)
1965: (4th round, l. Rafael Osuna)
1968: (semifinalist, l. Rod Laver)
1969: (semifinalist, l. Rod Laver)
1970: (4th round, l. Andrés Gimeno)
1971: (3rd round, l. Marty Riessen)
1974: (3rd round, l. Roscoe Tanner)
1975: (champion, d. Jimmy Connors)
1976: (4th round, l. Vitas Gerulaitis)
1978: (1st round, l. Steve Docherty)
1979: (1st round, l. Kris Kachel)

DAVIS CUP COMPETITION

1963: vs. Venezuela (d. Orlando Bracamonte)
1965: vs. Canada (d. Keith Carpenter and Harry Fauquier)
       vs. Mexico (d. Rafael Osuna and Antonio Palafox)
1966: vs. British West Indies (d. Lance Lumsden and Richard Russell)
       vs. Brazil (doubles, with Ralston, d. Thomas Koch and José Edison
         Mandarino)
1967: vs. Mexico (d. Marcelo Lara and Rafael Osuna)
       vs. Ecuador (l. Miguel Olvera and Pancho Guzman)
1968: vs. British West Indies (d. Lance Lumsden and Richard Russell)
       vs. Mexico (d. Rafael Osuna and Joaquín Loyo-Mayo)
       vs. Ecuador (d. Pancho Guzman and Miguel Olivera)
       vs. Spain (d. Juan Gisbert and Manuel Santana)
       vs. India (d. Premjit Lall and Ramanathan Krishnan)
       vs. Australia (d. Ray Ruffels, l. Bill Bowrey)
1969: vs. Romania (d. Ilie Nastase and Ion Tiriac)
1970: vs. West Germany (d. Wilhelm Bungert and Christian Kuhnke)
1975: vs. British West Indies (d. Richard Russell)

1977: vs. Mexico (d. Roberto Chávez, l. Raúl Ramírez)
1978: vs. Sweden (l. Bjorn Borg, d. Kjell Johansson)

Davis Cup Player Summary (1963–78)

27 wins, 5 losses, .844 winning percentage, 5 Davis Cups (1963, 1968, 1969, 1970, 1978); Doubles (1966), 1 win, 0 losses.

U.S. Davis Cup Captain Summary (1981–85)

13 wins, 3 losses, .812 winning percentage, 2 Davis Cups (1981, 1982)

NOTE ON ARCHIVAL SOURCES
AND INTERVIEWS

The largest and most important archival collection related to Arthur Ashe's life and career is the Arthur Ashe Papers (AAP), located at the Arthur Schomburg Center for Black Culture, a branch of the New York Public Library. Organized in a collection of forty-two boxes, the AAP contains newspaper and magazine clippings, correspondence, manuscripts, published writings, and miscellaneous documents, the majority of which deal with the years 1968 to 1997. Other significant collections of Ashe materials include: the Ashe Files at the library of the International Tennis Hall of Fame, in Newport, Rhode Island; the Ashe Vertical File at the Richmond, Virginia, Public Library; the Arthur Ashe File located at the UCLA Sports Information Office; the various collections dealing with Coach J. D. Morgan and the UCLA tennis program, located in the UCLA University Archive; and the Wimbledon Scrapbooks at the Kenneth Ritchie Wimbledon Library, Wimbledon, U.K. The research for this book also benefited from access to an extensive privately held collection in the possession of Jeanne Moutoussamy-Ashe, South Kent, Connecticut; and a smaller collection held by Al Schragis, Scarsdale, New York.

Oral history interviews also constituted an essential source of information on Ashe's life, the historical context of his career, his experiences as an African American, and the evolution of tennis both before and after the beginning of the Open era in 1968. Interviews were conducted both by phone and in person, and their length and character ranged from lengthy formal interview sessions to casual conversations. The following list of interviews includes Ashe family members, friends, players and other figures from the world of professional tennis, individuals associated with various institutions with which Ashe was involved, and miscellaneous others.

INTERVIEWS

Abraham, Seth, by Jackie Inman, January 26, 2014

Abram, D. A., by author, August 30, 2016

Adams, Katrina, by author, September 1, 2015

Allen, Leslie, by author, September 1, 2013

Amdur, Neil, by author, September 1, 2013

Anderson, Susan, by author, September 12, 2011

Ashe, Johnnie, by author, May 25, 2017

Beale, Sam, by author, July 18, 2013

Beck, Chris, by Dara Vance, July 2013

Bent, Timothy, by author, January 8, 2016

Bloom, Alex, by author, April 7, 2017

Blount, Renee, by Rachel Sanderson, January 27, 2014

Bonds, Steve, by author, August 27, 2016

Bollettieri, Nick, by author, September 1, 2013; by Dara Vance, July 2014

Boxser, Litten, by author, November 16, 2017

Buchholz, Butch, by Jackie Inman, December 9, 2013

Buchholz, Cliff, by author, August 30, 2013

Buchholz, Karin, by author, August 29, 2016

Burgess, Granville, by author, January 15, 2016

Burpee, Trey, by author, January 31, 2016

Cammack-Spencer, Doris, by author, August 9, 2009, October 7, 2015

Carrico, Lucretia, by author, March 31, 2017

Carrington, Arthur, by Jackie Inman, January 31, February 3, 2014

Carson, Clayborne, by author, May 19, 2016

Chewning, Tom, by Dara Vance, June 11, 2014; by author, March 14, 2017

Collins, Bud, by author, June 10, 2014

Crookenden, Ian, by Dara Vance, July 15, 2013; by author, March 26, 2018

Davis, Bobby, by Dara Vance, July 24, 2013

Davis, Jonathan, by author, March 14, 2017

Davis, Patricia Battles, and Billy Davis, by Dara Vance, July 2014

Dell, Donald, by author, August 30, 2013, March 26, 2014

Desdunes, Jean, by author, July 29, 2013

Dinkins, David, by Rachel Sanderson, January 27, 2014, by author, August 27, 2016

DiPasquale, Paul, by Dara Vance, August 2014; by author, March 15, 2017

Dittmann, Steve, by author, March 12, 2018

Dowdell, Kevin, by author, September 13, 2016

Drake, Veronica, by author, January 20, 2018

Drysdale, Cliff, by author, August 30, 2013

Ebner, Deb, by author, May 22, 2017

Edwards, Harry, by Nano Riley, February 17, 2018; by author, June 2018

Einwick, Lou, by author, March 13–15, 2017

Emerson, Roy, by Rachel Sanderson, January 24, 2014

Farrell, Robert, by author, August 23, 2005

Ferszt, Judith, by author, October 3, 2017

Fleming, Carlos, by Rachel Sanderson, February 27, 2014

Floyd, James Jr., by author, October 2011

Fox, Allen, by Dara Vance, July 18, 2013

Freeman, Marcel, by Jackie Inman, July 14, 2014

Freeman, Marcus, by author, July 29, 2013

Froehling, Frank, by Jackie Inman, December 26, 2013

Garrison, Zina, by Rachel Sanderson, March 26, 2014

Gates, Henry Louis, by author, August 9, 2009

Gewecke, Clifford George Jr., by Jackie Inman, July 12, 2014

Gottfried, Brian, by Jackie Inman, January 31, 2014

Graebner, Clark, by author, September 27, 2013

Green, Reginald, by author, August 11, 2005

Green, Traci, by Dara Vance, July 14, 2014

Grossman, James, by author, March 11, 2017

Grover, Shema, by author, March 14, 2017

Harmon, Rodney, by author, September 30, 2013

Harris, Don, by author, February 2007

Harris, Loretta Florence Ashe, by author, August 27, 2016

Harris, Ralph, by author, July 31, 2011

Hartman, Skip, by author, August 31, 2016

Henchman, Kate, by author, October 26, 2017

Hooper, Chip, by Jackie Inman, February 14, 2014

Irby, Robert E. Lee, by author, March 31, 2017

Jenks, Dennis, by author, February 22, 2018

Johnson, Willard, by Erin Hughes, April 9, 2015

Kaplan, Lynda, by author, April 7, 2010, October 21, 2017

Kelen, Leslie, by author, October 8, 2015

Koger, Anne, by Dara Vance, June 24, 2014

Lucas, Phil, by author, August 29, 2013

Mandelstam, Rodney, by Nano Riley, October 25, 2017

Mandeville, Eddie, by author, August 29, 2013

Mayer, Gene, by Arielle Stevenson, October 14, 2015
Mayfield, June, by Nano Riley, February 19, 2018
Maymi-Perez, Javier, by author, February 19, 2018
McEnroe, John, Jr., by author, September 1, 2015
McGuire, Kay and Kevin, by author, January 23, 2016
McNeil, Lori, by author, July 13, 2013
McNichols, Steve, by author, August 16, 2005
McPhee, John, by author, May 29, 2014
Michaels, Will, by author, February 17, 2018
Moore, Ray, by Dara Vance, August 12, 2013
Morris, Christopher, by author, November 12, 2015, April 6, 2017
Moutoussamy-Ashe, Jeanne, by author, Dec. 2009, August 29, 2015, January
    12–15, 2016, August 27, 2016, February 8–9, 2018
Muir, Toby, by author, March 27, 2018
Murray, Henry, by author, August 31, 2016
Myers, David, by author, March 21, 2018
Nagler, Larry, by Arielle Stevenson, July 27, 2017
Nash, Gary, by author, May 19, 2016
Nelson, Todd, by Jackie Inman, June 27, 2014
Newcombe, John, by Nano Riley, January 2, 2018
Newman, Butch, by Jackie Inman, January 15, 2014
Nicholson, Jim, by author, March 28, 2014
Northup, Steve, by author, May 24, 29, 2018
Norton, Mary Beth, by author, August 9, 2009
Pace, La Chandra Harris, by author, August 27, 2016
Pasarell, Charlie, by author, February 2016, March 27, 2018
Pearson, Martha McMasters, by author, August 10, 2015
Policinski, Gene, by Nano Riley, October 4, 2017
Price, Connie, by author, December 11, 2016
Ralston, Dennis, by Arielle Stevenson, October 5, 2015
Rampersad, Arnold, by author, October 31, 2017
Reed, David, by Dara Vance, July 19, 2013
Reid, Horace, by author, July 31, 2011
Reilly, Mike, by author, July 10, 2016, July 16, 2017
Reilly, Paul, by author, July 31, 2016, July 16, 2017
Reilly, Steve, by author, June 2016
Richey, Cliff and Nancy, by Jackie Inman, February 17, 2014
Ricks, Barbara Starling, by Dara Vance, 2014
Riessen, Marty, by Dara Vance, June 19, 2013; by Arielle Stevenson, July 2017
Robinson, Randall, by author, July 17, 2017
Rogers, Jefferson, by author, July 2013
Ryland, Robert, by author, September 1, 2013

Sammons, Jeffrey, by author, January 28, 2009

Sanderlin, David, by Dara Vance, August 8, 2013

Sands, Kim, by Jackie Inman, June 18, 2014

Sanger, Joan, by author, October 8, 2015

Savage, C. J., by author, May 29, 2014

Scherman, Rowland, by author, September 2017

Schragis, Al, by Jackie Inman, March 24, 2014; by author, August 31, 2016

Shelton, Bryan, by Dara Vance, June 14, 2014

Sherrod, Charles, by author, February 7, 2013

Shropshire, Diane, by Jackie Inman, February 12, 2014

Simons, Bill, by author, May 24, 29, 2018

Simpson, Lenny, by author, August 29, 2017

Sims, Fran and John, by author, July 10, 2016

Singleton, Robert, by author, September 13, 2011

Slaughter, Fred, by Arielle Stevenson, November 19, 2015

Smith, Bruce, by author, November 2016

Smith, Jolynn Johnson, by Dara Vance, August 2014

Smith, Rev. Paul, by Jackie Inman, December 5, 2013

Smith, Stan, by Jackie Inman, May 9, July 2014

Snyder, Sheridan, by author, June 2018

Spong, Jack, by author, August 5, 2016

Stockton, Dick, by Jackie Inman, April 12, 2014

Tanner, Roscoe, by Arielle Stevenson, November 19, 2015

Thomas, John Charles, by author, March 15, 2017

Thomas, Willis S., by author, July 29, 2013

Thompson, Douglas, by author, November 6, 14, 2015

Trabert, Tony, by Dara Vance, July 1, 2014

Turner, Pat, by author, August 29, 2016

Tuttle, Rick, by author, September 12, 2011

Wallace, Sally, by author, July 9, 2017

Wallace, William, by author, July 9, 2017

Washington, MaliVai, by Arielle Stevenson, July 2017

Wilkerson, John, by author, July 28, 2013

Williams, Charles, by author, January 2, 2014

Williams, Owen, by Dara Vance, July 1, 2014

Woodrum, Robert, by author, March 4, 2017

Yellin, Eric, by author, April 7, 2017

Young, Andrew, by author, August 7, 2015, March 28, 2018

NOTES

ABBREVIATIONS USED IN THE NOTES

AA Arthur Ashe Jr., as told to Clifford George Gewecke Jr., *Advantage Ashe* (New York: Coward-McCann, 1967).

AADJ Arthur Ashe daily journals; in private collection of Jeanne Moutoussamy-Ashe

AAP Arthur Ashe Papers, Schomburg Center for Research in Black Culture, New York Public Library

AATC Louie Robinson Jr., *Arthur Ashe: Tennis Champion* (Garden City, NY: Doubleday, 1970).

ASC Al Schragis Collection of Arthur Ashe Memorabilia, Scarsdale, New York

BAA *Baltimore Afro-American*

BATN Sundiata Djata, *Blacks at the Net: Black Achievement in the History of Tennis*, vol. 1 (Syracuse: Syracuse University Press, 2006).

BCHT Bud Collins, *The Bud Collins History of Tennis: An Authoritative Encyclopedia and Record Book* (second edition) (New York: New Chapter Press, 2011).

CD *Chicago Defender*

CTN Cecil Harris and Larryette Kyle-DeBose, *Charging the Net: A History of Blacks in Tennis from Althea Gibson and Arthur Ashe to the Williams Sisters* (Chicago: Ivan Dee, 2007).

DB *Daily Bruin* (UCLA)

DG Arthur Ashe and Arnold Rampersad, *Days of Grace: A Memoir* (New York: Alfred A. Knopf, 1993).

HRG Arthur R. Ashe Jr., *A Hard Road to Glory: A History of the African-American Athlete* (vol. 1, 1619–1918; vol. 2, 1919–1945; vol. 3, Since 1946) (New York: Warner Books, 1988).

int   interview
IRAA   Mike Towle, ed., *I Remember Arthur Ashe* (Nashville: Cumberland House, 2001).
ITHF   International Tennis Hall of Fame, Newport, Rhode Island
JMA   Jeanne Moutoussamy-Ashe
KRWL   Kenneth Ritchie Wimbledon Library
LAT   *Los Angeles Times*
LG   John McPhee, *Levels of the Game* (New York: Farrar, Straus & Giroux, 1969).
NYT   *New York Times*
OSC   Olympic Studies Center, Lausanne, Switzerland
OTC   Arthur Ashe, with Neil Amdur, *Off the Court* (New York: New American Library, 1981).
PIM   Arthur Ashe, with Frank Deford, *Arthur Ashe, Portrait in Motion* (Boston: Houghton Mifflin, 1975).
q, qs   quotation, quotations
RFP   *Richmond Free Press*
RNL   *Richmond News Leader*
RTD   *Richmond Times-Dispatch*
SI   *Sports Illustrated*
SSAA   *Tennis Channel Signature Series: Arthur Ashe.* Directed by Nitin Varma, 2014.
UCLASIO UCLA Sports Information Office
UCLAUA UCLA, University Archive
W   Doug Smith, *Whirlwind: The Godfather of Black Tennis: The Life and Times of Dr. Robert Walter Johnson* (Washington, DC: Blue Eagle Publishing, 2004).
WP   *Washington Post*
WT   *World Tennis* magazine

PREFACE

1   See Howard Bryant, *The Last Hero: A Life of Henry Aaron* (New York: Pantheon, 2010); David Remnick, *King of the World: Muhammad Ali and the Rise of an American Hero* (New York: Vintage, 1999); William J. Baker, *Jesse Owens: An American Life* (New York: Free Press, 1986); Randy Roberts, *Joe Louis: Hard Times Man* (New Haven: Yale University Press, 2010); David Maraniss, *Clemente: The Passion and Grace of Baseball's Last Hero* (New York: Simon & Schuster, 2007); James S. Hirsch, *Willie Mays: The Life, the Legend* (New York: Scribner, 2010); Larry Tye, *Satchel: The Life and Times of an American Legend* (New York: Random House, 2009); Jules Tygiel, *Baseball's Great Experiment: Jackie Robinson and His Legacy* (New York: Oxford University Press, 1983); Arnold Rampersad, *Jackie Robinson, A Biography* (New York: Alfred A. Knopf, 1997); Wil Haygood, *Sweet Thunder: The Life and Times of Sugar Ray Robinson* (New York: Alfred A. Knopf, 2009); and Aram Goudsouzian, *King of the Court: Bill Russell and the Basketball Revolution* (Berkeley: University of California Press, 2010).

2   Frank Deford, *Big Bill Tilden: The Triumphs and the Tragedy* (New York: Simon & Schuster, 1976); Susan Ware, *Game, Set, Match: Billie Jean King and the Revolution in Women's Sports* (Chapel Hill: University of North Carolina Press, 2011); and Chris Bowers, *Federer* (London: John Blake, 2016). Those seeking a greater understanding

of the personal side of tennis history can turn to: John McPhee, *Levels of the Game* (New York: Farrar, Straus & Giroux, 1969); Richard Evans, *McEnroe: A Rage for Perfection* (New York: Simon & Schuster, 1982); John Feinstein, *Hard Courts: Real Life on the Professional Tennis Tours* (New York: Villard, 1991); Stephen Tignor, *High Strung: Bjorn Borg, John McEnroe and the Untold Story of Tennis's Fiercest Rivalry* (New York: Harper, 2012); Marshall Jon Fisher, *A Terrible Splendor: Three Extraordinary Men, A World Poised for War, and the Greatest Tennis Match Ever Played* (New York: Broadway, 2010); Eric Hall, *Arthur Ashe: Tennis and Justice in the Civil Rights Era* (Baltimore: Johns Hopkins University Press, 2014; Peter Bodo, *Ashe vs Connors: Wimbledon 1975—Tennis That Went Beyond Centre Court* (London: Aurum Press, 2015); Frances Clayton Gray and Yanick Rice Lamb, *Born to Win: The Authorized Biography of Althea Gibson* (New York: John Wiley & Sons, 2004); Richard Evans, *Nasty: Ilie Nastase vs. Tennis* (New York: Stein & Day, 1979); Adrianne Blue, *Martina. The Lives and Times of Martina Navratilova* (New York: Birch Lane Press, 1995); Johnette Howard, *The Rivals: Chris Evert vs. Martina Navratilova—Their Rivalry, Their Friendship, Their Legacy* (New York: Yellow Jersey Press, 2005); Caroline Seebohm, *Little Pancho: The Life of Tennis Legend Pancho Segura* (Lincoln: University of Nebraska Press, 2009); and Chris Bowers, *Novak Djokovic and the Rise of Serbia: The Sporting Statesman* (London: John Blake, 2015).

3   Althea Gibson, edited by Ed Fitzgerald, *I Always Wanted to Be Somebody* (New York: Harper & Row, 1958); Althea Gibson, with Richard Curtis, *So Much to Live For* (New York: G. P. Putnam's Sons, 1968); Alice Marble, with Dale Leatherman, *Courting Danger: My Adventures in World-Class Tennis, Golden Age Hollywood, and High-Stakes Spying* (New York: St. Martin's, 1991); Rod Laver, with Bud Collins, *The Education of a Tennis Player* (New York: Simon & Schuster, 1971); Jack Kramer, *The Game: My Forty Years in Tennis* (New York: Putnam, 1979); Billie Jean King, with Frank Deford, *Billie Jean* (New York: Viking, 1982); Martina Navratilova, with George Vecsey, *Martina* (New York: Alfred A. Knopf, 1985); John McEnroe and James Kaplan, *You Cannot Be Serious* (New York: G. P. Putnam's Sons, 2002); Pete Sampras, with Peter Bodo, *A Champion's Mind: Lessons from a Life in Tennis* (New York: Three Rivers Press, 2009); Andre Agassi, *Open: An Autobiography* (New York: Alfred A. Knopf, 2009); Jimmy Connors, *The Outsider: A Memoir* (New York: Harper, 2013); Chris Evert, *Chrissie: My Own Story* (New York: Simon & Schuster, 1982); Zina Garrison, with Doug Smith, *Zina: My Life in Women's Tennis* (Berkeley: Frog Ltd., 2001); James Blake, with Andrew Friedman, *Breaking Back: How I Lost Everything and Won Back My Life* (New York: Harper, 2007); Rafael Nadal and John Carlin, *Rafa* (New York: Hachette, 2012); Andy Murray, *Andy Murray: Seventy-Seven* (London: Headline, 2015); Serena Williams, *My Life: Queen of the Court* (New York: Pocket Books, 2010); Serena Williams, with Daniel Paisner, *On the Line* (New York: Grand Central, 2009); Arthur Ashe Jr., as told to Clifford George Gewecke Jr., *Advantage Ashe* (New York: Coward-McCann, 1967); Arthur Ashe, with Frank Deford, *Arthur Ashe: Portrait in Motion* (Boston: Houghton Mifflin, 1975); Arthur Ashe, with Neil Amdur, *Off the Court* (New York: New American Library, 1981); and Arthur Ashe and Arnold Rampersad, *Days of Grace, A Memoir* (New York: Alfred A. Knopf, 1993). See also two fascinating memoir-style narratives: Bud Collins, *My Life with the Pros* (New York: E. P. Dutton, 1989); and Peter Bodo, *The Courts of Babylon: Tales of Greed and Glory in the Harsh New World of Professional Tennis* (New York: Scribner, 1995).

PROLOGUE

1   Doris Cammack-Spencer int. The entire Cammack family was prominent in ATA circles, and Doris's older brother, Bill Cammack, was one of the ATA's most talented young stars. Doris played on the Anacostia High School tennis team from 1955 to 1957.

2   *DG*, 262–65; *NYT*, September 5, 10, 1992; "Ex-Tennis Star Ashe Arrested in Protest of Haitian Policy," *USA Today*, September 10, 1992; Gary Lee and Molly Sinclair, "Refugee Policy Protested," *WP*, September 10, 1992; *Washington Times*, September 10, 1992; Robinson int. See the clippings and correspondence in folder 8, box 1, AAP.

CHAPTER 1: UNDER THE DOMINION

1   *OTC*, 19; *AA*, 13; Hall, *Arthur Ashe*, 7–8; *PIM*, 27; *LG*, 62; and Marvin Martin, *Arthur Ashe: Of Tennis and the Human Spirit* (New York: Franklin Watts, 1999), 13. On the history of Jim Crow segregation, see C. Vann Woodward, *The Strange Career of Jim Crow* (Commemorative Edition) (New York: Oxford University Press, 2001); and Jane Dailey, Glenda Elizabeth Gilmore, and Bryant Simon, eds., *Jumpin' Jim Crow: Southern Politics from Civil War to Civil Rights* (Princeton: Princeton University Press, 2000).

2   On the distinctive history and mythology of Virginia, see David Hackett Fischer, *Albion's Seed: Four British Folkways in America* (New York: Oxford University Press, 1989), 207–418; Carl Bridenbaugh, *Myths and Realities: Societies of the Colonial South* (New York: Atheneum, 1972); Wilbur J. Cash, *The Mind of the South* (New York: Alfred A. Knopf, 1941); Virginius Dabney, *Virginia: The New Dominion* (Garden City, NY: Doubleday, 1971); Virginius Dabney, *Virginius Dabney's Virginia: Writings on the Old Dominion* (Chapel Hill: Algonquin Books, 1986); Virginia Moore, *Virginia Is a State of Mind* (New York: E. P. Dutton, 1942); Jean Gottman, *Virginia at Mid-Century* (New York: Henry Holt, 1955); Jean Gottman, *Virginia in Our Century* (Charlottesville: University of Virginia Press, 1969); Parke Rouse Jr., *We Happy WASPS: Virginia in the Days of Jim Crow and Harry Byrd* (Richmond: R. Dietz Press, 1996); and Marshall Fishwick, *Virginia: A New Look at the Old Dominion* (New York: HarperCollins, 1959). On Richmond, see Virginius Dabney, *Richmond: The Story of a City* (Garden City, NY: Doubleday, 1976); Maurice Duke and David P. Jerdas, eds., *A Richmond Reader, 1733–1983* (Chapel Hill: University of North Carolina Press, 1983); Francis E. Lutz, *Richmond in World War II* (Richmond: R. Dietz Press, 1951); John A. Cutchins, *Memoir of Old Richmond* (Vernon, VA: McClure Press, 1973); Emily J. and John S. Salmon, *Remembering Richmond* (Nashville: Turner Publishing, 2010); Benjamin Campbell, *Richmond's Unhealed History* (Richmond: Brandylane, 2011); Walter S. Griggs Jr., *Hidden History of Richmond* (Mount Pleasant, SC: History Press, 2012); Walter S. Griggs Jr., *World War II Richmond, Military* (Mount Pleasant, SC: History Press, 2013); and Amy Waters Yarsinske, *Richmond Through the 20th Century* (Mount Pleasant, SC: Arcadia, 2016). On the historical and cultural significance of Monument Avenue, see Marie Tyler McGraw, "Southern Comfort Levels: Race, Heritage Tourism, and the Civil War in Richmond," in James Oliver Horton and Lois E. Horton, eds., *Slavery and Public History: The Tough Stuff of American Memory* (New York: New Press, 2006), 151–67; Robert Hodder, "Redefining a Southern City's Heritage: Historic Preservation Planning, Public Art, and Race in Richmond, Virginia," *Journal of Urban Affairs* 21 (1999): 437–53; Matthew Mace Barbee, "Race, Memory, and Communal Belonging in Narrative and Art: Richmond, Virginia's Monument Avenue,

1948–1996" (PhD thesis, Bowling Green State University, 2007); and Matthew Mace Barbee, *Race and Masculinity in Southern Memory: History of Richmond, Virginia's Monument Avenue* (New York: Rowman & Littlefield, 2016). For a discerning fictional treatment of current-day Richmond's Confederate mystique, see Lee Irby, *Unreliable* (New York: Doubleday, 2017).

3   *OTC*, 22 (third q), 23 (first and fourth qs), 27 (second q); *AA*, 17–18.

4   *OTC*, 15–16 (qs); *LG*, 12–13; Martin, *Arthur Ashe*, 13.

5   *OTC*, 16 (qs); *LG*, 11; Martin, *Arthur Ashe*, 13.

6   *AA*, 109–10 (first q); *OTC*, 16, 17 (second q), 18; "The Name and Family of Ash(e)," fourteen-page typescript prepared by Roots Research Bureau LTD (New York, 1984), in folder 1, box 1, AAP; *LG*, 11–12; Hall, *Arthur Ashe*, 10–11; Martin, *Arthur Ashe*, 13–14; Richard Steins, *Arthur Ashe: A Biography* (Westport, CT: Greenwood, 2005), 4.

7   *LG*, 61 62; *OTC*, 17 18; Martin, *Arthur Ashe*, 14; Christopher Silver and John V. Moeser, *Separate City: Black Communities in the Urban South, 1940–1968* (Lexington: University Press of Kentucky, 1995), 1–14, 24–30, 42–48. See also J. Douglas Smith, *Managing White Supremacy: Race, Politics, and Citizenship in Jim Crow Virginia* (Chapel Hill: University of North Carolina Press, 2002); and Michael P. Claibourn, "Blacks in Virginia: Demographic Trends in Historical Context," *Numbers Count: Analysis of Virginia Population* (Demographics of Workforce Group, Weldon Cooper Center, University of Virginia) (April 2012): 1–16.

8   *LG*, 62 (first q); *OTC*, 18 (second and third qs).

9   Griggs, *World War II Richmond, Military*; Rick Atkinson, *Day of Battle: The War in Sicily and Italy, 1943–44* (New York: Henry Holt, 2007); *OTC*, 19, 21; *LG*, 62–66. On the Double V campaign popular among African Americans during World War II, see Rawn James Jr., *The Double V: How Wars, Protest, and Harry Truman Desegregated America's Military* (New York: Bloomsbury, 2014).

10   *OTC*, 19; Silver and Moeser, *Separate City*, 25–30, 42–47; *LG*, 62; Thompson int. On Bill "Bojangles" Robinson, see Jim Haskins and N. R. Mitgang, *Mr. Bojangles: The Biography of Bill Robinson* (New York: William Morrow, 1990); and Meghan Cunningham, *Bill Bojangles Robinson* (New York: Cavendish Square, 2016).

11   *LG*, 64 (q); Raymond Pierre Hylton, *Virginia Union University* (Mount Pleasant, SC: Arcadia, 2014); Reginald Green and Thompson ints.

12   *OTC*, 19, 28; *LG*, 64–65 (qs); *AA*, 12–13, 16; Einwick int.

13   *OTC*, 17–18 (qs); *AA*, 110; Hall, *Arthur Ashe*, 10–11; Martin, *Arthur Ashe*, 17; *AATC*, 58.

14   *OTC*, 24 (q); *AATC*, 35; Chewning and Einwick ints.

15   *OTC*, 34–35 (q); *LG*, 35–36; *AATC*, 16, 25–35.

16   *OTC*, 35 (q); Martin, *Arthur Ashe*, 16; *AATC*, 26; Johnnie Ashe and Loretta Ashe Harris ints; Johnnie Ashe int, *SSAA*.

17   *OTC*, 24–26; *AA*, 17 (second q)–18 (first q); Martin, *Arthur Ashe*, 16–17; Johnnie Ashe int, *SSAA*.

18   *LG*, 62–66; *OTC*, 19–20 (qs); *AA*, 16; *DG*, 3–4, 48; Johnnie Ashe int, *SSAA*.

19   *OTC*, 20 (q); *AATC*, 13, 15.

20   *OTC*, 21 (q).

21   *DG*, 48 (first q), 50 (second q).

22   *OTC*, 22 (q), 24–25; *AA*, 16; *AATC*, 17–22; Martin, *Arthur Ashe*, 16. Olis W. Berry was born in Brunswick County, Virginia, in 1879, and died in Richmond in 1971. See Social Security Death Index, available on archives.com.

23   *DG*, 49–50 (first q); *LG*, 65–66; *OTC*, 14, 22, 25–26 (second q), 34, 36, 48; *AA*, 13, 31.

24   *AA*, 13 (first q); B. Drummond Ayres Jr., "Ashe Returns to the City He Disowned in Youth," *NYT*, May 7, 1992 (second q); *RFP*, April 16–18, 1992 (third q); *AATC*, 9–10, 30.

25   *RFP*, April 16–18, 1992 (q); *AA*, 14; *OTC*, 33, 35; *LG*, 37–38; *AATC*, 40–44. Gordon was one of the first blacks to graduate from the Univeristy of Virginia (1964) and went on to be the district manager of Bell Atlantic Telephone Company. See October 13, 2000, obituary in Legacy.com.

CHAPTER 2: PLAYING IN THE SHADOWS

1   *AA*, 12–15, 19 (qs); *OTC*, 33; *AATC*, 68.

2   *OTC*, 33 (first q); *AA*, 15 (second q); Einwick int; Eric Perkins, Tom Wood, and John Packett, *Richmond: One of America's Best Tennis Towns* (Richmond: Dementi Milestone Publishing, 2012), 5–6; John Packett, "Early Help Spurred Parrish to Greater Heights," October 8, 2013, available online at the Richmond Tennis Association website richmondtennis.org.

3   *BCHT*, 3–16; Heiner Gillmeister, *Tennis: A Cultural History* (New York: NYU Press, 1998), 191, 207–22; Allison Danzig and Peter Schwed, eds., *The Fireside Book of Tennis: A Complete History of the Game and Its Great Players and Matches* (New York: Simon & Schuster, 1972), 3–28; E. Digby Baltzell, *Sporting Gentlemen: Men's Tennis from the Age of Honor to the Cult of the Superstar* (New Brunswick, NJ: Transaction, 2013), 13–162; Eugene Scott, *Tennis: Game of Motion* (New York: Crown, 1973), 30–49; *HRG*, vol. 2, 59–60; *CTN*, 3; *W*, 42–43; Frank Deford int, *SSAA*.

4   Gillmeister, *Tennis*, 211; *BCHT*, 8; Danzig and Schwed, eds., *Fireside Book of Tennis*, 14–20; *CTN*, 106–9, 239–42; *W*, 4–5, 41–47; *BATN*, 1–27; *HRG*, vol. 2, 60–62.

5   *CTN*, 106–9, 239–42; *W*, 4–5, 41–47; *BATN*, 4–27. On the "Golden Age" of white tennis in the 1920s, see *BCHT*, 15–42; Danzig and Schwed, eds., *Fireside Book of Tennis*, 130–266; and Baltzell, *Sporting Gentlemen*, 163–218. For early coverage of black tennis in the black press, see *The Chicago Defender*; the *Baltimore Afro-American*; and *The Pittsburgh Courier*.

6   *CTN*, 108, 239, 242; *W*, 48; *BATN*, 5–8; *HRG*, vol. 2, 62–63; Ryland, Bobby Davis, and Willis Thomas ints; Ben Rothenberg, "African-American Tennis, Fostered for 100 Years," *NYT*, August 27, 2017.

7   See Baker, *Jesse Owens*; Chris Mead, *Champion: Joe Louis, Black Hero in White America* (New York: Penguin, 1986); Roberts, *Joe Louis*; LeRoy (Satchel) Paige, as told to David Lipman, *Maybe I'll Pitch for Ever* (Lincoln: University of Nebraska Press, 1993); and Tye, *Satchel*.

8   Ryland int; *W*, 92–97.

9   *W*, 1, 19, 28, 44, 58, 104; *CTN*, 3, 7, 95, 108–9; *BATN*, 6–9; Ryland int.

10   Ryland int. See Woody Strode and Sam Young, *Goal Dust: The Warm and Candid Memoirs of a Pioneer Black Athlete and Actor* (Aurora, IL: Madison Press Books, 1993); Robert W. Peterson, *Pigskin: The Early Years of Pro Football* (New York: Oxford University Press, 1997); Steve Bisheff, *Los Angeles Rams* (New York: Macmillan, 1973); Bob Oates, *The Los Angeles Rams* (Hollywood, CA: Murray & Gee, 1955); and Jules Tygiel, *Baseball's Great Experiment: Jackie Robinson and His Legacy* (New York: Oxford University Press, 1983), 3–9, 30–208. On the Marian Anderson controversy, see Raymond Arsenault, *The Sound of Freedom: Marian Anderson, the Lincoln Memorial, and the Concert That Awakened America* (New York: Bloomsbury, 2009).

11   *BATN*, 9–13; *BCHT*, 61–63, 66, 554–55; *CTN*, 110–11, 242; *W*, 46 (first q), 48; Steven
      M. Tucker, "Against All Odds," *Racquet* (Fall 1991): 58–60; Al Laney, "2,000 Ne-
      groes," *New York Herald Tribune*, July 30, 1940 (second q); *HRG*, vol. 2, 63–64.
12   *W*, 46.
13   *CTN*, 111 (q); *BATN*, 18; *W*, 59; *BCHT*, 586, 606–7; Ryland int. On Alice Marble, see
      Marble, with Leatherman, *Courting Danger*; and Alice Marble, *The Road to Wimble-
      don* (New York: Charles Scribner's Sons, 1947).
14   Ryland int; *CTN*, 110, 238; *W*, 58.
15   *NYT*, March 9, 1948 (q); *CTN*, 108–9; Trabert int.
16   *HRG*, vol. 3, 145 (q); *BATN*, 14–15; Trabert int.
17   *W*, xi–xv, 3, 7–41, 48–49 (q), 50–54, 64–72; *LG*, 36–41; *CTN*, 112–13; *AA*, 21–45;
      OTC, 39–41; *HRG*, vol. 3, 150–51; *BATN*, 18–21; Ben Rothenberg, "Bringing to
      Light a Seminal Figure," *NYT*, August 27, 2017; Jolyn Johnson Smith and Simpson
      ints.
18   *W*, 75–76, 78, 83; Jolyn Johnson Smith and Simpson ints.
19   *CTN*, 52–54, 64; *W*, 54–57; *BATN*, 28–30; *HRG*, vol. 3, 146; Hubert A. Eaton, *Every
      Man Should Try* (Wilmington, NC: Bonaparte Press, 1984); Gibson, *I Always Wanted
      to Be Somebody*, 36–39; Gibson, with Curtis, *So Much to Live For*, 17; Gray and Lamb,
      Born to Win, 34–36; Jennifer H. Lansbury, *A Spectacular Leap: Black Women Ath-
      letes in Twentieth-Century America* (Fayetteville: University of Arkansas Press, 2014),
      11–26, 74–100; *Althea* (PBS *American Masters* series, directed by Rex Miller, 2015).
20   Lansbury, *A Spectacular Leap*, 80–93; Gray and Lamb, *Born to Win*, 36–51; Gibson, *I
      Always Wanted to Be Somebody*, 40–57; *Althea*.
21   *HRG*, vol. 3, xxi, 1–7, 77, 162–64; Lansbury, *A Spectacular Leap*, 65–74; *CTN*, 54.
22   *BCHT*, 73, 86–88, 94, 581–82, 644. On Segura, see Seebohm, *Little Pancho*; and *NYT*,
      November 20, 2017 (obituary). On Gonzales, see Pancho Gonzales, *Man with the
      Racket: The Autobiography of Pancho Gonzales* (n.p.: Ulan Press, 2012); Doreen Gon-
      zales, *Tennis Legend: Pancho Gonzales* (Goodyear, AR: Gregory Gonzales Publishing,
      2007); Danzig and Schwed, eds., *Fireside Book of Tennis*, 294–306, 701–9; and *Pancho
      Gonzales: Warrior of the Court* (Spike/PBS television documentary by Higher Ground
      Entertainment, 2009); *RFP*, April 16–18, 1992 (q). Both Segura and Gonzales men-
      tored and practiced with Ashe during his years at UCLA. See *HRG*, vol. 3, 153–54.
23   Alice Marble, "A Vital Issue," *American Lawn Tennis* (July 1950): 14; *W*, 2, 58–60;
      CTN, 54–55; Lansbury, *A Spectacular Leap*, 93–94; Gibson, *I Always Wanted to Be
      Somebody*, 61–68; Gray and Lamb, *Born to Win*, 51–58; *BATN*, 30–31; *Althea*.
24   *CTN*, 55–56; *HRG*, vol. 3, 147–49 (q), 150; *BATN*, 15.
25   Gibson, *I Always Wanted to Be Somebody*, 68–75; Gray and Lamb, *Born to Win*, 41–42,
      58–67; *CTN*, 56–57 (q); Lansbury, *A Spectacular Leap*, 95–96, 100–101; *W*, 59–60;
      HRG, vol. 3, 150–51; Danzig and Schwed, eds., *Fireside Book of Tennis*, 710–11; *Al-
      thea*.

CHAPTER 3: DR. J AND THE LYNCHBURG BOYS

1   *W*, 1–2 (q); *LG*, 23, 26–27; George McGann, "'Doc' Johnson, Dedicated to Medicine
      and Junior Tennis, Wins July Marlboro Award," *WT* (July 1965): 32–34.
2   *W*, 3–4; *LG*, 23–27.
3   *W*, 3 (qs), 70; *LG*, 27–28.
4   *W*, 4 (q), 5, 71; Dell int.

5   *W*, 70–72.
6   *CTN*, 58 (q); *HRG*, vol. 3, 146, 151.
7   Simpson, Willis Thomas, and Bobby Davis ints; *CTN*, 94; *AA*, 26, 30–34.
8   *OTC*, 30 (q); *LG* 29–30; *AATC*, 44–47, 54–55.
9   *PIM*, 56, 57 (q); *AA*, 20–22.
10   *PIM*, 56 (q).
11   *CTN*, 112 (first q), 113; *AA*, 25 (second q); *OTC*, 40–41; *LG*, 41–42; *AATC*, 51–54.
12   *AA*, 24, (qs), 26 (last q); *OTC*, 40; *AATC*, 50; Willis Thomas and Bobby Davis ints.
13   *AA*, 25 (fourth q)–26 (first and second qs), 29 (third q); *LG*, 42–43.
14   *OTC*, 25 (q), 43; *DG*, 42, 262; *AA*, 18; *LG*, 55–57; Loretta Ashe Harris int; *AATC*,
      62–63.
15   *W*, 77–79.
16   Ibid., 80–81.
17   "Bringing to Light a Seminal Figure" (q); Koger and Jolyn Johnson Smith ints. On
      the gathering force of white supremacist resistance in Virginia in 1955, see Benjamin
      Muse, *Virginia's Massive Resistance* (Bloomington: Indiana University Press, 1961);
      Robbins Ladew Gates, *The Making of Massive Resistance: Virginia's Politics of Public
      School Desegregation, 1954–1956* (Chapel Hill: University of North Carolina Press,
      1964); J. Harvie Wilkinson, *Harry Byrd and the Changing Face of Virginia Politics*
      (Charlottesville: University of Virginia Press, 1968); Ronald L. Heinemann, *Harry
      Byrd of Virginia* (Charlottesville: University of Virginia Press, 1996); and Matthew
      Lassiter and Andrew B. Lewis, eds., *The Moderates' Dilemma: Massive Resistance to
      School Desegregation in Virginia* (Charlottesville: University of Virginia Press, 1998).
      On the murder of Emmett Till, see Stephen J. Whitfield, *A Death in the Delta: The
      Story of Emmett Till* (Baltimore: Johns Hopkins University Press, 1988); Dewey S.
      Anderson, *Emmett Till: The Murder That Shocked the World and Propelled the Civil
      Rights Movement* (Jackson: University of Mississippi Press, 2015); and Timothy B.
      Tyson, *The Blood of Emmett Till* (New York: Simon & Schuster, 2017).
18   *W*, 83–85 (qs); *LG*, 28–29; "Bringing to Light a Seminal Figure"; Simpson int.
19   *W*, 87 (q); *AATC*, 5; "Bringing to Light a Seminal Figure."
20   *AA*, 29 (first q), 32 (second q).
21   *W*, 80; *AA*, 30.
22   *OTC*, 42 (first q), 43; *AA*, 30 (second q); Simpson and Willis Thomas ints.
23   *HRG*, vol. 3, 4–14, 72–80. See Haygood, *Sweet Thunder*; Remnick, *King of the World*;
      Willie Mays, with Lou Sahadi, *Say Hey* (New York: Simon & Schuster, 1988); Hirsch,
      Willie Mays; Tygiel, *Baseball's Great Experiment*; Rampersad, *Jackie Robinson*; Steve
      Jacobson, *Carrying Jackie's Torch: The Players Who Integrated Baseball—and America*
      (Chicago: Lawrence Hill, 2007); Cal Fussman, ed., *After Jackie: Pride, Prejudice, and
      Baseball's Forgotten Heroes: An Oral History* (New York: ESPN Books, 2007); Roger
      Kahn, *Boys of Summer* (New York: Harper Perennial, 2006); Peter Golenbock, *Bums:
      An Oral History of the Brooklyn Dodgers* (New York: Dover, 2010); Joseph Thomas
      Moore, *Larry Doby: The Struggle of the American League's First Black Player* (New
      York: Dover, 2012); Douglas Branson, *Greatness in the Shadows: Larry Doby and the
      Integration of the American League* (Lincoln: University of Nebraska Press, 2016); Bry-
      ant, *The Last Hero*; and Marannis, *Clemente*.
24   *HRG*, vol. 3, 55–63, 116–19; Mike Freeman, *Jim Brown: The Fierce Life of an American
      Hero* (New York: William Morrow, 2006); J. Thomas Jable, "Jim Brown: Superlative
      Athlete, Screen Star, Social Activist," in David K. Wiggins, ed., *Out of the Shadows: A*

Biographical History of African American Athletes (Fayetteville: University of Arkansas Press, 2006), 241–61; Jimmy Brown with Myron Cope, *Off My Chest* (Garden City, NY: Doubleday, 1964); Lenny Moore and Jeffrey Jay Ellish, *All Things Being Equal: The Autobiography of Lenny Moore* (New York: Sports Publishing, 2005); Mike Burns, *Night Train Lane: Life of Hall of Famer Richard Night Train Lane* (Austin, TX: Eakin Press, 2001); Goudsouzian, *King of the Court*; William F. Russell and Taylor Branch, *Second Wind: The Memoirs of an Opinionated Man* (New York: Random House, 1979); Bill Reynolds, *Rise of a Dynasty: The '57 Celtics, The First Banner, and the Dawning of a New America* (New York: New American Library, 2010); Nelson George, *Elevating the Game: Black Men and Basketball* (New York: HarperCollins, 1992); and Ron Thomas, *They Cleared the Lane: The NBA's Black Pioneers* (Lincoln: University of Nebraska Press, 2002).

25   *HRG*, vol. 3, 151–52; Lansbury, *A Spectacular Leap*, 104–8; *CTN*, 59–69; Gray and Lamb, *Born to Win*, 81–111; Gibson, *I Always Wanted to Be Somebody*, 88–150; *Althea*.

26   *W*, 58–75; *HRG*, vol. 3, 151–52 (q); Gibson, *I Always Wanted to Be Somebody*, 151–57, 158 (q), 159–76; Gibson, *So Much to Live For*, 15–128; Gray and Lamb, *Born to Win*, 112–61; *Althea*.

27   *W*, 62 (first q); *AA*, 31–32 (second and third qs); Simpson, Willis Thomas, and Bobby Davis ints.

28   *AA*, 32–33 (first q), 38–39; *W*, 101 (second q), 102. On Baltimore's racial climate in the 1950s and 1960s, see Howell S. Baum, *Brown in Baltimore: School Desegregation and the Limits of Liberalism* (Ithaca: Cornell University Press, 2010); and Antero Pietila, *Not in My Backyard: How Bigotry Shaped a Great American City* (Chicago: Ivan R. Dee, 2010).

29   *AA*, 32 (q).

30   Ibid., 33 (q), 34; *W*, 101.

31   *AA*, 33 (q); *W*, 93–97.

32   *AA*, 29–30 (q); *AATC*, 60; Simpson, Willis Thomas, and Bobby Davis ints.

CHAPTER 4: THE ONLY RAISIN IN A RICE PUDDING

1   *AA*, 34 (first q), 35, 44–45 (third q); W, 87–88, 98–100; *LG*, 71 (second q); *CD*, February 12, June 7, September 6, 1958; *NYT*, August 2–3, 1958; Sanderlin and Simpson ints.

2   *AA*, 33–34; *LG*, 44–45; Chewning and Willis Thomas ints.

3   Benjamin Muse, *Ten Years of Prelude: The Story of Integration since the Supreme Court's 1954 Decision* (New York: Viking, 1964), 70–71, 146–50, 211; James Jackson Kilpatrick, *The Sovereign States of America: Notes of a Citizen of Virginia* (Washington, DC: Regnery, 1957); William P. Hustwit, *James J. Kilpatrick: Salesman for Segregation* (Chapel Hill: University of North Carolina Press, 2013); and Numan V. Bartley, *The Rise of Massive Resistance: Race and Politics in the South during the 1950's* (Baton Rouge: Louisiana State University Press, 1969).

4   *AA*, 35 (first q), 36 (fourth q); *OTC*, 37–38, 81 (third q); Ken Wright, "News Stirs Childhood Memories of a Determined Fighter," *Virginia Pilot-Ledger Star*, April 12, 1992 (second q); *AATC*, 63–64, 67; Gertrude Woodruff Marlowe, *A Right Worthy Grand Mission: Maggie Lena Walker and the Quest for Black Economic Empowerment* (Washington, DC: Howard University Press, 2013); *RNL*, November 10, 1938, and *Washington Afro-American*, January 14, 1939, clippings in "Richmond: Education

and Schools—Negro" folder, vertical files, Richmond Public Library; Patricia Battles Davis int; *DG*, 111; *AATC*, 29, 37–39, 47, 59–62; Robinson int; L. Spurlock and Johnnie Ashe ints, *SSAA*.

5   *AATC*, 63 (first and second qs), 64; *AA*, 33–34 (fifth q), 35 (third q); *OTC*, 37 (fourth q).

6   *AA*, 36–37, 60 (second q), 61, 148–50; *PIM*, 25 (first q); London *Times*, June 28, 1968 (third q); Danzig and Schwed, eds., *Fireside Book of Tennis*, 454; Pasarell, Dell, and Graebner ints; Charlie Pasarell int, *SSAA*. On the distinctive character of Miami's race relations, see Raymond Mohl, "Miami: The Ethnic Cauldron," in Richard M. Bernard and Bradley R. Rice, eds., *Sunbelt Cities: Politics and Growth Since World War II* (Austin: University of Texas Press, 1983), 58–99; Marvin Dunn, *Black Miami in the Twentieth Century* (Gainesville: University Press of Florida, 1997); and N. D. B. Connolly, *A World More Concrete: Real Estate and the Remaking of Jim Crow South Florida* (Chicago: University of Chicago Press, 2014). On Pasarell's career, see *BCHT*, 133–35, 139–40, 147–48, 704, 738; *NYT*, December 13, 1967.

7   *AA*, 37–38, 39–40 (q); *W*, 90–91; *CD*, May 9, 1959; Dr. R. Walter Johnson to William F. Riordan, July 10, 1959, folder 1, box 1, AAP.

8   *W*, 88 (q); *CD*, May 9, 1959. On the desegregation of the University of Virginia, see Bryan Kay, "The History of Desegregation at the University of Virginia, 1950–1969" (Undergraduate Honors Essay, University of Virginia, 1979); Peter Wallenstein, "Desegregation in Higher Education in Virginia," *Encyclopedia Virginia* (online at www.encyclopediavirginia.org/Desegregation_in_Higher_Education; nsstart_entry); Sarah Patton Boyle, *The Desegregated Heart: A Virginian's Stand in Time of Transition* (New York: William Morrow, 1962); Coy Barefoot, *The Corner: A History of Student Life at the University of Virginia* (Charlottesville: Howell Press, 2001); and Susan Tyler Hitchcock, *The University of Virginia: A Pictorial History* (Charlottesville: University of Virginia Press, 2012). See also Peter Wallenstein, ed., *Higher Education and the Civil Rights Movement: White Supremacy, Black Southerners, and College Campuses* (Gainesville: University Press of Florida, 2008).

9   *AA*, 38 (qs); *CD*, July 14, 1959; *NYT*, July 5, 1959; *W*, 101.

10   *DG*, 61 (first q); *NYT*, July 14, 19, 21, 1959; *WP*, July 1959, clipping in folder 1, box 35, AAP (second q); Simpson int.

11   *AA*, 19–20 (qs); *AATC*, 80; Chewning int; Tom Chewning int, *SSAA*.

12   *W*, 92–97.

13   *NYT*, September 4–5, 1959; *AA*, 40. In the 1959 U.S. National Championship singles competition, Laver lost to the American Ronald Holmberg in the quarterfinals. On Laver, see *BCHT*, 461, 600–601; Laver, with Collins, *The Education of a Tennis Player*; and Rod Laver, *Rod Laver: A Memoir* (Sydney: Allen & Unwin, 2014).

14   *AA*, 35–37; *OTC*, 19, 63–64, 80 (q); Loretta Ashe Harris, Patricia Battles Davis, and Johnnie Ashe ints.

15   *AA*, 40 (qs); *OTC*, 38.

16   *LG*, 64 (q); *OTC*, 28.

17   *OTC*, 37 (second q), 162 (first q).

18   *NYT*, February 21, 23, 1960; *RTD*, February 21–23, 1960; Silver and Moeser, *Separate City*, 75; Reginald Green and Sherrod ints.

19   Silver and Moeser, *Separate City*, 69–80; *RTD*, September 7–8, 1960; *AA*, 43. Arthur and Johnnie Ashe's cousin Horace was also a student at Marshall during the early years of the school's desegregation; Johnnie Ashe int. See Kenneth E. Whitlock Jr., "Segregation, Massive Resistance, and Desegregation: Personal Reflections on Growing

Up in Richmond, Virginia—1950–1967," January 21, 2013, typescript available online at www.mxschool.edu; "Negro Girls Enter John Marshall High School," *Southern School News* 8, No. 4 (October 1961): 4; Carol Swann-Daniels, in Juan Williams, *My Soul Looks Back in Wonder: Voices of the Civil Rights Experience* (New York: Sterling, 2004), 65–71. See also Robert A. Pratt, *The Color of Their Skin: Education and Race in Richmond, Virginia, 1954–1989* (Charlottesville: University of Virginia Press, 1993); and James W. Ely, *The Crisis of Conservative Virginia: The Byrd Organization and the Politics of Massive Resistance* (Knoxville: University of Tennessee Press, 1976).

20 *DG*, 116–17; *OTC*, 46 (first and fourth qs); *W*, 88 (second q); *AA*, 45 (third q); Koger and Simpson ints.

21 *AA*, 41 (q); *W*, 83–89; Simpson int.

22 *W*, 100–101 (first q); *AA*, 41 (second q), 42; *OTC*, 47.

23 *OTC*, 46 (first q); *CD*, May 28, September 3, 1960; *BAA*, August 23, 1960; *AA*, 10 (second q), 44.

CHAPTER 5: THE GATEWAY

1 *AA*, 46 (q); *OTC*, 47.

2 Cliff Buchholz int; *OTC*, 47; *W*, 104; *CTN*, 91; *BATN*, 6, 14; *AA*, 23 (first q), 45 (second and third qs), 46; *LG*, 139–40; *AATC*, 77–85; A. S. "Doc" Young, "Tennis Is Not a Stranger to Blacks," *LAT*, July 22, 1972. According to Ashe, the origin of the arrangement was based on a misunderstanding: "Mr. Hudlin had started the wheel turning almost by chance. . . . One day in 1960 he dropped by Washington University, near his home, to get assistance for Wilbur Jenkins, another Negro who was high-ranked in the ATA. Somebody there said, 'If you want to help somebody, why not Arthur Ashe?' They thought I'd already finished high school. Their idea was for me to live with the Hudlins and go to Washington University on a tennis scholarship. Mr. Hudlin was all for that—especially because he wanted his son to become a good tennis player, and he thought being around me might inspire Richard Jr. to practice more. He and Dr. Johnson decided I should move to St. Louis anyway, and go to Sumner High School there."

3 *AA*, 46 (q).

4 Ibid., 46 (q); *NYT*, September 4–6, 1960.

5 *AA*, 46–48 (qs); Hall, *Arthur Ashe*, 37.

6 *AA*, 48 (first q); *PIM*, 94 (second q). In 1974, Ashe offered a much more positive assessment of his St. Louis experience, writing, "I had a great year there." See also Hall, *Arthur Ashe*, 36–37. U.S. Bureau of the Census, *Eighteenth Census of the United States, 1960: Population* (Washington, DC: Government Printing Office, 1961). On segregation, civil rights, and race relations in twentieth-century St. Louis, see Clarence Lang, *Grassroots at the Gateway: Class, Politics and Black Freedom Struggle in St. Louis, 1936–75* (Ann Arbor: University of Michigan Press, 2009); Patricia A. Dowden-White, *Groping Toward Democracy: African American Social Welfare Reformers, 1910–1949* (Columbia: University of Missouri Press, 2011); Ann Morris, ed., *Lift Every Voice and Sing: St. Louis African Americans in the Twentieth Century* (Columbia: University of Missouri Press, 1999); John A. Wright Sr., *The Ville* (Mount Pleasant, SC: Arcadia, 2001); John A. Wright Sr., *African Americans in Downtown St. Louis* (Mount Pleasant, SC: Arcadia, 2003); and John A. Wright, *St. Louis's Disappearing Black Communities* (Mount Pleasant, SC: Arcadia, 2005). On the recent racial scene in St. Louis, see Paul

Kersey, *Bell Curve City: St. Louis, Ferguson, and the Unmentionable Racial Realities That Shape Them* (n.p.: CreateSpace, 2015).

7   Cliff Buchholz int; Wright, *The Ville*, passim; Carolyn Hewes Toft, *The Ville: The Ethnic Heritage of an Urban Neighborhood* (St. Louis: Landmarks Association of St. Louis, 1975). See also "The Ville: A Prosperous Black Community," *St. Louis Argus*, April 28, 1977; Cynthia Todd, "The Ville: Where We Live," *St. Louis Post-Dispatch*, undated clipping; "Annie Malone," undated clipping, all in "Black Neighborhoods in St. Louis" folder, vertical clipping file, St. Louis Public Library, St. Louis, MO. On the *Shelley v. Kraemer* case, which originated in St. Louis with the activism of Olivia Merriweather Perkins, see Jeffrey S. Copeland, *Olivia's Story: The Conspiracy of Heroes Behind* Shelley v Kraemer (St. Paul: Paragon House, 2010). On Richmond Heights, which adjoins the larger community of Clayton, see www.richmondheigts.org; *Our Storehouse of Missouri Place Names* (second edition) (Columbia: University of Missouri Press, 1973); and https://en.wikipedia.org/wiki/Richmond_Heights,_Missouri. The Hudlins lived at 1221 Laclede Station Road, a few blocks southwest of Forest Park. *St. Louis City Directory 1960* (Detroit: R. L. Polk, 1960).

8   *OTC*, 48 (first q); *AA*, 48–49 (second q); Hall, *Arthur Ashe*, 36–37; Cliff Buchholz int. Named for Charles Sumner, the nineteenth-century United States senator and abolitionist from Massachusetts, Sumner High was the alma mater of several musical and theatrical celebrities, including the noted comic and civil rights activist Dick Gregory, a member of the class of 1951 and a high school track star in the late 1940s and early 1950s; the legendary rock 'n' roller Chuck Berry, class of 1944; the singer Tina Turner (aka Anna Mae Bulloch), class of 1958; the actor Robert Guillaume, class of 1945; and the mezzo-soprano Grace Bumbry, class of 1955. See Dick Gregory, with Robert Lipsyte, *Nigger: An Autobiography* (New York: Pocket Books, 1976); Chuck Berry, *Chuck Berry: The Autobiography* (New York: Harmony, 1989); Bruce Pegg, *Brown-Eyed Handsome Man: The Life and Hard Times of Chuck Berry* (New York: Routledge, 2002); Tina Turner and Kurt Loder, *I, Tina* (New York: William Morrow, 1986); Robert Guillaume and David Ritz, *Guillaume, A Life* (Columbia: University of Missouri Press, 2002); and Peter Bailey, "Grace Bumbry: 'Singing Is Terrific, but Living Is an Art,'" *Ebony* (December 1973): 67–68, 73–75.

9   *AA*, 47 (q); Cliff and Butch Buchholz ints.

10   *NYT*, November 27–28, 1960; *BCHT*, 127 (first q), 162; *OTC*, 39; *AA*, 47 (second q); Hall, *Arthur Ashe*, 38; Froehling int. The win over Froehling earned Ashe his first mention in *Sports Illustrated*. See "Faces in the Crowd," *SI* (December 12, 1960): 12.

11   *AA*, 47 (first and fourth qs); *OTC*, 50 (second, third, fifth, and sixth qs); *PIM*, 94; Cliff Buchholz and Chewning ints.

12   *NYT*, December 25, 27, 1960; *OTC*, 49–50; *AA*, 42; *AATC*, 85; Mandelstam int. Mandelstam returned to Miami in the fall of 1960 to enroll at the University of Miami, where he assumed the number one singles position in 1962 and 1963, earning All-American honors. He later earned a law degree at the University of Miami, played intermittently on the men's tour until 1973, and eventually headed several Miami-based corporations, including Tennis Schools International, Inc. For a time, he built tennis courts, including one at the Ashes' Doral home. He and Arthur were close friends for three decades. See "All American Monday: Rodney 'Rod' Mandelstam," an online article posted December 3, 2012, at www.hurricanesports.com/ViewArticle.dbml?ATCHD=205819628.

13   Pasarell and Froehling ints; *OTC*, 51–52; *AA*, 49.

14 *OTC*, 51 (first and fourth qs); *AA*, 49–50 (second and third qs); *AATC*, 85.

15 *AA*, 39, 49.

16 Pasarell and Ralston ints; *OTC*, 51; *AA*, 49; http://www.NCAA.com/sports/tennis -men/history.

17 *AA*, 50–51; Pasarell int.

18 See "Athens of Athletics," Chapter 13 in Andrew Hamilton and John B. Jackson, *UCLA on the Move During the Fifty Golden Years, 1919–1969* (Los Angeles: Ward Ritchie Press, 1969), 169–86; Brian Urquhart, *Ralph Bunche: An American Odyssey* (New York: W. W. Norton, 1998), 37–43; Rampersad, *Jackie Robinson*, 56–82, 242–43; Rafer Johnson, with Philip Goldberg, *The Best That I Can Be* (New York: Doubleday, 1998); Slaughter int; *AA*, 50 (q).

19 *OTC*, 48 (qs); Cliff Buchholz int.

20 Raymond Arsenault, *Freedom Riders: 1961 and the Struggle for Racial Justice* (New York: Oxford University Press, 2006), 93–97, 106, 112–16; Charlotte Devree, "The Young Negro Rebels," *Harper's* 223 (October 1961): 133–38; Reginald Green int.

21 *LG*, 140 (first q); *OTC*, 51–52 (qs).

22 *OTC*, 48 (q); Cliff Buchholz int.

23 *AA*, 49 (first q), 80; *OTC*, 47 (second q), 51; *W*, 105; *AATC*, 71–73; *NYT*, June 23, 1961; *WP*, June 23, 1961; Harry Gordon, "Arthur Ashe Has to Be Aware That He is a Pioneer in Short White Pants," *NYT Magazine* (January 2, 1966): 164; *AATC*, 70–71; Pasarell and Cliff Buchholz (third q) ints.

24 "Ashe Takes Tennis Title," *NYT*, June 23, 1961; "Ashe Captures School Tennis," *WP*, June 23, 1961; "Tennis the Menace," *SI* (July 3, 1961): editorial (qs); "An Unfair Rap," unidentified clipping, July 1961, in folder 1, box 35, AAP; Paul M. Gaston, *Coming of Age in Utopia: The Odyssey of an Idea* (Montgomery: NewSouth Books, 2009), 193–94; Hall, *Arthur Ashe*, 38–39.

25 *NYT*, June 28, July 1, 9, August 7, 1961; Hall, *Arthur Ashe*, 39–40; Martin, *Arthur Ashe*, 54; *OTC*, 51–52; "Arthur Ashe, Tennis Star," *Life* (October 15, 1965): 64 (first q); *AA*, 94 (second q); *AATC*, 71; Cliff Buchholz, Graebner, and Pasarell ints.

26 *AA*, 51 (q); *NYT*, August 20, 1961.

27 *NYT*, August 30–September 3, 1961; *OTC*, 52 (q).

CHAPTER 6: THE GOLDEN LAND

1 See Kevin Starr's multivolume study of "Americans and the California Dream": *Americans and the California Dream, 1850–1915*; *Inventing the Dream: California Through the Progressive Era*; *Material Dreams: Southern California through the 1920s*; *Endangered Dreams: The Great Depression in California*; *The Dream Endures: California Enters the 1940s*; *Embattled Dreams: California in War and Peace, 1940–1950*; and *Golden Dreams: California in the Age of Abundance, 1950–1963* (New York: Oxford University Press, 1973, 1985, 1990, 1996, 1997, 2002, 2009).

2 U.S. Bureau of the Census, *Eighteenth Census of the United States, 1960: Population* (Washington, DC: Government Printing Office, 1961); Lawrence DeGraaf, "The City of Black Angels: The Emergence of the Los Angeles Ghetto, 1890–1930," *Pacific Historical Review* 59 (Spring 1970): 323–52; Lawrence DeGraaf, *Negro Migration to Los Angeles, 1930–1950* (San Francisco: R&E Research Associates, 1974); Scott Kurashige, *The Shifting Grounds of Race: Blacks and Japanese Americans in the Making of Multiethnic Los Angeles* (Princeton: Princeton University Press, 2008); Douglas Flamming,

Bound for Freedom: Black Los Angeles in Jim Crow America (Berkeley: University of California Press, 2005); Darnell Hunt and Ana-Christina Ramon, *Black Los Angeles: American Dreams and Racial Realities* (New York: NYU Press, 2010); Josh Sides, *L.A. City Limits: African American Los Angeles from the Great Depression to the Present* (Berkeley: University of California Press, 2004); R. J. Smith, *The Great Black Way: L.A. in the 1940s and the Lost African-American Renaissance* (New York: PublicAffairs, 2006); Lawrence B. DeGraaf, Kevin Mulroy, and Quintard Taylor, eds., *Seeking El Dorado: African Americans in California* (Seattle: University of Washington Press, 2001); Delilah Beasley, *The Negro Trail Blazers of California* (New York: Negro Universities Press, 1969); Kenneth Goode, *California's Black Pioneers: A Brief Historical Survey* (Santa Barbara: McNally & Lofton, 1973); Rudolph Lapp, *Afro-Americans in California* (San Francisco: Boyd & Fraser, 1979); *Black Angelenos: The Afro-American in Los Angeles, 1850–1950* (Los Angeles: California Afro-American Museum, 1989); Mike Garcia and Jerry Wright, "Race Consciousness in Black Los Angeles, 1886–1915," and Eugene J. Grigsby, "The Rise and Decline of Black Neighborhoods in Los Angeles" (Feature Series: Black Angelenos), *UCLA CAAS Report* 12 (Spring–Fall 1989): 4–5, 16–17, 42–44. See also James Fisher, "The History of the Political and Social Development of the Black Community in California, 1850–1950" (PhD thesis, UCLA, 1971); Frederick Anderson, "The Development of Leadership and Organization Building in the Black Community of Los Angeles from 1900 Through World War II" (PhD thesis, University of California, 1976); and Patricia Adler, "Watts: From Suburb to Black Ghetto" (PhD thesis, University of Southern California, 1977).

3   Singleton, Anderson, Slaughter, Willard Johnson, Nash, and Carson ints; Anne Allen, "This Way Out: Slum Youngsters Choose College, but It Takes Courage to Stick," *American Education* (July–August 1967): 2–4, 28–29.

4   Verne Stadtman, ed., *Centennial Record of the University of California* (Berkeley: University of California Press, 1968), 330–72; Ernest Carroll Moore, *I Helped Make a University* (Los Angeles: Dawson's Bookshop, 1952); William C. Ackerman, *My Fifty Year Love-in at UCLA* (Los Angeles: Fashion Press, 1969); Edward A. Dickson, *University of California at Los Angeles: Its Origin and Formative Years* (Los Angeles: Friends of the UCLA Library, 1955); and Hamilton and John Jackson, *UCLA on the Move During the Fifty Golden Years, 1919–1969*. On Murphy's tenure at UCLA, see Record Series #401, Chancellor's Office, Administrative Subject File of Franklin Murphy, 1935–71, in UCLAUA. "Image UCLA," *DB*, December 14, 1961, cites a magazine article by Martin Mayer, "UCLA: The College as a Country Club," and Steve Allen's television show *Campus USA*, both of which "portray the typical student as a screaming, faddish, amoralistic, uneducated boor who cuts Roy Harris and Willard Libby lectures to go surfing or dancing!"

5   See "Athens of Athletics," Chapter 13 in Hamilton and Jackson, *UCLA on the Move During the Fifty Golden Years, 1919–1969*, 169–86.

6   *AA*, 58; Hamilton and Jackson, *UCLA on the Move During the Fifty Golden Years, 1919–1969*, 171, 187; Ackerman, *My Fifty Year Love-in at UCLA*, 90–91; John Matthew Smith, *The Sons of Westwood: John Wooden, UCLA, and the Dynasty That Changed College Basketball* (Urbana: University of Illinois Press, 2013); Rampersad, *Jackie Robinson*, 62–83. On Washington and Strode, see Strode and Sam Young, *Goal Dust*; Charles K. Ross, *Outside the Lines: African Americans and the Integration of the National Football League* (New York: NYU Press, 2001); the documentary film *The Forgotten Four: The Integration of Pro Football* (EPIX, Ross Greenburg Productions, 2014); and

Cynthia Lee, "Forgotten Story of Four Who Broke Color Bar in Pro Football," *UCLA News*, August 21, 2014, available online at news.ucla.edu. On Rafer Johnson and C. K. Yang, see Johnson, with Goldberg, *The Best That I Can Be*; and David Marannis, *Rome 1960: The Olympics That Changed the World* (New York: Simon & Schuster, 2008), 10–12, 34–37, 101–2, 114–16, 265–90. Johnson's younger brother Jimmy played on the UCLA football team.

7   Willard Johnson and Beale ints; *AA*, 56 (q).

8   *AA*, 53, 55–56 (qs).

9   Pasarell int; Pasarell int, *SSAA*; *OTC*, 89–90 (qs), 101–3.

10   *AA*, 53, 54–55 (qs), 56–57, 61, 84; *AATC*, 87–91; Pasarell int (second q).

11   *OTC*, 54–55 (qs).

12   Ibid., 55–56.

13   Ibid., 53–54 (qs), 62; Pasarell int.

14   Slaughter int; *AA*, 57–58 (qs), 59; Danzig and Schwed, eds., *Fireside Book of Tennis*, 454.

15   *OTC*, 59 (q).

16   Ibid., 56–57 (qs); *AA*, 56.

17   *OTC*, 60 (first q); *AA*, 58 (second q).

18   *Arthur Ashe: Citizen of the World* (HBO Video/HBO Sports, directed by Julie Anderson, 1994); Edward Steichen, *The Family of Man* (New York: Museum of Modern Art, 1955); Singleton int; *OTC*, 58 (qs).

19   Singleton, Farrell, and McNichols ints.

20   Smith, *The Sons of Westwood*, 36–38, 39 (qs), 40–42; Pasarell, Singleton, and Slaughter ints.

21   *AA*, 59 (q), 115; *OTC*, 67; *BCHT*, 83–85, 99, 110, 117 (first q), 120 (second q), 121, 124–25, 581–82, 589, 597–98, 634–35. On Kramer and the professional tour from 1947 to 1962, see Kramer, *The Game: My 40 Years in Tennis*; and the Tennis Channel's Signature Series television documentary *Barnstormers* (Tennis Channel, directed by Heath Woodlief, 2016).

22   *OTC*, 63 (q); Pasarell int.

23   *NYT*, December 15, 1961; *AA*, 55; *Atlanta Daily World*, April 28, 1962 (qs), clipping in *AA* File, UCLASIO; *DB*, January–April 1961; Nagler int.

24   www.NCAA.com/history/tennis; John Hassan, ed., *1998 ESPN Sports Almanac* (New York: Hyperion ESPN Books, 1997), 832; *AA*, 52, 70; *OTC*, 67; *NYT*, June 24, 1962; *LAT*, June 24, 1962; Fox and Nagler ints.

25   *AA*, 78–79 (second q), 84, 93, 114, 121, 184 (first q); *CD*, July 14, 1962 (third q); Pasarell int; *NYT*, June 26, 28, July 15, 18, 20, 22, 24–26, 29–31, August 1–5, 7, 12, 14, 16 1962; *CTN*, 242; *W*, 106–7, notes the 1962 ATA national tournament was marred by a misunderstanding between Ashe and Ron Charity about a promise to defend their 1961 doubles title: "Though they agreed to defend their title for the next year, Ashe discovered that he had been teamed with Whirlwind instead of Charity, in the 1962 ATA national doubles competition. Whirlwind wanted only to enjoy the same sentimental trip that Charity took last year while playing with Ashe. He knew that Ashe probably would never play another ATA event after this year. He saw this as a last opportunity to play with the boy who had become as special as a son. But Charity didn't see it that way. 'I found Arthur and I said, "Hey man, what's going on?"' Charity said. "Mr. Charity—he never called me Ron—I don't know; you'll have to ask Dr. Johnson." . . . I couldn't blame Ashe; he was only a 17-year-old kid caught in the middle.

I thought it was the worst thing in the world to happen. So I played with John Mudd, and as fate would have it, we played Johnson and Ashe in the first round and beat the hell out of them, 6–0, 6–1. I didn't hit a single ball to Arthur.'"

26 *NYT*, September 1–4 (q), 8, 1962; *AA*, 130–31; Newman int. On Emerson, see *BCHT*, 574–75.

27 *OTC*, 64–65; *AA*, 55, 128, 148, 153.

28 *AA*, 44 (second q), 45, 53 (third q), 57 (first q), 58–59 (fourth q), 77, 94 (fifth q); *AATC*, 125–26; Pasarell, Reed, and Sanderlin ints; "Arthur Ashe, Tennis Star," *Life* (October 15, 1965): 61–66.

29 *OTC*, 78, 82–83 (qs); Pasarell int.

30 *OTC*, 83–84 (qs); Pasarell int.

31 *OTC*, 63 (third q), 64 (second q), 65, 90 (first q); *AATC*, 76; Pasarell int; Pasarell int, *SSAA; BCHT*, 581–82, 597–98, 615, 644.

32 *NYT*, April 14, December 29, 1963; *DB*, February–April 1963; *LAT*, April 17, 25–27, May 4, 8, 11, 18–19, 31, 1963; *AA*, 61, 116; Martin, *Arthur Ashe*, 68–69; Pasarell, Reed, Sanderlin, and Ralston ints; "1963 UCLA Tennis," UCLA Athletic News Bureau, typescript, April 1963, 5 (qs), Arthur Ashe File, UCLASIO.

33 *NYT*, May 8, 14, 1963; *WP*, May 8, 1963; *CD*, May 9, 13, 20, 1963; *AA*, 62–63 (qs); Richard Evans, *The Davis Cup: Celebrating 100 Years of International Tennis* (New York: Universe, 1998), 172. On the history of the Davis Cup competition, see Danzig and Schwed, eds., *Fireside Book of Tennis*, 28–45; Evans, *The Davis Cup*; and Alan Trengrove, *The Story of the Davis Cup* (London: David & Charles, 1986).

34 *NYT*, June 18–21, 22 (qs), 1963; *LAT*, June 18, 20, 22, 1963; *AA*, 63; Pasarell, Reed, and Sanderlin ints. On Allison "Al" Danzig (1898–1987), who covered tennis for *The New York Times* from 1923 to 1968, see *BCHT*, 568; *NYT*, January 28, 1987 (obituary); and Danzig and Schwed, eds., *Fireside Book of Tennis*.

35 *OTC*, 70–71 (qs); *LAT*, June 9, 1963.

36 Ibid., 68 (first and second qs), 69 (third and fourth qs).

37 *OTC*, 69, 70–71 (qs); Pasarell int; Deborah Haber, "Hollywood Tennis Does Socko Business," *SI* (March 2, 1971).

CHAPTER 7: TRAVELING MAN

1 *AA*, 116 (qs); Bob Funesti, "Area Tennis Players Give Ashe Boost," *WP*, June 23, 1963, copy in folder 1, box 35, AAP.

2 *OTC*, 76; *WT* (November 1963); Pasarell and Ralston ints.

3 *OTC*, 72–73 (qs).

4 Ibid., 73–74 (qs); *AA*, 117 (final q).

5 *AA*, 116–17 (qs).

6 Ibid., 118 (qs); *OTC*, 75.

7 *NYT*, June 26 (first q), 27–28, 1963; *AA*, 118–19; *OTC*, 74–75 (second q). For full coverage of the 1963 Wimbledon tournament, see the voluminous clippings in the "AELTC, The Championships, 1963" scrapbook, KRWL.

8 *AA*, 119; *NYT*, May 8 (first q), June 28, 1963 (third q); *CD*, July 3, 1963; *OTC*, 75 (second q).

9 See Wimbledon.com/archive/1963 draw; *NYT*, July 3–5, 1963; Fox int.

10 *OTC*, 72 (second q), 75 (first q).

11 *AA*, 120 (qs); *NYT*, July 14, 1963.

12 *NYT*, July 17 18, 21, 23–28 (qs), 1963; *AATC*, 95.

13 *AA*, 104, 113 (qs); Donald Dell int, *SSAA*.

14 Ibid., 115–16 (qs)

15 Ibid., 120–21(first q); 123 (second q).

16 *NYT*, August 2, 1963; *CD*, May 9, 13, 20, August 14, September 4, 1963; Shirley Povich, "This Morning," unidentified clipping, in folder 1, box 35, AAP; E. Culpepper Clark, *The Schoolhouse Door: Segregation's Last Stand at the University of Alabama* (New York: Oxford University Press, 1993), 168; Taylor Branch, *Parting the Waters: America in the King Years, 1954–63* (New York: Simon & Schuster, 1989), 738, 821–22, 888–901; Dan T. Carter, *The Politics of Rage: George Wallace, the Origins of the New Conservatism, and the Transformation of American Politics* (New York: Simon & Schuster, 1995), 108–9 (q),133–55; John Dittmer, *Local People: The Struggle for Civil Rights in Mississippi* (Urbana: University of Illinois Press, 1994), 163–69; Michael Vinson Williams, *Medgar Evers: Mississippi Martyr* (Fayetteville: University of Arkansas Press, 2011), 3–4, 267–304. On the 16th Street Baptist Church bombing, see Spike Lee's documentary *Four Little Girls* (DVD, HBO Studios, 2004).

17 *NYT*, August 2, 1963 (q); *AA*, 165–66; "First Negro Davis Cupper," *Ebony* (October 1963): 151–52; Sanderlin int.

18 *AA*, 166 (first q); 167 (second q); 1962 Davis Cup "Draws and Results," in www.daviscup.com.

19 *BCHT*, 128, 495–501; *AATC*, 96–100; *NYT*, August 15 (qs), September 4, 1963.

20 *NYT*, August 20–24, 31, September 1–2, 4 (q), 1963.

21 Riessen int; *AA*, 123, 168–69; *OTC*, 91–92; *NYT*, September 13, 15–16, 1963; Branch, *Parting the Waters*, 846–901.

22 *AA*, 120 (first q), 124, 169; *OTC*, 76 (second q); *LAT*, September 16, 1963; *NYT*, September 4, 9, 16, 21–23, 1963.

23 *AA*, 60–61 (qs); Pasarell (fourth q); and Nagler ints. Ashe bought both of his motorcycles from Nagler. Baker later became one of Haiti's most prominent businessmen and sports officials, serving as president of the Haitian Association of Industrialists (ADIH) and as the president of the Haitian National Olympic Committee from 1982 to 2013. "Jean-Edouard Baker Elected as Head of COH," IciHaiti.com, November 21, 2012; Baker's term as COH president ended in August 2013 when the COH executive committee removed him from office on charges of corruption. See touthaiti.com, December 11, 2013. See also William Over, *Human Rights in the International Public Sphere: Civic Discourse for the 21st Century* (New York: Praeger, 1999), 148.

24 *AA*, 63–64 (qs).

25 "1964 UCLA Tennis Press Booklet," "1964 Singles Record of Arthur Ashe, UCLA (As of May 21)," and "Thumbnail Sketches of UCLA's 1964 Varsity Tennis Players," typescripts in Arthur Ashe File, UCLASIO; *NYT*, February 16–17, 20–23, 1964; *LAT*, February 7–10, 20–23, 28, March 12, 15–16,1964; *DB*, February–March, 1964.

26 Smith, *Sons of Westwood*, 1–48 (first q), 49 (second q), 50–54 (third q); *DB*, January–March 1964.

27 "1964 UCLA Tennis Press Booklet"; *LAT*, March 21–22, 29, April 2–3, 10, 12, 18, 23, 25, May 2–3, 5–7, 9–11, 14–17, 22–24, June 16–21, 1964; *NYT*, June 16, 19–21, 1963; Ralston and Pasarell ints.

28 *AA*, 125 (qs); *NYT*, June 18, 22–23, 25–29; *LAT*, June 26–27, 1964.

29 *AA*, 98–99 (qs); *LAT*, June 27, 1964.

30 *AA*, 120, 125 (first q), 126–27 (qs); *OTC*, 76.

31 *NYT*, June 28, July 16, 21–31 (q), August 1–3, 1964; *LAT*, July 16, 22, 28, 30–31, August 2–3, 1964; *WT* (September 1964): 23.

32 *NYT*, August 3 (first q), 5, 25–29, 1964; *OTC*, 102 (second q); *DB*, September 1961–October 1964; *LAT*, August 5–8, 29 1964; Singleton, Carson, and Farrell ints; Taylor Branch, *Pillar of Fire: America in the King Years, 1963–65* (New York: Simon & Schuster, 1999), 343–509; Dittmer, *Local People*, 242–302; Nick Kotz, *Judgment Days: Lyndon Baines Johnson, Martin Luther King, Jr., and the Laws That Changed America* (Boston: Houghton Mifflin Harcourt, 2005), 156–222. On Hamer, see Kate Mills, *This Little Light of Mine: The Life of Fannie Lou Hamer* (Philadelphia: E. P. Dutton, 1993); Chana Kai Lee, *For Freedom's Sake: The Life of Fannie Lou Hamer* (Urbana: University of Illinois Press, 1999); and Danielle L. McGuire, *At the Dark End of the Street: Black Women, Rape, and Resistance—A New History of the Civil Rights Movement from Rosa Parks to the Rise of Black Power* (New York: Vintage, 2011), 191–95, 201, 210–11.

33 *NYT*, August 30, September 2, 6–10, 14 (qs), 1964; *LAT*, September 8–9, 1964; *AA*, 133; *AATC*, 104; *WT* (November 1964): 31 (last q).

34 *NYT*, September 16, 23, 25–28, 1964; *BCHT*, 130; *LAT*, August 19, September 16, 24, 1964.

35 *AA*, 60, 76 (q), 101–2, 130; and Pasarell int; Smith, *Sons of Westwood*, 64–67; Wendy Soderburg, "Al Scates: 50 Years of Bruin Volleyball," *UCLA Magazine*, April 1, 2012, available online at magazine.ucla.edu. On the popularity of the Ford Mustang, see Donald Farr, *Mustang: Fifty Years: Celebrating America's Only True Pony Car* (Concord, NC: Motorsports, 2013).

36 "UCLA Tennis Schedule and Results 1965," folder, box 74, Intercollegiate Sports Information Office Files, UCLASIO; and various 1965 typescripts, all in the Arthur Ashe File, UCLASIO; *LAT*, March 2, 7–8, 15, 17, 20–22, 24, April 4, 10–11, 15, 21–25, May 1–2, 4–8, 10, 12–16, 21, 24, 1965.

37 *AA*, 60, 62; *DG*, 171; Danzig and Schwed, eds., *Fireside Book of Tennis*, 453; Flink int, *SSAA*.

38 *NYT*, June 16, August 19, September 16, 23–28, 1964, March 9, 17, April 25, May 14, 16, 19, 23–24, 29, 1965; *LAT*, March 17, April 28, May 8, 29, June 1, 4–6, 1965; USTA Yearbook—Davis Cup, 5, available at www.usta.com; *DG*, 44, 61 (first q)–62; *AA*, 129 (third q), 168 (second q), 169–71; *AATC*, 99; Gordon, "Arthur Ashe Has to Be Aware"; Ralston and Dell ints. On Seixas, see *BCHT*, 645. MacCall and Ralston eventually reconciled, and the former USC star rejoined the team in July. On MacCall, see Collins, *My Life with the Pros*, 179–81; and *BCHT*, 141. See also the George MacCall Papers (1946–2005), Special Collections Library, Pennsylvania State University, State College, Pennsylvania.

39 *NYT*, June 3–6, 1965; *AA*, 170. Bakersfield was Ralston's hometown.

40 *NYT*, June 17, 20, 1965; *AA*, 129; Crookenden, Reed, and Sanderlin ints. There are numerous documents on the 1965 NCAA Tennis Championships, including the official program, in "1965 NCAA Tennis Championships" folder, box 57, Athletic Department, Administrative Files of Robert A. Fischer, UCLAUA; and J. D. Morgan's "Year-end Report—University Division Tennis" (Morgan to G. David Price, September 7, 1965), Arthur Ashe File, UCLASIO.

CHAPTER 8: FROM DIXIE TO DOWN UNDER

1 *BCHT*, 421, 623–24; *AA*, 129; *NYT*, June 17, 20–22, 23 (q), 24–26, 1966; Pasarell, Fox, and Ralston ints.

2 *NYT*, July 10, 12, 14–16, 1965; *AA*, 129 (q).

3   Kotz, *Judgment Days*, 329–37; *NYT*, July 29–31, August 1–7, 1965; "The Ace," *Time*
        (August 13, 1965)(first and third qs); Frank Deford, "An Understudy Takes Charge,"
        SI (August 9, 1965): 18 (second q); Hall, *Arthur Ashe*, 70–71 (fourth q); *AA*, 86 (fifth
        and sixth qs); *OTC*, 99; *AATC*, 109–16; Ralston, Morris, and Mayfield ints. On the ul-
        traconservative political climate in Dallas during the 1960s, see Edward H. Miller, *Nut
        Country: Right-Wing Dallas and the Birth of the Southern Strategy* (Chicago: University
        of Chicago Press, 2015).

4   *AA*, 129 (first q), 174 (third q), 175 (fourth q); Deford, "An Understudy Takes Charge,"
        19 (second q); *AATC*, 117; *NYT*, August 4, 15–18, 20, 1965; Froehling and Ralston ints.

5   See David J. Garrow, *Protest at Selma: Martin Luther King Jr. and the Voting Rights Act
        of 1965* (New Haven: Yale University Press, 1978); Taylor Branch, *At Canaan's Edge:
        America in the King Years, 1965–68* (New York: Simon & Schuster, 2006), Parts 1 and
        2; Robert E. Conot, *Rivers of Blood, Years of Darkness* (New York: Bantam, 1967); and
        Gerald Horne, *Fire This Time: The Watts Uprising and the 1960s* (Charlottesville: Uni-
        versity of Virginia Press, 1995).

6   *NYT*, September 3, 5, 1965; *AA*, 129–30 (q).

7   *NYT*, September 7–10, 1965; Emerson int. On Emerson, see *BCHT*, 129–34, 574–75.

8   *AA*, 130–31 (qs); *NYT*, September 11, 1965; *BCHT*, 133.

9   *AA*, 132–33 (q).

10   *NYT*, September 12–13, 1965; *AA*, 129–33. Santana was the first Spaniard to win the
        U.S. National singles title.

11   *AA*, 133 (qs).

12   *AA*, 86–88 (qs); *NYT*, September 21, 1965; *Fort Worth Star-Telegram*, September 15–
        21, 1965.

13   Scherman int; *Eye on the 60s: The Iconic Photography of Rowland Scherman* (docu-
        mentary produced and directed by Chris Szwedo, 2013); "Arthur Ashe: Negro Tennis
        Star," *Life* (October 15, 1965): 61–66.

14   *AA*, 176–77 (qs); *OTC*, 94; *NYT*, September 16, October 25, 1965.

15   *NYT*, September 16, 23–24, 27–28, 30, October 25, 1965; *BCHT*, 123–33 (q); Hall,
        Arthur Ashe, 72–73; *AATC*, 129. See also Allison Danzig, "Our Friends the 'Aussies,'"
        in Danzig and Schwed, eds., *Fireside Book of Tennis*, 38–43; Bodo, *Courts of Babylon*,
        29–36; and Laver, with Collins, *The Education of a Tennis Player*, 67–89.

16   *DB*, November–December 1965; *LAT*, November 1965, January 1966; *AA*, 124, 133–
        34, 140.

17   Frank Deford, "Arthur Ashe," in Danzig and Schwed, eds., *Fireside Book of Tennis*,
        449, 451–52 (q),; *IRAA*, 92.

18   *OTC*, 94 (qs), *AA*, 135; Frank Deford int, *SSAA*. On the Maori of New Zealand, see
        Michael King, *The Penguin History of New Zealand* (New York: Penguin, 2007); Cleve
        Barlow, *Tikanga Whakaaro: Key Concepts in Maori* (New York: Oxford University
        Press, 1991); and Christina Thompson, *Come on Shore and We Will Kill and Eat You
        All: A New Zealand Story* (New York: Bloomsbury USA, 2009).

19   *AA*, 134 (first q), 135; *OTC*, 94–95 (second q). On the racial and ethnic makeup of
        Fiji, see Rajendra Prasad, *Tears in Paradise: Suffering and Struggle of Indians in Fiji,
        1879–2004* (Windsor, Ontario: Glade Publishing, 2014); and Leonard Webberley,
        Fiji: Islands of Dawn (New York: Ives Washburn, 1964).

20   *AA*, 97 (first q), 98–99 (second q); *OTC*, 96–97; Arsenault, *Freedom Riders*, 511. On the
        history of Australian Aborigines, see Richard Broome, *Aboriginal Australia: A History
        Since 1788* (Sydney: Allen & Unwin, 2010); Josephine Flood, *The Original Australians:*

Story of the Aboriginal People (Sydney: Allen & Unwin, 2007); and Bill Gammage, *The Biggest Estate on Earth: How Aborigines Made Australia* (Sydney: Allen & Unwin, 2013).

21   *NYT*, October 31, November 1, 3–8, 1965; *Brisbane Courier-Mail*, October 30–November 8, 1965; *AA*, 135 (qs). On the Australians' passion for sports, see Wray Yamplew and Brian Stoddart, eds., *Sport in Australia: A Social History* (Cambridge: Cambridge University Press, 2008). For a sample of the Australians' reaction to Ashe in 1965–1966, see the sports coverage in the *Sydney Daily Telegraph*, the *Sydney Morning Herald*, the *Melbourne Herald Sun*, and the *Brisbane Courier-Mail*.

22   *AA*, 135–36 (qs).

23   *AA*, 136 (qs); Danzig and Schwed, eds., *Fireside Book of Tennis*, 453; *NYT*, November 13–17, 19–22, 1965; *Sydney Morning Herald*, November 13–22, 1965; Newcombe int.

24   *AA*, 136–37 (q); Newcombe int.

25   *AA*, 137 (q); *OTC*, 95–96; *NYT*, November 27–30, December 2–4, 8–12, 17, 19–20, 31, 1965, January 3, 5–10, 12–17, 1966; Emerson int.

26   Gordon, "Arthur Ashe Has to Be Aware," 7, 25, 27–28 (qs).

27   Ibid., 28 (first q); *AA*, 10 (second q); Hall, *Arthur Ashe*, 41, 76–77, 103–6, 139–40, 239; Bodo, *Courts of Babylon*, 251. On the complicated nature of the goodwill tours involving black celebrities, see Peggy M. von Eschen, *Satchmo Blows Up the World: Jazz Ambassadors Play the Cold War* (Cambridge: Harvard University Press, 2004); Damion L. Thomas, *Globetrotting: African American Athletes and Cold War Politics* (Urbana: University of Illinois Press, 2012); and Thomas Borstelmann, *The Cold War and the Color Line: American Race Relations in the Global Arena* (Cambridge: Havard University Press, 2003).

28   *BCHT*, 135–37, 360–61; *AA*, 138; *NYT*, January 23–30, 1966; *Sydney Morning Herald*, January 22–30, 1966.

29   *AA*, 138–39 (qs); *NYT*, February 1, 1966 (final q).

30   *AA*, 139 (first q); *OTC*, 95–96 (second q).

31   *AA*, 99 (first q), 139 (second q).

32   Ibid., 139; *OTC*, 91 (qs).

33   *AA*, 67, 70, 72–75, 77; Pasarell and Burgess ints; Dana Haddad, "Top of His Game Isn't Enough for Glass to Win in Semis," *LAT*, December 15, 1991.

CHAPTER 9: ADVANTAGE ASHE

1   Gewecke int.

2   Einwick int; Perkins, Hood, and Packett, *Richmond: One of America's Best Tennis Towns*, 5–6, 34–38, 44, 103–6; The *WT* Reporter, "A Visit to Richmond," *WT* (July 1968). Einwick was born in Norfolk, attended high school in Philadelphia, and earned degrees at the University of Virginia and the University of Richmond. *AATC*, 131–32 (second q), 133–34; *AA*, 9 (first and third qs), 10–11 (fourth and fifth qs), 12 (sixth through eighth qs), 13–15 (ninth q); *RNL*, February 3, 1966; *NYT*, February 6–7, 1966; Hall, *Arthur Ashe*, 72. Named for Chief Justice John Marshall, a Virginia native who moved to Richmond in 1782 at the age of twenty-seven, the John Marshall Hotel was the largest hotel in the South when it opened in 1929. The hotel's interior featured a grand St. Genevieve marble staircase and the Virginia Room, a ballroom that could accommodate 1,200 guests. See Robert P. Winthrop, *Architecture in Downtown Richmond* (Richmond: Junior Board of Historic Richmond Foundation, 1982). Following the meetings at the Marshall Hotel, Senator Harry F. Byrd Sr. announced the Massive

Resistance campaign on February 24, 1956. See Ely, *The Crisis of Conservative Virginia*; and Gates, *The Making of Massive Resistance*.

3   *HRG*, vol. 1, ix–xiv; *DG*, 174–75; box 9, AAP.

4   *Glory Road* (Walt Disney Pictures, directed by James Gartner, 2006); Don Haskins, with Dan Wetzel, *Glory Road* (New York: Hyperion, 2006); Charles H. Martin, *Benching Jim Crow: The Rise and Fall of the Color Line in Southern College Sports, 1890–1980* (Urbana: University of Illinois Press, 2010), 90–119; Frank Fitzpatrick, *And the Walls Came Tumbling Down: Kentucky, Texas Western, and the Game That Changed American Sports* (New York: Simon & Schuster, 1999); and Michael Wilbon, "A Win for Texas Western, A Triumph for Equality," *WP*, January 13, 2006.

5   *Atlanta Constitution*, March–April 1966; *Atlanta Daily World*, April 1966; Bryant, *The Last Hero*, 299–324, 336–39. On Atlanta's complex racial history in the twentieth century, see Ronald H. Bayor, *Race and the Shaping of Twentieth-Century Atlanta* (Chapel Hill: University of North Carolina Press, 2000); Kevin M. Kruse, *White Flight: Atlanta and the Making of Modern Conservatism* (Princeton: Princeton University Press, 2005); and Tomiko Brown-Nagin, *Courage to Dissent: Atlanta and the Long History of the Civil Rights Movement* (New York: Oxford University Press, 2011).

6   *Boston Globe*, April 19–June 2, 1966; *NYT*, May 2, 1966; *HRG*, vol. 3, 56–57; Curry Kirkpatrick, "The Celtics Stretch an Era," *SI* (April 11, 1966): 30–31; "Where the Negro Goes from Here in Sports," *Sport* (September 1966): 56–59, 87–88; Goudsouzian, *King of the Court*, 179–200; Thomas, *They Cleared the Lane*, 211–37; George, *Elevating the Game*, 47–48, 105–9, 148–53, 188–90; David Halberstam, *The Breaks of the Game* (New York: Ballantine, 1981), 35–36, 180–81, 186–87; Maureen M. Smith, "Bill Russell: Pioneer and Champion of the Sixties," in Wiggins, ed., *Out of the Shadows*, 223–39, especially 233–37; Bill Russell, as told to William McSweeney, *Go Up for Glory* (New York: Coward-McCann, 1966), 153–210; Bill Russell, with Alan Steinberg, *Red and Me: My Coach, My Lifelong Friend* (New York: Collins, 2009), 146–47; Russell and Branch, *Second Wind*. On the general relationship between race and sports in Boston, see Howard Bryant, *Shut Out: A Story of Race and Baseball in Boston* (New York: Routledge, 2002).

7   *NYT*, July 10, 1966. On Brown, see J. Thomas Jable, "Jim Brown: Superlative Athlete, Screen Star, Social Activist," in Wiggins, ed., *Out of the Shadows*, 241–61; and *HRG*, vol. 3, 118–20.

8   *DG*, 40, 43, 175. On Jack Johnson, see *HRG*, vol. 1, 30–42, 113–15; Geoffrey C. Ward, *Unforgivable Blackness: The Rise and Fall of Jack Johnson* (New York: Alfred A. Knopf, 2004); Randy Roberts, *Papa Jack: Jack Johnson and the Era of White Hopes* (New York: Free Press, 1983); and Gerald R. Gems, "Jack Johnson and the Quest for Racial Respect," in Wiggins, ed., *Out of the Shadows*, 58–77. On Joe Louis, see Roberts, *Joe Louis*; Mead, *Champion*; and Anthony O. Edmonds, "Joe Louis, Boxing, and American Culture," in Wiggins, ed., *Out of the Shadows*, 132–45. On Ali, see Muhammad Ali, *The Greatest: My Own Story* (New York: Random House, 1975), passim (qs); John Cottrell, *Man of Destiny: The Story of Muhammad Ali* (London: Frederick Muller, 1967); *HRG*, vol. 3, 82–87; Arthur Ashe, "Ali's Greatest Opponents Could Be the 'Jackals,'" *RTD*, September 14, 1980; Remnick, *King of the World*, 205–92; Gerald Early, "Muhammad Ali: Flawed Rebel with a Cause," in Wiggins, ed., *Out of the Shadows*, 269–72; and Branch, *At Canaan's Edge*, 226–28, 588–89, 603, 605, 627, 735, 769. See also Bill Russell, with Tex Maule, "I Am Not Worried About Ali," *SI* (June 19, 1967): 18–21. According to Pancho Gonzales, Ashe "worried about the Cassius Clay thing." See

Danzig and Schwed, eds., *Fireside Book of Tennis*, 453. *Clay v. United States* 403 U.S. 698 (1971).

9   *LAT*, November 10, 1965 (first q); *NYT*, November 10, 1965; *CD*, November 10, 1965; "Country Needs Men Like Him," *Redwood City Tribune*, November 12, 1965 (second q), copy in Arthur Ashe File, UCLASIO.

10   *AA*, 9–15; *NYT*, February 6–7, 10, 13–14, 16, 18–21, 25–27, 1966.

11   *AA*, 191; *DG*, 185 (q). Cullman was later instrumental in creating the Virginia Slims women's tour. See Bodo, *Courts of Babylon*, 272–79.

12   *AA*, 76 (q); Patricia Battles Davis/Billy Davis int.

13   *NYT*, March 19, 1966; *AA*, 76–77 (q); Pasarell int. At the time of the engagement, the young woman later known as Patricia Battles used the name Diane Seymour. Her father was Lloyd Seymour of Hartford, Connecticut, and her mother was Doris Battles of White Plains, New York. She was a graduate of Stamford Catholic High School. She had worked for the Southern New England Telephone Company for several years. See "First Negro Davis Cupper," *Ebony* (October 1963): 154.

14   *NYT*, February 22, March 27, 31, April 1, 2, 4, 1966; Pasarell int.

15   Chandler Brossard, "Arthur Ashe: Hottest New Tennis Star," *Look* 30 (April 19, 1966): 110–14; Claude Lewis, "Arthur Ashe: I Want to Be No. 1 Without an Asterisk," *Sport* (1966): 35, 96–98; Deford, "An Understudy Takes Charge"; *OTC*, 51 (q).

16   *OTC*, 61 (qs); Singleton, Slaughter, Carson, Nash, Anderson, McNichols, and Tuttle ints.

17   *OTC*, 61 (first and second qs), 62 (third and fourth qs); *DG*, 113; *AA*, 88 (fifth q). Carson and Singleton ints. On Karenga and his organization US ("Us Slaves"), see Scott Brown, *Fighting for US* (New York: NYU Press, 2003); and Maulana Ron Karenga, *The Quoteable Karenga* (Los Angeles: US Organization, 1967). See also Martha Biondi, *The Black Revolution on Campus* (Berkeley: University of California Press, 2014).

18   Rogers and Einwick ints; *AA*, 73–74, 88 (q), 185.

19   *AA*, 89–90 (qs); Mayfield int.

20   *AA*, 107–8 (qs).

21   *AA*, 95 (qs). On Carmichael, see Peniel Joseph, *Stokely: A Life* (New York: Basic Civitas, 2014); Stokely Carmichael, with Michael Thelwell, *Ready for Revolution: The Life and Struggles of Stokely Carmichael (Kwame Ture)* (New York: Scribner, 2005); and Stokely Carmichael and Charles V. Hamilton, *Black Power: The Politics of Liberation* (New York: Random House, 1967). On Brown, see H. Rap Brown (Jamil Abdullah al-Amin), *Die Nigger Die! A Political Autobiography of Jamil Abdullah al-Amin* (Chicago: Chicago Review Press, 2002). On the Black Panthers, see Josh Bloom and Waldo E. Martin Jr., *Black Against Empire: The History and Politics of the Black Panther Party* (Berkeley: University of California Press, 2013); and the excellent documentary *The Black Panthers: Vanguard of the Revolution* (Firelight Films, directed by Stanley Nelson Jr., 2015).

22   *DG*, 113 (qs). On the ideological gap between Du Bois and Washington, see W. E. B. Du Bois, *Souls of Black Folk: Essays and Sketches* (Chicago: A. C. McClurg, 1903); Booker T. Washington, *Up from Slavery: An Autobiography* (Garden City, NY: Doubleday, 1901); W. Fitzhugh Brundage, ed., *Booker T. Washington and Black Progress: Up from Slavery 100 Years Later* (Gainesville: University Press of Florida, 2003); David Levering Lewis, *W. E. B. Du Bois: Biography of a Race, 1868–1919* (New York: Henry Holt, 1993), 261–64, 273–77, 286–88, 302–4, 311–13, 336, 362, 369, 401, 407, 434, 439, 442, 479, 494, 501–3, 513, 563; and Robert J. Norrell, *Up from History: The Life*

of Booker T. Washington (Cambridge: Harvard University Press, 2009), 7–8, 14, 180, 224–33, 268, 276–80, 293–96, 316–32, 433–39.

23   Branch, *At Canaan's Edge*, 5–559; John Lewis, with Michael D'Orso, *Walking with the Wind: A Memoir of the Movement* (New York: Simon & Schuster, 1998), 363–69; Joseph, *Stokely*, 5–99.

24   Adam Goudsouzian, *Down to the Crossroads: Civil Rights, Black Power, and the Meredith March Against Fear* (New York: Farrar, Straus & Giroux, 2014), 3–62, 137–43 (second and third qs), 144–247; David J. Garrow, *Bearing the Cross: Martin Luther King, Jr., and the Southern Christian Leadership Conference* (New York: William Morrow, 1986), 484, 487 (first q); Joseph, *Stokely*, 1–2, 101–17 (fifth q), 127 (fourth q); Branch, *At Canaan's Edge*, 475–95; Adam Fairclough, *To Redeem the Soul of America: The Southern Christian Leadership Conference and Martin Luther King, Jr.* (Athens: University of Georgia Press, 1987), 308–22.

25   Joseph, *Stokely*, 123–37 (q), 138–47; Goudsouzian, *Down to the Crossroads*, 250–62.

26   Pasarell, Crookenden, and Riessen ints; *NYT*, June 15–23, 1966.

27   *DG*, 116–17,

28   *OTC*, 97–98 (qs).

29   Ibid., 97–98 (q); *AA*, 182; Hall, *Arthur Ashe*, 75–76.

30   *OTC*, 98 (qs); *AA*, 182–83; Nicholson and Johnnie Ashe ints; *Arthur and Johnnie* (ESPN Films, 30 for 30 documentary, directed by Tate Donovan, 2013).

31   *BCHT*, 135–37; *NYT*, September 1, 11, 1966.

32   *NYT*, August 16–30, 1966; *AA*, 108 (qs).

33   Frank Deford, "Service, But First a Smile," *SI* (August 29, 1966): 47 (qs). On Deford's long and distinguished career as a sportswriter, see Frank Deford, *Over Time: My Life as a Sportswriter* (New York: Grove, 2013); and *You Write Better than You Play: The Best of Frank Deford* (ESPN Classic Films, directed by Neil Leifer, 2005).

34   Deford, "Service, But First a Smile," 49–50 (qs).

35   *NYT*, August 28, 30–31, September 1–2, 4–5, 7 (q), 9–12, 1966; *BCHT*, 137–39, 460–61, 618–19; Newcombe and Graebner ints.

36   *NYT*, September 11 (q), 12, 18–19, 28–29, October 1, 3, 1966; Pasarell int.

37   *AA*, 179, 180 (first and second qs), 181 (fourth and fifth qs); *NYT*, October 14, 24–26, 28, 30–31, November 4–8 (third q), 1966; *BCHT*, 631–32, 706–7; Richey and Ralston ints.

38   *AA*, 181; *NYT*, November 8, 26–28, 30, December 1–2, 4–8, 10–11, 13, 15–19, 29, 1966; January 3–6, 11–12, 14–19, 21–22, 24–25 (q), 26–31, 1967; Dave Anderson, "U.S. Image in Tennis Turning Pale," *NYT*, November 8, 1966; Patricia Battles Davis/Billy Davis, Richey, Ralston, and Newcombe ints; *BCHT*, 139, 361.

39   Harry Gordon, "Memo from Down Under: What We Can Learn About Tennis," *NYT*, November 27, 1966 (qs).

40   *NYT*, February 3–6, 1966; Pasarell and Drysdale ints; Drysdale int, *SSAA*.

41   On the changing streetscape and social character of Jackson Ward and adjacent neighborhoods during the 1960s, see Robert P. Winthrop, *The Jackson Ward Historic District* (Richmond: Richmond Department of Planning and Community Development, 1978); "Jackson Ward Historic District," available online at dig.library.vcu.edu; Selden Richardson, *Built by Blacks: African American Architecture and Neighborhoods in Richmond* (Charleston: The History Press, 2008); Keshia A. Case, *Richmond (VA) (Then and Now)* (Charleston: Arcadia, 2006); and Robert P. Winthrop, *Richmond's Architecture* (Richmond: Richmond Times-Dispatch, 1981). See also Campbell, *Richmond's Unhealed History*, for a discussion of the city's social transformation and historical

legacies. Deford, "Service, But First a Smile," 49 (q); *LG*, 54–58; McPhee int. The ten-court complex at Battery Park eventually gained a reputation as the best cluster of public courts in Richmond and became an important venue for inner-city tennis programs such as the National Junior Tennis League. The courts and the adjoining community center have played a large role in the economic and cultural renewal of the Battery Park neighborhood in recent years, and local leaders marked Arthur Ashe's seventy-fourth birthday in July 2017 by adding a mural depicting his life. Perkins, Hood, and Packett, *Richmond: One of America's Best Tennis Towns*, 7, 24; Jonathan Davis and Grover ints; Courtney J. Cole, "Court Murals Honor Life and Legacy of RVA Native Arthur Ashe," www.wric.com, July 13, 2017.

42   *AA*, 69–70, 182 (qs), 183–92; Johnnie Ashe int; *Arthur and Johnnie*; "Arthur Ashe's Little Brother and the Sacrifice He Made," *RTD*, October 27, 2014; *NYT*, February 8, 10–21, 1966; Nicholson, Pasarell, and Gewecke ints.

43   Allison Danzig, "Ashe Urges Stress on Clay," *NYT*, February 12, 1967 (qs); *AA*, 184–85.

44   *AA*, 73 (fourth q), 75 (qs); Reed and Crookenden ints.

45   *AA*, 186 (first q), 187 (second and third qs), 190 (fourth q).

46   Ibid., 189 (first q); *IRAA*, 158–61; "Arthur Ashe and NJTL Legacy Lives on," *USTA News*, available at www.midwest.usta.com. In 2009, the National Junior Tennis League was renamed the National Junior Tennis and Learning Network (still known as NJTL). At that point, the NJTL had 550 chapters in forty-six states, with a total of 220,000 participants. Beck, Desdunes, Pasarell, Snyder, Karin Buchholz; Hartman, and Dowdell ints; David Dinkins int, *SSAA*.

CHAPTER 10: OPENINGS

1   *NYT*, February 22–23, 25, 28, March 1, 4–6, 1967.

2   *OTC*, 81 (qs); Pasarell and Patricia Battles Davis/Billy Davis ints.

3   *NYT*, March 12, 26–28, April 1–2, 1967; "Sheridan Snyder Given ITA Achievement Award" (2008), and "Sheridan Snyder Tennis Center" (2012), available online at www.virginiasports.com; "Sherry Snyder: Court Reform," *New York* (June 29, 1970). Later a biotech entrepreneur and philanthropist, Snyder continued his involvement with his alma mater, and in 2012 the University of Virginia's tennis center was re-named the Sheridan G. Snyder Tennis Center. Snyder int.

4   *NYT*, April 28–30, May 1–2, 19, 25, 1967.

5   Ibid., May 7, 1967; Pasarell and Young ints. On Maddox's demagogic career, see Robert Sherrill, *Gothic Politics in the Deep South: Stars of the New Confederacy* (New York: Ballantine, 1969), 277–301; and Bruce Galphin, *The Riddle of Lester Maddox* (Atlanta: Camelot Publishing, 1968).

6   *NYT*, May 25–27 (first and second qs), 28–30 (third q), 1967; *BCHT*, 141. Loyo-Mayo and Lara caused quite a stir at the 1966 U.S. Doubles Championships at Longwood when they outlasted the Spaniards Manolo Santana and Luis García in five sets—a marathon match that went a record-setting 105 games.

7   Nicholson int; *NYT*, May 31, June 7, 9–11, 18–20 (second q), 21, 1967; *El Universo*, June 21, 1967 (first q); *OTC*, 98–99; *BCHT*, 140–41. On Ecuador's distinctive national culture, see Carlos de la Torre and Steve Striffler, eds., *The Ecuador Reader: History, Culture, Politics* (Durham: Duke University Press, 2009).

8   *OTC*, 99 (q); Nicholson int.

9   Pasarell and Nicholson ints; Neil Amdur, "Conversations with Lt. Arthur Ashe: Part

1," *WT* (April 1968): 52–54; Neil Amdur, "Conversations with Lt. Arthur Ashe, Part 2," *WT* (May 1968): 28–29; *Arthur and Johnnie.*

10   *NYT*, July 19–24, 1967; Riessen int.

11   *NYT*, July 26–27, 29, 31 (qs), August 1, 1967; Hall, *Arthur Ashe*, 77. After leading Stanford to an undefeated season and a Rose Bowl victory in 1940, Frankie Albert (1920–2002) played quarterback for the San Francisco 49ers for seven seasons. He is widely considered to be the first T-formation quarterback in modern football history. *NYT*, September 9, 2002.

12   *NYT*, August 19, 1967 (q).

13   Ibid., August 31, September 1–2, 21, 29, 1967.

14   *BCHT*, 117, 120–21, 126, 138–39; Eugene L. Scott, "Volley for Open Tennis," *NYT*, December 10, 1967 (qs); Richard Evans, *Open Tennis, 1968–1989: The Players, the Politics, the Pressures, the Passions, and the Great Matches* (Lexington: Stephen Greene Press, 1990), 3–18. See also the Tennis Channel documentary *Barnstormers.*

15   Evans, *Open Tennis*, 3–5 (qs), 13, 17–18; *BCHT*, 138–39.

16   On Kelleher (1913–2012), who was appointed a federal judge in 1970, see *BCHT*, 594–95. *BCHT*, 139, 144; Evans, *Open Tennis*, 18–21 (first q), 22–25 (second q); Allison Danzig, "Tennis Faces Crisis," *NYT*, December 15, 1967.

17   *NYT*, December 13, 24, 26–27, 31, 1967. On Pilic, see *BCHT*, 704.

18   *NYT*, January 14–15, 22, 29–30, February 4–5, 11–12, 15–16, 18–19, 25, 28–29, March 3–4, 24–31, April 1, 1968.

19   On Lamar Hunt (1932–2006), see *BCHT*, 591; Michael MacCambridge, *Lamar Hunt: A Life in Sports* (Kansas City, MO: Andrews McNeel, 2012); and David A. F. Sweet, *Lamar Hunt: The Gentle Giant Who Revolutionized Professional Sports* (Chicago: Triumph Books, 2010). Evans, *Open Tennis*, 8–9 (q), 10–17; *BCHT*, 138, 141; Danzig and Schwed, eds., *Fireside Book of Tennis*, 849–52; Dell int.

20   Dell int; *BCHT*, 140, 152, 570; Bodo, *Ashe vs Connors*, 1; *IRAA*, 32, 104 Evans, *Open Tennis*, 7, 32–34; *OTC*, 103–6; *Arthur and Johnnie.* On Shriver, see Scott Stossel, *Sarge: The Life and Times of Sargent Shriver* (Washington, DC: Smithsonian Books, 2004).

21   Rogers int; *OTC*, 101, 103 (qs); *DG*, 114.

22   Rogers int; *WP*, March 6 (first q), 11, 1968; *DG*, 114–15 (qs), 145: Hall, *Arthur Ashe*, 84–86.

23   *WP*, March 11, 1968; *DG*, 114–15 (first q); Neil Amdur, "Ashe, Net Pro of Future, Prepares Civil Rights Talk," *NYT*, January 28, 1968; *OTC*, 102; Rogers and Nicholson ints.

24   *OTC*, 103 (first q); *DG*, 145–46 (second and third qs); Rogers int.

25   Phil Finch, "Ashe Isn't Afraid to Tell It Like It Is, Baby," *Washington Daily News*, March 18, 1968 (qs), copy in folder 1, box 35, AAP.

26   Finch, "Ashe Isn't Afraid to Tell It Like It Is, Baby" (qs); *NYT*, February 9, 12, March 26 (third q); *BAA*, April 16, 1968; Hall, *Arthur Ashe*, 86–87.

27   Rogers int; *NYT*, April 12, 1968; *OTC*, 102 (qs); *DG*, 113–15; Hall, *Arthur Ashe*, 86; Hugh McIlvanney, "Ashe Tries to Knock Down Racial Wall," *WP*, July 14, 1968.

28   *OTC*, 89, 103 (first q); Martin Luther King, Jr. to Arthur Ashe, February 7, 1968, folder 1, box 2 AAP; Young int.

29   Dell int; *NYT*, April 28, May 4–6 (second q), 24–25, 27, June 2–3, 6–7 (first q), 10; *OTC*, 104–5 (third q), 120–21, 138 (fourth q); *DG*, 114, 118; Evans, *Open Tennis*, 32–34. On the assassination of Robert F. Kennedy, see William W. Turner and John Christian, *The Assassination of Robert F. Kennedy* (New York: Basic Books, 2006); Mel

Ayton, *The Forgotten Terrorist: Sirhan Sirhan and the Assassination of Robert F. Kennedy* (Washington, DC: Potomac Books, 2007); and David Margolick, *The Promise and the Dream* (New York: Rosetta Books, 2018), chapter 14.

30   Johnnie Ashe and Nicholson ints; *Arthur and Johnnie.*

31   *NYT*, June 11–16, 19, 1968; Richey int.

32   *NYT*, June 19, 23–24 (first q), 27, 29–30, July 1 (second q), 2–4, 1968; various clippings in 1968 Wimbledon Scrapbook, KRWL; Newcombe and Graebner ints; McPhee, *Levels of the Game.*

33   *OTC*, 103–5 (first and last qs), 106, 146; *DG*, 103(second q), 104 (third, fourth, and fifth qs), 178–80; Dell and Pasarell ints; Drysdale int, *SSAA.*

34   Dell int; *NYT*, July 7, 10 (qs), 11, 13–16, 1968. See especially Eugene L. Scott, "Open Tennis: The Pros Now Respect the Amateurs," *NYT*, July 7, 1968.

35   *NYT*, July 17–22, 1968; Graebner int.

36   *NYT*, July 23–24, 27 (first and third qs), 28–29 (second q), 1968; Dell, Riessen, and Pasarell ints.

37   *NYT*, August 16–20, 1968.

38   Ibid., August 17–18, 21 (q), 22–26, 1968; *OTC*, 106.

39   *NYT*, August 20–21, 26 (first q), September 1, 1968; Arthur Daley, "A Rugged Assignment," *NYT*, August 28, 1968 (qs).

40   *OTC*, 100–101,108–9; *BCHT*, 146–147; Evans, *Open Tennis*, 44; *NYT*, August 31, September 1–4, 6 (q), 1968; Drysdale int.

41   McPhee and Graebner ints; McPhee, *Levels of the Game*, 3–23, 46–150; *BCHT*, 140; *OTC*, 106–7; Evans, *Open Tennis*, 44; *NYT*, September 5, 8–9, 1968; Dave Anderson, "Dell Offers 'Schizophrenic' Counsel," *NYT*, September 9, 1968 (qs).

42   *NYT*, September 9–11, 1968; *OTC*, 107–12; *BCHT*, 147.

43   *OTC*, 112 (qs).

44   "End of Tortuous Road: Arthur Robert Ashe, Jr.," *NYT*, September 10, 1968 (qs); Dave Anderson, "Significant Tennis Step," *NYT*, September 11, 1968, includes a comment by Donald Dell on the pro-amateur confrontation at the first U.S. Open: "The tournament seemed to be conducted of the pros, by the pros, and for the pros, and one of our Davis Cup players won it." Anderson followed up with the observation: "Ashe was fortunate, however, in not having to play any of the top four seeded players—Laver, Roche, Rosewall, and Newcombe—but he defeated two pros, Roy Emerson and Cliff Drysdale."

45   Arthur Daley, "Direct Confrontation," *NYT*, September 10, 1968 (qs).

46   *NYT*, September 12, 14, 1968; *OTC*, 114 (q). See also "Lt. Ashe Breaks Through," unidentified clipping, in folder 1, box 35, AAP; Kim Chapin, "Arthur All the Way," *SI* (September 16, 1968): 26–29; Louie Robinson Jr., "A Crown for King Arthur," *Ebony* 24 (November 1968): 64–68, 70–71; Louis Wolf, "Arthur, the New King of the Courts," *Life* 65 (September 20, 1968): 30–35; and H. W. Winn, "Sporting Scene," *New Yorker* 44 (September 28, 1968): 136+.

CHAPTER 11: MR. COOL

1   *OTC*, 113.

2   Robinson, "A Crown for King Arthur," 64–65; Martin, *Arthur Ashe*, 107; *NYT*, September 15, 1968; *Face the Nation* video clip, *SSAA.*

3   Wolf, "Arthur, the New King of the Courts," 35 (qs), copy in box 37 (Scrapbook 1968), AAP. The headline on the magazine cover read: "He topped the tennis world—THE

ICY ELEGANCE OF ARTHUR ASHE." The cover photograph showed an intense, bespectacled Ashe preparing to strike a ball near the net. Most of the article is devoted to photographs taken at the U.S. Open.

4 Robinson, "A Crown for King Arthur," 68 (first and second qs), 65 (third q).

5 *NYT*, October 17, 1968; *LAT*, October 18, 1968; *CD*, October 19, 1968; Deford int, *SSAA*; Edwards int.; David Hartmann, *Race, Culture, and the Revolt of the Black Athlete: The 1968 Olympic Protests and Their Aftermath* (Chicago: University of Chicago Press, 2004); Amy Bass, *Not the Triumph but the Struggle: The 1968 Olympics and the Making of the Black Athlete* (Minneapolis: University of Minnesota Press, 2004); Richard Hoffer, *Something in the Air: American Passion and Defiance in the 1968 Mexico City Olympics* (New York: Free Press, 2009); Tommie Smith and David Steele, *Silent Gesture: The Autobiography of Tommie Smith* (Philadelphia: Temple University Press, 2007); John Wesley Carlos and David Zirin, *The John Carlos Story: The Sports Moment That Changed the World* (Chicago: Haymarket Books, 2011); Harry Edwards, *The Revolt of the Black Athlete* (New York: Free Press, 1969); and Harry Edwards, *The Struggle That Must Be: An Autobiography* (New York: Macmillan, 1980). See also the excellent documentary film on the Smith-Carlos controversy and its context: *Fists of Freedom: The Story of the '68 Summer Games* (HBO Documentary Films, directed by George Roy, 1999). In 2008, Smith and Carlos received the Arthur Ashe Award for Courage at the ESPY Awards ceremony.

6 Wolf, "Arthur, the New King of the Courts," 34 (first q); Robinson, "A Crown for King Arthur," 70 (second and third qs).

7 For an overview of the tumult of 1968, see David Caute, *The Year of the Barricades: A Journey Through 1968* (New York: HarperCollins, 1988); Mark Kurlansky, *1968: The Year That Rocked the World* (New York: Random House, 2005); David Farber, *Chicago '68* (Chicago: University of Chicago Press, 1994); and Jeremi Suri, *The Global Revolutions of 1968* (New York: W. W. Norton, 2007). *AA*, 103, 220; *NYT*, November 8, 15, December 13, 1968. See also Chapin, "Arthur All the Way," 26–29; Darden, "Arthur, the New King of the Courts," 36; Winn, "Sporting Scene," 136+; "People Are Talking About," *Vogue* 152 (November 15, 1968): 132–33; and Robinson, "A Crown for King Arthur," 64–68, 70.

8 John McPhee, *A Sense of Where You Are: A Profile of Bill Bradley at Princeton* (New York: Farrar, Straus & Giroux, 1965); McPhee int.

9 McPhee and Graebner ints; Clifford Geertz, "Deep Play: Notes on the Balinese Cockfight," *Daedalus* 101 (Winter 1972): 1–37. See also Clifford Geertz, *The Interpretation of Cultures* (New York: Basic Books, 1973).

10 McPhee and Graebner ints; McPhee, *Levels of the Game*, back cover (first and second qs), 3–4 (third q); John McPhee, "Profiles," *New Yorker* 45 (June 7, 1969): 45–58+; and John McPhee, "Profiles," *New Yorker* 45 (June 14, 1968): 44–48+. On Graebner, see Neil Amdur, "The Graebner Few People Know," *NYT*, July 21, 1968.

11 "Pros Want Arthur Ashe," *Sepia* 17 (December 1968): 64–67; *OTC*, 113–14; *NYT*, July 1, 10, 29, August 28, September 11, October 20 (q), November 19, 28, 1968; *BCHT*, 144–45.

12 *NYT*, March 30, May 6, July 7 (first q), September 5, November 6, 17, 19 (second q), December 4, 1968; Dell int; *BCHT*, 144, 147, 149.

13 *NYT*, September 11, 12, 14–17, 19, 22–25, October 10, 1968; *OTC*, 114.

14 *NYT*, November 8–9, 10 (first q), 11, 12 (second q), 1968; McPhee, Dell, and Pasarell ints. Pasarell was an alternate limited to playing in a preliminary exhibition match.

15 Dell int; *NYT*, November 13, 15, 19, 21, 1968; *OTC*, 122–23 (q). See also "Diplomacy: The Liveliest Ambassador," *Time* 92 (November 1, 1968). Until 1971, the defending Davis Cup champion was guaranteed a place in the final tie, which was known as the Challenge Round. After 1971, the defending champion had to compete with the other teams in the earlier rounds.

16 Owen Williams, *Ahead of the Game: Memoir of a Trailblazer Who Had Serious Fun While Turning Tennis into Big Business* (Miami: Professional Press, 2013), 169–70 (qs), 171; Owen Williams and Dell ints; Arthur Ashe and Williams ints, *SSAA*.

17 *NYT*, October 8, December 5, 10–11, 13–14, 15 (q), 16, 18, 1968; Richard Evans int, *SSAA*.

18 *NYT*, December 15, 1968.

19 Ibid., December 17–19, 21–29, 1968; *OTC*, 115 (q); Dell, Collins, and Stan Smith ints; Hall, *Arthur Ashe*, 105–6.

20 *NYT*, January 6–9, 12–13, 1969; *OTC*, 120; Dell, Stan Smith, and Einwick ints; "Speech by Arthur Ashe, Ten Outstanding Young Men of America Congress, Syracuse, New York, January 1969," transcript (q); and Nomination Form for Arthur Ashe, Ten Outstanding Young Men of America, copies in possession of Lou Einwick, Richmond, Virginia.

21 Dell and Collins ints; *NYT*, January 13, 1969 (q).

22 Collins and Johnnie Ashe ints; *OTC*, 116–17 (qs); *Arthur and Johnnie*. On the Tet Offensive, see Don Oberdorfer, *Tet!: The Turning Point in the Vietnam War* (Baltimore: Johns Hopkins University Press, 2001).

23 Collins int; *OTC*, 117–18 (qs); *IRAA*, 141–44.

24 *OTC*, 118–19 (qs); Collins and Pasarell ints.

25 Dell int.

26 Collins int; *NYT*, February 2–3, 5 (q), 1969.

27 *NYT*, January 19, February 2, 6–8, 9 (qs), 1969; Dell int; *BCHT*, 149.

28 *OTC*, 97–99, 122; Nicholson, Dell, and McPhee ints; *NYT*, February 25 (qs), 27, 1969.

29 *NYT*, March 21 (qs), 22–24, 1969. On the growing awareness of the importance of money in the world of sports during the late 1960s, see Joseph Durso, "Big Money and Professional Sports: Vexing Problems Go with Affluence," *NYT*, February 9, 1969.

30 Wolf, "Arthur, the New King of the Courts," 34 (first q); *NYT*, March 21, 1969 (second and third qs). The 1969 St. Petersburg Masters International tournament was Ashe's last tournament as an amateur. Ashe played well in the early rounds but lost his semifinal match against Zeljko Franulovic of Yugoslavia 3–6, 6–1, 6–1. The tournament was held at the St. Petersburg Tennis Center, a city-owned public facility. *The Tenth Annual Masters Invitational Tennis Championships, March 18–23, 1969* (St. Petersburg: St. Petersburg Tennis Foundation, 1969), program; William P. Wallace, Steve Reilly, Paul Reilly, and Mike Reilly ints.

31 *NYT*, March 25–31, 1969.

32 Ibid., April 1, 4–7, 1969; Pasarell int.

33 *NYT*, April 9, 1969 (qs).

34 Ibid., April 15–18, 22, 24, 26, 29–30 (q).

35 Ibid., May 1, 10, 21, 27, 29, 31, June 1, 5, 1969; *BCHT*, 104–5, 152, 388–89, 400, 652.

36 *NYT*, June 10–13, 1969.

37 *OTC*, 225; *BCHT*, 150; Graebner and Dell ints; McPhee, "Profiles," *New Yorker* (June 7, 14, 1969).

38 *NYT*, June 17, 1969 (qs); Pasarell, Dell, and Riessen ints.

39 *NYT*, June 24, 1969 (qs); Dell int.

40   *NYT*, June 24 (qs), 29, 1969; Pasarell, Dell, and Collins ints; *BCHT*, 151.

41   *NYT*, May 28 (first and second qs), June 24, 30 (third and fourth qs), 1969; London *Times*, July 1, 1969; Drysdale and Dell ints.

42   *NYT*, July 2, 4, 1969; *BCHT*, 150, 152.

43   *NYT*, July 4, 1969 (q); *BCHT*, 149.

44   *NYT*, July 9, 1969 (qs); Dell int; Dell's Tennis Channel commentary, 2016 Citi Open, July 23, 2016.

45   *NYT*, July 10–14, 1969; *Washington Star*, July 10–14, 1969; "Don't Forget Arthur's Contribution to Washington," *Washington Times*, March 7, 1993; Dell int.

46   *BCHT*, 149; *NYT*, July 11–13, 1969; Dell int.

47   *NYT*, July 14, 20, 29 (first q), 30 (second q), 1969; Drysdale int.

48   *NYT*, July 30, 1969 (qs); Bodo, *Courts of Babylon*, 273–74; Drysdale, Dell, and Owen Williams ints. On Williams, see Robert Lipsyte, "The Promoter," *NYT*, August 23, 1969; and Williams, *Ahead of the Game*.

49   *NYT*, July 31, August 1–3, 16–17, 19–22, 1969.

50   *NYT*, August 27, 29 (qs), 1969; Williams and Stockton ints.

51   Arthur Daley, "A Patriarch Discourses," *NYT*, August 29, 1969.

52   *NYT*, August 29–31, September 1–2, 6–9, 1969. See especially Robert Lipsyte, "Looking for Heroes," *NYT*, August 30, 1969; *BCHT*, 150 (q), 151. On Laver's remarkable career, see Laver, with Bud Collins, *The Education of a Tennis Player*.

53   *NYT*, September 19–20, 21 (first q), 22 (second and third qs), 1969; *BCHT*, 149, 151, 161–62, 165, 615–16, 711; Bodo, *Courts of Babylon*, 25–26; Danzig and Schwed, eds., *Fireside Book of Tennis*, 886–88; Dell and Stan Smith ints.

CHAPTER 12: RACKET MAN

1   *NYT*, July 4, 11–13, September 14, 22, November 4, December 17, 1969; *BCHT*, 149.

2   *NYT*, February 25, 27, April 18, 22, 30, May 20, June 1–5, 10–13, 25–30, July 2–4, 8–14, 19, 22–28, 31, August 1–3, 10, 24, September 6–8, 28, October 6–12, 1969; Dell int.

3   Dell (q), Stan Smith, William P. Wallace, and Sally Wallace ints. On Mark McCormack (1930–2003) and the IMG sports management and media conglomerate, see Mark H. McCormack, *What They Didn't Teach You at Harvard Business School: Notes from a Street-Smart Executive* (New York: Bantam, 1984); and the websites IMG.com and IMGworld.com. Dell and his partner, Frank Craighill, formally incorporated ProServ in 1970. Craighill left ProServ in 1983 to form his own sports agency, Advantage, Inc. On the evolution of sports agencies such as ProServ and IMG, see Lisa P. Masteralexis, Carol A. Barr, and Mary Hums, *Principles and Practice of Sport Management* (New York: Jones & Bartlett Learning, 2011).

4   *OTC*, 125, 127–28 (q), 129; Martin, *Arthur Ashe*, 111–12; *DG*, 25, 184; Dell int. On Arnold Palmer as a sports and endorsement icon, see Thomas Hauser, with Arnold Palmer, *Arnold Palmer: A Personal Journey* (New York: NBC Books, 2012); and Howard Sounes, *The Wicked Game: Arnold Palmer, Jack Nicklaus, Tiger Woods, and the Story of Modern Golf* (New York: William Morrow, 2004). In recent decades, Palmer's endorsement record has been surpassed by a number of athletes, including Tiger Woods and Michael Jordan. On Jordan's commercialization, see Walter LaFeber, *Michael Jordan and the New Global Capitalism* (New York: Norton, 2002); and Roland Lazenby, *Michael Jordan: The Life* (Boston: Back Bay Books, 2015).

5   *OTC*, 128 (q); Dell int.

6   *OTC*, 128–29; Dell int.

7   *OTC*, 129–30; *DG*, 25, 184; *BCHT*, 185; Martin, *Arthur Ashe*, 112; Dell and M. C. Savage ints. On Howard Head, see *NYT*, March 4, 1991 (obituary).

8   *OTC*, 130 (q). On the colorful history of post-1969 tennis apparel and related player endorsements, see Bodo, *Courts of Babylon*, 175–97.

9   *OTC*, 131 (q)–132; *DG*, 185; Bollettieri int.

10   See the voluminous correspondence and documentation in folders 3–14, box 31, and folders 1–2, box 32, AAP. The first meeting of PEI was in Berkeley, California, on October 4, 1969. The five players added to the PEI roster were Tom Gorman, Brian Gottfried, Marty Riessen, Dick Stockton, and Roscoe Tanner. See also *DG*, 180.

11   *DG*, 179 (q); Dell int.

12   *DG*, 179 (third q), 180 (first q); Dell int (second q).

13   *DG*, 184; *OTC* 129; Dell int.

14   *OTC*, 130; *DG*, 25, 168–69, 184; Mandeville and Schragis ints. Howie Evans, "Ashe's Ace: Tennis Director at Doral," *New York Amsterdam News*, c. October 1970 (q); Howie Evans to Howard Kaskel, October 26, 1970; Alvin Schragis, "The Brotherhood of Al and Arthur" (undated typescript); and *Doral Newsletter* (October–November 1974), all in Al Schragis Collection, in possession of Al Schragis, Scarsdale, New York.

15   *DG*, 103. On Ali, see Remnick, *King of the World*; Michael Ezra, *Muhammad Ali: The Making of an Icon* (Philadelphia: Temple University Press, 2009); and Michael Marqusee, *Redemption Song: Muhammad Ali and the Spirit of the Sixties* (New York: Verso, 1999). On Brown, see Jim Brown and Steve Delsohn, *Jim Brown Out of Bounds* (New York: Zebra Books, 1989); and Freeman, *Jim Brown*. On Russell, see Goudsouzian, *King of the Court*; Russell and Branch, *Second Wind*; and John Taylor, *The Rivalry: Bill Russell, Wilt Chamberlain, and the Golden Age of Basketball* (New York: Ballantine, 2006). On Flood, see Curt Flood, *The Way It Is* (New York: Trident Press, 1971); Brad Snyder, *A Well-Paid Slave: Curt Flood's Fight for Free Agency in Professional Sports* (New York: Plume, 2007); Stuart Weiss, *The Curt Flood Story: The Man Behind the Myth* (Columbia: University of Missouri Press, 2007); and Alex Belth and Tim McCarver, *Stepping Up: The Story of All-Star Curt Flood and His Fight for Baseball Players' Rights* (New York: Persea, 2006). On White, see Bill White, *Uppity: My Untold Story About the Games People Play* (New York: Grand Central, 2011). See also James Blake, with Carol Taylor, *Ways of Grace: Stories of Activism, Adversity, and How Sports Can Bring Us Together* (New York: Amistad, 2017).

16   Eric Allen Hall, " 'I Guess I'm Becoming More and More Militant': Arthur Ashe and the Black Freedom Movement," *Journal of African American History* 96 (Fall 2011): 476 (first q), 488 (second q); Barry Lorge, "Inside the Heart and Mind of Arthur Ashe," *Tennis* (September 1988): 46; Bodo, *Courts of Babylon*, 260.

17   Rogers int; Hall, " 'I Guess I'm Becoming More and More Militant,' " 488–49; *OTC*, 102–6; *DG*, 115 (q); Eric J. Morgan, "Black and White at Center Court: Arthur Ashe and the Confrontation of Apartheid in South Africa," *Diplomatic History* 36 (November 2012): 815–41.

18   *NYT*, December 4 (first q), 6 (third and fourth qs), 1969; Morgan, "Black and White at Center Court," 819, 829 (second q); Drysdale int.

19   Morgan, "Black and White at Center Court," 820–21 (first q), 822–23; December 12, 16 (second and third qs), 18, 21, 1969; Dell int. On the long history of "constructive engagement" policies and South Africa, see Christopher Coker, *The United States and South Africa, 1968–1985: Constructive Engagement and Its Critics* (Durham, NC: Duke University Press, 1985).

20   *NYT*, November 2, 18, December 6, 20–22, 24, 1969, January 13, 1970; *BCHT*, 151, 156; *OTC*, 220; Stan Smith int, *SSAA*.

21   *NYT*, January 9, 12, 15–18, 1970.

22   Ibid., January 22, 1970; *BCHT*, 150.

23   *NYT*, January 21–23, 25–28 (q), 1970; *WP*, January 27, 1970; *BCHT*, 155–57, 361–62.

24   *NYT*, January 29, February 1, 1970 (qs).

25   Ibid., February 1 (Newcombe qs), 2, 6 (Turville q), 1970.

26   *NYT*, February 9 (q), 17, 1970.

27   Ibid., February 17, 1970 (q); Morgan, "Black and White on Center Court," 829–31.

28   *NYT*, February 22, 1970 (qs); Graebner, Riessen, and Richey ints.

29   *NYT*, February 10, 13, 15–16, 18, 27–28, March 1–2, 1970.

30   Ibid., February 1, 6, 8, March 8, 1970.

31   Ibid., March 6, 10–11, 1970; *BCHT*, 156–57, 169.

32   *NYT*, March 24 (Dell q), 25 (Ashe q), 1970; Dell and Moore ints. On Moore's opposition to apartheid and his friendship with Ashe, see "Visit by Ashe Was Biggest Tennis Boost Says Moore," unidentified clipping, c. December 1, 1973, in folder 7, box 1, AAP.

33   *NYT*, April 6, 13, 15 (q), 1970; Martin, *Arthur Ashe*, 115.

34   *NYT*, April 18, 1970 (q).

35   *BCHT*, 153–54; *NYT*, April 9, 1970 (q).

36   *BCHT*, 154 (qs); *NYT*, July 29, August 30, September 4 (Ashe qs), 1970.

37   *NYT*, August 26, September 1, 17 (qs), 1970; *BCHT*, 155–56.

38   *BCHT*, 154; *PIM*, 14 (q).

39   *OTC*, 220–21, 225, 228; *BCHT*, 155, 462; *NYT*, June 28–29, September 2–11, November 30, December 4, 1970.

40   *NYT*, August 18, 29–31, September 1, 1970; *WP*, August 15, 1970; *OTC*, 140, 224; *BCHT*, 156; Collins and Stan Smith ints. Held in Cleveland, the Challenge Match saw an American sweep, 5–0, as Ashe extended his Davis Cup singles record to 23–3.

41   Collins and Stan Smith ints; *IRAA*, 125–26. On Kenyatta and Kenya, see Jomo Kenyatta, *The Challenge of Uhuru: The Progress of Kenya, 1968 to 1970* (Nairobi: East African Publishing, 1971); Jomo Kenyatta, *Suffering Without Bitterness* (Nairobi: East African Publishing, 1971); and Guy Arnold, *Kenyatta and the Politics of Kenya* (London: Dent, 1974).

42   *NYT*, October 24, 1970; Collins and Stan Smith ints; *OTC*, 141 (qs); *IRAA*, 128. On Julius Nyerere and Tanzania, see Julius Nyerere, *Freedom and Socialism: A Selection from the Writing and Speeches, 1965–67* (Oxford: Oxford University Press, 1968); Julius Nyerere, *Freedom and Development: A Selection from the Writing and Speeches, 1968–73* (Oxford: Oxford University Press, 1974); and Raymond F. Hopkins, *Political Roles in a New State: Tanzania's First Decade* (New Haven: Yale University Press, 1971).

43   *NYT*, October 27, 1970 (qs); Collins and Stan Smith ints; *IRAA*, 128–29. On Zambia and Kenneth Kaunda, see Andrew Sardanis, *Africa: Another Side of the Coin: Northern Rhodesia's Final Years and Zambia's Nationhood* (London: I. B. Tauris, 2003); Andrew Roberts, *A History of Zambia* (New York: Africana Publishing, 1975); Richard Hall, *The High Price of Principles: Kaunda and the White South* (New York: Africana Publishing, 1969); and Fergus MacPherson, *Kenneth Kaunda: The Times and the Man* (New York: Oxford University Press, 1974).

44   *NYT*, August 17, November 1, 1970; Collins and Stan Smith ints; *OTC*, 142–43 (qs). On Uganda, see Phares Mutibwa, *Uganda Since Independence: A Story of Unfulfilled*

Hopes (Trenton, NJ: Africa World Press, 1992). General Idi Amin's brutal regime took power in 1971, the year after Ashe's visit. On Amin, see Andrew Rice, *The Teeth May Smile but the Heart Does Not Forget: Murder and Memory in Uganda* (New York: Picador, 2010). On Nigeria and the Biafran civil war, see Toyin Falola and Matthew M. Heaton, *A History of Nigeria* (Cambridge: Cambridge University Press, 2008); Chinua Achebe, *There Was a Country: A Personal History of Biafra* (New York: Penguin, 2012); Frederick Forsyth, *The Biafra Story* (Baltimore: Penguin, 1969); Luke N. Aneke, *The Untold Story of the Nigeria-Biafra War* (New York: Triumph, 2008); and Alfred Uzokwe, *Surviving in Biafra: The Story of the Nigerian Civil War* (New York: Writers Advantage, 2003).

45 Collins and Stan Smith ints. On Ghana and Nkrumah, see Basil Davidson, *Black Star: A View of the Life and Times of Kwame Nkrumah* (New York: Praeger, 1974); C. L. R. James, *Kwame Nkrumah and the Ghana Revolution* (Westport, CT: L. Hill, 1977); and David Birmingham, *Kwame Nkrumah: Father of African Nationalism* (Athens: Ohio University Press, 1998).

46 *NYT*, November 15, 16 (q), 1970; Riessen int.

47 *NYT*, November 17, 21–22, 24–27, 29–30, 1970; Stan Smith int.

48 *NYT*, December 2, 6, 1970; *BCHT*, 157.

49 *NYT*, November 6 (first q), 8 (second q), 1970.

50 Ibid., November 13, December 6, 9 (q), 1970; *BCHT*, 157.

51 *NYT*, December 8–11, 16, 1970; *BCHT*, 153 (qs), 157; Danzig and Schwed, eds., *Fireside Book of Tennis*, 899–909; Stan Smith and Richey ints. Jan Kodes replaced Richey to complete the six-man field. Stan Smith won the first-place prize money of $15,000. After four days of play, the tournament took a three-day break before resuming on Monday, December 14.

CHAPTER 13: DOUBLING DOWN

1 *NYT*, January 2, 1971.

2 Ibid., January 17–19 (qs), 1971.

3 Ibid., January 21, 22(q), 24, 29–30, February 6–7, 14, 18, 20, 22–23, 1971. When Laver defeated Ashe on January 28, it was his seventh straight victory in the series and his sixth consecutive victory over Ashe. Two weeks later, Ashe lost to Laver again in the semifinals of the Philadelphia International indoor tournament. In the Champion Classic series, Ashe made it to the quarterfinals, where he lost to Ralston (whom he had defeated the previous week in Philadelphia) on February 22.

4 Ibid., January 25, 1971.

5 *OTC*, 146; *IRAA*, 25 (first q), 33, 104 (second q); Angela Y. Davis, *Angela Davis: An Autobiography* (New York: International Publishers, 2013). Created by Don Cornelius, *Soul Train* first aired on WCIU-TV in Chicago in August 1970. On October 2, 1971, it went into national syndication and soon became "the black *American Bandstand.*" The popular show ran continuously until March 25, 2008. See the 2010 documentary *Soul Train: The Hippest Trip in America* (VH-1 Productions); and Nelson George, *The Hippest Trip in America: Soul Train and the Evolution of Culture and Style* (New York: William Morrow, 2014).

6 *DG*, 126–67, 157 (q); *OTC*, 215–16.

7 *DG*, 115 (qs); Young and Dell ints; Dell int, *SSAA*. Hall, *Arthur Ashe*, 83, incorrectly places the Atlanta episode in 1968 at Young's home. Donald Dell also remembered the

date as 1968, but Ashe did not meet Young until 1970; Hazzard moved to Atlanta in 1969. See *IRAA*, 66.

8   *NYT*, January 12–14, 16, February 11, 25 (qs), 1971; *OTC*, 146. South Africa's Population Registration Act of 1950 established four official racial groups: white, black, coloured, and Indian. Individuals were placed into one of these groups based on appearance, known ancestry, cultural lifestyle, and socioeconomic status. Deborah Posel, "Race as Common Sense: Racial Classification in Twentieth-Century South Africa," *African Studies Review* 44 (September 2001): 87–113.

9   *BCHT*, 158, 160–61, 582–83; *NYT*, February 25, 1971 (qs). See also Harry Gordon, "How the Daughter of an Ancient Race Made It Out of the Australian Outback," *NYT Magazine* (August 29, 1971): 10–11 and ff; and Bodo, *Courts of Babylon*, 104–17.

10   *BCHT*, 158–61, 362, 369; *NYT*, March 8, 10–15, 1971.

11   *BCHT*, 161–62, 396, 432, 562 (q); *OTC*, 221.

12   *BCHT*, 152, 157, 400, 436, 702, 776; *OTC*, 220–24; *IRAA*, 64; Riessen int.

13   *BCHT*, 159, 162; *NYT*, March 15, May 29, 30 (q), June 4–5, 1971; Riessen int.

14   Riessen and Stan Smith ints; *NYT*, June 4, 5 (qs), 1971; *BCHT*, 162.

15   *NYT*, February 14, April 15, June 16, 27 (qs), August 31, 1970; *BCHT*, 158–59, 162, 648; Stan Smith int.

16   *BCHT*, 159, 421, 436, *NYT*, June 30, July 1–4, 1971; Stan Smith, Newcombe, and Ralston ints. At the age of seventeen, Ralston, with Rafael Osuna as his partner, won the Wimbledon doubles title in 1960.

17   *NYT*, July 1, 1971; *PIM*, 3; *W*, 64–69, 74, 98, 106–7, 119, 125, 149–57, 166–67, 175–76, 152 (q); *DG*, 116; *CTN*, 112–13; *IRAA*, 4; Willis Thomas and Bobby Davis ints.

18   *DG*, 109–10; *OTC*, 147; *NYT*, June 18, 24 (q), 25, 1971. During the first round of the 1971 U.S. Open, played on June 17 at the Merion Golf Club in Ardmore, Pennsylvania, two members of the crowd heckled Gary Player with the chant "Arthur Ashe, Sharpeville," linking Ashe's visa denial to the infamous March 1960 massacre of black South Africans by white policemen. The actual site of the massacre, which left 69 dead and 180 wounded, was the African township of Vereeniging, in the Transvaal town of Sharpeville. See Jim Hoagland, *South Africa: Civilizations in Conflict* (Boston: Houghton Mifflin, 1972), 132–33.

19   *BCHT*, 159; *NYT*, January 10, February 3, 14, April 7, May 25, June 1, 16, 1971; *OTC*, 138; Dell int.

20   *NYT*, July 11, 14 (q), 1971; *BCHT*, 160, 568; Dell and Collins ints. On television's impact on tennis, see Mariah Gillespie, "Tennis and Television: The Impact of the Media on a Traditional Sport," October 8, 2011, available online at mariahgillespie1 .blogspot.com. The first televised tennis match took place in Rye, New York, in 1937. The experimental coverage by NBC was seen on primitive four-by-three-inch screens, and those watching could barely make out the flight of the ball. See *BCHT*, 65.

21   *NYT*, April 11, 1971 (q).

22   *OTC*, 144–49; *DG*, 101–4, 107, 109, 112–13; Morgan, "Black and White at Center Court," 833; Hoagland, *South Africa*, 340–59.

23   *DG*, 102–12; Ronald V. Dellums and H. Lee Hatterman, *Lying Down with the Lions* (Boston: Beacon, 2000); Raymond W. Copson, *The Congressional Black Caucus and Foreign Policy (1971–2002)* (Boston: Nova Science, 2003); Robert Singh, *The Congressional Black Caucus: Racial Politics in the US Congress* (New York: Sage, 1997). On the American anti-apartheid movement, see David Hostetter, *Movement Matters: American Antiapartheid Activism and the Rise of Multicultural Politics* (New York:

Routledge, 2009); Donald Culverson, *Contesting Apartheid: U.S. Activism, 1960–1987* (Boulder: Westview, 1999); and Francis N. Nesbitt, *Race for Sanctions: African Americans and Apartheid, 1946–1994* (Bloomngton: Indiana University Press, 2004). On the movement to boycott and isolate South African sports, see Peter Hain, *Don't Play with Apartheid: The Background to the Stop the Seventy Tour* (London: Allen & Unwin, 1971); and Robert Nixon, *Homelands, Harlem and Hollywood: South African Culture and the World Beyond* (New York: Routledge, 1994), 131–54. See also Hoagland, *South Africa*, 340–83.

24   Nesbitt, *Race for Sanctions*; *DG*, 107; *OTC*, 147–48; Morgan, "Black and White at Center Court," 818–19, 824–27.

25   Gordon, "How the Daughter of an Ancient Race Made It Out of the Australian Outback," 11, 45, 47.

26   *NYT*, October 2, 7, 12, 15, 19, November 1, 3, 5–8, 13–15, 19, December 5, 1971; *OTC*, 132.

27   Keesing's Research Report, *Africa Independent: A Study of Political Developments* (New York: Charles Scribner's Sons, 1972), 209–12, 222–24, 233–36. See also Tambi Eyongetah and Robert Brain, *A History of the Cameroon* (London: Longman, 1974); Meredith Terreta, *Nation of Outlaws, State of Violence: Nationalism, Grassfields Tradition, and State Building in Cameroon* (Athens: Ohio University Press, 2013); and William Mark Habeeb, *Ivory Coast* (Broomall, PA: Mason Crest, 2013). On Senegal and Senghor, see Janet Vaillard, *Black, French, and African: A Life of Léopold Segar Senghor* (Cambridge: Harvard University Press, 1990).

28   Ray Kennedy, "There's Bitter with the Sweet," *SI* (August 15, 1983): 54–60 (first q), 62–66; Barry Lorge, "The Sudden Rise of Noah's Arc," *Sport* (September 1983): 54–57 (second q), 58–61; *OTC*, 132 (third and fourth qs); *BCHT*, 619–20; Noah int, *SSAA*; Bodo, *Courts of Babylon*, 124, 132–33. On Noah, see Yannick Noah, *T'as Pas Deux Balles?* (Paris: Stock, 1984); and Yannick Noah, *Noah par Noah* (Paris: Cherche Midi, 2006).

29   *OTC*, 132 (qs), 133; *IRAA*, 44.

30   Ibid., 133 (q); *CTN*, 101, 114, 129–30, 164, 166, 206–10; *BATN*, 70–83, 142–61; *W*, 118, 165–66; Reid, Carrington, Desdunes, and Wilkerson ints.

31   Desdunes, Wilkerson, Allen, Reid, Carrington, McNeil, Sands, Harmon, and Nelson ints.

32   *AA*, 70–77; *CTN*, 72, 101 (second q), 113–14 (first and third qs), 115 (second and fourth qs), 136, 228; *W*, 108–9, 118, 135, 160, 164–65 (sixth q), 166 (fifth q), 167–68; Carrington, Wilkerson, Reid, and Desdunes ints.

33   *W*, 137–43, 148–49, 151, 164–65 (third q), 180; *CTN*, 101, 112, 115, 205 (first q), 206 (second q), 207–8, 226; *BATN*, 70–84; Harmon, Sands, Reid, Allen, Hooper, Shelton, Carrington, and Wilkerson ints.

34   Reid int (qs); *CTN*, 101, 245; *W*, 117–18, 164–65; *BATN*, 71–72.

35   *IRAA*, 108 (first q); Reid and Hooper ints (second q); *W*, 166–68; *BATN*, 81–84.

36   Hooper int; *CTN*, 115, 136, 167, 245; W, 141, 164, 180; *BATN*, 81–83.

37   Harmon, Thomas, and Wilkerson ints; *IRAA*, 4, 12–13, 14 (first q), 15, 17–19, 54–57, 80–81, 107–8, 117–18, 132–33, 158, 166–67; *CTN*, 41, 102, 115, 120, 155–56, 158–59, 161, 166 (second q)–168, 207, 214, 226, 230; W, 160, 162–63, 180; *BATN*, 83–84.

38   *IRAA*, 17 (fifth q), 80 (first q), 108 (fourth q), 118 (second q); *CTN*, 102 (third q); Harmon and Dell ints.

39   *NYT*, February 4, 6, 1972; Harmon and JMA ints; *IRAA*, 48, 60, 65, 72–73, 101–18.

CHAPTER 14: RISKY BUSINESS

1   *PIM*, 2–3 (q); Loretta Ashe Harris int.

2   George Herring, *The Longest War: The United States and Vietnam, 1950–1975* (New York: McGraw-Hill, 1979), 242–83; John Morton Blum, *Years of Discord: American Politics and Society, 1961–1974* (New York: W. W. Norton, 1991), 374–430; Andrew Young, *An Easy Burden: The Civil Rights Movement and the Transformation of America* (New York: HarperCollins, 1996), 504–20; Young, Johnnie Ashe, and Dell ints; George McGovern to Arthur Ashe, February 15, 1972, in folder 2, box 2, AAP.

3   *BCHT*, 160, 163–64; *NYT*, February 13 (q), March 15–16, 19, 1972; Dell int.

4   Dell int; *NYT*, April 12, 21, 27 (q), July 12–13, 18, 1972; *BCHT*, 160–61, 163; Connors, *The Outsider*, 79–81. On King and the women's tour in the 1970s, see Ware, *Game, Set, Match*, 1–178; Billie Jean King, with Kim Chapin, *Billie Jean: An Autobiography* (New York: Harper & Row, 1974); King, with Frank Deford, *Billie Jean*; Selena Roberts, *A Necessary Spectacle: Billie Jean King, Bobby Riggs, and the Tennis Match That Leveled the Game* (New York: Crown, 2005); and Grace Lichtenstein, *A Long Way Baby: The Inside Story of the Women in Pro Tennis* (New York: William Morrow, 1974).

5   *BCHT*, 161, 165, 169; *NYT*, April 12, 1972; Connors, *The Outsider*, 85–86; Evans, *The Davis Cup*, 173–200; Murray Janoff, *Game! Set! Match!* (New York: Stadia Sports, 1973), 111–22.

6   *NYT*, April 2 (q), July 13, 1972; *BCHT*, 174–75; Morgan, "Black and White at Center Court," 824, 833; *PIM*, 106; *DG*, 107.

7   *NYT*, June 10, 12, 18, July 1, 7–10, 19, 21, 27–31, August 1, 3–7, 9, 12–13, 17, 1972.

8   Ibid., May 28, June 10, 12, July 28 (q), August 1, 3–7, 9, 12–13, 17, 1972.

9   Ibid., June 27, August 6, 20, 1972.

10 Ibid., August 23, 27 (first q), August 30–September 2, 5–6, 8 (second q); *BCHT*, 164; Connors, *The Outsider*, 96.

11 *BCHT*, 165; *OTC*, 138–39; *DG*, 66, 267; Dell and Drysdale ints; *NYT*, September 8 (q), 10, 1972.

12 *NYT*, September 10 (first q), 11–12 (second q), 22, 1972; Wells Twombly, "Here Comes Nasty: In the Style of Bo Belinsky, Joe Namath, Lee Trevino, and Muhammad Ali," *NYT Magazine* (October 22, 1972): 42–43, 84–85 (third q), 86–88; Evans, *Nasty*, 74–82; *DG*, 72, 91; Collins int.

13 *NYT*, September 11, 14, 17–18, 1972.

14 Ibid., September 22, October 1–2, 26–27, 30, November 14, 16, 18, 23–24, 26–27 (first q), 28 (second q), 1972; Rampersad, *Jackie Robinson*, 444–61. On the presidential election of 1972, see Theodore H. White, *The Making of the President, 1972* (New York: Atheneum, 1973).

15 *NYT*, January 7, 1973 (first q); *BCHT*, 167 (second q), 168–71.

16 *BCHT*, 167–68; *NYT*, December 12, 1972, January 7, 1973.

17 *NYT*, January 24, 26–27, 30, February 11, 23, March 1, 5, 10, 20, 24–26, April 3, 5–6, 9, 11, 13–14, 18–23, 25, 29–30, 1973.

18 *BCHT*, 167–68; *NYT*, May 9–10, 12–14, 1973; *AA*, 87, 129, 171–74.

19 *NYT*, January 12, 1973 (qs).

20 Ibid., May 15, 18–20 (q), 1973; Richey and Gottfried ints.

21 *PIM*, passim; Patricia Battles Davis/Billy Davis and Dell ints; *AA*, 95, 105–6 (first q), 120 (second q); *OTC*, 81–84. On the *Loving* decision, see Peter Wallenstein, *Race, Sex, and the Freedom to Marry:* Loving v. Virginia (Lawrence: University Press of Kansas,

2014); the documentary film *The Loving Story* (HBO Documentary Films, directed by Nancy Buirski. 2011); and the acclaimed feature film *Loving* (Universal Studios, directed by Jeff Nichols, 2016).

22 *AA*, 95 (first and third qs), 106 (second and fourth qs).

23 See Wil Haygood, *In Black and White: The Life of Sammy Davis, Jr.* (New York: Alfred A. Knopf, 2003); Sammy Davis Jr., and Jane and Burt Boyar, *Yes I Can: The Story of Sammy Davis Jr.* (New York: Farrar, Straus & Giroux, 1990); Pearl Bailey, *The Raw Pearl* (New York: Harcourt, Brace & World, 1968); Pearl Bailey, *Talking to Myself* (New York: Harcourt, 1971); Roberts, *Papa Jack*; Ward, *Unforgivable Blackness*; William S. McFeely, *Frederick Douglass* (New York: W. W. Norton, 1991); Maria Diedrich, *Love Across Color Lines: Ottilie Assing and Frederick Douglass* (New York: Hill & Wang, 1999); and Jewel Parker Rhodes, *Douglass' Women: A Novel* (New York: Pocket Books, 2002).

24 *OTC*, 187–88; *PIM*, 3 (q), passim; Joseph Carroll, "Most Americans Approve of Interracial Marriages," Gallup News Service, August 16, 2007, available online.

25 *IRAA*, 93 (first q); *PIM*, vii (qs).

26 *PIM*, 1–2; *BCHT*, 389, 400; *NYT*, May 23–June 1, 1973.

27 *BCHT*, 168 (q), 169; *PIM*, 1–9; *NYT*, May 23, June 7, 1973; Dell int.

28 *NYT*, June 7, 1973; *PIM*, 1, 2 (first q), 3–4 (second q); *OTC*, 137 (third q); *IRAA*, 109.

29 *NYT*, June 20, 1973 (first q); *London Times*, June 20–23, 1973; *PIM*, 1(fifth q), 10–11 (second and third qs), 12 (fourth q); *OTC*, 139–40; *BCHT*, 168.

30 *NYT*, June 21, 1973 (q).

31 *BCHT*, 168–69; *PIM*, 5, 7–8, 14 (q), 15; London *Times*, June 17–30, 1973; *NYT*, June 21–July 3, 1973. See also the 1973 Wimbledon Scrapbook, KRWL.

32 *DG*, 66 (q); *PIM*, 48–52.

33 Ware, *Game, Set, Match*, 99–103; *BCHT*, 168, 170, 595, 744; *NYT*, May 31, June 23, July 3 (qs), 4, August 4, 5, 9, 28, September 10, 18, November 4, 11, 19, December 12, 14, 27, 1973.

34 *PIM*, 53 (first q); *DG*, 233–34, 235 (second q), 236; *OTC*, 191, 194–97; Ware, *Game, Set, Match*, 102, 202, 266; JMA and Dell ints.

35 *NYT*, July 3, 4 (first q), August 4 (second q), 5 (third q), 9, 28 1973; *BCHT*, 170. On Murphy, see Dennis Murphy and Richard Neil Graham, *Murph: The Sports Entrepreneur Man and His Leagues* (Los Angeles: Inline Hockey Central, 2013).

36 *NYT*, May 3, August 28 (first and second qs), 29–31, September 1–3, 1973; Carrington, Willis Thomas, and Wilkerson ints; *CTN*, 113–15; W, 92, 136–37; *BCHT*, 93–94, 579; *PIM*, 70–72, 73–74 (third q), 75 (fourth q).

37 Ware, *Game, Set, and Match*, 1–8, 14, 38–39, 43, 75, 118, 178, 207, 213; *PIM*, 72–73, 90; *BCHT*, 566–67, 595–96, 632; *NYT*, May 13 (first and second qs), 14 (third q), August 4, September 20, 1973.

38 *NYT*, September 21, 1973.

39 Ibid., September 22, 1973; *PIM*, 72 (first q), 86 (qs); Hall, *Arthur Ashe*, 188–92.

40 *PIM*, 90.

41 Ibid., 95, 102–4, 110 (q); *IRAA*, 41. On the rush of events during the fall of 1973, see the numerous current events articles in *Time*, September–December 1973. For an overview of the major events and trends of 1973, see Blum, *Years of Discord*, 431–60; and Peter N. Carroll, *It Seemed Like Nothing Happened: America in the 1970s* (New Brunswick: Rutgers University Press, 1990), 91–153.

42 *PIM*, 93 (q); Arthur Ashe, "Don't Tell Me What to Think," *Black Sports* (August 1975): 35–37. On James Meredith and the 1962 desegregation of the University of

Mississippi, see Charles Eagles, *The Price of Defiance: James Meredith and the Integration of Ole Miss* (Chapel Hill: University of North Carolina Press, 2009).

CHAPTER 15: SOUTH AFRICA

1   *OTC*, 146–48; *PIM*, 15–16 (q), 17, 22–24, 48; Hall, *Arthur Ashe*, 158–59; Drysdale, Dell, and Williams ints; Williams, *Ahead of the Game*, 169–72. On Suzman, see Joanna Strangwayes-Booth, *A Cricket in the Thorn Tree* (Bloomington: Indiana University Press, 1976); and Robin Renwick, *Helen Suzman: Bright Star in a Dark Chamber* (London: Biteback Publishing, 2014).

2   *PIM*, 18 (qs); Dell and Williams ints; Williams, *Ahead of the Game*, 170–71.

3   *PIM*, 22 (first and second qs), 23 (fourth q), 24, 42–43; *OTC*, 148; Young int; Hall, *Arthur Ashe*, 160–63. See the letters in folder 6, box 1, AAP, especially Barbara Jordan to Arthur Ashe, July 23, 1973 (third q); Nikki Giovanni to Arthur Ashe, July 25, 1973; and J. D. Morgan to Arthur Ashe, July 12, 1973.

4   *PIM*, 23 (first q), 42–43; Giovanni to Ashe, July 25, 1973 (second q); Morgan to Ashe, July 12, 1973 (third q).

5   *OTC*, 148; *PIM*, 107; *IRAA*, 75. On Terre'Blanche and the Afrikaner Resistance Movement, see Amos van der Merwe, *Eugene Terre'Blanche* (Capetown: Giffel Media, 2010); and obituary, *London Daily Mail*, April 4, 2010. In 2010 Terre'Blanche was "hacked to death" in his bedroom after a row with two black farmworkers. On the Vorster regime and the politics of apartheid in the early 1970s, see Herbert Adam, *Modernizing Racial Domination: The Dynamics of South African Politics* (Berkeley: University of California Press, 1971); and Nancy Clark and William Worger, *South Africa: The Rise and Fall of Apartheid* (New York: Routledge, 2013).

6   *PIM*, 97–98 (first q), 99–106 (second q); Williams, *Ahead of the Game*, 171 (third and fourth qs); Williams int; Dell and Deford ints, *SSAA*.

7   *PIM*, 107 (qs).

8   Ibid., 101 (seventh q), 107 (first q), 108 (qs), 112 (eighth q).

9   Ibid., 112, 113 (q), 114; Hall, *Arthur Ashe*, 162, 164; Deford int, *SSAA*.

10 *PIM*, 113–16 (q); Dell int.

11 *OTC*, 149; *PIM*, 116–17 (qs); Drysdale and Dell ints.

12 *PIM*, 117–18 (qs); *OTC*, 149–50; Hall, *Arthur Ashe*, 166.

13 *PIM*, 118.

14 Ibid.,119 (qs); *OTC*, 150.

15 *PIM*, 120–21 (qs).

16 Ibid., 121 (qs); *OTC*, 154–55; Williams, *Ahead of the Game*, 17. See Don Mattera's poem, "Anguished Spirit-Ashe," in folder 6, box 1, AAP. On Mattera, see Don Mattera, *Sophiatown: Coming of Age in South Africa* (Boston: Beacon, 1991); and Don Mattera, *Memory Is the Weapon* (Johannesburg: African Perspectives Publishing, 2010). On Foster and his 1973 visit to South Africa, see Eric Hall, "Foster v. Fourie: Race, Image, and Betrayal in Apartheid South Africa, 1973," paper presented at the annual meeting of the Organization of American Historians, Atlanta, Georgia, April 11, 2014; and Hall, *Arthur Ashe*, 167–69, 199–200, 204–6.

17 *PIM*, 120, 122 (q); Owen Williams int.

18 Mark Mathabene, *Kaffir Boy: The True Story of a Black Youth's Coming of Age in Apartheid South Africa* (New York: Free Press, 1986), 3–5, 208, 210 (first q), 230–31 (second q), 338–50.

19   Ibid., 215–32, 233–34 (qs); *PIM*, 122–23.

20   *PIM*, 123; Owen Williams int.

21   *PIM*, 123–24 (qs).

22   Ibid., 124–25 (q); *OTC*, 154.

23   *PIM*, 126–28 (qs); *OTC*, 155 (qs); Hall, *Arthur Ashe*, 170–72.

24   *PIM*, 129 (first q), 130 (second q), 131 (third q); *OTC*, 151; Hall, *Arthur Ashe*, 172; *BCHT*, 588–89.

25   *PIM*, 131 (first q), 132 (third q); *OTC*, 151 (second q); Hall, *Arthur Ashe*, 173; Arthur Ashe, "South Africa: Why I Felt That I Had to Go," London *Sunday Times*, November 18, 1973, copy in folder 7, box 1, AAP.

26   *PIM*, 132 (qs)–34. Alan Paton's novel *Cry, the Beloved Country* (New York: Charles Scribner's Sons, 1948) is widely regarded as a classic of African literature. On Paton (1903–88), see Peter F. Alexander, *Alan Paton: A Biography* (New York: Oxford University Press, 1994).

27   Drysdale int; *PIM*, 133.

28   *PIM*, 134, 137; Connors, *The Outsider*, 103, 107–8. For an excellent introduction to Connors's personal style and outlier image, see Bodo, *Ashe vs Connors*, 28–55.

29   *OTC*, 151 (first q); Connors, *The Outsider*, 107 (second q). In his memoir, Connors incorrectly identifies the year as 1974.

30   *OTC*, 151–52 (qs); *PIM*, 134; Williams, *Ahead of the Game*, 171; Williams int.

31   Mathabene, *Kaffir Boy*, 238–39 (first q); *PIM*, 135, 136 (third q); *OTC*, 155 (second q).

32   Ibid., 136 (qs); Owen Williams int, *SSAA*; "Soweto Elite Gives Ashe Big Welcome," unidentified clipping, November 1973; "Ashe Neither Shocked, Surprised at Conditions in South Africa," unidentified clipping, November 1973; "Weather Upsets Ashe's Schedule," *Cape Argus*, November 28, 1973, all in folder 7, box 1, AAP. Hall, *Arthur Ashe*, 175, identifies the hosts as "Dr. and Mrs. Methlane."

33   *PIM*, 137–38 (qs); *OTC*, 151; Connors, *The Outsider*, 107–8.

34   *PIM*, 139 (qs); "Weather Upsets Ashe's Schedule." On Buthelezi, see Ben Temkin, *Buthelezi: A Biography* (London: Routledge, 2002). Born in 1928, Buthelezi became South Africa's premier Zulu leader during the late twentieth century. In January 1974, he was instrumental in the formulation of the Mahlabatini Declaration of Faith, a five-point plan for racial peace. In 1975 he founded the Inkata Freedom Party, which refused to sanction the ANC's policy of "armed struggle." From 1994 to 2004, he served as South Africa's minister of home affairs.

35   *PIM*, 139–41 (qs); *OTC*, 152 (second q); Hall, *Arthur Ashe*, 177–78; *Cape Argus*, November 28, 1973, Arthur Ashe, "Parting Gifts Epitomised the Two Faces of SA," *Cape Argus*, December 3, 1973, clippings in folder 7, box 1, AAP.

36   *PIM*, 142 (qs); *Cape Times*, November 29, 1973, *Cape Argus*, December 3, 1973, clippings in folder 7, box I, AAP. On Barnard (1922–2001), see Christiaan Barnard, *Christiaan Barnard: One Life* (New York: Macmillan, 1970); and Chris Logan, *Christiaan Barnard, A Life* (Cape Town: Jonathan Ball, 2003).

37   *PIM*, 142–43; Hall, *Arthur Ashe*, 181–82; *Sunday Express*, December 2, 1973 (qs), and *Cape Argus*, November 29, 1973, clippings in folder 7, box 1, AAP.

38   *PIM*, 142–43; *OTC*, 158–59 (q); *DG*, 106 (q); Morgan, "Black and White at Center Court," 837; Mattera, "Anguished Spirit—Ashe"; "Knock-out for Prejudice," *Cape Town Argus*, December 3, 1973, clipping in folder 7, box 1, AAP.

39   *PIM*, 143–45 (qs); Williams int; Hall, *Arthur Ashe*, 203, 206. The foundation, known officially as the Black Tennis Foundation (BTF), became a reality in 1974, and during

the following decade it oversaw the construction of four hundred tennis courts in predominantly black or Coloured communities. The BTF ceased operation in 1991. Williams, *Ahead of the Game*, 174–75.

40   *OTC*, 159.

41   *PIM*, 147; *Cape Times*, November 29, 1973, clipping in folder 7, box 1, AAP; Dell and Collins ints; Dell int, *SSAA*.

42   *PIM*, 147; *NYT*, December 1, 1973; Stan Smith and Dell ints; Dan White, "Margie Gengler," *Princeton Alumni Weekly* 73 (June 20, 1973). Gengler and Smith had known each other since she was fifteen, and in 1973 and 1974 they teamed up to play mixed doubles at the U.S. Open. They married in November 1974. Iver Petersen, "As Princeton Changes, a Black Community Fears for Future," *NYT*, September 3, 2001; Jean Stratton, "Former Township Mayor Jim Floyd Is Committed to Change," *Princeton Town Topics*, May 19, 2004; Deborah Yaffe, "Across Nassau Street," *Princeton Alumni Weekly* 117 (April 26, 2017): 24–29; Floyd int.

43   *PIM*, 148–50 (qs), 151.

44   Ibid., 152 (q), 153.

45   Ibid., 153–54 (q).

46   Ibid., 155 (q)–57; *BATN*, 70–71.

47   *Cape Argus*, November 29, 1973, clipping in folder 7, box 1, AAP.

CHAPTER 16: PROS AND CONS

1   *BCHT*, 172–75; Connors, *The Outsider*, 106–34; Hall, *Arthur Ashe*, 193; *OTC*, 131–32, 173.

2   Connors, *The Outsider*, 113–14; *BCHT*, 339–40, 554–55, 600–601; *NYT*, January 18–20, 25, 27, February 15, 1974; Bodo, *Courts of Babylon, 132*.

3   *NYT*, February 15, 16 (q), 1974. On Chatrier, see *BCHT*, 558.

4   *BCHT*, 172–73, 389, 400, 702; *PIM*, 65, 248–52 (qs); *NYT*, May 31, June 13, 1974; Connors, *The Outsider*, 114–15.

5   *PIM*, 250–51; *BCHT*, 173, 175.

6   *PIM*, 52–54, 61, 77–79, 248–49.

7   Ibid., 78, 251 (q); Tanner int. On Tanner, see *BCHT*, 710; and Roscoe Tanner, with Mike Yorkey, *Double Fault: My Rise and Fall, and My Road Back* (Chicago: Triumph Books, 2005).

8   *PIM*, 252–53 (qs).

9   Ibid., 253–54 (qs). Hesse (1877–1962) was a German novelist, poet, and painter who won the Nobel Prize in Literature in 1946. During the 1960s and 1970s, his best-known novels, *Steppenwolf* and *Siddhartha*, became extremely popular among readers attracted to Eastern mysticism and the counterculture. See Joseph Mileck, *Hermann Hesse: Life and Art* (Berkeley: University of California Press, 1981).

10   *OTC*, 86 (qs). On Diana Ross, see Diana Ross, *Secrets of a Sparrow* (New York: Villard, 1993); and J. Randy Taraborelli, *Diana Ross: A Biography* (New York: Citadel, 2007). On Motown, see Nelson George, *Where Did Our Love Go? The Rise and Fall of the Motown Sound* (Urbana: University of Illinois Press, 2007).

11   *NYT*, June 21–July 2, 1974; *PIM*, 255–70; Tanner int.

12   *NYT*, July 2, 1974; *PIM*, 256–57, 268.

13   *PIM*, 256 (q); Connors, *The Outsider*, 115–17.

14   *PIM*, 257 (qs); Connors, *The Outsider*, 117.

15   *PIM*, 270 (qs); *NYT*, July 2–4, 1974; Tanner int.

16   *OTC*, 176–77; *PIM*, 272 (qs); Tanner int.

17   *PIM*, 27 (first q), viii (second q); Schragis int.

18   *IRAA*, 60, 166–67 (first q); *DG*, 176 (second q), 180–81; *PIM*, 27.

19   *NYT*, July 10–September 10, 1974; Connors, *The Outsider*, 117–18, 129, 131–34; *BCHT*, 172–73. For examples of the British press's fixation on the Connors-Evert relationship, see the 1974 Wimbledon Scrapbook, KRWL. On Evert, see Bodo, *Courts of Babylon*, 198–221.

20   Connors, *The Outsider*, 114–16,129; *DG*, 235; *BCHT*, 174; Dell int; *IRAA*, 75; Bodo, *Courts of Babylon*, 378–94.

21   *NYT*, October 5, 10, 20, 25, November 2, 8, 1974; *BCHT*, 174; Morgan, "Black and White at Center Court," 833–34; Hall, *Arthur Ashe*, 197–98. On Gandhi's career (1893–1914) in South Africa, see Paul F. Powell, "Gandhi in South Africa," *Journal of Modern African History* 7 (1969): 441–55; and Ashwin Desai and Goolem Vahed, *The South African Gandhi: Stretcher-Bearer of Empire* (Palo Alto: Stanford University Press. 2015).

22   *NYT*, October 5 (qs), 10, 20, November 2, 8, December 17, 1974; *CD*, December 17, 1974; *BAA*, December 28, 1974; *BCHT*, 174–75; Hall, *Arthur Ashe*, 198.

23   *NYT*, October 25, 1974; *BCHT*, 178.

24   *NYT*, October 17, 25 (q), 1974; Owen Williams int. On Ralston's tenure as U.S. Davis Cup Captain, see Janoff, *Game! Set! Match!*, 58, 70–83.

25   *NYT*, November 2, 10–11, 13, 1974.

26   *Rand Daily Mail*, November 18, 1974, clipping in scrapbook 1, box 39, AAP; "Sports Policy Is a Lesson," *Rand Daily Mail*, October 26, 1974, "Ashe: Why I'm Coming," *Rand Daily Mail*, c. October 1974 (second q), clippings in folder 7, box 1, AAP; *NYT*, October 25, 27 (first q), 1974.

27   Owen Williams int; "Ashe: Why I'm Coming" (first, third, and fourth qs); Sy Lerman, "Ashe's Plan to Help," *Rand Daily Mail*, c. October 1974 (second q), clipping in folder 7, box 1, AAP.

28   *OTC*, 159–61 (first q), 162 (second and third qs); Young int; Donald Dell int, *SSAA*; Hall, *Arthur Ashe*, 199–201. On Green, see Nat Serache, "Pledge of US Study Help," *The World*, November 27, 1974, clipping in scrapbook 2, box 39, AAP. See also Eric Mani, "Don't Lose Hope—Message from Black Americans," *The World*, c. November 27, 1974, and "Why Ashe Came to South Africa," *Durban Post*, December 1, 1974, clippings in scrapbook 2, box 39, AAP.

29   *OTC*, 154.

30   Ibid., 159–60 (qs); Patrick Laurence, "Sobukwe a True Leader, say Black Americans," *Rand Daily Mail*, November 30, 1974, clipping in scrapbook 2, box 39, AAP; Young int. On Sobukwe (1924–78), see Benjamin Pogrund, *Sobukwe and Apartheid* (New Brunswick, NJ: Rutgers University Press, 1991); and Benjamin Pogrund, *Robert Sobukwe: How Can Man Die Better* (Johannesburg: Jonathan Ball, 2012).

31   See clippings in scrapbooks 1 and 2, box 39, AAP; Owen Williams and Young ints.

32   "Ashe Beaten by Connors in SA Open," "King Connors," "Grudge Final," *Rand Daily Mail*, November 25, 1974, "Ashe on the Run," *Rand Daily Mail*, November 26, 1974 (first q), clippings in scrapbook 1, box 39, AAP; Sam Mirwis, "Connors and Ashe Feud Comes to Boil," *Sunday Express*, December 1, 1974 (second and third qs), clipping in scrapbook 2, box 39, AAP; *NYT*, November 26, 1974.

33   "Grudge final"; "Arthur Ashe Comes Under Fire," *Post*, December 1, 1974 (q), clipping in folder 7, box 1, AAP; "Visit Soweto: Our Tennis Players Need 10 Years: Ashe," *Rand Daily Mail*, November 27, 1974, clipping in scrapbook 1, box 39, AAP.

34   *NYT*, November 20, 1974; OwenWilliams int; "Ashe nets R10645," *The World*, December 1, 1974, clipping in scrapbook 2, box 39, AAP.

35   Laurence, "Sobukwe a True Leader, Say Black Americans," (qs); Young and Owen Williams ints.

36   *NYT*, December 17, 1974 (qs).

37   Ibid., December 24, 1974; *OTC*, 222; *PIM*, viii; Hall, *Arthur Ashe*, 193; Following Ashe's death, Seth Abraham, his close friend and former employer at HBO, remarked: "I think he lived every day as though it could be his last." *IRAA*, 111.

38   *OTC*, 168 (q); Norman Vincent Peale, *The Power of Positive Thinking* (New York: Ballantine, 1996).

39   *OTC*, 168 (q).

40   See John Hoberman, *Darwin's Athletes: How Sport Has Damaged Black America and Preserved the Myth of Race* (New York: Mariner Books, 1997); William C. Rhoden, *Forty Million Dollar Slaves: The Rise, Fall, and Redemption of the Black Athlete* (New York: Broadway, 2007); Shaun Powell, *Souled Out? How Blacks Are Winning and Losing in Sports* (Champaign, IL: Human Kinetics, 2007); Patrick Cooper, *Black Superman: A Cultural and Biological History of the People That Became the World's Greatest Athletes* (Austin: First Sahara, 2001); and Jon Entine, *Taboo: Why Black Athletes Dominate Sports and Why We Are Afraid to Talk About It* (New York: PublicAffairs, 2003). On Russell's coaching stint with the Boston Celtics, see Goudsouzian, *King of the Court*, 189–239. On Robinson's managerial debut, see Frank Robinson and Dave Anderson, *Frank: The First Year* (New York: Holt, Rinehart & Winston, 1976).

41   "He Teaches the Pros," *Ebony* (October 1977): 134–35 (second q), 136, 138; Bob Ruf, "Pro Track Star Has a New Teaching Approach," *Sarasota Herald-Tribune*, September 9, 1975 (first q); Henry Hines, *Quick Tennis* (New York: NAL/Dutton, 1977); *OTC*, 168–69; Pasarell int; *NYT*, January 14–19, 1975.

42   *NYT*, January 24–25, 29–31, February 2–3, 1975.

43   *BCHT*, 176 (first q); *OTC*, 221–22; *NYT*, March 3, 5, 8–10 (second and third qs), 15–18, 26, April 28, 1975.

44   *BCHT*, 176 (q); *OTC*, 169; *NYT*, April 3, 1975.

45   *NYT*, April 16, 1975 (qs). A college tennis star at Yale, Scott (1937–2006) founded *Tennis Week* magazine in 1974. *BCHT*, 641–42. See also Scott, *Tennis: Game of Motion*.

46   *NYT*, April 16, 1975 (qs); *OTC*, 156–57; Williams int.

47   *OTC*, 152; *NYT*, April 30 (qs), May 2, 5, 1975; *BCHT*, 588–89, 612.

48   *NYT*, April 30, May 5, 6, 8, 1975; Hall, *Arthur Ashe*, 209.

49   *NYT*, May 2, 4, 9–10, 12, 1975; Bud Collins, "Tennis Star of Many Faces: Arthur Ashe: Portrait in Motion," *NYT*, May 25, 1975 (q); Collins int.

50   *BCHT*, 176; *NYT*, May 8–12 (qs), 1975.

51   *NYT*, May 12, 1975 (first q); *OTC*, 169 (second and third qs); Bodo, *Courts of Babylon*, 225–46.

CHAPTER 17: WIMBLEDON 1975

1   *OTC*, 133.

2   *NYT*, June 10–15, 1975.

3   Ibid., June 17–20 (q), 21–22, 1975; *OTC*, 133.

4   *OTC*, 136–38; Marty Bell, "Arthur Ashe vs. Jimmy Connors Is No Love Match," *Sport* (September 1975): 34–38; Connors, *The Outsider*, 113, 155–56, 174–76.

5   *NYT*, June 22, 1975 (q); Bell, "Arthur Ashe vs. Jimmy Connors Is No Love Match," 35 (q); Curry Kirkpatrick, "By Hook or by Crook," *SI* 43 (August 25, 1975): 52; Joe Jares, "A Centre Court Case," *SI* 43 (July 14, 1975), 12; Evans, *Open Tennis*, 130; Bodo, *Ashe vs Connors*, 193, 199. Connors, *The Outsider*, 155, claims he knew nothing of the suit against Ashe prior to reading about it in the newspapers on June 22.

6   Bell, "Arthur Ashe vs. Jimmy Connors Is No Love Match," 38; *NYT*, June 22, 1975 (q); Evans, *Open Tennis*, 130–31.

7   *NYT*, June 19–20, 1975; Jares, "Centre Court Case," 13.

8   *OTC*, 133–34; Jares, "Centre Court Case," 14; *NYT*, June 24–29, 1975; Bodo, *Ashe vs Connors*, 206–7.

9   *NYT*, June 30, 1975; *OTC*, 134.

10   Jares, "Centre Court Case," 13 (q); Bell, "Arthur Ashe vs. Jimmy Connors Is No Love Match," 38; London *Times*, June 27–30, 1975; Connors, *The Outsider*, 159–61.

11   Jares, "Centre Court Case," 13–14; Bell, "Arthur Ashe vs. Jimmy Connors Is No Love Match," 35; *NYT*, July 2, 1975; Evans, *Open Tennis*, 150–51; Connors, *The Outsider*, 156, claims the injury suffered during the Lloyd match was much more serious than he revealed at the time: "Chasing a drop shot early in my first-round match on the damp grass of Centre Court, I slipped and hyperextended my knee. I didn't think much about it at the time. . . . But once the adrenaline rush of my first Wimbledon title defense was over, all that changed. I felt a degree of pain that I had never experienced before. I thought I would be OK after some rest, but when I woke up the next morning, the pain had intensified; my knee was completely swollen and unable to support my weight. . . . After they examined me, it turned out I had a couple of hairline fractures in my shin—painful but treatable. . . . The physiotherapist's advice was simple: rest. The timing could not have been worse. . . . The physiotherapist wrapped up my leg and off I went to practice. I knew that once I was on the court, I would forget about the medical warnings. After every match I won in those two weeks, I would immediately go for an intensive treatment of ultrasound, ice, and massage—and I wasn't above taking a fistful of painkillers, either. I kept the injury as secret as I could, refusing to wear even an Ace bandage; I wasn't going to give anyone an edge."

12   *NYT*, July 2, 1975; Evans, *Open Tennis*, 130–31; Bodo, *Ashe vs Connors*, 210–11. Borg would not lose another match at Wimbledon until 1981, when he finished second to John McEnroe after winning five consecutive Wimbledon singles titles. *BCHT*, 204, 422.

13   Jares, "Centre Court Case," 14 (q); *NYT*, July 2, 1975; *OTC*, 171.

14   *NYT*, July 2, 1975; *OTC*, 171; Evans, *Open Tennis*, 131. On Roche, see *BCHT*, 632–33.

15   *NYT*, July 4, 1975; London *Times*, July 4, 1975.

16   *NYT*, July 4, 1975; Jares, "Centre Court Case," 14; Bell, "Arthur Ashe vs. Jimmy Connors Is No Love Match," 34–38.

17   *NYT*, July 4, 1975 (first and second qs); London *Times*, July 4, 1975; Jares, "A Centre Court Case," 13; Evans, *Open Tennis*, 131 (third q); Bodo, *Ashe vs Connors*, 212–13; Tanner int. At the 1976 Wimbledon tournament, Connors lost to Tanner in the quarterfinals. Connors, *The Outsider*, 176.

18   Evans, *Open Tennis*, 131–32 (q); *OTC*, 171–72; Bell, "Arthur Ashe vs. Jimmy Connors Is No Love Match," 36; Bodo, *Ashe vs Connors*, 214–17; Dell, Riessen, and Ralston ints.

19   *OTC*, 171–72 (qs); Dell, Pasarell, Riessen, and Ralston ints.

20   *OTC*, 172 (q).

21   Ibid., 172–73 (qs); Dell int; Evans, *Open Tennis*, 132.

22   Jares, "A Centre Court Case," 14.

23   Steve Flink, "Wimbledon '75: The Art of Ashe," *WT* (July 1985):16 (q).

24   Ibid.; *NYT*, July 6, 1975; Connors, *The Outsider*, 158–59; Bodo, *Ashe vs Connors*, vii–xi.

25   Bell, "Arthur Ashe vs. Jimmy Connors Is No Love Match," 36; Jares, "A Centre Court Case," 13, 15; Flink, "Wimbledon '75: The Art of Ashe," 16; *NYT*, July 6, 1975; Connors, *The Outsider*, 159–61, 169–70.

26   *Wimbledon the Classic Match: Men's Final 1975, Connors v. Ashe* (DVD, All England Lawn Tennis, 2007) (first q); *BCHT*, 484–85; *NYT*, July 6, 1975 (second q); Connors, *The Outsider*, 157.

27   *NYT*, July 6, 1975 (q); Bodo, *Ashe vs Connors*, 224–35.

28   *Wimbledon the Classic Match: Men's Final 1975, Connors v. Ashe* (q); Evans, *Open Tennis*, 133–34; Bodo, *Ashe vs Connors*, 235–39.

29   Evans, *Open Tennis*, 134 (first q); Bodo, *Ashe vs Connors*, 240–44; *Wimbledon the Classic Match: Men's Final: 1975, Connors v. Ashe* (second and third qs); *BCHT*, 202; Dell int.

30   *Wimbledon the Classic Match: Men's Final 1975, Connors v. Ashe* (q).

31   *OTC*, 175 (first and second qs); *WP*, July 6, 1975 (third q); *NYT*, July 6, 1975; Connors, *The Outsider*, 157; Bodo, *Ashe vs Connors*, 244–45.

32   *BATN*, 49 (first q); *CTN*, 92 (second q); W, 166; Flink, "Wimbledon '75: The Art of Ashe," 17–18; Hall, *Arthur Ashe*, 214–15.

33   *Wimbledon the Classic Match: Men's Final 1975, Connors v. Ashe*; *WP*, July 6, 1975; *NYT*, July 6, 1975 (qs).

34   Evans, *Open Tennis*, 134 (first q); *NYT*, July 6, 1975 (second and third qs).

35   *NYT*, July 6, 1975 (q); Connors, *The Outsider*, 157–58, 161.

36   Barbara Jordan to Arthur Ashe, July 7, 1975, in folder 2, box 2, AAP (first q); *NYT*, July 8, 1975 (qs); Connors, *The Outsider*, 155, 158, 165.

37   *NYT*, July 8 (q), 16, 1975. Riordan predicted Connors would be sidelined for six to eight weeks. Nine days after his loss at Wimbledon, Connors appeared in Los Angeles with a cast on his right leg.

38   Connors, *The Outsider*, 165, 169; Evans, *Open Tennis*, 130, 137.

39   *NYT*, July 30, 31 (q), September 6, 7, 1975; Connors, *The Outsider*, 166; Ralston, Trabert, and Dell ints; *BCHT*, 178, 652–53.

40   Dave Anderson, "The Davis Cup Détente," *NYT*, September 7, 1975 (qs).

41   Ibid., (q); *NYT*, August 23, 1975; Evans, *Open Tennis*," 137. According to Evans: "Predictably enough, the Riordan lawsuit was settled out of court, but only after Kramer had counter-sued Riordan and Connors for three million dollars."

CHAPTER 18: KING ARTHUR

1   Connors, *The Outsider*, 161–241; *BCHT*, 178–179, 186–205, 608–10.

2   *BCHT*, 177, 180; *NYT*, August 28, September 2 (qs), 1975; Bell, "Arthur Ashe vs. Jimmy Connors Is No Love Match," 38. See also Dave Anderson, "The Grass Is Always Greener," *NYT*, September 4, 1975; Connors, *The Outsider*, 162–63; and Bodo, *Courts of Babylon*, 15.

3   *NYT*, September 2, 4, 8 (second and third qs), 1975; Connors, *The Outsider*, 163–64 (first q).

4   *OTC*, 175 (q); Flink, "Wimbledon '75: The Art of Ashe," 17.

5   Evans, *Open Tennis*, 134 (first q); Flink, "Wimbledon '75: The Art of Ashe," 16 (second q), 18 (third q).

6   *OTC*, 179 (first q); *St. Petersburg Times*, July 10, 1975 (second q).

7   *OTC*, 180 (q); Doug Smith, "Arthur Ashe: Businessman," *Black Enterprise* 6 (April 1976): 43.

8   Ibid., 179; Bell, "Arthur Ashe vs. Jimmy Connors Is No Love Match," 36.

9   *BCHT*, 177–78; *NYT*, September 11, 19, 21, 26, 30

10   *NYT*, October 28–29, 31, November 1–3, 6–8, 10–12, 14, 16, 18, 20–22, 24–26, 30, December 1–5, 7, 1975.

11   Ibid., October 29, 31, November 1–2 (q), 3, 1975.

12   Ibid., November 8, 11 (first q), 12 (second q), 1975; *BCHT*, 146.

13   *NYT*, November 19–22, 24–26, 1975; Gottfried int.

14   *NYT*, November 30, 1975 (qs). Ashe also told the reporters in Stockholm that he generally liked the life of nearly constant travel that the tennis tour required. The tour, in his words, was "the endless trip. You never play at home, you always play away. . . . I like constant travel. I haven't been three weeks at a time in one place for the last six years."

15   Evans, *Nasty*, 121 (qs); *IRAA*, 152, 168–69.

16   Ibid., 121 (first q), 122 (fourth, fifth, and sixth qs), 123–25; *NYT*, December 1, 1975 (second and third qs).

17   *NYT*, December 1 (first and third qs), 2 (second, fourth, and fifth qs), 1975; Evans, *Nasty*, 124–26.

18   *NYT*, December 5–6, 7 (qs), 1975; Evans, *Nasty*, 125–26.

19   Evans, *Nasty*, 117–19, 126–27, 202; *NYT*, December 9, 1975 (qs); *BCHT*, 183.

20   Ed Meyer, "A Mixed-Up Tennis World Needs a Czar," *NYT*, December 7, 1975 (second and third qs); *NYT*, December 9, 1975 (first q). See also Rich Coster, *The Tennis Bubble: Big Money Tennis—How It Grew and Where It's Going* (New York: Quadrangle, 1976).

21   *NYT*, December 10 (q), 18, 24, 1975, January 7, 15, 1976.

22   *BCHT*, 149–52, 182, 600–601, 634–35; *OTC*, 179–80.

23   Public references to Ashe as "King Arthur" began as early as 1965. See Joe Jares, "Arthur Was King for a Day," *SI* 21 (September 20, 1965), 36–37; Louie Robinson Jr., "A Crown for King Arthur," *Ebony* 24 (November 1968): 64–66; Norman Darden, "Arthur, the New King of the Courts," *Life* 65 (September 20, 1968), 30–35; Norman Darden, "Arthur Ashe: The New King of the Courts," *Encore* (September 8, 1975): 36; and *BCHT*, 176.

24   See Christopher Lasch, *The Culture of Narcissism: American Life in an Age of Diminishing Expectations* (New York: W. W. Norton, 1978); and Neil Postman, *Amusing Ourselves to Death: Public Discourse in the Age of Show Business* (20th anniversary edition) (New York: Penguin, 2004).

25   The term "superstar" was used as early as the 1920s by Canadian sportswriters describing contemporary hockey stars, and the artist Andy Warhol used the term in the 1960s. But it did not gain widespread currency until the release of the musical *Jesus Christ Superstar* in 1970. Televised "superstar" competitions—an idea first advanced by former Olympic ice skating champion Dick Button—were first shown on the BBC and ABC television networks in 1973. The popular television show *ABC Superstars* was on the air from 1973 to 1984 and again from 1991 to 1994. NBC ran a similar show from 1985 to 1990.

26   *BCHT*, 144–203; Evans, *Open Tennis*, 3–203; Judson Gooding, "The Tennis Industry," *Fortune* (June 1973): 124–33; Scott, *Tennis: Game of Motion*, 9–27; Coster, *The*

Tennis Bubble; Collins, *My Life with the Pros*, 227–358; Williams, *Ahead of the Game*, 191–242; Connors, *The Outsider*, 77–229; Renée Richards, *Second Serve* (New York: Stein & Day, 1992); Bodo, *Courts of Babylon*, 17–18.

27   See Judy Kutulas, *After Aquarius Dawned: How the Revolutions of the Sixties Became the Popular Culture of the Seventies* (Chapel Hill: University of North Carolina Press, 2017); and Sherrie A. Innes, ed., *Disco Divas: Women and Popular Culture in the 1970s* (Philadelphia: University of Pennsylvania Press, 2003).

28   *OTC*, 86 (first q), 87; Beverly Johnson, with Allison Samuels, *The Face That Changed It All, A Memoir* (New York: Atria, 2015), 109 (second and third qs), 110–11 (fourth through sixth qs), 112–19, 124.

29   See *HRTG*, vol. 3, 14–39; *NYT*, September–October 1975; Anthony Pascal and Leonard Rapping, *Racial Discrimination in Organized Baseball* (Santa Monica: RAND Corporation, 1976); Robinson and Anderson, *Frank: The First Year*; Schneider, *Frank Robinson*; George Plimpton, *One for the Record: The Inside Story of Hank Aaron's Chase for the Home Run Record* (Boston: Little, Brown, 2016); Bryant, *The Last Hero*, 321–401; Tom Stanton, *Hank Aaron and the Home Run That Changed America* (New York: William Morrow, 2004); Rod Carew and Ira Berkow, *Carew* (Minneapolis: University of Minnesota Press, 2010); and Joe Morgan and David Falkner, *Joe Morgan: A Life in Baseball* (New York: W. W. Norton, 1993).

30   *NYT*, June 1975; *CD*, June 1975; *HRTG*, vol. 3, 40–70; Leonard Koppett and Ken Shouler, *Total Basketball: The Ultimate Basketball Encyclopedia* (Wilmington: Sport Media, 2003); George, *Elevating the Game*; Kareem Abdul-Jabbar and Mignon McCarthy, *Kareem* (New York: Random House, 1990); Kareem Abdul-Jabbar and Peter Knobler, *Giant Steps: The Autobiography of Kareem Abdul-Jabbar* (New York: Bantam, 1983); S. H. Burchard, *Walt Frazier* (New York: Harcourt Brace Jovanovich, 1975).

31   *HRTG*, vol. 3, 119–30; *Official Encyclopedia of Professional Football* (New York: New American Library, 1977); J. Devaney, *O. J. Simpson: Football's Greatest Runner* (New York: Warner, 1976); Gary M. Pomerantz, *Their Life's Work: The Brotherhood of the 1970s Pittsburgh Steelers, Then and Now* (New York: Simon & Schuster, 2013); Chad Millman and Shawn Coyne, *The Ones Who Hit the Hardest: The Steelers, the Cowboys, the '70s, and the Fight for America's Soul* (New York: Gotham, 2011).

32   *HRTG*, vol. 3, 82–94; Ali, *The Greatest*; *When We Were Kings* (DVD, Universal Studios Home Entertainment, directed by Leon Gast, 2002).

33   Reid, Desdunes, and Ryland ints.

34   *NYT*, January 7, 15, 18, 30, February 15, March 8, 1976; *OTC*, 222.

35   *NYT*, January 8, 12, 16, 20, 23, 26, 28, 30, February 5–9, 1976; *BCHT*, 182; Gottfried int.

36   *NYT*, February 13, 16–23, 25 (q), 1976; *OTC*, 210 (qs)–211. In early April, Ashe and Dick Stockton played the final match of the Lagos tournament, with Stockton winning 6–3, 6–2. The match was played in Caracas, Venezuela. Stockton int; *NYT*, April 2, 1976.

37   *NYT*, February 26–29, March 1, 3–8 (qs), 1976; Newcombe int.

38   *BCHT*, 172–73; Connors, *The Outsider*, 272–82; *NYT*, February 26–29, 1976. See also Tony Kornheiser, "Single World Circuit Shapes Up in Tennis," *NYT*, May 12, 1976.

39   *NYT*, January 21, February 25, March 22, May 21–24, 1976; *BCHT*, 176–77, 183; Bodo, *Courts of Babylon*, 251.

40   Bill Riordan, "The Hows and Whys of Connors-Orantes," *NYT*, February 29, 1976.

41   Arthur Ashe, "A Professional Guide to Watching Tennis," *NYT*, February 22, 1976 (q).

42   Riordan, "The Hows and Whys of Connors-Orantes" (qs).

43   *NYT*, May 4–5, 7–15, 1976; Dell and Savage ints. On Ashe's earnings from his Head endorsement contract, see folder 2, box 31, AAP, especially "Ashe—Head Royalties, 1974–1980."

44   *NYT*, May 17, 21, 23, 1976; Evans, *Nasty*, 58–60.

45   Evans, *Nasty*, 128; Collins int; *NYT*, May 24, 1976 (qs). See also Robin Herman, "Are Tennis Rules Strong Enough to Stop Misconduct on Court?," *NYT*, August 3, 1976; and Bodo, *Courts of Babylon*, 22–23. Ashe favored the new Code of Conduct but did not want it to dampen the excitement of the game. As he told Herman, "We don't want robots on the court. I think Nastase's histrionics are great for the game. You have to allow some outlet for release of frustration and anger. But you can't have it open-ended."

46   *NYT*, June 2, 4–9, 11, 15, 20, 22–23, 25, 27 (first q), 28, 30, July 4, 1976; *BCHT*, 155, 182–85, 389, 422. "King Arthur Arrives at Court with His Beauty Queen," *Evening Standard*, June 22, 1976 (second and third qs); "Ashe Is So Right About the Girls," *Daily Express*, June 24, 1976; Laurie Pignon, "Threats Are Not the Right Way to Do It," *Daily Mail*, June 28, 1976 (fourth q); Peter Wilson, "Equal Pay? It's a Load of Rubbish," *Daily Mirror*, July 1, 1976, all in 1976 Wimbledon scapbook, KRWL.

47   *NYT*, July 10, 15, 17–18, August 3–5, 7, 8 (q), 1976; Dittmann int. Connors's 1976 pairing with Ashe was only his first adventure in North Conway. In July 1978, Connors's pregnant wife, Patti, went into labor during the Volvo tournament, just before her husband was scheduled to take the court against Eliot Teltscher. Two hours later, after defeating Teltscher in short order, Connors rented a Learjet at a small airfield nearby and flew to Los Angeles to be present at the birth of his first child. Connors, *The Outsider*, 223–25.

48   *NYT*, August 29, September 2, 4 (qs), 1976.

49   *OTC*, 222; *NYT*, September 25, 27, 29, October 3, 9, 14, 16, 27, 29, November 5, December 2, 9, 15–20, 1976, April 29–May 2, 1977.

50   *NYT*, September 14, 1976 (q); *DG*, 231–37; JMA and Allen ints. *BCHT*, 175; Ware, *Game, Set, Match*, 38, 209; Bodo, *Courts of Babylon*, 281; *IRAA*, 133. Wimbledon did not begin equalization of prize money until 2007, when Venus Williams became the first women's singles champion to receive the same prize money as the men's champion.

51   Young, Dell, and JMA ints; Sargent Shriver to Arthur Ashe, March 22, 1976, in folder 2, box 2, AAP; Andrew Young, "Why I Support Jimmy Carter," *Nation* (April 3, 1976): 397–98; Joseph Lelyveld, "Children of African Dissident Live with Rep. Young Family," *NYT*, December 18, 1976; Howard Zinn, *The Twentieth Century: A People's History* (New York: HarperCollins, 1998), 322–38; Carroll, *It Seemed Like Nothing Happened*, 161–206. On the 1976 presidential election and the Carter campaign, see Jules Witcover, *Marathon: The Pursuit of the Presidency, 1972–1976* (New York: Viking, 1977); and Patrick Anderson, *Electing Jimmy Carter: The Election of 1976* (Baton Rouge: Louisiana State University Press, 1994).

52   *OTC*, 156–57 (qs); Hall, *Arthur Ashe*, 208, 224–27; *DG*, 104. On the 1976 Soweto uprising, see Mosegomi Mosala, *Soweto Explodes: The Beginning of the End of Apartheid* (Dubuque: Kendall Hunt, 2007); Elsabe Brink et al., *Soweto 16 June 1976: Personal Accounts of the Uprising* (Cape Town: Kwela Books, 2006); and Robert Price, *The Apartheid State in Crisis: Political Transformation in South Africa, 1975–1990* (New York: Oxford University Press, 1991), 46–68.

CHAPTER 19: AFFAIRS OF THE HEART

1   *OTC*, 168, 198–99; *AA*, 23–64; Dell and Pasarell ints.

2   *OTC*, 81–87, 182–83 (q); Hall, *Arthur Ashe*, 220; Johnson, *The Face That Changed It All*, 110–17; Rampersad int.

3   *OTC*, 183–84 (qs), 188.

4   Ibid., 181–82 (qs); *DG*, 51; Kalia Brooks, "Jeanne Moutoussamy-Ashe," BOMBS Oral History Project, available online at http://bombmagazine.org/article/1000255/jeanne -moutoussamy-ashe; *NYT*, October 10, 15, 1976. The actor Cleavon Little and the comedian Bill Cosby served as co-chairmen of the event, which featured an exhibition doubles match in which Ashe was paired with Althea Gibson.

5   *OTC*, 182 (qs), 192; JMA int; Brooks, "Jeanne Moutoussamy-Ashe"; Johnson, *The Face That Changed It All*, 108–15 (last q), 116–19, 124.

6   *DG*, 295–96; *OTC*, 189, 196–197; Laura B. Randolph, "Jeanne Moutoussamy-Ashe: On Love, Loss and Life After Arthur," *Ebony* (October 1993): 27–34; Hall, *Arthur Ashe*, 220–21; *NYT*, September 3, 1977; JMA int (q).

7   Randolph, "On Love, Loss and Life After Arthur," 32(q); Hall, *Arthur Ashe*, 221; *OTC*, 183; JMA int; Brooks, "Jeanne Moutoussamy-Ashe."

8   *NYT*, October 27, 29, November 5, 1976; *OTC*, 183 (q).

9   *OTC*, 190 (qs).

10   Ibid., 191–92 (qs); JMA int.

11   Ibid., 181 (qs).

12   Ibid., 192, 224; *NYT*, December 15, 17–20, 27, 1976.

13   *NYT*, January 2, 5, 7, 13, 1977; *BCHT*, 187, 190, 373; *OTC*, 222; Pasarell int.

14   *OTC*, 192 (qs); Loretta Ashe Harris int.

15   *OTC*, 192–93; *NYT*, January 31, February 17, 1977; Young and JMA ints; *DG*, 14, 51.

16   *NYT*, February 11, 1977 (qs).

17   Ibid., February 17, 1977 (q).

18   Ibid., February 6, 1977 (qs); Hall, *Arthur Ashe*, 227–31. For responses to Ashe's open letter, see Marvin S. Dent, Jr., "An Open Letter to Arthur Ashe: Many Blacks Must Play Just to Get an Education," the letters in "Mailbox: Not for Blacks Only," and Ross Thomas Runfola, "Sports Called Opiate for Black Masses," in *NYT*, February 27, 1977. See also Walt Frazier, "Talk About Doctors Instead of Athletes," *NYT*, May 1, 1977; Joe Lapointe, "Ashe Urges Parents to Look at the Odds," *Chicago Sun-Times*, June 5, 1977, copy in folder 2, box 35, AAP; and Earl Graves to Arthur Ashe, February 10, 1977, in folder 2, box 2, AAP.

19   Dell int; JMA int; *NYT*, February 17, 21, 1976; *OTC*, 192–93 (q), 194; *DG*, 51–52.

20   *OTC*, 198, 209.

21   *NYT*, April 10, 1977 (qs); *OTC*, 156, 209; Williams and JMA ints.

22   *DG*, 106–7 (qs).

23   *NYT*, May 24, 1977 (q).

24   Robinson and Willard Johnson ints; Hall, *Arthur Ashe*, 227; *DG*, 110.

25   *NYT*, June 8, 1977.

26   Ibid., June 19, July 1–3, 1977; *BCHT*, 186–87, 422.

27   *NYT*, July 7, 19 (q), 1977.

28   Ibid., July 27, 29, August 1, 2, 5, 1977.

29   Ibid., August 26, 28, 1977; the Ashe quotation is in Neil Amdur, "The Stormy Summer of Controversy at Forest Hills," in *NYT*, August 28, 1977. See also Bud Collins, "Farewell to Forest Hills," *NYT Magazine*, September 11, 1977.

30   *NYT*, September 3, 1977.

31   Ibid., September 9, 1977 (qs); Bodo, *Courts of Babylon*, 359–62.

32   *NYT*, September 10, 1977 (q).

33   Ibid., September 9, 1977 (q).

34   Ibid., September 12, 1977 (qs).

35   Arthur Ashe, "South Africa's 'New' Interracial Sports Policy: Is It a Fraud?," *NYT*,
      October 2, 1977 (qs); Robinson and Williams ints. See also Hall, *Arthur Ashe*, 231–32.

36   "Ashe Is Back at Forest Hills—With a Wife but Without a Racquet," *NYT*, September
      3, 1977 (qs); JMA int.

37   *OTC*, 195 (qs); JMA and Dell ints.

38   *OTC*, 194–95 (qs).

39   Jeanne Moutoussamy-Ashe, *Daufuskie Island* (Columbia: University of South Caro-
      lina Press, 2007) (25th Anniversary Edition), 7–8 (q), 9–17; *OTC*, 195–97; *DG*, 55;
      JMA and Stan Smith ints. On the distinctive Gullah culture of the South Carolina Sea
      Islands, see Pat Conroy, *The Water Is Wide* (Boston: Houghton Mifflin, 1972); Guy
      and Candie Carawan, *Ain't You Got a Right to the Tree of Life?: The People of Johns
      Island, South Carolina—Their Faces, Their Words, and Their Songs* (Athens: University
      of Georgia Press, 1994); and Charles Joyner, *Shared Traditions: Southern History and
      Folk Culture* (Urbana: University of Illinois Press, 1999), 275–82.

40   *OTC*, 197–98 (q); Dell int.

41   Dell and Savage ints; *OTC*, 199; Hall, *Arthur Ashe*, 233; folders 1–10, box 31, AAP.

42   *DG*, 184–87.

43   *OTC*, 199 (q); *NYT*, December 10, 1977.

44   *NYT*, October 7, 1977; *OTC*, 198; Hall, *Arthur Ashe*, 233; Louie Robinson Jr., "Arthur
      Ashe: The Man Who Despite Age and an Operation Refused to Quit: He Comes Back
      as a Top Star," *Ebony* (April 1979): 74–76, 78, 80.

45   Tony Kornheiser, "Smile, Even Though You're Aching," *NYT*, November 22, 1977
      (qs).

CHAPTER 20: COMING BACK

1   *NYT*, January 5–7, 12, February 1 (q), 2, 1978.

2   Ibid., February 8, 20, 26, 27, March 2 (qs),1978.

3   Ibid., March 9, 1978 (qs). On the two Spinks-Ali fights of 1978, see Pat Putnam, "He's
     the Greatest, I'm the Best," *SI* (February 27, 1978): 14ff; and Vic Ziegel, "Ali, Spinks,
     and the Battle of New Orleans," *New York* (October 2, 1978), available online at
     nymag.com.

4   *NYT*, March 18–20, 1978; *Nashville Tennessean*, March 18–20, 1978; "South African
     Davis Cup Team Selection of Peter Lamb Discussed," *WP*, February 14, 1978; Jim
     Jerome, "Apartheid Critics Say He's Merely a Token, but Peter Lamb's Davis Cup
     Runneth Over," *People* (March 20, 1978): 28; Hall, *Arthur Ashe*, 206, 219; Douglas
     Booth, "Accommodating Race to Play the Game: South Africa's Readmission to Inter-
     national Sports," *Sporting Traditions* 8, no. 2 (1992): 182–209; Owen Williams int. See
     also Neil Amdur, "Davis Cup: Crucible of Race, Money, and Politics," *NYT*, March
     13, 1978; Evans, *Davis Cup*, 173–219; Douglas Booth, *The Race Game: Sport and Pol-
     itics in South Africa* (New York: Routledge, 1998); and John Nauright, *Long Run to
     Freedom: Sports, Cultures and Identities in South Africa* (Morgantown, WV: Fitness Info
     Tech, 2010).

5   *NYT*, March 20, April 2, 26, 29, 30, May 1, 1978.

6   Ibid., May 26, 1978. Solomon was the eighth seed in Rome.

7   Ibid., May 31 (first q), June 2, 4, 6 (second q); *BCHT*, 192, 390.

8   *NYT*, June 14, 20, 25–28 (q), July 1–2, 1978; Riessen and Stockton ints; *BCHT*, 185, 190, 192, 422; *IRAA*, 44–45. Borg won the 1978 Wimbledon men's singles championship, his third consecutive title. Having already won the 1978 Italian and French singles titles, he became the first player since Rod Laver in 1962 to win the "Old World Triple." The British press paid no attention to Ashe during the 1978 fortnight. See the press clippings in the 1978 Wimbledon scrapbook, KRWL.

9   *NYT*, July 14, 17, 20, August 1, 3, 1978. Mitton went on to win the 1978 Hall of Fame tournament, his first victory on the Grand Prix circuit.

10 Ibid., August 28–September 10, 1978.

11 Evans, *Davis Cup*, 173–200; Evans, *Open Tennis*, 178; *NYT*, December 8, 1978; Gottfried and Trabert ints. On Trabert as a Davis Cup captain, see Tony Trabert, *Trabert on Tennis: The View from Center Court* (Chicago: Contemporary Books, 1988).

12 *OTC*, 199 (q), 223–24; *NYT*, November 8, 10, 15, 18–19, December 3–4, 9, 11, 1978, January 7, 1979.

13 *OTC*, 199–200; *NYT*, December 20–22, 29–31, 1978, January 1–3, 1979; JMA int.

14 *NYT*, December 17, 1978, January 4–5, 7 (q), 10, 1979.

15 Ibid., January 11 (first q), 12–14 (second q), 1979; Gottfried int.

16 *NYT*, January 14 (first q), 15 (second and third qs), 1979; *OTC*, 200.

17 *NYT*, January 23–28 (first q), 29 (second and third qs), 1979; E. M. Swift, "It Was a Grave Ending for Arthur," *SI* 50 (February 5, 1979): 22–24+.

18 Ibid., February 4, 13, March 3–5, 1979.

19 Robinson, "Arthur Ashe: The Man Who Despite Age and an Operation Refused to Quit," 74–76; Mike Lupica, "Ashe Is Back," *WT* 26 (April 1979): 44–46+; Bodo, *Courts of Babylon*, 251.

20 Dell int; "Ashe Raps Black Students for Sad Values, Bad Habits," *Jet* (April 20, 1978): 48; Hall, *Arthur Ashe*, 230. See also "Ashe on Target . . ." *Jet* (May 11, 1978): 4; and *DG*, 150–51.

21 Arthur Ashe, "Sports Boycotts Are Against the Nature of Competition," *WP*, October 22, 1978; Hall, *Arthur Ashe*, 231.

22 Dell, Amdur, JMA, and Young ints.; *DG*, 43, 118–19; Neil Amdur, "Athletes Prospering in Political Arena," *NYT*, November 9, 1978; *IRAA*, 101.

23 Hall, *Arthur Ashe*, 232; *DG*, 152–53; Curtis Austin, "'I Support the Bakke Decision,' Ashe Says," *BAA*, March 24, 1979; Charles Williams and Dell ints. On the *Bakke* controversy, see Howard Ball, *The Bakke Case: Race, Education, and Affirmative Action* (Lawrence: University Press of Kansas, 2000); and Joel Dreyfuss and Charles Lawrence III, *The Bakke Case: The Politics of Inequality* (New York: Harcourt Brace, 1979).

24 *DG*, 181–82 (qs); *IRAA*, 88–89. On Tolbert, Taylor, and the carnage in Liberia, see Colin M. Waugh, *Charles Taylor and Liberia: Ambition and Atrocity in Africa's Lone Star State* (London: Zed Books, 2011); and Gabriel I. H. Williams, *Liberia: The Heart of Darkness* (Victoria, BC: Trafford Books, 2006).

25 *NYT*, May 10–11, 14, 29, 31, June 2, 1979; *BCHT*, 197, 389–90, 601–2; P. Taubman, "Working Out with Arthur Ashe," *Esquire* 91 (June 5, 1979): 33–35. On Lendl, see Bodo, *Courts of Babylon*, 46–64.

26 Evans, *Open Tennis*, 193–98; Dell, Butch Buchholz, and Drysdale ints. For a sharp critique of Dell's behavior, see *Bodo, Courts of Babylon*, 139–43, 261.

27 *NYT*, June 15, 17–18, 25–27, July 1–2, 1979; *DG*, 33; *OTC*, 3.

28 *OTC*, 3–4 (qs), 5–6; JMA int.

29 *DG*, 33 (q); *NYT*, July 29, 1979 (qs); *IRAA*, 97. See also W. Kalyn, "Television," *WT* 27 (August 1979): 62.

CHAPTER 21: OFF THE COURT

1 *DG*, 33, 52; *OTC*, 7, 9; Loretta Ashe Harris int; Arthur Ashe, "An Athlete Nearly Dying Young: A Tennis Champ Tells His History," *People* (September 21, 1981): 113; *IRAA*, 139. In August 1980, Ashe revealed he was receiving instruction in the art of broadcasting. He told his old friend the reporter Doug Smith: "Five years from now I expect to have completed this training program I'm going through with ABC to be a better sports broadcaster than I am." Doug Smith, "Arthur Ashe: The LI Interview," *LI* (August 3, 1980): 39, in folder 11, box 26, AAP.

2 *DG*, 33 (q); *OTC*, 9–10, 54; Ashe, "An Athlete Nearly Dying Young," 113; Arthur Ashe, "Ashe Heart Attack: Why Me?," *WT*, August 29, 1979, typescript in folder 3, box 26, AAP; *NYT*, August 1, 2, 4, 1979.

3 *DG*, 33–34; *OTC*, 10–11 (qs); Ashe, "An Athlete Nearly Dying Young," 113; Ashe, "Ashe Heart Attack: Why Me?"

4 *OTC*, 1–3, 11 (first q), 12, 201; Ashe, "Ashe Heart Attack: Why Me?" (second q).

5 *OTC*, 1 (second and third qs), 2–3 (first q), 4 (fourth q); JMA int.

6 Carole Kranepool, "Interview: Arthur Ashe," *Sportswise N.Y.* (May–June 1980): 16–17 (qs); *NYT*, March 10, 1980; *IRAA*, 165.

7 *OTC*, 201 (q); "It Couldn't Be a Heart Attack—But It Was," *SI* 51 (September 3, 1979): 24–25

8 Ashe, "Ashe Heart Attack: Why Me?" (qs).

9 Ashe, "An Athlete Nearly Dying Young," 113 (first q); Ashe, "Ashe Heart Attack: Why Me?" (second q); *DG*, 34 (third and fourth qs); Kranepool, "Interview: Arthur Ashe," 17.

10 *NYT*, November 26, December 10, 1979; R. Bookman, "Thinking About Arthur," *WT* 27 (October 1979): 6.

11 *OTC*, 201–2 (qs); Ashe, "An Athlete Nearly Dying Young," 114; *NYT*, December 6, 10, 1979; Pasarell int.

12 *NYT*, December 10, 14 22 (qs), 1979; *OTC*, 202; *DG*, 35; Ashe, "An Athlete Nearly Dying Young," 114.

13 *OTC*, 202–3 (q); JMA and Dell ints.

14 Dell and Pasarell ints; *DG*, 34 (first and third qs), 35, 41 (fourth q), 47–48; *OTC*, 204 (second q); *NYT*, December 10, 1979.

15 Kranepool, "Interview: Arthur Ashe," 17; *NYT*, November 26, 1979 (first q), January 6–7, 13, February 6, March 10, 17, 1980; *DG*, 58 (second q); *WT*, January 6, 9, 27, March 2, 1980; Frank Deford to Arthur Ashe, January 25, 1980, and *Westport News*, January 23, 1980, both in box 1, folder 14, AAP; Dell int.

16 *NYT*, March 10, 1980; *DG*, 36 (qs); Ashe, "An Athlete Nearly Dying Young," 114; JMA int.

17 *DG*, 36–38 (q); JMA int. According to Jeanne, Arthur's artistic sensibility was heavily laden with "logic," while hers was all about "art and emotion."

18 Barry Lorge, "Ashe Suffers Setback," *WT*, March 26, 1980; Donald Dell to Ashe, c. April 1980, in folder 14, box 1, AAP; Justice Lewis F. Powell to Ashe, March 26, 1980,

in folder 3, box 2, AAP; Arthur Ashe, "Owens Left Mark: Giant of His Time," *WT*, April 2, 1980, typescript in folder 3, box 26, AAP; *NYT*, April 17, 1980; Barry Lorge, "Ashe Ends Career as Player," *WT*, April 17, 1980 (q), copy in folder 3, box 35, AAP; Hall, *Arthur Ashe*, 237 (q).

19 *NYT*, April 17, 1980 (q); Lorge, "Ashe Ends Career as Player."

20 "Arthur Robert Ashe Jr.," biographical entry in *International Who's Who in Tennis* (Dallas: World Championship Tennis, 1983): 32; "Arthur Ashe," official International Tennis Hall of Fame profile, available online at tennisfame.com; Arthur Ashe career statistics, available online at atpworldtour.com; Nick White to Ashe, April 21, 1980, in folder 3, box 2, AAP; Hall, *Arthur Ashe*, 237–38; Lorge, "Ashe Ends Career as Player," (q); Peter Harris, "Ashe Retirement: A Move for Betterment," *BAA*, May 10, 1980; Jennings Culley, "A Champion, Retired," *RTD*, April 23, 1980, in scrapbooks, box 40, AAP; Henry "Bunny" Austin to Arthur and Jeanne Ashe, April 20, 1980, in folder 10, box 1, AAP; R. Bookman, "Arthur Ashe: Still Classy After All These Years," *WT* 28 (August 1980): 26–28.

21 Mayor Henry A. Marsh III to Ashe, May 22, 1980, in folder 3, box 2, AAP.

22 *NYT*, May 25, 30, June 1 (q), 1980.

23 Ibid., June 10, 1980; Dr. Stephen S. Scheidt to Ashe, July 24, 1980, in folder 3, box 2, AAP; Smith, "Arthur Ashe: The LI Interview," 17.

24 Arthur Ashe, "Don't Tell Me How to Think," *Black Sports* (August 1975): 35–37; Arthur Ashe, "What America Means to Me," *Reader's Digest* (March 1976): 119–20; Smith, "Arthur Ashe: The LI Interview"; *DG*, 100–101, 112–13, 127, 168–69, 194; Joseph Durso, "New Ashe Role," *NYT*, November 10, 1982 (first q); *OTC*, 205–14 (q), 215–19; Hall, *Arthur Ashe*, 238–39; Dell and JMA ints; Martin, *Arthur Ashe*, 10.

25 *DG*, 39–40 (qs); JMA int.

26 *DG*, 40 (q).

27 Ibid., 40 (qs); Edwards int; James Blake, with Carol Taylor, *Ways of Grace*. See also Remnick, *King of the World*, 285–91; and Harry T. Edwards to Arthur Ashe, January 12, 1982, in folder 4, box 2, AAP. In his letter, Edwards praised Ashe's recent inter- pretive piece on Smith and Carlos: "Just a quick note to say that I loved the piece on Smith-Carlos. I thought that it was a masterful job. It was one of the very few times that my relationship to Carlos and Smith has been accurately portrayed—mine was not the role of 'guru,' ideological or 'fanatic Black nationalist,' but teacher. Again, thanks for a job well done."

28 Amdur and Gewecke ints; *OTC*, vii; *DG*, 81; Hall, *Arthur Ashe*, 316; Jonathan Yardley, "Arthur Ashe Steps off the Court to Reveal the Man Behind the Player," *SI* (September 7, 1981).

29 *DG*, 45 (first q), 46–48 (second and third qs); *OTC*, 208; Daniel J. Levinson, with Maria H. Levinson, Charlotte N. Darrow, Edward B. Klein, and Braxton McKee, *The Seasons of a Man's Life* (New York: Random House, 1978). A disciple of the noted psychologists Erik Erickson and Gordon Allport, Levinson (1920–94) helped found the field known as "positive adult development." See Levinson's obituary in *NYT*, April 14, 1994.

30 JMA int (first q); Jeanne Moutoussamy-Ashe, *Viewfinders: Black Women Photogra- phers* (New York: Dodd & Mead, 1986); Schragis and Butch Buchholz ints; *DG*, 48 (second q), 169 (third q).

31 JMA, Dell, and Pasarell ints; *OTC*, 212–13, 217 (qs); *DG*, 185–86. Ashe's articles were published in the *WP* on February 4, March 17, April 8, 29, June 17, August 12, 29, September 1, 10, 30, October 20, December 2, 16, 1979; and on January 6, 9, 27, March

2, 16, April 2, 17, June 8, August 3, October 17, December 27, 1980. Martin, *Arthur Ashe*, 138–39; Bodo, *Courts of Babylon*, 268; Arthur Ashe, with Louie Robinson, *Getting Started in Tennis* (New York: Atheneum, 1979); Arthur Ashe, *Arthur Ashe's Tennis Clinic* (Norwalk: Golf Digest/Tennis, 1981); Arthur Ashe, with Alexander McNab, *Arthur Ashe on Tennis* (New York: Alfred A. Knopf, 1995).

32   *OTC*, 212 (fifth q), 215 (fourth q), 217 (first q); *DG*, 43, 117–18 (second q), 119, 121; Bodo, *Courts of Babylon*, 269 (third q); JMA, Dell, and Dinkins ints; *NYT*, September 26, October 30, 1980; Edward Kennedy to Arthur Ashe, February 15, 1980, folder 2, box 2; Edward Kennedy to Arthur Ashe, September 2, 1981, folder 3, box 2; Edward Kennedy to Arthur Ashe, February 26, 1982, folder 14, box 27; Jimmy Carter to Arthur Ashe, September 25, 1980, folder 1, box 2; Charles Robb to Arthur Ashe, January 22, 1982, folder 4, box 2; W. Wilson Goode to Arthur Ashe, October 24, 1983, folder 5, box 2; Tom Bradley to Arthur Ashe, September 9, 1982, folder 4, box 2; Edward Kennedy to Arthur and Jeanne Ashe, December 20, 1982, folder 4, box 2; Bill Bradley to Arthur Ashe, January 23, 1984, folder 6, box 2; Douglas Wilder to Arthur Ashe, November 4, 1985, folder 6, box 2; Lady Bird Johnson to Arthur Ashe, August 10, 1983, folder 5, box 2, all in AAP.

33   *DG*, 107 (q); Robinson and Young ints; Hall, *Arthur Ashe*, 227, 252–53; John Herbers, "Aftermath of Andrew Young Affair: Blacks, Jews, and Carter All Could Suffer Greatly," *NYT*, September 6, 1979; "The Andrew Young Affair," *Newsweek* (August 27, 1979): cover story; "Foreign Policy, Black America, and the Andrew Young Affair," *Ebony* (January 1980): 116–18, 120, 122; "The Fall of Andy Young," *Time* (August 27, 1979): 10; Carl Gershman, "The Andy Young Affair," *Commentary* (November 1, 1979): 25–33; Samih Fasoun, "Andrew Young: The Two-edged Sword," *Journal of Palestine Studies* 9 (March 1980): 139–45; Wiliam Minter and Sylvia Hill, "Anti-Apartheid Solidarity in United States-South Africa Relations from the Margins to the Mainstream," Chapter 9 in *The Road to Democracy in South Africa*, vol. 3 (2008), 782–83; "Lancaster House Agreement, 21 December 1979," available online at sas-space .sas.ac.uk. See also Nancy Mitchell, *Jimmy Carter and Africa: Race and the Cold War* (Palo Alto: Stanford University Press, 2016). On the fall of Rhodesia and the origins and evolution of Zimbabwe, see Alois Miambo, *A History of Zimbabwe* (Cambridge: Cambridge University Press, 2014); Sara Dorman, *Understanding Zimbabwe: From Liberation to Authoritarianism and Beyond* (New York: Oxford University Press, 2016. During the 1979 Wimbledon fortnight, Ashe met with Rhodesian leader Ian Smith's son at the home of Henry "Bunny" Austin, a Wimbledon singles finalist in 1932 and 1938 and a British tennis icon who befriended Ashe in the 1960s. Ashe also discussed the situation in Southern Africa with Young and Fiat auto magnate Gianni Agnelli during a private meeting in New York. JMA int.

34   On the 1980 U.S. presidential contest, see *NYT*, June–November 1980; and Andrew E. Busch, *Reagan's Victory: The Presidential Election of 1980 and the Rise of the Right* (Lawrence: University Press of Kansas, 2005). On the boycott of the 1980 Summer Olympics in Moscow, see Derick Hulme, *The Political Olympics: Moscow, Afghanistan, and the 1980 U.S. Boycott* (New York: Praeger, 1990); and Jerry and Tom Caraccioli, *Boycott: Stolen Dreams of the 1980 Moscow Olympic Games* (Chicago: New Chapter Press, 2008).

35   Young, JMA, and Dell ints; Tignor, *High Strung*, 79–82; *BCHT*, 200; McEnroe, with Kaplan, *You Cannot Be Serious*, 124–26.

CHAPTER 22: CAPTAIN ASHE

1   *DG*, 62 (first q), 63 (qs), 64 (last q); *NYT*, September 8, 1980; Trabert int; *BCHT*, 652–53; Trabert, with Cousins, *Trabert on Tennis.*

2   See the numerous letters congratulating Ashe on his appointment as U.S. Davis Cup captain in folder 7, box 29, AAP. Edward A. Turville to Arthur Ashe, November 19, 1980, in folder 3, box 2, AAP; Donald Dell to Arthur Ashe, November 30, 1980, in folder 2, box 31, AAP; *DG*, 65–68; and McEnroe, with Kaplan, *You Cannot Be Serious*, 129–30.

3   *DG*, 107–8 (qs); *NYT*, July 7, October 17, 1980; *BCHT*, 200–203; Tignor, *High Strung*, 16, 42–48, 55–58; McEnroe, with Kaplan, *You Cannot Be Serious*, 120–27; McEnroe and Robinson ints; Evans, *Open Tennis*, 158–59.

4   *DG*, 108 (first q); *NYT*, October 17, 1980 (second through fourth qs); Arthur Ashe, "McEnroe: 'No' to Borg Duel," *WP*, October 1, 1980 (qs); "Ashe Thwarts S. Africa in Bid for Tennis Plum," *BAA*, October 25, 1980; Hall, *Arthur Ashe*, 251–52; McEnroe, with Kaplan, *You Cannot Be Serious*, 126–27; McEnroe, JMA, and Robinson ints.

5   Goudsouzian, *King of the Court*, 189–237; Robinson, with Dave Anderson, *Frank: The First Year; DG*, 65 (q), 68.

6   *DG*, 67 (first q), 68 (second q), 71–72; *NYT*, October 8, 1980; Evans, *Open Tennis*, 180, 187.

7   McEnroe, with Kaplan, *You Cannot Be Serious*, 130 (q); Connors, *The Outsider*, 169–71, 283–84, 287; *DG*, 68; *NYT*, March 1, 10, 1981; Arthur Ashe to Stan Smith, May 8, 1981, Arthur Ashe to Bob Lutz, May 8, 1981, Bob Lutz to Arthur Ashe, May 13, 1981, all in folder 7, box 5, AAP; *BCHT*, 648; McEnroe, Stan Smith, and Riessen ints.

8   *DG*, 69 (qs); McEnroe int. On McEnroe and the Davis Cup, see Richard Evans, *McEnroe: Taming the Talent* (Lexington: S. Greene, 1990), 119–40.

9   *NYT*, March 7, 9 (first and second qs), 10, 1981; *DG*, 69, 70 (qs). See also folder 10, box 5, AAP.

10 *DG*, 70 (first q), 71 (second q); McEnroe int.

11 *DG* 72, 73(first q), 74–74 (second q); *NYT*, July 6–9, 13, 1981; McEnroe, with Kaplan, *You Cannot Be Serious*, 132–38; *BCHT*, 205; Tignor, *High Strung*, 62–66,144; Connors, *The Outsider*, 283–87; McEnroe int; 1981 Wimbledon Scrapbook, KRWL. See the numerous clippings and letters in folder 11, box 29, AAP; Frank Deford, "Cap'n Ashe and Crew Cancel the Czechs," *SI* (July 20, 1981): 16–19.

12 *DG*, 75–76 (qs), 77; *NYT*, October 3–5, 1981; McEnroe int. See folder 12, box 5, AAP, especially Donald Dell to Gordon Jorgensen, October 6, 1981; and Robert F. King to Sports Editor, *NYT*, October 16, 1981.

13 *DG*, 76 (q), 77; McEnroe, with Kaplan, *You Cannot Be Serious*, 129–30; Neil Amdur, "Ashe Sticking with McEnroe," *NYT*, October 5, 1981; Neil Amdur, "McEnroe Suspended, Still in Cup," *NYT*, November 17, 1981; McEnroe int.

14 *DG*, 77 (qs); Neil Amdur, "Connors Pulls Out of Cup," *NYT*, November 26, 1981; McEnroe, with Kaplan, *You Cannot Be Serious*, 140–41; Bodo, *Courts of Babylon*, 269–70.

15 *DG*, 78 (qs), 79 (last four qs); McEnroe with Kaplan, *You Cannot Be Serious*, 141–44; *NYT*, December 11–12, 1981; McEnroe int. See folder 13, box 5, AAP, especially Barry McDermott, "Troubled Doubles and a Singular Singles," *SI* (December 21, 1981): 24–25.

16 *NYT*, December 13, 1981 (first q); *DG*, 79 (second q), 80 (third, fourth, fifth, and seventh qs); McDermott, "Troubled Doubles and Singular Singles," 24 (sixth q); McEnroe, with Kaplan, *You Cannot Be Serious*, 145 (final q).

17   Neil Amdur, "McEnroe's Victory Clinches Davis Cup," *NYT*, December 14, 1981 (qs).

18   Stuart M. Butler to Arthur Ashe, December 14, 1981 (first q); Donald B. Keller to
      Arthur Ashe, December 16, 1981 (second q); Myers, "Question: What Does It Take to
      Absolve Outrageous Conduct?" (third q); Luther L. Terry to Arthur Ashe, December
      10, 1981 (fourth q), all in folder 13, box 29, AAP.

19   Dell and McEnroe ints; R. V. Baugus, "Davis Cup Comes Back to America," *International
      Tennis Weekly* (December 25, 1981), in folder 13, box 29, AAP; Donald Dell to
      Gordon Jorgensen (bcc. Captain Arthur Ashe), October 6, 1981 (first q), in folder 12,
      box 29, AAP; Donald Dell to Arthur Ashe, December 17, 1981 (second q), in folder 15,
      box 1, AAP.

20   "Ashe Says McEnroe Still with U.S. Team," *Cincinnati Enquirer*, December 14, 1981
      (qs), in folder 13, box 29, AAP.

21   *DG*, 82; see folder 1, box 30, AAP.

22   *NYT*, June 11, 20, 23, 24 (q), 27, 29, 1982; 1982 Wimbledon scrapbook, KRWL;
      McEnroe, with Kaplan, *You Cannot Be Serious*, 162–63. On the 1982 Hooper situa-
      tion, see Lawrence B. Hooper to William Simons, July 23, 1982; and William Simons
      to Arthur Ashe, August 20, 1982, both in folder 8, box 29, AAP. See also *BATN*, 82–83;
      and Ralph Wiley, "Serving Notice in a Big Way," *SI* (May 3, 1982): 61–63.

23   *DG*, 82–83; McEnroe, with Kaplan, *You Cannot Be Serious*, 163; McEnroe int; *NYT*,
      July 10–11, 12 (first and second qs), 13 (third through fifth qs), 1982. See the clippings
      and correspondence in folder 2, box 30, AAP. On Wilander, see *BCHT*, 209–13, 660.

24   David Butcher to Arthur Ashe, July 17, 1982 (first q); Briggs M. Austin to Arthur
      Ashe, July 15, 1982 (second q); Marshall J. Lech to Arthur Ashe, July 12, 1982 (third
      q); and Elizabeth Leonard to Arthur Ashe, July 13, 1982 (fourth q), all in folder 2, box
      30, AAP. On the decline of sportsmanship during the Open era, see Bodo, *Courts of
      Babylon*, 313–32.

25   *NYT*, September 8, 10, 1982; George Vecsey, "At Home with Jimmy Connors," *NYT*,
      September 12, 1982 (q); McEnroe and JMA ints.

26   *DG*, 81 (q), 90; JMA and McEnroe ints; Neil Amdur, "McEnroe: Caught Up in a
      Difficult Year," *NYT*, August 30, 1982; Connors, *The Outsider*, 1–76, 284, 286.

27   *DG*, 83–84; *NYT*, October 1, 2 (qs), 4, 1982; McEnroe int. See folder 3, box 30, AAP;
      Bernard L. Schmidt to Arthur Ashe, September 8, 1982; and Elaine Rawlings to Ar-
      thur Ashe, November 14, 1982, both in folder 8, box 29, AAP.

28   Joseph Durso, "New Ashe Role," *NYT*, November 10, 1982 (first q); Mike Zitz, "Ar-
      thur Ashe: Career Has Come Full Circle," *Fredericksburg Free Lance-Star*, July 17,
      1982, in folder 3, box 35, AAP; Donald Dell to James C. Bowling (Vice President,
      Philip Morris, Inc.), September 20, 1982, Raymond S. Benton to Arthur Ashe, Febru-
      ary 4, 1982, both in folder 15, box 1, AAP; Arthur Ashe to Governor Charles Robb, Au-
      gust 10, 1982 (mailgram), David K. McLoud to Arthur Ashe, August 11, 1982, Claude
      Lenfant (NIH) to Arthur Ashe, August 6, 1982, all in folder 14, box 27, AAP; Jonathan
      A. Bell (U.S. Military Academy) to Arthur Ashe, January 25, 1982, Mayor Henry L.
      Marsh III to Arthur Ashe, March 19, 1982, Henry A. Talbert Jr. to Arthur Ashe, April
      3, 1982, Senator Harry F. Byrd Jr. to Arthur Ashe, May 18, 1982, all in folder 4, box 2,
      AAP.

29   Rogers, Ricks, JMA, and Schragis ints; *DG*, 168–69 (second q), 170–73; Hall, *Arthur
      Ashe*, 255–56; "Professor Arthur Ashe: Tennis' Class Act Moves into the Classroom,"
      Ebony (July 1983): 79–80, 82. "Our History," fmuniv.edu, provides a history of Florida
      Memorial College, which moved to Miami in 1968, after many years in St. Augustine.

The school originated as the Florida Baptist Institute in Live Oak, Florida, in 1879, and changed its name to Florida Memorial University in 2004. On Howard Thurman (1900–1981), widely regarded as the Rev. Martin Luther King Jr.'s spiritual mentor, see Howard Thurman, *With Head and Heart: The Autobiography of Howard Thurman* (New York: Harcourt, Brace, Jovanovich, 1979); Howard Thurman, with Walter Earl Fluker et al., eds., *A Strange Freedom: The Best of Howard Thurman on Religious Experience and Public Life* (Boston: Beacon, 1999); and Luther E. Smith Jr., *Howard Thurman: The Mystic as Prophet* (Richmond, IN: Friends United Press, 2007).

30 *DG*, 173–74 (first q), 175; David K. Wiggins, "Symbols of Possibility: Arthur Ashe, Black Athletes, and the Writing of *A Hard Road to Glory*," *Journal of African American History* 99 (Fall 2014): 381–84; Hall, *Arthur Ashe*, 256–57; Murray int. See the various documents in folder 1, box 9, AAP. See especially Arthur Ashe, "First Draft Proposal," December 8, 1982 (qs); *IRAA*, 111 (last q).

31 *BCHT*, 46 (first q), 212, 499, 503; *DG*, 84 (second q); *NYT*, October 20, November 17 (third q), 25 (last two qs), 26, 1982; Dell int. See the clippings and correspondence in folder 4, box 30, AAP. See especially Neville Deed, "France Remains the Champion Nation," *American Lawn Tennis* (August 20, 1932): 7–12; Ed Turville to Arthur Ashe, November 29, 1982; Julius Hoyt to Arthur Ashe, December 13, 1982; and Curry Kirkpatrick, "He Cleaned Up on the Dirt," *SI* (December 6, 1982): 77–78.

32 *DG*, 84 (first q), 85 (third q); *IRAA*, 132, 137–38; *NYT*, November 26 (second q), 27–28; Donald Dell to Arthur Ashe, November 24, 1982, in folder 15, box 1, AAP; Rodney Harmon to Arthur Ashe, November 29, 1982, in folder 4, box 2, AAP; McEnroe and Mayer ints.

CHAPTER 23: BLOOD LINES

1 *DG*, 52–53 (first and second qs), 54 (third q); JMA int; *Jet* (January 3, 1983): 18; *Chicago Tribune*, December 20, 1982.

2 *AADJ*, January 1983.

3 *DG*, 170 (first q), 171 (second and third qs), 172 (fourth through ninth qs), 173 (tenth q); Rogers and Ricks ints.

4 *AADJ*, January 24–March 1, 1983; *DG*, 85–86; *BCHT*, 210, 218, 655; *NYT*, February 27, March 4, 1983. See the various clippings in folder 5 ("Davis Cup, Argentina, March 1983"), box 30, AAP.

5 Steve Flink, "Ashe Goes Ivy," *WT* (May 1983): 54–55 (qs), copy in folder 3, box 35, AAP; *DG*, 169–70; JMA, Dell, and Gates ints; *Yale Daily News*, February 9, 1983; Robin Winks to Arthur Ashe, February 14, 1983, in folder 5, box 2, AAP; *AADJ*, February 8–11, 1983; Hall, *Arthur Ashe*, 260–61; Arthur Ashe, "NCAA and Prop 48," *WP*, February 13, 1983; Chris Charles Winkler, "NCAA Academic Eligibility Standards for Competition in Division II" (PhD thesis, University of Texas, 2008), 1–13.

6 McEnroe int; folder 5, box 30, AAP; *NYT*, February 9, 27, March 4, 5 (qs), 1983; Edward Schumacher, "U.S. Task Slightly Uphill in Davis Cup," *NYT*, March 4, 1983; Maymi-Perez int.

7 *DG*, 86 (first and fifth qs), 87 (third and fourth qs); *NYT*, March 4, 7 (second q); McEnroe int. On the Falklands War, see Martin Middlebrook, *Argentine Fight for the Falklands* (Barnsley, UK: Pen & Sword, 2009); and Max Hastings and Simon Jenkins, *The Battle for the Falklands* (New York: W. W. Norton, 1984).

8 *NYT*, March 10, 1983; *DG*, 180, 253; Donald Dell to Arthur Ashe, April 13, 1983, in folder 15, box 1, AAP; Jane Leavy, "Dell's Firm's Breakup: Even Family Members

Were Surprised," *WP*, May 3, 1983 (first q); David Neil Prescott, "Advantage, Ashe," *Success* (July 1983): 43, copy in folder 4, box 35, AAP, and in Arthur Ashe Vertical File, ITHF; Evans, *Open Tennis*, 218 (second q); Bodo, *Courts of Babylon*, 260–61.

9   *AADJ*, April 1983; *DG*, 87; Hall, *Arthur Ashe*, 248.

10   *AADJ*, April 13, 1983; Hall, *Arthur Ashe*, 256; Wiggins, "Symbols of Possibility," 383; "Arthur Ashe Signs Contract for Major Book with Howard University Press," *Howard University Press News* (April 1983), in folder 1, box 9, AAP.

11   Wiggins, "Symbols of Possibility," 383 (qs); *Howard University Press News* (April 1983): 3 (last q), in folder 1, box 9, AAP; Joseph F. Cullman to Arthur Ashe, May 11, 1983, in folder 13, box 1, AAP.

12   "Collaboration Agreement, June 1, 1983," and "Outlines of the various deadlines and tasks . . . March–October 1983," typescripts in folder 1, box 9, AAP (q); Wiggins, "Symbols of Possibility," 384–85.

13   *AADJ*, April 12–May 30, 1983; *NYT*, June 10, 26, 1983; Arthur Ashe to Ladies and Gentlemen, Fellow Inductees, May 17, 1983; Tucker DiEdwardo (NCAA) to Arthur Ashe, June 27, 1983; and Vic Seixas to Arthur Ashe, June 27, 1983, all in folder 5, box 2, AAP; Arthur Ashe, "Peete: Green Jackets, Black Ironies at Masters," *WP* (May 1, 1983). Ashe was among the first sixteen inducted into the new ITA Men's Collegiate Tennis Hall of Fame. J. D. Morgan, Dennis Ralston, Rafael Osuna, and Alex Olmedo were also inducted in 1983. See www.itatennis.com/AboutITA/HOF/Mens.htm; and brochure for the ITA Men's Collegiate Tennis Hall of Fame's second annual Enshrinement Banquet, May 16, 1984, copy in folder 8, box 32, AAP.

14   *NYT*, June 6, 18, 22 (qs), 23 (last q), 1983; Dick Hobson to Arthur Ashe, June 5, 1983 (mailgram), in folder 5, box 2, AAP.

15   *NYT*, June 18 (first q), 21–22 (third q), 27–28 (fourth q), 1983; *DG*, 87 (second q); Murray int; Hall, *Arthur Ashe*, 248.

16   *DG*, 87 (qs). On the origins and early years of the AIDS epidemic, see Randy Shilts, *And the Band Played On: Politics, People, and the AIDS Epidemic* (New York: St. Martin's, 2007) (20th Anniversary Edition), 3–484; Jonathan Engel, *The Epidemic: A Global History of AIDS* (Washington, DC: Smithsonian Press, 2006), Prologue and Chapters 1–6; Victoria A. Harden, *AIDS at 30: A History* (Washington, DC: Potomac Books, 2012); Edward Hooper, *The River: A Journey to the Source of HIV and AIDS* (Boston: Little, Brown, 1999); and Jacques Pepin, *The Origins of AIDS* (Cambridge: Cambridge University Press, 2011). See also www.factlv.org/timeline.htm for "A Brief Timeline of AIDS"; and "History of HIV and AIDS Overview," at www.avert.org.

17   *NYT*, June 21, 1983; *DG*, 87 (qs); JMA and Dell ints; *AADJ*, July 1983; Bodo, *Courts of Babylon*, 65–66, 79–80.

18   National Council of Juvenile and Family Court Judges, 46th annual conference program, July 12, 1983 (q), copy in folder 8, box 32, AAP; JMA int; *DG*, 167, 281–92. On the Jones Institute and the beginnings of in vitro fertilization in the United States, see Dr. Howard W. Jones Jr. and Dr. Roger G. Gosden, *In Vitro Fertilization Comes to America: Memoir of a Medical Breakthrough* (James City County, VA: Jamestowne Bookworks, 2014). Dr. Howard W. Jones Jr. died in 2015 at the age of 104. His wife, Georgeanna, died in 2005 at the age of ninety-three.

19   Donald Dell to Arthur Ashe, June 27, 1983 (first q); and Donald Dell to Arthur Ashe, May 12, 1983 (second q), both in folder 15, box 1, AAP; David Falk to Arthur Ashe, June 2, 1983, in folder 5, box 2, AAP; Dell and Harmon ints.

20   Hall, *Arthur Ashe*, 256 (first q); Bob Lipper, "The Grace and Grit of Arthur Ashe,"

RTD, May 2, 989; Robert M. Thomas Jr., "Ashe Searches Past," *NYT*, June 27, 1983 (qs), copy in folder 3, box 35, AAP; Wiggins, "Symbols of Possibility," 385; miscellaneous documents in folders 1 and 2, box 9, AAP.

21   Arthur Ashe, "Tennis Everyone?," *Hemispheres* inflight magazine (July 1983): 101, 103; and Leslie Allen to Arthur Ashe, August 1, 1983 (qs), both in folder 5, box 2, AAP; Allen int.

22   Wiggins, "Symbols of Possibility," 384–85; "Outline of Deadlines and Tasks," in folder 1, box 9, AAP. See Ocania Chalk, *Pioneers of Black Sport: The Early Days of Black Professional Athletes in Baseball, Basketball, Boxing, and Football* (New York: Dodd, Mead, 1975); and Chalk, *Black College Sport* (New York: Dodd, Mead, 1976).

23   Barry Lorge, "The Sudden Rise of Noah's Arc," *Sport* (September 1983): 54–58 (first and second qs), 59–66; Ray Kennedy, "There's Bitter with the Sweet," *SI* (August 15, 1983): 54–65 (third q); Curry Kirkpatrick, "The French to a Frenchman," *SI* (June 13, 1983): 25–29; Evans, *Open Tennis*, 208.

24   Kennedy, "There's Bitter with the Sweet," 60 (first q); Lorge, "The Sudden Rise of Noah's Arc," 60 (second and third qs); *NYT*, August 29–September 10, 1983; *BCHT*, 214–17, 463, 619–20; Bodo, *Courts of Babylon*, 247.

25   Bud Collins, "For All Players Great and Small," *WT* (1983): 89 (first q), 91–92, and "Pressed Between the Pages," *WT* (1983): 74–76, both in folder 3, box 35, AAP; *NYT*, September 6 (second q), 12, 1983; David A. Superdock to Arthur Ashe, November 7, 1983, in folder 5, box 2, AAP; *BCHT*, 213, 218, 463, 601–2; Prescott, "Advantage, Ashe," 43; Ron Cobb, "When It Comes to Davis Cup, Jimbo No Patriot," *St. Louis Post-Dispatch*, March 7, 1983, in folder 5, box 30, AAP; McEnroe int; Connors, *The Outsider*, 140, 164, 176–79, 226, 241–43, 246–47, 259–60, 275–81.

26   Peter Alfano, "What Direction Is Tennis Going?," *NYT*, August 29, 1983 (q).

27   *NYT*, September 10 (second q), 11–12, 15 (first and third qs), 1983; Lexie Verdon, "Boycotting South Africa," *WP*, September 13, 1983; Clarke Taylor, "Entertainers, Athletes Join to End Apartheid," *LAT*, September 15, 1983; Hall, *Arthur Ashe*, 227, 252–54 (fourth q), 255; Simon Anekwe, "Cultural Boycott of So. Africa Launched on Both Coasts," *New York Amsterdam News*, October 8, 1983; "Tennis Keeps Ashe on the Run," *USA Today*, November 7, 1983, copy in Arthur Ashe Vertical File, ITHF; Robinson int. See also the materials in folder 5, box 27, AAP. On the Sullivan Principles, see Leon Howard Sullivan, *Moving Mountains: The Principles and Purposes of Leon Sullivan* (Valley Forge, PA: Judson Press, 1998).

28   Wiggins, "Symbols of Possibility," 385–87 (qs); John Hope Franklin to Arthur Ashe, September 19, 1983; Henry Louis Gates to Arthur Ashe, October 19, 1983; V. P. Franklin to Arthur Ashe, September 7, 1983; Sandra Jamison to Charles Harris, April 26, 1984; Benjamin Quarles to Sandra Jamison, May 31, 1984 (qs), all in folder 1, box 9, AAP. On Quarles, see August Meier, "Benjamin Quarles and the Historiography of Black America," *Civil War History* 26 (June 1980): 101–16.

29   See the clippings in "Davis Cup, Ireland, October 1983," in folder 6, box 30, AAP. See especially "Relax, John, You're at Your Granny's," *Sunday Press*, October 2, 1983 (first q); "The Style of a Champion," *Sunday Independent*, October 2, 1983; "Peter Bodo Reports from Ireland: McEnroe's Bizarre Davis Cup Homecoming," *Tennis* (December 1983): 116, 118, 121, 122; and Bodo, *Courts of Babylon*, 73. *DG*, 88–89 (second q); *NYT*, October 1–2, 1983; McEnroe int.

30   Sandra Jamison to Clifford Johnson, January 9, 1984; Sandra Jamison to Emily Dyer, May 29, 1984, both in folder 1, box 9, AAP; Evans, *Open Tennis*, 241–45; "Tennis Keeps Ashe on the Run," *USA Today*, November 7, 1983, copy in Arthur Ashe Vertical

File, ITHF; Bodo, *Courts of Babylon*, 148–49; folders 1 and 2, Tennis ITF folders for 1985 and 1986–1988, folder on Tennis/ITF Executive Bureau 1985–1988, all in ITF Files, OSC; IOC Executive Board Minutes, May 28–30, 1984, May 31–June 3, June 6, 1985, in Executive Board Files, OSC.

31   Bob Bednar to Arthur Ashe, September 29, 1983, in folder 5, box 2, AAP; Stan Smith and JMA ints; *AADJ*, October 6–8, 1983; Bodo, *Courts of Babylon*, 113–14.

32   *AADJ*, October 13–20, November 1, 1983; Beck and Abram ints; "Tennis Keeps Ashe on the Run."

33   Schragis int; *AADJ*, November–December 1983; Prescott, "Advantage, Ashe," 43 (qs). On the Hunger Project, see www.thp.org.

CHAPTER 24: HARD ROAD TO GLORY

1   *DG*, 194 (q).

2   Ibid., 89 (qs), 90; Steve Flink, "Rumble Looms in Romania: It's Now Connors and Mac in U.S. Davis Cup Attack," *Tennis USA* (February 1984): 1, 4, copy in folder 7, box 30, AAP; McEnroe and Dell ints.

3   On the ties in Bucharest (February 1984), Atlanta (July 1984), and Portland, Oregon (September 1984), see folders 7–9, box 30, AAP. *DG*, 90 (q); McEnroe int; *NYT*, July 14, September 28–30, 1984; Hall, *Arthur Ashe*, 249; and Bodo, *Courts of Babylon*, 23–24.

4   *DG*, 92 (qs), 93–94 (second q); *BCHT*, 222; see the clippings, letters, and programs related to the Goteborg tie in folder 10, box 30, AAP; McEnroe int; Connors, *The Outsider*, 283–87.

5   *DG*, 92 (first q), 93 (second through fifth qs); *BCHT*, 222; McEnroe int; Richard Evans, "Young Swedes Pound U.S.," *Tennis Week* (December 27, 1984): 4–5, 7; Neil Amdur, "A Swede Success," *WT* (December 1983): 16, 18, copies in folder 10, box 30, AAP; *NYT*, December 17–19, 1984; Hall, *Arthur Ashe*, 249–50; Connors, *The Outsider*, 286–87.

6   *DG*, 93 (first q), 94 (second and third qs), 95 (fourth through sixth qs), 96 (seventh q); Harry A. Merlo to Gordon Jorgensen, December 21, 1984, in folder 16, box 30, AAP; McEnroe int; *NYT*, January 11, 15, 1985; Hall, *Arthur Ashe*, 250; Bodo, *Courts of Babylon*, 264–67; Evans, *The Davis Cup*, 217–18; Evans, *McEnroe: Taming the Talent*, 141–62.

7   Dave Anderson, "Arthur Ashe's New Match," *NYT*, May 9, 1985. See the correspondence and clippings in folder 16, box 30, AAP. See especially Harry A. Merlo to Arthur Ashe, February 7, 1985; Harry A. Merlo to John McEnroe, February 6, 1985; Harry A. Merlo to Jimmy Connors, February 6, 1985; the numerous pro–Conduct Code letters received by Merlo; the USTA January 15, 1985, press release regarding the Code; William E. Simon, "America's Punks," *National Review* (March 22, 1985): 20; Bud Collins, "It's Time to Change, Baby," *Boston Globe*, January 25, 1985; Ann Liquori, "Raging Genius," *Inside Sports* (March 1985): 25–31; Curry Kirkpatrick, "What's Love Got to Do . . ." *SI* (1985): 42–43; and Peter Bodo, "Why the U.S. Davis Cup Team Is in Crisis," *Tennis* (August 1985): 70–76.

8   See folder 11, box 30, AAP, especially Mark McEnroe, "Rookies Lead U.S. to Davis Cup Victory," *Tennis USA* (April 1985): 1; and "New U.S. Team Performs for Captain Ashe," *International Tennis Weekly* (March 22, 1985). *BCHT*, 208, 212–13, 217, 219, 225–26, 228, 231.

9   JMA and Pace ints; "Ashe Buys House," Mount Kisco *Patent Trader* (c. April 1985)
     (first q), in folder1, box 1, AAP; Donald Dell and Raymond S. Benton to Arthur Ashe,
     February 13, 1986, in folder 15, box 1, AAP; Barry Lorge, "Inside the Heart and Mind
     of Arthur Ashe," *Tennis* (September 1988): 46 (second q), 48, 51, 53–55, copy in Arthur
     Ashe Vertical File, ITHF.

10   Thomas Boswell, unidentified clipping, January 1985 (q), in folder 4, box 35, AAP.
     Bodo, *Courts of Babylon*, 262, noted that Ashe "worked tirelessly for the cause of his
     people, but he did so mostly in boardrooms, Beltway offices, and other establishment
     venues."

11   *DG*, 101 (q).

12   *DG*, 111 (first q), 112 (second through fourth qs), 113 (fifth q), 117; *NYT*, November
     8, 30, 1984, January 12, 1985; Karlyn Barker, "Arthur Ashe Jailed in Apartheid Pro-
     test," *WP*, January 12, 1985; Karlyn Barker, "Apartheid Protestors' 'Show Trial' Can-
     celed," *WP*, February 26, 1985; Hall, *Arthur Ashe*, 255; "Marching Against Apartheid,"
     Time (December 10, 1984): 40; Robinson int.

13   Hartman, Desdunes, Pasarell, Dowdell, and Wilkerson ints; *NYT*, July 24 (first q),
     August 26 (qs), 1985; *W*, 163–64.

14   *NYT*, March 22, 1985; Anderson, "Arthur Ashe's New Match" (q).

15   Hooper, Harmon, and Blount ints; *W*, 160, 162–64, 180, 182; *CTN*, 115, 125–38, 155–
     56, 166–67, 191–92, 207, 214, 226, 230; *BATN*, 70–71, 75, 77, 81–84, 137–40, 142–45,
     149–50, 159, 168–70, 177–78, 197, 201, 205–9, 211, 215, 217; *BCHT*, 318, 463–65, 685–
     86. Blake lost a tough five-set match to Agassi 3–6, 3–6, 6–3, 6–3, 7–6. He also reached
     the U.S. Open quarterfinals in 2006, losing to the eventual champion Roger Federer
     7–6, 6–0, 6–7, 6–4.

16   Allen and Adams ints; *W*, 62, 113, 160–61, 164, 182; *CTN*, 15, 73, 75, 113, 116, 144,
     183–88, 224, 238; Bodo, *Courts of Babylon*, 249.

17   Wilkerson, Garrison, McNeil, and Washington ints; Garrison, with Doug Smith,
     Zina; Bodo, *Courts of Babylon*, 252–57; BCHT, 216, 227, 231, 235–36, 238, 241, 243,
     251–52, 260, 263, 269–71, 327, 689–90; *W*, 45, 62, 160–64, 182; *BATN*, 21, 30–31, 39,
     41, 73, 75, 78–79, 88–106, 108, 111, 118, 121, 144, 150, 170, 176–77, 180, 188, 194, 197,
     205–7; *CTN*, viii, 4, 15, 17, 22, 72–73, 77, 103, 106, 115–16, 119–21, 140–54, 161–62,
     183, 190, 197, 214, 223, 227–28, 232.

18   Sands, Washington, and Desdunes ints; *CTN*, 189 (q)–90; *BATN*, 72, 75, 77. Sands's
     highest world ranking in singles was #44 in 1984. See wwww.stevegtennis.com/draw
     -results/wta/French-Open for the women's draw at the 1985 French Open. McNeil
     was also in the singles draw but was unseeded.

19   *BCHT*, 224, 228, 390, 400; *NYT*, June 5–9, November 26, 1985; Christian Endemann,
     "Arthur Ashe: A Gentleman Graces the Tennis Scene with Candour and Courage,"
     Canadian Rackets (July 1985): 32–33, copy in folder 4, box 35, AAP.

20   *NYT*, June 23, 1985; "Ashe in the United Nations," *Secretariat News* (June 14, 1985),
     copy in folder 4, box 35, AAP; JMA int.

21   *DG*, 235 (qs)–36; JMA and Dell ints; Donald Dell to Arthur Ashe, July 5, 1985, in
     folder 15, box 1, AAP.

22   *BCHT*, 192, 201, 206, 208, 211, 217, 220, 222, 224–26, 240, 422, 546, 696–97; www
     .wimbledon.com/en_GB/scores/draws/archives/1985; 1985 Wimbledon scrapbook,
     KRWL; *DG*, 109–10; Simon Cambers, "Kevin Curren: 1985 Wimbledon Defeat by
     Boris Becker a Special Not Bitter Memory," *The Guardian* (June 25, 2015); Bodo,
     Courts of Babylon, 267, 333–51, 355; Arthur Ashe, "Kevin Curren," *WP*, July 7, 1985;

Bud Collins, "Class Act Makes It to Hall," *Boston Globe*, July 12, 1985. On the Kriek incident in Richmond, see *OTC*, 207. See also Johann Kriek, "Johan Kriek Remembers His Early Struggles in Tennis," Tennis.Prose.com, posted July 20, 2011.

23   For information on the history and evolution of PEI, see folders 3–14, box 31, and folders 1 and 2, box 32, AAP. On the dissolution, see especially Frank Craighill to Arthur Ashe, May 15, 1985, in folder 5, box 31, AAP; Minutes, PEI board meeting, July 11, 1985, and Draft of "Notice of Termination Plan," both in folder 1, box 32, AAP. Barbara Lloyd, "Ashe Enters the Hall of Fame," *NYT*, July 14, 1985; "Ashe Proud to Be First Black Male in Tennis Hall," *Jet* (August 12, 1985), copy in folder 4, box 35, AAP.

24   *DG*, 98–99; "Class Act Makes It to Hall," (first five qs); "Arthur Ashe, Class of 1985," ITHF Fact Sheet, April 10, 2001, Arthur Ashe Vertical File, ITHF; Bill Parrillo, "Arthur Ashe Earned His Place in History," *Providence Journal*, July 14, 1985 (sixth q), copy in folder 4, box 35, AAP; Frederick Waterman, "Arthur Ashe Entering Hall of Fame," *Taunton Gazette*, July 13, 1985 (last q), copy in Arthur Ashe Vertical File, ITHF.

25   Covering the induction ceremony for the *Richmond Times-Dispatch*, John Packett wrote: "Ashe was one of the best sportsmen to ever play the game and was thoroughly deserving of his moment in the sun yesterday." *RTD*, July 14, 1985; "Arthur Ashe Entering Hall of Fame" (first q); "Ashe Enters the Hall of Fame" (second q); Frederick Waterman, "For Ashe, Bottom Line Was Fun," *Newport News*, July 15, 1985 (third q); Sam Lacy, "Ashe's Aces," *BAA*, July 27, 1985; Marion Collins, "Arthur Ashe Quietly Ascends to Hall of Fame," New York *Daily News*, July 28, 1985 (qs); ITHF fact sheet; copies of each in Arthur Ashe Vertical File, ITHF.

26   *NYT*, July 18, August 2–5, 1985; *BCHT*, 224–26; *DG*, 97–98 (qs). On the Hamburg tie, see the clippings in folder 12, box 30, AAP. See especially Curry Kirkpatrick, "A Smash Hit on His Home Court," *SI* (August 12, 1985): 28–33.

27   On Ashe's resignation as Davis Cup captain, see the clippings in folder 17, box 30, AAP. *DG*, 98 (first q), 99 (second through fifth qs), 100 (last q); *NYT*, October 22–23, December 14, 17, 1985; Bodo, *Courts of Babylon*, 267.

28   *DG*, 100 (qs).

29   Ibid., 102 (first and second qs), 103 (third q).

30   Ibid., 103 (qs), 158–59; JMA and Young ints; Douglas Wilder to Arthur Ashe, November 4, 1985, in folder 6, box 2, AAP. On Jesse Jackson and the 1984 presidential campaign, see Jack W. Germond and Jules Witcover, *Wake Us When It's Over: Presidential Politics of 1984* (New York: Macmillan, 1984); and Lucius J. Barber and Ronald W. Walters, eds., *Jesse Jackson's 1984 Presidential Campaign: Challenge and Change in American Politics* (Urbana: University of Illinois Press, 1989). On the 1988 campaign, see Jack W. Germond and Jules Witcover, *What Broad Stripes and Bright Stars: The Trivial Pursuit of the Presidency, 1988* (New York: Warner, 1989).

31   Wiggins, "Symbols of Possibility," 387–88; Hall, *Arthur Ashe*, 257; *DG*, 174 (q), 175; *NYT*, March 8, November 8, 1986; Dell int. For a detailed survey of *A Hard Road to Glory*'s road to publication, see the miscellaneous documents in box 9, AAP. See especially Amistad Press, Inc., "President's Annual report—1988"; Amistad Press fact sheet; Charles Harris CV; and David O. Bernline to David B. Falk, August 11, 1988. On the *Amistad* mutiny and its aftermath, see Marcus Rediker, *The Amistad Rebellion: An Atlantic Odyssey of Slavery and Freedom* (New York: Viking, 2012). On the origins of the Craighill-Dell feud, see folders 4 and 5, box 31, and folders 1 and 2, box 32, AAP.

See especially the correspondence between Craighill and Dell, February 27, March 3, 1986, in folder 2, box 32, AAP. On the television documentary *A Hard Road to Glory* (directed by Stephen E. Goodrick), see www.imdb.com/title/tt3004992.

32   *NYT*, June 22 (first q), August 22, August 30–September 11, October 3–6, 1986; *BCHT*, 370, 433, 483, 474, 690; Bodo, *Courts of Babylon*, 248–51; Ira Berkow, "Hard Times for Garrison," *NYT*, April 12, 1986; Michael Lewellen, "Arthur Ashe," *Kappa Alpha Psi Journal* (February 1986): 9–10, copy in folder 4, box 35, AAP; Walt Hazzard to Arthur Ashe, July 25, 1986, in folder 7, box 2, AAP; Phil Patton, "The Selling of Michael Jordan," *NYT*, November 9, 1986 (second and third qs).

33   JMA, Pace, Loretta Ashe Harris, and Schragis ints; *DG*, 56 (first q), 57 (second and third qs), 58.

34   JMA int; *DG*, 57 (fourth q), 58 (first, third, and fifth qs); Hall, *Arthur Ashe*, 260 (second q); *Arthur Ashe: Citizen of the World* (King qs); Martin, *Arthur Ashe*, 144–45; Marian Christy, "They Are Living a Loving Match," Newport News *Daily Press*, October 10, 1980, copy in scrapbook, box 40, AAP.

35   List of Committee Members, National Organization on the Status of Minorities in Sport, typescript; Dr. Harry Edwards to Peter Roselle, April 22, 1987; Harry Edwards, "The Exploitation of Black Athletes," *Journal of the Association of Governing Boards of Universities and Colleges* 25 (November–December 1983): 37–46, all in folder 9, box 27, AAP; *NYT*, May 21, June 13 (q), 30, 1987; Edwards int; *DG*, 147–48, 165; Hall, *Arthur Ashe*, 228.

36   "Arthur Ashe Int: On Blacks and Tennis," *Tennis Industry* (April 1988): 88–91; "Words: Arthur Ashe Remembers the Forgotten Men of Sport—America's Early Black Athletes," unidentified 1988 article; "Around the World with Kim Cunningham," *WT* (September 1988): 6, copies in Arthur Ashe Vertical File, ITHF; Lorge, "Inside the Heart and Mind of Arthur Ashe," 46 (q), 48, 51, 53–55; *NYT*, September 6, November 21, 1987.

37   *DG*, 195–96; JMA and Dell ints.

CHAPTER 25: DAYS OF GRACE

1   *DG*, 195 (first q), 196 (second q); JMA int.
2   *DG*, 196 (first q), 197 (second and third qs), 198 (fourth q).
3   Ibid., 199 (qs).
4   Ibid., 200 (first, second, and third qs), 201 (fourth and fifth qs).
5   Mandeville and JMA ints; *DG*, 204 (first q), 201 (second and third qs). Shilts, *And the Band Played On*, is the best source on the early years of the AIDS pandemic.
6   *DG*, 202 (first and second qs), 203 (third q); Murray int.
7   *DG*, 203 (q); JMA, Pasarell, Stan Smith, and Dell ints.
8   Murray int (q); *DG*, 203–5.
9   Murray int; *DG*, 205, 206 (qs), 207.
10   *DG*, 207, 208 (first and second qs), 209 (third through sixth qs).
11   Ibid., 210 (qs), 211; Murray int (second and fifth qs).
12   Murray int; *DG*, 210, 211 (first and second qs), 212 (third q).
13   *DG*, 212 (first q), 213 (second and third qs), 214–15; Murray int. On the emergence of AZT as a primary medicine in the treatment of AIDS, see John Manuel Andriote, *Victory Deferred: How AIDS Changed Gay Life in America* (Chicago: University of Chicago Press, 1999), 176–77, 183–97, 203–4; Engel, *The Epidemic*, 48, 92, 106, 124,

129–31, 134, 140–41, 206, 231, 235, 238–46; and Elizabeth Fee and Daniel M. Fox, eds., *AIDS: The Burdens of History* (Berkeley: University of California Press, 1988), 327, 334–35.

14   Murray int (q).

15   Wiggins, "Symbols of Possibility," 388–89; copy of *NYT Book Review* advertisement, and "Amistad Press Fact Sheet," both in folder 1, box 9, AAP; Arthur Ashe, "Taking the Hard Road with Black Athletes: Success in Sports Became a Matter of Cultural Pride," *NYT*, November 13, 1988 (qs).

16   Barry Lorge, "Ashe Book Literary Labor of Love," *San Diego Union*, November 2, 1988 (qs), copy in folder 1, box 9, AAP; Wiggins, "Symbols of Possibility," 389. See also Lorge, "Inside the Heart and Mind of Arthur Ashe," 46ff.

17   Wiggins, "Symbols of Possibility," 389–92 (second q); Skp Myslenski, "A Race to Succeed: Trials and Dreams of America's Black Athletes," *Chicago Tribune*, November 27, 1988; Dave Anderson, "Thanksgiving Thank-Yous: Remembering Those Who Make the World a Better Place to Be," *NYT*, November 24, 1988 (first q). The book also received a favorable review in the February 1, 1989, issue of *Ebony*.

18   David Halberstam, "Champions We Never Knew," *NYT Book Review*, December 8, 1988 (qs), copy in folder 1, box 9, AAP.

19   Wiggins, "Symbols of Possibility," 390, 391, 392 (qs); Dave Nicholson, "Those Championship Seasons," *WP*, January 29, 1989; Nicolaus Mills, "On and Off the Playing Field," *Nation*, May 8, 1989; J. Milton Yinger, review in *Contemporary Sociology* 19 (March 1990): 286; Gary A. Sailes, review in *Sociology of Sport Journal* 6 (1989): 394.

20   Wiggins, "Symbols of Possibility," 389; "Amistad Press, Inc., Gross Profit, Title-to-Date, 1990," typescript; and "A Book Party, Hard Road to Glory," flier, both in folder 1, box 9, AAP; Mandeville and Don Harris ints.

21   Obituary, printed sheet in folder 1, box 1, AAP; *DG*, 54 (first q); Martin, *Arthur Ashe*, 148; Loretta Ashe Harris, Pace, and JMA ints; Bob Lipper, "The Grace and Grit of Arthur Ashe," *RTD*, May 21, 1989 (second q), copy in folder 4, box 35, AAP.

22   Lipper, "The Grace and Grit of Arthur Ashe," (first q); Bollettieri, Bobby Davis, and Dowdell ints; *DG*, 191 (second q); *IRAA*, 157–58; Hall, *Arthur Ashe*, 259; *IRAA*, 157, 162 (third q). On the ABC program, see the letters and documents, especially the brochure, "The Ashe-Bollettieri Cities Tennis Program," in folder 4, box 27, AAP; and Nick Bollettieri and Dick Schaap, *My Aces, My Faults* (New York: Avon, 1996); and Nick Bollettieri, *Bollettieri: Changing the Game* (Sarasota: New Chapter Press, 2014), Chapters 12 and 13. On IMG, see Bodo, *The Courts of Babylon*, 23, 88, 91–95, 140–43, 147–48, 164, 193, 213, 220, 258, 261, 287–88, 297, 308, 427.

23   Dowdell and JMA ints; *DG*, 192 (qs), 193 (fourth q).

24   *NYT*, January 19, 1989 (qs); *DG*, 147–51.

25   Arthur Ashe, "Coddling Black Athletes," *NYT*, February 10, 1989; "Is Prop 42 Racist?," *Ebony* (June 1989): 139–40, presents a point-counterpoint between Ashe and Dr. Joseph Johnston, president of Grambling State University (a historically black school in Louisiana) and chairman of the national Association for Equal Opportunity in Higher Education.

26   *DG*, 151 (first q), 152 (second q).

27   William C. Rhoden, "Golf Strikes Sensitive Nerve," *NYT*, August 5, 1990; Jaime Diaz, "Applying Lessons of the Civil Rights Movement," *NYT*, August 9, 1990 (q).

28   Jaime Diaz, "TV Executive Is First Black at Augusta," *NYT*, September 12, 1990 (first q); Paul S. Fein, "We've Come a Long Way, Racially—or Have We? Ashe on Tennis'

Shoal Creeks," *Tennis Week* (October 18, 1990): 8–9 (qs), copy in Arthur Ashe Vertical File, ITHF.

29 "Agenda for BE-Arthur Ashe Meeting, Halloween 1990"; Memorandum, Arthur Ashe to Luther Fagin, November 26, 1990; Memorandum on "BE, BET, Black Tennis and Sports Foundation Collaboration," Arthur Ashe to Earl Graves, c. November 1990, all in folder 4, box 29, AAP.

30 Lorge, "Inside the Heart and Mind of Arthur Ashe," 53; *DG*, 153–57 (q), 158–64; Dinkins and Young ints. On Lewis and the "beloved community," see John Lewis, with Michael D'Orso, *Walking with the Wind: A Memoir of the Civil Rights Movement* (New York: Simon & Schuster, 1998). See also Charles Marsh, *The Beloved Community: How Faith Shapes Social Justice, from Civil Rights to Today* (New York: Basic Books, 2004).

31 *DG*, 166 (fourth q), 282 (second and third qs), 283 (first q); *IRAA*, 109.

32 Ibid., 285–88 (first and second qs), 289 (third and fourth qs), 290 (fifth through seventh qs)–92; Rogers, Paul Smith, and Young ints; Howard Thurman, *Jesus and the Disinherited* (Boston: Beacon, 1996); Howard Thurman, *Meditations of the Heart* (Boston: Beacon, 1999).

33 *DG*, 132–36, 215; Murray int.

34 Dennis H. Osmond, "Epidemiology of HIV/AIDS in the United States" (compiled March 2003), available online at hivinsite.ucsf.edu; Andrew Sullivan, "A Right to Live," *NYT Book Review* (November 27, 2016): 1 (q), 22; Murray int. For a comprehensive and thoughtful survey of the war against AIDS, see David France, *How to Survive a Plague: The Inside Story of How Citizens and Science Tamed AIDS* (New York: Alfred A. Knopf, 2016).

35 Lipper, "The Grace and Grit of Arthur Ashe" (first q); Lorge, "Inside the Heart and Mind of Arthur Ashe," 51–52 (second q), 53, 56; "The Price of Greatness," *National Sports Journal* (November 2–3, 1990): 12, copy in folder 5, box 35, AAP; Murray, JMA, Schragis, and Butch Buchholz ints.

36 Lorge, "Inside the Heart and Mind of Arthur Ashe," 52–53. On the African American Athletic Association, Inc., see the extensive documentation in folder 2, box 27, AAP. See especially the printed program for the First Annual Student-Athlete Conference sponsored by the AAAA's Athletic Role Model Educational Institute, held at Madison Square Garden in November 1992. On the African American Sports Hall of Fame, see *DG*, 267; and folders 1–10, box 28, and folders 1–2, box 29, AAP.

37 Lorge, "Inside the Heart and Mind of Arthur Ashe," 53; *DG*, 182–83 (q), 184; Martin, *Arthur Ashe*, 148.

38 Martin, *Arthur Ashe*, 148 (q); JMA, Murray, and Dell ints.

39 *DG*, 120–22 (q); *NYT*, February 11–12, 1990; Donald Dell int, *SSAA*; Pauline H. Baker, *The United States and South Africa: The Reagan Years* (New York: Ford Foundation Press, 1989); Piero Gleijeses, *Visions of Freedom: Havana, Washington, Pretoria, and the Struggle for Southern Africa, 1976–1991* (Chapel Hill: University of North Carolina Press, 2016). On Mandela, see Nelson Mandela, *Long Walk to Freedom: The Autobiography of Nelson Mandela* (Boston: Back Bay Books, 1995); and Martin Meredith, *Mandela: A Biography* (New York: PublicAffairs, 2011). On de Klerk, see F. W. de Klerk, *The Last Trek—A New Beginning: The Autobiography* (New York: St. Martin's, 1999).

40 *DG*, 117 (qs); Robinson int; *NYT*, February 12, 1986; *Dartmouth Review*, November 13, 15, 18–19, 22, 1985, January 7, 14, 25, 1986; *Dartmouth Review*, December 11,

1985, January 29, 1986; Eloise Salholz, "Shanties on the Green," *Newsweek* (February 3, 1986): 63; Jon Weiner, "Students, Stocks, and Shanties," *Nation* (October 11, 1986): 337–40; Horace A. Porter, *The Making of a Black Scholar: From Georgia to the Ivy League* (Iowa City: University of Iowa Press, 2003), 129–34; Bradford Martin, *The Other Eighties: A Secret History of America in the Age of Reagan* (New York: Hill & Wang, 2011), 45–66.

41   *DG*, 119–20.

42   *DG*, 120 (first q), 121 (qs); *NYT*, June 20, 1990; Dinkins interview.

43   *DG*, 122 (first q), 123 (second and third qs); *NYT*, April 27–29, 1994; Anthony Sampson, *Mandela: The Authorized Biography* (New York: HarperCollins, 1999), 401–86; Robinson int. On TransAfrica's "Democracy Now" tour, see folder 9, box 27, AAP.

44   *DG*, 124 (q).

45   *DG*, 7–10 (qs); W, 174–76: Policinski int.

46   *DG*, 10–12; JMA int.

47   *DG*, 12, 13 (q), 14–15; JMA, Dell, Pasarell, and Abraham ints.

48   *DG*, 14 (q); JMA, Young and Dinkins ints.

49   *DG*, 6–8 (qs), 13.

50   *DG*, 15 (q); Smith, *W*, 175–76; JMA int.

51   Murray (q) and JMA ints; *DG*, 15.

52   *DG*, 15–18 (qs); JMA, Dell, Murray, Mandeville, and Pasarell ints. See the voluminous collection of clippings on Ashe's AIDS announcement in folder 6, box 35, AAP. See especially the multiple articles in the *WP* and the *NYT*, April 9, 1992.

CHAPTER 26: FINAL SET

1   Alex Jones, "Report of Ashe's Illness Raises an Old Issue for Editors," *NYT*, April 10, 1992; "Ashe Already Fostering AIDS Awareness," *NYT*, April 11, 1992 (qs); "A Hug for Arthur Ashe," *NYT*, April 14, 1992; Bill Carter, " 'Don't Worry,' Walters told Desiree Washington, 'I'll Help You,'" *NYT Magazine* (August 23, 1992): 22ff.

2   Jones, "Report of Ashe's Illness Raises an Old Issue for Editors" (qs); *DG*, 23.

3   *DG*, 22 (first q), 23; James Cox, "Pursuit of Ashe Story Brings Mixed Reviews," *USA Today*, April 10, 1992, copy in folder 7, box 35, AAP; Jonathan Yardley, "Arthur Ashe and the Cruel Volleys of the Media," *WP*, April 13, 1992 (second q), copy in folder 8, box 35, AAP. To gauge the range of press reaction immediately following the AIDS announcement, see the numerous clippings in folders 6–8, box 35, AAP. See also the clippings from the *Providence Journal-Bulletin* and the *Newport Daily News* in the Arthur Ashe Vertical File, ITHF.

4   Raymond R. Coffey, "Media Double-Faulted on Ashe Story," *Chicago Sun-Times*, April 16, 1992 (first q), copy in folder 8, box 35, AAP; Michael Olesker, "Ashe's Revelation Is Journalism's Shame," *Baltimore Sun*, April 9, 1992 (second q), copy in folder 6, box 35, AAP; *DG*, 22 (third q).

5   Robert Lipsyte, "None of Us Needs Other People's Fears," *NYT*, April 10, 1992 (qs).

6   *DG*, 22 (first q), 23 (second q); *NYT*, April 9–13, 1992.

7   *DG*, 19–20; Peter Prichard, "Arthur Ashe's Pain Is Shared by Public and Press," *USA Today*, April 13, 1992 (qs), copy in folder 8, box 35, AAP.

8   Carl Rowan, "Ashe Performed Public Service by Disclosing He Has AIDS," *Chicago Sun-Times*, April 15, 1992 (qs).

9   Bud Collins, "Ashe Gallantly Confronts Another Challenge," *Boston Globe*, April 9,

1992 (first q), copy in Arthur Ashe Vertical File, ITHF; Collins int; *DG*, 24 (second q), 25–26 (third q); Arthur Ashe, "Life Goes On," *Tennis* (July 1992): 42 (fourth q).

10 Sally Jenkins, "Another Battle Joined," *SI* 76 (April 20, 1992): 24 (first, second, and third qs), 25 (fourth q).

11 *DG*, 26–30, 284; Barry Lorge, "Tennis's Conspiracy of Compassion for Arthur Ashe," *NYT*, April 12, 1992 (third q); *RTD*, April 9, 1992, copy in folder 8, box 35, AAP. See Tracy Austin to Arthur and Jeanne Ashe, c. April 10, 1992; Dorothy Chambers to Arthur Ashe, May 6, 1992 (first q); Heidi J. Aronin to Arthur Ashe, April 10, 1992 (second q); and the rest of the correspondence in folder 1, box 3, AAP. See also folder 8, box 2, AAP.

12 "The Burden of Truth," *People* (April 20, 1992): 51 (first q); *DG*, 12 (third q), 17 (second q).

13 Calvin Sims, "AIDS Policy Coordinator Named by Mayor Dinkins," *NYT*, April 10, 1992 (qs); Dinkins int.

14 *NYT*, April 11, 1992 (qs); *DG*, 190 (qs). See Gregory Seay, "Ashe to Stand for Re-election as Member of Aetna Board," *Hartford Courant*, April 10, 1992; Victor Zonana, "Ashe's AIDS Disclosure Puts New Pressure on Insurers," *Chicago Sun-Times*, April 20, 1992; and "Ashe to Retain Aetna Seat," *RTD*, April 11, 1992, all in folder 1, box 27, AAP. See also Gregory Seay, "Ashe Won't Put Pressure on Aetna over AIDS," *Hartford Courant*, April 11, 1992, copy in folder 7, box 35, AAP.

15 *DG*, 191–93, 255–57; *NYT*, April 19, May 30, June 1, 1992. "Ashe to Speak Out—on His Terms," *Chicago Sun-Times*, April 28, 1992 (first q); Edward Colimore, "For Arthur Ashe, a Warm Welcome," *Philadelphia Inquirer*, April 25, 1992 (third q); Michael Farine, "Ashe Visits D.C. School, Answers AIDS Questions," *Washington Times*, April 28, 1992; Jack Moss, "It's Homecoming of Sorts for Ashe," *Kalamazoo Gazette*, April 30, 1992; Earlene McMichael, "Ashe's Next Match: Public vs. Private," *Kalamazoo Gazette*, May 1, 1992 (second q); Vartan Kupelian, "Ashe Addresses King Verdict: Learn to Organize," *Detroit News*, May 1, 1992; Greg Stoda, "Ashe Pursues Causes Despite Disclosure," *Detroit Free Press*, May 1, 1992; "Ashe Serves Another Ace," *Miami Herald*, May 2, 1992; all in folder 8, box 35, AAP. David O'Brien, "Equality Long Way Off—Ashe," *Fort Lauderdale Sun-Sentinel*, May 3, 1992, copy in folder 13, box 27, AAP; John M. Eisenberg to Arthur Ashe, April 29, 1992, in folder 3, box 29, AAP. Hall, *Arthur Ashe*, 259; Robinson and Dowdell ints.

16 "Arthur Ashe's Winning Spirit," "Arthur Coming Home May 6," and "City Council Salutes Hometown Hero" (first q), *RFP*, April 16–18, 1992; and "Arthur Back Home," *RFP*, May 14–16, 1992, all in folder 8, box 35, AAP. The naming of the Arthur Ashe Jr. Tennis Center was initiated by a Richmond school board resolution approved on May 9, 1980, which honored Ashe as "the first native born Virginian to be designated the world's number one athlete in any sport . . . tennis's first gentleman and noted author." See "Arthur Ashe Jr. Athletic Center," available online at newweb.richmond .k12.va.us. On Richmond's turn to heritage tourism, see Tyler-McGraw, "Southern Comfort Levels," 151–66 (second and third qs), 167. Hall, *Arthur Ashe*, 267; *OTC*, 80–81; B. Drummond Ayres Jr., "Ashe Returns to the City He Disowned in Youth," *NYT*, May 7, 1992 (fourth q); DiPasquale, JMA, and Chewning ints. On the gala planning and the early negotiations related to the proposed Hall of Fame, see Arthur Ashe to Walter T. Kenney, June 17, 1992 (qs); Joseph James to Arthur Ashe, September 25, 1992; Joseph James to Alonzo Monk, October 12, 1992; Arthur Ashe to Joseph James, October 28, 1992; Arthur Ashe to Frances and Sydney Lewis, December 18, 1992; Paul DiPasquale to Joseph James, December 22, 1992; Joseph James to Arthur

Ashe, December 29, 1992; Howard Owen, "African-American Sports Hall a Worthy Cause, Good for City," *RTD*, October 4, 1992; "Black Athletes' Hall of Fame Gains Impetus," *RTD*, November 17, 1992, all in folder 1, box 28, AAP.

17   *DG*, 256 (q).

18   Ayres, "Ashe Returns to the City He Disowned in Youth," (qs); Gwen Ifill, "Clinton's Platform Gets Tryouts Before Friends," *NYT*, May 20, 1992; JMA int.

19   *DG*, 257–58 (qs); JMA and Murray ints; Richard Marlink to Arthur Ashe, June 22, 1992; and "Ashe to Speak at HMS Class Day Ceremonies," *Focus* (Harvard University News Office for the Medical Area) (c. June 1, 1992), copies in folder 8, box 27, AAP. Richard Marlink, "AIDS, Entry to the U.S., and the Bush Administration's Dangerous Silence," typescript of article written for the *Boston Globe*, June 1992, copy in folder 10, box 3, AAP.

20   *DG*, 193, 252–54; JMA, Murray, Mandeville, and Abraham ints. Following Ashe's death, the name of the organization was changed to the Arthur Ashe Endowment for the Defeat of AIDS. See the c. 1995 AAEDA pamphlet in folder 10, box 35, AAP. See also the current AAEDA website: arthurashe.org/ . . . /arthur-ashe-endowment-for -the-defeat-of-aids.

21   *DG*, xi (q)–xii; Rampersad and Ferszt ints; Arnold Rampersad, "Arthur Ashe," Great Lives Lecture Series, University of Mary Washington, Fredericksburg, VA, February 2014, CD audio version in author's possession. Rampersad's publications include *The Life of Langston Hughes: Volume 1 (1902–1941): I, Too, Sing America* (New York: Oxford University Press, 1986); *The Life of Langston Hughes: Volume II (1941–1967): I Dream a World* (New York: Oxford University Press, 1988); *Jackie Robinson*; and *Ralph Ellison, A Biography* (New York: Alfred A. Knopf, 2007). The Ellison biography was a finalist for the National Book Award in Biography; Rampersad was awarded the National Humanities Medal in 2010. He is currently an emeritus professor of English and Humanities at Stanford University.

22   *DG*, ix (table of contents), 293 (q); JMA int.

23   *DG*, 261 (first four qs); Ayres, "Ashe Returns to the City He Disowned in Youth" (fifth q); Ashe, "Life Goes On," 42 (sixth q).

24   *DG*, 262 (qs); JMA and Loretta Ashe Harris ints.

25   *DG*, 260 (q); Mandeville int.

26   *DG*, 259 (qs), 260 (fourth q); *NYT*, June 9, 1992; Ashe, "Life Goes On," 43; Harvey W. Schiller to Arthur Ashe, October 19, 1992, in folder 9, box 2, AAP. Schiller offered "congratulations on your appointment as a Public Sector member of the USOC Board of Directors."

27   *DG*, 259 (first and fourth qs); Martin, *Arthur Ashe*, 144–45 (second and third qs).

28   *DG*, 260 (q); *BCHT*, 261–97, 421–24, 637–39, 666–67; Agassi, *Open*, 162–66; Sampras and Bodo, *A Champion's Mind*.

29   *BCHT*, 266, 277, 279, 281, 310, 317–18, 321, 323–26, 328, 331, 336, 679–81, 685–86, 712; *W*, 162–68, 180; *BATN*, 107, 114–16, 138, 144–45, 149–50, 161, 170, 194, 197, 200, 205, 209, 213–14; *CTN*, 9–45, 115, 124–29 (q), 130–39, 144, 162–68, 224–29; Washington int; Blake, with Friedman, *Breaking Back*; Blake, with Taylor, *Ways of Grace*. Bryan Shelton, with a #55 world ranking in 1991, was the only other top performer among the black players on the 1992 ATP tour. Shelton int.

30   *W*, 162–68; Reid, Carrington, Wilkerson, Shelton, Desdunes, Adams, Dowdell, and Hartman ints; *NYT*, July 20–21, 1992; *DG*, 193 (q); Bodo, *Courts of Babylon*, 258–59, 270–71.

31 *DG*, 128–31, 253–54 (q); *NYT*, August 17, 19, 27, 31, 1992: Richard Finn, "Tennis Rallies Round Ashe," *NYT*, August 27, 1992 (qs); David Dinkins to Arthur Ashe, June 8, 1992, in folder 3, box 29, AAP: Hall, *Arthur Ashe*, 267; John Jeansonne, "An Ace," *New York Newsday*, August 30, 1992, copy in folder 5, box 35, AAP. See also "Arthur Ashe AIDS Tennis Challenge," program; Arvelia Myers to Arthur Ashe, August 1992; "Mayor David Dinkins and the Family of Arthur Ashe Invite You to a Tribute and Celebration Honoring a True American Champion," August 28, 1992, all in folder 2, box 1, AAP.

32 *NYT*, September 5, 10, 1992; "Ex-Tennis Star Ashe Arrested in Protest of Haitian Policy," *USA Today*, September 10, 1992; Gary Lee and Molly Sinclair, "Refugee Policy Protested," *WP*, September 10, 1992; *Washington Times*, September 10, 1992; Robinson int; *DG*, 262–63 (qs), 264; *IRAA*, 145–46; S. L. Price, "Ashe, a Voice That Must Be Heeded," *Miami Herald*, September 11, 1992, copy in folder 5, box 35, AAP. See the letters and clippings in folder 11, box 2, AAP. See especially Ben Hooks to Arthur Ashe, September 22, 1992; and "Committee in Solidarity with the People of Haiti" to Arthur Ashe, October 3, 1992.

33 Price, "Ashe, a Voice That Must Be Heeded," (qs); JMA and Robinson ints; Steins, *Arthur Ashe*, 77–78; Lee and Sinclair, "Refugee Policy Protested": *DG*, 264–65.

34 *DG*, 266; Robert Lipsyte, "Concern in the Season of Jocklock," *NYT*, September 11, 1992; *NYT*, September 12, 13 (qs), 1992.

35 *NYT*, September 15, 1992; *DG*, 266 (qs), 267.

36 *DG*, 267–68 (first q); *NYT*, October 19, 1992 (second and third qs).

37 *DG*, 268; *NYT*, October 19 (second q), November 3–4, 1992; Doug Smith, "Ashe's Elegance Helps Ease the Anguish," *USA Today*, December 10, 1992; "Ninety-Two of '92," *USA Today*, December 29, 1992; Neil Rudenstine to Arthur Ashe, October 21, 1992, in folder 8, box 27, AAP; "Arthur Ashe Honored for AIDS Leadership," unidentified clipping, November 1992; and "Arthur: The Hero of Heroes," *RFP*, November 19–21, 1992, both in folder 5, box 35, AAP. Commonwealth Fund press release, c. November 26, 1992, in folder 1, box 1, AAP.

38 *DG*, 268 (first and second qs), 269 (third and fourth qs); Howard Lamar to Arthur Ashe, December 1, 1992; and Jay Oliva to Arthur Ashe, December 7, 1992, both in folder 10, box 2, AAP.

39 *DG*, 269–70; Paul Smith and Rogers ints.

40 Jeansonne, "An Ace" (first q); Robert Lipsyte, "A History of Hitting the Snooze Button," *NYT*, December 11, 1992 (second q); Smith, "Ashe's Elegance Helps Ease the Anguish" (third q); *DG*, 268; Richard Sandomir, "Even the Sportscasters Are Sort of Speechless," *NYT*, December 6, 1992; *IRAA*, 155.

41 See the letters and clippings in folder 10, box 2, AAP. See especially: "Ashe Is SI's Top Sportsman," *Philadelphia Daily News*, December 16, 1992 (first q); "Ashe Recognized as Top Sportsman," *Detroit Free Press*, December 16, 1992 (second q); Richard Finn, "'SI' Honoree Ashe Credits His Heroes," *USA Today*, December 16, 1992 (third q); "Ashe Is Honored as Sportsman of Year," *Albany Times-Union*, December 16, 1992; Mike Lupica, "Ashe Is Sportsman Who Will Not Quit," New York *Daily News*, December 16, 1992 (fourth and fifth qs); Bernie Miklasz, "Byrd and Ashe Pull Sports Fans to Higher Place," *St. Louis Post-Dispatch*, December 17, 1992 (sixth q); Anthony Carter Paige, "It's Still a Wonderful Life," *Brooklyn City Sun*, December 23, 1992–January 12, 1993; and Mike Celizic, "No Honor Is Too Great," *Bergen County Record*, December 16, 1992 (seventh q); *DG*, 270 (eighth q).

42   *DG*, 270 (first, second, third, and fifth qs), 271 (fourth and sixth qs); JMA int.

43   *DG*, 271–72 (first and second qs), 274 (third and fourth qs), 275 (fifth q); Murray, Butch Buchholz, and JMA ints.

44   Murray, JMA, Mandeville, Dell, Paul Smith, Young, Beck, Stan Smith, and Robinson ints; *DG*, 276–78 (first, second, and third qs), 279; Moore, "The Eternal Example," 27 (fourth q); Steins, *Arthur Ashe*, 81; *IRAA*, 134.

45   Steins, *Arthur Ashe*, 81; Hall, *Arthur Ashe*, 268; *DG*, 276–77, 280; *IRAA*, 116.

46   "You're Invited, for a Father/Daughter Valentines Dinner Dance," card in folder 9, box 1, AAP. Arthur and Camera were listed as the dance's official hosts.

47   DiPasquale (qs) and JMA ints; Robin Finn, "Arthur Ashe, Tennis Champion, Dies of AIDS," *NYT*, February 7, 1993; Martin Weil, "Tennis Legend Arthur Ashe Dies at 49," *WP*, February 7, 1993; *IRAA*, 136. Ashe's death also preempted a planned Long Island fishing trip with tennis journalist Peter Bodo. In lamenting this missed opportunity to spend time with a man he admired, Bodo commented on Ashe's selfless sense of duty: "Thinking about it later, I realized that the worst thing about being Arthur Ashe was not that he had to give up some things that he truly enjoyed, but that he had grown so accustomed to sacrifice that it hardly seemed to bother him. I shudder to think of how much of himself Ashe gave away as he trod his own hard road to glory." Bodo, *Courts of Babylon*, 271.

EPILOGUE: SHADOW'S END

1   Murray and JMA ints; Lawrence K. Altman, "Ashe Was Stricken Suddenly After Years of AIDS," *NYT*, February 8, 1993; George Vecsey, "America Loses a Hero," *NYT*, February 8, 1993; Richard Sandomir, "For a Very Long Year, His Days Were Full," *NYT*, April 30, 1993; Frank Rich, "Horror Stories," *NYT Magazine* (July 4, 1993): 38; *IRAA*, 119, 149. On the AIDS death toll during the first decade of the pandemic, see *DG*, 205–7; Shilts, *And the Band Played On*; Ronald Bayer, *Private Acts, Social Consequences: AIDS and the Politics of Public Health* (New York: Free Press, 1989); Engel, *The Epidemic*, 1–231; and "A Decade of Loss," *Newsweek* (July 18, 1993): 22–23. In 1992, the most celebrated case of an AIDS victim who had contracted the disease through a blood transfusion was Ryan White (1971–1990) of Kokomo, Indiana; see Ryan White and Ann Marie Cunningham, *My Own Story* (New York: Signet, 1992).

2   "Statement from the Family of Arthur Ashe, February 7, 1993," typescript, in folder 3, box 32, AAP (qs). Folder 2, box 34, AAP, contains a large file of condolence letters.

3   Robert McG. Thomas Jr., "Ashe, a Champion in Sport and Life," *NYT*, February 7, 1993 (q); William G. Rhoden, "Arthur Ashe: a Hero in Word and Deed," *NYT*, February 7, 1993; Vecsey, "America Loses a Hero"; "A Hero, Harbinger for Change," *NYT*, February 8, 1993; Robin Finn, "Arthur Ashe, Tennis Star, Is Dead at 49," *NYT*, February 8, 1993; Ira Berkow, "Ashe's Legacy Is the Gift for Inspiration," *NYT*, February 8, 1993.

4   Rhoden, "Arthur Ashe: a Hero in Word and Deed," (q).

5   Thomas, "Ashe, a Champion in Sport and Life," (qs). Dinkins and Ashe shared the same birthday, July 10. *NYT*, July 19, 1993; Dinkins int.

6   "A Celebration of the Life of Arthur Robert Ashe Jr., 1943–1993," Arthur Robert Ashe Jr. Athletic Center, February 10, 1993, program, in folder 3, box 32, AAP; Mike Allen, "Just Plain Better Than Most of Us," *RTD*, February 11, 1993 (first q); Michael Paul Williams, "'Your Spirit Lives On and On,'" *RTD*, February 11, 1993 (qs); Bob Lipper, "Ashe's Legacy: 'Stumbling Blocks into Steppingstones,'" *RTD*, February 11,

1993 (fourth q); Ira Berkow, "A 'Good Man' Transcending Sport," *NYT*, February 11, 1993; Tom Callahan, "To America and the World, Arthur Ashe Was a Gift," *WP*, February 11, 1993; Garrison int.; Bodo, *Courts of Babylon*, 263, notes that Zina Garrison was the only active player to attend the service in Richmond: "She broke a tournament obligation in order to attend, a sacrifice that none of her male or female peers saw fit to make."

7   "Memorial Service Program, Cathedral of St. John the Divine," February 12, 1993, in folder 3, box 32, AAP; William C. Rhoden, "A Cold Day to Say a Last Farewell," *NYT*, February 13, 1993 (qs); Martin, *Arthur* Ashe, 156 (q); *Arthur Ashe: Citizen of the World*; Ronald Akin, "A Final Service for Arthur Ashe," *The Observer*, in *Arthur Ashe, A Tribute* (June 27, 1993): 20–21, 23, copy in Arthur Ashe Vertical File, ITHF; Pasarell, Stan Smith, Dell, JMA, and McNeil ints; Bodo, *Courts of Babylon*, 263, 267–68. Bodo notes that he "saw only one active pro player in attendance, Lori McNeil."

8   Neil Amdur, "Arthur Ashe—A Man of Artistry and Letters," *NYT*, February 14, 1993 (qs); *AA*, 94.

9   Frank Deford, "Lessons from a Friend," *Newsweek* (February 22, 1993): 60 (first q), 61; Bodo, *Courts of Babylon*, 259–60 (second q), 262 (third q); *IRAA*, 151; Dave Anderson, " 'People Don't Listen to Losers,' " *NYT*, February 9, 1993.

10   Robin Finn, "Some Absences Make Hearts Grow Fonder," *NYT*, February 21, 1993; "Arthur Ashe Honors Presented Posthumously," typescript, in folder 8, box 32, AAP; Steins, *Arthur Ashe*, 91; Martin, *Arthur Ashe*, 157. Rachel Shuster, "Ashe's Impact Is Now Painfully Obvious," *USA Today*, May 29, 1993 (q); Gordon Parks to JMA, February 9, 1993, both in folder 3, box 32, AAP; "Man of Grace and Glory," *People* (February 22, 1993): 66–72; Kenny Moss, "He Did All He Could," *SI* (February 15, 1993): 12–15; *NYT*, April 14, May 14, 20, 25, June 4, 1993. Charles S. Farrell, "Academics, Athletes Remember Contributions of Arthur Ashe," *Black Issues in Higher Education* (February 25, 1993): 29, 34; Kenneth I. Chenault, "Accepting Award for Arthur Ashe, the One to One Partnership, June 18, 1993," typescript; "Arthur Ashe Jr., 1943–1993: Maxwell Finland Award Recipient, 1993"; "Barnard Medal of Distinction, Citation for Arthur Ashe," May 18, 1993; John Henry "Pop" Lloyd Humanitarian Award citation; Luchia Ashe, 1993 speech in Texas, transcript; and Margaret E. Mahoney, "Remembering Arthur Ashe," typescript of remarks at USTA dinner, White Plains, New York, November 13, 1993, all in folder 8, box 32, AAP.

11   Jim Memmott, "ASHE: A Symbol of Hope," *Alliance* (Fall 1994): 9–10, copy in folder 4, box 28, AAP; *NYT*, March 9, 24, July 10, 12 (q), 1993; *Newport Daily News*, February 8, 1993; "International Tennis Community Rallies to Support the Arthur Ashe Foundation for the Defeat of AIDS, Inc.," press release, July 1993, copy in Arthur Ashe Vertical File, ITHOF.

12   Richard Sandomir, "HBO Must Carry On Without Ashe," *NYT*, June 21, 1993; Abraham int. On September 27, 1993, many of Arthur's Wimbledon friends attended "an evening at Grosvenor House, Park Lane, to honour the life of one of sport's greatest ambassadors." Donald Dell and Charlie Pasarell served as the honorary co-chairmen, and Jeanne was the "guest of honour." See "Arthur Ashe: A Tribute," twenty-nine-page program, Arthur Ashe Vertical File, ITHF.

13   Charlie Pasarell, "Unforgettable Arthur Ashe," *Reader's Digest* (September 1993): 35, 36 (second q), 40 (first q); Pasarell int.

14   *NYT*, December 2, 1993 (qs); JMA int; Claudia Glen Dowling, and Jeanne Moutoussamy-Ashe, "Daddy and Me," *Life* (November 1993): 61–64, 66, 68–69;

Jeanne Moutoussamy-Ashe, *Daddy and Me: A Photo Story of Arthur Ashe and His Daughter Camera* (New York: Alfred A Knopf, 1993); Randolph, "On Love, Loss and Life After Arthur," 27–28, 30, 32, 34. For drafts, galleys, clippings, and correspondence related to *Daddy and Me*, see folders 12 and 13, box 26, AAP.

15   *NYT*, August 26–27, 2005; *BATN*, 66; Robert Lipsyte, "Are Four Jock Heroes So Saintly After All?," *NYT*, December 5, 1993 (qs).

16   *Arthur Ashe: Citizen of the World*; Abraham int.

17   Doug Smith, "Ashe's Work, Legacy Live On in His Family, Foundation," *USA Today*, August 5, 1997; JMA, Turner, Schragis, Mandeville, Murray, Dell, and Pasarell ints; "Artists and Athletes for Arthur," 1995 typescript, in folder 7, box 32, AAP; Mayor James Sharpe to JMA, February 10, 1993, in folder 8, box 32, AAP; Odom Fanney, "NIH's Hail to a Hero," *WP*, 1995, copy in folder 10, box 35, AAP; *NYT*, May 23, August 9, 18, 30, September 5, 9, 1993; *IRAA*, 150; www.arthurashe.org. See also Jeanne Moutoussamy-Ashe (photographs) and Petra Richterova (Preface), *Arthur Ashe: Out of the Shadow* (New York: Arthur Ashe Learning Center, 2011). In 2017, the AALC changed its name to the Arthur Ashe Legacy Center and moved its headquarters to UCLA.

18   Robinson, Karin Buchholz, Hartman, Dowdell, Desdunes, Wilkerson, Willis Thomas, Chewning, Dell, and Pasarell ints; Michael Kimmelman, "In the Bronx, Tennis for Everyone," *NYT*, April 29, 2017. See also the following online sites: transafrica.org; aptworldtour.com; ustafoundation.com/njtl; safepassageyouthtennis.com; Richmond .com/news/local/city-of-richmond/photos-years-of-virginia-heroes/collection; and ar thurashe.org/blog/lasting-legacy-virginia heroes-continues-to-achieve.

19   Dowdell int; Williams, *Ahead of the Game*, 174–75.

20   A. L. Nellum to Douglas Wilder, February 19, 1993, in folder 2, box 28, AAP; "Implementation Strategy for the Hard Road to Glory Project, March 1993," in folder 3, box 28, AAP; Harrison Wilson to JMA, February 29, 1996, in folder 8, box 28, AAP. See also the correspondence in folder 2, box 29, AAP. On the Ashe statue controversy that complicated and transformed Richmond's racial politics from 1993 to 1996, see Hodder, "Redefining a Southern City's Heritage," 437–53; Barbee, "Race, Memory, and Communal Belonging in Narrative and Art"; Barbee, *Race and Masculinity in Southern Memory*; and Tyler-McGraw, "Southern Comfort Levels," 151–67.

21   DiPasquale, John Charles Thomas, Chewning, and Einwick ints; Paul DiPasquale to JMA, February 16, 1993, folder 2, box 28; Paul DiPasquale to JMA, April 1, 1993, folder 4, box 28; JMA to Paul DiPasquale, March 15, 1993, folder 3, box 28; Paul DiPasquale to JMA, March 31, 1995, folder 5, box 28; all in AAP.

22   Chewning, DiPasquale, and Einwick ints; *RFP*, December 8–10, 1994; *RTD*, December 6, 1994; "In Steel and Stone," ed., *RTD*, December 15, 1994; Paul DiPasquale to JMA, December 16, 1994, in folder 4, box 28, AAP; *NYT*, June 18, 1995 (q).

23   JMA and DiPasquale ints. Paul DiPasquale to JMA, February 13, 27, July 20, 1995; JMA to Paul DiPasquale, February 27, 1995, in folder 5, box 28, AAP; "Hard Road Not Over for Ashe," *Chicago Sun-Times*, February 5, 1995; Cassandra Cossitt, "Ashe Statue Near Expressway on Monument Avenue," *Style Weekly*, June 17, 1995; "On Street Where Confederates Reign, Arthur Ashe May, Too," *NYT*, June 18, 1995; "Ashe Joining Dixie Heroes," *NYT*, June 20, 1995; Peter Baker, "Landmark Decision in Richmond," *WP*, June 20, 1995; "Race-Tinged Furor Stalls Arthur Ashe Memorial," *NYT*, July 9, 1995; Mike Allen, "Return to Square One," *RTD*, June 28, 1995; Gordon Hickey, "Panel Asserts Ashe Site Authority," *RTD*, July 4, 1995; Michael Paul

Williams, "Ashe Monument Could Be Symbol of Reconciliation," *RTD*, June 26, 1995; Paul DiPasquale to JMA, July 26, 1995 (q), all in folder 5, box 28, AAP; Harrison Wilson to JMA, May 29, 1996, in folder 1, box 29, AAP

24 John Charles Thomas (last q) int; Michael Paul Williams, "Arthur Ashe Deserves Place on Monument," *RTD*, December 12, 1994; *WP*, December 9, 1994; Robert A. Carter to Councilwoman Viola Baskerville, July 17, 1995, in folder 5, box 28, AAP. See also the clippings in folder 5, box 28, AAP. See especially *RTD*, June 28, 29, July 1, 11, 16–19, 1995; Margaret Edds, "Clashing Views on Ashe Memorial, *RFP*, July 13–15, 1995; and John Maloney, "We Can Do This: Finding Common Ground in Honoring Arthur Ashe," *Style Weekly*, July 19, 1995.

25 DiPasquale, Einwick, and Chewning ints; Tom Chewning to JMA, January 24, 1996, in folder 7, box 28, AAP; Paul DiPasquale to JMA, July 26, 1995, in folder 5, box 28, AAP; Hodder, "Redefining a Southern City's Heritage," 446 (second q), 447 (first q), 448; John Bryan, "The Aesthetics of DiPasquale's Ashe," *Style Weekly*, January 30, 1996, copy in folder 8, box 28, AAP. See also Michael Kammen, *Visual Shock: A History of Art Controversies in American Culture* (New York: Alfred A. Knopf, 2006), 335–37.

26 Jeanne Moutoussamy-Ashe, "A 'New Year's Wish for Richmond: Accept Gift of Arthur's Vision," *RTD*, January 1, 1996 (qs). See also a preliminary draft of the op-ed in folder 7, box 28, AAP. JMA int; "Arthur Ashe's Widow Says She Is Not in Accord with Husband's Statue Being Erected Among Civil War Heroes," *Jet* (January 22, 1996): 34–35.

27 Hodder, "Redefining a Southern City's Heritage," 448; *RTD*, January 3–6, 9, 14, February 11, 20, 24, 1996; *RFP*, January 4–6, February 28–March 2, 1996; Harrison Wilson to JMA, January 4, 1996, and Tom Chewning to JMA, January 8, 23, 1996, all in folder 7, box 28, AAP; Tom Chewning to JMA, February 2, 1996, and Jay Poole to Harrison Wilson, February 9, 1996, both in folder 8, box 28, AAP; Tom Chewning to JMA, May 14, 28, 1996, in folder 1, box 29, AAP; Mike Allen, "Integration Must Wait on Dixie Heroes Avenue," *NYT*, January 4, 1996; "Honoring Arthur Ashe," ed., *Christian Science Monitor*, January 12, 1996; Frank Deford, "Arthur Ashe's Dream of Hall Lives On," *National Public Radio Morning Edition*, January 5, 1996, transcript, in folder 7, box 28, AAP; Harrison Wilson, "Richmond Will Benefit by Making Ashe's Dream a Reality," *RTD*, March 29, 1996, op-ed. See also correspondence in folder 9, box 28, AAP.

28 Chewning (first q), John Charles Thomas, and DiPasquale ints; *NYT*, July 5, 7, 11, 1996; Hodder, "Redefining a Southern City's Heritage," 436, 448–49; Gordon Hickey, "Council Again Gives OK to Ashe Statue Site," *RTD*, February 27, 1996; Dedication Program, "Virginia Heroes Inc. and Dominion Resources Inc. Celebrate the Life of Arthur Ashe," July 10, 1996, Arthur Ashe Vertical File, ITHF; *RTD*, July 11, 1996; Doug Smith, "Statue Saluting Ashe Unveiled on Historic Avenue in Hometown," *USA Today*, July 11, 1996 (second, third, and fourth qs); John Charles Thomas, *Poetry on the Wings of the Morning* (Richmond: privately printed, 2013), 28–29 (fifth q).

29 DiPasquale (q), Chewning, Einwick, John Charles Thomas, Carrico, and Irby ints; *RTD*, July 11, 1996; Tyler-McGraw, "Southern Comfort Levels," 159–67; Hodder, "Redefining a Southern City's Heritage," 449–51; Josh Sanburn, "A Confederate Monument Solution, with Context," *Time* (July 3, 2017): 17–18.

30 Bill Simons int; William G. Simons, "A Call from the Heart," and "The People's Choice—Ashe Stadium," *Inside Tennis* (March 1997): 6–10; William G. Simons, "Arthur Ashe: The True Test," *Inside Tennis* (September 1997): 10–11; Dwight Chapin, "Ashe Gets His Due in Drive to Rename U.S. Open Stadium," *San Francisco Examiner*,

August 17, 1997; Doug Smith, "USTA Rethinks Naming of New U.S. Open Stadium," *USA Today*, February 14, 1997; Doug Smith, "USTA Names Open Stadium After Ashe," *USA Today*, February 19, 1997; Dave Anderson, "Ashe's Name on Stadium Is an Ace," *NYT*, February 20, 1997; Michael Hiestand, "Sport Counts on USTA Center for Lift," *USA Today*, August 21, 1997; George Vecsey, "Ashe's Image Well Served at New Joint," *NYT*, August 24, 1997; Doug Smith, "Stadium Dedication Tonight Culminates Ashe Celebrations," *USA Today*, August 25, 1997; Lisa Olson, "Thinking-Man's Champ," New York *Daily News*, August 22, 1997, all in folder 10, box 35, AAP; JMA, Dell, and DiPasquale ints; *NYT*, December 30, 1933, January 9, 1934; September 23, 1935; July 8, 1936, April 11, 1966; February 19, 1997, August 30, 2000, August 28–31, 2006; *IRAA*, 167 (q); Vincent F. Seyfried, *Corona: From Farmland to Suburb, 1650–1935* (New York: n.p., 1986); F. Scott Fitzgerald, *The Great Gatsby* (New York: Charles Scribner's Sons, 1925), 28; ericfischl.com/arthur-ashe-memorial; J. A. Adande, "It's Art, but It's Sure Not Arthur," *LAT*, August 30, 2000; Jerry Magee, "It May Be Art, but It's Not Arthur," *San Diego Union-Tribune*, February 24, 2004; Ron Turner, "Fans Don't Like Naked Arthur Ashe Statue," September 1, 2000, available online at groups .google.com; *BATN*, 66; Koger int; Kammen, *Visual Shock*, 337.

31   JMA int; *BATN*, 66; *NYT*, April 30, 1993; espn.go.com/espys/arthurasheaward.

32   Allen, McNeil, Garrison, and Washington ints; Khoe Dominguez, "Yannick Noah pour les 20 ans de 'fete le mur': 'la lute continue,'" *Paris Match*, November 11, 2016; fetelemur.com; enfantsdelaterre.com; "Zina Garrison: Conscious Leader, Humanitarian," entry on arthurashe.org notes the creation of the Zina Garrison Foundation for the Homeless in 1988 and the Houston-based Zina Garrison All-Court Tennis Program; zinagarrison.org/programs; lorimcneiltennisfoundation.org; jamesblaketennis .com/foundation; malwashington.com/youthfoundation; *NYT*, August 18, 22, 1993; Lisa Harris, "A Friend Recalls a Legend," *RTD*, February 5, 1995.

33   Karin Buchholz, Dowdell, Hartman, and Adams ints; *BATN*, 79–80, 170, 199–215; *CTN*, 144, 149–50, 232; "Tennis: A Great Match for Katrina Adams," *Northwestern Magazine* (Winter 2004); Harvey Araton, "She Stumbled Into Tennis, but Strode Into a Top Post: Katrina Takes Helm of U.S.T.A. After Long Ascent," *NYT*, January 16, 2015.

34   Willis Thomas, Bobby Davis, Desdunes, Sands, Hartman, Abram, Dowdell, Beck, Washington, Wilkerson, Harmon, Shelton, Karin Buchholz, Koger, Pasarell, Nagler, Drysdale, McEnroe, and Stan Smith ints; Skip Hartman, "Tennis in the Nation's Service," November 11, 1993, typescript in folder 13, box 27, AAP; George Vecsey, "Where Are Next Gibsons And Ashes?," *NYT*, August 29, 1997; *IRAA*, 134, 152–54, 163–64. On the foundations and related philanthropy of today's top tennis players, see Joanna Tilley, "The Charitable Side of Tennis Stars," November 9, 2013, available online at Aljazeera.com; rogerfedererfoundation.org; Les Roopanarine, "Roger Federer Foundation Aiming for Maximum Impact with Minimum Spin," *The Guardian* (November 30, 2012); fundacionrafanadal.org; Laura Pedley, "The Charitable Giving of Andy Murray," July 10, 2013, available online at cause4.co.uk; novakdjokovic foundation.org; the serenawilliamsfoundation.org; and elevenbyvenuswilliams.com. The best source on Billie Jean King's political and social activism is Ware, *Game, Set, Match*.

35   "A Conversation with the President: Sports, Race, and Achievement," ESPN Forum, October 11, 2016 (qs), available on YouTube. See also Bill Simons, "The Great Goodness of Arthur Ashe," *Inside Tennis* (March 2018): 6–7.

PHOTO CREDITS

1. Photo by the Browns' Studio
2. Courtesy of Ashe Family
3. Photo by Scott L. Henderson
4. AP Images
5. Photo by Ed Fernberger
6. Photo by Maurice Sorrell/*Ebony* and *Life* magazines
7. Getty Images
8. AP Images
9. Photo by Sam Troutman/Courtesy of UCLA Sports Information Office
10. AP Images
11. Photo by Rowland Scherman
12. AP Images
13. Photo by Bob Schutz/AP Images
14. Getty Images
15. Photo by Marty Lederhandler/AP Images
16. AP Images
17. Getty Images
18. Photo by Thomas Monaster/Getty Images
19. AP Images
20. Getty Images
21. Photo by Marty Lederhandler/AP Images

22. Photo by Ron Gallella/Getty Images
23. Popperfoto Collection/Getty Images
24. Photo by Gerry Cranham/Getty Images
25. Photo by Ed Fernberger/International Tennis Hall of Fame
26. Getty Images
27. Getty Images
28. Getty Images
29. Getty Images
30. Getty Images
31. AP Images
32. Getty Images
33. AP Images
34. Getty Images
35. Getty Images
36. Photo by Michael Lipchitz/AP Images
37. Getty Images
38. Getty Images
39. Photo by G. Paul Barnett/AP Images
40. Getty Images
41. Photo by Lana Harris/AP Images
42. Photo by Robin Platzer/Getty Images
43. AP Images
44. Photo by Renaud Giroud/Getty Images
45. Getty Images
46. Photo by Ken Bennett/AP Images
47. Photo by Raymond Arsenault
48. Getty Images
49. Photo by Bryan Bedder/Getty Images

INDEX